WOMEN'S VOICES, FEMINIST VISIONS

Classic and Contemporary Readings

SUSAN M. SHAW   JANET LEE
Oregon State University

Mc Graw Hill **Higher Education**

Boston   Burr Ridge, IL   Dubuque, IA   New York   San Francisco   St. Louis
Bangkok   Bogotá   Caracas   Kuala Lumpur   Lisbon   London   Madrid   Mexico City
Milan   Montreal   New Delhi   Santiago   Seoul   Singapore   Sydney   Taipei   Toronto

The **McGraw·Hill** Companies

Higher Education

Published by McGraw-Hill, an imprint of The McGraw-Hill Companies, Inc., 1221 Avenue of the Americas, New York, NY 10020. Copyright © 2009, 2007, 2004. All rights reserved. No part of this publication may be reproduced or distributed in any form or by any means, or stored in a database or retrieval system, without the prior written consent of The McGraw-Hill Companies, Inc., including, but not limited to, in any network or other electronic storage or transmission, or broadcast for distance learning.

1 2 3 4 5 6 7 8 9 0 FGR/FGR 0 9 8

ISBN: 978-0-07-351228-0
MHID: 0-07-351228-1

Editor in chief: *Michael Ryan*
Publisher: *Frank Mortimer*
Sponsoring editor: *Gina Boedeker*
Development editor: *Kate Scheinman*
Marketing manager: *Leslie Oberhuber*
Production editor: *Anne Fuzellier*
Art director: *Thomas Preston*
Art manager: *Robin Mouat*
Design manager: *Ashley Bedell*
Photo manager: *Brian J. Pecko*
Photo researcher: *Christine A. Pullo*
Production supervisor: *Louis Swaim*
Production service: *The Left Coast Group, Inc.*
Composition: *10/12 Minion Web by Aptara®, Inc.*
Printing: *45# New Era Matte Plus by Quebecor World*

Cover image: *"Red Abstraction" by Alma Woodsey Thomas © Smithsonian American Art Museum, Washington, D.C., Art Resource*

Credits: *The credits section for this book begins on page C-0 and is considered an extension of the copyright page.*

Library of Congress Cataloging-in-Publication Data
Women's voices, feminist visions : classic and contemporary readings / [edited by] Susan M. Shaw, Janet Lee.—4th ed.
    p. cm.
Includes bibliographical references and index.
ISBN-13: 978-0-07-351228-0
ISBN-10: 0-07-351228-1
    1. Women's studies 2. Feminism. I. Shaw, Susan M. (Susan Maxine), 1960– II. Lee, Janet, 1954–
    HQ1180.W689 2009
    305.42–dc22   2008027946

The Internet addresses listed in the text were accurate at the time of publication. The inclusion of a Web site does not indicate an endorsement by the authors or McGraw-Hill, and McGraw-Hill does not guarantee the accuracy of the information presented at these sites.

www.mhhe.com

*Dedicated to all our WS 223 "Women: Self
and Society" students
with thanks for all they have taught us.*

Contents

2 Systems of Privilege and Inequality in Women's Lives   59

3 Learning Gender in a Diverse Society   124

Preface

We decided to create this book after finding our students were increasingly not reading the assigned material in our introductory women's studies course. Our students found the texts to be mostly inaccessible, or alternatively, they enjoyed reading the more testimonial first-person accounts included in some texts but were not getting the theoretical framework necessary to make sense of these more experiential readings. We were tired of creating packets of readings, and students were tired of having to access alternative readings on top of purchasing a textbook. This book was crafted to include a balance of recent contemporary readings with historical and classic pieces as well as both testimonial and more theoretical essays that would speak to the diversity of women's experiences. Each chapter has an introduction that provides an overview of the topic and provides a framework for the readings that follow. Additionally, each chapter provides a variety of learning activities, activist profiles, ideas for activism, and other sidebars that can engage students with the material in various ways.

Although students of women's studies in the early 2000s are in many ways like the students who have preceded them, they are also characterized by certain distinctions from the students of the 1980s and 1990s. Many of today's students come to our classes believing the goals of the women's movement have already been accomplished, and, although most will say they believe in gender equity of some sort, few identify with feminism as a political theory or social movement. Even among students who are supportive of feminist thought, there is a distinct sense of a "third wave" of feminism that reflects the interests of young women who have come of age benefiting from the gains made by their feminist foremothers. Moreover, as women's studies has become institutionalized on college campuses and is fulfilling baccalaureate core requirements, more students are being exposed to women's studies than ever before. Many of these students "choose" women's studies from a menu of options and come to the discipline with varying levels of misunderstanding and resistance. Some of these students have been influenced by the backlash efforts of the 1980s and 1990s and by conservative religious ideologies that seek a return to traditional gender relations. All of these distinctions call for a new, relevant, and accessible introductory women's studies text.

As is typical of contemporary students, students in women's studies today are the kind of visual learners who often prefer reading and interacting in front of a computer screen or watching video clips to reading traditional texts. They are unlikely to wade through long, dense, theoretical readings because they deem them "boring" and "irrelevant." We know from experience that a large percentage of students in introductory women's studies classes only read a fragment of the required readings and that our required readings end up as "fragmented texts."

Our intention in this book is to address these challenges by presenting a student-friendly text that provides short, accessible readings which reflect the diversity of women's experiences and offer a balance of classic/contemporary and theoretical/experiential pieces. The goal is to start where students are rather than where we hope they might be, and to provide a text that enriches their thinking, encourages them to read, and relates to their everyday experiences. We have chosen accessible articles that we hope are readable. They are relatively short, to the point, and interesting in terms of both topics and writing styles. Although most articles are quite contemporary, we have also included several earlier classic articles that are "must-reads." And although the articles we have chosen cover the breadth of issues and eras in women's studies, we hope students will read them and enjoy reading them because of their accessibility, style of presentation, and relevance to their lives. Many are written by young feminists, many are testimonial in format, and, on the whole, they avoid dense, academic theorizing. The cartoons, we hope, bring humor to this scholarship.

We also structure opportunities for students to reflect on their learning throughout the text, and, in this sense, the book is aimed at "teaching itself." It includes not only articles and introductions but also a number of features designed to engage students in active learning around the content. For example, we address students' tendencies to lose interest by creating a format that presents smaller, self-contained, more manageable pieces of knowledge that hold together through related fields and motifs that are woven throughout the larger text as boxes. This multiple positioning of various forms of scholarship creates independent but related pieces that enable students to read each unit in its entirety and make connections between the individual units and the larger text. We see this subtext as a way to address students' familiarity and comfort with contemporary design, multiple windows (as on Web pages), and "sound bytes." By also presenting material in these familiar formats, we intend to create a student-friendly text that will stimulate their interest. We encourage them to actually read the text and then be actively engaged with the material.

Pedagogy is embedded within the text itself. In addition to the textual narrative, we include in each chapter learning activities, activism ideas that provide students with examples and opportunities for the practical implementation of the content, questions for discussion that help students explore chapter themes critically, and suggestions for further reading. Instructors will be able to utilize the various pedagogical procedures suggested in the text (and those in the accompanying instructor's manual) to develop teaching plans for their class sessions. By embedding the pedagogy within the text, we are creating a classroom tool that enables a connection between content and teaching procedure, between assigned readings and classroom experience. Thus, students and instructors should experience the text as both a series of manageable units of information and a holistic exploration of the larger topics.

We hope that this text will address the needs and concerns of students and instructors alike by speaking to students where they are in relation to feminist issues. Our hope is that the innovations included in this book will invite students into productive dialogue with feminist ideas and encourage personal engagement in feminist work.

Like other women's studies text-readers, this book covers the variety of issues that we know instructors address in the introductory course. We do not isolate race and racism and other issues of difference and power as separate topics, but thoroughly integrate them throughout the text into every issue addressed. We have also chosen not to present groups of chapters in parts or sections but to let the individual chapters stand alone. Pragmatically, this facilitates instructors being able to decide how they want to organize their own courses. At the same time, however, the chapters do build on each other. For example, after introducing students to women's studies, Chapter 2 presents the systems of privilege and inequality that form the context of women's lives and then Chapter 3 explores the social construction of gender, building on the previous chapter by introducing the plurality of sex/gender systems. The following chapters then examine how sex/gender systems are expressed and maintained in social institutions.

For this new edition, we have revised chapter framework essays to reflect the most up-to-date research and theory in the field. We've also included new readings that are contemporary and exciting. With each new edition, we strive to keep the textbook fresh and interesting for our students.

ACKNOWLEDGMENTS

Writing a textbook is inevitably a community project, and without the assistance of a number of people this project would have been impossible. We would particularly like to thank Mehra Shirazi for the many hours of tedious library and Internet research she put into this book. Our office coordinator, Lisa Lawson, also provided invaluable help with the clerical tasks of preparing a manuscript. Additionally, we thank our graduate teaching assistants for their input at various stages throughout the writing and editing process—Sriyanthi Gunewardena, Fabiola Sanchez-Sandoval, Susan Wood, Tracy Clow, Rebecca Farrow, Evy Cowan, Michelle Kilkenny, Dawn Cuellar, Katie Atwood, Melanie Love, Melissa Warming, Amy Leer, Hoa Nguyen, Emily Wingard, Heather Ebba Maib, and Elle Bublitz. We would especially like to thank November Papaleo for her assistance with revisions to Chapter 9.

We also would like to acknowledge the work of the many reviewers who provided insights and suggestions for this edition:

Anita Anantharam, University of Florida

Laurie Bernstein, Rutgers University

Julie Goldman Caran, James Madison University

Audrey Fessler, The University of Wisconsin–Eau Claire

Kate Miller, Western Washington University

Sujatha Moni, California State University, Sacramento

Kathleen Butterly Nigro, University of Missouri–St. Louis

Finally, we want to thank Gina Boedeker and Kate Scheinman, our editors at McGraw-Hill, who have provided invaluable support and encouragement. We'd also like to thank Serina Beauparlant, who initiated the first edition of the book with us when she was an editor at Mayfield Publishing.

About the Authors

SUSAN M. SHAW is associate professor and director of women studies and director of the Difference, Power, and Discrimination program at Oregon State University. Her research interests are in women and rock 'n' roll, women and HIV/AIDS, and women in religion, and she teaches courses in systems of oppression, women and sexuality, feminist theology, and women and pop culture. She is author of *Storytelling in Religious Education* (Religious Education Press, 1999) and *God Speaks to Us, Too: Southern Baptist Women on Church, Home, and Society* (University Press of Kentucky, 2008), and coauthor of *Girls Rock! Fifty Years of Women Making Music* (University Press of Kentucky, 2004). She is an avid racquetball player, reader of murder mysteries, and hot tubber.

JANET LEE is professor of women studies at Oregon State University where she teaches a variety of courses on gender and feminism. Research interests include women's history and biography, feminist theories and pedagogy, and issues concerning women and the body. She is author of *War Girls: The First Aid Nursing Yeomanry* (FANY) in the First World War (Manchester University Press, 2005), *Comrades and Partners: The Shared Lives of Grace Hutchins and Anna Rochester* (Rowman and Littlefield, 2000), and coauthor of *Blood Stories: Menarche and the Politics of the Female Body in Contemporary U.S. Society* (Routledge, 1996). She enjoys gardening, riding her horses, and playing tennis.

Janet Lee and Susan Shaw are currently working on a new text, *Women Worldwide: Transnational Feminist Perspectives on Women,* forthcoming from McGraw-Hill. It brings global perspectives to the study of women, gender, and feminism.

Women's Studies:
Perspectives and Practices

WHAT IS WOMEN'S STUDIES?

Women's studies is an interdisciplinary academic field devoted to topics concerning women, gender, and feminism. As a body of knowledge, it examines women's status in society and seeks to improve the condition of women's lives, both in the United States and globally. Women's studies puts women (in all our diversity) at the center of inquiry and focuses on our reality as subjects of study, informing knowledge through this lens. This inclusion implies that traditional notions regarding men as "humans" and women as "others" must be challenged and transcended. Such a confusion of maleness with humanity, putting men at the center and relegating women to outsiders in society, is called *androcentrism*. By making women the subjects of study, we assume that our opinions and thoughts about our own experiences are central in understanding human society generally. Adrienne Rich's "Claiming an Education" articulates this demand for women as subjects of study. It also encourages you as a student to take seriously your right to be taken seriously and invites you to understand the relationship between your personal biography and the wider forces in society that affect your life. As authors of this text, we also invite your participation in knowledge creation, hoping it will be personally enriching and vocationally useful.

Women's studies involves the study of gender as a central aspect of human existence. Gender concerns what it means to be a woman or a man in society. Gender involves the way society creates, patterns, and rewards our understandings of femininity and masculinity. In other words, *gender* can be defined as the way society organizes understandings of sexual difference. Women's studies explores our gendered existence: how we perform femininity and masculinity and how this interacts with other aspects of our identities, such as race, ethnicity, socioeconomic status, and sexuality.

HOW DID WOMEN'S STUDIES COME ABOUT?

Women's studies emerged as concerned women and men noticed the absence, misrepresentation, and trivialization of women in the higher education curriculum, as well as the ways women were systematically excluded from many positions of power

Copyright © 1991 by Nicole Hollander. Used by permission of Nicole Hollander.

and authority as college faculty and administrators. This was especially true for women of color. In the late 1960s and early 1970s, students and faculty began demanding that the knowledge learned and shared in colleges around the country be more inclusive of women's issues, and they asked to see more women in leadership positions on college campuses. It was not unusual, for example, for entire courses in English or American literature to include not one novel written by a woman, much less a woman of color. Literature was full of men's ideas about women—ideas that often continued to stereotype women and justify their subordination. History courses often taught only about men in wars and as leaders, and sociology courses primarily addressed women in the context of marriage and the family. Similarly, entire departments often consisted exclusively of men with perhaps a small minority of (usually White) women in junior or part-time positions. Although there have been important changes on most college campuses as women's issues are slowly integrated into the

MAPPING WOMEN'S AND GENDER STUDIES   **About Women's Studies**

- There are 652 women's and gender studies programs at community colleges, colleges, and universities in the United States, based upon survey responses
- Undergraduate women's studies courses enrolled nearly 89,000 students in 2005–2006, and 85% of women's and gender studies courses fulfilled general education requirements
- Undergraduate majors enrolled nearly 4,300 students, while undergraduate minors enrolled nearly 10,500 students in 2005–2006
- Graduate courses had a total enrollment of nearly 2,700, with 1,076 students registered in doctoral courses in 2005–2006
- 30.4% of women's studies faculty are faculty of color, compared with 19% of faculty nationally, based upon a National Center for Education Statistics (NCES) 2003 report on postsecondary faculty at degree-granting institutions

Source: http://nwsa.org/projects/database/index.php.

curriculum and advances have been made in terms of women in leadership positions, these problems still do, unfortunately, exist in higher education today.

It is important to note that making women subjects of study involves two strategies that together resulted in changes in the production of knowledge in higher education. First, it rebalanced the curriculum. Women as subjects of study were integrated into existing curricula through the development of new courses about women. This shifted the focus on men and men's lives in the traditional academic curriculum and gave some attention to women's lives and concerns by developing, for example, courses such as "Women and Art" and "Women in U.S. History" alongside "regular" courses that sometimes claimed to be inclusive but focused on (usually White) men. In addition, not only did traditional academic departments (like Sociology or English) offer these separate courses on women, but the development of women's studies programs and departments offered curricula on a variety of issues that focused specifically on (initially, usually White) women's issues.

Second, the integration of women as subjects of study resulted in a transformation of traditional knowledge. People began questioning the nature of knowledge, how knowledge is produced, and the applications and consequences of knowledge in wider society. This means that claims to "truth" and objective "facts" are challenged by new knowledge integrating the perspectives of marginalized people. It recognizes, for example, that a history of the American West written by migrating Whites is necessarily incomplete and differs from a history written from the perspective of indigenous native people who had their land taken from them. Although the first strategy was an "add women and stir" approach, this second involved a serious challenge to traditional knowledge and its claims to truth. In this way, women's studies aimed not only to create programs of study where students might focus on women's issues and concerns, but also to integrate a perspective for looking at things that would challenge previously unquestioned knowledge. This perspective questions how such knowledge reflects women's lives and concerns, how it maintains patterns of male privilege and power, and how the consequences of such knowledge affect women and other marginalized people.

Women's studies as a discipline has its origins in the women's movement of the 1960s and 1970s (known as the "second wave" to distinguish it from "first wave" mid-nineteenth-century women's rights and suffrage activity and "third wave" contemporary feminism) and is often named as its academic wing. As an academic discipline, women's studies was influenced by the American studies, and ethnic studies programs of the late 1960s. The demand to include women and other marginalized people as subjects of study in higher education was facilitated by a broad societal movement in which organizations and individuals (both women and men) focused on such issues as work and employment, family and parenting, sexuality, reproductive rights, and violence against women. The objective was to improve women's status in society and therefore the conditions of women's lives. The U.S. women's movement emerged at a moment of widespread social turmoil as various social movements questioned traditional social and sexual values, racism, poverty and other inequities, and U.S. militarism. These social movements, including the women's movement and the civil rights movement, struggled for the rights of people of color, women, the poor, gays and lesbians, the aged and the young, and the disabled, and fought to transform society through laws and policies as well as changes in attitudes and consciousness. The focus on women's issues from a global

HISTORICAL MOMENT   **The First Women's Studies Department**

Following the activism of the 1960s, feminists in the academy worked to begin establishing a place for the study of women. In 1970 women faculty at San Diego State University (SDSU) taught five upper-division women's studies classes on a voluntary overload basis. In the fall of that year, the SDSU senate approved a women's studies department, the first in the United States, and a curriculum of 11 courses. The school hired one full-time instructor for the program. Other instructors included students and faculty from several existing departments. Quickly, many other colleges and universities around the nation followed suit, establishing women's studies courses, programs, and departments. In 1977 academic and activist feminists formed the National Women's Studies Association (NWSA) to further the development of the discipline. NWSA held its first convention in 1979. Presently, more than 600 women's studies programs, departments, research centers, and libraries exist in the United States.

perspective has encouraged women's studies scholars to understand the similarities and differences among women worldwide.

Two aspects of the women's movement—a commitment to personal change and to societal transformation—have helped establish women's studies as a discipline. In terms of the personal, the women's movement involved women asking questions about the cultural meanings of being a woman in U.S. society. Intellectual perspectives that became central to women's studies as a discipline were created from the everyday experiences of women both inside and outside the movement.

Women and Education

Education is a basic right. It is essential for development, as education can help people to find solutions to their problems and can provide new opportunities. It opens chances to participate in labor markets or to look for more decent employment opportunities. Still, almost 800 million adults have not had the opportunity to learn how to read and write, about two-thirds of whom are women. In addition, 60 percent of school drop-outs are girls, as they often have to leave school at early ages to help in households or to work. Moreover, there are often cultural restrictions that prevent girls from finishing even basic education, severely limiting their chances to determine their own future.

The lowest literacy rates for women can be found in South and West Asia, sub-Saharan Africa, and the Arab States. Even though these have increased in recent times, their comparatively low levels reflect the disadvantages faced by women in these regions.

Unfortunately, basic education does not always translate into better employment opportunities. This is why it is important for women to continue to gain knowledge and skills beyond those acquired during youth. An underlying reason for the discrepancy in decent work opportunities between adult men and women could well be the lack of lifelong learning opportunities for many women.

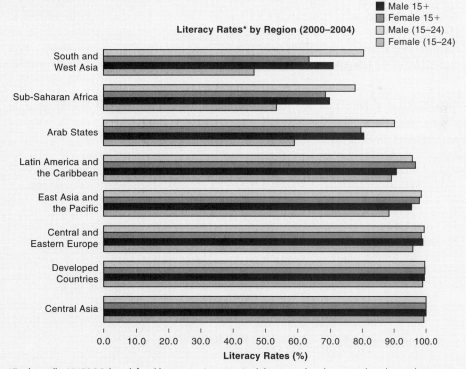

*Traditionally, UNESCO has defined literacy as "a person's ability to read and write, with understanding, a simple statement about one's everyday life." The grouping of countries into regions is taken as provided by UNESCO and differs slightly from the groupings used in this publication.
Source: UNESCO Institute for Statistics, September 2006, *http://www.uis.unesco.org/ev.php?ID=5020 _ 201&ID2=DO_TOPIC.*

Through consciousness-raising groups and other situations where women came together to talk about their lives, women realized that they were not alone in their experiences. Problems they thought to be personal (like working outside the home all day and then coming home to work another full day doing the domestic tasks that are involved with being a wife and mother) were actually part of a much bigger picture of masculine privilege and female subordination. Women began to make connections and coined the phrase *the personal is political* to explain how things taken as personal or idiosyncratic have broader social, political, and economic causes and consequences. In other words, situations that we are encouraged to view as personal are actually part of broader cultural patterns and arrangements. Note that the idea that the personal is political has relevance for men's lives as they understand the connections between patterns of gender in societal institutions and personal experiences of gender privilege and entitlement. In "The Movement That Has No Name," Deborah Siegel writes of a contemporary disconnect between many young women's understandings of their personal lives and awareness of wider social structures in which those personal lives are embedded. She points to the ways individualism and consumerism have "trumped collective action" and calls for a reexamination of this connection. The title of this reading reflects on feminist writer Betty Friedan's famous phrase about women's inequality as "the problem that has no name."

A key term for women's studies writers and activists is *patriarchy*, defined as a system where men dominate because power and authority are in the hands of adult men. It is important to remember that many men are supporters of women's rights and that many of the goals of the women's movement benefit men as well, although

Educational Attainment of the Population 25 Years and over by Sex and Age: 2006

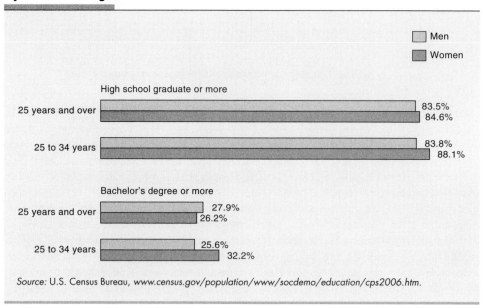

Source: U.S. Census Bureau, www.census.gov/population/www/socdemo/education/cps2006.htm.

being a supporter of women's rights does not necessarily translate into men understanding how everyday privileges associated with masculinity maintain entitlements in a patriarchal society. It is one thing to feel indignant about inequality or compassion for marginalized people, and another to recognize that your privilege is connected to the oppression of others. Connecting with the personal as political encourages men to potentially function as allies on a deeper, more authentic level.

In terms of societal change, the U.S. women's movement, for example, continues to be successful in bringing about various legal and political changes that increase women's status in society and in higher education. These legal changes of the second wave include the passage of the Equal Pay Act in 1963 that sought equal pay for individuals performing the same work, Title VII of the 1964 Civil Rights Act that forbade workplace discrimination, and the creation of the Equal Employment Opportunity Commission (EEOC) to enforce antidiscrimination laws in the early 1970s. Affirmative action as a legal mechanism to combat discrimination was first utilized in 1961 and was extended to women in 1967, although it is increasingly under attack. Similarly, though legislation such as *Roe v. Wade* legalized abortion and provided reproductive choices for women, such gains are under attack as well. In terms of legal changes directly aimed at higher education, Title IX of the Education Amendments Act of 1972 supported equal education and forbade gender discrimination in schools. This includes women's access to sports in the context of schooling and most recently covers the right of school officials to sue in cases of retaliation as a result of Title IX school officials' complaints.

Legal changes in the United States have been accompanied by relatively significant increases in women running for political office and taking positions of authority in government, business, education, science, and the arts. Women have become visible and active in all societal institutions. These societal changes have strengthened the demand for alternative educational models: Not only is it the right thing to include women in college life, but it is illegal to prevent their participation. Jennifer Baumgardner and Amy Richards encourage you to think about these second wave gains in the reading "A Day Without Feminism."

WHAT WERE THE ORIGINS OF WOMEN'S RIGHTS ACTIVISM IN THE UNITED STATES?

Although women's studies emerged out of the second wave of mid- to late-twentieth-century social activism, that activism itself was a part of an ongoing commitment for women's liberation that had its roots in late-eighteenth-century and nineteenth-century struggles for gender equity. Women had few legal, social, and economic rights in nineteenth-century U.S. society. They had no direct relationship to the law outside of their relationships as daughters or wives; in particular, married women lost property rights upon marriage. Women were also mostly barred from higher education until women's colleges started opening in the mid-nineteenth century.

Most early women's rights activists (then it was referred to as "woman's" rights) in the United States had their first experience with social activism in the abolition movement, the struggle to free slaves. These activists included such figures as Elizabeth Cady Stanton, Lucretia Mott, Susan B. Anthony, Sojourner Truth, Sarah M. and Angelina Grimké, Henry Blackwell, Frederick Douglass, and Harriet Tubman.

ACTIVIST PROFILE   **Susan B. Anthony**

Born in Massachusetts in 1820, Susan B. Anthony grew up in a Quaker family in which she learned justice and activism. In the 1840s she became involved with the temperance movement, campaigning for stricter liquor laws to address the ill effects of drunkenness on families. In 1853 she was denied the right to speak at the New York Sons of Temperance meeting because she was a woman. That year she joined with Elizabeth Cady Stanton in founding the Women's State Temperance Society. The society gathered 28,000 signatures urging the state legislature to pass a law limiting the sale of liquor, but, because most of the signatures were from women and children, the legislature rejected the petition. As a result of this experience, Anthony realized that women needed the vote in order to have political influence.

From that point on, Anthony campaigned vigorously for women's suffrage. In 1866 she and Stanton founded the American Equal Rights Association and in 1868 began to publish *The Revolution,* with the masthead "Men, their rights, and nothing more; women, their rights, and nothing less." In 1872 Anthony was arrested in Rochester, New York, for voting. At her trial, the judge ordered the jury to find her guilty, and then he fined her $100 plus court fees. Although she refused to pay, he did not imprison her, thereby denying her the opportunity to appeal and force the issue before the Supreme Court.

In 1877 she gathered 10,000 signatures from 26 states, but Congress ignored them. She appeared before every Congress from 1869 to 1906 to ask for passage of a suffrage amendment. Even in her senior years, Anthony remained active in the cause of suffrage, presiding over the National American Women Suffrage Association from 1892 to 1900. Anthony died in 1906, 14 years before American women won the vote with the Nineteenth Amendment, also known as the Susan B. Anthony Amendment.

LEARNING ACTIVITY   **The National Women's Hall of Fame**

How many significant American women can you name? Most students cannot name 20 women from American history. To learn more about some of the women who have made important contributions in the United States, visit the National Women's Hall of Fame at *www.greatwomen.org*. What is the mission of the Hall of Fame? Who are this year's inductees and why were they inducted? What do you think is the significance of having a National Women's Hall of Fame?

Many abolitionists became aware of inequities elsewhere in society. Some realized that to improve women's status a separate social movement was required. In this way, for many abolitionists, their experiences with abolition inspired their desire to improve the conditions of all women's lives.

English philosopher Mary Wollstonecraft's book *A Vindication of the Rights of Woman* (1792) is seen as the first important expression of the demand for women's equality, although the beginning of the women's movement in the United States is usually dated to the Seneca Falls Convention of 1848. This convention was conceived as a response to the experience of Lucretia Mott and Elizabeth Cady Stanton, who, as delegates to the World Anti-Slavery Convention in London in 1840, were refused seating, made to sit behind a curtain, and not allowed to voice their opinions because they were women. Their experience fueled the need for an independent women's movement in the United States and facilitated the convention at Seneca Falls, New York, in July 1848. An important document, the "Declaration of Sentiments and Resolutions," came out of this convention. Authored primarily by Elizabeth Cady Stanton, it used the language of the U.S. Declaration of Independence and included a variety of demands to improve women's status in the family and in society. Woman's suffrage, the right of women to vote, was included. Other conventions occurred across the country, and national organizations were organized to promote women's rights generally and suffrage in particular. These organizations included the National Woman Suffrage Association (NWSA) formed in 1869 and the National American Woman Suffrage Association (NAWSA) in 1890. NAWSA was formed from the merging of NWSA and the American Woman Suffrage Association and continues today as the League of Women Voters. These organizations fought for women's political personhood—a struggle that continues today. The "Anthony Amendment," the women's suffrage amendment, was introduced into Congress in 1878; it took another 42 years for this amendment to be ratified as the Nineteenth Amendment in 1920, granting women the right to vote.

WHAT IS THE STATUS OF WOMEN'S STUDIES ON COLLEGE CAMPUSES TODAY?

Over the last several decades, women's studies has steadily become institutionalized, or established as a regular custom, on many college campuses. From a scattering of courses (often taught for free by committed faculty when colleges did not want to

Stone Soup © 1992 Jan Eliot. Reprinted with permission of Universal Press Syndicate. All Rights Reserved.

spend money on these courses) have come whole programs and departments with minors and majors of study and graduate degrees at both the master's and doctoral levels. Although most campuses have adopted women's studies, some have gone with gender studies and others with feminist studies. These different names reflect different perspectives concerning knowledge about and for women. How is women's studies institutionalized on your campus?

Professors of women's studies might teach only women's studies, or they might do most of their work in another department like anthropology or history. This illustrates the multidisciplinary nature of women's studies: It can be taught from the point of view of many different disciplines. For the most part, however, women's studies is *interdisciplinary;* that is, it combines knowledge and methodologies from across many academic disciplines. Knowledge integration has occurred at a more rapid rate in the humanities and social sciences than in the biological and physical sciences. This is primarily because these sciences are considered "objective" (free of values), with topics of study immune from consideration of issues of gender, race, and class. However, as scholars have pointed out, science is a cultural product and its methodologies are grounded in historical practices and cultural ideas. There are now courses on many campuses examining the history and current practices of science that integrate knowledge about science as a human (gendered and racialized) product.

A list of the goals or objectives of women's studies might look like this:

• To understand the social construction of gender and the intersection of gender with other systems of inequality in women's lives
• To learn about the status of women in society and ways to improve that status through individual and collective action for social change
• To experience how institutions in society affect individual lives and to be able to think critically about the role of patterns of privilege and discrimination in our own lives
• To improve writing and speaking skills, gain new insights, and empower self and others

WHAT DOES WOMEN'S STUDIES HAVE TO DO WITH FEMINISM?

Women's studies is generally associated with feminism as a paradigm for understanding self and society. Although there are many definitions of feminism and some disagreement concerning a specific definition, there is agreement on two core principles underlying any concept of feminism. First, feminism concerns equality and justice for all women, and it seeks to eliminate systems of inequality and injustice in all aspects of women's lives. Because feminism is politics of equality, it anticipates a future that guarantees human dignity and equality for all people, women and men. Second, feminism is inclusive and affirming of women; it celebrates women's achievements and struggles and works to provide a positive and affirming stance toward women and womanhood. Feminism is a personal perspective as well as a political theory and social movement. Put this way, feminism is hardly a radical notion. Most people, if asked, will say they support equal rights; fewer will identify themselves as feminists. (See What Are the Myths Associated with Feminism? later in the chapter.)

Various kinds of feminisms (while embracing the two core concepts listed above) differ in terms of their specific explanations for understanding the social organization of gender and their ideas for social change. An important distinction is that between liberal feminism and radical feminism. Liberal feminists believe in the viability of the present system (meaning, the system is okay), and work within this context for change in such public areas as education and employment. Liberal feminists attempt to remove obstacles to women's full participation in public life. Strategies include education, federal and state policies, and legal statutes.

Although liberal feminists want a piece of the pie, radical feminists (sometimes known as radical cultural feminists or difference feminists) want a whole new pie. Radical feminists recognize the oppression of women as a fundamental political oppression wherein women are categorized as inferior based upon their gender. It is not enough to remove barriers to equality; rather, deeper, more transformational changes need to be made in societal institutions (like the government or media) as well as in people's heads. Patriarchy, radical feminists believe, shapes how women and men think about the world, their place in it, and their relationships with one another. Radical feminists assert that reformist solutions like those liberal feminism would enact are problematic because they work to maintain rather than undermine the system. Not surprisingly, although the focus of liberal feminism is on the public sphere, the focus of this radical approach is the private sphere of everyday individual consciousness and change. Radical feminist offshoots include lesbian feminism, which focuses on how compulsory heterosexuality (the cultural norm that assumes and requires heterosexuality) and heterosexual privilege (the rights and privileges of heterosexuality, such as legal marriage and being intimate in public) function to maintain power in society. Radical feminist thought also includes ecofeminism, a perspective that focuses on the association of women with nature and the environment and the simultaneous relationships among patriarchy, global economic expansion, and environmental degradation.

Other perspectives within the general rubric of feminism include Marxist feminism, a perspective that uses economic explanations from traditional Marxist theory to

Thank a Feminist

Thank a feminist if you agree that . . .

- Women should have the right to vote.
- Women should have access to contraceptives.
- Women should have the right to work outside the home.
- Women should receive equal pay for equal work.
- Women should have the right to refuse sex, even with their husbands.
- Women should be able to receive a higher education.
- Women should have access to safe, legal abortion.
- Women should be able to participate in sports.
- Women should be able to hold political office.
- Women should be able to choose any career that interests them.
- Women should be free from sexual harassment in the workplace.
- Women should be able to enter into legal and financial transactions.
- Women should be able to study issues about women's lives and experiences.

One hundred years ago, none of these statements was possible for women in the United States. Only through the hard work and dedication of women in each decade of the twentieth century did these rights become available to women.

Imagine a world without feminism. If you are a woman, you would not be in college. You would not be able to vote. You could not play sports. Contraception is illegal. So is abortion. You're expected to marry and raise a family. If you must work, the only jobs available to you are in cleaning, clerical services, or teaching. And you have no legal protection on the job if your boss pressures you for sex or makes lewd comments. Your husband can force you to have sex, and, if you were sexually abused as a child, most likely no one will believe you if you tell. If you are sexually attracted to women, you are considered mentally ill and may be subjected to an array of treatments for your illness.

Today, young women who claim, "I'm not a feminist, but . . ." benefit from the many gains made by feminists through the twentieth century. So, the next time you go to class or vote or play basketball, thank a feminist!

understand women's oppression. For Marxist feminists, the socioeconomic inequities of the class system are the major issues. This can be distinguished from socialist feminism, a perspective that integrates both Marxist and radical feminism. Socialist feminists use the insights of class analysis alongside radical feminist explanations of gender oppression. Socialist feminists seek to understand the workings of capitalist patriarchal institutions and societies. All these feminist approaches have been critiqued by the perspectives of women of color, who require that these approaches be inclusive of *all* women's lives. Multiracial feminism is among the most essential of all influences in asserting that gender is constructed by a range of interlocking inequalities that work simultaneously to shape women's experience. It brings together understandings drawn from the lived experiences of diverse women and influences all feminist writing today. The reading by bell hooks fits into this genre. Finally, some feminists have utilized a postmodern perspective to emphasize that truth is a relative concept and that identity

IDEAS FOR ACTIVISM **Two-Minute Activist**

Many important legislative issues related to women come before elected officials regularly. You can make your voice to support women heard by contacting your senators and representatives. To become a two-minute activist ("one minute to read, one minute to act"), visit the website of the American Association of University Women (AAUW) at *www.aauw.org*. Follow the "Issue Advocacy" link to find the Two-Minute Activist link. There, you'll find links to information about the latest issues before Congress and to prewritten AAUW messages that you can personalize and send to your representatives.

is more multifaceted than we often imagine. This approach pays attention to how language constructs reality. It emphasizes that humans actively construct or shape our lives in the context of various social systems, and often in the face of serious constraints.

Many writers now refer to a current "third wave" of feminist activity that is influenced by postmodernism and multiracial feminism and which problematizes the universality and potential inclusivity of the term *woman*. Third wave feminism has its origins in the 1990s and reflects the thinking, writing, and activism of women and men who tended to come of age taking for granted the gains of second wave feminism, as well as the resistance or backlash to it. Third wave perspectives are shaped by the material conditions created by globalization and technoculture, and tend to focus on issues of sexuality and identity. Contemporary third wave activity has been important in fueling feminist activism, especially through musical and art forms, various "rages" or "zines" (consciousness-raising magazines produced locally and usually shared electronically), and the use of electronic information and entertainment and virtual technologies generally. The reading by Rebecca Walker (the writer Alice Walker's daughter) titled "We Are Using This Power to Resist" discusses third wave feminism and the founding of the Third Wave Foundation, and Deborah Siegel's article on "The Movement That Has No Name" is written from this perspective. Despite the advantages of using a "wave" metaphor to characterize the developments in feminism, the metaphor distracts attention from the continuity of feminist activity and runs the risk of setting up distinctions and potential intergenerational divisiveness between a more stodgy, second wave generation, devoid of sexuality and unwilling to share power, and a younger, self-absorbed generation obsessed with popular culture and uncritically sexualized. Neither of these extremes reflects reality; it is enough to say that just as feminism encompasses diversity, so feminists do not all agree on what equality looks like or how to get there. As a social movement, feminism has always thrived on differences of ideology and practice. In "A Day Without Feminism," third wavers Jennifer Baumgardner and Amy Richards actively claim feminism as relevant to their lives and underscore the gains of second wave feminist activism.

Finally, feminists recognize both the similarities and differences in women's status worldwide. Women's status in developing and nonindustrialized countries is often very low, especially in societies where strict religious doctrines govern gendered behaviors. Although women in various countries around the world often tend to be in subordinate positions, the form this subordination takes varies. As a result, certain issues, like the ability of women to maintain subsistence agriculture and feed their families—matters of personal survival—take priority over the various claims to autonomy that characterize women's issues in the West. What are considered feminist issues in the United States are not necessarily the most important concerns of women in other parts of the world. It is important to understand this in order to avoid overgeneralizing about feminism's usefulness globally, even though the notion of global feminism or transnational feminism is real and useful for political alliances across national borders. It is also important to recognize that any claims for Western feminism are necessarily interpreted internationally in the context of U.S. militarism, a history of colonialism, and international "development," as well as in regard to the power of U.S.-based corporations, consumerism, and popular culture. Nonetheless, global feminism underscores the similarities women share across the world and seeks strategies that take into account the interdependence of women globally. And, as communication technologies have advanced, the difficulties of organizing women in all parts of the world have lessened. International feminist groups have worked against militarism, global capitalism, and racism, and they have worked for issues identified by local women. Such actions were reflected in the United Nations Fourth World Conference on Women held in Beijing, China, in 1995 and the post-Beijing gatherings of the last decade. More than 30,000 women attended the Beijing conference, and 181 governments signed the "Platform for Action." This platform was a call for concrete action to include the human rights of women and girls as part of universal human rights, thus eradicating poverty of women, removing the obstacles to women's full participation in public life and decision making, eliminating all forms of violence against women, ensuring women's access to educational and health services, and promoting actions for women's economic autonomy. The reading by Estelle B. Freedman titled "The Global Stage and the Politics of Location" focuses on the historical development of the global women's movement.

Currently, much transnational feminist emphasis is on the passage of CEDAW (Convention on the Elimination of All Forms of Discrimination Against Women), adopted by the United Nations (UN) General Assembly in 1979, and already ratified by 185 countries (over 90 percent of UN countries). CEDAW prohibits all forms of discrimination against women by legally binding the countries that ratify it to incorporate equality of men and women into their legal systems. Measures include abolishing discriminatory laws and adopting new ones, establishing tribunals to ensure the protection of women, and eliminating acts of discrimination against women by persons, organizations, or enterprises. The United States is the only industrial society that has not yet (as of this writing) ratified the convention because of a fear among those in authority that it would give the UN power over U.S. legal statutes and institutions.

WHAT ARE THE MYTHS ASSOCIATED WITH FEMINISM?

Recent national polls show a marked increase in women identifying as feminists: 56 percent did so in 2003, up from 51 percent in 1995. It is important to mention that when respondents in the 2003 poll were given the dictionary definition of *feminist* as "someone who supports the political, economic, and social equality of women," the percentage of women identifying as feminists rose to 77 percent. There was also an increase in support for the women's movement, with 83 percent in 2003 having a favorable opinion, compared with 57 percent in a 1998 poll. Note again that respondents in the 2003 poll were asked their opinion of the movement to strengthen women's rights, not the "women's rights movement." The misleading and negative connotations associated with the word "feminism" play a central role in backlash, or organized resistance, and encompass what some call the "battered-word syndrome." The organized backlash to feminism also involves, for example, the ways certain groups who believe they would lose from a redistribution of power have worked hard to discredit and destroy the feminist movement and brand feminists in negative ways. This perspective is known as anti-feminism. Although such anti-feminist activity includes conservative groups and politicians, it also involves women who claim to be feminists yet are resistant to its core principles. These women, whose careers in part have been fueled by the gains brought about by the feminist movement, include such successful female academics as Christina Hoff Summers, Camille Paglia, Daphne Patai, Katie Roiphe, and Rene Denfield, and syndicated journalists like Mona Charen. The reading by Deborah L. Rhode, an excerpt from *Speaking of*

LEARNING ACTIVITY   **The Dinner Party**

In *Manifesta: Young Women, Feminism, and the Future,* Jennifer Baumgardner and Amy Richards tell the story of a dinner party they had, reminiscent of the consciousness-raising meetings of the 1970s during which women shared the stories and frustrations of their lives, most of which were directly related to sexism. The point of consciousness raising was to radicalize women, to help them develop the consciousness and motivation needed to make personal and political change in the world. One night in 1999, Jennifer and Amy brought together six of their friends around a dinner table to talk about current issues for women and directions needed for the contemporary women's movement. They found that the conversation wound its way around personal experiences and stories and their political implications and strategies. Their dinner party offered the beginnings of a revolution. They write, "Every time women get together around a table and speak honestly, they are embarking on an education that they aren't getting elsewhere in our patriarchal society. And that's the best reason for a dinner party a feminist could hope for."

Have a dinner party! Invite five or six of your friends over for dinner to discuss issues related to women. What are the experiences of the people around the table in terms of sexuality, work, family, body image, media, religion? What are the political implications of these experiences? What can be done to make the world better around these issues?

After your dinner party, write about what happened. What issues came up? What did various guests have to say about the issues? What strategies for change did the group identify? What plans for action did the group make? What did you learn from the experience?

Sex: The Denial of Gender Inequality, focuses on the backlash that denies the existence of gender inequality despite the concrete realities of women's lives.

One result of this backlash has been the coining of the term *postfeminism* by those who recognize feminism as an important perspective but believe its time has passed, and it is now obsolete. "We're already liberated" is the stance they take. Like other broad generalizations, there is some truth to this: Things have improved for some women in some areas. Although generally it is accurate to say that women's status in the United States at the beginning of the twenty-first century is markedly improved, we still have a long way to go to reach equality. In terms of the issues of poverty, violence, pornography, and HIV/AIDS (to name just a few), things are worse for many women than they ever have been. There are still many areas in which women's status might be enhanced, and, for the majority of the world's women, life is very difficult indeed.

The idea that women have achieved equality is reinforced by the capitalist society in which we live. Surrounded by consumer products, we are encouraged to confuse liberation with the freedom to purchase products or to choose among a relatively narrow range of choices. Often personal style is mistaken for personal freedom as the body becomes a focus for fashion, hair, piercing, exercise, tattoos, and so forth. We are often encouraged to confuse such freedoms of expression with freedom in the sense of equality and social justice. Of course, popular culture and media play a large part in this. We are encouraged to enjoy the freedoms that, in part, feminism has brought, often without recognition of this struggle or allegiance to maintaining such freedoms. Feminist writers such as Ariel Levy (her article, "Female Chauvinist Pigs," from the book by the same name, is included in Chapter 9) explain that cultural changes exacerbated by virtual technologies have encouraged young women to participate in their own objectification (being made into objects for male pleasure) in such practices as "Girls Gone Wild." Levy emphasizes that these young women (who often consider themselves feminists) confuse their freedom to objectify themselves with authentic freedom.

Many people, groups, and institutions have attempted to discredit feminism (and therefore women's studies) in other ways. Feminism has been subject to the following associations: (1) feminists are angry, whiny women who have an axe to grind, no sense of humor, and who exaggerate discrimination against women; (2) feminists hate men or want to be like men and selfishly want to create new systems of power *over* men; (3) all feminists are said to be lesbians, women who choose romantic relationships with other women; (4) feminists are said to reject motherhood, consider children a burden, and have rejected all things feminine; and (5) feminism is dismissed as a White, middle-class movement that draws energy away from attempts to correct social and economic problems and discourages coalition building.

While several of these myths contain grains of truth, as a whole they can easily be shattered. First, although there are some feminists who respond, some would say rightly, to societal injustices with anger, most feminists work patiently with little resentment. Men as a social group demonstrate much more anger than women, feminists included. Even though male rage comes out in numerous acts of violence, wars, school shootings, and so on, men's anger is seen merely as a human response to circumstance. Note the androcentrism at work here. Because a few angry feminists get much more publicity than the majority of those working productively to change the status quo, a better question might be why women are

Yes, I Am

Ashley Judd   Margaret Cho   Camryn Manheim   Whoopi Goldberg

not more angry, given the levels of injustice against women both in the United States and worldwide. Feminists do not exaggerate this injustice; injustice is a central organizing principle of contemporary society. We should also ask why women's anger provokes such a negative response. The cause of the relatively intense reaction to women's anger is grounded in a societal mandate against female anger that works to keep women from resisting their subordination—that is, it keeps them passive. Anger is seen as destructive and inappropriate, going against what we imagine to be feminine. As a result, organized expressions of anger are interpreted as hostile.

Second, it is often said that feminists hate men. It is accurate to say that, in their affirmation of women and their desire to remove systems of inequality, feminists ask men to understand how gender privilege works in men's lives. Many men are more than willing to do this because the same social constructions of masculinity that privilege men also limit them. Because the demand for the examination of gender privilege is not synonymous with hating men, we might ask why these different concepts are so easily conflated. A more interesting question is why men are not accused more often of hating women. Certainly the world is full of *misogyny,* the hatred of, or contempt for, women, and every day we see examples of the ways misogyny influences, and sometimes destroys, the lives of women. The reality, of course, is that most feminists are in relationships with men, and some feminists *are* men. Some men eagerly call themselves pro-feminist because feminism is a perspective on life (even though some feminists would argue that just as people of color are better prepared to understand racial inequality, so women are in a better place to understand how gender works). Nonetheless, the man-hating myth works to prevent many women who want to be in relationships with men from claiming feminism. They are encouraged to avoid a political stance that suggests antagonism toward men.

Feminists often respond to the declaration that they hate men with the observation that the statement illustrates a hypersensitivity about the possibility of

*"I'm really proud of my daughter. She's
a thorn in the side of the patriarchy."*

exclusion and loss of power on the part of men. Only in a patriarchal society would the inclusion of women be interpreted as a potential threat or loss of men's power. It is a reflection of the fact that we live in a competitive patriarchal society that it is assumed that the feminist agenda is one that seeks to have power over men. Only in an androcentric society where men and their reality is center stage would it be assumed that an inclusion of one group must mean the exclusion of another. In other words, male domination encourages the idea that affirming women means hating men and interprets women's request for power sharing as a form of taking over. This projection of patriarchal mentality equates someone's gain with another's loss.

In response to the assertion that feminists want to be men, it is true to say that feminists might like to share some of the power granted to men in society. However, feminism is not about encouraging women to be like men; it's about valuing women for being women. People opposed to feminism often confuse *sameness* and *equality* and say that women will never be equal to men because they are different (less physically strong, more emotional, etc.) or they say that equality is dangerous because women will start being like men. Feminism of course affirms and works to maintain difference; it merely asks that these differences are valued equally.

Third, feminists are accused of being lesbians in an effort to discredit feminism and prevent women both from joining the movement and from taking women's studies classes. The term for this is *lesbian baiting*. Feminism affirms women's choices to be and love whomever they choose. Although some lesbians are feminists, many lesbians are not feminists, and many feminists are heterosexual. Feminists do not interpret an association with lesbianism as an insult. Nonetheless, *homophobia,* the societal fear or hatred of lesbians and gay men, functions to maintain this as an insult. There is considerable fear associated with being called a lesbian, and this declaration that all feminists are lesbians serves to keep women in line, apart from one another, and suspicious of feminism and women's studies. Note that this myth is related to the above discussion on men-hating because it is assumed that lesbians hate men too. Again, although lesbians love women, this does not necessitate a dislike of men.

Fourth, feminism has never rejected motherhood but instead has attempted to improve the conditions under which women mother. Contemporary legislation to improve working mothers' lives and provide safe and affordable health care, child-care, and education for children (to name just a few examples) has come about because of the work of feminists. In terms of rejecting femininity, feminists have rejected some of the constraints associated with femininity such as corsets and hazardous beauty products and practices. Mostly they strive to reclaim femininity as a valuable construct that should be respected.

Fifth, feminism has been critiqued as a White, middle-class perspective that has no relevance to the lives of women of color. The corollary of this is that women's studies is only about the lives of White, bourgeois women. This critique is important because throughout the history of the women's movement there have been examples of both blatant and subtle racism, and White women have been the ones to hold most of the positions of power and authority. Similarly, working-class women have been underrepresented. This is also reflected in the discipline of women's studies as faculty and students have often been disproportionately White and economically privileged. Much work has been done to transform the women's movement into an inclusive social movement that has relevance for all people's lives. Women's studies departments and programs today are often among the most diverse units on college campuses, although most still have work to do. It is absolutely crucial that the study of women as subjects both recognizes and celebrates diversity and works to transform all systems of oppression in society. In "Feminist Politics," bell hooks claims back feminism as the movement to do just that. She emphasizes that any call to sisterhood must involve a commitment on the part of White women to examine White privilege and understand the interconnections among gender, race, and class domination. Likewise, Rebecca Walker in "We Are Using This Power to Resist" makes a similar plea for young women. She uses the term *queer* in this essay as a way to affirm and celebrate the diversity of sexual identities. Her hope is for solidarity among all groups.

Although the women's movement has had a profound impact on the lives of women in the United States and great strides have been made toward equality, real problems still remain. Women continue to face discrimination and harassment in the workplace, domestic violence, rape and abuse, inequities in education, poverty, racism, and homophobia. Anna Quindlen responds to this in the short reading "Still Needing the F Word." Women's studies provides a forum for naming the problems women face, analyzing the root causes of these problems, envisioning a just and equitable world, and developing strategies for change. As you read the following articles, keep these questions in mind: What does the author identify as problems women face? What does the author suggest is the root of these problems? What strategies does the author suggest for bringing about change to improve the lives of women?

U.S. Suffrage Movement Timeline

1792	British author Mary Wollstonecraft argues for the equality of the sexes in her book, *A Vindication of the Rights of Woman*.
1840	The World's Anti-Slavery Convention is held in London, England. When the women delegates from the United States are not allowed to participate, Lucretia Mott and Elizabeth Cady Stanton determine to have a women's rights convention when they return home.
1845	Margaret Fuller publishes *Woman in the Nineteenth Century,* which has a profound influence on the development of American feminist theory.
1848	
July 19	The first woman's rights convention is called by Mott and Stanton. It is held on July 20 at the Wesleyan Chapel in Seneca Falls, NY.
August 2	A reconvened session of the woman's rights convention is held at the Unitarian Church in Rochester, NY. Amelia Bush is chosen chair and becomes the first woman to preside over a meeting attended by both men and women. New York State Legislature passes a law which gives women the right to retain possession of property they owned prior to their marriage.
1851	Elizabeth Cady Stanton and Susan B. Anthony meet and begin their 50-year collaboration to win for women their economic, educational, social, and civil rights.
	Sojourner Truth delivers her "And Ain't I a Woman" speech at the Woman's Rights Convention in Akron, OH.

1855	Elizabeth Cady Stanton makes an unprecedented appearance before the New York State Legislature to speak in favor of expanding the Married Woman's Property Law.
1863	Stanton and Anthony organize the Women's Loyal National League and gather 300,000 signatures on a petition demanding that the Senate abolish slavery by constitutional amendment.
1866	The American Equal Rights Association is founded with the purpose to secure for all Americans their civil rights irrespective of race, color, or sex. Lucretia Mott is elected president. To test women's constitutional right to hold public office, Stanton runs for Congress receiving 24 of 12,000 votes cast.
1867	Stanton, Anthony, and Lucy Stone address a subcommittee of the New York State Constitutional Convention requesting that the revised constitution include women's suffrage. Their efforts fail.
	Kansas holds a state referendum on whether to enfranchise Blacks and/or women. Stone, Anthony, and Stanton traverse the state speaking in favor of women's suffrage. Both Black and women's suffrage is voted down.
1868	Stanton and Anthony launch their women's rights newspaper, *The Revolution,* in New York City.
	Anthony organizes the Working Women's Association, which encourages women to form unions to win higher wages and shorter hours.
	The Fourteenth Amendment to the U.S. Constitution is adopted. The amendment grants suffrage to former male African American slaves, but not to women. Anthony and Stanton bitterly oppose the amendment, which for the first time explicitly restricts voting rights to "males." Many of their former allies in the abolitionist movement, including Lucy Stone, support the amendment.
1869	National Woman Suffrage Association (NWSA) is founded with Elizabeth Cady Stanton as president.
	American Woman Suffrage Association (AWSA) is founded with Henry Ward Beecher as president.
	Wyoming Territory grants suffrage to women.
1870	Utah Territory grants suffrage to women.
	First issue of the *Woman's Journal* is published with Lucy Stone and her husband, Henry Blackwell, as editors.
1871	Victoria Woodhull addresses the Judiciary Committee of the House of Representatives arguing that women have the right to vote under the Fourteenth Amendment. The Committee issues a negative report.

(continued)

1872	In Rochester, NY, Susan B. Anthony registers and votes contending that the Fourteenth Amendment gives her that right. Several days later she is arrested.
1873	At Anthony's trial the judge does not allow her to testify on her own behalf, dismisses the jury, rules her guilty, and fines her $100. She refuses to pay.
1874	In *Minor v. Happersett,* the Supreme Court decides that citizenship does not give women the right to vote and that women's political rights are under the jurisdiction of each individual state.
1876	Stanton writes a "Declaration and Protest of the Women of the United States" to be read at the centennial celebration in Philadelphia. When the request to present the Declaration is denied, Anthony and four other women charge the speakers' rostrum and thrust the document into the hands of Vice President Thomas W. Ferry.
1880	New York State grants school suffrage to women.
1882	The House of Representatives and the Senate appoint Select Committees on Woman Suffrage.
1887	The first three volumes of the *History of Woman Suffrage,* edited by Susan B. Anthony, Matilda Joslyn Gage, and Elizabeth Cady Stanton, are published.
1890	After several years of negotiations, the NWSA and the AWSA merge to form the National American Woman Suffrage Association (NAWSA) with Elizabeth Cady Stanton, Susan B. Anthony, and Lucy Stone as officers.
	Wyoming joins the union as the first state with voting rights for women. By 1900 women also have full suffrage in Utah, Colorado, and Idaho.
	New Zealand is the first nation to give women suffrage.
1892	Susan B. Anthony becomes president of the NAWSA.
1895	Elizabeth Cady Stanton publishes *The Woman's Bible,* a critical examination of the Bible's teaching about women. The NAWSA censures the work.
1900	Anthony resigns as president of the NAWSA and is succeeded by Carrie Chapman Catt.
1902	
October 26	Elizabeth Cady Stanton dies.
	Women of Australia are enfranchised.
1903	Carrie Chapman Catt resigns as president of the NAWSA and Anna Howard Shaw becomes president.

1906	
March 13	Susan B. Anthony dies. Women of Finland are enfranchised.
1907	Harriet Stanton Blatch, daughter of Elizabeth Cady Stanton, founds the Equality League of Self-Supporting Women, later called the Women's Political Union.
1910	The Women's Political Union holds its first suffrage parade in New York City.
1911	National Association Opposed to Woman Suffrage is founded.
1912	Suffrage referendums are passed in Arizona, Kansas, and Oregon.
1913	Alice Paul organizes a suffrage parade in Washington, D.C., the day of Woodrow Wilson's inauguration.
1914	Montana and Nevada grant voting rights to women.
	Alice Paul and Lucy Burns organize the Congressional Union for Woman Suffrage. It merges in 1917 with the Woman's Party to become the National Woman's Party.
1915	Suffrage referendum in New York State is defeated.
	Carrie Chapman Catt is elected president of the NAWSA.
	Women of Denmark are enfranchised.
1916	Jeannette Rankin, a Republican from Montana, is elected to the House of Representatives and becomes the first woman to serve in Congress.
	President Woodrow Wilson addresses the NAWSA.
1917	Members of the National Woman's Party picket the White House. Alice Paul and ninety-six other suffragists are arrested and jailed for "obstructing traffic." When they go on a hunger strike to protest their arrest and treatment, they are force-fed.
	Women win the right to vote in North Dakota, Ohio, Indiana, Rhode Island, Nebraska, Michigan, New York, and Arkansas.
1918	Women of Austria, Canada, Czechoslovakia, Germany, Hungary, Ireland, Poland, Scotland, and Wales are enfranchised.
	House of Representatives passes a resolution in favor of a woman suffrage amendment. The resolution is defeated by the Senate.
1919	Women of Azerbaijan Republic, Belgium, British East Africa, Holland, Iceland, Luxembourg, Rhodesia, and Sweden are enfranchised.
	The Nineteenth Amendment to the Constitution granting women the vote is adopted by a joint resolution of Congress and sent to the states for ratification.
	New York and twenty-one other states ratify the Nineteenth Amendment.

(continued)

| 1920 | Henry Burn casts the deciding vote that makes Tennessee the thirty-sixth, and final, state to ratify the Nineteenth Amendment. |
| August 26 | The Nineteenth Amendment is adopted and the women of the United States are finally enfranchised. |

Source: Anthony Center for Women's Leadership: US Suffrage Movement Timeline, prepared by Mary M. Huth, Department of Rare Books and Special Collections, University of Rochester Libraries, February 1995. Obtained from *http://www.rochester.edu/SBA/timeline1.html,* August 2002.

Claiming an Education

Adrienne Rich (1979)

For this convocation, I planned to separate my remarks into two parts: some thoughts about you, the women students here, and some thoughts about us who teach in a women's college. But ultimately, those two parts are indivisible. If university education means anything beyond the processing of human beings into expected roles, through credit hours, tests, and grades (and I believe that in a women's college especially it *might* mean much more), it implies an ethical and intellectual contract between teacher and student. This contract must remain intuitive, dynamic, unwritten; but we must turn to it again and again if learning is to be reclaimed from the depersonalizing and cheapening pressures of the present-day academic scene.

The first thing I want to say to you who are students is that you cannot afford to think of being here to *receive* an education; you will do much better to think of yourselves as being here to *claim* one. One of the dictionary definitions of the verb "to claim" is *to take as the rightful owner; to assert in the face of possible contradiction.* "To receive" is *to come into possession of; to act as receptacle or container for; to accept as authoritative or true.* The difference is that between acting and being acted-upon, and for women it can literally mean the difference between life and death.

One of the devastating weaknesses of university learning, of the store of knowledge and opinion that has been handed down through academic training, has been its almost total erasure of women's experience and thought from the curriculum, and its exclusion of women as members of the academic community. Today, with increasing numbers of women students in nearly every branch of higher learning, we still see very few women in the upper levels of faculty and administration in most institutions. Douglass College itself is a women's college in a university administered overwhelmingly by men, who in turn are answerable to the state legislature, again composed predominantly of men. But the most significant fact for you is that what you learn here, the very texts you read, the lectures you hear, the way your studies are divided into categories and fragmented one from the other—all this reflects, to a very large degree, neither objective reality, nor an accurate picture of the past, nor a group of rigorously tested observations about human behavior. What you can learn here (and I mean not only at Douglass but any college in any university) is how *men* have perceived and organized their experience, their history, their ideas of social relationships, good and evil, sickness and health, etc. When you read or hear about "great issues," "major texts," "the mainstream of Western thought," you are hearing about what men, above all white men, in their male subjectivity, have decided is important.

Black and other minority peoples have for some time recognized that their racial and ethnic experience was not accounted for in the studies broadly labeled human; and that even the sciences can be racist. For many reasons, it has been more difficult for women to comprehend our exclusion, and to realize that even the sciences can be sexist. For one thing, it is only within the last

This talk was given at the Douglass College Convocation, September 6, 1977, and first printed in *The Common Woman*, a feminist literary magazine founded by Rutgers University women in New Brunswick, New Jersey.

hundred years that higher education has grudgingly been opened up to women at all, even to white, middle-class women. And many of us have found ourselves poring eagerly over books with titles like *The Descent of Man; Man and His Symbols; Irrational Man; The Phenomenon of Man; The Future of Man; Man and the Machine; From Man to Man; May Man Prevail?; Man, Science and Society;* or *One-Dimensional Man*—books pretending to describe a "human" reality that does not include over one-half the human species.

Less than a decade ago, with the rebirth of a feminist movement in this country, women students and teachers in a number of universities began to demand and set up women's studies courses—to *claim* a woman-directed education. And, despite the inevitable accusations of "unscholarly," "group therapy," "faddism," etc., despite backlash and budget cuts, women's studies are still growing, offering to more and more women a new intellectual grasp on their lives, new understanding of our history, a fresh vision of the human experience, and also a critical basis for evaluating what they hear and read in other courses, and in the society at large.

But my talk is not really about women's studies, much as I believe in their scholarly, scientific, and human necessity. While I think that any Douglass student has everything to gain by investigating and enrolling in women's studies courses, I want to suggest that there is a more essential experience that you owe yourselves, one which courses in women's studies can greatly enrich, but which finally depends on you, in all your interactions with yourself and your world. This is the experience of *taking responsibility toward your selves*. Our upbringing as women has so often told us that this should come second to our relationships and responsibilities to other people. We have been offered ethical models of the self-denying wife and mother; intellectual models of the brilliant but slapdash dilettante who never commits herself to anything the whole way, or the intelligent woman who denies her intelligence in order to seem more "feminine," or who sits in passive silence even when she disagrees inwardly with everything that is being said around her.

Responsibility to yourself means refusing to let others do your thinking, talking, and naming for you; it means learning to respect and use your own brains and instincts; hence, grappling with hard work. It means that you do not treat your body as a commodity with which to purchase superficial intimacy or economic security; for our bodies and minds are inseparable in this life, and when we allow our bodies to be treated as objects, our minds are in mortal danger. It means insisting that those to whom you give your friendship and love are able to respect your mind. It means being able to say, with Charlotte Brontë's *Jane Eyre:* "I have an inward treasure born with me, which can keep me alive if all the extraneous delights should be withheld or offered only at a price I cannot afford to give."

Responsibility to yourself means that you don't fall for shallow and easy solutions: predigested books and ideas, weekend encounters guaranteed to change your life, taking "gut" courses instead of ones you know will challenge you, bluffing at school and life instead of doing solid work, marrying early as an escape from real decisions, getting pregnant as an evasion of already existing problems. It means that you refuse to sell your talents and aspirations short, simply to avoid conflict and confrontation. And this, in turn, means resisting the forces in society which say that women should be nice, play safe, have low professional expectations, drown in love and forget about work, live through others, and stay in the places assigned to us. It means that we insist on a life of meaningful work, insist that work be as meaningful as love and friendship in our lives. It means, therefore, the courage to be "different"; not to be continuously available to others when we need time for ourselves and our work; to be able to demand of others—parents, friends, roommates, teachers, lovers, husbands, children—that they respect our sense of purpose and our integrity as persons. Women everywhere are finding the courage to do this, more and more, and we are finding that courage both in our study of women in the past who possessed it, and in each other as we look to other women for comradeship, community, and challenge. The difference between a life lived actively, and a life of passive drifting and dispersal of energies, is an immense difference. Once we begin to feel committed to our lives, responsible to ourselves, we can never again be satisfied with the old, passive way.

Now comes the second part of the contract. I believe that in a women's college you have the right to expect your faculty to take you seriously. The education of women has been a matter of debate for centuries, and old, negative attitudes about women's role, women's ability to think and take leadership, are still rife both in and outside the university. Many male professors (and I don't mean only at Douglass) still feel that teaching in a women's college is a second-rate career. Many tend to eroticize their women students—to treat them as sexual objects—instead of demanding the best of their minds. (At Yale a legal suit [*Alexander* v. *Yale*] has been brought against the university by a group of women students demanding a stated policy against sexual advances toward female students by male professors.) Many teachers, both men and women, trained in the male-centered tradition, are still handing the ideas and texts of that tradition on to students without teaching them to criticize its antiwoman attitudes, its omission of women as part of the species. Too often, all of us fail to teach the most important thing, which is that clear thinking, active discussion, and excellent writing are all necessary for intellectual freedom, and that these require *hard work*. Sometimes, perhaps in discouragement with a culture which is both antiintellectual and antiwoman, we may resign ourselves to low expectations for our students before we have given them half a chance to become more thoughtful, expressive human beings. We need to take to heart the words of Elizabeth Barrett Browning, a poet, a thinking woman, and a feminist, who wrote in 1845 of her impatience with studies which cultivate a "passive recipiency" in the mind, and asserted that "women want to be made to *think actively*: their apprehension is quicker than that of men, but their defect lies for the most part in the logical faculty and in the higher mental activities." Note that she implies a defect which can be remedied by intellectual training—*not* an inborn lack of ability.

I have said that the contract on the student's part involves that you demand to be taken seriously so that you can also go on taking yourself seriously. This means seeking out criticism, recognizing that the most affirming thing anyone can do for you is demand that you push yourself further, show you the range of what you *can* do. It means rejecting attitudes of "take-it-easy," "why-be-so-serious," "why-worry-you'll-probably-get-married-anyway." It means assuming your share of responsibility for what happens in the classroom, because that affects the quality of your daily life here. It means that the student sees herself engaged *with* her teachers in an active, ongoing struggle for a real education. But for her to do this, her teachers must be committed to the belief that women's minds and experience are intrinsically valuable and indispensable to any civilization worthy [of] the name; that there is no more exhilarating and intellectually fertile place in the academic world today than a women's college—*if* both students and teachers in large enough numbers are trying to fulfill this contract. The contract is really a pledge of mutual seriousness about women, about language, ideas, methods, and values. It is our shared commitment toward a world in which the inborn potentialities of so many women's minds will no longer be wasted, raveled-away, paralyzed, or denied.

A Day Without Feminism

Jennifer Baumgardner and Amy Richards (2000)

We were both born in 1970, the baptismal moment of a decade that would change dramatically the lives of American women. The two of us grew up thousands of miles apart, in entirely different kinds of families, yet we both came of age with the awareness that certain rights had been won by the women's movement. We've never doubted how important feminism is to people's lives—men's and women's. Both of our mothers went to consciousness-raising-type groups. Amy's mother raised Amy on her own, and Jennifer's mother, questioning the politics of housework, staged laundry strikes.

With the dawn of not just a new century but a new millennium, people are looking back and taking stock of feminism. Do we need new strategies? Is feminism dead? Has society changed so much that the idea of a feminist movement is obsolete? For us, the only way to answer these questions is to imagine what our lives would have been if the women's movement had never happened and the conditions for women had remained as they were in the year of our births.

Imagine that for a day it's still 1970, and women have only the rights they had then. Sly and the Family Stone and Dionne Warwick are on the radio, the kitchen appliances are Harvest Gold, and the name of your Whirlpool gas stove is Mrs. America. What is it like to be female?

Babies born on this day are automatically given their father's name. If no father is listed, "illegitimate" is likely to be typed on the birth certificate. There are virtually no child-care centers, so all preschool children are in the hands of their mothers, a baby-sitter, or an expensive nursery school. In elementary school, girls can't play in Little League and almost all of the teachers are female. (The latter is still true.) In a few states, it may be against the law for a male to teach grades lower than the sixth, on the basis that it's unnatural, or that men can't be trusted with young children.

In junior high, girls probably take home ec; boys take shop or small-engine repair. Boys who want to learn how to cook or sew on a button are out of luck, as are girls who want to learn how to fix a car. *Seventeen* magazine doesn't run feminist-influenced current columns like "Sex + Body" and "Trauma-rama." Instead, the magazine encourages girls not to have sex; pleasure isn't part of its vocabulary. Judy Blume's books are just beginning to be published, and *Free to Be . . . You and Me* does not exist. No one reads much about masturbation as a natural activity; nor do they learn that sex is for anything other than procreation. Girls do read mystery stories about Nancy Drew, for whom there is no sex, only her blue roadster and having "luncheon." (The real mystery is how Nancy gets along without a purse and manages to meet only white people.) Boys read about the Hardy Boys, for whom there are no girls.

In high school, the principal is a man. Girls have physical-education class and play half-court basketball, but not soccer, track, or cross country; nor do they have any varsity sports teams. The only prestigious physical activity for girls is cheerleading, or being a drum majorette. Most girls don't take calculus or physics; they plan the dances and decorate the gym. Even when girls get better grades than their male counterparts, they are half as likely to qualify for a National Merit Scholarship because many of the test questions favor boys. Standardized tests refer to males and male experiences much more than to females and their experiences. If a girl "gets herself pregnant," she loses her membership in the National Honor Society (which is still true today) and is expelled.

Girls and young women might have sex while they're unmarried, but they may be ruining their chances of landing a guy full-time, and they're probably getting a bad reputation. If a pregnancy happens, an enterprising gal can get a legal abortion only if she lives in New York or is rich enough to fly there, or to Cuba, London, or Scandinavia. There's also the Chicago-based Jane Collective, an underground abortion-referral service, which can hook you up with an illegal or legal termination. (Any of these options are going to cost you. Illegal abortions average $300 to $500, sometimes as much as $2,000.) To prevent pregnancy, a sexually active woman might go to a doctor to be fitted for a diaphragm, or take the high-dose birth-control pill, but her doctor isn't likely to inform her of the possibility of deadly blood clots. Those who do take the Pill also may have to endure this contraceptive's crappy side effects: migraine headaches, severe weight gain, irregular bleeding, and hair loss (or gain), plus the possibility of an increased risk of breast cancer in the long run. It is unlikely that women or their male partners know much about the clitoris and its role in orgasm unless someone happens to fumble upon it. Instead, the myth that vaginal orgasms from penile penetration are the only "mature" (according to Freud) climaxes prevails.

Lesbians are rarely "out," except in certain bars owned by organized crime (the only businessmen who recognize this untapped market), and if lesbians don't know about the bars, they're less likely to know whether there are any other women like them. Radclyffe Hall's depressing early-twentieth-century novel *The Well of Loneliness* pretty much indicates their fate.

The Miss America Pageant is the biggest source of scholarship money for women. Women can't be students at Dartmouth, Columbia, Harvard, West Point, Boston College, or the Citadel, among other all-male institutions. Women's colleges are referred to as "girls' schools." There are no Take Back the Night marches to protest women's lack of safety after dark, but that's okay because college girls aren't allowed out much after dark anyway. Curfew is likely to be midnight on Saturday and 9 or 10 p.m. the rest of the week.

Guys get to stay out as late as they want. Women tend to major in teaching, home economics, English, or maybe a language—a good skill for translating someone else's words. The women's studies major does not exist, although you can take a women's studies course at six universities, including Cornell and San Diego State College. The absence of women's history, black history, Chicano studies, Asian-American history, queer studies, and Native American history from college curricula implies that they are not worth studying. A student is lucky if he or she learns that women were "given" the vote in 1920, just as Columbus "discovered" America in 1492. They might also learn that Sojourner Truth, Mary Church Terrell, and Fannie Lou Hamer were black abolitionists or civil-rights leaders, but not that they were feminists. There are practically no tenured female professors at any school, and campuses are not racially diverse. Women of color are either not there or they're lonely as hell. There is no nationally recognized Women's History Month or Black History Month. Only 14 percent of doctorates are awarded to women. Only 3.5 percent of MBAs are female.

Only 2 percent of everybody in the military is female, and these women are mostly nurses. There are no female generals in the U.S. Air Force, no female naval pilots, and no Marine brigadier generals. On the religious front, there are no female cantors or rabbis, Episcopal canons, or Catholic priests. (This is still true of Catholic priests.)

Only 44 percent of women are employed outside the home. And those women make, on average, fifty-two cents to the dollar earned by males. Want ads are segregated into "Help Wanted Male" and "Help Wanted Female." The female side is preponderantly for secretaries, domestic workers, and other low-wage service jobs, so if you're a female lawyer you must look under "Help Wanted Male." There are female doctors, but twenty states have only five female gynecologists or fewer. Women workers can be fired or demoted for being pregnant, especially if they are teachers, since the kids they teach aren't supposed to think that women have sex. If a boss demands sex, refers to his female employee exclusively as "Baby," or says he won't pay her unless she gives him a blow job, she has to either quit or succumb—no pun intended. Women can't be airline pilots. Flight attendants are "stewardesses"—waitresses in the sky—and necessarily female. Sex appeal is a job requirement, wearing makeup is a rule, and women are fired if they exceed the age or weight deemed sexy. Stewardesses can get married without getting canned, but this is a new development. (In 1968 the Equal Employment Opportunity Commission—EEOC—made it illegal to forcibly retire stewardesses for getting hitched.) Less than 2 percent of dentists are women; 100 percent of dental assistants are women. The "glass ceiling" that keeps women from moving naturally up the ranks, as well as the sticky floor that keeps them unnaturally down in low-wage work, has not been named, much less challenged.

When a woman gets married, she vows to love, honor, and obey her husband, though he gets off doing just the first two to uphold his end of the bargain. A married woman can't obtain credit without her husband's signature. She doesn't have her own credit rating, legal domicile, or even her own name unless she goes to court to get it back. If she gets a loan with her husband—and she has a job—she may have to sign a "baby letter" swearing that she won't have one and have to leave her job.

Women have been voting for up to fifty years, but their turnout rate is lower than that for men, and they tend to vote right along with their husbands, not with their own interests in mind. The divorce rate is about the same as it is in 2000, contrary to popular fiction's blaming the women's movement for divorce. However, divorce required that one person be at fault, therefore if you just want out of your marriage, you have to lie or blame your spouse. Property division and settlements, too, are based on fault. (And at a time when domestic violence isn't a term, much less a crime, women are legally encouraged to remain in abusive marriages.) If fathers ask for custody of the children, they get it in 60 to 80 percent of the cases. (This is still true.) If a husband or a lover hits his partner, she has no shelter to go to unless she happens to live near the one in northern California or the other in upper Michigan. If a

woman is downsized from her role as a housewife (a.k.a. left by her husband), there is no word for being a displaced homemaker. As a divorcée, she may be regarded as a family disgrace or as easy sexual prey. After all, she had sex with one guy, so why not *all* guys?

If a woman is not a Mrs., she's a Miss. A woman without makeup and a hairdo is as suspect as a man with them. Without a male escort she may be refused service in a restaurant or a bar, and a woman alone is hard-pressed to find a landlord who will rent her an apartment. After all, she'll probably be leaving to get married soon, and, if she isn't, the landlord doesn't want to deal with a potential brothel.

Except among the very poor or in very rural areas, babies are born in hospitals. There are no certified midwives, and women are knocked out during birth. Most likely, they are also strapped down and lying down, made to have the baby against gravity for the doctor's convenience. If he has a schedule to keep, the likelihood of a cesarean is also very high. *Our Bodies, Ourselves* doesn't exist, nor does the women's health movement. Women aren't taught how to look at their cervixes, and their bodies are nothing to worry their pretty little heads about; however, they are supposed to worry about keeping their little heads pretty. If a woman goes under the knife to see if she has breast cancer, the surgeon won't wake her up to consult about her options before performing a Halsted mastectomy (a disfiguring radical procedure, in which the breast, the muscle wall, and the nodes under the arm, right down to the bone, are removed). She'll just wake up and find that the choice has been made for her.

Husbands are likely to die eight years earlier than their same-age wives due to the stress of having to support a family and repress an emotional life, and a lot earlier than that if women have followed the custom of marrying older, authoritative, paternal men. The stress of raising kids, managing a household, and being undervalued by society doesn't seem to kill off women at the same rate. Upon a man's death, his beloved gets a portion of his Social Security. Even if she has worked outside the home for her entire adult life, she is probably better off with that portion than with hers in its entirety, because she has earned less and is likely to have taken time out for such unproductive acts as having kids.

Has feminism changed our lives? Was it necessary? After thirty years of feminism, the world we inhabit barely resembles the world we were born into. And there's still a lot left to do.

R E A D I N G **3**

The Movement That Has No Name

Deborah Siegel (2007)

On February 15, 1969, the day I was born, the newly formed women's liberation movement launched its national attack on domesticity. In New York City, members of the Women's International Terrorist Conspiracy from Hell—WITCH—stormed a Madison Square Garden bridal fair. They marched among the faux flowers, folded napkins, and lamé bridesmaid dresses and hexed the vendors (whom they dubbed "manipulator-exhibitors") as they advanced. "Always a Bride, Never a Person!" they chanted. "Here Comes the Slave, Off to Her Grave!" they sang. Meanwhile, their movement sisters in San Francisco picketed a bridal fair and passed out leaflets printed with similar warnings to stunned brides-to-be.[1]

That previous September, some one hundred young radicals protested the Miss America pageant in Atlantic City, throwing aprons, high heels, bras, and hair rollers into a "Freedom Trashcan." Pictures from that day show images of young women with long hair parted in the middle standing behind a poster of a naked women whose body is labeled like meat: Rump. Rib. Chuck. Round. "Welcome to the Miss America Cattle Auction," banners proclaimed. "Atlantic City is a town with class—they raise your morals and they judge your ass!" Suddenly, just as the oldest members of the future Generation X were entering the world, all the commonplace assumptions about femininity, sexuality, and domesticity that a baby girl could expect to inherit were under siege. Everyday choices, like wearing stilettos or tying

the knot, now had significant political implications. Family life, standards of beauty, and relations with men were no longer private matters of individual choice or social custom but issues of national import.

The personal became political.

It was an age of unprecedented action. During the late 1960s and early 1970s, a hundred women took over the offices of *Ladies' Home Journal* and suggested retitling the magazine's famous monthly column, "Can This Marriage Be Saved?" to "Can This Marriage." Women in Seattle created pamphlets on women's reproductive health with titles like "Have Intercourse without Getting Screwed." Women in Boston created a 138-page booklet that later became *Our Bodies, Ourselves.* Valerie Solanas, author of the man-hating tract known as the S.C.U.M. (Society for Cutting Up Men) Manifesto, shot Andy Warhol. The National Organization for Women celebrated Mother's Day by organizing demonstrations nationwide for "Rights, Not Roses" and dumping piles of aprons on the White House lawn—near the exact spot where a group of suffragists had chained themselves to a White House fence fifty years earlier—to symbolize their rejection of the 1950s housewife role. The National Black Feminist Organization organized black women nationwide. Mothers staged a mother-and-baby sit-in at the office of the Secretary of Health, Education, and Welfare. Lesbian women formed a guerrilla group called "Lavender Menace" and staged "zap" actions (a combination of disruptive protest and street theater). Single women and others disrupted Senate hearings on the safety of the birth control pill, which was released less than a decade earlier. Women in New York disrupted a legislative hearing on abortion—then still illegal—overseen by a panel of so-called objective witnesses comprising fourteen men and one nun.

To women of the Baby Boomer generation, these opening salvos of a revolution are moments of canonical—and personal—feminist history. But to women born circa 1969, many of them raised by feminists, these momentous occasions that have shaped us forever are shrouded in a collective amnesia. Feminism is not yet dead, but our memory of its past is dying. Younger women run from the word "feminist" without quite knowing why, or what the word has stood for. The movement's architects are aging, some are dying, and the names of others are hardly known. In 2007, we hardly know the history that surrounded our births and gave us our identity. We are barely acquainted with the story of the movement that has shaped our lives.

. . .

Women fighting for rights, power, and parity generally share some rudimentary goals, hopes, and dreams. But from its inception, the movement known as feminism has been one of the most internally fragmented and outwardly controversial—perhaps because so many have so much to gain. Today many of the conflicts that characterize public debates about the meaning and relevance of feminism are generational, with yesterday's flaming radicals and today's cool girl bloggers rarely recognizing each other as fellow travelers in the fight for social equality and personal satisfaction. "Where are the younger feminists?" cry founders of women's organizations, now approaching retirement, as they e-mail each other about their often unformulated succession plans. "Why don't older women get us?" ask younger women on social networking Web sites like MySpace—women who may know more about the life of Bettie Page than that of Betty Friedan.

With little awareness of a shared history, younger women seeking to rally their peers and continue the forward march toward advancement are stuck reinventing the wheel. At the same time, framers of the 1960s and 1970s women's movement (commonly known as the second wave) are proving increasingly blind to interpretations of empowerment that they didn't themselves initiate. Blocked by their own inability to see members of the next generation as sisters in a struggle that they themselves inherited from members of an earlier wave, second-wave movement mothers worry that they have failed younger women. Or that younger women, ungrateful daughters, have in turn failed them. Have they? Have we?

In spite of our differences, older and younger women concerned with women's continued progress have much more in common than we think. But a mounting generation gap—fueled by divergent understandings of power and empowerment—obscures the larger war. How can younger women relate to their movement mothers and narrow the chasm between their mothers' style of empowerment and their own? Instead of brushing aside generational differences in the name of an abstract concept once known fondly as sisterhood, women young and old must appreciate where the alienation is coming from and seek first, as the old adage implores us, to understand.

The age gap is not, of course, the only chasm preventing women concerned with equity and continued advancement from uniting in common cause. Today as in the past, lack of sensitivity to race and class, and other markers, often precludes any shot at solidarity. But against this already divisive landscape, age is fast becoming an unnecessary divider.

Why don't younger women call themselves feminists? Perhaps, in part, it is a matter of spin. Feminism the movement and feminist the identity have never been an easy sell. The question of how to "fix" feminism's meaning and sell revolution to a critical mass of American women has plagued popularizers and would-be popularizers of the movement for forty years. The current sales quandary—that of "selling" the movement to the young—is but the latest in a long line of attempts to mainstream a hotly contested cause. Across the generations and at the heart of the battle to articulate feminism as a movement with mass appeal has been that singular tagline: *The Personal Is Political.* These words more than any others link the far-flung battles of women fighting for equality—including the ones we are in the midst of today.

In 2007, veteran feminists accuse younger women of turning their backs on feminism's history and turning back the clock. For many women in their twenties and thirties, "politics" refers to elections or politicians—not necessarily the underlying currents that shape their personal lives. For them, the conditions shaping individual trajectories and private lives no longer seem political, at least not in the way they seemed to be for the Boomer women who preceded them.

But the disconnect between personal life and social context is not solely the fault of younger women. Individualism seems to have trumped collective action—not just among women, but throughout American culture more generally during the past thirty years. Recent decades have seen the decline of liberalism and a decline in social commitment to collective, progressive change more broadly, though the emergence of Internet activism around recent elections offers a propitious sign for the future of citizen movements. Still, from a historical perspective, civic participation in general has been on the wane.[2] Liberals have lost political power as conservatives have gained it, and the social movements that historically have dominated progressive politics—including those for women, labor, and civil rights—have less overall impact on politics today. Collective social movements decrease in political relevance when high finance trumps grassroots organizing, and this is exactly what we have seen happening of late. Political parties once dependent on the number of volunteers on the ground are now media-driven and depend less on foot soldiers than on massive television buys. For women, the fallout from these shifts is profound.

Although women's organizations and activism certainly still exist, younger women today do not always experience the direct support of a movement behind them. And without a movement behind them, the reasons women still can't have it all—fulfilling career, committed relationships,

kids—seem, as in the days before Betty Friedan's *Feminine Mystique,* merely "personal." Many of women's social problems once again have no public names. The word "revolution" itself has lost its political edge. Google the words "women" and "revolution" and you are likely to dredge up stories about the "opt-out revolution"—a headline-making term for what happens when well-heeled, well-educated daughters of feminists drop out of their careers. This so-called trend, cavalierly dubbed so by prominent newspapers, is neither revolutionary nor counterrevolution, but rather the adjustment of a privileged few to a workplace that doesn't make room for mothers. Even though it is often framed as such, a well-off women's choice to stay home is hardly the pinnacle of broad-scale empowerment. Elite women's sense that their only option is to opt out is a copout—but it is hardly the fault of the individual women who cannot find a way to make it all work. Rather, it signals our common failure to see the shared themes in women's personal struggles, across race and class and geography, as connected to larger structural issues or addressable by collective formulas for change. Instead of questioning what's wrong with "the system," a younger woman struggling today for "balance" (or, on the other end of the economic spectrum, to "get by") more typically asks herself: What's wrong with *me?* The result? A series of parallel individual meltdowns where instead a *real* revolution should be.

It is ironic, perhaps, that members of a generation raised on the Barbie slogan, "You Can Do Anything," and philosophies that emanated from hit albums like *Free to Be You and Me* today demonstrate scant awareness of women's collective power. Younger women, who are more likely to be single, are portrayed on television, in Hollywood, and in the news as being more concerned with dating than changing the world. Polls proclaimed that 22 million unmarried women did not vote in the 2000 presidential election.[3] Popular culture reinforces, by amplification, this assumed image of apathy. On shows like *Laguna Beach,* or as starlets-turned-role models like Paris Hilton and Jessica Simpson, younger women are portrayed as more obsessed with lip gloss, Manolo Blahniks, and "hotness" than liberation, critical mass, and social change. What has happened to us, the daughters of women's liberation? This is hardly the world the architects of a movement for women's social, political, and economic equality envisioned. It's no wonder the aging visionaries seem upset.

But it's not as if women of a younger generation are sitting on their duffs. They are coming of age in a world that has changed—though, as many of them recognize, not enough. Yes, women of Generations X and Y live in a different environment, but it is no less complex than the one Boomer women faced. The difference, and the problem, is that they often lack an awareness that many of their conflicts are shared. In a recent book on how the stakes have changed for a new generation, *Midlife Crisis at Thirty*, Gen X-ers Lia Macko and Kerry Rubin offer their personal anxiety attacks as evidence of a broader generational angst. That angst, they argue, is a response to the lingering social and economic contradictions that continue to affect women of all ages—or, as they put it, the gap between women's progress and old-school corporate structures and rigid social conventions. It's the gap between What Has Changed and What Has Stayed the Same. In this breach, confusion is born: We've come a long way . . . maybe.

So where do we go from here?

The trendy notion that we are living in a "postfeminist" era has lulled many young women into inertia. Younger women assume their equality and take it for granted, but they aren't the first to dismiss the movement prematurely. The word "postfeminist" was first uttered in 1919—just a few decades after the coining of the word "feminist"—by a group of female literary radicals in Greenwich Village who rejected the feminism of their mothers, one year before women won the right to vote.[4] To the generation that came of age in the 1920s—many of them dancing, bobbed-haired fun-seekers—feminism seemed unfashionable and obsolete. The word "postfeminist" was resurrected in the backlash 1980s to describe an era in which feminism was, once again, deemed unhip and unnecessary. In a *New York Times Magazine* article published in 1982, Susan Bolotin popularized the idea that women in their twenties were fast becoming "postfeminists."[5] The media ran with this term, as did conservative pundits, who were all too happy to dance gleefully once again on feminism's so-called grave.

If "postfeminists" is a word twice coined to describe an era that is past patriarchy, surely the word—though popular—is woefully premature. Without a doubt, second-wave feminists opened doors. Title IX. *Roe v. Wade*. Later, the Violence against Women Act. But today, two of these crowning and hard-won achievements are in danger of being yanked away. Having made tremendous inroads in politics, business, and law, in 2007, still only 16 of 100 U.S. senators and 71 of 435 representatives are women. Following the 2006 midterm elections, there are more women in Congress than ever before, but the percentage only went up from 15.4 to 16.4. The number of female Supreme Court justices has recently been reduced by 50 percent (from 2 to 1), and the only female president this country has seen is Geena Davis, the doe-eyed movie star who played President MacKenzie Allen on ABC's short-lived drama *Commander in Chief*. Despite the significantly high numbers of women receiving law degrees, PhDs, and MBAs—more, in some cases, than men—women are only 20 percent of full professors and 17 percent of partners at law firms. Thirteen years after feminists switched the voice boxes of Teen Talk Barbie doll ("Math is hard!") and Talking Duke G. I. Joe ("Eat lead, Cobra!"), we have Harvard's then-president, Lawrence Summers, telling us that women might be biologically inferior in science, and one of the world's leading advertising executives, Neil French, telling us that women creative directors are "crap."[6] Only 10 Fortune 500 CEOs are women, and, according to The White House Project, an organization that tracks women's political influence and authority, women make up only 14 percent of guests on the five Sunday morning talk shows.[7]

Equal pay for equal work is still a joke. For every dollar a man earns, a woman still earns only 77 cents—an increase from the 59 cents she earned when the second wave of feminism began, but still far from equal. Women own only

1 percent of the world's assets. We continue to make up the majority of the world's poor.[8] We are disproportionately victims of violent crime. We are still, forty years after Simone de Beauvoir coined the term, the "second sex."

In de Beauvoir's day, the question was not whether women were oppressed but who, and what, was to blame. Today, in spite of the evidence, women are arguing over the question of whether women are oppressed at all. And therein lies the rub: How do younger women reconcile the gap between the tremendous opportunities they've been given and the inequalities that persist? How do they continue the fight for equality when they are constantly told—by the media, by each other, and often by their leaders—how good they already have it? These are the ironies younger women inhabit today.

It's true: Younger women shy away from the "f-word," as Karen Rowe-Finkbeiner called it, in her book of that title. But they do so for a reason. As Jennifer Baumgardner and Amy Richards write in *ManifestA: Young Women, Feminism, and the Future,* some younger women flee from the feminist label "because they don't want to be associated with spooky stereotypes about feminists and their freaky excesses, or because they resist being identified solely as feminists. You know this rap: *some feminists think all sex is rape, all men are evil, you have to be a lesbian to be a feminist, you can't wear girlie clothes or makeup, married women are lame, et cetera.*"[9] To the women who believe the rap, the specter they call Feminism is scary. And it's small wonder, as the capital "F" version of the cause has been scarily framed.

From its debut on the public stage of history, feminism has been blamed by opponents for going too far and by advocates for not going far enough. The women's movement has been lambasted by dreamers for failing to transform women's lives, damned by detractors for failing to make women happy, and blamed by everyone for failing to institutionalize enough profound and lasting change. In the 1990s, right-wing ideologue Pat Robertson charged feminists with encouraging women to leave their husbands, kill their children, practice witchcraft, become lesbians, and destroy capitalism, while conservative talk show host Rush Limbaugh coined that unflattering term, "feminazi."[10] The antifeminist fervor surrounding Hillary Clinton in her 2000 bid for the U.S. Senate makes the 1970s stereotype of a feminist as a hairy-lipped man-eater seem quaint. A line in *Bridget Jones's Diary* tells us "Nothing is more unattractive to a man than a feminist." Actress Jennifer Aniston, who directed a film for a series sponsored by *Glamour* magazine as part of a project to address the paucity of female directors working in Hollywood, anxiously reassured an interviewer that she wasn't, like, "a bleeding heart feminist," while twenty-six-year-old singer-songwriter Kelis recently told *Essence* not to call her one: "Whenever you say that word, people think of some crazy, hairy lesbian."[11] In television shows like *Desperate Housewives* and spooky Hollywood remakes like *Stepford Wives,* feminists are portrayed as wily or deviant examples of contemporary womanhood run amok.

. . .

We are left, instead, with vacuous images that fuel and perpetuate misunderstandings. For instance, when the words "young women" and "feminism" appear yoked together in a sentence these days, it's increasingly in reference to Girls-Gone-Wild types who fight valiantly for their right to bare their breasts on camera and flash their thongs. If most brands of feminism are framed as taboo or outré, the one form that the media loves to play up as popular and even ultra-hip—"bimbo feminism"—is, in many ways, an anachronistic throwback to an earlier time. In her provocative book *Female Chauvinist Pigs: Women and Raunch Culture,* thirty-something *New York* magazine writer Ariel Levy describes how many young women have internalized the bad news about old feminism and end up projecting the old patriarchy instead. They are now "empowered" enough to get Brazilian bikini waxes and install stripping poles in their living rooms. Is this what our foremothers had in mind when they threw out their bras?

. . . Most younger women are neither the self-hating sexual throwbacks nor the postfeminists and antifeminists they are made out to be.

Although they may be far less visible because they are not out there flashing for tv cameras, there are younger women who grapple intensely with issues of parity in their relationships and their workplaces, if not on Capitol Hill. Younger women volunteer in record numbers, throwing their creativity and, when possible, their wallets behind a range of causes. Younger women's membership in the National Organization for Women may be down because they consider the organization old-fashioned, but the number of younger women founding their own organiztions is on the rise. In 2005, 130 women from 42 states attended a Meet-Up to found the Younger Women's Task Force, a grassroots movement that now boasts 11 chapters and a membership over 1,000. A 2005 poll by the Partnership for Public Service found that, following 9/11, many young people are turning causes into careers.[12] There are models for young activism within mainstream culture—consider Jehmu Greene (former president of Rock the Vote), Wendy Kopp (founder of Teach for America, whose program continues to receive record numbers of applications from recent college grads seeking to teach in urban and rural public schools), Zainab Salbi (whose Women for Women International helps women in wartorn regions rebuild their lives and who has appeared on *Oprah* seven times), or the Woodhull Institute for Ethical Leadership, a training ground for ethical, pro-woman leaders. There are many more. Young women are organizing and championing social causes in spirited and imaginative ways—like the women behind The Real Hot 100, a campaign to redefine "hotness" and counter the impossible beauty standards informing *Maxim* magazine's Hot 100 list (which ranks women for their sex appeal) by refiguring the criteria to honor women for their guts and not just their glam. Pro-woman activism scans younger and younger. In an action reminiscent of an earlier day, in 2005, twenty-four teenage girls from Allegheny waged a national "Girlcott" against Abercrombie & Fitch after the popular clothing company came out with a line of female T-shirts with sexist and racist messages like

"Who needs brains when you have these?" Apparently, there *are* younger women who still wrestle with feminism, whether they call it by its name or not.

. . . According to a March 2006 Lifetime Women's Pulse poll, 51 percent of Generation Y women believe that there are more advantages today to being a man. And in a 2003 report *Progress and Perils: New Agenda for Women* by the Center for the Advancement of Women, a majority of the 3,300 women surveyed believed more effort should be made to improve the status of women in the United States today. More than six in ten agreed that "the United States continues to need a strong women's movement to push for changes that benefit women." A poll conducted by the Peter Harris Research Group for *Ms.* magazine that same year found that 83 percent of all women queried said they approved of the movement to strengthen women's rights. Among eighteen-to-twenty-four-year-olds, a full 92 percent rated the women's movement favorably.[13] Younger women's support for social causes remains strong. They may be perceived as politically disengaged, but this caricature masks a more complicated reality. The low turnout among young female voters during the 2004 election doesn't mean that *all* women under thirty-five are apathetic but rather, perhaps, that many are turned off and disillusioned by politicians who fail to take on their issues. And their rejection of the "f-word" does not mean that feminism is dead.

So, then, the questions remain: Does it matter that droves of young women reject the f-word? What, for that matter, *is* "feminism"? Who decides? Does sisterhood have a future, or only a short-lived past? Is feminism today a culture, an identity, or a cause? The problem or the cure?

These very questions have plagued and stymied—but also propelled and shaped—the modern American women's movement from the start. Despite myriad attempts over the past four decades to fix feminism's meaning, despite media caricatures that younger generations continue to internalize and movement veterans continue to deplore, "a feminist" has never been a frozen or static classification. The very act of defining one has led to a fragmentation that has become as predictable as it is inevitable. Today, as soon as one woman says "sister," another woman turns away.

But conflict has long been feminism's lifeblood, and for a good number of reasons—many of which are covered in this book. Women invested in changing the status quo often encounter ruthless resistance not only from other women but from the establishment they wish to change. Perhaps this is one reason why feminism's most public warriors have held each other up to such intense scrutiny. Regardless of why, the fact remains that the fight for women's social, economic, and political equality remains one of the most dynamic movements—the most debated, negotiated, fought over and fought for, owned, disowned, blamed, and reclaimed—of the last forty years. Since the days when the Women's International Terrorist Conspiracy from Hell crashed the Madison Square Garden bridal fair and young radicals protested Miss America, raising eyebrows and tempers within their own nascent movement, internal battles over the nature of feminist politics, its tactics, the sources of women's oppression, and the paths for "true" and lasting change have engaged a broad swath of women in an ongoing conversation about what it means for women to be powerful and empowered. The deep tension between change as internal and change as institutional has animated most of these fights. These fights did not begin in 1969, nor have they ended with the emergence of a more individualistic generation. They rage on now with more intensity, and greater consequence, than ever before.

FIGHTING FOR FEMINISM

American culture is obsessed with the girlfight. Images of women fighting are sexualized, sensationalized, and manufactured to titillate—think of the cultural obsession with female mud wrestling. In recent years, women's fighting has become a cottage industry, with movies, studies, and books. In the early 1990s, female fighting became the subject of psychological inquiry, led by Harvard educational psychologist Carol Gilligan and Lyn Mikel Brown.[14] Gilligan stressed the importance of relationships and social networks to girls' development, noting that our fighting is not martial but social, and more backchannel. The girlfight, Gilligan-style, was memorialized in the 1989 Hollywood spoof *Heathers* and explored dramatically in the more recent *Mean Girls*. Books on women's fighting abound. New ones about girl's physical animosity, like *See Jane Fight*, vie for shelf space with earlier explorations of grown women's mutual social aggression, such as Leora Tannenbaum's *Catfight* and Phyllis Chesler's *Woman's Inhumanity to Woman*. The spectacle of moms facing off about their choices in print and online is by now de rigueur. And now, as women slowly rise within the professional ranks, we are reading more and more about competition among women and female fighting at work.[15] But the most publicly celebrated fight remains the one among feminists. Hear us roar.

. . . Feminism has always been a fight, and a public one at that. As media critic Susan Douglas puts it, the American public—or rather, the media—loves a dirty catfight, *Dynasty*-style, where women slog it out in the mud. Yet as Douglas also writes, "The media referees insist on putting feminism in one corner and antifeminism in the other, as if feminism could never be in the middle, but what they fail to recognize is that feminism *is* this middle ground. It may be filled with ambivalence and compromise, tradition and rebellion, but the space between the two cats—the space where we, the girls, are—is what feminism is all about."[16]

A preliminary word on some terms: The word "feminism" came into being in late-nineteenth-century France. It was adopted by a segment of the U.S. movement for women's right to vote in the 1910s, women who sought cultural as well as legal change.

. . . Feminist history is often explained through the metaphor of waves. In the oceanography of the U.S. and British women's movements, "first wave" usually refers to the surge of activism that began in the 1830s and culminated with women's suffrage in 1920 in the United States (1928 in the United Kingdom). To launch their movement, "first wavers" borrowed theories, tactics, and language from the abolitionist debates around them. At the Seneca Falls women's rights convention in 1848, for starters, activists demanded full participation in public and civic life for women, calling for higher education and professional opportunities, the right to divorce, own property, claim inheritance, win custody of children, and vote. In parallel, they worked to enact the Thirteenth Amendment, which abolished slavery in 1865. After 1920, the year the Nineteenth Amendment granted women the right to vote, the first wave is widely assumed to have ebbed. In the following years, the successful "suffragist" coalition scattered and its members joined other social justice and activist causes, including unionization, antipoverty, and antimilitarist campaigns. Daughters of first-wave feminists generally rejected the suffragists' feminism wholesale, and it wasn't until a few generations later that women collectively identified with an organized women's movement again.

The "second wave" describes the resurgence of women's organizing beginning in the mid-1960s and, in the United States, ending—or at least suffering major setbacks—with the defeat of the Equal Rights Amendment and the advent of the Reagan-Bush era. The term was first used by Martha Lear in a 1968 *New York Times* magazine article to connect the new women's movement to the past. Historians of that era tend to refer to two distinct branches of the second-wave movement, alternately characterized by generation ("older" or "younger"), vision ("women's rights" or "women's liberation"), attitude ("liberal/reformist" or "radical/revolutionary"), or mode of organization ("bureaucratic" or "collectivist").[17] The "third wave" generally refers to the period beginning with the Clinton-Gore era in 1993 and continues, though the term is much debated, today.

. . .

Although some of the most vibrant debates about feminism today are now taking place on a global scale, I am amazed at the paucity of histories written about the U.S. women's movement—first, second, or third wave. I am equally amazed at how much in the histories that *do* exist still seems to be news—as, for instance, the fact that sex-positive feminism was part and parcel of the early second wave and not an invention of today's younger generation, or the fact that the idea that women needed their own civil rights organization was first articulated by an African American woman. Gerda Lerner once said that the only constant in feminist history seems to be a constant forgetting of our past. I remain both intrigued and disheartened by the way that past battles over rhetoric and theory (in particular, the question of "What is feminism?") are uncannily reenacted by my own generation—reluctant heiresses of a vision as yet only partially fulfilled.

. . .

Feminism itself has a layered and remarkably cyclical past. From WITCH to *Bitch*—a popular third-wave magazine critiquing a still-sexist culture—much has changed in the world of feminism, its rhetorics, and its fights. But far more has stayed the same. The personal remains political. Women young and old sometimes lose sight of how and why, or fail to see each other as engaged in the same larger battle. Instead, we are left fighting ourselves.

But there is too much at stake to let such fights continue to derail women's continued social, political, and economic evolution. Although women who care about women's collective future may never stop fighting over the means and the methods of change, we can learn to fight with a deeper awareness of shared goals, a greater appreciation of our history, and a greater respect for new ways of doing things.

NOTES

1. In San Francisco, the flyers denounced "mass media images of the pretty, sexy, passive, childlike vacuous woman." See Ruth Rosen, *The World Split Open: How the Modern Women's Movement Changed America*, 205.
2. For an account and criticism of the decline of civic participation and its consequences for politics, see Robert D. Putnam's *Bowling Alone: The Collapse and Revival of American Community*.

3. Fewer single women than married women vote (52 percent as compared to 68 percent in the 2000 election), and more young women today are likely to be single. See "Women's Voices, Women Vote: National Survey Polling Memo," Lake, Snell, and Perry Associates, October 19, 2004.

4. Nancy Cott, *The Grounding of Modern Feminism*, 365, quoting *Judy* 1:1 (June 1919): 2:3.

5. Academics Deborah Rosenfelt and Judith Stacey are also credited for reintroducing the term "postfeminist" during this time. See their "Second Thoughts on the Second Wave," 341–361.

6. Summers's remarks were made at the NBER Conference on Diversifying the Science & Engineering Workforce in Cambridge, Massachusetts on January 14, 2005. At an industry conference in Toronto on October 21, 2005, French said, "Women don't make it to the top because they don't deserve to. They're crap." He added that women inevitably "wimp out and go suckle something." See Tom Leonard, "Advertising Chief Loses Job over French Maid and Sexist Insults."

7. See The White House Project, *Who's Talking Now: A Follow-Up Analysis of Guest Appearances by Women on the Sunday Morning Talk Shows.*

8. For more on the current status of women worldwide, see the National Council for Research on Women, *Gains and Gaps: A Look at the World's Women.*

9. Jennifer Baumgardner and Amy Richards, *ManifestA: Young Women, Feminism, and the Future,* 62.

10. In August 1992, television evangelist Pat Robertson wrote a letter to help raise money to defeat Amendment I, an Iowa ballot initiative that would extend the protections of the state constitution to women. In it, he wrote, "The feminist agenda is not about equal rights for women. It is about a socialist, anti-family political movement that encourages women to leave their husbands, kill their children, practice witchcraft, destroy capitalism and become lesbians." See Maralee Schwartz and Kenneth J. Cooper, "Equal Rights Initiative in Iowa Attacked."

11. Helen Fielding, *Bridget Jones' Diary,* 20; Julie Bosman, "Glamour's Hollywood Side: Films by and About Women"; Akiba Solomon, "Boss Lady," 69.

12. According to the May 2–5, 2005, poll: "College students said 9/11 jolted them out of their complacency about life in general and made them more serious about making a contribution to society through their work." See Celinda Lake and Kellyanne Conway, *What Women Really Want: How American Women Are Quietly Erasing Political, Racial, Class, and Religious Lines to Change the Way We Live,* 163.

13. See Lifetime Women's Pulse Poll, "Generation Why?" March 2006. Generation Y was defined as those aged eighteen to twenty-nine. Generation X, ages thirty to forty-four, and Baby Boomers, age forty-five to fifty-nine. The poll, conducted by Kellyanne Conway and Celinda Lake, looked at women's attitudes regarding sex, men, marriage and career. Center for the Advancement of Women, *Progress and Perils: New Agenda for Women.* Lorraine Dusky, "*Ms.* Poll: Feminist Tide Sweeps in as the 21st Century Begins," 56–61. Young women are most appreciative of the impact of the women's movement on their careers, with 84 percent of those under twenty-five and 85 percent of working women ages twenty-six to thirty reporting a positive effect, according to Business and Professional Women and the Institute for Women's Policy Research, "Working Women Speak Out."

14. See Lyn Mikel Brown and Carol Gilligan, *Meeting at the Crossroads: Women's Psychology and Girls' Development* and Jill McLean Taylor, Carol Gilligan, and Amy M. Sullivan, *Between Voice and Silence: Women and Girls, Race and Relationships.*

15. See, for instance, Beth Brykman, *The Wall Between Women;* Leslie Morgan Steiner, *Mommy Wars;* and Nan Mooney, *I Can't Believe She Did That! Women Sabotaging Women at Work.*

16. Susan Douglas, *Where the Girls Are: Growing Up Female with the Mass Media,* 244.

17. See Joan Cassell, *A Group Called Women: Sisterhood and Symbolism in the Feminist Movement;* Jo Freeman, "The Origins of the Women's Liberation Movement," and *The Politics of Women's Liberation;* J. Rothschild-Whitt, "The Collectivist Organization: An Alternative to Rational-Bureaucratic Models"; and Myra Marx Ferree and Beth B. Hess, *Controversy and Coalition: The New Feminist Movement Across Four Decades of Change,* esp. 58–59.

Feminist Politics
Where We Stand

bell hooks (2000)

Simply put, feminism is a movement to end sexism, sexist exploitation, and oppression. This was a definition of feminism I offered in *Feminist Theory: From Margin to Center* more than 10 years ago. It was my hope at the time that it would become a common definition everyone would use. I liked this definition because it did not imply that men were the enemy. By naming sexism as the problem it went directly to the heart of the matter. Practically, it is a definition which implies that all sexist thinking and action is the problem, whether those who perpetuate it are female or male, child or adult. It is also broad enough to include an understanding of systemic institutionalized sexism. As a definition it is open-ended. To understand feminism it implies one has to necessarily understand sexism.

As all advocates of feminist politics know, most people do not understand sexism, or if they do, they think it is not a problem. Masses of people think that feminism is always and only about women seeking to be equal to men. And a huge majority of these folks think feminism is anti-male. Their misunderstanding of feminist politics reflects the reality that most folks learn about feminism from patriarchal mass media. The feminism they hear about the most is portrayed by women who are primarily committed to gender equality—equal pay for equal work, and sometimes women and men sharing household chores and parenting. They see that these women are usually white and materially privileged. They know from mass media that women's liberation focuses on the freedom to have abortions, to be lesbians, to challenge rape and domestic violence. Among these issues, masses of people agree with the idea of gender equity in the workplace—equal pay for equal work.

Since our society continues to be primarily a "Christian" culture, masses of people continue to believe that god has ordained that women be subordinate to men in the domestic household. Even though masses of women have entered the workforce, even though many families are headed by women who are the sole breadwinners, the vision of domestic life which continues to dominate the nation's imagination is one in which the logic of male domination is intact, whether men are present in the home or not. The wrongminded notion of feminist movement which implied it was anti-male carried with it the wrongminded assumption that all female space would necessarily be an environment where patriarchy and sexist thinking would be absent. Many women, even those involved in feminist politics, chose to believe this as well.

There was indeed a great deal of anti-male sentiment among early feminist activists who were responding to male domination with anger. It was that anger at injustice that was the impetus for creating a women's liberation movement. Early on most feminist activists (a majority of whom were white) had their consciousness raised about the nature of male domination when they were working in anti-classist and anti-racist settings with men who were telling the world about the importance of freedom while subordinating the women in their ranks. Whether it was white women working on behalf of socialism, black women working on behalf of civil rights and black liberation, or Native American women working for indigenous rights, it was clear that men wanted to lead, and they wanted women to follow. Participating in these radical freedom struggles awakened the spirit of rebellion and resistance in progressive females and led them towards contemporary women's liberation.

As contemporary feminism progressed, as women realized that males were not the only group in our society who supported sexist thinking and behavior—that females could be sexist as well—anti-male sentiment no longer shaped the movement's consciousness. The focus shifted to an all-out effort to create gender justice. But women could not band together to further feminism without confronting our sexist thinking. Sisterhood could not be powerful as long as women were competitively at war with one another. Utopian visions of sisterhood based solely on the awareness of the reality that all women were in some way victimized by male domination were disrupted by discussions of class and race. Discussions of class differences occurred early on in contemporary feminism, preceding discussions of race. Diana Press published revolutionary insights about class divisions between women as early as the mid-'70s in their collection of essays *Class and Feminism*. These discussions did not trivialize the feminist insistence that "sisterhood is powerful," they simply emphasized that we could only become sisters in struggle by confronting the ways women—through sex, class, and race—dominated and exploited other women, and created a political platform that would address these differences.

Even though individual black women were active in contemporary feminist movement from its inception, they were not the individuals who became the "stars" of the movement, who attracted the attention of mass media. Often individual black women active in feminist movement were revolutionary feminists (like many white lesbians). They were already at odds with reformist feminists who resolutely wanted to project a vision of the movement as being solely about women gaining equality with men in the existing system. Even before race became a talked about issue in feminist circles it was clear to black women (and to their revolutionary allies in struggle) that they were never going to have

equality within the existing white supremacist capitalist patriarchy.

From its earliest inception feminist movement was polarized. Reformist thinkers chose to emphasize gender equality. Revolutionary thinkers did not want simply to alter the existing system so that women would have more rights. We wanted to transform that system, to bring an end to patriarchy and sexism. Since patriarchal mass media was not interested in the more revolutionary vision, it never received attention in mainstream press. The vision of "women's liberation" which captured and still holds the public imagination was the one representing women as wanting what men had. And this was the vision that was easier to realize. Changes in our nation's economy, economic depression, the loss of jobs, etc., made the climate ripe for our nation's citizens to accept the notion of gender equality in the workforce.

Given the reality of racism, it made sense that white men were more willing to consider women's rights when the granting of those rights could serve the interests of maintaining white supremacy. We can never forget that white women began to assert their need for freedom after civil rights, just at the point when racial discrimination was ending and black people, especially black males, might have attained equality in the workforce with white men. Reformist feminist thinking focusing primarily on equality with men in the workforce overshadowed the original radical foundations of contemporary feminism which called for reform as well as overall restructuring of society so that our nation would be fundamentally anti-sexist.

Most women, especially privileged white women, ceased even to consider revolutionary feminist visions, once they began to gain economic power within the existing social structure. Ironically, revolutionary feminist thinking was most accepted and embraced in academic circles. In those circles the production of revolutionary feminist theory progressed, but more often than not that theory was not made available to the public. It became and remains a privileged discourse available to those among us who are highly literate, well-educated, and usually materially privileged. Works like *Feminist Theory: From Margin to Center* that offer a liberatory vision of feminist transformation never receive mainstream attention. Masses of people have not heard of this book. They have not rejected its message; they do not know what the message is.

While it was in the interest of mainstream white supremacist capitalist patriarchy to suppress visionary feminist thinking which was not anti-male or concerned with getting women the right to be like men, reformist feminists were also eager to silence these forces. Reformist feminism became their route to class mobility. They could break free of male domination in the workforce and be more self-determining in their lifestyles. While sexism did not end, they could maximize their freedom within the existing system. And they could count on there being a lower class of exploited subordinated women to do the dirty work they were refusing to do. By accepting and indeed colluding with the subordination of working-class and poor women, they not only ally themselves with the existing patriarchy and its concomitant sexism, they give themselves the right to lead a double life, one where they are the equals of men in the workforce and at home when they want to be. If they choose lesbianism they have the privilege of being equals with men in the workforce while using class power to create domestic lifestyles where they can choose to have little or no contact with men.

Lifestyle feminism ushered in the notion that there could be as many versions of feminism as there were women. Suddenly the politics was being slowly removed from feminism. And the assumption prevailed that no matter what a woman's politics, be she conservative or liberal, she too could fit feminism into her existing lifestyle. Obviously this way of thinking has made feminism more acceptable because its underlying assumption is that women can be feminists without fundamentally challenging and changing themselves or the culture. For example, let's take the issue of abortion. If feminism is a movement to end sexist oppression, and depriving females of reproductive rights is a form of sexist oppression, then one cannot be anti-choice and be feminist. A woman can insist she would never choose to have an abortion while affirming her support of the right of women to choose and still be an advocate of feminist politics. She cannot be anti-abortion and an advocate of feminism. Concurrently there can be no such thing as "power feminism" if the vision of power evoked is power gained through the exploitation and oppression of others.

Feminist politics is losing momentum because feminist movement has lost clear definitions. We have those definitions. Let's reclaim them. Let's share them. Let's start over. Let's have T-shirts and bumper stickers and postcards and hip-hop music, television and radio commercials, ads everywhere and billboards, and all manner of printed material that tells the world about feminism. We can share the simple yet powerful message that feminism is a movement to end sexist oppression. Let's start there. Let the movement begin again.

We Are Using This Power to Resist

Rebecca Walker (2004)

Life is plurality, death is uniformity.

—*Octavio Paz*

I

Imagine. It's 1992, and I am a graduating senior at Yale University, the school my mother warned me about. I have spent much of my time there protesting: the university's investment in South Africa under apartheid, the paucity of students and faculty of color, the racist-sexist-classist-homophobic characterization and content of my courses. I have attended speak-outs against date rape and sexual harassment and for the creation of a teachers' union, and sat on the founding board of the first paper to bring together voices from the Asian and Asian-American, African and African-American, Native American, Puerto Rican, and Mexican-American communities under the controversial new term "people of color." For two years I have been directing a documentary on these same "people of color," looking at socioeconomic and ideological diversity among allegedly monolithic communities. When I am not reading queer theorists like Judith Butler (fluidity and performative aspects of gender and sexuality) and cultural critics like Michel Foucault (hegemony and the language of power), or studying with bell hooks (the white supremacist capitalist patriarchy), I am waiting in line to hear the Dalai Lama. When I am not reading Paolo Freire (*Pedagogy of the Oppressed*) and Thich Nhat Hanh (*Peace Is Every Step*), I am being dismissed from lecture halls for asking world-renowned professors why their classes are called The History of Art and not The History of White Western Male Art, and why African women are viciously murdered in so many "postcolonial" texts. When I am not reading Audre Lorde (*Sister Outsider*) and Trinh T. Minh-ha (*Woman, Native, Other*), I am talking with brilliant young black female poets who speak of suicide, and soulful Lebanese philosophers who speak angrily and with great longing of Beirut before the invasion.

Outside my ivory tower, rampant police brutality has been captured on home video (LAPD versus Rodney King), Bush I has signed legislation which continues to erode access to reproductive choice to all but the well-heeled and urban (the gag rule, twenty-four-hour notification, and parental consent laws), AIDS deaths mount while the acronym never crosses the administration's lips, and environmental racism perpetuates the dumping of runoff toxins from power plants and factories into poor urban and rural communities around the country. Though it is pre-NAFTA, pre-GATT, and pre-WTO, there are still plenty of international abominations in play—the invasion and interminable bombing of Iraq, for example, and the burgeoning number of women laboring under intolerable conditions at the *maquiladoras,* for another.

Even though almost everyone I know is involved in some form of social change work, from teaching after-school programs for disadvantaged kids to building houses for poor people in inner cities and starting "cheap art" revolutions à la the Guerrilla Girls, the media scream incessantly that ours is the most apathetic and least politicized of any known generation. Feminism is dead, the civil rights movement is not happening, communism is taking its last gasp, and educated twenty-somethings, traditionally the most radical of all demographics, are apparently content to sit back and reap the benefits of our parents' world-changing labor. While some young activists are able to use this distinction to their advantage, incorporating the need to contradict the media into their mission statements, the public hears that the racist, capitalist status quo is acceptable: even the youth have acquiesced.

While my community includes queer-fabulous Chicanos and ACT UP–affiliated lipstick lesbians, budding black revolutionaries and brilliant baby art stars, neo-utopian Marxist bohemians and well-meaning trust-fund recluses, sensuously defiant womanists and politicized Muslim academics, it seems a rare event to see any of these individuals breaking rank and communicating meaningfully with one another. I certainly never see this happening within the walls of the campus Women's Center, and it's not because I haven't looked. I enter this cramped home of Feminism on the Old Campus once as a freshman and once again as a sophomore, both times looking for resonance and both times finding only the now-too-often cited group of well-off white women, organizing Take Back the Night marches and lectures on eating disorders, neither of which, in the face of all that is going on, manages to capture my imagination.

I am not alone in my assessment that capital *F* Feminism needs an overhaul. By 1992 Feminism has been roundly critiqued by the majority of the world's women, including but not limited to indigenous women, Third World women, American women of color, and working-class women. Even among the privileged and/or converted, there is a resistance to identifying with its rebel yell. Sure, there are those "I am not a feminist but . . ." girls who don't have a clue, but then there are the rest of us, who are feminist but not Feminists. We came to our radical consciousness in the heady postmodern matrix of womanist texts, queer culture, postcolonialist discourse, Buddhism, direct action, sex positivity, and so much more. We are intimate with racist feminists, sexist postcolonialists, and theorists who are so far removed from the street they can't organize their own

wallets, let alone a rally. We find that the nexuses of power and identity are constantly shifting, and so are we. We find that labels which seek to categorize and define are historical constructs often used as tools of oppression. We find that many of our potential allies in resistance movements do feminism but do not, intuitively, embrace Feminism.

In the context of all this, to call oneself a Feminist without a major disclaimer seems not only reductive but counterproductive. While this complexity makes for meetings full of fervor and supreme sensitivity to differences of all kinds, it also leaves many of us at the forefront of a movement with no name.

II

Shannon Liss, a young organizer of the Anita Hill conference in New York City, reads an article I have written in *Ms.* magazine titled "Becoming the Third Wave" and telephones me in New Haven to ask if I might be interested in doing something together. In fact, I have been trying to figure out how to organize the two hundred or so young women from around the country who have written me passionate letters echoing my sentiments that "I am not a post-feminism feminist, I am the third wave." To what organization can I refer them? What books can I suggest they read? The book that you are holding in your hands did not exist. There are no articles in *Ms.* magazine about young women doing brave new things. There is not yet a W.E.R.I.S.E., a Black Grrrl Movement, a Shakti, a Third Wave Foundation, an Active Element Foundation. There has not been a "Just do it" Nike campaign for women, an Urban Outfitters chain catering to the earthy, funky DIY young woman, and no WTO protests flying in the face of both. There has been no twenty-something-year-old Julia Butterfly Hill living in a tree for a year to protect it from loggers and then writing a best-selling memoir about the experience. There is no WNBA. Politicians are not trying to win our vote on MTV. There is bell hooks, Queen Latifah, Susie Bright, and the Indigo Girls, but there is no Erykah Badu, no India.Arie, no Ani DiFranco, no asha bandele, no La Bruja on Def Jam Poetry Slam.

In our first of many marathon conversations, Shannon brings her organizing acumen and knowledge of the "Gen X" activism she sees in New York and contextualizes the article and its response within something larger. I bring all of my frustration with identity politics, all of my desires to do social change work that is vibrant and creative and not prone to divisive infighting. Three or four estrogen-packed, burrito-and-margarita-filled meetings later, we decide to found a direct action organization devoted to cultivating young women's leadership and activism in order to bring the power of young women to bear on politics as usual. We want to flex the muscle of young women's might, to make it visible not just to the media and the progressive left but also to the older female activists whose lives have so profoundly shaped our own.

From our first conversation we know that Third Wave Direct Action Corporation will be multiracial, multicultural, and multi-issue. It will consist of people of varying abilities and sexual preferences. It will include men. We hope it will be international. While we have strong opinions about what issues we want to begin to work around, we believe strongly that young women and men will articulate their own concerns, and that it is not our job to decide which are worthy of being included. Our job is to support young activists in whatever ways we can, by connecting them to resources, tools, or most important, one another. The young woman who wants to organize against sweatshop labor or homophobia or toxic dumping in her backyard can call and be connected to other young women with similar foci; groups of young women and men can start chapters (independently acting cells), which can be mobilized for a product boycott, an action, a support group. Because we believe that change is also internal, we plan to initiate projects that bring people of different backgrounds and perspectives together; participants will unite around a common

agenda, working interpersonally through issues of difference in the process and learning how to build communities based on mutual respect and understanding.

We pride ourselves on being utopic but also pragmatic. We want to extend the parameters of the "feminist" community and include even those who do not identify with Feminism, and so we make a conscious decision to avoid the use of the word in our mission statement, press releases, and other organizing materials, choosing instead to use "young women's empowerment." We want to be linked with our foremothers and centuries of women's movement, but we also want to make space for young women to create their own, different brand of revolt, and so we choose the name Third Wave. We don't want to be exploited in the name of social change, and so we vow to factor salaries for ourselves into our budgets and call ourselves a corporation. We do not want to be marginalized as we have seen so many activist groups become, and so we vow, too, to be unafraid of both large sums of money and the media, and aggressively seek both out, determined to market our empowerment message.

I speak of marketing social change, and actually feel hopeful when young advertising executives show up at my talks armed with yellow legal pads. They peer at my seemingly incongruous work boots and short dresses, my suit jackets and long dreadlocks, and ask me questions about how young women want to see themselves in the media. I am young and naïve enough to believe that these smart and fresh-faced white women are only on our side, and that by marketing us to ourselves they will help young woman–power of all kinds to grow.

III

What I don't know then is that even though there is no Us and Them, and we need to move beyond binarism and labels and to have compassion for all, including the heads of heinous multinational corporations and the executives at the IMF, the truth is that there is a clear line in the sand. That line is global hypercapitalism, that line is greed, that line is human exploitation, that line is the utter disregard for the delicate balance of the earth. Either you believe that the system that ensures 50 percent of the world's resources for 6 percent of its population by any and all means necessary is leading us to annihilation one cancer case at a time, or you do not. Whether or not you are able to act in opposition to this reality in every instance is beside the point. Do you see it?

What I [didn't] understand in 1992 is that it is this line that separates a system designed to colonize and homogenize from one that seeks to honor and cultivate the diversity that is our birthright as human beings. Those of us who dare, toil not to force our way upon others but simply to make a space in which all are honored: capitalism and communalism, the patriarch and the matriarch, the exiled settler and the indigenous nomad, and so on. It is this imperative for true pluralism that runs through and connects, however tenuously, all of our different activisms, all of our different feminisms. It is this place where we all may rest that snakes through our dreams. We can barely imagine now what this world fueled by real right to self-determination will look like, and yet we know it must be born. As we belong to it, this planet must belong to all of us.

While I believe that Shannon and I were right about some things—decentralized, multifront, multilingual, and multi-aesthetic movement for one, and working with men and families for another—we were wrong about some other things, like the very real risk of our own complacency, our own tendency to get more cynical and pessimistic with age, more removed from the cultural and political work there is to be done instead of more radical. I think that we were right about pushing our sensibility and ideas into the marketplace of the mainstream but we were shortsighted in that we did not anticipate that

young women and men would think buying books or magazines, or supporting films and fashion that reflected their diverse beauty and beliefs, could replace the many important struggles still to be waged against an unjust system. And finally, while we were right to found an organization, we had no idea just how much effort and endurance was necessary to build an institution, let alone a movement.

Third Wave Direct Action had a fairly successful run spearheading projects, building a national network, and raising awareness about the existence of some incredible young women. Ultimately, however, then-Chairwoman of the Board Amy Richards and I decided to reenvision its original scope and, with the cofounders Catherine Gund and Dawn Lundy Martin, to throw ourselves into the Third Wave Foundation, the only national, activist, philanthropic organization serving women aged fifteen to thirty. In other words, we realized we had to get out of the business of direct action and into the business of redistributing wealth, of moving it from one side of the line to the other. We had to get real about what was essential and what we, a group of privileged, educated women born and raised in the United States, could provide.

And yet, I cannot adequately describe here the tremendous pride and gratitude I feel in the knowledge that our dreams for revitalized, multipronged movement are being realized. Whether the work is called third wave, young feminism, hip-hop womanism, humanist global activism, or anything else matters very little. What matters is that this work is being done by women and men from various communities who slowly, step by step, find themselves working alongside those who previously may have been seen only as Other.

There is a fire this time, burning, and it cannot, will not, go out, because that would mean the end of life as we know it. And we, those of us who love this planet and one another, are not yet ready to let that happen.

The Global Stage and the Politics of Location

Estelle B. Freedman (2002)

To talk feminism to a woman who has no water, no food and no home is to talk nonsense.

—NGO Forum '80, Denmark, 1980

Everything is a woman's issue.

—Charlotte Bunch, United States, 1985

In her 1984 essay "Notes Toward a Politics of Location," the American poet Adrienne Rich reevaluated her earlier use of the category "woman" in light of the writings of women of color. Acknowledging her own "politics of location" as a North American, white, Jewish lesbian, Rich named "the faceless, raceless classless category of all women as a creation of white, western, self-centered women." Because national and political location affected women throughout the world, Rich reconsidered Virginia Woolf's statement that "as a woman I have no country; as a woman my country is the whole world." One's country, she suggested, deeply influenced one's view of the world and of womanhood.[1]

Other Western feminists, stimulated by women of color and women outside the West, were also recognizing the "politics of location." In 1978, for example, a special issue of the radical feminist journal *Quest* on international feminism asked readers, "Can we talk about the global oppression of women—its causes and lives—in any universal terms?" In an influential 1988 essay, sociologist Chandra Mohanty argued persuasively against the Western feminist assumption of "a commonality of the category of women."[2] Mohanty called on Western feminists to understand how local contexts created gender relations that differed from those in the West. Neither oppression nor liberation looked the same from the perspective of women in Asia, Africa, Latin America, and the Middle East. Just as women of color transformed U.S. feminism, so too exchanges across nations placed Western women's rights movements within the contexts of racial and social justice as well as national sovereignty.

. . .

In addition, international organizations provided a forum for both communication and conflict among diverse women's movements. A key locus of these discussions was the Decade for Women, declared by the United Nations from 1975 to 1985. Subsequent regional and international gatherings, including the UN's Fourth World Conference on Women, held in Beijing in 1995, facilitated transnational feminist organizing across regions. By the end of the twentieth century, women's movements had expanded to all parts of the world—in rural and urban settings, in liberal or conservative states. From a history of colonial encounters to a growing transnational movement, the politics of location have taken both common and diverse paths to gender equality.

. . .

THE ORIGINS OF INTERNATIONAL FEMINISM

Because diverse local contexts forged women's politics, early efforts to create an international movement faced formidable challenges. European and U.S. feminists had corresponded and met since the 1840s. Beginning in the 1880s they built organizations to promote goals ranging from temperance and pacifism to socialism and suffrage. Until World War I, the movement was international in name only. Western European and American women initiated the groups and then encouraged local chapters to form in other parts of the world. As European world domination declined after the war, however, women in Latin America, Asia, and Africa increasingly took part in the International Woman Suffrage Alliance, the International Council of Women, and the Women's International League for Peace and Freedom. The leadership remained dominated by elite, white, Christian women from northern and western Europe. Anti-Semitism placed limits on the roles of European Jewish women, while Huda Sha'arawi from Egypt was the only Muslim among leaders of the suffrage alliance. Significantly, although Sha'arawi aligned with Western feminists on suffrage, she chastised these allies when they supported colonialism. Aware of the limitations of European women's "universalism," she also fostered pan-Arab women's movements, including the establishment of the regional Arab Feminist Union in 1945.

The earliest efforts to create an international women's movement often reproduced colonial relations. When European women spoke of aiding "primitives," for example, they relied on the same stereotypes of passive, helpless others that characterized missionary and colonialist rhetoric. Just as women of color within the United States challenged white feminists to recognize their racial biases, so too women from Asia, Africa, and the Middle East took issue with what scholars later termed "feminist orientalism," the tendency to view all women outside the West as exotic, sexually oppressed others.[3] In 1920 black women from the United States and Africa responded to comments demeaning to them by forming the International Council of Women of the Darker Races. At an international conference in 1935, Shareefeh Hamid Ali of India spoke for women "of the East" when she explained to "you of the west" that "any arrogant assumption of superiority or of patronage on the part of Europe or America" would alienate "the womanhood of Asia and Africa."[4] These women expected support from Western feminists in their dual struggle for personal and national independence.

Some Western feminists understood that they could learn a great deal from other women, many of whom already enjoyed privileges not available in Europe and North America. In the early 1900s the *Jus Suffragii*, the international suffrage journal, reported on the economic and political rights that women enjoyed as traders in Africa or as municipal voters in Burma. The U.S. suffrage leader Carrie Chapman Catt could be patronizing about the need to "uplift" women outside the West, but she also recognized that millions of these women "have always enjoyed more personal freedom than was accorded to most European women a century ago, and more than is now permitted to thousands of women under our boasted Western civilization."[5] Articles in the suffrage journal also pointed out how European efforts had eroded women's customary authority, and they acknowledged that Islam was not necessarily oppressive to women. Eventually the international women's movement recognized that women outside the West were perfectly capable of establishing their own women's movements, which could meet on equal terms with European and American organizations.

Most of the European women involved in international feminist organizing espoused liberal goals of educational, property, and voting rights; many shared maternalist sympathies for improving women's family lives through temperance and antiprostitution movements. In addition, socialist women influenced international movements, largely in those countries with strong Marxist politics. The Socialist Women's International organized by Clara Zetkin in 1907 favored woman suffrage for all classes along with social justice. After World War II a Communist Party women's international backed by Moscow raised women's issues but avoided the word *feminist*.

World War II represented a turning point for women's organizing, as it did for international relations generally. Aside from women's cooperative relief efforts, the war gave rise to political institutions, such as the United Nations, that fostered international feminism. In the decades after the war, the rhetoric of democratic rights first articulated two centuries earlier during the European Enlightenment extended far beyond its original geographic boundaries. The remaining colonial empires soon gave way to independent states. This expansion of the ideals of human rights had important implications for both the former colonies and women's movements.

Despite the extension of national self-determination beyond the West, the postcolonial world faced huge economic disparities. Former colonies, termed the "Third World," "developing nations," or the "South," remained dependent on the advanced industrial nations for financial and technological investments. They also became a battleground in the Cold War struggle for alliance with either the "First World" of the West or the "Second World" of the Communist bloc. True independence—for countries or for individuals—required not only national sovereignty but also economic stability and international security.

The United Nations provided a potential global forum for discussing human rights, economic justice, and international security. The 1945 UN charter incorporated both Enlightenment ideals and the language of liberal feminism when it reaffirmed "faith in fundamental human rights, in the dignity and worth of the human person, in the equal rights of men and women." The document repeatedly called for rights, freedoms, and respect for all "without distinctions to race, sex, language, or religion."

In 1947, as part of its mechanisms to foster economic and social progress, the UN established the Commission on the Status of Women. Two years later the General Assembly agreed upon the Declaration of Human Rights, which applied the principle of equal rights to thought, opinions, privacy, education, work, leisure, and peace. Significantly, it also incorporated the domestic concerns of maternalist reformers such as Eleanor Roosevelt, who provided the driving force behind its adoption. Along with adult men and women sharing "equal rights as to marriage, during marriage and at its dissolution," the declaration proclaimed that "motherhood and childhood are entitled to special care and assistance," whether a child was born "in or out of wedlock."[6] However idealistic these pronouncements, the

UN has had a wide-reaching practical impact on the kinds of health and welfare issues long championed by maternalist reformers. Nongovernmental organizations (NGOs) such as the World Health Organization (WHO) and the United Nations International Children's Emergency Fund (UNICEF) have both channeled aid and nurtured cross-cultural communication among those concerned about the status of women.

These networks expanded after the UN declared 1975 to be International Women's Year, launching the Decade for Women. Three international conferences on women's issues punctuated the decade. Delegates from 133 nations gathered in Mexico City in 1975; in 1980, 145 nations were represented in Copenhagen; and in 1985 representatives from 157 countries met in Nairobi. These conferences provided a critical intersection where Western feminists encountered the political and material realities of women's lives outside the West.

Although a majority of the participants were women, men dominated the speeches and leadership at Mexico City in 1975. The official delegates often represented the interests of their governments, not necessarily those of women's organizations. At Copenhagen, for example, a male delegate from the USSR declared that there was no discrimination against women in the Soviet Union because the law forbade such discrimination, and there was no such thing as sexism in his country because there was no such word in the Russian language. As women at the UN pressed for equality, however, the conferences included more female leadership and the discussions turned to the gaps between male and female opportunities.

Equally important, women from around the world who were not official delegates gathered at parallel meetings held during each of the UN conferences. A tribune outside the Mexico City meeting attracted six thousand activists; the forums at Copenhagen and Nairobi grew from ten thousand in 1980 to fifteen thousand in 1985. Though Western-dominated at first, 65 percent of the participants at Nairobi came from developing countries, and women of color from the West now played leading roles. With no formal governmental agendas, these forums provided opportunities for intense communications, at times quite heated. Representatives of NGOs ran workshops and panels to share their efforts to combat poverty, violence against women, female genital cutting, and illiteracy. Each topic provoked conflict over political strategies. In Copenhagen women spontaneously organized sessions every day, such as one sponsored by Norwegian women called "Sisterhood—A Myth?" A daily free newspaper announced workshops and criticized the politics of the official conference, whose delegates could not avoid the radical ferment around them.

The political tensions that reverberated through each meeting reflected the imbalance of power between advanced industrial and developing nations. When U.S. feminists arrived in Mexico City to talk about equal rights, for example, they immediately encountered criticism from delegates who did not want to discuss gender outside the context of movements for national self-determination. The U.S. government did not want the politics of apartheid in South Africa or the Israeli-Palestinian conflict on the agenda. Greek delegate Margaret Papandreou called this U.S. position "antifeminist" for trying to separate politics from women's issues.[7]

At the NGO forums women did debate international politics as well as economic development policies. Western feminists arrived with a focus on equal rights to education, property, and political authority. For women from Asia, Africa, and Latin America, however, rural and urban poverty represented the most pressing challenges to human rights. "To talk feminism to a woman who has no water, no food and no home is to talk nonsense," the *NGO Forum* newspaper at Copenhagen explained.[8] Responding to this sentiment, the 1985 NGO Forum in Nairobi convened workshops to discuss the variety of regional contexts that feminism must address.

The exchanges at the official UN conference and the unofficial NGO meetings proved highly educational for Western feminists. Delegates learned about the daily problems that confronted women globally: living under apartheid in South Africa; struggling for self-determination in Palestine; bringing water, sewers, and electricity to poor Brazilian women; trying to feed families throughout the world. The NGO gatherings especially convinced many Western women that world poverty and national liberation were feminist issues because they affected women's lives around the globe. After attending the Copenhagen conference, Charlotte Bunch, a radical lesbian feminist in the United States during the 1970s, began to address international women's issues. In preparing for the 1985 NGO forum in Nairobi, she came to the conclusion that "the beginning point at both conferences must be that *everything* is a woman's issue. That means racism is a woman's issue, just as is anti-Semitism, Palestinian homelessness, rural development, ecology, the persecution of lesbians, and the exploitative practices of global corporations."[9]

Women from developing nations also felt the profound effects of these conferences. Valsa Verghese, who came from India to attend the Copenhagen conference, initially felt "frustration and confusion" at the multitude of choices at the NGO Forum. By the end she found it "heartening to realize that in spite of cultural differences there was so much in common to unite us, to feel the bond of sisterhood, to break the isolation of women and to feel the growing power within us."[10] The meetings also exposed women to the potential of feminism for their own local politics. A Latin American woman who was "not at all interested in feminism" before attending the Copenhagen conference wrote that "after seeing how governments and the UN treat women and what has and has not happened in the Forum, I am now considering the potential of feminism seriously."[11]

. . .

RETHINKING FEMINISM IN THE POSTCOLONIAL WORLD

Creating a transnational women's movement requires that feminists overcome the legacies of colonialism. That challenging task means reaching across cultures without imposing Western notions of superiority and acknowledging the multiple forms that both injustice and emancipation may take. Two international issues embody the tensions inherent in women's global encounters. The first, international development programs, highlights the dilemmas of liberal feminist politics, which founder over the role of gender difference in efforts to achieve gender equality. The second, the notion of "global feminism," highlights the weaknesses of both liberalism and a radical feminism that overlooks class and race distinctions among women. Both serve as reminders that economic and political strategies must take into account the particular strengths of women's local heritage.

During the 1970s and 1980s the United Nations and other international organizations began to rethink the role of women in economic development programs. The international efforts to stimulate economic growth in the developing regions begun after World War II had failed to undermine the extensive poverty in these countries. Along with the earlier goal of expanding national productivity, UN agencies turned their attention to the growing inequalities of wealth. The impoverishment of women represented a major obstacle to economic justice, and the UN Decade for Women provided a forum for reviewing development policy through the lens of gender.

In *Woman's Role in Economic Development* (1970) Ester Boserup argued that most development programs had failed to take into account women's productive roles. In the rush to increase productivity in developing nations, planners and lenders such as the World Bank and the International Monetary Fund concentrated on male workers. Foreign aid provided men with land, credit, and tools and expected wives to provide domestic labor. As a result, the gender gap in technology, wealth, and status widened. Describing West Africa in the mid-twentieth century, Boserup observed that "men ride the bicycle and drive the lorry, while women carry head loads, as did their grandmothers. In short, men represent modern farm-

ing in the village, women represent the old drudgery."[12] When development programs considered women at all it was usually in their capacity as mothers targeted by family planning efforts to reduce population growth.

In the past, African women had contributed to the economy, especially as producers of food. Boserup and other scholars wanted to integrate rural women into new forms of production through education and training. A school of thought termed Women in Development (WID) made the case that full economic development required a recognition of women's contributions to the economy and their integration into production. Rather than viewing women as dependents in families, WID argued, they should be encouraged to generate income, either as small entrepreneurs or as factory laborers.

WID advocates helped extend modernization policies to women in the developing regions by drawing women into the market economy. As several scholars have noted, WID represented "liberal feminism writ global," for it rested upon liberal values of individualism, self-interest, and private property.[13] To an extent, this approach succeeded in adding gender to the policy debates on international development. In practical terms, WID also laid the groundwork for the influx of young Latin American and Asian women into manufacturing jobs in the free-trade zones where multinational corporations established factories. It also lent support for efforts to educate girls.

Even as international development programs began to integrate women into national productivity goals, criticisms of WID emerged. The South Asian feminist scholar Naila Kabeer summarized the problem: WID recognized women's productive potential at the expense of appreciating their unpaid work in the household. Ignoring reproductive and household labor placed women in a double bind. Women workers could not earn enough money to purchase the household and child care services they needed in order to be able to leave their homes to work for pay. By assuming a similarity between female and male workers, WID overlooked important differences, particularly the realities of motherhood. Without taking into account both women's biological capacity for childbearing and the structural inequalities of race and class, WID could not contribute to solving the problems of women's, and world, poverty.

Moreover, simply mobilizing women as workers did not necessarily empower them, a lesson that women of color in the West long realized. In her study of Malaysian factory workers, anthropologist Aihwa Ong concluded that these women may have exchanged patriarchal control within their families for industrial surveillance and discipline in the factory. As one worker complained of her foremen, "They give this job, that job, and even before my task is done they say do that, do this, and before that is ready, they say do some other work." In the words of another Malaysian factory worker, "It would be nice working here if the foremen, managers, all the staff members and clerks understand that the workers are not under their control."[14]

The flaws of merely drawing women into the labor force became apparent by the end of the UN Decade for Women. During the period when WID policies dominated, women's economic resources had declined, not improved. In response to the shortcomings of WID, feminists recommended a new approach known as Gender and Development, or GAD. Since the 1980s GAD advocates have attempted to take into account women's customary economic and family responsibilities when they implement development policies. GAD addresses issues such as the relationships of men and women to natural resources and the impact of male migration on women's work and responsibilities. Rather than exclude women from, or integrate them into, a male model, the GAD approach builds upon rural women's practices, such as their traditional knowledge about agriculture. In projects that recognize female expertise in native plant diversity, development agencies turn to local women as authorities for seed selection. As Mona Khalaf, of the Institute for Women's Studies in the Arab World in Beirut, Lebanon, explains, GAD has broadened development analysis to discuss "sus-

tainable human development, a development achieved by people and not for them."[15] The UN has adopted the goal of "stimulating growth with equity" by providing resources to both women and men in sustainable development projects.

[Another] feminist dilemma concerns the controversial notion of a "universal sisterhood" that presumes the relevance of Western politics to the rest of the world, regardless of local conditions. In Amrita Basu's terms, the "challenge of local feminisms" complicates sisterhood.[16] Although patriarchy may subordinate women all over the world, as a group of African women scholars explains, "women are also members of classes and countries that dominate others. . . . Contrary to the best intentions of 'sisterhood,' not all women share identical interests."[17] Just as women of color in the West testified about their racially specific identities, women outside the West have explained why gender cannot be the sole determinant of their politics. Peasant and working-class women in Africa, Asia, and Latin America have been adamant that for them, economic justice, along with cultural and national sovereignty, must become a priority of feminism. In contrast to European and North American drives for individual rights, these local activists often stress women's domestic identities and the needs of family and community. At times they turn to innovative cooperative structures rather than purely individualistic ones, building upon women's mutual support networks.

. . .

Western feminist politics achieved its earliest victories by calling for the extension to women of men's growing political and economic rights. Transnational women's movements recognize as well the political importance of alternative strategies that draw on women's heritage of raising their families, maintaining their cultures, and empowering themselves. Women throughout the world developed these survival skills under patriarchy; before a politics of rights, they often relied on reciprocal family and social obligations to maintain a balance of power between men and women. By insisting on adequate care for women's families, these strategies complement equal rights arguments and broaden the reach of women's movements.

REDEFINING FEMINISM

By the end of the UN Decade for Women, women in the developing world had redefined feminism, rejecting the myth of global sisterhood in favor of a more heterogeneous and flexible framework. As participants at the Nairobi conference explained in 1985, feminism "constitutes the political expression of the concerns and interests of women from different regions, classes, nationalities, and ethnic backgrounds. . . . There is and must be a diversity of feminisms, responsive to the different needs and concerns of different women, and defined by them for themselves."[18] For Western women, the myth of global sisterhood had to give way to the politics of location. The result has been a more realistic notion of transnational feminism. In this model, an understanding of historical and cultural differences among women provides the base for alliances across those differences.

NOTES

1. Adrienne Rich, "Notes Towards a Politics of Location," *Blood, Bread, and Poetry* (New York W. W. Norton, 1986), 210–31.
2. Chandra Mohanty, "Under Western Eyes: Feminist Scholarship and Colonial Discourses," *Feminist Review* 30 (1988), 61–85.
3. Joyce Zonana, "The Sultan and the Slave: Feminist Orientalism and the Structure of *Jane Eyre*," *Signs* 18:3 (1993), 592–617; Leila Rupp, *Worlds of Women: The Making of an International Women's Movement* (Princeton, N.J.: Princeton University Press, 1977), 75ff.
4. Quoted in Rupp, *Worlds of Women,* 80.
5. Ibid., 77.
6. Ibid., 224–25: "Universal Declaration of Human Rights," in *Human Rights Documents* (Washington, D.C.: U.S. Government Printing Office, 1983), 61–67.
7. Quoted in Barry Schlachter, "International News," Associated Press, Nairobi, Kenya, July 15, 1985.
8. NGO *Forum* '80 newsletter (Copenhagen), quoted in Charlotte Bunch, *Passionate Politics: Feminists Theory in Action* (New York: St. Martin's Press, 1987), 299.
9. Charlotte Bunch, "U.N. World Conference in Nairobi: A View from the West," *Ms.* 13:12 (1985), 79–82, reprinted in Bunch, *Passionate Politics.* 325.
10. Quoted in Arvonne S. Fraser, *The U.N. Decade for Women: Documents and Dialogue* (Boulder: Westview Press, 1987), 155.
11. Quoted in Bunch, *Passionate Politics,* 300.
12. Ester Boserup, *Woman's Role in Economic Development* (New York: St. Martin's Press, 1970), 56.
13. Naila Kabeer, *Reserved Realities: Gender Hierarchies in Development Thought* (London: W. W. Norton, 1994), 27.
14. Aihwa Ong, *Spirits of Resistance and Capitalist Discipline* (New York: State University of New York Press, 1999), 163–68.
15. "The 25 Year Life Story of the Institute for Women's Studies in the Arab World," *Al-Raida* 57 (1998). 83–84. See also Helen Zweifel, "The Gendered Nature of Biodiversity Conservation," *National Women's Studies Association Journal* 9:3 (1997), 106–16.
16. The term comes from Amrita Basu, ed., *The Challenge of Local Feminisms: Women's Movements in Global Perspective* (Boulder: Westview Press, 1995).
17. Association of African Women for Research and Development, "A Statement on Genital Mutilation," in *Third World, Second Sex: Women's Struggle and National Liberation/Third World Woman Speak Out,* ed. Miranda Device (London: Zed Books, 1983), vol. 2, 217–19.
18. Nilufer Cagatay, Caren Grown, and Aida Santiago, "Nairobi Women's Conference: Toward a Global Feminism?" (1986), quoted in Johnson-Odim, "Common Thomas," 925.

Denials of Inequality

Deborah L. Rhode (1997)

Americans' most common response to gender inequality is to deny its dimensions. A widespread perception is that once upon a time, women suffered serious discrimination, but those days are over. Barriers have been coming down, women have been moving up, and full equality is just around the corner. If anything, many men believe that women are now getting undeserved advantages. In a series of recent articles with titles like "The Decline and Fall of the White Male," commentators air their view that "merit is out," "special privileges" are in, and the only group that can't claim equal protection under law is white men. "Pale males eat it again," announces a character in Michael Crichton's popular film *Disclosure.* This perspective is widely shared. According to recent polls, close to half of all men think that they are subject to unfair penalties for advantages that others had in the past. Two-thirds of men and three-quarters of male business leaders do not believe that women encounter significant discrimination for top positions in business, professions, or government.

Such views are difficult to square with the facts. White males account for about 40 percent of the population but about 95 percent of senior managers, 90 percent of newspaper editors, 80 percent of the *Forbes* list of richest Americans, and 80 percent of congressional legislators. Significant sex-based disparities in employment salaries and status persist, even when researchers control for objective factors such as education, experience, and hours worked. As *Newsweek*'s article "White Male Paranoia" points out, the pale male certainly appears to be "holding his own (and most of everybody else's) in the world of hard facts"; it's only in the "world of images and ideas . . . [that] he's taking a clobbering."

What explains this gap between popular perceptions and concrete data on gender inequality? Part of the explanation lies with selective perception. Men often deny bias because they fail to recognize it. They usually don't need to, it does not significantly affect their lives. As with race, part of the privilege of dominance is the privilege of accepting without noticing its benefits.

. . .

For obvious reasons, women are more sensitive to gender inequality than men are, but some perceptual blinders persist among both sexes. Not all women encounter all forms of bias, and those who lack personal experience sometimes fail to appreciate collective problems. What sociologists label the "Queen Bee Syndrome" is common among some professionally successful women. Their attitude is "I managed, why can't you?"

Many women also are unable to see patterns of discrimination because important parts of the picture are missing or murky. Salary, hiring, and promotion data that compare similarly qualified men and women are hard to come by, and the most overt sexism has gone underground. As a 1989 Supreme Court case revealed, male employers may still penalize a woman who they think needs courses in "charm school." But that is no longer what they say in mixed company or in personnel records. Moreover, gender is only one of the characteristics, and not always the most important one, that disadvantages women. Race, ethnicity, class, disability, and sexual orientation often overshadow or interact with gender.

. . .

Self-interest complicates the process. For some men, the increasing unacceptability of sexism, coupled with the inconvenience of eliminating it, encourages various strategies of self-deception. These techniques frequently surface on issues of household work. Employed men, who average only half as much time as employed women on family tasks, generally manage not to notice the disparity. In one recent poll, over two-thirds of surveyed husbands reported that they shared childrearing duties equally with their wives, an assessment wildly inconsistent with that of most wives and virtually all reported research.

Moreover, even men who acknowledge disparities often view women's extra tasks as matters of personal choice, not joint responsibility. Rather than accept an equal division of cleaning, cooking, or childcare obligations, some men redefine their share as unnecessary; they don't mind a little mess or a fast-food dinner, and their infants will do just fine with extra time among their "friends" at daycare. Other men seem not to notice when some of their assigned tasks need doing, or else mismanage key parts of the job. Rather than broadcast constant reminders or complaints, many women simply pick up pieces that their partners don't even realize have been dropped. As one wife wearily noted, "I do my half, I do half of [my husband's half], and the rest doesn't get done."

. . .

Part of what keeps men, and often women, from recognizing that gap is their choice of reference groups. Where gender appears to be a relevant characteristic, most individuals compare themselves to members of their own sex. In assessing domestic burdens, husbands look to other husbands or their own fathers rather than to wives. From this perspective, unequal divisions of labor become easy to rationalize because they remain the norm rather than the exception.

Women also tend to compare their family burdens to those of members of their own sex. As a result, many wives deny that their husbands do less than their "fair share" around the home, even when responsibilities are grossly unequal. Cultural attitudes reinforce such perceptions. As Anna Quindlen notes, "When men do the dishes it's called helping. When women do dishes, that's called life." Most women are not fully aware of how much time they or their partners spend on family work and generally believe that their arrangements are far more equal than they truly are.

This is not to imply that women totally fail to notice gender inequalities in household burdens. How much help they receive (or don't receive) from their male partners shows up in opinion surveys as one of the greatest sources of resentment. Yet even women who are most resentful often do not expect an equal division of household work. It is only their partner's refusal to help with particular jobs or his inability to justify refusing, that triggers conflict. And for many women, avoiding conflict is more important than achieving equality. They, like their male counterparts, use selective perception as a form of self-protection.

Similar patterns operate in other contexts. According to workplace surveys, even when women recognize gender discrimination as a problem or where objective evidence points to that conclusion, most individuals still do not believe that they personally have been targets. Although many critics denounce feminism for encouraging women to exaggerate their own victimization, recent research finds that individuals generally are reluctant to see themselves in that light. Acknowledging vulnerability carries a cost: it erodes individuals' sense of control and self-esteem, and involves the unpleasantness of identifying a perpetrator. Many women understandably are unwilling to alienate men whose approval is important personally and professionally.

Although some individuals enjoy nursing grievances and claiming the moral leverage of victim status, most do not. As Hillary Clinton once noted, "Who wants to walk around constantly with clenched fists?" Particularly where women feel powerless to avoid inequality, they are likely to avoid acknowledging it.

Still Needing the F Word

Anna Quindlen (2003)

Let's use the F word here. People say it's inappropriate, offensive, that it puts people off. But it seems to me it's the best way to begin, when it's simultaneously devalued and invaluable.

Feminist. Feminist, Feminist, Feminist.

Conventional wisdom has it that we've moved on to a postfeminist era, which is meant to suggest that the issues have been settled, the inequities addressed, and all is right with the world. And then suddenly from out of the South like Hurricane Everywoman, a level 03 storm, comes something like the new study on the status of women at Duke University,* and the notion that we're post-anything seems absurd. Time to use the F word again, no matter how uncomfortable people may find it.

Fem-i-nism *n. 1. Belief in the social, political and economic equality of the sexes.*

That wasn't so hard, was it? Certainly not as hard as being a female undergraduate at Duke, where apparently the operative ruling principle is something described as "effortless perfection," in which young women report expending an enormous amount of effort on clothes, shoes, workout programs and diet. And here's a blast from the past: they're expected "to hide their intelligence in order to succeed with their male peers."

"Being 'cute' trumps being smart for women in the social environment," the report concludes.

That's not postfeminist. That's prefeminist. Betty Friedan wrote *The Feminine Mystique* exactly 40 years ago, and yet segments of the Duke report could have come right out of her book. One

17-year-old girl told Friedan, "I used to write poetry. The guidance office says I have this creative ability and I should be at the top of the class and have a great future. But things like that aren't what you need to be popular. The important thing for a girl is to be popular."

Of course, things have changed. Now young women find themselves facing not one, but two societal, and self-imposed, straitjackets. Once they obsessed about being the perfect homemaker and meeting the standards of their male counterparts. Now they also obsess about being the perfect professional and meeting the standards of their male counterparts. In the decades since Friedan's book became a best seller, women have won the right to do as much as men do. They just haven't won the right to do as little as men do. Hence, effortless perfection.

While young women are given the impression that all doors are open, all boundaries down, empirical evidence is to the contrary. A study from Princeton issued at the same time as the Duke study showed that faculty women in the sciences reported less satisfaction in their jobs and less of a sense of belonging than their male counterparts. Maybe that's because they made up only 14 percent of the faculty in those disciplines, or because one out of four reported their male colleagues occasionally or frequently engaged in unprofessional conduct focusing on gender issues.

Californians were willing to ignore Arnold Schwarzenegger's alleged career as a serial sexual bigot, despite a total of 16 women coming forward to say he thought nothing of reaching up your skirt or into your blouse. (Sure, they're only allegations. But it was Arnold himself who said that where there's smoke, there's fire. In this case,

---

*In the Fall, 2003, Duke University published a comprehensive Women's Initiative Report that documented the full range of women's experiences at the university.

there was a conflagration.) The fact that one of the actor's defenses was that he didn't realize this was objectionable—and that voters were OK with that—speaks volumes about enduring assumptions about women. What if he'd habitually publicly humiliated black men, or Latinos, or Jews? Yet the revelation that the guy often demeaned women with his hands was written off as partisan politics and even personal behavior. Personal behavior is when you have a girlfriend. When you touch someone intimately without her consent, it's sexual battery.

The point is not that the world has not changed for women since Friedan's book lobbed a hand grenade into the homes of pseudohappy housewives who couldn't understand the malaise that accompanied sparkling Formica and good-looking kids. Hundreds of arenas, from government office to the construction trades, have opened to working women. Of course, when it leaks out that the Vatican is proposing to scale back on the use of altar girls, it shows that the forces of reaction are always waiting, whether beneath hard hats or miters.

But the world hasn't changed as much as we like to tell ourselves. Otherwise, *The Feminine Mystique* wouldn't feel so contemporary. Otherwise Duke University wouldn't find itself concentrating on eating disorders and the recruitment of female faculty. Otherwise, the governor-elect of California wouldn't be a guy who thinks it's "playful" to grab and grope, and the voters wouldn't ratify that attitude. Part fair game, part perfection: that's a tough standard for 51 percent of everyone. The first women's-rights activists a century ago set out to prove, in Friedan's words, "that woman was not a passive empty mirror." How dispiriting it would be to those long-ago heroines to read of the women at Duke focused on their "cute" reflections in the eyes of others. The F word is not an expletive, but an ideal—one that still has a way to go.

DISCUSSION QUESTIONS FOR CHAPTER 1

1. Why are you taking a women's studies course?

2. What are your expectations, fears, anxieties, and hopes about taking a women's studies class?

3. Why did women's studies emerge in the academic community?

4. What are negative stereotypes of feminism? Where do they come from? How do these stereotypes serve to perpetuate the dominant social order?

5. Do you think that, on the whole, equality has been achieved? Why or why not? Are there places where you see room for improvement or the need for drastic change?

SUGGESTIONS FOR FURTHER READING

Berger, Melody, ed. *We Don't Need Another Wave: Dispatches from the Next Generation of Feminists.* Emeryville, CA: Seal Press, 2006.

Bystydzienski, Jill, and Sharon Bird, eds. *Removing Barriers: Women in Academic Science, Technology, Engineering, and Mathematics.* Bloomington, IN: Indiana University Press, 2006.

Freedman, Estelle B. *No Turning Back: The History of Feminism and the Future of Women.* New York: Ballantine, 2002.

Henry, Astrid. *Not My Mother's Sister: Generational Conflict and Third-Wave Feminism.* Bloomington: Indiana University Press, 2004.

Hercus, Cheryl. *Stepping Out of Line: Becoming and Being Feminist.* New York: Routledge, 2005.

Hernandez, Daisy, and Bushra Rheman, eds. *Colonize This! Young Women of Color on Today's Feminism.* New York: Avalon, 2002.

hooks, bell. *Feminism Is for Everybody: Passionate Politics.* Boston: South End, 2000.

—. *Teaching to Transgress: Education as the Practice of Freedom.* New York: Routledge, 1994.

Levy, Ariel. *Female Chauvinist Pigs: Women and the Rise of Raunch Culture.* New York: Free Press, 2006.

MacDonald, Amie, and Susan Sanchez, eds. *Twenty-First Century Feminist Classrooms: Pedagogies of Identity and Difference.* New York: St. Martin's, 2002.

Messer-Davidow, Ellen. *Disciplining Feminism: How Women's Studies Transformed the Academy and Was Transformed by It.* Durham, NC: Duke University Press, 2002.

Peril, Lynn. *College Girls: Bluestockings, Sex Kittens, and Co-Eds, Then and Now.* New York: W. W. Norton, 2006.

Rogers, Mary F., and C. D. Garrett. *Who's Afraid of Women's Studies? Feminisms in Everyday Life.* Walnut Creek, CA: Alta Mira Press, 2002.

Rowe-Finkbeiner, Kristin. *The F Word: Feminism in Jeopardy: Women, Politics, and the Future.* Emeryville, CA: Seal Press, 2004.

Siegel, Deborah, and Jennifer Baumgardner. *Sisterhood, Interrupted: From Radical Women to Girls Gone Wild.* New York: Palgrave Macmillan, 2007.

Valenti, Jessica. *Full Frontal Feminism: A Young Woman's Guide to Why Feminism Matters.* Emeryville, CA: Seal Press, 2007.

CHAPTER 2

Systems of Privilege and Inequality in Women's Lives

Women are as different as we/they are alike. Although sharing some conditions, including having primary responsibility for children and being victims of male violence, women's lives are marked by difference. This is a result of the varying conditions and material practices of women's existence in global communities and the societies in which these communities are embedded. We inhabit different cultures whose norms or cultural expectations prescribe different ways of acting as women and impose different sanctions if these norms are broken. It is therefore important to recognize difference and, as already discussed in Chapter 1, avoid using "woman" as a universal or homogeneous category that assumes sameness. The readings in this chapter are classic essays written in the last 25 years that illustrate how power in society works, how differences are ranked or valued differently, and how privilege and discrimination operate. They make suggestions for change in both personal and social lives. They emphasize that what it means to be a woman is a complex interaction of multiple identities.

In the United States our differences are illustrated by the material conditions of our lives; the values, cultures, behavioral practices, and legal structures of the communities in which we live; and even the geographic region of the country we inhabit. In particular, we inhabit different identities in terms of race and ethnicity, religion, age, looks, sexual identity, socioeconomic status, and ability. Just as it is important to question the homogenizing notions of sameness in terms of the category "woman" across societies, it is also important to understand that these universalizing tendencies work against our understanding of women in the United States as well. Often we tend to think of women in comparison to a *mythical norm:* White, middle-class, heterosexual, abled, thin, and a young adult, which is normalized or taken for granted such that we often forget that Whites are racialized and men are gendered. Asking the question "Different from what?" reveals how difference gets constructed against what people think of as "normal." "Normality" tends to reflect the identities of those in power.

It is important to recognize that the *meanings* associated with differences are socially constructed. These social constructions would not be problematic were they not created against the notion of the mythical norm. Being a lesbian would not be a "difference" that invoked cultural resistance if it were not for *compulsory heterosexuality,* the notion that everyone should be heterosexual and have relationships with the opposite sex. This concept is illustrated in "The Social Construction of Disability" by Susan Wendell. She makes the case that *ableism,* discrimination against the mentally and physically disabled, is a direct result of social factors that actively create standards of normality against which ability/disability is constructed. In this chapter we focus on differences among women and explore the ways systems of privilege and inequality are created out of these differences.

DIFFERENCE, HIERARCHY, AND SYSTEMS OF PRIVILEGE AND INEQUALITY

Society recognizes the ways people are different and assigns group membership based on these differences; at the same time, society also ranks the differences and institutionalizes them into the fabric of society (Figure 2.1). *Institutionalized* means

Figure 2.1
Intersecting Axes of Privilege, Domination, and Oppression

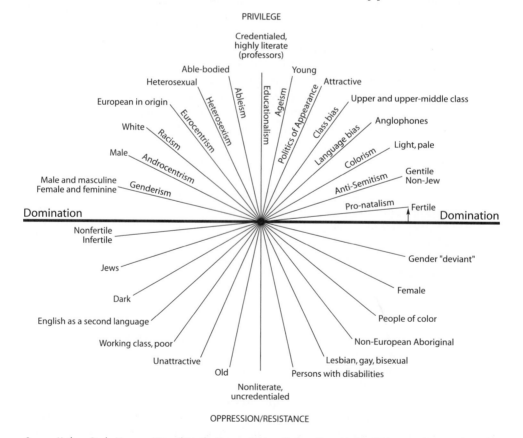

Source: Kathryn Pauly Morgan, "Describing the Emperor's New Clothes: Three Myths of Educational (In)Equality." *The Gender Question in Education: Theory, Pedagogy & Politics,* Ann Diller et al., Boulder, CO: Westview, 1996.

LEARNING ACTIVITY　**Unpack Your Knapsack**

Peggy McIntosh lists a number of ways that she experiences White privilege. Based on your various nontarget statuses, make lists of the ways you experience the following categories of privilege:

White	Male	Heterosexual
Middle or upper class	Young	Able-bodied

officially placed into a structured system or set of practices. This implies that meanings associated with difference exist beyond the intentions of individual people. In this ranking, masculine is placed above feminine, thin above fat, economically privileged above poor, and so forth. These rankings of groups and their members create a hierarchy in which some ways of being, like being abled or heterosexual, are valued more than others, like being disabled or gay or lesbian. Some have advantages in accessing resources while others are disadvantaged by unequal access to economic opportunities; some are unable to exercise the rights of citizenship while others have clearer access to right to life and happiness. For example, U.S. rights of citizenship include equal participation in the political process to ensure that laws reflect the will of the people with the knowledge that the government exists to serve the people, and to serve all equally. Although civil rights legislation removed many of the barriers set up to prevent non-Whites from voting, intimidation (such as discarding votes for various reasons and requiring different ID for certain votes) and restructuring (drawing voting district lines in a way that neutralizes the power of non-White voters) still occur.

The hierarchical ranking of difference is constructed through social processes such that patterns of difference become systems of privilege and inequality. Inequality for some and privilege for others is the consequence of these processes. *Privilege* can be defined as advantages people have by virtue of their status or position in society. This can be distinguished from earned privilege that results, for example, from earning a degree or fulfilling responsibilities. In "White Privilege and Male Privilege," Peggy McIntosh writes that White privilege is the "invisible package of unearned assets" that White people can count on cashing in every day. And, as McIntosh explains, it is easier to grant that others are disadvantaged than to admit being privileged. Men might be supportive of women's rights but balk at the suggestion that their personal behavior is in need of modification. Whites might be horrified by the stories of racial injustice but still not realize that taken-for-granted White privilege is part of the problem. This is similar to the discussion in Chapter 1 where being supportive of women's rights does not necessarily translate into an understanding of how the entitlements of masculine privilege work.

Systems that facilitate privilege and inequality, subordination and domination, include *racism* based upon racial/ethnic group membership (African American, Asian American, Latino/a, Native American—note this also includes anti-Semitism, or discrimination against Jews, as well as discrimination against Arab Americans and/or those who are Muslim [especially a problem after the bombing of the World Trade Center and

LEARNING ACTIVITY   **Test for Hidden Bias**

Go to the website for Southern Poverty Law Center's Teaching Tolerance at *www.tolerance.org.* Click on "Explore your hidden biases" to take a series of tests to uncover unconscious biases you may have. Even though most of us believe we view everyone equally, we still may hold stereotypes and biases of which we are unaware. These tests can check to see if perhaps you hold hidden biases of race, sexual orientation, age, gender, or body image. After you finish the tests, take a few minutes to write about what you learned about yourself. Were there any surprises? Do you hold hidden biases? How do you feel about your test results? Now that you know about your hidden biases, what can you do?

the consequences of the War in Iraq]); *sexism* based upon gender; *classism* associated with socioeconomic status; *heterosexism,* concerning sexual identity; *ageism* relating to age; *looksism* and *sizeism,* concerning body size and looks; and *ableism,* about physical and mental ability. Systems of oppression can be defined as systems that discriminate and privilege based on perceived or real differences among people. Given this, sexism discriminates and privileges on the basis of gender, resulting in gender stratification, racism discriminates and privileges on the basis of racial and ethnic differences, and so forth for classism, heterosexism, ageism, looksism, and ableism.

Every woman is in multiple places vis-à-vis these systems. She might not have access to race and gender privilege because she is African American and a woman; she might have access to heterosexual privilege because she is heterosexual and class privilege because she lives in a family that is financially secure. This is the *confluence,* the flowing together of various identities. As Patricia Hill Collins explains in "Toward a New Vision," it is not as useful to think of these various identities as being stacked or arranged in a cumulative manner. Lives are not experienced as "Here I'm a woman, here I'm abled, here I'm poor," as if all our various statuses are all stacked up; we experience ourselves as ordinary people who struggle daily with the inequities in our lives and who usually take the privileges for granted. Various identities concerning these systems of equality and privilege are usually thoroughly blended and potentially shifting depending on subjective orientation and cultural context. This means that cultural forces of race and class, and others such as age and ability, are all determinants of gender. It is important to emphasize that people experience race, class, gender, and sexual identity differently depending on their social location in various structures of inequality and privilege. This means that people of the same race or same age, for example, will experience race or age differently depending on their location in gendered structures (whether they are women or men), class structures (such as working class, professional class, or unemployed, etc.), as well as structures associated with sexual identity (whether they identify as heterosexual, bisexual, lesbian, gay, or "queer"), and so on. In "Report from the Bahamas," June Jordan illustrates the multilayered tensions associated with intersecting identities in the context of global inequality, and the shifting limitations/privileges that shift again when a citizen of a "First World" country visits colonized, westernized locations outside the United States.

Challenging Your Assumptions

Read the following sentences and identify the assumptions inherent in each regarding age, ability, appearance, ethnicity, gender, race, religion, sexual identity, and socioeconomic power or status.

Identify the "norm" (a standard of conduct that should or must be followed; a typical or usual way of being or behaving, usually said of a certain group), and discuss how the assumptions reflect this norm.

Discuss how these assumptions operate in your cultural situation. How are you affected by cultural assumptions about the "norm"?

Our founding fathers carved this great state out of the wilderness.

Mrs. Imoto looks remarkably good for her age.

Fashion Tights are available in black, suntan, and flesh color.

Someday I intend to visit the third world.

We need more manpower.

Our facilities all provide handicapped access.

I'm just a person.

The network is down again. We'd better get Kevin in here to do his voodoo on it.

Our boys were having a rough time of it, and the black regiment was, too.

How Neandertal man existed for so long is a mystery. He must have had the ability to adapt to his environment.

I see she forgot to sign her time sheet. She's acting a little blonde today.

Mitochondrial DNA testing should help us determine when our race split off from the lower creatures.

Confined to a wheelchair, Mr. Garcia still manages to live a productive life.

Pat really went on the warpath when the budget figures came out.

I won't be associated with you and your pagan behaviors!

The Academy now admits women and other minorities.

We have a beautiful daycare center where women can leave their children while they work.

See if you can Jew him down to $50.

Personally, I don't think it's right that the foreign students come in here before term and buy up all the insignia bags. Our kids don't get a chance at them.

I completely forgot where I put my car keys. I must be having a senior moment.

Win a fabulous lovers' weekend in Hawaii! Prizes include a day at the spa for her and a relaxing game of golf for him.

That is not a very Christian attitude.

We welcome all guests, their wives, and their children.

May I speak to Mr. or Mrs. Williams?

Source: Janet Lockhart and Susan Shaw, *Writing for Change: Raising Awareness of Issues of Difference, Power, and Discrimination, www.teachingtolerance.org.*

LEARNING ACTIVITY   **Combating Hate**

Many web pages provide valuable information about hate, hate crimes, and hate groups in the United States. Go to the Southern Poverty Law Center's homepage at *www.splcenter.org*. Click on "Intelligence Project" and then on "Hate Incidents." Put in your state to see a list of hate crimes where you live. You may also want to visit these websites as well: *www.wiesenthal.com, www.adl.org, www.stopthehate.org, www.hrc.org,* and *www.hatewatch.org.* Using information from these sites, make a list of ways you can help stop hate.

Systems of inequality like racism, sexism, and classism interconnect and work together to enforce inequality and privilege, each mostly supporting the other. The intersections of racism and classism are demonstrated by the fact that 25 percent of African Americans compared to 9 percent of White Americans were living in poverty in 2006. As Baba Copper explains in her article on ageism, age discrimination is very much connected to sexism as well as to looksism. Women learn to "age pass"; that is, we do not want to be mistaken for 40 when we are in our 30s, or mistaken for 70 when only 60. This is part of the pursuit for youth and beauty that encourages women to participate as agents of ageism as we fulfill the expectations of gender. Similarly, Suzanne Pharr writes about the ways homophobia functions as a weapon of sexism. *Homophobia* is the fear and dislike of lesbians and gay men. Pharr emphasizes that homophobia functions as a threat to keep women apart from one another and under male power, thus reinforcing sexism.

INSTITUTIONS

Institutions are social organizations that involve established patterns of behavior organized around particular purposes. They function through social norms (cultural expectations) and established rules and/or laws. Major institutions in our society include the family, marriage, the economy, government and criminal justice systems, religion, education, science, health and medicine, mass media, the military, and sports. Usually patterns of rules and practices implicit in major societal institutions have a historical component and reflect political, military, legal, and socioeconomic decisions made over decades and centuries. Although institutions are intended to meet the needs of society generally, or people in particular, they meet some people's needs better than others. These social organizations are central in creating systems of inequality and privilege because they pattern and structure differences among women in relatively organized ways. Institutions are important channels for the perpetuation of what Hill Collins calls "structures of domination and subordination." Note that institutions may resist systems of inequality and privilege through, for example, positive portrayal of women and marginalized people in media or the activities of some churches for civil rights.

LEARNING ACTIVITY **Women in Science and Engineering**

In 2005 Harvard University President Lawrence H. Summers created an uproar when he made the comment at an academic conference that the reasons fewer women than men succeed in science and math may be more related to innate differences than to socialization or discrimination. Many feminists responded by pointing to the wealth of research that indicates that girls and women are just as capable but their performances are often affected by social factors.

Certainly, the numbers do indicate a persistent dearth of women in science and engineering careers, although more women than ever are completing degrees in these areas. A 2004 report by the National Science Foundation found that from 1994 to 2001 the numbers and percentages of women declined in computer science and the numbers and percentages of minorities declined in engineering. Additionally, studies demonstrate that few White women are in tenured and tenure-track faculty positions in science, technology, and engineering, and the numbers are even bleaker for women of color.

Why do you think White women and women and men of color are underrepresented in science, technology, and engineering?

Visit the websites of the professional organizations listed below that are dedicated to increasing the success of White women and women and men of color in various science, technology, and engineering fields. What do these sites suggest about the reasons for underrepresentation? How do they suggest addressing the problem of underrepresentation?

Society of Women Engineers *www.swe.org*

Association for Women in Computing *www.awc-hq.org*

Association for Women in Mathematics *www.asm-math.org*

Association for Women in Science *www.awis.org*

National Action Council for Minorities in Engineering *www.nacme.org*

Marilyn Frye focuses on the institutional aspect of systems of inequality and privilege in her article "Oppression." She emphasizes that people who suffer under systems of inequality are oppressed by these systems. Frye writes about the difference between being oppressed and being limited and goes on to explain that a fundamental aspect of oppression is the double bind: All potential options have limitations. She uses the metaphor of a birdcage to explain the networks of related barriers that function in systems of oppression. One wire might be like an individual-level prejudice; a bird could simply move around it and escape. But a birdcage involves patterns of wires, systematically arranged so that escape is thwarted. The wires of the cage symbolically become institutionalized into a system of oppression.

Institutions encourage the channeling of various systems of gendered inequality to all aspects of women's lives. In terms of the patterning of resources and practices, institutions function to support systems of inequality and privilege. First, institutions assign various roles to women and men and are also places of employment where people perform gendered work. Educational institutions, for example, employ a considerable number of women. However, as the prestige of the teaching position increases, the number of White males in these positions increases, along with higher salaries. Additionally, it is very difficult for openly lesbian teachers to find employment in schools, and many states are attempting to pass laws preventing lesbians and gay men from teaching in state-funded educational establishments.

Second, institutions distribute resources and extend privileges differentially to different groups. Sports are a good example of this. As an institution, athletics has traditionally been male dominated. Men's sports are more highly valued than women's sports and are a major focus for sports entertainment. Compared to men's professional sports, women's are grossly underrepresented. Despite Title IX of the 1972 Educational Amendments Act, which barred discrimination in education, many colleges still are not in compliance and spend considerably more money on men's sports than on women's. Female athletes on some campuses complain that men receive better practice times in shared gymnasiums and more up-to-date equipment. And, within women's sports, some are more "White" than others. Examples that immediately come to mind are gymnastics, ice skating, equestrian sports, tennis, golf, and to some extent soccer (all relatively expensive pursuits). Most women's sports—

HISTORICAL MOMENT   **Women of Color Feminism**

Acutely aware of the intersections of gender, race, sexual identity, and social class were women of color who daily experienced the material realities of the confluence of oppressions. From the beginning of the women's movement, women of color participated actively, although their specific concerns were often overlooked by some of the middle-class White women in the movement. In the early 1970s, women of color spoke out about their experiences of racism, sexism, and heterosexism. Barbara Smith co-founded the Combahee River Collective, a Black feminist group that confronted racism and homophobia in the women's, gay, and Black movements. The Collective took its name from a river in South Carolina where Harriet Tubman led a military action that freed hundreds of slaves.

In the late 1970s, Smith joined forces with Cherríe Moraga to found Kitchen Table/Women of Color Press when Moraga and Gloria Anzaldúa could not find a publisher for *This Bridge Called My Back: Writings by Radical Women of Color*. Kitchen Table/Women of Color Press was the first independent press to publish exclusively works by feminists of color. *This Bridge Called My Back* won an American Book Award from the Columbus Foundation.

In 1983 poet and novelist Alice Walker coined the term *womanism* to describe Black feminism in contrast to *feminism*, which has generally been associated with White women. Walker situates womanists in a long line of Black women who have struggled for social change and liberation. Womanists are, in her words, "outrageous, audacious, courageous, and willful, responsible, in charge, serious." They love Black women's culture, Black women's beauty, and themselves.

outside of basketball and track—are dominated by White women. In this way, sports and athletics are an example of an institution where resources are inequitably distributed.

Stark Intersections: Gender, Race, Class, and HIV/AIDS

"We must address power imbalances in every single policy, strategy, and programme related to prevention, treatment and care if we seriously want to tackle this global challenge. [Gender] equality is not simply a matter of justice or fairness. Gender inequality is fatal."

—*Noeleen Heyzer, UNIFEM*

Gender inequality is fueling the HIV/AIDS epidemic: it deprives women of the ability to say no to risky practices, leads to coerced sex and sexual violence, keeps women uninformed about prevention, puts them last in line for care and life-saving treatment, and imposes an overwhelming burden for the care of the sick and dying. These fundamental threats to women's lives, health, and well-being are critical human rights issues—when women's human rights are not promoted, protected, and fulfilled, gender inequality is the dangerous result. Guaranteeing women's human rights is an indispensable component of the international struggle to combat HIV/AIDS. To combat today's scourge, we must understand the multiple intersections between gender, racial and ethnic discrimination, and the epidemiology of HIV/AIDS.

This intersectional approach derives from the realization that discriminations based on gender, race, ethnicity, caste, and class are not discrete phenomena, but compound one another in almost all socio-economic circumstances.[1] Nine points are critical with regard to HIV/AIDS:

- Economic dependence and social subordination limit the ability of women and members of racial and ethnic minorities to demand safe and responsible sexual practices, including the use of condoms.
- Groups already subject to socioeconomic discrimination—including racial and ethnic minorities, migrant populations, and refugees—rank high among those most vulnerable to HIV infection. In all these groups, women are hardest hit.
- Racial and ethnic identities operate in complicated ways to increase women's vulnerability to sex trafficking, a major factor in women's growing infection rates.
- The culture of silence that surrounds female sexuality in many societies prevents women and girls from accessing information and services for protection or treatment.
- In many countries, especially among racial and ethnic minorities, men receive preferential treatment in anti-retroviral therapies.
- Gender-based violence, both inside and outside the household, increases women's vulnerability to HIV/AIDS. HIV-positive women are frequently shunned by families and communities—and often subjected to further violence.
- This vulnerability mounts because of practices such as polygamy and wife-inheritance, as well as mistaken beliefs, such as that sex with a virgin can cure AIDS.
- Because women are primarily responsible for caregiving, caring for people with HIV/AIDS typically falls to widows and grandmothers or older girl children.

(continued)

Caregiving responsibilities increase as health and social services decrease and increasingly privatized services require a higher proportion of household income.

- Because women often care for communities as well as families, their illness or absorption in sheer survival activities weakens the vital informal support systems on which poor and marginalized communities depend, deepening and perpetuating poverty.[2]

These intersections are more alarming in light of the gender dimensions of HIV/AIDS:[3]

- Worldwide, of the 17.5 million adults who have died of the disease, 9 million have been women. Approximately 47 percent of all new adult infections afflict women.
- In sub-Saharan Africa, 61 percent of HIV-positive adults are women. In Mozambique, HIV infection is twice as prevalent among girls as boys.[4]
- Of the 1.3 million cases in Eastern Europe and Central Asia reported in 2000, at least half are estimated to be female.
- In parts of Latin America and the Caribbean, the proportion has reached 45 percent, a rapidly rising figure.

Moreover, these statistics represent underestimations due to the personal reluctance to report the disease as well as government reluctance to acknowledge its extent. In addition, medical studies often do not disaggregate data according to race and gender, nor do they examine the specific health issues affecting women from racial and ethnic minorities or indigenous women as a matter of course. Thus, they may fail to uncover medical problems specific to particular groups of women.[5]

[1]For discussion of the concept of intersectionality, see *Gender and Racial Discrimination: Report of the Expert Group Meeting,* November 2000, Zagreb. UN Division for the Advancement of Women, 2001.
[2]Mercedes González de la Rocha and Alejandro Grinspun, "Private Adjustments: Household, Crisis and Work," in Grinspun, ed., *Choices for the Poor: Lessons from National Poverty Strategies.* New York: UNDP, 2001.
[3]Unless otherwise noted, statistics are taken from the UNAIDS *AIDS Epidemic Update,* December 2000, or the UNAIDS *Report on the Global HIV Epidemic,* June 2000.
[4]Dr. Pascoal Macumbi, prime minister of Mozambique, quoted in *Conference News Daily,* UN Special Session on HIV/AIDS, June 25, 2001.
[5]UNIFEM, 2000. "Integrating Gender into the Third World Conference Against Racism, Racial Discrimination, Xenophobia and Related Intolerance." Background Paper prepared for the *Gender and Racial Discrimination: Report of the Expert Group Meeting,* November 2000, Zagreb, Croatia.

Source: www.unaids.org.

Another blatant example of inequitable distribution concerns the economic system. Other than inherited wealth, the major way our economic system distributes resources is in terms of remuneration for the work that we do. Women tend to work in jobs that are heavily occupied by women; examples include clerical work, service and retail sales, and professional occupations like teaching and nursing. These jobs are undervalued in our society, contributing to the fact that a woman's average salary generally for all occupations tends to be less than a man's average salary. Some women work under deplorable conditions at minimum wage levels; some work with hazardous chemicals or have to breathe secondhand smoke throughout their workday. Old women and women of color own a tiny percentage of the wealth in this society—another example of the inequitable distribution of resources by a confluence of multiple identities.

Third, major institutions in society are interconnected and work to support and maintain one another. Often this means that personnel are shared among major institutions; more likely it means that these institutions mutually support one another in terms of the ways they fulfill (or deny) the needs of people in society. For example, close ties to economic institutions include the military (through the military-industrial complex), the government (corporate leaders often have official positions in government and rely on legislative loopholes and taxation systems to maintain corporate profits), health and medicine (with important ties to pharmaceutical companies), the media (whose content is controlled in part by advertising), and sports (through corporate sponsorship). Finally, institutions produce ideas and values that shape meanings associated with different identities. It is to this that we now turn.

IDEOLOGY AND LANGUAGE

Alongside the distribution of roles and resources and as they connect with each other through a variety of social practices, institutions also produce messages that shape our understandings of social life. Importantly, ideas and values (like stereotypes and jokes) or sets of beliefs (often called ideologies) provide the rationale for injustice. Hill Collins calls this the "symbolic dimension" of systems of domination and subordination. For example, media often reinforce stereotypes about women like dumb blondes, passive Asian Americans, or pushy African Americans. Another example of gendered messages comes from the institution of religion. This institution is especially powerful because it implies the notion of divine sanction. Traditional religious texts tell stories (for example, Eve's behavior that led to the banishment from the Garden of Eden or the chaste role of the Virgin Mary) that convey important messages about moral thought and behavior as well as women's place in society. These messages tend to be strongly gendered and often support different behaviors for women and men. A central code of such religious teaching is that women should be subordinate to men in their spiritual and everyday lives.

An example of an ideology that is supported by various institutions and that affects women's lives is the *bootstrap myth* concerning economic success. Propagated by the economic system, it paints economic success as a result of hard work and ambition and asserts that people, if properly motivated and willing to work hard, can pull themselves up by their bootstraps. Given this set of ideas, those individuals who are not able to provide for their families must have deficiencies. Perhaps they were unmotivated, did not work hard enough, or were not smart enough. Such ideas encourage blaming the poor for their poverty rather than understanding the wider societal forces that shape people's existence and maintain classism. Notwithstanding the fact that of course hard work and ambition may facilitate some measure of success in the short term, it does not guarantee such success, nor does it tend to transform the bigger picture of structural inequalities. Notice that a particular ideology need not be supported unanimously for it to influence society. Many people would disagree vehemently with the bootstrap

Copyright © Judy Horacek. www.horacek.com.au. Reprinted with permission.

myth; yet, still, this is a key part of the ideology of capitalist countries. In this way, institutions perpetuate sets of ideas and practices and use them to justify the institution.

Classism is also addressed in the article by Donna Langston titled "Tired of Playing Monopoly?" Here she explains how class is not just about socioeconomic status, that is, how much wealth you have access to or how much you earn. She writes,

> Class is also culture. As a result of the class you were born into and raised in, class is your understanding of the world and where you fit in; it's composed of ideas, attitudes, values, and language; class is how you think, feel, act, look, dress, talk, move, walk; class is what stores you shop at, restaurants you eat in; class is the schools you attend, the education you attain; class is the jobs you will work at throughout your adult life. Class even determines when we marry and become mothers.

Stereotypes and ideologies that support systems of inequality involve prejudices. *Prejudice* means, literally, to prejudge and involves making premature judgments without adequate information or with inaccurate information. Often these ideas support systems of inequality and privilege because prejudice is often adopted when there is no other basis for understanding. For example, many White people have little contact with people of color, and many young people do not interact on an everyday basis with old people. As a result, there is a lack of accurate information, and stereotypes or images from movies or other media are used instead. This kind of ignorance and misinformation breeds prejudice. In "Something About the Subject Makes It Hard to Name," Gloria Yamato writes about different kinds of prejudice: aware/blatant, aware/covert, unaware/unintentional, and unaware/self-righteous. In this article she emphasizes that much prejudice comes from misinformation and is very often unintentional. She also notes that social norms against racism have pushed some racism underground and made it covert (hidden) rather than overt (blatant).

Prejudices are *internalized* (assimilated, integrated, or incorporated into our thoughts and behavior) by all of us. However, since humans have active agency and will, they can be resisted. Generally we can say that individuals negotiate these ideologies, accepting, resisting, and/or modifying them. If we are members of the *target group,* the group against whom the prejudice is aimed, it can lead to low self-esteem, self-loathing, and shame. Sadly, it can mean individuals are encouraged to believe they are not worthy of social justice and therefore are less likely to seek equality. Although members of target groups may internalize negative messages, members of *nontarget groups,* groups (often part of the mythical norm) against whom the prejudice is not aimed, also internalize these messages as well as messages about their own privilege. This can encourage or justify hostility against target groups.

Internalizing oppression means that we not only police ourselves but also police one another, encouraging compliance with institutions that may oppress. When individuals direct the resentment and anger they have about their situation onto those who are of equal or of lesser status, this process is called *horizontal hostility.* As a strategy, it is similar to the military notion of "divide and conquer" in which groups are encouraged to fight with one another in order to avoid alliances that might collaboratively overpower an enemy. Women might do this when they are in competition about each other's looks or put other women down with verbal and/or nonverbal behavior. Baba Copper remarks on horizontal conflict when she writes about woman-to-woman ageism, how women want to "age pass," and in the ways women compete "for the crumbs of social power."

Language, or the symbolic means by which we communicate, is a key aspect of what makes us human and central to ideologies that support systems of inequality and privilege. Language is an incredibly sophisticated process of symbols that we learn at an early age and mostly take for granted unless we are confronted with trying to communicate in a language not our own. Because language allows us not only to name the objects of our experience but also to typify them (experience them as similar to something of a similar type), it creates as well as reflects our reality. It shapes as well as expresses thought. And because language helps us sort and anticipate our experiences, it has a primary influence on our lives.

The English language is structured in such a way that it maintains sexism and racism. Lois Keith's poem "Tomorrow I'm Going to Rewrite the English Language" suggests how the English language helps shape our understandings of gender and limits women's options for self-definition. This poem encourages us to think about the ways that language shapes our reality and helps structure the everyday realities of women's lives. When you grow up knowing 20 different words synonymous with

ACTIVIST PROFILE **Fannie Lou Hamer**

She began life in Mississippi in 1917 as the granddaughter of slaves and the daughter of share-croppers, but Fannie Lou Hamer was to become one of the most important leaders of the civil rights movement in the United States. Although Hamer became a share-cropper herself, by 1962 she'd had enough of the second-class life of the segregated South. She joined 17 other African Americans taking a bus to the county seat to register to vote. On the way home, they were stopped by police and arrested. After Hamer returned home, she was visited by the plantation owner, who told her that if she insisted on voting, she would have to get off his land, which she did that same day.

The next year, when Hamer joined other civil rights workers in challenging the "Whites only" policy at a bus terminal diner, she was arrested and jailed. The police ordered two other African American prisoners to beat her with a metal-spiked club. Hamer was blinded in one eye from the beating and suffered permanent kidney damage.

In 1964 Hamer helped organize the Mississippi Freedom Democratic Party (MFDP) to challenge the all-White Mississippi delegation to the Democratic Convention. Hamer spoke to the credentials committee of the convention, and although her live testimony was preempted by a presidential press conference, it was aired by national networks in its entirety later that evening. The MFDP and the credentials committee reached a compromise, giving voting and speaking rights to two MFDP delegates and seating the others as honored guests. Hamer responded, "We didn't come all this way for two seats when all of us is tired." In 1968 the Mississippi Democratic Party did seat an integrated delegation.

Throughout her life, Hamer continued to work for justice, supporting Head Start for Black schools and jobs for poor African Americans, opposing the Vietnam War, and helping to convene the National Women's Political Caucus in the 1970s.

Hamer died in 1977 and was buried in Mississippi. Her tombstone reads, "I am sick and tired of being sick and tired."

IDEAS FOR ACTIVISM

- Find out how your university ensures access for people with disabilities. If some structures on your campus are inaccessible, advocate with your administration to create accessibility.
- Plan a celebration of Black women during Black History Month.
- Find out what programs your university offers to recruit and retain students and faculty of color. If programs are not in place, advocate with your administration to develop such programs.
- Find out if your university's antidiscrimination policy includes sexual identity as a protected classification, and find out if your university provides benefits for domestic partners. If not, advocate with your administration to include sexual identity in its policy and/or to provide domestic partner benefits.

slut, you learn something powerful about gender and female sexuality. The English language also maintains racism. For example:

> Some may blackly (angrily) accuse me of trying to blacken (defame) the English language, to give it a black eye (a mark of shame) by writing such black words (hostile). They may denigrate (to cast aspersions; to darken) me by accusing me of being black hearted (malevolent), of having a black outlook (pessimistic, dismal) on life, of being a blackguard (scoundrel)—which will certainly be a black mark (detrimental act) against me. Some may black-brow (scowl) at me and hope that a black cat crosses in front of me because of this black deed. I may become a black sheep (one who causes shame or embarrassment because of deviation from the expected standards), who will be black-balled (ostracized) by being placed on a black list (list of undesirables) in an attempt to blackmail (to force or coerce into a particular action) me to retract my words. . . . The preceding is of course a white lie (not intended to cause harm), meant only to illustrate some examples of racist terminology in the English language.*

In this chapter we focus on the social construction of difference and how systems of inequality and privilege based upon these differences function and are maintained. While we have emphasized that systems of inequality and privilege are maintained through the presence and power of institutions and the interrelated workings of ideologies and language, negotiated by individuals, it is also important to recognize the way hate crimes are central to these power relations. Hate crimes include the threat of coercion and violence as well as the actual practice of it, and their motives are hate and bigotry. Evidence shows that perpetrators of hate crimes are most likely to be heterosexual White males. For example, there has been a substantial increase in hate crimes in the last decade, especially against people of

---

*Robert B. Moore, "Racism in the English Language." Excerpted in *Experiencing Race, Class, and Gender in the U.S.*, Virginia Cyrus, ed. (Mountain View, CA: Mayfield, 1993), p. 152.

Challenging the Pseudogeneric "Man"

Examine the following phrases that use male nouns as "generic." Describe the mental image created for you by each phrase. Do you see yourself and people like you in the images?

Next, choose a term representing a group of people of a specific age, religion, class, or ethnicity, and substitute that term for the male noun (example: "childkind"). Does use of the new, specific term sound incongruous or unusual? Why?

Describe the mental images created by using the substitute terms. Do you see yourself and people like you in the images?

Finally, suggest a gender-free, inclusive term for each (example: for "mankind," "humanity" or "people").

For the benefit of all mankind

"All men are created equal"

May the best man win

Prehistoric man

Man the pumps!

The first manned mission to Mars

Chairman of the Board

We need more manpower

Not fit for man or beast

The relationship between men and machines

Man's best friend

"To boldly go where no man has gone before"

Man of the Year

"Peace on Earth, goodwill toward men"

The founding fathers

"Crown thy good with brotherhood"

"Friends, Romans, countrymen; lend me your ears"

Source: Janet Lockhart and Susan M. Shaw, Writing for Change: Raising Awareness of Difference, Power, and Discrimination, *www.teachingtolerance.org.*

color, lesbians, gays, and transgendered and transsexual people (see Chapters 3 and 4), although improved reporting systems are also increasing awareness of this social problem and providing hate-crime statistics. Hate groups include the Ku Klux Klan, racist Skinhead, Christian Identity Movement, Neo-Confederate, and Neo-Nazi (including Aryan Nations). One of the best sources for understanding hate crimes is the

Southern Poverty Law Center at *www.splcenter.org*. It is important to emphasize that gender as a category is omitted from most hate-crime statutes despite the fact that women suffer from the crimes of misogyny. Women are often hurt and killed because they are women; if these figures were included, hate-crime statistics would skyrocket. The United Nations now recognizes crimes against women, and the United States is starting to recognize crimes against non-U.S. women as basis for asylum. Hate crimes against women just because they are women, as well as hate against, for example, lesbians or women of color, often involve *sexual terrorism,* the threat of rape and sexual assault that controls a woman's life whether or not she is actually physically or sexually violated.

In concluding this chapter we underscore the need for social change and transformation to improve the conditions of women's lives. Almost all the readings focus on this need. Patricia Hill Collins, for example, writes about awareness and education, the need to build empathy with each other, and the need to work to form coalitions for structural change around common causes. June Jordan also writes of the power of empathy and the possibilities of friendship for alliance building and social transformation. Peggy McIntosh suggests we recognize our privilege and work on our internalized prejudices and privileges. Baba Copper writes about identifying and acknowledging sources of inequality and specifically the ways we have been taught contempt for old women. She also hopes for alliances across our differences. Suzanne Pharr points out the homophobia of the women's movement and its failure to achieve solidarity when the rights of all women are not recognized. Donna Langston presents ways to challenge classism that involve confronting the behavior in ourselves, making demands on behalf of poor communities, and learning from the skills and strengths of working-class people. Similarly, Gloria Yamato has good ideas for Whites who want to be allies to people of color. The message in all these classic articles is the need to recognize difference, to understand how the meanings associated with difference and the material conditions of everyday lives get translated into privilege and inequality, and to celebrate difference through coalitions for social justice and other expressions of personal and social concern.

Toward a New Vision

Race, Class, and Gender as Categories of Analysis and Connection

Patricia Hill Collins (1993)

The true focus of revolutionary change is never merely the oppressive situations which we seek to escape, but that piece of the oppressor which is planted deep within each of us.

—*Audre Lorde,* Sister Outsider, *123*

Audre Lorde's statement raises a troublesome issue for scholars and activists working for social change. While many of us have little difficulty assessing our own victimization within some major system of oppression, whether it be by race, social class, religion, sexual orientation, ethnicity, age or gender, we typically fail to see how our thoughts and actions uphold someone else's subordination. Thus, White feminists routinely point with confidence to their oppression as women but resist seeing how much their White skin privileges them. African-Americans who possess eloquent analyses of racism often persist in viewing poor White women as symbols of white power. The radical left fares little better. "If only people of color and women could see their true class interests," they argue, "class solidarity would eliminate racism and sexism." In essence, each group identifies the type of oppression with which it feels most comfortable as being fundamental and classifies all other types as being of lesser importance.

Oppression is full of such contradictions. Errors in political judgment that we make concerning how we teach our courses, what we tell our children, and which organizations are worthy of our time, talents and financial support flow smoothly from errors in theoretical analysis about the nature of oppression and activism. Once we realize that there are few pure victims

or oppressors, and that each one of us derives varying amounts of penalty and privilege from the multiple systems of oppression that frame our lives, then we will be in a position to see the need for new ways of thought and action.

. . .

[This discussion] addresses this need for new patterns of thought and action. I focus on two basic questions. First, how can we reconceptualize race, class and gender as categories of analysis? Second, how can we transcend the barriers created by our experiences with race, class and gender oppression in order to build the types of coalitions essential for social exchange? To address these question[s] I contend that we must acquire both new theories of how race, class and gender have shaped the experiences not just of women of color, but of all groups. Moreover, we must see the connections between these categories of analysis and the personal issues in our everyday lives, particularly our scholarship, our teaching and our relationships with our colleagues and students. As Audre Lorde points out, change starts with self, and relationships that we have with those around us must always be the primary site for social change.

HOW CAN WE RECONCEPTUALIZE RACE, CLASS, AND GENDER AS CATEGORIES OF ANALYSIS?

To me, we must shift our discourse away from additive analyses of oppression (Spelman 1982; Collins 1989). Such approaches are typically based on two key premises. First, they depend on either/or, dichotomous thinking. Persons, things and ideas are conceptualized in terms of their opposites. For example, Black/White, man/woman, thought/feeling, and fact/opinion are defined in oppositional terms. Thought and feeling are not seen as two different and interconnected ways of approaching truth that can coexist in scholarship and teaching. Instead, feeling is defined as antithetical to reason, as its opposite. In spite of the fact that we all have "both/and" identities (I am both a college professor and a mother—I don't stop being a mother when I drop my child off at school, or forget everything I learned while scrubbing the toilet), we persist in trying to classify each other in either/or categories. I live each day as an African-American woman—a race/gender specific experience. And I am not alone. Everyone has a race/gender/class specific identity. Either/or, dichotomous thinking is especially troublesome when applied to theories of oppression because every individual must be classified as being either oppressed or not oppressed. The both/and position of simultaneously being oppressed and oppressor becomes conceptually impossible.

A second premise of additive analyses of oppression is that these dichotomous differences must be ranked. One side of the dichotomy is typically labeled dominant and the other subordinate. Thus, Whites rule Blacks, men are deemed superior to women, and reason is seen as being preferable to emotion. Applying this premise to discussions of oppression leads to the assumption that oppression can be quantified, and that some groups are oppressed more than others. I am frequently asked, "Which has been most oppressive to you, your status as a Black person or your status as a woman?" What I am really being asked to do is divide myself into little boxes and rank my various statuses. If I experience oppression as a both/and phenomenon, why should I analyze it any differently?

Additive analyses of oppression rest squarely on the twin pillars of either/or thinking and the necessity to quantify and rank all relationships in order to know where one stands. Such approaches typically see African-American women as being more oppressed than everyone else because the majority of Black women experience the negative effects of race, class and gender oppression simultaneously. In essence, if you add together separate oppressions, you are left with a grand oppression greater than the sum of its parts.

I am not denying that specific groups experience oppression more harshly than others—lynching is certainly objectively worse than being held up as a sex object. But we must be careful not to confuse this issue of the saliency of one type of oppression in people's lives with a theoretical stance positing the interlocking nature of oppression. Race, class and gender may all structure a situation but may not be equally visible and/or important in people's self-definitions. In certain contexts, such as the antebellum American South and contemporary South America, racial oppression is more visibly salient, while in other contexts, such as Haiti, El Salvador and Nicaragua, social class oppression may be more apparent. For middle class White women, gender may assume experiential primacy unavailable to poor Hispanic women struggling with the ongoing issues of low-paid jobs and the frustrations of the welfare bureaucracy. This recognition that one category may have salience over another for a given time and place does not minimize the theoretical importance of assuming that race, class and gender as categories of analysis structure all relationships.

In order to move toward new visions of what oppression is, I think that we need to ask new questions. How are relationships of domination and subordination structured and maintained in the American political economy? How do race, class and gender function as parallel and interlocking systems that shape this basic relationship of domination and subordination? Questions such as these promise to move us away from futile theoretical struggles concerned with ranking oppressions and towards analyses that assume race, class and gender are all present in any given setting, even if one appears more visible and salient than the others. Our task becomes redefined as one of reconceptualizing oppression by uncovering the connections among race, class and gender as categories of analysis.

1. Institutional Dimension of Oppression

Sandra Harding's contention that gender oppression is structured along three main dimensions—the institutional, the symbolic, and the individual—offers a useful model for a more comprehensive analysis encompassing race, class and gender oppression (Harding 1986). Systemic relationships of domination and subordination structured through social institutions such as schools, businesses, hospitals, the workplace, and government agencies represent the institutional dimension of oppression. Racism, sexism and elitism all have concrete institutional locations. Even though the workings of the institutional dimension of oppression are often obscured with ideologies claiming equality of opportunity, in actuality, race, class and gender place Asian-American women, Native American men, White men, African-American women, and other groups in distinct institutional niches with varying degrees of penalty and privilege.

Even though I realize that many . . . would not share this assumption, let us assume that the institutions of American society discriminate, whether by design or by accident. While many of us are familiar with how race, gender and class operate separately to structure inequality, I want to focus on how these three systems interlock in structuring the institutional dimension of oppression. To get at the interlocking nature of race, class and gender, I want you to think about the antebellum plantation as a guiding metaphor for a variety of American social institutions. Even though slavery is typically analyzed as a racist institution, and occasionally as a class institution, I suggest that slavery was a race, class, gender specific institution. Removing any one piece from our analysis diminishes our understanding of the true nature of relations of domination and subordination under slavery.

. . .

A brief analysis of key American social institutions most controlled by elite White men should convince us of the interlocking nature of race, class and gender in structuring the institutional dimension of oppression. For example, if you are from an American college or university, is your campus a modern plantation? Who controls your university's political economy? Are elite White men overrepresented among the upper administrators and trustees controlling your university's finances and policies? Are elite White men being joined by growing numbers of elite White women helpmates? What kinds of people are in your classrooms grooming the next generation who will occupy these and other decision-making positions? Who are the support staff that produce the mass mailings, order the supplies, fix the leaky pipes? Do African-Americans, Hispanics or other people of color form the majority of the invisible workers who feed you, wash your dishes, and clean up your offices and libraries after everyone else has gone home?

If your college is anything like mine, you know the answers to these questions. You may be affiliated with an institution that has Hispanic women as vice-presidents for finance, or substantial numbers of Black men among the faculty. If so, you are fortunate. Much more typical are colleges where a modified version of the plantation as a metaphor for the institutional dimension of oppression survives.

2. The Symbolic Dimension of Oppression

Widespread, societally-sanctioned ideologies used to justify relations of domination and subordination comprise the symbolic dimension of oppression. Central to this process is the use of stereotypical or controlling images of diverse race, class and gender groups. In order to assess the power of this dimension of oppression, I want you to make a list, either on paper or in your head, of "masculine" and "feminine" characteristics. If your list is anything like that compiled by most people, it reflects some variation of the following:

Masculine	Feminine
aggressive	passive
leader	follower
rational	emotional
strong	weak
intellectual	physical

Not only does this list reflect either/or, dichotomous thinking and the need to rank both sides of the dichotomy, but ask yourself exactly which men and women you had in mind when compiling these characteristics. This list applies almost exclusively to middle class White men and women. The allegedly "masculine" qualities that you probably listed are only acceptable when exhibited by elite White men, or when used by Black and Hispanic men against each other or against women of color. Aggressive Black and Hispanic men are seen as dangerous, not powerful, and are often penalized when they exhibit any of the allegedly "masculine" characteristics. Working-class and poor White men fare slightly better and are also denied the allegedly "masculine" symbols of leadership, intellectual competence and human rationality. Women of color and working class and poor White women are also not represented on this list, for they have never had the luxury of being "ladies." What appear to be universal categories representing all men and women instead are unmasked as being applicable to only a small group.

It is important to see how the symbolic images applied to different race, class and gender groups interact in maintaining systems of domination and subordination. If I were to ask you to repeat the same assignment, only this time, by making separate lists for Black men, Black women, Hispanic women and Hispanic men, I suspect that your gender symbolism would be quite different. In comparing all of the lists, you might begin to see the interdependence of symbols applied to all groups. For example, the elevated images of White womanhood need devalued images of Black womanhood in order to maintain credibility.

. . .

Assuming that everyone is affected differently by the same interlocking set of symbolic images allows us to move forward toward new analyses. Women of color and White women have different relationships to White male authority, and this difference explains the distinct gender symbolism applied to both groups. Black women encounter controlling images such as the mammy, the matriarch, the mule and the whore, that encourage others to reject us as fully human people. Ironically, the negative nature of these images simultaneously encourages us to reject them. In contrast, White women are offered seductive images, those that promise to reward them for supporting the status quo. And yet seductive images can be equally controlling. Consider, for example, the views of Nancy White, a 73-year-old Black woman, concerning images of rejection and seduction:

> My mother used to say that the black woman is the white man's mule and the white woman is his dog. Now, she said that to say this: we do the heavy work and get beat whether we do it well or not. But the white woman is closer to the master and he pats them on the head and lets them sleep in the house, but he ain't gon' treat neither one like he was dealing with a person. (Gwaltney 1980, 148)

Both sets of images stimulate particular political stances. By broadening the analysis beyond the confines of race, we can see the varying levels of rejection and seduction available to each of us due to our race, class and gender identity. Each of us lives with an allotted portion of institutional privilege and penalty, and with varying levels of rejection and seduction inherent in the symbolic images applied to us. This is the context in which we make our choices. Taken together, the institutional and symbolic dimensions of oppression create a structural backdrop against which all of us live our lives.

3. The Individual Dimension of Oppression

Whether we benefit or not, we all live within institutions that reproduce race, class and gender oppression. Even if we never have any contact with members of other race, class and gender groups, we all encounter images of these groups and are exposed to the symbolic meanings attached to those images. On this dimension of oppression, our individual biographies vary tremendously. As a result of our institutional and symbolic statuses, all of our choices become political acts.

Each of us must come to terms with the multiple ways in which race, class and gender as categories of analysis frame our individual biographies. I have lived my entire life as an African-American woman from a working-class family, and this basic fact has had a profound impact on my personal biography. Imagine how different your life might be if you had been born Black, or White, or poor, or of a different race/class/gender group than the one with which you are most familiar. The institutional treatment you would have received and the symbolic meanings attached to your very existence might differ dramatically from what you now consider to be natural, normal and part of everyday life. You might be the same, but your personal biography might have been quite different.

I believe that each of us carries around the cumulative effect of our lives within multiple structures of oppression. If you want to see how much you have been affected by this whole thing, I ask you one simple question—who are your close friends? Who are the people with whom you can share your hopes, dreams, vulnerabilities, fears and victories? Do they look like you? If they are all the same, circumstance may be the cause. For the first seven years of my life I saw only low-income Black people. My friends from those years reflected the composition of my community. But now that I am an adult, can the defense of circumstance explain the patterns of people that I trust as my friends and colleagues? When given other alternatives, if my friends and colleagues reflect the homogeneity of one race, class and gender group, then these categories of analysis have indeed become barriers to connection.

I am not suggesting that people are doomed to follow the paths laid out for them by race, class and gender as categories of analysis. While these three structures certainly frame my opportunity structure, I as an individual always have the choice of accepting things as they are, or trying to change them. As Nikki Giovanni points out, "we've got to live in the real world. If we don't like the world we're living in, change it. And if we can't change it, we change ourselves. We can do something" (Tate 1983, 68). While a piece of the oppressor may be planted deep within each of us, we each have the choice of accepting that piece or challenging it as part of the "true focus of revolutionary change."

HOW CAN WE TRANSCEND THE BARRIERS CREATED BY OUR EXPERIENCES WITH RACE, CLASS, AND GENDER OPPRESSION IN ORDER TO BUILD THE TYPES OF COALITIONS ESSENTIAL FOR SOCIAL CHANGE?

Reconceptualizing oppression and seeing the barriers created by race, class and gender as interlocking categories of analysis is a vital first step. But we must transcend these barriers by moving toward race, class and gender as categories of connection, by building relationships and coalitions that will bring about social change. What are some of the issues involved in doing this?

1. Differences in Power and Privilege

First, we must recognize that our differing experiences with oppression create problems in the relationships among us. Each of us lives within a system that vests us with varying levels of power and privilege. These differences in power, whether structured along axes of race, class, gender, age or sexual orientation, frame our relationships. African-American writer June Jordan describes her discomfort on a Caribbean vacation with Olive, the Black woman who cleaned her room:

> . . . even though both "Olive" and "I" live inside a conflict neither one of us created, and even though both of us therefore hurt inside that conflict, I may be one of the monsters she needs to eliminate from her universe and, in a sense, she may be one of the monsters in mine. (1985, 47)

Differences in power constrain our ability to connect with one another even when we think we are engaged in dialogue across differences. . . .

In extreme cases, members of privileged groups can erase the very presence of the less privileged. When I first moved to Cincinnati, my family and I went on a picnic at a local park. Picnicking next to us was a family of White Appalachians. When I went to push my daughter on the swings, several of the children came over. They had missing, yellowed and broken teeth, they wore old clothing and their poverty was evident. I was shocked. Growing up in a large eastern city, I had never seen such awful poverty among Whites. The segregated neighborhoods in which I grew up made White poverty all but invisible. More importantly, the privileges attached to my newly acquired social class position allowed me to ignore and minimize the poverty among Whites that I did encounter. My reactions to those children made me realize how confining phrases such as "well, at least they're not Black," had become for me. In learning to grant human subjectivity to the Black victims of poverty, I had simultaneously learned to demand White victims of poverty. By applying categories of race to the objective conditions confronting me, I was quantifying and ranking oppressions and missing the very real suffering which, in fact, is the real issue.

One common pattern of relationships across differences in power is one that I label "voyeurism." From the perspective of the privileged, the lives of people of color, of the poor, and of women are interesting for their entertainment value. The privileged become voyeurs, passive onlookers who do not relate to the less powerful, but who are interested in seeing how the "different" live. Over the years, I have heard numerous African-American students complain about professors who never call on them except when a so-called Black issue is being discussed. The students' interest in discussing race or qualifications for doing so appear unimportant to the professor's efforts to use Black students' experiences as stories to make the material come alive for the White student audience. Asking Black students to perform on cue and provide a Black experience for their White classmates can be seen as voyeurism at its worst.

Members of subordinate groups do not willingly participate in such exchanges but often do so because members of dominant groups control the institutional and symbolic apparatuses of oppression. Racial/ethnic groups, women, and the poor have never had the luxury of being voyeurs of the lives of the privileged. Our ability to survive in hostile settings has hinged on our ability to learn intricate details about the behavior and worldview of the powerful and adjust our behavior accordingly. I need only point to the difference in perception of those men and women in abusive relationships. Where men can view their girlfriends and wives as sex objects, helpmates and a collection of stereotyped categories of voyeurism—women must be attuned to every nuance of their partners' behavior. Are women "naturally" better in relating to people with more power than themselves, or have circumstances mandated that men and women develop different skills? . . .

Coming from a tradition where most relationships across difference are squarely rooted in relations of domination and subordination, we have much less experience relating to people as different but equal. The classroom is potentially one powerful and safe space where dialogues among individuals of unequal power relationships can occur. . . .

2. Coalitions Around Common Causes

A second issue in building relationships and coalitions essential for social change concerns knowing the real reasons for coalition. Just what brings people together? One powerful catalyst fostering group solidarity is the presence of a common enemy. African-American, Hispanic, Asian-American, and women's studies all share the common intellectual heritage of challenging what passes for certified knowledge in the academy. But politically expedient relationships and coalitions like these are fragile because, as June Jordan points out:

> It occurs to me that much organizational grief could be avoided if people understood that partnership in misery does not necessarily provide for partnership for change: When we get the monsters off our backs all of us may want to run in very different directions. (1985, 47)

Sharing a common cause assists individuals and groups in maintaining relationships that transcend their differences. Building effective coalitions involves struggling to hear one another and developing empathy for each other's points of view. The coalitions that I have been involved in that lasted and that worked have been those where commitment to a specific issue mandated collaboration as the best strategy for addressing the issue at hand.

. . .

None of us alone has a comprehensive vision of how race, class and gender operate as categories of analysis or how they might be used as categories of connection. Our personal biographies offer us partial views. Few of us can manage to study race, class and gender simultaneously. Instead, we each know more about some dimensions of this larger story and less about others. . . . Just as the members of the school had special skills to offer to the task of building the school, we have areas of specialization and expertise, whether scholarly, theoretical, pedagogical or within areas of race, class or gender. We do not all have to do the same thing in the same way. Instead, we must support each other's efforts, realizing that they are all part of the larger enterprise of bringing about social change.

3. Building Empathy

A third issue involved in building the types of relationships and coalitions essential for social change concerns the issue of individual accountability. Race, class and gender oppression form the structural backdrop against which we frame our relationship—these are the forces that encourage us to substitute voyeurism . . . for fully human relationships. But while we may not have created this situation, we are each responsible for making individual, personal choices concerning which elements of race, class and gender oppression we will accept and which we will work to change.

One essential component of this accountability involves developing empathy for the experiences of individuals and groups different than ourselves. Empathy begins with taking an interest in the facts of other people['s] lives, both as individuals and as groups. If you care about me, you should want to know not only the details of my personal biography but a sense of how race, class and gender as categories of analysis created the institutional and symbolic backdrop for my personal biography. How can you hope to assess my character without knowing the details of the circumstances I face?

Moreover, by taking a theoretical stance that we have all been affected by race, class and gender as categories of analysis that have structured our treatment, we open up possibilities for using those same constructs as categories of connection in building empathy. For example, I have a good White woman friend with whom I share common interests and beliefs. But we know that our racial differences have provided us with different experiences. So we talk about them. We do not assume that because I am Black, race has only affected me and not her or that because I am a Black woman, race neutralizes the effect of gender in my life while accenting it in hers. We take those same categories of analysis that have created cleavages in our lives, in this case, categories of race and gender, and use them as categories of connection in building empathy for each other's experiences.

Finding common causes and building empathy is difficult, no matter which side of privilege we inhabit. Building empathy from the dominant side of privilege is difficult, simply because individuals from privileged backgrounds are not encouraged to do so. For example, in order for those of you who are White to develop empathy for the experiences of people of color, you must grapple with how your white skin has privileged you. This is difficult to do, because it not only entails the intellectual process of seeing how whiteness is elevated in institutions and symbols, but it also involves the often painful process of seeing how your whiteness has shaped your personal biography. Intellectual stances against the institutional and symbolic dimensions of racism are generally easier to maintain than sustained self-reflection about how racism has shaped all of our individual biographies. Were and are your fathers, uncles, and grandfathers really more capable than mine, or can their accomplishments be explained in part by the racism members of my family experienced? Did your mothers stand silently by and watch all this happen? More importantly, how have they passed on the benefits of their whiteness to you?

These are difficult questions, and I have tremendous respect for my colleagues and students who are trying to answer them. Since there is no compelling reason to examine the source and meaning of one's own privilege, I know that those who do so have freely chosen this stance. They are making conscious efforts to root out the piece of the oppressor planted within them. To me, they are entitled to the support of people of color in their efforts. Men who declare themselves feminists, members of the middle class who ally themselves with antipoverty struggles, heterosexuals who support gays and lesbians, are all trying to grow, and their efforts place them far ahead of the majority who never think of engaging in such important struggles.

Building empathy from the subordinate side of privilege is also difficult, but for different reasons. Members of subordinate groups are understandably reluctant to abandon a basic mistrust of members of powerful groups because this basic mistrust has traditionally been central to their survival. As a Black woman, it would be foolish for me to assume that White women, or Black men, or White men or any other group with a history of exploiting African-American women have my best interests at heart. These groups enjoy varying amounts of privilege over me and therefore I must carefully watch them and be prepared for a relation of domination and subordination.

Like the privileged, members of subordinate groups must also work toward replacing judgments by category with new ways of thinking and acting. Refusing to do so stifles prospects for effective coalition and social change. Let me use another example from my own experiences. When I was an undergraduate, I had little time or patience for the theorizing of the privileged. My initial years at a private, elite institution were difficult, not because the course work was

challenging (it was, but that wasn't what distracted me) or because I had to work while my classmates lived on family allowances (I was used to work). The adjustment was difficult because I was surrounded by so many people who took their privilege for granted. Most of them felt entitled to their wealth. That astounded me.

I remember one incident of watching a White woman down the hall in my dormitory try to pick out which sweater to wear. The sweaters were piled up on her bed in all the colors of the rainbow, sweater after sweater. She asked my advice in a way that let me know that choosing a sweater was one of the most important decisions she had to make on a daily basis. Standing knee-deep in her sweaters, I realized how different our lives were. She did not have to worry about maintaining a solid academic average so that she could receive financial aid. Because she was in the majority, she was not treated as a representative of her race. She did not have to consider how her classroom comments or basic existence on campus contributed to the treatment her group would receive. Her allowance protected her from having to work, so she was free to spend her time studying, partying, or in her case, worrying about which sweater to wear. The degree of inequality in our lives and her unquestioned sense of entitlement concerning that inequality offended me. For a while, I categorized all affluent White women as being superficial, arrogant, overly concerned with material possessions, and part of my problem. But had I continued to classify people in this way, I would have missed out on making some very good friends whose discomfort with their inherited or acquired social class privileges pushed them to examine their position.

Since I opened with the words of Audre Lorde, it seems appropriate to close with another of her ideas. . . .

Each of us is called upon to take a stand. So in these days ahead, as we examine ourselves and each other, our works, our fears, our differences, our sisterhood and survivals, I urge you to tackle what is most difficult for us all, self-scrutiny of our complacencies, the idea that since each of us believes she is on the side of right, she need not examine her position. (1985)

I urge you to examine your position.

REFERENCES

Collins, Patricia Hill. 1989. "The Social Construction of Black Feminist Thought." *Signs.* Summer 1989.

Gwaltney, John Langston. 1980. *Drylongso: A Self-Portrait of Black America.* New York: Vintage.

Harding, Sandra. 1986. *The Science Question in Feminism.* Ithaca, NY: Cornell University Press.

Jordan, June. 1985. *On Call: Political Essays.* Boston: South End Press.

Lorde, Audre. 1984. *Sister Outsider.* Trumansberg, New York: The Crossing Press.

———. 1985 "Sisterhood and Survival." Keynote address, conference on the Black Woman Writer and the Diaspora, Michigan State University.

Spelman, Elizabeth. 1982. "Theories of Race and Gender: The Erasure of Black Women." *Quest* 5: 36–32.

Tate, Claudia, ed. 1983. *Black Women Writers at Work.* New York: Continuum.

R E A D I N G   **10**

Oppression

Marilyn Frye (1983)

It is a fundamental claim of feminism that women are oppressed. The word "oppression" is a strong word. It repels and attracts. It is dangerous and dangerously fashionable and endangered. It is much misused, and sometimes not innocently.

The statement that women are oppressed is frequently met with the claim that men are oppressed too. We hear that oppressing is oppressive to those who oppress as well as to those they oppress. Some men cite as evidence of their oppression their much-advertised inability to cry. It is tough, we are told, to be masculine. When the stresses and frustrations of being a man are cited as evidence that oppressors are oppressed by their oppressing; the word "oppression" is being stretched to meaninglessness; it is treated as though its scope includes any and all human experience of limitation or suffering, no matter the cause, degree or consequence. Once such usage has been put over on us, then if ever we deny that any person or group is oppressed, we seem to imply that we think they never suffer and have no feelings. We are accused of insensitivity, even of bigotry. For women, such accusation is particularly intimidating, since sensitivity is one of the few virtues that has been assigned to us. If we are found insensitive, we may fear we have no redeeming traits at all and perhaps are not real women. Thus are we silenced before we begin: the name of our situation drained of meaning and our guilt mechanisms tripped.

But this is nonsense. Human beings can be miserable without being oppressed, and it is perfectly consistent to deny that a person or group is oppressed without denying that they have feelings or that they suffer. . . .

The root of the word "oppression" is the element "press." *The press of the crowd; pressed into military service; to press a pair of pants; printing press; press the button.* Presses are used to mold things or flatten them or reduce them in bulk, sometimes to reduce them by squeezing out the gasses or liquids in them. Something pressed is something caught between or among forces and barriers which are so related to each other that jointly they restrain, restrict or prevent the thing's motion or mobility. Mold. Immobilize. Reduce.

The mundane experience of the oppressed provides another clue. One of the most characteristic and ubiquitous features of the world as experienced by oppressed people is the double bind—situations in which options are reduced to a very few and all of them expose one to penalty, censure or deprivation. For example, it is often a requirement upon oppressed people that we smile and be cheerful. If we comply, we signal our docility and our acquiescence in our situation. We need not, then, be taken note of. We acquiesce in being made invisible, in our occupying no space. We participate in our own erasure. On the other hand, anything but the sunniest countenance exposes us to being perceived as mean, bitter, angry or dangerous. This means, at the least, that we may be found "difficult" or unpleasant to work with, which is enough to cost one one's livelihood; at worst, being seen as mean, bitter, angry or dangerous has been known to result in rape, arrest, beating and murder. One can only choose to risk one's preferred form and rate of annihilation.

Another example: It is common in the United States that women, especially younger women, are in a bind where neither sexual activity nor sexual inactivity is all right. If she is heterosexually active, a woman is open to censure and punishment for being loose, unprincipled or a whore. The "punishment" comes in the form of criticism, snide and embarrassing remarks, being treated as an easy lay by men, scorn from her more restrained female friends. She may have to lie and hide her behavior from her parents. She must juggle the risks of unwanted pregnancy and dangerous contraceptives. On the other hand, if she refrains from heterosexual activity, she is fairly constantly harassed by men who try to persuade her into it and pressure her to "relax" and "let her hair down"; she is threatened with labels like "frigid," "uptight," "man-hater," "bitch" and "cock-tease." The same parents who would be disapproving of her sexual activity may be worried by her inactivity because it suggests she is not or will not be popular, or is not sexually normal. She may be charged with lesbianism. If a woman is raped, then if she has been heterosexually active she is subject to the presumption that she liked it (since her activity is presumed to show that she likes sex), and if she has not been heterosexually active, she is subject to the presumption that she liked it (since she is supposedly "repressed and frustrated"). Both heterosexual activity and heterosexual nonactivity are likely to be taken as proof that you wanted to be raped, and hence, of course, weren't *really* raped at all. You can't win. You are caught in a bind, caught between systematically related pressures.

Women are caught like this, too, by networks of forces and barriers that expose one to penalty, loss or contempt whether one works outside the home or not, is on welfare or not, bears children or not, raises children or not, marries or not, stays married or not, is heterosexual, lesbian, both or neither. Economic necessity; confinement to racial and/or sexual job ghettos; sexual harassment; sex discrimination; pressures of competing expectations and judgments about *women, wives* and *mothers* (in the society at large, in racial and ethnic subcultures and in one's own mind); dependence (full or partial) on husbands, parents or the state; commitment to political ideas; loyalties to racial or ethnic or other "minority" groups; the demands of self-respect and responsibilities to others. Each of these factors exists in complex tension with every other, penalizing or prohibiting all of the apparently available options. And nipping at one's heels, always, is the endless pack of little things. If one dresses one way, one is subject to the assumption that one is advertising one's sexual availability; if one dresses another way, one appears to "not care about oneself" or to be "unfeminine." If one uses "strong language," one invites categorization as a whore or slut; if one does not, one invites categorization as a "lady"—one too delicately constituted to cope with robust speech or the realities to which it presumably refers.

The experience of oppressed people is that the living of one's life is confined and shaped by forces and barriers which are not accidental or occasional and hence avoidable, but are systematically related to each other in such a way as to catch one between and among them and restrict or penalize motion in any direction. It is the experience of being caged in: all avenues, in every direction, are blocked or booby trapped.

Cages. Consider a birdcage. If you look very closely at just one wire in the cage, you cannot see the other wires. If your conception of what is before you is determined by this myopic focus, you could look at that one wire, up and down the length of it, and be unable to see why a bird would not just fly around the wire any time it wanted to go somewhere. Furthermore, even if, one day at a time, you myopically inspected each wire, you still could not see why a bird would have trouble going past the wires to get anywhere. There is no physical property of any one wire, *nothing* that the closest scrutiny could discover, that will reveal how a bird could be inhibited or harmed by it except in the most accidental way. It is only when you step back, stop looking at the wires one by one, microscopically, and take a macroscopic view of the whole cage, that you can see why the bird does not go anywhere; and then you will see it in a moment. It will require no great subtlety of mental powers. It is perfectly *obvious* that the bird is surrounded by a network of systematically

related barriers, no one of which would be the least hindrance to its flight, but which, by their relations to each other, are as confining as the solid walls of a dungeon.

It is now possible to grasp one of the reasons why oppression can be hard to see and recognize: one can study the elements of an oppressive structure with great care and some good will without seeing the structure as a whole, and hence without seeing or being able to understand that one is looking at a cage and that there are people there who are caged, whose motion and mobility are restricted, whose lives are shaped and reduced.

. . .

As the cageness of the birdcage is a macroscopic phenomenon, the oppressiveness of the situations in which women live our various and different lives is a macroscopic phenomenon. Neither can be *seen* from a microscopic perspective. But when you look macroscopically you can see it—a network of forces and barriers which are systematically related and which conspire to the immobilization, reduction and molding of women and the lives we live.

R E A D I N G **11**

Tomorrow I'm Going to Rewrite the English Language

Lois Keith (1996)

Tomorrow I am going to rewrite the English
    Language.
I will discard all those striving ambulist
    metaphors of power and success
And construct new ways to describe my strength.
My new, different strength.

Then I won't have to feel dependent
Because I can't stand on my own two feet.
And I'll refuse to feel a failure

When I don't stay one step ahead.
I won't feel inadequate if I can't
Stand up for myself
Or illogical when I don't
Take it one step at a time.
I will make them understand that it is a very
    male way
To describe the world.
All this walking tall
And making great strides.

Yes, tomorrow I am going to rewrite the English
　Language
Creating the world in my own image.
Mine will be a gentler, more womanly way

To describe my progress.
I will wheel, cover and encircle.
Somehow I will learn to say it all.

Homophobia
A Weapon of Sexism

Suzanne Pharr (1997)

Homophobia—the irrational fear and hatred of those who love and sexually desire those of the same sex. Though I intimately knew its meaning, the word *homophobia* was unknown to me until the late 1970s, and when I first heard it, I was struck by how difficult it is to say, what an ugly word it is, equally as ugly as its meaning. Like racism and anti-Semitism, it is a word that calls up images of loss of freedom, verbal and physical violence, death.

In my life I have experienced the effects of homophobia through rejection by friends, threats of loss of employment, and threats upon my life; and I have witnessed far worse things happening to other lesbian and gay people: loss of children, beatings, rape, death. Its power is great enough to keep ten to twenty percent of the population living lives of fear (if their sexual identity is hidden) or lives of danger (if their sexual identity is visible) or both. And its power is great enough to keep the remaining eighty to ninety percent of the population trapped in their own fears.

　. . .

Homophobia works effectively as a weapon of sexism because it is joined with a powerful arm, heterosexism. Heterosexism creates the climate for homophobia with its assumption that the world is and must be heterosexual and its display of power and privilege as the norm. Heterosexism is the systemic display of homophobia in the institutions of society. Heterosexism and homophobia work together to enforce compulsory heterosexuality and that bastion of patriarchal power, the nuclear family. The central focus of the right-wing attack against women's liberation is that women's equality, women's self-determination, women's control of our own bodies and lives will damage what they see as the crucial societal institution, the nuclear family. The attack has been led by fundamentalist ministers across the country. The two areas they have focused on most consistently are abortion and homosexuality, and their passion has led them to bomb women's clinics and to recommend deprogramming for homosexuals and establishing camps to quarantine people with AIDS. To resist marriage and/or heterosexuality is to risk severe punishment and loss.

It is not by chance that when children approach puberty and increased sexual awareness they begin to taunt each other by calling these names: "queer," "faggot," "pervert." It is at puberty that the full force of society's pressure to conform to heterosexuality and prepare for marriage is brought to bear. Children know what we have taught them, and we have given clear messages that those who deviate from standard expectations are to be made to get back in line.

The best controlling tactic at puberty is to be treated as an outsider, to be ostracized at a time when it feels most vital to be accepted. Those who are different must be made to suffer loss. It is also at puberty that misogyny begins to be more apparent, and girls are pressured to conform to societal norms that do not permit them to realize their full potential. It is at this time that their academic achievements begin to decrease as they are coerced into compulsory heterosexuality and trained for dependency upon a man, that is, for economic survival.

There was a time when the two most condemning accusations against a woman meant to ostracize and disempower her were "whore" and "lesbian." The sexual revolution and changing attitudes about heterosexual behavior may have led to some lessening of the power of the word *whore,* though it still has strength as a threat to sexual property and prostitutes are stigmatized and abused. However, the word *lesbian* is still fully charged and carries with it the full threat of loss of power and privilege, the threat of being cut asunder, abandoned, and left outside society's protection.

To be a lesbian is to be *perceived* as someone who has stepped out of line, who has moved out of sexual/economic dependence on a male, who is woman-identified. A lesbian is perceived as someone who can live without a man and who is therefore (however illogically) against men. A lesbian is perceived as being outside the acceptable, routinized order of things. She is seen as someone who has no societal institutions to protect her and who is not privileged to the protection of individual males. Many heterosexual women see her as someone who stands in contradiction to the sacrifices they have made to conform to compulsory heterosexuality. A lesbian is perceived as a threat to the nuclear family, to male dominance and control, to the very heart of sexism.

Gay men are perceived also as a threat to male dominance and control, and the homophobia expressed against them has the same roots in sexism as does homophobia against lesbians. Visible gay men are the objects of extreme hatred

and fear by heterosexual men because their breaking ranks with male heterosexual solidarity is seen as a damaging rent in the very fabric of sexism. They are seen as betrayers, as traitors who must be punished and eliminated. In the beating and killing of gay men we see clear evidence of this hatred. When we see the fierce homophobia expressed toward gay men, we can begin to understand the ways sexism also affects males through imposing rigid, dehumanizing gender roles on them. The two circumstances in which it is legitimate for men to be openly physically affectionate with one another are in competitive sports and in the crisis of war. For many men, these two experiences are the highlights of their lives, and they think of them again and again with nostalgia. War and sports offer a cover of all-male safety and dominance to keep away the notion of affectionate openness being identified with homosexuality. When gay men break ranks with male roles through bonding and affection outside the arenas of war and sports, they are perceived as not being "real men," that is, as being identified with women, the weaker sex that must be dominated and that over the centuries has been the object of male hatred and abuse. Misogyny gets transferred to gay men with a vengeance and is increased by the fear that their sexual identity and behavior will bring down the entire system of male dominance and compulsory heterosexuality.

If lesbians are established as threats to the status quo, as outcasts who must be punished, homophobia can wield its power over all women through lesbian baiting. Lesbian baiting is an attempt to control women by labeling us as lesbians because our behavior is not acceptable, that is, when we are being independent, going our own way, living whole lives, fighting for our rights, demanding equal pay, saying no to violence, being self-assertive, bonding with and loving the company of women, assuming the right to our bodies, insisting upon our own authority, making changes that include us in society's decision-making; lesbian baiting occurs when women are called lesbians because we resist male dominance and control. And it has little or nothing to do with one's sexual identity.

To be named as lesbian threatens all women, not just lesbians, with great loss. And any woman who steps out of role risks being called a lesbian. To understand how this is a threat to all women, one must understand that any woman can be called a lesbian and there is no real way she can defend herself: there is no way to credential one's sexuality. ("The Children's Hour," a Lillian Hellman play, makes this point when a student asserts two teachers are lesbians and they have no way to disprove it.) She may be married or divorced, have children, dress in the most feminine manner, have sex with men, be celibate—but there are lesbians who do all those things. *Lesbians look like all women and all women look like lesbians.* There is no guaranteed method of identification, and as we all know, sexual identity can be kept hidden. (The same is true for men. There is no way to prove their sexual identity, though many go to extremes to prove heterosexuality.) Also, women are not necessarily born lesbian. Some seem to be, but others become lesbians later in life after having lived heterosexual lives. Lesbian baiting of heterosexual women would not work if there were a definitive way to identify lesbians (or heterosexuals).

We have yet to understand clearly how sexual identity develops. And this is disturbing to some people, especially those who are determined to discover how lesbian and gay identity is formed so that they will know where to start in eliminating it. (Isn't it odd that there is so little concern about discovering the causes of heterosexuality?) There are many theories: genetic makeup, hormones, socialization, environment, etc. But there is no conclusive evidence that indicates that heterosexuality comes from one process and homosexuality from another.

We do know, however, that sexual identity can be in flux, and we know that sexual identity means more than just the gender of people one is attracted to and has sex with. To be a lesbian has as many ramifications as for a woman to be heterosexual. It is more than sex, more than just the bedroom issue many would like to make it: it is a woman-centered life with all the social interconnections that entails. Some lesbians are in long-term relationships, some in short-term ones, some date, some are celibate, some are married to men, some remain as separate as possible from men, some have children by men, some by alternative insemination, some seem "feminine" by societal standards, some "masculine," some are doctors, lawyers and ministers, some laborers, housewives and writers: what all share in common is a sexual/affectional identity that focuses on women in its attractions and social relationships.

If lesbians are simply women with a particular sexual identity who look and act like all women, then the major difference in living out a lesbian sexual identity as opposed to a heterosexual identity is that as lesbians we live in a homophobic world that threatens and imposes damaging loss on us for being *who we are,* for choosing to live whole lives. Homophobic people often assert that homosexuals have the choice of not being homosexual; that is, we don't have to act out our sexual identity. In that case, I want to hear heterosexuals talk about their willingness not to act out their sexual identity, including not just sexual activity but heterosexual social interconnections and heterosexual privilege. It is a question of wholeness. It is very difficult for one to be denied the life of a sexual being, whether expressed in sex or in physical affection, and to feel complete, whole. For our loving relationships with humans feed the life of the spirit and enable us to overcome our basic isolation and to be interconnected with humankind.

. . .

What does a woman have to do to get called a lesbian? Almost anything, sometimes nothing at all, but certainly anything that threatens the status quo, anything that steps out of role, anything that asserts the rights of women, anything that doesn't indicate submission and subordination. Assertiveness, standing up for oneself, asking for more pay, better working conditions, training for and accepting a nontraditional (you mean a man's?) job, enjoying the company of women, being financially independent, being in control of one's life, depending first and foremost upon oneself, thinking that one can do whatever needs to be done, but above all, working for the rights and equality of women.

In the backlash to the gains of the women's liberation movement, there has been an increased effort to keep definitions man-centered. Therefore, to work on behalf of women must mean to work against men. To love women must mean that one hates men. A very effective attack has been made against the word *feminist* to make it a derogatory word. In current backlash usage, *feminist* equals *man-hater,* which equals *lesbian.* This formula is created in the hope that women will be frightened away from their work on behalf of women. Consequently, we now have women who believe in the rights of women and work for those rights while from fear deny that they are feminists, or refuse to use the word because it is so "abrasive."

So, what does one do in an effort to keep from being called a lesbian? She steps back into line, into the role that is demanded of her, tries to behave in such a way that doesn't threaten the status of men, and if she works for women's rights, she begins modifying that work. When women's organizations begin doing significant social change work, they inevitably are lesbian baited; that is, funders or institutions or community members tell us that they can't work with us because of our "man-hating attitudes" or the presence of lesbians. We are called too strident, told we are making enemies, not doing good.

The battered women's movement has seen this kind of attack: the pressure has been to provide services only, without analysis of the causes of violence against women and strategies for ending it. To provide only services without political analysis or direct action is to be in an approved "helping" role; to analyze the causes of violence against women is to begin the work toward changing an entire system of power and control. It is when we do the latter that we are threatened with the label of man-hater or lesbian. For my politics, if a women's social change organization has not been labeled lesbian or communist, it is probably not doing significant work; it is only "making nice."

Women in many of these organizations, out of fear of all the losses we are threatened with, begin to modify our work to make it more acceptable and less threatening to the male-dominated society which we originally set out to change. The work can no longer be radical (going to the root cause of the problem) but instead must be reforming, working only on the symptoms and not the cause. Real change for women becomes thwarted and stopped. The word *lesbian* is instilled with the power to halt our work and control our lives. And we give it its power with our fear.

In my view, homophobia has been one of the major causes of the failure of the women's liberation movement to make deep and lasting change. (The other major block has been racism.) We were fierce when we set out, but when threatened with the loss of heterosexual privilege, we began putting on brakes. Our best-known nationally distributed women's magazine was reluctant to print articles about lesbians, began putting a man on the cover several times a year, and writing articles about women who succeeded in a man's world. We worried about our image, our being all right, our being "real women" despite our work. Instead of talking about the elimination of sexual gender roles, we stepped back and talked about "sex role stereotyping" as the issue. Change around the edges for middle-class white women began to be talked about as successes. We accepted tokenism and integration, forgetting that equality for all women, for all people—and not just equality of white middle-class women with white men—was the goal that we could never put behind us.

But despite backlash and retreats, change is growing from within. The women's liberation movement is beginning to gain strength again because there are women who are talking about liberation for all women. We are examining sexism, racism, homophobia, classism, anti-Semitism, ageism, ableism, and imperialism, and we see everything as connected. This change in point of view represents the third wave of the women's liberation movement, a new direction that does not get mass media coverage and recognition. It has been initiated by women of color and lesbians who were marginalized or rendered invisible by the white heterosexual leaders of earlier efforts. The first wave was the 19th and early 20th century campaign for the vote; the second, beginning in the 1960s, focused on the Equal Rights Amendment and abortion rights. Consisting of predominantly white middle-class women, both failed in recognizing issues of equality and empowerment for all women. The third wave of the movement, multi-racial and multi-issued, seeks the transformation of the world for us all. We know that we won't get there until everyone gets there; that we must move forward in a great strong line, hand in hand, not just a few at a time.

We know that the arguments about homophobia originating from mental health, and biblical/religious attitudes can be settled when we look at the sexism that permeates religious and psychiatric history. The women of the third wave of the women's liberation movement know that *without the existence of sexism, there would be no homophobia.*

Finally, we know that as long as the word *lesbian* can strike fear in any woman's heart, then work on behalf of women can be stopped; the only successful work against sexism must include work against homophobia.

R E A D I N G   **13**

White Privilege and Male Privilege

Peggy McIntosh (1988)

Through work to bring materials and perspectives from Women's Studies into the rest of the curriculum, I have often noticed men's unwillingness to grant that they are overprivileged in the curriculum, even though they may grant that women are disadvantaged. Denials that amount to taboos surround the subject of advantages that men gain from women's disadvantages. These denials protect male privilege from being fully recognized, acknowledged, lessened, or ended.

Thinking through unacknowledged male privilege as a phenomenon with a life of its own, I realized that since hierarchies in our society are interlocking, there was most likely a phenomenon of white privilege that was similarly denied and protected, but alive and real in its effects. As a white person, I realized I had been taught about racism as something that puts others at a disadvantage, but had been taught not to see one of its corollary aspects, white privilege, which puts me at an advantage.

I think whites are carefully taught not to recognize white privilege, as males are taught not to recognize male privilege. So I have begun in an untutored way to ask what it is like to have white privilege. This paper is a partial record of my personal observations and not a scholarly analysis. It is based on my daily experiences within my particular circumstances.

I have come to see white privilege as an invisible package of unearned assets that I can count on cashing in each day, but about which I was "meant" to remain oblivious. White privilege is like an invisible weightless knapsack of special provisions, assurances, tools, maps, guides, codebooks, passports, visas, clothes, compass, emergency gear, and blank checks.

Since I have had trouble facing white privilege, and describing its results in my life, I saw parallels here with men's reluctance to acknowledge male privilege. Only rarely will a man go beyond acknowledging that women are disadvantaged to acknowledging that men have unearned advantage, or that unearned privilege has not been good for men's development as human beings, or for society's development, or that privilege systems might ever be challenged and *changed.*

I will review here several types or layers of denial that I see at work protecting, and preventing awareness about, entrenched male privilege. Then I will draw parallels, from my own experience, with the denials that veil the facts of white privilege. Finally, I will list forty-six ordinary and daily ways in which I experience having white privilege, by contrast with my African American colleagues in the same building. This list is not intended to be generalizable. Others can make their own lists from within their own life circumstances.

Writing this paper has been difficult, despite warm receptions for the talks on which it is based.[1] For describing white privilege makes one newly accountable. As we in Women's Studies work [to] reveal male privilege and ask men to give up some of their power, so one who writes about having white privilege must ask, "Having described it, what will I do to lessen or end it?"

The denial of men's overprivileged state takes many forms in discussions of curriculum change work. Some claim that men must be central in the curriculum because they have done most of what is important or distinctive in life or in civilization. Some recognize sexism in the curriculum but deny that it makes male students seem unduly important in life. Others agree that certain *individual* thinkers are male oriented but deny that there is any *systemic* tendency in disciplinary frameworks or epistemology to overempower men as a group. Those men who do grant that male privilege takes institutionalized and embedded forms are still likely to deny that male hegemony has opened doors for them personally. Virtually all men deny that male overreward alone can explain men's centrality in all the inner sanctums of our most powerful institutions. Moreover, those few who will acknowledge that male privilege systems have overempowered them usually end up doubting that we could dismantle these privilege systems. They may say they will

work to improve women's status, in the society or in the university, but they can't or won't support the idea of lessening men's. In curricular terms, this is the point at which they say that they regret they cannot use any of the interesting new scholarship on women because the syllabus is full. When the talk turns to giving men less cultural room, even the most thoughtful and fair-minded of the men I know will tend to reflect, or fall back on, conservative assumptions about the inevitability of present gender relations and distributions of power, calling on precedent or sociobiology and psychobiology to demonstrate that male domination is natural and follows inevitably from evolutionary pressures. Others resort to arguments from "experience" or religion or social responsibility or wishing and dreaming.

After I realized, through faculty development work in Women's Studies, the extent to which men work from a base of unacknowledged privilege, I understood that much of their oppressiveness was unconscious. Then I remembered the frequent charges from women of color that white women whom they encounter are oppressive. I began to understand why we are justly seen as oppressive, even when we don't see ourselves that way. At the very least, obliviousness of one's privileged state can make a person or group irritating to be with. I began to count the ways in which I enjoy unearned skin privilege and have been conditioned into oblivion about its existence, unable to see that it put me "ahead" in any way, or put my people ahead, overrewarding us and yet also paradoxically damaging us, or that it could or should be changed.

My schooling gave me no training in seeing myself as an oppressor, as an unfairly advantaged person, or as a participant in a damaged culture. I was taught to see myself as an individual whose moral state depended on her individual moral will. At school, we were not taught about slavery in any depth; we were not taught to see slaveholders as damaged people. Slaves were seen as the only group at risk of being dehumanized. My schooling followed the pattern which Elizabeth Minnich has pointed out: whites are taught to think of their lives as morally neutral, normative, and average, and also ideal, so that when we work to benefit others, this is seen as work that will allow "them" to be more like "us." I think many of us know how obnoxious this attitude can be in men.

After frustration with men who would not recognize male privilege, I decided to try to work on myself at least by identifying some of the daily effects of white privilege in my life. It is crude work, at this stage, but I will give here a list of special circumstances and conditions I experience that I did not earn but that I have been made to feel are mine by birth, by citizenship, and by virtue of being a conscientious law-abiding "normal" person of goodwill. I have chosen those conditions that I think in my case *attach somewhat more to skin-color privilege* than to class, religion, ethnic status, or geographical location, though these other privileging factors are intricately intertwined. As far as I can see, my Afro-American co-workers, friends, and acquaintances with whom I come into daily or frequent contact in this particular time, place, and line of work cannot count on most of these conditions.

1. I can, if I wish, arrange to be in the company of people of my race most of the time.
2. I can avoid spending time with people whom I was trained to mistrust and who have learned to mistrust my kind or me.
3. If I should need to move, I can be pretty sure of renting or purchasing housing in an area which I can afford and in which I would want to live.
4. I can be reasonably sure that my neighbors in such a location will be neutral or pleasant to me.
5. I can go shopping alone most of the time, fairly well assured that I will not be followed or harassed by store detectives.
6. I can turn on the television or open to the front page of the paper and see people of my race widely and positively represented.
7. When I am told about our national heritage or about "civilization," I am shown that people of my color made it what it is.
8. I can be sure that my children will be given curricular materials that testify to the existence of their race.
9. If I want to, I can be pretty sure of finding a publisher for this piece on white privilege.
10. I can be fairly sure of having my voice heard in a group in which I am the only member of my race.
11. I can be casual about whether or not to listen to another woman's voice in a group in which she is the only member of her race.
12. I can go into a book shop and count on finding the writing of my race represented, into a supermarket and find the staple foods that fit with my cultural traditions, into a hairdresser's shop and find someone who can deal with my hair.
13. Whether I use checks, credit cards, or cash, I can count on my skin color not to work against the appearance that I am financially reliable.
14. I could arrange to protect our young children most of the time from people who might not like them.
15. I did not have to educate our children to be aware of systemic racism for their own daily physical protection.
16. I can be pretty sure that my children's teachers and employers will tolerate them if they fit school and workplace norms; my chief worries about them do not concern others' attitudes toward their race.
17. I can talk with my mouth full and not have people put this down to my color.
18. I can swear, or dress in secondhand clothes, or not answer letters, without having people attribute these choices to the bad morals, the poverty, or the illiteracy of my race.
19. I can speak in public to a powerful male group without putting my race on trial.
20. I can do well in a challenging situation without being called a credit to my race.
21. I am never asked to speak for all the people of my racial group.
22. I can remain oblivious to the language and customs of persons of color who constitute the world's majority without feeling in my culture any penalty for such oblivion.
23. I can criticize our government and talk about how much I fear its policies and behavior without being seen as a cultural outsider.

24. I can be reasonably sure that if I ask to talk to "the person in charge," I will be facing a person of my race.

25. If a traffic cop pulls me over or if the IRS audits my tax return, I can be sure I haven't been singled out because of my race.

26. I can easily buy posters, postcards, picture books, greeting cards, dolls, toys, and children's magazines featuring people of my race.

27. I can go home from most meetings of organizations I belong to feeling somewhat tied in, rather than isolated, out of place, outnumbered, unheard, held at a distance, or feared.

28. I can be pretty sure that an argument with a colleague of another race is more likely to jeopardize her chances for advancement than to jeopardize mine.

29. I can be fairly sure that if I argue for the promotion of a person of another race, or a program centering on race, this is not likely to cost me heavily within my present setting, even if my colleagues disagree with me.

30. If I declare there is a racial issue at hand, or there isn't a racial issue at hand, my race will lend me more credibility for either position than a person of color will have.

31. I can choose to ignore developments in minority writing and minority activist programs, or disparage them, or learn from them, but in any case, I can find ways to be more or less protected from negative consequences of any of these choices.

32. My culture gives me little fear about ignoring the perspectives and powers of people of other races.

33. I am not made acutely aware that my shape, bearing, or body odor will be taken as a reflection on my race.

34. I can worry about racism without being seen as self-interested or self-seeking.

35. I can take a job with an affirmative action employer without having my co-workers on the job suspect that I got it because of my race.

36. If my day, week, or year is going badly, I need not ask of each negative episode or situation whether it has racial overtones.

37. I can be pretty sure of finding people who would be willing to talk with me and advise me about my next steps, professionally.

38. I can think over many options, social, political, imaginative, or professional, without asking whether a person of my race would be accepted or allowed to do what I want to do.

39. I can be late to a meeting without having the lateness reflect on my race.

40. I can choose public accommodation without fearing that people of my race cannot get in or will be mistreated in the places I have chosen.

41. I can be sure that if I need legal or medical help, my race will not work against me.

42. I can arrange my activities so that I will never have to experience feelings of rejection owing to my race.

43. If I have low credibility as a leader, I can be sure that my race is not the problem.

44. I can easily find academic courses and institutions that give attention only to people of my race.

45. I can expect figurative language and imagery in all of the arts to testify to experiences of my race.

46. I can choose blemish cover or bandages in "flesh" color and have them more or less match my skin.

I repeatedly forgot each of the realizations on this list until I wrote it down. For me, white privilege has turned out to be an elusive and fugitive subject. The pressure to avoid it is great, for in facing it I must give up the myth of meritocracy. If these things are true, this is not such a free country; one's life is not what one makes it; many doors open for certain people through no virtues of their own. These perceptions mean also that my moral condition is not what I had been led to believe. The appearance of being a good citizen rather than a troublemaker comes in large part from having all sorts of doors open automatically because of my color.

A further paralysis of nerve comes from literary silence protecting privilege. My clearest memories of finding such analysis are in Lillian Smith's unparalleled *Killers of the Dream* and

Margaret Andersen's review of Karen and Mamie Fields' *Lemon Swamp*. Smith, for example, wrote about walking toward black children on the street and knowing they would step into the gutter; Andersen contrasted the pleasure that she, as a white child, took on summer driving trips to the south with Karen Fields' memories of driving in a closed car stocked with all necessities lest, in stopping, her black family should suffer "insult, or worse." Adrienne Rich also recognizes and writes about daily experiences of privilege, but in my observation, white women's writing in this area is far more often on systemic racism than on our daily lives as light-skinned women.[2]

In unpacking this invisible knapsack of white privilege, I have listed conditions of daily experience that I once took for granted, as neutral, normal, and universally available to everybody, just as I once thought of a male-focused curriculum as the neutral or accurate account that can speak for all. Nor did I think of any of these perquisites as bad for the holder. I now think that we need a more finely differentiated taxonomy of privilege, for some of these varieties are only what one would want for everyone in a just society, and others give license to be ignorant, oblivious, arrogant, and destructive. Before proposing some more finely tuned categorization, I will make some observations about the general effects of these conditions on my life and expectations.

In this potpourri of examples, some privileges make me feel at home in the world. Others allow me to escape penalties or dangers that others suffer. Through some, I escape fear, anxiety, insult, injury, or a sense of not being welcome, not being real. Some keep me from having to hide, to be in disguise, to feel sick or crazy, to negotiate each transaction from the position of being an outsider or, within my group, a person who is suspected of having too close links with a dominant culture. Most keep me from having to be angry.

I see a pattern running through the matrix of white privilege, a pattern of assumptions that were passed on to me as a white person. There was one main piece of cultural turf; it was my own turf, and I was among those who could control the turf. I could measure up to the cultural standards and take advantage of the many options I saw around me to make what the culture would call a success of my life. *My skin color was an asset for any move I was educated to want to make.* I could think of myself as "belonging" in major ways and of making social systems work for me. I could freely disparage, fear, neglect, or be oblivious to anything outside of the dominant cultural forms. Being of the main culture, I could also criticize it fairly freely. My life was reflected back to me frequently enough so that I felt, with regard to my race, if not to my sex, like one of the real people.

Whether through the curriculum or in the newspaper, the television, the economic system, or the general look of people in the streets, I received daily signals and indications that my people counted and that others *either didn't exist or must be trying, not very successfully, to be like people of my race.* I was given cultural permission not to hear voices of people of other races or a tepid cultural tolerance for hearing or acting on such voices. I was also raised not to suffer seriously from anything that darker-skinned people might say about my group, "protected," though perhaps I should more accurately say *prohibited,* through the habits of my economic class and social group, from living in racially mixed groups or being reflective about interactions between people of differing races.

In proportion as my racial group was being made confident, comfortable, and oblivious, other groups were likely being made unconfident, uncomfortable, and alienated. Whiteness protected me from many kinds of hostility, distress, and violence, which I was being subtly trained to visit in turn upon people of color.

For this reason, the word "privilege" now seems to me misleading. Its connotations are too positive to fit the conditions and behaviors which "privilege systems" produce. We usually think of privilege as being a favored state, whether earned or conferred by birth or luck. School graduates are reminded they are privileged and urged to use their (enviable) assets well. The word "privilege" carries the connotation of being something everyone must want. Yet some of the conditions I have described here work to systemically overempower certain groups. Such privilege simply *confers dominance,* gives permission to control, because of one's race or sex. The kind of privilege that gives license to some people to be, at best, thoughtless and, at worst, murderous should not continue to be referred to as a desirable attribute. Such "privilege" may be widely desired without being in any way beneficial to the whole society.

Moreover, though "privilege" may confer power, it does not confer moral strength. Those who do not depend on conferred dominance have traits and qualities that may never develop in those who do. Just as Women's Studies courses indicate that women survive their political circumstances to lead lives that hold the human race together, so "underprivileged" people of color who are the world's majority have survived their oppression and lived survivors' lives from which the white global minority can and must learn. In some groups, those dominated have actually become strong through *not* having all of these unearned advantages, and this gives them a great deal to teach the others. Members of so-called privileged groups can seem foolish, ridiculous, infantile, or dangerous by contrast.

I want, then, to distinguish between earned strength and unearned power conferred systemically. Power from unearned privilege can look like strength when it is, in fact, permission to escape or to dominate. But not all of the privileges on my list are inevitably damaging. Some, like the expectation that neighbors will be decent to you, or that your race will not count against you in court, should be the norm in a just society and should be considered as the entitlement of everyone. Others, like the privilege not to listen to less powerful people, distort the humanity of the holders as well as the ignored groups. Still others, like finding one's staple foods everywhere, may be a function of being a member of a numerical majority in the population. Others have to do with not having to labor under pervasive negative stereotyping and mythology.

We might at least start by distinguishing between positive advantages that we can work to spread, to the point where they are not advantages at all but simply part of the normal civic and social fabric, and negative types of advantage that unless rejected will always reinforce our present hierarchies. For example, the positive "privilege" of belonging, the feeling that one belongs within the human circle, as Native Americans say, fosters development and should not be seen as privilege for a few. It is, let us say, an entitlement that none of us should have to earn; ideally it is an *unearned entitlement.* At present, since only a few have it, it is an *unearned advantage* for them. The negative "privilege" that gave me cultural permission not to take darker-skinned Others seriously can be seen as arbitrarily conferred dominance and should not be desirable for anyone. This paper results from a process of coming to see that some of the power that I originally saw as attendant on being a human being in the United States consisted in *unearned advantage* and *conferred dominance,* as well as other kinds of special circumstance not universally taken for granted.

In writing this paper I have also realized that white identity and status (as well as class identity and status) give me considerable power to choose whether to broach this subject and its trouble. I can pretty well decide whether to disappear and avoid and not listen and escape the dislike I may engender in other people through this essay, or interrupt, answer, interpret, preach, correct, criticize, and control to some extent what goes on in reaction to it. Being white, I am given considerable power to escape many kinds of danger or penalty as well as to choose which risks I want to take.

There is an analogy here, once again, with Women's Studies. Our male colleagues do not have a great deal to lose in supporting Women's Studies, but they do not have a great deal to lose if they oppose it either. They simply have the power to decide whether to commit themselves to more equitable distributions of power. They will probably feel few penalties whatever choice they make; they do not seem, in any obvious short-term sense, the ones at risk, though they and we are all at risk because of the behaviors that have been rewarded in them.

Through Women's Studies work I have met very few men who are truly distressed about systemic, unearned male advantage and conferred dominance. And so one question for me and others like me is whether we will be like them, or whether we will get truly distressed, even outraged, about unearned race advantage and conferred dominance and if so, what we will do to lessen them. In any case, we need to do more work in identifying how they actually affect our daily lives. We need more down-to-earth writing by people about these taboo subjects. We need more understanding of the ways in which white "privilege" damages white people, for these are not the same ways in which it damages the victimized. Skewed white psyches are an inseparable part of the picture, though I do not want to confuse the kinds of damage done to the holders of special assets and to those who suffer the deficits. Many, perhaps most, of our white students in the United States think that racism doesn't affect them because they are not people of color; they do not see "whiteness" as a racial identity. Many men likewise think that Women's Studies does not bear on their own existences because they are not female; they do not see themselves as having gendered identities. Insisting on the universal "effects" of "privilege" systems, then, becomes one of our chief tasks, and being more explicit about the *particular* effects in particular contexts is another. Men need to join us in this work.

In addition, since race and sex are not the only advantaging systems at work, we need to similarly examine the daily experience of having age advantage, or ethnic advantage, or physical ability, or advantage related to nationality, religion, or sexual orientation. Professor Marnie Evans suggested to me that in many ways the list I made also applies directly to heterosexual privilege. This is a still more taboo subject than race privilege: the daily ways in which heterosexual privilege makes some persons comfortable or powerful, providing supports, assets, approvals, and rewards to those who live or expect to live in heterosexual pairs. Unpacking that content is still more difficult, owing to the deeper embeddedness of heterosexual advantage and dominance and stricter taboos surrounding these.

But to start such an analysis I would put this observation from my own experience: the fact that I live under the same roof with a man triggers all kinds of societal assumptions about my worth, politics, life, and values and triggers a host of unearned advantages and powers. After recasting many elements from the original list I would add further observations like these:

1. My children do not have to answer questions about why I live with my partner (my husband).
2. I have no difficulty finding neighborhoods where people approve of our household.
3. Our children are given texts and classes that implicitly support our kind of family unit and do not turn them against my choice of domestic partnership.
4. I can travel alone or with my husband without expecting embarrassment or hostility in those who deal with us.
5. Most people I meet will see my marital arrangements as an asset to my life or as a favorable comment on my likability, my competence, or my mental health.
6. I can talk about the social events of a weekend without fearing most listeners' reactions.
7. I will feel welcomed and "normal" in the usual walks of public life, institutional and social.
8. In many contexts, I am seen as "all right" in daily work on women because I do not live chiefly with women.

Difficulties and dangers surrounding the task of finding parallels are many. Since racism, sexism, and heterosexism are not the same, the advantages associated with them should not be seen as the same. In addition, it is hard to isolate aspects of unearned advantage that derive chiefly from social class, economic class, race, religion, region, sex, or ethnic identity. The oppressions are both distinct and interlocking, as the Combahee River Collective statement of 1977 continues to remind us eloquently.[3]

One factor seems clear about all of the interlocking oppressions. They take both active forms that we can see and embedded forms that members of the dominant group are taught not to see.

In my class and place, I did not see myself as racist because I was taught to recognize racism only in individual acts of meanness by members of my group, never in invisible systems conferring racial dominance on my group from birth. Likewise, we are taught to think that sexism or heterosexism is carried on only through intentional, individual acts of discrimination, meanness, or cruelty, rather than in invisible systems conferring unsought dominance on certain groups. Disapproving of the systems won't be enough to change them. I was taught to think that racism could end if white individuals changed their attitudes; many men think sexism can be ended by individual changes in daily behavior toward women. But a man's sex provides advantage for him whether or not he approves of the way in which dominance has been conferred on his group. A "white" skin in the United States opens many doors for whites whether or not we approve of the way dominance has been conferred on us. Individual acts can palliate, but cannot end, these problems. To redesign social systems, we need first to acknowledge their colossal unseen dimensions. The silences and denials surrounding privilege are the key political tool here. They keep the thinking about equality or equity incomplete, protecting unearned advantage and conferred dominance by making these subjects taboo. Most talk by whites about equal opportunity seems to me now to be about equal opportunity to try to get into a position of dominance while denying that *systems* of dominance exist.

Obliviousness about white advantage, like obliviousness about male advantage, is kept strongly inculturated in the United States so as to maintain the myth of meritocracy, the myth that democratic choice is equally available to all. Keeping most people unaware that freedom of confident action is there for just a small number of people props up those in power and serves to keep power in the hands of the same groups that have most of it already. Though systemic change takes many decades, there are pressing questions for me and I imagine for some others like me if we raise our daily consciousness on the perquisites of being light-skinned. What will we do with such knowledge? As we know from watching men, it is an open question whether we will choose to use unearned advantage to weaken invisible privilege systems and whether we will use any of our arbitrarily awarded power to try to reconstruct power systems on a broader base.

NOTES

I have appreciated commentary on this paper from the Working Papers Committee of the Wellesley College Center for Research on Women, from members of the Dodge seminar, and from many individuals, including Margaret Andersen, Sorel Berman, Joanne Braxton, Johnnella Butler, Sandra Dickerson, Marnie Evans, Beverly Guy-Sheftall, Sandra Harding, Eleanor Hinton Hoyt, Pauline Houston, Paul Lauter, Joyce Miller, Mary Norris, Gloria Oden, Beverly Smith, and John Walter.

1. This paper was presented at the Virginia Women's Studies Association conference in Richmond in April 1986, and the American Educational Research Association conference in Boston in October 1986, and discussed with two groups of participants in the Dodge seminars for Secondary School Teachers in New York and Boston in the spring of 1987.

2. Andersen, Margaret, "Race and the Social Science Curriculum: A Teaching and Learning Discussion." *Radical Teacher,* November 1984, pp. 17–20. Smith, Lillian, *Killers of the Dream,* New York: W. W. Norton, 1949.

3. "A Black Feminist Statement," The Combahee River Collective, pp. 13–22 in G. Hull, P. Scott, B. Smith, Eds., *All the Women Are White, All the Blacks Are Men, But Some of Us Are Brave: Black Women's Studies,* Old Westbury, NY: The Feminist Press, 1982.

Something About the Subject Makes It Hard to Name

Gloria Yamato (1991)

Racism—simple enough in structure, yet difficult to eliminate. Racism—pervasive in the U.S. culture to the point that it deeply affects all the local town folk and spills over, negatively influencing the fortunes of folk around the world. Racism is pervasive to the point that we take many of its manifestations for granted, believing "that's life." Many believe that racism can be dealt with effectively in one hellifying workshop, or one hour-long heated discussion. Many actually believe this monster, racism, that has had at least a few hundred years to take root, grow, invade our space, and develop subtle variations . . . this mind-funk that distorts thought and action, can be merely wished away. I've run into folks who really think that we can beat this devil, kick this habit, be healed of this disease in a snap. In a sincere blink of a well-intentioned eye, presto—poof—racism disappears. "I've dealt with my racism . . . (envision a laying on of hands) . . . Hallelujah! Now I can go to the beach." Well, fine. Go to the beach. In fact, why don't we all go to the beach and continue to work on the sucker over there? Cuz you can't even shave a little piece off this thing called racism in a day, or a weekend, or a workshop.

When I speak of *oppression,* I'm talking about the systematic, institutionalized mistreatment of one group of people by another for whatever reason. The oppressors are purported to have an innate ability to access economic resources, information, respect, etc., while the oppressed are believed to have a corresponding negative innate ability. The flip side of oppression is *internalized oppression.* Members of the target group are emotionally, physically, and spiritually battered to the point that they begin to actually believe that their oppression is deserved, is their lot in life, is natural and right, and that it doesn't even exist. The oppression begins to feel comfortable, familiar enough that when mean ol' Massa lay down de whip, we got's to pick up and whack ourselves and each other. Like a virus, it's hard to beat racism, because by the time you come up with a cure, it's mutated to a "new cure-resistant" form. One shot just won't get it. Racism must be attacked from many angles.

The forms of racism that I pick up on these days are (1) aware/blatant racism, (2) aware/covert racism, (3) unaware/unintentional racism, and (4) unaware/self-righteous racism. I can't say that I prefer any one form of racism over the others, because they all look like an itch needing a scratch. I've heard it said (and understandably so) that the aware/blatant form of racism is preferable if one must suffer it. Outright racists will, without apology or confusion, tell us that because of our color we don't appeal to them. If we so choose, we can attempt to get the hell out of their way before we get the sweat knocked out of us. Growing up, aware/covert racism is what I heard many of my elders bemoaning "up north," after having escaped the overt racism "down south." Apartments were suddenly no longer vacant or rents were outrageously high, when black, brown, red, or yellow persons went to inquire about them. Job vacancies were suddenly filled, or we were fired for very vague reasons. It still happens, though the perpetrators really take care to cover their tracks these days. They don't want to get gummed to death or slobbered on by the toothless laws that supposedly protect us from such inequities.

Unaware/unintentional racism drives usually tranquil white liberals wild when they get called on it, and confirms the suspicions of many people of color who feel that white folks are just plain crazy. It has led white people to believe that it's just fine to ask if they can touch my hair (while reaching). They then exclaim over how soft it is, how it does not scratch their hand. It has led whites to assume that bending over backwards and speaking to me in high-pitched (terrified), condescending tones would make up for all the racist wrongs that distort our lives. This type of racism has led whites right to my doorstep, talking 'bout, "We're sorry/we love you and want to make things right," which is fine, and further, "We're gonna give you the opportunity to fix it while we sleep. Just tell us what you need. 'Bye!!"—which *ain't* fine. With the best of intentions, the best of educations, and the greatest generosity of heart, whites, operating on the misinformation fed to them from day one, will behave in ways that are racist, will perpetuate racism by being "nice" the way we're taught to be nice. You can just "nice" somebody to death with naïveté and lack of awareness of privilege. Then there's guilt and the desire to end racism and how the two get all tangled up to the point that people, morbidly fascinated with their guilt, are immobilized. Rather than deal with ending racism, they sit and ponder their guilt and hope nobody notices how awful they are. Meanwhile, racism picks up momentum and keeps on keepin' on.

Now, the newest form of racism that I'm hip to is unaware/self-righteous racism. The "good white" racist attempts to shame Blacks into being blacker, scorns Japanese-Americans who don't speak Japanese, and knows more about the Chicano/a community than the folks who make up the community. They assign themselves as the "good whites," as opposed to the "bad whites," and are often so busy telling people of color what the issues in the Black, Asian, Indian, Latino/a communities should be that they don't have time to deal with their errant sisters and brothers in the white community. Which means that people of color are still left to deal with what the "good whites" don't want to . . . racism.

Internalized racism is what really gets in my way as a Black woman. It influences the way I see or don't see myself, limits what I expect of myself or others like me. It results in my acceptance of mistreatment, leads me to believe that being treated with less than absolute respect, at least this once, is to be expected because I am Black, because I am not white. "Because I am (*you fill in the color*), you think, "Life is going to be hard." The fact is life may be hard, but the color of your skin is not the cause of the hardship. The color of your skin may be used as an excuse to mistreat you, but there is no reason or logic involved in the mistreatment. If it seems that your color is the reason, if it seems that your ethnic heritage is the cause of the woe, it's because you've been deliberately beaten down by agents of a greedy system until you swallowed the garbage. That is the internalization of racism.

Racism is the systematic, institutionalized mistreatment of one group of people by another based on racial heritage. Like every other oppression, racism can be internalized. People of color come to believe misinformation about their particular ethnic group and thus believe that their mistreatment is justified. With that basic vocabulary, let's take a look at how the whole thing works together. Meet "the Ism Family," racism, classism, ageism, adultism, elitism, sexism, heterosexism, physicalism, etc. All these ism's are systematic, that is, not only are these parasites feeding off our lives, they are also dependent on one another for foundation. Racism is supported and reinforced by classism, which is given a foothold and a boost by adultism, which also feeds sexism, which is validated by heterosexism, and so it goes on. You cannot have the "ism" functioning without first effectively installing its flip side, the internalized version of the ism. Like twins, as one particular form of the ism grows in potency, there is a corresponding increase in its internalized form within the population. Before oppression becomes a specific ism like racism, usually all hell breaks loose. War. People fight attempts to enslave them, or to subvert their will, or to take what they consider theirs, whether that is territory or dignity. It's true that the various elements of racism, while repugnant, would not be able to do very much damage, but for one generally overlooked key piece: power/privilege.

. . .

So, what can we do? Acknowledge racism for a start, even though and especially when we've struggled to be kind and fair, or struggled to rise above it all. It is hard to acknowledge the fact that racism circumscribes and pervades our lives. Racism must be dealt with on two levels, personal and societal, emotional and institutional. It is possible—and most effective—to do both at the same time. We must reclaim whatever delight we have lost in our own ethnic heritage or heritages. This so-called melting pot has only succeeded in turning us into fast-food-gobbling "generics" (as in generic "white folks" who were once Irish, Polish, Russian, English, etc. and "black folks," who were once Ashanti, Bambara, Baule, Yoruba, etc.). Find or create safe places to actually *feel* what we've been forced to repress each time we were a victim of, witness to, or perpetrator of racism, so that we do not continue, like puppets, to act out the past in the present and future. Challenge oppression. Take a stand against it. When you are aware of something oppressive going down, stop the show. At least call it. We become so numbed to racism that we don't even think twice about it, unless it is immediately life-threatening.

Whites who want to be allies to people of color: You can educate yourselves via research and observation rather than rigidly, arrogantly relying solely on interrogating people of color. Do not expect that people of color should teach you how to behave non-oppressively. Do not give into the pull to be lazy. Think, hard. Do not blame people of color for your frustration about racism, but do appreciate the fact that people of color will often help you get in touch with that frustration. Assume that your effort to be a good friend is appreciated, but don't expect or accept gratitude from people of color. Work on racism for your sake, not "their" sake. Assume that you are needed and capable of being a good ally. Know that you'll make mistakes and commit yourself to correcting them and continuing on as an ally, no matter what. Don't give up.

People of color, working through internalized racism: Remember always that you and others like you are completely worthy of respect, completely capable of achieving whatever you take a notion to do. Remember that the term "people of color" refers to a variety of ethnic and cultural backgrounds. These various groups have been oppressed in a variety of ways. Educate yourself about the ways different peoples have been oppressed and how they've resisted that oppression. Expect and insist that whites are capable of being good allies against racism. Don't give up. Resist the pull to give out the "people of color seal of approval" to aspiring white allies. A moment of appreciation is fine, but more than that tends to be less than helpful. Celebrate yourself. Celebrate yourself. Celebrate the inevitable end of racism.

R E A D I N G **15**

Tired of Playing Monopoly?

Donna Langston (1988)

I. Magnin, Nordstrom, The Bon, Sears, Penneys, Kmart, Goodwill, Salvation Army. If the order of this list of stores makes any sense to you, then we've begun to deal with the first question which inevitably arises in any discussion of class here in the U.S.—huh? Unlike our European allies, we in the U.S. are reluctant to recognize class differences. This denial of class divisions functions to reinforce ruling class control and domination. America is, after all, the supposed land of equal opportunity where, if you just work hard enough, you can get ahead, pull yourself up by your boot-straps. What the old bootstraps theory overlooks is that some were born with silver shoe horns. Female-headed households, communities of color, the elderly, disabled and children find themselves, disproportionately, living in poverty. If hard work were the sole determinant of your ability to support yourself and your family, surely we'd have a different outcome for many in our society. We also, however, believe in luck and, on closer examination, it certainly is quite a coincidence that the "unlucky" come from certain race, gender and class backgrounds. In order to perpetuate racist, sexist and classist outcomes, we also have to believe that the current economic distribution is unchangeable, has always existed, and probably exists in this form throughout the known universe; i.e., it's "natural." Some people explain or try to account for poverty or class position by focusing on the personal and moral merits of an individual. If people are poor, then it's something they did or didn't do; they were lazy, unlucky, didn't try hard enough, etc. This has the familiar ring of blaming the victims. Alternative explanations focus on the ways in which poverty and class position are due to structural, systematic, institutionalized economic and political power relations. These power relations are based firmly on dynamics such as race, gender and class.

In the myth of the classless society, ambition and intelligence alone are responsible for success. The myth conceals the existence of a class society, which serves many functions. One of the main ways it keeps the working class and poor locked into a class-based system in a position of servitude is by cruelly creating false hope. It perpetuates the false hope among the working class and poor that they can have different opportunities in life. The hope that they can escape the fate that awaits them due to the class position they were born into. Another way the rags-to-riches myth is perpetuated is by creating enough visible tokens so that oppressed persons believe they, too, can get ahead. The creation of hope through tokenism keeps a hierarchical structure in place and lays the blame for not succeeding on those who don't. This keeps us from resisting and changing the class-based system. Instead, we accept it as inevitable, something we just have to live with. If oppressed people believe in equality of opportunity, then they won't develop class consciousness and will internalize the blame for their economic position. If the working class and poor do not recognize the way false hope is used to control them, they won't get a chance to control their lives by acknowledging their class position, by claiming that identity and taking action as a group.

The myth also keeps the middle class and upper class entrenched in the privileges awarded in a class-based system. It reinforces middle- and upper-class beliefs in their own superiority. If we believe that anyone in society really can get ahead, then middle- and upper-class status and privileges must be deserved, due to personal merits, and enjoyed—and defended at all costs. According to this viewpoint, poverty is regrettable but acceptable, just the outcome of a fair game: "There have always been poor people, and there always will be."

Class is more than just the amount of money you have; it's also the presence of economic security. For the working class and poor, working and eating are matters of survival, not taste. However, while one's class status can be defined in important ways in terms of monetary income, class is also a whole lot more—specifically, class is also culture. As a result of the class you are born into and raised in, class is your understanding of the world and where you fit in; it's composed of ideas, behavior, attitudes, values, and language; class is how you think, feel, act, look, dress, talk, move, walk; class is what stores you shop at, restaurants you eat in; class is the schools you attend, the education you attain; class is the very jobs you will work at throughout your adult life. Class even determines when we marry and become mothers. Working-class women become mothers long before middle-class women receive their bachelor's degrees. We experience class at every level of our lives; class is who our friends are, where we live and work, even what kind of car we drive, if we own one, and what kind of health care we receive, if any. . . .

Class affects what we perceive as and what we have available to us as choices. Upon graduation from high school, I was awarded a scholarship to attend any college, private or public, in the state of California. Yet it never occurred to me or my family that it made any difference which college you went to. I ended up just going to a small college in my town. It never would have occurred to me to move away from my family for school, because no one ever had and no one would. I was the first person in my family to go to college. I had to figure out from reading college catalogs how to apply—no one in my family could have sat down and said, "Well, you take this test and then you really should think about . . ." Although tests and high school performance had shown I had the ability to pick up white middle-class lingo, I still had quite an adjustment to make—it was lonely and isolating in college. I lost my friends from high school—they were at the community college, vo-tech school, working, or married. I lasted a year and a half in this foreign environment before I quit college, married a factory worker, had a baby and resumed living in a community I knew. . . .

If class is more than simple economic status but one's cultural background as well, what happens if you're born and raised middle class, but spend some of your adult life with earnings below a middle-class income bracket—are you then working class? Probably not. If your economic position changes, you still have the language, behavior, educational background, etc., of the middle class, which you can bank on. You will always have choices. Men who consciously try to refuse male privilege are still male; whites who want to challenge white privilege are still white. I think those who come from middle-class backgrounds need to recognize that their class privilege does not float out with the rinse water. Middle-class people can exert incredible power just by being nice and polite. The middle-class way of doing things is the standard—they're always right, just by being themselves. Beware of middle-class people who deny their privilege. Many people have times when they struggle to get shoes for the kids, when budgets are tight, etc. This isn't the same as long-term economic conditions without choices. . . .

How about if you're born and raised poor or working class, yet through struggle, usually through education, you manage to achieve a different economic level: do you become middle class? Can you pass? I think some working-class people may successfully assimilate into the middle class by learning to dress, talk, and act middle class—to accept and adopt the middle-class way of doing things. It all depends on how far they're able to go. To succeed in the middle-class world means facing great pressures to abandon working-class friends and ways.

Contrary to our stereotype of the working class—white guys in overalls—the working class is not homogeneous in terms of race or gender. If you are a person of color, if you live in a female-headed household, you are much more likely to be working class or poor. The experience of Black, Latino, American Indian or Asian American working classes will differ significantly from the white working classes, which have traditionally been able to rely on white privilege to provide a more elite position within the working class. Working-class people are often grouped together and stereotyped, but distinctions can be made among the working class, working poor, and poor. Many working-class families are supported by unionized workers who possess marketable skills. Most working-poor families are supported by non-unionized, unskilled men and women. Many poor families are dependent on welfare for their income.

Attacks on the welfare system and those who live on welfare are a good example of classism in action. We have a "dual welfare" system in this country whereby welfare for the rich in the form of tax-free capital gain, guaranteed loans, oil depletion allowances, etc., is not recognized as welfare. Almost everyone in America is on some type of welfare; but, if you're rich, it's in the form of tax deductions for "business" meals and entertainment, and if you're poor, it's in the form of food stamps. The difference is the stigma and humiliation connected to welfare for the poor, as compared to welfare for the rich, which is called "incentives." . . . The "dual welfare" system also assigns a different degree of stigma to programs that benefit women and children, such as AFDC, and programs whose recipients are primarily male, such as veterans' benefits. The implicit assumption is that mothers who raise children do not work and therefore are not deserving of their daily bread crumbs.

Anti-union attitudes are another prime example of classism in action. At best, unions have been a very progressive force for workers, women and people of color. At worst, unions have reflected the same regressive attitudes which are out there in other social structures: classism, racism and sexism. Classism exists within the working class. The aristocracy of the working class—unionized, skilled workers—have mainly been white and male and have viewed themselves as being better than unskilled workers, the unemployed and the poor, who are mostly women and people of color. The white working class must commit itself to a cultural and ideological transformation of racist attitudes. The history of working people, and the ways we've resisted many types of oppressions, are not something we're taught in school. Missing from our education is information about workers and their resistance.

Working-class women's critiques have focused on the following issues:

Education: White middle-class professionals have used academic jargon to rationalize and justify classism. The whole structure of education is a classist system. Schools in every town reflect class divisions: like the store list at the beginning of this article, you can list schools in your town by what classes of kids attend, and in most cities you can also list by race. The classist system is perpetuated in schools with the tracking system, whereby the "dumbs" are tracked into homemaking, shop courses and vocational school futures, while the "smarts" end up in advanced math, science, literature and college-prep courses. If we examine these groups carefully, the coincidence of poor and working-class backgrounds with "dumbs" is rather alarming. The standard measurement of supposed intelligence is white middle-class English. If you're other than white

middle class, you have to become bilingual to succeed in the educational system. If you're white middle class, you only need the language and writing skills you were raised with, since they're the standard. To do well in society presupposes middle-class background, experiences and learning for everyone. The tracking system separates those from the working class who can potentially assimilate to the middle class from all our friends and labels us "college bound."

After high school, you go on to vocational school, community college, or college—public or private—according to your class position. Apart from the few who break into middle-class schools, the classist stereotyping of the working class as being dumb and inarticulate tracks most into vocational and low-skilled jobs. A few of us are allowed to slip through to reinforce the idea that equal opportunity exists. But for most, class position is destiny—determining our educational attainment and employment. Since we must overall abide by middle-class rules to succeed, the assumption is that we go to college in order to "better ourselves"—i.e., become more like them. I suppose it's assumed we have "yuppie envy" and desire nothing more than to be upwardly mobile individuals. It's assumed that we want to fit into their world. But many of us remain connected to our communities and families. Becoming college educated doesn't mean we have to, or want to, erase our first and natural language and value system. It's important for many of us to remain in and return to our communities to work, live, and stay sane.

Jobs: Middle-class people have the privilege of choosing careers. They can decide which jobs they want to work, according to their moral or political commitments, needs for challenge or creativity. This is a privilege denied the working class and poor, whose work is a means of survival, not choice. . . . Working-class women have seldom had the luxury of choosing between work in the home or market. We've generally done both, with little ability to purchase services to help with this double burden. Middle- and upper-class women can often hire other women to clean their houses, take care of their children, and cook their meals.

Guess what class and race those "other" women are? Working a double or triple day is common for working-class women. Only middle-class women have an array of choices such as: parents put you through school, then you choose a career, then you choose when and if to have babies, then you choose a support system of working-class women to take care of your kids and house if you choose to resume your career. After the birth of my second child, I was working two part-time jobs—one loading trucks at night—and going to school during the days. While I was quite privileged because I could take my colicky infant with me to classes and the day-time job, I was in a state of continuous semi-consciousness. I had to work to support my family; the only choice I had was between school or sleep: Sleep became a privilege. A white middle-class feminist instructor at the university suggested to me, all sympathetically, that I ought to hire someone to clean my house and watch the baby. Her suggestion was totally out of my reality, both economically and socially. I'd worked for years cleaning other peoples' houses. Hiring a working-class woman to do the shit work is a middle-class woman's solution to any dilemma which her privileges, such as a career, may present her.

Mothering: The feminist critique of families and the oppressive role of mothering has focused on white middle-class nuclear families. This may not be an appropriate model for communities of class and color. Mothering and families may hold a different importance for working-class women. Within this context, the issue of coming out can be a very painful process for working-class lesbians. Due to the homophobia of working-class communities, to be a lesbian is most often to be excommunicated from your family, neighborhood, friends and the people you work with. If you're working class, you don't have such clearly demarcated concepts of yourself as an individual, but instead see yourself as part of a family and community that forms your survival structure. It is not easy to be faced with the risk of giving up ties which are so central to your identity and survival.

. . .

WAYS TO AVOID FACING CLASSISM

Deny Deny Deny: Deny your class position and the privileges connected to it. Deny the existence or experience of the working class and poor. You can even set yourself up (in your own mind) as judge and jury in deciding who qualifies as working class by your white middle-class standards. So if someone went to college, or seems intelligent to you, not at all like your stereotypes, they must be middle class.

Guilt Guilt Guilt: "I feel so bad, I just didn't realize!" is not helpful, but is a way to avoid changing attitudes and behaviors. Passivity—"Well, what can I do about it, anyway?"—and anger—"Well, what do they want?"—aren't too helpful either. Again, with these responses, the focus is on you and absolving the white middle class from responsibility. A more helpful remedy is to take action. Donate your time and money to local foodbanks. Don't cross picket lines. Better yet, go join a picket line.

HOW TO CHALLENGE CLASSISM

If you're middle class, you can begin to challenge classism with the following:

1. Confront classist behavior in yourself, others and society. Use and share the privileges, like time or money, which you do have.

2. Make demands on working-class and poor communities' issues—anti-racism, poverty, unions, public housing, public transportation, literacy and day care.

3. Learn from the skills and strength of working people—study working and poor people's history; take some Labor Studies, Ethnic Studies, Women Studies classes. Challenge elitism. There are many different types of intelligence: white middle-class, academic, professional intellectualism being one of them (reportedly). Finally, educate yourself, take responsibility and take action.

If you're working class, just some general suggestions (it's cheaper than therapy—free, less time-consuming and I won't ask you about what your mother said to you when you were five):

1. Face your racism! Educate yourself and others, your family, community, any organizations you belong to; take responsibility and take action. Face your classism, sexism, heterosexism, ageism, ablebodiness, adultism. . . .

2. Claim your identity. Learn all you can about your history and the history and experience of all working and poor peoples. Raise your children to be anti-racist, anti-sexist and anti-classist. Teach them the language and culture of working peoples. Learn to survive with a fair amount of anger and lots of humor, which can be tough when this stuff isn't even funny.

3. Work on issues which will benefit your community. Consider remaining in or returning to your communities. If you live and work in white middle-class environments, look for working-class allies to help you survive with your humor and wits intact. How do working-class people spot each other? We have antenna.

We need not deny or erase the differences of working-class cultures but can embrace their richness, their variety, their moral and intellectual heritage. We're not at the point yet where we can celebrate differences—not having money for a prescription for your child is nothing to celebrate. It's not time yet to party with the white middle class, because we'd be the entertainment ("Aren't they quaint? Just love their workboots and uniforms and the way they cuss!"). We need to overcome divisions among working people, not by ignoring the multiple oppressions many of us encounter, or by oppressing each other, but by becoming committed allies on all issues which affect working people: racism, sexism, classism, etc. An injury to one is an injury to all. Don't play by ruling-class rules, hoping that maybe you can live on Connecticut Avenue instead of Baltic, or that you as an individual can make it to Park Place and Boardwalk. Tired of Monopoly? Always ending up on Mediterranean Avenue? How about changing the game?

R E A D I N G **16**

Voices
On Becoming Old Women

Baba Copper (1986)

When we ask for a chance to live our old age in comfort, creativity and usefulness, we ask it not for ourselves alone, but for you. We are not a special interest group. We are your roots. You are our continuity. What we gain is your inheritance.

—Irene Pauli, Some Ironies of Aging

How can old women define the subjects of age and ageism so that false understanding of these issues does not dominate the interactions be-

tween women and keep us forever separate? Aging is a natural and universal personal experience that begins the day we are born. It is a process of challenge—not necessarily growth and development when we are young as opposed to loss and deterioration when we are old—but learning through change. Ageism is the negative social response to different stages in the process of aging and it is a political issue. The ageism that old women experience is firmly embedded in sexism—an extension of the male power to define, control values, erase, disempower, and divide. Woman-to-woman ageism is an aspect of the horizontal conflict that usurps the energies of the colonized—part of the female competition for the crumbs of social power.

How can the same word be used for the experience of teenagers, old women, and the most powerful men in the world? Yet we say that all these are subject to *ageist* attitudes—stereotyping and denigration because of age. But each age group—children, teens, midlife women, old women, old men—have radically different expectations of their due, their rightful social place. For an old woman, ageism is a killer, because her sense of worth has been eroded by a lifelong pursuit of youth/beauty. Age passing—passing for young enough—is part of all female experience. The foundation of lies built into passing and the fear and loathing of female aging are what keep the generations of women—decade by decade—divided from each other.

I believe that age passing is one of the primary learning arenas of female competition, as well as an apprenticeship to hatred of old women. When women pass easily, we gain comfort knowing that we do not have to identify with the woman who, in our view, is not passing. "I am not like her" translates easily into "I am better than her." In our thirties, we do not want to be mistaken for forty. In our forties, we do not want anyone to assume we are fifty. Somewhere in our fifties, the mass of anxieties about age, and the increase of rejection and invisibility we are experiencing, becomes critical. This is often a time when our trained inability to identify with women older than ourselves reaches its climax. Old women cannot rely upon the midlife woman as ally. The midlife woman, in her rage and fear, may unconsciously discharge all kinds of covert aggression against the old woman as the personification of what is threatening her.

Can women afford to ignore issues that surround the aging process? When I have asked younger women what they thought ageism was all about, they talked about the aura of death and decay which permeates age for them, the oppressive

power/over of the mythic Mother figure, and the deplorable neglect exhibited by the authorities in making adequate institutional responses to age. None have seen ageism as a problem of prejudice or bigotry on their part. With a righteousness reminiscent of the anchorman on the evening news, most of my young informants have advocated more and better government support for the old. But government subsidies for medicine and institutional care have created a highly profitable industry of geriatric technology, with the elderly aid recipients captive to the modern Grail, longevity. Just staying alive is a false goal. Acceptance of age in women has not kept pace with our increasing life expectancy. It is the quality of that extra time that is important. As long as women allow themselves to be brainwashed into worshiping youth and plasticized beauty, increased life expectancy (and the institutionalized responses to it) will remain a burden for both the young and the old.

How can ageism be defined by women; how can we develop clear vocabulary and theory; can we afford to ignore it? For me these questions are more than rhetorical. I am an old woman living in a highly politicized community of women. I find struggle and change taking place in relation to all the differences between women except age. I need to divert some of that political consciousness toward ageism.

I am an *old* woman. I am sixty-six. Part of the reason I self-identify as *old* is a need to escape the prissy category of "older woman." This label claims descriptive power over women from eighteen to eighty, depending upon the age and consciousness of the user. . . . After lots of internal arguments, I found a rationalization that made me comfortable with the label. Calling myself an old woman was the radical way out of my dilemma. At sixty-six, it may be presumptuous of me to assume a label that is descriptive of women in their nineties, but I have noticed that many of them avoid the term. Like other words that feminists are reclaiming by proud usage, I would take to myself the word everyone seems to fear. My *real* circumstances would not suffer more than they have from the visual impact of my years. Nobody but radical women would stand there beside me, honest and angry about the distortions that surround the time of life all women dread. I would walk through the door-of-no-return and from the other side name the politics of age instead of waltzing around pretending I am just an "older woman." The lies of age passing would not save me from the stigma of age. In fact, it has been my experience that the invention and practice of feminine lies keep women forever in harness, laboring to be someone who fits in, who pleases, who is chosen, who earns (and therefore deserves) love. I have grown sick of the harness.

. . .

Young and midlife women tend to see ageism as a continuing oppression of women throughout their lives. The point of view I tried to voice as an old woman sprang from my new experience, which revealed abrupt changes in the degree or intensity of stigma, when, for whatever reasons, one could no longer pass as middle-aged. I am uncomfortable with the absence of differentiation between the kind of ageism I can remember experiencing as a teenager and what I am experiencing in my sixties.

I felt confused. I did not know how to integrate these concepts into my present circumstances. Was the pain over the ageism I experience intensified by the fact that my youth privilege had been augmented by the privileges of being white, able, thin, blond, tall, middle class? And how did all this relate to age passing, for many women try— and some even succeed by the use of repeated plastic surgery—to appear forever middle-aged? For instance, the small, thin old woman— especially one who plays the "cute" social role— does not receive the same direct hostility that big "motherly" women do. Was the pain of ageism relative also, or was there a pall that settled over an old woman (the year varying for different women) which was similar for all whether or not they had been pretty or middle class?

. . .

Death is an extremely important subject that our culture has mystified, professionalized, sensationalized—and at the same time, made taboo. Everyone needs to make his or her peace with the meaning of death. However, the assumption that death is a preoccupation, or subject of expertise, of midlife or old women is ageist. I understood that we might want to talk about death. But the old should not be seen as standing with death at their elbow. Nor should they be expected to help others on the subject or allow the subject to be age segregated. Repeatedly, younger women make assumptions about my relationship to death. One woman said that she shared identity with me because she had had many losses of people close to her in her life. She assumed that I had too. In reality, other than the death of my mother when she was ninety-three, no one I loved has ever died.

. . .

Here it was, that virulent stereotype—the age/death connection. . . . Apparently only old people die. Death does not hover near the cradle, the motorcycle, the toxic workplace, high bridges, or battlefields. But around old women, everyone is reminded that they have given their own possible mortality insufficient attention. Death is a forbidden subject with all but the old, who are expected to bear the burden of this social suppression. Since my own demise is as distant from my conscious mind as it was when I was twenty, I have come to recognize that it is my looks that evoke the age/death connection in others. Death has become a private buzzword for me, warning me of the shoals of ageism before me.

Talking about choice in relation to dying always makes me very nervous. I reminded the group that we were at the beginning of a worldwide demographic boom of old women. It is easy to predict that our society will soon be subject to all kinds of "new looks" at death and dying. I read a clipping from a futurist magazine suggesting that a demise pill be available to the elderly (but not the young, of course). The old are seen as half dead already. Old women, like everyone else, buy into the prevailing concepts surrounding both worth and death—we are as easy to brainwash as the next. When one believes that one has done everything one wants to do, it may be a way of expressing the feeling that what one has to contribute from a wheelchair, for example, is not valuable.

. . .

How can old women begin to change this? First, we have to name our circumstances more clearly, identifying the root sources of our denigrated place in society. Feminist analysis and the concept of ageism are not used as tools by most old women to explain the increased negative content of our experience. Old women tend to see problems as personal—interpersonal or physical or economic—instead of political. The time of life that should be a final ripening, a meaningful summation, a last chance for all the risks and pleasures of corporeal existence, is all too often deadened by emotional isolation and self-doubts. As the average life expectancy for women keeps creeping upward—almost into the eighties now—the quality of that life-to-be-expected keeps deteriorating.

The "natural alliance" that old women have a right to expect with midlife women will not emerge until all women begin to recognize the pitfalls of age passing. Separating the perspective of the barely-passing older woman from some of my concerns as one-who-no-longer-is-able-to-pass has taken all my confidence and a great deal of hindsight. The midlife woman feels increasing pressure—internal and external—about aging as well as the rejections of ageism. It is natural that she rushes forward to define the problem. In asserting her power over the insights of the old woman—the complaints, the accusations of ageism, the naming of the universal hatred of the Old Woman—she unconsciously silences the inherent radicalism of the only one who can tell her how it really is.

The problem for old women is a problem of power. First, power over the circumstances and directions of our own lives and identity. Second, power as an influence upon the world we live in—the world we have served, in which we have such a large, unrecognized vested interest. This is, of course, the rub. Patriarchal institutions are, without exception, designed to exclude the vision of old women. Most old women have little experience in leadership, influence, or even respect. Mostly, old women know how to serve. The roles reserved and expected of women in old age—grandmothers, self-effacing volunteers to the projects and priorities designed by others, or caretakers of old men—are custom fit to our powerless status.

But there are ways that all women can begin to prepare the way for the empowerment of themselves in the future, when they are old. These changes can first be brought about in the women's community, among lesbians and political women. The first step is for women to recognize that they have been programmed to hate old women and to deny them power. This brainwashing is so subtle that its eradication will take an effort equal to that which we have made and still must expend upon sexism. Further, this brainwashing extends down through our lives, making us fear the processes of our own bodies within time, so that our energies and attention are constantly undermined by ageist competition and self-doubts. These are attitudes and expectations that we can change now, if we decide to. Empowerment of women will come when we identify with women older than we are and not before.

The Social Construction of Disability

Susan Wendell (1996)

I maintain that the distinction between the biological reality of a disability and the social construction of a disability cannot be made sharply, because the biological and the social are interactive in creating disability. They are interactive not only in that complex interactions of social factors and our bodies affect health and functioning, but also in that social arrangements can make a biological condition more or less relevant to almost any situation. I call the interaction of the biological and the social to create (or prevent) disability "the social construction of disability."

Disability activists and some scholars of disability have been asserting for at least two decades that disability is socially constructed. Moreover, feminist scholars have already applied feminist analyses of the social construction of the experience of being female to their analyses of disability as socially constructed. Thus I am saying nothing new when I claim that disability, like gender, is socially constructed. Nevertheless, I understand that such an assertion may be new and even puzzling to many readers, and that not everyone who says that disability is socially constructed means the same thing by it. Therefore, I will explain what I mean in some detail.

I see disability as socially constructed in ways ranging from social conditions that straightforwardly create illnesses, injuries, and poor physical functioning, to subtle cultural factors that determine standards of normality and exclude those who do not meet them from full participation in their societies. I could not possibly discuss all the factors that enter into the social construction of disability here, and I feel sure that I am not aware of them all, but I will try to explain and illustrate the social construction of disability by discussing what I hope is a representative sample from a range of factors.

SOCIAL FACTORS THAT CONSTRUCT DISABILITY

First, it is easy to recognize that social conditions affect people's bodies by creating or failing to prevent sickness and injury. Although, since disability is relative to a person's physical, social, and cultural environment, none of the resulting physical conditions is necessarily disabling, many do in fact cause disability given the demands and lack of support in the environments of the people affected. In this direct sense of damaging people's bodies in ways that are disabling in their environments, much disability is created by the violence of invasions, wars, civil wars, and terrorism, which cause disabilities not only through direct injuries to combatants and noncombatants, but also through the spread of disease and the deprivations of basic needs that result from the chaos they create. In addition, although we more often hear about them when they cause death, violent crimes such as shootings, knifings, beatings, and rape all cause disabilities, so that a society's success or failure in protecting its citizens from injurious crimes has a significant effect on its rates of disability.

The availability and distribution of basic resources such as water, food, clothing, and shelter have major effects on disability, since much disabling physical damage results directly from malnutrition and indirectly from diseases that attack and do more lasting harm to the malnourished and those weakened by exposure. Disabling diseases are also contracted from contaminated water when clean water is not available. Here too, we usually learn more about the deaths caused by lack of basic resources than the (often life-long) disabilities of survivors.

Many other social factors can damage people's bodies in ways that are disabling in their environments, including (to mention just a few) tolerance of high-risk working conditions, abuse and neglect of children, low public safety standards, the degradation of the environment by contamination of air, water, and food, and the overwork, stress, and daily grinding deprivations of poverty. The social factors that can damage people's bodies almost always affect some groups in a society more than others because of racism, sexism, heterosexism, ageism, and advantages of class background, wealth, and education.

Medical care and practices, traditional and Western-scientific, play an important role in both preventing and creating disabling physical damage. (They also play a role in defining disability. . . .) Lack of good prenatal care and dangerous or inadequate obstetrical practices cause disabilities in babies and in the women giving birth to them. Inoculations against diseases such as polio and measles prevent quite a lot of disability. Inadequate medical care of those who are already ill or injured results in unnecessary disablement. On the other hand, the rate of disability in a society increases with improved medical capacity to save the lives of people who are dangerously ill or injured in the absence of the capacity to prevent or cure all the physical damage they have incurred. Moreover, public health and sanitation measures that increase the average lifespan also increase the number of old people with disabilities in a society, since more people live long enough to become disabled.

The *pace of life* is a factor in the social construction of disability that particularly interests me, because it is usually taken for granted by non-disabled people, while many people with disabilities are acutely aware of how it marginalizes or threatens to marginalize us. I suspect that increases in the pace of life are important social causes of damage to people's bodies through rates of accident, drug and alcohol abuse, and illnesses that result from people's neglecting their needs for rest and good nutrition. But the pace of life also affects disability as a second form of social construction, the social construction of disability through expectations of performance.

When the pace of life in a society increases, there is a tendency for more people to become disabled, not only because of physically damaging consequences of efforts to go faster, but also because fewer people can meet expectations of 'normal' performance; the physical (and mental) limitations of those who cannot meet the new pace become conspicuous and disabling, even though the same limitations were inconspicuous and irrelevant to full participation in the slower-paced society. Increases in the pace of life can be counterbalanced for some people by improvements in accessibility, such as better transportation and easier communication, but for those who must move or think slowly, and for those whose energy is severely limited, expectations of pace can make work, recreational, community, and social activities inaccessible.

Let me give a straightforward, personal illustration of the relationship between pace and disability. I am currently just able (by doing very little else) to work as a professor three-quarter time, on one-quarter disability leave. There has been much talk recently about possible increases in the teaching duties of professors at my university, which would not be accompanied by any reduction in expectations for the other two components of our jobs, research and administration. If there were to be such an increase in the pace of professors' work, say by one additional course per term, I would be unable to work more than half-time (by the new standards) and would have to request half-time disability leave, even though there had been no change in my physical condition. Compared to my colleagues, I would be more work-disabled than I am now. Some professors with less physical limitation than I have, who now work full-time, might be unable to work at the new full-time pace and be forced to go on part-time disability leave. This sort of change could contribute to disabling anyone in any job.

Furthermore, even if a person is able to keep up with an increased pace of work, any increase in the pace of work will decrease the energy available for other life activities, which may upset the delicate balance of energy by which a person manages to participate in them and eventually exclude her/him from those activities. The pace of those other activities may also render them inaccessible. For example, the more the life of a society is conducted on the assumption of quick travel, the more disabling are those physical conditions that affect movement and travel, such as needing to use a wheelchair or having a kind of epilepsy that prevents one from driving a car, unless compensating help is provided. These disabling effects extend into people's family, social, and sexual lives and into their participation in recreation, religious life, and politics.

Pace is a major aspect of expectations of performance; non-disabled people often take pace so much for granted that they feel and express impatience with the slower pace at which some people with disabilities need to operate, and accommodations of pace are often crucial to making an activity accessible to people with a wide range of physical and mental abilities. Nevertheless, expectations of pace are not the only expectations of performance that contribute to disability. For example, expectations of individual productivity can eclipse the actual contributions of people who cannot meet them, making people unemployable when they can in fact do valuable work. There are often very definite expectations about *how* tasks will be performed (not the standards of performance, but the methods). For example, many women with disabilities are discouraged from having children because other people can only imagine caring for children in ways that are impossible for women with their disabilities, yet everything necessary could be done in other ways, often with minor accommodations. Furthermore, the expectation that many tasks will be performed by individuals on their own can create or expand the disability of those who can perform the tasks only in cooperative groups or by instructing a helper.

Expectations of performance are reflected, because they are assumed, in the social organization and physical structure of a society, both of which create disability. Societies that are physically constructed and socially organized with the unacknowledged assumption that everyone is healthy, non-disabled, young but adult, shaped according to cultural ideals, and, often, male, create a great deal of disability through sheer neglect of what most people need in order to participate fully in them.

Feminists talk about how the world has been designed for the bodies and activities of men. In many industrialized countries, including Canada and the United States, life and work have been structured as though no one of any importance in the public world, and certainly no one who works outside the home for wages, has to breast-feed a baby or look after a sick child. Common colds can be acknowledged publicly, and allowances are made for them, but menstruation cannot be acknowledged and allowances are not made for it. Much of the public world is also structured as though everyone were physically strong, as though all bodies were shaped the same, as though everyone could walk, hear, and see well, as though everyone could work and play at a pace that is not compatible with any kind of illness or pain, as though no one were ever dizzy or incontinent or simply needed to sit or lie down. (For instance, where could you rest for a few minutes in a supermarket if you needed to?) Not only the architecture, but the entire physical and social organization of life tends to assume that we are either strong and healthy and able to do what the average young, non-disabled man can do or that we are completely unable to participate in public life.

A great deal of disability is caused by this physical structure and social organization of society. For instance, poor architectural planning creates physical obstacles for people who use wheelchairs, but also for people who can walk but cannot walk far or cannot climb stairs, for people who cannot open doors, and for people who can do all of these things but only at the cost of pain or an expenditure of energy they can ill afford.

Some of the same architectural flaws cause problems for pregnant women, parents with strollers, and young children. This is no coincidence. Much architecture has been planned with a young adult, non-disabled male paradigm of humanity in mind. In addition, aspects of social organization that take for granted the social expectations of performance and productivity, such as inadequate public transportation (which I believe assumes that no one who is needed in the public world needs public transportation), communications systems that are inaccessible to people with visual or hearing impairments, and inflexible work arrangements that exclude part-time work or rest periods, create much disability.

When public and private worlds are split, women (and children) have often been relegated to the private, and so have the disabled, the sick, and the old. The public world is the world of strength, the positive (valued) body, performance and production, the non-disabled, and young adults. Weakness, illness, rest and recovery, pain, death, and the negative (devalued) body are private, generally hidden, and often neglected. Coming into the public world with illness, pain, or a devalued body, people encounter resistance to mixing the two worlds; the split is vividly revealed. Much of the experience of disability and illness goes underground, because there is no socially acceptable way of expressing it and having the physical and psychological experience acknowledged. Yet acknowledgement of this experience is exactly what is required for creating accessibility in the public world. The more a society regards disability as a private matter, and people with disabilities as belonging in the private sphere, the more disability it creates by failing to make the public sphere accessible to a wide range of people.

Disability is also socially constructed by the failure to give people the amount and kind of help they need to participate fully in all major aspects of life in the society, including making a significant contribution in the form of work. Two things are important to remember about the help that people with disabilities may need. One is that most industrialized societies give non-disabled people (in different degrees and kinds, depending on class, race, gender, and other factors) a lot of help in the form of education, training, social support, public communication and transportation facilities, public recreation, and other services. The help that non-disabled people receive tends to be taken for granted and not considered help but entitlement, because it is offered to citizens who fit the social paradigms, who by definition are not considered dependent on social help. It is only when people need a different kind or amount of help than that given to 'paradigm' citizens that it is considered help at all, and they are considered socially dependent. Second, much, though not all, of the help that people with disabilities need is required because their bodies were damaged by social conditions, or because they cannot meet social expectations of performance, or because the narrowly-conceived physical structure and social organization of society have placed them at a disadvantage; in other words, it is needed to overcome problems that were created socially.

Thus disability is socially constructed through the failure or unwillingness to create ability among people who do not fit the physical and mental profile of 'paradigm' citizens. Failures of social support for people with disabilities result in inadequate rehabilitation, unemployment, poverty, inadequate personal and medical care, poor communication services, inadequate training and education, poor protection from physical, sexual, and emotional abuse, minimal opportunities for social learning and interaction, and many other disabling situations that hurt people with disabilities and exclude them from participation in major aspects of life in their societies.

. . .

CULTURAL CONSTRUCTION OF DISABILITY

Culture makes major contributions to disability. These contributions include not only the omission of experiences of disability from cultural representations of life in a society, but also the cultural stereotyping of people with disabilities, the selective stigmatization of physical and mental limitations and other differences (selective because not all limitations and differences are stigmatized, and different limitations and differences are stigmatized in different societies), the numerous cultural meanings attached to various kinds of disability and illness, and the exclusion of people with disabilities from the cultural meanings of activities they cannot perform or are expected not to perform.

The lack of realistic cultural representations of experiences of disability not only contributes to the 'Otherness' of people with disabilities by encouraging the assumption that their lives are inconceivable to non-disabled people but also increases non-disabled people's fear of disability by suppressing knowledge of how people live with disabilities. Stereotypes of disabled people as dependent, morally depraved, super-humanly heroic, asexual, and/or pitiful are still the most common cultural portrayals of people with disabilities. Stereotypes repeatedly get in the way of full participation in work and social life. For example, Francine Arsenault, whose leg was damaged by childhood polio and later by gangrene, describes the following incident at her wedding:

> When I got married, one of my best friends came to the wedding with her parents. I had known her parents all the time I was growing up; we visited in each other's homes and I thought that they knew my situation quite well.
>
> But as the father went down the reception line and shook hands with my husband, he said, "You know, I used to think that Francine was intelligent, but to put herself on you as a burden like this shows that I was wrong all along."

Here the stereotype of a woman with a disability as a helpless, dependent burden blots out, in the friend's father's consciousness, both the reality that Francine simply has one damaged leg and the probability that her new husband wants her for her other qualities. Moreover, the man seems to take for granted that the new husband sees Francine in the same stereotyped way (or else he risks incomprehension or rejection), perhaps

because he counts on the cultural assumptions about people with disabilities. I think both the stigma of physical 'imperfection' (and possibly the additional stigma of having been damaged by disease) and the cultural meanings attached to the disability contribute to the power of the stereotype in situations like this. Physical 'imperfection' is more likely to be thought to 'spoil' a woman than a man by rendering her unattractive in a culture where her physical appearance is a large component of a woman's value; having a damaged leg probably evokes the metaphorical meanings of being 'crippled,' which include helplessness, dependency, and pitifulness. Stigma, stereotypes, and cultural meanings are all related and interactive in the cultural construction of disability. . . .

SOCIAL DECONSTRUCTION OF DISABILITY

In my view, then, disability is socially constructed by such factors as social conditions that cause or fail to prevent damage to people's bodies; expectations of performance; the physical and social organization of societies on the basis of a young, non-disabled, 'ideally shaped,' healthy adult male paradigm of citizens; the failure or unwillingness to create ability among citizens who do not fit the paradigm; and cultural representations, failures of representation, and expectations. Much, but perhaps not all, of what can be socially constructed can be socially (and not just intellectually) deconstructed, given the means and the will.

A great deal of disability can be prevented with good public health and safety standards and practices, but also by relatively minor changes in the built environment that provide accessibility to people with a wide range of physical characteristics and abilities. Many measures that are usually regarded as helping or accommodating people who are now disabled, such as making buildings and public places wheelchair accessible, creating and respecting parking spaces for people with disabilities, providing American Sign Language translation, captioning, and Telephone Devices for the Deaf, and making tapes and Descriptive

Video services available for people who are visually impaired, should be seen as preventive, since a great deal of disability is created by building and organizing environments, objects, and activities for a too-narrow range of people. Much more could be done along the same lines by putting people with a wide variety of physical abilities and characteristics in charge of deconstructing disability. People with disabilities should be in charge, because people without disabilities are unlikely to see many of the obstacles in their environment. Moreover, they are likely not to see them *as obstacles* even when they are pointed out, but rather as 'normal' features of the built environment that present difficulties for 'abnormal' people.

Disability cannot be deconstructed by consulting a few token disabled representatives. A person with a disability is not likely to see all the obstacles to people with disabilities different from her/his own, although s/he is likely to be more aware of potential inaccessibility. Moreover, people with disabilities are not always aware of the obstacles in our environment *as obstacles,* even when they affect us. The cultural habit of regarding the condition of the person, not the built environment or the social organization of activities, as the source of the problem, runs deep. For example, it took me several years of struggling with the heavy door to my building, sometimes having to wait until someone stronger came along, to realize that the door was an accessibility problem, not only for me, but for others as well. And I did not notice, until one of my students pointed it out, that the lack of signs that could be read from a distance at my university forced people with mobility impairments to expend a lot of energy unnecessarily, searching for rooms and offices. Although I have encountered this difficulty myself on days when walking was exhausting to me, I interpreted it, automatically, as a problem arising from my illness (as I did with the door), rather than as a problem arising from the built environment having been created for too narrow a range of people and situations. One of the most crucial factors in the deconstruction of disability is the change of perspective that causes us to look in the environment for both the source of the problem and the solutions.

. . .

OBSTACLES TO THE DECONSTRUCTION OF DISABILITY

. . .

Attitudes that disability is a personal or family problem (of biological or accidental origin), rather than a matter of social responsibility, are cultural contributors to disability and powerful factors working against social measures to increase ability. The attitude that disability is a personal problem is manifested when people with disabilities are expected to overcome obstacles to their participation in activities by their own extraordinary efforts. The public adoration of a few disabled heroes who are believed to have 'overcome their handicaps' against great odds both demonstrates and contributes to this expectation. The attitude that disability is a family matter is manifested when the families of people with disabilities are expected to provide whatever they need, even at great personal sacrifice by other family members. Barbara Hillyer describes the strength of expectations that mothers and other caregivers will do whatever is necessary to 'normalize' the lives of family members, especially children, with disabilities—not only providing care, but often doing the work of two people to maintain the illusion that there is nothing 'wrong' in the family.

These attitudes are related to the fact that many modern societies split human concerns into public and private worlds. Typically, those with disabilities and illnesses have been relegated to the private realm, along with women, children, and the old. This worldwide tendency creates particularly intractable problems for women with disabilities; since they fit two 'private' categories, they are often kept at home, isolated and overprotected. In addition, the confinement of people with disabilities in the private realm exploits women's traditional caregiving roles in order to meet the needs of people with disabilities, and it hides the need for measures to make the public realm accessible to everyone.

There also seem to be definite material advantages for some people (people without disabilities who have no disabled friends or relatives for whom they feel responsible) to seeing disability as a biological misfortune, the bad luck of individuals, and a personal or family problem. Accessibility and creating ability cost time, energy, and/or money. Charities for people with disabilities are big businesses that employ a great many non-disabled professionals; these charities depend upon the belief that responding to the difficulties faced by people with disabilities is superogatory for people who are not members of the family—not a social responsibility to be fulfilled through governments, but an act of kindness. Moreover, both the charities and most government bureaucracies (which also employ large numbers of non-disabled professionals) hand out help which would not be needed in a society that was planned and organized to include people with a wide range of physical and mental abilities. The potential resistance created by these vested interests in disability should not be underestimated.

The 'personal misfortune' approach to disability is also part of what I call the 'lottery' approach to life, in which individual good fortune is hoped for as a substitute for social planning that deals realistically with everyone's capabilities, needs and limitations, and the probable distribution of hardship. In Canada and the United States, most people reject the 'lottery' approach to such matters as acute health care for themselves and their families or basic education for their children. We expect it to be there when we need it, and we are (more or less) willing to pay for it to be there. I think the lottery approach persists with respect to disability partly because *fear,* based on ignorance and false beliefs about disability, makes it difficult for most non-disabled people to identify with people with disabilities. If the non-disabled saw the disabled as potentially themselves or as their future selves, they would want their societies to be fully accessible and to invest the resources necessary to create ability wherever

possible. They would feel that 'charity' is as inappropriate a way of thinking about resources for people with disabilities as it is about emergency medical care or basic education.

The philosopher Anita Silvers maintains that it is probably impossible for most non-disabled people to imagine what life is like with a disability, and that their own becoming disabled is unthinkable to them. Certainly many people without disabilities believe that life with a disability would not be worth living. This is reflected in the assumption that potential disability is a sufficient reason for aborting a fetus, as well as in the frequent statements by non-disabled people that they would not want to live if they had to use a wheelchair, lost their eyesight, were dependent on others for care, and so on. The belief that life would not be worth living with a disability would be enough to prevent them from imagining their own disablement. This belief is fed by stereotypes and ignorance of the lives of people with disabilities. For example, the assumption that permanent, global incompetence results from any major disability is still prevalent; there is a strong presumption that competent people either have no major physical or mental limitations or are able to hide them in public and social life.

It seems that the cultural constructions of disability, including the ignorance, stereotyping, and stigmatization that feed fears of disability, have to be at least partly deconstructed before disability can be seen by more people as a set of social problems and social responsibilities. Until that change in perspective happens, people with disabilities and their families will continue to be given too much individual responsibility for 'overcoming' disabilities, expectations for the participation of people with disabilities in public life will be far too low, and social injustices that are recognized now (at least in the abstract), such as discrimination against people with disabilities, will be misunderstood.

To illustrate, let me look briefly at the problem of discrimination. Clearly, when considering whether some action or situation is an instance of discrimination on the basis of ability, the trick is to distinguish ability to do the relevant things from ability to do irrelevant things. But, given that so many places and activities are structured for people with a narrow range of abilities, telling the two apart is not always easy. No one has to walk to be a typist, but if a company is housed in a building that is inaccessible to wheelchairs, and therefore refuses to hire a competent typist who uses a wheelchair because it would be expensive to fix the building, has it discriminated against her on the basis of her disability? Laws may say yes, but people will resist the laws unless they can see that the typist's inability to work in that office is not solely a characteristic of her as an individual. Most people will be ready to recognize refusal to hire her to work in a wheelchair-accessible office, provided she is the most competent typist who applied, as discrimination against her because of her disability; they will regard her disability (like her race) as a personal characteristic irrelevant in the circumstances. But will they be ready to require a company to create wheelchair accessibility so that it can hire her? This is being tested now in the United States by the 1990 Americans with Disabilities Act. Although I expect the Act to have an invaluable educational function, I predict that it will be very difficult to enforce until more people see accessibility as a public responsibility. Only then will they be able to recognize inabilities that are created by faulty planning and organization as irrelevant.

Consider these sentiments expressed in the Burger King case, as described in *The Disability Rag and Resource:*

> When deaf actress Terrylene Sacchetti sued Burger King under the ADA for refusing to serve her when she handed the cashier a written order at the pickup window instead of using the intercom, Stan Kyker, executive vice-president of the California Restaurant Association, said that those "people (with disabilities) are going to have to accept that they are not 100 percent whole and they can't be made 100 percent whole in everything they do in life."

Had a woman been refused service because she used a cane to walk up to the counter, her treatment would, I think, have been recognized at once as discrimination. But since Ms. Sacchetti was refused service because she was unable to perform the activity (ordering food) in the way (orally) that the restaurant required it to be performed, the refusal to serve her was not immediately recognized as discrimination. Indeed, the representative of the restaurant association apparently felt comfortable defending it on the grounds that her individual characteristics were the obstacles to Ms. Sacchetti's being served.

When I imagine a society without disabilities, I do not imagine a society in which every physical and mental 'defect' or 'abnormality' can be cured. On the contrary, I believe the fantasy that someday everything will be 'curable' is a significant obstacle to the social deconstruction of disability. Instead, I imagine a fully accessible society, the most fundamental characteristic of which is universal recognition that all structures have to be built and all activities have to be organized for the widest practical range of human abilities. In such a society, a person who cannot walk would not be disabled, because every major kind of activity that is accessible to someone who can walk would be accessible to someone who cannot, and likewise with seeing, hearing, speaking, moving one's arms, working for long stretches of time without rest, and many other physical and mental functions. I do not mean that everyone would be able to do everything, but rather that, with respect to the major aspects of life in the society, the differences in ability between someone who can walk, or see, or hear, and someone who cannot would be no more significant than the differences in ability among people who can walk, see, or hear. Not everyone who is not disabled now can play basketball or sing in a choir, but everyone who is not disabled now can participate in sports or games and make art, and that sort of general ability should be the goal in deconstructing disability.

I talk about accessibility and ability rather than independence or integration because I think that neither independence nor integration is always an appropriate goal for people with disabilities. Some people cannot live independently because they will always need a great deal of help from caregivers, and some people with disabilities, for example the Deaf, do not want to be integrated into non-disabled society; they prefer their own, separate social life. Everyone should, however, have access to *opportunities* to develop their abilities, to work, and to participate in the full range of public and private activities available to the rest of society.

R E A D I N G   **18**

Report from the Bahamas

June Jordan (1985)

I am staying in a hotel that calls itself The Sheraton British Colonial. One of the photographs advertising the place displays a middle-aged Black man in a waiter's tuxedo, smiling. What intrigues me most about the picture is just this: while the Black man bears a tray full of "colorful" drinks above his left shoulder, both of his feet, shoes and trouserlegs, up to ten inches above his ankles, stand in the also "colorful" Caribbean salt water. He is so delighted to serve you he will wade into the water to bring you Banana Daquiris while you float! More precisely, he will wade into the water, fully clothed, oblivious to the ruin of his shoes, his trousers, his health, and he will do it with a smile.

I am in the Bahamas. On the phone in my room, a spinning complement of plastic pages offers handy index clues such as CAR RENTAL and CASINOS. A message from the Ministry of Tourism appears among these travellers tips. Opening with a paragraph of "WELCOME," the message then proceeds to "A PAGE OF HISTORY," which reads as follows:

> New World History begins on the same day that modern Bahamian history begins—October 12, 1492. That's when Columbus stepped ashore—British influence came first with the Eleutherian Adventurers of 1647—After the Revolutions. American Loyalists fled from the newly indepen-

dent states and settled in the Bahamas. Confederate blockade-runners used the island as a haven during the War between the States, and after the War, a number of Southerners moved to the Bahamas.

There it is again. Something proclaims itself a legitimate history and all it does is track white Mr. Columbus to the British Eleutherians through the Confederate Southerners as they barge into New World surf, land on New World turf, and nobody saying one word about the Bahamian people, the Black peoples, to whom the only thing new in their island world was this weird succession of crude intruders and its colonial consequences.

This is my consciousness of race as I unpack my bathing suit in the Sheraton British Colonial. Neither this hotel nor the British nor the long ago Italians nor the white Delta airline pilots belong here, of course. And every time I look at the photograph of that fool standing in the water with his shoes on I'm about to have a West Indian fit, even though I know he's no fool; he's a middle-aged Black man who needs a job and this is his job—pretending himself a servile ancillary to the pleasures of the rich. (Compared to his options in life, I am a rich woman. Compared to most of the Black Americans arriving for this Easter weekend on a three nights four days' deal of bargain rates, the middle-aged waiter is a poor Black man.)

We will jostle along with the other (white) visitors and join them in the tee shirt shops or, laughing together, learn ruthless rules of negotiation as we, Black Americans as well as white, argue down the price of handwoven goods at the nearby straw market while the merchants, frequently toothless Black women seated on the concrete in their only presentable dress, humble themselves to our careless games:

"Yes? You like it? Eight dollar."

"Five."

"I give it to you. Seven."

And so it continues, this weird succession of crude intruders that, now, includes me and my brothers and my sisters from the North.

This is my consciousness of class as I try to decide how much money I can spend on Bahamian gifts for my family back in Brooklyn. No matter that these other Black women incessantly weave words and flowers into the straw hats and bags piled beside them on the burning dusty street. No matter that these other Black women must work their sense of beauty into these things that we will take away as cheaply as we dare, or they will do without food.

We are not white, after all. The budget is limited. And we are harmlessly killing time between the poolside rum punch and "The Native Show on the Patio" that will play tonight outside the hotel restaurant.

This is my consciousness of race and class and gender identity as I notice the fixed relations between these other Black women and myself. They sell and I buy or I don't. They risk not eating. I risk going broke on my first vacation afternoon.

We are not particularly women anymore; we are parties to a transaction designed to set us against each other.

"Olive" is the name of the Black woman who cleans my hotel room. On my way to the beach I am wondering what "Olive" would say if I told her why I chose The Sheraton British Colonial; if I told her I wanted to swim. I wanted to sleep. I did not want to be harassed by the middle-aged waiter, or his nephew. I did not want to be raped by anybody (white or Black) at all and I calculated that my safety as a Black woman alone would best be ensured by a multinational hotel corporation. In my experience, the big guys take customer complaints more seriously than the little ones. I would suppose that's one reason why they're big; they don't like to lose money anymore than I like to be bothered when I'm trying to read a god-damned book underneath a palm tree I paid $264 to get next to. A Black woman seeking refuge in a multinational corporation may seem like a contradiction to some, but there you are. In this case it's a coincidence of entirely different self-interests: Sheraton/cash = June Jordan's short run safety.

Anyway, I'm pretty sure "Olive" would look at me as though I came from someplace as far away as Brooklyn. Then she'd probably allow herself one indignant query before righteously removing her vacuum cleaner from my room; "and why in the first place you come down here without your husband?"

I cannot imagine how I would begin to answer her.

My "rights" and my "freedom" and my "desire" and a slew of other New World values; what would they sound like to this Black woman described on the card atop my hotel bureau as "Olive the Maid"? "Olive" is older than I am and I may smoke a cigarette while she changes the sheets on my bed. Whose rights? Whose freedom? Whose desire?

And why should she give a shit about mine unless I do something, for real, about hers?

It happens that the book that I finished reading under a palm tree earlier today was the novel *The Bread Givers,* by Anzia Yezierska. Definitely autobiographical. Yezierska lays out the difficulties of being both female and "a person" inside a traditional Jewish family at the start of the twentieth century. . . .

. . .

I am thinking about the boy who loaned this novel to me. He's white and he's Jewish and he's pursuing an independent study project with me, at the State University where I teach whether or not I feel like it, where I teach without stint because, like the waiter, I am no fool. It's my job and either I work or I do without everything you need money to buy. The boy loaned me the novel because he thought I'd be interested to know how a Jewish-American writer used English so that the syntax, and therefore the cultural habits of mind expressed by the Yiddish language, could survive translation. He did this because he wanted to create another connection between us on the basis of language, between his knowledge/his love of Yiddish and my knowledge/my love of Black English.

He has been right about the forceful survival of the Yiddish. And I had become excited by this further evidence of the written voice of spoken language protected from the monodrone of "standard" English, and so we had grown closer on this account. But then our talk shifted to student affairs more generally, and I had learned that this student does not care one way or the other about currently jeopardized Federal Student Loan Programs because, as he explained it to me, they do not affect him. He does not need financial help outside his family. My own son, however, is Black. And I am the only family help available to him. . . .

. . .

It's time to pack it up. Catch my plane. I scan the hotel room for things not to forget. There's that white report card on the bureau.

"Dear Guests:" it says, under the name "Olive." "I am your maid for the day. Please rate me: Excellent. Good. Average. Poor. Thank you."

I tuck this momento from the Sheraton British Colonial into my notebook. How would "Olive" rate *me?* What would it mean for us to seem "good" to each other? What would that rating require?

But I am hastening to leave. Neither turtle soup nor kidney pie nor any conch shell delight shall delay my departure. I have rested, here, in the Bahamas, and I'm ready to return to my usual job, my usual work. But the skin on my body has changed and so has my mind. On the Delta flight home I realize I am burning up, indeed.

So far as I can see, the usual race and class concepts of connection, or gender assumptions of unity, do not apply very well. I doubt that they ever did. Otherwise, why would Black folks forever bemoan our lack of solidarity when the deal turns real. And if unity on the basis of sexual

oppression is something natural, then why do we women, the majority people on the planet, still have a problem?

The plane's ready for takeoff. I fasten my seatbelt and let the tumult inside my head run free. Yes: race and class and gender remain as real as the weather. But what they must mean about the contact between two individuals is less obvious and, like the weather, not predictable.

And when these factors of race and class and gender absolutely collapse is whenever you try to use them as automatic concepts of connection. They may serve well as indicators of commonly felt conflict, but as elements of connection they seem about as reliable as precipitation probability for the day after the night before the day.

It occurs to me that much organizational grief could be avoided if people understood that partnership in misery does not necessarily provide for partnership for change: *When we get the monsters off our backs all of us may want to run in very different directions.*

And not only that: even though both "Olive" and "I" live inside a conflict neither one of us created, and even though both of us therefore hurt inside that conflict, I may be one of the monsters she needs to eliminate from her universe and, in a sense, she may be one of the monsters in mine.

I am reaching for the words to describe the difference between a common identity that has been imposed and the individual identity any one of us will choose, once she gains that chance.

That difference is the one that keeps us stupid in the face of new, specific information about somebody else with whom we are supposed to have a connection because a third party, hostile to both of us, has worked it so that the two of us, like it or not, share a common enemy. *What happens beyond the idea of that enemy and beyond the consequences of that enemy?*

I am saying that the ultimate connection cannot be the enemy. The ultimate connection must be the need that we find between us. It is not only who you are, in other words, but what we can do for each other that will determine the connection.

I am flying back to my job. I have been teaching contemporary women's poetry this semester. One quandary I have set myself to explore with my students is the one of taking responsibility without power. We had been wrestling ideas to the floor for several sessions when a young Black woman, a South African, asked me for help, after class.

Sokutu told me she was "in a trance" and that she'd been unable to eat for two weeks.

"What's going on?" I asked her, even as my eyes startled at her trembling and emaciated appearance.

"My husband. He drinks all the time. He beats me up. I go to the hospital. I can't eat. I don't know what/anything."

In my office, she described her situation. I did not dare to let her sense my fear and horror. She was dragging about, hour by hour, in dread. Her husband, a young Black South African, was drinking himself into more and more deadly violence against her.

Sokutu told me how she could keep nothing down. She weighed 90 lbs. at the outside, as she spoke to me. She'd already been hospitalized as a result of her husband's battering rage.

I knew both of them because I had organized a campus group to aid the liberation struggles of Southern Africa.

Nausea rose in my throat. What about this presumable connection: this husband and this wife fled from that homeland of hatred against them, and now what? He was destroying himself. If not stopped, he would certainly murder his wife.

She needed a doctor, right away. It was a medical emergency. She needed protection. It was a security crisis. She needed refuge for battered wives and personal therapy and legal counsel. She needed a friend.

I got on the phone and called every number in the campus directory that I could imagine might prove helpful. Nothing worked. There were no institutional resources designed to meet her enormous, multifaceted, and ordinary woman's need.

I called various students. I asked the Chairperson of the English Department for advice. I asked everyone for help.

Finally, another one of my students, Cathy, a young Irish woman active in campus IRA activi-

ties, responded. She asked for further details. I gave them to her.

"Her husband," Cathy told me, "is an alcoholic. You have to understand about alcoholics. It's not the same as anything else. And it's a disease you can't treat any old way."

I listened, fearfully. Did this mean there was nothing we could do?

"That's not what I'm saying," she said. "But you have to keep the alcoholic part of the thing central in everybody's mind, otherwise her husband will kill her. Or he'll kill himself."

She spoke calmly. I felt there was nothing to do but to assume she knew what she was talking about.

"Will you come with me?" I asked her, after a silence. "Will you come with me and help us figure out what to do next?"

Cathy said she would but that she felt shy: Sokutu comes from South Africa. What would she think about Cathy?

"I don't know," I said. "But let's go."

We left to find a dormitory room for the young battered wife.

It was late, now, and dark outside.

On Cathy's VW that I followed behind with my own car, was the sticker that reads BOBBY SANDS FREE AT LAST. My eyes blurred as I read and reread the words. This was another connection: Bobby Sands and Martin Luther King Jr. and who would believe it? I would not have believed it; I grew up terrorized by Irish kids who introduced me to the word "nigga."

And here I was following an Irish woman to the room of a Black South African. We were going to that room to try to save a life together.

When we reached the little room, we found ourselves awkward and large. Sokutu attempted to treat us with utmost courtesy, as though we were honored guests. She seemed surprised by Cathy, but mostly Sokutu was flushed with relief and joy because we were there, with her.

I did not know how we should ever terminate her heartfelt courtesies and address, directly, the reason for our visit: her starvation and her extreme physical danger.

Finally, Cathy sat on the floor and reached out her hands to Sokutu. "I'm here," she said quietly,

"Because June has told me what has happened to you. And I know what it is. Your husband is an alcoholic. He has a disease. I know what it is. My father was an alcholic. He killed himself. He almost killed my mother. I want to be your friend."

"Oh," was the only small sound that escaped from Sokutu's mouth. And then she embraced the other student. And then everything changed and I watched all of this happen so I know that this happened: this connection.

And after we called the police and exchanged phone numbers and plans were made for the night and for the next morning, the young South African woman walked down the dormitory hallway, saying goodbye and saying thank you to us.

I walked behind them, the young Irish woman and the young South African, and I saw them walking as sisters walk, hugging each other, and whispering and sure of each other and I felt how it was not who they were but what they both know and what they were both preparing to do about what they know that was going to make them both free at last.

And I look out the windows of the plane and I see clouds that will not kill me and I know that someday soon other clouds may erupt to kill us all.

And I tell the stewardess No thanks to the cocktails she offers me. But I look about the cabin at the hundred strangers drinking as they fly and I think even here and even now I must make the connection real between me and these strangers everywhere before those other clouds unify this ragged bunch of us, too late.

DISCUSSION QUESTIONS FOR CHAPTER 2

1. How do different forms of prejudice affect your life?

2. How do ideologies undergird institutions? How do these ideologies show up in the institutions that most affect your life?

3. How do institutions maintain gender inequality? Have you experienced gender inequality in particular institutions?

4. How do institutions work together to support and maintain one another?

5. How do hate crimes help maintain systems of inequality? What images of hate crimes do you recall? What effects do these images have on you?

SUGGESTIONS FOR FURTHER READING

Allison, Dorothy. *Trash*. Ithaca, NY: Firebrand, 1989.

Anzaldúa, Gloria. *Borderlands/La Frontera: The New Mestiza*. San Francisco: Aunt Lute, 1987.

Blee, Kathleen M. *Inside Organized Racism: Women in the Hate Movement*. Berkeley: University of California Press, 2002.

Cole, Johnetta, and Beverly Guy-Sheftall. *Gender Talk: The Struggle for Women's Equality in African American Communities*. New York: One World/Ballantine, 2003.

Collins, Patricia. *From Black Power to Hip-Hop: Racism, Nationalism, and Feminism*. Philadelphia: Temple University Press, 2006.

hooks, bell. *Where We Stand: Class Matters*. New York: Routledge, 2002.

Jones, Charisse, and Kumea Shorter-Gooden. *Shifting: The Double Lives of Black Women in America*. New York: HarperCollins, 2003.

Lorde, Audre. *Sister Outsider*. Freedom, CA: Crossing Press, 1984.

Mihesuah, Devon A. *Indigenous American Women: Decolonization, Empowerment, Activism*. Lincoln, NE: Bison Books, 2003.

Pough, Gwendolyn, et al., eds. *Home Girls Make Some Noise!: Hip-Hop Feminism Anthology*. Mira Loma, CA: Parker Publishing, LLC, 2007.

Smith, Bonnie G., and Beth Hutchison. *Gendering Disability*. New Brunswick, NJ: Rutgers University Press, 2004.

Stein, Arlene. *The Stranger Next Door: The Story of a Small Community's Battle over Sex, Faith, and Civil Rights*. Boston: Beacon Press, 2002.

Wehbi, Samantha. *Community Organizing Against Homophobia and Heterosexism*. San Francisco: Harrington Park Press, 2004.

Wilson, Shamillah, Anasuya Sengupta, and Kristy Evans, eds. *Defending Our Dreams: Global Feminist Voices for a New Generation*. London: Zed Books, 2006.

Learning Gender
in a Diverse Society

Our typical in-class exercise while teaching a unit on the social construction of gender is to ask how many among the large number of women students present identified as "tomboys" when they were growing up. A sea of hands usually results as women remember their early years as girls resisting traditional notions of femininity. When male students are asked whether they had been called "sissies" when they were young, usually the whole group laughs as one lone male sheepishly raises his hand and remarks that he's always been a sissy. Why is it so easy to say you were a tomboy and so difficult to admit to being a sissy? This has a lot to do with the meanings associated with masculinity and femininity and the ways these are ranked in society. In this chapter we focus specifically on gender and sexism, keeping in mind two important points: First, how gender is constructed in connection to other differences among women like race, ethnicity, and class, and second, how sexism as a system of oppression is related to other systems of inequality and privilege.

BIOLOGY AND CULTURE

In Chapter 1 we explained gender as the way society creates, patterns, and rewards our understandings of femininity and masculinity, or the process by which certain behaviors and performances are ascribed to women and men. Gender, in other words, can be understood as the social organization of sexual difference. Although biological distinctions create female and male humans, society interprets these differences and gives us "feminine" and "masculine" people. These adjectives are intentionally placed in quotation marks to emphasize that notions of femininity and masculinity are socially constructed—created by social processes that reflect the various workings of power in society. Therefore these notions are culturally and historically changeable. There is nothing essential, intrinsic, or static about femininity or masculinity; rather, they are social categories that might mean different things in different societies and in different historical periods. Society shapes notions of femininity and masculinity through the subtle interactions between nature and nurture.

LEARNING ACTIVITY   **Tomboys and Sissies**

Take an informal poll on your campus. Ask the women if they ever wanted to be a boy when they were growing up. Note their reaction to the question. Then ask why or why not. Also ask the women if they were considered tomboys growing up and how they felt about it if they were. Record responses and observations in a research journal.

Ask men on your campus if they ever wanted to be a girl when they were growing up. Again, note their reaction to the question. Ask why or why not. Then ask if they were considered sissies growing up and, if so, how they felt about it. Record responses and observations.

Once you've completed your poll, compare and contrast the responses you received from women and men. What do you notice? Why do you think responses may have been the way they were? What do responses suggest about gender in American society?

However, the relationship between biology (female/male) and culture (feminine/masculine), is more complicated than the assertion that sex is a biological fact and gender is the societal interpretation of that fact. First, as new scholarship points out, there is greater gender diversity in nature than once thought. As Joan Roughgarden suggests in *Evolution's Rainbow* (2004), many species are not just female or male, but can be both female and male at the same time, or be one or the other at different times. Second, while biology may imply some basic physiological facts, culture gives meaning to these in such a way that we must question whether biology can exist except within the society that gives it meaning in the first place. This implies that sex, in terms of raw male or female, is already gendered by the culture within which these physiological facts of biology exist. In other words, although many people make a distinction between biological sex (female/male) and learned gender (feminine/masculine), it is really impossible to speak of a fixed biological sex category outside of the sense that a culture makes of that category.

An example that highlights how biology is connected to culture concerns the processes by which ambiguous sex characteristics in children are handled. When hermaphrodites (individuals with both female and male genitalia) or "intersex" children (without distinct genitalia to characterize them as either girls or boys) are born health professionals and the family tend to make an immediate sex determination. Hormone therapy and surgeries follow to make such a child fit the constructed binary categories our society has created, and gender is taught in accordance with this decision. This is an example of the way a breakdown in the taken-for-granted tight connection between natural biology and learned gender is seen as a medical and social emergency. Indeed, anthropologists have questioned this connection and used, for example, the Native American "berdache" status that entailed varying gender identities with behaviors encompassing social and economic roles, religious specialization, and temperament, to demonstrate the range of gender identity on the American continent. Along these lines, Anne Fausto-Sterling questions the tidy

"Why does he always get to be the boy?"

organization of human sex into the two categories female and male, emphasizing that sex is not as easy as genetics and genitalia and arguing for theories that allow for human variation. In the reading "Two Sexes Are Not Enough," Fausto-Sterling comments on an article she wrote in 1993 (published in *The Sciences,* vol. 33, 20–24 that suggested replacing the two-sex system with a five-sex system to reflect this diversity.

Gender is one of the most important features of a person's identity, shaping social life and informing attitudes, behavior, and the individual's sense of self. Its pervasiveness is also a theme of Judith Lorber's article "The Social Construction of Gender." She explains that gender is a process that involves multiple patterns of interaction and is created and re-created constantly in human interaction. Lorber also makes the important point that because gender is so central in shaping our lives, much of what is gendered we do not even recognize; it's made normal and ordinary and occurs on a subconscious level. In other words, the differences between femininity (passive, dependent, intuitive, emotional) and masculinity (strong, independent, in control, out of touch emotionally) are made to seem natural and inevitable despite the fact that gender is a social script that individuals learn. Importantly, many of the skills and practices associated with gender involve privilege and entitlements. They also involve limitations.

In reality, gender is a practice in which all people engage; it is something we perform over and over in our daily lives. In this sense, gender is something that we "do" rather than "have." Through a process of *gender socialization,* we are taught and learn the appropriate thinking and behaviors associated with being a boy or girl in this culture. We actively learn the skills and practices of gender, and most of us become very accomplished in these various performances. For example, in sports, the way that girls tend naturally to throw a ball is often the object of derision. Throwing the way boys do, however, is actually an act that is learned, then performed again and again until it becomes a skill. Girls can learn to throw like boys if they are taught. Men are not necessarily better athletes than women; rather, sports as an institution has developed to reflect the particular athletic

LEARNING ACTIVITY   **Speaking of Women and Men**

Think about the adjectives we typically use to describe women and men and list these words in the columns below. A couple of examples are provided to get you started.

WOMEN	MEN
Passive	Active
Nurturing	Strong

What do you notice about the words we use to describe women and men? How does our language reinforce stereotypical notions about women and men?

Think about the words we use to designate women and list these names in the columns below. Also, try to find parallel names for women and men. And think about the profanities we use as well. Again, a couple of examples are provided.

WOMEN	MEN
Slut	Stud
Chick	

What do you notice here about the terms we use to name women and men? What is the significance of the words for which you could not identify parallels?

How do you think language plays a role in shaping the ways we think about and "do" gender?

competencies of men. For example, if long-distance swimming or balance beam (activities where women generally outperform men) were popular national sports, then we might think differently about the athletic capabilities of women and men. In addition to sports, there are many other major U.S. institutions that support gendered practices. You only need go to a toy store and cruise the very different girls' and boys' aisles to witness the social construction of gender in contemporary U.S. society. What does it mean to get a child-size ironing board instead of a toy gun, and what kinds of behaviors and future roles do these toys help create and justify?

Cathy © 1996 Cathy Guisewite. Reprinted with permission of Universal Press Syndicate. All rights reserved.

This discussion of gender identity and practices does not imply that all men in contemporary North American society are ambitious and independent and all women domestic and emotional. However, this discussion clarifies the social norms or shared values associated with the two kinds of human beings our society has created. Gender norms provide the standards or parameters through which thoughts and behaviors are molded. If we created a continuum with "feminine" on one end and "masculine" on the other, we would find mostly women on one end and mostly men on the other, and a mixture in between. This means that women and men learn the practices of gender, internalize the norms associated with masculinity and femininity, are rewarded for appropriate behaviors and sanctioned for inappropriate behaviors, and learn to perform the ones that are expected of them.

It is important to emphasize that gender is embedded in culture and that what it might mean to be "feminine" or "masculine" in one culture is different from meanings in another culture. This means that people growing up in different societies in different parts of the world at different historical moments will learn different notions of gender. As the boxed insert in this chapter called "Rites of Passage" suggests, gender performances vary around the world. In addition, as discussed in the reading "Masculinities and Globalization" by R. W. Connell, contemporary life in the early twenty-first century, which involves global systems of production, consumption, and communication, means that patterns of gender in the United States

HISTORICAL MOMENT   **Gender Testing**

In 1966 the European Athletics Championships in Budapest required the first sex testing of women athletes. Earlier, charges had been leveled suggesting that some women competitors were really men. In 1966 the first sex test was a visual examination of the naked athletes. Later, this test was replaced by a test that detected the athletes' chromosomal pattern (XX for female and XY for male).

In 1967 Polish sprinter Ewa Klobukowska failed the sex test and was banned from competition. Later, doctors found that she had a condition that once identified would have allowed her to compete.

In 1985 Spanish hurdler Maria Patino expected to compete in the World University Games in Kobe, Japan. Patino had lived her entire life as a woman, and her body type and sex characteristics were typically female. Unfortunately, for Patino, however, her sex test revealed that she did not have two X chromosomes. She was barred from the competition. A few months later, she competed in Spain and won her event. Following her win, however, she was kicked off the Spanish national team, stripped of her titles, and banned from all future competition. Her fight to be reinstated by the International Amateur Athletics Federation took 2½ years.

While our society generally operates under the assumption that people are either male or female, variations from typical biological patterns are common. Some form of intersexuality may occur in as many as 1 in 100 births. Generally, 1 in 400 female athletes will fail the sex test. For many years, women athletes engaged in activism to stop the sex test. Finally, the test was suspended for the 2000 Olympics, although the Olympic Committee reserved the right to reinstate the test at any point in the future.

Notice that sex testing has been used only for female athletes. Why do you suppose this is true? How does the existence of people who do not fit neatly into one or the other of the biological categories of male and female disrupt notions of fixed sexes and fixed genders?

are exported worldwide and are increasingly linked to patterns of global economic restructuring. This encourages us to consider the ways the social and economic dynamics of globalization (including economic and political expansion, militarism and colonial conquest and settlement, disruption/appropriation of indigenous peoples and resources, exportation of ideas through world markets, etc.) have shaped global gender arrangements and transformed gender relations between people based on these politics.

There are some people who consider themselves *transgendered* or who claim a gender identity or expression different from the one usually associated with the sex at their birth. Identifying oneself as transgendered involves resisting the social construction of gender into two distinct categories, masculinity and femininity, and working to break down these constraining, and polarized, categories. Transgendered people push at the boundaries of gender and help reveal its constructed nature. Being transgendered illustrates the ways a person's gender identity does not match the assigned gender

Calvin and Hobbes   by Bill Watterson

identity given at birth based upon physical or genetic sex characteristics. Transgender does not imply any specific form of sexual identity: transgendered people may identify as heterosexual, gay, lesbian, bisexual, or asexual. It is important not to confuse gender and sexuality here: Transgendered identities are about gender performance and might involve any sexual identity. It can be confusing, however, because on many campuses there are LGBTQ (Lesbian/Gay/Bisexual/Trans/Queer) alliances or centers where resources for transgendered students are incorporated into a coalition about sexual rights. In addition, the new term *genderqueer* has combined alternative gender identities and sexualities, although you might see it used to imply someone who is transgendered without concern for sexual identity. Generally, genderqueer describes a person who is a nonconformist in challenging existing constructions and identities. You might also see it used to describe a social movement resisting the traditional categories of gender. Specifically, it implies attempts to challenge the binary models of both gender (male/female) and sexual identity (straight/gay). Use of the term *queer* and other issues associated with sexual identity are discussed in more detail in Chapter 4. However, although genderqueer focuses on the integration of gender and sexual identities and therefore is a useful concept both in terms of individual empowerment and social commentary and political change, it is important to understand that, conceptually, these identities (gender and sexuality) are distinct from each other.

The constructed aspect of gender is illustrated in the reading by Judy Wajcman titled "Virtual Gender." She encourages us to consider the ways the Internet and other virtual technologies have facilitated transgendered identities through a disruption of the expected relationship between self and body ("feminine" identity/"female" body). These technologies remove physical, bodily cues and allow "gender swapping," or the creation of identities that attempt to avoid the binaries of "femininity" and "masculinity." This supports the postmodern view of gender as performative and identity as multiple and fluid. Wajcman also alludes to the limits of separation between cyborg subject and body as she describes an example of masquerade and betrayal.

The term *transgendered* is often used interchangeably with the term *transsexual* (and simply labeled *trans*. Some scholars are more likely to describe transsexuals as transgendered people who believe they are born with the bodies of the wrong sex and who desire chemical or surgical altering in the form of hormone therapies or sex reassignment surgeries. They transition from female to male (FtM, F2M, or "transman") and male to female (MtF, M2F, or "transwoman"). The reading by Debra Rosenberg, "(Rethinking) Gender," discusses transgender issues. As a category, transgender overlaps with *cross-dressing,* the practice of wearing the clothes of the opposite sex, or the sex different from that to which a person was assigned in childhood. Cross-dressing is different from *fetishistic transvestism* (also known as transvestic fetishism), which involves occasional wearing of the other sex's clothes for sexual self-arousal or pleasure. In addition, the category of transgendered cross-dressers does not necessarily include impersonators who look upon dressing as solely connected to their livelihood or actors undertaking roles. Similarly, drag performances that involve makeup and clothing worn on special occasions for theatrical or comedic purposes are not necessarily transgender behavior, although within the genre of drag there are gender illusionists who do try to pass as another gender and are very active in the transgender community. Drag queens are men doing female impersonation and drag kings are women doing male impersonation.

As a concept, transgendered is different from androgyny, although in practice, one performance of a transgendered identity might be androgyny. *Androgyny* can be defined as a lack of gender differentiation or a balanced mixture of recognizable feminine and masculine traits. This blurring or balancing is not the only consequence of an attempt to break down or rebel against gender categories. It is interesting to note that contemporary ideas about androgyny tend to privilege the "andro" (male) more than the "gyny" (female), with the presentation of androgyny looking a lot more like a young male than a mature female. The trappings of femininity seem to be the first things that are shed when a body tries to redo itself as androgynous. This is related to androcentrism and the ways masculinity more closely approximates our understanding of (nongendered) "human."

MASCULINITY

In mainstream contemporary North American society, *masculinity* has been constructed from the classical traits of intelligence, courage, and honesty, with the addition of two other key dimensions. One of these dimensions revolves around potent sexuality and an affinity for violence: the machismo element. *Machismo* involves breaking rules, sexual potency contextualized in the blending of sex and violence, and contempt for women (*misogyny*). To be a man is to *not* be a woman. Weakness, softness, and vulnerability are to be avoided at all costs. It is no coincidence that the symbol of male ♂ represents Mars, the Roman god of war. A second dimension of masculinity is the *provider role,* composed of ambition, confidence, competence, and strength. Early research by Deborah David and Robert Brannon characterized four dictates of masculinity that encompass these key dimensions. The dictates include (1) "no sissy stuff," the rejection of femininity; (2) the "big wheel," ambition and the

Rites of Passage

In almost every culture, adolescents participate in some rite of passage to mark entry into adulthood. Quite often, these rites reinforce gender distinctions. Most rites of passage share four basic elements: (1) separation from society, (2) preparation or instruction from an elder, (3) transition, and (4) welcoming back into society with acknowledgment of changed status.* Notice in the following examples how gender is reinforced through rites of passage:

- Among the Okrika of Africa, girls participate in the Iria, a rite that begins in the "fatting rooms" where the girls are fed rich foods to cause the body to "come out." The girls learn traditional songs from the elderly women, and these songs are used to free the girls from their romantic attachments to water spirits so they can become marriageable and receive mortal suitors. On the final day of their initiation, the water spirits are expected to try to seize the girls, but the Osokolo (a male) strikes the girls with sticks and drives them back to the village, ensuring their safety and future fertility.*

- The Tukuna of the Amazon initiate girls into womanhood at the onset of menstruation through the Festa das Mocas Novas. For several weeks, the girl lives in seclusion in a chamber in her family's home. The Tukuna believe that during this time, the girl is in the underworld and in increasing danger from demons, the Noo. Near the end of the initiation period, the girl is painted with black genipa dye for 2 days to protect her from the Noo, while guests arrive, some wearing masks to become incarnations of the Noo. On the third day, she leaves the chamber to dance with her family until dawn. The shaman gives her a firebrand to throw at the Noo to break the Noo's power and allow her to enter into womanhood.*

- In Ohafia in Nigeria, a father provides his son with a bow and arrows around age 7 or 8. The boy practices shooting at targets until he develops the skill to kill a small bird. When this task is accomplished, the boy ties the dead bird to the end of his bow and marches through his village singing that his peers who have not yet killed their first bird are cowards. His father, then, dresses him in finery and takes him to visit, often for the first time, his maternal family. His new social role distinguishes him from the "cowards" and marks his entrance into manhood.†

What are some rites of passage in the United States? How do these rites reinforce gender? How might rites of passage be developed that acknowledge entrance into adulthood without reinforcing gender distinctions?

* Cassandra Halle Delaney, "Rites of Passage in Adolescence," *Adolescence* 30 (1995): 891–987.
† *www.siu.edu/~anthro/mccall/children.html.*

LEARNING ACTIVITY   **Performing Gender in the Movies**

Many movies offer gender-bending performances. Choose one or more of the following movies to watch. During the movie, record your observations about how the various characters learn and perform gender. Also note the ways race intersects with gender in these performances. How does sexual identity get expressed in the performance of gender?

- *Victor/Victoria*
- *Tootsie*
- *Mrs. Doubtfire*
- *To Wong Foo, Thanks for Everything! Julie Newmar*
- *The Adventures of Priscilla, Queen of the Desert*
- *Switch*
- *The Birdcage*
- *Orlando*
- *Shakespeare in Love*
- *Boys Don't Cry*
- *Big Momma's House*
- *Sorority Boys*
- *Nutty Professor*
- *Nutty Professor II: The Klumps*
- *Connie and Carla*
- *White Chicks*

pursuit of success, fame, and wealth; (3) the "sturdy oak," confidence, competence, stoicism, and toughness; and (4) "give 'em hell," the machismo element.* Although these scripts dictate masculinity in a broad sense, there are societal demands that construct masculinity differently for different kinds of men. Middle-class masculinity puts an emphasis on the big-wheel dimension, the dictates of White masculinity often involve the sturdy oak, and men of color often become associated with the machismo element (with the exception of Asian American men, who are often feminized).

The last decades have seen changes in the social construction of contemporary masculinity. Although the machismo element is still acted out by countless teenage boys and men, it is also avoided by many men who genuinely do not want to be constrained by its demands. Often these men have realized that moving away from the machismo does not necessarily imply a loss of power. In fact, it seems contemporary women may prefer men who are a little more sensitive and vulnerable. In part, these changes have come about as a result of the focus on gender provided by the women's movement and as a result of the work of such organizations as the National Organization of Men Against Sexism (NOMAS) and groups like Dads and Daughters. As feminist writer and activist Gloria Steinem once said, gender is a prison for both women and men. The difference, she said, is that for men it's a prison with wall-to-wall

* Deborah S. David and Robert Brannon, eds., *The Forty-Nine Percent Majority: The Male Sex Role* (Reading, MA: Addison-Wesley, 1976), pp. 13–35.

carpeting and someone to bring you coffee. Understanding the limitations associated with masculine social scripts has encouraged many men to transform these scripts into more productive ways of living. Many pro-feminist men and men's organizations have been at the forefront of this work.

Some men have responded to the limitations of masculinity and the advances of women brought about by feminism by focusing on themselves as victims, as demonstrated by the mytho-poetic men's movement, which encourages men to bond and reclaim their power. While this may empower individual men, private solutions to social problems do little to transform patriarchal social structure. Other men more overtly express their desire to take back the power they believe they have lost as a result of changes in contemporary notions of femininity and the gains of the women's movement. These include the Promise Keepers, a group of Christian-affiliated men who want to return men to their rightful place in the family and community through a strong re-assertion of traditional gender roles. They believe that men are to rule and women are to serve within the traditional family system.

FEMININITY

Adjectives associated with traditional notions of femininity in contemporary mainstream North American society include soft, passive, domestic, nurturing, emotional, dependent, sensitive, as well as delicate, intuitive, fastidious, needy, fearful, and so forth. These are the qualities that have kept women in positions of subordination and encouraged them to do the domestic and emotional work of society. Again, no surprise that the symbol of female ♀ represents Venus, the goddess of love. "Doing gender" in terms of femininity involves speaking, walking, looking, and acting in certain ways: in feminine ways. The performative quality involved in being a drag queen (a man who is acting out normative femininity) highlights and reveals the taken-for-granted (at least by women) affectations of femininity. Yet, femininity, like masculinity, varies across cultures and groups. For example, due to historical and cultural factors, many African American women have not internalized the association of femininity with passivity and dependency characteristic of White women. Asian American women, on the other hand, often have to deal with societal stereotypes that construct femininity very much in terms of passivity and dependence: the "exotic gardenia" or "oriental chick" described in Nellie Wong's poem "When I Was Growing Up."

A key aspect of femininity is its bifurcation or channeling into two opposite aspects. These aspects involve the chaste, domestic, caring mother or madonna and the sexy, seducing, fun-loving playmate or whore (known in popular mythology as women you marry and women with whom you have sex). These polar opposites cause tension as women navigate the implications of these aspects of femininity in their everyday lives. This is an example of the double bind that Marilyn Frye wrote about in her article "Oppression" included in Chapter 2. A woman often discovers that neither sexual activity nor sexual inactivity is quite right. If she is too sexually active, she will be censured for being too loose, the whore; if she refrains from sexual activity, she might similarly be censured for being a prude or frigid. Notice there are many slang words for both kinds of women: those who have too much sex and those who do not have enough. This is the double bind: You're damned if you do and

ACTIVIST PROFILE **Gloria Steinem**

Gloria Steinem didn't set out to become one of the key spokespersons for feminism. Growing up in poverty and with a mentally ill mother, Steinem often found herself in the role of her mother's caretaker. Despite the difficulties at home, she succeeded at school and was eventually accepted to Smith College, where her interest in women's rights began to take hold. After graduating from Smith, Steinem received a fellowship to do graduate studies at the University of Delhi and University of Calcutta, India. While in India, she did some work as a freelance writer and, upon returning to the United States, began a career in journalism.

As a woman in journalism, Steinem was rarely given serious assignments. Her most famous article resulted from a 1963 undercover assignment as a Playboy Bunny. Steinem saw the article as an opportunity to expose sexual harassment, but following its publication she had a difficult time being taken seriously as a journalist, despite the excellent reviews the article received.

She finally got her chance for key political assignments in 1968 when she came on board *New York Magazine* as a contributing editor. One assignment sent her to cover a radical feminist meeting, and following that meeting she moved to the center of the women's movement, co-founding the National Women's Political Caucus and the Women's Action Alliance.

In 1972 she co-founded *Ms.* magazine. Although Steinem believed there should be a feminist magazine, she had not intended to start it herself. Originally, she had thought she'd turn over the editorship once the magazine got on its feet. But with the success of *Ms.*, Steinem became one of the nation's most visible and important proponents of feminism.

The first issue of *Ms.* featured Wonder Woman on the cover, and its entire first printing of 300,000 copies sold out in 8 days. Steinem remained editor for 15 years and is still involved with the magazine today.

potentially damned if you don't. These contradictions and mixed messages serve to keep women in line. The article by Pamela J. Bettis and Natalie Guice Adams, "Short Skirts and Breast Juts," on cheerleading in the schools, addresses the (hetero)sexualized dimension of cheerleading as a sport and illustrates the ways gender performances help provide frameworks for sexual behaviors. These frameworks, known as *sexual scripts,* are discussed in Chapter 4.

Unlike contemporary masculinity, which is exhibiting very small steps into the realms of the feminine, femininity has boldly moved into areas that were traditionally off-limits. Today's ideal woman (perhaps from a woman's point of view) is definitely more androgynous than the ideal woman of the past. The contemporary ideal woman

LEARNING ACTIVITY   **Gender Swapping on the Web**

As discussed in the reading by Judy Wajcman, the virtual world of the Internet has provided a fascinating environment in which people often play with gender, although, given the social relations of power in contemporary society, this virtual world can also be a place where individuals use gender as a source of power over, or harassment against, other people. Still, in many text-based virtual environments, Web users are able to take on another gender. Men create "feminine" identities for themselves, and women create "masculine" identities for themselves. As Web users engage in this process of gender swapping, they are able to explore the ways that human interactions are structured by gender and to experience in some ways what life is like as another gender.

Create a virtual identity for yourself as another gender and join a chat room or game on the Web as that person. How does it feel to experience the world as another gender? Do you notice ways you act or are treated differently as this gender? What do your experiences suggest to you about how gender structures the ways humans interact with one another?

Men, by far, gender swap on the Web more than women. Why do you think this is true? Do you think gender swapping on the Web has the potential to challenge gender stereotypes? Or do you think it reinforces them? How might the technology of the Internet be used to challenge the limitations of gender? How might the technology of the Internet be used to reinforce male dominance?

Learn more: The following books offer in-depth exploration of these issues. What do these authors suggest about the nature of gender on the Web?

Cherny, Lynn, and Elizabeth Reba Weise, eds. *Wired Women: Gender and New Realities in Cyberspace.* Seattle, WA: Seal Press, 1996.

Kendall, Lori. *Hanging Out in the Virtual Pub: Masculinities and Relationships Online.* Berkeley: University of California Press, 2002.

Paasonen, Susanna. *Figures of Fantasy: Internet, Women, and Cyberdiscourse.* New York: Peter Lang, 2005.

Spender, Dale. *Nattering on the Net: Women, Power, and Cyberspace.* North Melbourne: Spinifex Press, 1995.

might be someone who is smart, competent, and independent, beautiful, thin, athletic, and sexy, yet also loving, sensitive, competent domestically, and emotionally healthy. Note how this image has integrated characteristics of masculinity with traditional feminine qualities at the same time that it has retained much of the feminine social script. The contemporary ideal woman is strong, assertive, active, and independent rather than passive, delicate, and dependent. The assumption is that she is out in the public world rather than confined to the home. She has not completely shed her domestic, nurturing, and caring dimension, however, or her intuitive, emotional, and sensitive aspects. These attributes are important in her success as a loving and capable partner to a man, as indeed are her physical attributes concerning looks and body size.

LEARNING ACTIVITY   **Walk Like a Man, Sit Like a Lady**

One of the ways we perform gender is by the way we use our bodies. Very early, children learn to act their gender in the ways they sit, walk, and talk.

Try this observation research:

- Observe a group of schoolchildren playing. Make notes about what you observe concerning how girls and boys act, particularly how they use their bodies in their play and communication.
- Find a place where you can watch people sitting or walking. A public park or mall may offer an excellent vantage point. Record your observations about the ways women and men walk and sit.

Also try this experiment: Ask a friend of the opposite sex to participate in an experiment with you. Take turns teaching each other to sit and to walk like the other sex. After practicing your newfound gender behaviors, write your reflections about the experience.

To be a modern woman today (we might even say a "liberated woman") is to be able to do *everything*: the superwoman. It is important to ask who is benefiting from this new social script. Women work in the public world (often in jobs that pay less, thus helping employers and the economic system) and yet still are expected to do the domestic and emotional work of home and family as well as stay fit and "beautiful." In many ways, contemporary femininity tends to serve both the capitalist economic system and individual men better than the traditional, dependent, domestic model.

GENDER RANKING

Gender encompasses not only the socially constructed differences prescribed for different kinds of human beings but also the values associated with these differences. Recall the sissy/tomboy exercise at the beginning of this chapter. Those traits assigned as feminine are less valued than those considered masculine, illustrating why men tend to have more problems emulating femininity and trans people moving into femininity are viewed with somewhat more hostility than those transitioning toward masculine identities. It is okay to emulate the masculine and act like a boy, but it is not okay to emulate the feminine. This is *gender ranking* (the valuing of one gender over another), which sets the stage for sexism. Judith Lorber writes, "When genders are ranked, the devalued genders have less power, prestige, and economic rewards than the valued genders." Just as White is valued above Brown or Black, and young (though not too young) above old, and heterosexual above homosexual, masculinity tends to be ranked higher than femininity. To be male is to have privileges vis-à-vis gender systems; to be female means to be a member of a target group. As already discussed, the social system here that discriminates and privileges on the basis of gender is sexism. It works by viewing the differences between women and men as important for determining access to social, economic, and political resources. As defined in Chapter 2, *sexism* is the system that discriminates and privileges on the basis of gender and that results in gender stratification. Given the ranking of gender in our society, sexism works to privilege men and limit women. In other words, men receive entitlements and privilege in a society that ranks masculinity over femininity.

Although all women are limited by sexism as a system of power that privileges men over women, the social category "woman," as you recall from Chapter 2, is hardly homogeneous. Location in different systems of inequality and privilege shapes women's lives in different ways; they are not affected by gender in the same ways. Other systems based on class, race, sexual identity, and so forth interact with gender to produce different experiences for individual women. In other words, *the effects of gender and understandings of both femininity and masculinity are mediated by other systems of power*. This is another way that gender ranking occurs: the ranking of identities within the same gender. Forms of gender-based oppression and exploitation depend in part on other social characteristics in people's lives, and gender practices often enforce other types of inequalities. This reflects the confluence that occurs as gender categories are informed/constructed through social relations of power associated with other identities and accompanying systems of inequality and privilege (like racial identities and racism, sexual identities and heterosexism, and so forth). These identities cannot be separated, and certainly they are lived and performed through a tangle of multiple (and often shifting) identities. In this way, then, ranking occurs both *across* gender categories (masculinity is valued over femininity) and *within* gender categories (for example, as economically privileged women are represented differently than poor women and receive economic and social entitlements, or as abled women live different lives than disabled women, and so forth).

Other examples of this latter type of gender ranking include the ways African American women are often characterized as promiscuous or matriarchal and African American men are described as hyperathletic and sexually potent. Jewish women are painted as materialistic and overbearing, whereas Jewish men are supposedly very ambitious, thrifty, good at business, yet still tied to their mothers' apron strings. Latinas and Chicanas are stereotyped as sexy and fun loving, and, likewise, Latinos and Chicanos are seen as oversexed, romantic, and passionate. Native American women are portrayed as silent and overworked or exotic and romantic, whereas Native American men are stereotyped as aloof mystics, close to nature, or else as savages and drunks. Asian Americans generally are often portrayed as smart and good at science and math while Asian American women have also been typed as exotic, passive, and delicate. All these problematic constructions are created against the norm of Whiteness and work to maintain the privileges of the mythical norm. This concept is illustrated in Nellie Wong's poem. She longed to be White, something she saw as synonymous with being a desirable woman. Although there are ethnic and regional stereotypes for White women (like the dizzy blonde, Southern belle, sexually liberated Scandinavian, or hot-tempered Irish), for the most part White women tend not to have discrete stereotypes associated with their race. This reflects the fact that White people are encouraged not to see White as a racial category although it is just as racialized as any other racial group. The fact that being White

IDEAS FOR ACTIVISM

- Be a gender traitor for a day. Act/dress in ways that are not generally considered to be appropriate for your gender.
- Develop and perform on campus a street theater piece about gender performance.
- Plan, create, publish, and distribute a zine challenging traditional gender roles.
- Examine how masculinity is valued above femininity on your campus. Write a letter about your findings to your campus newspaper.

can be claimed the mythical norm strips Whiteness from the historical and political roots of its construction as a racial category. As discussed in Chapter 2, this ability for nontarget groups to remain relatively invisible is a key to maintaining their dominance in society.

In this way, diverse gendered experiences implies that the expression of femininity, or the parameters of femininity expected and allowed, is related to the confluence of gender with other systems. Historically, certain women (the poor and women of color) were regarded as carrying out appropriate womanhood when they fulfilled the domestic labor needs of strangers. Upper-class femininity meant that there were certain jobs such women could not perform. This demonstrates the interaction of gender with class and race systems. Old women endure a certain brand of femininity that tends to be devoid of the playmate role and is heavy on the mother aspect. Sexually active old women are violating the norms of femininity set up for them: This shows the influence of ageism in terms of shaping gender norms. Other stereotypes that reveal the interaction of gender with societal systems of privilege and inequality include disabled women's supposedly relatively low sexual appetite or lesbians' lack of femininity (they are presumed to want to be like men at the same time they are said to hate them). In this way the expression of femininity is dependent on other intersecting systems of inequality and privilege and the beliefs, stereotypes, and practices associated with these systems.

Two Sexes Are Not Enough

Anne Fausto-Sterling (2000)

In 1843 Levi Suydam, a 23-year-old resident of Salisbury, Connecticut, asked the town's board of selectmen to allow him to vote as a Whig in a hotly contested local election. The request raised a flurry of objections from the opposition party, for a reason that must be rare in the annals of American democracy: It was said that Suydam was "more female than male," and thus (since only men had the right to vote) should not be allowed to cast a ballot. The selectmen brought in a physician, one Dr. William Barry, to examine Suydam and settle the matter. Presumably, upon encountering a phallus and testicles, the good doctor declared the prospective voter male. With Suydam safely in their column, the Whigs won the election by a majority of one.

A few days later, however, Barry discovered that Suydam menstruated regularly and had a vaginal opening. Suydam had the narrow shoulders and broad hips characteristic of a female build, but occasionally "he" felt physical attractions to the "opposite" sex (by which "he" meant women). Furthermore, "his feminine propensities, such as fondness for gay colors, for pieces of calico, comparing and placing them together, and an aversion for bodily labor and an inability to perform the same, were remarked by many." (Note that this 19th-century doctor did not distinguish between "sex" and "gender." Thus he considered a fondness for piecing together swatches of calico just as telling as anatomy and physiology.) No one has yet discovered whether Suydam lost the right to vote. Whatever the outcome, the story conveys both the political weight our culture places on ascertaining a person's correct "sex" and the deep confusion that arises when it can't be easily determined.

European and American culture is deeply devoted to the idea that there are only two sexes. Even our language refuses other possibilities, thus to write about Levi Suydam I have had to invent conventions—s/he and h/er to denote individuals who are clearly neither/both male and female or who are, perhaps, both at once. Nor is the linguistic convenience an idle fancy. Whether one falls into the category of man or woman matters in concrete ways. For Suydam—and still today for women in some parts of the world—it meant the right to vote. It might mean being subject to the military draft and to various laws concerning the family and marriage. In many parts of the United States, for example, two individuals legally registered as men cannot have sexual relations without breaking antisodomy laws.

But if the state and legal system has an interest in maintaining only two sexes, our collective biological bodies do not. While male and female stand on the extreme ends of a biological continuum, there are many other bodies, bodies such as Suydam's, that evidently mix together anatomical components conventionally attributed to both males and females. The implications of my argument for a sexual continuum are profound. If nature really offers us more than two sexes, then it follows that our current notions of masculinity and femininity are cultural conceits. Reconceptualizing the category of "sex" challenges cherished aspects of European and American social organization.

Indeed, we have begun to insist on the male–female dichotomy at increasingly early stages, making the two-sex system more deeply a part of how we imagine human life and giving it the appearance of being both inborn and natural. Nowadays, months before the child leaves the comfort of the womb, amniocentesis and ultrasound identify a fetus's sex. Parents can decorate the baby's room in gender-appropriate style, sports wallpaper—in blue—for the little boy, flowered designs—in pink—for the little girl. Researchers have nearly completed development of technology that can choose the sex of a child at the moment of fertilization. Moreover, modern surgical techniques help maintain the two-sex system. Today children who are born "either/or—neither/both"— a fairly common phenomenon—usually disappear from view because doctors "correct" them right away with surgery. In the past, however, intersexuals (or hermaphrodites, as they were called until recently) were culturally acknowledged.

HERMAPHRODITIC HERESIES

In 1993 I published a modest proposal suggesting that we replace our two-sex system with a five-sex one. In addition to males and females, I argued, we should also accept the categories herms (named after "true" hermaphrodities), merms (named after male "pseudohermaphrodites"), and ferms (named after female "pseudohermaph-rodites"). [*Editor's note:* A "true" hermaphrodite bears an ovary and a testis, or a combined gonad called an ovo-testis. A "pseudohermaphrodite" has either an ovary or a testis, along with genitals from the "opposite" sex.] I'd intended to be pro-vocative, but I had also been writing tongue in cheek and so was surprised by the extent of the controversy the article unleashed. Right-wing Christians somehow connected my idea of five sexes to the United Nations–sponsored Fourth World Conference on Women, to be held in Beijing two years later, apparently seeing some sort of global conspiracy at work. "It is maddening," says the text of a *New York Times* advertisement paid for by the Catholic League for Religious and Civil Rights, "to listen to discussions of 'five genders' when every sane person knows there are but two sexes, both of which are rooted in nature."

[Sexologist] John Money was also horrified by my article, although for different reasons. In a new edition of his guide for those who counsel intersexual children and their families, he wrote:

"In the 1970s nurturists . . . became . . . 'social constructionists.' They align themselves against biology and medicine. . . . They consider all sex differences as artifacts of social construction. In cases of birth defects of the sex organs, they attack all medical and surgical interventions as unjusti-fied meddling designed to force babies into fixed social molds of male and female. . . . One writer has gone even to the extreme of proposing that there are five sexes . . . (Fausto-Sterling)."

Meanwhile, those battling against the con-straints of our sex/gender system were delighted by the article. The science fiction writer Melissa Scott wrote a novel entitled *Shadow Man,* which includes nine types of sexual preference and sev-eral genders, including fems (people with testes, XY chromosomes, and some aspects of female genitalia), herms (people with ovaries and testes), and mems (people with XX chromosomes and some aspects of male genitalia). Others used the idea of five sexes as a starting point for their own multi-gendered theories.

Clearly I had struck a nerve. The fact that so many people could get riled up by my proposal to revamp our sex/gender system suggested that change (and resistance to it) might be in the off-ing. Indeed, a lot *has* changed since 1993, and I like to think that my article was one important stimulus. Intersexuals have materialized before our very eyes, like beings beamed up onto the Starship Enterprise. They have become political organizers lobbying physicians and politicians to change treatment practices. More generally, the debate over our cultural conceptions of gender has escalated, and the boundaries separating masculine and feminine seem harder than ever to define. Some find the changes under way deeply disturbing; others find them liberating.

I, of course, am committed to challenging ideas about the male/female divide. In chorus with a growing organization of adult intersexuals, a small group of scholars, and a small but grow-ing cadre of medical practitioners, I argue that medical management of intersexual births needs to change. *First,* let there be no unnecessary infant surgery (by *necessary* I mean to save the infant's life or significantly improve h/er physical well-being). *Second,* let physicians assign a provisional sex (male or female) to the infant (based on existing knowledge of the probability of a particular gender identity formation—penis size be damned!). *Third,* let the medical care team provide full information and long-term counseling to the parents and to the child. However well-intentioned, the methods for managing intersexuality, so entrenched since the 1950s, have done serious harm.

R E A D I N G   **20**

The Social Construction of Gender

Judith Lorber (1994)

Talking about gender for most people is the equivalent of fish talking about water. Gender is so much the routine ground of everyday activities that questioning its taken-for-granted assumptions and presuppositions is like thinking about whether the sun will come up.[1] Gender is so pervasive that in our society we assume it is bred into our genes. Most people find it hard to believe that gender is constantly created and re-created out of human interaction, out of social life, and is the texture and order of that social life. Yet gender, like culture, is a human production that depends on everyone constantly "doing gender" (West and Zimmerman 1987).

And everyone "does gender" without thinking about it. Today, on the subway, I saw a well-dressed man with a year-old child in a stroller. Yesterday, on a bus, I saw a man with a tiny baby in a carrier on his chest. Seeing men taking care of small children in public is increasingly common—at least in New York City. But both men were quite obviously stared at—and smiled at, approvingly. Everyone was doing gender—the men who were changing the role of fathers and the other passengers, who were applauding them silently. But there was more gendering going on that probably fewer people noticed. The baby was wearing a white crocheted cap and white clothes. You couldn't tell if it was a boy or a girl. The child in the stroller was wearing a dark blue T-shirt and dark print pants. As they started to leave the train, the father put a Yankee baseball cap on the child's head. Ah, a boy, I thought. Then I noticed the gleam of tiny earrings in the child's ears, and as they got off, I saw the little flowered sneakers and lace-trimmed socks. Not a boy after all. Gender done.

. . .

For the individual, gender construction starts with assignment to a sex category on the basis of what the genitalia look like at birth.[2] Then babies are dressed or adorned in a way that displays the category because parents don't want to be constantly asked whether their baby is a girl or a boy. A sex category becomes a gender status through naming, dress, and the use of other gender markers. Once a child's gender is evident, others treat those in one gender differently from those in the other, and the children respond to the different treatment by feeling different and behaving differently. As soon as they can talk, they start to refer to themselves as members of their gender. Sex doesn't come into play again until puberty, but by that time, sexual feelings and desires and practices have been shaped by gendered norms and expectations. Adolescent boys and girls approach and avoid each other in an elaborately scripted and gendered mating dance. Parenting is gendered, with different expectations for mothers and fathers, and people of different genders work at different kinds of jobs. The work adults do as mothers and fathers and as low-level workers and high-level bosses, shapes women's and men's life experiences, and these experiences produce different feelings, consciousness, relationships, skills—ways of being that we call feminine or masculine.[3] All of these processes constitute the social construction of gender.

. . .

To explain why gendering is done from birth, constantly and by everyone, we have to look not only at the way individuals experience gender but at gender as a social institution. As a social institution, gender is one of the major ways that human beings organize their lives. Human society depends on a predictable division of labor, a designated allocation of scarce goods, assigned responsibility for children and others who cannot care for themselves, common values and their systematic transmission to new members, legitimate leadership, music, art, stories, games, and other symbolic productions. One way of choosing people for the different tasks of society is on the basis of their talents, motivations, and competence—their demonstrated achievements. The other way is on the basis of gender, race, ethnicity—ascribed membership in a category of people. Although societies vary in the extent to which they use one or the other of these ways of allocating people to work and to carry out other responsibilities, every society uses gender and age grades. Every society classifies people as "girl and boy children," "girls and boys ready to be married," and "fully adult women and men," constructs similarities among them and differences between them, and assigns them to different roles and responsibilities. Personality characteristics, feelings, motivations, and ambitions flow from these different life experiences so that the members of these different groups become different kinds of people. The process of gendering and its outcome are legitimated by religion, law, science, and the society's entire set of values.

GENDER AS PROCESS, STRATIFICATION, AND STRUCTURE

As a social institution, gender is a process of creating distinguishable social statuses for the assignment of rights and responsibilities. As part of a stratification system that ranks these statuses unequally, gender is a major building block in the social structures built on these unequal statuses.

As a *process,* gender creates the social differences that define "woman" and "man." In social interaction throughout their lives, individuals learn what is expected, see what is expected, act and react in expected ways, and thus simultaneously construct and maintain the gender order. . . .

Gendered patterns of interaction acquire additional layers of gendered sexuality, parenting, and work behaviors in childhood, adolescence, and adulthood. Gendered norms and expectations are enforced through informal sanctions of gender-inappropriate behavior by peers and by formal punishment or threat of punishment by those in authority should behavior deviate too far from socially imposed standards for women and men.

. . .

As part of a *stratification* system, gender ranks men above women of the same race and class. Women and men could be different but equal. In practice, the process of creating difference depends to a great extent on differential evaluation. . . . The dominant categories are the hegemonic ideals, taken so for granted as the way things should be that white is not ordinarily thought of as a race, middle class as a class, or men as a gender. The characteristics of these categories define the Other as that which lacks the valuable qualities the dominants exhibit.

In a gender-stratified society, what men do is usually valued more highly than what women do because men do it, even when their activities are very similar or the same. In different regions of southern India, for example, harvesting rice is men's work, shared work, or women's work: "Wherever a task is done by women it is considered easy, and where it is done by [men] it is considered difficult" (Mencher 1988, 104). A gathering and hunting society's survival usually depends on the nuts, grubs, and small animals brought in by the women's foraging trips, but when the men's hunt is successful, it is the occasion for a celebration. Conversely, because they are the superior group, white men do not have to do the "dirty work," such as housework; the most inferior group does it, usually poor women of color (Palmer 1989).

. . .

When gender is a major component of structured inequality, the devalued genders have less power, prestige, and economic rewards than the valued genders. In countries that discourage gender discrimination, many major roles are still gendered; women still do most of the domestic labor and child rearing, even while doing full-time paid work; women and men are segregated on the job and each does work considered "appropriate"; women's work is usually paid less than men's work. Men dominate the positions of authority and leadership in government, the military, and the law; cultural productions, religions, and sports reflect men's interests.

In societies that create the greatest gender difference, such as Saudi Arabia, women are kept out of sight behind walls or veils, have no civil rights, and often create a cultural and emotional world of their own (Bernard 1981). But even in societies with less rigid gender boundaries, women and men spend much of their time with people of their own gender because of the way work and family are organized. This spatial separation of women and men reinforces gendered differences, identity, and ways of thinking and behaving (Coser 1986).

Gender inequality—the devaluation of "women" and the social domination of "men"—has social functions and social history. It is not the result of sex, procreation, physiology, anatomy, hormones, or genetic predispositions. It is produced and maintained by identifiable social processes and built into the general social structure and individual identities deliberately and purposefully. The social order as we know it in Western societies is organized around racial, ethnic, class, and gender inequality. I contend, therefore, that the continuing purpose of gender as a modern social institution is to construct women as a group to be the subordinates of men as a group.

THE PARADOX OF HUMAN NATURE

To say that sex, sexuality, and gender are all socially constructed is not to minimize their social power. These categorical imperatives govern our lives in the most profound and pervasive ways, through the social experiences and social practices of what Dorothy Smith calls the "everday/evernight world" (1990, 31–57). The paradox of human nature is that it is *always* a manifestation of cultural meanings, social relationships, and power politics; "not biology, but culture, becomes destiny" (J. Butler 1990, 8). Gendered people emerge not from physiology or sexual orientations but from the exigencies of the social order, mostly, from the need for a reliable division of the work of food production and the social (not physical) reproduction of new members. The moral imperatives of religion and cultural representations guard the boundary lines among genders and ensure that what is demanded, what is permitted, and what is tabooed for the people in each gender is well known and followed by most (C. Davies 1982). Political power, control of scarce resources, and, if necessary, violence uphold the gendered social order in the face of resistance and rebellion. Most people, however, voluntarily go along with their society's prescriptions for those of their gender status, because the norms and expectations get built into their sense of worth and identity as [the way we] think, the way we see and hear and speak, the way we fantasy, and the way we feel.

There is no core or bedrock in human nature below these endlessly looping processes of the social production of sex and gender, self and other, identity and psyche, each of which is a "complex cultural construction" (J. Butler 1990, 36). *For humans, the social is the natural. . . .*

NOTES

1. Gender is, in Erving Goffman's words, an aspect of *Felicity's Condition*: "any arrangement which leads us to judge an individual's . . . acts not to be a manifestation of strangeness. Behind Felicity's Condition is our sense of what it is to be sane" (1983:27). Also see Bem 1993; Frye 1983, 17–40; Goffman 1977.
2. In cases of ambiguity in countries with modern medicine, surgery is usually performed to make the genitalia more clearly male or female.
3. See J. Butler 1990 for an analysis of how doing gender is gender identity.

REFERENCES

Bem, Sandara Lipsitz. 1993. *The Lenses of Gender: Transforming the Debate on Sexual Inequality.* New Haven: Yale University Press.

Bernard, Jessie. 1981. *The Female World.* New York: Free Press.

Butler, Judith. 1990. *Gender Trouble: Feminism and the Subversion of Identity.* New York and London: Routledge.

Coser, Rose Laub. 1986. "Cognitive structure and the use of social space." *Sociological Forum* 1:1–26.

Davies, Christie. 1982. "Sexual taboos and social boundaries." *American Journal of Sociology* 87:1032–63.

Dwyer, Daisy, and Judith Bruce (eds.). 1988. *A Home Divided: Women and Income in the Third World.* Palo Alto, Calif.: Stanford University Press.

Frye, Marilyn. 1983. *The Politics of Reality: Essays in Feminist Theory.* Trumansburg, N.Y.: Crossing Press.

Goffman, Erving, 1977. "The arrangement between the sexes." *Theory and Society* 4:301–33.

Mencher, Joan. 1988. "Women's work and poverty: Women's contribution to household maintenance in South India." In Dwyer and Bruce 1988.

Palmer, Phyllis. 1989. *Domesticity and Dirt: House-wives and Domestic Servants in the United States, 1920–1945.* Philadelphia: Temple University Press.

Smith, Dorothy. 1990. *The Conceptual Practices of Power: A Feminist Sociology of Knowledge.* Toronto: University of Toronto Press.

West, Candace, and Don Zimmerman. 1987. "Doing gender." *Gender & Society* 1:125–51.

R E A D I N G   **21**

Short Skirts and Breast Juts
Cheerleading, Eroticism and Schools

Pamela J. Bettis and Natalie Guice Adams (2006)

INTRODUCTION

During fall 2003 in Elma, Washington, a community controversy arose over cheerleading attire, specifically the length of the high school cheerleader and drill teams' skirts (*Spokesman Review*, 2003). The Elma school district's administration banned the wearing of these skirts to school since the length did not adhere to school dress regulations for the rest of the student body; in the past this regulation had been waived for cheerleaders and drill team members. School Superintendent Tami Hickle said 'What the high school decided is that the dress code would apply to everyone equally.' However, the new regulations did allow members of the all female cheerleading and drill squad to wear these skirts to cheer and perform during sports events.

A mother of one of the team members said that parents were told by administrators that the short skirts were a distraction in the classroom, particularly for the boys. She responded that 'Boys will always be horn toads no matter what girls wear.' Furthermore, she commented that the school district's new rule implied that 'Cheerleaders are not nice girls.' One young woman was so incensed with the new regulations that she chose to wear 'very ugly' warm-up pants and her team sweater to school on game day as a form of protest against the administrative edict.

This recent school controversy speaks to the erotic tensions embedded in cheerleading, an activity in which 3.8 million people participate in the United States and an ever-increasing popular activity in over 50 countries, including England, Scotland and Wales (Elias, 2002; Roenigk, 2002).

References to 'horn toads' and 'nice girls' illustrate the narrow pathway of appropriate femininity that adolescent girls must tread, particularly in very public activities such as cheerleading. In this article, we explore the erotic tensions in contemporary school cheerleading through an analysis of how US adolescent girls, cheerleading coaches and those associated with the business facets of cheerleading construct the meaning of cheerleading. Insights gained from a study of cheerleading's erotic tensions in its nation of origin have significance for all countries in which cheerleading has been introduced because cheerleading, whether it be in the United States, England, Sweden or Costa Rica, offers girls one of the only adult sanctioned and mainstream vehicles for them to try out a sexualized identity in a public space.

SEXUALITY AND CHEERLEADING: A LITERATURE REVIEW

A Brief History

Cheerleading became institutionalized on college campuses in the United States in the late nineteenth and early twentieth centuries. At this time, cheerleaders were all male, and the activity itself was seen as a masculine activity that was highly respected (Adams & Bettis, 2003). However, as early as the 1920s, one can find cheerleaders, albeit male cheerleaders, being described in very sensual terms.

> A contemporary of Pericles, strolling into one of our football stadiums would . . . delight in those lithe, white-sweatered and flannel-trousered youths in front of the bleachers, their mingled force and grace, their gestures at the same time hieratic and apparently jointless, that accompanied the spelling out of the locomotive cheer. And even an ancient Greek pulse would halt for a moment at that final upward leap of the young body, like a diver into the azure, as the stands thundered out the climatic 'Stanford!' (Cited in Hanson, 1995, p. 2)

Cheerleading remained an activity primarily for males until the 1940s. Females began to dominate cheerleading squads when male cheerleaders left campuses to fight during World War II, and by the 1950s the activity, particularly at the high school level, had become completely feminized. With the feminization of cheerleading came a new kind of sexualization of the activity as seen in Arturo Gonzales's (1956) description of female cheerleaders:

> No report on cheerleaders over the past three decades could be complete, of course, without reference to the coeds. Pretty young things in vestigial skirts, amply-filled sweaters and wearing baby shakos, they've burbled and twirled to the intense enjoyment of those fans easily distracted from the male carnage at the midfield by a few well-placed curves. (p. 104)

That focus on female sexuality and the erotic elements of cheerleading was amplified during the 1970s when professional cheerleading squads associated with professional athletic teams, particularly football, emerged. The Dallas Cowboys Cheerleaders, with their patented hot pants and low-cut cowgirl vests and shirts, was the first such squad to make explicit the sexual element of cheerleading. Performing routines more akin to Las Vegas showgirls, the Dallas Cowboys Cheerleaders, as described by three of its former cheerleaders, epitomized the ultimate male fantasy:

> How do you tap into the paradox of the sexy, wholesome girl, the girl you'd like to take home to mother but make love to on the way over there? Well, take Miss America and dress her in hot pants and a halter top. Then put her out on a football field grinding out a lot of provocative dances, but the whole time keep telling the fans that these are good girls, wholesome girls. (Scholz *et al.*, 1991, p. 143)

Because cheerleading represents simultaneously the 'sexy, wholesome girl,' as the Scholz sisters observe, the cheerleader, according to Kurman (1986), has evolved into 'a disturbing erotic icon . . . She incarnates, in a word, a basic male-voyeuristic fantasy' (p. 58).

Yet, most secondary, collegiate and competitive squads bear little resemblance to the Dallas Cowboys Cheerleaders, and most work hard to disassociate themselves from this image. However, as we argue in this article, the erotic tensions already described creep into the language, practices and policies of cheerleading squads at all levels, from preadolescent All-Star squads to collegiate competitive squads. What then does this sexualization reveal about growing up feminine in today's society? Davis (1990) argued that today the cheerleader symbolizes 'dominant ideology about how females should look and act in our society' (p. 155). Embedded in this ideology are the contradictory positions in which girls and women are located. They, meaning both females and cheerleaders, are to embody simultaneously the virtuous, 'good girls' and the sexually provocative 'bad girls.' Navigating these tensions becomes the work, albeit unacknowledged, of all cheerleaders.

Sexuality and Adolescent Girls at the Turn of this Century

Martin (1996) points out that the plethora of research published about adolescent girls in the late 1980s and 1990s failed to adequately address female sexuality and its effects on girls' self-esteem. In the twenty-first century, we have seen a marked change in the silencing of female sexuality with the publication of several popular press books, including *The Secret Lives of Girls* (Lamb, 2001); *Fast Girls* (White, 2002); *Flirting with Danger* (Phillips, 2000) and *Dilemmas of Desire* (Tolman, 2002). What all of these books reveal is that adolescent females think about and engage in sexual activity of a wider variety than dominant society is ready to admit. The strength of these books is that they open the discussion of adolescent and prepubescent female sexuality that has often been overlooked. However, the findings of these authors focus on what girls think about and do in private.

Several researchers (Fine, 1988; Walkerdine, 1990) have pointed out that the erotic is rarely allowed to enter schools, at least in the formal curriculum and practices. Furthermore, schools provide little space for girls to claim any sense of sexual agency, the formal sexual education curriculum being but one of many places in which female sexual desire and agency are silenced (Fine, 1988; Tolman, 2002). Yet, the erotic does sneak into schools—in private bathroom and cafeteria discussions, in the visible embraces among students in the hall and in the public display of dress. The erotic also enters in the form of extracurricular activities. In *Prom Night,* Best (2000) notes that the prom is one space in which girls are allowed to 'negotiate the sexual terrain of school' (p. 60). We assert in this article that cheerleading is another.

Cheerleaders as Sexy Tease and Good Girl

Cheerleading is an activity that is found in almost every middle-level, secondary-level and university level school in the United States. In the United States, cheerleading is often perceived as the highest status activity for girls in middle and high school, and girls who cheer occupy positions of power, prestige and privilege (Eder, 1985, 1995; Kurman, 1986; Eder & Parker, 1987; Lesko, 1988; Eckert, 1989; Adler *et al.,* 1992; Adler & Adler, 1995; Merten, 1996, 1997; Kinney, 1999; Bettis & Adams, 2003). Furthermore, it is an activity that is typically supported by the school administration and other adults in the community since it represents a mainstream understanding of the role of females; in this perspective, cheerleading equates with 'youthful prestige, wholesome attractiveness, peer leadership and popularity' (Hanson, 1995, p. 2). As Eckert (1989) notes, extracurricular activities typically become the exclusive domain of those students who are supportive of school and what it represents to adults. For example, 'Burnouts' or those affiliated with drugs and/or those who are hostile to school rarely choose to become cheerleaders nor would they typically be selected to join the squad since a positive attitude towards school is a central facet of the activity.

However, at the same time, in the society at large and in the eyes of many adolescents, cheerleading operates as an activity that symbolizes 'objectified sexuality and promiscuous availability' (Hanson, 1995, p. 2). The short skirts, the sometimes sexually provocative moves of a cheerleading routine, the bright red lipstick and the public gaze of adult men and boys all contribute to a cultural activity that openly celebrates female sexuality. However, female sexuality is typically unacknowledged in schools, and the connection between the erotic and cheerleading is silenced by most adults associated with cheerleading (i.e. coaches, parents, camp instructors). Instead, most of the formal public discussion focuses on whether cheerleading is a sport or activity and its lack of status and financial support by school administrators. This eschewal of the erotic in cheerleading runs counter to representations of cheerleaders in popular culture venues. For example, in the award winning film, *American Beauty* (Universal Studios, 1999), a mid-life crisis for the lead male character, Lester Burnham, manifests itself in his desire for his daughter's best friend, an adolescent cheerleader. Furthermore, professional cheerleading squads who cheer for professional sports teams, such as the Dallas Cowboy Cheerleaders and Laker girls, are viewed as sexual icons in the country at large, and *Debbie Does Dallas* (Pussycat Cinema, 1978), a film that narrates a high school cheerleaders squad's sexual escapades, remains one of the top selling adult movies in the United States and has even been remade into an off-Broadway play (Nutt, 2001; Zinoman, 2002).

Hence, cheerleading operates symbolically at the intersection of the all-American good-girl next door who exemplifies peer leadership and the vamp who teases with her short skirt. How then do adolescent girls make sense of the contradictory status of cheerleading, one that embodies both wholesome and erotic tensions?

SETTING, METHODS AND PARTICIPANTS OF THE STUDY

This qualitative case study is part of a larger study that we began in a middle school located in a Midwestern state in the United States. The focus of this school ethnography was how adolescent girls understood leadership and the ways in which schools foster leadership in young girls. We became acquainted with this particular school and its principal during our work as teacher educators in mentoring first-year teachers. The principal's interest and support of our study along with the racial/ethnic and social class diversity of the student population encouraged us to conduct our study at this particular school.

The school was located in Witchita, a town of 26,000 whose origins lay in an oil boom in the 1930s and a town that was known throughout the state as a highly stratified community. Approximately 5700 students were enrolled in the school district and approximately 430 attended the middle school, which consisted of two sixth-grade classes and all of the district's seventh graders. The school district's demographics were 75% White, 14% American Indian, 5% African American, 5% Latino and 1% Asian or Pacific Islander.

Each of us observed a full day in the school on a weekly basis for the entire school year, and both attended after school events such as talent night and cheerleading tryouts. After observing in a variety of classrooms and informal school settings such as lunch at the beginning of the year, we solicited girls who represented a variety of peer groups, social classes, racial and ethnic backgrounds, and academic interests to participate in our interviews. Of the approximately 75 girls we solicited, 61 agreed to be interviewed. During the first round of formal interviews with these 61 girls and throughout our accumulating field notes, cheerleaders were mentioned frequently as leaders, and we began to explore in these initial interviews why cheerleaders were considered both leaders and the most popular girls in the school. We asked the girls to describe the various peer groups in school, where cheerleaders fit in this scheme, and why the participants might want to become a cheerleader or not. Then, beginning in the second semester, we observed on a weekly basis two cheer preparation classes that the school had instituted to prepare girls for cheerleading tryouts. Initial cheerleading interviews were conducted with 22 of the girls before the tryouts, and we explored why girls wanted to become cheerleaders, what the judges were looking for in the selection of the cheerleading squad and who they thought might make the squad. Another round of interviews was conducted with 16 of the girls following the tryouts where we asked about the tryout process itself, selection of the squad and, if they did not try out, why that was the case. Of these 16 girls who were enrolled in the cheerleading preparation class, eight did not try out—and the eight who did try out made the squad. The racial composition of the girls interviewed specifically about cheerleading consisted of 14 Whites, five Native Americans and three African Americans. Data for this case study were also derived from interviews of girls who did not participate in the cheerleading tryouts plus the cheer preparation teacher, Louise, who was responsible for the cheerleading classes and tryouts.

Separate from the ethnography, further data were gathered from observations of two 2002 Universal Cheerleaders Association (UCA) Cheer Camps for middle and secondary cheerleaders over a combined five-day period and from informal interviews conducted with camp coaches. One of these camps was located in Alabama and the other in Idaho. These observations consisted of watching the girls practice new cheers that were being taught during the camp, listening to their informal talk during breaks, and noting the talk and actions of the instructors as they presented the material. We also conducted formal interviews with 10 officials of Varsity Spirit Corporation, the world's largest distributor of cheerleading uniforms and paraphernalia and organizer of UCA Cheer Camps. We asked questions about the change in uniform design over the past 25 years as well as the criteria for judging the UCA competitions. Such questions engendered discussions ranging from the introduction of spandex into cheerleading uniforms to the deduction of points for 'slashy' or sexually suggestive movements during competitive cheerleading contests that UCA sponsors. Another major source of data for this study was derived from popular culture literature, videos, television and radio programs, and media discussions of cheerleading.

'CUTE WOMEN IN SHORT SKIRTS': RESULTS AND DISCUSSION

I'm sexy; I'm cute.
I'm popular to boot.
I'm bitchin', great hair,
The boys all love to stare.
I'm wanted; I'm hot.
I'm everything you're not.
I'm pretty; I'm cool.
I dominate this school.

(Opening cheer from the movie Bring It On; *Universal studios, 2000)*

This opening cheer in *Bring it On,* an enormously popular cheerleading movie both in the United States and in Europe, speaks to the sexual tensions embedded in not only contemporary cheerleading but also contemporary girlhood. All adolescent girls must find ways to negotiate the landscape of girlhood where they are expected to be nice, confident girls who are neither sluts nor snobs. However, cheerleaders find that pathway even more treacherous since they occupy a public position that situates them both as a wholesome girl and a sexy tease.

As representatives or ambassadors of their schools, cheerleaders are expected to be role models, and their morals are expected to be beyond reproach. Drinking, smoking, cursing and having sex while in one's uniform are strictly forbidden, but even out of uniform cheerleaders are to be the moral leaders. Most cheerleaders must sign a contract or constitution that prescribes in detail what is acceptable and unacceptable behavior as illustrated by these guidelines:

Cheerleaders should never use cheers that are the least bit suggestive, or have phrases that rhyme with swear words. Cheers of this nature discourage many rooters in the stands from cooperating and encourage others to carry on with crude and inappropriate responses. (*Saturday Review,* 1962)

Corny as it sounds, cheerleaders do represent their school, so we have to act properly wherever we're likely to meet anyone who knows us in that capacity. Our squad works under a system of demerits, which are handed out for reasons, ranging from wearing too much makeup to smoking or drinking in uniform. (Norton, 1977)

Each 8th grade (cheerleading) candidate is to wear a plain white shirt with red shorts and each 9th grade candidate is to wear a plain white shirt with navy shorts. Also, hair should be pulled away from the face. The girls will not be able to wear jewelry of any kind. (1998)

This final guideline was issued for those girls trying out for cheerleading at Wichita Middle School (WMS). The cheerleading coach repeatedly reminded the girls who wanted to be cheerleaders that they were expected to have high morals. They were told that whether they were selected or not, girls were to have 'class—to win with grace and to lose with grace.' In most of our conversations with the girls interested in trying out for cheerleader, they echoed the sentiments of the coach. For example, Sadie answered this way when asked about the meaning of cheerleading:

It means that you're going to have a lot of people looking up to you, and so you're going to have to do, be, have like a big responsibility and you're going to have to like do right things and if you do something bad, like if you make a mistake, you're going to have to have big responsibility and like be responsible basically.

Responsibility, good grades, and being nice to everyone were all mentioned as part of being a cheerleader, and certainly fit its good-girl image. However, the girls were also intrigued by the sexual tensions inherent in cheerleading.

One of the primary reasons girls wanted to be a cheerleader was because they believed that cheerleading was a route to instant popularity, which increased the likelihood of getting a boyfriend, a high-status marker for adolescent girls. Hence, cheerleading operated as a discursive practice that affirmed heterosexualized femininity. Milea, a Native American girl who was selected as cheerleader, explains the perennial appeal of cheerleading at her school and why

she wants to be part of this activity: 'Boys like cheerleaders so that makes you popular. I want more boys to like me.' Shanna, another Native American girl who participated in the cheerleading preparation class but did not try out for the squad, similarly notes, 'Some girls think the boys will like you if you're a cheerleader 'cause boys like the cheeriest people.' Finally, Daneka, a Native American girl who wanted to be a cheerleader but eventually did not try out, explained why so many girls, including herself, want to be a cheerleader: 'Girls want to be cheerleaders because they believe that guys will like them more—they will see them as cute women in short skirts.'

Daneka's use of 'girls' and 'women' in the same sentence reflects a primary attraction of cheerleading for many girls: it allows girls to try on a womanly (i.e. sexualized) identity in a school-sanctioned space. Girls have the opportunity to wear short skirts and often tight fitting vests that highlight their womanly physical attributes. When asked why she wanted to be a cheerleader, Julie, a White girl who eventually made the squad, immediately answered, 'Well, I like wearin' those cute little uniforms . . . Oh, they're really cute. They fit the level . . .' Julie is intrigued by the shortness of the skirt, and she is aware that the length does meet school regulations, in that 'they fit the level.'

Furthermore, since many of the contemporary cheerleading moves are sexually suggestive, girls have the opportunity to move their bodies in ways that are not typically permitted on school campuses. Trying out for cheerleader allowed the girls numerous opportunities to use their bodies in sexually provocative ways and to draw attention to their physically maturing bodies. While learning a dance during their cheerleading preparation class, the girls practiced thrusting their hips from side to side while jutting their breasts prominently outward in moves reminiscent of Brittany Spears' music videos. At first, their faces were intense as they assumed the look of a sexually mature woman. However, within seconds, many of them, suddenly feeling self-conscious with their new persona, erupted into girlish giggles, thus breaking the spell of sexuality and womanhood that appeared to envelop them. This was obviously a space for girlhood to meet womanhood with no boys around, but it was also practice for the time in which they would be expected to be the object of the male gaze. Once a girl is selected cheerleader, she is given ample opportunities at pep rallies and athletic events to perform (literally) her femininity (Walkerdine, 1993) in front of her peers, her adult teachers and administrators, and the larger community. Thus, cheerleading is a vehicle through which girls can try on various sexual facets of what it means to be a woman in contemporary US society and do so with a large audience and without the fear of being labeled a slut or a 'skank,' a derogatory term used at this school to designate girls who were sexually promiscuous.

For many girls, such as Julie, a White girl who was selected cheerleader, this opportunity to play with a sexualized identity was a primary reason why cheerleading was so appealing. She explains, 'I'm in it for the short skirts, the guys, getting in front of everybody and making a total fool of myself.' Lisa, a White girl who scored the most points during the tryouts, noted rather nonchalantly that the players were much more interested in cheerleaders' bodies rather than their cheers: 'they're not paying any attention to the cheerleaders anyways except looking at their legs or something.' Both girls focus on the fact that cheerleading provides a public space in which to be gazed upon, particularly by males. In fact, for girls at most schools, it is the most visible space for them, and visibility is the cornerstone of popularity. Therefore, cheerleading embodies the two things that many adolescent girls desire: to be visible and to showcase their femininity. Because cheerleading has been one of the only spaces in which females could enjoy high status and visibility, Milea, a Native American girl who made the squad, states 'I've been waitin' for it [cheerleading] my whole life.'

Walkerdine (1993) argues that in most accounts of girls' experiences in schools, the schoolgirl is typified as the girl who follows rules and is deferential, loyal, quiet and works hard. This image of the schoolgirl, Walkderdine asserts, has been constructed as a 'defense against being the object

of male fantasies. The erotic is displaced [in school accounts] as too dangerous. But it re-enters, it enters in the spaces that are outlawed in the primary school: popular culture' (1993, p. 20). However, as seen earlier and contrary to Walkerdine's assertion, cheerleading does allow the erotic to enter into school-sanctioned space for girls to play with or try on the identity of the all-American nice girl next door and the sexually provocative woman simultaneously. Cheerleaders are allowed to wear short skirts and tight fitting vests that often violate school dress codes, as seen in the Elma, Washington case, while performing sexually provocative dance moves such as pelvic thrusts to popular music not allowed elsewhere in school.

Although adults involved in cheerleading tend to downplay the sexualized elements of cheerleading, they are not immune to the erotic tensions of cheerleading. In preparing the girls for the middle school competition, Louise, the cheerleading preparation instructor, on several occasions instructed the girls to play up their sexuality, 'When you make that turn, give the judges a sexy look.' 'Dazzle them. Give them goosebumps.' On the day before tryouts, Louise offered make-up advice that speaks poignantly to the expectation that cheerleaders are to be sexy, but not sexual: 'Put Vaseline on your teeth and put on a little extra makeup, but not too much. Don't come looking like someone who could stand on the street [meaning a prostitute].'

. . .

CHEERLEADING AND ITS IMPLICATIONS FOR EDUCATORS: SOME INITIAL RECOMMENDATIONS

Girl power posters rarely show girls dressing up like the Spice Girls and prancing around with their midriffs showing, preferring instead to show girls doing science behind test tubes or girls on the soccer field celebrating a goal. (Lamb, 2001, p. 40)

Lamb's point is an important one to consider in understanding the perennially popular nature of US cheerleading and its growing numbers in the

United Kingdom. Adults typically construct cheerleaders as girls who are 'good' girls and whose sole rationale for joining the squad has to do with school spirit and motivation. Louise, the WMS cheer coach, emphasized the support that cheerleaders were to provide the athletic teams:

> My school spirit comes from the heart, and these young women need to learn how to be loyal. They need to learn how to take the eyes off themselves. We're there for other people; we're not there for ourselves . . . If it weren't for the athletes in the building, there would be no reason for us; we're to give of ourselves; we are serving our athletes.

Instead, as the girls in this study have attested, their desire to be a part of the activity of cheerleading is as much about 'dressing up like the Spice Girls and prancing around with their midriffs showing' as it was about leading the fans and players to victory. . . .

[Cheerleading] is a ubiquitous institution found in almost every middle and high school across this country, and its status, although in flux in some schools, typically remains high. Second, its history delineates changing gender roles in American society, and, finally, its sexual image is found in popular culture films, videos, television, and in the popular vernacular (Adams & Bettis, 2003). Discussions of why cheerleading is still considered an activity for popular girls or not, how cheerleading has changed over its 135-year history, and how cheerleaders are used symbolically in music videos, films and popular culture, would all provide fertile ground for an exploration of sexuality and cheerleading. . . .

Kim Irwin, originator of the performance art piece 'WANTED: The X Cheerleaders Project', has organized a curriculum for public school girls aged 9–12 and their teachers that uses cheerleading as a vehicle to explore a wide range of topics pertinent to girls' lives. In conjunction with the Institute for Labor and the Community, Kim conducts workshops that discuss gender inequality, racism, body image, stereotypes and sports. The girls engage in research about these topics, share their findings with their peers and then construct cheers that speak to some of the tensions of contemporary girls' lives. They share these cheers in public fora with teachers and parents in attendance. Therefore, they simultaneously receive the public visibility that cheerleaders have and most adolescents covet while critiquing facets of dominant femininity. In fact, Radical Cheerleaders whose squad numbers have grown exponentially across North America and Europe also use the vehicle of cheerleading to protest sexism and promote different dialogues about women's issues, including sexuality.

What might it mean to involve adolescent girls themselves in conversations that interrogate the sexuality of cheerleading? We answer that question with two cheers, composed by early adolescent girls. The first one was constructed by an Idaho girl who playfully challenges stereotypical images of the cheerleader and confidently portrays what she considers important attributes for girls:

> Totally, for sure,
> As if I need a manicure.
> My hair's, a mess,
> But I can ace most any test.
> 98s to 99s,
> My grades are looking really fine.
> I DON'T LIKE BOYS!
> They just make a lot of noise.
> Gooooooo GIRLS!

This second cheer was created by a group of girls from New York who were involved in Kim Irwin's after-school program for children 9–12 years old. Their cheer also demonstrates how girls can become actively involved (if asked) in breaking traditional feminine stereotypes.

> G-I-R-L-S
> Girls, girls, we RULE
> We can play sports, we're tired of your lies
> And we don't have to stay home baking
>   cherry pies.
> We can beat you any day.
>   We're fast; we're strong,
>   And we know how to play.

Both cheers speak to what is on the minds of preadolescent and adolescent girls, trying out what it means to be a female in the twenty-first century. Constructing cheers and exploring the image of cheerleading in the society at large and in the schools that they inhabit, whether it is in physical education classes, in sex education classes or in the regular classroom, offers girls a non-threatening and fun way to talk about sexuality, desire, the female body and what it means to be 'feminine.' ...

REFERENCES

Adams, N. G. & Bettis, P. J. (2003) *Cheerleader! An American icon* (New York, Palgrave/Macmillan).

Adler, P. A. & Adler, P. (1995) Dynamics of inclusion and exclusion in preadolescent cliques, *Social Psychology Quarterly,* 58(3), 145–162.

Adler, P. A., Kless, S. & Adler, P. (1992) Socialization to gender roles: popularity among elementary school boys and girls, *Sociology of Education,* 65, 169–187.

Best, A. (2000) *Prom night* (New York, Routledge).

Bettis, P. J. & Adams, N. G. (2003) The power of the preps and a cheerleading equity policy, *Sociology of Education,* 76, 128–142.

Davis, L. (1990) Male cheerleaders and the naturalization of gender, in: M. Messner & D. Sabo (Eds) *Sports, men, and the gender order* (Champaign, IL, Human Kinetics Books).

Eckert, P. (1989) *Jocks and burnouts* (New York, Teachers College Press).

Eder, D. (1985) The cycle of popularity: interpersonal relations among female adolescents, *Sociology of Education,* 58, 154–165.

Eder, D. (1995) *School talk: gender and adolescent culture* (New Brunswick, NJ, Rutgers University Press).

Eder, D. & Parker, S. (1987) The cultural production and reproduction of gender: the effects of extracurricular activities on peer group culture, *Sociology of Education,* 60, 200–213.

Elias, M. (2002) Cheerleading leaps into dangerous-sport camp. *USA Today,* 22 October.

Fine, M. (1988) Sexuality, schooling, and adolescent females: the missing discourse of desire, *Harvard Educational Review,* 58, 29–53.

Gonzales, A. (1956) The first college cheer, *American Mercury,* 83, 101–104.

Hanson, M. E. (1995) *Go! Fight! Win! Cheerleading in American culture* (Bowling Green, OH, Bowling Green State University Press).

Irvine, J. (2002) *Talk about sex: the battles over sex education in the United States* (Berkeley, CA, University of California Press).

Kinney, D. (1999) From 'headbangers' to 'hippies': delineating adolescent active attempts to form alternative peer culture, *New Directions for Child and Adolescent Development,* 84, 21–35.

Kurman, G. (1986) What does girls' cheerleading communicate?, *Journal of Popular Culture,* 20, 57–64.

Lamb, S. (2001) *The secret lives of girls: what good girls really do—sex play, aggression, and their guilt* (New York, The Free Press).

Lesko, N. (1988) 'We're leading America': the changing organization and form of high school cheerleading, *Theory and Research in Social Education,* 16, 139–161.

Martin, K. (1996) *Puberty, sexuality, and the self: girls and boys at adolescence* (New York, Routledge).

Merten, D. (1996) Burnout as cheerleader: the cultural basis for prestige and privilege in Junior High School, *Anthropology and Education,* 27, 51–70.

Merten, D. (1997) The meaning of meanness: popularity, competition, and conflict among junior high school girls, *Sociology of Education,* 70, 175–191.

Norton, G. (1977) Cheerleading doesn't deserve a bad image, *Seventeen,* 36, 64.

Nutt, S. T. (2001) More cheerleaders! *Adult DVD Empire,* 28 August. Available online at: http://www.pornpopdvd.com/exec/news/article.as?media_id=114 (accessed 9 January 2003).

Phillips, L. (2002) *Flirting with danger: young women's reflections on sexuality and domination* (New York, New York University Press).

Pussycat Cinema (1978) *Debbie does Dallas* (New York, Pussycat Cinema).

Roenigk, A. (2002) It's a cheer world after all, *American Cheerleader,* February. Available online at: wysiwyg://76/http://www.americancheerleader.com/backissues/feb02/cheerworld.html (accessed 14 October 2002).

Saturday Review (1962) On the art of cheerleading, *Saturday Review,* 20 October, p. 73.

Scholz, S., Scholz, S. & Scholz, S. (1991) *Deep in the heart of Texas: reflections of former Dallas Cowboys Cheerleaders* (New York, St Martins Press).

Spokesman Review (2003) Cheerleaders brought up short by dress code, *The Spokesman Review,* 9 September, p. B5.

Tolman, D. (2002) *Dilemmas of desire: teenage girls talk about sexuality* (Cambridge, MA, Harvard University Press).

Universal Studios (1999) *American beauty* (Los Angeles, Universal Studios).

Universal Studios (2000) *Bring it on* (Los Angeles, Universal Studios).

Walkerdine, V. (1990) *Schoolgrl fictions* (London, Verso).

Walkerdine, V. (1993) Girlhood through the looking glass, in: M. De Ras & M. Lunenberg (Eds) *Girls, girlhood, and girls' studies in transition* (Amsterdam, Het Spinhuis).

White, E. (2002) *Fast girls: teenage tribes and the myth of the slut* (New York, Scribner).

Zinoman, J. (2002) Debbie's doing New York, but rate her PG, *The New York Times,* 27 October.

R E A D I N G   **22**

When I Was Growing Up

Nellie Wong (1981)

I know now that once I longed to be white.
How? you ask.
Let me tell you the ways.

when I was growing up, people told me
I was dark and I believed my own darkness
in the mirror, in my soul, my own narrow vision

when I was growing up, my sisters
with fair skin got praised
for their beauty, and in the dark
I fell further, crushed between high walls

when I was growing up, I read magazines
and saw movies, blonde movie stars,
white skin,
sensuous lips and to be elevated, to become
a woman, a desirable woman, I began to wear
imaginary pale skin

when I was growing up, I was proud
of my English, my grammar, my spelling
fitting into the group of small children
smart Chinese children, fitting in,
belonging, getting in line

when I was growing up and went to
high school,
I discovered the rich white girls, a few
yellow girls,

their imported cotton dresses, their
cashmere sweaters,
their curly hair and I thought that I too
should have
what these lucky girls had

when I was growing up, I hungered
for American food, American styles,
coded: white and even to me, a child
born of Chinese parents, being Chinese
was feeling foreign, as limiting,
was unAmerican

when I was growing up and a white man
wanted
to take me out, I thought I was special,
an exotic gardenia, anxious to fit
the stereotype of an oriental chick

when I was growing up, I felt ashamed
of some yellow men, their small bones,
their frail bodies, their spitting
on the streets, their coughing,
their lying in sunless rooms,
shooting themselves in the arms

when I was growing up, people would ask
if I were Filipino, Polynesian, Portuguese.

They named all colors except white, the shell
of my soul, but not my dark, rough skin

> when I was growing up, I felt
> dirty. I thought that god
> made white people clean
> and no matter how much I bathed,
> I could not change, I could not shed
> my skin in the gray water

> when I was growing up, I swore
> I would run away to purple mountains,

houses by the sea with nothing over
my head, with space to breathe,
uncongested with yellow people in an area
called Chinatown, in an area I later
   learned
was a ghetto, one of many hearts
of Asian America

I know now that once I longed to be white.
How many more ways? you ask.
Haven't I told you enough?

R E A D I N G **23**

Virtual Gender

Judy Wajcman (2004)

The idea that the Internet can transform conventional gender roles, altering the relationship between the body and the self via a machine, is a popular theme in recent postmodern feminism. The message is that young women in particular are colonizing cyberspace, where gender inequality, like gravity, is suspended. In cyberspace, all physical, bodily cues are removed from communication. As a result, our interactions are fundamentally different, because they are not subject to judgments based on sex, age, race, voice, accent or appearance, but are based only on textual exchanges. In *Life on the Screen,* Sherry Turkle enthuses about the potential for people "to express multiple and often unexplored aspects of the self, to play with their identity and to try out new ones . . . the obese can be slender, the beautiful plain, the 'nerdy' sophisticated."[1] It is the increasingly interactive and creative nature of computing technology that now enables millions of people to live a significant segment of their lives in virtual reality. Moreover, it is in this computer-mediated world that people experience a new sense of self, which is decentred, multiple and fluid. . . .

Interestingly, the gender of Internet users features mainly in Turkle's chapter about virtual sex. Cyberspace provides a risk-free environment where people can engage in the intimacy they both desire and fear. Turkle argues that people find it easier to establish relationships on-line and then pursue them off-line. Yet, for all the celebration of the interactive world of cyberspace, what emerges from her discussion is that people engaging in Internet relationships really want the full, embodied relationship. Like many other authors, Turkle argues that gender swapping, or virtual cross-dressing, encourages people to reflect on the social construction of gender, to acquire "a new sense of gender as a continuum."[2] However she does not reflect upon the possibility that gender differences in the constitution of sexual desire and pleasure influence the manner in which cybersex is used.

In a similar vein, Allucquére Rosanne Stone celebrates the myriad ways in which modern technology is challenging traditional notions of gender identity. Complex virtual identities rupture the cultural belief that there is a single self in a single body. Stone's discussion of phone and virtual sex, for example, describes how female sex workers disguise crucial aspects of identity and can play at reinventing themselves. She takes seriously the notion that virtual people or selves can exist in cyberspace, with no necessary link to a physical body. As an illustration of this, Stone recounts the narrative about the cross-dressing psychiatrist that has become an apocryphal cyberfeminist tale. Like many stories that become legends, it is a pastiche of fiction and fact, assembled from diverse sources, including real events.[3]

It is the story of a middle-aged male psychiatrist called Lewin who becomes an active member of a CompuServe chat line, a virtual place where many people can interact simultaneously in real time. One day Lewin found he was conversing with a woman who assumed he was a female psychiatrist. Lewin was stunned by the power and intimacy of the conversation. He found that the woman was more open to him than were his female patients and friends in real life. Lewin wanted more, and soon began regularly logging on as Julie Graham, a severely handicapped and disfigured New York resident. Julie said it was her embarrassment about her disfigurement that made her prefer not to meet her cyberfriends in person.

Over time, Julie successfully projected her personality and had a flourishing social life on the Internet, giving advice to the many women who confided in her. Lewin acquired a devoted following and came to believe that it was as Julie that he could best help these women. His on-line female friends told Julie how central she had become to their lives. Indeed, the elaborate details of Julie's life gave hope particularly to other disabled women as her professional life flourished and, despite her handicaps, she became flamboyantly sexual, encouraging many of her friends to engage in Net sex with her. Her career took her around the world on the conference circuit, and she ended up marrying a young police officer.

Julie's story is generally taken to show that the subject and the body are no longer inseparable; that cyberspace provides us with novel free choices in selecting a gender identity irrespective of our material body. Stone argues that by the time he was exposed, Lewin's responses had

ceased to be a masquerade, that he was in the process of *becoming* Julie. However, this story can be read in a radically different manner, one that questions the extent to which the cyborg subject can escape the biological body. Although Julie's electronic manifestation appears at first sight to subvert gender distinctions, it can be just as forcefully argued that it ultimately reinforced and reproduced these differences. For the women seeking Julie's advice, her gender was crucial. They wanted to know that there was a woman behind the name; this is what prompted their intimacies. Julie's gender guided their behaviour and their mode of expression. "It rendered her existence, no matter how intangible and 'unreal' Julie appeared at first, extremely physical and genuine."[4] When Julie was unmasked as a cross-dressing man years later, many women who had sought her advice felt deeply betrayed and violated.

It was the "real" disabled women on-line who first had suspicions about the false identity, indicating that there are limits on creating sustainable new identities in cyberspace. Relationships on the Internet are not as free of corporeality as Stone and Turkle suggest. Although computer-mediated communication alters the nature of interaction by removing bodily cues, this is not the same as creating new identities. Just because all you see is words, it does not mean that becoming a different person requires only different words, or that this is a simple matter. Choosing words for a different identity is problematic.[5] The choice of words is the result of a process of socialization associated with a particular identity. It is therefore very difficult to learn a new identity without being socialized into that role. Although mimicry is possible, it is limited and is not the same as creating a viable new identity.

Research on artificial intelligence and information systems now emphasizes the importance of the body in human cognition and behaviour. Moreover, the sociology of scientific knowledge has taught us that much scientific knowledge is tacit (things people know but cannot explain or specify in formal rules) and cannot be learned explicitly. So it is with becoming a man or a woman. Lewin's false identity was discovered by people who had been socialized in the role that Lewin adopted: namely, that of a disabled woman. Bodies play an important part in what it means to be human and gendered.

That this narrative is about a man posing as a woman is not merely incidental as there is evidence that many more men adopt a female persona than vice versa. The masculine discursive style of much communication on the Web is well recognized. "Flaming" or aggressive on-line behaviour, including sexual harassment, is rife, and has a long lineage all the way back to the original hackers who developed the first networked games such as the notorious Dungeons and Dragons/MUD games. These games were designed by young men for the enjoyment of their peers. This reflected the computer science and engineering "nerd" technoculture that produced the Internet and excluded women from participation.

Cyberspace first appeared as "a disembodied zone wilder than the wildest West, racier than the space race, sexier than sex, even better than walking on the moon" in cyberpunk fiction.[6] It promised to finally rupture the boundaries between hallucination and reality, the organic and the electronic. For cyberpunks, technology is inside the body and the mind itself. Textual and visual representations of gendered bodies and erotic desire, however, proved less imaginative. It was new technology with the same old narratives. Here was a phallocentric fantasy of cyberspace travel infused with clichéd images of adolescent male sex, with console cowboys jacking into cyberspace.

. . .

A popular, contemporary version of these adventure games does feature a female character—notably Lara Croft, in the popular Tomb Raider game, alternatively seen as a fetish object of Barbie proportions created by and for the male gaze or as a female cyberstar. The orthodox feminist view of Lara Croft sees her as a pornographic technopuppet, an eternally young female automaton. By contrast, postmodern gender and queer theorists stress the diverse and subversive readings that Lara Croft is open to.[7] For some she is a tough, capable, sexy adventurous female heroine. For others, Lara as drag queen enables men to experiment with 'wearing' a feminine identity, echoing the phenomenon of gender crossing in Internet chat rooms.

While Lara may offer young women an exciting way into the male domain of computer games, much of the desire projected on to this avatar is prosaic. The game even features a Nude Raider patch that removes Lara's clothing. To cast her as a feminist heroine is therefore a long bow to draw. Perhaps we should let her creator Toby Gard have the last word: "Lara was designed to be a tough, self-reliant, intelligent woman. She confounds all the sexist clichés apart from the fact that she's got an unbelievable figure. Strong, independent women are the perfect fantasy girls—the untouchable is always the most desirable."[8]

NOTES

1. Sherry Turkle, *Life on the Screen: Identity in the Age of the Internet* (New York: Simon & Schuster, 1995), p. 12.
2. Ibid., p. 314.
3. Allucquére Rosanne Stone, *The War of Desire and Technology at the Close of the Mechanical Age* (Cambridge, Mass.: MIT Press, 1995), ch. 3.
4. Ruth Oldenziel, "Of old and new cyborgs: Feminist narratives of technology," *Letterature D' America*, 14, 55 (1994), p. 103.
5. Edgar A. Whitley, "In cyberspace all they see is your words: A review of the relationship between body, behaviour and identity drawn from the sociology of knowledge," *OCLC Systems and Services*, 13, 4 (1997), pp. 152–63.
6. Sadie Plant, *Zeros and Ones: Digital Women and the New Technoculture* (London: Fourth Estate, 1998), p. 180.
7. Anne-Marie Schleiner, "Does Lara Croft wear fake polygons? Gender and gender-role subversion in computer adventure games," *Leonardo*, 34, 4 (2001), pp. 221–26.
8. Justine Cassell and Henry Jenkins, "Chess for girls? Feminism and computer games," in Justine Cassell and Henry Jenkins (eds), *From Barbie to Mortal Kombat: Gender and Computer Games* (Cambridge, Mass.: MIT Press, 1998), p. 30.

(Rethinking) Gender

Debra Rosenberg (2007)

Growing up in Corinth, Mississippi, J. T. Hayes had a legacy to attend to. His dad was a well-known race-car driver and Hayes spent much of his childhood tinkering in the family's greasy garage, learning how to design and build cars. By the age of 10, he had started racing in his own right. Eventually Hayes won more than 500 regional and national championships in go-kart, midget and sprint racing, even making it to the NASCAR Winston Cup in the early '90s. But behind the trophies and the swagger of the racing circuit, Hayes was harboring a painful secret: he had always believed he was a woman. He had feminine features and a slight frame—at 5 feet 6 and 118 pounds he was downright dainty—and had always felt, psychologically, like a girl. Only his anatomy got in the way. Since childhood he'd wrestled with what to do about it. He'd slip on "girl clothes" he hid under the mattress and try his hand with makeup. But he knew he'd find little support in his conservative hometown.

In 1991, Hayes had a moment of truth. He was driving a sprint car on a dirt track in Little Rock when the car flipped end over end. "I was trapped upside down, engine throttle stuck, fuel running all over the racetrack and me," Hayes recalls. "The accident didn't scare me, but the thought that I hadn't lived life to its full potential just ran chill bumps up and down my body." That night he vowed to complete the transition to womanhood. Hayes kept racing while he sought therapy and started hormone treatments, hiding his growing breasts under an Ace bandage and baggy T shirts.

Finally, in 1994, at 30, Hayes raced on a Saturday night in Memphis, then drove to Colorado the next day for sex-reassignment surgery, selling his prized race car to pay the tab. Hayes chose the name Terri O'Connell and began a new life as a woman who figured her racing days were over. But she had no idea what else to do. Eventually, O'Connell got a job at the mall selling women's handbags for $8 an hour. O'Connell still hopes to race again, but she knows the odds are long: "Transgendered and professional motor sports just don't go together."

To most of us, gender comes as naturally as breathing. We have no quarrel with the "M" or the "F" on our birth certificates. And, crash diets aside, we've made peace with how we want the world to see us—pants or skirt, boa or blazer, spiky heels or sneakers. But to those who consider themselves transgender, there's a disconnect between the sex they were assigned at birth and the way they see or express themselves. Though their numbers are relatively few—the most generous estimate from the National Center for Transgender Equality is between 750,000 and 3 million Americans (fewer than 1 percent)—many of them are taking their intimate struggles public for the first time. In April 2007, *L.A. Times* sportswriter Mike Penner announced in his column that when he returned from vacation, he would do so as a woman, Christine Daniels. Nine states plus Washington, D.C., have enacted antidiscrimination laws that protect transgender people, and an additional three states have legislation pending, according to the Human Rights Campaign. And in May 2007 the U.S. House of Representatives passed a hate-crimes prevention bill that included "gender identity." Today's transgender Americans go far beyond the old stereotypes (think "Rocky Horror Picture Show"). They are soccer moms, ministers, teachers, politicians, even young children. Their push for tolerance and acceptance is reshaping businesses, sports, schools and families. It's also raising new questions about just what makes us male or female.

What is gender anyway? It is certainly more than the physical details of what's between our legs. History and science suggest that gender is more subtle and more complicated than anatomy. (It's separate from sexual orientation, too, which determines which sex we're attracted to.) Gender helps us organize the world into two boxes, his and hers, and gives us a way of quickly sizing up every person we see on the street. "Gender is a way of making the world secure," says feminist scholar Judith Butler, a rhetoric professor at University of California, Berkeley. Though some scholars like Butler consider gender largely a social construct, others increasingly see it as a complex interplay of biology, genes, hormones and culture.

. . .

Now, as transgender people become more visible and challenge the old boundaries, they've given voice to another debate—whether gender comes in just two flavors. "The old categories that everybody's either biologically male or female, that there are two distinct categories and there's no overlap, that's beginning to break down," says Michael Kimmel, a sociology professor at SUNY-Stony Brook. "All of those old categories seem to be more fluid." Just the terminology can get confusing. "Transsexual" is an older term that usually refers to someone who wants to use hormones or surgery to change their sex. "Transvestites," now more politely called "cross-dressers," occasionally wear clothes of the opposite sex. "Transgender" is an umbrella term that includes anyone whose gender identity or expression differs from the sex of their birth—whether they have surgery or not.

Gender identity first becomes an issue in early childhood, as any parent who's watched a toddler lunge for a truck or a doll can tell you. That's also when some kids may become aware that their bodies and brains don't quite match up. Jona Rose, a 6-year-old kindergartner in northern California, seems like a girl in nearly every way—she wears dresses, loves pink and purple, and bestowed female names on all her stuffed animals. But Jona, who was born Jonah, also has a penis. When she was 4, her mom, Pam, offered to buy Jona a dress, and she was so excited she nearly hyperventilated. She began wearing dresses every day to preschool and no one seemed to mind. It wasn't easy at first. "We wrung our hands about this every night," says her dad, Joel. But finally he and Pam decided to let their son live as a girl. They chose a private kindergarten where Jona wouldn't have to hide the fact that he was born a boy, but could comfortably dress like a girl and even use the girls' bathroom. "She has been pretty adamant from the get-go: 'I am a girl,'" says Joel.

Male or female, we all start life looking pretty much the same. Genes determine whether a particular human embryo will develop as male or female. But each individual embryo is equipped to be either one—each possesses the Müllerian ducts that become the female reproductive system as well as the Wolffian ducts that become the male one. Around eight weeks of development, through a complex genetic relay race, the X and the male's Y chromosomes kick into gear, directing the structures to become testes or ovaries. . . .

After birth, the changes keep coming. In many species, male newborns experience a hormone surge that may "organize" sexual and behavioral traits, says Nirao Shah, a neuroscientist at UCSF. In rats, testosterone given in the first week of life can cause female babies to behave more like males once they reach adulthood. "These changes are thought to be irreversible," says Shah. Between 1 and 5 months, male human babies also experience a hormone surge. It's still unclear exactly what effect that surge has on the human brain, but it happens just when parents are oohing and aahing over their new arrivals.

Here's where culture comes in. Studies have shown that parents treat boys and girls very differently—breast-feeding boys longer but talking more to girls. That's going on while the baby's brain is engaged in a massive growth spurt. "The brain doubles in size in the first five years after birth, and the connectivity between the cells goes up hundreds of orders of magnitude," says Anne Fausto-Sterling, a biologist and feminist at Brown University who is currently investigating whether subtle differences in parental behavior could influence gender identity in very young children. "The brain is interacting with culture from day one."

So what's different in transgender people? Scientists don't know for certain. Though their hormone levels seem to be the same as non-trans levels, some scientists speculate that their brains react differently to the hormones, just as men's differ from women's. But that could take decades of further research to prove. . . . For now, transgender issues are classified as "Gender Identity Disorder" in the psychiatric manual DSM-IV. That's controversial, too—gay-rights activists spent years campaigning to have homosexuality removed from the manual.

Gender fluidity hasn't always seemed shocking. Cross-dressing was common in ancient Greece and Rome, as well as among Native Americans and many other indigenous societies, according to Deborah Rudacille, author of "The Riddle of Gender." Court records from the Jamestown settlement in 1629 describe the case of Thomas Hall, who claimed to be both a man and a woman. Of course, what's considered masculine or feminine has long been a moving target. Our Founding Fathers wouldn't be surprised to see men today with long hair or earrings, but they might be puzzled by women in pants.

Transgender opponents have often turned to the Bible for support. Deut. 22:5 says: "The woman shall not wear that which pertaineth unto a man, neither shall a man put on a woman's garment: for all that do so are abomination unto the Lord thy God." When word leaked in February 2007 that Steve Stanton, the Largo, Florida, city manager for 14 years, was planning to transition to life as a woman, the community erupted. At a public meeting over whether Stanton should be fired, one of many critics, Ron Sanders, pastor of the Lighthouse Baptist Church, insisted that Jesus would "want him terminated." (Stanton did lose his job and later appeared as Susan Stanton on Capitol Hill to lobby for antidiscrimination laws.) Equating gender change with homosexuality, Sanders says that "it's an abomination, which means that it's utterly disgusting."

Not all people of faith would agree. Baptist minister John Nemecek, 56, was surfing the Web one weekend in 2003, when his wife was at a baby shower. Desperate for clues to his long-suppressed feelings of femininity, he stumbled across an article about gender-identity disorder on WebMD. The suggested remedy was sex-reassignment surgery—something Nemecek soon thought he had to do. Many families can be ripped apart by such drastic changes, but Nemecek's wife of 33 years stuck by him. His employer of 15 years, Spring Arbor University, a faith-based liberal-arts college in Michigan, did not. Nemecek says the school claimed that transgenderism violated its Christian principles, and when it renewed Nemecek's contract—by then she was taking hormones and using the name Julie—it barred her from dressing as a woman on campus or even wearing earrings. Her workload and pay were cut, too, she says. She filed a discrimination claim, which was later settled through mediation. (The university declined to comment on the case.) Nemecek says she has no trouble squaring her gender change and her faith. "Actively expressing the feminine in me has helped me grow closer to God," she says.

Others have had better luck transitioning. Karen Kopriva, now 49, kept her job teaching high school in Lake Forest, Illinois, when she shaved her beard and made the switch from Ken. When Mark Stumpp, a vice president at Prudential Financial, returned to work as Margaret in 2002, she sent a memo to her colleagues (subject: Me) explaining the change. "We all joked about wearing pantyhose and whether 'my condition' was contagious," she says. But "when the dust settled, everyone got back to work." Companies like IBM and Kodak now cover trans-related medical care. And 125 Fortune 500 companies now protect transgender employees from job discrimination, up from three in 2000. Discrimination may not be the worst worry for transgender people: they are also at high risk of violence and hate crimes.

Perhaps no field has wrestled more with the issue of gender than sports. There have long been accusations about male athletes' trying to pass as women, or women's taking testosterone to gain a competitive edge. In the 1960s, would-be female Olympians were required to undergo gender-screening tests. Essentially, that meant baring all before a panel of doctors who could verify that an athlete had girl parts. That method was soon scrapped in favor of a genetic test. But that quickly led to confusion over a handful of genetic disorders that give typical-looking women chromosomes other than the usual XX. Finally, the International Olympic Committee ditched mandatory lab-based screening, too. "We found there is no scientifically sound lab-based technique that can differentiate between man and woman," says Arne Ljungqvist, chair of the IOC's medical commission.

The IOC recently waded into controversy again: In 2004 it issued regulations allowing transsexual athletes to compete in the Olympics if they've had sex-reassignment surgery and have taken hormones for two years. After convening a panel of experts, the IOC decided that the surgery and hormones would compensate for any hormonal or muscular advantage a male-to-female transsexual would have. (Female-to-male athletes would be allowed to take testosterone, but only at levels that wouldn't give them a boost.) So far, Ljungqvist doesn't know of any transsexual athletes who've competed. Ironically, Renee Richards, who won a lawsuit in 1977 for the right to play tennis as a woman after her own sex-reassignment surgery, questions the fairness of the IOC rule. She thinks decisions should be made on a case-by-case basis.

Richards and other pioneers reflect the huge cultural shift over a generation of gender change. Now 70, Richards rejects the term transgender along with all the fluidity it conveys. "God didn't put us on this earth to have gender diversity," she says. "I don't like the kids that are experimenting. I didn't want to be something in between. I didn't want to be trans anything. I wanted to be a man or a woman."

But more young people are embracing something we would traditionally consider in between. Because of the expense, invasiveness, and mixed results (especially for women becoming men), only 1,000 to 2,000 Americans each year get sex-reassignment surgery—a number that's on the rise, says Mara Keisling of the National Center for Transgender Equality. Mykell Miller, a Northwestern University student born female who now considers himself male, hides his breasts under a special compression vest. Though he one day wants to take hormones and get a mastectomy, he can't yet afford it. But that doesn't affect his self-image. "I challenge the idea that all men were born with male bodies," he says. "I don't go out of my way to be the biggest, strongest guy."

Nowhere is the issue more pressing at the moment than a place that helped give rise to the feminist movement a generation ago: Smith College in Northampton, Massachusetts. Though Smith was one of the original Seven Sisters women's colleges, its students have now taken to calling it a "mostly women's college," in part because of a growing number of "transmen" who decide to become male after they've enrolled. In 2004, students voted to remove pronouns from the student government constitution as a gesture to transgender students who no longer identified with "she" or "her." (Smith is also one of 70 schools that have antidiscrimination policies protecting transgender students.) For now, anyone who is enrolled at Smith may graduate, but in order to be admitted in the first place, you must have been born a female. Tobias Davis, class of '03, entered Smith as a woman, but graduated as a "transman." When he first told friends over dinner, "I think I might be a boy," they were instantly behind him, saying "Great! Have you picked a name yet?" Davis passed as male for his junior year abroad in Italy even without taking hormones; he had a mastectomy last fall. Now 25, Davis works at Smith and writes plays about the transgender experience. (His work "The Naked I: Monologues From Beyond the Binary" is a trans take on "The Vagina Monologues.")

As kids at ever-younger ages grapple with issues of gender variance, doctors, psychologists, and parents are weighing how to balance immediate desires and long-term ones. Like Jona Rose, many kids begin questioning gender as toddlers, identifying with the other gender's toys and clothes. Five times as many boys as girls say their gender doesn't match their biological sex, says Dr. Edgardo Menvielle, a psychiatrist who heads a gender-variance outreach program at Children's National Medical Center. (Perhaps that's because it's easier for girls to blend in as tomboys.) Many of these children eventually move on and accept their biological sex, says Menvielle, often when they're exposed to a disapproving larger world or when they're influenced by the hormone surges of puberty. Only about 15 percent continue to show signs of gender-identity problems into adulthood, says Ken Zucker, who heads the Gender Identity Service at the Centre for Addiction and Mental Health in Toronto.

In the past, doctors often advised parents to direct their kids into more gender-appropriate clothing and behavior. Zucker still tells parents of unhappy boys to try more-neutral activities—say, chess club instead of football. But now the thinking is that kids should lead the way. If a child persists in wanting to be the other gender, doctors may prescribe hormone "blockers" to keep puberty at bay. (Blockers have no permanent effects.) But they're also increasingly willing to take more lasting steps: Isaak Brown (who started life as Liza) began taking male hormones at 16; at 17 he had a mastectomy.

For parents like Colleen Vincente, 44, following a child's lead seems only natural. Her second child, M. (Vincente asked to use an initial to protect the child's privacy), was born female. But as soon as she could talk, she insisted on wearing boy's clothes. Though M. had plenty of dolls, she gravitated toward "the boy things" and soon wanted to shave off all her hair. "We went along with that," says Vincente. "We figured it was a phase." One day, when she was 2-1/2, M. overheard her parents talking about her using female pronouns. "He said, 'No—I'm a him. You need to call me him,'" Vincente recalls. "We were shocked." In his California preschool, M. continued to insist he was a boy and decided to change his name. Vincente and her husband, John, consulted a therapist, who confirmed their instincts to let M. guide them. Now 9, M. lives as a boy and most people have no idea he was born otherwise. "The most important thing is to realize this is who your child is," Vincente says. That's a big step for a family, but could be an even bigger one for the rest of the world.

R E A D I N G   **25**

Masculinities and Globalization

R. W. Connell (1999)

[In this article] I offer a framework for thinking about masculinities as a feature of world society and for thinking about men's gender practices in terms of the global structure and dynamics of gender. . . .

THE WORLD GENDER ORDER

Masculinities do not first exist and then come into contact with femininities; they are produced together, in the process that constitutes a gender order. Accordingly, to understand the masculinities on a world scale, we must first have a concept of the globalization of gender.

This is one of the most difficult points in current gender analysis because the very conception is counterintuitive. We are so accustomed to thinking of gender as the attribute of an individual, even as an unusually intimate attribute, that it requires a considerable wrench to think of gender on the vast scale of global society. Most relevant discussions, such as the literature on women and development, fudge the issue. They treat the entities that extend internationally (markets, corporations, intergovernmental programs, etc.) as ungendered in principle—but affecting unequally gendered recipients of aid in practice, because of bad policies. Such conceptions reproduce the familiar liberal-feminist view of the state as in principle gender-neutral, though empirically dominated by men.

But if we recognize that very large scale institutions such as the state are themselves gendered, in quite precise and specifiable ways (Connell 1990), and if we recognize that international relations, international trade, and global markets are inherently an arena of gender formation and gender politics (Enloe 1990), then we can recognize the existence of a world gender order. The term can be defined as the structure of relationships that interconnect the gender regimes of institutions, and the gender orders of local society, on a world scale. That is, however, only a definition. The substantive questions remain: what is the shape of that structure, how tightly are its elements linked, how has it arisen historically, what is its trajectory into the future?

Current business and media talk about globalization pictures a homogenizing process sweeping across the world, driven by new technologies, producing vast unfettered global markets in which all participate on equal terms. This is a misleading image. As Hirst and Thompson (1996) show, the global economy is highly unequal and the current degree of homogenization is often overestimated. Multinational corporations based in the three major economic powers (the United States, European Union, and Japan) are the major economic actors worldwide.

The structure bears the marks of its history. Modern global society was historically produced, as Wallerstein (1974) argued, by the economic and political expansion of European states from the fifteenth century on and by the creation of colonial empires. It is in this process that we find the roots of the modern world gender order. Imperialism was, from the start, a gendered process. Its first phase, colonial conquest and settlement, was carried out by gender-segregated forces, and it resulted in massive disruption of indigenous gender orders. In its second phase, the stabilization of colonial societies, new gender divisions of labor were produced in plantation economies and colonial cities, while gender ideologies were linked with racial hierarchies and the cultural defense of empire. The third phase, marked by political decolonization, economic neo-colonialism, and the current growth of world markets and structures of financial control, has seen gender divisions of labor remade on a massive scale in the "global factory" (Fuentes and Ehrenreich 1983), as well as the spread of gendered violence alongside Western military technology.

The result of this history is a partially integrated, highly unequal and turbulent world society, in which gender relations are partly but unevenly linked on a global scale. The unevenness becomes clear when different substructures of gender (Connell 1987; Walby 1990) are examined separately. [These substructures include:]

The Division of Labor. A characteristic feature of colonial and neocolonial economies was the restructuring of local production systems to produce a male wage worker–female domestic worker couple (Mies 1986). This need not produce a "housewife" in the Western suburban sense, for instance, where the wage work involved migration to plantations or mines (Moodie 1994). But it has generally produced the identification of masculinity with the public realm and the money economy and of femininity with domesticity, which is a core feature of the modern European gender system (Holter 1997).

Power Relations. The colonial and postcolonial world has tended to break down purdah systems of patriarchy in the name of modernization, if not of women's emancipation (Kandiyoti 1994). At the same time, the creation of a westernized public realm has seen the growth of large-scale organizations in the form of the state and corporations, which in the great majority of cases are culturally masculinized and controlled by men. In *comprador* capitalism, however, the power of local elites depends on their relations with the metropolitan powers, so the hegemonic masculinities of neocolonial societies are uneasily poised between local and global cultures.

Emotional Relations.   Both religious and cultural missionary activity has corroded indigenous homosexual and cross-gender practice, such as the Native American *berdache* and the Chinese "passion of the cut sleeve" (Hinsch 1990). Recently developed Western models of romantic heterosexual love as the basis for marriage and of gay identity as the main alternative have now circulated globally—though as Altman (1996) observes, they do not simply displace indigenous models, but interact with them in extremely complex ways.

Symbolization.   Mass media, especially electronic media, in most parts of the world follow North American and European models and relay a great deal of metropolitan content; gender imagery is an important part of what is circulated. A striking example is the reproduction of a North American imagery of femininity by Xuxa, the blonde television superstar in Brazil (Simpson 1993). In counterpoint, exotic gender imagery has been used in the marketing strategies of newly industrializing countries (e.g., airline advertising from Southeast Asia)—a tactic based on the long-standing combination of the exotic and the erotic in the colonial imagination (Jolly 1997).

Clearly, the world gender order is not simply an extension of a traditional European-American gender order. That gender order was changed by colonialism, and elements from other cultures now circulate globally. Yet in no sense do they mix on equal terms, to produce a United Colours of Benetton gender order. The culture and institutions of the North Atlantic countries are hegemonic within the emergent world system. This is crucial for understanding the kinds of masculinities produced within it.

THE REPOSITIONING OF MEN AND THE RECONSTITUTION OF MASCULINITIES

The positioning of men and the constitution of masculinities may be analyzed at any of the levels at which gender practice is configured: in relation to the body, in personal life, and in collective social practice. At each level, we need to consider how the processes of globalization influence configurations of gender.

Men's bodies are positioned in the gender order, and enter the gender process, through body-reflexive practices in which bodies are both objects and agents (Connell 1995)—including sexuality, violence, and labor. The conditions of such practice include where one is and who is available for interaction. So it is a fact of considerable importance for gender relations that the global social order distributes and redistributes bodies, through migration, and through political controls over movement and interaction.

The creation of empire was the original "elite migration," though in certain cases mass migration followed. Through settler colonialism, something close to the gender order of Western Europe was reassembled in North America and in Australia. Labor migration within the colonial systems was a means by which gender practices were spread, but also a means by which they were reconstructed, since labor migration was itself a gendered process—as we have seen in relation to the gender division of labor. Migration from the colonized world to the metropole became (except for Japan) a mass process in the decades after World War II. There is also migration within the periphery, such as the creation of a very large immigrant labor force, mostly from other Muslim countries, in the oil-producing Gulf states.

These relocations of bodies create the possibility of hybridization in gender imagery, sexuality, and other forms of practice. The movement is not always toward synthesis, however, as the race/ethnic hierarchies of colonialism have been re-created in new contexts, including the politics of the metropole. Ethnic and racial conflict has been growing in importance in recent years, and as Klein (1997) and Tillner (1997) argue, this is a fruitful context for the production of masculinities oriented toward domination and violence. Even without the context of violence, there can be an intimate interweaving of the formation of masculinity with the formation of ethnic identity, as seen in the study by Poynting, Noble, and Tabar (1997) of Lebanese youths in the Anglo-dominant culture of Australia.

At the level of personal life as well as in relation to bodies, the making of masculinities is shaped by global forces. In some cases, the link is indirect, such as the working-class Australian men caught in a situation of structural unemployment (Connell 1995), which arises from Australia's changing position in the global economy. In other cases, the link is obvious, such as the executives of multinational corporations and the financial sector servicing international trade. The requirements of a career in international business set up strong pressures on domestic life: almost all multinational executives are men, and the assumption in business magazines and advertising directed toward them is that they will have dependent wives running their homes and bringing up their children.

At the level of collective practice, masculinities are reconstituted by the remaking of gender meanings and the reshaping of the institutional contexts of practice. Let us consider each in turn.

The growth of global mass media, especially electronic media, is an obvious "vector" for the globalization of gender. Popular entertainment circulates stereotyped gender images, deliberately made attractive for marketing purposes. International news media are also controlled or strongly influenced from the metropole and circulate Western definitions of authoritative masculinity, criminality, desirable femininity, and so on. But there are limits to the power of global mass communications. Some local centers of mass entertainment differ from the Hollywood model, such as the Indian popular film industry centered in Bombay. Further, media research emphasizes that audiences are highly selective in their reception of media messages, and we must allow for popular recognition of the fantasy in mass entertainment. Just as economic globalization can be exaggerated, the creation of a global culture is a more turbulent and uneven process than is often assumed (Featherstone 1995).

More important, I would argue, is a process that began long before electronic media existed, the export of institutions. Gendered institutions not only circulate definitions of masculinity (and femininity), as sex role theory notes. The functioning of gendered institutions, creating specific conditions for social practice, calls into existence specific patterns of practice. Thus, certain patterns of collective violence are embedded in the organization and culture of a Western-style army, which are different from the patterns of precolonial violence. Certain patterns of calculative egocentrism are embedded in the working of a stock market; certain patterns of rule following and domination are embedded in a bureaucracy.

Now, the colonial and postcolonial world saw the installation in the periphery, on a very large scale, of a range of institutions on the North Atlantic model: armies, states, bureaucracies, corporations, capital markets, labor markets, schools, law courts, transport systems. These are gendered institutions and their functioning has directly reconstituted masculinities in the periphery. This has not necessarily meant photocopies of European masculinities. Rather, pressures for change are set up that are inherent in the institutional form.

To the extent that particular institutions become dominant in world society, the patterns of masculinity embedded in them may become global standards. Masculine dress is an interesting indicator: almost every political leader in the world now wears the uniform of the Western business executive. The more common pattern, however, is not the complete displacement of local patterns but the articulation of the local gender order with the gender regime of global-model institutions. Case studies such as Hollway's (1994) account of bureaucracy in Tanzania illustrate the point; there, domestic patriarchy articulated with masculine authority in the state in ways that subverted the government's formal commitment to equal opportunity for women.

We should not expect the overall structure of gender relations on a world scale simply to mirror patterns known on the smaller scale. In the most vital of respects, there is continuity. The world gender order is unquestionably patriarchal, in the sense that it privileges men over women. There is a patriarchal dividend for men arising from unequal wages, unequal labor force participation, and a highly unequal structure of ownership, as well as cultural and sexual privileging. This has been extensively documented by feminist work on women's situation globally (e.g., Taylor 1985), though its implications for masculinity have mostly been ignored. The conditions thus exist for the production of a hegemonic masculinity on a world scale, that is to say, a dominant form of masculinity that embodies, organizes, and legitimates men's domination in the gender order as a whole.

The conditions of globalization, which involve the interaction of many local gender orders, certainly multiply the forms of masculinity in the global gender order. At the same time, the specific shape of globalization, concentrating economic and cultural power on an unprecedented scale, provides new resources for dominance by particular groups of men. This dominance may become institutionalized in a pattern of masculinity that becomes, to some degree, standardized across localities. I will call such patterns *globalizing masculinities,* and it is among them, rather than narrowly within the metropole, that we are likely to find candidates for hegemony in the world gender order.

. . .

MASCULINITIES OF POSTCOLONIALISM AND NEOLIBERALISM

. . .

With the collapse of Soviet communism, the decline of postcolonial socialism, and the ascendancy of the new right in Europe and North America, world politics is more and more organized around the needs of transnational capital and the creation of global markets.

The neoliberal agenda has little to say, explicitly, about gender: it speaks a gender-neutral language of "markets," "individuals," and "choice." But the world in which neoliberalism is ascendant is still a gendered world, and neoliberalism has an implicit gender politics. The "individual" of neoliberal theory has in general the attributes and interests of a male entrepreneur, the attack on the welfare state generally weakens the position of women, while the increasingly unregulated power of transnational corporations places strategic power in the

hands of particular groups of men. It is not surprising, then, that the installation of capitalism in Eastern Europe and the former Soviet Union has been accompanied by a reassertion of dominating masculinities and, in some situations, a sharp worsening in the social position of women.

We might propose, then, that the hegemonic form of masculinity in the current world gender order is the masculinity associated with those who control its dominant institutions: the business executives who operate in global markets, and the political executives who interact (and in many contexts, merge) with them. I will call this *transnational business masculinity*. This is not readily available for ethnographic study, but we can get some clues to its character from its reflections in management literature, business journalism, and corporate self-promotion, and from studies of local business elites (e.g., Donaldson 1997).

As a first approximation, I would suggest this is a masculinity marked by increasing egocentrism, very conditional loyalties (even to the corporation), and a declining sense of responsibility for others (except for purposes of image making). Gee, Hull and Lankshear (1996), studying recent management textbooks, note the peculiar construction of the executive in "fast capitalism" as a person with no permanent commitments, except (in effect) to the idea of accumulation itself. Transnational business masculinity is characterized by a limited technical rationality (management theory), which is increasingly separate from science.

Transnational business masculinity differs from traditional bourgeois masculinity by its increasingly libertarian sexuality, with a growing tendency to commodify relations with women. Hotels catering to businessmen in most parts of the world now routinely offer pornographic videos, and in some parts of the world, there is a well-developed prostitution industry catering for international businessmen. Transnational business masculinity does not require bodily force, since the patriarchal dividend on which it rests is accumulated by impersonal, institutional means. But corporations increasingly use the exemplary bodies of elite sportsmen as a marketing tool (note the phenomenal growth of corporate "sponsorship" of sport in the last generation) and indirectly as a means of legitimation for the whole gender order.

MASCULINITY POLITICS ON A WORLD SCALE

Recognizing global society as an arena of masculinity formation allows us to pose new questions about masculinity politics. What social dynamics in the global arena give rise to masculinity politics, and what shape does global masculinity politics take?

The gradual creation of a world gender order has meant many local instabilities of gender. Gender instability is a familiar theme of poststructuralist theory, but this school of thought takes as a universal condition a situation that is historically specific. Instabilities range from the disruption of men's local cultural dominance as women move into the public realm and higher education, through the disruption of sexual identities that produced "queer" politics in the metropole, to the shifts in the urban intelligentsia that produced "the new sensitive man" and other images of gender change.

One response to such instabilities, on the part of groups whose power is challenged but still dominant, is to reaffirm *local* gender orthodoxies and hierarchies. A masculine fundamentalism is, accordingly, a common response in gender politics at present. A soft version, searching for an essential masculinity among myths and symbols, is offered by the mythopoetic men's movement in the United States and by the religious revivalists of the Promise Keepers (Messner 1997). A much harder version is found, in that country, in the right-wing militia movement brought to world attention by the Oklahoma City bombing (Gibson 1994), and in contemporary Afghanistan, if we can trust Western media reports, in the militant misogyny of the Talibaan. It is no coincidence that in the two latter cases, hardline masculine fundamentalism goes together with a marked anti-internationalism. The world system—rightly enough—is seen as the source of pollution and disruption.

Not that the emerging global order is a hotbed of gender progressivism. Indeed, the neoliberal agenda for the reform of national and international economics involves closing down historic possibilities for gender reform. I have noted how it subverts the gender compromise represented by the metropolitan welfare state. It has also undermined the progressive-liberal agendas of sex role reform represented by affirmative action programs, antidiscrimination provisions, child care services, and the like. Right-wing parties and governments have been persistently cutting such programs, in the name of either individual liberties or global competitiveness. Through these means, the patriarchal dividend to men is defended or restored, without an *explicit* masculinity politics in the form of a mobilization of men.

Within the arenas of international relations, the international state, multinational corporations, and global markets, there is nevertheless a deployment of masculinities and a reasonably clear hegemony. The transnational business masculinity described above has had only one major competitor for hegemony in recent decades, the rigid, control-oriented masculinity of the military, and the military-style bureaucratic dictatorships of Stalinism. With the collapse of Stalinism and the end of the cold war, Big Brother (Orwell's famous parody of this form of masculinity) is a fading threat, and the more flexible, calculative, egocentric masculinity of the fast capitalist entrepreneur holds the world stage.

We must, however, recall two important conclusions of the ethnographic moment in masculinity research: that different forms of masculinity exist together and that hegemony is constantly subject to challenge. These are possibilities in the global arena too. Transnational business masculinity is not completely homogeneous; variations of it are embedded in different parts of the world system, which may not be completely compatible. We may distinguish a Confucian variant, based in East Asia, with a stronger commitment to hierarchy and social consensus, from a secularized Christian variant, based in North America, with more hedonism and individualism and greater tolerance for social conflict. In certain arenas, there is already conflict between the business and political leaderships embodying these forms of masculinity: initially over human rights versus Asian values, and more recently over the extent of trade and investment liberalization.

If these are contenders for hegemony, there is also the possibility of opposition to hegemony. The global circulation of "gay" identity (Altman 1996) is an important indication that nonhegemonic masculinities may operate in global arenas, and may even find a certain political articulation, in this case around human rights and AIDS prevention.

REFERENCES

Altman, Dennis. 1996. Rupture or continuity? The internationalisation of gay identities. *Social Text* 48 (3): 77–94.

Connell, R. W. 1987. *Gender and power.* Cambridge, MA: Polity.

———. 1990. The state, gender and sexual politics: Theory and appraisal. *Theory and Society* 19:507–44.

———. 1995. *Masculinities.* Cambridge, MA: Polity.

Donaldson, Mike. 1997. Growing up very rich: The masculinity of the hegemonic. Paper presented at the conference Masculinities: Renegotiating Genders, June, University of Wollongong, Australia.

Enloe, Cynthia. 1990. *Bananas, beaches and bases: Making feminist sense of international politics.* Berkeley: University of California Press.

Featherstone, Mike. 1995. *Undoing culture: Globalization, postmodernism and identity.* London: Sage.

Fuentes, Annette, and Barbara Ehrenreich. 1983. *Women in the global factory.* Boston: South End.

Gee, James Paul, Glynda Hall, and Colin Lankshear. 1996. *The new work order: Behind the language of the new capitalism.* Sydney: Allen & Unwin.

Gibson, J. William. 1994. *Warrior dreams: Paramilitary culture in post-Vietnam America.* New York: Hill and Wang.

Hinsch, Bret. 1990. *Passions of the cut sleeve: The male homosexual tradition in China.* Berkeley: University of California Press.

Hirst, Paul, and Grahame Thompson. 1996. *Globalization in question: The international economy and the possibilities of governance.* Cambridge, MA: Polity.

Hollway, Wendy. 1994. Separation, integration and difference: Contradictions in a gender regime. In *Power/gender: Social relations in theory and practice,* edited by H. Lorraine Radtke and Henderikus Stam, 247–69. London: Sage.

Holter, Oystein Gullvag. 1997. Gender, patriarchy and capitalism: A social forms analysis. Ph.D. diss., University of Oslo, Faculty of Social Science.

Jolly, Margaret. 1997. From point Venus to Bali Ha'i: Eroticism and exoticism in representations of the Pacific. In *Sites of desire, economies of pleasure: Sexualities in Asia and the Pacific,* edited by Lenore Manderson and Margaret Jolly, 99–122. Chicago: University of Chicago Press.

Kandiyoti, Deniz. 1994. The paradoxes of masculinity: Some thoughts on segregated societies. In *Dislocating masculinity: Comparative ethnographies,* edited by Andrea Cornwall and Nancy Lindisfarne, 197–213. London: Routledge.

Klein, Uta. 1997. Our best boys: The making of masculinity in Israeli society. Paper presented at UNESCO expert group meeting on Male Roles and Masculinities in the Perspectives of a Culture of Peace, September, Oslo.

Messner, Michael A. 1997. *The politics of masculinities: Men in movements.* Thousand Oaks, CA: Sage.

Mies, Maria. 1986. *Patriarchy and accumulation on a world scale: Women in the international division of labour.* London: Zed.

Moodie, T. Dunbar. 1994. *Going for gold: Men, mines, and migration.* Johannesburg: Witwatersand University Press.

Poynting, S., G. Noble, and P. Tabar. 1997. "Intersections" of masculinity and ethnicity: A study of male Lebanese immigrant youth in Western Sydney. Paper presented at the conference Masculinities: Renegotiating Genders, June, University of Wollongong, Australia.

Simpson, Amelia. 1993. *Xuxa: The mega-marketing of a gender, race and modernity.* Philadelphia: Temple University Press.

Taylor, Debbie. 1985. Women: An analysis. In *Women: A world report,* 1–98. London: Methuen.

Tillner, Georg. 1997. Masculinity and xenophobia. Paper presented at UNESCO meeting on Male Roles and Masculinities in the Perspective of a Culture of Peace, September, Oslo.

Walby, Sylvia. 1990. *Theorizing patriarchy.* Oxford, U.K.: Blackwell.

Wallerstein, Immanuel. 1974. *The modern world-system: Capitalist agriculture and the origins of the European world-economy in the sixteenth century.* New York: Academic Press.

DISCUSSION QUESTIONS FOR CHAPTER 3

1. How do notions of sex and gender take shape within a cultural context? In what ways has your cultural context shaped your notions of sex and gender?

2. How would you describe the dominant notions of masculinity and femininity in U.S. society? How do these dominant notions help maintain systems of inequality?

3. How do people learn to "do" gender? Can you think of ways you've learned to do gender? From what sources did you learn to do gender?

4. How does gender ranking reinforce sexism?

5. How is the experience of sexism shaped by the confluences of other systems of oppression?

SUGGESTIONS FOR FURTHER READING

Bornstein, Kate. *My Gender Workbook.* New York: Routledge, 1998.

Boylan, Jennifer Finney. *She's Not There: A Life in Two Genders.* New York: Broadway, 2003.

Browne, Jude, ed. *The Future of Gender.* New York: Cambridge University Press, 2007.

Butler, Judith. *Undoing Gender.* New York: Routledge, 2004.

Fausto-Sterling, Anne. *Sexing the Body: Gender Politics and the Construction of Sexuality.* New York: Basic Books, 2000.

Feinberg, Leslie. *Transgender Warriors.* Boston: Beacon, 1996.

Green, Eileen, *Virtual Gender: Technology, Consumption and Identity.* London: Taylor & Francis, 2007.

Howey, Noelle. *Dress Codes: Of Three Girlhoods—My Mother's, My Father's, and Mine.* New York: St. Martin's Press, 2002.

Roughgarden, Joan. *Evolution's Rainbow: Diversity, Gender, and Sexuality in Nature and People.* Berkeley: University of California Press, 2004.

CHAPTER 4

Sex, Power, and Intimacy

Sexuality is a topic of great interest to most people. It entertains and intrigues and is a source of both personal happiness and frustration. Over the centuries men have struggled to control women's sexuality through a variety of physical and emotional means; controlling a woman's sexuality has often meant controlling her life. The flip-side of this is that sexuality has the potential to be a liberating force in women's lives. To enjoy and be in control of one's sexuality and to be able to seek a mutually fulfilling sexual relationship can be an empowering experience. This chapter begins with a discussion of the social construction of sexuality and provides definitions for key terms. Following is a focus on two themes associated with sexuality: first, the politics of sexuality, and second, intimacy, romance, and interpersonal communication.

THE SOCIAL CONSTRUCTION OF SEXUALITY

Human sexuality involves erotic attractions, identity, and practices, and it is constructed by and through societal sexual scripts. *Sexual scripts* reflect social norms, practices, and workings of power, and they provide frameworks and guidelines for sexual feelings and behaviors. There is often embarrassment, shame, and confusion associated with these sexual scripts, and they easily become fraught with potential misunderstandings.

Sexual scripts vary across cultures and through time and are almost always heavily informed by societal understandings of gender and power. As the reading "Women, Sexuality, and Social Change in the Middle East" by Pinar Ilkkaracan suggests, in this age of globalization, women's bodies and sexuality are increasingly becoming arenas of intense conflict. The article by Pepper Schwartz and Virginia Rutter, "Sexual Desire and Gender," emphasizes two key points: Sexuality is about society as much as it is about biological urges, and that the most significant dimension of sexuality is gender. For example, as discussed in Chapter 3, feminine sexual scripts have often involved a double bind: To want sex is to risk being labeled promiscuous and to not want sex means potentially being labeled frigid and a prude. For many women, sexuality is shrouded in shame and fear, and, rather than seeing

Rainbow Trivia

1. At what New York bar did the modern gay liberation movement begin?
   a. Studio 54
   b. Stonewall
   c. Club 57
   d. Scandals

2. What were homosexuals required to wear to identify them in concentration camps during World War II?
   a. A yellow star
   b. A lavender H
   c. A pink star
   d. A pink triangle

3. What Greek letter symbolizes queer activism?
   a. Lambda
   b. Alpha
   c. Delta
   d. Sigma

4. What is the name of the religious organization that supports queer Catholics?
   a. Spirit
   b. Celebration
   c. Dignity
   d. Affirmation

5. What is the country's largest political organization working specifically for queer rights?
   a. Human Rights Campaign
   b. ACT-UP
   c. NOW
   d. Christian Coalition

6. What famous athlete came out at the 1993 March on Washington?
   a. Greg Louganis
   b. Reggie White
   c. Tonya Harding
   d. Martina Navratilova

7. What show made television history by having the first gay lead character?
   a. *Soap*
   b. *Roseanne*
   c. *Ellen*
   d. *All in the Family*

8. Who of the following is not a famous lesbian performer?
   a. Sarah McLachlan
   b. Melissa Etheridge
   c. k.d. lang
   d. Indigo Girls

(continued)

9. Which of the following is a must-read for any good lesbian?
   a. *The Well of Loneliness* by Radclyffe Hall
   b. *Rubyfruit Jungle* by Rita Mae Brown
   c. Anything by Dorothy Allison
   d. All of the above

10. Which of the following movies did *not* have a lesbian character?
   a. *Boys on the Side*
   b. *Personal Best*
   c. *Desert Hearts*
   d. None of the above
   Answers: 1. b 2. d 3. a 4. c 5. a 6. d 7. c 8. a 9. d 10. d

themselves as subjects in their own erotic lives, women may understand themselves as objects, seen through the eyes of others. This can be compared to sexual potency which involves the power to initiate and enjoy being the center of one's erotic experience, a key aspect of masculinity in contemporary Western societies.

Within the context of sexual scripts, individuals develop their own sexual self-schemas. *Sexual self-schemas* can be defined as identities or cognitive generalizations about sexual aspects of the self that are established from past and present experiences and that guide sexual feelings and behavior. What is desirable or acceptable to one person may be unacceptable or even disgusting to another. Note that sexual scripts are societal-level guidelines for human sexuality, whereas sexual self-schemas are individual-level understandings of the self.

Sexual scripts vary across such differences as race, class, age, and ability. The short story by Emily Oxford, "Prue Shows Her Knickers," tells of the empowerment of an adolescent girl with disabilities as well as the constraints associated with her physical condition. The relentless youth-oriented culture of contemporary U.S. society sees "older" ("older than whom?" you may ask—note how this term encourages a mythical norm associated with young adulthood) people or people with disabilities as less sexual, or interprets their sexuality as humorous or out of place. Much of this is learned from the media and enacted in peer groups.

There have also been strong mandates in U.S. society (such as anti-miscegenation laws) that have maintained racial superiority by outlawing interracial dating and marriage. In addition, there are class and race differences associated with interpersonal relationships that reflect the norms of specific communities. For example, Chicana lesbians have spoken out about intense homophobia that is related to the sexual scripts identifying women as wives and mothers in their communities. In "La Güera," Cherríe Moraga describes how coming out as a lesbian helped her connect with the inequities of race. She is a light-skinned Chicana who had learned to pass as White. She writes, "The joys of looking like a white girl haven't been so great since I realized I could be beaten on the street for being a dyke." Paula Gunn Allen's poem, "Some Like Indians Endure," also makes the connections between racism and heterosexism. Both Indians and lesbians have endured and survived oppression.

World Report 2007: Lesbian, Gay, Bisexual, and Transgender Rights

Although the visibility of lesbian, gay, bisexual, and transgender people throughout the world continued to rise in 2007, their increased visibility was accompanied by attacks based on sexual orientation and gender identity. Human rights activists who sought to use the human rights framework to call to account states that participated in these rights abuses or condoned them also came under attack. In virtually every country in the world people suffered from de jure and de facto discrimination based on their actual or perceived sexual orientation. In some countries, sexual minorities lived with the very real threat of being deprived of their right to life and security of person. A small number of countries continued to impose the death penalty for private sexual acts between consenting adults. In several others, sexual minorities were targeted for extrajudicial executions. In many countries, police or other members of the security forces actively participated in the persecution of lesbian, gay, bisexual, and transgender people, including their arbitrary detention and torture. Pervasive bias within the criminal justice system in many countries effectively precluded members of sexual minorities from seeking redress.

. . .

[The following examples suggest the enormity of discrimination faced by lesbian, gay, bisexual, and transgender people worldwide:]

Uganda Publication of identifying information of 45 alleged homosexuals in the tabloid paper *Red Pepper* in August 2006 raised concerns of an escalation in the government's long-standing campaign of harassment of lesbian, gay, bisexual, and transgender Ugandans. Homophobic allegations by the same tabloid in 2002 that two women had married led to their arrest and detention.

Russia After a court upheld Moscow Mayor Yuri Luzkhov's ban on a gay and lesbian pride march, on May 27, 2006, several dozen gay activists and supporters attempted to hold two protest rallies in support of freedoms of assembly and expression. Hundreds of anti-gay protesters, including skinheads, nationalists, and Orthodox followers, attacked the participants, beating and kicking many, and chanted threats. The mayor's office had earlier made homophobic statements and circulated directives to restrict gay and lesbian rights.

Poland In January 2006 the European Parliament, motivated in part by rising homophobia in Poland, adopted a resolution calling on EU member states "firmly to condemn homophobic hate speech or incitement to hatred and violence." But overtly homophobic rhetoric from Polish government officials, coupled with attacks on lesbian, gay, bisexual, and transgender (LGBT) activists, continued during 2006.

Guatemala [A] transgender woman was murdered and another was critically wounded on December 17, 2005, when they were gunned down on a street in Guatemala City. Eyewitnesses reported that the gunmen were uniformed police officers.

Nepal The initial committee in charge of guiding the [constitutional] constituent assembly was composed only of men, but was broadened after protests to include women as well as those from so-called untouchable castes, or Dalits. But other groups continue to be sidelined; for instance, Nepal's beleaguered population of lesbian, gay, bisexual, and transgender people.

Papua New Guinea Police target street vendors as well as female sex workers, men, and boys suspected of homosexual conduct for beatings and rape. Police also extort money from such individuals, using the threat of arresting them for illegal activities.

Source: http://www.hrw.org/wr2k7/index.htm.

Sexual identity is a person's attraction to, or preference for, people of a given sex. It is an individual's romantic and/or sexual (also called erotic) identity and behavior toward other people. Note that sexual identity does not necessarily require sexual experience. *Heterosexuality* is a sexual identity where romantic and/or sexual attachments are between people of the opposite sex (popularly termed *straight*). *Homosexuality* is a sexual identity where romantic and/or sexual attachments are between people of the same sex. Because the term *homosexual* is stigmatized and because the term seems to emphasize sexual behavior, homosexual communities have preferred the term *gay*. *Gay* and *homosexual* are terms inclusive of women, although they are used mainly to describe men. The term *lesbian* means the romantic and/or sexual attachment and identification between women, specifically. Bisexuality implies a sexual identification with both women and men. There are derogatory social connotations of bisexuality as hypersexualized: Not only do these people have sex all the time, but they are doing it with both women and with men, simultaneously. Of course, to be bisexual does not imply this at all; it just means the choice of lover can be either a woman or a man. Nonetheless, these connotations reflect the fact that there are many stigmas associated with bisexuality from both the straight and the lesbian and gay communities. Jennifer Baumgardner answers the question, "What is bisexuality?" in the reading with the same name.

The word *queer,* traditionally meaning out of the ordinary or unusual, and historically an insult when used in the context of sexualities (most often as a derogatory term for effeminate and/or gay boys and men), has in recent times taken on new meaning. It has been reclaimed as a source of self-empowerment by those who reject the distinct categories of straight, gay, lesbian, and bisexual, and who seek to live alternative sexual identities. As discussed in Chapter 3, *genderqueer* also challenges the rules associated with sex and gender, as transgendered individuals of any sexual identity may claim this term. You might also hear the terms *dyke, butch,* and *femme. Dyke* is synonymous with *lesbian,* although it connotes a masculine or mannish lesbian. Like *queer, dyke* is a word that is used against lesbians as an insult and has been appropriated or reclaimed by lesbians with pride. This means that if you are not a member of the lesbian, gay, or queer communities, you should use these terms with care. *Butch* and *femme* are roles associated with gender that have been adopted by some lesbians, especially in the past. Butch means acting as the masculine partner, and femme means acting in a feminine role. Although today many lesbians avoid these role types because there is little incentive to mimic traditional heterosexual relationships, others enjoy these identities and appropriate them to suit themselves.

Finally, the term *coming out* refers to someone adopting a gay, lesbian, bisexual, trans, or queer identity. Coming out is a psychological process that tends to involve two aspects: first, recognizing and identifying this to oneself, and second, declaring oneself in a "public" (broadly defined) way. In terms of this second aspect, individuals usually come out to affirming members in their own community before they (if ever) face a general public. Some never come out to families or co-workers for fear of rejection, reprisals, and retaliation. For some, coming out means becoming part of an identifiable political community; for others, it means functioning for the most part as something of an outsider in a straight world. The phrase *in the closet* means not being out at all. In the closet can imply that a person understands her-/himself to be lesbian or gay but is not out to others. It can also imply that a person is in denial about her/his own sexuality and is not comfortable claiming a nonheterosexual identity.

THE POLITICS OF SEXUALITY

The term *politics* used here implies issues associated with the distribution of power in sexual relationships. There are politics in sexual relationships because they occur in the context of a society that assigns power based on gender and other systems of inequality and privilege. As discussed in Chapter 1, the personal is political: Issues and problems taken as personal or idiosyncratic within sexuality or relationships generally have broader social, political, and economic causes and consequences.

When people get together romantically, what results is more than the mingling of two idiosyncratic individuals. The politics of this relationship implies that people bring the baggage of their gendered lives and other identities into relationships. We negotiate gender and other identities associated with systems of inequality and privilege that inform sexual scripts and shape our lives through internalized self-schemas. Although much of this baggage is so familiar that it is thoroughly normalized and seen as completely natural, the baggage of differently gendered lives implies power. As many feminists have pointed out, heterosexuality is organized in such a way that the power men have in society gets carried into relationships and can encourage women's subservience, sexually and emotionally. Practically, this might mean that a woman sees herself through the eyes of men, or a particular man, and strives to live up to his image of who she should be. It might mean that a woman feels that men, or again, a particular man, owns or has the right to control her body or sexuality, or that she should be the one to ease the emotional transitions of the household or tend to a man's daily needs—preparing his meals, cleaning his home, washing his clothes, raising his children—while still working outside the home. Even though she might choose this life and enjoy the role she has, feminists would argue that this is still an example of male domination in the private sphere where individual men benefit. They have their emotional and domestic needs filled by women and are left free to work or play at what they want. Of course, their part of the bargain for these services is that they should provide for women economically. This is an arrangement that many women choose rationally in both North America and other parts of the world.

We know that heterosexual relationships are a source of support and strength for many women; it is not heterosexuality that is faulted but the context in which heterosexual coupling takes place. When heterosexual intimacies are grounded in unequal power relationships, it becomes more and more difficult for women and men to love in healthy ways. The politics of sexuality also come into play in lesbian and bisexual relationships. Women come together with the baggage of femininity to work out and often internalized homophobia as well. These relationships also have fewer clear models for successful partnering. An example of this is the "Are we on a date?" syndrome that occurs as two women attempt to deal with the boundaries between being platonic girlfriends and being romantically interested in each other. These relationships also occur in the context of _heteronormativity,_ the way heterosexuality is constructed as the norm. A related concept is *compulsory heterosexuality,* as already

ACTIVIST PROFILE **Emma Goldman**

According to J. Edgar Hoover, she was one of the most dangerous women in America in the early twentieth century. Emma Goldman came to the United States from Russia as a teenager in 1885, but for a Jewish immigrant, America was not the land of opportunity she had envisioned. Rather, she found herself in slums and sweatshops, eking out a living. Goldman had witnessed the slaughter of idealist political anarchists in Russia, and in 1886 she saw the hangings of four Haymarket anarchists who had opposed Chicago's power elite. As a result of these experiences, Goldman was drawn to anarchism and became a revolutionary.

Goldman moved to New York, where she met anarchist Johann Most, who advocated the overthrow of capitalism. Most encouraged Goldman's public speaking, although she eventually began to distance herself from him, recognizing the need to work for practical and specific improvements such as higher wages and shorter working hours. In 1893 she was arrested and imprisoned for encouraging a crowd of unemployed men to take bread if they were starving.

In New York, Goldman also worked as a practical nurse in New York's ghettos where she witnessed the effects of lack of birth control and no access to abortion. She began a campaign to address this problem, and her views eventually influenced Margaret Sanger and Sanger's work to make contraception accessible. Goldman was even arrested for distributing birth control literature.

Goldman was particularly concerned about sexual politics within anarchism. She recognized that a political solution alone would not rectify the unequal relations between the sexes. Rather, she called for a transformation of values, particularly by women themselves—by asserting themselves as persons and not sex commodities, by refusing to give the right over her body to anyone, by refusing to have children unless she wants them.

Her involvement in no conscription leagues and rallies against World War I led to her imprisonment and subsequent deportation to Russia. There she witnessed the Russian Revolution and then saw the corruption of the Bolsheviks as they amassed power. Her experience led her to reassess her earlier approval of violence as a means to social justice. Instead, she argued that violence begets counterrevolution.

Goldman remained active in Europe and continued to exercise influence in the United States. In 1922 *Nation* magazine named her one of the 12 greatest living women. In 1934 she was allowed to lecture in the United States, and in 1936 she went to Spain to participate in the Spanish Revolution. Goldman died in 1940 and was buried in Chicago near the Haymarket martyrs.

LEARNING ACTIVITY   **As the World Turns**

Tune into your favorite soap opera each day for a week. As you watch, record observations about the depictions, roles, and interactions of women and men. If all anyone knew about heterosexual relationships was what she or he saw on the soaps, what would this person believe?

Work with one or two other people in your class to devise an episode of a feminist soap opera. Who would be the characters? What dilemmas would they face? How would they resolve them? What would you call your soap opera? Is feminist soap opera possible? Would anyone watch?

discussed in previous chapters: that heterosexuality is the expected and desirable sexual identity. For example, various institutions support and encourage heterosexual coupling and dating. Schools offer dances and proms, the entertainment industry generally assumes heterosexual dating, and there is a public holiday (Valentine's Day) that celebrates it. Public displays of heterosexual intimacy are seen on the Internet, on billboards, magazine covers, television shows and in the movies.

Finally, there is marriage, an institution that historically has recognized two committed people only if one is a woman and the other a man. Currently, gay marriage is only available in Massachusetts and a case is pending in Iowa. Several states (Vermont, Connecticut, New Jersey, and New Hampshire) have civil union laws that provide same-sex couples with the rights, benefits, and responsibilities of opposite-sex civil marriage. Others (Hawaii, Maine, the District of Columbia, California, Washington, and Oregon provide domestic partnership laws that have similar, although in some cases more limited, impact. The federal government does not recognize these unions and under the U.S. Defense of Marriage Act (DOMA) of 1996, other U.S. states are not obliged to recognize them.

Nonheterosexual couples often encounter obstacles when adopting children, raising their biological children (products of previous heterosexual relationships, planned heterosexual encounters with the goal of conception, or artificial insemination), as well as gaining custody of these children. This is because these sexual identities are often constructed by society as an immoral and abnormal "choice" that could have negative consequences on children. It has generally been assumed by the dominant culture that children of homosexual parents will grow up to be homosexual, although all the evidence shows that this is indeed not the case. Despite research that suggests that lesbians make fine mothers and lesbian couples fine parents, there are strong social imperatives against lesbian child rearing. A related prejudice is the notion that homosexuals abuse or recruit children. These negative and misinformed stereotypes reinforce homophobia and help maintain heterosexism. Research shows overwhelmingly that it is heterosexual males who are the major predators of children. Nonetheless, because of these societal stigmas, lesbians and "queers" encounter many obstacles concerning voluntary parenting, and, in addition, are often not welcome in occupations involving children.

LEARNING ACTIVITY **Heteronormativity: It's Everywhere**

Heterosexism is maintained by the illusion that heterosexuality is the norm. This illusion is partly kept in place by the visibility of heterosexuality and the invisibility of other forms of sexuality. To begin to think about the pervasiveness of heterosexuality, grab a clipboard, pen, and paper and keep a tally.

- Go to a card store and peruse the cards in the "love" and "anniversary" sections. How many depict heterosexual couples? How many depict same-sex couples? What options are there for customers who wish to buy a card for a same-sex partner?
- Look at the advertisements in one of your favorite magazines. How many pictures of heterosexual couples do you find? How many pictures of same-sex couples? If a photo is of a man or woman alone, do you automatically assume the person is heterosexual? Or is that assumption so deep-seated that you don't even think about it at all?
- Watch the commercials during your favorite hour of television. How many images of heterosexual couples do you see? Of same-sex couples?
- Go to the mall or a park and people-watch for an hour. How many heterosexual couples holding hands do you see? How many same-sex couples?

In this way, sexual self-schemas develop in a social context and are framed by the various workings of power in society. This section has emphasized how politics—the distribution of power—influence and shape every aspect of sexual relationships. On the macro (societal) level these politics are often represented in the forms of public debates about sexuality (like gay marriage, reproductive rights, sex education, interpersonal violence) that are also experienced on the individual level. This micro (individual-level) analysis is the topic of the next section of this chapter.

INTIMACIES

Courtship is that period when two people are attracted to each other, develop intimacy, enjoy each other's company, and identify as a couple. In contemporary U.S. society this period usually involves dating, although what "dating" means changes across time and place and is heavily influenced by popular culture and the technologies of the time. Cell phones, for example, have influenced communication in relationships, altering notions of public and private conversations, and encouraging the accessibility of individuals to each other. An essential aspect of courtship and dating is the development of romantic love: a mainstay of our culture and one of the most important mythologies of our time. *Romantic love* is about a couple coming together, sharing the excitement of an erotic relationship, and feeling united with the other in such a way that the other is unique and irreplaceable. The clichés of love abound: Love is blind; love is painful; love means never having to say you're sorry; love

LEARNING ACTIVITY   **It's in the Cards**

Go to a local card shop and browse through the cards in the "love" or "romance" sections. What are their messages about heterosexual relationships? How do cards targeted toward women differ from cards targeted toward men?

Now get creative. Design a feminist romance greeting card. How does it differ from the ones you saw at the card shop? How do you think the recipient will feel about this card? Now, if you're really brave, mail it to the one you love.

conquers all; and so forth. bell hooks comments on this phenomenon in the reading "Romance: Sweet Love." "Gate C22," the poem by Ellen Bass, counters the idea that love happens only for young, "beautiful" people, and shows how expressions of love move us as humans.

Cultural constructions of love would have us believe that romantic love has always been around, but it is possible to trace the history of romantic love in U.S. society as a cultural phenomenon. There is a tight relationship between romantic love as an ideology and consumer culture as an industrial development. Prior to the twentieth century, dating as we know it did not exist. As dating developed after the turn of the twentieth century, it quickly became associated with consuming products and going places. The emerging movie industry glamorized romance and associated it with luxury products; the automobile industry provided those who could afford it with the allure of travel, get-aways, and private intimacy; and dancehalls allowed close contact between men and women in public. Romance became a commodity that could be purchased, and it made great promises. Women were (and still are) encouraged to purchase certain products with the promise of romantic love. Fashion and makeup industries began revolving around the prospect of romantic love, and the norms associated with feminine beauty became tied to glamorous, romantic images. Romantic love came to be seen as women's special domain; women were encouraged to spend enormous emotional energy, time, and money in the pursuit and maintenance of romantic love.

Romantic love is fun; it can be the spice of life and perhaps one of the most entertaining features of women's lives. In particular, it often contrasts starkly with our working lives because romance is associated with leisure, entertainment, and escape. At the same time, however, romantic love and its pursuit have become the means by which women are encouraged to form relationships and the justification for tolerating inequities in interpersonal relationships.

When it comes to sexuality, romantic love plays a large part in feminine sexual scripts. Research suggests that women make sense of sexual encounters in terms of the amount of intimacy experienced; love becomes a rationale for sex. If I am in love, women often reason, sex is okay. Men more easily accept sex for its own sake, with no emotional strings necessarily attached. In this way, sexual scripts for men have involved more of an *instrumental* (sex for its own sake) approach, whereas for women it tends to be more *expressive* (sex involving emotional attachments). There is evidence to suggest that women are moving in the direction of sex as an end in itself without the normative constraints of an emotional relationship. By and large, however, women are still more likely than men to engage in sex as an act of love. Many scholars suggest that romance is one of the key ways that sexism is maintained in society.

As romantic relationships develop, individuals may become physically intimate and sexually active. These sexual practices can include kissing, hugging, petting, snuggling, caressing, oral sex (oral stimulation of genital area), penis in vagina sex, and anal sex (sexual stimulation of the anus with fingers, penis, or other object). Note how "foreplay" (in this case meaning heterosexual behaviors before "the act" of vaginal penetration) is often not defined as "sex," although, ironically, "foreplay" often is expressed as the sexual activity heterosexual women most enjoy. Lesbians do many of the same things as straight couples, although there is no penis-vagina sex. Some women, straight and lesbian, use dildos (penis-shaped objects that can be inserted into a bodily opening) when they are having sex or during masturbation (sexual self-stimulation), and some straight women use dildos to penetrate male partners during sexual intercourse.

In heterosexual relationships, sexual scripts tend to encourage men to be sexual initiators and sexually more dominant. Although this is not always the case, women who do initiate sex often run the risk of being labeled with terms that are synonymous with *slut*. Having one person in the relationship more sexually assertive and the other more passive is different from sado-masochistic sexual practices (S and M) where one person takes a domineering role and the other becomes dominated. There are both heterosexuals and homosexuals who enjoy sado-masochistic practices. Although usually consensual, S and M can also be coercive, in which case it functions as a form of violence.

LEARNING ACTIVITY **Cybersex**

The growth of technology has created a new form for sexual expression: cybersex. You can create a persona, meet someone online, and have cybersex—with no risk of disease, no commitment, no regrets in the morning. Right? Maybe, but maybe not. On the one hand, cybersex does present an opportunity for a different kind of sexual exploration. On the other, cybersex may raise real problems of isolation, harassment, addiction, and infidelity. Spend a little time surfing the Web for information about cybersex. Then make a list of the pros and cons. How might cybersex be different for women and men? What role does gender play in cybersex? What role does race play? How does sexual identity come into play? How do you think feminists might evaluate cybersex? Would they see it as potentially liberating for women? Or might it reinforce male sexual dominance?

Consider organizing a faculty panel to talk about these issues on your campus. Be sure to include a variety of disciplinary perspectives—women's studies, sociology, psychology, ethnic studies, philosophy, communication, computer science, religion, anthropology, disability studies.

HISTORICAL MOMENT **The Faked Orgasm**

From "Venus Observed" by Ruth Davis in *Women: A Journal of Liberation,* 1972, Davis, CA.

In the early days of the second wave of the Women's Movement, women gathered in small consciousness-raising groups to talk about their experiences as women, and, of course, sooner or later, the conversation turned to sex. What surprised most women as they began to talk openly was that they were not the only ones ever to fake orgasm. While the sexual revolution was rolling on for men, opening greater and greater access to sexual exploits with lots of women, women were finding themselves continuing to fall into the role prescribed by their gender—pleasing men sexually even when they themselves were not being satisfied. But as the Women's Movement began to have an impact, women came to expect to be equal partners in the sexual revolution . . . and that meant no longer faking orgasms.

In 1968 Anne Koedt wrote "The Myth of the Vaginal Orgasm," denouncing Freud's construction of the vaginal orgasm as the truly mature sexual response and denigrating the clitoral orgasm as "infantile." She argued that by marginalizing the clitoris, Freud and other doctors and scientists had controlled women's sexuality and had made women feel sexually inadequate for not achieving vaginal orgasm. Soon, the "faked orgasm" became a metaphor for women's sexual exploitation.

And feminists offered a variety of solutions, from sex toys to celibacy. In 1970, Shulamith Firestone argued that sex, not social class, was the root of all oppression. In *The Dialectic of Sex,* she argued that reproductive technologies should be pursued to deliver women from the tyranny of their biology.

Germaine Greer, author of *The Female Eunuch,* contended that all women should become sexually liberated, and she advocated a strike, the withdrawal of women from sexual labor. She said that women should have the same sexual freedom as men and, if need be, should use men for sexual pleasure.

The debate about sexuality swirled among feminists through the 70s, encompassing issues ranging from pornography to rape, abortion to prostitution. And while the question of the dangers and/or pleasures of sex remained an open one, the raising of the question itself had made an important mark on the consciousness of American women.

Source: Ruth Rosen, *The World Split Open* (New York: Viking, 2000).

Emotional intimacy can be defined as sharing aspects of the self with others with the goal of mutual understanding. Intimacy can sometimes be a source of conflict in heterosexual relationships because women tend to be more skilled at intimacy than men, as the title of John Gray's popular book *Men Are from Mars, Women Are from Venus* suggests. Traditionally, women have been socialized to be emotional and emotionally expressive, and men have been socialized to put their energy into shaping culture and society and to be more reserved about interpersonal emotional issues.

Some scholars have suggested that women are inherently better at connecting with others and that this skill is rooted in early childhood psychosexual development that reflects the fact that girls have a continuous relationship and identification with a maternal figure, unlike boys, who have to break from the mother to identify with the masculine. Others have focused on the social context of childhood skill acquisition. They suggest that the interpersonal skills girls learn at an early age are a result of social learning. Certainly these skills are useful for women in terms of intimacy generally, and in terms of their role as keepers of heterosexual relationships in particular. For example, girls are more likely to play games that involve communication: talking and listening, as well as taking the role of the other through imaginary role-playing games. Boys, on the other hand, are more likely to play rule-bound games where the "rights" and "wrongs" of the game are predetermined rather than negotiated. As a result, girls learn to notice and are trained to be perceptive. They learn to be sensitive of others' feelings, and become more willing to do emotional work. Boys are often raised to repress and deny their inner thoughts and ignore their fears. Often they are taught that feelings are feminine or are for sissies. Girls become more comfortable with intimacy, and boys learn to shy away from it because intimacy is often seen as synonymous with weakness. Boys learn to camouflage feelings under a veneer of calm and rationality because fears are not manly. Importantly, as boys grow up they learn to rely on women to take care of their emotional needs, and girls learn that this request is part of being a woman.

Because emotional intimacy is about self-disclosure and revealing oneself to others, when people are intimate with each other, they open themselves to vulnerability. In the process of becoming intimate, one person shares feelings and information about her-/himself, and then the other person (if that person wants to maintain and develop intimacy) responds by sharing too. In turn each gives away little pieces of her-/himself, and, in return, mutual trust, understanding, and friendship develop. Given the baggage of gender, however, what can happen is that one person does more of the giving away, and the other reveals less; one opens up to being vulnerable, and the other maintains personal power. The first person also takes on the role of helping the other share, drawing that person out, translating ordinary messages for their hidden emotional meanings, and investing greater amounts of energy into interpersonal communication. The first person has taken the role prescribed by femininity and the latter the role that masculinity endorses. The important point here is that intimacy is about power. Men who take on masculine scripts tend to be less able to open themselves up because of anxiety associated with being vulnerable and potentially losing personal power.

Central in understanding masculine sexual scripts and issues around emotional intimacy is the mandate against homosexuality. Because boys and men may play

Copyright © 1992 by Nicole Hollander. Used by permission of Nicole Hollander.

rough and work closely together—touching each other physically in sports and other masculine pursuits—there are lots of opportunities for *homoeroticism* (arousal of sexual feelings through contact with people of the same sex). In response to this, strong norms against homosexuality regulate masculine behavior—norms fed by homophobia and enforced by such institutions as education, sports, media, family, the military, and the state. These norms discourage men from showing affection with each other and thus discourage intimacy between men. As an aside, they also encourage male bonding where women may function as objects in order for men to assert sexual potency as "real" heterosexuals. Examples of this include women as entertainment for various kinds of stag parties, women as pinups in places where men live and/or work together, and, in the extreme, gang rape. Homophobia serves to keep women apart too, of course. In particular, women are encouraged to give up the love of other women in order to gain the approval of men. However, compared with men, women in the United States tend to have more opportunities for intimacies between friends. This is also demonstrated in language about friendships: Women friends call each other "girlfriend" with no sexual innuendo, while men tend not to call their platonic male friends "boyfriend."

A key aspect of intimacy, and thus sexuality, is interpersonal communication. Again, the ways we communicate in relationships have a lot to do with gender; these different styles help to maintain gender differences in status and power. Feminine and masculine speech varies in the following ways: First, in terms of speech patterns,

IDEAS FOR ACTIVISM

- Work with various women's groups on your campus to develop, publish, and distribute a "Check Up on Your Relationship" brochure. This brochure should contain a checklist of signs for emotional/physical/sexual abuse and resources to get help.
- Organize and present a forum on healthy dating practices.
- Organize a clothes drive for your local women's shelter.
- Research gay rights, such as protection against discrimination in employment or housing, domestic partner benefits, or hate crimes legislation in your city or state. If you find that gay, lesbian, bisexual, or transgender people in your area do not enjoy full civil rights, write your government officials to encourage them to enact policies providing civil rights for queer people.
- Organize a National Coming Out Day celebration on your campus.
- Organize an event on your campus in recognition of World AIDS Day, which is December 1.
- Become a member of the Human Rights Campaign. For more information see *www.hrc.org.*

feminine speech is more polite, less profane, and uses more standard forms. More fillers like "uhm," hedges like "sort of" and "I guess," and intensifiers like "really" and "very" are used. In addition, feminine speech involves tag questions on statements like "It's hot today, isn't it?" and often turns an imperative into a question: "Would you mind opening the door?" rather than "Open the door!" All these forms of speaking are less authoritative. Note that although women in U.S. society are more likely to use feminine speech and men to use masculine speech, anyone can learn these speech patterns. Indeed, women are often trained in masculine speech to function effectively in authority positions or careers in which an assertive communication style is necessary or most productive.

Second, feminine speech tends to use different intonations with a higher pitch that is recognized as less credible and assertive than a lower pitch. This speech has more emotional affect and is more likely to end with a raised pitch that sounds like a question and gives a hesitant quality to speaking.

Third, feminine speech differs from masculine speech in that the latter involves more direct interruptions of other speakers. Listening to real people talking, we find that although men and women interrupt at about the same rate in same-sex conversations (women interrupting women, and men interrupting men), in mixed groups men interrupt other speakers more than women do, and men are more likely to change the subject in the process, whereas women tend to interrupt to add to the story with their own experiences and thoughts. Although there are cultural differences around interruptions, it is clear that who interrupts and who gets interrupted is about power.

Fourth, feminine speech patterns involve more confirmation and reinforcement, such as "Yes, go on" or "I hear you" or "uh-hum." Examples of nonverbal confirmation of the speaker include leaning forward, eye contact, and nodding.

Finally, feminine speech and masculine speech fulfill different functions. Feminine speech tends to work toward maintaining relationships, developing rapport, avoiding conflict, and maintaining cooperation. Masculine speech, on the other hand, is more likely oriented toward attracting and maintaining an audience, asserting power and dominance, and giving information. Given these gendered differences in communication, it is easy to see how problems might arise in interpersonal interaction generally and in sexual relationships in particular, and how these issues are related to the give-and-take of interpersonal power.

In this way, sexual intimacy is as much about sexual scripts taught by society as it is about physiology. Sexuality is wound up with our understandings of gender, and these norms channel our sense of ourselves as sexual persons. These social constructs encourage us to feel desire and enjoy certain sexual practices and relationships, and they guide the meanings we associate with our experiences.

Sexual Desire and Gender

Pepper Schwartz and Virginia Rutter (1998)

The gender of the person you desire is a serious matter seemingly fundamental to the whole business of romance. And it isn't simply a matter of whether someone is male or female; how well the person fulfills a lover's expectations of masculinity or femininity is of great consequence. . . .

. . . Although sex is experienced as one of the most basic and biological of activities, in human beings it is profoundly affected by things other than the body's urges. Who we're attracted to and what we find sexually satisfying is not just a matter of the genital equipment we're born with. . . .

Before we delve into the whys and wherefores of sex, we need to come to an understanding about what sex is. This is not as easy a task as it may seem, because sex has a number of dimensions.

On one level, sex can be regarded as having both a biological and a social context. The biological (and physiological) refers to how people use their genital equipment to reproduce. In addition, as simple as it seems, bodies make the experience of sexual pleasure available—whether the pleasure involves other bodies or just one's own body and mind. It should be obvious, however, that people engage in sex even when they do not intend to reproduce. They have sex for fun, as a way to communicate their feelings to each other, as a way to satisfy their ego, and for any number of other reasons relating to the way they see themselves and interact with others.

Another dimension of sex involves both what we do and how we think about it. *Sexual behavior* refers to the sexual acts that people engage in. These acts involve not only petting and intercourse but also seduction and courtship. Sexual behavior also involves the things people do alone for pleasure and stimulation and the things they

do with other people. *Sexual desire,* on the other hand, is the motivation to engage in sexual acts. It relates to what turns people on. A person's *sexuality* consists of both behavior and desire.

The most significant dimension of sexuality is *gender.* Gender relates both to the biological and social contexts of sexual behavior and desire. People tend to believe they know whether someone is a man or a woman not because we do a physical examination and determine that the person is biologically male or biologically female. Instead, we notice whether a person is masculine or feminine. Gender is a social characteristic of individuals in our society that is only sometimes consistent with biological sex. Thus, animals, like people, tend to be identified as male and female in accordance with the reproductive function, but only people are described by their gender, as a man or a woman.

When we say something is *gendered* we mean that social processes have determined what is appropriately masculine and feminine and that gender has thereby become integral to the definition of the phenomenon. For example, marriage is a gendered institution: The definition of marriage involves a masculine part (husband) and a feminine part (wife). Gendered phenomena, like marriage, tend to appear "naturally" so. But as recent debates about same-sex marriage underscore, the role of gender in marriage is the product of social processes and beliefs about men, women, and marriage. In examining how gender influences sexuality, moreover, you will see that gender rarely operates alone: Class, culture, race, and individual differences also combine to influence sexuality.

. . .

DESIRE: ATTRACTION AND AROUSAL

The most salient fact about sex is that nearly everybody is interested in it. Most people like to have sex, and they talk about it, hear about it, and think about it. But some people are obsessed with sex and willing to have sex with anyone or anything. Others are aroused only by particular conditions and hold exacting criteria. For example, some people will have sex only if they are positive that they are in love, that their partner loves them, and that the act is sanctified by marriage. Others view sex as not much different from eating a sandwich. They neither love nor hate the sandwich; they are merely hungry, and they want something to satisfy that hunger. What we are talking about here are differences of desire. As you have undoubtedly noticed, people differ in what they find attractive, and they are also physically aroused by different things.

Many people assume that differences in sexual desire have a lot to do with whether a person is female or male. In large representative surveys about sexual behavior, the men as a group inevitably report more frequent sex, with more partners, and in more diverse ways than the women as a group do. . . . First, we should consider the approaches we might use to interpret it. Many observers argue that when it comes to sex, men and women have fundamentally different biological wiring. Others use the evidence to argue that culture has produced marked sexual differences among men and women. We believe, however, that it is hard to tease apart biological differences and social differences. As soon as a baby enters the world, it receives messages about gender and sexuality. In the United States, for example, disposable diapers come adorned in pink for girls and blue for boys. In case people aren't sure whether to treat the baby as masculine or feminine in its first years of life, the diaper signals them. The assumption is that girl babies really are different from boy babies and the difference ought to be displayed. This different treatment continues throughout life, and therefore a sex difference at birth becomes amplified into gender differences as people mature.

Gendered experiences have a great deal of influence on sexual desire. As a boy enters adolescence, he hears jokes about boys' uncontainable desire. Girls are told the same thing and told that their job is to resist. These gender messages have power not only over attitudes and behavior (such as whether a person grows up to prefer sex with a lover rather than a stranger) but also over physical and biological experience. For example, a girl may be discouraged from vigorous competitive activity, which will subsequently influence how she develops physically, how she feels about her body, and even how she relates to the adrenaline rush associated with physical competition. Hypothetically, a person who is accustomed to adrenaline responses experiences sexual attraction differently from one who is not.

What follows are three "competing" explanations of differences in sexual desire between men and women: a biological explanation, sociobiological and evolutionary psychological explanations, and an explanation that acknowledges the social construction of sexuality. We call these competing approaches because each tends to be presented as a complete explanation in itself, to the exclusion of other explanations. Our goal, however, is to provide a clearer picture of how "nature" and "nurture" are intertwined in the production of sexualities.

THE BIOLOGY OF DESIRE: NATURE'S EXPLANATION

Biology is admittedly a critical factor in sexuality. Few human beings fall in love with fish or sexualize trees. Humans are designed to respond to other humans. And human activity is, to some extent, organized by the physical equipment humans are born with. Imagine if people had fins instead of arms or laid eggs instead of fertilizing them during intercourse. Romance would look quite different.

Although biology seems to be a constant (i.e., a component of sex that is fixed and unchanging), the social world tends to mold biology as much as biology shapes humans' sexuality. Each society has its own rules for sex. Therefore, how people experience their biology varies widely. In some societies, women act intensely aroused and active during sex; in others, they have no concept of orgasm. In fact, women in some settings, when told about orgasm, do not even believe it exists, as anthropologists discovered in some parts of Nepal. Clearly, culture—not biology—is at work, because we know that orgasm is physically possible, barring damage to or destruction of the sex organs. Even ejaculation is culturally dictated. In some countries, it is considered healthy to ejaculate early and often; in others, men are told to conserve semen and ejaculate as rarely as possible. The biological capacity may not be so different, but the way bodies behave during sex varies according to social beliefs.

Sometimes the dictates of culture are so rigid and powerful that the so-called laws of nature can be overridden. Infertility treatment provides an example: For couples who cannot produce children "naturally," a several-billion-dollar industry has provided technology that can, in a small proportion of cases, overcome this biological problem. Recently, in California, a child was born to a 63-year-old woman who had been implanted with fertilized eggs. The cultural emphasis on reproduction and parenthood, in this case, overrode the biological incapacity to produce children. Nevertheless, some researchers have focused on the biological foundations of sexual desire. They have examined the endocrine system and hormones, brain structure, and genetics. Others have observed the mechanisms of arousal. What all biological research on sex has in common is the proposition that many so-called sexual choices are not choices at all but are dictated by the body. A prominent example comes from the study of the biological origins of homosexuality. However, contradictory and debatable findings make conclusions difficult.

The Influence of Hormones

Biological explanations of sexual desire concentrate on the role of hormones. *Testosterone,* sometimes called the male sex hormone, appears to be the most important hormone for sexual function.

Numerous research studies identify testosterone as an enabler for male sexual arousal. But we cannot predict a man's sexual tastes, desires, or behavior by measuring his testosterone. Although a low level of testosterone in men is sometimes associated with lower sexual desire, this is not predictably the case. Furthermore, testosterone level does not always influence sexual performance. Indeed, testosterone is being experimented with as a male contraceptive, thus demonstrating that desire and the biological goal of reproduction need not be linked to sexual desire.

Testosterone has also been implicated in nonsexual behaviors, such as aggression. Furthermore, male aggression sometimes crosses into male sexuality, generating sexual violence. But recent research on testosterone and aggression in men has turned the testosterone-aggression connection on its head: Low levels of testosterone have been associated with aggression, and higher levels have been associated with calmness, happiness, and friendliness.

Testosterone is also found in women, although at levels as little as one-fifth those of men. This discrepancy in levels of testosterone has incorrectly been used as evidence for "natural" gender differences in sex drives. However, women's testosterone receptors are simply more sensitive than men's to smaller amounts of testosterone.

Estrogen, which is associated with the menstrual cycle, is known as the female hormone. Like testosterone, however, estrogen is found in both women and men. Furthermore, estrogen may be the more influential hormone in human aggression. In animal research, male mice whose ability to respond to estrogen had been bred out of them lost much of their natural aggressiveness. Researchers are currently investigating the association between adolescents' moodiness and their levels of estrogen. Of course, many social factors—such as changes in parental behavior toward their teenagers—help explain moodiness among adolescents.

Some biological evidence indicates that a woman's sexual desire may be linked to the impact of hormones as levels change during her reproductive cycle. (No evidence shows men's sexual desire to be cyclical.) Some scientists believe that women's sexual arousal is linked to the fertile portion of their cycle. They believe that sexual interest in women is best explained as the product of thousands of years of natural selection. Natural selection would favor for survival those women who are sexually aroused during ovulation (the time women are most likely to become pregnant). These women would be reproductively successful and therefore pass on to their children the propensity for arousal during ovulation. Neat though this theory is, it doesn't fit all the data. Other research finds no evidence of increased sexual interest among women who are ovulating. Instead, the evidence suggests that women's sexual interest actually tends to peak well before ovulation. Still other evidence finds no variation in sexual desire or sexual activity in connection to the menstrual cycle.

. . . [T]estosterone and estrogen are not clearly linked to either men's desire or women's. Research shows a complicated relationship between hormones and sexuality. Hormonal fluctuations may not be the central cause of sexual behavior or any social acts; instead, social circumstances may be the cause of hormonal fluctuation. A famous series of experiments makes the point. One animal experiment took a dominant rhesus monkey out of his environment and measured [his] testosterone level. It was very high, suggesting that he had reached the top of the monkey heap by being hormonally superior. Then the monkey was placed among even bigger, more dominant monkeys than himself. When his testosterone was remeasured, it was much lower. One interpretation is that social hierarchy had influenced the monkey's biological barometer. His testosterone level had adjusted to his social status. In this case, the social environment shaped physiology.

. . .

SOCIOBIOLOGY AND EVOLUTIONARY PSYCHOLOGY

The past few decades of research on sexuality have produced a new school of human behavior—*sociobiology* and a related discipline, *evolutionary*

psychology—that explains most gender differences as strategies of sexual reproduction. According to evolutionary psychologist David Buss, "evolutionary psychologists predict that the sexes will differ in precisely those domains in which women and men have faced different sorts of adaptive problems." By "those domains," Buss refers to reproduction, which is the only human function that depends on a biological difference between men and women.

The key assumption of sociobiological/evolutionary theory is that humans have an innate, genetically triggered impulse to pass on their genetic material through successful reproduction: This impulse is called *reproductive fitness*. The human species, like other species that sociobiologists study, achieves immortality by having children who live to the age of reproductive maturity and produce children themselves. Sociobiologists and evolutionary psychologists seek to demonstrate that almost all male and female behavior, and especially sexuality, is influenced by this one simple but powerful proposition.

Sociobiologists start at the species level. Species are divided into *r* and *K reproductive categories*. Those with *r* strategies obtain immortality by mass production of eggs and sperm. The *r* species is best illustrated by fish. The female manufactures thousands of eggs, the male squirts millions of sperm over them, and that is the extent of parenting. According to this theory, the male and female fish need not pair up to nurture their offspring. Although thousands of fertilized fish eggs are consumed by predators, only a small proportion of the massive quantity of fertilized eggs must survive for the species to continue. In the *r* species, parents need not stay together for the sake of the kids.

In contrast, humans are a *K*-strategy species, which has a greater investment in each fertilized egg. Human females and most female mammals have very few eggs, especially compared to fish. Moreover, offspring take a long time to mature in the mother's womb and are quite helpless when they are born, with no independent survival ability. Human babies need years of supervision before they are independent. Thus, if a woman wants to pass on her genes (or at least the half her child will inherit from her), she must take good care of her dependent child. The baby is a scarce resource. Even if a woman is pregnant from sexual maturation until menopause, the number of children she can produce is quite limited. This limitation was particularly true thousands of years ago. Before medical advances of the nineteenth and twentieth centuries, women were highly unlikely to live to the age of menopause. Complications from childbirth commonly caused women to die in their 20s or 30s. Where the food supply was scarce, women were less likely to be successful at conceiving, further reducing the possibility of generating offspring.

Sociobiologists and evolutionary psychologists say that men inseminate, women incubate. The human female's reproductive constraints (usually one child at a time, not so many children over a life cycle, and a helpless infant for a long period of time) shape most of women's sexual and emotional approaches to men and mating. According to their theory, women have good reason to be more selective than men about potential mates. They want to find a man who will stick around and continue to provide resources and protection to this child at least until the child has a good chance of survival. Furthermore, because a woman needs to create an incentive for a man to remain with her, females have developed more sophisticated sexual and emotional skills specifically geared toward creating male loyalty and commitment to their mutual offspring.

Sociobiologists and evolutionary psychologists say that differences in reproductive capacity and strategy also shape sexual desire. Buss asserts that reproductive strategies form most of the categories of desire: Older men generally pick younger women because they are more fertile; younger women seek older men who have more status, power, and resources (a cultural practice known as *hypergamy*) because such men can provide for their children. Furthermore, health and reproductive capacity make youth generally sexier, and even certain shapes of women's bodies (such as an "ideal" hip-to-waist ratio epitomized by an hourglass figure, which correlate with ability to readily reproduce), are widely preferred—

despite varying standards of beauty across cultures. Likewise, men who have demonstrated their fertility by producing children are more sought after than men who have not.

According to evolutionary psychologists, men's tastes for recreational sex, unambivalent lust, and a variety of partners are consistent with maximizing their production of children. Men's sexual interest is also more easily aroused because sex involves fewer costs to them than to women, and the ability for rapid ejaculation has a reproductive payoff. On the other hand, women's taste for relationship-based intimacy and greater investment in each sexual act is congruent with women's reproductive strategies.

In a field that tends to emphasize male's "natural" influence over reproductive strategies, evolutionary anthropologist Helen Fisher offers a feminist twist. Her study of hundreds of societies shows that divorce, or its informal equivalent, occurs most typically in the third or fourth year of a marriage and then peaks about every four years after that. Fisher hypothesizes that some of the breakups have to do with a woman's attempt to obtain the best genes and best survival chances for her offspring. In both agrarian and hunter-gatherer societies, Fisher explains, women breast-feed their child for three or four years—a practice that is economical and sometimes helps to prevent further pregnancy. At the end of this period, the woman is ready and able to have another child. She reenters the mating marketplace and assesses her options to see if she can improve on her previous mate. If she can get a better guy, she will leave the previous partner and team up with a new one. In Fisher's vision, unlike the traditional sociobiological view . . . , different male and female reproductive strategies do not necessarily imply female sexual passivity and preference for lifelong monogamy.

Sociobiologists and evolutionary psychologists tell a fascinating story of how male and female reproductive differences might shape sexuality. To accept sociobiological arguments, one must accept the premise that most animal and human behavior is driven by the instinct to reproduce and improve the gene pool. Furthermore, a flaw of sociobiology as a theory is that it does not provide a unique account of sexual behavior with the potential to be tested empirically. Furthermore, other social science explanations for the same phenomena are supported by more immediate, close-range evidence.

Consider hypergamy, the practice of women marrying men slightly older and "higher" on the social status ladder than they are. Sociobiologists would say women marry "up" to ensure the most fit provider for their offspring. But hypergamy makes little sense biologically. Younger men have more years of resources to provide, and they have somewhat more sexual resources. Empirically, however, hypergamy is fact. It is also a fact that men, overall and in nearly every subculture, have access to more rewards and status than women do. Furthermore, reams of imagery—in movies, advertising, novels—promote the appeal of older, more resourceful men. Why not, when older, more resourceful men are generating the images? Social practice, in this case, overrides what sociobiologists consider the biological imperative.

THE SOCIAL ORIGINS OF DESIRE

Your own experience should indicate that biology and genetics alone do not shape human sexuality. From the moment you entered the world, cues from the environment were telling you which desires and behaviors were "normal" and which were not. The result is that people who grow up in different circumstances tend to have different sexualities. Who has not had their sexual behavior influenced by their parents' or guardians' explicit or implicit rules? You may break the rules or follow them, but you can't forget them. . . .

The Social Construction of Sexuality

Social constructionists believe that cues from the environment shape human beings from the moment they enter the world. The sexual customs, values, and expectations of a culture, passed on to the young through teaching and by example, exert a powerful influence over individuals. When Fletcher Christian sailed into Tahiti in Charles

Nordhoff's 1932 account, *Mutiny on the Bounty,* he and the rest of his nineteenth-century English crew were surprised at how sexually available, playful, guilt free, and amorous the Tahitian women were. Free from the Judeo-Christian precepts and straight-laced customs that inhibited English society, the women and girls of Tahiti regarded their sexuality joyfully and without shame. The English men were delighted and, small wonder, refused to leave the island. Such women did not exist in their own society. The women back in England had been socialized within their Victorian culture to be modest, scared of sex, protective of their reputation, and threatened by physical pleasure. As a result, they were unavailable before marriage and did not feel free to indulge in a whole lot of fun after it. The source of the difference was not physiological differences between Tahitian and English women; it was sexual *socialization* or the upbringing that they received within their differing families and cultures.

If we look back at the Victorian, nineteenth-century England that Nordhoff refers to, we can identify *social structures* that influenced the norms of women's and men's sexuality. A burgeoning, new, urban middle class created separate spheres in the division of family labor. Instead of sharing home and farm or small business, the tasks of adults in families became specialized: Men went out to earn money, women stayed home to raise children and take care of the home. Although this division of labor was not the norm in all classes and ethnicities in England at the time, the image of middle-class femininity and masculinity became pervasive. The new division of labor increased women's economic dependence on men, which further curbed women's sexual license but not men's. When gender organizes one aspect of life—such as men's and women's position in the economy—it also organizes other aspects of life, including sex.

In a heterogeneous and individualistic culture like North America, sexual socialization is complex. A society creates an "ideal" sexuality, but different families and subcultures have their own values. For example, even though contemporary society at large may now accept premarital sexuality, a given family may lay down the law: Sex before marriage is against the family's religion and an offense against God's teaching. A teenager who grows up in such a household may suppress feelings of sexual arousal or channel them into outlets that are more acceptable to the family. Or the teenager may react against her or his background, reject parental and community opinion, and search for what she or he perceives to be a more "authentic" self. Variables like birth order or observations of a sibling's social and sexual expression can also influence a person's development.

As important as family and social background are, so are individual differences in response to that background. In the abstract, people raised to celebrate their sexuality must surely have a different approach to enjoying their bodies than those who are taught that their bodies will betray them and are a venal part of human nature. Yet whether or not a person is raised to be at ease with physicality does not always help predict adult sexual behavior. Sexual sybarites and libertines may have grown up in sexually repressive environments, as did pop culture icon and Catholic-raised Madonna. Sometimes individuals whose families promoted sex education and free personal expression are content with minimal sexual expression.

. . .

To summarize, social constructionists believe that a society influences sexual behavior through its norms. Some norms are explicit, such as laws against adult sexual activity with minors. Others are implicit, such as norms of fidelity and parental responsibility. In a stable, homogeneous society, it is relatively easy to understand such rules. But in a changing, complex society like the United States, the rules may be in flux or indistinct. Perhaps this ambiguity is what makes some issues of sexuality so controversial today.

AN INTEGRATIVE PERSPECTIVE ON GENDER AND SEXUALITY

Social constructionist explanations of contemporary sexual patterns are typically pitted against the biology of desire and the evolutionary understanding of biological adaptations. Some social constructionists believe there is no inflexible biological reality; everything we regard as either female or male sexuality is culturally imposed. In contrast, *essentialists*—those who take a biological, sociobiological, or evolutionary point of view—believe people's sexual desires and orientations are innate and hard-wired and that social impact is minimal. Gender differences follow from reproductive differences. Men inseminate, women incubate. People are born with sexual drives, attractions, and natures that simply play themselves out at the appropriate developmental age. Even if social constraints conspire to make men and women more similar to each other (as in the 1990s, when the sensitive and nurturing new man [was] encouraged to get in touch with his so-called feminine, emotional side), people's essential nature is the same: Man is the hunter, warrior, and trailblazer, and woman is the gatherer, nurturer, and reproducer. To an essentialist, social differences, such as the different earning power of men and women, are the consequence of biological difference. In short, essentialists think the innate differences between women and men are the cause of gendered sexuality; social constructionists think the differences between men and women are the result of gendering sexuality through social processes.

Using either the social constructionist or essentialist approach to the exclusion of the other constrains understanding of sexuality. We believe the evidence shows that gender differences are more plausibly an outcome of social processes than the other way around. But a social constructionist view is most powerful when it takes the essentialist view into account. . . . [W]e describe this view of gender differences in sexual desire as *integrative*. Although people tend to think of sex as primarily a biological function—tab B goes into slot A—biology is only one part of the context of desire. Such sociological factors as family relationships and social structure also influence sex. A complex mix of anatomy, hormones, and the brain provides the basic outline for the range of acts and desires possible, but biology is neither where sexuality begins nor where it ends. Social and biological contexts link to define human sexual possibilities.

The integrative approach follows from a great deal that sexuality researchers have observed. Consider the following example: A research project, conducted over three decades ago, advertised for participants stating that its focus was how physical excitement influences a man's preference for one woman over another. The researchers connected college men to a monitor that allowed them to hear their heartbeats as they looked at photographs of women models. The men were told that they would be able to hear their heartbeat when it surged in response to each photograph. A greater surge would suggest greater physical attraction. The participants were then shown a photograph of a dark-haired woman, then a blonde, then a redhead. Afterward, each man was asked to choose the picture that he would prefer to take home. In each case, the man chose the photograph of the woman who, as he believed from listening to his own speeding heartbeat, had most aroused him. Or at least the man thought he was choosing the woman who had aroused him most. In reality, the men had been listening to a faked heartbeat that was speeded up at random. The men thus actually chose the women whom they believed had aroused them most. In this case, the men's invented attraction was more powerful than their gut response. Their mind (a powerful sexual organ) told them their body was responding to a specific picture. The participants' physiological experience of arousal was eclipsed by the social context. When social circumstances influence sexual tastes, are those tastes real or sincere? Absolutely. The social world is as much a fact in people's lives as the biological world.

Romance: Sweet Love

bell hooks (2000)

Sweet Love say
Where, how and when
What do you want of me? . . .

Yours I am, for You I was born:
What do you want of me? . . .

—*Saint Teresa of Avila*

To return to love, to get the love we always wanted but never had, to have the love we want but are not prepared to give, we seek romantic relationships. We believe these relationships, more than any other, will rescue and redeem us. True love does have the power to redeem but only if we are ready for redemption. Love saves us only if we want to be saved. So many seekers after love are taught in childhood to feel unworthy, that nobody could love them as they really are, and they construct a false self. In adult life they meet people who fall in love with their false self. But this love does not last. At some point, glimpses of the real self emerge and disappointment comes. Rejected by their chosen love, the message received in childhood is confirmed: Nobody could love them as they really are.

Few of us enter romantic relationships able to receive love. We fall into romantic attachments doomed to replay familiar family dramas. Usually we do not know this will happen precisely because we have grown up in a culture that has told us that no matter what we experienced in our childhoods, no matter the pain, sorrow, alienation, emptiness, no matter the extent of our dehumanization, romantic love will be ours. We believe we will meet the girl of our dreams. We believe "someday our prince will come." They show up just as we imagined they would. We wanted the lover to appear, but most of us were not really clear about what we wanted to do with them—what the love was that we wanted to make and how we would make it. We were not ready to open our hearts fully.

In her first book, *The Bluest Eye,* novelist Toni Morrison identifies the idea of romantic love as one "of the most destructive ideas in the history of human thought." Its destructiveness resides in the notion that we come to love with no will and no capacity to choose. This illusion, perpetuated by so much romantic lore, stands in the way of our learning how to love. To sustain our fantasy we substitute romance for love.

When romance is depicted as a project, or so the mass media, especially movies, would have us believe, women are the architects and the planners. Everyone likes to imagine that women are romantics, sentimental about love, that men follow where women lead. Even in nonheterosexual relationships, the paradigms of leader and follower often prevail, with one person assuming the role deemed feminine and another the designated masculine role. No doubt it was someone playing the role of leader who conjured up the notion that we "fall in love," that we lack choice and decision when choosing a partner because when the chemistry is present, when the click is there, it just happens—it overwhelms—it takes control. This way of thinking about love seems to be especially useful for men who are socialized via patriarchal notions of masculinity to be out of touch with what they feel. In the essay "Love and Need," Thomas Merton contends: "The expression to 'fall in love' reflects a peculiar attitude toward love and life itself—a mixture of fear, awe, fascination, and confusion. It implies suspicion, doubt, hesitation in the presence of something unavoidable, yet not fully reliable." If you do not know what you feel, then it is difficult to choose love; it is better to fall. Then you do not have to be responsible for your actions.

Even though psychoanalysts, from Fromm writing in the fifties to Peck in the present day, critique the idea that we fall in love, we continue to invest in the fantasy of effortless union. We continue to believe we are swept away, caught up in the rapture, that we lack choice and will. In *The Art of Loving,* Fromm repeatedly talks about love as action, "essentially an act of will." He writes: "To love somebody is not just a strong feeling—it is a decision, it is a judgment, it is a promise. If love were only a feeling, there would be no basis for the promise to love each other forever. A feeling comes and it may go." Peck builds upon Fromm's definition when he describes love as the will to nurture one's own or another's spiritual growth, adding: "The desire to love is not itself love. Love is as love does. Love is an act of will—namely, both an intention and action. Will also implies choice. We do not have to love. We choose to love." Despite these brilliant insights and the wise counsel they offer, most people remain reluctant to embrace the idea that it is more genuine, more real, to think of choosing to love rather than falling in love.

Describing our romantic longings in *Life Preservers,* therapist Harriet Lerner shares that most people want a partner "who is mature and intelligent, loyal and trustworthy, loving and attentive, sensitive and open, kind and nurturant, competent and responsible." No matter the intensity of this desire, she concludes: "Few of us evaluate a prospective partner with the same objectivity and clarity that we might use to select a household appliance or a car." To be capable of critically evaluating a partner we would need to be able to stand back and look critically at ourselves, at our needs, desires, and longings. It was difficult for me to really take out a piece of paper and evaluate myself to see if I was able to give the love I wanted to receive. And even more difficult to make a list of the qualities I wanted to find in a mate. I listed ten items. And then when I applied the list to men I had chosen as potential partners, it was painful to face the discrepancy between what I wanted and what I had chosen to accept. We fear that evaluating our needs and then carefully choosing partners will reveal that there is no one for us to love. Most of us prefer to have a partner who is lacking than no partner at all. What becomes apparent is that we may be more interested in finding a partner than in knowing love.

Time and time again when I talk to individuals about approaching love with will and intentionality, I hear the fear expressed that this will bring an end to romance. This is simply not so. Approaching romantic love from a foundation of care, knowledge, and respect actually intensifies romance. By taking the time to communicate with a potential mate we are no longer trapped by the fear and anxiety underlying romantic interactions that take place without discussion or the sharing of intent and desire. I talked with a woman friend who stated that she had always been extremely fearful of sexual encounters, even when she knew someone well and desired them. Her fear was rooted in a shame she felt about the body, sentiments she had learned in childhood. Previously, her encounters with men had only intensified that shame. Usually men made light of her anxiety. I suggested she might try meeting with the new man in her life over lunch with the set agenda of talking to him about sexual pleasure, their likes and dislikes, their hopes and fears. She reported back that the lunch was incredibly erotic; it laid the groundwork for them to be at ease with each other sexually when they finally reached that stage in their relationship.

Erotic attraction often serves as the catalyst for an intimate connection between two people, but it is not a sign of love. Exciting, pleasurable sex can take place between two people who do not even know each other. Yet the vast majority of males in our society are convinced that their erotic longing indicates who they should, and can, love. Led by their penis, seduced by erotic desire, they often end up in relationships with partners with whom they share no common interests or values. The pressure on men in a patriarchal society to "perform" sexually is so great that men are often so gratified to be with someone with whom they find sexual pleasure that they ignore everything else. They cover up these mistakes by working too much, or finding playmates they like

outside their committed marriage or partnership. It usually takes them a long time to name the lovelessness they may feel. And this recognition usually has to be covered up to protect the sexist insistence that men never admit failure.

Women rarely choose men solely on the basis of erotic connection. While most females acknowledge the importance of sexual pleasure, they recognize that it is not the only ingredient needed to build strong relationships. And let's face it, the sexism of stereotyping women as caregivers makes it acceptable for women to articulate emotional needs. So females are socialized to be more concerned about emotional connection. Women who have only named their erotic hunger in the wake of the permission given by the feminist movement and sexual liberation have always been able to speak their hunger for love. This does not mean that we find the love we long for. Like males, we often settle for lovelessness because we are attracted to other aspects of a partner's makeup. Shared sexual passion can be a sustaining and binding force in a troubled relationship, but it is not the proving ground for love.

This is one of the great sadnesses of life. Too often women, and some men, have their most intense erotic pleasure with partners who wound them in other ways. The intensity of sexual intimacy does not serve as a catalyst for respect, care, trust, understanding, and commitment. Couples who rarely or never have sex can know lifelong love. Sexual pleasure enhances the bonds of love, but they can exist and satisfy when sexual desire is absent. Ultimately, most of us would choose great love over sustained sexual passion if we had to. Luckily we do not have to make this choice because we usually have satisfying erotic pleasure with our loved one.

The best sex and the most satisfying sex are not the same. I have had great sex with men who were intimate terrorists, men who seduce and attract by giving you just what you feel your heart needs then gradually or abruptly withholding it once they have gained your trust. And I have been deeply sexually fulfilled in bonds with loving partners who have had less skill and know-how. Because of sexist socialization, women tend to put sexual satisfaction in its appropriate perspective. We acknowledge its value without allowing it to become the absolute measure of intimate connection. Enlightened women want fulfilling erotic encounters as much as men, but we ultimately prefer erotic satisfaction within a context where there is loving, intimate connection. If men were socialized to desire love as much as they are taught to desire sex, we would see a cultural revolution. As it stands, most men tend to be more concerned about sexual performance and sexual satisfaction than whether they are capable of giving and receiving love.

Even though sex matters, most of us are no more able to articulate sexual needs and longings than we are able to speak our desire for love. Ironically, the presence of life-threatening sexually transmitted diseases has become the reason more couples communicate with each other about erotic behavior. The very people (many of them men) who had heretofore claimed that "too much talk" made things less romantic find that talk does not threaten pleasure at all. It merely changes its nature. Where once knowing nothing was the basis for excitement and erotic intensity, knowing more is now the basis. Lots of people who feared a loss of romantic and/or erotic intensity made this radical change in their thinking and were surprised to find that their previous assumptions that talk killed romance were wrong.

Cultural acceptance of this change shows that we are all capable of shifting our paradigms, the foundational ways of thinking and doing things that become habitual. We are all capable of changing our attitudes about "falling in love." We can acknowledge the "click" we feel when we meet someone new as just that—a mysterious sense of connection that may or may not have anything to do with love. However, it could or could not be the primal connection while simultaneously acknowledging that it will lead us to love. How different things might be if, rather than saying "I think I'm in love," we were saying "I've connected with someone in a way that makes me think I'm on the way to knowing love." Or, if instead of saying "I am in love," we said "I am loving" or "I will love." Our patterns around romantic love

are unlikely to change if we do not change our language.

We are all uncomfortable with the conventional expressions we use to talk about romantic love. All of us feel that these expressions and the thinking behind them are one of the reasons we entered relationships that did not work. In retrospect we see that to a grave extent the way we talked about these bonds foreshadowed what happened in the relationship. I certainly changed the way I talk and think about love in response to the emotional lack I felt within myself and in my relationships. Starting with clear definitions of love, of feeling, intention, and will, I no longer enter relationships with the lack of awareness that leads me to make all bonds the site for repeating old patterns.

Although I have experienced many disappointments in my quest to love and be loved, I still believe in the transformative power of love. Disappointment has not led me to close my heart. However, the more I talk with people around me I find disappointment to be widespread and it does lead many folks to feel profoundly cynical about love. A lot of people simply think we make too much of love. Our culture may make much of love as compelling fantasy or myth, but it does not make much of the art of loving. Our disappointment about love is directed at romantic love. We fail at romantic love when we have not learned the art of loving. It's as simple as that. Often we confuse perfect passion with perfect love. A perfect passion happens when we meet someone who appears to have everything we have wanted to find in a partner. I say "appears" because the intensity of our connection usually blinds us. We see what we want to see. In *Soul Mates,* Thomas Moore contends that the enchantment of romantic illusion has its place and that "the soul thrives on ephemeral fantasies." While perfect passion provides us with its own particular pleasure and danger, for those of us seeking perfect love it can only ever be a preliminary stage in the process.

We can only move from perfect passion to perfect love when the illusions pass and we are able to use the energy and intensity generated by intense, overwhelming, erotic bonding to heighten self-discovery. Perfect passions usually end when we awaken from our enchantment and find only that we have been carried away from ourselves. It becomes perfect love when our passion gives us the courage to face reality, to embrace our true selves. Acknowledging this meaningful link between perfect passion and perfect love from the onset of a relationship can be the necessary inspiration that empowers us to choose love. When we love by intention and will, by showing care, respect, knowledge, and responsibility, our love satisfies. Individuals who want to believe that there is no fulfillment in love, that true love does not exist, cling to these assumptions because this despair is actually easier to face than the reality that love is a real fact of life but is absent from their lives.

R E A D I N G **28**

What Is Bisexuality?

Jennifer Baumgardner (2007)

I have a recurring dream where I'm at a family wedding and I can hear my mother's voice ringing out over the throng, "Jenny's a bi*sex*ual. Jenny's a bi*sex*ual," while I smile wanly. Of course, I want my loved ones to know who I am. The act of admitting who you are not only invites others to do that too, but it also frees you from living a double life—or worse, a vague life. Therefore, no sooner had my lips met another woman's than I wanted my family to be up on my evolution. I hadn't been in New York City for much more than a year when I wrote my mother, in a letter she received the day before Mother's Day, to say that I was *bisexual*. Mother remembers it this way:

> I have always said that I don't care about a gift, I just want a Mother's Day card and I want it to be there on time. But that year you all missed the date and instead I got this letter and no cards. I was a little surprised by your letter, but I wasn't completely bowled over because at Christmastime you girls had been asking me whether *I* had ever wanted to kiss a girl. And when I said, "No," you insisted, "Oh, you must have wanted to at some sleepover or at some point." But I really hadn't.

Contemplating this maternal recollection some years later, I think I had been terrified that my experience might not be common—and I would be marginalized and alone. I recall that I meant the confessional letter to be casual: *This is not a bombshell.* I was committed to setting the tone, and the tone was instructive and confident. I didn't want this to be *that* coming-out story where the girl tells her parents and they are disappointed and kick her out of the house, nor did I want it to be the one where the parents show tearful acceptance and go run the local chapter of PFLAG. I wanted everything to be the same as it was before, just with my girlfriend in the picture. Besides, 90 percent of me believed that my making out with a woman was no big deal and that I should *not* encourage any parental weirdness by asking how they felt, as if I were waiting for approval. But, of course, in a way I *was* waiting for acceptance. Ten percent of me was afraid of my parents' disapproval, as indicated by my writing my mother a letter as if it were 1875 and the telephone hadn't been invented yet.

. . .

Mom's response to my revelation when we finally spoke on Mother's Day was interesting.

"Do you have a problem with your dad?" she asked. It was an old-fashioned notion, which my mother told me later had to do with having never thought about bisexuality before in her life. Then, she said, "Are you rejecting the kind of life I chose?" And, then, as the conversation moved from her to me: "The only bisexual I can think of is . . . Elton John," she said, in a mulling-it-over tone. "And he seems so *unstable.*"

. . .

Mom's other fears I could dispense with confidently. I didn't have a problem with my dad and I didn't disrespect my mother. In a way, the stability of their marriage was part of what made me feel I could eschew a more conventional path. I didn't need to make up for what they hadn't given me. Despite my quick—even pat—answers to Mom's instinctive concerns, I now realize that her real questions were What is bisexuality? What does it mean?

. . .

Webster's dictionary is not so helpful, the first two definitions are essentially "hermaphrodite" and the third is "sexually attracted by both sexes." I Googled *bisexual* and learned from the BiNet Web site that "a bisexual is someone who has the ability to be sexually attracted to men and women." According to Robyn Ochs, the editor of *Getting Bi: Voices of Bisexuals Around the World* and an activist for more than twenty-five years, "a bisexual person has the potential to be sexually and/or romantically attracted to more than one sex, but not necessarily at the same time or to the same extent." A more social definition of bisexuality is provided by bisexual icon Lani Ka'ahumanu, in *The Reader's Companion to U.S. Women's History*: "Bisexuals are a part of as well as apart from heterosexual society and the lesbian and gay community."

Rather than defined, bisexuals have been "treated," as in therapized, since the Victorian Era. No one examined bisexuality—or at least bisexuals—more than Sigmund Freud. Feminists have critiqued Freud's sexism, and feminist relational psychologists have shown that despite Freud's assertions, physical drives aren't simply or exclusively what motivate human beings. Still, when it comes to bisexuality, Freud was there early, and his style—talk therapy—enabled him to learn that sexuality was much more complex than polite company would allow, and that both sexual abuse and sexual "deviance" were very common.

Born May 6, 1856, in Freiberg, Germany, Freud was not just the father of psychoanalysis but also the doting mother of bisexuality. If it's true (as Nietzsche believed) that philosophers tend to write their memoirs in their theories, Freud, the man, was not unfamiliar with the concept of looking both ways himself. His friend Wilhelm Fliess was the object of Freud's most breathless and profound correspondence—and the provocateur of his greatest insights. Freud referred to Fliess as his only Other, his Daemon, and breathlessly declared Fliess's praise "nectar and ambrosia" to him.[1]

. . .

I like to think of Freud as the mother of bisexuality because he nurtured and further developed Fliess's initial seed of bisexuality in his own fertile psyche. The version of bisexuality Fliess described to Freud was closer to what we now understand as androgyny, applied literally. For instance, Fliess said that there is a masculine and a feminine side to each of us, which might explain why some people feel an invitation to be attracted to either sex. Psychosexual health comes from males suppressing the feminine in themselves and females the masculine. Freud then brought the theory of innate bisexuality to the world, elaborating on it for the rest of his life, and denying paternity to Fliess (as the birth mother can do), "forgetting" that it was his friend who first uttered such a potent concept. Any casual student of Freud knows, though, that he believed one never forgets; one represses.

When Fliess first mentioned his theory of bisexuality to Freud in 1898, the great analyst balked at it. Within a few years, though, there was a spate of writing in European intellectual circles on the topic. In typical sexist fashion, bisexuality was used to rationalize why those few women who managed to have a creative or intellectual life were able to do so. Their masculine side was dominant, of course—blessedly, though neurotically, so. Adopting masculine traits was also seen as a way to avoid the feminine role and thus avoid having to be the helpmate rather than the main event. Otto Weininger, one such fashionable theorist, was a young, depressed misogynist and anti-Semitic scholar of Freud's acquaintance who wrote a 1904 book, *Sex and Character,* that imagined bisexuality as men and women fusing to find a perfect "whole." . . .

According to Garber, both Weininger's and Fliess's theories gave primacy to heterosexuality even while identifying masculine and feminine principles in all of us.[2] Fliess saw in Weininger's work a near carbon copy of the theory he had shared only with Freud and that he, Fliess, had wanted to make into an historic book. When Fliess confronted his loose-lipped friend (who had indeed mentioned Fliess's insight to Weininger), Freud had already absorbed how consequential bisexuality was to the study of neurosis and the understanding of "sexuality, repression, and desire."[3] He wrote to Fliess on August 7, 1901, with clueless hubris, "And now, the main thing! As far as I can see, my next work will be called 'Human Bisexuality.' It will go to the root of the problem and say the last word it may be granted me to say—the last and the most profound."[4]

Although Freud never underwent analysis himself—something he felt everyone else needed—he did acknowledge that he had "homosexual" feelings for his former friend and suspected that Fliess's "paranoia" (stemming from the fact that Freud had purloined his best idea) was in fact Fliess's homosexual passion for Sigmund sublimated.[5]

Freud's theories about bisexuality progressed through three phases. The first was a version of Fliess's biological bisexuality: we are all born bisexual, but mature adults repress their homosexual desire and get together with opposite-sex partners. Later, he believed the root of bisexuality was in culture, not biology. Eventually, he described it as the unfixed nature of attraction and sexual identity, alluding to the fluid description of bisexuality (indeed, all sexuality) that most of today's theorists now embrace. Freud ultimately believed that sexuality changes and evolves throughout one's life, imagining that even the

term *bisexuality,* as broad as it's meant to be, is inadequate to describe the drives for sex and love, as well as the deep connections we feel to certain people at certain times.

Freud's most radical legacy is the one that is the least actualized. After years of evolution on the topic, he came to the conclusion that any exclusive monosexual interest—regardless of whether it was hetero- or homosexual—was neurotic. In a sense Freud is saying what second-wave critic Kate Millett said a half century later: "Homosexuality was invented by a straight world dealing with its own bisexuality."[6] By the end of his writings, in 1937, Freud was downright blithe about bisexuality: "Every human being['s] . . . libido is distributed, either in a manifest or a latent fashion, over objects of both sexes."[7]

A decade or so later, Alfred Kinsey took Freud's idea of a distribution of the libido and converted it into the famous Kinsey Scale. Many other experts have pondered bisexuality, from Weininger to Fritz Klein to Robyn Ochs, but Freud's and Kinsey's ideas have had the deepest impact on mainstream culture. The second major codifier of bisexuality, Kinsey was a zoologist and gall wasp specialist who taught at Indiana University in the thirties and forties. Born June 23, 1894, Kinsey was presumably forming his Oedipal complex around the time Freud was learning about bisexuality. When some female co-eds at Indiana asked if their youngish prof would teach a course on marriage and sex, he decided to give it a go.

As Kinsey researched reading materials upon which to base the course, he found that there were enormous holes in what was known about the psychological, physical, and medical understanding of sexuality. He developed a series of 350 questions and began collecting the sexual histories of his students, via face-to-face interviews rather than questionnaires. In doing so, he got their stories, instead of just their labels of sexual identity, and from this data he developed the Kinsey Scale, which rates three elements of sexuality—sexual desires, sexual practices, and sexual identity—on a continuum from 0 (exclusively straight) to 6 (exclusively gay). There are five spots on the scale that represent bisexuality. In the center sits the

"Kinsey 3," representing those equally straight and gay.

Initially, Kinsey's work focused on men, for whom he found that a full 50 percent had had some bisexual experience. In 1948, he published *Sexual Behavior in the Human Male,* which was called the "least-read bestseller" because of its controversial and shockingly explicit content. Five years later, he published *Sexual Behavior in the Human Female,* finally filling the void in sexology. His study of females caused a lot more controversy than the male report, largely because it refuted assumptions about women's frigidity and virginity and demonstrated how common it was for a woman to have had an abortion. Half of the six thousand women who provided him with sexual histories said they weren't virgins when they got married, and 35 percent had had some bisexual experience.

. . .

All of the bisexuality theorists I have come across do what Millett, Freud, and Kinsey (not to mention Margaret Mead and Ani DiFranco) do. They assert that while bisexuality is natural and common perhaps to every individual, we live in a straight world that rewards coupling with the opposite sex and thus also rewards the denial of our more fluid erotic instincts. Feminists—both activists and therapists—built upon that insight, defanging some of Kinsey's and Freud's more sexist assumptions and popularizing the liberating elements of the work of Masters and Johnson.

Anne Koedt was one such popularizer. As a member of the Redstockings, an early and influential feminist group in New York, she helped develop the idea of consciousness-raising among women and organized the first abortion speakouts. Koedt's most significant contribution to us all, though, was to debunk the fact that female pleasure is derived ideally from penetration. In 1968, she began analyzing the writings of Freud, a much-reviled figure for the ways he had dismissed women's complaints of dissatisfaction and abuse as psychological delusions. Koedt also studied the work of Masters and Johnson (published in 1966) whose examination of human sexual response asserted that the female orgasm originated in the clitoris and that women were, by

and large, multi-orgasmic. (Freud had stated that clitoral orgasms existed but were only immature, and that getting pleasure from the clitoris was emulating masculine sexuality. Evolved women, according to Freud, had "vaginal orgasms.") In a few brisk paragraphs and one title that summed it all up—"The Myth of the Vaginal Orgasm"—Koedt's essay reaffirmed Masters and Johnson's "finding." Furthermore, she asserts women's *right* to have orgasms and concludes that there is no such thing as a frigid female, just inept male partners. . . . At the time of Koedt's article, when feminism was new and the media was hungry for their next bold statement, the work of do-it-yourself debunkers such as Koedt traveled fast and far.

Bisexuality, so clearly a major component in human sexuality, was studied again and again—so why does being bisexual remain denied or diminished? In the beginning was the word, and when the word is *bisexual,* you are already screwed. Or, as writer Jenny Weiss put it in *Girlfriends* magazine, "Of all the words for bisexual, the worst is probably bisexual." As a label, *bisexual* sounds pathological, academic, and a little embarrassed—like the identities "stay-at-home mom" and "runner-up." The synonyms that have been coined are far from positive—*fence-sitter, waffler, heartbreaker, disease vector.* The only one that can be construed as complimentary (or at least useful) is AC/DC—which is, after all, an adapter. Meanwhile, the one jaunty nickname, *bi,* sounds sort of half-assed, since *het* isn't used, nor is *homo* by any one other than Archie Bunker and modern-day fag bashers. *Lesbian, gay,* and *straight* are all more substantial terms. They have gravitas.

The term *bisexual* has ended up as the ugly stepchild of *sexuality,* both in name and meaning. Its fate is symptomatic of the bisexual's own lot in life: to be as common as can be, but unacknowledged. The term *lesbian* is derived from the Greek isle of Lesbos, in the northeastern Aegean Sea, where the lyric poet Sappho lived and wrote of her many female liaisons. But Sappho had male lovers as well, so to be accurate, not just *lesbian* (first coined in 1591) but the adjective or noun *Sapphic* should describe bisexuals. The ancient Roman poet Catullus writes of "Lesbia," that she is a woman with so much power over him that he is destroyed.[8] It is safe to assume that Lesbia had that power not as a woman who lived on a separatist commune, but as a woman who engaged with men but was not subservient to them.

Many people who might feasibly be described as bisexual do not choose to describe themselves that way. Not just because it sounds clinical or compromised, but because it sounds limiting. "Unlabelled experience can be strong stuff," writes Elise Mattheson, a self-identified bi from Minneapolis, on her Web site. The zine-maker Sabrina Margarita Alcantara-Tan, who is married and "queer," insists on the term *omnisexual* to indicate her sexuality. She is attracted to transgendered people and gay men, too, and for her, *bisexuality,* as it is currently understood, doesn't convey that scope.[9] Alcantara-Tan's verve in using a more self-made term is appealing. After all, even *lesbian* is a term made up by male sexologists, not women involved in same-sex relationships, according to the historian Lillian Faderman, who traced the history of women's romantic relationships in her book *Odd Girls and Twilight Lovers.* And then there are bisexuals such as Anne Heche, who "fall in love with a person," as she told Barbara Walters, and "don't put a label on it." Or the once-married Sapphic folkie Ani DiFranco, who famously sings, "I've got no criteria for sex or race/ I just want to hear your voice/ I just want to see your face."

The word *bisexual* makes me cringe at times, but saying I'm heterosexual or a lesbian feels inaccurate—regardless of who I am in a relationship with. So, cringing all the while, I use the label. Because of my relationship to the term *feminist,* I have learned that cringing is often a sign of unfinished political business: the label *bi* sounds bad because, at least in some ways, bisexuals are an unliberated, invisible, and disparaged social group.

For many, though, finding a word such as *bisexuality* is at least a start toward being seen and laying claim to an identity. "I can't categorize myself as just being a lesbian; it doesn't tell the whole story," says Natalie, one of the interviewees in *The Bisexual Spouse,* a 1989 book featuring six compelling case studies of spouses who had

drives toward same-sex relationships. "And I've never considered myself to be a straight heterosexual either." Natalie's history is dialectic, a constant conversation between her relationships with men and those with women. The way that our culture has developed, if you take a bisexual woman and remove her life story from the picture, her identity suddenly makes no sense. It appears aberrant or a phase. In her thorough treatise on bisexuality, *Vice Versa: Bisexuality and the Eroticism of Everyday Life,* the Harvard English professor Marjorie Garber underscores the importance of storytelling in understanding bisexuality. She describes Tiresias—the "seer" in classic Greek texts. Tiresias had been both male and female at different times, and had "heterosexual" sex as a woman and as a man. "Tiresias mark[s] the place of a story rather than a body," writes Garber. "It is not any one state or stage of life but the whole life, the whole life 'story.'" Bisexuality, then, is a label that alludes to a life of changes and complexity in the most positive sense. It doesn't imply abnormal flux as opposed to normal fixed identity, but rather a human being's singular physical and emotional evolution.

As a culture, however, we seem to recognize only two homes for love and sex: gay and straight. The general presumption is that the vast majority of people are privileged to be straight, while a proud, growing minority is gay. Barbara Ehrenreich refers to this as the "gay-as-ethnic-group" approach to sexuality. In her May 1993 column in *Time* magazine, she noted that reducing sexuality to simply gay and straight:

> denies the true plasticity of human sexuality and, in so doing, helps heterosexuals evade that which they really fear. And what heterosexuals really fear is not that "they"—an alien subgroup with perverse tastes in bedfellows—are getting an undue share of power and attention, but that "they" might well be us.

. . .

In the face of the jokes and the disbelief in bisexual women's existence and the fact that very few people use the term *bisexual* to describe themselves . . . is the plain fact that many, many women of my generation and those older and younger, while not identifying as lesbian, choose to have sexual and romantic relationships with other women. And these women often end up married, or were once married, or went on to have a boyfriend, or had only girlfriends but simply still felt attracted to men in emotional and sexual ways, too. When you consider how many of these women looked both ways, it seems clear that bisexuality is, in fact, ubiquitous.

The cover of *The Bisexual Spouse* asserts that "there are 25 million bisexual spouses in this country."[10] Meanwhile, the fact that "being bisexual automatically doubles your chance of a date on a Saturday night," as Woody Allen joked, is played out at some matchmaking services. At Spring Street, the successful personals arm of Nerve.com, all those looking for love are asked to specify whether it is a man, a woman, or either that they seek. Thirty-five percent of women in the Nerve.com system are seeking women or either—which corresponds, incidentally, with the percentage of women who reported bisexual experience in the Kinsey interviews—leaving only 65 percent who are full-on straight. A full 19 percent of the women say "either," which is 3 percent more than say they want only women.

Twenty-five percent of those "either" women are ages eighteen to twenty-four, and the percentage of women who want "either" goes up markedly the younger the woman. In my estimation, this is due to the fact that younger women are the daughters of both an active gay rights revolution and of second-wave feminism. They feel more freedom to have same-sex relationships without risk and harbor high expectations of equality in relationships. In my social group alone, more than half of the women either consider themselves bisexual or have conducted their love lives that way. Even my sister (who is straight but spent most of her teen years in the bathroom with her best friend doing god knows what) has had a blush-provoking crush on a go-go dancer and zine writer named Christine Doza. My former colleague Sandy's first love was her junior high best friend, with whom she knew mysterious passion on the shag rug after school. Shortly after the girl

broke up with her, Sandy went on a family trip to Mexico, where older cousins tried to transform her from a gawky teen with braces, bushy hair, and defeated posture into a hot *mamacita*. No one knew that her dejectedness wasn't just a thirteen-year-old's being awkward—she was brokenhearted. A woman whom I met while I was on a date with Steven but who went on to pursue me with flowers and other gallantries dated women exclusively until her twenty-sixth year, at which point she started dating men exclusively. She's now married and refers to being with women as like living in London: "I want to really *be* in America," she says now, "but I will always love and miss London. It's wonderful to visit London." Anyone reading this book could possibly take her own inventory of her friends and come up with a paragraph just as full of acquaintances who have "looked both ways."

  . . .

. . . [A]mong the reasons the legitimacy of bisexual women is so in dispute is the fact that we haven't put good enough descriptions or images out in the world yet of who and what we are. This is a version of the problem Ellen DeGeneres alludes to when she speaks about the dearth of out lesbians in Hollywood as role models. As for bisexuals, without any other bisexuals (besides Elton John) to point to in mainstream culture, without any visible presence, it's easy to think that we're in denial. It's easy to write off a three-year relationship during which Anne bought a house with Ellen and called her "my wife" ad nauseum as just a phase. In a critical way, people's sexuality is viewed not by who they are but by which gender they sleep with at the present moment—as if there is no heart, no core, to *their* human sexuality.

There are analogies to corelessness in other groups, such as transgendered people . . . or biracial people. For example, the third-wave writer Rebecca Walker was supposed to be a manifestation of integration—her mother, Alice, southern black; her father, Mel Leventhal, East Coast Jew. Her parents came together as the civil rights movement was cresting and had biracial love child Rebecca in 1969. Then the seventies happened—with feminism and black power and separatism, leaving Rebecca to be the "black-white Jewish" kid shuffled from one broken home to another. With her mother, she was never seen as Jewish. Spending time in Westchester with her father, who had remarried a white woman with whom he had two younger children, Rebecca wasn't even assumed to be part of the family. In fact, she was often mistaken for the nanny. Never—or rarely—was she seen as her integrated whole self.

Walker herself has had male and female lovers, among them the bisexual single mother and singer-songwriter Meshell Ndegeocello. Walker worked for several years on a never-published anthology of bisexual writing called *Having Our Cake,* but it is in her memoir, *Black, White, and Jewish,* that she organically and unselfconsciously incorporates attraction to her childhood girlfriends and her burgeoning sense of heterosexuality. Her attractions are presented as natural— full-fledged—and don't create for Walker the same lack of visibility that race and culture do (which is probably why she didn't need to title the book *Black, White, Jewish, Straight, and Gay*). Her mother, too, has had male and female lovers, so perhaps Walker's confidence is enhanced by having plural sexuality be so familiar. . . .

   . . .

Rosie the Riveter and the heroines of *Lysistrata* and all the girls at the Ani DiFranco concert aren't just about politics and negotiations to confront our oppression. Looking both ways is also about crazy, overwhelming, cue-the-orchestra *love.* "Perhaps it is time to acknowledge that the potential to fall in love with a person of the same sex," wrote Barbara Ehrenreich in that *Time* op-ed in 1993, "is widespread among otherwise perfectly conventional people." . . .

NOTES

1. Peter Gay, *Freud: A Life of Our Time* (New York: Norton, 1998).
2. Garber, *Vice Versa,* pp. 56–57, 101, 190–91.
3. Ibid., p. 181.
4. As quoted in ibid., p. 169.
5. Ibid., pp. 274–75.
6. Millett, quoted in her telegram-like memoir, *Flying* (New York: Simon & Schuster, 1990). I wouldn't have found this quote without first seeing it on page 2 of the anthology *Bi Any Other Name: Bisexual People Speak Out,* edited by Loraine Hutchins and Lani Ka'ahumanu (New York: Alyson Books, 1991).
7. As quoted in Garber, *Vice Versa,* p. 204.
8. Marilyn French, *Beyond Power: On Women, Men, and Morals* (New York: Ballantine Books, 1986), p. 519.
9. See Sabrina Margarita Alcantara-Tan's essay in *Young Wives' Tales: New Adventures in Love and Partnership* (Seattle: Seal Press, 2001).
10. The book doesn't say how Ivan Hill, the ethicist and professor who edited *The Bisexual Spouse,* came to that large number.

READING **29**

Gate C22

Ellen Bass (2007)

At gate C22 in the Portland airport
a man in a broad-band leather hat kissed
a woman arriving from Orange County.
They kissed and kissed and kissed. Long after
the other passengers clicked the handles of their
    carry-ons
and wheeled briskly toward short-term parking,

the couple stood there, arms wrapped around
    each other
like he'd just staggered off the boat at Ellis Island,
like she'd been released at last from ICU, snapped
out of a coma, survived bone cancer, made it down
from Annapurna in only the clothes she was
    wearing.

Neither of them was young. His beard was gray.
She carried a few extra pounds you could
    imagine
her saying she had to lose. But they kissed
    lavish
kisses like the ocean in the early morning,
the way it gathers and swells, sucking
each rock under, swallowing it
again and again. We were all watching—
passengers waiting for the delayed flight
to San Jose, the stewardesses, the pilots,
the aproned woman icing Cinnabons, the man
    selling
sunglasses. We couldn't look away. We could
taste the kisses crushed in our mouths.

But the best part was his face. When he drew back
and looked at her, his smile soft with wonder,
    almost
as though he were a mother still open from giv-
    ing birth,
as your mother must have looked at you, no matter
what happened after—if she beat you or left you or
you're lonely now—you once lay there, the varnix
not yet wiped off, and someone gazed at you
as if you were the first sunrise seen from the Earth.
The whole wing of the airport hushed,
all of us trying to slip into that woman's middle-
    aged body,
her plaid Bermuda shorts, sleeveless blouse, glasses,
little gold hoop earrings, tilting our heads up.

R E A D I N G   **30**

La Güera

Cherríe Moraga (1979)

*It requires something more than personal experi-
ence to gain a philosophy or point of view from any
specific event. It is the quality of our response to
the event and our capacity to enter into the lives of
others that help us to make their lives and experiences our own.*

—*Emma Goldman*[1]

I am the very well-educated daughter of a woman
who, by the standards in this country, would be
considered largely illiterate. My mother was born
in Santa Paula, Southern California, at a time when
much of the central valley there was still farm land.
Nearly thirty-five years later, in 1948, she was the
only daughter of six to marry an Anglo, my father.

I remember all of my mother's stories, probably much better than she realizes. She is a fine
story-teller, recalling every event of her life with
the vividness of the present, noting each detail
right down to the cut and color of her dress. I

remember her stories of her being pulled out of
school at the ages of five, seven, nine, and eleven
to work in the fields, along with her brothers and
sisters; stories of her father drinking away whatever small profit she was able to make for the
family; of her going the long way home to avoid
meeting him on the street, staggering toward the
same destination. I remember stories of my mother
lying about her age in order to get a job as a hat-
check girl at Agua Caliente Racetrack in Tijuana.
At fourteen, she was the main support of the family. I can still see her walking home alone at 3 A.M.,
only to turn all of her salary and tips over to her
mother, who was pregnant again.

The stories continue through the war years and
on: walnut-cracking factories, the Voit Rubber factory, and then the computer boom. I remember
my mother doing piecework for the electronics
plant in our neighborhood. In the late evening,
she would sit in front of the TV set, wrapping

copper wires into the backs of circuit boards, talking about "keeping up with the younger girls." By that time, she was already in her mid-fifties.

Meanwhile, I was college-prep in school. After classes, I would go with my mother to fill out job applications for her, or write checks for her at the supermarket. We would have the scenario all worked out ahead of time. My mother would sign the check before we'd get to the store. Then, as we'd approach the checkstand, she would say—within earshot of the cashier—"Oh honey, you go 'head and make out the check," as if she couldn't be bothered with such an insignificant detail. No one asked any questions.

I was educated, and wore it with a keen sense of pride and satisfaction, my head propped up with the knowledge, from my mother, that my life would be easier than hers. I was educated; but more than this, I was *la güera*: 'fair-skinned.' Born with the features of my Chicana mother, but the skin of my Anglo father, I had it made.

No one ever quite told me this (that light was right), but I knew that being light was something valued in my family (who were all Chicano, with the exception of my father). In fact, everything about my upbringing (at least what occurred on a conscious level) attempted to bleach me of what color I did have. Although my mother was fluent in it, I was never taught much Spanish at home. I picked up what I did learn from school and from overheard snatches of conversation among my relatives and mother. She often called the other lower-income Mexicans *braceros,* or 'wet-backs,' referring to herself and her family as "a different class of people." And yet, the real story was that my family, too, had been poor (some still are) and farmworkers. My mother can remember this in her blood as if it were yesterday. But this is something she would like to forget (and rightfully), for to her, on a basic economic level, being Chicana meant being "less." It was through my mother's desire to protect her children from poverty and illiteracy that we became "Anglo-ized"; the more effectively we could pass in the white world, the better guaranteed our future.

From all of this, I experience daily a huge disparity between what I was born into and what I was to grow up to become. Because, as Goldman suggests, these stories my mother told me crept under my *güera* skin. I had no choice but to enter into the life of my mother. *I had no choice.* I took her life into my heart, but managed to keep a lid on it as long as I feigned being the happy, upwardly mobile heterosexual.

When I finally lifted the lid to my lesbianism, a profound connection with my mother was reawakened in me. It wasn't until I acknowledged and confronted my own lesbianism in the flesh that my heartfelt identification with and empathy for my mother's oppression—due to being poor, uneducated, and Chicana—was realized. My lesbianism is the avenue through which I have learned the most about silence and oppression, and it continues to be the most tactile reminder to me that we are not free human beings.

You see, one follows the other. I had known for years that I was a lesbian, had felt it in my bones, had ached with the knowledge, gone crazed with the knowledge, wallowed in the silence of it. Silence *is* like starvation. Don't be fooled. It's nothing short of that, and felt most sharply when one has had a full belly most of her life. When we are not physically starving, we have the luxury to realize psychic and emotional starvation. It is from this starvation that other starvations can be recognized—if one is willing to take the risk of making the connection—if one is willing to be responsible to the result of the connection. For me, the connection is an inevitable one.

What I am saying is that the joys of looking like a white girl haven't been so great since I realized I could be beaten on the street for being a dyke. If my sister's being beaten because she's black, it's pretty much the same principle. We're both getting beaten any way you look at it. The connection is blatant; and in the case of my own family, the differences in the privileges attached to looking white instead of brown are merely a generation apart.

In this country, lesbianism is poverty—as is being brown, as is being a woman, as is being just plain poor. The danger lies in ranking the oppressions. *The danger lies in failing to acknowledge the specificity of the oppression.* The danger lies in attempting to deal with oppression purely from a theoretical base. Without an emotional, heart-felt grappling with the source of our own oppression, without naming the enemy within ourselves and outside of us, no authentic, nonhierarchical connection among oppressed groups can take place.

When the going gets rough, will we abandon our so-called comrades in a flurry of racist/heterosexist/what-have-you panic? To whose camp, then, should the lesbian of color retreat? Her very presence violates the ranking and abstraction of oppression. Do we merely live hand to mouth? Do we merely struggle with the "ism" that's sitting on top of our own heads?

The answer is: yes, I think first we do; and we must do so thoroughly and deeply. But to fail to move out from there will only isolate us in our own oppression—will only insulate, rather than radicalize us.

. . .

Within the women's movement, the connections among women of different backgrounds and sexual orientations have been fragile, at best. I think this phenomenon is indicative of our failure to seriously address ourselves to some very frightening questions: How have I internalized my own oppression? How have I oppressed? Instead, we have let rhetoric do the job of poetry. Even the word *oppression* has lost its power. We need new language, better words that can more closely describe women's fear of and resistance to one another; words that will not always come out sounding like dogma.

I don't really understand first-hand what it feels like being shit on for being brown. I understand much more about the joys of it—being Chicana and having family are synonymous for me. What I know about loving, singing, crying, telling stories, speaking with my heart and hands, even having a sense of my own soul comes from the love of my mother, aunts, cousins. . . .

But at the age of twenty-seven, it is frightening to acknowledge that I have internalized a racism and classism where the object of oppression is not only someone outside of my skin, but the someone inside my skin. In fact, to a large degree,

the real battle with such oppression, for all of us, begins under the skin. I have had to confront the fact that much of what I value about being Chicana, about my family, has been subverted by Anglo culture and my own cooperation with it. This realization did not occur to me overnight. For example, it wasn't until long after my graduation from the private college I'd attended in Los Angeles that I realized the major reason for my total alienation from and fear of my classmates was rooted in class and culture. *Click*.

Three years after graduation, in an apple-orchard in Sonoma, a friend of mine (who comes from an Italian working-class family), says to me, "Cherríe, no wonder you felt like such a nut in school. Most of the people there were white and rich." It was true. All along I had felt the difference, but not until I had put the words *class* and *culture* to the experience did my feelings make any sense. For years, I had berated myself for not being as "free" as my classmates. I completely bought that they simply had more guts than I did—to rebel against their parents and run around the country hitchhiking, reading books and studying "art." They had enough privilege to be atheists, for chrissake. There was no one around filling in the disparity for me between their parents, who were Hollywood filmmakers, and my parents, who wouldn't know the name of a filmmaker if their lives depended on it (and precisely because their lives didn't depend on it, they couldn't be bothered). But I knew nothing about "privilege" then. White was right. Period. I could pass. If I got educated enough, there would never be any telling.

Three years after that, another click. In a letter to a friend, I wrote:

> I went to a concert where Ntozake Shange was reading. There, everything exploded for me. She was speaking a language that I knew—in the deepest parts of me—existed, and that I had ignored in my own feminist studies and even in my own writing. What Ntozake caught in me is the realization that in my development as a poet, I have, in many ways, denied the voices of my brown mother—the brown in me. I have acclimated to the sound of a white language which, as my father represents it, does not

speak to the emotions in my poems—emotions which stem from the love of my mother.

The reading was agitating. Made me feel uncomfortable. Threw me into a week-long terror of how deeply I was affected. I felt that I had to start all over again. That I had turned only to the perceptions of white middle-class women to speak for me and all women. I am shocked by my own ignorance.

Sitting in that auditorium chair was the first time I had realized to the core of me that for years I had disowned the language I knew best—ignored the words and rhythms that were the closest to me. The sounds of my mother and aunts gossiping—half in English, half in Spanish—while drinking cerveza in the kitchen. And the hands—I had cut off the hands in my poems. But not in conversation; still the hands could not be kept down. Still they insisted on moving.

The reading had forced me to remember that I knew things from my roots. But to remember puts me up against what I don't know. Shange's reading agitated me because she spoke with power about a world that is both alien and common to me: "the capacity to enter into the lives of others." But you can't just take the goods and run. I knew that then, sitting in the Oakland auditorium (as I know in my poetry), that the only thing worth writing about is what seems to be unknown and therefore fearful.

The "unknown" is often depicted in racist literature as the "darkness" within a person. Similarly, sexist writers will refer to fear in the form of the vagina, calling it "the orifice of death." In contrast, it is a pleasure to read works such as Maxine Hong Kingston's *Woman Warrior,* where fear and alienation are described as "the white ghosts." And yet, the bulk of literature in this country reinforces the myth that what is dark and female is evil. Consequently, each of us—whether dark, female, or both—has in some way *internalized* this oppressive imagery. What the oppressor often succeeds in doing is simply *externalizing* his fears, projecting them into the bodies of women, Asians, gays, disabled folks, whoever seems most "other."

> call me
> roach and presumptuous
> nightmare on your white pillow
> your itch to destroy
> the indestructible
> part of yourself   —*Audre Lorde*[2]

But it is not really difference the oppressor fears so much as similarity. He fears he will discover in himself the same aches, the same longings as those of the people he has shit on. He fears the immobilization threatened by his own incipient guilt. He fears he will have to change his life once he has seen himself in the bodies of the people he has called different. He fears the hatred, anger, and vengeance of those he has hurt.

This is the oppressor's nightmare, but it is not exclusive to him. We women have a similar nightmare, for each of us in some way has been both the oppressed and the oppressor. We are afraid to see how we have taken the values of our oppressor into our hearts and turned them against ourselves and one another. We are afraid to admit how deeply "the man's" words have been ingrained in us.

To assess the damage is a dangerous act. I think of how, even as a feminist lesbian, I have so wanted to ignore my own homophobia, my own hatred of myself for being queer. I have not wanted to admit that my deepest personal sense of myself has not quite "caught up" with my "woman-identified" politics. I have been afraid to criticize lesbian writers who choose to "skip over" these issues in the name of feminism. In 1979, we talk of "old gay" and "butch and femme" roles as if they were ancient history. We toss them aside as merely patriarchal notions. And yet, the truth of the matter is that I have sometimes taken society's fear and hatred of lesbians to bed with me. I have sometimes hated my lover for loving me. I have sometimes felt "not woman enough" for her. I have sometimes felt "not man enough." For a lesbian trying to survive in a heterosexist society, there is no easy way around these emotions. Similarly, in a white-dominated world, there is little getting around racism and our own internalization of it. It's always there, embodied in someone we least expect to rub up against.

When we do rub up against this person, *there* then is the challenge. *There* then is the opportunity to look at the nightmare within us. But we usually shrink from such a challenge.

. . .

As Lorde suggests in the passage I cited earlier, it is in looking to the nightmare that the dream is found. There, the survivor emerges to insist on a future, a vision, yes, born out of what is dark and female. The feminist movement must be a movement of such survivors, a movement with a future.

NOTES

1. Alix Kates Shulman, ed., "Was My Life Worth Living?" *Red Emma Speaks* (New York: Random House, 1972), p. 388.
2. From "The Brown Menace or Poem to the Survival of Roaches," *The New York Head Shop and Museum* (Detroit: Broadside, 1974), p. 48.

R E A D I N G   **31**

Prue Shows Her Knickers

Emily Oxford (1996)

Prue was just a teenager. She was skinny and lean but two budding breasts made faint bumps under her clothes. Boys teased her and Andy kept asking for a flash.

The once-soft face of childhood was harder now, her jaw jutted forward a little, a physical sign of her stubbornness. Circumstance had made her wilful, wary and nervous of the world she lived in, but somewhere the indomitable spirit of her optimism still burned.

She was not normal. She was a cripple, she was handicapped, she was a Special pre-pubescent.

Her legs were unique maps of her illness, stiff and unbending, her knees decorated with tiny craters and variously swelling bumps. She didn't walk on them much and used a wheelchair at times she called simply "agony" days. Her neck, though rarely painful, bent to one side and stayed there. These were her bodily impairments which attracted the labels of doctors, and consequently categorised her neatly for the rest of the world.

The labels attached to her had done their work; her psyche suffered its own impairments as a result, and as she approached adolescence, she found herself nervous about a world which had once seemed a dazzling dance of magic.

She never thought much about her situation, she just accepted that she was these things other people placed on her, and if it kept the peace with her anxious, fretting mother, then she played by the rules that meant she saw lots of white-coats, went to a Special school in a Special bus and didn't expect to do a whole array of things in the hostile, anti-cripple world.

But even these rules had begun to change of late.

Now she was expected to play the Independence game—a game with a particular definition. Lectures on "Personal Independence" featured in her life these days with growing regularity. She had to go to "Buttons and Bows" classes, where groups of bored teenagers were grilled about how to tie shoe laces; tackle buckles, poppers, buttons, zips; pull this on, pull that off; and sundry other activities. With her twig-like fingers curving at bulbous joints that neither bent very far nor had the strength to stay straight, most of these tasks were to Prue a punishment in ritualised boredom. She knew her own limits, just as she knew what challenges were worth taking on. These activities were pointless and demoralising as she failed at every attempt. The "teachers"—in fact blue-coats serving under the Head's baleful glare—would tut at her and admonish her to try harder.

The enforced ideas about Independence were suffocating shadows closing in on her life. She had to be taught to do everything in her life herself, absolutely, in readiness for adulthood when there would be no kind mum to wait on you, no teachers and Care ladies, oh no. It seemed to Prue it was the sort of Independence you might only need if you were the only person left alive on some fantastic, civilised desert island; and it was the sort of Independence which she knew she could never actually achieve.

What being Independent meant, of course, was being able to present to their real world an approximation of Normality. You wouldn't ever have to bother a nice Normal person with your nasty difficulties, you'd never have to ask for anything. It didn't matter how many hopeless hours of pain and toil were involved.

But who was she to argue? She was just a cripple kid, told every day that she didn't know what was best for herself, in her Special situation. . . .

If you didn't play the game of Independence by their rules, they made fearful threats about putting you in a Home when you reached sixteen. It was up to you, they would shrug, as if they had no say in the decision. If you tried your hardest and were Independent, then you didn't have to worry. You would be allowed into their world.

. . .

Prue had to draw on every ounce of her hard-won reserve of strength today because two traumas were facing her at school. The white-coat prodders had decided to send her away to a new place for "better treatment," so this was her last day for God knows how long. She would be going to another hospital. They all kept insisting that it wasn't hospital—even her mother—but a special residential centre for children and young adults with arthritis; just what she needed. But Prue was not calmed by their explanations. She

had grown weary and resigned towards their soothing platitudes and downright lies. With a churning in her stomach, she braced herself for the worst.

But although this imminent event lay in her mind like a heavy, dulling ache, there was a more pressing engagement awaiting her at school.

She had been half dared, half coaxed into promising Andy Easter a look down her knickers—as long as she was allowed a look down his. She and Sally had giggled over the prospect all week, and in high bravado she had announced the forthcoming exploit for days. Now the whole class knew about it, and boys and girls alike laughed and chattered expectantly as she entered the classroom.

Sally was excited and anxious, a great bubbling jitter of worry.

"What if you're caught? What if they tell your mum?"

"Mum won't care, she knows I'm not stupid. I'd say it was just a silly game. Anyway, we won't get caught—he's only getting a few seconds look! That's the dare!"

Sammy Smith, one of their gang, a small compact tomboy of a girl with twisting wiry hair, pulled a face.

"You'll have to watch him, 'e's a bugger! Don't let him touch nothin'! If 'e does I'll whack him for year!"

Sammy was tough, renowned for hurtling down the corridors on her three-wheeled walking frame, scattering unwary younger pupils as she went.

"Oh blimey, no touching, 'course not!" Prue laughed, hiding the lurch in her stomach which reminded her suddenly not only of the present embarrassing scrape she was in, but also of her appointment with new white-coats tomorrow. She could hardly believe that she was leaving all her friends, Miss Tobin, and her mum and brother, for who knew how long. And thoughts of her mum brought back the painful scene at breakfast.

Andy was grinning at her across the classroom, tapping his flies with the palm of his hand, a swanking display for his sniggering mates. She pulled a disgusted face at him before turning back to the gang. At least there was a morning full of lessons before she had to Do It.

No one was allowed to watch, they both insisted on that, meeting inside the stationery cupboard, at the edge of the assembly hall. Their friends waited outside, giggling and hushing each other, keeping a sharp watch for teachers or prowling Snotty Scott.

Prue had worked herself up into a perfect state of arrogant devilry, deciding this was the only way she could get through the ordeal. Anyhow, her mother had taught her not to be ashamed of anything to do with her private parts (although she didn't like Prue to display her bumpy lumpy legs), saying that they were hers and she should be proud to be a woman.

Now here she was, wearing her best pink knickers, facing Andy and staring him in the eye, allowing him no chance to renege on his part of the dare. He looked up at her, sheepish now the door was shut, his grin not so swanky.

"Well?" said Prue, keen to get it over with. Mum might have told her to be proud of her "Miss Mary" but at this instant she felt silly and embarrassed.

"Who's going to go first, then?" he asked uncertainly, playing with the top of his trousers.

"We'll do it together. Let's count to three, then—then show ourselves—only for five seconds—we'll count together."

Her stomach was doing somersaults. A tiny voice somewhere asked her why she was being so childish. It was too late to answer that.

Andy had his hands ready at his zip. Prue hooked her stiff fingers with some difficulty into her knickers. Looking down at him, a pang of pity hit her. What a sorrowful sight he was. He was terrified! But being a boy he couldn't let on, could he? She felt strong and in charge. Why was she afraid? She'd seen a willy, on Rory and in books. His couldn't be any more peculiar or strange. She decided to display herself with a flourish.

"Right then . . . get ready, let's count together . . . one . . . two . . . three!"

A quick extra second of struggle with unwieldy clothes and there they stood.

"One chim-pan-zee, TWO chim-pan-zee . . ." Prue stared hard at the grey-pink length of flesh that lay limp and wrinkled in Andy's hand. She wanted to laugh but managed a less insulting smile instead, noticing that Andy was avidly looking down as she held her dress under her chin. She stepped back slightly, her legs moving apart. His willy looked like a sagging sausage that was going off she decided, and those straggles of hair around it, yuck!

". . . FIVE chim-pan-zee!" they chorused together before hastily covering themselves. Outside the others were growing restless. Andy still looked nervous.

"Er . . . it's not very big, is it? I mean, my brother has got a really huge one."

Prue wanted to laugh out loud. She was going away from all this tomorrow, and she knew how much she would miss it. She would even miss Andy.

"Well, I don't really know. It looked just the same as the others I've seen," Prue remarked airily, amazed at how timid he had become in displaying his prized part to her. 'How did I do?'

She didn't actually care much what he thought but was interested in what he might say.

He looked up at her, taller as she was, and smiled shyly.

"You're great, Prue. I really like you. You're pretty."

Prue was flabbergasted by this response, expecting something rude and smart. But she was in control and she knew it. She also knew now that the great, bragging, flashy bugger Andy Easter had never seen a woman's private part before. She glowed and smiled.

"You're all right too, mate." There was a little devil suddenly inside her. Tomorrow this would all be gone . . . for a long time, she just knew it.

"Give us a kiss, then." The words came out of her mouth, a dancing request half-filled with laughter, half with blank nerve. She bent down to him, put her hand on his shoulder, and pressed her lips against his.

She didn't want him to forget her in a hurry while she was away.

Some Like Indians Endure

Paula Gunn Allen (1998)

i have it in my mind that
dykes are indians

they're a lot like indians
they used to live as tribes
they owned tribal land
it was called the earth

they were massacred
lots of times
they always came back
like the grass
like the clouds
they got massacred again

they thought caringsharing
about the earth and each other
was a good thing
they rode horses
and sang to the moon

but i don't know
about what was so longago
and it's now that dykes
make me think i'm with indians
when i'm with dykes

because they bear
witness bitterly
because they reach
and hold
because they live every day
with despair laughing
in cities and country places
because earth hides them
because they know
the moon
because they gather together
enclosing
and spit in the eye of death

indian is an idea
some people have
of themselves
dyke is an idea some women
have of themselves
the place where we live now
is idea
because whiteman took
all the rest
because father
took all the rest
but the idea which
once you have it
you can't be taken
for somebody else
and have nowhere to go
like indians you can be
stubborn

the idea might move you on,
ponydrag behind
taking all your loves and
children maybe downstream

maybe beyond the cliffs
but it hangs in there
an idea
like indians
endures

it might even take your
whole village with it
stone by stone
or leave the stones
and find more
to build another village
someplace else

like indians
dykes have fewer and fewer

someplace elses to go
so it gets important
to know
about ideas and
to remember or uncover
the past
and how the people
traveled
all the while remembering
the idea they had
about who they were
indians, like dykes
do it all the time

dykes know all about dying
and that everything belongs
to the wind
like indians
they do terrible things
to each other
out of sheer cussedness
out of forgetting
out of despair
so dykes
are like indians
because everybody is related
to everybody
in pain
in terror
in guilt
in blood
in shame
in disappearance
that never quite manages

to be disappeared
we never go away
even if we're always
leaving

because the only home
is each other
they've occupied all
the rest
colonized it; an
idea about ourselves is all
we own

and dykes remind me of indians
like indians dykes
are supposed to die out
or forget
or drink all the time
or shatter
go away
to nowhere
to remember what will happen
if they don't

they don't anyway—even
though the worst happens

they remember and they
stay
because the moon remembers
because so does the sun
because the stars
remember
and the persistent stubborn grass
of the earth

Women, Sexuality, and Social Change in the Middle East

Pinar Ilkkaracan (2002)

INTRODUCTION

In this age of globalization, women's bodies and sexuality are increasingly becoming arenas of intense conflict. Conservative and religious right political forces are fiercely trying to maintain or reinforce traditional mechanisms of control over women's sexuality and even create new ones. Four UN conferences held in the 1990s—the 1994 International Conference on Population and Development (ICPD) in Cairo, the 1995 Beijing Conference, the 1999 five-year review of the ICPD (ICPD+5), and the 2000 five-year review of the Beijing Conference (Beijing+5)—witnessed the Catholic and Muslim religious right engaging in unprecedented cooperation to oppose and restrict women's right to control their bodies and sexuality.

At the same time, in the last decade, women around the globe have joined forces to counter these moves from the conservative and religious right and have engaged in an international struggle against violations of their sexual and reproductive rights—a struggle transcending national borders as well as real or constructed North–South and East–West dichotomies. A visible sign of the success of this struggle is the significant change in the way international agencies use language. As the global women's movement has become stronger and the "rights" approach has gained credibility, "reproductive rights" discourse has increasingly replaced reproductive "health" and "sexual health" and become a focus of interest and a part of common terminology. The shift from "sexual health" to "sexual rights" constitutes the last link in this chain of global change as introduced by the global women's movement.

In this context, several traditional cultural practices—such as honor crimes, the stoning of women accused of adultery, virginity tests, or female genital cutting—in Muslim societies, including the Middle East, have increasingly drawn the attention of the Western media and public in recent years as human rights abuses. The lack of information on Islam and on the wide diversity of Muslim societies, the parallel rise of the Islamic religious right, which claims such customary practices to be Islamic, and the tendency to "essentialize" Islam are some of the factors that have led to the incorrect portrayal in the West of such practices as Islamic. This depiction is not only misleading, but also stands in sharp contrast to the efforts of women's movements in Muslim societies, which, in their fight against such practices, are campaigning to raise public consciousness that these practices are against Islam. In fact, the incorrect depiction contributes to the Islamic religious right's cause of vigorously trying to create extreme forms of control over women and their sexuality by incorporating and universalizing the worst customary practices in the name of religion.

. . .

SEXUALITY IN THE QUR'AN AND THE EARLY FIQH TEXTS: THE INITIAL ROOTS OF CONTROVERSY

Several researchers have pointed to the contradiction between the notion of gender equality in the Qur'an and the patriarchal misinterpretation of it by male religious authorities in the early and medieval canonical texts traditionally accepted as establishing Islam's normative practices (Mernissi, 1987; Sabbah, 1984; An-Naim, 1990;

Ahmed, 1991, 1992; Hassan, n.d.; Wadud, 1999; Mir-Hosseini, 2001). As in other monotheistic religions, the classical *fiqh* texts—that is, texts of early Islamic legal jurisprudence—ignored gender equality as it was presented in the Qur'an and introduced interpretations in line with the prevailing patriarchal social order. Thus, one can find several logical contradictions in the classical *fiqh* texts since they reflect two dissenting voices: an egalitarian voice inspired by revelation (*wahy*) and a patriarchal voice incorporating the social order and the social, cultural, and political pragmatisms of the time and place where Islam was trying to ensure its survival (Mir-Hosseini, 2001). An analysis of discourses based on the Qur'an and the early literature of Islamic legal jurisprudence leads to contradictory conclusions about the construction of women's sexuality in Islam.

Mir-Hosseini (2001), for example, asserts that this contradiction is most evident in the rules that classical jurists devised for regulating the formation and the termination of the marriage contract—a product of tension in which the voice of the patriarchal social order outweighs the egalitarian voice of the revelation (*wahy*). Her analysis of the classical *fiqh* texts on marriage shows that the model of gender relations in the early texts of Islamic jurisprudence is grounded in the patriarchal ideology of pre-Islamic Arabia, which continued into the Islamic era in a modified form through a set of male-dominated theological, legal, and social theories and assumptions, such as "women are created of and for men."

These theories stood in sharp contradiction to the Qur'an, which holds that the relationship of men and women is one of equality, mutuality, and cordiality. In the Qur'an, Eve is not a delayed product of Adam's rib, as in the Christian and Jewish traditions; instead, the two were born from a single soul: "O mankind! Be careful of your duty to your Lord, who created you from a single soul and from it created its mate and from them twain hath spread abroad a multitude of men and women" (Surah 4:1).[1] It was not just Eve, but both Adam and Eve, who let the Devil convince them to eat the forbidden fruit.[2] Islam has recognized that both women and men have sex drives and the right to sexual fulfillment and has also acknowledged that women, like men, experience orgasms. The Islamic view of love and sexuality—in which pleasure and responsibility are coexistent—removes any guilt from the sexes (Bouhdiba, 1998). Marital intercourse does not need the justification of reproduction and is based on the right to sexual fulfillment; contraception is permitted and abortion tolerated (Musallam, 1989). Women's ejaculation was recognized in the *hadiths*, the traditional body and texts of knowledge and memories about the Prophet's life, his custom and his words, where female sexuality is regarded as active, like male sexuality (Ahmed, 1989).

. . .

Some Qur'anic verses, especially the story of Zuleikha and Yusuf, have laid the foundation for interpretations of women as capable of greater sexual desire and temptation than men—casting women as beguiling seductresses and men as susceptible to seduction but rational and capable of self-control.[3] Yet, several of the customary practices aimed at controlling women's sexuality, like honor crimes, stoning for adultery, or female genital cutting, cannot be justified by appeal to the Qur'an. The Qur'an forbids adultery,[4] like the other two main monotheistic religions, Judaism and Christianity, and foresees heavy punishment (100 lashes) for both women and men guilty of adultery or fornication.[5] It requires, however, four witnesses to the act.[6] Otherwise, if a woman denies the accusation, then it is her word that must be accepted rather than that of her husband.[7] Thus, according to the Qur'an, the punishment for adultery, meant both for women and men, can only be carried out if conviction is based on the testimony of a minimum of four witnesses. In addition, although it foresees a stern punishment of 100 lashes, it is not stoning or execution—contrary to the customary practices of honor crimes or stoning as carried out in some Muslim countries. Stoning as a punishment in cases of adultery has only recently been introduced as an "Islamic" practice by the Islamic religious right in Iran, Pakistan, and Nigeria.

. . .

Islam has set consent of both the woman and the man as a precondition of marriage. In the main classical schools of legal jurisprudence of Islam (*Hanafi* or *Shi'a* law, for example), a girl who has attained majority age is free to contract marriage without the consent of her father or any other relative and cannot be forced into a marriage by her male relatives (Carroll, 2000). Accordingly, the practice of "forced marriages" in Muslim societies constitutes a clear violation of the basic premise of marriage as specified in the Qur'an.

The diversity of Muslim societies shows that Islam does not have a static or monolithic tradition. Islam has absorbed not only the practices and traditions of the two other monotheistic religions—Judaism and Christianity—from the region of its birth, but also other pre-Islamic practices and traditions from the geographic location in which it strove to survive and gain power as a cultural and political system. Thus, it is very difficult to define what is intrinsic to Islam in shaping sexual behavior. The issue becomes even more complicated when we attempt to analyze its interaction with various socioeconomic and political systems. In the following, I will explore some of these factors, which affect the norms governing and practices of women's sexuality in the Middle East and Maghreb.

GENDER INEQUALITY AND SEXUALITY IN THE MIDDLE EAST AND THE MAGHREB

. . .

The Middle East shows a great degree of diversity in the formulation of legal codes and their application to women's everyday lives, which is also the case in the rest of the Muslim world. The extent of the legal reforms redefining gender relations varies greatly between countries. While in Turkey, for example, modernization included the adoption of Western legal codes and aimed at complete secularization,[8] [and] most Gulf countries preserved their interpretation of Islamic legal jurisprudence as the fundamental law in all juridical areas. . . .

Despite the positive impact of all modern legal, educational, and economic reforms on the position of women and the growing strength of feminist movements, the majority of women living in the region have not benefited from the opportunities created, especially in the economic and political spheres. The United Nations Development Program (UNDP) 2002 report, *Arab Human Development,* states that the Arab world shows the fastest improvement in female education of any region, with female literacy expanding threefold since 1970, and primary and secondary enrollment doubling. However, in terms of the Gender Empowerment Measure, which the UNDP introduced in 1995, the Arab region's ranking is lower than any region except sub-Saharan Africa. Arab countries have the lowest rate of women's participation in the workforce and the lowest rate of representation in parliaments. More than half of Arab women are illiterate. The maternal mortality rate is double that of Latin American and the Caribbean and four times that of East Asia (UNDP, 2002). The collective mechanisms aimed at controlling women's bodies and sexuality continue to be one of the most powerful tools of patriarchal management of women's sexuality and a root cause of gender inequality in the region.

THE CONTRADICTORY IMPACT OF MODERNIZATION ON WOMEN'S SEXUAL LIVES

Modernization movements and efforts occupied a central place in the regional political discourses of the nineteenth and early twentieth centuries in the Middle East. Women's status has also occupied a central place in the modernization efforts in the region; for decades, the modernists argued that reforms in the position of women in the economic, educational, and legal spheres would lead to more "modernization," and consequently, to greater gender equality in all spheres. Women were among the first who recognized the complex and contradictory nature of modernity and that modernization projects did not necessarily lead to real gender equality for all or in every sphere.

. . .

Mervat Hatem (1997) illustrates a good example of the contradictory effects of modernization on women's sexual lives in her research on the professionalization of health in nineteenth-century Egypt. The school of *Hakimahs*, which was established in the early nineteenth century and was the first modern state school for women in Egypt, aimed at replacing local midwifery practices with modern female professionals. While the local Egyptian midwives (*dayas*) performed circumcisions on girls, thus implementing patriarchal control of women's sexuality, they also provided women with folk-based means to control their reproductive capacities, such as supplying them with information on fertility and providing quick and effective abortions. Although the establishment of the *Hakimahs* school established an opportunity for middle-class women to become professionals, it also led to a loss of power for traditional midwives, contributed to the extinction of women's indigenous knowledge, and to a state policy of criminalizing abortion. Moreover, the new midwives from the middle class were given the task of policing working class midwives (*dayas*) and their middle and working class clients.

. . .

THE NATIONALIST IDEOLOGIES AND WOMEN'S SEXUALITY

Nationalist movements and ideologies that accompanied the foundation of nation-states in the Middle East have posed contradictory roles for women. On the one hand, they allowed women—especially those from the middle and upper classes—to participate more fully in social and political life, as they disrupted traditional gender roles and relations. On the other hand, they redefined women's roles as mothers and bearers of the nation and its newly constructed legacy (Kandiyoti, 1996; Mehdid, 1996; Pettman, 1996; Saigol, 2000). This led to the emergence of new strategies to control women, and especially their sexuality, which was meant to serve the reproduction and maintenance of the newly constructed "national identity" and "uniqueness" of community.

In Turkey, for example, the foundation of a secular nation-state and the "modern" Turkish Republic set revolutionary changes in gender roles as a priority in order to destroy the links to the Ottoman Empire and to strike at the foundations of religious hegemony. However, nationalist discourses almost competed with Islamic discourses in their zeal to regulate the sexual identity and behavior of Turkish women. The leaders and the ideologues of the Turkish nationalist movement took great pains to establish a new nationalist morality regarding women's sexuality in which the new rights gained by women in the public sphere could be justified as an integral part of so-called Turkish culture (Kandiyoti, 1988). The leading ideologue of the newly constructed Turkish identity, Ziya Gökalp, went so far as to construct the principal virtue of Turkish women as chastity, *iffet*. In fact, this construction has been so powerful that Turkish women are still faced with the human rights violations it causes. The Statute for Awards and Discipline in High School Education, enacted in January 1995, states that "proof of unchastity" is a valid reason for expulsion from the formal educational system. This statute, which served to institutionalize a customary practice, led to suicides of girls whom school authorities sent for so-called virginity tests. Female students were forced to undergo "virginity tests" even in such cases where a girl was merely seen walking with a male classmate on the playground. As a result of the Turkish women's movement's protests and campaigns, the Ministry of Justice banned virginity testing in January 1999.[9] However, in July 2001, the tests were reinstated for student nurses through a decree of the health minister, who is from the far-right National Action Party. The reinstatement of the tests led to extensive protests by the Turkish women's movement and international human rights organizations. Finally, in 2002, the Ministry of Education changed the Statute for Awards and Discipline and deleted the provision that stated "proof of unchastity" as a reason for expulsion from the formal educational system.

. . .

THE RISE OF THE ISLAMIC RELIGIOUS RIGHT AND ITS EFFORTS TO CONTROL WOMEN'S SEXUALITY

In the decades since World War II, several factors have contributed to the creation of a rather difficult and unfavorable atmosphere regarding the extension of liberal reforms, including reforms in the area of sexuality; these factors have also encouraged the growth of religious right-wing movements in the region. The failure of attempted social and economic reforms resulted in an increasing gap between the Westernized elite and the majority, leading to disillusionment with Westernized rulers. The widening gap of economic and political power between Muslim societies and the West, along with urbanization, migration, and increasing poverty, has contributed to the creation of an atmosphere where religious right-wing movements have gained the support of the masses. The founding of Israel and the resulting occupations and war have contributed to an increasingly hostile atmosphere against the West and facilitated the construction by fundamentalist groups of the West and its perceived culture as an "enemy."

The religious and nationalist fundamentalists make utmost use of this perceived threat against "Muslim" identity by constructing a "Muslim" or "national" female identity as a last sphere of control against the "enemy": the West. Thus, pressure on women to become bearers of constructed group identities and the control of women's sexuality are currently at the heart of many fundamentalist agendas. Their strategies are multifold; here I will attempt to outline some of them. The dress code, the most perceptible form of identity creation, has been high on the agenda of the Muslim religious right, which wanted to use the code's visibility as a demonstration of its political power. . . .

Aware of the power of the imagery of *hijab* as a demonstration of its influence and authority, the Islamic religious right has sought to prescribe or violently enforce extreme forms of veiling that were specific to certain communities (for instance, the *chador* or *burqa*); veiling is intended to be a universal uniform for Muslim women, not only in the region but throughout the world, even in places where they were previously unheard of, such as Uzbekistan, Kashmir, or Senegal. . . .

. . .

In the last two decades, the rise of the Islamic religious right has caused women in countries such as Iran, Algeria, and South Yemen to suffer the loss of previously gained legal rights, especially within the family. In 1979, two weeks after the overthrow of the Pahlavi dynasty through the Islamic revolution in Iran, the Family Protection Act of 1967—which restrained men's legal right to polygamous marriage by requiring either the court's or the first wife's permission, enforced a woman's right to divorce with mutual consent, and improved women's chances of retaining the custody of their children or at least visiting rights—was scrapped as un-Islamic (Hoodfar, 1996). Women were dismissed and barred from the judiciary and higher education (Najmabadi, 1998). In Algeria, in July 1984, the government adopted a repressive family law that legalized polygyny and rescinded Algerian women's rights in the family. Algerian women were quick to mobilize wide and fierce opposition but their strong resistance remained ineffective (Mahl, 1995; Moghadam, 1993). In 1990, the unification of North and South Yemen, which had fostered hopes for political openness and democracy in the country, resulted in a major disappointment for Yemeni women, both from the south and the north. Yemeni women in the north had hoped to profit from the egalitarian laws of the socialist regime in the south. These were basically secular in orientation, defining marriage as a contract with equal rights and responsibilities for men and women, including financial responsibility; they also abolished polygyny, made women's consent a basis of engagement for marriage, ended a man's right to unilateral divorce, and set the minimum age of marriage at 15 for girls and 16 for boys. However, because of tribal rebellion, urban terrorism, sharp cuts in Western and Gulf countries aid programs (in response to Yemen's refusal to join the anti-Iraq coalition after Iraq's invasion of Kuwait in

1990), the two factions in Yemen were usurped by open warfare, which contributed to the rise of the Islamic religious right. As is very often the case in war, the losers were women. Upon unification, the progressive family laws of the south were abolished. Not only did the women in southern Yemen lose the legal rights they had enjoyed since 1974, but the women of North Yemen, who had hoped for the incorporation of the greater degree of gender equality enshrined in the southern codes, had to bury their hopes (Boxberger, 1998; al-Basha, 2001).

THE IMPACT OF CHANGING SOCIAL VALUES AND FEMINIST ACTIVISM AROUND WOMEN'S SEXUAL RIGHTS

The violent imposition of practices leading to the Islamic religious right's violations of women's sexual rights presents a contradictory picture of the changing social values regarding sexuality in the region. Although premarital sex is still strongly prohibited in many countries, there is evidence, for example from Morocco, Lebanon, Tunisia, and Turkey, that it increasingly forms part of the experience of young people and that this change has created a social conflict between the patriarchal control of women's sexuality and the socioeconomic changes taking place in the region (Obermeyer, 2000; Khair Badawi, 2001; Belhadj, 2001; Mernissi, 1982; Cindoglu, 1997). Female genital cutting, which clearly has nothing to do with Islam, is now outlawed as a result of the efforts of women's advocacy groups in Egypt (al-Dawla, 2000). In recent years, activism against honor crimes in Palestine, Jordan, Pakistan, Egypt, and Turkey has grown, and women's NGOs have succeeded in putting the issue onto the agenda of national and international bodies (Albadeel Coalition, 2000; Yirmisbesoglu, 2000; Rouhana, 2001; Tadros, 2002; International Women's Health Coalition, 2000; Clarke, 2001). A popular Friday night television program in Lebanon, *Al-Chater Yehki* (*Let the Brave Speak Out*), topped the ratings with its live debates on sexuality,

with issues ranging from masturbation to incest or homosexuality (Foster, 2000). . . .

Alongside the legal setbacks in Iran, Algeria, and Yemen must be set the advocacy and lobbying by national women's movements that have led to legal reforms for greater gender equality in the family in Turkey, Egypt, and Jordan. In Turkey, the reform of the civil code in 2001 ended the supremacy of men in marriage by removing a clause defining the man as the head of the family. Through the reform of its civil code, Turkey has become the only predominantly Muslim country that has legally established the full equality of men and women in the family. The new Turkish civil code raises the legal age for marriage to 18 for both women and men (it was previously 17 for men and 15 for women) and makes the equal division of property acquired during marriage as the default property regime. The concept of "illegitimate children"—that is, children born out of wedlock—has been abolished, and the custody of these children is given to their mothers.[10] In addition, in October 2001, Article 41 of the Turkish constitution was amended, redefining the family as an entity that is based on equality between spouses. . . .

The last two decades have also witnessed the emergence of a reformist discourse that argues for equality in Islam on all fronts. This reformist discourse seeks to analyze "women's sexuality as defined by social circumstances, not by nature and divine will" (Mir-Hosseini, 2001: 12). As such, it removes the issue of sexuality or women's status from the domain of *fiqh* rulings to social practices and norms, which are neither sacred nor immutable but human and changing. This new movement is opening new windows by bridging the gap between the traditional divide of the so-called traditionalists—ranging from conservatives to the religious right—and the so-called progressives, including the feminists, blurring the traditional fixed fronts in Muslim societies as constructed in the last century. In addition, women are increasingly daring to participate and invade the domain of production of religious knowledge, a domain of power traditionally owned by men.

CONCLUSION

The sexual oppression of women in the Middle East and elsewhere in the Muslim world is not the result of an oppressive vision of sexuality based on Islam, but a combination of historical, sociopolitical, and economic factors. Although an analysis of the Qur'an and the literature traditionally accepted as establishing the normative practices of Islam leads to contradictory conclusions about the construction of women's sexuality in early Islam, several customary practices that allow violations of women's human rights in the region—honor crimes, stoning, female genital cutting, or virginity tests—have no Koranic basis, as women researchers and activists in the region point out. Moreover, the prevalence of these practices varies greatly among the countries in the region.

. . .

The changing social values in the region and the increasing activity of women's groups in the last decade have begun to act as powerful agents of change that have led to new attitudes toward sexuality, especially among young people, and to new progressive legal and social reforms. These have established the basis of new rights regarding women's sexuality and their status in the family in, for example, Turkey, Egypt, and Jordan. The last two decades also witnessed the emergence of a reformist discourse that argues for equality in Islam on all fronts. This reformist discourse seeks to analyze "women's sexuality as defined by social circumstances, not by nature and divine will" (Mir-Hosseini, 2001: 12). As such, it removes the issue of sexuality or women's status from the domain of *fiqh* rulings to social practices and norms. This approach builds a bridge between the old fixed fronts in their struggles of power over the construction of women's sexuality as constructed in the last century. Another factor that also promises change in the sexual domain is the increasing participation of women in the traditionally male-dominated production of religious knowledge.

NOTES

1. All references to the Qur'an in this article use the translation by Pickthall (1953).

2. "And We said: O Adam! Dwell thou and thy wife in the Garden and eat ye freely (of the fruits) thereof where ye will; but come not nigh this tree lest ye* become wrongdoers. But Satan caused them to deflect therefrom and expelled them from the (happy) state in which they were; and We said: Fall down**, one of you a foe onto the other! There shall be for you on earth a habitation and provision for a time." (Surah 2:35–36). (*Here, the command is in the dual, as addressed to Adam and his wife; **here, the command is in the plural, as addressed to Adam's race.)

3. For an analysis of the discussion about the story of Zuleikha and Yusuf in the Islamic tradition, and the need for and possibilities of alternative feminist readings of the story, see Merguerian and Najmabadi (1997).

4. "And come not near unto adultery. Lo! It is an abomination and an evil way" (Surah 17:32).

5. "The adulterer and the adulteress, scourge ye each one of them (with) a hundred stripes. And let not pity for the twain withhold you from obedience to Allah, if ye believe in Allah and the Last Day. And let a party of believers witness their punishment." (Surah 24:2)

6. "And those who accuse honourable women but bring not four witnesses, scourge them (with) eighty stripes and never (afterward) accept their testimony—They indeed are evildoers." (Surah 24:4)

7. "As for those who accuse their wives but have no witnesses except themselves; let the testimony of one of them be four testimonies (swearing by Allah that he is of those who speak the truth;

   And yet a fifth, invoking the curse of Allah on him if he is of those who lie.

   And it shall avert the punishment from her if she bear witness before Allah four times that the thing he saith is indeed false,

   And a fifth (time) that the wrath of Allah be upon her if he speaketh truth. . . .

   Why did they not produce four witnesses? Since they produce not witnesses, they verily are liars in the sight of Allah" (Surah 24: 6, 7, 8, 9, 13).

8. The Turkish Civil Code was translated and adapted from the Swiss Civil Code of the time and the Turkish Penal Code was adapted from the Italian Penal Code.

9. For a discussion of the virginity tests in Turkey from a human rights perspective, see Human Rights Watch (1994) and Seral (2000).

10. For a more comprehensive analysis and description of the reform of the Turkish Civil Code, see Women for Women's Human Rights–New Ways (2002).

REFERENCES

Ahmed, Leila. "Arab Culture and Writing Women's Bodies." *Feminist Issues* 9:1 (Spring 1989): 41–55. Rpt. in Ilkkaracan, ed. (2000): 51–65.

————. "Early Islam and the Position of Women: The Problem of Interpretation." *Women in Middle Eastern History: Shifting Boundaries in Sex and Gender.* Eds. Nikki R. Keddie and Beth Baron. New Haven: Yale University Press, 1991: 58–73.

————. *Women and Gender in Islam.* New Haven: Yale University Press, 1992.

Albadeel Coalition. "Albadeel Coalition Against 'Family Honor' Crimes." In Ilkkaracan, ed. (2000): 399–401.

al-Basha, Amal. "Reproductive Health in Yemen: Aspirations and Reality in Applications of Human Rights to Reproductive and Sexual Health." Paper presented at the international meeting on "Women, Sexuality and Social Change in the Middle East and the Mediterranean," organized by Women for Women's Human Rights (WWHR)–New Ways, Istanbul, Sept. 28–30, 2001.

An-Naim, Abdullah. *Toward an Islamic Reformation.* Cairo: American University in Cairo Press, 1990.

Belhadj, Ahlem. "Le Comportement Sexuel des Femmes en Tunisie." Paper presented at the international meeting on "Women, Sexuality and Social Change in the Middle East and the Mediterranean," organized by Women for Women's Human Rights (WWHR)–New Ways, Istanbul, Sept. 28–30, 2001.

Bouhdiba, Abdelwahab. *Sexuality in Islam.* London: Saqi Books, 1998 [1975].

Boxberger, Linda. "From Two Sisters to One: Women's Lives in the Transformation of Yemen." *Women in Muslim Societies: Diversity within Unity.* Boulder: Lynne Riener Publishers, 1998: 119–133.

Carroll, Lucy. "Law, Custom and the Muslim Girl in the U.K." *Dossier 20.* Montpellier: Women Living Under Muslim Laws, n.d.: 68–75. Rpt. in Ilkkaracan, ed. (2000): 245–252.

Cindoglu, Dilek. "Virginity Tests and Artificial Virginity in Modern Turkish Medicine." *Women's Studies International Forum* 20:2 (1997): 253–261. Rpt. in Ilkkaracan, ed. (2000): 215–228.

Clarke, Lisa. "Beijing+5 and Violence against Women." *Holding on to the Promise: Women's Human Rights and the Beijing+5 Review.* Ed.

Cynthia Meillon in collaboration with Charlotte Bunch. New Jersey: Center for Women's Global Leadership, 2001: 147–155.

al-Dawla, Aida Seif. "The Story of the FGM Task Force: An Ongoing Campaign against Female Genital Mutilation." In Ilkkaracan, ed. (2000): 427–433.

Foster, Angel M. "Conference Report: Sexuality in the Middle East, Oxford, June 23–25, 2000." Oxford: St. Anthony's College, The Middle East Center, 2000.

Hassan, Riffat. "The Role and Responsibilities of Women in the Legal and Ritual Tradition of Islam (Shari'ah)." *Riffat Hassan: Selected Articles.* Montpellier: Women Living Under Muslim Laws, n.d.

Hatem, Mervat F. "The Professionalization of Health and the Control of Women's Bodies as Modern Governmentalities in Nineteenth-Century Egypt." *Women in the Ottoman Empire: Middle Eastern Women in the Early Modern Era.* Ed. Madeline C. Zilfi. Leiden: Brill, 1997: 66–80. Rpt. in Ilkkaracan, ed. (2000): 67–79.

Hoodfar, Homa. "The Women's Movement in Iran: Women at the Crossroad of Secularization and Islamization." Paper presented at the conference on "Women's Solidarity Beyond All Borders," organized by Women for Women's Human Rights (WWHR), Istanbul, Oct. 11–12, 1996.

Human Rights Watch. *A Matter of Power: State Control of Women's Virginity in Turkey.* New York: Human Rights Watch, 1994.

Ilkkaracan, Pinar. *A Brief Overview of Women's Movements in Turkey: The Influence of Political Discourses.* Instanbul: Women for Women's Human Rights (WWHR), 1996. Rpt. in *Dossier 16.* Montpellier: Women Living Under Muslim Laws, n.d.: 93–103.

————. "Introduction." In Ilkkaracan, ed. (2000): 1–15.

————. "Conference on Women, Sexuality and Social Change in the Middle East and the Mediterranean." *Women's Global Network for Reproductive Rights Newsletter* 75:1 (2002).

Ilkkaracan, Pinar, ed. *Women and Sexuality in Muslim Societies.* Istanbul: Women for Women's Human Rights (WWHR)–New Ways, 2000.

International Women's Health Coalition. "Beijing+5: Analysis of Negotiations and Final 'Further Actions' Document." Comp. Francoise Girard. New York: International Women's Health Coalition, 2000 <www.iwhc.org/uploads/FutherActions%2Epdf>.

Kandiyoti, Deniz. "Contemporary Feminist Scholarship and Middle East Studies." *Gendering the Middle East.* Ed. Deniz Kandiyoti. London: I. B. Tauris, 1996: 1–27.

————. "Slave Girls, Temptresses and Comrades: Images of Women in the Turkish Novel." *Feminist Issues* 8:1 (Spring 1988): 35–50. Rpt. in Ilkkaracan, ed. (2000): 91–106.

Khair Badawi, Marie-Therese. "Le Désir Amputé, Sexual Experience of Lebanese Women." Paper presented at the international meeting on "Women, Sexuality and Social Change in the Middle East and the Mediterranean," organized by Women for Women's Human Rights (WWHR)–New Ways, Istanbul, Sept. 28–30, 2001.

Mahl. "Women on the Edge of Time." *New Internationalist* 270 (August 1995) <www.newint.org/issue270/270edge.html>.

Mehdid, Malika. "En-Gendering the Nation State: Women, Patriarchy and Polities in Algeria." *Women and the State: International Perspectives.* Eds. Shirin M. Rai and Geraldine Lievesley. London: Taylor and Francis, 1996: 78–102.

Merguerian, Gayane Karen, and Afsanah Najmabadi. "Zuleykha and Yusuf: 'Whose Best Story'?" *International Journal of Middle East Studies* 29 (1997): 485–508.

Mernissi, Fatima. "Virginity and Patriarchy." *Women's Studies International Forum* 5:2 (1982): 183–194. Rpt. in Ilkkaracan, ed. (2000): 203–214.

————. *Beyond the Veil: Male-Female Dynamics in a Modern Muslim Society.* Bloomington: Indiana University Press, 1987 [1975].

Mir-Hosseini, Ziba. "The Construction of Gender in Islamic Legal Thought and Strategies for Reform." Paper presented for the workshop on "Islamic Family Law and Justice for Muslim Women," organized by Sisters in Islam, Kuala Lumpur, June 8–10, 2001.

Moghadam, Valentine M. *Modernizing Women: Gender and Social Change in the Middle East.* Boulder: Lynne Riener Publishers, 1993.

Musallam, Basim F. *Sex and Society in Islam.* Cambridge: Cambridge University Press, 1989 [1983].

Najmabadi, Afsaneh. "Feminism in an Islamic Republic." *Islam, Gender and Social Change.* Eds. Yvonne Yazbeck Haddad and John L. Esposito. New York: Oxford University Press, 1998. 59–84.

Obermeyer, Carla Makhlouf. "Sexuality in Morocco: Changing Context and Contested Domain." *Culture, Health and Sexuality* 2:3 (2000): 239–254.

Pettman, Jan Jindy. "Boundary Politics: Women, Nationalism and Danger." *New Frontiers in Women's Studies: Knowledge, Identity and Nationalism.* Eds. Mary Maynard and June Purvis. London: Taylor and Francis, 1996: 187–202.

Pickthall, Mohammed Marmaduke, trans. *The Meaning of the Glorious Koran.* New York: Mentor Books, 1953.

Rouhana, Zoya. "Obedience: A Legalized Social Custom." Paper presented at the international meeting on "Women, Sexuality and Social Change in the Middle East and the Mediterranean," organized by Women for Women's Human Rights (WWHR)–New Ways, Istanbul, Sept. 28–30, 2001.

Sabbah, Fatna A. *Woman in the Muslim Unconscious.* New York: Pergamon Press, 1984.

Saigol, Rubina, "Militarisation, Nation and Gender: Women's Bodies as Arenas of Violent Conflict." In Ilkkaracan, ed. (2000): 107–120.

Seral, Gülsah. "Virginity Testing in Turkey: The Legal Context." Women and Sexuality in Muslim Societies. In Ilkkaracan, ed. (2000): 413–416.

Tadros, Mariz. "Like a Match Stick." *Al-Ahram Weekly Online.* No. 573 (14–20 February 2002) <www.ahram.org.eg/weekly/2002/573/lil.htm>.

United Nations Development Program (UNDP). *The Arab Human Development Report 2002.* New York: UNDP, 2002 <www.undp.org/rbas/ahdr/english.html>.

Wadud, Amina. *Qur'an and Woman: Rereading the Sacred Text from a Woman's Perspective.* Oxford: Oxford University Press, 1999.

Women for Women's Human Rights (WWHR)–New Ways. *The New Legal Status of Women in Turkey.* Istanbul: WWHR–New Ways, 2002.

Yirmisbesoglu, Vildan. "Sevda Gök: Killed for Honor." Rpt. in Ilkkaracan, ed. (2000): 389–391.

DISCUSSION QUESTIONS FOR CHAPTER 4

1. In what ways is the personal political for you in your relationships?

2. How is the personal political in heterosexual relationships generally?

3. How does socialization into gender affect intimacy in relationships?

4. How does homophobia discourage intimacy? Have there been instances in your life when homophobia has prevented you from developing intimacy with someone?

5. How would you describe women's and men's different ways of communicating? How do women's and men's different ways of communicating affect relationships?

6. How is romantic love related to consumerism? Give some examples.

SUGGESTIONS FOR FURTHER READING

Collins, Patricia Hill. *Black Sexual Politics: African Americans, Gender, and the New Racism*. New York: Routledge, 2004.

Freedman, Estelle. *Feminism, Sexuality, and Politics: Essays by Estelle B. Freedman*. Chapel Hill, NC: The University of North Carolina Press, 2006.

Hite, Shere. *The Hite Report: A National Study of Female Sexuality*. New York: Seven Stories Press, 2005.

Kamen, Paula. *Her Way: Young Women Remake the Sexual Revolution*. New York: Broadway Books, 2002.

Stoltenberg, John. *Refusing to Be a Man: Essays on Sex and Justice,* revised ed. London: UCL Press, 1999.

White, Emily. *Fast Girls: Teenage Tribes and the Myth of the Slut*. New York: Penguin, 2003.

Wolf, Naomi. *Promiscuities: A Secret History of Female Desire*. London: Random House, 2000.

CHAPTER 5

Inscribing Gender on the Body

In contemporary U.S. society we are surrounded by images of beautiful, thin (although fit and sculpted, large breasted, and sometimes full bottomed), young, abled, smiling women. Most of these bodies are White, and when women of color are depicted, they tend to show models with more typically White features or hair. These images set standards for appearance and beauty that are internalized—standards that affect how we feel about our own bodies. As a result, most of us grow up disliking our bodies or some parts of them. Many women are especially troubled by those parts of their bodies they see as larger than societal ideals.

It is distressing that women often experience their bodies as sources of despair rather than joy and celebration. This is especially true as we age and measure our bodies against notions of youthful "beauty." These images of perfect bodies are fabricated by a male-dominated culture and are reinforced by multi-billion-dollar industries that serve to maintain both corporate profits and patriarchal social relations. The images we are given are flawless and give the illusion of absolute perfection. In reality these images tend to be airbrushed and computer enhanced or completely computer generated. These digital representations integrate all the "positive" features associated with contemporary North American "beauty" in one image. Fashion models today weigh more than 20 percent less than the average woman; only about 5 percent of the female population in our society weighs the average fashion model's weight given her height. Obviously, real women come in all shapes and sizes. Our diversity is part of our beauty!

Although the body is an incredibly sophisticated jumble of physiological events, our understanding of the body cannot exist outside of the society that gives it meaning. Even though bodies are biophysical entities, what our bodies mean and how they are experienced is intimately connected to the meanings and practices of the society in which we reside. This is clearly demonstrated in the reading by Amy Bloom on intersexuals and the cultural consequences for children born with "ambiguous genitalia." In "Hemaphrodites with Attitude," Bloom discusses the culturally mediated process of gender reassignment. In this way, bodies are like cultural artifacts; culture becomes embodied and is literally inscribed or represented through the body at the same time

LEARNING ACTIVITY **Considering Body Size, Shape, and Movement**

Take a tour examining the public facilities of your school or campus, which may include:

Telephone booths or stalls

Drinking fountains

Bleachers

Sinks and stalls in public restrooms

Curbs, ramps, and railings

Chairs and tables

Turnstiles

Elevators and escalators

Stairs and staircases

Vending machines

Doors and doorways

Fire alarm boxes

Answer the following questions:

What assumptions about the size and shape of the users (height, weight, proportionate length of arms and legs, width of hips and shoulders, hand preference, mobility, etc.) are incorporated into the designs?

How do these design assumptions affect the ability of you and people you know to use the facilities satisfactorily?

How would they affect you if you were significantly:

Wider or narrower than you are?

Shorter or taller?

Heavier or lighter?

Rounder or more angular?

More or less mobile/ambulatory?

Identify any access or usage barriers to people with physical disabilities. Answer the following questions:

Are classrooms accessible to people who can't walk up or down stairs?

Are emergency exit routes usable by people with limited mobility?

Are amplification devices or sign language interpreters available for people with hearing impairments?

Are telephones and fire alarms low enough to be reached by people who are seated in wheelchairs or who are below average height?

Are audiovisual aids appropriate for people with hearing or vision impairments?

Describe the experience of a person in your class or school who has a mobility, vision, speech, or hearing impairment.

Variation 1. Identify one assumption incorporated into the design of one of the facilities (drinking fountain, phone booth, etc.). Gather formal or informal data about the number of people on campus that might not be able to use the facility satisfactorily, based on the design assumption. Suggest one or two ways to make the facility more useful to those people.

Variation 2. Choose one of the access or usage barriers you have identified and suggest a way to remove the barrier. Research the cost involved. Identify one or two ways of funding the access strategy you have suggested.

Source: Janet Lockhart and Susan M. Shaw, *Writing for Change: Raising Awareness of Difference, Power, and Discrimination, www.teachingtolerance.org.*

that the *objectification* of women's bodies (seeing the body as an object and separate from its context) is supported by the media and entertainment industries. Note how these norms about the body rely on a notion of the healthy and/or abled body.

Bodies, however, are not only reflections of social norms and practices but also sites of *identity, self-expression,* and *performance.* As our lives become more complex and we have less power over the way we live them, we are encouraged to focus more on the body as something we *can* control and as something we can use to express our identity. As a result, the body becomes something to be fashioned and controlled; at the same time, this control over body—and the ability to shape, clothe, and express it—becomes synonymous with personal freedom. We might question whether the ability to change and adorn the body in new ways is really "freedom," as is political or economic freedom. Indeed, scholars discussing backlash (organized resistance) have emphasized that the contemporary preoccupation with the body illustrates the ways society encourages us (members of marginalized groups in particular) to focus on the body and its management as a "distraction" from real economic and political concerns.

Tattoos and piercing among young women are examples of a trend toward self-expression in the context of mass-market consumerism. Having a tattoo or multiple tattoos—traditionally a masculine or an outlaw, rebellious act—is a form of self-expression for women. Similarly, multiple piercing of many body parts, including erogenous and sexually charged areas of the body, can be seen as a form of rebellion against the constraints of gender and sexuality. This expression is certainly less rebellious from society's point of view than activities for real social and political change, especially when trends involve the purchase of products and services that support the capitalist economy and make someone rich. Indeed, both tattooing and piercing can also be interpreted as reactionary trends and as examples of the many ways women are encouraged to mutilate and change parts of their bodies. Note that these "rebellious" practices have now been appropriated as relatively ordinary fashion practices. You can buy nose and belly-button rings, for example, that clip on without ever having to pierce anything, just as you can buy temporary tattoos. In fact, the self-consciousness involved in the parody of the real thing is now a form of self-expression all its own. This issue of body image and its consequences for women's lives is a central issue for third wave feminism, mobilizing many young women and men.

Although men are taught to be concerned with their bodies and looks (and increasingly so, given the advertising industry's desire to create a new market for beauty products), women are particularly vulnerable to the cultural preoccupation with the body. There is a *double standard* of beauty for women and men: Physical appearance is more important in terms of the way women are perceived and treated. This is especially true in terms of the aging body; there is a much stronger mandate for women than for men to keep their bodies looking young.

We want to focus on two issues associated with the cultural preoccupation of women and the body: (1) the close relationship between women and nature and bodily functions, and (2) norms associated with appearance and beauty that help determine women's identity and worth. We examine these two issues next and then discuss eating disorders and methods for resisting the beauty ideal.

BODIES, NATURE, AND WOMEN

Although both women and men have bodies, an obvious aspect of the social construction of the body is that what female and male bodies stand for, or signify, implies different things in different cultures. Women have been associated with *nature:* the body, earth, and the domestic, whereas men, because of historical and mythological associations with the spirit and sky, have been associated with *culture:* the mind rather than the body and abstract reason rather than earthly mundane matters. Importantly, Western civilizations have incorporated not only a distinction between nature and culture but also a domination of culture and mind over nature and body. In particular, Western societies' notions of progress have involved the taming and conquering of nature in favor of civilization. As a result, the female/nature side of this dichotomy is valued less and often denigrated and/or controlled.

A prime example of this is the way the normal processes of the female body have been seen as smelly, taboo, and distasteful. Menstruation is regarded negatively and described with a multitude of derogatory euphemisms like "the curse" and "on the rag," and girls are still taught to conceal menstrual practices from others (and men in particular). As Gloria Steinem suggests in the reading "If Men Could Menstruate," the experience would be something entirely different if it was men who menstruated. Advertisements abound in magazines and on television about tampons, pads, douches, feminine hygiene sprays, and yeast infection medicines that give the message that women's bodies are constantly in need of hygienic attention. Notice we tend not to get ads for jock itch during prime-time television like we do ads for feminine "ailments." In this way, there is a strange, very public aspect to feminine bodily processes at the same time that they are coded as very private.

These notions about women and the body have helped shape gender ideologies and reinforce *biological determinism,* a tendency that sees women in terms of their reproductive and biological selves and allows the male body to avoid such constraints. Men as a group have been able to project their fears and anxieties about (?)

ACTIVIST PROFILE   **Maggie Kuhn**

Most people are getting ready to retire at 65. Maggie Kuhn began the most important work of her life at that age. In 1970 Kuhn was forced to retire from her career with the Presbyterian Church. In August of that year, she convened a group of five friends, all of whom were retiring, to talk about the problems faced by retirees—loss of income, loss of social role, pension rights, age discrimination. Finding new freedom and strength in their voices, they also concerned themselves with other social issues, such as the Vietnam War.

The group gathered in Philadelphia with college students opposed to the war at the Consultation of Older and Younger Adults for Social Change. A year later, more than 100 people joined the Consultation. As this new group began to meet, a New York television producer nicknamed the group the Gray Panthers, and the name stuck.

In 1972 Kuhn was asked at the last minute to fill in for someone unable to speak during the 181st General Assembly of the United Presbyterian Church. Her stirring speech launched the Gray Panthers into national prominence, and calls began to flood the organization's headquarters. Increased media attention came as the Gray Panthers became activists. They co-sponsored the Black House Conference on Aging to call attention to the lack of African Americans at the first White House Conference on Aging, and they performed street theater at the American Medical Association's 1974 conference, calling for health care as a human right. At the core of Panther activities was the belief that older people should seize control of their lives and actively campaign for causes in which they believe.

The Gray Panthers have been instrumental in bringing about nursing home reform, ending forced retirement provisions, and combating fraud against the elderly in health care. Kuhn, who was active with the Panthers until her death at age 89, offered this advice to other activists: "Leave safety behind. Put your body on the line. Stand before the people you fear and speak your mind—even if your voice shakes. When you least expect it, someone may actually listen to what you have to say. Well-aimed slingshots can topple giants."

Body Art

Across practically all times and cultures, humans have practiced various forms of body modification for such differing reasons as warding off or invoking spirits, attracting sexual partners, indicating social or marital status, identifying with a particular age or gender group, and marking a rite of passage (Lemonick, et al.). People all over the world have pierced, painted, tattooed, reshaped, and adorned their bodies, turning the body itself into an artistic canvas.

The earliest records of tattoos were found in Egypt around the time of the building of the pyramids. Later, the practice was adopted in Crete, Greece, Persia, Arabia, and China. The English word *tattoo* comes from the Polynesian *tatau*, a practice observed by James Cook when he visited Tahiti on his first voyage around the world. In the Marquesas, Cook noted that the men had their entire bodies tattooed, but women tattooed only their hands, lips, shoulders, ankles, and the area behind the ears.

Today, many of the Maori men of New Zealand are returning to the practice of wearing the elaborate tattoos of their ancestors. In Morocco, henna designs on the hands and feet are an integral part of significant celebrations, such as weddings and religious holidays. In Ethiopia, Hamar men earn raised scars made by cutting with a razor and then rubbing ash into the wounds for killing a dangerous animal or enemy. Surma girls have their earlobes stretched by clay plates and paint their faces during courtship season.

As you may have noted, body art is a gendered practice. Tattooing, piercing, painting, and reshaping the body also serve the purpose of marking gender. What are common body modification practices in the United States? How do these practices express and reinforce gender?

Sources: Monica Desai, "Body Art: A History," *Student BMJ* 10 (2002):196–97. Michael Lemonick et al., "Body Art," *Time South Pacific* (12/13/99), 66–68. Pravina Shukla, "The Human Canvas," *Natural History* 108 (1999): 80.

LEARNING ACTIVITY **On the Rag**

Collect a wide variety of women's magazines such as *Cosmopolitan, Glamour, Vogue, Elle, Mirabella,* and so on. Identify advertisements for "feminine hygiene products"—tampons, pads, douches, feminine hygiene sprays, yeast infection medicines. What do the visual images in the ads suggest? What do the words tell readers? What messages do these advertisements send about women's bodies? Now collect a variety of men's magazines such as *GQ, Maxim, Men's Journal,* and so on. Identify advertisements for "masculine hygiene products." What do you find? What does the difference imply about women's bodies in contrast to men's bodies? How does this implication reinforce structures of gender subordination?

frailty and mortality onto women's flesh and imagined women as more controlled by their biology (as evident in mythology, art, and philosophy). Biological determinism assumes that a person's biology (rather than culture or society) determines that person's destiny. You will recall from Chapter 3 that culture does indeed shape human destiny in tandem with human physiology and chemistry, a rejection of the myth of biological determinism. Despite the fact that these notions about biological determinism affect everyone in Western societies, it is important to understand that the body and its expressions have stronger repercussions in women's lives.

THE "BEAUTY" IDEAL

In this section we discuss four points associated with the "beauty" ideal. First, contemporary images of female beauty are changeable. What is considered beautiful in one society is different from standards in others: Practices in one society might ostracize you—or might certainly prevent your getting a date—in another. Some societies encourage the insertion of objects into earlobes or jawline or other mechanics to increase neck length or head shape. Others consider large women especially attractive and see their fat as evidence of prosperity; again, in most contemporary Western societies, thin is closer to standards of ideal beauty, although there are differences within specific ethnic communities within the United States. In other words, what is considered beautiful is culturally produced and changes across different cultures and historical periods. Most adult women can clearly see these changes in feminine "beauty" even within their own lifetimes. In addition, Western standards of body appearance are exported along with the exportation of fashion and other makeup products. A poignant example of this is in the reading by Jonathan Watts titled "China's Cosmetic Surgery Craze." He discusses a procedure that aims to bring Chinese women closer to Western ideals of beauty through leg-lengthening operations.

A focus on standards of Western female beauty over time reveals that in the nineteenth century White, privileged women were encouraged to adopt a delicate, thin, and fragile appearance and wear bone-crushing (literally) corsets that not only gave them the hourglass figure but also cramped and ruptured vital organs. These practices made women faint, appear frail, delicate, dependent, and passive—responses to nineteenth-century notions of middle-class femininity. Victorian furniture styles accommodated this ideal with special swooning chairs. Standards for weight and body shape changed again in the early twentieth century when a sleek, boyish look was adopted by the flappers of the 1920s. Women bound their breasts to hide their curves. Although more curvaceous and slightly heavier bodies were encouraged through the next decades, body maintenance came to dominate many women's lives. Fueled by the fashion industry, the 1960s gave us a return to a more emaciated, long-legged look, but with very short skirts and long hair. At the beginning of this new century, we see a more eclectic look and a focus on health and fitness, but norms associated with ideal female beauty still construct the thin, large-breasted, White (tanned, but not too brown) body as the most beautiful. Note the body type that has a slender, thin frame with large breasts is quite rare and represents a very small minority of women in the United States. Nonetheless it is still the standard of beauty to which most women aspire. This is reflected in the increasing numbers

HISTORICAL MOMENT   **Protesting Miss America**

In 1921 a group of hotel owners in Atlantic City came up with the idea to stage a bathing beauty contest to get tourists to stay in town after the Labor Day holiday. Eight finalists were chosen from photo entries in newspapers, and Margaret Gorman, representing Washington, D.C., was crowned the first "Miss America" at the age of 16.

Throughout the rest of the twentieth century, the Miss America pageant continued to reinforce norms of the ideal woman. By 1968 the women's movement had begun to challenge beauty ideals and the ways women were judged by their appearance. In the days leading up to the 1968 pageant, members of the New York Radical Women made known their intentions to protest the oppressive image of the beauty queen. On September 7, as the winner paraded onstage, activists in the auditorium unfurled a women's liberation banner and chanted slogans. While people in the hall barely noticed the protest, network TV picked it up and broadcast it to the nation.

Outside the hall, 200 women protested. In a mock mini-pageant, protestors led out a sheep which they crowned as Miss America. Into a "Freedom Trash Can," they threw "instruments of torture"—girdles, curlers, false eyelashes, cosmetics, issues of *Cosmopolitan* and *Playboy,* and bras. While they had originally planned to set a fire in the can, they chose to comply with local fire regulations and did not. When a reporter asked Robin Morgan why, she explained that the mayor had been concerned about fire safety. She added, "We told him we wouldn't do anything dangerous—just a symbolic bra-burning." While the *New York Times* correctly reported no fire had been lit, only a few weeks later the paper referred to "bra-burning" as if it had actually taken place. The image caught on with the media, and, without reference to any reality, the media promoted the myth of the bra-burning feminist.

Source: Ruth Rosen, *The World Split Open: How the Modern Women's Movement Changed America* (New York: Viking, 2000).

of cosmetic surgeries involving breast augmentation among fashion models and the general population.

A second point concerning the beauty ideal is that the ideal reflects various relations of power in society. Culture is constructed in complex ways, and groups with more power and influence tend to set the trends, create the options, and enforce the standards. As Courtney Martin in the reading "Love Your Fat Self" suggests, sizeism and the discrimination against fat people "remains the only truly socially acceptable form of discrimination." These standards about body size and beauty tend not to be created by the ordinary women whose lives these beauty ideals affect. In our culture, beauty standards are very much connected to the production and consumption of various products, and, indeed, the beauty product and fashion industries are multi-billion-dollar enterprises. As the reading excerpted from Joan Jacobs Brumberg's *The Body Project* explains, garment industries in the United States helped sexualize women's breasts through their development of the bra. Corporate powers, advertising, and the fashion, cosmetics, and entertainment industries all help create standards for us and reinforce gender relations. Even the "natural look" is sold to us as something to be tried on, when obviously the real natural look is devoid of marketing illusions in the first place. Most of these industries are controlled by White males or by other individuals who have accepted what many scholars call ruling-class politics. The main point is that most of us get offered beauty and fashion options constructed by other people. Although we have choices and can reject them, lots of resources are involved in encouraging us to adopt the standards created by various industries. However, as the reading "Body Ethics and Aesthetics Among African American and Latina Women" by Lisa R. Rubin, Mako L. Fitts, and Anne E. Becker suggests, college-educated African American and Latina women found ways to reject the thin, White body aesthetic and actively created alternative constructions of beauty. It is important to understand the ways the slender body has been constructed as a White aesthetic.

In this way, beauty ideals reflect White, abled, and middle-class standards. Such standards of beauty can humiliate fat or non-White women as well as the poor, the aged, and the disabled. These norms help enforce racism, classism, ableism, ageism, and fat oppression, as well as sexism generally. Many ethnic communities, however, have alternative notions of feminine beauty and actively resist the normalizing standards of Anglo culture. Lisa Miya-Jervis understands the racial politics of appearance and explains in "Hold That Nose" why she avoided surgery to change the shape of her nose.

The third point concerning beauty practices is that standards are enforced in complex ways. Of course, "enforcement" does not mean, as Sandra Bartky has said, that someone marches you off to electrolysis at gunpoint. Instead, we adopt various standards, integrate them as "choices" we make for ourselves, and sometimes "police" one another in a general sense. The policing of women by other women around body issues (such as imposing standards and sanctions like negative talk, withdrawing friendship, or exclusion from a group or party) is an example of horizontal hostility (see Chapter 2). Norms (cultural expectations) of female beauty are produced by all forms of contemporary media and by a wide array of products. For example, Victoria's Secret, a lingerie company, sells more than underwear. Models are displayed in soft-porn poses and the company's advertisements shape ideas about gender, sexuality, and the body. Other companies, such as the producer of Dove brand soap and beauty products, have emphasized body acceptance, paralleling a surge in the acceptance of "plus size" models. It is interesting to note that these models, although called "plus size," more closely mirror average U.S. women's bodies than do traditional fashion models.

Beauty norms are internalized, and we receive various positive and negative responses for complying with or resisting them. This is especially true when it comes to hair. Hair plays significant roles in women's intimate relationships, as the reading "What We Do for Love" by Rose Weitz on women and their hair suggests. It is interesting to think about these everyday behaviors that maintain the body: the seemingly trivial routines, rules, and practices. Some scholars call these *disciplinary body practices*. They are "practices" because they involve taken-for-granted routinized behaviors such as shaving legs, applying makeup, or curling/straightening/coloring hair; and they are "disciplinary" because they involve social control in the sense that we spend time, money, and effort, and imbue meaning in these practices. Again, disciplinary beauty practices are connected to the production and consumption of various products. Of particular concern is the connection between practices associated with weight control and smoking. A study from the National Institutes of Health reported that weight concerns and a "drive for thinness" among both Black and White girls at ages 11 to 12 years were the most important factors leading to subsequent daily smoking (*www.nih.gov*).

You can probably think of many disciplinary beauty practices that you or your friends take part in. Men have their practices too, although these tend to be simpler and involve a narrower range of products. Alongside fashion and various forms of cosmetics and body sculpting, women are more likely to get face-lifts, eye tucks, nose jobs, collagen injections to plump up lips, liposuction, tummy tucks, stomach bands and stapling, and, of course, breast implants as well as breast reductions. The American Society of Plastic Surgeons reports that in 2007 there were twice as many women electing to have their breasts enlarged through cosmetic surgery as there were a decade earlier. In particular, the number of African American women electing cosmetic surgery generally quadrupled (with most favored procedures being rhinoplasty [nose reshaping], liposuction, and breast reduction), reflecting the imposition of White standards of beauty as well as the increase in disposable income and acceptance of cosmetic surgery among some groups in the African American community. Although rhinoplasty is the most common cosmetic operation for teenage girls, there has also been a very significant increase in the numbers of teenage girls getting breast implants, with a tripling of the numbers between 2002 and 2003 from 3,800 to just over 11,000 such surgeries.

The enormous popularity of shows like "Extreme Makeover," "The Swan," and MTV's "I Want a Famous Face," plus the increased number of websites encouraging young girls to change the way they look, have fueled these changes. The U.S. FDA (Food and Drug Administration) has been concerned about the safety of both silicone gel-filled and saline-filled breast implants for many years and banned the widespread use of silicone gel-filled implants some years ago. Known risks involve leakage and rupture, loss of sensation in the nipples, permanent scarring, problems with breast-feeding, potential interference with mammography that may delay cancer diagnoses, and fibrositis, or pain and stiffness of muscles, ligaments, and tendons. Breast implants require ongoing maintenance and often need periodic operations to replace or remove the devices. In 2006 the FDA again approved the marketing of silicone gel-filled implants by two companies for breast reconstruction in women of

In Six Chix, May 31, 2001. Reprinted with the author's permission.

all ages and breast augmentation in women aged 22 years and older. The companies are required to conduct post-approval studies of potential health risks.

Another surgery that has increased in popularity is vaginal cosmetic surgery. It includes labiaplasty (a procedure to change the shape and size of the labia minora [inner lips of the vagina] and/or labia majora [outer lips], although most often it involves making the labia minora smaller), vaginoplasty (creating, reshaping, or tightening the vagina; the latter procedure is often called "vaginal rejuvenation"), and clitoral unhooding (exposing the clitoris in an attempt to increase sexual stimulation). There is no agreement, for example, on what is the "normal" size for labia and no reliable studies on the impact of labia size on sexual functioning and sexual pleasure. The American Society of Plastic Surgeons has only recently started collecting data about cosmetic vaginal surgeries from the 793 "vaginal rejuvenation" procedures reported in 2005. By 2006, the number had shown a 30 percent increase. Although these surgeries are performed for medical reasons, their increase is related to what has been called "aesthetic" motivations. It is important to understand that the aesthetics of the pelvic area are related to norms about gender, the body, and sexuality, and especially norms created by media and contemporary pornography. Simone Weil Davis discusses labiaplasty in the reading "Designer Vaginas." She discusses the politics of these surgeries and relates this to the typically non-Western practice of female genital cutting.

As mentioned, an interesting development is the popularity of "reality" television shows that take people (especially women) out of communities, isolate them, and then transform their bodies through surgery, cosmetics, and other technologies of body management, before reintroducing them into their communities as radically transformed people (implying that their lives will now be better, more successful, happier, etc.). Such shows encourage people to pass for a younger age and to consider

Body Image Quiz

INTRODUCTION

When was the last time you looked in the mirror and liked what you saw? Most women have to think long and hard before answering this question. Whether or not we admit it, women are active players in the beauty game, which requires us to think looks and body weight are the true sources of our happiness. The truth is, women are their own worst critics when it comes to their bodies. Yet experts tell us that self-esteem is closely tied to body image, even more so than our actual physical appearance. Take this quiz to learn more about body image and self-esteem.

1. In a national survey in which 200 women were asked, "If you could change one thing about your body, what would it be?" how many women said they would leave their bodies unchanged?
   a. 50
   b. 25
   c. 10
   d. 0

2. What percentage of American women overestimate their body size?
   a. 20 percent
   b. 35 percent
   c. 50 percent
   d. 95 percent

3. Which of the following do psychologists call "eating disorder breeding grounds" for women?
   a. Sports teams
   b. Dance troupes
   c. High schools and colleges
   d. Commercial weight-loss programs
   e. All of the above

4. In a national survey, women were asked what they thought was the "peak age" for attractiveness. Which was the most frequent age answer from the following choices?
   a. 16
   b. 22
   c. 33
   d. 45

5. How many women in the United States suffer from eating disorders?
   a. 200,000
   b. 2 million
   c. 4 million
   d. 5 million
   e. 12 million

ANSWERS

1. d. 0. In a body image survey, conducted by Rita Freeman, Ph.D., the author of *Bodylove: Learning to Like Our Looks—And Ourselves,* not a single woman out of 200 was willing to leave her body

alone. Body areas and/or conditions that women seem most dissatisfied with run from head to toe. Some of the body changes women wish for include wider eyes, freckles, longer legs, smaller feet, better posture, firmer thighs, thinner ankles, longer nails, and bigger breasts. Above all else, American women want to lose weight. Two-thirds of the women surveyed wanted to drop weight, particularly in the area between their waist and knees. Why such an obsession with weight loss? Psychologists say the reasons abound. Obviously American society sets unrealistic, even ridiculous, standards by glorifying models who are dangerously thin. Psychologists say there is also a social tendency to associate good looks and thinness with success. It's called "looksism," and it is a form of stereotyping.

2. d. 95 percent. The condition of not being satisfied with one's weight is far more prevalent in women than men, and it includes American women of all races, ethnic groups, religions, professions, and economic classes. Most women who weigh in the normal, healthy range for their age and height still tend to consider themselves overweight. Many remain in a lifelong, futile diet mentality, thinking that life would be bliss if only they could lose 10 pounds. Two-thirds of all American women list fear of getting fat on their list of life's worst fears. Finally, women over age 60 report that gaining weight is their second most serious concern; losing their memory is first.

   Many health care experts believe that women have a poor notion of what a healthy weight should be for themselves. Health care providers say that a healthy weight is based on several factors, including weight history (your weight, age, and activity level over several years), genetic factors, age, activity level, as well as other factors such as hormonal changes, stress, and use of nicotine and/or alcohol.

3. c. High schools and colleges. It is during the teenage years that many women first begin their unhealthy preoccupation with their body and appearance. On the brink of puberty, many girls describe a tremendous pressure to be feminine, which, sadly, often equates to being beautiful like a movie star and having an emaciated look. For this reason, eating disorders, such as anorexia and bulimia, are detected more frequently in high school girls and college women than in any other group.

4. c. 33. The good news in the results of this survey is that most women didn't check off the earliest age. Still, 33 is less than half the age expectancy for most women, and psychologists say that women should strive to accept themselves at every age and to see themselves as continuously attractive in a different, more mature way.

   A couple of myths exist on women and aging. Dispelling these myths may help women come to a better acceptance of themselves and their bodies.

   Myth 1: As time passes, more women become increasingly unhappy with their bodies. In reality, a survey showed that women in their 20s, 30s, and 40s said they felt no different about their bodies than they had earlier in life.

   Myth 2: With age women become even more self-conscious of their looks and minor imperfections. In reality, women become less self-conscious. Again, good news!

5. d. 5 million. Eating disorders are devastating mental illnesses that affect more than 5 million American women. Ninety percent of the people who suffer from anorexia nervosa and bulimia nervosa are women, according to the National Association of Anorexia Nervosa and Associated Disorders. Although they revolve around eating and body weight, eating disorders aren't about food, but about feelings and self-expression. Women with eating disorders use food and dieting as ways of coping with life's stresses. For some, food becomes a source of comfort and nurturing or a way to control or release stress. For others, losing weight is a way to gain the approval of friends and family. Eating disorders are not diets, signs of personal weakness, or problems that will go away without treatment. And although the teenage years are considered a high-risk period for these eating disorders, women of all ages can experience the problem or have a relapse later in life.

   Anorexia is a condition of self-induced starvation. The desire to lose weight becomes an obsession because the woman has a distorted body image and cannot see herself as anything but fat. Ten percent of women with anorexia die from it.

(continued)

Bulimia is an eating disorder that involves bingeing and purging. A bulimic woman will eat a large quantity of food and then take separate measures to purge herself of the food by vomiting, taking laxatives, or heavy exercising.

If you think you may have an eating disorder, you should consult a health care provider. Eating disorders are complex medical and psychological conditions, but with therapy and medical intervention, they can be treated.

Source: www.electra.com/electraquiz/admin/Body_Image_Quiz.html.

cosmetic surgery (especially breast implants and argumentation) something women of all ages should seek and want. Though these shows are often entertaining and seductive in their voyeuristic appeal, it is important to recognize the role they play in the social construction of "beauty," the advertising of products and body-management technologies, and the social relations of power in society. In considering these practices—from following fashion and buying clothes, accessories, and makeup to breast enhancement and all the practices in between—we need to keep in mind how much they cost, how they channel women's energies away from other (perhaps more productive) pursuits, and how they may affect the health and well-being of people and the planet.

The body and the various practices associated with maintaining the female body are probably the most salient aspects of what we understand as femininity, and they are crucial in social expressions of sexuality. Note how many bodily practices of contemporary femininity encourage women to stay small, not take up space, and stay young. Maturity in the form of body hair is unacceptable; we are encouraged to keep our bodies sleek, soft, and hairless—traits that some scholars identify with youth and powerlessness. The trend among some women to shave and remove pubic hair so that the genitalia appear prepubertal is an example of this. Such hair removal, mimicking the display of female genitalia in pornography, sends the message that the mature female body is "gross" or should be altered. It also sexualizes children's bodies.

The final point regarding the beauty ideal is that while it shapes women's bodies and lives, it is a huge aspect of corporate capitalism and U.S. consumerism. Enormous profits accrue to the fashion, cosmetics, beauty, and entertainment industries yearly. It is important to remember that gendered beauty practices are related to specific products and commodities that women are encouraged to purchase. And, of course, the underlying message is that women are not good enough the way they are but need certain products to improve their looks or their relationships. This is not good for women's self-esteem in most cases. In addition, there is also a huge weight-loss industry in the United States. Millions of dollars are spent every year by people who seek to cram their bodies into smaller sizes. Of course, many individuals want to make their bodies smaller out of a concern for better health and mobility, and the weight and exercise industries help them attain these goals. But as Courtney Martin in the reading "Love Your Fat Self" emphasizes, it is possible to be both fit and fat, and many people have learned to despise flesh and fat and participate in these industries' profits out of a desire to more closely fit the cultural standard. Again, there is a double standard here whereby fat women have a harder time than fat men in our

LEARNING ACTIVITY　**Feminism and Plastic Surgery**

In recent years, technology has made plastic surgery more successful and more accessible for a large number of American women. Women are having nearly every body part resized and reconstructed. Televisions shows such as *The Swan*, *Extreme Makeover*, and *Nip/Tuck* have popularized the notion of creating a new self through surgery. Beyond nose and breast jobs, however, women are now also having all sorts of plastic surgery to have their labia reduced or their hymen "repaired." Put the word *labiaplasty* or *vaginoplasty* in your Web search engine. Visit the sites of some of the doctors who offer these forms of plastic surgery. What are these surgeries? Why do these sites suggest women might want these surgeries? Why do you think so many women are choosing these surgeries? Read Elizabeth Haiken's *Venus Envy: A History of Cosmetic Surgery* (Baltimore: Johns Hopkins University Press, 1999) for one feminist's take on the issue of plastic surgery.

Eating Disorder Information

The following organizations provide information about eating disorders. Visit their websites to learn more about anorexia, bulimia, and other forms of disordered eating.

Academy for Eating Disorders　Telephone: 703-556-9222　Website: *www.aedweb.org*

National Association of Anorexia Nervosa and Associated Disorders　Telephone: 847-831-3438　Website: *www.anad.org*

National Eating Disorder Information Center (Canada)　Toll-free: 866-633-4220 Website: *www.nedic.ca*

National Eating Disorders Association　Toll-free: 800-931-2237　Website: *www.NationalEatingDisorders.org*

culture. This is not to say that fat men have an easy time; certainly, as already mentioned, prejudice against large-size people of all genders is one of the last bulwarks of oppression in U.S. society. Many people have no qualms about blatantly expressing their dislike and disgust for fat people even when they might keep sexist or racist attitudes hidden. However, fat women have an especially difficult time because of the interaction between sexism and fat phobia. In this way the beauty ideal supports the weight-loss industry and encourages looksism and fat oppression.

Finally, at the very same time that we are bombarded with messages about being thin, the food industry in the United States (the third largest industry nationally) has considerable clout. Never before have North Americans (and, increasingly, people in developing countries) been bombarded with advertising for cheap and often toxic (high in sugar, fat, salt, or preservatives) food to such a degree. Children, for example, watch over 10,000 food ads per year on television, 90 percent of which are for four types of "food": sugar-coated cereals, soft drinks, fast food, and candy. A 2007 study from the United Kingdom found that the more overweight a child was, the more she or he would eat when exposed to advertisements following a television show. Obese children increased food intake by 134 percent and normal-weight children by 84 percent. Chocolate was the food source of choice. The need for healthy nutrition is underscored by a study at Brigham and Women's Hospital in which researchers found that though as many as 1 in 4 children under the age of 14 years diet, these behaviors were not only ineffective but often tended to lead ultimately to weight gain.

EATING DISORDERS

Contemporary eating disorders are compulsive disorders that include a variety of behaviors. Among these are *anorexia nervosa* (self-starvation), *bulimia nervosa* (binge eating with self-induced vomiting and/or laxative use), *compulsive eating* (uncontrolled eating or binge eating), and *muscle dysmorphia* (fear of being inadequately muscled). Alongside these diagnostic categories are general eating-disordered behavior that may include occasional binge eating and fasting, overly compulsive food habits such as eating only certain foods, not being able to eat in public, and general problems associated with compulsive dieting and/or compulsive over-exercising (sometimes called *anorexia athletica,* although at this time this is not recognized as a formal diagnosis). The latter catchall category of generalized disordered eating/exercising seems to be widespread among North American women. These disorders are culturally mediated in that they are related to environmental conditions associated with the politics of gender and sexuality. It appears that the number of eating-disordered women in any given community is proportional to the number of individuals who are dieting to control weight. Dieting seems to trigger the onset of an eating disorder in vulnerable individuals. According to a 2007 British study, teenage girls who diet even "modestly" are five times more likely to become anorexic or bulimic than those who do not diet. Those on strict diets were 18 times more likely to develop an eating disorder.

Anorexics can become very thin and emaciated by refusing to maintain a healthy body weight, having intense fears of gaining weight, and tending to strive for perfection. Bulimics eat large amounts of food in a short time (binge) and then make themselves vomit, or they purge with laxatives or overexercising, or they may purge through diuretics and/or amphetamines. Bulimics are more likely to be of normal weight than anorexics, although they both share emotions and thoughts associated with self-punishment, or feelings of being overwhelmed because they feel fat, or feelings of frustration and/or anger with other factors in their lives. Compulsive eating (which may involve bingeing) is understood as an addiction to food and often involves using food as comfort and includes eating to fill a void in life, hide emotions, or cope with problems. Compulsive eaters often have low self-esteem and feel shame about their weight. Individuals with muscle dysmorphia believe that their physiques are too small and unmuscular rather than too large. They participate in maladaptive exercise and dietary practices, and many use performance-enhancing substances. Although

WIDE GIRL WEB **The Best Plus-Sized Sites Taking Up Space on the Internet**

Tired of endless diet blather and media misrepresentation, young fat women are making themselves seen and heard in pop culture like never before, thanks to the Internet. From blogs to activist networks to YouTube rants, big girls are creating their own media in a big way. So put these six sassy sites in your feed reader, and treat your mind to some righteous food for thought.

What happens when the funny fat chick stops playing sidekick and starts kicking ass? You get **Joy Nash's "A Fat Rant"** on YouTube (*www.youtube.com/watch?v= yUTJQlBl1oA*). Rallying viewers to be open about their weight (even if it's—*gasp!*— over 200 pounds), to ditch stores that don't carry plus sizes, and to stop using fat as an excuse, this diatribe proves that the revolution just might be televised.

For more fat-positive video, check out **Nation of Size** (*www.nationofsize.com*), a site showcasing the talents of big, beautiful performing artists. More than a dozen talented peeps are featured here, in short but inspiring documentary clips, so you can see for yourself that there's more to being an ample show-stopper than what you've seen on *Fat Actress*.

The ladies on the **Big Fat Deal** blog (*www.bfdblog.com*) look at body-image issues through the fun-house mirror of pop culture, discussing the good, the bad, and the *Ugly Betty* with hilarious commentary. Typical headline: "Beth Ditto Jams Out With Her Ham Out." Hell yeah!

"We defy those who tell us our bodies are wrong," reads the manifesta of **NOLOSE** (*www.nolose.org*), an organization dedicated to creating a fat, fabulous queer community through conferences, workshops, and shindigs like My Big Fat Queer Prom. Visit their blog (community.Livejournal.com/nolose) to find out about upcoming events—or to plan your own big fat queer thing.

Fat is also a feminist issue, and that's why Kate Harding and her co-bloggers at **Shapely Prose** (*www.kateharding.net*) write witty, fierce daily posts challenging bullshit assumptions made by health statistics, popular media, and any other dumbass who thinks you should diet.

So those jeans make you look fat. So what? Talk it out at **Fatshionista** (*community .livejournal.com/fatshionista*), a LiveJournal community devoted to plus-sized style. Filled with links, recommendations, sales, and swaps, it's like a fashion show, slumber party, and fat-girl flea market all in one.

Source: Wendy McClure, "Wide Girl Web: The Best Plus-Sized Sites Taking Up Space on the Internet." Reprinted with permission from *BUST* Magazine.

early studies focused on male bodybuilders, recent scholarship suggests that such symptoms can appear in the general population and that women are increasingly demonstrating this disorder. Similarly, while boys and men tend to use steroids more than women to increase athletic performance, new scholarship has shown that girls and women are also using steroids. A 2005 study at Oregon Health and Science

University found that two-thirds of female steroid use was not by athletes but by women hoping to improve their body image, look more toned, and control their weight.

Eating disorders (with the exception of muscle dysmorphia) affect women primarily; the ratio of women to men among anorexia nervosa and bulimia sufferers is 10:1 and the figure is 3:1 for binge eating. In Western society, these disorders primarily affect young (aged 15 to 25 years) women. Current statistics suggest that about 1 percent of female adolescents have anorexia, 4 percent have bulimia (with about half of the former also developing bulimic patterns), and approximately 3.5 percent experience binge eating in any 6-month period. Accurate numbers associated with generalized eating problems are unknown, although it is assumed that the number of women who indulge in disordered eating patterns of some kind is quite substantial. While these disorders occur in all populations in the United States, White women and those with higher socioeconomic status are somewhat more likely to suffer these problems, although as the reading by Rubin et al. suggests, while African American and Latina women's beauty ethics are more nurturing and self-accepting, this does not necessarily protect them from eating disorders. In addition, reporting bias occurs as reported statistics in part reflect the ways "incidence" is tied to resource availability for treatment in various communities. We do not know the incidence of unacknowledged or untreated eating disorders that occur in communities where treatment resources are scarce or unavailable. Finally, while eating disorders tend to be Western phenomena not usually manifested in countries with food scarcity, Asian countries have recently experienced a surge in the incidence of eating disorders as a result of increased westernization and urbanization.

There are often serious physical and emotional complications with these disorders, and up to 20 percent of people with serious eating disorders die from the disorder, usually of complications associated with heart problems and chemical imbalances, as well as suicide. With treatment, mortality rates fall to 2–3 percent; about 60 percent recover and maintain healthy weight and social relationships; 20 percent make only partial recoveries and remain compulsively focused on food and weight; and approximately 20 percent do not improve. The latter often live lives controlled by weight- and body-management issues, and they often experience depression, hopelessness, and loneliness. Chronic obesity that may follow compulsive eating also has important consequences for health and illness.

Many students who live in dorms and sororities report a high incidence of eating disorders; perhaps you have struggled with an eating disorder yourself or have had a close friend or sister similarly diagnosed. If the huge number of women who have various issues with food—always on a diet, overly concerned with weight issues, compulsive about what they do or do not eat—are also included in the figures on eating disorders, then the number of women with these problems increases exponentially. Indeed, although teenage boys are actually more likely to be overweight than girls, they are less likely to diet. A 2007 study published in the *American Journal of Health Promotion* found that 21 percent of the teenage girls in the study were overweight, 55 percent said they were dieters, and 35 percent were consistent dieters. Although more teenage boys in the study were overweight, only a quarter said they were dieters and only 12 percent were consistent dieters. An early study some years ago reported 80 percent of fifth-grade girls telling researchers that they were on a diet, highlighting the ways cultural ideas about weight and the body are internalized at young ages. Because food and bodies are central preoccupations in so many women's lives, we might ask, why women and why food?

IDEAS FOR ACTIVISM

- Organize an eating disorders awareness event. Provide information about eating disorders and resources for help. Invite a therapist who specializes in treating eating disorders to speak. Create awareness posters to hang around your campus.
- Organize a letter-writing campaign to protest the representation of such a small range of women's shapes and sizes in a particular women's magazine.
- Organize a speak-out about beauty ideals.
- Organize a tattoo and piercing panel to discuss the politics of tattooing and piercing. Have a tattoo and piercing fashion show, and discuss the meaning of the various tattoos/piercings.

First, women have long been associated with food and domestic pursuits; food preparation and focus on food is a socially accepted part of female cultural training. Given that women have been relegated to the private sphere of the home more than the public world, food consumption is easily accessible and unquestioned. Second, food is something that nourishes and gives pleasure. In our culture, food has been associated with comfort and celebration, and it is easy to see how eating can be a way of dealing with the anxieties and unhappiness of life. Put these two together, and we get food as the object of compulsion; when we add the third factor, the "beauty" ideal, with all the anxieties associated with closely monitoring the size and shape of women's bodies, the result can be eating disorders.

Scholars also emphasize that eating disorders reflect the ways women desire self-control in the context of limited power and autonomy. In other words, young women turn to controlling their bodies and attempt to sculpt them to perfection because they are denied power and control in other areas of their lives. Central in understanding eating disorders, however, is the pressure in our society for women to measure up to cultural standards of beauty and attractiveness, what is often called the "culture of thinness." These standards infringe on all our lives whether we choose to comply with them or to resist them. Messages abound telling women that they are not good enough or beautiful enough, encouraging us to constantly change ourselves, often through the use of various products and practices. The result is that girls learn early on that they must aspire to some often-unattainable standard of physical perfection. Such bombardment distracts girls and women from other issues, "disciplining" them to focus energy on the body, affecting their self-esteem and constantly assaulting the psyche as the body ages. In this way, eating disorders can be read as cultural statements about gender.

RESISTING "BEAUTY" IDEALS

Although many women strive to attain the "beauty" ideal on an ongoing, daily basis, some actively resist such cultural norms. These women are choosing to not participate in the beauty rituals, not support the industries that produce both images and products, and to create other definitions of beauty. Some women are actively appropriating

Learn to Love Your Body

Do you ever stand in front of the mirror dreaming about where you'd get a few nips and tucks? Or feeling like life would be better if only you had smaller thighs, a flatter tummy, or there was simply less of you? These are all signs of a not-so-hot body image.

It's important that you feel good about who you are. And until you like yourself as is, trying to change your body shape will be a losing proposition. High self-esteem is important for a healthy, balanced lifestyle—and it's a definite must if successful weight loss is one of your goals. So it's time to smile back at that image in the mirror and value all the wonderful characteristics about the person reflected there. Try these techniques:

1. *Recognize your special qualities.* Make a list of all your positive qualities—not including your physical traits. Are you kind? Artistic? Honest? Good in business? Do you make people laugh? Post your list near the mirror or another place where you'll see it every day.
2. *Put your body back together.* Most of us with negative body images have dissected our bodies into good and bad parts. "I hate my thighs and butt." "My butt's okay, but my stomach is fat and my arms are flabby." Reconnect with your body by appreciating how it all works to keep you going. Try stretching or yoga—the fluid movements are great for getting in touch with the wonders of the human body.
3. *Remember the kid inside you.* Give yourself permission not to be perfect. Inside all of us is the kid we used to be—the kid who didn't have to be perfect and worry about everything. Remember that kid, and give yourself a break. Place a photo of yourself as a child in your bedroom or at your desk at work so that you can see it each day and remember to nurture yourself and laugh a little.
4. *Enjoy your food.* Eating is pleasurable. So enjoy it! Food gives us energy and sustains life. Don't deprive yourself or consider eating an evil act. If you allow yourself to enjoy some of the foods you like, you'll be less likely to overeat. In turn, your body won't feel bloated and uncomfortable.
5. *Indulge in body pleasures.* One step toward being kind to your body, and inevitably yourself, is to indulge yourself. Get a massage, take a long, hot bath, use lotions that smell good, or treat yourself to a manicure or pedicure.
6. *Speak positively.* Pay attention to your self-talk. It's amazing how often we put ourselves down throughout the day. Each time you catch yourself making critical comments, fight back by immediately complimenting yourself.
7. *See the world realistically.* It's common to compare ourselves to people in magazines or movies, but this can make you feel self-conscious. If you want to compare yourself to others, look at the real people around you. They come in different shapes and sizes—and none of them are airbrushed or highlighted.
8. *Dress in clothes that fit.* When we feel badly about our bodies, we often dress in shabby clothes, waiting until we lose weight before we buy something we like. But why? Feel good now! Find attractive clothes that fit your current size. Treating yourself will make you feel renewed.
9. *Be active.* Movement and exercise can make you and your body feel terrific. Not only does exercise help boost your mood, it stimulates your muscles, making you feel more alive and connected to your body.
10. *Thrive!* Living well will help you feel better about who you are and how you look. Strive to make your personal and professional life fulfilling. You are a unique, amazing person. A healthy, happy life can be all yours!

Source: www.thriveonline.com/shape/countdown/countdown.feature2.week7.html.

these standards by highlighting and/or exaggerating the very norms and standards themselves. They are carving out their own notions of beauty through their use of fashion and cosmetics. For them, empowerment involves playing with existing cultural standards. Most women comply with some standards associated with the beauty ideal and resist others. We find a place that suits us, criticizing some standards and practices and conforming to others, usually learning to live with the various contradictions that this implies.

A question that might be raised in response to ideas about resisting beauty ideals and practices is: What's wrong with being beautiful? In response, feminists say that it is not beauty that is a problem but, rather, the way that beauty has been constructed by the dominant culture. This construction excludes many beautiful women and helps maintain particular (and very restricted) notions of femininity. Maya Angelou's poem "Phenomenal Woman" celebrates female beauty and encourages women to rejoice in themselves and their looks. In "Love Your Fat Self," Courtney Martin also asks us to love our bodies and especially to understand the cultural loathing of fat that many women in the United States have internalized.

Another common question is: Can you wear makeup and enjoy the adornments associated with femininity and still call yourself a feminist? Most feminists (especially those who identify as third wave) answer with a resounding yes. In fact, you can reclaim these trappings and go ultra-femme in celebration of your femininity and your right to self-expression. What is important from a feminist perspective is that these practices are *conscious*. In other words, when women take part in various reproductions of femininity, it is important to understand the bigger picture and be aware of the ways "beauty" ideals work to limit and objectify women, encourage competitiveness (Is she better looking than me? Who is the cutest woman here? How do I measure up?), and ultimately to lower women's self-worth. Understand also how many beauty products are tested on animals, how the packaging of cosmetics and other beauty products encourages the use of resources that end up polluting the environment, and how many fashion items are made by child and/or sweatshop global labor. The point is for us to make conscious and informed choices about our relationships to the "beauty" ideal and to love and take care of our bodies.

Hermaphrodites with Attitude

Amy Bloom (2002)

Beautiful, the doctor says. Ten fingers, ten toes, and the mother's beautiful blond curls. Baby and parents crying with relief, three weary, joyful travelers. They place the baby on the mother's stomach, clamp the cord, and hand the father a pair of slim scissors to cut it. The parents expect both these things—they've seen it done in the Lamaze video, they've seen it on the Lifetime channel. The OB nurse cleans and swaddles the baby quickly while the aide washes the mother's face and changes the bloody sheet under her for a fresh one. They give the baby the Apgar test, a visual assessment taken minutes after birth—a nice experience in most cases, since a baby will get a gratifyingly high score, 8 or 9 out of 10, just by being his or her healthy baby self. It is a high score in this case too, but the doctor shakes his head, in such a small gesture that the father doesn't even see it. The mother sees it, through the anaesthetic, through the sweat, right past the sight of her beautiful baby held tight in the nurse's arms.

Finally, the baby is in the mother's arms. The doctor is thinking fast and trying to hide it. As Dr. Richard Hurwitz instructs in *Surgical Reconstruction of Ambiguous Genitalia in Female Children*, a 1990 training videotape produced by the American College of Surgeons, "The finding of ambiguous genitalia in the newborn is a medical and social emergency." A hundred years ago, midwives examined babies and assigned gender in doubtful cases, or they brought the babies to priests or doctors and the team consulted and assigned gender, and little was made of it until the occasional married, childless woman went to her doctor for a hernia and discovered she had testes, or the married, childless farmer went to the doctor and discovered he had ovaries. Today many physicians regard "genital anomaly" as a dire matter. "After stillbirth, genital anomaly is the most serious problem with a baby, as it threatens the whole fabric of the personality and life of the person," one doctor wrote in 1992; only slightly worse to be dead than intersexed.

The baby is taken to the nursery. The next day the doctor comes in and sits down, and speaks softly. "Your baby will be fine," he says. The parents brace themselves: a faulty valve, a hole where there should be none, something invisible but terrible. "Somehow your baby's genitals haven't finished developing, so we don't quite know right now what sex it is. We're going to run a couple of tests and we'll know very soon. Don't worry. It may be that some cosmetic surgery is required, but don't worry," the doctor tells the parents, who are already well past worrying. "This will all be okay. We can solve this in just a few days. The sooner, the better." As the doctor leaves, he is already calling a pediatric urologist for a consult, getting a pediatric endocrinologist to come over and take a look, getting a geneticist to come on board, to help assign sex and then do what is medically necessary to have the baby's genitals resemble the standard form of that sex.

This scene occurs about two thousand times a year in hospitals all over America. Far from being an exceptionally rare problem, babies born with "genitals that are pretty confusing to all the adults in the room," as medical historian and ethicist Alice Dreger puts it, are more common than babies born with cystic fibrosis. Or, to think of it differently, there are probably at least as many intersexed people in the United States as there are members of the American College of Surgeons.[1]

Imagine a baby born with an oddly shaped but functional arm. Would one choose an invasive, traumatizing pediatric surgery that almost inevitably produces scarring and loss of sensation, just to make the arm conform more closely to the standard shape? Yet parents believe there must be tests that will show their baby's true sex, and surgery that will ensure and reinforce their baby's true sex, and parents want it to happen, quickly. A few days, even a few hours, of having Baby X is too long. One cannot raise a nothing; when people say, "What a beautiful baby! Boy or girl?" one cannot say, "We don't know." In a culture that's still getting used to children who are biracial and adults who are bisexual, the idea of a baby who is neither boy nor girl, or both boy and girl, is unbearable. How do you tell the grandparents? How do you deliver the happy news that you have a healthy it?

The parents hold the baby, still beautiful, still raw but shapely, and they peer at what is under the diaper. Let's say that what they see is a tiny—even for a baby—tiny penis, technically, a microphallus, both misshapen and far smaller than the standard (less than about two centimeters when stretched out from the body). The prevailing approach for the last fifty years has been to declare that a baby boy with such a small and inadequate penis is better off as a girl. In the straightforward words of surgeons, "Easier to make a hole than build a pole," and the collective medical wisdom has been that a boy without much of a pole, and even more, a man without much of a pole, is doomed to live ashamed, apart, and alone. In the face of the assumption that suicide is likely and profound depression inevitable, a physician with the best intentions and the support of his peers might well declare the boy a girl, remove the micropenis and the testes, fashion labia and a small vagina, and tell the parents as little as possible so as to spare the entire family further anxiety and troubling questions of gender (parents who don't know that their little girl was born a boy are less likely to wring their hands over persistent play with trucks and a refusal to wear dresses). . . .

Or let's say that what the parents see is a baby girl with a larger than standard clitoris (more than one centimeter in length). You might not think that this is a problem of "doubtful sex" or confusing genitals, but in infants the gap between clitoris and penis is only about half a centimeter, so the large clitoris that doctors fear will worry her parents every time they change the diaper, and will alarm or even dissuade her future husband, also requires the surgical solution, as early as possible. The surgeries include "clitoral reduction," and if necessary, some enlargement of the vaginal cavity by metal dilators inserted by the parents daily for six months, beginning two weeks postoperatively. Monthly dilation of the seven-or eight-year-old continues into adolescence to prevent narrowing or closure of the vaginal cavity. (The standard for a "good" vagina is one that can be penetrated adequately.) And then, perhaps, following the early vaginoplasty, further molding of delicate and cosmetically pleasing labia may be required.

"Ambiguous genitals," "doubtful sex," "intersexed babies," "male and female pseudohermaphroditism," "true hermaphroditism"—these phrases sometimes describe the same conditions, sometimes very different conditions. Some conditions require hormonal treatment or surgery or both; some require no treatment at all except counseling and time. Symptoms range from the physical anomaly—an unusual-looking set of genitals—to symptoms that will not become apparent until adolescence, to symptoms that will never be apparent from the outside. Some anomalies are defects in the plumbing; others are simply unusual fixtures.

There is a range of medical conditions that fall under the umbrella term "congenital anomalies of the reproductive and sexual system." Boys may suffer from hypospadias, meaning in mild cases that the urethral opening (the "pee hole"), which is supposed to be at the tip of the penis, is perhaps in the glans, on the underside of the penis, or in more severe cases is open from mid-shaft out to the glans, or is even entirely absent, with urine exiting the bladder from behind the penis. Hypospadias sometimes results in ambiguity as to sexual organs, as does Klinefelter's syndrome, which is quite common, occurring in one in five hundred to one in a thousand male births. Most men inherit a single X chromosome from their mother and a single Y chromosome from their father. Men with Klinefelter's inherit an extra X chromosome from either father or mother, and their testes often produce smaller than average quantities of testosterone, so that they don't virilize (develop facial and body hair, muscles, deep voice, larger penis and testes) as strongly as other boys at puberty. (Many also develop small breasts, one of Nature's variations that is often found in those with no intersex conditions at all.) Despite an absence of sperm in their generally small, firm testes, many men with Klinefelter's are never diagnosed because their genitals are typical in appearance.

In androgen insensitivity syndrome (AIS), the body of an XY individual lacks a receptor that enables it to decode messages from androgens (virilizing hormones). AIS results in people with male chromosomes and obviously female bodies; although they produce male hormones, their cells are not sensitive to those hormones, and their bodies never masculinize. There is also partial androgen insensitivity syndrome (PAIS), which typically results in "ambiguous genitalia." The clitoris is large or, alternatively, the penis is small and hypospadic (two different ways of labeling the same anatomical structure). PAIS seems to be quite common, and has been suggested as the cause of infertility in many men whose genitals are typically male.

Among the most prevalent causes of intersexuality among XX (usually female) people is congenital adrenal hyperplasia (CAH), in which the adrenal gland produces an excess of androgens but feminizing occurs at puberty because the ovaries function normally. When excess androgens are produced in utero (sometimes not because of CAH but because an unborn XX baby's metabolism converts hormonal drugs such as progestin, which was frequently administered to prevent miscarriage in the 1950s and 1960s, into an androgen), the female baby may be born with an enlarged clitoris and fused labia that look very much like a scrotum. Sometimes the genitals look typically female, with barely perceptible variations. Sometimes the babies appear to be healthy boys

without testes, and it may be that no one in the delivery room thinks anything is amiss. And less often, the babies' genitals are not just misleading but the hallmark of what has historically been called hermaphroditism: truly ambiguous genitals, both male and female, although not a complete set of either.

. . .

In modern America, we have done our own disappearing act on hermaphrodites: we have turned a lot of baby boys into baby girls, and a lot of healthy baby girls into traumatized ones. A number of scientists and academics have written about this in the last ten years (most notably, the gifted researcher Dreger, the eminently readable and imaginative Fausto-Sterling, the less readable, provocative Judith Butler, and the psychologist Suzanne Kessler), but the person who has almost single-handedly changed both the dialogue on the subject and the surgical practice itself is Cheryl Chase, businesswoman turned activist. . . . In a world of megacorporations, tobacco-sponsored rock concerts, and vast, unsavory alliances, Cheryl Chase, perceived as a "true hermaphrodite," first declared a girl, then a boy, then not much of a boy, then operated upon to make her a more suitable girl by removing her "too large" clitoris (what was too large as a clitoris was, of course, terminally too small as a penis), is a modest, relentless, sleepless army of one.

In 1993, she was just an angry woman, distressed and puzzled by the little she knew of her own traumatic history, and anxious to move past it by offering support to people born intersexed (that is, people who have historically been called, with mystery but not much meaning, "hermaphrodites"). She did outreach and information-sharing and complained to anyone who would listen about the unnecessary and usually damaging surgery routinely visited upon babies born with ambiguous genitals—five babies every day, as a conservative estimate, to state the incidence in another way. She picketed; she fired off press releases from her home in the name of her fledgling group, the Intersex Society of North America (ISNA); she organized support meetings and sent out an indignant and well-informed newsletter (now the *ISNA Newsletter,* formerly and more compellingly called *Hermaphrodites with Attitude*). Cheryl Chase and her lieutenants, volunteers all . . . , have changed the terms of discussion about surgery and treatment for intersexed babies. The head of pediatric endocrinology at Oakland Hospital now supports the ISNA point of view, the American Medical Association's *Archives of Pediatrics and Adolescent Medicine* has run articles that mirror ISNA's position, and Chase herself has been invited to give talks at the Albert Einstein College of Medicine in New York City, at Denver Children's Hospital, and at the 2000 meeting of the Lawson Wilkins Pediatric Endocrine Society, as the honored closing speaker.

It may be that if you can tell the right story, at the right moment, even people who don't wish to hear will hear. The story of intersex babies is medically complicated, but ISNA simplified it. . . . Through careful study and the pained honesty of intersexed adults, ISNA has undermined the standard argument of good-hearted people ("Surgery may not be a great solution, but it's the only one we have, and it would be worse to raise those poor children as 'nothings'"), and it has undone the peculiar psychological argument that many pediatricians made (parents would be so upset every time they changed a diaper that they would not be able to love the child, and a child with inadequate genitals, especially a boy, would not be able to survive the scrutiny of other children). As common sense dictates, ISNA supports surgery when a medical condition requires it, and encourages families to consult with endocrinologists, knowledgeable psychotherapists, and, if appropriate, the best surgeons they can find. . . .

. . .

"No lying," Philip Gruppuso says. "No delusions of grandeur on the part of the doctor."

Gruppuso is both a doctor and a dad. He's a bearded, fatherly middle-aged man with twin daughters, now twenty-one years old. When sexual orientation comes up over drinks or at conferences, he tells his colleagues that he wouldn't care if either or both of his girls were lesbians. The straight men around him eye him dubiously, and he's not sure whether they're wondering why

he's saying something that couldn't possibly be true, or whether they're wondering if it *is* true—which makes them wonder what kind of normal middle-aged physician and family man from the Bronx would feel that way.

"Physicians, like everyone else, find it hard to change. Not just because of habit but because, in the history of treating these kids, there is an element of homophobia. It doesn't make my colleagues happy when I say this. If you look back at the standard texts of the fifties and sixties, the underlying concern was that people who were 'really' male but looked female would want to have sex with males, and the same for females who appeared male. Homosexual sex was the underlying fear. Not worrying about sexual orientation allows me to think about what's best for the patient and what's good medical practice."

If this criticism has not endeared Gruppuso to his pediatric colleagues, neither has his straightforward assessment of the most common treatment for intersexed babies, and of why it's still more common than what ISNA recommends: "This isn't complicated, it's simple. There are a million ways to screw this up, and most of them have to do with doctors being too sure of themselves, imagining that they control the outcome for sexual orientation and gender identity, and then doing irreversible surgery."

Ten years ago, Phil Gruppuso, now director of research in pediatrics at Rhode Island Hospital and professor of pediatrics and biochemistry at Brown University, was a doctor just like that.

"I was a pediatric endocrinologist and very much in the mainstream. Anne Fausto-Sterling was a colleague and became a friend. I started thinking: I'm a scientist, look at the evidence, look at the follow-ups. I looked at the evidence, and the evidence that this genital surgery is a good idea is just—junk. There's no such evidence that doing surgery on infant genitals for appearance's sake, surgery without consent and which frequently results in sexual dysfunction—there's no evidence at all that this is a good thing. And I am unwilling to harm patients to protect the reputations of physicians who are fine academicians and thoughtful men, but who were—mistaken."

And his advice to doctors confronting their first intersexed baby? "Get a specialist and don't do anything irreversible. Be willing to say, 'It may take a month for us to have a diagnosis and a determination of gender.' Help the parents, help the grandparents, and always, always—it's the first thing we learn as doctors—do no harm. This surgery, and intersexed babies treated by people who don't know what they're doing, does harm."

At the other end of the debate on the treatment of the intersexed are Drs. Richard Hurwitz and Harry Applebaum, creators of the American College of Surgeons training videotape on ambiguous genitals in female children. The tape begins with Vivaldi and a statement of goals: reduce the size of the clitoris, exteriorize the vagina (making it penetrable), and make the genitals cosmetically normal. There is no mention at all of either function or feeling. Hurwitz looks into the camera and says, with quiet confidence, "The treatment of the clitoris depends on its size and the preference of the surgeon." I'm sure it is so; I'm surprised that he says it. "If the clitoris is very large, however," Hurwitz continues as the camera carefully follows the scalpel and the removal of erectile tissue from the clitoris until it folds back into itself, accordionlike, "it may need to be taken care of for social reasons."

It is hard to imagine what social reasons a baby girl might have. It's harder still to imagine how the odd results, described repeatedly in the videotape as cosmetically pleasing, could be anything other than a source of shame and discomfort. Not only are the results not cosmetically pleasing, they're not even good. The surgically altered vaginas and reduced clitorises are painful to contemplate (and even more painfully, the vaginas will probably close and require dilation in the course of the patients' childhood). And according to U.K. research reported in the *Lancet,* follow-up studies of intersexed children show more sexual and psychological dysfunction among those who have had these pull-through vaginoplasties and clitoral reductions than among those who have had no surgery at all. To watch the surgery is to wonder who in their right mind could think that stripping away and excising nerves protects sexual

function or that this surgery is not only preferable but essential and urgent—far more so than helping parents help their child to live with a large clitoris, or with a tiny penis, or even with other, more puzzling anomalies.

Not monsters, nor marvels, nor battering rams for gender theory, people born intersexed have given the rest of the world an opportunity to think more about the odd significance we give to gender, about the elusive nature of truth, about the understandable, sometimes dangerous human yearning for simplicity—and we might, in return, offer them medical care only when they need it, and a little common sense and civilized embrace when they don't.

NOTE

1. In a 1998 article in *The Hastings Center Report,* Dreger writes, "Most people . . . assume the phenomenon of intersexuality to be exceedingly rare. It is not. But how common is it? The answer depends, of course, on how one defines it. Broadly speaking, intersexuality constitutes a range of anatomical conditions in which an individual's anatomy mixes key masculine anatomy with key feminine anatomy. One quickly runs into a problem, however, when trying to define 'key' or 'essential' feminine and masculine anatomy. In fact, any close study of sexual anatomy results in a loss of faith that there is a simple, 'natural' sex distinction that will not break down. . . . For our purposes, it is simplest to put the question of frequency pragmatically: How often do physicians find themselves unsure which gender to assign at birth? One 1993 gynecology text estimates that 'in approximately 1 in 500 births, the sex is doubtful because of the external genitalia.' I am persuaded by more recent, well-documented literature that estimates the number to be roughly 1 in 1,500 live births." The authors of a peer-reviewed 2000 article in the *American Journal of Human Biology* write, "We surveyed the medical literature from 1955 to the present for studies of the frequency of deviation from the ideal of male or female. We conclude that this frequency may be as high as 2% of live births. The frequency of individuals receiving 'corrective' genital surgery, however, probably runs between one and two per 1,000 live births (0.1 to 0.2%)." The Intersex Society of North America bases its

estimate of one in 2,000 (which, given about four million births a year, yields an annual total of two thousand births) on "statistics of how many newborn babies are referred to 'gender identity teams' in major hospitals." By any of these reckonings, intersexuality is significantly more common than cystic fibrosis, which has an incidence of one in 2,300 live births, according to the Cystic Fibrosis Research website, and affects some forty thousand children and adults in the United States. The number of fellows of the American College of Surgeons fluctuates a bit from year to year but is about fifty thousand.

R E A D I N G **35**

Breast Buds and the "Training" Bra

Joan Jacobs Brumberg (1997)

In every generation, small swellings around the nipples have announced the arrival of puberty. This development, known clinically as "breast buds," occurs before menarche and almost always provokes wonder and self-scrutiny. "I began to examine myself carefully, to search my armpits for hairs and my breasts for signs of swelling," wrote Kate Simon about coming of age in the Bronx at the time of World War I. Although Simon was "horrified" by the rapidity with which her chest developed, many girls, both in literature and real life, long for this important mark of maturity. In Jamaica Kincaid's fictional memoir of growing up in Antigua, *Annie John,* the main character, regarded her breasts as "treasured shrubs, needing only the proper combination of water and sunlight to make them flourish." In order to get their breasts to grow, Annie and her best friend, Gwen, lay in a pasture exposing their small bosoms to the moonlight.

Breasts are particularly important to girls in cultures or time periods that give powerful meaning or visual significance to that part of the body. Throughout history, different body parts have been eroticized in art, literature, photography, and film. In some eras, the ankle or upper arm was the ultimate statement of female sexuality. But breasts were the particular preoccupation of Americans in the years after World War II, when voluptuous stars, such as Jayne Mansfield, Jane Russell, and Marilyn Monroe, were popular box-office attractions. The mammary fixation of the 1950s extended beyond movie stars and shaped the experience of adolescents of both genders. In that era, boys seemed to prefer girls who were "busty," and American girls began to worry about breast size as well as about weight. This elaboration of the ideal of beauty raised expectations about what adolescent girls should look like. It also required them to put even more energy and resources into their body projects, beginning at an earlier age.

The story of how this happened is intertwined with the history of the bra, an undergarment that came into its own, as separate from the corset, in the early twentieth century. In 1900, a girl of twelve or thirteen typically wore a one-piece "waist" or camisole that had no cups or darts in front. As her breasts developed, she moved into different styles of the same garment, but these had more construction, such as stitching, tucks, and bones, that would accentuate the smallness of her waist and shape the bosom. In those days, before the arrival of the brassiere, there were no "cups." The bosom was worn low; there was absolutely no interest in uplift, and not a hint of cleavage.

The French word *brassière,* which actually means an infant's undergarment or harness, was used in *Vogue* as early as 1907. In the United States, the first boneless bra to leave the midriff bare was developed in 1913 by Mary Phelps Jacobs, a New York City debutante. Under the name Caresse Crosby, Jacobs marketed a bra made of two French lace handkerchiefs suspended from the shoulders. Many young women in the 1920s, such as Yvonne Blue, bought their first bras in order to achieve the kind of slim, boyish figure that the characteristic chemise (or flapper) dress required. The first bras were designed simply to flatten, but they were superseded by others intended to shape and control the breasts. Our current cup sizes (A, B, C, and D), as well as the idea of circular stitching to enhance the roundness of the breast, emerged in the 1930s.

Adult women, not adolescents, were the first market for bras. Sexually maturing girls simply moved into adult-size bras when they were ready—and if their parents had the money. Many women and girls in the early twentieth century still made their own underwear at home, and some read the advertisements for bras with real longing. When she began to develop breasts in the 1930s, Malvis Helmi, a midwestern farm girl, remembered feeling embarrassed whenever she wore an old summer dimity that pulled and gaped across her expanding chest. As a result, she spoke to her mother, considered the brassieres in the Sears, Roebuck catalog, and decided to purchase two for twenty-five cents. However, when her hardworking father saw the order form, he vetoed the idea and declared, "Our kind of people can't afford to spend money on such nonsense." Although her mother made her a makeshift bra, Malvis vowed that someday she would have store-bought brassieres. Home economics teachers in the interwar years tried to get high school girls to make their own underwear because it saved money, but the idea never caught on once mass-produced bras became widely available.

The transition from homemade to mass-produced bras was critical in how adolescent girls thought about their breasts. In general, mass-produced clothing fostered autonomy in girls because it took matters of style and taste outside the dominion of the mother, who had traditionally made and supervised a girl's wardrobe. But in

the case of brassieres, buying probably had another effect. So long as clothing was made at home, the dimensions of the garment could be adjusted to the particular body intended to wear it. But with store-bought clothes, the body had to fit instantaneously into standard sizes that were constructed from a pattern representing a norm. When clothing failed to fit the body, particularly a part as intimate as the breasts, young women were apt to perceive that there was something wrong with their bodies. In this way, mass-produced bras in standard cup sizes probably increased, rather than diminished, adolescent self-consciousness about the breasts.

Until the 1950s, the budding breasts of American girls received no special attention from either bra manufacturers, doctors, or parents. Girls generally wore undershirts until they were sufficiently developed to fill an adult-size bra. Mothers and daughters traditionally handled this transformation in private, at home. But in the gyms and locker rooms of postwar junior high schools, girls began to look around to see who did and did not wear a bra. Many of these girls had begun menstruating and developing earlier than their mothers had, and this visual information was very powerful. In some circles, the ability to wear and fill a bra was central to an adolescent girl's status and sense of self. "I have a figure problem," a fourteen-year-old wrote to *Seventeen* in 1952: "All of my friends are tall and shapely while my figure still remains up-and-down. Can you advise me?"

In an era distinguished by its worship of full-breasted women, interest in adolescent breasts came from all quarters: girls who wanted bras at an earlier age than ever before; mothers who believed that they should help a daughter acquire a "good" figure; doctors who valued maternity over all other female roles; and merchandisers who saw profits in convincing girls and their parents that adolescent breasts needed to be tended in special ways. All of this interest coalesced in the 1950s to make the brassiere as critical as the sanitary napkin in making a girl's transition into adulthood both modern and successful.

The old idea that brassieres were frivolous or unnecessary for young girls was replaced by a national discussion about their medical and psychological benefits. "My daughter who is well developed but not yet twelve wants to wear a bra," wrote a mother in Massachusetts to *Today's Health* in 1951. "I want her to wear an undervest instead because I think it is better not to have anything binding. What do you think about a preadolescent girl wearing a bra?" That same year a reader from Wilmington, Delaware, asked *Seventeen:* "Should a girl of fourteen wear a bra? There are some older women who insist we don't need them." The editor's answer was an unequivocal endorsement of early bras: "Just as soon as your breasts begin to show signs of development, you should start wearing a bra." By the early 1950s, "training" or "beginner" bras were available in AAA and AA sizes for girls whose chests were essentially flat but who wanted a bra nonetheless. Along with acne creams, advertisements for these brassieres were standard fare in magazines for girls.

Physicians provided a medical rationale for purchasing bras early. In 1952, in an article in *Parents' Magazine,* physician Frank H. Crowell endorsed bras for young girls and spelled out a theory and program of teenage breast management. "Unlike other organs such as the stomach and intestines which have ligaments that act as guywires or slings to hold them in place," Crowell claimed, the breast was simply "a growth developed from the skin and held up only by the skin." An adolescent girl needed a bra in order to prevent sagging breasts, stretched blood vessels, and poor circulation, all of which would create problems in nursing her future children. In addition, a "dropped" breast was "not so attractive," Crowell said, so it was important to get adolescents into bras early, before their breasts began to sag. The "training" that a training bra was supposed to accomplish was the first step toward motherhood and a sexually alluring figure, as it was defined in the 1950s.

In the interest of both beauty and health, mothers in the 1950s were encouraged to check their daughters' breasts regularly to see if they were developing properly. This was not just a matter of a quick look and a word of reassurance.

Instead, Crowell and others suggested systematic scrutiny as often as every three months to see if the breasts were positioned correctly. One way to chart the geography of the adolescent bustline was to have the girl stand sideways in a darkened room against a wall covered with white paper. By shining a bright light on her and having her throw out her chest at a provocative angle, a mother could trace a silhouette that indicated the actual shape of her daughter's bosom. By placing a pencil under her armpit, and folding the arm that held it across the waist, mothers could also determine if their daughter's nipples were in the right place. On a healthy breast, the nipple was supposed to be at least halfway above the midway point between the location of the pencil and the hollow of the elbow.

Breasts were actually only one part of a larger body project encouraged by the foundation garment industry in postwar America. In this era, both physicians and entrepreneurs promoted a general philosophy of "junior figure control." Companies such as Warners, Maidenform, Formfit, Belle Mode, and Perfect Form (as well as popular magazines like *Good Housekeeping*) all encouraged the idea that young women needed both lightweight girdles and bras to "start the figure off to a beautiful future."

The concept of "support" was aided and abetted by new materials—such as nylon netting and two-way stretch fabrics—developed during the war but applied afterward to women's underwear. By the early 1950s, a reenergized corset and brassiere industry was poised for extraordinary profits. If "junior figure control" became the ideal among the nation's mothers and daughters, it would open up sales of bras and girdles to the largest generation of adolescents in American history, the so-called baby boomers. Once again, as in the case of menstruation and acne, the bodies of adolescent girls had the potential to deliver considerable profit.

There was virtually no resistance to the idea that American girls should wear bras and girdles in adolescence. Regardless of whether a girl was thin or heavy, "junior figure control" was in order, and that phrase became a pervasive sales mantra. "Even slim youthful figures will require foundation assistance," advised *Women's Wear Daily* in 1957. In both *Seventeen* and *Compact*, the two most popular magazines for the age group, high school girls were urged to purchase special foundation garments such as "Bobbie" bras and girdles by Formfit and "Adagio" by Maidenform that were "teen-proportioned" and designed, allegedly, with the help of adolescent consultants. The bras were available in pastel colors in a variety of special sizes, starting with AAA, and they were decorated with lace and ribbon to make them especially feminine. In addition to holding up stockings, girdles were intended to flatten the tummy and also provide light, but firm, control for hips and buttocks. The advertisements for "Bobbie," in particular, suggested good things about girls who controlled their flesh in this way; they were pretty, had lots of friends, and drank Coca-Cola. As adults, they would have good figures and happy futures because they had chosen correct underwear in their youth.

By the mid-1950s, department stores and specialty shops had developed aggressive educational programs designed to spread the gospel of "junior figure control." In order to make young women "foundation conscious," Shillito's, a leading Cincinnati department store, tried to persuade girls and their mothers of the importance of having a professional fitting of the first bra. Through local newspaper advertisements, and also programs in home economics classes, Shillito's buyer, Edith Blincoe, promoted the idea that the purchase of bras and girdles required special expertise, which only department stores could provide. (*Seventeen* echoed her idea and advised a "trained fitter" for girls who wanted a "prettier" bosom and a "smoother" figure.) Blincoe acknowledged that teenage girls were already "100% bra conscious," and she hoped to develop the same level of attention to panty girdles. In order to attract junior customers and get them to try on both items, she had the corset department place advertising cards on the walls of dressing rooms in sections of the store where teenagers and their mothers shopped. Strapless bras were suggested on cards in the dress and formal wear departments; light-weight girdles were suggested in the sportswear and bathing suit sections.

In home economics classes, and also at the local women's club, thousands of American girls saw informational films such as *Figure Forum* and *Facts About Your Figure*, made by the Warner Brassiere Company in the 1950s. Films like these stressed the need for appropriate foundation garments in youth and provided girls with scientific principles for selecting them. They also taught young women how to bend over and lean into their bras, a maneuver that most of us learned early and still do automatically. Most middle-class girls and their mothers embraced the code of "junior figure control" and spent time and money in pursuit of the correct garments. Before a school dance in 1957, Gloria James, a sixteen-year-old African-American girl, wrote in her diary: "Mommy and I rushed to Perth Amboy [New Jersey] to get me some slacks, bras and a girdle. I don't even know how to get it [the girdle] on."

In the postwar world, the budding adolescent body was big business. Trade publications, such as *Women's Wear Daily*, gave special attention to sales strategies and trends in marketing to girls. In their reports from Cincinnati, Atlanta, and Houston, one thing was clear: wherever American girls purchased bras, they wanted to be treated as grown-ups, even if they wore only a AAA or AA cup. In Atlanta, at the Redwood Corset and Lingerie Shop, owner Sally Blye and her staff spoke persuasively to young customers about the importance of "uplift" in order "not to break muscle tissue." And at Houston's popular Teen Age Shop, specially trained salesgirls allowed young customers to look through the brassieres on their own, and then encouraged them to try on items in the dressing room without their mothers. Although many girls were shy at first, by the age of fourteen and fifteen most had lost their initial self-consciousness. "They take the merchandise and go right in [to the dressing room]," Blincoe said about her teenage clientele. Girls who could not be reached by store or school programs could send away to the Belle Mode Brassiere Company for free booklets about "junior figure control" with titles such as "The Modern Miss—Misfit or Miss Fit" and "How to Be Perfectly Charming." In the effort to help girls focus on their figures,

Formfit, maker of the popular "Bobbies," offered a free purse-size booklet on calorie counting.

Given all this attention, it's not surprising that bras and breasts were a source of concern in adolescents' diaries written in the 1950s. Sandra Rubin got her first bra in 1951, when she was a twelve-year-old in Cleveland, but she did not try it on in a department store. Instead, her mother bought her a "braziere" while she was away on a trip and sent it home. "It's very fancy," Sandra wrote. "I almost died! I ran right upstairs to put it on." When she moved to New York City that September and entered Roosevelt Junior High School, Sandra got involved with a clique of seven girls who called themselves the "7Bs." Their name was not about their homeroom; it was about the cup size they wanted to be. "Flat, Flat! The air vibrates with that name as my friends and I walk by," Sandra wrote in a humorous but self-deprecating manner. By the time she was sixteen, Sandra had developed amply, so that her breasts became a source of pride. One night she had an intimate conversation with a male friend about the issue of chests: "We talked about flat-chested women (of which, he pointed out, I certainly am not [one])."

Breasts, not weight, were the primary point of comparison among high school girls in the 1950s. Although Sandra Rubin called herself a "fat hog" after eating too much candy, her diary reportage was principally about the bosoms, rather than the waistlines, she saw at school. Those who had ample bosoms seemed to travel through the hallways in a veritable state of grace, at least from the perspective of girls who considered themselves flat-chested. "Busty" girls made desirable friends because they seemed sophisticated, and they attracted boys. In December 1959, when she planned a Friday-night pajama party, thirteen-year-old Ruth Teischman made a courageous move by inviting the "gorgeous" Roslyn, a girl whom she wrote about frequently but usually only worshiped from afar. After a night of giggling and eating with her junior high school friends, Ruth revealed in her diary the source of Roslyn's power and beauty: "Roslyn is very big. (Bust of course.) I am very flat. I wish I would get

bigger fast." Many girls in the 1950s perused the ads, usually in the back of women's magazines, for exercise programs and creams guaranteed to make their breasts grow, allegedly in short order.

The lament of the flat-chested girl—"I must, I must, I must develop my bust"—was on many private hit parades in the 1950s. There was a special intensity about breasts because of the attitudes of doctors, mothers, and advertisers, all of whom considered breast development critical to adult female identity and success. Although "junior figure control" increased pressure on the entire body, and many girls wore waist cinches as well as girdles, it was anxiety about breasts, more than any other body part, that characterized adolescent experience in these years. As a result, thousands, if not millions, of girls in early adolescence jumped the gun and bought "training bras" at the first sight of breast buds, or they bought padded bras to disguise their perceived inadequacy. In the 1950s, the bra was validated as a rite of passage: regardless of whether a girl was voluptuous or flat, she was likely to purchase her first bra at an earlier age than had her mother. This precocity was due, in part, to biology, but it was also a result of entrepreneurial interests aided and abetted by medical concern. By the 1950s, American society was so consumer-oriented that there were hardly any families, even among the poor, who would expect to make bras for their daughters the way earlier generations had made their own sanitary napkins.

Training bras were a boon to the foundation garment industry, but they also meant that girls' bodies were sexualized earlier. In contemporary America, girls of nine or ten are shepherded from undershirts into little underwear sets that come with tops that are protobrassieres. Although this may seem innocuous and natural, it is not the same as little girls "dressing up" in their mother's clothing. In our culture, traditional distinctions between adult clothing and juvenile clothing have narrowed considerably, so that mature women dress "down," in the garments of kids, just as often as little girls dress "up." While the age homogeneity of the contemporary wardrobe helps adult women feel less matronly, dressing little girls in adult clothing can have an insidious side effect. Because a bra shapes the breasts in accordance with fashion, it acts very much like an interpreter, translating functional anatomy into a sexual or erotic vocabulary. When we dress little girls in brassieres or bikinis, we imply adult behaviors and, unwittingly, we mark them as sexual objects. The training bras of the 1950s loom large in the history of adolescent girls because they foreshadowed the ways in which the nation's entrepreneurs would accommodate, and also encourage, precocious sexuality.

R E A D I N G   **36**

If Men Could Menstruate

Gloria Steinem (1978)

A white minority of the world has spent centuries conning us into thinking that a white skin makes people superior—even though the only thing it really does is make them more subject to ultraviolet rays and to wrinkles. Male human beings have built whole cultures around the idea that penis-envy is "natural" to women—though having such an unprotected organ might be said to make men vulnerable, and the power to give birth makes womb-envy at least as logical.

In short, the characteristics of the powerful, whatever they may be, are thought to be better than the characteristics of the powerless—and logic has nothing to do with it.

What would happen, for instance, if suddenly, magically, men could menstruate and women could not?

The answer is clear—menstruation would become an enviable, boast-worthy, masculine event:

Men would brag about how long and how much.

Boys would mark the onset of menses, the longed-for proof of manhood, with religious ritual and stag parties.

Congress would fund a National Institute of Dysmenorrhea to help stamp out monthly discomforts.

Sanitary supplies would be federally funded and free. (Of course, some men would still pay for the prestige of commercial brands such as John Wayne Tampons, Muhammad Ali's Rope-a-dope Pads, Joe Namath Jock Shields—"For Those Light Bachelor Days," and Robert "Barretta" Blake Maxi-Pads.)

Military men, right-wing politicians, and religious fundamentalists would cite menstruation ("*men*struation") as proof that only men could serve in the Army ("you have to give blood to take blood"), occupy political office ("can women be aggressive without that stead-fast cycle governed by the planet Mars?"), be priests and ministers ("how could a woman give her blood for our sins?"), or rabbis ("without the monthly loss of impurities, women remain unclean").

Male radicals, left-wing politicians, and mystics, however, would insist that women are equal, just different; and that any woman could enter their ranks if only she were willing to self-inflict a major wound every month ("you *must* give blood for the revolution"), recognize the preeminence of menstrual issues, or subordinate her selfness to all men in their Cycle of Enlightenment.

Street guys would brag ("I'm a three-pad man") or answer praise from a buddy ("Man, you lookin' *good!*") by giving fives and saying, "Yeah, man, I'm on the rag!"

TV shows would treat the subject at length. ("Happy Days": Richie and Potsie try to convince

Fonzie that he is still "The Fonz," though he has missed two periods in a row.) So would newspapers. (SHARK SCARE THREATENS MENSTRUATING MEN. JUDGE CITES MONTHLY STRESS IN PARDONING RAPIST.) And movies. (Newman and Redford in "Blood Brothers"!)

Men would convince women that intercourse was *more* pleasurable at "that time of the month." Lesbians would be said to fear blood and therefore life itself—though probably only because they needed a good menstruating man.

Of course, male intellectuals would offer the most moral and logical arguments. How could a woman master any discipline that demanded a sense of time, space, mathematics, or measurement, for instance, without that in-built gift for measuring the cycles of the moon and planets—and thus for measuring anything at all? In the rarefied fields of philosophy and religion, could women compensate for missing the rhythm of the universe? Or for their lack of symbolic death-and-resurrection every month?

Liberal males in every field would try to be kind: the fact that "these people" have no gift for measuring life or connecting to the universe, the liberals would explain, should be punishment enough.

And how would women be trained to react? One can imagine traditional women agreeing to all these arguments with a staunch and smiling masochism. ("The ERA would force housewives to wound themselves every month": Phyllis Schlafly. "Your husband's blood is as sacred as that of Jesus—and so sexy, too!": Marabel Morgan.) Reformers and Queen Bees would try to imitate men, and *pretend* to have a monthly cycle. All feminists would explain endlessly that men, too, needed to be liberated from the false idea of Martian aggressiveness, just as women needed to escape the bonds of menses-envy. Radical feminists would add that the oppression of the non-menstrual was the pattern for all other oppressions. ("Vampires were our first freedom fighters!") Cultural feminists would develop a bloodless imagery in art and literature. Socialist feminists would insist that only under capitalism would men be able to monopolize menstrual blood. . . . In fact, if men could menstruate, the power justifications could probably go on forever.

If we let them.

Body Ethics and Aesthetics Among African American and Latina Women

Lisa R. Rubin, Mako L. Fitts, and Anne E. Becker (2003)

INTRODUCTION

This paper reports on an investigation of the relationships among ethnicity, self-representation, and body aesthetics among a sample of college-educated black and Latina women. Until recently, there has been a clinical and lay misperception that body image and weight-related concerns predominantly affect white upper- and middle-class girls and women. Because the ideal of thinness for women is viewed as a European American aesthetic preference, women of color—particularly African American and Latina women—have been considered relatively "protected" from the development of body dissatisfaction and disordered eating common among white women. Contemporary research among women of color has challenged the myth that ethnic minority women in the United States are "immune" from body dissatisfaction and disordered eating (Root 1990). However, within this growing body of research are suggestions that the nature and expression of these concerns may in many cases be distinct from symptom patterns described within the established eating disorders literature (Kuba and Harris 2001).

... Clinical research on sociocultural contributions to disordered eating and body image has produced a literature with a relatively narrow focus on the relationship between body satisfaction and culturally-promoted aesthetic body ideals. Clinical research has also been dominated by quantitative methods. Moreover, its exclusive use of measures developed and validated among predominantly White, Northern American, and Western European samples has limited the scope of understanding of more diverse experiences of eating and embodiment (Davis and Yager 1992). Indeed, the clinical significance attributed to body aesthetics among other populations may be misguided, and may in fact have obscured other important protective and risk factors for eating disorders in ethnically diverse populations. This provides insight into the clinical paradox that the greater body satisfaction reported among African American women as compared with white or Latina women (Akan and Grilo 1995; Altabe 1998) has not conferred the expected protection from disordered eating. That is, several studies among African American subjects have found equivalent rates of purging behavior and notably higher rates of laxative and diuretic abuse relative to white girls and women (Emmons 1992; Pumariega et al. 1994). Similarly, whereas Latina girls and women have been found to report larger (i.e., less thin) aesthetic body ideals (Winkleby et al. 1996) and less concern about weight than whites (Crago et al. 1996), research suggests that disordered eating among Hispanic youth is equivalent to that among whites (Crago et al. 1996; Smith and Krejci 1991).... These data strongly suggest that there is a different relationship among aesthetic ideals, body satisfaction, and disordered eating among women of color than has been found among white women.

...

Representation and Resistance

Bordo argues that mainstream Western media imagery tends to homogenize female beauty, removing racial, ethnic, and sexual differences that "disturb Anglo-Saxon, heterosexual expectations and identifications" (1993:25). These beauty ideals become models against which women measure, judge, and discipline their bodies. Whereas these models typically represent an unhealthful ideal for any woman to achieve, they may be particularly oppressive for many women of color, whose body size, shape, and features may differ significantly from mainstream representations of female beauty (see Becker et al. 2002). Their looks are either denigrated or simply erased from mainstream cultural imagery. Although women of color are now more likely to be represented in beauty and fashion magazines, these representations rarely subvert the dominant imagery. Rather, they typically reinscribe prevailing stereotypes by featuring women with lighter skin and "Anglo" features to the exclusion of other women, and by exoticizing and eroticizing racial difference (hooks 1992).

...

Black feminist appeals to women of color to resist hegemony echo a growing interest in the examination of how cultural representations oppress individuals and whether and how this oppression can be resisted. Collins argues that "the controlling images applied to black women are so uniformly negative that they almost necessitate resistance" (2000:100)....

Culture and Embodiment

...

Previous research suggests important differences in the concepts of body and beauty ideals among both African American and white working-class girls and their white middle- and upper-class counterparts. Mimi Nichter (2000) examined culturally-valued forms of self-presentation, as identified by African American girls, and, in particular, the context and motivation in which these forms are exhibited. She found that while white girls in the study maintained a fixed concept of beauty, "a living manifestation of the Barbie doll" (Parker et al. 1995:106), the African American girls defined beauty through attitude, style, personality, and presence rather than through attaining the "perfect" look. This finding parallels statements from Collins (1990), who argues that while Eurocentric beauty is rigid, Afrocentric beauty is "not based solely on physical criteria" (1990:89). Similarly, participants in Lyn Mikel Brown's (1998) study of white working-class adolescent girls recognized the "perfect" look as a culturally constructed fiction, mocking it (even as they admired it), and ultimately identifying qualities such as trust and attitude as valued over physical appearance. Although this work provides a beginning framework for understanding beauty ideals among girls of diverse social backgrounds, further research is needed to explore these concerns among White working-class women and African American women of all classes.

. . .

METHODS

Narrative data generated in focus group discussions were used to investigate relationships among ethnicity, self-representation, and body aesthetic ideals among ethnically diverse women. . . .

A total of 18 women participated in this study, eight who self-identified as black or African American and ten who self-identified as Latina or Chicana. Five of the women participating in the Latina focus groups were born outside of the United States, in Mexico and Central America, and five were born in the United States. Among participants in the black women's focus group, two were born in the Virgin Islands and the rest were born in the United States. All participants had been living in the United States for several years. Participants ranged in age from 18 to 60 years old, with a mean age of 25. All participants had at least some college education, and four were graduate students. Most participants were raised in middle- and working-class family

households and had already exceeded their parents' educational attainment.

. . .

RESULTS

Study participants described embodied experiences that in many ways resonate with familiar theoretical discourse regarding women's bodies, such as encountering bodily objectification or engaging in social comparison processes. However, their ethnic identities—including cultural values regarding the care and presentation of the body, as well as personal and political commitments—provided alternative, often more positive ways of experiencing their bodies and cultural norms and practices. Inasmuch as participants felt that their ethnic identities also problematized body image, they described strategies for identifying affirming images of women of color and fostering positive self-image against the backdrop of powerful dominant cultural ideals. Several themes relating to ethnic identity and self-representation through the body emerged and are presented below.

Body Aesthetic Ideals Versus Body Ethics

Citing research indicating that African American and Latina girls and women are, on average, heavier than their white counterparts, some investigators have questioned whether African American and Latino/a cultures support different aesthetic body ideals from the dominant Euro-American ideal of a "lean, svelte, almost prepubescent body" (Chamorro and Flores-Ortiz 2000:126; see also Parnell et al. 1996). However, focus group participants resisted identifying a uniform African American or Latina body ideal. Throughout the group discussions, study participants expressed acceptance and appreciation of diverse body types. In fact, data from these focus groups suggest that rather than endorsing different particular *body aesthetic ideals* per se, respondents endorsed a set of *body ethics*—values and beliefs regarding care and presentation of the body—different than those documented among

Euro-American White women. Unlike the dominant culture, in which thinness has arguably become a key defining aspect of beauty, participants in both focus groups endorsed a multifaceted beauty ideal that promotes personal style, self-care, and spirituality.

Styling the Body, the Self

African American participants described style as a key aspect of community aesthetic ideals. One African American participant, a graduate student in her mid-twenties, raised in a mostly black urban community, explained,

> I'm gonna have to say for our community, like for us growing up . . . the emphasis was not on your body. Like you can see someone who is huge, but as long as they're dressed, like it's more [a matter] of dress to present yourself. If you're dressed, and you know how to dress, and you know how to wear your clothes, and you know how to comb your hair and present yourself, you're OK.

For this study participant, looking good is defined through a style that communicates respect and care for one's body and appearance. . . .

One African American study participant, a college student in her mid-twenties who was born and had lived most of her life in the U.S. Virgin Islands, described similar acceptable modes of self-presentation in her culture:

> You're attractive, like people are attracted to you because how you [dress]. . . . Over there, ironing is the huge thing. Like you have to have seams in your pants. . . . You sit just to try not to wrinkle your shirt, like you would not lean up sometimes, just so you won't wrinkle your shirt. And it's like, if you don't have that, you're not attractive. . . . I remember, it would be times where the popular girls who got all the guys would like come to school one day wrinkled, and that was it for them. It was like, "Did you see Tiffany today?" "Oh yeah, her shirt was wrinkled huh, I don't know what happened to her." Like it was like a huge thing. . . . So I think in a lot of ways, like for us, it wasn't a big thing in how your body looked, but it was a big thing with how you presented yourself in terms of clothes and your hair. I don't know, hygiene kind of stuff, it was huge. You can be as ugly as a beast. It didn't matter.

The valuation of style and grooming *over* bodily control and manipulation emerged as a shared theme among these participants, despite their being raised in radically different cultural settings, and resonates with findings from other studies on women in the Caribbean and Latin America (Cohen et al. 1996; Wilk 1996).

Cultural messages about the relative importance of hygiene and grooming were also noted by Latina study participants, such as this early-twenties college student, born in Mexico and raised in the southwestern U.S., who recalls a premium placed on grooming in her household during childhood.

> [My mom] always just took care of her[self]. She was very clean . . . so we grew up—my sisters, my siblings—we grew up with that. Like we had to take a shower every day, you know, just that hygiene type of thing and keep our clothes clean . . . be dressed nice, have our hair clean.

Cherishing God's Temple

In contemporary Western culture, the emphasis on "seeming" (Bourdieu 1984:200) encourages the deliberate reshaping and aesthetic manipulation of the body as a means of projecting qualities of the self (Becker 1995). Women are especially vulnerable to the illusion that the body not only *is* malleable, but that it *should* be cultivated to achieve a particular body size and shape (Becker and Hamburg 1996). By contrast, participants were far less invested in attaining a specific aesthetic ideal through cultivation of their bodies and, instead, espoused an ethic of body acceptance. Religion and spirituality provided a rationale for body acceptance and a rejection of body modification, particularly modifications to accommodate mainstream, dominant aesthetic values. Several participants explained how religion and personal spirituality helped them frame their relationships to their bodies in terms of being the custodian of something precious. One African American participant explained,

> There's a scripture in The Word that talks about [how] you're wonderfully and fearfully made. When I became a Christian and I read that I was like, oh God! It did something for me, you know. I'm fearfully and wonderfully made in the sight of God . . . it empowered me. It really did . . . it really empowered me to know that there's a high being, if you will, that values me the way I am.

In a similar vein, a Latina participant explained,

> I'm real happy with the way God gave me whatever he gave me, you know, and . . . that's okay with me. . . . I don't want to be this way or that way, I'm fine with what I've got.

Whereas the previous two comments demonstrate how spirituality has helped them accept their body, one African American participant describes how spirituality actively influences how she treats her body. She explains,

> Spiritually, I believe that there's a verse in the Bible, in the New Testament, that says your body is a temple, a temple of God. When I think in that way, I'm more careful about what I eat . . . about what I put in my body, I'm careful how I adorn myself. Not to the point of being fanatical, but to the point of treating what I have as something that's precious even when other people don't value it . . . and it's hard sometimes finding [food that's] . . . organic.

Her qualifier, "even when other people don't value it," again suggests that this orientation toward self-nurturance may signal resistance to dominant cultural aesthetic ideals and may comprise a strategic response to negative representations of women of color in the consciousness of white America.

Self-Representation, Dignity, and Self-Respect

In addition to examining the devaluation of black women's beauty, focus group participants discussed troubling cultural representations and stereotypes of African American women's manners and styles of behavior. Similar to participants in Nichter's (2000) study, participants in the present study discussed strategies of self-representation as an important aspect of beauty; in the present study, however, participants explicitly linked these values with the need to counter negative cultural stereotypes, resist hegemonic imagery, and promote self-determination. As one participant explained,

> I think that [looking ghetto] is more, I think that, come on now, you guys know. . . . That's more of an issue [than weight] though, I think. That you don't wanna be ghetto. Unless you're ghetto because you don't know.

Johnson et al. define "ghetto" as "a mode of acting, dressing, or speaking, that comes off as abrasive, and well, ghetto" (2001:205). These comments lend support to the earlier discussion of body ethics: beauty is described here as more than a static image or aesthetic ideal—it is how one carries and cares for oneself. However, in contrast to the girls in Nichter's study, for whom the ideal girl embodied attitude and spontaneity, as adult women negotiating various life roles and cultural contexts, participants in the present study explained how they sometimes monitored their own behavior, reining in some of their spontaneity in particular contexts. The following exchange between two study participants highlights how they have learned to manage self-representation in order to gain respect in the dominant culture and resist cultural stereotypes that portray African American women as loud and abrasive:

> P1: I think too, in the black community, there's a stereotype, that black people are loud.

> P2: Right, so trying to like turn that stereotype around whatever, we're kinda taught not to be loud.

The second participant further explained,

> We were at IHOP and people were turning around because we were laughing. . . . The first thing that you think is, they're looking at us like

that because we're black. And we know that people are gonna think we're gonna be loud anyway, just because we are black. And we know we're not supposed to be loud because we are black. That's another issue that [goes] beyond the health and beauty . . . you're not loud in public places like this, because you're gonna be looked at.

In the paper "Those Loud Black Girls," based on an ethnography of a predominantly African American urban high school, Signithia Fordham argues that, for African American girls, being invisible, "dissociating oneself from the image of 'those loud Black girls'" (1993:22), is a prerequisite for academic (and professional) success, though at the cost of disconnection from one's self and community. As the African American women in this study have all achieved considerable academic success, it is not surprising that struggles regarding management of visibility and representation emerged as an important theme. . . .

Latinas: Achieving Health, Fighting Disease

Whereas among African American participants, self-nurturance was described as the embodiment of self-respect, Latina study participants provided a somewhat different rationale for their self-care practices. Among Latinas in this study, self-care practices were described as being motivated by their desire to be healthy and their concerns about health and disease, rather than a desire to control body size or shape. Data demonstrating that Latino/as have significantly higher body mass index (BMI) and prevalence of overweight than whites (Winkleby et al. 1996) provide a tangible and substantial basis for concern about a healthy body weight. Indeed, several Latina study participants had friends and family with diabetes, hypertension, or other potentially weight-related diseases, or had one of these conditions themselves.

As one Latina participant, a woman in her late thirties who attended the group in her workout clothing, explained,

Mine's become more of a health issue now. Because I have to do it because I have diabetes, and in order to stay alive with all my limbs and stuff,

[maybe] be able to see for the rest of my life, I gotta do it. So yeah, it's just for me now.

For this participant, changing her lifestyle—eating more healthful foods and exercising—was literally a matter of life and limb. . . .

Several group members described their orientation towards eating and exercise as a departure from their families' eating and exercise practices. According to several participants, it was not uncommon for their mothers to complain about their own weight, and several discussed "fad" diets, teas and other strategies their mothers and aunts would use to lose weight. The participant in workout clothes in her late thirties, quoted above, explained,

My mama and my aunt were very vain about their weight. . . . My mom would drink like these laxative teas and stuff, like that's gonna help her lose weight. . . . There was these chocolates they would eat, okay, they were called AYDS, I think, A-Y-D-S, ask your moms, or whoever. . . . They were suppose to suppress the appetite. . . . Now I never saw them exercise a day in their life. I never saw them eating differently, salads and stuff. . . . If it was, it was for a week and that was it.

In contrast to these descriptions of their mothers' quick-fix diets and diet aids, Latina participants in this study did not place a high value on food restriction, as this participant in her late twenties explained,

I just wanna be healthy. I mean I still eat what I want to, and I will, just because if I'm gonna exercise I'm gonna still eat you know, I mean I'll eat sensibly, I won't go and eat tons of junk. Although I do sometimes do that.

. . .

Study participants' emphasis on body ethics over aesthetics—of working with the body instead of trying to fight it, of caring for the body rather than trying to control it—mirrors the results of a study recently completed by Anderson-Fye examining cultural change processes among adolescent girls in Belize. The "central ethnopsychological tenet"

(Anderson-Fye 2002:159) expressed among girls in this study was the importance of staying true to oneself, honestly experiencing and responding to one's thoughts, emotions and bodily needs, summarized by the expression "never leave yourself" (2002:161). Like the girls in Anderson-Fye's study, the African American and Latin women participating in this study expressed values of self-acceptance, self-nurturance, and self-care in the face of, and perhaps as a response to, an onslaught of messages, images, and representations devaluing and discouraging these moral and ethical ideals.

Contesting Cultural Representations

Study respondents' efforts to accept and nurture their bodies are certainly an extraordinary achievement, given the negative representations of women of color in the media and the countless products available to help women alter and reshape their appearances to accommodate mainstream beauty ideals. In fact, a central theme that emerged in every focus group was the perceived devaluation of "ethnic" looks by the dominant culture. Whether addressing overt racism, such as exclusionary practices or the exoticization of women of color in the media, or more subtle forms of othering, such as the commercial co-opting of cultural identities, most respondents were concerned with cultural representations of women of their shared ethnic background. Participants describe a very conscious and deliberate struggle with the mainstream cultural representations and aesthetic ideals, marked by tremendous pressure confronting women of color to accommodate mainstream beauty ideals in order to be accepted within society.

Cultural Representations of Black Women

In the African American women's focus groups, participants expressed their dissatisfaction and frustration with the lack of affirming images of black women in mainstream and black media sources. Participants expressed their opinion that, despite a small degree of tokenism, black women are rarely represented in mainstream iconography. Two participants in the same focus group, both in their early thirties, one a graduate

student and one a nondegree student quoted earlier, described their alienation from mainstream representations, stating,

> Most of the images in this culture are, you gotta be thin, white, what else, young. As a black woman, I look at those images and I don't see me.

And

> That white Caucasian look thing, it's not real to me, and it totally ignores the black woman's experience, and other women of color.... Of course they throw a little tokenism in there, but their basic images is still thin, Anglo-Saxon.

. . .

Numerous studies have documented the pernicious effects of exposure to media imagery on indices of disordered eating (e.g., Field et al. 1999; Stice and Shaw 1994), including body dissatisfaction among American women. Similarly, cultural representations of African American women in media imagery powerfully influence self-concept and body image among black women in Western culture. One African American participant, the nondegree student quoted above, describes the insidious and noxious nature of these controlling images and messages as "the new kind of slavery," stating,

> You don't have to shackle a person physically if you already have them convinced they're not anything, that they have no value.

. . . Several women participating in the African American focus groups grew up with familial messages regarding appearance that accommodated or even reproduced the dominant culture's aesthetic values, such as preferences for lighter skin and straighter hair. One subject now in her early sixties, who grew up a generation ahead of the others, explained,

> I come from a family where it was something about being dark-skinned with nappy hair, versus being light with Caucasian features and straight hair. . . . I didn't have straight hair or really kinky hair. . . . My mom, she made me feel like my look, African look, was not acceptable,

and I felt bad for a long time about that. . . . She would always be sure that my hair was straightened . . . and don't get in the sun, you know. So it was a negative experience, and it took me a long time to overcome those things.

. . .

The aesthetics of hairstyle and presentation has considerable sociopolitical relevance among African American women (Banks 2000; Byrd and Tharps 2002; Caldwell 1997). For instance, several of the participants seemed to have chosen to "go natural" or "do locks" while in college as a way to celebrate Afrocentric aesthetic ideals and resist the white aesthetic norms imposed on African American women. Study participants described their personal strategies for resisting, challenging, and overcoming mainstream aesthetic ideals. As the 60-year-old returning student explained,

It took me a long time to overcome those things . . . to accept my African features, nappy hair . . . like you said it was a struggle. But one day you say, this don't make no sense for me to be worrying about something that I had nothing to do with. . . . I didn't have anything to do with my hair being nappy, my nose being big. It must be alright. . . . So then I decided to think to myself, hey I'm beautiful just the way I am. I don't like to sit in the beauty parlor for three hours getting my hair relaxed, scalp burns and all those things. I'm so off that now. It's just over and I feel so free.

The participant mentioned earlier who was growing dreadlocks explained,

[My mother will] just fall out when she sees my hair now because I did these [dreadlocks] myself . . . I had my hair in braids, and I liked the braids and everything, but it was just time out, it's time for something new and I had been thinking about doing locks for a while, so I said you know what, I'm just gonna do it.

Russell et al. argue that "a certain level of black consciousness would seem to be necessary before a woman dares go natural" (1992, 87).

. . .

For African American study participants, strategies of self-representation were experienced as linked to one's social location (e.g., student versus corporate employee). Study participants negotiated their own self-interests against the backdrop of the interests of their community. Thus, while hair-straightening may be considered to perpetuate racist and classist notions of "good hair" and "bad hair," it may also be critical to attaining a high-paying job after college. One participant, an early-twenties college senior, explained,

Unless you're trying to achieve something . . . that's when you start [thinking] I have to look this way and I have to act this way, and I can't, you know, if I'm gonna do this certain activity I can't have my typical friends with me because then I'm gonna look bad. But it's only when . . . it's only when black people are really trying to achieve something in their life . . . whether it's going for a job . . . you've gotten a job and you're trying to live that lifestyle . . . then that's when the rest of the world comes into play.

The comments of this participant, herself about to leave college to find a job, suggest that economic success often necessitates accommodating dominant white, middle-class aesthetic and cultural values.

Latinas in the Media: Celebrating and Contesting Imagery

Latina participants expressed fewer concerns regarding the negative messages embedded in cultural representations, but rather were concerned with the lack of representations of Latinas in mainstream iconography. Historically, Latino/as were conspicuously underrepresented in the mainstream media, despite their growing numbers in the United States. . . .

. . .

Participants had somewhat polarized opinions about cultural representations of Latinas. Given the paucity of images, some study participants felt that any representation was positive, as this participant, a student from Central America, explained,

> Like even now, but I remember when I was really young, a teenager, I would see a Latina in a magazine or someone that looked Latina, even though they were probably from Europe or something, I would get excited. I'm like there's a Latina in this magazine! Or even in the movies, I probably would wanna go watch the movie just because there's another Latino in there.

Other participants were concerned that the Latinas that are represented in popular media merely reified mainstream aesthetic values, such as this participant in her mid-twenties who was born in Mexico.

> And even with the models, they still pick the stereotype. They might be colored, but still thin. They still look beautiful. And it's like, what happened to the others? . . . Selena is one of my faves, and she wasn't like very stereotypical thin. She looked more like a real person. I really like her because of that. Then there's Jennifer Lopez, and I'm like okay, she's kinda real, but then at the same time I see that her image has changed to fit some of those rules—the skimpy clothing and dyeing your hair. It's like hmmmm? . . . Because if you don't fit that, the stereotypical, you don't cross over.

Another participant, a theatre major, remarked, "There's one image of being a Latina, and it's Jennifer Lopez," provoking laughter from the group. As these focus group participants suggest, it is difficult for Latino/a actors and musicians to "cross over," or be accepted by the dominant cultural group, without changing their look to be more "Anglo." Like the group member that contrasted the "real" Selena to the "kinda real" Jennifer Lopez, the laughter that follows this remark may point to the discrepancy between "trendy" commercial representations of Latinas and this focus group participant's own personal definitions of Latina identity.

However, some participants, noting the insufficient representation of Latinas in the media, felt that "even just" seeing Jennifer Lopez made them happy, and offered a compassionate reading of the position of this singer/actress. One remarked,

> I get so happy when I see even just Jennifer Lopez on the screen. You know, good. Lopez, Lopez! I mean she's got her music, and then I think she's gonna be taking out a line of clothes too . . . at least she's promoting her own thing. She growing, and it's hard for a person who is a minority to be at the top.

Still, others were pleased with the increasing diversity of Latinas represented in the media, as is suggested in the following remark made by a graduate student in her late twenties:

> I think the good part about the media right now [is] the Latinas that are coming out. . . . The variety of them is unbelievable.

Participants' complex reactions to these images suggest that they are still grappling with their somewhat ambivalent feelings towards current representations of Latinas in popular culture. These participants expressed satisfaction with the increasing social and political power of Latinas but concern regarding the commodification and dilution of their ethnic heritage. . . . Similarly to the black women participating in these focus group discussions, Latina participants are grappling with how to negotiate mainstream and local cultural values and ideals and how to stay true to themselves and their cultural heritage.

CONCLUSION

Ethnically based differences in aesthetic body ideals have previously been suggested as the key underpinning for the reportedly greater body shape satisfaction experienced by women of color. However, contrary to this notion, African American and Latina women participating in these focus groups did *not* endorse specific alternative body aesthetic ideals that could be contrasted with the prevailing aesthetic ideal favoring slimness promoted and disseminated by the commercial media. More notably, study participants' emphasis of body ethics rather than body aesthetic ideals suggests the need for an important reframing of a presumed core orientation toward the body—one that is perhaps recognizable and dominant among Euro-American cultures but is by no means universal. Specifically, narrative data from both black and Latina subjects presented in this study reflect a central concern with body care and nurturance—glossed here as body *ethics,* as contrasted with the central *aesthetic* concerns that have previously been described among women in Euro-American culture.

. . .

Among the women participating in this study, staying "true to oneself," one's own personal values and ideals as well as one's cultural heritage, was itself considered a sign of this well-being (cf. Anderson-Fye 2002). These sentiments are echoed in the lyrics of the African American soul singer/songwriter India.Arie, who sings about learning to "love myself unconditionally," by fashioning herself according to "whatever feels good in my soul" (India.Arie 2001). For black and Latina women, and likely for other women of color negotiating two distinct cultural worlds, embodying an ethic of self-valuation and self-acceptance is a positive and strategic means to resist cultural aesthetic ideals that oppress virtually all women but which can be particularly oppressive to women of color. Hurtado argues, "White women, as a group, are subordinated through seduction, women of color, as a group, through rejection" (1990: 12). For women who maintain an ethic of self-acceptance and nurturance, such rejection necessitates resistance, a cherishing of one's body and self-rooted in both spiritual and political ideologies "even when other people don't value it," perhaps *especially* because other people do not value it.

In addition to comprising a strategic response to ethnically and racially based oppression, we propose that the ethic of self-acceptance exhibited by the participants in this study may also modulate risk for the body dissatisfaction that is associated with disordered eating. We further hypothesize that women of color who are economically and/or socially marginalized and who are disconnected from their cultural roots may be less able to call upon an ethic of

self-acceptance and consequently are at greater risk for the body- and self-disparagement associated with eating disorders. Indeed, this may explain the equivalent or even higher rates of eating disorder symptoms among some women of color compared with white women. Pumariega et al.'s (1994) finding that a strong black identity may play a protective role against eating disorder risk factors supports this hypothesis, as does the association between acculturation and higher prevalence of eating disorders found in numerous studies (Anderson-Fye and Becker in press).

Insofar as this study presents perspectives from African American and Latina women with a critical consciousness of culture, body, and health, it suggests and elaborates new avenues for investigating the nexus of embodiment, ethnicity, and disordered body image and eating. Further research will be important for probing the dimensions of body ethics and aesthetics, identity and self-representation in larger, more representative samples of black and Latina women. Such research will be instrumental in exploring whether the alternative body ethics described in this study may actually confer protection from the development of eating or weight disorders among ethnically diverse populations of women. . . .

REFERENCES

Akan, G., and C. Grilo. 1995. Sociocultural Influences on Eating Attitudes and Behaviors, Body Image, and Psychological Functioning: A Comparison of African-American, Asian-American, and Caucasian College Women. *International Journal of Eating Disorders* 18:181–187.

Altabe, M. 1998. Ethnicity and Body Image: Quantitative and Qualitative Analysis. *International Journal of Eating Disorders* 23:153–159.

Anderson-Fye, E. 2002. Never Leave Yourself: Belizean Schoolgirls' Psychological Development in Cultural Context. Unpublished Dissertation, Harvard University.

Anderson-Fye, E., and A. E. Becker. In press. *Cultural Dimensions of Eating Disorders.* TEN: Trends in Evidence-Based Neuropsychiatry.

Banks, I. 2000. *Hair Matters: Beauty, Power, and Black Women's Consciousness*. New York: New York University Press.

Becker, A. E. 1995. *Body, Self and Society: The View From Fiji*. Philadelphia: University of Pennsylvania Press.

Becker, A. E., R. A. Burwell, S. Gilman, D. B. Herzog, and P. Hamburg. 2002. Eating Behaviours and Attitudes Following Prolonged Television Exposure Among Ethnic Fijian Adolescent Girls. *British Journal of Psychiatry* 180:509–514.

Becker, A. E., and P. Hamburg. 1996. Culture, the Media, and Eating Disorders. *Harvard Review of Psychiatry* 4:163–167.

Bordo, S. 1993. *Unbearable Weight: Feminism, Western Culture, and the Body*. Berkeley, CA: University of California Press.

Bourdieu, P. 1984. *Distinction*. Cambridge, MA: Harvard University Press.

Brown, L. M. 1998. *Raising Their Voices: The Politics of Girls' Anger*. Cambridge, MA: Harvard University Press.

Byrd, A. D., and L. L. Tharps. 2002. *Hair Story: Untangling the Roots of Black Hair in America*. New York: St. Martin's Press.

Caldwell, P. 1997. *A Hair Piece: Perspectives on the Intersection of Race and Gender*. Pp. 297–305 in *Critical Race Feminism: A Reader*. A. K. Wing, ed. New York: New York University Press.

Chamorro, R., and Y. Flores-Ortiz. 2000. Acculturation and Disordered Eating Patterns Among Mexican-American Women. *International Journal of Eating Disorders* 28:125–129.

Cohen, C., R. Wilk, and B. Stoeltje, eds. 1996. *Beauty Queens on a Global Stage: Gender, Contests, and Power*. New York: Routledge.

Collins, P. H. 1990. *Black Feminist Thought: Knowledge, Consciousness, and the Politics of Empowerment*. Boston: Unwin Hyman.

———. 2000. *Black Feminist Thought: Knowledge, Consciousness, and the Politics of Empowerment*. New York: Routledge.

Crago, M., C. M. Shisslak, and L. S. Estes. 1996. Eating Disturbances Among American Minority Groups: A Review. *International Journal of Eating Disorders* 19:239–248.

Davis, C., and J. Yager. 1992. Transcultural Aspects of Eating Disorders: A Critical Literature Review. *Culture, Medicine and Psychiatry* 16:377–394.

Emmons., L. 1992. Dieting and Purging Behavior in Black and White High School Students. *Journal of the American Dietetic Association* 92:306–312.

Field, A. E., L. Cheung, A. M. Wolf, D. B. Herzog, S. L. Gortmaker, and G. A. Colditz. 1999. Exposure to the Mass Media and Weight Concerns Among Girls. *Pediatrics* 103 (3): 36.

Fordham, S. 1993. "Those Loud Black Girls": (Black) Women, Silence, and Gender "Passing" in the Academy. *Anthropology and Education Quarterly* 24:3–32.

hooks, b. 1992. *Black Looks: Race and Representation*. Boston: South End Press.

Hurtado, A. 1990. Relating to Privilege: Seduction and Rejection in the Subordination of White Women and Women of Color. *Signs* 14:833–855.

India.Arie. 2001. Video. *Acoustic Soul*. New York: Motown Record Company.

Johnson, K., T. Lewis, K. Lightfoot, and G. Wilson. 2001. *The BAP Handbook: The Official Guide to the Black American Princess*. New York: Broadway Books.

Kuba, S. A., and D. J. Harris. 2001. Eating Disturbances in Women of Color: An Exploratory Study of Contextual Factors in the Development of Disordered Eating in Mexican-American Women. *Health Care for Women International* 22:281–298.

Nichter, M. 2000. *Fat Talk*. Cambridge, MA: Harvard University Press.

Parker, S., M. Nichter, N. Vukovic, C. Sims, and C. Ritenbaugh. 1995. Body Image and Weight Concerns Among African-American and White Adolescent Females: Differences That Make a Difference. *Human Organization* 54:103–114.

Parnell, K., R. Sargent, S. H. Thompson, S. F. Duhe, R. F. Valois, and R. C. Kemper. 1996. Black and White Adolescent Females' Perceptions of Ideal Body Size. *Journal of School Health* 66:112–118.

Pumariega, A. J., C. R. Gustavson, J. C. Gustavson, P. Motes, and S. Ayres. 1994. Eating Attitudes in African-American Women: The Essence Eating Disorders Survey. *Eating Disorders* 2:5–16.

Root, M. 1990. Disordered Eating in Women of Color. *Sex Roles* 22:525–536.

Russell, K., M. Wilson, and R. Hall. 1992. *The Color Complex*. New York: Anchor Books.

Smith, J. E., and J. Krejci. 1991. Minorities Join the Majority: Eating Disturbances Among Hispanic and Native American Youth. *International Journal of Eating Disorders* 10:179–186.

Stice, E., and H. Shaw. 1994. Adverse Effects of the Media Portrayed Thin-Ideal on Women and Linkages to Bulimic Symptomatology. *Journal of Social and Clinical Psychology* 13:288–308.

Wilk, R. 1996. Connections and Contradictions: From the Crooked Tree Cashew Queen to Miss World Belize. Pp. 217–232 in *Beauty Queens on the Global Stage: Gender, Contests, and Power*. C. Cohen, R. Wilk, and B. Stoeltje, eds. New York: Routledge.

Winkleby, M., C. Gardner, and C. Barr Taylor. 1996. The Influence of Gender and Socioeconomic Factors on Hispanic/White Differences in Body Mass Index. *Preventive Medicine* 25:203–211.

R E A D I N G   **38**

What We Do for Love

Rose Weitz (2004)

Rapunzel's life turned around the day a prince climbed up her hair and into her stairless tower. The rest of us sometimes suspect that, as was true for Rapunzel, our hair offers us the key to finding a prince who'll bring us love and happiness. Yet surprisingly often, when we talk about hair and romance, we talk not only about love but also about power—the ability to obtain desired goals through controlling or influencing others. Power exists not only when a politician fixes an election or an army conquers a country, but also when we style our hair to get boyfriends or to keep men away, and when our boyfriends browbeat us into cutting our hair or growing it longer.

CATCHING A MAN

Hair plays a central role in romantic relationships, from start to finish. If we're in the mood for love (or sex), from the moment we meet someone, we begin an internal calculus, reckoning how attractive we find him and how attractive he seems to find us. If he finds us attractive, our power will increase, for in any relationship, whoever wants the relationship most holds the least power.[1]

Attractiveness, of course, means many different things. A man might be attracted to a woman because of her income, interest in sports, or good sense of humor. But when it comes to dating—especially first dates—pretty women, like pretty girls, usually come out ahead. In a recent experiment, researchers placed bogus personal ads for two women, one a "beautiful waitress," the other an "average looking, successful lawyer." The waitress received almost three times more responses than the lawyer. (The reverse was true for men: the "successful lawyer" received four times more responses from women than did the "handsome cabdriver.") Other studies also have found that men choose their dates based more on women's looks than on women's earning potential, personality, or other factors.[2]

In a world where beautiful waitresses get more dates than do successful women lawyers, it makes perfect sense for women to use their looks to catch and keep men. Although some writers imply that women who do so are merely blindly obeying cultural rules for feminine appearance and behavior—acting as "docile bodies," in the words of the French philosopher Michel Foucault—most women are acutely aware of those rules and know exactly what they are doing and why.[3]

The first step in getting a man is catching his eye. A classic way to do so is with the "hair flip." Of course, the flip can be an innocent gesture, intended only to get the hair out of our eyes or move a tickling strand off our cheeks. But often it's consciously used to get men's attention while on dates, in classes, stopped at red lights, and elsewhere. If you want to see it in action, sit at any bar. Sooner or later a woman will look around the room, find a man who interests her, wait until he turns toward her, and then—ever so nonchalantly—flip her hair.

Hair flipping can be an amazingly studied act. In response to an e-mail query on the subject that I sent to students at my university, a white undergraduate female replied,

> I have very long hair and do use the hair flip, both consciously and unconsciously. When I do it [consciously], I check the room to see if anyone is looking in my direction, but never catch a guy's eye first. I just do it in his line of vision. [I] bend over slightly (pretending to get something from a bag or pick something up) so that some of my hair falls in front of my shoulders. Then I lean back and flip my hair out, and then shake my head so my hair sways a little. I make sure that the hair on the opposite side ends up in front of my shoulder. I keep that shoulder a little bit up with my head tilted and lean on the hand that I used to flip my hair.

Similarly, in the film *Legally Blonde,* the lead character, Elle, instructs her dumpy friend Paulette how to "bend and snap"—bending over so her hair will fall forward, then standing up while snapping her head and hair back to catch men's attention.

Other times the hair flip is less studied, but the motivation is the same. A Mexican-American student writes:

> I tend to flip my hair when I see an attractive male, but I do it unconsciously. I don't think, "Okay, here he comes, so now I have to flip my hair," It's more of a nervous, attention-getting thing. When I see a good-looking guy and get that uneasy feeling in my stomach, I run my fingers through my hair and flip it to make it look fuller and to attract his eye as he passes. If there isn't enough room to flip my hair, I'll play with a strand of hair instead.

Whether conscious or unconscious, hair flipping works. In a world that expects women to speak in a low tone, keep eyes down, and sit quietly with legs together and elbows tucked in, the hair flip says, "Look at me." This in itself makes it sexy. It's also inherently sexy: the back of the hand rubbing upward against the neck, then caressing the underside of the hair, drawing it out and away from the body, while the chin first tucks down into the shoulder and then tilts up, arching the neck back.

Even when a man finds neither long hair nor the flip inherently attractive, flipping hair can whet his interest. The gesture itself draws the eyes by taking up space and causing motion. Perhaps more important, men know the flip can be a form of flirtation. As a result, they pay close attention to any woman who flips her hair to see whether she's flirting with them, flirting with someone else, or simply getting the hair out of her eyes.

This use of the hair flip doesn't escape notice by women with short hair. An undergraduate writes:

> In Hispanic culture hair is very important for a woman. It defines our beauty and gives us power over men. Now that I cut my hair short, I miss the feeling of moving my hair around and the power it gave me. . . . It is kind of a challenge [to other women] when a woman flips her hair. [She's] telling me that she has beautiful healthy hair and is moving it to get attention from a male or envy from me.

The hair flip is especially aggravating for those black women whose hair will not grow long. As one black graduate student explains,

> As an African-American woman, I am very aware of non-African-American women "flipping" their hair. . . . I will speak only for myself here (but I think it's a pretty global feeling for many African-American women), but I often look at women who can flip their hair with envy, wishfulness, perhaps regret? . . . With my "natural" hair, if I run my fingers through it, it's going to be a mess [and won't] gracefully fall back into place.

She now wears long braided extensions and, she says, flips her hair "constantly."

In the same way that women use their hair's motion to catch men, they use its style and color.

Cecilia told how she dyed her hair Kool-Aid bright to horrify others in her small Southern town. These days her hair decisions serve very different purposes:

> I can think of an occasion where I changed my hair while I was dating this guy. I had this feeling that he was losing attraction for me and I'd just been feeling the need to do something to my appearance. And my hair is always the easiest way to go. It's too expensive to buy a new wardrobe. There's nothing you can do about your face. So your hair, you can go and have something radically done to it and you'll look like a different person.

With this in mind, Cecilia cut off about seven inches of her hair:

> It was kind of a radical haircut, shaved, kind of asymmetrical, and [dyed] a reddish maroon color. When he saw me, [he] was like, "Whoa! . . . Oh, my God, look at it!" He just couldn't stop talking about it. . . . He said, "I don't know, there's just something about you. I really want to be with you."

When I ask how she felt about his rekindled interest in her, she replies, "I was pretty pleased with myself."

Few women would cut their hair asymmetrically and dye it maroon to capture a man's interest, but millions try to do so by dyeing their hair blonde. Of the 51 percent of women who dye their hair, about 40 percent dye it blonde.[4] (Most of the rest dye it brunette shades simply to cover any gray.) Several women I've talked to, when asked why they dye their hair blonde, responded by singing the old advertising ditty: "Is it true blondes have more fun?" These women, like many others, have found blonde hair a sure way to spark men's interest.

But being a blonde can be a mixed blessing: Remember Marilyn Monroe. To catch men's attention without being labeled dumb, passive, or "easy" (stereotypes that haunt all blondes, dyed or natural), about 20 percent of women who dye their hair instead choose shades of red. Red hair, they believe, draws men's interest while calling on a different set of stereotypes, telling men that they are smart, wild, and passionate.[5] Brenda, a quiet, petite twenty-eight-year-old, for many years envied her golden-blonde sister's popularity. A few years ago she began dyeing her hair red to "let people know I'm a competent person, independent, maybe a little hotheaded—or maybe a lot hotheaded, [even] fiery." Dyeing her hair red, she believes,

> *made* people see me. . . . Before I dyed my hair, my sister and I would go out and all these guys would ask her to dance and talk to her and ask for her number and I would just be standing there. And after I started dyeing my hair, I started getting noticed a little bit more. I also stopped waiting to be asked.

Brenda credits her marriage in part to her red hair; her husband approached her initially because he "always wanted to date a redhead."

Using our hair to look attractive is particularly important for those of us whose femininity is sometimes questioned. Since Jane Fonda began selling her fitness videos in 1982, women (or at least middle-class women) have been expected to look as though they "work out." Yet those whose broad shoulders and muscular arms and legs announce them as dedicated athletes are still often stigmatized as unfeminine, or denigrated as suspected lesbians. Since most true athletes can't have manicured nails (which can break during sports) or wear makeup (which can smear from sweat), those who want to look attractively feminine often rely on their hair. The tennis-playing Williams sisters and the U.S. women's soccer team won the hearts of Americans not only through their athletic skills but also because their beaded braids and ponytails, respectively, told us they were still feminine and heterosexual (an image bolstered by constant news coverage about the Williamses' fashion sense and the soccer players' boyfriends and husbands). Similarly, most professional female bodybuilders counterbalance their startlingly muscular bodies with long, curled, and dyed blonde hair. Those who don't do so risk losing contests, no matter how large and well-sculpted their muscles.[6]

Similar pressures weigh on black women. Although it is far less true today than in the past, many people—whites and blacks, men and women—still regard black women as less feminine and less attractive than white women. For example, when I asked 270 white undergraduates in 2003 to choose from a list all the adjectives they felt described the "average" white, non-Hispanic woman, 75 percent chose "feminine" and 48 percent chose "attractive." In contrast, when asked to describe the average black woman, only 33 percent chose "feminine" and only 21 percent chose "attractive."

As a result of such attitudes, black women often feel especially obligated to do what they can to increase their attractiveness. Within the black community attractiveness still primarily centers on having light skin and long, straight hair.[7] Since there's little one can do about one's skin color (Michael Jackson notwithstanding), much of black women's attention to their looks focuses on their hair. Norma explains,

> If you are an African-American woman and you have long hair, you are automatically assumed to be pretty, unless your face is just awful! [But if you have short, tightly curled hair like mine,] African-American males [will] say "I'm not going out with her, her head is as bald as mine!" Or they will call [you] "nappy head."

To avoid such treatment without subjecting herself to the difficulties and expense of straightening her hair, Norma now wears a wig with shoulder-length straight hair. Her husband approves. Many other black women do the same, creating a substantial market in the black community for wigs (ads for which appear regularly in the major black magazines), while many others rely on purchased hair extensions.

But each of these options carries a price. In choosing straightened hair, wigs, or extensions over natural hair, black women obtain hair that *looks* good in exchange for hair that *feels* good to the touch. If your lover starts stroking your wig, it might fall off or come askew. If he strokes your extensions, expensive hair that took hours to attach may come out. If you've got a weave, his fingers will hit upon the web of thread holding the hair in. And if he tries to stroke your carefully coiffed straightened hair, not only will it lose its style, but it will feel stiff and oily or, if it hasn't been moisturized in a while, like brittle straw. Or it might just break off. To avoid these problems, black women teach the men and boys around them never to touch a woman's hair. Stephen, a twenty-three-year-old black student, told me:

> The same way you learn as a kid not to touch that cookie in the cookie jar, you learn not to touch that hair. I remember once trying to touch my mother's hair and having her slap my hands away....
>
> You learn at beauty parlors, too. When I was a kid, my mom would go to the beauty parlor every two weeks. And it would take six hours to do her hair sometimes, and we would have to sit around the whole time. So we saw how long it took and how important it was for them. And then you'd hear the stylists tell the little girls not to touch their hair afterwards. And you'd hear all the women talking about their own hair, and how they would have to sleep sitting up to keep from messing it. Or they'd say, "That man better not try to touch my head, I just paid $200 for this hair!"

When black women date either white men or the rare black man who hasn't been properly trained, the women keep the men's hands away by covering their hair before coming to bed, relying on quick maneuvers to keep their hair out of harm's way, saying they need to get their hair done and it's not fit to be touched, or saying they just had their hair done and don't want it ruined.[8]

Like black women, overweight and disabled women also can rely on their hair to make themselves seem more feminine and attractive. Although many famous beauties of the late nineteenth century, such as the actress Lillian Russell, were admired for their voluptuous curves, and still today in some African beauty contests no women under 200 pounds need apply, in contemporary America overweight women are often ridiculed as unattractive and asexual. So, too, are disabled women, leaving them more likely than either disabled men or nondisabled women to remain single, to marry at later ages, and to get divorced.[9]

When I interviewed Debra, who became quadriplegic in a car accident when she was twenty, she was sitting in her kitchen. Her hair was immaculately styled: dyed and frosted shades of blonde, with perfectly placed bangs and neat waves falling below her shoulders.

Although Debra always cared about her appearance, her disability has heightened its importance for her. As she explains,

> When people first see someone in a wheelchair, the image they have [is] like a "bag of bones" or something toting urine. They expect the person to not have a high level of hygiene. . . . People will actually say things to me like "You are so much cleaner than I expected," and will give me shampoo as gifts because they assume I need the help. I'm trying to beat that image.

For Debra, keeping her hair nicely styled is a point of pride. It also offers her the pleasure of feeling more feminine and feeling at least partly in control of her body. Like other disabled and overweight women, this is particularly important for her because in other ways she can't make her body do what she wants. Controlling her hair also takes on special significance because it's difficult for her to find attractive, nicely fitting clothes suitable for someone who spends her days in a wheelchair and who can't dress herself.

At the same time, Debra's hair remains "a point of great frustration" that sometimes causes her a "huge amount of stress." Because she can't lift her arms high enough to style her own hair, she must rely on her personal attendant to do so. But in choosing a personal attendant, her first priority must be selecting someone she feels comfortable trusting with the most intimate details of her life and her body, not selecting someone who both has hairstyling skills and will follow her styling

wishes. In addition, because the work of a personal attendant is poorly paid, emotionally stressful, and physically draining, few attendants stay long. Consequently, Debra frequently must find and train new attendants, ratcheting up her anxiety levels and diminishing her sense of control over her body and her appearance anew each time.

But even able-bodied, slender white women take risks when they rely on their appearance to bolster their self-confidence and their attractiveness. Attractiveness offers only a fragile sort of power, achieved one day at a time through concentrated effort and expenditures of time and money. As a result, the occasional "bad hair day" can seem a catastrophe. From the moment we realize our hair just isn't going to cooperate, things start going badly. We spend extra time trying to style our hair in the morning, then have to run out the door because we're late. By the time we get to work or school, we're feeling both frazzled and self-conscious about our appearance. Throughout the day, a small voice in the back of our head may nag, berating us either for not having our act together or for worrying what others are thinking. As a result, we lose self-confidence and the ability to concentrate, as well as prospects for male approval. In the long run, too, if a man is interested in us only because of our looks, his interest likely won't last. (It may not even survive the morning after, when we awake with bleary eyes, no makeup, and "bed head.") And attractiveness must decline with age, as more than one middle-aged society woman dumped for a younger "trophy wife" has discovered.

HAIR IN RELATIONSHIPS

Once we are in a relationship, hair can bring pleasure to our partners and ourselves. If our hair is long enough, we can drape it over our partner's chest to form a silky curtain, or swing it from side to side to tease and caress him. And whether our hair is long or short, our partner can enjoy the pleasure of brushing it, washing it, smoothing his hands over it, or weaving his fingers through it. In addition, caring for our hair enables the men in our lives to show their love and affection without having to put their feelings into words.

Eva's relationship with her husband, Stanley, epitomizes this dynamic. After more than forty years of marriage, it's clear that he's still smitten. While I am interviewing Eva, Stanley seems unable to stay out of the room. Once in the room, his eyes linger on her. His hand grazes her hair and keeps drifting to her shoulder. Although to me Eva's hair seems ordinary, he makes more than one comment about its beauty.

Ever since he retired, Stanley has dyed Eva's hair for her. They describe this as a way to save time and money, and I'm sure it does. But they're retired and wealthy, so I'm convinced that Stanley cares for Eva's hair primarily as a way of caring for Eva.

Sometimes, though, the pleasures of hair turn to perils if our partners come to view our hair as an object for their own pleasure. Learning to do so begins early, when boys realize they can pull girls' braids in schoolyards and classes and touch girls' hair against their will, with few if any repercussions. Once in relationships, some boys and men will come to think of their girlfriend's or wife's hair as their property or as a reflection on them. When this happens, our hair becomes an object for a man to critique or control. For example, when Debra met her first boyfriend, a couple of years before her accident, her hair was waist-length. The boyfriend had previously dated a hairstylist who taught him how to style hair and gave him his own haircutting equipment. Although Debra wasn't happy about it, he quickly took charge of her hair and began cutting it shorter and shorter with each passing month. "It ended up being a control feature in our relationship," she says. "He always wanted it worn very spiky and short, and I hated that look." He also took control of dyeing her hair. "It ended up being a trust game," she recalls, "where he'd say, 'I'm going to go get a hair color, and you're not going to know what color it is. So you have to trust me that I will not make you ugly'. . . . In retrospect, the relationship really was very controlling."

At the extreme, men's control of women's hair can become violent. In a recent study, the sociologist Kathryn Farr looked at thirty consecutive reported cases of woman-battering that escalated to attempted homicides. In three of those cases, the police noted in the record that the man had cut the woman's hair by force during the attack. (The men may well have done so in additional cases without the police noting it.) The attitude of these men toward their wives and girlfriends comes through clearly in a fourth case that did not quite meet Farr's definition of attempted homicide. After the man in that case finished punching and kicking his girlfriend, he forced her to kneel on the floor and began cutting her hair. When she asked why he was doing this, he replied, "You belong to me and I can do anything I want."[10]

But if men can demonstrate their power over us by controlling our hair, we can demonstrate our own power within a relationship by asserting control over it. Until recently, Stacy, who is twenty-two, wore her hair falling loosely to her waist. She now wears it parted in the middle and just long enough to pull back into a ponytail. Surprisingly, she cut her hair *because* her boyfriend liked it long. Irritated by his frequent remarks about how her hair made her so attractive, she says, "I deliberately cut it off, a little bit spitefully, to say I'm more than my hair." Doing so made her feel "powerful," she explains, "in the sense that I feel that they [men] prefer long hair, that I wasn't ruled by that, and that I could set my own standards." (Their relationship continued anyway.)

. . .

CELEBRATING INDEPENDENCE FROM MEN

In the same way we sometimes use our hair to attract men, we also can use our hair to proclaim our independence from a particular man or from men in general. Darla first met her husband on a blind date in 1949, when she was fifteen. Normally before a date Darla would wash her hair, set it, and leave it to dry in curlers for three hours before combing it out and styling it. This time, though, to show that she "was not the kind of girl who went out on blind dates, [and] was just not impressed with that idea at all," she didn't set her hair until right before he arrived.

When the doorbell rang, Darla went to greet her date with her hair in curlers and wrapped in a bandanna. She immediately realized she'd made a big mistake:

> Here was this young god standing there. Black wavy hair, way better [looking] than James Dean. And not only that, he was all dressed up. He had on a white shirt and tie. And there was nothing I could do about my hair.

To compensate for her hair faux pas, Darla excused herself so she could triple-check her makeup and swap her pedal-pushers for a pretty skirt. Then they went out, as if there were nothing unusual about going on a date wearing curlers:

> He did not say anything [about my hair]. And he didn't seem to be turned off. . . . I think he found me attractive. . . . The fact that I had my hair up in curlers didn't seem to bother him at all, which impressed me.

When he called for a second date, Darla made sure her hair looked great. They've now been married more than fifty years.

Although few of us would, like Darla, use our hair to signal our lack of interest in a man at the beginning of a relationship, many of us do so when a relationship breaks up. After Roxanne got divorced, she dated a man who loved her hair and who took great pleasure in braiding, brushing, and especially washing it. But they had "a very bad breakup," leading Roxanne to decide to cut her hair. When I ask her why, she replies by singing the lyric from *South Pacific:* "I'm gonna wash that man right out of my hair." As she explains, "I had to get rid of everything that he liked, and I started with my hair." She "felt great" afterward.

Dana tells a similar story. Twenty-six years old, she now wears her hair past her waist and favors "vintage" clothing and dramatic makeup. A few years ago she broke up with a long-term boyfriend. Afterward, she recalls, "I wanted to do

something different, . . . to completely shut off that old self and be somebody new. . . . I wanted to appear sexier [and to] regain confidence in myself." Although fear kept her from making any drastic changes, a slight change to her hairstyle allowed her to feel better about herself and to feel like a new person.

Although both Roxanne and Dana used their hair to reject their former partners, neither wanted to reject men in general and both continued to use their hair to attract men's attention. But other women use their hair, at least occasionally, to *reduce* men's interest in them. For example, LaDonna, a black woman who [has] described the attention her hair brought her as a child, usually enjoys the power her naturally long and wavy hair now gives her over black men. Nonetheless, her hair is a mixed blessing, because she can't control who will be attracted to it (her handsome neighbor or her married boss?) or why (because he simply likes long hair or because he thinks hair that looks "white" is superior?). As a result, she says, "It's kind of funny, because I know it [my hair] will get me attention, and I do things to make it look nice that I know will get me attention, but sometimes I don't wear my hair down because I *don't* want the attention. I don't feel like dealing with this."

Susan goes to even greater lengths to avoid male attention. She's probably the prettiest woman I interviewed, with the prettiest hair. Her blue eyes and cascade of naturally curling dark hair contrast attractively with her pale skin, giving her a girl-next-door sort of appeal that matches her outgoing nature. Susan met her husband, who is an Egyptian Muslim, when they were both studying in England. Once she began dating him, the other Arab men in the school seemed to consider her "fair game." So long as her boyfriend was around she felt safe, but her fears grew when he left the school six weeks before she did. During those weeks, she recalled, "The Arab men were all over me, constantly bugging me. . . . I was afraid I would get raped by one of them one night."

After they returned to the United States, Susan and her boyfriend married. As she began to learn more about Islam, her interest in it grew, and she decided to convert. A few months later they went to visit her husband's family home. Expecting the men there to treat her as they would any Muslim woman, she was appalled when they instead treated her as a "loose" American. To convince others that she was a chaste Muslim and to protect herself from sexual harassment or worse when her husband was absent, she began wearing a hijab (a traditional robe) and covering her hair in Muslim fashion. Her husband, aghast, told her that if he'd wanted a traditional Muslim bride, he would have married one. Moreover, in his city only the oldest women still wore head coverings, which were now considered old-fashioned, ugly, and "backward." It's not surprising, then, that, as Susan describes, "He flipped out. He got so upset. He *wants* my hair to show, because . . . he wants to show me off."

Still, feeling that her physical safety was at risk, Susan ignored his wishes and began covering her head. Her strategy succeeded:

> If you are not born Muslim and you are American, [and] you're not dressed the way they [Arab men] think is best for a Muslim women, and covering your head, . . . they'll think you're loose [and] treat you disrespectfully. . . . But when I put the hijab on and covered my head, . . . everybody changed how they treated me.

After they got back to the United States, Susan decided to continue veiling. Like other Muslim-American women who veil, she enjoyed the sense of empowerment the veil brought her by reminding her of her religion and her God.[11] And, even though she no longer felt physically at risk, she continued to appreciate the protection from men's eyes that the veil afforded her. Without the veil, she says, "You feel like you're naked. . . . Men would look at me and smile and I'd know that they thought I was beautiful. I don't want that. I just want my husband to think that."

Susan's husband objected even more vociferously to her desire to veil herself once they returned to the United States. After a series of fights, they compromised and agreed that she

could cover most of her hair with a turban if he was with her in public, and could veil more completely if he wasn't.

For Susan, the fights and the eventual compromise were worth it. She recognizes that women gain rewards for displaying attractive hair, but feels that the power she gets from *covering* her hair is greater:

> Men open doors for you. Not just Arabic men but, even more, American men. What must be going through their heads is exactly what you are trying to put across: that I am . . . a person of God, someone who is chaste. And they're very helpful, very respectful. And I don't think it's that they think you are submissive, because I don't appear submissive. I talk, I stand tall. I'm by myself. It's not like I'm with my husband and I don't say anything.

Most tellingly, she notes, "It's hard for Americans to think that a woman could be empowered without using her body and beauty to do it. [But] my power comes from within."

At the same time, Susan has paid a price for her choice. Her husband remains unhappy about her veiling, which strains their marriage. She's also sentenced herself to a hot, uncomfortable head covering, given up the pleasure of playing with personal ornamentation, and foresworn the myriad benefits—in addition to those that occur within intimate relationships—that come to those who look attractive to the world in general.

Still, because Susan is married and doesn't work outside the home, she can afford to make this choice. Women who have paid jobs, on the other hand, must style their hair in ways that balance relationship issues with career requirements—or pay the consequences.

· · ·

NO MORE BAD HAIR DAYS

There's no getting around it: As it was for Rapunzel, hair is central to our identities and our prospects. Whenever we cut our hair short or grow it long, cover the gray or leave it alone, dye it blonde or dye it turquoise, curl it or straighten it, we decide what image we want to present to the world. And the world responds in kind, deciding who we are and how to treat us based in part on what our hair looks like.

At one level, this is perfectly natural. Whenever we first meet someone, we need to figure out what sort of person he or she is (a threat? a potential friend? a new boss? a new client?), and often need to do so quickly. As a result, we use any clues available to decipher whether that person is wealthy, middle-class, or poor; friendly or aloof; athletic or bookish; and so on. Hair offers one of the most visible clues. This is why people who have no hair typically look less individualistic; although their bald heads are distinctive, their faces often seem vaguely alike.

But for all its naturalness, this process of defining ourselves and others through hair is also a product of culture. As we've seen, girls have to be taught to consider their hair central to their identities and to use their hair to manipulate both their self-identity and the image they project to others. And although it's probably true that humans are innately attracted to beauty, the definition of beautiful hair varies across time and culture—how many beautiful women these days sport six-inch-high beehives?—and so girls must learn how beauty is defined in their particular social world. Once they do, they quickly also learn that a wide variety of rewards accrue to those who most closely meet beauty norms.

In part because our hair plays such a large role in how we view ourselves and are viewed by others, it offers us many opportunities for pleasure. Each day our hair provides us with the means to create ourselves anew—at least until our perm, relaxer, or hair dye grows out. And in comparison to losing weight, affording a better-looking wardrobe, or finding true love, changing our lives by changing our hair seems downright easy. Styling our hair also offers the artistic and, at times, intellectual pleasure of sculpting a highly malleable substance. Often, too, hairstyling is a community affair, involving friends, relatives, or stylists and bringing us the pleasures of laughing, joking, working, talking, and sharing our lives with other women. What's more, the results of our efforts bring sensual and sexual pleasures to us and to our lovers, be they male or female.

But each of these pleasures of hair also carries dangers. As girls learn the importance of attractive hair (and of attractiveness in general); start spending time, energy, and money on their appearance; and come to evaluate both themselves and other girls on their appearance and on their ability to attract the opposite sex, they help perpetuate the idea that only a limited range of female appearance are acceptable. More insidiously, their actions make it seem as if focusing on appearance is something that girls do naturally, rather than something girls must learn to do. This in turn limits the life chances both of girls who succeed at attractiveness and of those who don't, for those who succeed sometimes must struggle to be seen as more than just a pretty image and those who fail are often denigrated not only as unattractive but also as lazy, unintelligent, and incompetent. At the same time, the focus on appearance teaches girls to view each other as competitors and limits the potential for true friendship between them.

By the time we reach adulthood, all of us have, at least to some extent, absorbed these lessons. Yet this does not mean that we docilely internalize them and blindly seek male approval for our appearance, as some writers seem to suggest.[12] Rather, each of us chooses daily how far she will go to meet beauty expectations. As we've seen, some of us choose hairstyles for convenience, some to project a professional image, some to reject notions of proper femininity or to reject male approval altogether. Moreover, those of us whose main goal in styling our hair is to attract men typically know perfectly well what we're doing. Far from meekly and unconsciously following cultural scripts, we actively use our appearance to get what we want: wearing long extensions, dyeing our hair blonde or red, flipping it off our shoulders to catch men's eyes, spiking it with gel to suggest sexy rebelliousness, and so on. In a world that still all too often holds women back and expects them to accept passively whatever life brings, those of us who manipulate our appearance to manipulate men and to create opportunities that might otherwise be denied us—whether getting a promotion or marrying well—can sometimes seem like rebels, resisting the narrow role in which others would place us.

That said, it would be equally wrong to overstate the extent to which, in manipulating our appearance, we manipulate our social position and so resist those who would constrain our lives and options.[13] Whether we wear our hair in blonde curls to attract men's interest or in short, professional styles to move ahead in the corporate world, we're still limited by social stereotypes regarding women's nature and capabilities. Although our hair can help us achieve our personal goals, it cannot change those stereotypes. Rather, such strategies *reinforce* stereotypes by reinforcing the idea that appearance is central to female identity. In the long run, therefore, they limit all girls' and women's opportunities. Even those hair strategies that seem most to embody resistance, like "lesbian power cuts" and voluntary baldness, have limited ability to change women's position since, like Afros, they either stigmatize their wearers and reduce their ability to achieve their goals or evolve into mere fashions that lack political effect.

The truth, then, lies somewhere in between these two positions. In our decisions about hair, we actively and rationally make choices based on a realistic assessment of how we can best obtain our goals, given cultural expectations regarding female appearance and given our personal resources. As this suggests, girls and women are far from free agents. If we ignore cultural expectations for female appearance we pay a price in lost wages, diminished marital prospects, lowered status, and so on. If we attempt to follow cultural expectations, we pay a price in time, money, and energy when we obsess about our hair; in low self-esteem when our hair fails us; and in low esteem from others when we are considered little more than the sum total of our hair and our appearance.

Is this double-bind inevitable? Is there a way to stop setting up ourselves and our daughters for more "bad hair days"?

As we've seen, from birth girls are taught to emphasize their appearance. No parent—or, for that matter, teacher, lover, or friend—can fully counteract all these cultural pressures. But we can make those pressures tolerable, and at least plant the seeds for a better future. For better or worse, all of us serve as role models for the girls and younger women around us. When we allow our lovers or spouses to dictate our hairstyles, we teach our children to value their hair primarily for its effect on others. When we obsess over our hair, we teach them to do the same. Conversely, when we joke about our hair "flaws" and move on with our life or enjoy the pleasures our hair brings us without worrying what others think about it, we help create an environment in which an alternative message can begin to take root. This doesn't mean that we should dismiss our children's concerns about appearance—all children need to feel that they fit in, and having a socially acceptable appearance is part of that—but it does mean we shouldn't reinforce those concerns (through such actions as paying for modeling lessons or arranging birthday parties at hair salons).

As teachers, parents, aunts, scout leaders, and youth group leaders, we also have the opportunity to expose children to alternative ways of thinking about appearance. Several books are now on the market that teach young black girls to take pride in their natural hair, including Carolivia Herron's *Nappy Hair,* bell hooks's *Happy to Be Nappy,* and Natasha Tarpley's *I Love My Hair.* The only equivalent book I've seen for white girls is *This Is My Hair,* by Todd Parr; more such books are definitely needed. We also have the power to begin pressuring the media to change how it portrays girls and women. Write a letter asking why *InStyle* uses so few black models, why *Ebony* uses so few models with natural hair, or why *Ladies' Home Journal* uses almost no models with graying hair. Even better, organize those in your church, synagogue, Girl Scout troop, or women's group to do the same.

None of this means that we should keep girls from playing with their hair, or stop playing with our own hair. Nor do I mean to suggest that there's anything inherently bad or good, sexist or feminist, rebellious or conformist, about blonde, turquoise, gray, dreadlocked, curled, or straightened hair. These styles are only problematic when they are forced "choices," prices we must pay to keep a job, find romance, or be accepted by the incrowd at our school. We don't want to lose the pleasure of changing our hair color or style any more than we would want to lose the pleasure of changing the color or style of our bedroom. But we *do* want to make sure that hair play is voluntary and fun.

For this to happen, we need to consider not only what we teach girls, but also how we live our own lives. We need to explore honestly how we interact with other women. When do we compliment others on their hair? When do we withhold compliments? Why? What do we say (and think) when a friend decides to let her hair go gray, or decides to dye it hot pink, blonde, or black? In our remarks, are we honoring our friend's individuality? Recognizing the constraints under which she lives? Or reinforcing the pressures on her to use her appearance to bolster her identity, self-esteem, and life chances? Conversely, we need to recognize that a friend who routinely criticizes our appearance is not much of a friend. The same issues apply in the work world. Do we assume that coworkers, employees, and underlings who have long hair aren't professional, or that those with short hair aren't feminine? And do our thoughts and actions limit the potential of other women?

By altering our behavior in response to these questions and issues, we can start to chip away at the prison bars of the beauty culture. But although such actions are crucial for improving the lives of individual girls and women, they can bring only limited change. In the long run, the only way to truly break the hold of the beauty culture is to change girls' and woman's position in society.

For minority girls and women, that change must include improving the social and economic positions of their ethnic communities. We can already see this happening. Although white women with frizzy "Jewish" hair and black women with Afros still raise eyebrows and sometimes lose jobs for leaving their hair in its natural state, their

hair is no longer the mark of shame it once was. And in some circles it's considered downright attractive. In the same fashion, if disparaging stereotypes of overweight and disabled people decline, overweight and disabled girls and women will no longer have to rely on their hair to "prove" their femininity.

More broadly, only when all girls and women are freed from stereotypical expectations about our natures and abilities will we also be freed from the bonds of the beauty culture. Again, we can see those effects already. Girls whose athletic, creative, or academic interests are nurtured, taking into account and valuing all levels of abilities; whose special talents are rewarded with approval from parents and teachers; who attend schools and universities where their particular skills and talents are appreciated; and who believe that their futures hold myriad intriguing possibilities are far less likely than other girls to center their identities on their appearance. In such environments, too, others are more likely to evaluate girls on their personality and achievements and less likely to evaluate them on their looks. By the same token, women whose social and economic positions are based not on their looks but on their intellect, personality, skills, talents, and achievements can afford to regard their hair as a personal pleasure rather than as a tool for pleasing or manipulating others.

Rapunzel had only one way to change her life: attracting a prince through her hair and her beauty. All of us these days have more options than that. Still, as it was for Rapunzel, our hair remains an almost magical substance: both uniquely public, open to others' interpretations, and uniquely personal, growing out of our bodies and molded (if imperfectly) to our individual desires. For this reason, hair will continue to serve as a marker of our individual identity throughout our lives. Yet our hair can also be simply fun: an idle amusement, a sensuous pleasure, an outlet for creativity, a means for bonding with others, and a way of playing with who we are and who we might become. The more control we gain over our lives as girls and women, the more freedom we will have to truly enjoy and celebrate our hair.

NOTES

1. On the social psychology of relationships, see Judith A. Howard, "Social Psychology of Identities," *Annual Review of Sociology* 26 (2000): 367–93.

   Physical appearance also, of course, plays a role in romantic relationships between women. However, existing data on this topic are very mixed. Some studies suggest that lesbians find a broader range of appearance acceptable than do heterosexuals, and other studies indicate that mainstream appearance norms are equally important in the lesbian community. See Dawn Atkins, ed., *Looking Queer: Body Image and Identity in Lesbian, Bisexual, Gay, and Transgender Communities* (New York: Haworth, 1998); and Jeanine C. Cogan, "Lesbians Walk the Tightrope of Beauty: Thin Is In But Femme Is Out," *Journal of Lesbian Studies* 3, no. 4 (1999): 77–89. This topic deserves a fuller treatment than I can give in this [reading], and so I have chosen only to discuss heterosexual relationships here.

2. David M. Buss, Todd K. Shackelford, Lee A. Kirkpatrick, and Randy J. Larsen, "A Half Century of Mate Preferences: The Cultural Evolution of Values," *Journal of Marriage and the Family* 62 (2001): 491–503; Susan Sprecher, "The Importance to Males and Females of Physical Attractiveness, Earning Potential, and Expressiveness in Initial Attraction," *Sex Roles* 21 (1989): 591–607; Erich Goode, "Gender and Courtship Entitlement: Responses to Personal Ads," *Sex Roles* 34 (1996): 141–69.

3. Michel Foucault, *Discipline and Punish: The Birth of the Prison* (New York: Vintage, 1979), and *History of Sexuality* (New York: Pantheon, 1980). For critiques of feminist writings that emphasize women's docility, see Lyn Mikel Brown, *Raising Their Voices: The Politics of Girls' Anger* (Cambridge, Mass.: Harvard University Press, 1998); Kathy Davis, "Remaking the She-Devil: A Critical Look at Feminist Approaches to Beauty," *Hypatia* 6, no. 2 (1991): 21–42; and Lois McNay, "The Foucauldian Body and the Exclusion of Experience," *Hypatia* 6, no. 3 (1991): 125–39.

4. *DSN Retailing Today,* "Salon-Inspired Hair Products Weave Their Way into Mass Market," 40 (5): 17 (2001), and Victoria Wurdinger, "The Haircolor Report," *Drug and Cosmetic Industry* 161 (4): 38–47 (1997). In contrast, about 10 percent of men dye their hair (a sharp increase over previous years), with most doing so to impress other young men with their "coolness." See Dana Butcher, "More than a Shave and a Haircut," *Global Cosmetic Industry* 166, no. 1 (2000): 45–48.

5. For stereotypes of blondes and redheads, see Wendy Cooper, *Hair: Sex, Society, and Symbolism* (New York: Stein and Day, 1971); Saul Feinman and George W. Gill, "Sex Differences in Physical Attractiveness Preferences," *Journal of Social Psychology* 105 (1978): 43–52; Druann Maria Heckert and Amy Best, "Ugly Duckling to Swan: Labeling Theory and the Stigmatization of Red Hair," *Symbolic Interaction* 20 (1997): 365–84; Dennis E. Clayson and Micol R. C. Maughan, "Redheads and Blonds: Stereotypic Images," *Psychological Reports* 59 (1986): 811–16; and Diana J. Kyle and Heike I. M. Mahler, "The Effects of Hair Color and Cosmetic Use on Perceptions of a Female's Ability," *Psychology of Women Quarterly* 20 (1996): 447–55.

6. For further discussion of this process (referred to in the scholarly literature as a "feminine apologetic"), see Dan C. Hilliard, "Media Images of Male and Female Professional Athletes: An Interpretive Analysis of Magazine Articles," *Sociology of Sport Journal* 1 (1984): 251–62; and Maria R. Lowe, *Women of Steel: Female Body Builders and the Struggle for Self-Definition* (New Brunswick, N.J.: Rutgers University Press, 1998). Quote is from Lowe, 123–24.

7. For data on the prevalence and nature of attitudes toward black women, see Rose Weitz and Leonard Gordon, "Images of Black Women among Anglo College Students," *Sex Roles* 28 (1993): 19–45. Numerous books discuss attitudes toward black women's bodies and hair, including Ingrid Banks, *Hair Matters: Beauty, Power, and Black Women's Consciousness* (New York: New York University Press, 2000); Patricia Hill Collins, *Black Feminist Thought: Knowledge, Consciousness, and the Politics of Empowerment* (London: Routledge, 1991), 67–90; Maxine Craig, *Ain't I a Beauty Queen?: Black Women, Beauty, and the Politics of Race* (Berkeley: University of California Press, 2002); Noliwe M. Rooks, *Hair Raising: Beauty, Culture, and African American Women* (New Brunswick, N.J.: Rutgers University Press, 1996); and Ayana D. Byrd and Lori L. Tharps, *Hair Story: Untangling the Roots of Black Hair in America* (New York: St. Martin's Press, 2001).

8. Cherilyn Wright, "If You Let Me Make Love to You, Then Why Can't I Touch Your Hair?" in

Tenderheaded: A Comb-Bending Collection of Hair Stories, edited by Juliette Harris and Pamela Johnson (New York: Pocket Books, 2001), 64–165.

9. Regarding the importance of fatness in African beauty contests, see Norimitsu Onishi, "Maradi Journal: On the Scale of Beauty, Weight Weighs Heavily," *New York Times,* February 12, 2001. Regarding stereotypes and experiences of disabled women, see Michelle Fine and Adrienne Asch, eds., *Women with Disabilities: Essays in Psychology, Culture, and Politics* (Philadelphia: Temple University Press, 1988); Adrienne Asch and Michelle Fine, "Nurturance, Sexuality, and Women with Disabilities: The Example of Women and Literature," in *Disability Studies Reader,* edited by Lennard J. Davis (New York: Routledge, 1997); and William John Hanna and Betsy Rogovsky, "Women with Disabilities: Two Handicaps Plus," in *Perspectives on Disability,* 2nd ed., edited by Mark Nagler (Palo Alto, Calif.: Health Markets Research, 1993).

10. Kathryn Farr, Department of Sociology, Portland State University, personal communication with the author.

11. Jen'nan Ghazal Read and John P. Bartkowski, "To Veil or Not to Veil? A Case Study of Identity Negotiation among Muslim Women in Austin, Texas," *Gender & Society* 14 (2000): 395–417.

12. Writers who have been criticized for emphasizing women's docility include Sandra Lee Bartky,

"Foucault, Femininity, and the Modernization of Patriarchal Power," in *Feminism and Foucault,* edited by Irene Diamond and Lee Quinby (Boston: Northeastern University Press, 1988), and Susan R. Bordo, "The Body and the Reproduction of Femininity: A Feminist Appropriation of Foucault," in *Gender/Body/Knowledge,* edited by Alison M. Jaggar and Susan R. Bordo (New Brunswick, N.J.: Rutgers University Press, 1989).

13. Writers who have been criticized for overstating women's resistance include Lyn Mikel Brown, *Raising Their Voices: The Politics of Girls' Anger* (Cambridge, Mass.: Harvard University Press, 1998); Kathy Davis, "Remaking the She-Devil: A Critical Look at Feminist Approaches to Beauty," *Hypatia* 6, no. 2 (1991): 21–42; Kathy Davis, *Reshaping the Female Body: The Dilemma of Cosmetic Surgery* (New York: Routledge, 1995); and Lois McNay, "The Foucauldian Body and the Exclusion of Experience," *Hypatia* 6, no. 3 (1991): 125–39. Among those who have criticized such research are Scott Davies, "Leaps of Faith: Shifting Currents in Critical Sociology of Education," *American Journal of Sociology* 100 (1995): 1448–78; Joan Ringelheim, "Women and the Holocaust," *Signs: A Journal of Women in Society* 10 (1985): 741–61; and Myra Dinnerstein and Rose Weitz, "Jane Fonda, Barbara Bush and Other Aging Bodies: Femininity and the Limits of Resistance," *Feminist Issues* 14 (1994): 3–24.

R E A D I N G   **39**

Hold That Nose

Lisa Miya-Jervis (2003)

I'm a Jew. I'm not even slightly religious. Aside from attending friends' bat mitzvahs, I've been to temple maybe twice. I don't know Hebrew; my junior-high self, given the option of religious education, easily chose to sleep in on Sunday mornings. My family skips around the Passover Haggadah to get to the food faster. Before I dated someone from an observant family, I wouldn't have known a mezuzah if it bit me on the butt. I was born assimilated.

But still, I'm a Jew, an ethnic Jew of a very specific variety: a godless, New York City–raised, neurotic middle-class girl from a solidly liberal-Democratic family, who attended largely Jewish, "progressive" schools. When I was growing up, almost everyone around me was Jewish; I was stunned when I found out that Jews make up only 2 percent of the American population. For me, being Jewish meant that on Christmas Day my family went out for Chinese food and took in the new Woody Allen movie. It also meant that I had a big honkin' nose.

And I still do. By virtue of my class and its sociopolitical trappings, I always knew I had the option to have my nose surgically altered. From adolescence on, I've had a standing offer from my mother to pay for a nose job.

"It's not such a big deal."

"Doctors do such individual-looking noses these days, it'll look really natural."

"It's not too late, you know," she would say to me for years after I flat-out refused to let someone break my nose, scrape part of it out, and reposition it into a smaller, less obtrusive shape. "I'll still pay." As if money were the reason I was resisting.

My mother thought a nose job was a good idea. See, she hadn't wanted one either. But when she was 16, her parents demanded that she get that honker "fixed," and they didn't take no for an answer. She insists that she's been glad ever since, although she usually rationalizes that it was good for her social life. (She even briefly dated a guy she met in the surgeon's waiting room, a boxer having his deviated septum corrected.)

Even my father is a believer. He says that without my mother's nose job, my sister and I wouldn't exist, because he never would have gone out with Mom. I take this with an entire salt lick. My father thinks that dressing up means wearing dark sneakers; that pants should be purchased every 20 years—and then only if the old ones are literally falling apart; and that haircuts should cost $10 and take as many minutes. The only thing he says about appearances is, "You have some crud . . ." as he picks a piece of lint off your sleeve. But he cared about the nose? Whatever.

Even though my mother is happy with her tidy little surgically altered nose, she wasn't going to put me through the same thing, and for that I am truly grateful. I'm also unspeakably glad that her comments stayed far from the "you'd be so pretty if you did" angle. I know a few people who weren't so lucky. Not that they were dragged kicking and screaming to the doctor's office; no, they were coerced and shamed into it. Seems it was their family's decision more than their own—usually older female relatives: mothers, grandmothers, aunts.

What's the motivation for that kind of pressure? Can it be that for all the strides made against racism and anti-Semitism, Americans still want to expunge their ethnicity from their looks? Were these mothers and grandmothers trying to fit their offspring into a more white, gentile mode? Possibly. Well, definitely. But on purpose? Probably not. Their lust for the button nose is probably more a desire for a typical femininity than for any specific de-ethnicizing. But given the society in which we live, the proximity of WASPy white features to the ideal of beauty is no coincidence. I think that anyone who opts for a nose job today (or who pressures her daughter to get one) would say that the reason for the surgery is to look "better" or "prettier." But when we scratch the surface of what "prettier" means, we find that we might as well be saying "whiter" or "more gentile" (I would add "bland," but that's my personal opinion).

Or perhaps the reason is to become unobtrusive. The stereotypical Jewish woman is loud and pushy—qualities girls really aren't supposed to have. So is it possible that the nose job is supposed to usher in not only physical femininity but a psychological, traditional femininity as well? Bob your nose, and become feminine in both mind and body. (This certainly seems to be the way it has worked with Courtney Love, although her issue is class more than ethnicity. But it's undeniable that her new nose comes with a Versace-shilling, tamed persona, in stark contrast to her old messy, outspoken self.)

Even though I know plenty of women with their genetically determined schnozzes still intact, sometimes I still feel like an oddity. From what my mother tells me, nose jobs were as compulsory a rite of passage for her peers as multiple ear-piercings were for mine. Once, when I was still in high school, I went with my mother to a Planned Parenthood fund-raiser, a cocktail party in a lovely apartment, with lovely food and drink, and a lovely short speech by Wendy Wasserstein. But I was confused: We were at a lefty charity event in Manhattan, and all the women had little WASP noses. (Most of them were blond, too, but that didn't really register. I guess hair dye is a more universal ritual.)

"Why are there no Jewish women here?" I whispered to my mother. She laughed, but I think she was genuinely shocked. "What do you mean?" she asked. "All of these women are Jewish." And then it hit me: It was wall-to-wall rhinoplasties. And worse, there was no reason to be surprised. These were women my mother's age or older who came of age in the late '50s or before, when anti-Semitism in this country was much more overt than it is today. Surface assimilation was practically the norm back then, and those honkers were way too, ahem, big a liability on the dating and social scenes. Nose jobs have declined since then. They're no longer among the top five plastic surgeries, edged out by liposuction and laser skin resurfacing.

I don't think it's a coincidence that, growing up in New York, I didn't consider my nose an "ethnic" feature. Almost everyone around me had that ethnicity, too. It wasn't until I graduated from college and moved to California that I realized how marked I was. I also realized how much I like being instantly recognizable to anyone who knows how to look. I once met another Jewish woman at a conference in California. In the middle of our conversation, she randomly asked, "You're Jewish, right?" I replied, "With this nose and this hair, you gotta ask?" We both laughed. The question was just a formality, and we both knew it.

Only once did I feel uneasy about being "identified." At my first job out of college, my boss asked, after I mentioned an upcoming trip to see my family, "So, are your parents just like people in Woody Allen movies?" I wondered if I had a sign on my forehead reading "Big Yid Here." His comment brought up all those insecurities American Jews have that, not coincidentally, Woody Allen loves to emphasize for comic effect: Am I *that* Jewish? I felt conspicuous, exposed. Still, I'm glad I have the sign on my face, even if it's located a tad lower than my forehead.

Judaism is the only identity in which culture and religion are supposedly bound closely: If you're Irish and not a practicing Catholic, you can still be fully Irish; being Buddhist doesn't specify race or ethnicity. To me, being a Jew is cultural, but it's tied only marginally—even hypothetically—to religion, and mostly to geography (New York Jews are different from California Jews, lemme tell ya). So what happens when identity becomes untied from religion? I don't know for sure. And that means I'll grab onto anything I need to keep that identity—including my nose.

R E A D I N G   **40**

Love Your Fat Self

Courtney E. Martin (2008)

Gareth looks up from her crochet project just as the train pulls into the Brooklyn Jay Street station, where she must get off and switch across the platform for the A train to Manhattan. She stuffs the yarn into her new orange leather clutch and positions herself in front of the door, waiting for it to open.

"Yeah, that's right, get off the train, you fat bitch!" yells a man sitting nearby. He looks to be in his 40s or 50s, dressed in jeans and a leather coat, possibly drunk but not obviously so. His words hang in the air like a noxious gas. A woman nearby gasps, clearly offended. An older man with white hair and a friendly, wrinkled face shakes his head silently. Two schoolkids in puffy jackets muffle their giggles with their hands.

It feels like it takes the doors a year to open. Gareth has heard this kind of thing so often that the effect is dulled at first. Later she will relive this moment in her head many times over, articulating the multitude of sassy responses she could have spat back, but ultimately this reflection will do nothing except give her the sharp stab of familiar pain. It is loneliness so deep that she must turn it into anger in order to survive.

Gareth is my best friend, and, yes, she is obese by clinical standards. She is also brilliant, kind, popular, magnetic, and in a loving relationship. She dresses up to go out on Saturday nights, dances her ass off, gets the occasional free drink from a hopeful guy. She is a powerhouse at the office, blazing through her daily tasks with efficiency and conscientiousness. She is an activist and an actor—mentoring a little girl with AIDS, marching in prochoice rallies, writing and performing monologues in off-Broadway productions.

There is nothing atypical about Gareth's biography. In fact, even at her present size, she is certainly not unusual: 66 percent of U.S. adults age 20 and older are overweight or obese. She grew up in Connecticut in a divorced, middle-class family, made it to New York City as soon as she could, excelled in college, moved to Brooklyn, and got an administrative job at a nonprofit. This is not a woman who has "checked out," contrary to what so many thin people assume about those who are fat. She doesn't sit at home and lament her size. She isn't passive or embarrassed. She certainly isn't lazy. She spends her time trying to make the world a better place and figuring out how the hell she fits into it.

On paper, she is a perfect girl. To the ignorant, naked eye, she is flawed.

Sizeism remains the only truly socially acceptable form of discrimination on the planet. We see living in a fat body as an insurmountable disability. Nearly a decade ago, the feminist therapist Mary Pipher wrote that "fat is the leprosy of the 1990s." Today fat is the death penalty of the 21st century. Skinny girls, counting their carrot sticks for lunch, can't imagine being lovable at that size, applying for a job at that size, even living at that size. When I asked 14-year-old Manhattanites how their lives would be different if they were fat, they were struck silent. After a few moments, one responded, "I would be dead."

Paradoxically, we as a society make it a catastrophe to be fat, but we have little awareness of the pain of a woman like Gareth's internal world. We dramatize fatness through news segments on the obesity epidemic, but our awareness of the emotional and psychological pain of fatness remains virtually nonexistent.

We are deathly afraid of fat. In some ways, we should be. According to the World Health Organization, there are 1 billion overweight and 300 million obese adults around the globe. Fatness is linked to an increased risk for heart disease, stroke, type 2 diabetes, and some forms of cancer. According to the National Institutes of Health (NIH), health care costs for treating diseases associated with obesity are estimated at more than $100 billion a year and rising, just within the United States (inexplicably, the NIH spends just 2 percent of its annual budget on obesity research). The physical, psychological, and economic implications of widespread obesity are undeniably frightening.

There is evidence, though, that our approach to fatness is as unhealthy as fatness itself. In an *ELLEgirl* poll of 10,000 readers, 30 percent said they would rather be thin than healthy. Dieting is ineffective 95 percent of the time. That means, in America alone, we pump some $40 billion a year into a crapshoot industry with only a 5 percent chance of payoff. Besides being hard on our pocketbooks, dieting is hard on our bodies and hard on our psyches. Many women are pushed to use diet pills that damage their organs; 23-year-old Janet admits, "Even after my friend had a mini-stroke from taking ephedra, I sometimes wonder if I can search the Internet and find some on the black market. Crazy, right?"

Political scientist J. Eric Oliver, an expert in obesity, argues in his 2005 book *Fat Politics: The Real Story Behind America's Obesity Epidemic* that the health risks of obesity have been grossly exaggerated. Being fat, he maintains, is not equivalent to being unfit. Fitness, not weight, is actually the most accurate measure of a person's health and life expectancy. Even a group of researchers at the Centers for Disease Control and Prevention acknowledge that "evidence that weight loss improves survival is limited."

Thirty-five percent of those who diet go on to yo-yo diet, dragging their bodies through a cycle of weight gains and losses; 25 percent of those who diet develop partial- or full-syndrome eating disorders. As the mindfulness expert Susan Albers writes: "The dieting mind-set is akin to taking a knife and cutting the connection that is your body's only line of communication with your head." There is little hope for long-term improvement in health when this vital line is severed.

In fact, studies show that prolonged weight loss is more often the result of psychological work. In a two-year study conducted by nutrition researchers at the University of California, Davis, behavior change and self-acceptance were far more effective in achieving long-term health improvements in obese women than America's most lucrative scam: dieting.

Conflating obesity with laziness or stupidity is an inaccurate habit of linking a physical trait, in this case fatness, with personality. This is equivalent to believing that all smokers or anorexics are incompetent. Just the fact that someone is genetically predisposed to fatness and struggles with the complex psychological implications of food and body image does not disqualify her from being brilliant, talented, and effective. As obvious as this sounds, many of the health professionals I spoke to about this issue aired an unmistakable tone of disdain for fat patients. While they were able to empathize with women who undereat, the idea of overeating sent them into a dispassionate laundry list of how to decrease input and increase output—as if people were machines.

As a society, we seek answers: black-and-white declarations, either-or cures. Fatness is not so sim-

ple. Gareth is fat because she has a genetic predisposition to fat, because she grew up with a father who sells chocolate for a living and often showed his affection through tarts and candy bars, because her mother—however well-intentioned she was—restricted Gareth's food and, as a result, made love feel conditional. She is fat because she is fascinated by food, generously cooks for others, and enjoys a good hamburger. She is fat because she refuses to live a watered-down life—cutting out carbs or sugars or meat, becoming one of those difficult dinner guests or boring picnic companions—so that she can be thin. She is fat because, like so many of the rest of us, she sometimes uses food to fill an emotional void. She is fat because she lives in an age when advertising preys on every potential craving, insecurity, and discomfort.

Most programs designed to curb obesity neglect the complicated causes of fat. Janell Lynn Mensinger, a psychology professor and expert on both eating disorders and obesity in women, has been continually frustrated by medical doctors' culturally ignorant, gender-blind, and usually unsuccessful interventions to reduce obesity. "There is such an emphasis on the body as this biological organism that must be controlled in a completely medical way," she explains. "Emotions get completely pushed aside because most physicians have very little psychological training."

At a recent conference on pediatric obesity, Mensinger sat next to a tiny black exercise physiologist who was lamenting the low success rate of programs meant to teach children to maintain a healthy weight. Mensinger recalls that "she segued right into talking about how she used to be a size nine and now she is a size five, thanks to two hours a day of rigorous exercise. She acted like size nine was an atrocity! And this is [a person with whom] obese children from poor backgrounds are supposed to identify?"

There is only one rational reason to fear fatness: health risks. The other reasons, which play unconscious and insidious roles in our negative perception of fat people, are profoundly American. Obesity is rampant in the heartland of America, in the sprawling suburbs of the Midwest and the South, the farm towns of Texas. But it is rarely admitted that our struggle over the meaning of fat is at the heart of our national identity.

Our all-or-nothing nation is built on foundations of fantasy. Our imaginations are harnessed to America's favorite adolescent fantasy: how much prettier, thinner, richer, and more successful we will be one day. This perpetual American daydream is written in the language of "somedays." Someday whispers us to sleep at night, gets us through a boring workday, makes our little lives bearable. The hundreds of ads the average American sees every day brainwash us into believing that we need more shiny, new things and, of course, food—glorious piles of chocolate chip cookies, decadent ice cream, burgers the size of elephants. "Someday" soothes insecurities, numbs discomfort, and keeps perfect girls running obediently in the hamster wheel of preoccupation with their weight. Someday we will be thin. Translation: Someday we will be happy, loved, and powerful.

But even those precious few who get to this someday destination aren't happy or better. If you live fat in your head, then you are fat. If you believe you are unattractive, you will experience the world as an unattractive woman. If you hound yourself about everything you put in your mouth, you won't enjoy eating. Regardless of the number on the scale, if the number inside your head is large, insurmountable, and loaded with meaning, then you will feel weighed down by its implications.

This is the heart of the matter: A starving person can ache just as deeply inside a thin body. Our dissatisfaction is never, at its deepest, about our bodies. This is why fat women and thin women often experience the world in similar ways. If a thin woman feels inadequate and "thinks fat," she may endure less hate coming from the outside in than a fat woman does, but just as much criticism and sadness from the inside out. Likewise, if a woman of any size is able to stop her negative self-talk and accept herself, she may experience the world with a little peace of mind.

Gareth is onstage, the shadow of her voluptuous silhouette on the wall behind her. I am watching it, instead of her, during her monologue, because it's too hard to look her in the eye when she is speaking such brave and brutal truths. Her words start out celebratory but quickly become accusatory:

In a way it is easy to be proud of my body. I'm proud of what it does for me and what it can do for other people. But every time I get dressed I think about how other people will see my body and I can't help but hear the words "fat bitch" in my head. I've been hearing them most of my life. It's as if people feel the need to make a judgment on my character as well as my body all at once. And it works. It makes me feel huge and obtrusive and grotesque, deformed.

It's true. I am fat. I am not attractive to most people. Most of the time, I am not attractive to myself. Where does that leave me? Angry with myself? Yes. Angry with society? No.

I think that's a cop-out, and it's not a cop-out for me. It's a cop-out for the people who judge my size. It's like, at this point, we all know that the media, old white men, corporations, the fashion industry, and all sorts of bad people or things out there shape the way we view ourselves and others. Okay, I get it. But don't you think, at some point, knowing all this, we should start taking some responsibility for our thoughts and words? I mean, isn't that the point of all this higher education, all this enlightenment?

As she reaches the end, she starts screaming her questions at the stunned audience: "So what's going on, people? Why do I still feel like crap? Huh? Who can tell me? Do you know? Can someone please explain it to me?"

I can almost hear the audience members' brains buzzing with rationalizations: But fat is unhealthy. I don't date fat women, but I have nothing against them. Why is she complaining? She's one of those beautiful fat women. When is this going to be over? It's torture.

Gareth pulls herself together, takes a deep breath, and says calmly, "I know what you are all thinking, and it's OK," then ends, cool as ice, "You want the fat bitch to shut up," and struts out of the spotlight and off the stage.

Gareth is beautiful, especially tonight. She's dressed in a knee-length black skirt, cut in uneven triangles on the bottom. Her shirt is a rainbow of reds, oranges, and yellows—as fiery as her monologue—cut low, revealing the tops of her breasts, freckled with beauty marks. Her eyes are outlined in dark pencil, making them seem even bigger than they are, even more striking. The spotlight bathes her in an ethereal light.

But most of the audience members instead focus on her anger. They are not used to being called on the carpet for their judgment of obesity. They feel attacked, misunderstood, perhaps defensive. They have fat friends. They aren't narrow-minded, just concerned about the obesity epidemic. They thought that was the right way to be. They feel unmoored, the first phase of a new consciousness.

Gareth's monologue provokes a storm of self-reflection. I would never say anything rude to a fat man or woman about his or her weight, but would I think it? I preach tolerance, but would I consider dating someone who is overweight? When I compliment Gareth on her new haircut, is there a part of me that feels relieved that she is undeniably beautiful despite being fat? Do I identify her anger more quickly than I would a thinner friend's? Do I patronize her by complimenting her eyes, her sense of humor, her determination—as if the rest of her doesn't exist?

Just as racism is not primarily about frightened white women clutching their purses but about the seemingly mundane, unconscious voices in our heads—Why do black girls have to be so loud? That Latina woman is probably a great nanny. This new Asian guy is probably really smart—sizeism is not about the drunken man who screams "fat bitch" at Gareth on the subway as much as it is about the march of hateful inner monologues: That girl would be so pretty if she would just lose some weight. I wonder what's wrong with her, must be lazy. This fat bitch is taking up more than her share of the bus seat.

When I started to pay attention to the voices in my own head, I was frankly horrified. It wasn't only fat women on whom I unconsciously commented, it was thin women, too: That skinny girl looks like such a bitch; I bet she's vacuous and vain. That woman shouldn't be eating that muffin. I feel sorry for that little girl; she's going to be lonely if she doesn't lose some weight.

Seriously humbled by my own judgmental nature, I realized that thinking this way about other people creates an inner climate of suspicion. If I think this way about her, what is she thinking about me? Like a chronic gossip suddenly aware that other people probably talk about her behind her back too, I woke up to the fact that I was sealing my own fate of mercilessly judging and being judged, even if my participation was unspoken.

That understanding is Gareth's gift to me. It is a daily struggle not to listen to the voices—the furtive whispers, the outdated instincts—that try to slip under the radar. But it makes me feel more generous. It makes me feel less scrutinized myself. Sometimes I sit on a subway car and look at every woman purposefully and lovingly—as if she were my mother or my best friend. It is breathtaking how beautiful they all are when I see like this.

R E A D I N G   **41**

Phenomenal Woman

Maya Angelou (1978)

Pretty women wonder where my secret lies.
I'm not cute or built to suit a fashion model's
   size
But when I start to tell them,
They think I'm telling lies.

I say,
It's in the reach of my arms,
The span of my hips,
The stride of my step,
The curl of my lips.

I'm a woman
Phenomenally.
Phenomenal woman,
That's me.

I walk into a room
Just as cool as you please,
And to a man,
The fellows stand or
Fall down on their knees.
Then they swarm around me,
A hive of honey bees.
I say,
It's the fire in my eyes,
And the flash of my teeth,
The swing in my waist,
And the joy in my feet.
I'm a woman
Phenomenally.
Phenomenal woman,
That's me.

Men themselves have wondered
What they see in me.
They try so much
But they can't touch
My inner mystery.
When I try to show them

They say they still can't see.
I say,
It's in the arch of my back,
The sun of my smile,
The ride of my breasts,
The grace of my style.
I'm a woman
Phenomenally.
Phenomenal woman,
That's me.

Now you understand
Just why my head's not bowed.
I don't shout or jump about
Or have to talk real loud.
When you see me passing
It ought to make you proud.
I say,
It's in the click of my heels,
The bend of my hair,
The palm of my hand,
The need for my care.
Cause I'm a woman
Phenomenally.
Phenomenal woman,
That's me.

R E A D I N G   **42**

China's Cosmetic Surgery Craze

Jonathan Watts (2004)

The expression "no pain, no gain" has long been used in association with cosmetic surgery, but it has perhaps never been as appropriate as in today's China, where men and women are increasingly willing to undergo expensive and painful operations to change their appearances.

According to the local media, consultants report a 25% increase in women seeking nips and tucks. The most popular operation puts an extra fold in eyelids. Like nose-lengthening, jaw reshaping, and breast enlargements, the procedure aims to bring women closer to western ideals of beauty.

But the most dramatic—and agonising—operation is leg-lengthening, which involves breaking a patient's legs and stretching them over several months using an external cage.

In part, the popularity of such surgery can be explained by the surge of interest in fashion and beauty as an increasingly affluent urban middle class shakes off a dowdy communist legacy.

Good looks are becoming increasingly important. During the cultural revolution, beauty pageants were banned as the "nonsense" of a decadent west, but late last year, China hosted its first Miss World competition.

With the economy surging forward at the rate of more than 8% per year, more and more people who are dissatisfied with their appearance can afford to change their physical appearance.

For a minimum US$4000 price tag, doctors are offering to make people up to 10 cm taller. The leg-lengthening procedure has three stages. First, the legs are broken and steel pins—27 cm long and 8 mm in diameter—are pushed through the tibiae. These are fixed to an external frame by eight or so screws, each of which is 4 mm in diameter. Next comes the stretching, which is done over several months (depending on how much the customer wants to grow) by turning the screws each day and lengthening the bone at the point where it was broken. When the stretching is complete the external frame is removed. In the final stage, the steel pins are left in place for about a year as a support for the newly regenerated bone. Once it has hardened, the pins are removed.

The complex procedure was initially developed in Russia for people with stunted growth, mismatched legs, or disfigurements. But at one Beijing clinic, which undertakes 150 such operations per year, doctors say customers are increasingly driven by cosmetic motivations.

Height has long been socially important in China. It is often listed among the criteria required on job advertisements. To get a post in the foreign ministry, for instance, male applicants need not bother applying unless they are at least 5 ft 7 in., while women must be at least 5 ft 3 in. Chinese diplomats are expected to be tall to match the height of their foreign counterparts.

For more glamorous positions the conditions are even tougher: air stewardesses must be over 5 ft 5 in. But height discrimination is evident even at ground level: in some places, people under 5 ft 3 in. are not even eligible to take a driving test. To get into many law schools, women students need to be over 5 ft 1 in. and men over 5 ft 5 in.

The surgery can help people find jobs and marriage partners. But if not done carefully, the dangers are considerable. Bones stretched too rapidly will not grow strong enough to support the body's weight. Legs extended at different speeds can become misshapen and nerves can be damaged. Horror stories about other less capable surgeons appear from time to time in the Chinese media. Young women have reportedly been left with their feet splayed outwards on weirdly twisted legs; others' bones have never properly healed and continue to break at the slightest knock. In one of the worst cases, a 31-year-old woman was left in the frame for a year because her bones proved so brittle that they could not support her weight after being stretched. Her feet still point in odd directions and she is unable to squat.

But despite the risks involved, surgeons and consultants report an increase in demand for cosmetic procedures among the increasingly affluent urban populations. In Shanghai, there are five large cosmetic surgery outfits and about 100 smaller clinics that offer specialised procedures.

The fascination with such makeovers has created at least two cosmetic surgery celebrities. Last summer, the domestic media was filled with stories about Hao Lulu, a 24-year-old fashion writer who is undergoing a 7-month marathon of face and body altering procedures costing $US24,000 so that she can work as a spokeswoman for the industry.

Soon after, Shanghai newspapers announced the winner of what they dubbed the "grey girl" competition—to select the girl in the city most in need of a makeover. Despite the unflattering moniker, more than 50 women applied for the contest, in which the victor was awarded a prize of $US12,000 worth of cosmetic surgery.

Designer Vaginas

Simone Weil Davis (2002)

Perhaps you noticed some of the articles in women's magazines that came out in 1998; *Cosmopolitan, Marie Claire,* and *Harper's Bazaar* each carried one, as did *Salon* on-line, articles with titles like "Labia Envy," "Designer Vaginas," and "The New Sex Surgeries." More recently, *Jane* magazine covered the topic, and Dan Savage's nationally syndicated advice column, "Savage Love," stumbled explosively upon it as well. These pieces all discussed labiaplasty, a relatively recent plastic surgery procedure that involves trimming away labial tissue and sometimes injecting fat from another part of the body into labia that have been deemed excessively droopy. In contrast to the tightening operation known as "vaginal rejuvenation," labiaplasty is sheerly cosmetic in purpose and purports to have no impact on sensation (unless something were to go terribly awry).[1] Throughout coverage here and in Canada, the aptly named Doctors Alter, Stubbs, and Matlock shared much of the glory and the public relations. In the name of consumer choice, these articles provoke consumer anxiety. The *Los Angeles Times* quotes Dr. Matlock: "The woman is the designer . . . the doctor is just the instrument. . . . Honestly, if you look at *Playboy,* those women, on the outer vagina area, the vulva is very aesthetically appealing, the vulva is rounded. It's full, not flat. . . . Women are coming in saying, I want something different, I want to change things. They look at *Playboy,* the ideal women per se, for the body and the shape and so on. You don't see women in there with excessively long labia minora."[2]

All the popular articles about the "new sex surgeries" that I've reviewed also include remarks from skeptical colleagues and from polled readers who feel okay about their labia. (In an unfortunate turn of phrase, one plastic surgeon describes Dr. Matlock as a bit too "cutting edge.") Despite this apparently balanced coverage, a brand-new worry is being planted, with the declaration in *Salon* that "many women had been troubled for years about the appearance of their labia minora," and with the use of words like "normal" and "abnormal" to describe nonpathological variations among genitalia. The November 1998 article in *Cosmopolitan* has an eye-catching blurb: "My labia were so long, they'd show through my clothes!" Having taken *that* in, the reader suddenly looks up at the accompanying photo with new eyes: the photograph is of a slim woman in fairly modest underwear; because of the picture's cropping, she is headless, but the posture is distinctive, awkward. She's somewhat hunched forward, her hands are both crotch-bound, and one finger slips beneath the edge of her panties. Having read the caption, you think, "My God, she's tucking in her labia!"[3]

Ellen Frankfort's 1972 book, the women's liberationist *Vaginal Politics,* begins with the following scene.[4] Carol from the Los Angeles Self-Help Clinic "slips out of her dungarees and underpants," hops onto a long table in an old church basement and inserts a speculum into her vagina. The 50 other women present file up and look with a flashlight, and learn, too, how to self-examine with a speculum and a dimestore mirror. This self-exploration of what has been referred to as "the dark continent" or just "down there" seemed the perfect symbol for the early claim of women's liberation that "the personal is political." How could a woman call for sexual autonomy without self-awareness? To reverse the phrasing of one of Second Wave feminism's most famous by-products, how could we know "our selves" without knowing "our bodies" first?[5] This image of women using a well-placed mirror to demystify and reclaim their own bodies is rooted dimly in my teen-years memory. I found it eerily resurrected when the *Salon* piece by Louisa Kamps came up on my computer screen. Kamps starts off like this: "'Ladies, get out your hand mirrors,' begins a curious press release I find at my desk one Monday morning. 'Yes, it is true . . . the newest trend in surgically enhanced body beautification: Female Genital Cosmetic Surgery.'" The hand mirror this time is used to alert the would-be vagina shopper to any deficiencies "down below" that she may have been blithely ignoring. From 1970s' consciousness-raising groups and Judy Chicago's dinner plates, through Annie Sprinkle's speculum parties of the 1980s, and on to Eve Ensler's collaborative *Vagina Monologues*,[6] we came at the end of the 1990s to Dr. Alter and Dr. Stubbs. What's the trajectory from Second Wave feminist "self-discovery and celebration" to the current almost-craze for labiaplasty? And does the fact of this trajectory provide us with a warning?

. . .

These days, in part because of the video dissemination and the mainstreaming of pornography, women, regardless of gender preference, can see the vaginas of a lot of different other women. They may desire those vaginas, they may simultaneously identify with them, but if they are rich enough or have great credit, they can definitely have them built.[7] A 1997 article in the Canadian magazine *See* interviews a patient of Dr. Stubbs in Toronto. Deborah "has had her eyes done and had breast implants and some liposuction. She says that she started thinking about her labia when her first husband brought home porn magazines and she started comparing herself. 'I saw some other ones that were cuter than mine' and I thought, 'Hey, I want that one,' she laughs."[8] Of course, the images we relish or bemoan in pornography are almost always tweaked technically. As Deborah did her "catalog shopping," the women she was admiring were perhaps themselves surgically "enhanced," but additionally, they were posed, muted with makeup and lighting, and the resultant photographic images were then edited with an airbrush or the digital modifications of Photoshop.

This is especially true of pornography that presents itself as "upscale," whether soft or hard core. As Laura Kipnis helps us realize, there's a crucial link between *Hustler*'s targeting of a working-class market and its being the first of the big three glossy "wank mags" to show what it called "the pink."[9] *Hustler*'s aggressive celebration of vulgarity informed its initial rejection of soft-core decorum about genitals; thus, its representations of vaginas were matter-of-fact, and often enough contextualized with very explicit, poorly lit Polaroid shots sent in by readers. When the vagina finally came to the pages of *Penthouse*, by contrast, it was as flaw-free and glossy as the rest of the models' figures. In "The Pussy Shot: An Interview with Andrew Blake," sex writer Susie Bright discusses the classed aesthetics of this pornographer, whose trademarks are his lavish sets (straight out of *Architectural Digest*, Bright remarks) and high-end production values: in this posh setting, it comes as no surprise that the star's labia are small and her "pussy is perfectly composed, with every hair in place."[10]

. . .

In part because of the prevalence of a mainstreamed *Penthouse* and *Playboy* aesthetic, labias in pornography are often literally tucked away (in the most low-tech variant of body modification).[11] If you review enough porn, however, especially lesbian porn or that which is unsqueamishly "déclassé" as in *Hustler*, you will see a wide variety in the female genitalia on display—wide enough to evoke the "snowflake uniqueness" analogy that is bandied around in popular coverage of the new cosmetic enhancement surgeries. And indeed the before-and-after shots available at some of the surgeons' web sites that I've found so far do reveal, unsurprisingly, that the single favored look for these "designer vaginas" is . . . the clean slit. Louisa Kamps of *Salon* magazine agrees: "What strikes me in the 'after' shots is the eerie similarity between the women . . . their genitalia are carbon copies of each other."

. . .

Bodies do change with the passage of time, of course. If the living body is to approximate sculpture, change itself must be managed, *fixed.* Reading the following quote from Dr. Alter's web site, one is reminded of the Renaissance theory of the wandering womb, whereby female hysteria and misbehavior were deemed the results of a uterus that had dislodged and begun to storm about internally, wreaking havoc. A woman's "womb was like a hungry animal; when not amply fed by sexual intercourse or reproduction, it was likely to wander about her body, overpowering her speech and senses."[12] In Dr. Alter's prose, the older woman, "in dialogue with gravity,"[13] may find her previously pleasing vagina dangerously "on the move": "The aging female may dislike the descent of her pubic hair and labia and desire re-elevation to its previous location," Dr. Alter warns. So, it is woman's work to make sure her genitalia are snug, not wayward.

We are talking about vaginal aesthetics, and aesthetic judgments almost always evidence socially relevant metaphors at work on the material and visual planes. Ideas about feminine beauty are ever-changing: the classic example is a comparison of Rubens's fleshy beauties and the wraithlike super-model Kate Moss (who succeeded Twiggy). But, in a world where many women have never thought about judging the looks of their genitals, even if they care about their appearance more generally, we should ask what criteria make for a good-looking vagina, and who is assigned as arbiter. These (mutating) criteria should tell us something about the value system that generates them. To tease out some answers to these questions, this article goes on to put the labiaplasty phenomenon in a contextual frame with other vaginal modifications.

MODIFYING/CLASSIFYING

What representations of vulvas circulate in our society? And who, beyond Dr. Tight, is modifying the female genitalia, how and why? For one, among alternative youth (and the not-so-alternative, not-so-youthful, too) piercings are being sought to modify and decorate the labia, sometimes to extend them, and, ideally, to add to clitoral stimulation. What sensibilities mark these changes?

Among body modifiers on the Web, conversation about body image, self-mutilation, and, contrarily, healing, is common, with an accepted understanding that many turn to piercing as a means of overcoming perceived past abuse. "'Most folks use BodMod to get back in touch with the parts of themselves that were hurt or misused by others. BodMod has helped me undemonize pain. . . . I was able to handle [childbirth] better, knowing that I'd survived . . . two ten-gauge labial piercings. . . .'" Changing one's relationship to one's genitalia by becoming their "modifier" leads here to an aesthetic reassessment: "'You know, I never liked to look at [myself] until I got my rings. I have well-developed inner labia that always show, and I was always envious of those women who seemed to [be neat] with everything tucked inside. So one reason I *know* I wasn't mutilating myself when I got my privates pierced was how much I liked to look at myself after the work was done. You might actually say I'm *glad* my labia are the way they are now.'"[14]

"Glad" is what the cosmetic surgeons do *not* want you to be about prominent labia minora. If you look at the opening paragraph of Ensler's *Vagina Monologues,* you begin to wonder if the unruliness now coming under the governance of the cosmetic surgeon isn't at least as symbolic as it is aesthetic. This is Ensler, introducing her project (interviews with real women, transcribed, performed onstage, and then collected in a book):

> I was worried about vaginas. I was worried about what we think about vaginas, and even more worried that we don't think about them. . . . So I decided to talk to women about their vaginas, to do vagina interviews, which became vagina monologues. I talked with over two hundred women. I talked to old women, young women, married women, single women, lesbians, college professors, actors, corporate professionals, sex workers, African American women, Hispanic women, Asian American women, Native American women, Caucasian women, Jewish women. At first women were reluctant to talk. They were a little shy. But once they got going, you couldn't stop them.[15]

Just as Ensler's own catalog of interviewees seems to burgeon and proliferate, so too the women with whom she spoke were "unstoppable." With a similar metaphoric expansion, in the cosmetic surgeons' promotional material, not only are women's *labia* depicted as in danger of distention, but one woman customer also described her *"hang-up"* about her preoperative labia as "just growing and growing," until the doctor cut it short, that is. Loose lips sink ships.

. . .

CONFOUNDING THE BOUNDARIES

The U.S. Congress passed a measure criminalizing the circumcision of a minor female in 1996, and nine or ten states have passed anti-FGO acts since 1996 as well. In Illinois, Minnesota, Rhode Island, and Tennessee, this legislation felonizes operations performed on adults as well as on minors. But *which* operations? Anti-FGO laws that now exist in a number of U.S. states describe procedures that would definitely include those practiced by Drs. Alter and Matlock, but they use only language that addresses the "ritual" or custom and belief-based cutting of African immigrant bodies. Meanwhile, this legal language either elides or okays both the "corrective" cutting of the intersexed child and the surgery sought by the unsettled consumer who has been told by plastic surgeons that her labia are unappealing and aberrant. Thus American law marks out relations between the state and its citizen bodies that differ depending on birthplace, cultural context, and skin color.

In fact, however, it is a (prevalent) mistake to imagine a quantum distinction between Euro-American and African reshapings of women's bodies: far too often, they are measured with entirely different yardsticks, rather than on a continuum. Nahid Toubia, executive director of the advocacy group Rainbo, remarks that "[t]he thinking of an African woman who believes that 'FGM is the fashionable thing to do to become a real woman' is not so different from that of an American woman who has breast implants to appear more feminine."[16] . . .

Soraya Miré, Somali maker of the film *Fire Eyes,* remarks in Inga Muscio's (wo)manifesto, *Cunt: A Declaration of Independence:* "[Western women] come into conversations waving the American flag, forever projecting the idea that they are more intelligent than I am. I've learned that American women look at women like me to hide from their own pain. . . . In America, women pay *the money that is theirs and no one else's* to go to a doctor who cuts them up so they can create or sustain an image men want. Men are the mirror. Western women cut themselves up voluntarily."[17] Significantly, in Miré's construction, consent to genital surgery does *not* okay it so much as it marks the degrading depths of women's oppression. Although consent is at the heart of the issue of genital operations on children, a topic both urgent and not to be downplayed, we must also look at the social and cultural means whereby consent is manufactured, regardless of age, in the West as well as in African and other countries engaging in FGOs. In the North American popular imagination, the public address of advertising is not understood as infringing upon our power of consent. Indeed, the freedom to "pay the money that is [one's] own" is too often inscribed as the quintessential exemplar of life in a democracy. Perhaps due to that presumption, beauty rituals hatched on Madison Avenue or in Beverly Hills do not bear the onus of "barbarism" here, despite the social compulsions, psychological drives, and magical thinking that impel them.

. . .

SURGERY, SISTERLINESS, AND THE "RIGHT TO CHOOSE"

Among the key motivating factors raised by African women who favor female genital surgeries are beautification, transcendence of shame, and the desire to conform; these clearly matter to American women seeking cosmetic surgery on their labia, as well. Thus, the motivations that impel African-rooted FGOs and American labiaplasties should not be envisioned as radically distinct. Not only does such oversimplification lead to a dangerous reanimation of the un/civilized binary, but it also leaves the feminist with dull tools for analysis of either phenomenon. There are aesthetic parallels between the Western and the African procedures. The enthusiasm for the clean slit voiced so vigorously by the American plastic surgeon I consulted is echoed among a group of Egyptian mothers discussing female genital operations for their daughters in the 1990 documentary *Hidden Faces*. Although several of the women laughingly nudge each other and say they wouldn't want the excisers to interfere much with "the front" (showing a clear zest for clitoral pleasure), one woman voices an aesthetic principle about which she feels strongly. Energetically, she decries the ugliness of dangling labia, and explains to the filmmaker, with appropriate hand gestures, "Do you want her to be like a boy, with this floppy thing hanging down? Now, it should be straight. Shhh. Smooth as silk." This aesthetic judgment is in keeping not only with the views of labiaplasters in the United States but also with the vocabulary of Mauritanian midwives: one such woman, who has argued to her colleagues for a milder version of circumcision in place of vigorous excision, "use[s] two words to refer to female circumcision, 'tizian,' which means to make more beautiful, and 'gaaad,' which means to cut off and make even."[18]

The group of women chatting on a rooftop in *Hidden Faces* invokes another continuum between African and American women's approaches to feminine beauty rituals and vaginal modifications. Simplistic depictions of a global patriarchy, wherein men curb, cow, cut, and dominate "their" women, may drive home the ubiquity of female subjugation, but they leave out an important factor at the same time: although both labiaplasties and African female circumcision should be (and are here) investigated through a feminist lens, that feminism should be informed by an awareness of women's agency. A knee-jerk celebration of that agency misleads, but its disavowal in the name of victimhood leads to dangerous blind sports. Across many different cultural contexts, female genital operations are contemplated and undergone by girls and women in a social and psychological framework shaped *in part* by other women.

The plastic surgeon whose office I visited provided me with two referrals, patients who had had the procedure done by him. As part of what seemed a well-worn sales pitch, he referred often to "self-help groups," a network of supportive, independent women helping each other find the professional care they wanted and deserved, in the face of an unfeeling, disbelieving medical profession. I was interested by what seemed an invocation of rather feminist sensibilities and wondered about this swelling, grassroots support group he seemed to be conjuring up for me. And, indeed, the image of the surgery consumer as a liberated woman and an independent self-fashioner did provide a crucial spin for the doctor, throughout his consultation. The consumer-feminist in support of other women he condoned; by contrast, he expressed an avowed disapproval of the women who came to him solely to please a domineering partner. He brought up this posited bad, weak, man-centric woman three times as we spoke, and each time his face clouded, he frowned, and his brow furrowed: he said that it was only this type of woman who complained of pain after the procedure, for instance, just to get the attention of her partner, whereas for most women, he insisted, the pain was minimal. He seemed to use these diverging models of female behavior to answer in advance any reservations the prospective client might have about a cosmetic operation on the genitalia (such as, "Should I really do something so drastic to my body just to please men?"). By insisting on his antipathy toward women who kowtowed to the male perspective, and celebrating the fearless vision of the pioneer consumer of "cutting edge" surgery, the doctor tried, I suspect, to ward off potential surges of feminist resistance to the procedure.

In the same spirit, one web site advertising the surgery fuels itself on a long-standing feminist call for a more responsive medical establishment by contrasting the surgeon being advertised with other doctors less sensitive to the needs of women.

"Very few physicians are concerned with the appearance of the female external genitalia. A relative complacency exists that frustrates many women."[19] Rachel Bowlby has addressed the theoretical conflations between feminist freedom and the "freedom" to choose as a consumer.[20] The surgeon to whose sales pitch I listened and the creators of the web site noted here certainly understood that the feminist discourse of choice can be appropriated, funneled toward the managed choosing-under-duress of the consumer, becoming saturated along the way with commodity culture's directives.

One goal of this article is to raise the question of this ready appropriation. In *States of Injury: Power and Freedom in Late Modernity,* Wendy Brown examines some of the liabilities of the Left's reliance on the rhetoric of identity, injury, and redress, suggesting that it can result in a politics of state domination.[21] From Bakke on, we have certainly seen the language of affirmative action hauled into the arena of "reverse racism." Perhaps by the same token, the language of choice, as central to the feminist project in this country as we could imagine, sprang up in a culture where the glories of consumer "choice" had already been mythologized. Revisiting and perhaps refiguring the conceptual framework behind "choice" in the face of manufactured consent, then, is to enable, not critique, feminism. The hand mirror that allowed feminists of the 1960s and 1970s to get familiar with "our bodies, our selves" is positioned again so that we can see our vaginas. Only, it comes now with the injunction to look critically at what we see and to exert our selfhood through expenditure and remodeling of a body that is not "ourself" any longer but which is "ours," commodified and estranged, to rebuild.

Although the approach of the doctor I visited seemed agenda-driven and rather theatricalized, when I talked with the women to whom he referred me, I was struck by how very friendly and supportive they *did* seem. I had found the doctor likable but showy, like a much rehearsed salesman, but these women were engaged, candid, and genuinely warm. They were generous with their time (and with their permission to be cited anonymously in the present article), and they made it clear that they really did want to help other women with their "experience, strength, and hope." Perhaps these women were "incentivized" to speak well of the doctor (about whose care they raved): maybe they received discounted work in exchange for talking with prospective clients. Even with this possibility in mind they seemed sincerely ready to assume a common perspective, in fact an intimacy, between women discussing their bodies and body image. To overlook their candor, generosity, and *sisterliness* in order to critique the misogynist judgments that may have driven them to surgery would be to mischaracterize the phenomenon of gender display. We typically learn about and develop a gendered bodily performance, not in isolation, but as members of both real and imagined female "communities."[22] And in 2002, one senses the cultural shading that twentieth-century feminism has, ironically, brought to this community building: the rhetoric of choice making and of solidarity developed during the Second Wave ghosts through our conversations. It's a stereotypical joke that women *really* dress for each other—a deeper look at how this female-to-female hodgepodge of peer pressure and peer support really manifests itself is useful. And again, a look at the web of relations among women is helpful in understanding African female genital operations as well.

One online World Health Organization report discusses the impact of female circumcisions on girls' psychological health. Importantly, it mentions not only "experiences of suffering, devaluation and impotence" but also the "desirability of the ceremony for the child, with its social advantage of peer acceptance, personal pride and material gifts." Claire Robertson points out that among the functions of the circumcision ceremony in Central Kenya is the role female initiation plays in maintaining the social strength of organizations of older women.[23] The flip side of approving support, of course, is peer pressure. "When girls of my age were looking after the lambs, they would talk among themselves about their circumcision experiences and look at each other's genitals to see who had the smallest opening. If there was a girl in the group who was still uninfibulated, she would always feel ashamed since she had nothing to show the others."[24]

A reminiscent bodily shame lurks behind the support for labial modifications that my American patient contacts expressed. One (heterosexual) woman explained to me that although none of her boyfriends had ever remarked on her labia, "ever since I was fourteen, I felt like I had this abnormalcy; I felt uncomfortable changing in front of girlfriends." She went on to say that she felt she had to hide her vagina around other women and could never enjoy skinny-dipping because of her concerns about other women judging her appearance. Another labiaplasty patient reported a "120% shift" in her "mental attitude," and a "night-and-day" improvement in the looks of her genitalia, thanks to the surgery. "As sad as it is, it makes you feel inferior," she commented.[25] Her use of the second person (or the ethical dative, as it's known), so intimate in its extension of subjectivity, meant that her language included me. . . . I too felt sad, I too felt inferior. And for a fee, the kind doctor was there to correct me.

. . .

It is probably obvious from this piece that, even in the age where both informational and medical technology have led to bodies being reshaped, extended, reconfigured, and reconceptualized like never before, I believe that erotic tissue is far better enjoyed than removed.[26] In approaching the politics of female genital operations, however, I would argue that it is imperative that both consent issues and vaginal modifications themselves be considered *on a continuum* that is not determined along hemispheric, national, or racial lines. . . .

In "Arrogant Perception, World-Traveling, and Multicultural Feminism: The Case of Female Genital Surgeries," Isabelle R. Gunning attempts to define and model a responsible approach to thinking about genital operations across cultures. She urges activists "to look at one's own culture anew and identify [. . .] practices that might prove 'culturally challenging' or negative to some

other," and "to look in careful detail at the organic social environment of the 'other' which has produced the culturally challenging practice being explored."[27] I have tried, in this article, to meet her first criterion, and I hope that rendering American cosmetic surgery strange through a heedful look at this latest, not-yet-naturalized procedure can aid us in contextualizing and understanding genital surgeries born in other contexts as well.

. . .

NOTES

Thanks to former students Jenn Sanders and Wacuka Mungai for their help in developing this article.

1. Things certainly can happen. See Louisa Kamps, "Labia Envy," 16 Mar. 1998, <http://www.salon.com/mwt/feature/1998/03/16feature.html> (9 Dec. 2001).

2. *Los Angeles Times,* 5 Mar. 1998. See, too, the following Internet resources on labiaplasty: Dr. Alter: "Female Cosmetic and Reconstructive Genital Surgery," <http://www.altermd.com/female/index.html> (9 Dec. 2001); Julia Scheeres, "Vaginal Cosmetic Surgery," 16 Apr. 2001, <http://thriveonline.oxygen.com/sex/sexpressions/vaginal-cosmetic-surgery.html> (9 Dec. 2001); Dr. Stubbs, <http://psurg.com>; Laser Rejuvenation Center of LA, <http://www.drmatlock.com>; Dan Savage, "Long in the Labia," 16 Dec. 1999, <http://www.the stranger.com/1999-12-16/savage.html> (13 Dec. 2001); iVillage.com Archive Message Board, "Cosmetic Surgery," 7 Jan. 2000, <http://boards.allhealth.com/messages/get/bhcosmeticsx2.html> (13 Dec. 2001); Patients' chatboard, <http://boards.allhealth.com/messages/get/bhcosmeticsx2.html>.

3. See Kamps. Also, see Carrie Havranek, "The New Sex Surgeries," *Cosmopolitan,* November 1998, 146.

4. Ellen Frankfort, *Vaginal Politics* (New York: Quadrangle, 1972). See, too, Julia Scheeres, "Vulva Goldmine: How Cosmetic Surgeons Snatch Your Money," *Bitch* 11 (January 2000): 70–84.

5. Boston Women's Health Collective, *Our Bodies, Ourselves* (New York: Simon & Schuster, 1973). Updated editions have continued to be released. See Boston Women's Health Collective, *Our Bodies, Ourselves for the New Century: A Book by and for Women* (New York: Simon & Schuster, 1998).

6. See Amelia Jones, ed., *Sexual Politics: Judy Chicago's Dinner Party in Feminist Art History* (Berkeley: University of California Press, 1996); Shannon Bell, "Prostitute Performances: Sacred Carnival Theorists of the Female Body," from her *Reading, Writing, and Rewriting the Prostitute Body* (Bloomington: Indiana University Press, 1994), 137–84; and Eve Ensler, *The Vagina Monologues* (New York: Villard Press, 1998).

7. On the thin line between identification and desire, between wanting to be like someone and wanting to bed down with them (so exploited in consumer culture), see Diana Fuss, "Fashion and the Homospectatorial Look," in *On Fashion,* ed. Shari Benstock and Suzanne Ferriss (New Brunswick, N.J.: Rutgers University Press, 1994), 211–32; and Judith Butler, *Gender Trouble: Feminism and the Subversion of Identity* (New York: Routledge, 1990), esp. 57–72.

8. Josey Vogels, "My Messy Bedroom," *See,* 10 July 1997, <http://www.greatwest.ca/SEE/Issues/1997/970710/josey.html> (13 Dec. 2001).

9. Laura Kipnis, *Bound and Gagged: Pornography and the Politics of Fantasy in America* (New York: Grove, 1996).

10. Susie Bright, "The Pussy Shot: An Interview with Andrew Blake," *Sexwise* (New York: Cleis Press, 1995), 82.

11. See Nedahl Stelio, "Do You Know What a Vagina Looks Like?" *Cosmopolitan,* August 2001, 126–28, on sex magazines' doctoring of vaginas and the increased prevalence of labiaplasty.

12. Natalie Zemon Davis, "Women on Top," in her *Society and Culture in Early Modern France* (Stanford: Stanford University Press, 1975), 124–31.

13. Denise Stoklos, remark made in Solo Performance Composition, her course offered by the Performance Studies Department, New York University, Spring 2000. "Our primary dialogue is with gravity," Stoklos says.

14. See Ambient, Inc., "Body Modification: Is It Self-Mutilation—Even if Someone Else Does It for You?" 2 Feb. 1998, <http://www.ambient.on.ca/bodmod/mutilate.html> (13 Dec. 2001). Another Web site dealing with body modification is <http://www.perforations.com> (13 Dec. 2001).

15. Ensler, 3–5.

16. Nahid Toubia, *Female Genital Mutilation: A Call for Global Action,* 3d ed. (New York: Women, Ink, 1995), 35.

17. Inga Muscio, *Cunt: A Declaration of Independence* (Toronto: Seal Press, 1998), 134–35.

18. Claire Hunt and Kim Longinotto, with Safaa Fathay, *Hidden Faces,* videorecording (New York: Twentieth Century Vixen Production/Women Make Movies, 1990). And see Elizabeth Oram, introduction to Zainaba's "Lecture on Clitoridectomy to the Midwives of Touil, Mauritania" (1987), in *Opening the Gates: A Century of Arab Feminist Writing,* ed. Margot Badran and Miriam Cooke (Bloomington: Indiana University Press, 1990), 63–71.

19. See <http://www.altermd.com/female/index.html> (13 Dec. 2001).

20. See Rachel Bowlby, in *Shopping with Freud: Items on Consumerism, Feminism, and Psychoanalysis* (New York: Routledge, 1993), on theoretical conflations between feminist freedom and the "freedom" to choose as a consumer.

21. Wendy Brown, *States of Injury: Power and Freedom in Late Modernity* (Princeton: Princeton University Press, 1995).

22. Anonymous telephone interviews with two West Coast labiaplasty patients, August 1999. For an on-line example of this, see the fascinating archived chat between women about cosmetic surgery at iVillage, "Cosmetic Surgery Archive Board," 7 Jan. 2001, <http://boards.allhealth.com/messages/get/ bhcosmeticsx2.html> (13 Dec. 2001).

23. See Claire Robertson, "Grassroots in Kenya: Women, Genital Mutilation, and Collective Action, 1920–1990," *Signs* 21 (Spring 1996): 615–42.

24. Anab's story, from "Social and Cultural Implications of Infibulation in Somalia," by Amina Wasame, in *Female Circumcision: Strategies to Bring about Change* (Somali Women's Democratic Organization), quoted in Toubia, 41.

25. Anonymous telephone interview with author, August 1999.

26. An important caveat: As the transgendered community has made clear, for some individuals, erotic enjoyment is enhanced via the genital modification that comes along with reassigning gender, even if that surgery has resulted in a reduction in nerve endings or sensation.

27. Isabelle R. Gunning, "Arrogant Perception, World Traveling, and Multicultural Feminism: The Case of Female Genital Surgeries," *Columbia Human Rights Law Review* 23 (Summer 1992): 213.

DISCUSSION QUESTIONS FOR CHAPTER 5

1. How are power relations reflected and reinforced in beauty norms?

2. How do beauty norms affect women and men differently? How have beauty norms affected you?

3. Two of your readings talk about women's connections with particular aspects of their bodies—vaginas, hair, and noses. What aspects of your body reflect key elements of your sense of self?

4. What are some of the connections between beauty standards and women's health?

5. How can women resist the beauty ideal?

SUGGESTIONS FOR FURTHER READING

Bordo, Susan, and Leslie Haywood. *Unbearable Weight: Feminism, Western Culture, and the Body, Tenth Anniversary Edition.* Berkeley: University of California Press, 2004.

Crawley, Sara, Lara Foley, and Constance Shehan. *Gendering Bodies.* Walnut Creek, CA: AltaMira Press, 2007.

Gimlin, Debra L. *Body Work: Beauty and Self-Image in American Culture.* Berkeley: University of California Press, 2002.

Holmlund, Chris. *Impossible Bodies: Femininity and Masculinity at the Movies.* New York: Routledge, 2002.

Mintz, Susannah. *Unruly Bodies: Life Writing by Women with Disabilities.* Chapel Hill, NC: The University of North Carolina Press, 2007.

Solovay, Sondra. *Tipping the Scales of Justice: Fighting Weight-Based Discrimination.* Amherst, NY: Prometheus, 2000.

Weitz, Rose. *Rapunzel's Daughters: What Women's Hair Tells Us About Women's Lives.* New York: Farrar, Straus and Giroux, 2004.

CHAPTER **6**

Health and Reproductive Rights

HEALTH AND WELLNESS

Health is a central issue in women's lives. Ask parents what they wish for their newborns and they speak first about hoping the baby is healthy; quiz people about their hopes for the new year and they speak about staying healthy; listen to politicians debate their positions before an election and health care is almost always a key issue. In contemporary U.S. society, good health is generally understood as a requirement for happy and productive living. Because women are prominent as both providers and consumers of health care, health issues and the health care system affect us on many levels. To make sense of the complexities of women's relationships to health care systems, we will discuss five concepts: equity, androcentrism, medicalization, stereotyping, and corporate responsibility.

First, medical institutions in the United States provide different levels of service based on health insurance status and the general ability to pay. Poor women are less healthy than those who are better off, whether the benchmark is mortality, the prevalence of acute or chronic diseases, or mental health. This is the issue of *equity*. Some people have better health care than others because of a two-tiered system that has different outcomes for those who can pay or who have health insurance and those who cannot afford to pay and do not have health insurance through their jobs or are not covered by welfare programs. This is a special problem as health care costs continue to rise. Some states are providing less coverage for low-income people, a problem because the United States, unlike most Western industrialized societies, does not yet have a nationalized health care system. The issue of equity affects all aspects of health care, including access to fertility, contraceptive, and abortion facilities.

A National Health Survey conducted by the U.S. Centers for Disease Control and Prevention (CDC) found that more than 40 million people of all ages went without insurance at some point in 2005 (about 16 percent of the U.S. population). Women are more likely than men to be uninsured because they are poorer. They are also more likely to be employed in part-time or full-time work without health insurance

296

LEARNING ACTIVITY   **Women, Heart Disease, and Cancer in Your State**

- To learn more about the prevalence of heart disease among women in your state, visit the CDC's website at *www.cdc.gov/nccdphp/cvd/womensatlas/factsheets/index.htm* and click on your state's name.
- To learn about the prevalence of cancer in your state, go to *www.cdc.gov/cancer/dbdata.htm* and select your state.

benefits. In 2007 over 17 million adult women (almost one-fifth of those between 18 and 64 years) were without health insurance. Of those, almost half reported in a 2004 survey that they had gone without care in the last year because of health care costs. Employment does not necessarily provide access to health insurance, as two-thirds of uninsured women live in families in which they or a partner are working full time. As a result, low-income women (who are disproportionately women of color) are more likely to postpone care and delay preventive procedures such as mammograms and pap smears. Uninsured children are at greater risk of experiencing health problems such as obesity, heart disease, and asthma that continue to affect them as (potentially uninsured) adults, resulting in increased costs for public health care services. Such adverse effects of health care inequity carry long-term implications for families and society.

As low-income families struggle to cover basic needs such as food, shelter, and the increasing cost of energy, the spiraling cost of health insurance becomes more difficult to afford. Health club memberships and healthy foods are outside the reach of most low-income people, who also tend to live in neighborhoods that provide unhealthy environments. As a result, low-income women are more susceptible to chronic conditions as well as acute problems that might have been avoided had preventive care been available. These cost the state millions of dollars annually and are not a fiscally responsible way to provide health care services. Women of color are especially at risk for not having health care coverage and for receiving substandard care when they enter the system. They have higher maternal and infant mortality rates, higher rates of HIV infection, and their reproductive health is threatened by limited access to basic reproductive health care, including family planning services and abortion care. The reading by Jael Silliman and colleagues, "Women of Color and Their Struggle for Reproductive Justice," touches on these issues in the context of reproductive health.

Professional health-related organizations (such as the American Medical Association [AMA]), health maintenance organizations (HMOs), insurance companies, pharmaceutical companies, and corporations representing other medical products and practices, have enormous influence over health politics. In addition, health is not just about medical services. Health conditions, including incidence and mortality rates, are related to such socioeconomic factors as poverty, poor nutrition, interpersonal violence, substandard housing, and lack of education. Many of the social issues that affect women on a daily basis and that contribute to increased tobacco use, chemical addictions, stress, and poor nutrition among women have their consequence in increased rates of heart disease, cancer, chronic obstructive pulmonary disease, diabetes, and obesity, to name just a few. Health problems are compounded by the aging of the population, such that by the year 2030, women (who are likely to have fewer economic resources than men) will represent approximately 81 percent of people who are over 85 years old. As suggested in the reading "American Women and Health Disparities" by former U.S. Surgeon General David Satcher, MD, while strides have been made in dealing with many women's health issues, more activism is still needed to ensure equity in health care, especially for women of color. These strides are reported in the reading by Linda Gordon titled "Is Nothing Simple about Reproduction Control?" as she discusses the history of the women's health movement. Vivian M. Dickerson, MD, president of the American College of Obstetricians and Gynecologists, also reports on activism that is necessary to ensure equity and justice in the reading "The Tolling of the Bell: Women's Health, Women's Rights."

Globally, women's health access is one of the most important issues determining justice and equity for women. The reading by Agnes R. Howard and Nicholas D. Kristof, "Cursed by God?: Two Essays on a Theme," discusses medical access for women in Africa suffering from the stigmatizing, although preventable and easily treatable, condition of obstetric fistula are a case in point. The HIV/AIDS global pandemic is also an important illustration of issues of gender and racial/ethnic equity both nationally and globally. As the box below shows, in 2005 the rate of AIDS

HIV/AIDS Among Women

Early in the epidemic, HIV infection and AIDS were diagnosed for relatively few women. Today, the HIV/AIDS epidemic represents a growing and persistent health threat to women in the United States, especially young women and women of color. In 2004, HIV infection was the leading cause of death for African American women aged 25–34 years and was among the four leading causes of death for African American women aged 35–44 years and 45–54 years, as well as Hispanic women aged 35–44 years.[1] Overall, in the same year, HIV infection was the sixth leading cause of death among all women aged 25–34 years and the fifth leading cause of death among all women aged 35–44 years.

CUMULATIVE EFFECTS OF HIV INFECTION AND AIDS (THROUGH 2005)

- Through 2005, 181,802 women were given a diagnosis of AIDS, a number that represents about one-fifth of the total 984,155 AIDS diagnoses.[2]
- An estimated 85,844 women with AIDS died. These women account for 16 percent of the 550,394 deaths of persons with AIDS.[2]
- Women with AIDS made up an increasing part of the epidemic. In 1992, women accounted for an estimated 14 percent of adults and adolescents living with AIDS.[3] By the end of 2005, this percentage had grown to 23 percent.[2]

- From 2001 through 2005, the annual number of estimated AIDS diagnoses increased 7 percent among women and increased 7 percent among men.[2]
- According to a recent CDC study of more than 19,500 patients in ten U.S. cities, HIV-infected women were 12 percent less likely than infected men to receive prescriptions for the most effective treatments for HIV infection.[3]

AIDS IN 2005

- An estimated 10,774 women had a diagnosis of AIDS, a number that represents 36 percent of the 29,766 AIDS diagnoses.[2]
- The rate of AIDS diagnoses for African American women (45.5/100,000 women) was approximately 22 times the rate for White women (2.0/100,000) and 4 times the rate for Hispanic women (11.2/100,000).[2]
- African American and Hispanic women together represented about 25 percent of all U.S. women,[4] yet they account for 82 percent of AIDS diagnoses reported in 2005.[2]
- An estimated 95,959 women were living with AIDS, representing 23 percent of the estimated 421,873 people living with AIDS.[2]
- An estimated 4,128 women with AIDS died, representing 24 percent of the 17,011 deaths of persons with AIDS.[2]
- Heterosexual contact was the source of almost 70 percent of these HIV infections.[2]
- Women accounted for 30 percent of the estimated 35,107 diagnoses of HIV infection.[2]

For more information on HIV and AIDS, contact

CDC National STD & AIDS Hotlines:1-800-342-AIDS; Spanish: 1-800-344-SIDA; Deaf: 1-800-243-7889

CDC National Prevention Information Network: P.O. Box 6003, Rockville, MD 20849-6003; 1-800-458-5231

Web Resources

NCHSTP: *www.cdc.gov/nchstp*

DHAP: *www.cdc.gov/hiv*

NPIN: *www.cdcnpin.org*

REFERENCES

1. *http://www.cdc.gov/nchs/data/nvsr/nvsr56/nvsr56_05.pdf.*
2. *http://www.cdc.gov/hiv/topics/surveillance/resources/reports/2005report/default.htm.*
3. McNaghten AD, Hanson DL, Aponte Z, Sullivan P, Wolfe MI. Gender disparity in HIV treatment and AIDS opportunistic illnesses (OI). XV International Conference on AIDS; July 2004; Bangkok, Thailand. Abstract MoOrC1032.
4. U.S. Census Bureau. Census Brief: Women in the United States: a profile. March 2000. Available at *http://www.census.gov/prod/2000pubs/cenbr001.pdf.* Accessed August 27, 2004.

For Better or For Worse®   **by Lynn Johnston**

diagnoses for African American women was approximately 22 times the rate for White women and 4 times the rate for Latinas. Although globally men make up a larger proportion of AIDS patients than women, the relative increase is greater for women. Risk factors for women, both in the United States and globally, include the lack of power in relationships (as reflected by sexual violence against women; the woman's lack of input into decisions such as whether a male partner wears a condom, visits a prostitute, or has multiple sexual partners, etc.), the lack of education about body and sexuality, and the biological vulnerability of women during sexual intercourse that provides more sources of entry for the virus.

Although there has been increased funding for HIV/AIDS prevention, treatment, and care in Africa and the Caribbean, a U.S. "global gag rule" on the U.S. Agency for International Development (USAID) population-control program has restricted foreign nongovernmental organizations (NGOs) that receive USAID family-planning funds from using their own, non-U.S. funds to provide legal abortion services, lobby their own governments for abortion law reform, or even provide accurate medical counseling or referrals regarding abortion. Such a policy has undermined funding for other, related health issues (as well as health and infant screening, nutritional programs, and health education) and encouraged narrow, often religious, and abstinence-based approaches to HIV/AIDS prevention that exclude condom use. It is important to consider the ways anti-choice policies in the United States are threatening the quality of women's lives around the world.

The second theme of this chapter is *androcentrism* or male centeredness (see Chapter 1). Men's bodies are the norm, and much medical research has focused on men (mostly White men) and has been overgeneralized to others. Baseline data for heart monitors, for example, were based on middle-aged White men, causing serious complications for patients who did not fit this description. Until recently, women often were not included in clinical trials to determine the safety and effectiveness of drugs and other medical devices because it was thought that women's hormonal cycling or other factors peculiar to being female might constitute variables that could skew trial results. It was declared that excluding women protected them, because a woman might be pregnant or the drug might prevent future fertility. Drug companies did not want to get sued. Over the last decade it has become increasingly clear that research from male-only trials may not apply equally to women, or may not provide data on important effects of drugs on women. Originally, researchers believed most sex differences in terms of reactions to drugs were most likely a result of differences in hormones, height, and/or weight. Scientists now know that these differences are more complex. Differences in the livers of men and women may explain why most women seem to metabolize drugs differently than men, for example. There may also be sex differences in pain tolerance and the ways individuals respond to pain medications.

Additionally, more money has been spent on diseases that are more likely to afflict men. Related to this is the notion of "anatomy is destiny" (an example of biological determinism, discussed in Chapter 5) whereby female physiology, and especially reproductive anatomy, is seen as central in understanding women's behavior. Social norms about femininity have come to guide medical and scientific ideas about women's health, and female genital organs have long been seen as sources of special emotional as well as physical health problems.

In terms of women as health care providers, androcentrism has supported sexism and encouraged systems where men have more positions of power and influence in the health care system. Although nursing is still overwhelmingly a feminine occupation, more women are becoming physicians, even though some prestigious specialties are still dominated by men. It remains to be seen whether this increase in female physicians will change the face of medicine as we know it.

Third, *medicalization* is the process whereby normal functions of the body come to be seen as indicative of disease. This tends to be the model by which modern medicine works. This affects women in two ways. One, because women have more episodic changes in their bodies as a result of childbearing (for example, menstruation, pregnancy, childbirth, lactation, and menopause), they are more at risk for medical personnel interpreting these natural processes as problematic. Note how this tends to reinforce the argument that biology is destiny. Two, medicalization supports business and medical technologies. It tends to work against preventive medicine and encourages sophisticated medical technologies to "fix" problems after they occur. Medical services are dominated by drug treatments and surgery, and controlled by pharmaceutical companies, HMOs, and such professional organizations as the American Medical Association.

Fourth, *stereotyping* encompasses how notions about gender, race/ethnicity, and other identities inform everyday understanding of health care occupations and - influence how medical practitioners treat their patients. For example, patients often assume that white-coated White male orderlies are doctors and call women doctors "nurse." Women tend to interact differently with the health care system and are treated differently, often to the detriment of women's health. For example, research suggests that physicians generally are more likely to consider emotional factors when diagnosing women's problems, and they are more likely to assume that the cause of illness is psychosomatic when the patient involved is female. It is well known that physicians also prescribe more mood-altering medication for women than they do for men. In addition, physicians attribute stereotypical notions of ethnicity, as well as gender, to patients, expecting Latinas/os, for example, to be more nervous and excitable. Homophobia prevents lesbians from receiving fully

Alcohol Abuse

Alcohol/substance abuse and alcohol/substance dependence are complicated illnesses that present unique threats to women's health. Medical research is showing that women who abuse alcohol and other drugs may develop addictions and substance-related health problems faster than men.

Recent surveys show that alcohol consumption is most common among

- Women between the ages of 26 and 34
- Women who are divorced or separated

Binge drinking (consumption of four or more drinks at one sitting) is most common among women between the ages of 18 to 25. And drinking is more prevalent among Caucasian women than other ethnic/racial groups, although African American women are more likely to drink heavily. It is binge drinking, as opposed to drinking in general, that causes most of the alcohol-associated harm occurring on our campuses and in students' lives.

Results of a major, eight-year study involving the drinking habits of thousands of college students were reported in the March 2002 edition of the *Journal of American College Health*. The 2001 Harvard School of Public Health College Alcohol Study surveyed students at 119 four-year colleges that participated in the 1993, 1997, and 1999 studies. Responses in the four survey years were compared to determine trends in heavy alcohol use, alcohol-related problems, and encounters with college and community prevention programs.

The findings revealed that, despite efforts to curb binge drinking on our campuses through the implementation of alcohol-prevention programs, services, activities, and policies, we have not yet solved the problem. Here are the key findings:

- In 2001 approximately two in five (44.4 percent) college students reported binge drinking, a rate almost identical to rates in the previous three surveys.
- Very little change in overall binge drinking occurred at the individual college level.
- A sharp rise (from 5.3 percent in 1993 to 11.9 percent in 2001) in frequent binge drinking was noted among women attending all-women's colleges, and a lesser, but still significant, increase of the same behavior for women in coeducational schools.
- The percentages of abstainers and frequent binge drinkers increased, indicating a polarization of drinking behavior first noted in 1997.
- Other significant changes included increases in immoderate drinking and harm among drinkers.
- More students lived in substance-free housing and encountered college educational efforts and sanctions resulting from their alcohol use.
- The prevalence of drinking among underage students is lower (77.4 percent) than that among 21- to 23-year-old students (85.6 percent). In addition, underage students drink less frequently than do their "legal age" peers, and the percentage of underage students who binge drink (43.6 percent) is lower than that of students who are over the age of 21 who do (50.2 percent).
- Half of the underage students who were studied reported obtaining alcohol easily; other students are their primary source. But since 1993, the use of fake identification cards to obtain alcohol illegally has declined, whereas the role of parents as providers of alcohol to underage students has increased.
- Having more laws restricting underage drinking or governing the volume of sales and consumption of alcohol in effect is associated with less drinking among underage students.

All of these statistics aside, the latest word from the National Institute on Alcohol Abuse and Alcoholism is that all women are more vulnerable to alcohol-related organ damage, trauma, and interpersonal difficulties:

- Liver damage: Women develop alcohol-induced liver disease in a shorter time period than men even if they consume less alcohol. And, women are more likely to develop alcohol hepatitis and die from cirrhosis (liver disease).
- Brain damage: Studies of brains, as seen via magnetic resonance imaging (MRI), show that women may be more vulnerable to brain damage due to alcohol consumption than men.
- Heart disease: Among heavy drinkers, women develop heart disease at the same rate as men, despite the fact that women consume 60 percent less alcohol than men over their lifetimes.
- Breast cancer: Some studies have shown a link between moderate or heavy alcohol consumption and an increased risk for breast cancer.
- Violence: College women who drink are more likely to be the victims of sexual abuse. And high school girls who use alcohol are more likely to be the victims of dating violence.
- Traffic crashes: Although women are less likely than men to drive after drinking, they have a higher risk of dying in a vehicle crash.
- Women are more likely than men to use a combination of alcohol and prescription drugs.
- Women may begin to abuse alcohol and drugs following depression, to relax on dates, to feel more adequate, to lose weight, to decrease stress, or to help them sleep at night.

Poor self-esteem is a major issue for most women who develop problems with drugs and alcohol. The following conditions may also increase their risk for developing substance abuse problems:

- A history of physical or sexual abuse. Physical and sexual violence against women is common when one or both partners have been drinking or using drugs. Women also are more likely to drink or use drugs when their partners use.
- Depression, panic disorder, and post-traumatic stress disorder. Researchers now know that there is a strong family (genetic) component to addiction. If you have a family history of addiction, you should be aware of the risk for developing dependency, especially during stressful periods in your life.

So, why are women more vulnerable to the effects of alcohol?

- Alcohol is absorbed faster in women's bodies than in men's bodies because of stomach enzyme differences. After a woman drinks, alcohol is delivered into her bloodstream more rapidly because a stomach enzyme that works to break down alcohol before it enters the bloodstream is less active in women, especially in alcoholic women, than in men. Women have a smaller ratio of water to fat than men. Alcohol circulates in the water and therefore alcohol is more concentrated. Your blood alcohol level will be higher and you will get drunker faster by drinking the same amount of alcohol as a man your own size.
- Hormonal fluctuations in women may affect how alcohol is metabolized. Some women report feeling the effects of alcohol more quickly or strongly when they drink at certain times during their cycle. Postmenopausal women who take hormone replacement therapy (HRT) have higher blood alcohol levels when they drink.

Source: www.healthywomen.org.

informed care as also do accusations of deviance associated with trans individuals that affect their options for health care and their access to these options. A 2008 Institute of Medicine report found that while emergency room waiting times increased by about 36 percent between 1997 and 2004, African Americans waited about 13 minutes longer, Latinos/as 14 minutes longer, and women generally 5 minutes longer.

LEARNING ACTIVITY   **Bad Science**

Should health policy decisions be based on science or philosophical positions? In 2004 a group of more than 60 scientists, including Nobel laureates, criticized the Bush administration for ignoring or suppressing scientific analysis and recommendations in its decision making. They cited as one example the suppression of an FDA study that reported that the Senate's Clear Air bill would be more effective in reducing mercury contamination in fish and preventing more deaths than the Clear Skies Act proposed by the administration. Despite all scientific evidence to the contrary, the administration has continued to increase funding for abstinence-only programs, although they have been demonstrated to be ineffective in preventing sexual activity and disease transmission.

How might political decisions that ignore science affect women's health? Visit the following websites and create a list of decisions and policies that have been made in contradiction to the scientific evidence about women's health. Find out what decisions related to women's health are pending in Congress or various government agencies, and write letters to your representatives encouraging them to base decisions on scientific evidence rather than political positions.

Reproductive Health Technologies Project *http://rhtp.org/index.htm*

Coalition to Protect Research *www.cossa.org/CPR/cpr.html*

American Association for the Advancement of Science
www.aaas.org/port_policy.shtml

American Foundation for AIDS Research *www.amfar.org/cgi-bin/iowa/
programs/publicp/index.html*

Association of Reproductive Health Professionals
www.arhp.org/advocacy/index.cfm

Society for Women's Health Research *www.womens-health.org/policy/home.htm*

Union of Concerned Scientists *www.ucsusa.org/global_environment/rsi/
index.cfm*

Finally, a focus on women's health must discuss the issue of *corporate responsibility* and the role of the state in guiding and establishing that responsibility. This relates to how national and global corporations with strong profit motives affect our lives in terms of environmental degradation and toxic exposure, food additives, and problematic medical practices, and the ways decisions at the state and federal level affect these practices. Examples include concern with greenhouse gases and global warming, use of pesticides and herbicides, genetically modified food and corporate control of bioresources, and growth hormones in beef and dairy food products. All these issues are related to the corporatization of life and the global economy, the stresses of life in postindustrial societies, and ultimately the quality of life on the planet.

LEARNING ACTIVITY **Obsessed with Breasts**

Go to the web page of the Breast Cancer Fund's "Obsessed with Breasts" ad campaign at *www.breastcancerfund.org/campaign.htm*. What are the goals of the campaign? Why is the campaign necessary? Now go to the Fund's "Facts, News, and Opinions" page. Identify five facts about breast cancer that are new to you.

There is increasing interest in exploring the role of stress in our lives, as well as the connections between mind and body in terms of illness. Scientists have long known about these connections and have emphasized that it is less stress per se (of work, relationships, trauma, etc.) that affects the immune system, but more how individuals interpret or make meaning of that stress. It seems that stresses we choose evoke different responses from those we cannot control, with feelings of helplessness being worse than the stressor itself. While stress affects everyone, there is differential impact based on where a person lives, the kind of work s/he performs, the food s/he can afford to eat, and so forth.

Environmental racism reflects the fact that people of color in the United States are disproportionately exposed to toxic environments due to the dumping of chemical and other waste on Native American lands and urban areas where more people of color live. Environmental waste tends not to be dumped in areas populated by people of high socioeconomic status or where property values are high. The dumping of radioactive waste at Yucca Mountain, Nevada, despite the impact of this on the Western Shoshone tribe that considers the mountain sacred, is a case in point. *Environmental justice* is the social movement to remedy the problem of environmental racism. People in developing countries who work in factories and sweatshops within the global economy (especially young women, who are often hired because they are cheap, dispensable, and easily controlled workers) are particularly at risk for occupational disease.

Breast cancer is one important health issue closely tied to environmental problems and therefore to corporate responsibility. Every 3 minutes a woman in the United States is diagnosed with breast cancer as the incidence over a woman's lifetime has increased from 1 in 20 in 1960 to 1 in 8 in 2007. The relative increase in women living longer does not explain this increase in breast cancer incidence. It is the most common form of cancer in women and the number-two cause of cancer death (lung and bronchial cancer causes the most deaths), except in the case of Latinas, for whom breast cancer is the number-one cause of cancer death. Approximately 41,000 women die from breast cancer every year; men also can have the disease. Although African American women are not more susceptible to breast cancer, they are over twice as likely to die from it. This is because they tend to have more advanced tumors as a result of poorer screening and reduced access to health care services. Breast cancer research works to find a "cure," despite the fact that a focus on environmental contributors could work effectively to prevent breast cancer.

The pink ribbon campaign for the cure, while a formidable support for breast cancer research and the empowerment of survivors, inadequately addresses environmental links to breast cancer. This is especially important because less than 10 percent of breast cancer cases have a genetic cause and the rates of breast cancer have more than doubled in the last thirty-five years. About half of all breast cancer cases cannot be explained by known risk factors, encouraging scientists to suspect toxic chemicals in the environment playing a role in breast cancer risk. In particular, it has been hypothesized that environmental estrogens may play a role in the increasing incidence of breast cancer, testicular cancer, and other problems of the human reproductive system.

Environmental estrogens (also known as xenoestrogens) mimic the effects of human estrogen or affect its level in the body indirectly by disrupting the ways human estrogen is produced or used. Although some are naturally occurring (for example, phytoestrogens in plants such as soybeans), the greatest concern is synthetic estrogens that are not easily broken down and can be stored in the body's fat cells. Over thirty years ago, researchers showed that organochlorines, a family of compounds including the pesticide DDT and the industrial chemicals known as polychlorinated biphenyls (PCBs), could mimic human estrogen and induce mammary tumors in laboratory animals. Organochlorines are organic compounds containing chlorine bonded to carbon. Virtually unknown in nature, they are primarily products or by-products of the chemical industry. Their largest single use is in the manufacture of polyvinyl chloride (PVC) plastics, but they are also used in bleaching, disinfection, dry cleaning, fire prevention, refrigeration, and such pesticides as DDT and atrazine. Although PCBs and DDT were banned years ago, they are still with us because they persist in the environment. An EPA (Environmental Protection Agency) report on dioxin, another highly toxic organochlorine, reports that Americans have far higher levels of dioxin in their systems than was previously thought, raising new questions about the chemical's relationship to breast cancer and other health problems. Focusing on environmental issues necessarily involves addressing the effects of U.S. corporations and businesses on environmental quality. Even if exposure to toxic chemicals in the environment was shown to be associated with only 10 to 20 percent of breast cancer cases (a very conservative estimate, because, as already mentioned, about half of all breast cancer cases cannot be explained by known risk factors), policy enforced by the U.S. government to control individual and corporate use of toxic chemicals could prevent between 9,000 and 36,000 women and men from contracting the disease every year. In this way the "cure" is much more within reach than is acknowledged. The reading "Eyes on the Prize" by Seldon McCurrie shares the story of a breast cancer survivor.

These environmental toxins are also affecting men's health too, of course, and not only because men are also diagnosed with breast cancer. In particular, as well as other cancer risks, environmental estrogens are linked to the decrease in testosterone levels among men today (other causes include increased weight and decreased smoking). In 2006, researchers reported that the average 50-year-old man has almost 20 percent less testosterone than his father did 20 years ago.

"All I really want is control over my own body!"

REPRODUCTIVE CHOICE

Reproductive choice involves being able to have safe and affordable birthing and parenting options; reliable, safe, and affordable birth control technologies; freedom from forced sterilization; and the availability of abortion. In other words, a key aspect of reproductive rights is the extent to which women can control their reproduction and therefore shape the quality and character of their lives. As Linda Gordon emphasizes in the reading "Is Nothing Simple about Reproduction Control?", the struggle over birth control "does not stem from an inevitably tragic march toward an overly high-tech civilization. Rather, the problems are primarily political. Access, motivation, and technological development are all shaped by political conflicts and negotiations, sometimes personal, sometimes so far out of individual control that most people are unaware that decisions are being made" (p. 347). Reproductive choice is increasingly under attack in contemporary society. For women of color in particular, as the reading "Women of Color and Their Struggle for Reproductive Justice" by Silliman and colleagues emphasizes, "Resisting population control while simultaneously claiming their right to bodily self-determination, including the right to contraception and abortion or the right to have children, is at the heart of their struggle for reproductive control" (p. 361).

Sterilization Practices

Female sterilization includes tubal ligation, a surgical procedure in which the fallopian tubes are blocked ("having the tubes tied"), and hysterectomy, in which the uterus is removed. A less invasive alternative to tubal ligation is a springlike device called *Essure* that blocks the fallopian tubes. Although hysterectomy (the removal of the uterus) is usually performed for medical reasons not associated with a desire for sterilization, this procedure results in sterilization. Vasectomy is permanent birth control for men, or male sterilization. It is effective and safe and does not limit male sexual pleasure. Countless women freely choose sterilization as a form of permanent birth control, and it is a useful method of family planning for many. "Freely choose," however, assumes a range of options not available to some women. In other words, "freely choose" is difficult in a racist, class-based, and sexist society that does not provide all women with the same options from which to choose. As a result, women on welfare are more likely

HISTORICAL MOMENT **The Women's Health Movement**

From the beginnings of the medical industry, women often suffered from the humiliation and degradation of medical practitioners who treated women as hysterical and as hypochondriacs, who medicalized normal female body functions, and who prevented women from controlling their own health. In 1969, as the women's movement heightened consciousness about other issues, women also began to examine the ways they had been treated and the ways women's biology and health had been largely unexplored. In the spring of that year, several women participated in a workshop on "women and their bodies" at a Boston conference. As they vented their anger at the medical establishment, they also began to make plans to take action. Although most of them had no medical training, they spent the summer studying all facets of women's health and the health care system. Then they began giving courses on women's bodies wherever they could find an audience. These women became known as the Boston Women's Health Collective and published their notes and lectures in what would eventually be known as *Our Bodies, Ourselves*.

Their efforts resulted in a national women's health movement. In March 1971, 800 women gathered for the first women's health conference in New York. Women patients began to question doctors' authority and to bring patient advocates to their medical appointments to take notes on their treatment by medical professionals. Feminists questioned established medical practices such as the gendered diagnosis and treatment of depression, the recommendation for radical mastectomies whenever breast cancer was found, and the high incidence of cesarean deliveries and hysterectomies.

Although the original members of the women's health movement tended to be well-educated, middle-class White women, the movement quickly expanded to work with poor women and women of color to address the inequities caused by the intersections of gender with race and social class. Together, these women worked on reproductive rights, recognizing that for many poor women and women of color, the right to abortion was not as paramount as the right to be free from forced sterilization. Their work shaped the agenda of the National Women's Health Network, founded in 1975 and dedicated to advancing the health of women of all races and social classes.

Source: Ruth Rosen, *The World Split Open: How the Modern Women's Movement Changed America* (New York: Viking, 2000).

to be sterilized than women who are not on welfare, and women of color and women in nonindustrialized countries are disproportionately more likely to receive this procedure. Although Medicaid pays for sterilization, it does not pay for some other birth control options. Lingering here is the racist and classist idea that certain groups have more right to reproduce than others, a belief and social practice called *eugenics*. Policies providing support for sterilization that make it free or very accessible obviously no longer force women to be sterilized. Rather, policies like these make the option attractive at a time when other options are limited.

One of the unfortunate legacies of reproductive history is that some women have been sterilized against their will, usually articulated as "against their full, informed consent." In the 1970s it was learned that many poor women—especially women of color, and Native American women in particular, as well as women who were mentally retarded or incarcerated—had undergone forced sterilization. Situations varied, but often they included women not giving consent at all, not knowing what was happening, believing they were having a different procedure, being strongly pressured to consent, or being unable to read or to understand the options told to them. The latter was especially true for women who did not speak or read English. Forced sterilization is now against the law, although problems remain.

Parenting Options and Birth Control Technologies

In considering reproductive choice, it is important to think about the motivations for having children as well as the motivations for limiting fertility. Most people, women and men, assume they will have children at some point in their lives, and, for some, reproduction and parenting are less of a choice than something that people just do. Although in many nonindustrial societies children can be economic assets, in contemporary U.S. society, for the most part, children consume much more than they produce. Some women do see children as insurance in their old age, but generally today we have children for emotional reasons such as personal and marital fulfillment, and for social reasons like carrying on the family name and fulfilling religious mandates.

Childbirth is an experience that has been shared by millions of women the world over. Women have historically helped other women at this time, strengthening family and kinship bonds and the ties of friendship. As the medical profession gained power and status and developed various technologies (forceps, for example), women's traditional authority associated with birthing was eclipsed by an increasing medicalization of birthing. Again, the medicalization of childbirth regards birthing as an irregular episode that requires medical procedures, often including invasive forms of "treatment." As these trends gained social power, women who could afford it started going to hospitals to birth their children instead of being attended at home by relatives, friends, or midwives. Unfortunately, in these early days, hospitals were relatively dangerous places where sanitation was questionable and women in childbirth were attended by doctors who knew far less about birthing than did midwives. As the twentieth century progressed and birthing in hospitals became routine, women gave birth lying down in the pelvic exam position with their feet in stirrups, sometimes with their arms strapped down; they were given drugs and episiotomies (an incision from the vagina toward the anus to prevent tearing) and were routinely shaved in the pubic area. By the late twentieth century, thanks to a strong consumer movement, women were giving birth under more humane conditions. Birthing centers now predominate in most hospitals, and doctors no longer perform the routine procedures and administer the drugs that they used to. Nonetheless, a large number of pregnant women (especially women of color) do not receive any health care at all, and a larger number still receive inadequate health care, some resorting to emergency rooms to deliver babies and having their first contact with the medical establishment at this time. As you can imagine, this scenario results in increased complications and potential unhealthy babies, and costs society much more financially than if routine health screening and preventive health care had been available.

Why might women want to control their fertility? The first and obvious answer concerns health. Over a woman's reproductive life, she could potentially birth many children and be in a constant state of pregnancy and lactation. Such a regimen compromises maximum health. Second, birthing large numbers of children might be seen as irresponsible in the context of world population and a planet with finite resources. Third, birthing is expensive and the raising of children even more expensive. Fourth, given that in contemporary Western societies women have primary responsibility for childcare and that the organization of mothering tends to isolate women in their homes, it is important to consider the emotional effects of constant child rearing. And, finally, if women had unlimited children, the constant caretaking of these children would preempt women's ability to be involved in other productive work outside

Exorcizing the Witch, Midwife, and Healer

By Amy Leer

Women have always been healers. They were the unlicensed doctors and anatomists of ancient history. They were abortionists, nurses, and counselors. They were pharmacists, cultivating healing herbs and revealing their clandestine uses. They were midwives, traveling from home to home and village to village. For centuries women were doctors without degrees, barred from books and lectures, learning from each other, and passing on experience from neighbor to neighbor and mother to daughter. They were called wise women by the people, witches or charlatans by the church and authorities. Medicine is part of our heritage as women, our history, our birthright.

Women's position in the health system today is not "natural." Femininity has become a diseased condition which is medically explained and "fixed." The question remains: How did women arrive at their current position of subservience from their former positions of leadership and power in health and healing? The historical antagonist of the female lay healer is the patriarchal medical profession. The rise of androcentric medicine and female medicalization was not the inevitable triumph of right over wrong, fact over myth; it began with a bitter conflict that set Pagan against Christian, woman against man, class against class. The notion of medicine as a profession was in some ways progressive over the unexamined tradition of female healing: A profession requires systematic training and, at least in theory, some formal methods of accountability. But a profession is also defined by its exclusiveness. While the female lay healer operated within a network of information sharing, and mutual sustainability, the male professional hoarded up his knowledge as a kind of property, to be dispensed to affluent patrons or sold on the market as a commodity. His goal was not to distribute the proficiency of healing, but to concentrate medicine within the elite interest group that the profession came to represent.

The triumph of the male medical profession is of crucial significance in our story. It involved the destruction of women's sovereignty and authority—leaving women in positions of isolation and dependency. Today, we are living in the aftermath of the social and economic oppression of masculinist medicine. In consciousness-raising groups and women's studies classrooms, women are questioning scientific "facts" about health, refusing to remain on the margins of society, refusing the patriarchal social order, and insisting that the values of women become equal organizing principles of health and medicine once again.

---

the home. This "indirect cost" concept involves the loss or limitation of financial autonomy, work-related or professional identity, and creative and ego development.

Although today women are as likely to have children as they ever were, three facts stand out. First, the average family size decreased as the twentieth century progressed. Second, women are having children later in life than they did in earlier times in our society. Both of these trends are related to changes in health care technologies that have raised health care standards and encouraged parenting at later ages, the availability of birth control and abortion, and the increase in women's education and participation in paid labor with subsequent postponement of marriage and child rearing. Third, there has been a large increase in the number of children born to single women, especially among non-White populations. The numbers of families headed by single mothers has increased by 25 percent since 1990. In 2004 approximately a third of all babies were born to unmarried women who may or may not have been partnered. Of these unwed births, only about a quarter were teen births. The teen pregnancy rate has been falling through the last decade, although 2006 data show this figure leveling off. Unwed births, especially among teenagers, may result from lack of knowledge and support about reproduction and contraception in the context of an increasing sexually active population, poverty and lack of opportunities for education and employment, failure of family and school systems to keep young people in school, the increased use of alcohol and other drugs, and increasing restrictions on access to abortion services. Some girls see motherhood as a rite of passage into adulthood, as a way to escape families of origin, or as a way to connect with another human being whom they may believe will love them unconditionally. Because the largest increase in unmarried births has been among women between 25 and 29 years, these changes also reflect changing norms about raising a child out of wedlock, either alone or in a heterosexual or lesbian cohabiting, or living together, arrangement, and the fact that some women are wary of marriage and/or choose and have the resources to maintain families outside of legal marriage.

Birth control technologies have been around for a long time. Many preindustrial societies used suppositories coated in various substances that blocked the cervix or functioned as spermicides; the condom was used originally to prevent the spread of syphilis, although it was discovered that it functioned as a contraceptive; and the concept of the intrauterine device was first used by Bedouins who hoped to prevent camels from conceiving during long treks across the desert by inserting small pebbles into the uterus. Nineteenth-century couples in the United States used "coitus interruptus" (withdrawal before ejaculation), the rhythm method (sexual intercourse only during nonfertile times), condoms, and abstinence. Although technologies of one kind or another have been around for generations, the issue for women has been the control of, and access to, these technologies. Patriarchal societies have long understood that to control women's lives it is necessary to control women's reproductive options. In this way, information about, access to, and denial of birth control technologies are central aspects of women's role and status in society.

In the 1880s, the Comstock Law (statutes supposed to control pornography) limited contraception because these technologies were considered obscene. At the same time, however, women realized that the denial of contraception kept them in the domestic sphere and, more importantly, exposed them to repetitive and often dangerous pregnancies. In response, a social movement emerged that was organized around reproductive choice. Called "voluntary motherhood," this movement not only involved giving women access to birth control, but also worked to facilitate reproduction and parenting under the most safe, humane, and dignified conditions. Margaret Sanger was a leader of this movement and in 1931 wrote *My Fight for Birth Control* about her decision to become involved in the struggle for reproductive choice.

One unfortunate aspect, however, was the early birth control movement's affiliation with an emerging eugenics movement. Following Charles Darwin's theory of the survival of the fittest, eugenics argued that only the "fit" should be encouraged to reproduce and that birth control was necessary to prevent the "unfit" from unlimited reproduction. The "unfit" included poor and immigrant populations, the

ACTIVIST PROFILE **Margaret Sanger**

Margaret Sanger completed her nursing training in 1900 at the age of 21. Following her marriage and the birth of three children, Sanger returned to work as a visiting nurse in some of the worst slums in New York City. A great deal of her work involved assisting poor women in giving birth, and she began to see the impact of bearing too many children on the health and welfare of these women. She also saw the suffering and near fatality of many women who obtained unsafe, illegal abortions to avoid having even more children. Often these women would beg Sanger to tell them how to prevent pregnancy, but by law Sanger was forbidden to share this knowledge with them. When at last a young woman who had pleaded with Sanger for this information died from giving birth to yet another baby, Sanger decided to take action.

Convinced that women had a right to know how to prevent pregnancy and that the improvement of women's lives depended on family planning, Sanger began to educate herself about birth control. Armed with her newfound information, Sanger began her real life's work. Her plan was to educate the public about birth control, form a birth control organization to help raise awareness and money, seek to overturn the Comstock Law, which prevented sending birth control information through the U.S. mail, and lobby Congress to allow doctors to prescribe birth control devices, which were illegal even for married couples.

In 1914 Sanger started the *Woman Rebel,* a magazine encouraging women to think for themselves and promoting family planning. Under the Comstock Law, the magazine was banned by the U.S. Postal Service, and Sanger was charged with

(*continued*)

nine counts of obscenity. She fled to England for 2 years until the charges were dropped. Upon her return to New York, she founded the National Birth Control League, which later became Planned Parenthood. In 1916 she opened a birth control clinic in a poor section of Brooklyn. After only 9 days in operation, the clinic was raided and shut down. Sanger was sentenced to 30 days in a workhouse. Upon her release, Sanger reopened the clinic out of her home.

In 1921 Sanger moved her battle to the national level and started *The Birth Control Review.* During the first 5 years of its publication, she received more than a million letters from women detailing the horrors of poverty and unwanted pregnancy. In 1928 Sanger organized 500 of the letters into a book, *Mothers in Bondage,* which became highly influential in the fight for birth control. Throughout the 1930s Sanger continued her fight, speaking and lobbying. At last, the Supreme Court overturned the Comstock Law in 1936, and the American Medical Association reversed its position, giving doctors the right to distribute birth control devices. After her victory, Sanger persisted in her work for affordable and effective contraceptives. Her tireless efforts to secure research funding at last led to the development of the most significant contraceptive of the century—the birth control pill. Only a few months before Sanger died in 1966, the U.S. Supreme Court, in *Griswold v. Connecticut,* made birth control legal for married couples.

"feeble-minded," and criminals. Using a rationale grounded in eugenics, birth control proponents were able to argue their case while receiving the support of those in power in society. Nonetheless, although contraceptive availability varied from state to state, it was not until a Supreme Court decision (*Griswold v. Connecticut*) in 1965 that married couples were allowed rights to birth control. The Court's ruling said that the prohibition of contraceptive use by married people was unconstitutional in that it violated the constitutional right to privacy. This right was extended to single people in 1972 and to minors in 1977.

Today there are a variety of contraceptive methods available. Their accessibility is limited by the availability of information about them, by cost, and by health care providers' sponsorship. As you read about these technologies, consider the following questions: Whose body is being affected? Who gets to deal with the side effects? Who is paying for these methods? Who will pay if these methods fail? Who will be hurt if these side effects become more serious? These questions are framed by gender relations and the context of the U.S. economy and its health organizations. For example, since hitting the market in 1998, prescriptions for Viagra (a male impotence medication) were covered by more than half of health insurance plans, whereas most plans did not cover birth control pills. Fury over this has created bills passed in over 20 states to date to require insurers to provide contraceptive coverage. Citing the violation of the 1978 Pregnancy Discrimination Act, debate continues as of this writing.

Other than tubal ligation where women are surgically sterilized and vasectomy where men are surgically sterilized, birth control methods include, first, the intrauterine device (IUD), a small, t-shaped device made of flexible plastic that is inserted into the uterus and prevents the implantation of a fertilized egg. IUDs are available only by prescription, must be inserted by a clinician, and are a popular form of reversible birth control. Trade names include *ParaGard;* the *Progestasert* and *Mirena* are IUDs that contains hormones. They generally last up to 10 years, can result in heavier periods (although IUDs with hormones claim to reduce menstrual cramping and flow), and may increase the risk of pelvic inflammatory disease among women with multiple sexual partners. It is important to remember that IUDs do not protect against HIV/AIDS and other sexually transmitted infections.

Second are hormone regulation contraceptive methods. The pill is an oral contraceptive that contains a combination of two hormones: progestin and estrogen. It became widely available in the United States in the 1960s and quickly became the most popular means of contraception despite such side effects as nausea, weight gain, breast tenderness, and headaches. Combination pills usually work by preventing a woman's ovaries from releasing eggs (ovulation). They also thicken the cervical mucus, which keeps sperm from joining with an egg. The minipill contains no estrogen and a small dose of progestin and has fewer side effects than the regular pill, and it works by thickening cervical mucus and/or preventing ovulation. Taking the pill daily maintains the level of hormone that is needed to prevent pregnancy. The birth control pill trademarked as *YAZ* is marketed to appeal to young women through its claims to treat emotional and physical premenstrual symptoms and control moderate acne. *Norplant* is a contraceptive device that is implanted under the skin of the upper arm and releases a small amount of the hormone progestin through the inserted capsules for up to 5 years. As a result of lawsuits associated with unanticipated side effects, the maker of *Norplant* no longer markets this device in the United States, although it is available worldwide. *Depo-Provera* also uses progestin that is injected into the muscle every 11 weeks. It inhibits the secretion of hormones that stimulate the ovaries and prevents ovulation. It also thickens cervical mucus to prevent the entrance of sperm into the uterus. Risks include loss of bone density and side-effects generally associated with the pill, such as weight gain, irregular, heavy, or no bleeding, headaches, depression, and mood changes. In addition, it may take up to a year after discontinuing use of *Depo-Provera* before a woman is fertile again. A device marketed under the name *NuvaRing* was approved in 2001. It is a flexible, transparent ring about 2 inches in diameter that women insert vaginally once a month. The ring releases a continuous dose of estrogen and progestin. The ring remains in the vagina for 21 days and is then removed, discarded, and a new ring inserted. Other hormone regulation methods include hormone patches such as *Ortho Evra* that must be changed weekly and work by preventing ovulation. Since its introduction in 2002, there have been a substantial number of lawsuits by plaintiffs citing serious blood clot–related injuries. This resulted in a warning from the Food and Drug Administration (FDA) for *Ortho Evra* in 2005. None of the hormone methods protect against HIV/AIDS and other sexually transmitted infections.

Next are the barrier methods. The diaphragm, cervical cap, and shield are barrier methods that are inserted into the vagina before sexual intercourse, fit over the cervix, and prevent sperm from entering the uterus. They work in conjunction with spermicidal jelly that is placed along the rim of the device. Some women use them in conjunction with spermicidal foam that is inserted into the vagina with a small plunger. Unlike the other methods, spermicides are available at any drugstore. Also available at drugstores are vaginal sponges that are coated with spermicide, inserted into the vagina, and work to block the cervix and absorb sperm. All these barrier

Sexually Transmitted Diseases

Every year more than 12 million cases of sexually transmitted diseases (STDs) are reported in the United States. These infections result in billions of dollars in preventable health care spending. In addition, the health impact of STDs is particularly severe for women. Because the infections often cause few or no symptoms and may go untreated, women are at risk for complications from STDs, including ectopic (tubal) pregnancy, infertility, chronic pelvic pain, and poor pregnancy outcomes.

CHLAMYDIA

Chlamydia is the most common bacterial sexually transmitted disease in the United States. It causes an estimated 4 million infections annually, primarily among adolescents and young adults. In women, untreated infections can progress to involve the upper reproductive tract and may result in serious complications. About 75 percent of women infected with chlamydia have few or no symptoms, and without testing and treatment the infection may persist for as long as fifteen months. Without treatment, 20–40 percent of women with chlamydia may develop pelvic inflammatory disease (PID). An estimated one in ten adolescent girls and one in twenty women of reproductive age are infected.

PELVIC INFLAMMATORY DISEASE

PID refers to upper reproductive tract infection in women, which often develops when STDs go untreated or are inadequately treated. Each year, PID and its complications affect more than 750,000 women. PID can cause chronic pelvic pain or harm to the reproductive organs. Permanent damage to the fallopian tubes can result from a single episode of PID and is even more common after a second or third episode. Damage to the fallopian tubes is the only preventable cause of infertility. As much as 30 percent of infertility in women may be related to preventable complications of past STDs.

One potentially fatal complication of PID is ectopic pregnancy, an abnormal condition that occurs when a fertilized egg implants in a location other than the uterus, often in a fallopian tube. It is estimated that ectopic pregnancy has increased about fivefold over a twenty-year period. Among African American women, ectopic pregnancy is the leading cause of pregnancy-related deaths. The economic cost of PID and its complications is estimated at $4 billion annually.

GONORRHEA

Gonorrhea is a common bacterial STD that can be treated with antibiotics. Although gonorrhea rates among adults have declined, rates among adolescents have risen or remained unchanged. Adolescent females aged 15–19 have the highest rates of gonorrhea. An estimated 50 percent of women with gonorrhea have no symptoms.

Without early screening and treatment, 10–40 percent of women with gonorrhea will develop PID.

HUMAN IMMUNODEFICIENCY VIRUS

Human immunodeficiency virus (HIV) is the virus that causes AIDS. The risk of a woman acquiring or transmitting HIV is increased by the presence of other STDs. In particular, the presence of genital ulcers, such as those produced by syphilis and herpes, or the presence of an inflammatory STD, such as chlamydia or gonorrhea, may make HIV transmission easier.

HERPES SIMPLEX VIRUS (HSV)

Genital herpes is a disease caused by herpes simplex virus (HSV). The disease may recur periodically and has no cure. Scientists have estimated that about 30 million persons in the United States may have genital HSV infection. Most infected persons never recognize the symptoms of genital herpes; some will have symptoms shortly after infection and never again. A minority of those infected will have recurrent episodes of genital sores. Many cases of genital herpes are acquired from people who do not know they are infected or who had no symptoms at the time of the sexual contact. Acyclovir is a drug that can help to control the symptoms of HSV, but it is not a cure. HSV is frequently more severe in people with weakened immune systems, including people with HIV infection.

HUMAN PAPILLOMA VIRUS (HPV)

HPV is a virus that sometimes causes genital warts but in many cases infects people without causing noticeable symptoms. Concern about HPV has increased in recent years after several studies showed that HPV infection is associated with the development of cervical cancer. Approximately twenty-five types of HPV can infect the genital area. These types are divided into high-risk and low-risk groups based on whether they are associated with cancer. Infection with a high-risk type of HPV is one risk factor for cervical cancer, which causes 4,500 deaths among women each year. No cure for HPV infection exists.

SYPHILIS

Syphilis is a bacterial infection that can be cured with antibiotics. Female adolescents are twice as likely to have syphilis as male adolescents. African American women have syphilis rates that are seven times greater than the female population as a whole.

Such infections among infants are largely preventable if women receive appropriate diagnosis and treatment during prenatal care. Death of the fetus or newborn infant occurs in up to 40 percent of pregnant women who have untreated syphilis.

(continued)

CONDOM EFFECTIVENESS AND RELIABILITY

When used consistently and correctly, latex condoms are very effective in preventing a variety of STDs, including HIV infection. Multiple studies have demonstrated a strong protective effect of condom use. Because condoms are regulated as medical devices, they are subject to random testing by the Food and Drug Administration. Every latex condom manufactured in the United States is tested electronically for holes before packaging. Condom breakage rates are low in the United States—no higher than 2 per 100 condoms used. Most cases of condom failure result from incorrect or inconsistent use.

For further information, contact the Office of Women's Health, Centers for Disease Control and Prevention, 1600 Clifton Road, MS: D-51, Atlanta, GA 30033; phone: (404) 639-7230.

Source: www.cdc.gov/od/owh/whstd.htm.

methods work best when used in conjunction with a condom and are much less effective when used alone. The male condom is a latex rubber tube that comes rolled up and is unrolled on the penis. The female condom is a floppy polyurethane tube with an inner ring at the closed end that fits over the cervix and an outer ring at the open end that hangs outside the vagina. Condoms block sperm from entering the vagina and, when used properly in conjunction with other barrier methods, are highly effective in preventing pregnancy. Another very important aspect of condoms is that they are the only form of contraception that offers prevention against sexually transmitted diseases (STDs) generally and HIV/AIDS in particular. All health care providers emphasize that individuals not in a mutually monogamous sexual relationship should always use condoms in conjunction with other methods.

Finally, emergency contraception (EC) used after unprotected heterosexual intercourse is available. Commonly known as the "morning-after pill," this hormonal contraception was approved by the FDA in 1997. EC is effective if taken up to 120 hours after unprotected intercourse, although it is most effective if taken within 12 hours. EC provides a high dose of the same hormones as are in birth control pills to prevent ovulation and fertilization. A *New England Journal of Medicine* study reported that about 1.7 million of the approximately 3 million unintended pregnancies a year might be prevented if emergency contraception was more readily available. In addition, a new study in the *Journal of the American Medical Association* reported that women with easy access to emergency contraception were not more likely to engage in unprotected heterosexual contact or abandon the use of other forms of birth control. The FDA has approved EC for over-the-counter sales for individuals aged 18 years and older, but women still face barriers when trying to obtain the medication in some communities. EC is different from the drug mifiprex (also known as *RU-486* and discussed in the following section) that works by terminating an early pregnancy and is known as a "medical abortion." Emergency contraception does not terminate a pregnancy but prevents one from occurring. In very low doses, however, mifiprex can be used as a method of emergency contraception.

Abortion

Although induced abortion, the removal of the fertilized ovum or fetus from the uterus, is only one aspect of reproductive choice, it has dominated discussion of this topic. This is unfortunate because reproductive rights are about much more than abortion. Nonetheless, this is one topic that generates unease and often heated discussion. *Pro-choice* advocates believe that abortion is women's choice, women should not be forced to have children against their will, a fertilized ovum should not have all the legal and moral rights of personhood, and all children should be wanted children. Pro-choice advocates tend to believe in a woman's right to have an abortion even though they might not make that decision for themselves. *Pro-life* advocates believe that human personhood begins at conception and a fertilized ovum or fetus has the right to full moral and legal rights of personhood. They believe that rights about the sanctity of human life outweigh the rights of mothers. Some pro-life advocates see abortion as murder and doctors and other health care workers who assist in providing abortion services as accomplices to a crime.

According to a 2007 Gallup poll, 49 percent of Americans consider themselves "pro-choice" (defined as in favor of women's choice to access abortion facilities), 45 percent "pro-life" (against abortion under varying circumstances), and the rest uncertain. Six in 10 people surveyed believed abortion should be either limited or illegal in all circumstances and 4 in 10 thought it should be legal in all or most circumstances. Another way to look at this is that relatively few Americans are positioned at either extreme of the spectrum of beliefs—that abortion should be legal in all circumstances (26 percent) or illegal in all circumstances (18 percent). The majority falls somewhere in the middle. Despite this "middle ground" position among most people, the public debate on abortion tends to be highly polarized.

There are exceptions, most notably the Feminists for Life of America organization. Their motto is "Pro Woman Pro Life" and they advocate opposition to all forms of violence, characterizing abortion as violence. But most people who consider themselves feminists tend to be pro-choice. There are several issues raised by this perspective. The first issue is the moral responsibilities associated with requiring the birth of unwanted children, because the forces attempting to deny women safe and legal abortions are the very same ones that call for reductions in the social, medical, educational, and economic support of poor children. Does "pro-life" include being "for life" of these children once they are born? "Pro-life" politicians often tend to vote against increased spending for services for women and families. The second issue raised includes the moral responsibilities involved in requiring women to be mothers against their will. If you do grant full personhood rights to a fertilized ovum or fetus, then at what point do these rights take priority over the rights of another fully established person, the mother? What of fathers' rights? Third, several studies have shown that between two-thirds and three-quarters of all women accessing abortions would have an illegal abortion if abortion were illegal. Illegal abortions have high mortality rates; issues do not go away just by making them illegal.

In the years since *Roe v. Wade* was decided, thousands of American women's lives have been saved by access to legal abortion. It is estimated that before 1973, 1.2 million U.S. women resorted to illegal abortions each year and that botched illegal abortions caused as many as 5,000 annual deaths. Barriers to abortion endanger women's

88% in 1st trimester
1/3 of this number abort w/in first 3 wks
3rd trimester accounts for 1%

health by forcing women to delay the procedure, compelling them to carry unwanted pregnancies to term, and leading them to seek unsafe and illegal abortions.

Each year, almost half of all pregnancies among U.S. women are unintended, and about half of these end in abortion (approximately 1.3 million). It is estimated that 1 in 3 women will have an abortion by the time they reach age 45. Most abortions (88 percent) are obtained in the first trimester of pregnancy, with over half of all abortions taking place in the first 8 weeks. Less than 2 percent occur at 21 weeks or later. Women who have abortions come from all racial, ethnic, socioeconomic, and religious backgrounds and their motivations vary. Among women obtaining abortions, approximately half of these are younger than 25 years and 19 percent are teenagers. The abortion rate is highest among women who are 18 to 19 years old. African American women are 3 times more likely to have an abortion than White women, and Latinas are twice as likely, reflecting in part socioeconomic issues associated with raising children and, possibly, reduced adoption opportunities for children of color compared with White children. Approximately two-thirds of all abortions are obtained by never-married women, and the same number (although not necessarily the same women) intend to have children in the future.

In the United States, abortion was not limited by law or even opposed by the church until the nineteenth century. Generally, abortion was allowed before "quickening," understood as that time when the fetus's movements could be felt by the mother (usually between 3 and 4 months). In the 1820s, however, laws in New England declared abortion of an unquickened fetus a misdemeanor, and of a quickened fetus, second-degree manslaughter. As the century progressed, more restrictive laws were passed in various states, and in 1860 the Catholic Church officially ruled against abortion. Nonetheless, abortion continued. By the early twentieth century, abortion of any kind was illegal in the United States. In the reading "The Way It Was," Eleanor Cooney writes about her attempt to have an abortion in the 1960s, before the procedure was legal.

The major abortion decision came in January 1973 with the Supreme Court ruling of *Roe v. Wade.* Although some states such as California and New York had reformed their abortion laws before this time, the Supreme Court ruling overturned all states' bans on abortion. The ruling used the *Griswold v. Connecticut* decision in arguing that abortion must be considered part of privacy rights in deciding whether to have children. It did not, however, attempt to decide the religious or philosophical decisions about when life begins. The Court did agree that, under the law, a fetus is not treated as a legal person with civil rights. The ruling went on to divide pregnancy into three equal stages, or trimesters, and explained the differential interventions that the state could make during these different periods. The *Roe v. Wade* ruling held that the U.S. Constitution protects a woman's decision to terminate her pregnancy and allowed first-trimester abortions on demand. It declared that only after the fetus is viable, capable of sustained survival outside the woman's body with or without artificial aid, may the states control abortion. Abortions necessary to preserve the life or health of the mother must be allowed, however, even after fetal viability. Prior to viability, states can regulate abortion, but only if the regulation does not impose a "substantial obstacle" in the path of women.

Although there has been a general chipping away of women's rights to abortion since *Roe v. Wade* that involve legislation making abortion access more difficult and dangerous, there has been no ruling yet that says life begins at conception and

LEARNING ACTIVITY   **Walk in Her Shoes**

Go to the California Abortion Rights Action League (CARAL) homepage at *www.caral.org* and follow the links to "Walk in the Shoes" of a woman deciding about having an abortion in the time before choice was legal. Explore the barriers women faced in seeking an abortion before *Roe v. Wade.* Now go to the homepage of the International Planned Parenthood Federation (IPPF) at *www.ippf.org.* Follow the links to resources and then country profiles. Click on a country to find out the status of women's reproductive rights in that nation. Return to the IPPF homepage and follow the links to resources and then the IPPF Charter on Sexual and Reproductive Rights to learn what basic rights IPPF is demanding for women. Go to the homepage for the National Abortion Rights Action League (NARAL) at *www.naral.org* and click on "100 Ways to Fight 4 Choice" under "Take Action" to discover things you can do to help protect freedom to choose. To find out about your state's abortion and reproductive rights, select "Access to Abortion & Reproductive Rights" under "Get Informed About Reproductive Rights Issues." Then under "Facts and Information," select "NARAL Report: Who Decides? A State-by-State Review of Abortion and Reproductive Rights."

therefore no complete overturning of *Roe v. Wade.* Such an incident would cause abortion policy to revert to the states. However, as discussed below, there has been legislation that declares a fetus of any gestational age a "person" with legal rights. In terms of specific restrictions on abortion rights, these include, first, the Hyde Amendment, sponsored by Henry Hyde, a Republican senator from Illinois. It was an amendment to the 1977 Health, Education, and Welfare Appropriations Act and gave states the right to prohibit the use of Medicaid funds for abortion, thus limiting abortion to those women who could afford to pay. Note that this was accompanied by Supreme Court rulings (*Beal v. Doe,* 1977) that said that states could refuse to use Medicaid funds to pay for abortions and that Congress could forbid states to use federal funds (including Medicaid) to pay for abortion services (*Harris v. McRae,* 1980). The latter ruling also allowed states to deny funds even for medically necessary abortions.

Second, the 1989 *Webster v. Reproductive Health Services,* sponsored by Missouri State Attorney William Webster, upheld a state's right to prevent public facilities or public employees from assisting with abortions, to prevent counseling concerning abortion if public funds were involved, and to allow parental notification rights. Third, *Planned Parenthood v. Casey,* although upholding *Roe v. Wade* in 1992, also upheld the state's right to restrict abortion in various ways: parental notification, mandatory counseling and waiting periods, and limitations on public spending for abortion services. Refusal clauses and counseling bans limit women's access to honest information and medical care, making it virtually impossible for some women to access abortion services altogether. Refusal clauses permit a broad range of individuals and/or institutions—hospitals, hospital employees, health care providers, pharmacists, employers, and insurers—to refuse to provide, pay for, counsel, or even give referals for medical treatment that they personally oppose. Counseling bans, also known as "gag rules," prohibit health care providers, including individuals, under certain

Facts About Abortion, Choice, and Women's Health

- Between 1973, when abortion was made legal in the United States, and 1990, the number of deaths per 100,000 legal abortion procedures declined tenfold. By 1990, the risk of death from legal abortion had declined to 0.3 death per 100,000. (This rate is half the risk of a tonsillectomy and one-hundredth the risk of an appendectomy.)
- The mortality rate associated with childbirth is ten times higher than for legal abortion.
- Worldwide, 125,000 to 200,000 women die each year from complications related to unsafe and illegal abortions.
- In 87 percent of the counties in the United States, no physicians are willing or able to provide abortions.
- Only 12 percent of ob-gyn residency programs in the United States offer routine training in abortion procedures.
- Eighty-eight percent of abortions are performed before the end of the first trimester of pregnancy.
- Sixty-four percent of states prohibit most government funding for abortion, making access to the procedure impossible for many poor women.
- Thirty-eight states have enacted parental consent or notice requirements for minors seeking abortions.
- Abortion has no overall effect on the risk of breast cancer.
- Abortion does not increase the risk of complications during future pregnancies or deliveries.
- Emergency contraceptives reduce a woman's chance of becoming pregnant by 75 percent when taken within 72 hours of unprotected sex with a second dose 12 hours after the first.
- Emergency contraceptives do not cause abortions; they inhibit ovulation, fertilization, or implantation before a pregnancy occurs.
- Use of emergency contraceptives could reduce the number of unintended pregnancies and abortions by half annually.
- Eighty-nine percent of women aged 18 to 44 have not heard of or do not know the key facts critical to the use of emergency contraceptives.

Sources: NARAL Publications: *www.naral.org;* Reproductive Health and Rights Center: *www.choice.org.*

circumstances, from counseling or referring women for abortion care, preventing doctors from treating their patients responsibly, and severely limiting women's ability to make informed decisions. Congress has also imposed restrictions on abortion care for women who depend on the government for their health care needs, including women serving in the military. With very rare exceptions, almost all women who obtain health care through federal programs are subject to additional restrictions on their right to choose. Unlike women who can use their own funds or private health insurance to pay for abortion care, women insured by federal health plans often lack the means to pay for an abortion. These include low-income women who receive health care through Medicare or Medicaid, federal employees and military personnel and their dependents, residents of the District of Columbia, and women in federal prisons.

IDEAS FOR ACTIVISM   **Ten Things You Can Do to Protect Choice**

1. *Volunteer for a pro-choice organization.* Pro-choice organizations need volunteers. There are dozens of organizations working in various ways to help women get the services they need. For pro-choice organizations nationwide, check *www.choice.org.*
2. *Write a letter to a local clinic or abortion provider thanking them for putting themselves on the line for women.* Doctors and clinic workers hear vociferously from those opposed to abortion. Hearing a few words of thanks goes a long way.
3. *Monitor your local paper for articles about abortion.* Write a letter to the editor thanking them for accurate coverage or correcting them if coverage is biased.
4. *Find out how your elected representatives have voted on abortion.* Call and ask for their voting records, not just on bills relating to legality of abortion, but also on related issues such as funding for poor women, restrictions meant to impede a woman's access to services (such as waiting periods and informed consent), and contraceptives funding and/or insurance coverage. Whether or not you agree with the votes of your elected officials, write and let them know that this is an issue on which you make voting decisions. Anti-choice activists don't hesitate to do this; you should do it too.
5. *Talk to your children now about abortion.* Explain why you believe it's a decision only a woman can make for herself.
6. *If you have had an abortion, legal or illegal, consider discussing it with people in your life.* Over 40 percent of American women will have at least one abortion sometime during their lives. More openness about the subject might lead to less judgment, more understanding, and fewer attempts to make it illegal.
7. *Volunteer for a candidate whom you know to be pro-choice.*
8. *Be an escort at a clinic that provides abortions.*
9. *Vote!*
10. *Hold a house meeting to discuss choice with your friends.* You could show one or all of Dorothy Fadiman's excellent documentaries from the trilogy, *From the Back Alleys to the Supreme Court and Beyond. When Abortion Was Illegal* is a good conversation starter. For information on obtaining these videos, contact the CARAL ProChoice Education Fund or *Concentric Media.*

Source: *www.choice.org.*

Webster v. Reproductive Health Services and *Planned Parenthood v. Casey* both gave states the right to impose parental involvement laws. Attempts to mandate parental involvement often seem reasonable, but unfortunately may endanger vulnerable teenagers. Some young women cannot involve their parents because they come from homes where physical violence or emotional abuse is prevalent, because their pregnancies are the result of incest, or because they fear parental anger and disappointment. In these circumstances, some young women feel they cannot involve their parents in the decision to terminate a crisis pregnancy. Mandatory parental involvement laws (both notice and consent: "notice" requires notification of intent to terminate a pregnancy; "consent" requires the permission of one or both biological parents) do not solve the problem of troubled family communication; they only exacerbate a potentially dangerous situation.

Fourth, in September 2000, the FDA approved mifepristone (*mifeprex*), formerly known as *RU-486,* an antiprogesterone drug that blocks receptors of progesterone, a key hormone in the establishment and maintenance of human pregnancy. Used in conjunction with a prostaglandin such as misoprostol, mifepristone induces abortion when administered early in a pregnancy, providing women with a medical alternative to aspiration (suction) abortion. Although this drug has proven to be a safe and effective option for women seeking an abortion during the first few weeks of a pregnancy since its approval in France in 1988, it has been the target for anti-choice lobbying and activism to block access to the drug (for example, in the Bartlett/DeMint bill, as of this writing in debate). FDA approval in the United States of *RU-486* requires that a doctor administer and supervise the use of the drug for use as an abortifacient. Research in Europe suggests that the availability of this drug has not increased abortion rates generally.

Fifth, in November 2003, the Federal Abortion Ban (also known as the *Partial Birth* Abortion Ban) was passed and signed by President George W. Bush. This ban focused on *partial birth* abortion, a political term for the medical procedure named intact dilation and extraction (D&X). This is a very controversial topic. Proponents of the ban argue that it is a gruesome procedure and not medically necessary. Opponents of the ban emphasize that it is an infrequently performed procedure, done mostly when the life or health of the mother is at risk or when the baby is too malformed (for example, in severe cases of hydrocephalus where the baby cannot live and a normal delivery would kill the mother), and that anti-choice organizations and politicians have been using this issue to galvanize opposition to abortion and facilitate the banning of all abortions. In addition, opponents of the ban (including the American Medical Association, which recently withdrew support for the ban, the American College of Obstetricians and Gynecologists, the American Medical Women's Association, the American Nurses Association, and others, as well as pro-choice groups like Planned Parenthood and NARAL Pro-Choice America) describe the law as too broad in scope, emphasizing that it will dramatically curb the availability of second-trimester abortions that become necessary as a consequence of parental notification and consent laws that delay young women accessing a first-trimester abortion, or as a result of diagnostic tests that can be done only at a certain gestational age.

Opponents also believe the law is too punitive in that it results in jail time for medical practitioners assisting in such procedures. Finally, opponents of the federal ban say that it lacks a health exemption for women as set up in *Roe v. Wade*. Indeed, immediately after passing, the law's constitutionality was challenged on this item and three district judges (in New York, Nebraska, and California) had declared the ban unconstitutional. The U.S. Supreme Court had already overturned a Nebraska state "partial birth" abortion law in 2000 because it did not provide a health clause or an exemption to protect a woman in the event that she would suffer serious medical consequences if she were denied an abortion. In addition, the court found that it constituted undue burden on women's rights to access second-trimester abortions. However, the federal government then appealed the district court rulings, which were then affirmed by three courts of appeal. Finally, the U.S. Supreme Court agreed to hear the cases and in April 2007 ruled in a 5 to 4 decision in *Gonzales v. Carhart* and *Gonzales v. Planned Parenthood* to uphold the federal abortion ban as signed by President Bush in 2003. Justice Anthony Kennedy wrote for the majority and Justice Ruth Bader Ginsburg for the dissent. Surprisingly, and reversing three decades of legal rulings, the federal ban does not allow an exception when women's health is in danger. The court's decision gives the go-ahead to the states to restrict abortion services and paves the way for new legislation to enact additional bans on abortion, including those that doctors say are safe and medically necessary. It potentially allows for a criminal ban on abortions as early as 12 weeks of pregnancy. The reading by Eleanor Cooney comments on the "partial birth" abortion debate.

Sixth, in April 2004, President George W. Bush signed the Unborn Victims of Violence Act into law, giving the zygote, embryo, or fetus the same legal rights as a person and preparing the groundwork for further restrictions on abortion access. Also known as the Laci Peterson Law, in reference to the murder of a woman and her unborn child, this law creates the notion of double homicide in the case of the murder of a pregnant woman, although the law has jurisdiction only for homicides committed on federal property. This law is somewhat controversial for women's rights supporters. Though written to support survivors of violence by establishing that a fetus of any gestational age has equal personhood with a woman, it jeopardizes women's rights to safe and legal abortions.

Finally, in April 2005, the Child Interstate Abortion Notification Act passed the House of Representatives. It seeks to make it a crime to take a minor woman (under 18 years of age) residing in a state with parental notification and/or consent laws across state lines to access an abortion. It also seeks to create a national requirement for parental notification for underage women wanting to terminate a pregnancy and requires a 24-hour waiting period for a minor's abortion. Doctors and others could be prosecuted under the legislation. Supporters of the bill declare it necessary to protect young women because an adult predator could impregnate a girl and then force her to have an abortion to hide the crime. Opponents say the bill is too far-reaching, explaining that it sets up more roadblocks for women who have the right to safe and legal abortion, and could further isolate young women by making it a crime for a family member or other caring adult to provide assistance. Major medical and public health organizations, including the American Medical Association and the American Academy of Pediatrics, oppose such efforts to prevent young women from receiving confidential health services.

As of this writing, abortion in the United States remains legal, but its availability and accessibility have been limited. Approximately 87 percent of U.S. counties have no abortion provider and only 12 percent of ob-gyn medical residency programs offer routine training in abortion procedures. Further, some lawmakers and agencies use distorted scientific information, claiming, for example, that abortion causes breast cancer or mental illness, both untrue. All of these obstacles and limitations in access disproportionately affect poor women, women of color, and young women. One piece of legislation, however, was passed in 1994 to safeguard women's right to access their legal rights. After the public outcry associated with the public harassment, wounding, and death of abortion services providers, and the vandalism and bombing of various clinics, the Supreme Court ruled in *Madsen et al. v. Women's Health Center, Inc.* to allow a buffer zone around clinics to allow patients and employees access and to control noise around the premises. The same year, the Freedom of Access to Clinic Entrances (FACE) Act made it a federal crime to block access, harass, or incite violence in the context of abortion services.

American Women and Health Disparities

David Satcher, MD (2001)

In the last century, American women have been given 30 bonus years of life, thanks to such sweeping public health initiatives as sanitation and immunization programs. The America of the next century, however, presents us with new, more complex, and exceedingly interesting public health challenges.

Nearly 40 million of America's 140 million women are now members of racial and ethnic minority groups.[1] These women represent many diverse populations, but encompass 4 major groups: African Americans represent 13% of the total population of US women; Hispanic women, 11%; Asian-American/Pacific Islander women, 4%; and American Indian/Alaska Native women, just under 1%. The remaining 71% of American women are white.[2]

Although these women experience many of the same health problems as white women, as a group, they are in poorer health, use fewer health services, and continue to suffer disproportionately from premature death, disease, and disabilities. Many also face tremendous social, economic, cultural, and other barriers to optimal health.

It is a growing national challenge. The US Census Bureau estimates that by the year 2050, barely 53% of America's women will be classified as non-Hispanic white, and 25% will be Hispanic, 14% non-Hispanic black, 9% Asian and Pacific Islander, and just under 1% American Indian and Alaska Native.[3] Reclassification standards under the new 2000 census have blurred these categories somewhat, but it remains clear that if we are to leave our children and grandchildren a healthier nation, we must address health disparities immediately. The challenge grows more difficult when we consider the aging population. By the year 2050, nearly 1 in 4 adult women will be 65 years old or older, and an astonishing 1 in 17 will be 85 years old or older.[4]

For public health leaders, the mission of eliminating disparities among a diverse, aging population is daunting. Each group of minority women is made up of subgroups, who have diverse languages, cultures, degrees of acculturation, and histories. African-American women have a common African heritage, but they may also have roots in the United States, Great Britain, the Caribbean, or other countries. Hispanic women, or Latinas, have the distinction of being a multiracial ethnic group. Many Hispanic women in the United States are recent immigrants; most are of Mexican, Puerto Rican, Cuban, Central American, or South American descent. Asian-American/Pacific Islander women may be of Chinese, Japanese, Vietnamese, Cambodian, Korean, Filipino, Native Hawaiian, or other ancestry. Nearly 75% of this population group are foreign born, including an increasing number of immigrants and refugees from Southeast Asia.[5] American Indian/Alaska Native women are members of more than 500 federally or state-recognized tribes or unrecognized tribal organizations. Major subgroups of this population are American Indians, Eskimos, and Aleuts.[5]

These seemingly impersonal statistics have faces. A potpourri of cultures, traditions, beliefs, challenges, and family styles has always been America's greatest strength. Our challenge for the next century is to close the disparities gap, without compromising the uniqueness and richness of each culture.

We see disparities among these racial and ethnic groups and subgroups in almost every area of health. In breast cancer, for example, white women have a higher incidence rate (114 per 100,000) than African-American women (100), but black women have a higher mortality rate (31 v 25). This likely reflects lower rates of early detection as well as treatment disparities, but there could also be undiscovered physiological factors. Hispanic women have an incidence rate of 69 and a death rate of 15, compared to 75 and 11 for Asian and Pacific Islander women, and 33 and 12 for American Indian women.[6]

For these statistics to be meaningful, we need to take a closer look at each subgroup. Native Hawaiian women, for example, have an unusually high death rate from breast cancer (25 per 100,000), although the overall rate for Asian-American women is lower than average.[6] American Indian women in New Mexico report the lowest incidence (32 per 100,000) and the lowest death rate (9), but much higher rates are reported in many other Indian Health Service areas. There is no clear explanation for this phenomenon.[5(p74)]

When we look at cervical cancer, we see different trends. The incidence rate of invasive cervical cancer is higher among Asian-American than among white women (10.3 v 8.1 per 100,000). The incidence rate is nearly 5 times higher in Vietnamese women than in white women, yet we cannot explain the causes of this unusually high rate.[6]

If we look at death rates for diseases of the heart, African-American women are clearly at risk, with a staggering 147 deaths per 100,000, compared to 88 for white women, 70 for American Indian/Alaska Native women, and 63 each for Hispanic women and Asian-American/Pacific Islanders. This reflects rates of obesity and the lack of access to preventive health care services, including blood pressure screening and management.[7]

We cannot make assumptions about the health status of any particular racial group. Asian Americans are often viewed as a "model" minority because of their low unemployment and disease rates. Asian-American/Pacific Islander women age 65 and older, however, have the highest death rate from suicide (8 per 100,000) of all women in their age group, 4 times higher than the rate

among elderly black women and twice the rate of white women.[5(p32)]

Disparities are perhaps most striking when we look at the human immunodeficiency virus (HIV) and acquired immune deficiency syndrome (AIDS) rates among women. Twenty percent of Americans currently living with HIV are women, and 77% of those are African American or Hispanic. Many people are shocked to learn that AIDS is the second leading cause of death among African-American women age 25 to 44, their peak childbearing years, which leaves untold numbers of children motherless[8] and affects entire communities.

Not surprisingly, we also see disparities in key risk factors for disease. *The Surgeon General's Report on Women and Smoking,* released March 2001, reported that Alaska Native women have the highest rate of smoking at a discouraging 35%, compared to 24% for white women, 22% for African-American women, 14% for Hispanic women, and 11% for Asian and Pacific Islander women.[9]

In obesity, another major risk factor, we see significant disparities that clearly affect rates of disease. Non-Hispanic black women have the highest rate of obesity, 38%, compared to 35% for Mexican-American women, and 22% for non-Hispanic whites.[7(p247)] We know that cultural and lifestyle factors play a role in these disparities.

We have begun to address these differences through Healthy People 2010, the nation's health agenda for the next decade. Healthy People 2010 has 2 overarching goals: to increase the quality and years of life and to eliminate health disparities. Healthy People 2010 has 220 objectives relevant to women's health, including cancer, heart disease, stroke, diabetes, and access to quality health services. Goals for most ethnic groups are equal, even though some are starting from different baselines. For example, we want to reduce the death rate from breast cancer to 22.3 per 100,000, regardless of baseline disparities.

At the heart of Healthy People 2010 is improved access to such clinical preventive services as mammography and Papanicolaou tests. We also need improved access to high-quality health education and mental health and support services at the community level, so specific ethnic and cultural needs can be addressed. Health providers must use the clinical setting to better educate underserved women about risk factors they can modify, such as smoking and obesity, using culturally and linguistically appropriate approaches.

This cannot be done without change in the structure of the U.S. health care system, including the increasing influence of market forces, changes in payment and delivery systems, and welfare reform. Reinventing health care delivery is nearly useless without evaluating how these systemic changes will affect the most vulnerable and at-risk populations. Federal, state, and local public health agencies must redouble their efforts to address language and other access barriers and reduce disparities for these underserved Americans.

Throughout the federal health agencies, strategies are being developed to address health disparities. One model to watch is the Breast and Cervical Cancer Early Detection Program sponsored by the Centers for Disease Control and Prevention. It has grown from 8 states in 1991 to 50 states, 6 US territories, the District of Columbia, and 12 American Indian/Alaska Native organizations in 2000. More than 2.7 million breast and cervical cancer screening tests have been provided to more than 1.7 million underserved women from inception through March 2000. Federal and state programs now are addressing how to provide appropriate treatment for the women who are screened.

We have also increased our educational efforts. In 1998 the Health and Human Services Office on Women's Health (OWH) launched the National Women's Health Information Center Website and toll-free telephone service (www.4woman.gov or 1-800-994WOMAN, TDD: 1-888-220-5446). Women who cannot use the Internet can call information specialists, including Spanish-speaking experts, to get referrals to public and private organizations that can offer culturally appropriate information about specific health problems. The OWH has also launched an educational campaign that specifically targets women of each racial and ethnic group. *Pick Your Path to Health* offers simple-to-understand, culturally appropriate, weekly action steps to improve health status.[10]

The OWH-sponsored National Centers of Excellence in Women's Health[11] and Community Centers of Excellence in Women's Health[12] have taken a leadership role in developing model minority outreach programs and services.

Another good model is the work being done at the National Cancer Institute (NCI). Last spring the NCI launched a special populations network to address the unequal burden of cancer; 18 grants at 17 institutions will create or implement cancer control programs in minority and underserved populations.[13] The NCI, as well as many other institutes at the National Institutes of Health, have created centers and offices designed specifically to reduce health disparities.[14]

Another innovative program is the Reducing Health Care Disparities National Project at the Centers for Medicare and Medicaid Services (formerly known as the Health Care Financing Administration), which works at the state level to reduce health care disparities.[15] Descriptions and details of many other health disparities programs can be found on the websites of individual health agencies. I also recommend the *Women of Color Health Data Book*[5]; it is rich with information on the health, lives, and backgrounds of many ethnic groups of women.

Of course, when we discuss the elimination of health disparities, it must be emphasized that disparities take many forms: racial, ethnic, gender, geographic, income, educational, cultural, and others. Many of these disparities are interlinked. For example, some of the worst health outcomes are experienced by poor, undereducated, African-American women in the rural southern United States. Looking at data from specific racial and ethnic groups, however, is an important place to start as we develop strategies to encourage state and local health care experts to focus on our Healthy People 2010 objectives. Clearly, the one-size-fits-all approach to public health that was so effective for expanding the lifespan of women in the last century will not meet the challenges of the new century.

REFERENCES

1. U.S. Census Bureau, Population Division, Population Estimates Program. *Resident Population Estimates of the United States by Age and Sex: April 1, 1990 to October 1, 1999.* Available at www.census. gov/population/estimates/nation/intfile2-1.txt. Internet release date: November 26, 1999.
2. U.S. Census Bureau, Population Division, Population Estimates Program. *Projections of the Population by Age, Sex, Race and Hispanic Origin for the United States: 1990–1999.* Available at www.census.gov/population/www/estimates/nation3.html.
3. U.S. Census Bureau, Population Division, Population Estimates Program. *Projections of the Population by Age, Sex, Race and Hispanic Origin for the United States: 1999–2100 (middle series).* Available at www.census.gov/population/projections/nation/detail/d2041_50.pdf.
4. U.S. Census Bureau, Population Division, Population Estimates Program. *Resident Population Estimates of the United States by Age and Sex: 2035–2050.* Available at www.census.gov/population/projections/nation/detail/d2041_50.pdf.
5. *Women of Color Health Data Book.* Available at www4.od.nih.gov/orwh/WOCEnglish.pdf.
6. *Cancer Facts & Figures 2001.* Atlanta, Ga.: American Cancer Society; 2001:28.
7. *Health, U.S. 2000.* Available at www.cdc.gov/nchs/products/pubs/pubd/hus/hus.htm.
8. Healthy People 2010. Available at www.health.gov/healthypeople.
9. *Women and Smoking: A Report of the US Surgeon General.* Available at www.cdc.gov/tobacco.
10. Pick Your Path to Health Educational Campaign. Available at www.4woman.gov/PYPTH/index.htm.
11. National Centers of Excellence available at www.4woman.gov/COE/index.htm.
12. Community Centers of Excellence available at www.4woman.gov/owh/CCOE/index.htm.
13. Minority Health Initiative formerly available at www1.od. nih.gov/ormh/mhi.html.
14. The NCI Strategic Plan to Eliminate Health Disparities. Available at http://ospr.nci.nih.gov/healthdisprpt.pdf.
15. Reducing Health Care Disparities National Project. Available at www.hcfa.gov/quality/3x.htm.

R E A D I N G   **45**

The Tolling of the Bell
Women's Health, Women's Rights

Vivian M. Dickerson, MD (2004)

As physicians for women's health, we are inextricably involved in women's lives. We cannot be less than fully engaged. The poet John Donne expressed this most eloquently in his poem "For Whom the Bell Tolls": ". . . And therefore, never send to know for whom the bell tolls; It tolls for thee."

A tenet of leadership is to seek the truth and embrace it. As the third female President of the American College of Obstetricians and Gynecologists (ACOG), the truth is that my years in ACOG have coincided with the coming of age of women in our society, in the workplace, in leadership roles, and in this fellowship.

Over time, I have watched female physicians grow in number, acceptance, and distinction as they achieve fulfillment of their goals. Today, however, the truth is that who we are transcends gender. Our future must be based on active membership and leadership by both male and female colleagues. It is time to embrace our wholeness rather than to dwell on our differences.

The truth is that not only has our membership changed, but so has the world of health care. The provision of health care today requires new definitions, new roles, and a markedly expanded scope. My own awareness was born of a brief sojourn into public health in Togo, West Africa, before I became a physician. Working with women and children in clinics, schools, and communities, it was overwhelming to see the poverty, the treatment of women in society, the ubiquitous illness and suffering, and most of all, the futility. The sense of helplessness was pervasive. For me, it emphasizes the true definition of women's health, namely a coalescence of emotional, social, cultural, spiritual, and physical well-being. Thus, it is determined not only by biology but by the milieu in which women live their lives.[1]

With time and professional growth, the political and social underpinnings for what I had experienced in that little village in Togo have become increasingly clear. That clarity has resulted in my belief that resolution of many women's health problems in our own country mandates our collective involvement as physicians in the social and political arenas that impact change in a democratic society.

ACOG prescribes such an advocacy role in health care by stating: "Fellows should exercise their responsibility to improve the status of women and their offspring both in the traditional patient–physician relationships, and by working within their community, and at the state and national levels to assure access to high-quality programs meeting the health needs of women."[2]

Many physicians may be reluctant to participate in the "policy and politics" arena of health care. In our pluralistic society, socioeconomic and political issues do polarize advocates, create dissension among competing interests, and divide colleagues including physicians such as ourselves. Nonetheless, the truth is that many women are not receiving their fair share of the benefits or the bounty of this great nation. This pertains not just to their reproductive health care but to the care they receive in society, politics, science, research, and the workplace. If we as physicians limit our involvement to our individual clinical practices, we cannot effect the changes that must happen for women in this country.

I therefore propose that we embrace a Women's Health Bill of Rights for the purpose of improving the overall quality of women's lives as well as their health care. I do so in the conviction that the women for whom we care, and those whom we have yet to see, are entitled to these 10 rights.

NUMBER 1: SAFETY AND ACCOUNTABILITY IN HEALTH CARE

Physicians are now acting upon recommendations from academicians, government officials, and health care experts to improve the safety of patients under their care. Ever since the Institute of Medicine published its report "To Err Is Human,"[3] there is a public imperative as well. Unfortunately, much of the response has been that of finger pointing and blame. Physicians, already under severe stress over liability insurance issues, have feared a disconnect, that is, admitting a mistake is tantamount to a lawsuit. The truth of course is that most medical errors are systems errors, not individual ones. The increasingly troubled relationship between the tort system and patient safety makes it apparent that one cannot be resolved without addressing the other.[4] Self-assessment of normative behaviors, assessment of interactive processes and procedures, maintenance of certification, and programs of lifelong learning are assuredly in order. In the name of safety, society must in turn create a protected no-fault environment in which errors may be identified and corrected without threat of litigation and with the sole goal of patient protection. Just as "first do no harm" is our oath as physicians, the right to safety is the first right in the women's health bill of rights.

NUMBER 2: FREEDOM FROM DOMESTIC AND SOCIOPOLITICAL VIOLENCE BOTH HERE AND THROUGHOUT THE WORLD

As specialists, obstetrician–gynecologists have brought the epidemic of violence against women in this country into national focus. The vigilance must continue, making sure that every patient is asked: "Are you safe?" "Is anyone hurting you?" Physicians cannot truly be vigilant, however, if concerns are limited to clinical practice. We must also look at what we can do in society to reduce the potential for violence.

Social and economic inequalities contribute to increased violence and abuse against women, a fact that has been documented world-round.[5] We must recognize and remember that when we vote, campaign, or espouse any social legislation or candidate, we can and should examine how it may impact the ongoing violence against women in our world.

As an example, data show that women in this country are disproportionately victims of firearm homicides. A recent analysis of 25 high-income nations shows the United States to be an outlier, having the highest level of household gun ownership of any nation studied. And while only 32% of the females studied came from the United States, the United States accounted for 70% of the female homicides and 84% of female homicides by firearms.[6]

Addressing issues that contribute to societal violence throughout the world is part and parcel of health policy. We must look at the price that women in the war-torn countries of the world are now paying and have paid throughout history. The deaths, rapes, undiagnosed and untreated sexually transmitted infections, forced pregnancies, loss of family and home, and injuries have all taken an unacknowledged and often unreported toll on women's lives.

Fellows of the College must voice their concerns and stand up for women who cannot stand up for themselves. Who better to carry the banner than those who have dedicated themselves to the health and well-being of women?

NUMBER 3: APPROPRIATE AND EFFECTIVE INSURANCE COVERAGE

ACOG has worked long and hard to bring about universal health care coverage. Our efforts have been particularly directed toward maternal bene-fits and will continue to be a high priority in the year to come.

Similarly, seniors must be assured that Medicare will indeed cover the cost of their care and that they will not be marginalized because the government chooses not to provide for them. Reimbursement for services performed on women versus those same or analogous services performed on men are often inequitable. Such discrimination is inexcusable and hurts both women and the physicians who care for them.

We have other opportunities to promote appropriate insurance coverage for the truly disenfranchised: for the undocumented pregnant woman, for the uninsured working poor mother, for the physically and mentally disabled, for the morbidly obese patient whose insurance refuses to recognize obesity as a medical entity, for the elderly who choose palliative services in their final days, and for the chronically ill who require supportive therapies when cures for their extraordinary and life-long morbidities have eluded the medical establishment. Universal health care coverage and access are a woman's right.

NUMBER 4: EQUITY IN GENDER-SPECIFIC RESEARCH

Gender equity in research has always been an ACOG priority. Research protocols have come a long way from the days when female participation was denied, either because women might become pregnant or because they were "inherently biologically unstable." The inclusion of women in clinical trials, a policy of the National Institutes of Health since 1986, has been implemented slowly and incrementally amidst significant political maneuvering.[7]

As physicians continue to advocate for equitable funding and the prioritization of women's health research, we also must be instrumental in defining that research. This includes a multitude of unresolved questions in reproduction, in gynecologic disease, and even the dosing of pharmacological therapies as modified by the metabolism of the aging.[8,9] Equity in the allocation of research is a basic woman's right that all must embrace.

NUMBER 5: FREEDOM FROM DISCRIMINATION BASED ON GENDER, GENDER IDENTITY, SEXUAL ORIENTATION, AGE, RACE, OR ETHNICITY

According to the U.S. Census Bureau, by 2030 women will represent 53% of the population and 81% of the population over the age of 85 will be female. These women will be more likely to live alone and be poorer than older men.[10] Thus, as health problems increase with age, they will occur at a time when many women have fewer resources.

By 2050, 47% of the U.S. female population will be members of racial or ethnic minorities. The racial disparities in health outcomes for these women will likely increase rather than improve. While mortality rates for women are decreasing overall, there is an increasing gap between those rates and the rates for minority women, independent of risk behaviors and health care access. However, the lack of equal opportunities in education and employment for women—particularly women of color—results in discrimination via disproportionate exposures to environmental toxins, dangers, and risks.[11] Advocacy for change demands a clearer understanding of these sociopolitical dynamics. The Institute of Medicine, in a comprehensive treatise on the issues of racial inequity, examined the effects of racism and racial biases on the U.S. health care system.[12] Their recommendations include increased awareness, regulatory and policy interventions, and health system changes. Issues of discrimination based on sexual orientation often stem from lack of knowledge or information and have no place in the care of patients. Increasingly, physicians groups such as ACOG are educating and addressing issues germane to sensitive and appropriate care for all women, regardless of gender identity. Physicians must be increasingly aware of the diversity of patients for whom we care and support progressive changes to guarantee the right of all women to be free from discrimination.

NUMBER 6: SOCIOECONOMIC AND POLITICAL EQUALITY

Socioeconomic status is a predictor of health. This fact is unchallenged in the public health literature. Socioeconomic inequalities for women are well documented. Eight percent of all families living in poverty consist of single women and their children.[13] Many heads of these households are women (with children) on public assistance whose income doesn't cover expenses; only about one-third are ever extricated from poverty under the current welfare system.[14] Women in general have double responsibilities: their jobs in the workplace and their roles in the home.[15] While some women choose this dual role, others have no choice. Dual roles result in working women earning about 30% less than their male counterparts.[16] Indeed, men often earn more than women for similar occupations even when women have higher educational levels. There remain significant disparities between men and women in income and job prestige. Depression, lack of job satisfaction, and inability to support family needs economically and socially are common ramifications with all of their health consequences.[17]

Such facts are important to society in terms of law and public policy, and they are important to us as physicians because low-income status along with subordinate occupations and lack of socioeconomic prestige affects growth and development prenatally, throughout childhood, into young adulthood, and beyond. In short, socioeconomic issues shape health, health habits, and health decision-making.[18] Social equality is a health goal. It won't eliminate disparity, but it will contribute to further understanding of women's health determinants and protection of women's health status. Physicians must face these inequalities and work to empower women to have control of their own lives.

NUMBER 7: ACCESSIBLE, AFFORDABLE, AND SAFE FORMS OF CONTRACEPTION INCLUDING POSTCOITAL CONTRACEPTIVES

The care of the pregnant woman must include taking measures to insure that every pregnancy is a wanted and planned pregnancy. It means addressing the issues of sexual politics, rape, forced conception, and forced abandonment of contraception. It requires recognizing that an unintended or unwanted pregnancy can happen to anyone. The issues surrounding the decision to terminate such a pregnancy are profoundly divisive. Obstetrician–gynecologists cannot be less than engaged and cannot believe that the only entity that resonates in this debate is the embryo or fetus. The woman counts, too.

As intelligent and compassionate individuals, physicians may agree to disagree about abortion. As a profession, the only way not to become mired in an irresolvable debate about when life begins and the moral constructs of abortion is to give women the ability to protect themselves, physically, emotionally, and with appropriate contraceptive measures. The only way to prevent abortions is to prevent the pregnancy in the first place with long-term, carefully constructed family planning programs.

Teaching and advocating abstinence is certainly an important component of the prevention of unintended pregnancy. But it does not serve our young women well to teach abstinence ONLY, without concomitant education about sexually transmitted infections, contraceptive options, sexual assault, and empowerment to take reproductive control.

Accidents and coercion happen, and postcoital contraception must be made available to reduce unintended pregnancy and abortion rates. It is a travesty that the United States has the highest rate of teen pregnancy in the industrialized world. Teens in particular need affordable postcoital contraception. Members of ACOG must continue to support the Executive Board policy to seek over-the-counter status for emergency contraceptives.

NUMBER 8: FREEDOM OF REPRODUCTIVE CHOICE

Reproductive choice, despite the current vernacular, is not limited to the decision to carry a pregnancy or to have an abortion. A woman's right to choose abortion is only one aspect of control over reproductive choice. Reproductive choice is a much broader issue.

There are many reproductive choices that are denied to women. For example, choice may be denied through discrimination against women who are incarcerated, women who are single, or women who choose women as their partners. Women's health care providers must be alert to their own ethical dilemmas. How do obstetrician–gynecologists care for the woman seeking fertility services who is HIV positive, or indigent, or 55 years old?

Other questions remain. Is it fair for a gag rule to have been perpetrated on poor women in the United States during the first Bush administration, or on women internationally in the current administration? Is it fair to pay for Viagra and not for oral contraceptives? Reproductive choice is complex and must rest in the hands of the women herself. It is she, after all, who bears the risk and the ultimate responsibility for the birth of her children. We must speak out and reach out to support women's rights to reproductive choice.

NUMBER 9: CULTURALLY SENSITIVE EDUCATION AND INFORMATION

How to best and most effectively communicate with patients is not addressed simply. This country continues to be a haven for the world's displaced populations. The result is tremendous cultural diversity of the patient population. Patients are diverse not only in genetic predispositions and racially determined risks but also in how they understand and process both disease and cure. This diversity affects their access to physicians and their ability to comprehend the care that is offered when access is available.

Fourteen million Americans are not able to speak English proficiently. In addition, almost 1 in 5 American women cannot read and 1 in 4 are functionally illiterate.[18] Many more women do not understand written instructions either from physicians or in pharmaceutical inserts. They cannot interpret lab tests and do not know what they are signing in terms of Medicare rights or Health Insurance Portability and Accountability Act disclosures, let alone surgical procedure consents.

Our endeavors to address this goal are well served by the Agency for Healthcare Research and Quality as it continues its efforts to develop evidence-based strategies for the improvement of health outcomes across diverse populations.[19]

NUMBER 10: ACCESS TO HEALING ENVIRONMENTS AND INTEGRATIVE APPROACHES TO HEALTH AND HEALTH CARE

The patient whom we treat may or may not be cured, but there must be opportunity for each one to be healed. We may have medical knowledge about her disease, but frequently do not understand her illness. We have modalities for relief of pain, but may not be able to help her cope with nor understand her suffering.

What are the differences between curing and healing, disease and illness, and pain and suffering? Curing, disease, and pain are the traditional concerns of the physician. But the other half of each dyad—healing, illness, and suffering—represent the perspective of the patient and her family. A patient does not come to us and say, "I am diseased." No, she says, "I am ill." Similarly, while physicians focus on pain and pain management, the broader concern of suffering represents the social, emotional, psychological, financial, and spiritual ramifications of illness, both for the patient and for those who care for and about her. Cure has been the dominant focus of our training. But the truth is that sometimes, to do so is not in our power. We all have patients in whom the surgery or therapy fails. But health and quality of life are about more than cure; they are also very much about caring and healing.[20]

As the population ages and is beset by chronic disease, physicians must begin to look at what heals patients and how an environment can be created that speaks to the harmony and balance between mind, body, and spirit. It is time to commit research into identifying and enhancing the components of an optimal healing environment.[21] Medicine cannot advance if it attends only to pathogenesis as a road to the understanding of treatment and disease. We must seek further understanding of and research in salutogenesis— the process of health and healing.[22] This tenth item in my Women's Health Bill of Rights addresses the very basis for the quality of life that we all pursue.

In conclusion, I am asking a great deal of all of us. I know that we have precious little time to spend with our patients. In the clinical setting, we cannot possibly accomplish all of these things single-handedly. Nevertheless, I am asking you to become political and to be advocates for women in venues that are not traditionally a part of our role as health care providers.

As in Togo, West Africa, health care in the United States will not succeed if physicians maintain the normative biophysical view of medicine and fail to participate in the social and political system. We must face the fact that we are dealing with women who often have limited power, even over their own lives. We must redefine the frontiers, redefine care, and redefine advocacy. By adopting this Women's Health Bill of Rights, we bring together the two most basic tenets of ACOG: that in this world, physicians matter . . . and in this world, women matter.

REFERENCES

1. Women's Health Office–McGill University. Women's health in obstetrics and gynecology: their relationship and suggestions for a practical integration. J Soc Obstet Gynecol Can 1996;18:589–98.
2. Statement of Policy: Access to Women's Health Care. Washington, DC: American College of Obstetricians and Gynecologists. 2003.
3. Institute of Medicine. To err is human. Washington, DC: National Academy Press; 2001.
4. Mello MM, Brennan TA. Deterrence of medical errors: theory and evidence for malpractice reform. Texas Law Review 2002;80:1595–637.

5. Adler N, Boyce T, Chesney M, Cohen S, Folkman S, Kahn RL, et al. Socioeconomic status and health: the challenge of the gradient. Am J Psychol 1994;49:15–24.

6. Hemenway D, Shinoda-Tagawa T, Miller M. Firearm availability and female homicide victimization rates among 25 populous high-income countries. J Am Med Womens Assoc 2002;57:100–4.

7. U.S. General Accounting Office, National Institutes of Health: Problems in implementing policy on women in study populations. Statement of Mark V. Nadel, Associate Director of National and Public Health Issues, Human Resources Division, before the Subcommittee on Health and the Environment, Committee on Energy and Commerce, U.S. House of Representatives (GAO/T-HRD-90-80), June 18, 1990.

8. Lazarou J, Pomeranz H, Corey PN. Incidence of adverse drug reactions in hospitalized patients: a meta-analysis of prospective studies. JAMA 1998;279:1200–5.

9. Cohen JS. Do standard doses of frequently prescribed drugs cause preventable adverse effects in women? J Am Med Womens Assoc 2002;57:105–10.

10. Rowland Hogue CJ. Gender, Race and Class: From Epidemiologic Association to Etiologic Hypotheses. In: Goldman M, Hatch M, editors. Women and Health. San Diego (CA): Academic Press; 2000.

11. Williams DR. Race and health: basic questions emerging directions. Ann Epidemiol 1997;7:322–2.

12. Institute of Medicine. Unequal treatment-confronting racial and ethnic disparities in health-care. Smedley BD, Stith AY, Nelson AR, editors; 2003. Available at www.nap.edu/books/030908265X/html/.

13. Williams DR, Collins C. U.S. socioeconomic and racial differences in health: patterns and explanations. Annu Rev Soc 1995;21:349–86.

14. U.S. Bureau of the Census. Populations by age, sex, race and origin: 2000. Washington, DC: The Bureau; 2001.

15. McGuire GM, Reskin B. Authority hierarchies at work: the impacts of race and sex. Gender Soc 1993;7:487–506.

16. Burkhauser R, Duncan GJ. Economic risks of gender roles: income loss and life events over the life course. Soc Sci Q 1998;70:3–23.

17. Tennstedt S, Cafferata GL, Sullivan L. Depression among caregivers of impaired elders. J Aging Health 1992;4:58–76.

18. Baker DW, Parker RM, Williams MV, et al. The relationship of patient reading ability to self-reported health and health services. Am J Public Health 1997;87:1027–30.

19. www.ahcpr.gov/research.

20. Lerner M. Choices in healing: integrating the best of conventional and complementary approaches to cancer. Cambridge (MA): MIT Press; 1994.

21. Jonas WB, Chez RA, Duffy B, Strand D. Investigating the impact of optimal healing environments. Altern Ther Health Med 2003;9:58–64.

22. Malterun K, Hollnagel H. Talking with women about personal health resources in general practice: key questions about salutogenesis. Scand J Prim Health Care 1998;16:66–71.

Is Nothing Simple about Reproduction Control?

Linda Gordon (2007)

Everything about reproductive rights must be seen in a political context. Reproduction control brings into play not only the gender system but also the race and class system, the structure of medicine and prescription drug development and production, the welfare system, the educational system, foreign aid, and the question of gay rights and minors' rights. . . .

Major social and political conflicts intersected with these systems to revise the meanings of birth control at several points during its modern history. In the second half of the twentieth century, these conflicts were primarily oriented by the clash between the Left movements of the 1950s–1970s and the Right countermovements. Because the revival of feminism changed the social and political significance of reproduction control, the subject came to evoke basic ideologies about gender, family, and sex. The feminist/ antifeminist contest focused most intensely on abortion. . . . Although oral contraceptives predated the legalization of abortion by approximately a decade, by 1973 abortion discourse permeated debate about the Pill.

. . .

THE WOMEN'S HEALTH MOVEMENT

Within the women's movement, perhaps the most important achievement of reproductive rights activity was the establishment of an enduring women's health movement. An estimated twelve hundred groups considered themselves part of this movement by 1973.[1] The movement addressed a wide range of health issues—notably, transforming conditions of childbirth—but it also grew in large part out of birth control activism. . . . Equally important, it grew up simultaneously with a community health movement, centered in the black, Chicano, Asian, and Puerto Rican neighborhoods of several big cities, concerned with providing health services to the poor and with giving health care consumers a voice in the policies of medical institutions. Three organizations stand out as emblematic of the women's health movement: the Boston Women's Health Book Collective (BWHBC), author of the now famous *Our Bodies, Ourselves;* the National Women's Health Network (NWHN); and the National Black Women's Health Project (NBWHP).

The story of the BWHBC might be told as a fairy tale, a rags-to-riches adventure, and the collective's success might appear miraculous if we disregard the intense material needs and powerful social movement from which the group arose. In 1969, at a women's liberation conference in Boston, a group of women found themselves together in a discussion group focused on "women and their bodies." Discovering their common anger at many frustrating and humiliating experiences with physicians, they decided to continue meeting in order to prepare a list of "good doctors." When they found that list too short to be helpful, they decided to do their own research on women's health issues and began to offer health courses for groups of women. The results of their work, *Our Bodies, Ourselves* (first called *Women and Their Bodies*), was published by the New England Free Press, a small New Left publisher, in 1970. The book was most important to birth control precisely because it was *not* specialized on that topic but informed people about contraception and abortion in the overall context of health education. It encouraged its readers to respect their own desires and to think critically.

Printed on the cheapest newsprint paper, sold for seventy-five cents, and advertised primarily by word of mouth and in the burgeoning feminist underground press, the manual had sold 250,000 copies by 1973. Then the collective authors negotiated a publishing agreement with Simon and Schuster with the understanding that they would have editorial and advertising control and that clinics and other nonprofit health organizations could order the book at a 70 percent discount. Thirty years after its origins, the BWHBC remains stable and has used its substantial profits from book sales (now more than two million copies sold in the United States alone) to support the women's health movement. It has revised the book at least five times, produced and distributed a Spanish-language version for Hispanic Americans, and produced a book on health and sex education for teenagers and another for women entering menopause. It also established a health information center in Boston that is open to the public, subsidized free distribution of *Our Bodies, Ourselves* among various groups, distributed health information packets to some seven hundred women's groups, and saw *Our Bodies, Ourselves* translated into many foreign languages.[2] Rarely has such a small group had so much influence.

. . .

At the beginning of the 1980s, the women's health movement remained overwhelmingly white and middle class and was often insensitive to minority and poor women's needs. Reproductive rights politics had been singularly influential in creating this segregation. Birth control and abortion advocates were often insensitive to black fears about population control—51 percent of black women surveyed in the early 1970s believed that the survival of black people depended on increasing black births, and 37 percent believed that birth control programs were genocidal in intent. (Black men were even more suspicious.)[3] Indeed,

throughout the 1960s and 1970s fears of genocide were prominent in black commentary on birth control. Endorsements of family planning seemed to come only from conservative black sources and to recall the Booker T. Washington tradition of emphasis on self-improvement as opposed to that of challenging discrimination.[4] Indeed, black opposition to birth control, like white opposition, often arose from conservative sexual and gender attitudes.

But among African Americans, as in all groups, there was always female resistance to the anti-birth control perspective. Already in the late 1960s a powerful pro–birth control statement from the Black Women's Liberation Group of Mt. Vernon, New York, circulated throughout the women's movement:

> Black women are being asked by militant black brothers not to practice birth control because it's a form of Whitey committing genocide on black people. Well, true enough, but it takes two to practice genocide and black women are able to decide for themselves. . . . Poor black men won't support their families, won't stick by their women—all they think about is the street, dope and liquor, women, a piece of ass, and their cars. . . . Poor black women would be foolish to sit up in the house with a whole lot of children and eventually go crazy. . . . Middle-class white men have always done this to their women—only more sophisticated-like. . . . For us, birth control is the freedom to fight genocide of black women and children.[5]

Under the influence of the radical women's liberation movement, new groups began to define reproductive freedom so as to include the concerns of women across class and race lines, as we shall see. Unfortunately, the intensity of the anti-abortion attack in the 1980s produced a double narrowing of the politics of abortion rights defense: first to abortion alone, ignoring the many other needs involved in reproductive choice; and second to legal, individual rights, treating the cutbacks in funding and other obstacles to making rights usable with much less intensity. But this exclusion was increasingly challenged as black feminists seized the initiative to criticize sexual conservatism and male dominance. As Dr. Dorothy Brown, a pioneering black physician and feminist, argued in 1983, genocide in the United States "'dates back to 1619 and continues today'" but not through abortion; the issue of abortion is choice.[6]

. . .

[B]irth control has made substantial progress internationally. In the 1960s an estimated 10 percent of couples worldwide used birth control; in 1995 the figure was 55 percent. The average number of children born to each woman has fallen from six to three. These gains correlate well with gains in the percentage of women enrolled in secondary school. Infant and maternal mortality rates also fell significantly.[7] Birth rates have fallen dramatically, and as a result some conservatives now strengthen their arguments against population control with the claim that there is no longer an overpopulation problem.[8] Even population control supporters report that the world population in 2050 will be half a billion less than previously thought.

Ideal population size is, of course, a debatable and indeterminate matter, but there can be no doubt about the need for better reproductive health. Almost 600,000 women die of pregnancy-related causes each year, mostly from postpartum hemorrhage. Of the 50 million abortions performed annually, 75,000 result in death of the patient, overwhelmingly from illegal abortions. Where abortion is legal, there is an average of just 0.2–1.2 deaths per 100,000 abortions; but in developing regions, where abortion is often illegal or highly restricted, mortality rates are hundreds of times higher, averaging 330 deaths per 100,000 abortions.[9]

The number of children desired by women fell considerably in the past thirty years, and most couples say they want smaller families than is traditional in their culture. Six of ten women worldwide either want no more children or want to delay their next birth at least two years.[10] Women's grievances against birth control are overwhelmingly about the means of delivery—coercion, disrespectful treatment, long hours of waiting in uncomfortable waiting rooms, and dismissive responses to their complaints of side effects.[11]

Despite these needs, U.S. birth control aid was drastically reduced starting in 1996. The omnipresent abortion conflict has further reduced the efficiency of the aid that is given. The population controllers who argue that family planning has become "wrongly embroiled in the divisive politics of abortion" are understandably trying to find a noncontroversial ground on which to stand, but their analysis is wrong.[12] Contraception and abortion will not stay separated, and those who oppose both increasingly dominate antiabortion policy. President Reagan imposed a "gag rule" in 1984 prohibiting U.S. funds from going to any birth control service abroad that provided abortions or even informed women about the availability of abortions elsewhere. President Clinton rescinded this rule as one of his first official acts, but his successor, George W. Bush, reinstated it on his first day in office. This policy not only conflicts with U.S. law (which makes abortion legal) and public opinion (which supports legalized abortion), it not only conflicts with the laws of thirty-nine of the countries receiving the aid, but it also deprives foreign beneficiaries of the very freedoms that we enjoy in the United States—the rights to legal abortion and to free speech.

Of particular relevance here is the fact that the gag rule policy undermines contraception as well as abortion because providing contraception and abortion in the same clinic is the most efficient practice. For example, one of the most successful occasions on which to instruct clients in contraception is immediately after an abortion. In other words, not only does contraception help reduce abortion, but abortion can be used to promote contraception and thereby reduce the number of future abortions. Moreover, the gag rule exclusively targets contraception: U.S. aid for other medical uses flows freely to hospitals and clinics providing abortions. It is only contraception that may not be provided in the same setting as abortion.[13] The policy also works to weaken a woman-centered approach to birth control because clinics run by women and oriented to serving women's needs are those most likely to provide both contraception and abortion services or information.

CONTRACEPTION

Within the United States the polarization between feminist and antifeminist perspectives, so prominent in abortion struggles, has become muted with respect to contraception. Instead, contraceptive politics had its own peculiar dynamics. These arose, first, from the fact that contraception remained legitimate and not legally restricted, at least for married people, among most sectors of the U.S. population. While abortion politics rests on a dichotomy between social liberals and social conservatives, some of the major disagreements about contraceptive policy occurred among groups that shared a positive view of reproduction control and even of women's rights. Second, the system of development, testing, manufacture, and distribution of contraceptives in the United States pitted critics of particular contraceptives as consumers against big corporations and the Food and Drug Administration in a conflict not primarily defined by gender interests or sexual morality.

The first political battle about contraception concerned the safety of the Pill, and it aligned the new feminists of the late 1960s against the birth control establishment, the pharmaceutical companies, and even the federal government. The feminist challenge helped to create lasting improvements in drug safety and consumers' right to information.[14]

Soon after the Pill became available in the continental United States, women who took it began to complain in large numbers of the same side effects that had been reported in Puerto Rico, where it was first tested. . . . bloating, weight gain, nausea, vomiting, stomach pain, headaches, and rashes. As in the Puerto Rico trials, physicians, population controllers, and researchers trivialized or even discounted these complaints. Many women quit using the Pill, but many others started, so there was no economic incentive for

Searle, the lone U.S. manufacturer, to question its product, and the population control establishment had no political incentive to do so.

In 1961 came the first reports of Pill-related deaths from pulmonary embolisms (blood clots traveling to the lungs). Then four more deaths were reported in the *British Medical Journal.* Norway banned the Pill. Searle, Gregory Pincus (who had conducted the Puerto Rico trials), and the Population Council responded, first by denying the connection between health dangers and the Pill and then by saying that if there was a connection it was a 1-in-500,000 event. The Food and Drug Administration accepted these responses. By the end of 1962 there had been 272 reported cases of blood clots, thrombophlebitis, or strokes among Pill users, a ratio at least 135 times greater than that which Searle had allowed. Still, it was not until 1969 that the FDA conducted a study and found that women using the Pill were more than four times as likely to develop blood clots as nonusers.

These suspicions and denials occured just as the women's movement was inspiring challenges rather than deference to professionals (overwhelmingly male) who claimed to be authorities on women. One of the first manifestos in that challenge was Barbara Seaman's book *The Doctors' Case against the Pill,* published in 1969. This journalist did such masterful research and so carefully scrutinized the scientific research that her case—confirming the severe risks of high-dose oral contraceptives—could not be impeached (although it is revealing of the still developing confidence of the new feminism that in her title she felt she had to draw on traditional expertise, the "doctors' case," to legitimate her findings). Seaman soon had a large social movement behind her, raising questions and demanding public answers.

The fight was in part a consumer rights struggle, and Seaman has been called the women's Ralph Nader. The public outcry led Wisconsin Democratic senator Gaylord Nelson, chairman of the Subcommittee on Monopoly of the Select Committee on Small Business, to hold hearings in 1970 on the dangers of the Pill and whether consumers were getting adequate information about those dangers. The hearings provided one of the first stages on which the new women's movement could command attention. Frustrated by Nelson's refusal to let even a single woman testify as a consumer of contraception, the Washington, D.C.–based Women's Liberation seized the floor and the attention of the media, disrupting the proceedings and demanding to be heard. One poll found that an astonishing 87 percent of American women between the ages of twenty-one and forty-five followed the hearings. They heard politicians such as Bob Dole, then a Republican senator from Kansas, joke that reporting the dangers of the Pill would make women so terrified they would need tranquilizers as well as birth control. "'We must not frighten millions of women into disregarding the considered judgments of their physicians about the use of oral contraceptives,'" he declaimed.[15] Still, the FDA stalled; and it did not agree to require informative patient inserts in prescription drug packaging until 1978.

Debate about the Pill may have overemphasized the danger of death and illness but it underemphasized the discomforts. The "harmless" side effects such as nausea, rashes, weight gain, and bloating, belittled by physicians and researchers,[16] were more influential than long-term health risks in reducing oral contraceptive use. For example, the Pill "dropout" began in 1967, before there was much publicity about its dangers. Most women who had stopped using oral contraceptives by 1982 had done so on their own initiative—only one-third had been advised by a doctor to discontinue use.[17] Women were "saved" from the Pill's dangers not primarily by health professionals but mainly by their own feelings and the efforts of feminist organizations. . . . Debate about the Pill ended by making it safer.

. . .

As the antiabortion movement's target expanded to encompass contraception, the strategy of distinguishing abortion from contraception had to give way. The movement particularly opposed measures that spread *access* to contraception. Make contraception too easily available,

right-to-lifers argued, and it would license sex outside of marriage, especially among the young. These antiabortion advocates have the same objection to "emergency contraception," a high dosage of birth control hormones that, if taken within seventy-two hours after intercourse, prevents pregnancy. Several reproductive rights organizations have called for making emergency contraception available without a prescription, important because of the short window of opportunity. (Several counties in Oregon already allow pharmacists to dispense emergency contraception over the counter.) Advocates insist that emergency contraception is completely different from the abortifacient RU-486, but that distinction is shaky: mifepristone, the drug in RU-486, can also be used as emergency contraception. Since the body's reproductive processes are all part of a continuum, positioning a line between abortion and contraception is arbitrary.[18]

Antiabortion forces in the 1980s and 1990s consistently worked to cut public funding for birth control. During the Reagan and Bush Sr. presidencies, Title X funding for birth control (in real dollars) fell by 72 percent and total public funding by 27 percent, while the costs of contraception grew faster than inflation.[19] New regulations to Title X proposed by the Reagan administration in 1987 and 1988 not only prohibited funding of family planning projects that offered abortion counseling, referrals, or services but no longer required that they offer a "broad range of acceptable and effective . . . family-planning methods" (the old requirement). Instead, they defined family planning as "natural family-planning methods, adoption, infertility services and general reproductive health care, abstinence and contraception"—in that order. "Clinics" that offered only abstinence as a form of "natural" birth control could be funded under these regulations.[20]

The forms of contraception available in the United States have been influenced strongly by international and national political and economic structures. What U.S. consumers can get has been partly determined by the priorities of marketing in the Third World, because of the potential profits there and because the testing of new methods is skewed by the funding priorities of the international population control agencies—which push long-term hormonal and/or physician-controlled contraception over the "old-fashioned" barrier methods because they doubt that women in poor countries have the necessary skills and conditions to use diaphragms. (Today, some population experts have joined feminists in support of barrier methods, calculating that diaphragms may be more "effective" than pills or IUDs because of their greater "continuation rate"—that is, women who do not stop using them because of the discomfort. Population experts are also beginning to interrogate their use of the concept of "effectiveness," which has usually been based only on laboratory or clinical test results rather than on the evidence of actual and prolonged experience.[21] Moreover, the education of the U.S. public about oral contraceptives, and the successful pressure on drug companies to develop low-dosage pills, was a product of the intersection of the U.S. women's movement and the British National Health Service. Britain blew the whistle about the dangers of birth control pills because its medical system is less obligated to the large drug companies and directly responsible for women's medical bills. Had the United States had a public health insurance program, there might have been an incentive to develop safer pills more quickly. In other ways the internationalization of the contraceptive business by the multinational manufacturers pits the interests of women in the developed and undeveloped worlds against each other: for example, American women's victories at lowering hormonal doses in pills led to the dumping of the old high-dosage pills in third-world countries.

. . .

Although feminist health experts have long argued for a greater emphasis on barrier methods of contraception, it took the HIV/AIDS epidemic to produce a major effect in that direction, emphasizing condoms, which are the only form of birth control that can also protect against sexually transmitted diseases. In the 1980s the proportion of unmarried people using condoms increased

from 9 percent to 16 percent (though there was no apparent increase in use among married couples), while the proportion of those using diaphragms declined.[22] Through the mid-1990s, condom use rose to 19 percent among all women and to 34 percent among women not living with a partner. Encouraging but far from good enough, since 75 percent of women who had had sex with more than one partner in the previous year or whose partner had done likewise were not using condoms.[23]

Given the trade-offs, the diaphragm remains an excellent form of birth control, provided there is legal abortion as a backup. This relation between contraception and abortion must be emphasized, for it is inaccurate to see them as alternatives. No method of contraception yet developed can eliminate the need for legal abortion. Indeed, from a historical perspective, contraception at first may have increased the clientele for abortion because it accustoms people to planning reproduction and makes them unlikely to accept loss of control. Paradoxically, legalized abortion probably increased the use of contraception because most high-quality abortion services promote contraception among clients. For example, Planned Parenthood of New York City doubled its contraception caseload after the legalization of abortion because those who came in for abortions and those who proved not to be pregnant began using contraception.[24] The continued attack on abortion serves only to discourage the use of barrier methods and keep alive hopes for the perfect contraceptive.

. . .

. . . In some respects recent patterns of contraceptive development actually discouraged the taking of personal responsibility—another drawback of "magic-bullet" thinking. The orientation toward a technological solution de-emphasized the reforms needed to create the economic and social preconditions for contraceptive use, reforms designed to ameliorate poverty, reduce power differentials between men and women, provide women with more educational and work opportunities, and lessen sexual shame. In recreating contraception not as a human action but as a commodity, the "magic bullet" approach also discouraged personal responsibility and led contraceptive users to think of themselves as consumers waiting for the perfect product. The mid-twentieth-century gangbusters approach to technological development, driven in the case of drugs by the scramble of multinational pharmaceutical companies for the huge markets that make their expensive research labs profitable, provided no incentive to consider the long-term health consequences and/or discomforts of new chemicals and devices, and these dangers in turn discouraged active contracepting. Finally, the female-only focus of high-tech contraception reinforced the view of birth control as women's responsibility and avoided the discussion and sharing of sexual as well as birth control planning that barrier methods encourage.

. . .

STERILIZATION AND ITS ABUSES

Disappointment in high-tech contraception also promoted a turn to sterilization, which has been the most common form of birth control for U.S. women over the age of twenty-five since the late 1970s.[25] The women's health movement has not been a particularly strong proponent of sterilization, preferring temporary methods that allow women to change their minds about reproduction. Furthermore, widespread patterns of coercive sterilization provoked a strong movement against sterilization abuse.

Forcible sterilization is not new. The first eugenic sterilization programs, adopted by thirty states during the 1920s, forcibly sterilized some 64,000 "feebleminded" or "genetically defective" people. Disproportionately used in southern states, sterilization was imposed on many blacks, American Indians, and poor whites whose alleged "feeblemindedness," if any symptoms of it actually existed, was more likely the result of poor health and little or no education. Yet even in these overtly, nakedly eugenical programs, some of the sterilized women were willing, even eager clients. As one study shows, among women deprived of access to other forms of birth control,

often so poor that their existing children were malnourished, ill clothed, and uneducated, approximately 6 percent of those sterilized had requested the surgery. During the 1960s that figure rose to 20 percent.[26]

Even in the textbook case of sterilization abuse that occurred in Puerto Rico, it is not always easy to distinguish voluntary from forced sterilization. Starting in the 1920s, sterilization was heavily promoted in Puerto Rico as a primary form of birth control. By 1949, 18 percent of childbirths were followed by sterilization. Between the 1930s and the 1970s, one-third of Puerto Rican women of childbearing age had been sterilized.[27] Many women welcomed the opportunity to acquire a reliable form of birth control, but their choices were limited—by the availability of cheap or free sterilization in contrast to expensive contraception; by a creative rewriting of Catholic doctrine that treated contraception as a vice but blinked at sterilization; by the fact that sterilization required no cooperation from husbands and could even be hidden from men. One study showed that 22 percent of unmarried Puerto Rican women knew about *la operación* but only 1 percent had heard of the diaphragm and only 12 percent knew anything about condoms.[28] In Puerto Rico sterilization became legitimated more than contraception because it was medicalized—surgery performed in a hospital while under anesthesia. Conversely, contraception became associated with prostitutes and thus doubly immoral. But aren't all birth control choices constrained? Perhaps for the majority of the world's people, constraint is a matter of degree.

Many politicized Puerto Ricans denounced the sterilization campaign as a tool of colonialism. They saw it as a eugenics as well as a population control policy, a judgment difficult to contest. Prior to attaining commonwealth status and the right to elect its own governor, Puerto Rico was led by a governor appointed by the U.S. government. In 1932 he declared that Puerto Rico's population problem was a matter not only of high quantity but also of low quality.[29] No one could argue that the purpose of U.S. public and private investment in population control in Puerto Rico was to increase Puerto Rican women's reproductive autonomy.

Women of higher class, race, and national status faced paternalism of another kind. While impoverished Puerto Rican women were being pressured into sterilization, many prosperous white women in the United States were denied sterilization as a birth control option. Most doctors stuck to the indications for sterilization recommended by the American College of Obstetricians and Gynecologists (ACOG), which relied on a formula (the woman's age multiplied by the number of children she had) to determine whether a woman was a candidate for sterilization. If the result was 120 or more, she was approved, but only if two doctors plus a psychiatrist also recommended the surgery. Responding to pressure from women, ACOG liberalized its guidelines in 1969–70 and sterilizations increased substantially. Left unchallenged were the medical establishment's assumption of authority to decide when women could be sterilized and the refusal of most medical insurance providers to pay for elective sterilization. The liberalization also reflected the general cultural shifts of the post–World War II period toward a more positive view of small families and marital sexual activity, combined with the impact of population control arguments.[30] A 1982 study showed that 30 percent of former users of the Pill had turned to sterilization as their birth control alternative.[31]

Was the increase in surgical sterilization a net gain for reproductive and sexual freedom? Not necessarily, because even when the surgery was voluntary the context often constrained women's choices. Many women enjoyed being free from the hassle of using contraceptives, but they preferred contraception over sterilization because it left open the option of further childbearing.

The ambiguity of the meanings of sterilization can be seen in class, race, and sex differences. Overall, 11 percent of American men in the mid-1990s had chosen surgical sterilization compared to 28 percent of women. Among couples, approximately 5 percent relied on vasectomy for contraception, while 15 percent relied on female sterilization.[32] Female sterilization is a poor person's

birth control, most commonly relied on by women with less than a high school education or a household income below 150 percent of the federal poverty level. Vasectomy, by contrast, is more common among middle- and higher-income men and twenty-nine times more common among whites than blacks. Among whites, the more education a woman has received, the less likely she is to be sterilized for contraceptive purposes; with men, the correlation with education is reversed.[33] Overall, female sterilizations are medically more complex, and class differences influence how invasive the sterilization surgery will be: poor women are more likely to have hysterectomies than tubal ligations.[34] Public funds can be used to cover most of the cost of sterilizations for the poor, while there is little public funding for abortion or contraception. These differentials raise troubling questions. Vasectomies are safer, simpler, and generally easier to reverse than tubal ligations, and certainly safer and simpler than hysterectomies, so why aren't they the dominant method? Does the preponderance of poor and less well educated women suggest that sterilization might not be their method of choice if they had full access to the information, training, medical care, and money that contraception and abortion require?

. . .

TEENAGE PREGNANCY AND OUT-OF-WEDLOCK CHILDBEARING

In the 1980s a new reproductive issue moved to the center of political debate in the United States. The alarm about teenage pregnancy and out-of-wedlock childbearing supported the condemnation of welfare and an "underclass" who allegedly lacked good moral values and work ethic. The alarm demonstrated that contemporary sexual and reproductive assumptions, as in the nineteenth century, formed an important part of social definitions of respectability. Most directly relevant here were the parallel controversies about whether birth control or sexual abstinence, abortion or adoption, were better approaches to the problem, and this has remained a relatively dichotomous discussion between liberals and social conservatives even into the twenty-first century. A feminist approach, integrating the gendered experience of girls into the discussion of poverty and sex, remains rare.

Despite a great deal of research and publicity about teenage pregnancy, much of the popular discussion in the 1980s relied on the mistaken assumption that teenage fertility rates were rising. The fact is that these rates have been declining since 1960. . . .

So what prompted the 1980s panic that teenage pregnancies and childbearing were increasing? One reason is that adult births were falling even more than teenage births.[35] More significant, however, is that the same cluster of conservative political attitudes expressed in antiabortion campaigns, now applied to the issue of teenage pregnancy, led to an unnoticed misunderstanding. Accepting the rhetoric of Christian social conservatism, commentators fell into the mistake of not noticing teenage childbearing when the teenagers were *married*. In the 1950s, the birth rate for teenagers was higher than that of today, but those teenagers were much more often married. More recently, while teen births overall were decreasing, the proportion of teen births to the *unmarried* was increasing. . . .

In other words, the discourse about teenage childbearing typically rests on the hidden assumption that pregnancy among married teenagers is not objectionable—or, rather, that marriage somehow instantly makes teenagers into grownups. In fact, most of the negative consequences of teenage pregnancy pertain equally to the married and unmarried: teenagers have more-difficult childbirths and less-healthy babies, are worse parents, create more-unstable marriages, and achieve less education and lower earning power and status. Ironically, during the 1960s both scholarly and popular writing identified teenage marriage as the problem; by the 1980s the focus was on teenage pregnancy, with early marriage no longer considered problematic. In fact, some conservative commentators recommend early marriage as a remedy, failing to recognize that for many poor young women marriage is unlikely to increase stability or standard of living.[36] It is worth considering that while the rise of nonmarital pregnancies creates problems, the decline in early marriage is not a bad thing.

The racial subtext in the concern with pregnancy among unwed teenagers also fosters misunderstandings. While the percentage of out-of-wedlock births among all black women was higher during this period than among white women, it was only slightly higher than among whites of the same poverty level. Furthermore, white rates of out-of-wedlock (not necessarily teenage) pregnancy were rising while black rates were falling, among adults and teenagers.[37] African American attitudes about teenage and out-of-wedlock pregnancies went through particularly noticeable changes between the 1960s and the 1980s. Following publication in 1965 of the notorious "Moynihan Report," which blamed black poverty on "pathological" family patterns, many African American leaders responded critically, emphasizing the strengths of black extended-family networks and intergenerational child-raising and criticizing the report for diverting attention away from basic racial discrimination. As Joyce Ladner put it, there was a "closing of the ranks" behind black families, making open discussion of teen pregnancy or single-mother families appear disloyal, much like exposing one's weaknesses to the enemy. Indeed, the anger created by Moynihan's report probably impeded examination of these problems.[38] Since then, however, more black organizations have campaigned against teenage pregnancy, although they are as divided about solutions as are white organizations.

We can understand more by examining teenage pregnancy in a global context. The United States has substantially higher levels of teenage pregnancy, childbearing, and abortion than any of twenty-seven other industrialized countries. Teenagers in the United States are less likely to use contraception than those in other comparable countries. Furthermore, teenage birth rates have declined less steeply in the United States . . . than in other developed countries over the last three decades. These high rates in the United States are most correlated with the high rates of poverty and inequality in the United States, which on the individual level means less hope for upward mobility among the poorest teenagers who have most of the babies.

. . .

Single motherhood, poverty, and welfare receipt created difficulties for both mothers and children, but the three factors must be distinguished. Some lone mothers were prosperous, some chose this kind of family, and many suffered negligibly if at all from lack of husbands. The children of these mothers generally do very well. Single motherhood in general was highly correlated with poverty—especially where single mothers were heads of household—and it is overwhelmingly because of poverty that female-headed households were correlated with lasting disadvantages for children.[39] Moreover, while early pregnancy certainly added to the mothers' problems, they were poor mainly because they started off poor. Few would have done much better even if they had avoided early pregnancy; besides, pregnancies did not occur randomly among teenagers but affected those with the fewest resources and hopes for the future. Moreover, poor girls of all races were more likely to carry out-of-wedlock pregnancies to term than were more-prosperous girls.[40] This should not be construed as minimizing the damages of teenage pregnancy and parenthood. Many girls may have "chosen" to bear children, either passively (by their lack of attention to birth control) or actively (as a means of gaining status), but their "choices" emerged from a very limited range. For example, a far higher proportion of teenage girls than of adults described their pregnancies as unwanted, and this was the case three times as often among blacks as among whites.[41]

Teenage pregnancy was unusual among reproduction control issues in that nearly everyone thought it was a bad idea. But this consensus did little to promote agreement on policy. Liberals argued for promoting contraception and increasing access to it, but social conservatives feared that contraception would encourage teenage sexual activity, which they considered immoral and harmful in itself. . . .

. . . Among the 70 percent of public school districts that teach sex education, the vast majority

(86 percent) require that abstinence be promoted, either as the preferred option for teenagers (51 percent) or as the only option outside of marriage (35 percent). Only 14 percent address abstinence in a broader educational program to prepare adolescents to become sexually responsible adults. In one-third of school districts, information about contraception is either prohibited entirely or limited to emphasizing its ineffectiveness in protecting against unplanned pregnancy and sexually transmitted diseases. . . .

By contrast, providing contraception in high schools does seem to work.[42] An evaluation of five different pregnancy prevention programs found that the two that showed results were the two that were most active in providing access to contraceptive services.[43] Moreover, there is wide public support for such programs, and twenty-three states have adopted legislation that gives minors the authority to consent to contraceptive services for themselves.

. . .

Another aspect of the debate over teenage pregnancy is the tendency to discuss it without thinking about gender. This silence about the actual conditions of femaleness has characterized liberal as well as conservative discourse. In fact, throughout the 1980s most of the discussion of teenage pregnancy was entirely silent regarding boys, as if these pregnancies arose from immaculate conceptions. Very little anti–teenage pregnancy work was directed at boys, and in practice those who lobbied for abstinence education were challenging the double standard that accepts boys' sexual adventures. Also, the liberal teenage pregnancy discourse usually ignored pressures on girls to submit sexually, even though it is known that the sexual partners of teenage girls are often significantly older and that coercion in sex can take many forms short of rape with a weapon.

Birth control worked, historically, under two conditions: when women could take charge of their own sexual activity, resisting sexual pressure or violence while honoring their own sexual feelings; and when women had realizable aspirations beyond motherhood. Yet very few discussions of teenage pregnancy have touched on these issues. . . . Teenage pregnancy, like many reproductive issues, is problematic largely because of the social inequalities it thrives upon and helps to reproduce, and solutions are unlikely to be found if sex inequality is ignored.

HIV/AIDS AND BIRTH CONTROL

The HIV/AIDS epidemic born in the 1980s exposed similar inequalities. At first labeled a "gay disease," it has now become overwhelmingly a disease of heterosexual poor people of color, disproportionately female, both in the United States and abroad. The politics of HIV/AIDS has shifted somewhat in accord with the progress of the epidemic, but only slightly, and its basic alignment continues to parallel that regarding abortion and teen pregnancy.

The impact of HIV/AIDS on birth control in the United States mirrors that of venereal disease in the World War I era. . . . Like V.D., HIV/AIDS led to increased condom use but also provoked a backlash. Moreover, after appearing initially as a men's problem, it soon began disproportionately victimizing women—an effect magnified by public policy. . . .

Between 1985 and 1999, AIDS cases among women more than tripled, from 7 percent to 23 percent. The most dramatic increases occurred among women of color: African Americans and Hispanics together constituted 77 percent of AIDS cases among women, although they make up less than one-fourth of the female population in the United States. The most dramatic increase occurred among African American and Hispanic teenage girls. . . . Among women in general, the most frequently reported cause of infection was heterosexual intercourse, followed by drug injection (approximately 27 percent). High proportions of infected women were unaware of the risks associated with their partners.

. . .

Structures of economic and racial inequality create this disproportionate infection rate among poor, young people of color, who are less likely to have access to medical care and sex education and who, if they become infected, are more likely to die. People already afraid of the law because of their status as drug users, welfare recipients, or illegal immigrants have an incentive to avoid testing or any other contact with officials. But sex and gender are also front and center. Poor young women are more vulnerable to rape, less likely to get help from the police if they are threatened, and less able to resist the pressure to have sex with older men or to insist that they use condoms. That so many infected women report not knowing that their partners were putting them at risk points to the failure of education, women's intimidation by their partners, and/or their partners' dishonesty or irresponsibility. Among all groups homophobia leads men to engage in unsafe sex because safe sex requires accepting and taking responsibility for one's sexual activities. Unrealistic sexual moralism creates the same unsafe sexual activity among women.

The opposition to effective HIV/AIDS policy has been shaped by much the same ideologies and interests that oppose birth control. In the past, fear of veneral disease sometimes spurred birth control and sexual responsibility. Condoms gained their modern legitimacy as protection against gonorrhea, and their use has been widely approved since the HIV/AIDS epidemic began. In theory that approval should have advanced the cause of birth control. But conservative moralists have opposed wide distribution of condoms for much the same reason they did so during World War I, and for much the same reason they oppose wide distribution of any contraceptives—namely, in their view easy access to any contraceptive not only encourages but signals acceptance of nonmarital, nonreproductive sex. Moreover, condoms have seemed to many sexual conservatives to be one of the most objectionable contraceptives because they are so nonmedical, so easily procured and carried, so easy to use—and so difficult to restrict because of their tradition as a male privilege. The same logic infuses conservative opposition to the distribution of clean needles—namely, that doing so encourages drug use.

When HIV/AIDS seemed a "gay disease," it was easier for sexual conservatives to label it a punishment for, in their words, "the sin of homosexuality." Opposing condom distribution carried the not-so-subtle message that gays should be cast out of society, or worse. Some proponents of abstinence-only approaches disguised their own murderous impulses by broadcasting the failure rate of condoms in order to scare people away from sex. It became politically riskier, however, even among homophobes, to maintain that HIV/AIDS is deserved punishment once heterosexuals became infected in increasing numbers—although the fact that many of them were drug users, poor, and nonwhite made it easier to withhold sympathy.

Sexual conservatives now protest condom distribution more cautiously because, at least when HIV/AIDS is the issue, they face overwhelming opposition. Even among Americans with conservative views about birth control, a majority support promoting condoms for protection against disease. But Christian Coalition–type threats have cowed those who should be leading safe-sex campaigns, and HIV/AIDS remains an issue about which private-sector executives are resisting what the public wants. A majority of Americans favor placing condom ads on network as well as cable TV, for example.[44] Yet little progress has been made since the first ads aired in 1996. Such ads are few and are allowed only in very restricted time slots.[45]

CONCLUSION

Trying to control reproduction has been a human activity from as far back as historians can trace it. Reproduction control efforts constitute part of the evidence that biology has never been destiny, that even those functions most often described as "natural," such as reproduction, have always been formed by cultural and social organizations. In the twentieth century there was rapid, if intermittent, progress in birth control but also some disappointment. Methods became safer and more efficient, and their use became more widespread. But many people have been excluded from this progress. Women continue to suffer, even die, from birth control efforts, especially abortion—casualties that are due more to prohibitions and criminalization than to necessary risks.

. . .

The birth control problem does not stem from an inevitable, tragic march toward an overly high-tech civilization. Rather, the problems are primarily political. . . . Access, motivation, and technological development are all shaped by political conflicts and negotiations, sometimes personal, sometimes so far out of individual control that most people are unaware that decisions are being made.

. . .

Each historical campaign for birth control tried to enact a vision of a more democratic society, including not only its gender system but also its class divisions. Each campaign achieved its goals only partially, although each succeeding campaign achieved more than the previous one. Heady with their camaraderie and their new understandings, each group of feminists underestimated the emotional and political grip of the then-dominant sex/gender system and how radical a change their vision appeared to be. This was, in each case, a vision of egalitarian, voluntary family without coercive, permanent marriage as its necessary core; of public responsibility for the general welfare and for equal opportunity for children; of sexual experiences free of coercion; and of reproduction as a freely chosen human activity. It was foolish to think that such a program would fail to produce an intense resistance.

But radical as that feminist vision may have been and still is, it was not utopian; indeed, in the United States parts of that vision are being acted on, even as inequalities of class and race grow. However distant this vision appears, reproduction cannot be free of coercion without it. Throughout its history, the cause of reproduction control has been sometimes more attached to, sometimes more detached from, a feminist vision of family and society. The historical evidence suggests that the cause did better, and individuals did better, when birth control was sought after as part of an overall movement toward social equality and women's rights.

REFERENCES

1. Helen I. Marieskind and Barbara Ehrenreich, "Toward Socialist Medicine: The Women's Health Movement," *Social Policy* 6:2 (Sept.–Oct. 1975): 34–42; Rachel Fruchter et al., "The Women's Health Movement: Where Are We Now?," *Healthright* 1:1 (1974): 4.

2. Barbara Beckwith, "Boston Women's Health Book Collective: Women Empowering Women," *Women and Health* 10:1 (Spring 1985): 1–7; interview with Norma Swenson, June 27, 1988.

3. Castellano B. Turner and William A. Darity, "Fears of Genocide among Black Americans as Related to Age, Sex, and Region," *American Journal of Public Health* 63:12 (Dec. 1973): 1029–34, quoted in Willard Cates Jr., "Abortion Attitudes of Black Women," *Women and Health* 2:3 (Nov.–Dec. 1977): 3; A. O. Harrison, "Family Planning Attitudes among Black Females," *Journal of Social and Behavior Sciences* 22:3 (Winter 1977): 136–45; interview with Dr. Vicki Alexander, Aug, 2, 1988. According to Harrison, black women's use of birth control, just like white women's, was highly correlated with urban and middle-class living conditions.

4. For example, Vernon Davies, "Fertility versus Welfare: The Negro American Dilemma," *Phylon* 27:3 (Fall 1966): 226–32; Loretta Ross, "African-American Women and Abortion," in *Abortion Wars: A Half Century of Struggle, 1950–2000*, ed. Rickie Solinger (Berkeley: University of California Press, 1998), 161–207.

5. Quoted in Ros Baxandall and Linda Gordon, eds., *Dear Sisters: Dispatches from the Women's Liberation Movement* (New York: Basic Books, 2000), 135.

6. Quoted in *Women Wise*, Fall 1983, p. 2.

7. Alan Guttmacher Institute, "The Cairo Consensus" ("Issues in Brief"), Mar. 1995, New York; Family Health International, "Contraception Influences Quality of Life," *Network* 18:4 (Summer 1998); Rockefeller Foundation, *High stakes: The United States, Global Population, and Our Common Future* (report; New York: Rockefeller Foundation, 1997).

8. Nicholas Eberstadt, "The Population Implosion," *Foreign Policy*, Mar–Apr. 2001, pp. 42–53.

9. Online at <http://www.agi-usa.org/pubs/fb_0599.html>.

10. Alan Guttmacher Institute, *Sharing Responsibility: Women, Society, and Abortion Worldwide* (report; New York, 1999); Rockefeller Foundation, *High Stakes*.

11. Family Health International, "Contraception Influences Quality of Life," *Network* 18:4 (Summer 1998).

12. Rockefeller Foundation, *High Stakes*, 11.

13. Susan A. Cohen, "Global Gag Rule: Exporting Antiabortion Ideology at the Expense of American Values," *Guttmacher Report on Public Policy* 4:3 (June 2001).

14. My synopsis of the political battles over oral contraceptives is indebted to Andrea Tone, *Devices and Desires: A History of Contraceptives in America* (New York: Hill and Wang, 2001); Paul Vaughan, *The Pill on Trial* (New York: Coward-McCann, 1970); and Elizabeth Siegel Watkins, *On the Pill: A Social History of Oral Contraceptives, 1950–1970* (Baltimore: Johns Hopkins University Press, 1998).

15. Quoted in Tone, *Devices and Desires*, 249–50.

16. Judith Bruce, "User's Perspectives on Contraceptive Technology and Delivery Systems: Highlighting Some Feminist Issues," *Technology in Society: An International Journal* 9:3–4 (1987): 359–83. Bruce quotes Bernard Berelson, president of the Population Council in the 1960s: "'When uninformed women encountered minor difficulties they tended to discontinue. . . . dissatisfied women have spread adverse gossip and encouraged others to discontinue'" (359–60).

17. William F. Pratt and Christine A. Bachrach, "What Do Women Use When They Stop Using the Pill?," *Family Planning Perspectives* 19:6 (Nov.–Dec. 1987): 257–65; Rosalind Pollack Petchesky, *Abortion and Women's Choice: The State, Sexuality, and Reproductive Freedom* (New York: Longman, 1984), 188. By contrast, Jacqueline Darroch Forrest and Stanley K. Henshaw, in "What U.S. Women Think and Do about Contraception," *Family Planning Perspectives* 15:4 (July–Aug. 1983): 157–66, attribute the decline of oral contraceptive use to the impact of "adverse propaganda." The situation was substantially different in the Third World, where high-dosage pills were urged and sometimes dumped upon women often lacking any other contraceptive alternatives.

18. Charlotte Ellertson, "History and Efficacy of Emergency Contraception: Beyond Coca-Cola," *Family Planning Perspectives* 22:2 (June 1996): 52–56; "NARAL Urges FDA to Make Emergency Contraceptive Pills Available Over-the-Counter," online at <http://www.naral.org/mediaresources/press/pro62900_ecp.html>; "In Seven Oregon

counties . . . ," *Family Planning Perspectives* 31:5 (Sept. 1999): 211.

19. Harrison and Rosenfield, *Contraceptive Research and Development,* 227.

20. Jeannie I. Rosoff, "Taking Family Planning Out of Title X: The Impact of the Proposed New Regulations," *Family Planning Perspectives* 19:5 (Sept.–Oct. 1987): 222–26; *The U.S. International Family Planning Program under Siege,* PPFA Pamphlet, 1987; Michael Klitsch, "Courts Sink New Title X Regulations," *Family Planning Perspectives* 20:2 (Mar.–Apr. 1988): 96–98.

21. Malcolm Potts and Robert Wheeler, "The Quest for a Magic Bullet," *Family Planning Perspectives* 13:6 (Nov.–Dec. 1981): 269.

22. Jacqueline Darroch Forrest and Richard R. Fordyce, "U.S. Women's Contraceptive Attitudes and Practice: How Have They Changed in the 1980s?," *Family Planning Perspectives* 20:3 (May–June 1988): 112–18.

23. Akinrinola Bankole, Jacqueline E. Darroch, and Susheela Singh, "Determinants of Trends in Condom Use in the United States, 1988–1995," *Family Planning Perspectives* 31:6 (Nov.–Dec. 1999): 264–71.

24. Bruce, "User's Perspectives on Contraceptive Technology."

25. Forrest and Fordyce, "U.S. Women's Contraceptive Attitudes and Practice"; Rosalind Pollack Petchesky, "'Reproductive Choice' in the Contemporary United States: A Social Analysis of Female Sterilization," in *And the Poor Get Children: Radical Perspectives on Population Dynamics,* ed. Karen Michaelson (New York: Monthly Review Press, 1981), 51; Forrest and Henshaw, "What U.S. Women Think and Do." Thanks to Susan Jew at the Alan Guttmacher Institute for information used in this discussion.

26. The figures are from a North Carolina study by Johanna Schoen, summarized in "Between Choice and Coercion: Women and the Politics of Sterilization in North Carolina, 1929–1975," *Journal of Women's History* 13:1 (Spring 2001): 132–56.

27. Annette B. Ramírez de Arellano and Conrad Seipp, *Colonialism, Catholicism, and Contraception: A History of Birth Control in Puerto Rico* (Chapel Hill: University of North Carolina Press, 1983).

28. Cited in Jennifer A. Nelson, "'Abortions under Community Control': Feminism, Nationalism, and the Politics of Reproduction among New York City's Young Lords," *Journal of Women's History* 13:1 (Spring 2001): 167.

29. Ibid., 168.

30. Some critics have suggested as a further incentive that gynecologists and obstetricians were short of work, and especially surgical work, as a result of the falling birth rate and that residents needed more surgical practice. See Robert E. McGarrah, "Voluntary Female Sterilization: Abuses, Risks and Guidelines," *Hastings Center Report,* June 1974, p. 6, quoted in Barbara Caress, "Sterilization," *Health/PAC Bulletin* 62 (Jan.–Feb. 1975): 4.

31. Pratt and Bachrach, "What Do Women Use?," 263.

32. This information was found online at <http://www.nichd.nih.gov/publications/pubs/vasect/htm>.

33. Online at <http://www.agi-usa.org/pubs/teen_preg_sr_0699.html>.

34. Petchesky, "'Reproductive Choice' in the Contemporary United States."

35. Christopher Jencks, "What Is the Underclass—and Is It Growing?," *Focus* (University of Wisconsin Institute for Research on Poverty) 12:1 (Spring–Summer 1989): 14–26.

36. For example, Douglas J. Besharov and Alison J. Quinn, "Not All Female-Headed Families Are Created Equal," *The Public Interest* 89 (Fall 1987): 48–56; Maris A. Vinovskis, "Teenage Pregnancy and the Underclass," *The Public Interest* 93 (Fall 1988): 87–96.

37. *Family Planning Perspectives* 19:2 (Mar.–Apr. 1987): 83–84; Joyce Ladner, "Teenage Pregnancy: The Implication for Black Americans," in *The State of Black America 1986* (New York: National Urban League, 1986), 70.

38. Ladner, "Teenage Pregnancy," 69. The "Moynihan Report" was officially titled *The Negro Family: The Case for National Action* but became best known by the name of its author, Daniel P. Moynihan, at the time an assistant secretary in the Office of Policy Planning and Research at the U.S. Department of Labor.

39. There is no space here even to begin to summarize the voluminous literature about single mothers and their children, but see, for example, Kristen Luker, *Abortion and the Politics of Motherhood* (Berkeley: University of California Press, 1984); Irwin Garfinkel and Sara S. McLanahan, *Single Mothers and Their Children: A New American Dilemma* (Washington, D.C.: Urban Institute Press, 1986). On single mothers and the underclass, see

Jencks, "What Is the Underclass?," and Sara McLanahan and Irwin Garfinkel, "Single Mothers, the Underclass, and Social Policy," *Annals of the American Academy* 501 (Jan. 1989): 92–104.

40. According to a study published in 1994, 83 percent of teens who give birth are from poor families, compared to 61 percent of teens who have abortions and 38 percent of teens overall (Alan Guttmacher Institute, *Sex and America's Teenagers* [New York, 1994], 58). See also Petchesky, *Abortion and Woman's Choice*, 148–55. The claim that there is a "market" for adoptive babies is false when it comes to nonwhite babies.

41. W. C. Pratt and M. C. Horn, "Wanted and Unwanted Childbearing: United States, 1973–1982," *Advance Data from Vital and Health Statistics* 108 (1985), summarized in *Family Planning Perspectives* 17:6 (Nov.–Dec. 1985): 274–75.

42. Ladner, "Teenage Pregnancy," 80; Michelle Fine, "Sexuality, Schooling, and Adolescent Females: The Missing Discourse of Desire," *Harvard Education Review* 58:1 (Feb. 1983): 44; Neely Tucker, "Factions Spur Hodgepodge of Separately Funded Clinics," *Florida Today*, Oct. 26, 1986.

43. D. Kirby et al., "School-based Programs to Reduce Sexual Risk Behaviors: A Review of Effectiveness," *Public Health Reports* 109 (1994): 339–60; K. A. Moore et al., "Adolescent Pregnancy Prevention Programs: Interventions and Evaluations," *Child Trends* (Washington, D.C.), June 1995.

44. Three-fourths of those polled in 2001 said they would be comfortable with anti-HIV/AIDS condom ads on TV, while only 60 percent said they would support ads for contraceptives if HIV/AIDS was not mentioned. Moreover, when HIV/AIDS was mentioned in the poll, religious differences in support for contraceptive advertising diminished: without mention of the disease, there was a 25 percent difference between high levels of Jewish and lower levels of Protestant support, with Catholics in between; mentioning HIV/AIDS produced an 11 percent difference. (It is interesting that Catholics object less than Protestants to TV ads for contraceptives even though Catholics are 10 percent more likely to have religious objections to using contraceptives.) See Louis Harris and Associates, *Attitudes about Television, Sex, and Contraceptive Advertising* (New York: Planned Parenthood, 1987), 46–47 (tables 19a and 19b), 67–70 (tables 30b, 31a, and 31b). In evaluating these figures, it should be noted that the survey was contracted by Planned Parenthood in order to develop evidence to convince television networks and individual stations to accept contraceptive ads; it was hardly a disinterested inquiry. Still, a more recent—and disinterested—poll found the same thing (online at <http://dailynews.yahoo.com/h/nm/20010619/hl/ads-1.html>).

45. Associated Press, July 1, 2001.

Eyes on the Prize

Selden McCurrie (2004)

On July 29th I was initiated into a vast unwilling sisterhood—I was diagnosed with breast cancer. . . .

. . .

"I'm sorry, Selden." My doctor's husky voice was inordinately gentle. "You have cancer in both breasts. The left breast shows extensive ductal carcinoma in situ [DCIS], almost three centimeters. The right is infiltrating ductal carcinoma, around a centimeter. They're both highly treatable, though I'd like it better if the right wasn't infiltrating. I've taken the liberty of making an appointment with a surgeon for you. I'll fax you the biopsy results."

. . .

[After my diagnosis I tried] to assemble an emotionally charged clinical jigsaw puzzle, but the pieces kept multiplying. Lumpectomies vs. mastectomies. Mastectomies were becoming a very real option. Mastectomies without reconstruction. "Reconstruction" was a term I had come to loathe for signifying that mastectomy was the ultimate de-construction. Implants were out because of my track record of allergies. . . . Reconstruction would always be an option. Nonetheless, I called our health insurance companies. If I wanted reconstruction at a later date, it would be covered but would require a letter of medical necessity from my doctor. I pondered that—letter of medical necessity. Losing your breasts to mastectomies wasn't enough on its own? What would make it a *necessity*? Nervous breakdown? Severe back problems?

For now, my choice was mastectomies without reconstruction vs. lumpectomies [to just remove the tumors]. . . . Statistics, studies, and medical opinions couldn't put a human face on mastectomies, so I wanted to go straight to the source. Early on, I had started going to a breast cancer support group at The Wellness Community. I felt an instant bond of sisterhood when I walked into the room.

These were the human faces behind the statistics. There were five women there that first day and I listened in awe as we went around the circle and told our stories. Theirs were the faces of choices: lumpectomy with radiation, lumpectomy with chemotherapy, mastectomy with reconstruction, and recurrence. Hope. These women were the embodiment of coping and hope. Yet there was no face for the choice of mastectomy *without* reconstruction.

I had put the word out that I was facing this decision and wanted to talk with women who had had double mastectomies—bilateral mastectomy in medical jargon. I discovered that this is the quietest group within this sisterhood to which I had been unwillingly initiated. There were women out there, granted not a lot, who were unreconstructed, but they were silent. I prayed for help. My prayers were answered.

Alice, a friend of a sister-in-law, called from her family's beach house one Sunday afternoon. Like me, she'd had cancer in both breasts. Unlike me, she had been a DD-cup before her mastectomies. She had forgone reconstruction. What's it like? I had asked.

"It's more comfortable than before and in fact, my back problems have gotten better," she said with a trace of a Boston accent. "I decided that I had to be consistent—either I was going to wear the prostheses all the time or not. So when I leave the house, I have them on. I hated the first prostheses and I loathed the mastectomy bras. I'm happier now that I've found this sports bra. It took some trial and error, so be sure you get measured by a certified fitter.

"I've lost part of my sexuality—my breasts, but my husband has been great. It will take you some time to get used to it."

Susan. I never knew how she found me—she left a message on my voice-mail. She told me she was a tall, athletic woman, and had also had a bi-lateral mastectomy without reconstruction.

"I was an A-cup before the surgery and now I can choose. For example, today, I wore B-cup prostheses, but tonight I'm going out and I'll wear C-cups. My insurance pays for a pair every year, so I've got several pairs. I like the ones that stick to your skin. They feel like a part of my body. I don't even think about it anymore," she said in a soft voice.

Jan, a geek like me—a computer project manager for a Fortune 500 company—also called one evening.

"I was small," Jan said. "I didn't even wear prostheses for the first two years. Nobody ever noticed. In fact, one day at work I mentioned my mastectomies to a programmer in the next cube who was a lean, tall, marathon runner. We stood side by side and you couldn't tell the difference. She was muscular and flat. I was short and flat.

"Then my husband started telling me my posture was changing. So I told him that for Christmas, I wanted a pair of boobs. I hit a department store that stocked prostheses and bought a pair.

It did make a difference in my posture, and now I even wear them around the house."

. . .

Three surgeons were steering me toward bilateral mastectomy. Only the oncologist had said the survival odds at five years were the same for lumpectomies as mastectomies. A Mayo Clinic paper in Medline had turned up a slightly different outlook at ten years in favor of mastectomies. All four doctors had mentioned the hereditary potential of my cancer. In addition to my mother's breast cancer, my father had colon cancer at age seventy-eight. So had two of his brothers. I had had a colonoscopy in January so I knew I was clean. For now.

Back to assembling my clinical puzzle. My emotions nibbled at the edges of the pieces, making a good fit difficult. Where did my feelings go—in the middle or on the edges of the puzzle? And what were my feelings? Every time I thought about a bilateral mastectomy, I felt a sickening thud in the pit of my stomach. Yet, intellectually, I was leaning in that direction.

Snap. A genetic piece of the puzzle. My Medline queries had turned up papers implicating the hereditary aspects of breast cancer, which all my physicians had discussed with me.

Snap. A surgical piece of the puzzle. The surgeons who looked at my films, when pushed for an opinion on lumpectomies, had said it would be difficult to remove the entire duct. They could take the tumor out, but because of my dense, fibrous breasts could not be certain they would get the entire duct. I worried about what they could not see. The tumor was growing in a duct that had never been biopsied.

Snap. An anatomical piece of the puzzle. Breast cancer, especially DCIS, follows the duct. The oncologist said if I opted for lumpectomies, she would want to irradiate both breasts. Irradiation of my dense, heavy, elongated breasts, even with the best technology, carried a small chance of setting me up for potential heart disease. My mother had died of a heart attack—her seventh. I knew there were advances in radiation treatments, but I recalled a friend who had undergone radiation for his Hodgkin's disease, only to die twenty years

later from leukemia. With mastectomies, at least I could duck radiation if the cancer wasn't in the lymph nodes.

Snap. A chemotherapy piece of the puzzle. We went to see the oncologist—a deceptively gentle woman whose businesslike demeanor hid a scientist's analytical mind. I walked away from her convinced she never forgot a single thing you ever told her. Despite multiple drug allergies and my complex medical history of chemical sensitivities, she was certain she could manage chemotherapy if I needed it. This hurdle was still an unknown—my final pathology report would determine whether or not I needed chemotherapy. I was operating under the assumption that I would. If not, then it would be a pleasant surprise.

Snap. A radiological piece of the puzzle. The radiologist who had diagnosed me said that only 40 percent of DCIS showed on mammograms. Who knew what else was cooking in my breast ducts?

Snap. A pathological piece of the puzzle. Most of what I read indicated that the woman most likely to get breast cancer was a woman who *had* breast cancer. If I chose lumpectomies, what were my odds of recurrence with cancer already in both breasts?

So much for medical and scientific opinions. Where did the human factors fit? How could I gauge what it would be like to lose my breasts? How would I know unless I had mastectomies? Would it be comfortable? Would I turn into the Hunchback of Notre Dame? If I had lumpectomies, would the cancer come back? Could I live with the stress of the three-month, six-month interval mammograms and ultrasounds? Could I face additional surgery? Did I want to gamble and take that chance? How would I handle all of this? How was I going to learn how to be a cancer patient?

I sat on the screened-in porch, in total darkness. . . . I now owned my cancer, my enemy, and knew it well, but decided it would not *own* me. . . .

. . .

The painful realization dawned: bilateral mastectomy was my best option, but I wanted to see my radiologist one more time to ask about lumpectomies. I would have to live with my decision a long time. The only way I would have peace was to know all my questions had been answered.

"So what have you decided after your travels?" she said, walking into the examining room.

"I'm thinking about lumpectomies. Tell me how hard detection would be, given the way I scar?" I asked.

She clipped my mammograms on the light box, sighed, and turned to catch my eyes.

"If you want lumpectomies, we're here for you 24/7. We'd do mammograms and ultrasounds every six months for the rest of your life. But I want to tell you about a patient I had like you with cancer in both breasts. She chose lumpectomies and had chemo. She was fine until she developed ovarian cancer a few years later. Once again, she had surgery and did chemo. A few years after that, she developed breast cancer again, and even with careful monitoring, by the time we caught it, it was advanced. She died a few months later. Now I'm not saying that would be you. We can treat this breast cancer, but it's your potential for another breast cancer that I worry about. It's a chance you have to be willing to take."

"Thanks," I said with a sigh because she had crystallized what I had been afraid of. "I'm going to have a bilateral mastectomy."

The decision was made. I was ready to tell the family and friends who had been calling since the news of my diagnosis. I debated about going public with the mastectomies, but I decided if by being open, I could help one woman, even if it was through word of mouth, it would be worth it.

I told my brother-in-law one afternoon when he called. "You've got a great pair, but they ain't worth dying over," was his succinct response.

. . .

All too quickly, the time before surgery passed and suddenly it was the night before. My surgery was scheduled for 2:00 p.m. on September 3—five years and one day to the day my father had died.

By now, my anxiety had channeled into "what ifs?" Ever prepared, I keyed in a one-page list of instructions for my friend Abby, who would wait with Sam [author's husband] during the surgery and then stay with me in the hospital. My cousin Amy was coming from Alabama and would stay until the surgery was over.

The years of experience in information processing showed in my list. It was a decision tree of "if-then" statements. If the surgery goes well, stop here. If the surgery doesn't go well, call Sam's brother—he can be here in three hours, then call my shrink—here's her emergency number, here's the phone number of a friend who is also a shrink if you can't get my shrink, and by the way, here's a bottle of tranquilizers for Sam, if it's real bad.

"Take care of Sam, first. He's got to take care of me. I like to think the doctors will be looking after me," I told Abby as we talked one last time that night. "I left a twenty-dollar bill, so once surgery starts, go feed him. I've packed a kit bag for him—munchies and bottled water, but he'll need to eat. I'm leaving you my cell phone to make calls. Also, promise me you won't tell anybody if I wake up screaming in the recovery room, 'Put 'em back on!'"

There was one more thing left on my list that only my husband and I could do. Although reconstruction was out for the time being, I wanted to document my breasts. That way, down the road, if I wanted reconstruction, a plastic surgeon could see what the originals looked like.

I slipped my shirt off and my husband took pictures. Pictures from all angles—front, side, three-quarter profile. Grabbing a yardstick and standing with my back flat against the bathroom wall, we measured my D-cup breasts, both in a bra and without. From my back to my nipple was exactly twelve inches.

"I love your breasts," Sam said, hugging me when we finished. "But I love *you* so much more."

The next morning, the nurse handed me a pen. I opened my hospital gown and wrote "yes" on both breasts, careful not to come near the mark made earlier that would guide the surgeon to the sentinel lymph node. I remembered writing "no" on my mother's right breast seven years earlier. They couldn't make a mistake with me. I was going to lose both breasts. I was tempted to draw smiley frowns. I said goodbye to my breasts.

A few minutes later, as I climbed on the operating table, I prayed for strength. When the anesthesiologist injected something into my IV line, I closed my eyes. My last conscious thought was: it all does end in the blink of an eye.

They tell me I woke up in the recovery room wailing, "Nodes?" "No nodes," was the response. The wonder drug I'd been given didn't just mask pain but made you forget it. "Nodes?" I couldn't remember from one second to the next. "No nodes?" It finally registered. The sentinel node biopsy had shown my lymph nodes were clean.

. . .

Three days after surgery, I couldn't resist peeling back the edge of a bandage for a peek at where my right breast had been. My breast was replaced by a long row of silver, surgical staples. It looked exactly like a zipper.

I sniffed as I pushed the bandage back in place. No deodorant and I was ripe. I had not had a shower or bath since the morning before my surgery. My hair was so oily even the cats were trying to clean it.

I healed and passed the days. I was so grateful just to be alive that, for the time being, the loss of my breasts seemed insignificant. I had jumped one hurdle in this race—surgery. The next would come with the pathology results.

A week after surgery and it was time for the drains to come out. I felt like a caged animal that had finally been freed. I had not wanted to leave the house until the drains were gone. I threw a shirt on over my T-shirt and drove myself to the doctor's office. Sam followed me there so he could go on to work.

It took just seconds for the surgeon to remove the drains, and I didn't feel a thing. We talked while he was doing it. It would still be a few more days before the final pathology would be in, but he explained the preliminary report.

He told me it was good. The infiltrating tumor in the right breast was only 1.2 centimeters (about the size of a dime) with no sign of vascular or lymphatic involvement, encircled by fibrosis— my body had started to wall it off with scar tissue.

The most frightening part of the pathology was the left breast. One phrase leapt out at me from the report: "A 2.3 centimeter by 1.8 centimeter by 1.8 ill-defined mass. . . . The mass shows finger-like projections." Finger-like projections—tentacles holding an area about the size of a quarter. I shuddered, thinking DCIS had been reaching out to grasp the entire breast.

Walking out of the doctor's office, I decided to own my flatness. If traffic wasn't bad, I could just make the breast-cancer support group meeting at The Wellness Community. I was interested in seeing what other women thought.

"Am I flat or what?" I said as I walked into the meeting room.

"You look great," said the facilitator.

"How long has it been?" asked one of the women.

"A week," I said proudly.

"Lookin' good," said another.

"Nodes?" one woman questioned.

"No nodes," I said.

"Go, girl!" two women said in unison, as we made high-fives.

"You know, I think this is the first time I've seen the top of my stomach since puberty," I said, looking down and laughing.

They all laughed with me. Then one by one they offered their support and encouragement, knowing I was waiting for the final pathology report. The group was emotionally validating. It was safe. These women were further ahead of me in this race and had clocked many laps. I had only jumped the first hurdle: surgery. The next hurdle would come with the final pathology—the question of chemotherapy.

. . .

A week later, the final pathology report was in, and bleary-eyed at 8:00 a.m., Sam and I sat waiting in the oncologist's office.

"How are you healing?" the oncologist asked as she strode into the room.

"I'm good. So what's the verdict? Do I need chemo?" I took a deep breath.

"No," she said, smiling, looking very pleased. "We caught this early enough. It was a small tumor, slow growing, and highly hormone receptive. I want to put you on tamoxifen for five years."

"I'll do it," I said, thrilled. In my mind I sailed over a major hurdle.

So, what is it like losing your breasts? It was the unspoken question from friends and family. It's not uncomfortable, though it feels like my body's center of gravity has shifted. My posture has changed, but not to the shoulders-hunched-in "protective" posture that I had expected. I keep trying to tuck my pelvis under to compensate for the shift but those muscles won't cooperate. With or without prostheses, weighted or not, I think I stand straighter. I have to, and I make a conscious effort to monitor my posture, taking every opportunity to catch my reflection in a mirror. I refuse to become the Hunchback of Notre Dame.

. . .

Before surgery, I had bought a mastectomy bra and a weighted inexpensive pair of swimmer's B-cup prostheses. The bra's cups were seamed, not smooth like my regular bras, and it was heavily reinforced. A soft fabric was sewn to the back of the cup and would hold the prosthesis in place. It had been the best looking of the lot I had seen that day in the mastectomy boutique.

The first time I put on the bra and prostheses, I pulled on a cotton turtle neck, a staple of my fall wardrobe. Examining myself in the mirror, I decided my bust looked like something out of the 1950s—pointy breasts with bra seams showing through the cotton fabric. So not me. And what's worse, the prostheses I had bought were seamed and pointy, too. Their seams came together in the center of the prostheses to form a totally unnatural looking pseudo-erect nipple. Think June Cleaver with erect nipples wearing a tight sweater. Or today, Madonna in a cone bra. But I had bought the pointy guys so I was stuck with them—no returns on prostheses. I would have to make do until I could get a proper pair. Pointy nipples and all, I headed off to the nearest fabric shop. A little soft padding and a cover would work for the time being.

I had my sewing basket out and was working on a prosthesis when Sam came home that evening.

"Ah, my industrious little wife," he chuckled, bending down to kiss me. "Some women do needlepoint, you make boobs." He eyed the prosthesis and plopped down his laptop.

I wasn't shy about letting Sam see my incision scars; in fact, we made a point of checking them periodically in the beginning. The surgeon had been proud of his work—the scars were perfectly symmetrical. My battle scars. Of course, the scars are numb, just like the area under my right arm where the surgeon removed the sentinel node. Nerves were severed and may not grow back.

There's a long mirror in the foyer at the foot of the stairs in our house. Every time I go up or down the steps, I make a point of glancing in it. I check to see if I am hunched over and then correct my posture. The more time that passes since the surgery, the easier it is to maintain a good posture. There's a mirror in the antique sideboard in the kitchen, and I check my reflection there. Are the prostheses riding "high," up near my shoulders, or at an appropriate height?

The only problem has been the bras. I keep reminding myself that I had to experiment to find comfortable bras before the surgery. It's no different now. Problem is I can't tell if a bra works until I've worn it for a day or two, so returns are impossible. After spending fifty dollars for a "seamless, smooth cup" mastectomy bra that was miserably uncomfortable and rode up, I have forsworn mastectomy bras.

I have made an art of studying bras. I have found some that I like and that go with a new pair of prostheses. Rounder, softer, more natural. I'm comfortable.

It's now been several months since my surgery, and I have no regrets about my choice. It may seem odd, but I'm thankful for everything that has happened and especially for the women I've met. Breast cancer creates a powerful bond. I still tear up when I think of all the women who opened their hearts and their shirts to me, as I made a difficult decision.

I heard from one of my cousins recently who had a blip on her mammogram and was worried. She's scheduled for another mammogram and an ultrasound. I hope her doctor is just being hypervigilant because of my diagnosis. But if this turns out to be breast cancer, I envision myself offering her a hand at the starting line of the race, as so many women did for me. Side by side we'll run her first lap together, keeping our eyes on the prize.

Cursed by God?

Two Essays on a Theme

Agnes R. Howard and Nicholas D. Kristof (2007)

Americans generally think of pregnancy and birth in terms of natural processes that call for a healthy diet, doctor's appointments, ultrasounds, and pain management during labor. But as *New York Times* columnist Nicholas D. Kristof reported February 25, giving birth can prove nothing short of disastrous for many women in Africa.

That's because a large number of African women are stricken with obstetric fistula, a complication in childbirth that can leave the woman incontinent and socially isolated. With little recourse to corrective surgery, many of these women come to see themselves as cursed by God.

Obstetric fistula is the development of an abnormal body cavity that can allow uncontrolled leaking of urine and feces. For afflicted women, this can mean social ostracism and eventual abandonment. Their appearance, odor, and likely inability to bear more children can lead to their being shunned and to early death. While worldwide figures for postlabor fistula are hard to come by, partly because of the shame often associated with the condition, the United Nations Population Fund estimates that 2 million women live with the condition. There are a hundred thousand new cases each year.

In 2005, the World Health Organization (WHO) showcased a program called Great Expectations. Its aim was to draw attention to maternal-and-child health worldwide. It traced the lives of six women, from pregnancy through their infant's birth and first year. The women were from Bolivia, Egypt, Ethiopia, Laos, India, and the United Kingdom, and they differed in age, wealth, marital circumstances, and number of previous pregnancies. But their pictures were beautiful and luminous, conveying the women's struggles in pregnancy and their joy in their healthy newborns. The point was to underscore that women should be honored for carrying life and helped to do so safely.

International disparities in maternal morbidity and mortality make clear what a difficult undertaking motherhood can be. According to WHO, about half a million women die from pregnancy complications each year, and another 300 million experience short- or long-term problems related to pregnancy and childbirth.

Since the nineteenth century, obstetric fistula has become so rare in the West that it is almost unknown. As a result, it has dropped from our radar screen as a medical condition that merits public attention. This is unfortunate since it is comparatively easy and inexpensive to prevent or remedy. Dr. Catherine Hamlin, who runs fistula hospitals in Ethiopia, reckons that $450 covers the cost for repair surgery, "high-quality postoperative care, a new dress, and bus fare home." The procedure can mean the difference between a return to normal life and ostracism or even death. At Hamlin's hospitals, the success rate for the surgery is 93 percent.

Kristof faults the Bush administration for cutting spending on global maternal-and-child health programs. And Kristof is not alone. Supporters of population control and abortion have long lamented the reduction of international funds for reproductive health. But maternal-and-child health policy does not consist only of limiting or avoiding babies. Healthy pregnancy and childbirth should also be of interest to policymakers opposed to abortion and population control. Efforts to treat obstetric fistula need not be drawn into the abortion controversy.

As Kristof notes, though, neither Democrats nor Republicans have shown much interest in the problem. He credits the work of several organizations (most of them operating on shoestring budgets) like Hamlin's Fistula Foundation. . . .

Those who pride themselves on their concern for babies *and* women should not forget the plight of millions of African women who suffer from a condition that is easily remedied. Left unassisted, their lives can seem "cursed by God."

***

Meet Simeesh Segaye.

Ms. Simeesh, a warm 21-year-old Ethiopian peasant with a radiant smile, married at 19 and quickly became pregnant. After she had endured two days of obstructed labor, her neighbors carried her to a road and packed her into a bus, but it took another two days to get to the nearest hospital.

By then the baby was dead. And Ms. Simeesh awakened to another horror: She began leaking urine and feces from her vagina, a result of a childbirth injury called obstetric fistula.

Ms. Simeesh's family paid $10 for a public bus to take her to a hospital that could repair her fistula. But the other passengers took one whiff of her and complained vociferously that they shouldn't have to share the vehicle with someone who stinks. The bus driver ordered her off.

Mortified, Ms. Simeesh was crushed again when her husband left her. Her parents built a separate hut for her because of her smell, but they nursed her and brought her food and water.

In that hut, she stayed—alone, ashamed, helpless, bewildered. She barely ate, because the more she ate or drank, the more wastes trickled down her legs.

"I just curled up," she said. "For two years."

Ms. Simeesh was, in a sense, lucky. She wasn't one of the 530,000 women who die each year in pregnancy and childbirth—a number that hasn't declined in 30 years. Here in Ethiopia, a woman has one chance in 14 of dying in childbirth at some point in her life.

For every woman who dies in childbirth worldwide, another 20 are injured. But because the victims are born with three strikes against them—they are poor, rural and female—they are invisible and voiceless, receiving almost no help either from poor countries or from the developed world.

So Ms. Simeesh huddled in a fetal position on the floor of her hut for two years, thinking about killing herself. Finally, last month, Ms. Simeesh's parents sold all their farm animals and paid a driver to take her to the hospital in a vehicle with no other passengers present to complain.

So now Ms. Simeesh is lying in a bed here in the Addis Ababa Fistula Hospital (www.fistulafoundation.org). The hospital is run by an Australian gynecologist, Dr. Catherine Hamlin.

The doctors here will try to repair the fistula, but first they must strengthen Ms. Simeesh, who is skeletal. Her legs have withered and are permanently bent into a fetal position, so that she can't straighten them or move them.

. . . At a time when we're proposing further cuts in our negligible budget for maternal and child health, I was deeply moved by the sight of Ruth Kennedy, a British midwife at the fistula hospital, comforting Ms. Simeesh and bringing a lovely smile to her lips.

"They think they've been cursed by God," Ms. Kennedy explained. "And we tell them that they haven't been cursed by God and that they're beautiful and that the only reason that they got a fistula is because we failed them as health professionals."

My Fight for Birth Control

Margaret Sanger (1931)

Mrs. Sacks was only twenty-eight years old; her husband, an unskilled worker, thirty-two. Three children, aged five, three and one, were none too strong nor sturdy, and it took all the earnings of the father and the ingenuity of the mother to keep them clean, provide them with air and proper food, and give them a chance to grow into decent manhood and womanhood.

Both parents were devoted to these children and to each other. The woman had become pregnant and had taken various drugs and purgatives, as advised by her neighbors. Then, in desperation, she had used some instrument lent to her by a friend. She was found prostrate on the floor amidst the crying children when her husband returned from work. Neighbors advised against the ambulance, and a friendly doctor was called. The husband would not hear of her going to a hospital, and as a little money had been saved in the bank a nurse was called and the battle for that precious life began.

It was in the middle of July. The three-room apartment was turned into a hospital for the dying patient. Never had I worked so fast, never so concentratedly as I did to keep alive that little mother. Neighbor women came and went during the day doing the odds and ends necessary for our comfort. The children were sent to friends and relatives, and the doctor and I settled ourselves to outdo the force and power of an outraged nature.

Never had I known such conditions could exist. July's sultry days and nights were melted into a torpid inferno. Day after day, night after night, I slept only in brief snatches, ever too anxious about the condition of that feeble heart bravely carrying on, to stay long from the bedside of the patient....

At the end of two weeks recovery was in sight, and at the end of three weeks I was preparing to leave the fragile patient to take up the ordinary duties of her life, including those of wifehood and motherhood. Everyone was congratulating her on her recovery. All the kindness of sympathetic and understanding neighbors poured in upon her in the shape of convalescent dishes, soups, custards, and drinks. Still she appeared to be despondent and worried. She seemed to sit apart in her thoughts as if she had no part in these congratulatory messages and endearing welcomes. I thought at first that she still retained some of her unconscious memories and dwelt upon them in her silences.

But as the hour of my departure came nearer, her anxiety increased, and finally with trembling voice she said: "Another baby will finish me, I suppose."

"It's too early to talk about that," I said, and resolved that I would turn the question over to the doctor for his advice. When he came I said: "Mrs. Sacks is worried about having another baby."

"She well might be," replied the doctor, and then he stood before her and said: "Any more such capers, young woman, and there will be no need to call me."

"Yes, yes—I know, Doctor," said the patient with trembling voice, "but," and she hesitated as if it took all of her courage to say it, "*what* can I do to prevent getting that way again?"

"Oh ho!" laughed the doctor good naturedly, "You want your cake while you eat it too, do you? Well, it can't be done." Then, familiarly slapping her on the back and picking up his hat and bag to depart, he said: "I'll tell you the only sure thing to do. Tell Jake to sleep on the roof!"

With those words he closed the door and went down the stairs, leaving us both petrified and stunned.

Tears sprang to my eyes, and a lump came in my throat as I looked at the face before me. It was stamped with sheer horror. I thought for a moment she might have gone insane, but she conquered her feelings, whatever they may have been, and turning to me in desperation said: "He can't understand, can he?—he's a man after all—but you do, don't you? You're a woman and you'll tell me the secret and I'll never tell it to a soul."

She clasped her hands as if in prayer, she leaned over and looked straight into my eyes and beseechingly implored me to tell her something— something *I really did not know*. It was like being on a rack and tortured for a crime one had not committed. To plead guilty would stop the agony; otherwise, the rack kept turning.

I had to turn away from that imploring face. I could not answer her then. I quieted her as best I could. She saw that I was moved by the tears in my eyes. I promised that I would come back in a few days and tell her what she wanted to know. The few simple means of limiting the family like *coitus interruptus* or the condom were laughed at by the neighboring women when told these were the means used by men in the well-to-do families. That was not believed, and I knew such an answer would be swept aside as useless were I to tell her this at such a time.

A little later when she slept I left the house, and made up my mind that I'd keep away from those cases in the future. I felt helpless to do anything at all. I seemed chained hand and foot, and longed for an earthquake or a volcano to shake the world out of its lethargy into facing these monstrous atrocities.

The intelligent reasoning of the young mother— how to *prevent* getting that way again—how sensible, how just she had been—yes, I promised myself I'd go back and have a long talk with her and tell her more, and perhaps she would not laugh but would believe that those methods were all that were really known.

But time flew past, and weeks rolled into months. That wistful, appealing face haunted me day and night. I could not banish from my mind memories of that trembling voice begging so humbly for knowledge she had a right to have. I was about to retire one night three months later when the telephone rang and an agitated man's voice begged me to come at once to help his wife who was sick again. It was the husband of Mrs. Sacks, and I intuitively knew before I left the telephone that it was almost useless to go.

I dreaded to face that woman. I was tempted to send someone else in my place. I longed for an accident on the subway, or on the street—anything to prevent my going into that home. But on I went just the same. I arrived a few minutes after the doctor, the same one who had given her such noble advice. The woman was dying. She was unconscious. She died within ten minutes after my arrival. It was the same result, the same story told a thousand times before—death from abortion. She had become pregnant, had used drugs, had then consulted a five-dollar professional abortionist, and death followed.

The doctor shook his head as he rose from listening for the heart beat. I knew she had already passed on; without a groan, a sigh or recognition of our belated presence she had gone into the Great Beyond as thousands of mothers go every year. I looked at that drawn face now stilled in death. I placed her thin hands across her breast and recalled how hard they had pleaded with me on that last memorable occasion of parting. The gentle woman, the devoted mother, the loving wife had passed on leaving behind her a frantic husband, helpless in his loneliness, bewildered in his helplessness as he paced up and down the room, hands clenching his head, moaning "My God! My God! My God!"

The Revolution came—but not as it has been pictured nor as history relates that revolutions have come. It came in my own life. It began in my very being as I walked home that night after I had closed the eyes and covered with a sheet the body of that little helpless mother whose life had been sacrificed to ignorance.

After I left that desolate house I walked and walked and walked; for hours and hours I kept on, bag in hand, thinking, regretting, dreading to stop;

fearful of my conscience, dreading to face my own accusing soul. At three in the morning I arrived home still clutching a heavy load the weight of which I was quite unconscious.

I entered the house quietly, as was my custom, and looked out the window down upon the dimly lighted, sleeping city. As I stood at the window and looked out, the miseries and problems of that sleeping city arose before me in a clear vision like a panorama: crowded homes, too many children; babies dying in infancy; mothers overworked; baby nurseries; children neglected and hungry—mothers so nervously wrought they would not give the little things the comfort nor care they needed; mothers half sick most of their lives—"always ailing, never failing"; women made into drudges; children working in cellars; children aged six and seven pushed into the labor market to help earn a living; another baby on the way; still another; yet another; a baby born dead—great relief; an older child dies—sorrow, but nevertheless relief—insurance helps; a mother's death—children scattered into institutions; the father, desperate, drunken; he slinks away to become an outcast in a society which has trapped him. . . .

. . . For hours I stood, motionless and tense, expecting something to happen. I watched the lights go out, I saw the darkness gradually give way to the first shimmer of dawn, and then a colorful sky heralded the rise of the sun. I knew a new day had come for me and a new world as well.

It was like an illumination. I could now see clearly the various social strata of our life; all its mass problems seemed to be centered around uncontrolled breeding. There was only one thing to be done: call out, start the alarm, set the heather on fire! Awaken the womanhood of America to free the motherhood of the world! I released from my almost paralyzed hand the nursing bag which unconsciously I had clutched, threw it across the room, tore the uniform from my body, flung it into a corner, and renounced all palliative work forever.

I would never go back again to nurse women's ailing bodies while their miseries were as vast as the stars. I was now finished with superficial cures, with doctors and nurses and social workers who were brought face to face with this overwhelming truth of women's needs and yet turned to pass on the other side. They must be made to see these facts. I resolved that women should have knowledge of contraception. They have every right to know about their own bodies. I would strike out—I would scream from the housetops. I would tell the world what was going on in the lives of these poor women. I *would* be heard. No matter what it should cost. *I would be heard.*

R E A D I N G   **50**

Women of Color and Their Struggle for Reproductive Justice

Jael Silliman, Marlene Gerber Fried, Loretta Ross, and Elena R. Gutiérrez (2004)

REDEFINING REPRODUCTIVE RIGHTS

Women of color in the U.S. negotiate their reproductive lives in a system that combines various interlocking forms of oppression. As activist, scholar, and co-author Loretta Ross puts it: "Our ability to control what happens to our bodies is constantly challenged by poverty, racism, environmental degradation, sexism, homophobia, and injustice in the United States."[1] . . . It is because of these intersections that women of color advance a definition of reproductive rights beyond abortion. Their critique of "choice" does not deny women of color agency; rather, it shows the constraints within which women of color navigate their reproductive lives and organizing.

Early in the abortion rights struggle, . . . , women of color resisted the coercion that masqueraded as "choice." In a 1973 editorial that was supportive of the *Roe v. Wade* Supreme Court decision legalizing abortion, the National Council of Negro Women sounded this important cautionary note:

> The key words are "if she chooses." Bitter experience has taught the black woman that the administration of justice in this country is not colorblind. Black women on welfare have been forced to accept sterilization in exchange for a continuation of relief benefits and others have been sterilized without their knowledge or consent. A young pregnant woman recently arrested for civil rights activities in North Carolina was convicted and told that her punishment would be to have a forced abortion. We must be ever vigilant that what appears on the surface to be a step forward, does not in fact become yet another fetter or method of enslavement.[2]

Twenty-five years later, in her introduction to *Policing the National Body,* co-author Jael Silliman expands their critique:

> The mainstream movement, largely dominated by white women, is framed around choice: the choice to determine whether or not to have children, the choice to terminate a pregnancy, and the ability to make informed choices about contraceptive and reproductive technologies. This conception of choice is rooted in the neoliberal tradition that locates individual rights at its core, and treats the individual's control over her body as central to liberty and freedom. This emphasis on individual choice, however, obscures the social context in which individuals make choices, and discounts the ways in which the state regulates populations, disciplines individual bodies, and exercises control over sexuality, gender, and reproduction.[3]

"Choice" implies a marketplace of options in which women's right to determine what happens to their bodies is legally protected, ignoring the fact that for women of color, economic and institutional constraints often restrict their "choices." For example, a woman who decides to have an abortion out of economic necessity does not experience her decision as a "choice." Native American activist Justine Smith writes: In the Native context, where women often find the only contraceptives available to them are dangerous, where they live in communities in which unemployment rates can run as high as 80 percent, and where their life expectancy can be as low as 47 years, reproductive "choice" defined so narrowly is a meaningless concept.[4]

. . .

FIGHTING FOR THE RIGHT TO HAVE —OR NOT HAVE—CHILDREN

Women of color have had no trouble distinguishing between population control—externally imposed fertility control policies—and voluntary birth control—women making their own decisions about fertility. For women of color, resisting population control while simultaneously claiming their right to bodily self-determination, including the right to contraception and abortion or the right to have children, is at the heart of their struggle for reproductive control.

Although there has never been an official policy to reduce the growth of the US population, controlling fertility has been a persistent feature of other domestic policies directed at men and women of color, sometimes attempting to increase their fertility, but most often aiming to limit it. For example, during the colonization of the United States, Native American women were intentionally given blankets infected with smallpox. Population control during slavery took the form of brutal and coercive efforts to increase African American women's reproduction, with slave owners using rape and forced marriages to achieve this end. However, since then, population control efforts have been intended to prevent women of color from having children. Eugenics laws, immigration restrictions, sterilization abuses, targeted family planning, and welfare reform have all been vehicles for population control.

Since the 19th century, all of these population control strategies have been employed using racist ideologies as justifications. For example, efforts to maintain white "racial purity" underlie private and publicly funded efforts to control the fertility of those deemed "unfit" and "defective," understood by policy-makers to mean poor or not white. The mid-20th century saw advocates for domestic and international population control promulgating alarmist time bomb theories with strong racist overtones and raising fears among whites of people of color overrunning the Western world. In 1970, President Nixon supported establishing federal family planning services by appealing to whites' fears about population explosions that would make governance of the world in general—and inner cities in particular—difficult. Nixon's policy advisors assembled statistics that pointed to a "bulge" in the number of black Americans between the ages of five and nine, claiming the cohort was 25 percent larger than ten years before.[5] Population alarmists warned that this group of youngsters soon entering their teens was "an age group with problems that can create social turbulence."[6]

Recognizing the relationship between numbers of people and political power,[7] white politicians favored "helping" racial minorities limit their fertility. Determined to lower population growth in African American and Latino communities, many pro-segregation Southern politicians—both Republicans and Democrats—who had formerly opposed family planning, suddenly favored it as a way of regulating the reproduction of these groups. Opposition to welfare and the commitment to reduce welfare rolls by supplying free birth control services to poor women were joined in a race and class direct social policy. In one of the more overt expressions of this position, Leander Perez, a Louisiana judge, revealed in 1965 the link between coercive birth control and racism: "The best way to hate a nigger is to hate him before he is born."[8]

In the 1980s and 90s, fertility control remained a centerpiece of the nation's welfare program and

continued to undermine the rights of low-income women and women of color to have children. Federal welfare reform policies such as family caps, institutionalized in President Clinton's 1996 Personal Responsibility and Work Opportunity Reconciliation Act (PRWORA), deny additional benefits to women who have more children while receiving public assistance. Women of color in the economic justice and reproductive rights movements have criticized family caps and other aspects of welfare reform, such as marriage promotion and funding for abstinence-only sexual education. These policies punish women for being poor by attacking their fertility while not offering any substantive relief from structural poverty.[9]

Although rooted in racism, population control programs did at times, at least in part, meet the needs and desires of women of color for birth control, thus creating a complicated political dynamic. This was the case when Nixon's federally funded family planning and contraceptive program was created in 1970s.[10] African American communities provided the majority of family planning clinic clients in the Deep South because, since slavery, controlling one's own fertility had been associated with upward mobility. Despite the racist motivations of some proponents of the family planning–birth control movement, anthropologist Martha Ward, who researched federal population policies, notes: "Family planning became synonymous with the civil rights of poor women to medical care."[11]

Nevertheless, attempts to use family planning clinics to limit the population growth of communities of color were so blatant that they aroused a strong response from Nationalist movements that came to the conclusion that birth control and abortion were genocide. African American and Chicana women supporting birth control and abortion rights as part of their civil rights activism continually faced opposition from Nationalists who felt that the best way to fight racism and xenophobia was to encourage black and Latino communities to expand their population base. Thus, while women of color frequently worked with mainstream and Nationalist civil rights organizations, they had to criticize these organizations when they supported positions hostile to reproductive freedom.[12] In 1970, Frances Beal, coordinator of the Black Women's Liberation Committee of the Student Non-Violent Coordinating Committee (SNCC), made clear her support for both reproductive rights and civil rights:

> We are not saying that black women should not practice birth control. Black women have the right and the responsibility to determine when it is [in] the interest of the struggle to have children or not to have them, and this right must not be relinquished to anyone. It is also her right and responsibility to determine when it is in her own best interests to have children, how many she will have and how far apart. The lack of the availability of safe birth control methods, the forced sterilization practices, and the inability to obtain legal abortions are all symptoms of a decadent society that jeopardizes the health of black women (and thereby the entire black race) in its attempts to control the very life processes of human beings.[13]

Almost 20 years later, in 1989, activist and scholar Dorothy Roberts encountered the same issues when she spoke about threats to abortion rights at a neighborhood meeting, and a man in the audience took her to task: "He said that reproductive rights was a 'white woman's issue,' and advised me to stick to traditional civil rights concerns, such as affirmative action, voting rights, and criminal justice."[14]

However, women of color have refused to divide civil rights from reproductive rights. Rather, they have transformed the fight for both by creating an ever expanding comprehensive reproductive justice agenda. Their agenda includes fighting against two of the methods frequently employed by the racially motivated family planning apparatus that have undermined women of color's right to have children: coercive sterilization and invasive long-term birth control technologies.

In the 20th century, Native American, Mexican American,[15] African American, and Puerto Rican women and other women of color were denied the right to have children through systematic and widespread sterilization abuses[16] practiced by the U.S. government and by private doctors (who were more often than not subsidized by the U.S. government). Women of color responded by taking up the fight against sterilization abuse. Native American, African American, and Latina groups documented and publicized sterilization abuses in their communities in the 1960s and 70s, showing that women had been sterilized without their knowledge or consent. They demonstrated that women who spoke only Spanish were asked to sign consent forms in English, and sometimes pressured to do so during labor and childbirth. Native American women were given hysterectomies by Indian Health Service without their permission.

In the 1970s, a group of women, which included Dr. Helen Rodríguez-Trías, founded the Committee to End Sterilization Abuse (CESA) to stop this racist population control policy begun by the federal government in the 1940s—a policy that had resulted in the sterilization of over one-third of all women of childbearing age in Puerto Rico.[17] CESA helped to create the Advisory Committee on Sterilization, a coalition of groups that developed regulations to protect women using public hospitals in New York City.[18]

Native American and African American women were also active on this issue. Norma Jean Serena, of Creek-Shawnee ancestry, filed the first civil suit of its kind in 1973, addressing sterilization abuse as a civil rights violation.[19] In 1974, another successful lawsuit advanced by the National Welfare Rights Organization and the Southern Poverty Law Center demanded restitution for the involuntary sterilization of the Relf sisters. These 12- and 14-year-old African American sisters were sterilized in Alabama without their parents' knowledge or consent.[20] By 1978, the federal government was forced to establish guidelines regarding sterilization. These included required waiting periods and authorization forms in a language understood by the woman, to prevent women from being sterilized without their knowledge or informed consent.[21]

Despite these efforts, new forms of coercion have arisen. In the 1990s, the Committee on

Women, Population, and the Environment (CWPE) initiated a campaign to raise awareness about and to challenge CRACK (Children Requiring a Caring Kommunity), now called Project Prevention, a privately funded organization that pays women who are addicted to drugs $200 to be sterilized or to use long-acting contraceptives. Although private, CRACK is in fact implementing the same racist agenda manifest in the government policies previously discussed, namely, preventing "undesirable" women, overwhelmingly women of color, from having children.[22] Such continuing reproductive abuses of women of color lead CWPE to argue that a meaningful reproductive health agenda must include explicit opposition to policies that are disproportionately directed at controlling the reproductive capacity of women of color. The rights to bodily and reproductive autonomy are fundamental human rights.

While the resistance of women of color to oppressive reproductive restrictions has been focused on the government and private population control organizations, they have also had to contend with those white pro-choice activists in the mainstream movements for contraception and abortion who have been unable see how what may be reproductive freedom for them is reproductive tyranny for others. The mainstream movements have not linked policies and practices dressed in the benign language of family planning and welfare reform to restrictions on reproductive freedom. Thus, they were not the allies of women of color and sometimes were even at odds with women of color struggling for racial, economic, and reproductive justice.

Activist and philosopher Angela Davis wrote about this failure to confront racism:

> Birth control—individual choice, safe contraceptive methods, as well as abortions when necessary—is a fundamental prerequisite for the emancipation of women. Since the right of birth control is obviously advantageous to women of all classes and races, it would appear that even vastly dissimilar women's groups would have attempted to unite around this issue. In reality, however, the birth control movement has seldom succeeded in uniting women of different social backgrounds, and rarely have the movement's leaders popularized the genuine concerns of working-class women. Moreover, arguments advanced by birth control advocates have sometimes been based on blatantly racist premises.[23]

The fact that these views generally went unchallenged—and were sometimes embraced or not even recognized as racist—by the mainstream movements meant that women of color who opposed population control could not rely on these movements to counter such policies.

Further, Davis notes that the priorities of women of color are different from those of white women because of their different experiences. Thus, the reproductive rights agendas are shaped by the dynamics of class and race. The failure of white women to address their internalized racism and classism, and to appreciate the power of race and class dynamics to influence activist agendas, has sometimes had disastrous political results—specifically when initiatives promoted by the mainstream movement have actually turned out to limit the reproductive rights of women of color and poor women.[24]

For example, in the 1970s, when the major pro-choice and feminist organizations did not join women of color in demanding sterilization guidelines it was because their experiences with sterilization were radically different. While women of color were targets for coercive sterilization, white middle-class women had trouble persuading doctors to perform voluntary sterilizations, and often had to obtain permission from medical committees to do so.[25] Pro-choice organizations perceived guidelines regulating sterilization as infringing on women's choices, not enhancing them. While the National Organization for Women (NOW) did not take a position on the issue, the National Abortion and Reproductive Rights Action League (NARAL)[26] and other groups that had traditionally supported abortion rights, such as Planned Parenthood, Zero Population Growth, and the Association for Voluntary Surgical Contraception, opposed the sterilization regulations on the grounds that they deprived women of "freedom of choice." In general, mainstream white feminists believed the guidelines were unnecessary and paternalistic and interfered with the doctor-patient relationship.[27]

More recently, we have seen a similar divergence in views regarding hormonal contraception. Population groups and mainstream pro-choice organizations enthusiastically greeted the development of Norplant and Depo-Provera as an expansion of reproductive choice for women. Depo-Provera injections were promoted in their joint campaigns as "highly effective, long-acting . . . and [offering] privacy to the user since the woman has no need to keep contraceptive supplies at home."[28] Their endorsement came despite the risk that Depo-Provera causes menstrual cycle irregularities, principally amenorrhea (the absence of periods), and increases the risk of endometrial and breast cancer.[29]

In contrast, along with progressive women's health groups around the world, women of color have been more skeptical of provider-controlled hormonal methods of contraception whose side effects and risks were unclear.[30] For example, they have criticized Norplant (subdermal implants) and Depo-Provera (injectibles), the two methods most aggressively marketed to young African American, Latina, and Native American women. In 1991, NBWHP [National Black Women's Health Project], NAWHERC [Native American Women's Health Education Resource Center], and NLHO [National Latina Health Organization] issued warnings of the potential for Norplant abuses.[31] Their concerns were validated merely two days after the contraceptive implant was approved by the United States Food and Drug Administration, when the *Philadelphia Inquirer* newspaper published an editorial advocating its use "as a tool in the fight against black poverty."[32] Although the newspaper later apologized for its racist editorial, judges and state legislatures continued to advocate for the use of Norplant among disadvantaged women.

There was a similar although much less publicized division in 1988, when mainstream pro-choice groups developed a campaign to introduce mifepristone into the United States. Also known as RU 486, mifepristone is taken orally and is a non-surgical option for ending a pregnancy up to 49 days after the beginning of the last menstrual period. These organizations were not concerned that mifepristone had not been sufficiently tested on women of color in the United States, nor was attention given to the fact that women of color were less likely to have access to the follow-up care that is necessary for safe usage. The major pro-choice groups were universally enthusiastic about the campaign. Any criticisms that there might be a problematic side to mifepristone tended to be discouraged or dismissed as playing into the hands of the anti-abortion movement. It seemed that once again, in the drive to expand choice, women of color and their particular concerns were being ignored.

. . .

IDENTITY-BASED ORGANIZING

. . .

Women of color understood that white women and men of color, even with the best of intentions, could not speak to the uniqueness of their issues or represent the authenticity of their experiences. Women of color needed to claim leadership for themselves. By establishing organizations that were racially and ethnically specific and separate from white organizations, women of color created the visions and gained the support necessary to raise the visibility of their reproductive health concerns in their communities and in the broader society. Placing race and class at the center of their reproductive freedom agenda has allowed many of the groups studied to recruit supporters from other social justice movements, such as the civil rights, immigrant rights, economic justice, and environmental justice movements. This has also led to building support bases in communities of color for reproductive health issues. By grounding their organizing in community-identified needs, women of color do not have to isolate or separate themselves from the day-to-day concerns of their communities.

Women of color are subjected to racist and sexist stereotypes which send messages that they should not be in charge of their own reproductive and sexual destinies. When women of color internalize these stereotypes, it is damaging psychologically and a barrier to their activism. Groups based on racial and gender identities help participants overcome important barriers to activism by combating their internalized oppression. Toni Bond, founder and executive director of African American Women Evolving, writes about the toll of internalized oppression:

> Many of us have so internalized [racial] oppression that it has transformed into a self-hatred and seeps into and impedes even our ability to work together collectively, resulting in organizational upheaval and our further disenfranchisement. . . . So emotionally bruised are women of color from racist oppression and our internalization of that oppression that we have trouble letting our guards down to share personal stories about our experiences around health or any other issue.[33]

Eveline Shen, director of Asians and Pacific Islanders for Reproductive Health, echoes Bond's point when she talks about the need to confront stereotypes just to make activism possible. She says, "Asian women are supposed to be docile and obedient. This model is not compatible with fighting for women's rights."[34] For women of color, challenging these myths and stereotypes is part of the process of reclaiming their humanity and redefining their own identities.

Women from all four racial/ethnic groups have faced and challenged racial stereotyping. For African American women, the images of Mammy and Sapphire emphasize maternalism and promiscuity.[35] Asian women are also portrayed in contradictory ways, as concubines, prostitutes, or model minorities, deriving unfair advantage from affirmative action.[36] Racist descriptions represent the Native American woman as a willing squaw, an alcoholic, or "a brown lump of drudge."[37] Reservation Indians are said to "wallow in welfare, food stamps, free housing and medical care, affirmative action programs, and gargantuan federal cash payments."[38] Latinas are stereotyped as oversexed "hot tamales" or as illegal immigrants wanting to have babies in the United States so they can obtain citizenship and welfare benefits. Some social scientists describe Latinas as "ideally submissive, unworldly, and chaste" or "at the command of the husband who keeps her as he would a coveted thing, free from the contacts of the world, subject to his passions, ignorant of life."[39]

These myths and stereotypes are part of the larger system of oppression and play an important part in perpetuating it. Characterizing women of color as sexually promiscuous and too irresponsible to make their own reproductive decisions and be good mothers serves as the rationale for enacting and legitimizing discriminatory policies, programs, and laws. For example, the 1950s image of the lazy "welfare queen" was rejuvenated during the 1970s and 80s to fuel cutbacks in public assistance. President Reagan referred to a woman on welfare as a "pig at the trough."[40] Images of hyper-fertile Mexican women crossing the border to bear their children on United States soil so that their children could secure social benefits helped to pass restrictive legislation such as Proposition 187 in California, which denied undocumented immigrants educational and health benefits.[41] Continuing the assaults against Latinos, Harvard professor Samuel Huntington's new book, *Who Are We? The Challenges to America's National Identity*,[42] suggests that Hispanic immigrants are undermining the "greatness" of the United States by diluting our national identity as an "Anglo-Protestant" country, a diatribe offered by someone who has been a lifelong Democrat.

Reproductive rights organizing by women of color challenges both the stereotypes and the policies that undermine reproductive autonomy. Through activism, women of color assert the value and dignity of their lives, the lives of their children, and their roles as mothers.

NOTES

1. Loretta Ross et al., "Just Choices: Women of Color, Reproductive Health, and Human Rights," in *Policing the National Body*, ed. Jael Silliman and

Anannya Bhattacharjee (Cambridge, MA: South End Press, 2002), 147.

2. *Black Woman's Voice* 2, no. 2 (Jan/Feb, 1973).

3. Jael Silliman, "Introduction," in *Policing,* x–xi.

4. Justine Smith quoted in Andrea Smith "Better Dead Than Pregnant: The Colonization of Native Women's Reproductive Health," in *Policing,* 141.

5. Thomas B. Littlewood, *The Politics of Population Control* (Notre Dame, IN: University of Notre Dame Press, 1977), 56.

6. Ibid.

7. Ibid., 3.

8. Martha C. Ward, *Poor Women, Powerful Men: America's Great Experiment in Family Planning* (Boulder, CO: Westview Press, 1986), 31.

9. COLOR, *The Impact of Welfare Reform on Latina Reproductive Health,* Policy Position Paper (Denver: COLOR, September 2003).

10. A series of legislative reforms set the stage for federal support for family planning. Under the Economic Opportunity Act of 1964, known as the War on Poverty and launched by President Johnson, federal funds were used to increase the number of people eligible for public assistance. The Office of Economic Opportunity (OEO) was created to provide grants for public and private agencies for social programs to address poverty. When Congress passed the Voting Rights Act of 1965, which made it possible for more African Americans and Latinos to participate in the political process, some elected officials felt it was urgently necessary to minimize the impact and effectiveness of minority voters. The 1965 Immigration Reform Act, which removed the national-origins quotas on immigration, also added to the pressure to limit minority political strength. The first direct OEO grant for family planning services went to Corpus Christi, Texas, in 1964 to target low-income Mexican American families. Despite some congressional opposition, OEO support for family planning grew rapidly under the Johnson administration. Even more importantly, in terms of available funding, the Social Security Act governing Aid for Families with Dependent Children (AFDC) was modified to require that at least 6 percent of all funds available for maternal and infant care be spent on family planning. Moreover, states were authorized to purchase services from nongovernmental providers, such as Planned Parenthood, which created open-ended funding by the federal government for family planning.

11. Ward, *Poor Women, Powerful Men,* xiii.

12. For example, in the late 1980s when leading civil rights organizations wanted to expand support for affirmative action in the Civil Rights Restoration Act legislation, they compromised with Catholic anti-abortion groups who wanted Catholic colleges and universities exempted from the provisions of the legislation that would have made it illegal to discriminate against women faculty and students who supported abortion rights. For more on this see Loretta Ross's article "Blacks and Fertility" in the magazine of the Congressional Black Caucus, *Point of View,* Winter 1988, 12.

13. Frances Beal, "Double Jeopardy: To Be Black and Female," in *The Black Woman,* ed. Toni Cade (New York: Signet, 1970) quoted in Jennifer Nelson, *Women of Color and the Reproductive Rights Movement* (New York: New York University Press, 2003), 80.

14. Dorothy Roberts, *Killing the Black Body* (New York: Pantheon Books, 1997), 5.

15. Elena R. Gutiérrez, "Policing Pregnant Pilgrims: Situating the Sterilization Abuse of Mexican Origin Women in Los Angeles County," in *Women, Health and Nation: Canada and the United States Post–WW II,* ed. Molly Ladd-Taylor et al. (Toronto: McGill-Queens University Press, 2003).

16. See chapter two of *Killing the Black Body* and Angela Davis's chapter "Women Under Attack: Victories, Backlash and the Fight for Reproductive Freedom," in her *Women, Race, and Class* (New York: Vintage Books, 1983).

17. Davis, *Women, Race, and Class,* 14.

18. Nelson, *Women of Color,* 140–143.

19. Sally Torpy, "Endangered Species: Native American Women's Struggle for Their Reproductive Rights and Racial Identity: 1970–1990" (master's thesis, University of Nebraska, 1998), 38.

20. Nelson, *Women of Color,* 66–67.

21. Suzanne Staggenborg, *The Pro-Choice Movement: Organization and Activism in the Abortion Conflict* (New York: Oxford University Press, 1991), 111; Roberts, *Killing the Black Body,* 95; Susan E. Davis and the Committee for Abortion Rights and Against Sterilization Abuse (CARASA), *Women Under Attack: Victories, Backlash and the Fight for Reproduction Freedom* (Boston: South End Press, 1988).

22. Judith A. M. Scully, "Killing the Black Community: A Commentary on the United States War on Drugs," in *Policing,* 55–80.

23. Davis, *Women, Race, and Class,* 204–206.

24. While in this [reading] we focus on race and class, we acknowledge that sexual orientation, disability, and age also play critical roles in determining a woman's reproductive experience. It is important to note that historically the struggle for abortion rights had significant participation and leadership from lesbians who were not "out" in the organizations. Issues of sexual orientation did not become explicitly part of the pro-choice agenda until the late 1980s and still have not been fully incorporated into the pro-choice agenda. Neither the pro-choice nor the disability rights movement has consolidated around a position on "choice" and disability, and young people continue to struggle for recognition of their issues and for leadership in the mainstream movement.

25. Lucinda Cisler, "Unfinished Business: Birth Control and Women's Liberation," in *Sisterhood Is Powerful: An Anthology of Writings from the Women's Liberation Movement,* ed. Robin Morgan (New York: Vintage Books, 1970), 255–256.

26. NARAL has gone through three name incarnations. It was founded in 1969 as the National Association for the Repeal of Abortion Laws. With the legalization of abortion in 1973, it became the National Abortion and Reproductive Rights Action League. In 2003, it became NARAL Pro-Choice America. This book uses all three depending on which time period is referenced.

27. Davis and CARASA, *Women Under Attack,* 29.

28. Robert Hatcher, ed., *Contraceptive Technology: International Edition* (Atlanta, GA: Printed Matter Inc., 1989), 301.

29. Ibid.

30. Women and Pharmaceuticals Project, Women's Health Action Foundation, and WEMOS, *Norplant: Under Her Skin* (Delft, The Netherlands: Eburon Press, 1993), 3.

31. Ibid., 108.

32. Asoka Bandarage, *Women, Population and Global Crisis* (London: Zed Books, 1997), 85.

33. Toni Bond, "Barriers Between Black Women and the Reproductive Rights Movement," *Political Environments* 8 (Winter/Spring 2001): 1–5.

34. Eveline Shen, interview by Marlene Gerber Fried, January 2001, APIRH office, Oakland, CA.

35. Deborah Gray White, *Too Heavy a Load: Black Women in Defense of Themselves, 1894–1994* (New York: W. W. Norton, 1999), 19.

36. Huping Ling, *Surviving on the Gold Mountain: A History of Chinese American Women and Their Lives* (New York: State University of New York Press, 1998), 167.

37. Shirley Hill Witt, "Native Women Today: Sexism and the Indian Woman," *Civil Rights Digest* 6 (Spring 1974): 29.

38. Center for Democratic Renewal, "Indian Issues and Anti-Indian Organizing," in *When Hate Groups Come to Town: A Handbook of Effective Community Responses* (Atlanta: CDR, 1992), 138.

39. Adaljiza Sosa Riddell, "Chicanas and El Movimiento," in *Chicana Feminist Thought: The Basic Historical Writings,* ed. Alma M. Garcia (New York: Routledge, 1997), 93.

40. Found in Solinger, *Beggars and Choosers,* 156; originally quoted in Johnnie Tillmon, "Welfare Is a Woman's Issue," *Liberation News Service,* February 26, 1972, reprinted in *America's Working Women,* ed. Rosalyn Baxandall, Linda Gordon, and Susan Reverby (New York: Random House, 1976), 357.

41. Elena R. Gutiérrez, "Policing Pregnant Pilgrims."

42. Samuel Huntington, *Who Are We? The Challenges to America's National Identity* (New York: Simon & Schuster, 2004).

The Way It Was

Eleanor Cooney (2004)

In 1959, when I was a precocious smarty-pants still in grade school, I wrote a fake letter to Doris Blake, the *New York Daily News* advice columnist. I pretended to be a teenage girl "in trouble." I spun a tale of a liquor-soaked prom night and passing out in the back of a car. I included a cast of entirely fictional characters—a worthless boyfriend, a mentally unstable mother, a strict, brutal father. I ended my letter with: "Now I think I am pregnant. Please help me. I am desperate."

I'm not sure what I expected, but my letter was not printed, and no advice was forthcoming. The silence was utter. Possibly Miss Blake, like Nathanael West's Miss Lonelyhearts, had a drawer where such letters were tossed. If so, the other letters in that drawer were no doubt a lot like mine— except that they were not written by wiseass children. They were real. And for the writers of those letters, the silence was real. And I remember thinking: *Gee,* what if I really were that girl I made up? What would I do?

One summer night some years later, when I was not quite 18, I got knocked up. There was nothing exciting or memorable or even interestingly sordid about the sex. I wasn't raped or coerced, nor was I madly in love or drunk or high. The guy was another kid, actually younger than I, just a friend, and it pretty much happened by default. We were horny teenagers with nothing else to do.

Nature, the ultimate unsentimental pragmatist, has its own notions about what constitutes a quality liaison. What nature wants is for sperm and egg to meet, as often as possible, whenever and wherever possible. Whatever it takes to expedite that meeting is fine with nature. If it's two people with a bassinet and a nursery all decorated and waiting with a shelf full of baby books, fine. If it's a 12-year-old girl who's been married off to a 70-year-old Afghan chieftain, fine. And if it's a couple of healthy young oafs like my friend and me, who knew perfectly well where babies come from but just got stupid for about 15 minutes, that's fine, too.

In the movies, newly pregnant women trip, fall down the stairs, and "lose the baby." Ah. If only it were that easy. In real life, once that egg is fertilized and has glided on down the fallopian tube, selected its nesting place, and settled in, it's notoriously secure, behaves like visiting royalty. Nature doesn't give a fig about the hostess's feelings of hospitality or lack of them. If the zygote's not defective, and the woman is in good health, almost nothing will shake it loose. Anyone who's been pregnant and didn't want to be knows this is so.

On November 5, 2003, three decades after *Roe v. Wade* established a woman's constitutional right to terminate a pregnancy, President George W. Bush signed the Partial Birth Abortion Ban bill into law. We've all seen the photograph: The president sits at a table with a modest little smile on his lips. Nine guys—senators and congressmen—stand behind him, watching that signature go onto the paper, giddy grins on their faces. They look almost goofy with joy.

Two of these happy fellows are actually Democrats: Jim Oberstar and Bart Stupak. The rest are Republicans to their marrow: the bill's sponsor, Rick Santorum, as well as Steve Chabot, Orrin Hatch, Henry Hyde, Tom DeLay, Mike DeWine, and Dennis Hastert.

Be assured that it's not just "partial-birth" abortion they're so happy about passing a law against. It's all the law heralds. Like some ugly old wall-to-wall carpeting they've been yearning to get rid of, they finally, *finally* loosened a little corner of *Roe*. Now they can start to rip the whole thing up, roll it back completely, and toss it in the dumpster.

For with the PBAB, Bush and Co. have achieved the first federal legal erosion of *Roe v. Wade* since its adoption in 1973. *Roe* states that a woman may terminate a pregnancy up to the point of "viability," approximately 24 weeks. After that, states may prohibit or restrict abortion, but exceptions must be made to preserve "the life or health of the woman." The PBAB has been around the block before—in 1995, 1997, 1999, and 2000. What stopped it before was always the debate over allowances for women's health. President Clinton vetoed it three times because it disallowed exceptions to prevent serious disabling injury to the woman. But when the bill came up again in 2002, allowances for prevention of disabling injury to the mother were left out, as were those for rape and incest. A "partial-birth" abortion would be permitted only as a last resort to save the mother's life, or if the fetus was already dead. In other words, the risk of permanent injury to the woman if she proceeds with the pregnancy is not a good enough reason to perform one—not in Santorum's book. She has to be literally on death's doorstep. A couple of Democrats tried to offer an amendment that brought up that pesky women's health issue again. The bill's authors objected. Women and their doctors will just use the amendment as a loophole! Chabot worried it would create "a phony ban" and Santorum predicted it would be defeated. It was.

One Democratic senator proposed a nonbinding resolution, expressing ". . . the sense of the Senate that . . . *Roe v. Wade* was appropriate and secures an important constitutional right and should not be overturned." This amendment passed in the Senate by a 52-46 vote. The House version of the PBAB lacked any such amendment. In conference, the Republicans quickly took care of that feeble bleat on behalf of *Roe:* They simply deleted it. When the bill landed on Bush's desk, the resolution to reaffirm *Roe* was gone.

What, you might ask, is "partial-birth" abortion? Most of us know that the term is not a medical one. Invented by the pro-life folks in the last decade or so, it's a vague reference to "intact dilation and extraction," or D&X. Introduced in 1992, D&X is a variation on a similar, well-established second- (and sometimes third-) term procedure—"dilation and evacuation," or D&E—used after the fetus has grown too large to be vacuumed or scraped out in a simple D&C, or "dilation and curettage."

In a D&E, the fetus is usually dismembered inside the uterus and extracted in pieces. Old obstetrics books from as far back as the 1700s have disquieting illustrations of the various tools of yore used for fetal dismemberment. Nowadays, powerful gripping forceps are used, making the procedure much less dangerous for the women.

The D&X was developed with the same objective. An inherent hazard of D&E—aside from potential damage by the instruments themselves and the risk of leaving tissue behind, increasing the chances of infection—is that fetal bones begin to calcify at about 13 weeks. As they are broken up, the sharp bone ends can puncture, scrape, and perforate. Hence the "intact" dilation and extraction. The fetus is brought out whole instead of being pulled apart bit by bit. The head is punctured and then collapsed by suction or compression so that it will fit through the partially dilated cervix. The fetus is dead, but in one piece. This, specifically, is the procedure the PBAB has sought to criminalize—when the fetus is killed while its body is outside the uterus, therefore "partially born."

Under the PBAB of 2003, a D&X would be permitted only to save the woman's life or if the fetus is dead. It would require a girl who'd been impregnated by her uncle, father, or brother, and who, out of shame, ignorance, and fear had hidden her condition until it was obvious to the world, to carry the fetus to term and give birth. If a woman discovers, late in her pregnancy, that the fetus has, say, anencephaly—a brain stem but no actual brain—then she must carry it to term, give birth, and let it die on its own.

Since lurid descriptions of partial-birth abortion have been so effective in rallying support for the bill, perhaps some balance is needed. I've read and heard hundreds of accounts of pre-*Roe* abortion, and there was a wide range of danger, squalor, sanitary conditions, provider skill, follow-up care. The well-heeled and well-connected often flew to Puerto Rico or Sweden and checked into clinics. Of the ones who couldn't do that, some were lucky enough to find competent, compassionate doctors. Some were treated kindly and recovered without incident. The other extreme was pain, terror, and death worthy of the Inquisition. A typical picture emerges, though, and it matches up just about perfectly with a story told to me by a woman I know.

After a date rape (by a "poet") during a trip to Paris in 1967 when she was 23, she found herself pregnant. She tried the usual "remedies"—scalding hot baths, violent jumping, having someone walk on her belly. When she got home to Minnesota, she was two months along. A doctor friend there said he couldn't help her himself, but sent her to a local prostitute who did abortions.

The prostitute had her own speculum. The procedure was done on the prostitute's bed: The catheter was inserted through the cervix and left there. After four days of high fever, chills, bleeding, and passing big chunks of tissue, she landed in the hospital. They said her uterus was perforated, that she had acute peritonitis and an "incomplete" abortion. She was given a huge dose of penicillin and treated as if she were some sort of contemptible lower-life form. The emergency-room doctor snarled, "What have you done to yourself?" Later, she realized that the first doctor—her friend—had known all along that she'd probably get desperately ill. Only then could a hospital legally give her a D&C.

She recovered—sterile, violently allergic to penicillin, and so "paralyzed and ashamed" by the experience that she stayed away from men for four years. Who says deterrence doesn't work?

Then there's the famous 1964 police photograph of a woman's corpse on a motel-room floor in Connecticut. She's kneeling naked, facedown as if to Mecca, legs bent to her chest, bloody towels bunched under her. The case had made local headlines, but the picture wasn't seen by the

general public until *Ms. Magazine* ran it in a 1973 article lauding the ruling of *Roe v. Wade.* Details emerged about the woman's life and death: She was 27, married with two young daughters, but estranged from her violent husband. Her lover had performed the abortion, using borrowed instruments and a textbook. When she started hemorrhaging, he panicked, fled the motel, and left her there.

Compared to those two women, I got off easy. By the middle of September, I'd missed two periods and my cigarettes were tasting peculiar. I was bound for freshman year at college in Boston, though, so I just ignored the facts and went off to school. It took a third missed period and almost throwing up in the backseat of a car packed with kids to penetrate my adolescent thickheadedness.

I had a savvy friend in New York, Kat, who only dated rich older men. I figured she'd be the one to call. Soon a long ride on buses and trains took me out to a house in a Boston suburb. The doctor's wife answered the door. There was no waiting room, no magazines, no other patients. The house was completely ordinary, perhaps a touch rundown. She showed me into a room off the front hall and vanished.

Except for a small sink, the office was just a regular room, a parlor, with green walls and venetian blinds and a worn rug on the floor. A tall, battered, glass-doored porcelain cabinet stood in a corner. Through the glass, I could see on the shelves a dusty disorderly jumble of stethoscopes, hypodermics, bottles, little rubber hammers, basins, forceps, clamps, speculums, wads of cotton. There were rust stains in the sink and a tired old examining table.

The doctor, a little nervous man with glasses and a bald head, came in. I explained my problem. I have to examine you, he said. And he said: Everything has to be clean, very clean. He went to the sink and washed and washed his hands.

He finished and stood there without saying anything. His eyes were sort of glittering behind his glasses, and he acted as if I was supposed to know what to do next. I glanced around for a gown, but he was looking impatient, so I just took off my underwear and climbed onto the table.

He didn't bother with a glove. He poked around a while, then told me that I'd waited too long, I was too far gone, it would be too risky for him, and that would be $25.

And I was back out on the suburban street, the door shut firmly behind me.

Kat told me to come to New York and bring $500. I slept on the couch in her apartment. Kat's roommate, Elaine, gave me the address of a doctor over in Jersey City. I took a train and walked 10 blocks to a street of old brownstones, some of them with their windows boarded up. There had been no calling ahead for an "appointment"; you were supposed to just show up.

This doctor had a waiting room, with dark walls and a very high ceiling, the front room of the brownstone. It was full of people, facing each other along opposite walls, sitting in old, cracked, brown leather parlor chairs with stand-up ashtrays here and there, like in a bus station. A set of tall sliding wooden doors stood closed between that room and the next. Everyone was smoking, including me. The air was blue.

Several Puerto Rican–looking women chattered away in Spanish and seemed perfectly cheerful. There were a few men, who looked as if they might be accompanying somebody, and some more women who sat silent and staring.

And there was a couple who stood out like a pair of borzoi among street mutts: a man and woman, tall, slim, expensively dressed WASPS, faces grim, looking like people who'd taken a seriously wrong turn off the highway. I remember feeling sorry for them.

The tall wooden doors separated. A potbellied man in shirtsleeves who resembled Harpo Marx minus the fun stood there. His eyes moved around the room. He looked at the Puerto Rican women, the tall WASP woman, then at me, then the WASP woman again, considered for a moment, turned back to me, and pointed.

You, he said.

I got up and went in. He slid the doors shut. We were alone.

The windows in here had been nailed over with plywood, and the floor was ancient linoleum. There was a smell of insecticide. Boxes and bundles of paper were piled high in the dim corners and on a rolltop desk, and along the walls were shelves crammed messily with stethoscopes, hypodermics, speculums. The examining table was the centerpiece of the room, antique and massive, from the last century, dark green leather, steel and ceramic, designed so that the patient did not lie flat but in a semi-reclining position. Instead of stirrups, there were obstetrical leg supports. A tall old-fashioned floor lamp with a rose silk shade and a fringe, the only light in the room, stood next to the table alongside a cylinder of gas. An unlit crystal chandelier dangled in the overhead shadows.

The doctor had a trace of some sort of European accent. German, I guessed. He was about a foot shorter than I was, and behaved with obsequious deference, as if I had dropped in for an afternoon sherry. He gestured toward the examining table with a courtly flourish. I sat between the leg supports while he stood close and asked questions: Last period, how many times had I had sex, was I married, how many men had I had sex with, did they have large or small penises, were they circumcised, what positions, did I like it?

He moved the floor lamp closer. I put my legs in the apparatus and looked up at the chandelier.

He didn't bother with a glove, either. He thrust several fingers in, hard, so I could feel the scrape of his nails.

Ouch! I said politely.

Ouch, he mocked. Never mind your ouch. He pushed his fingers in harder and pressed down on my belly with his other hand.

You are very far along, he said. It will be a very difficult procedure. Come back tomorrow. Be here at seven o'clock in the evening. Give me one hundred dollars now because this will be difficult. You can pay the rest when you come back. Bring cash. Five hundred more.

I borrowed the extra hundred from Kat, and enlisted someone I knew to ride out to Jersey City with me on the train, a guy who was something of an ex-boyfriend. Even though I was enigmatic about why we were going to Jersey City at night, he guessed what was up, and seemed fairly entertained at the prospect.

This time, there was no one in the waiting room. The doctor looked very annoyed when he saw that I wasn't alone. My friend stayed out there while I went into the office. The doctor locked the door behind us.

When I was on the table, he stood between my legs and pressed and ground his pelvis against me and then put his fingers in for a while.

Then he said: You are too far gone. I cannot do it.

I put my legs down and sat up. He stood next to me, leaned on me heavily, and rubbed his two hands up my thigh, all the way up, so that his fingertips collided with my crotch. I understood then that he'd known perfectly well on my last visit that he wasn't going to go through with it.

You are a beautiful girl, a beautiful girl, he breathed moistly onto my face as his hands slid up and down, up and down. It is too late. Take my advice. Have the baby. Have the baby.

He unlocked the sliding doors and beckoned my friend in.

Get married, he said. Have the baby.

Hey, I'm not the guy, said my friend.

What about my hundred dollars? I asked.

Get out of here, the doctor said, and turned his back.

When we got to my friend's train stop, he walked off whistling a jaunty tune. Good luck, he said, and was gone.

Today, chat rooms and message boards related to abortion show a disturbing trend among some young people: Not only is disinformation rife ("The only reason abortion is still legal," writes one correspondent, "is becuz the babies organs are prossed and some of that money is forwarded to the libral party."), but many young people haven't the remotest notion of pre-*Roe* reality. Abortion's been legal since before they were born. Some even believe that abortion was invented with *Roe v. Wade.*

Abortion was not always illegal before *Roe.* Into the 19th century, what a woman did with her early pregnancy was considered a purely domestic matter. Until "quickening," when the fetus was perceived to be alive and kicking, it wasn't even considered a pregnancy, but a "blocking" or an "imbalance," and women regularly "restored the menses," if they so chose, through plants and potions. Abortifacients became commercially available by the mid-1700s.

Quality control was not great, and the earliest abortion legislation in the 1820s and '30s appears to have been an effort to curtail poisoning rather than abortion itself. According to several historians of the issue, as abortion—both through drugs and direct procedures—became a bigger and bigger commercial venture, "orthodox" physicians, who were competing with midwives, homeopaths, and self-styled practitioners of all stripes, pushed to make abortion illegal. The nascent American Medical Association established its dominance over lay practitioners through abortion laws, and women were kept in their place. Eugenics played a role, too: With "undesirables" breeding prolifically, motherhood was hailed as a white woman's patriotic duty, abortion a form of treason. By the mid-1800s, most of the "folk" knowledge had been lost and abortion became "infanticide." Between 1860 and 1880, antiabortion laws spread city by city, state by state. Now there was a ruthlessly pragmatic aspect: In the aftermath of the slaughter of half a million men during the Civil War, the births were needed. First the men were conscripted, then the women.

Demand for abortion continued to grow in spite of the laws. Periods of relative tolerance gave way to periods of stricter enforcement, which inevitably corresponded to periods of women's activism. In the late 19th century, it was when they demanded a voice in politics. After World War II and through the 1960s, it was when they demanded sexual freedom. All kinds of change, rebellion, and upheaval were busting out then, and the reflexive reaction of the authorities was to crack down. For women getting illegal abortions, this era was particularly marked by fear, secrecy, ignorance, shame, and danger. This was the era that put the rusty coat hanger into the collective consciousness.

The day after I returned from Jersey City, there was another doctor in a seedy little basement office in

New York who didn't even touch me. He said the only way to do it at this point would be to perform a miniature caesarean, not something he could do in his office.

Kat and Elaine were plainly getting tired of having me and my problem on their couch. They came up with a phone number in Florida. I called. A male voice said I should fly to Miami. They'd meet me and take me to one of the islands, to a clinic. Give us the telephone number of where you're staying now in New York. We'll call you back and confirm the arrangements.

He called back within an hour. It was set: Fly to Miami next Thursday, between the hours of noon and five. Wear something bright red so we'll know you when you get off the plane. And bring eight hundred dollars, in cash.

One last thing, he said. You must not tell anyone where you're going.

They understand that I'm over three months, right? I said.

Yeah, yeah. They know. It's all set.

I hung up. This didn't feel good at all. Florida, the islands, wads of cash, distant voices.

I thought about doing what I should have done in the first place: calling my mother.

Not calling her in the beginning wasn't because my mother was a prude or religious or anything like that. Hardly. It was because I was naturally secretive, had wanted to take care of things on my own. I just wanted it to go away. But there was a limit to even my pigheadedness. I thought about how sad it would make my mother if I just disappeared. My mother, who was right there in the city, swung into action instantly. She made arrangements with a doctor she knew, and borrowed the $1,500 it would cost because of the added risk.

This doctor had a clean, modern office in Midtown. He drew a diagram showing the difference between a first-trimester D&C and what I'd be having. After three months, he said, the placenta and the blood vessels that feed it grow too complex to simply be scraped out. To do so would be to just about guarantee a hemorrhage. In a normal birth or miscarriage, he said, the uterus contracts, shearing off the placenta and pinching off the connecting blood vessels. We induce a miscarriage, he said, by injecting a saline solution into the amniotic sac. The fetus dies. The uterus rejects it by contracting. That way, no hemorrhage. Then we go in and take it out. If it were done any other way, it could easily kill you.

A date was made for the following week. I was off of Kat and Elaine's couch and on my mother's.

One evening, my mother's phone rang. It was the man in Florida. He'd tracked me down through Kat, and he was angry. What the hell had happened? Where was I? They'd waited all day at the airport in Miami, met every plane. I apologized, told him I'd made other arrangements here at home. He said I was a fucking bitch who owed money to him and a lot of other people, told me to go fuck myself, and hung up.

Maybe everything would have been peachy if I'd gone to the islands. Maybe I'd have come back with a tan and heartwarming stories of kindness and caring that I'd remember fondly through the years. A rather different picture always comes to mind, though, and it involves a morgue in a run-down little hospital with heat and flies, and then a dinghy with an outboard, or maybe a fishing boat with a rumbling, smoky diesel engine, heading out into the Caribbean at night bearing a largish canvas bag weighted with cinder blocks. . . .

That year in the 1960s, several thousand American women were treated in emergency rooms for botched abortions, and there were at least 200 known deaths. Comparing my story with others from the pre-*Roe* era, what impresses me is how close I veered to mortal danger in spite of not living under most of the usual terrible strictures. Unlike so many of the women I've read about and talked to, especially the teenagers, I was quite unburdened by shame and guilt. I'd never, ever had the "nice girls don't do it" trip laid on me. I came from a religion-free background. I wasn't worried in the least about "sin," was not at all ambivalent about whether abortion was right or wrong. I wasn't sheltered or ignorant. I didn't face parental disapproval or stigmatization of any kind. I had no angry husband. My mother would have leapt in and helped me at any point. There was no need at all to keep my condition secret and to procrastinate, but

I did it anyway. What does this say about how it was for other young girls and women who didn't have my incredible luck? I was luckier than most in another department, too—being raped by the abortionist was a major hazard of the era. I merely got diddled by a couple of disgusting old men. It was nasty and squalid, but it certainly didn't kill me. As I said, I got off easy.

Ironically, it was the medical profession, which had made abortion illegal in the first place, that started to speak out. Doctors treating the desperately sick women who landed in hospitals with raging peritonitis, hemorrhages, perforated uteruses, and septic shock often had to futilely watch them die, because the women had waited too long to get help—because they were confused and terrified, because what they had done was "illegal" and "immoral."

One doctor's "awakening" is vividly described in *The Worst of Times,* a collection of interviews with women, cops, coroners, and practitioners from the illegal abortion era. In 1948, when this doctor was an intern in a Pittsburgh hospital, a woman was admitted with severe pelvic sepsis after a bad abortion. She was beautiful, married to someone important and wealthy, and already in renal failure. Over the next couple of days, despite heroic efforts to save her, a cascade of systemic catastrophes due to the overwhelming infection culminated with the small blood vessels bursting under her skin, bruises breaking out everywhere as if some invisible fist were punching her over and over, and she died. Being well-to-do didn't always save you.

Her death was so horrible that it made him, he recalls, physically ill. He describes his anger, but says he didn't quite know with whom to be angry. It took him another 20 years to understand that it was not the abortionist who killed her—it was the legal system, the lawmakers who had forced her away from the medical community, who "... killed her just as surely as if they had held the catheter or the coat hanger or whatever. I'm still angry. It was all so unnecessary."

All so unnecessary.

In the same book, a man who assisted in autopsies in a big urban hospital, starting in the mid-1950s, describes the many deaths from botched abortions that he saw. "The deaths stopped overnight in 1973." He never saw another in the 18 years before he retired. "That," he says, "ought to tell people something about keeping abortion legal."

In February 2004, seven abortion doctors in four states sued Attorney General John Ashcroft, claiming that D&X was indeed a medically necessary procedure. Ashcroft retaliated by subpoenaing their hospitals for the records of all patients who'd had late-term abortions in the past five years—most long before the PBAB—to determine, ostensibly, if any D&Xs had actually been prompted by health risk. In June, a federal judge in San Francisco declared the PBAB to be unconstitutional—saying it was vague, placed an "undue burden" on abortion rights, and contained no exception for a woman's health—but she did not, in deference to other cases wending their way through the legal system, completely lift the ban.

One doctor, writing about D&X, said something that particularly struck me—that the actual practice of medicine, the stuff that goes on behind closed doors, is often gruesome, gory, and messy. Saws whine, bones crack, blood spatters. We outside of the profession are mostly shielded from this reality. Our model is white sheets, gleaming linoleum, and Dr. Kildare. Face-lift, hip replacement, bypass, liver transplant—many people would faint dead away at a detailed description of any of these. Doctors roll up their sleeves, plunge in, and do tough, nervy, drastic, and risky things with our very meat-bone-and-gristle bodies, under occasionally harrowing circumstances.

The gruesome aspect of D&X has been detailed and emphasized, but as a procedure, it's in line with the purpose of medicine: to get a hard flesh-and-blood job done. What makes it different from other procedures is that it can involve a live fetus. This puts it in a class by itself. But the woman undergoing a D&X knows this. If she's doing it, there will be powerfully compelling reasons, and it's not for anyone else to decide if those reasons are compelling enough.

. . .

Teenagers—especially those who are poor and uneducated—are by far the group having the most elective late-term abortions. If we truly wish to protect the young and vulnerable, promote a "culture of life," as President Bush said so grandly in his signing speech, then we must make teenage girls a top priority. Make sure they don't get pregnant in the first place, and not just by preaching "abstinence only." If they do get pregnant, don't throw a net of fear, confusion, and complication over them that will only cause them to hide their conditions for as long as they can. Because that's exactly what they'll do. You could argue that "partial-birth" abortion is the price a society pays when it calculatedly keeps teenage girls ignorant instead of aggressively arming them with the facts of life and, if necessary, the equipment to protect themselves from pregnancy.

. . . When a woman does not want to be pregnant, the drive to become unpregnant can turn into a force equal to the nature that wants her to stay pregnant. And then she *will* look for an abortion, whether it's legal or illegal, clean or filthy, safe or riddled with danger. This is simply a fact, whatever our opinion of it. And whether we like it or not, humans, married and unmarried, will continue to have sex—wisely, foolishly, violently, nicely, hostilely, pleasantly, dangerously, responsibly, carelessly, sordidly, exaltedly—and there will be pregnancies: wanted, unwanted, partly wanted, partly unwanted.

A society that does not accept the facts is a childish society, and a society that makes abortion illegal—and I believe that the PBAB is a calculated step in exactly that direction—is a cruel and backward society that makes being female a crime. It works in partnership with the illegal abortionist. It puts him in business, sends him his customers, and employs him to dispense crude, dirty, barbaric, savage punishment to those who break the law. And the ones who are punished by the illegal abortionist are always women: mothers, sisters, daughters, wives.

It's no way to treat a lady.

DISCUSSION QUESTIONS FOR CHAPTER 6

1. How do patriarchal norms constitute a threat to women's health?

2. How are women treated differently in the health care system? What is the effect of this differential treatment? How does racism have an impact on the gendered experiences of women of color in the health care system? Have you ever had a negative experience based on gender in the health care system?

3. Why is reproductive choice important for women?

4. What have been the consequences of women's loss of control of their reproductive processes?

5. How does the chipping away of abortion rights threaten the achievements of *Roe v. Wade?*

SUGGESTIONS FOR FURTHER READING

Arnold, Carrie, and Timothy Walsh. *Next to Nothing: A Firsthand Account of One Teenager's Experience with an Eating Disorder.* New York: Oxford University Press, 2007.

Boston Women's Health Book Collective, *Our Bodies, Ourselves for the New Century.* New York: Simon & Schuster, 1998.

Ehrenreich, Nancy, ed. *The Reproductive Rights Reader: Law, Medicine, and the Construction of Motherhood.* New York: NYU Press, 2008.

Eisenstein, Zillah. *Manmade Breast Cancers.* Ithaca, NY: Cornell University Press, 2001.

Gorney, Cynthia. *Articles of Faith: A Frontline History of the Abortion Wars.* New York: Touchstone, 2000.

Houck, Judith. *Hot and Bothered: Women, Medicine, and Menopause in Modern America.* Cambridge, MA: Harvard University Press, 2006.

Morgen, Sandra. *Into Our Own Hands: The Women's Health Movement in the United States, 1969–1990.* New Brunswick, NJ: Rutgers University Press, 2002.

Nelson, Jennifer. *Women of Color and the Reproductive Rights Movement.* New York: New York University Press, 2003.

Rawlinson, Mary, and Shannon Lundeen, eds. *The Voice of Breast Cancer in Medicine and Bioethics.* Dordrecht: Springer, 2006.

Weddington, Sarah. *A Question of Choice.* New York: Penguin, 1993.

CHAPTER 7

Family Systems, Family Lives

The title of this chapter reflects the reality of the family as both a major societal institution and a place where individuals experience intimate relationships. Using the definition of institution as established patterns of social behavior organized around particular purposes, the family is constituted through general patterns of behavior that emerge because of the specific needs and desires of human beings and because of the societal conditions of our lives. At the institutional level, the family maintains patterns of privilege and inequity and is intimately connected to other institutions in society such as the economy, the political system, religion, and education. At the level of experience, the family fulfills basic human needs and provides most of us with our first experiences of love and relationship as well as power and conflict. Scholarship on the family has demonstrated that family forms are historically and culturally constructed and that family is a place for the reproduction of power relations in society. In this way, the family is a primary social unit that maintains other institutions and reinforces existing patterns of domination. At the same time, however, family networks provide support systems that can reduce the indignities and/or challenge the inequities produced by various systems of inequality in society.

DEFINITIONS OF FAMILY

Families are part of what social scientists call kinship systems, or patterns of relationships that define family forms. Kinship systems vary widely around the world and determine matters such as family descent or claims to common ancestry (for example, through the line of the father [*patrilineal*], mother [*matrilineal*], both parents [*bilateral*], or either parent [*unilateral*] line) and distribution of wealth. Kinship rules also govern norms about the meanings of marriage and the numbers of marriage partners allowed. *Monogamy* involves one wife and one husband, *polygamy* means multiple spouses, and *cenogamy*, group marriage. *Polygyny*, multiple wives, is a more common form of polygamy than *polyandry*, or multiple husbands. The family is a central

378

The World's Women: Women and Families

Some important findings:

- Women are generally marrying later, but more than a quarter of women aged 15 to 19 are married in 22 countries—all in developing regions.
- Informal unions are common in developed regions and in some countries of the developing regions.
- Birthrates continue to decline in all regions of the world.
- Births to unmarried women have increased dramatically in developed regions.
- More people are living alone in the developed regions, and the majority are women.
- In many countries of the developed regions, more than half of mothers with children under age 3 are employed.

Source: http://unstats.un.org/unsd/demographic/ww2000/wm2000.htm.

organizing principle among humans around the world and, as a result, the status and role of women in families not only is dependent on women's access to power in society generally, but also is related to the status of families within a society—especially their access to economic resources. As the reading "Cheaper than a Cow" by Miranda Kennedy, a journalist based in New Delhi writing for *Ms.* magazine, demonstrates, in countries where many families are in poverty, and where male power is granted over women in these families, women are sold and traded as commodities. This is exacerbated by the dowry system (the money or goods given to a groom's family by the bride's family). In the United States, there is no "normal" family, though such tends to be constructed as the nuclear family of the middle-class, White, married, heterosexual couple with children. *Nuclear* family implies a married couple residing together with their children, and it can be distinguished from an *extended* family in which a group of related kin, in addition to parents and children, live together in the same household. The nuclear family arose as a result of Western industrialization that separated the home from productive activities. In pre- and early-industrial times, the family was relatively self-sufficient in producing goods for family consumption and exchange with other families. As industrial capitalism developed, family members increasingly worked outside the home for wages that were spent on goods for family consumption. In this era of global expansion and production/consumption, family labor is both utilized by and central to maintaining corporate profits.

Traditional myths about the normative family hide the reality of the wide diversity of family life. There has been a significant drop in the number of legally married heterosexual couples in the last few decades, with (a) more women cohabiting; (b) delaying marriage; (c) divorcing and remarrying; (d) living alone or in single female-headed households; and (e) in lesbian partnerships. For example, (a) in 2006, the Census Bureau reported that only about one-fifth of households involved married-couple families with children. The American Community Survey also found that the number of cohabiting heterosexual couples had increased substantially, from half a

LEARNING ACTIVITY   **What Makes a Family?**

Conduct an informal survey of the people on your dorm floor or in an organization to which you belong about the structure of their family of origin. Whom do they consider to be in their family? What relation do these people have to them? Did all of these people live in the same house? Who had primary responsibility for caring for them as children? Who was primarily responsible for the financial well-being of the family? For the emotional well-being of the family? Was the family closely connected to extended family? If so, which extended family members and in what ways?

Compare your findings with those of your classmates. What do your findings lead you to surmise about what makes a family? How closely do the families of your interviewees resemble the dominant notion of the nuclear family—a husband and wife (in their first marriage) and their two or three children? What do you think is the impact of our stereotype of the nuclear family on social policy? How do you think this stereotype affects real families dealing with the real problems of everyday family life?

million in 1960 to 5 million in 2005, and that 1 in 3 children is born to unmarried parents who may or may not be living together. The number of unmarried-partner households (both heterosexual and gay) has increased by 72 percent in the last decade and only about two-thirds of the nation's children live with two married parents. In terms of (b), the median age of first marriage is 27 years for men and 26 years for women, up from 23 and 21 years, respectively, in 1980; (c) approximately 40 to 50 percent of marriages end in divorce. Although remarriage rates are high, half of all U.S. children will live in a single-parent household at some point in childhood. More than half of Americans today have been, are, or will be in one or more stepfamily situations; (d) the proportion of households consisting of one person living alone increased from 17 percent in 1970 to 26 percent in 2005, and single parents account for about 27 percent of family households. Finally, (e) estimates show that about 2 million children are raised by lesbian and gay parents and one-third of lesbian and one-fifth of gay male households have children. It is difficult to reliably estimate the percentage of lesbian and gay households, although as individuals they make up approximately 10 percent of the U.S. population.

In this way, the diversity of families includes single parents, extended and multigenerational families, lesbian and gay families with and without children, people (single or not and with or without children) living in community with other adults, grandparents raising grandchildren or nieces and nephews, and so forth. These families represent all social classes, sexualities, and racial and ethnic groups, and 1 in 5 children in the United States speak a language other than English in their homes. Globally, family structure is affected by the consequences of the global economy as well as by militarism and colonial expansion. These consequences for families and children are poignantly illustrated in the short story reading "Broken Transformers" by Bi Shumin.

Myths and Facts About Lesbian Families

MYTH 1: Lesbians don't have lasting relationships.

FACT: Many lesbians are in long-term partnerships. Unfortunately, social supports and civil rights are not accorded to lesbian partnerships as they are to heterosexual marriages. Only Massachusetts recognizes gay marriage, and in 1999 the Vermont Supreme Court ruled that denying lesbian and gay couples the benefits of marriage was unconstitutional and ordered the legislature to develop a form of civil union to allow lesbian and gay partnerships the same rights and responsibilities as married couples in Vermont. Since then, a number of other states have followed.

MYTH 2: Lesbians don't have children.

FACT: The American Bar Association estimates that at least 6 million American children have lesbian or gay parents. Many lesbians have children from previous heterosexual relationships before they came out. Others have children through artificial insemination, and others adopt children. Unfortunately, because the courts may believe stereotypes about lesbians, lesbian mothers often lose custody of their children in a divorce, despite research indicating the fitness of lesbian mothers. In many states, adoption is difficult for lesbians, and rarely can both partners in a lesbian relationship legally adopt a child together.

MYTH 3: Children of lesbian parents develop psychological disorders.

FACT: Research indicates that there is no difference in the development or frequency of pathologies between children of heterosexual parents and children of homosexual parents. In fact, study after study suggests that children in lesbian families are more similar to than different from children in heterosexual families. Studies of separation-individuation, behavior problems, self-concept, locus of control, moral judgment, and intelligence have revealed no major differences between children of lesbian mothers and children of heterosexual mothers.

MYTH 4: Children of lesbian parents become gay themselves.

FACT: Research indicates no difference between children raised in lesbian families and children raised in heterosexual families with respect to gender identity, gender role behavior, and sexual orientation. Studies suggest that children in lesbian families develop along the same lines as children in heterosexual families; they are as likely to be happy with their gender, exhibit gender role behaviors, and be heterosexual as children of heterosexual mothers.

"You just wait until your other mother gets homes, young man!"

Despite such diversity among U.S. families, legislation such as the Defense of Marriage Act (DOMA) passed in 1996 and subsequent state mandates have restricted the legality of unions beyond the male/husband and female/wife relationship. Still, Massachusetts does recognize gay marriage and other states recognize civil unions (Vermont, Connecticut, New Jersey, and New Hampshire) and domestic partnerships (Hawaii, Maine, District of Columbia, California, Washington, and Oregon) as of this writing. The reading "Partners as Parents: Challenges Faced by Gays Denied Marriage" by Charlene Gomes discusses these issues in the context of parenting, adoption, and custody legislation. The ongoing political debate concerning "family values" illustrates how supporters of the *status quo* (or existing power relations) in society have made the term *family values* synonymous with traditional definitions of the family and its role in society. This includes seeing women defined in terms of their domestic and reproductive roles, men as the rightful sources of power and authority, and married heterosexual families as the only legitimate family. Many people are offended by this narrow construction of family and its association with a repressive political agenda, and reject such values as *their* family values. Determining what kinds of families get to be counted as "real" families and determining whose "family values" are used as standards for judging others are heated topics of debate in the United States.

The notion of family—with all its connotations of love, security, connectedness, and nurturing—is a prime target for nostalgia in the twenty-first century. As economic forces have transformed the ways that families function, we yearn for a return to the "traditional" family, with its unconditional love and acceptance, to escape from the complexities and harsh realities of society. Although many families do provide this respite, dominant ideologies about the family have idealized and sometimes glorified the family, and women's roles in the family, in ways that hide underlying conflict and violence. In addition, these ideologies present a false dichotomization between public (society) and private (family) spheres. Poor and non-White families have rarely enjoyed the security and privacy assumed in this split between family and society. For example, the state, in terms of both social welfare policies and criminal justice statutes, has stronger impact and more consequences on poor families than on middle-class families. This is the topic of the next section: the connections between the family and other social institutions.

INSTITUTIONAL CONNECTIONS

The family interacts with other institutions in society and provides various experiences for family members. For example, economic forces shape women's family roles and help construct the balance between work and family responsibilities. As discussed in Chapter 8, women perform over two-thirds of household labor—labor that is constructed as family work and often not seen as work. In addition, the family work that women do in the home is used to justify the kinds of work women are expected to perform in the labor force. It is no coincidence that women are congregated in a small number of occupations known for their caretaking, educating, and servicing responsibilities. In addition, the boundaries are more fluid between women's paid work and home life than between men's. This is structured into the very kinds of jobs women tend to perform, as well as part of the expectations associated with hiring women. These assumptions can be used against women very easily as they attempt to advance in careers. At the same time, the more rigid boundaries between work and home for male-dominated jobs mean that men have a more difficult time negotiating parenting responsibilities when they want to be more actively involved in their children's lives.

The economic system impacts families in many ways; in turn, families support and impact economic systems. Women care for and maintain male workers as well as socialize future generations of workers, thus supporting economic institutions that rely on workers to be fed, serviced, and able to fulfill certain work roles. Although in contemporary U.S. society some families are still productive units in that they produce goods directly for family consumption or for exchange on the market, most families are consumptive units in that they participate in the market economy through goods purchased for family consumption. As a result, advertisers target women as family shoppers. The family is a consumptive unit that provides the context for advertising, media, and other forms of entertainment. In these ways family systems are intimately connected to economic forces in society.

The impact of shifting economies and changing technologies on families varies considerably by gender, class, sexuality, and race, such that a family's placement in the larger political economy directly influences diverse patterns of family organization. Economic factors impact single-headed families such that households headed by women have about half the income and less than a third of the wealth (assets) of other U.S. households and are about three times as likely to be at or below the poverty level. Most recent census data show that the poverty rate for single mothers (34 percent) is twice as high as the rate for single fathers (17 percent). Almost half of children living in single-headed households live in poverty. Race impacts this

LEARNING ACTIVITY **Families and Poverty**

> Go to the website of the 2000 U.S. Census at *www.census.gov/main/www/cen2000.html*. Click on the link to the American FactFinder. In the "Basic Facts" box, select "Economic Characteristics: Employment, Income, Poverty, and more." Select your state and town to find out more information about income and families in poverty where you live.

economic situation such that households headed by women of color are the most likely to experience poverty. It is well known that the most effective antipoverty program for families is one that includes educational opportunities, a living wage with benefits, and quality childcare. In this way families are shaped by their relationship to systems of inequality in society. This means, for example, that working-class women's lack of flexible work scheduling affects how families are able to meet their needs, as does the lower pay of working-class women, making them less able to afford quality daycare. Similarly, higher unemployment among men of color as compared to White men impacts families and pushes women in family relationships with unemployed men to work outside the home full time while also taking care of young children. Charlene Gomes, attorney and women's rights activist, focuses on heterosexism and the challenges facing gay couples in "Partners as Parents." Jobs with different incomes and levels of authority and seniority affect access to such family-friendly benefits as flextime, on-site childcare, and company-sponsored tax breaks for childcare. For example, although unpaid parenting leave is a legal right of all U.S. employees, many companies provide better family benefits for their higher level and better paid employees than they do for their lower level employees.

The family experience is also affected by the state and its legal and political systems. The government closely regulates the family and provides certain benefits to legally married couples. Couples need a license from the state to marry, and the government says they may file a joint tax return, for example. Lesbian and gay couples who jointly own property and share income and expenses may not have the privileges of marriage, joint tax filing, and domestic partner benefits. Benefits accrue to certain family members and not to people who, even though they might see themselves as family, are not recognized as such by the state. Lisa Miya-Jervis makes this very clear in the reading "Who Wants to Marry a Feminist?" She makes the case that in choosing marriage, feminists understand the oppressive roots of marriage as an institution and actively work to "forge a new vision of what marriage is" (p. 404). Although an advanced industrial society, the United States has no national funding of daycare centers. This lack affects the social organization of the family and the experience of parenting. Federal and state policies also impact the family through legal statutes that regulate marriage and divorce legislation, reproductive choice, and violence in families.

Indeed, the family has connections to all societal institutions, and these connections help shape the kind and quality of experiences that we have as family members.

Religion and the family are closely tied as social institutions. Religious socialization of children occurs in the family through religious and moral teachings, and religious institutions often shape societal understandings of families as well as provide rituals that help symbolize family and kin relations (such as baptisms, weddings, and funerals). Educational institutions rely on the family as a foundation for the socialization, care, and maintenance of children. Health systems rely on parents (and women in particular) to nurse and care for sick and elderly family members, as well as provide adequate nutrition and cleanliness to prevent disease. Military institutions need the family as a foundation for ideologies of combat and for socialization and support of military personnel. Sports and athletics are tied to the family through gender socialization, the purchase of certain equipment and opportunities, and the consumption and viewing of professional sports in the home. Although we might like to think of the family as an "oasis" apart from society, nothing could be further from the truth.

POWER AND FAMILY RELATIONSHIPS

At the direct level of experience, the family is the social unit where most people are raised, learn systems of belief, experience love and perhaps abuse and neglect, and generally grow to be a part of social communities. It is in the family where most of us internalize messages about ourselves, about others, and about our place in the world. Some learn that love comes with an abuse of power as large people hit little people, all in the name of love. Some also learn that love means getting our own way without responsibility—a lesson that may detract from the hopes of a civil society where individuals care about one another and the communities of which they are a part. Others learn that love is about trust, care, compassion, and responsibility.

Family is where many of us first experience gender because societal understandings of the differences between girls and boys are transferred through early teachings by family members. Parents bring home baby girls and boys, dress them in gender-"appropriate" colors, give them different toys, and decorate their bedrooms in different ways. As Chapter 3 emphasized, the family is a primary institution for teaching about gender. Experiences of gender are very much shaped by the gender composition of family members. A girl growing up in a family of brothers and a boy growing up with only women and girls in his family have different experiences of gender.

Central in any discussion of family is a focus on power. Power in families is understood as access to resources (tangible or intangible) that allows certain family members to define the reality of others, have their needs met, and access more resources. In most U.S. families today, power is distributed according to age and gender. Older family members (although not always the aged, who often lose power in late life) tend to have more power than children and young people, who are often defined as "dependents." Men have more power in the family than women do if this is measured in resource management and allocation and decision-making authority. Women, however, do have power if this is defined as day-to-day decisions about the running of the household and how certain household chores get done. Sociologists, however, tend to emphasize that this latter sort of "power" is vulnerable to changes in broader family dynamics and subject to decisions by men in positions as major economic providers or heads of household.

ACTIVIST PROFILE **Hannah Solomon**

Hannah Greenbaum Solomon believed that "woman's sphere is the whole wide world" and her first responsibility was to her family. Solomon worked tirelessly in turn-of-the-century Chicago for social reform. Laboring alongside Jane Addams at Hull House, Solomon worked to improve child welfare. She reformed the Illinois Industrial School for Girls, established penny lunch stations in the public schools, and led efforts for slum clearance, low-cost housing, child labor laws, mothers' pensions, and public health measures.

In 1876 Solomon became the first Jewish member of the Chicago Woman's Club, where she developed a sense of women's ability to work together for social good. In 1893 she organized the Jewish Women's Congress at the Chicago World's Fair, which led to her founding the National Council of Jewish Women (NCJW) to enhance social welfare and justice. Solomon saw her commitment to justice as a part of her responsibility as a Jew, a woman, and an American.

Under Solomon's leadership, the NCJW sponsored programs for the blind, formed the Port and Dock Department to assist immigrant women in finding housing and jobs, established a permanent immigrant aid station on Ellis Island, supported Margaret Sanger's National Birth Control League, raised relief dollars during World War I, and participated in the presidential effort to create jobs during the Depression.

Solomon's legacy has continued in the NCJW since her death in 1942. Following World War II, the NCJW provided assistance to Holocaust survivors in Europe and Israel. During the McCarthy era, NCJW organized the Freedom Campaign to protect civil liberties. Additionally, the organization was the first national group to sponsor Meals on Wheels, built the Hebrew University High School in Jerusalem, helped establish the Court Appointed Advocate Project (CASA) to protect the rights of children in court cases, and launched a national campaign to try to ensure that children were not harmed by changes in welfare law.

Currently, the National Council of Jewish Women has 90,000 members and continues the work of Hannah Solomon by bringing her vision of justice to bear in the world.

The United States has among the highest marriage and the highest divorce rates of any industrialized country. Although a large number of people get divorced, this does not seem to indicate disillusionment with marriage because large numbers of people also remarry. Marriage traditionally has been based on gender relations that prescribe authority of husbands over wives and that entail certain norms and expectations that are sanctioned by the state. The traditional marriage contract assumes the husband will be the head of household with responsibilities to provide a family wage and the wife will take primary responsibility for the home and the raising of children and integrate her personal identity with that of her husband. As in "Mrs. John Smith" and "Dr. and Mrs. John Smith," Mrs. Smith easily can become someone who loses her identity to her husband. The declaration of "man and wife" in the traditional marriage ceremony illustrates how men continue to be men under this contract and women become wives.

As Lisa Miya-Jervis writes in "Who Wants to Marry a Feminist?", these norms are increasingly being challenged by contemporary couples who have moved from this traditional contract to one whereby women are expected to contribute financially and men are expected to fulfill family roles. Despite these modifications, husbands still tend to hold more power in families and women do the majority of physical and emotional family work. The rituals of marriage ceremonies illustrate these normative gender relations: the father "giving away" his daughter, representing the passage of the woman from one man's house to another; the wearing of white to symbolize purity and virginity; the engagement ring representing a woman already spoken for; and the throwing of rice to symbolize fertility and the woman's obligation to bear and raise children. Finally, as already mentioned, the traditions of naming are illustrative of power in families: Approximately 9 out of 10 women take the name of their husband and among those who keep their name, most give their children their husband's name and not their own. A study at Harvard University points to a more conservative view of marriage in the last decade to explain a finding that among college-educated women in their 30s, the number keeping their names dropped from 23 percent in 1990 to 17 percent in 2000.

It is especially in the family where many girls and women experience gender oppression; in close relationship with men, they often experience gender domination. In other words, it is in the home and family where many girls and women feel the consequences of masculine power and privilege. Writing in 1910, socialist anarchist Emma Goldman saw marriage as an economic transaction that binds women into subservience to men (through love and personal and sexual services) and society (through unpaid housework). In the reading "Marriage and Love," she advocated "free love" that is unconstrained by marriage and relations with the state. Goldman believed love found in marriages occurred in spite of the institution of marriage and not because of it.

Sexism in interpersonal relationships among family members reduces female autonomy and lowers women's and girls' self-esteem. Consequences of masculine privilege in families can mean that men dominate women in relationships in subtle or not-so-subtle ways, expecting or taking for granted personal and sexual services, making and/or vetoing important family decisions, controlling money and expenditures, and so forth. In addition, power in family and marital relationships may lead to psychological, sexual, and/or physical abuse against women and children. Often

LEARNING ACTIVITY   **Divorce Law: Who Benefits in My State?**

Research your state's divorce laws. How is property divided in a divorce? How is custody determined? How are alimony and child support determined? How do these laws affect women and children in actuality in your state? What are the poverty rates for divorced women and their children in your state? How many fathers do not pay child support as ordered by the court? How does your state deal with nonpaying fathers? What can you do to challenge the legal system in your state to be more responsive to women's and children's needs following divorce?

IDEAS FOR ACTIVISM

- Become a Court Appointed Special Advocate (CASA) for children.
- Offer to babysit for free for a single mother one evening a month.
- Lobby your state lawmakers to enact legislation recognizing lesbian and gay unions.
- Organize an educational activity on your campus around alternative family models.

the double standard of sexual conduct allows boys more freedom and autonomy compared to girls. Also, girls are very often expected to perform more household duties than boys, duties that may include cleaning up after their brothers or father. A recent study by the University of Michigan's Institute for Social Research shows that boys aged 6 through 17 years spend an average of 30 percent less time doing chores and are more likely than girls to get paid or receive an allowance for doing the work. Mirroring the housework data for adults (see Chapter 8), chores such as dishwashing and cooking, often regarded as routine and performed for free, are more likely to be done by girls than boys. This sets up gender inequities in the family and impacts the amount of free time girls can enjoy.

In particular, the balance of power in marriage (or any domestic partnership) depends in part on how couples negotiate paid labor and family work in their relationships. Marriages or domestic partnerships can be structured according to different models that promote various ways that couples live and work together. These models include "head–complement," "junior partner/senior partner," and "equal partners"—relationships that each have different ways of negotiating paid work and family work, and, as a result, provide different balances of power within these relationships.

The "head–complement" model reflects the traditional marriage contract as discussed previously whereby the head/husband has responsibilities to provide a family wage and the complement/wife takes primary responsibility for the home and the raising of children. In addition the complement sees (usually her) role as complementing the head's role by being supportive and encouraging in both emotional and

HISTORICAL MOMENT   **The Feminine Mystique**

In 1963 Betty Friedan, a housewife and former labor activist, published the results of a series of interviews she had conducted with women who had been educated at Smith College. Despite their picture-perfect lives, these women reported extreme despair and unhappiness and, unaware that others shared this experience, blamed themselves. To deal with this "problem that has no name," these women turned to a variety of strategies, ranging from using tranquilizers to having affairs to volunteering with church, school, and charitable organizations.

What had happened to these educated women? Following World War II, when women had found a prominent role in the workforce, a national myth emerged that the place for (middle-class, White) women was in the home. To conform to this ideal, women sublimated their dreams and desires and fell in line with "the feminine mystique."

When Friedan's book, *The Feminine Mystique*, appeared in 1963, it spoke loudly to the unspoken misery of millions of American housewives. In its first year, it sold 3 million copies. Unfortunately, during the era just immediately following the repressive, anti-Communist McCarthy years, Friedan feared that were she to push the envelope in her book to include an analysis of race and social class, her work would be discredited. So, rather than choosing to address the more complex problems of working-class women and women of color and likely be dismissed, she chose to be heard and addressed the safer topic of middle-class housewives.

Despite its shortcomings, *The Feminine Mystique* found a readership that needed to know that they were not alone in believing that something was seriously wrong with their lives. Friedan suggested that that something wrong was a conspiracy of social institutions and culture that limited the lives of women. She challenged women to find meaningful and purposeful ways of living, particularly through careers.

While Friedan did not go so far as to question the need for men to move into equitable work in the home as she was encouraging women to move out into the workforce or to examine the social and economic, as well as psychological, forces at work in limiting women's lives, she did bring to national attention the problem of women's circumscribed existence and offered a call for women to begin to examine the limitations imposed on them.

Source: Ruth Rosen, *The World Split Open: How the Modern Women's Movement Changed America* (New York: Viking, 2000).

material ways. The balance of power in this family system is definitely tilted in the direction of the "head" of the head–complement couple. Power for the complement is to a large extent based on the goodwill of the head as well as the resources (educational and financial in particular) that the complement brings into the relationship. Although the complement does tend to have control over the day-to-day running of the household, this power may disappear with divorce or other internal family disruption.

"Yes, this is a two career household.
Unfortunately I have both careers."

Reprinted with permission from Carol Simpson Labor Cartoons.

In 2003, families consisting of breadwinner fathers and stay-at-home mothers accounted for only 10 percent of all households. Only 3 percent of stay-at-home parents in the United States are fathers, although this number has tripled in the last decade. However, in the reading "Don't Give Up Your Day Job," Heidi Bruggink shares an interview with Leslie Bennetts who provides evidence for a new trend in educated women choosing to give up their careers and live the head–complement lifestyle. She does not dispute the longitudinal trend of an increasing number of women with children entering the workplace since 1950; rather, she points out the slight decrease in this trend in the last five years among affluent couples. These choices reflect the difficulties in juggling the demands of work and home and the fact that these families can afford for wives not to work outside the home.

The "junior partner/senior partner" model is one in which the traditional marriage contract has been modified. Both members of the couple work outside the home, although one member (usually the wife or female domestic partner) considers her work to be secondary to the senior partner's job. She also takes primary responsibility for the home and childcare. This means that the junior partner has taken on some of the provider role while still maintaining responsibility for the domestic role. In practice this might mean that if the senior partner is transferred or relocated because of (usually his) work, the junior partner experiences a disruption in her work to follow. If someone is contacted when the children come home from school sick, it is the junior partner. She might enter and leave the labor force based on the needs of the children and family. This model, the most frequently occurring structure for marriage or domestic partnerships today, encourages the *double day* of work for women, in which they work both inside and outside the home.

In terms of power, there is a more equitable sharing in this model than in the head–complement model because the junior partner is bringing resources into the family and has control over the day-to-day running of the household. Note in both models described here, the head and senior partner loses out to a greater or lesser degree on the joys associated with household work—especially the raising of children. Junior partners tend to fare better after divorce than the "complements" of the head–complement model. But junior partners do have the emotional stress and physical burdens of working two jobs. These stresses and burdens are affected by how much the senior partner helps out in the home.

The "equal partners" model is one in which the traditional marriage contract is completely disrupted. Neither partner is more likely to perform provider or domestic roles. In practice this might mean both jobs or careers are valued equally such that one does not take priority over the other and domestic responsibilities are shared equally. Alternatively, it might mean an intentional sharing of responsibilities such that one partner agrees to be the economic provider for a period of time and the other agrees to take on domestic responsibilities, although neither is valued more than the other, and this is negotiated rather than implied. In this model financial power is shared, and the burdens and joys of domestic work and childcare are also shared. Although this arrangement gives women the most power in marriage or domestic partnerships, not surprisingly it is a relatively infrequent arrangement among contemporary couples. This is because, first, most men in domestic relationships have been socialized to expect the privileges associated with having women service their everyday needs or raise their children, and most women expect to take on these responsibilities. Both men and women rarely question this taken-for-granted gendered division of labor. Second, men's jobs are more likely to involve a separation of home and work, and it is more difficult for them to integrate these aspects of their lives. Third, men tend to earn more money than women do on the average, and although it might be relatively easy to value women's paid work equally in theory, it is difficult to do so in practice if one job brings in a much higher salary than the other. For example, imagine an equal partner relationship between a dentist and a dental hygienist. These occupations are very gender segregated, with the majority of dentists being men and dental hygienists women. On average among dual-career families generally, wives contribute about one-third of family income. Although the couple may value each other's work equally, it might be difficult for a family to make decisions concerning relocation and so forth in favor of the one partner who works as the dental hygienist because she makes a small percentage of her partner's salary as a dentist.

It is important to emphasize that despite these various arrangements and the differential balance of power in marriage or domestic partnerships, for many women the family is where they feel most empowered. Many women find the responsibilities of maintaining a household or the challenges of child rearing fulfilling and come to see the family as a source of their competency and happiness. Sometimes this involves living in traditional family forms, and sometimes it means devising new ways of living in families. In this way the family is a positive source of connection, community, and/or productive labor. These diverse experiences associated with family life suggest how family relationships are a complex tangle of compliance with and resistance against various forms of inequities. Mothering, in particular, is one experience that often brings women great joy and shapes their experiences of family relations at the very same time that in patriarchal societies it may function as a form of behavioral constraint. This is the topic to which we now turn.

MOTHERING

Scholars who research the family identify three types of childcare associated with mothering: activities to meet children's basic physical needs; work that attends to children's emotional, cognitive, and recreational needs; and activities for maintaining children's general well-being. Mothers tend to be involved with children more than fathers in all these ways except being involved with their recreational activities. The latter is especially true for fathers with male children, illustrating how gender informs parenting behaviors. Indeed, our understanding of motherhood is conflated with notions of innate, biologically programmed behavior and expectations of unconditional love and nurturance. In other words, even though the meanings associated with motherhood vary historically and culturally, women are expected to want to be mothers, and mothers are expected to take primary responsibility for the nurturing of children. Unlike the assumptions associated with "to father," "to mother" implies nurturing, comforting, and caretaking. You might mother a kitten or a friend without the assumption of having given birth to them. To have fathered a kitten implies paternity: You are its parent; you did not cuddle and take care of it. Similarly, to father a friend makes no sense in this context. In contemporary U.S. society, there is a cultural construction of "normal motherhood" that is class and race based, and sees mothers as devoted to, and sacrificing for, their children. In addition, as global societies have developed and the expectations associated with the role of motherhood have been framed by patterns of consumption in "First World" postindustrial societies, the role of the "perfect" middle-class mother has transformed to include managing a child's life and providing social and educational opportunities as well as managing their own careers. This scenario may cause stress for both mothers and children.

This primary association between women and the nurturing aspects of mothering has brought joys and opportunities for empowerment as well as problems and hardships. It has justified the enormous amount of work women do in the home and encouraged girls to set their sights on babies rather than on other forms of productive work, or, more likely today, on both babies *and* jobs, without enough conversation about the sharing of responsibilities or an understanding of the often exhausting consequences of attempting to juggle the needs of families and careers. It has justified the types of labor women have traditionally done in the labor force as well as women's lower pay, it has kept women out of specific positions such as in the military where they might be involved in taking life rather than giving life, and it has encouraged all kinds of explanations for why men are, and should be, in control in society. For example, research published by sociologist Shelley Correll in 2007 asked volunteers to evaluate a pool of equally qualified job applicants and found that mothers were consistently viewed as less competent and less

Facts About Singles

SINGLE LIFE

89.8 million
Number of unmarried and single Americans in 2005. This group comprised 41 percent of all U.S. residents age 18 and older.

54%
Percentage of unmarried and single Americans who are women.

60%
Percentage of unmarried and single Americans who have never been married. Another 25 percent are divorced and 15 percent are widowed.

14.9 million
Number of unmarried and single Americans age 65 and older. These older Americans comprise 14 percent of all unmarried and single people.

86
Number of unmarried men age 18 and older for every 100 unmarried women in the United States.

55 million
Number of households maintained by unmarried men or women. These households comprise 49 percent of households nationwide.

29.9 million
Number of people who live alone. These persons comprise 26 percent of all households, up from 17 percent in 1970.

PARENTING

32%
Percentage of births in 2004 to unmarried women.

12.9 million
Number of single parents living with their children in 2005. Of these, 10.4 million are single mothers.

40%
Percentage of opposite-sex, unmarried-partner households that include children.

672,000
Number of unmarried grandparents who were caregivers for their grandchildren in 2004. They comprised nearly 3 in 10 grandparents who were responsible for their grandchildren. (Source: American FactFinder.)

UNMARRIED COUPLES

4.9 million
Number of unmarried-partner households in 2005. These households consist of a householder living with someone of the opposite sex who was identified as an unmarried partner.

(continued)

DATING

904

The number of dating service establishments nationwide as of 2002. These establishments, which include Internet dating services, employed nearly 4,300 people and pulled in $489 million in revenues.

VOTERS

36%

Percentage of voters in the 2004 presidential election who were unmarried.

EDUCATION

82%

Percentage of unmarried people age 25 or older in 2004 who were high school graduates.

23%

Percentage of unmarried people age 25 or older with a bachelor's degree or more education.

committed, and they were held to higher performance and punctuality standards than other female or male candidates. Mothers were 79 percent less likely to be hired and, if hired, would be offered a starting salary $11,000 lower than nonmothers. Fathers, by contrast, were offered the highest salaries of all. In addition, the nonmothers were more than twice as likely as equally qualified mothers to be called back for interviews.

The close relationship between womanhood and mothering has caused pain for women who are not able to have children as well as for those who have intentionally chosen to not have any. Mothering a disabled child brings its own challenges and joys: Ableism and the normatively abled notion of childhood construct institutional responses that affect the experience of mothering.

In this way, contemporary constructions of mothering, like the family, tend to be created around a mythical norm that reflects a White, abled, middle-class, heterosexual, and young adult experience. But, of course, mothers come in all types, shapes, and sizes, and reflect the wide diversity of women in the United States. Their understandings of their roles and their position within systems of inequality and privilege are such that mothering is a diverse experience. This is because society has different expectations of mothers depending on class and culture and other differences at the same time that these differences create different attitudes toward the experience of mothering. For example, although society often expects poor mothers to work outside the home rather than accept welfare, middle-class mothers might be made to feel guilty for "abandoning" their babies to daycare centers. Because of class, ethnicity, and/or religious orientation, some women experience more ambivalence than others when it comes to combining work and family roles. About a third of all births in the United States are to single mothers, and many more women become single in the process of raising children. Motherhood for single mothers is often constructed through societal notions of stigma.

Interracial or lesbian couples or people who adopt a child of another race are often accused of not taking into account the best interests of their children. Of course, it is society that has these problems and the families are doing their best to cope. Lesbian mothers in particular have to deal with two mutually exclusive categories that have been constructed as contradictory: mother and lesbian. This illustrates the narrow understandings of motherhood as well as the stereotypes associated with being a mother and with being a lesbian. In addition, as discussed in the Gomes reading, in most states lesbian mothers (although often mothering with a female partner who also parents) are legally understood as single mothers: women parenting with an absent father. As a result, they must deal with that stigma too. Audre Lorde goes one step further and focuses on the stigma and difficulties of raising male children in lesbian families. This classic article encourages all acts of mothering to be guided by feminist anti-racist practices.

In this way, American families are increasingly diverse forms of social organization that are intricately connected to other institutions in society. The family is a basic social unit around which much of society is built; it is fundamental to the processes of meeting individual and social needs. The centrality of the family in U.S. society encourages us to think about the way the family reproduces and resists gender relations and what it means to each of us in our everyday lives.

Marriage and Love

Emma Goldman (1910)

The popular notion about marriage and love is that they are synonymous, that they spring from the same motives, and cover the same human needs. Like most popular notions this also rests not on actual facts, but on superstition.

Marriage and love have nothing in common; they are as far apart as the poles; are, in fact, antagonistic to each other. No doubt some marriages have been the result of love. Not, however, because love could assert itself only in marriage; much rather is it because few people can completely outgrow a convention. There are today large numbers of men and women to whom marriage is naught but a farce, but who submit to it for the sake of public opinion. At any rate, while it is true that some marriages are based on love, and while it is equally true that in some cases love continues in married life, I maintain that it does so regardless of marriage, and not because of it.

On the other hand, it is utterly false that love results from marriage. On rare occasions one does hear of a miraculous case of a married couple falling in love after marriage, but on close examination it will be found that it is a mere adjustment to the inevitable. Certainly the growing-used to each other is far away from the spontaneity, the intensity, and beauty of love, without which the intimacy of marriage must prove degrading to both the woman and the man.

Marriage is primarily an economic arrangement, an insurance pact. It differs from the ordinary life insurance agreement only in that it is more binding, more exacting. Its returns are insignificantly small compared with the investments. In taking out an insurance policy one pays for it in dollars and cents, always at liberty to discontinue payments. If, however, woman's premium is a husband, she pays for it with her name, her privacy, her self-respect, her very life, "until death doth part." Moreover, the marriage insurance condemns her to life-long dependency, to parasitism, to complete uselessness, individual as well as social. Man, too, pays his toll, but as his sphere is wider, marriage does not limit him as much as woman. He feels his chains more in an economic sense.

Thus Dante's motto over Inferno applies with equal force to marriage. "Ye who enter here leave all hope behind."

. . .

From infancy, almost, the average girl is told that marriage is her ultimate goal; therefore her training and education must be directed towards that end. Like the mute beast fattened for slaughter, she is prepared for that. Yet, strange to say, she is allowed to know much less about her function as wife and mother than the ordinary artisan of his trade. It is indecent and filthy for a respectable girl to know anything of the marital relation. Oh, for the inconsistency of respectability, that needs the marriage vow to turn something which is filthy into the purest and most sacred arrangement that none dare question or criticize. Yet that is exactly the attitude of the average upholder of marriage. The prospective wife and mother is kept in complete ignorance of her only asset in the competitive field—sex. Thus she enters into life-long relations with a man only to find herself shocked, repelled, outraged beyond measure by the most natural and healthy instinct, sex. It is safe to say that a large percentage of the unhappiness, misery, distress, and physical suffering of matrimony is due to the criminal ignorance in sex matters that is being extolled as a great virtue.

Nor is it at all an exaggeration when I say that more than one home has been broken up because of this deplorable fact.

If, however, woman is free and big enough to learn the mystery of sex without the sanction of State or Church, she will stand condemned as utterly unfit to become the wife of a "good" man, his goodness consisting of an empty brain and plenty of money. Can there be anything more outrageous than the idea that a healthy, grown woman, full of life and passion, must deny nature's demand, must subdue her most intense craving, undermine her health and break her spirit, must stunt her vision, abstain from the depth and glory of sex experience until a "good" man comes along to take her unto himself as a wife? That is precisely what marriage means. How can such an arrangement end except in failure? This is one, though not the least important, factor of marriage, which differentiates it from love.

Ours is a practical age. The time when Romeo and Juliet risked the wrath of their fathers for love, when Gretchen exposed herself to the gossip of her neighbors for love, is no more. If, on rare occasions, young people allow themselves the luxury of romance, they are taken in care by the elders, drilled and pounded until they become "sensible."

The moral lesson instilled in the girl is not whether the man has aroused her love, but rather it is, "How much?" The important and only God of practical American life: Can the man make a living? Can he support a wife? That is the only thing that justifies marriage. Gradually this saturates every thought of the girl; her dreams are not of moonlight and kisses, of laughter and tears; she dreams of shopping tours and bargain counters. This soul poverty and sordidness are the elements inherent in the marriage institution. The State and the Church approve of no other ideal, simply because it is the one that necessitates the State and Church control of men and women.

Doubtless there are people who continue to consider love above dollars and cents. Particularly is this true of that class whom economic necessity has forced to become self-supporting. The tremendous change in woman's position, wrought by that mighty factor, is indeed phenomenal when we reflect that it is but a short time since she has entered the industrial arena. Six million women wage workers; six million women, who have the equal right with men to be exploited, to be robbed, to go on strike; aye, to starve even. Anything more, my lord? Yes, six million wage workers in every walk of life, from the highest brain work to the mines and railroad tracks; yes, even detectives and policemen. Surely the emancipation is complete.

Yet with all that, but a very small number of the vast army of women wage workers look upon work as a permanent issue, in the same light as does man. No matter how decrepit the latter, he has been taught to be independent, self-supporting. Oh, I know that no one is really independent in our economic treadmill; still, the poorest specimen of a man hates to be a parasite; to be known as such, at any rate.

The woman considers her position as worker transitory, to be thrown aside for the first bidder. That is why it is infinitely harder to organize women than men. "Why should I join a union? I am going to get married, to have a home." Has she not been taught from infancy to look upon that as her ultimate calling? She learns soon enough that the home, though not so large a prison as the factory, has more solid doors and bars. It has a keeper so faithful that naught can escape him. The most tragic part, however, is that the home no longer frees her from wage slavery; it only increases her task.

According to the latest statistics submitted before a Committee "on labor and wages, and congestion of population," ten percent of the wage workers in New York City alone are married, yet they must continue to work at the most poorly paid labor in the world. Add to this horrible aspect the drudgery of housework, and what remains of the protection and glory of the home? As a matter of fact, even the middle-class girl in marriage can not speak of her home, since it is the man who creates her sphere. It is not important whether the husband is a brute or a darling. What I wish to prove is that marriage guarantees woman a home only by the grace of her husband.

There she moves about in *his* home, year after year, until her aspect of life and human affairs becomes as flat, narrow, and drab as her surroundings. Small wonder if she becomes a nag, petty, quarrelsome, gossipy, unbearable, thus driving the man from the house. She could not go, if she wanted to; there is no place to go. Besides, a short period of married life, of complete surrender of all faculties, absolutely incapacitates the average woman for the outside world. She becomes reckless in appearance, clumsy in her movements, dependent in her decisions, cowardly in her judgment, a weight and a bore, which most men grow to hate and despise. . . .

The institution of marriage makes a parasite of woman, an absolute dependent. It incapacitates her for life's struggle, annihilates her social consciousness, paralyzes her imagination, and then imposes its gracious protection, which is in reality a snare, a travesty on human character.

R E A D I N G   **53**

Cheaper than a Cow

Miranda Kennedy (2004)

On a muggy monsoon morning in Kufurpur village, north India, Pornita Das is making tea for the man who owns her.

She is a pretty girl in her late teens, wearing a *choli*, or short blouse, and a long underskirt—the typical underclothes of the region. She had come here believing she would be married, but instead she's become part of a sad demographic: a growing number of girls sold by their families in India's poorest states and bought for as little as $10 by men in prosperous parts of the country.

When young women such as Pornita arrive in their new village, their trafficker often displays them under a tree in the main market, like a slave on an auction block, and takes bids. Those bids can range up to $400, depending on the girl's age and the degree of abuse already inflicted on her by the trafficker. The girls are almost always virgins, and they are usually sold for less than the price of a cow.

In their new home, the girls often become a combination of family sex slave and domestic servant. Some girls are found chained in their owner's house; others are repeatedly raped and tortured. Even those who are better treated are expected to give birth to a son, considered a prize in Indian culture. If they fail to, they are often resold.

India's newest flesh trade is different from the trafficking of girls into brothels, although that still takes place across India. This form of trafficking emerged from the common and perfectly legal practice of finding brides in far-flung areas of the country. But when people realized how cheaply they could get girls from underprivileged West Bengal, Bihar, and the more remote string of northeastern states, they started buying young women for uses besides marriage, such as providing sexual favors to the men in a family. For propriety's sake, the eldest son will call the woman his wife, but rarely bothers with the expense—and official interference—of a wedding. Most Indian marriages are arranged, and after marriage the bride usually goes to live with her husband's family, which makes it difficult to detect girls exploited in this way.

Pappu Singh Ahir, the man Pornita calls her husband, has never married her, probably because she was underage when he bought her and he didn't want to alert the authorities. He is around 40—at least double her age, although it is hard to know for certain because his family is deliberately vague about how old Pornita is. Marriage under the age of 18 is illegal in India, although in rural areas it is still common practice. Buying girls and using them as sex slaves, however, was never common in India—until recently, when villagers became desperate for brides, and for sons.

Like many buyers, Pappu and his family refuse to admit that money exchanged hands. They say the only money they paid was the cost of transporting Pornita from her village in Assam state, in the far east of India. But Pappu Singh is not new to this business: He is accused of previously buying another young girl, Kanika, who mysteriously disappeared soon after he purchased her. As the tea boils, Pappu's mother steps into the room to warn Pornita, Kanika's replacement, not to speak openly.

It takes less than an hour to get to Kufurpur village from New Delhi, India's cosmopolitan political capital. Yet in almost every way, the villages in this region seem centuries behind the capital's world of frappuccinos and brand-name malls. There are few paved roads; during the long monsoon season, the surrounding "highways" are lined with trucks flipped on their sides in thick mud. This isn't a poor area, though: Kufurpur lies in Haryana state, the center of north India's prosperous and fertile "Hindi belt." Many farmers tend their fields with tractors here, rather than with the water buffaloes used in less affluent regions. Yet few men attend school past the age of 16, and women rarely attend at all. The attitudes are deeply feudal, and every other household includes a girl known as a *paro,* or outsider bride.

"Although it is one of the most economically affluent areas of the country, there is basically no social sensitization here," says Ravi Kant, director of Shakti Vahini, an organization fighting for sex workers' rights. "The villagers are not even aware that trafficking is a problem. They think it is their right to purchase girls and bring them back to their homes."

The Kufurpur men, hearing word of visitors, gather in the courtyard of Pappu Singh's house. The haunting sound of a peacock's mating cry echoes through the village as rain pours down.

The men have rough, weathered faces; although it is barely midday, most of them are swaying from the effects of cheap liquor. Like Pappu, they are landowners, and do not have to work much. They are more than happy to gather and give their opinions on Pappu Singh's *paro.* "Pappu had to marry a girl from outside because time had passed. He was too old and no one here wanted him," one explains. "There are no girls here for us to marry," shouts another, who says he is 25 but looks more like a ragged 45. "So we bring girls from outside, what's wrong with that?"

The problem for Indian men, says Vina Mazumdar of the Center for Women's Development Studies in New Delhi, is a shocking gender gap—"an acute shortage of brides for young men. That's the result of the steadily declining proportion of girls being born across India."

In the decade between 1991 and 2001, the number of girls (up to age 6) per 1,000 boys dropped from 945 to 927. In certain Indian regions, the problem is far worse: In one part of Haryana state, for example, the ratio has plummeted to 770 girls per 1,000 boys. Meanwhile, the population of India has ballooned above the 1 billion mark and is expected to surpass China by midcentury.

"A stage may soon come when it would become extremely difficult, if not impossible, to make up for the missing girls," predicts the United Nations Fund for Population Activities.

This dramatic differential has been created by the purposeful abortion of female fetuses, and even girl infanticide. According to the Campaign Against Female Feticide, 90 percent of the estimated 3.5 million abortions done annually in India are for the purpose of preventing the birth of girl children.

"In places like Punjab and Haryana, if you go into the village and ask people how many children they have, they say two, and they mean two sons, not two children," says Mohan Rao, a professor in the social medicine department at Jawaharlal Nehru University in New Delhi. Aborting a fetus because of its sex is illegal (standard abortions are legal in India), and the government recently toughened laws against prenatal gender screening. Nonetheless, an extremely high demand for the screening tests remains, and little can be done to stop doctors from using ultrasound machines for sex determination. "Unqualified doctors are doing ultrasounds," affirms J.B. Babbar, head medical officer at the Family Planning Association of India. "It's an easy way to make money, because we have such a strong preference for the male child in our culture."

Even poor parents often prefer to front the hefty expense of a sex determination test and abortion rather than to raise a girl. Daughters are commonly viewed as a burden in India, even among the educated classes. It's a belief facilitated by the dowry system—the illegal, but still prevalent practice of the bride's family giving money to the groom—and by the Hindu belief that a father's last rites must be carried out by his son. Many parents perceive girls to be more expensive than boys because girls require dowry money, do not support their parents in their old age, and are traditionally not earners.

"The social belief that sons are the only way to continue the family lineage perpetuates the falling sex ratio," says Indian health minister Sushma Swaraj, who insists her ministry is committed to correcting the problem. Swaraj recently proposed that the government begin an advertising campaign warning that there would not be enough women for men to marry if the trend continued.

But the Indian government is largely unwilling to recognize the connection between the ratio of male to female children and the purchasing of girls.

One woman who certainly grasps that connection is Deepa Das, suspected to have trafficked both Pornita and Kanika to Haryana state. Deepa, a 30-something woman who modestly covers her face in the company of men, was herself bought from Assam 10 years ago by her "husband." Now she lives on a large property dotted with cattle and, according to social workers in the Haryana area, runs a flourishing trade in Assamese girls. Deepa regularly travels back to her home state and convinces villagers to let her take their daughters, jangling her gold bangles and boasting about the buffalo she now owns. Then, she allegedly sells them, at a profit, to families who need brides.

Deepa freely acknowledges that she brings girls to be married in Haryana, but denies that money is involved. "I am doing a social good to bring them here," she insists. "I would have died of poverty if I had not come here. My life is so much better now."

Pornita's story begins some 1,300 miles east of Kufurpur, in a lush green village fed by the Brahmaputra, one of India's largest rivers. She grew up in a house made of bamboo and mud plaster, surrounded by waterlogged rice paddies and groves of coconut palms. Rural Assam is desperately poor, devastated by annual floods, economic isolation and a violent separatist insurgency that has ravaged the region for more than 20 years. Discrimination in greater India against the ethnically distinct Assamese is widespread, and most Assamese do not even speak India's national language, Hindi. Pornita is one of six children, so when a strange woman and man came to her village in search of a girl to take back to their rich land, her parents thought they were lucky and were happy to oblige—especially after they were offered a little money.

"Most parents who live below the poverty line believe that getting their girls married into a good family is the best thing they can give them," explains Hasina Kharbhih, a social worker who rehabilitates girls trafficked from the northeast. "What they don't realize is that these marriages are about exploitation more than anything else."

Pornita's parents had never educated their daughter, and they saw few prospects for her in their depressed village. But they had no idea they were sending her off with a man who would never actually marry her. On a bright afternoon in their village, they sat in their mud courtyard, their cows grazing nearby on freshly cut grass in wicker baskets. Pornita's father's bare legs were spattered with mud from working in the fields, and his teeth stained orange from chewing betelnut *paan*. The frames of his thick glasses were twisted. "I know nothing of Pappu Singh marrying another girl," he crowed. "Pornita is his wife now. She told us she lives in a concrete house. She has three meals a day. What else can matter?"

His wife was more emotional. A photo of their young daughter in her new house in Haryana, wearing the strange new Haryani dress, made her weep. The red *bindi* mark on her forehead smeared into a bloody-looking mark as she wiped her tears. Pornita had recently come back to visit them, bringing her new son, but then she had been dressed in Assamese clothes. She didn't complain to her family about her new life—but that's to be expected. Marriage is seen by many as part of a person's preordained destiny, and the wife's position in her in-laws' house is traditionally very low. Pornita did look a little weaker, her mother recalled. She told them she had recently had her kidney removed, although she had no history of kidney trouble. Rishi Kant of Shakti Vahini suspects that Pappu Singh sold Pornita's kidney for the money. Singh had told his neighbors he needed 10,000 rupees (about $200), and that's just about the price of a kidney on the black market.

Nonetheless, back in Kufurpur, Pornita clearly states that she doesn't want to return permanently to Assam. "I have a child and live with a family," she says as if by rote, her mother-in-law watching her carefully.

"In the villages [of Assam], poor means having no clothes to wear, no food to eat, no house to live in," says Arnab Deka, a superintendent of police for a district in Assam. "So these girls are lured, and their parents think this is an offer from god. By the time that they realize they have been cheated, that this girl has been sold, maybe one year has passed. Then, it is not possible for us to do anything."

Three years ago, Deepa Das showed up in Kanika's village in Assam. Kanika's mother, Omari, a widow, had six daughters and no sons. She barely managed to support her children by weaving saris in her dark one-room shack and working as a maid in a nearby village. It didn't take much to convince her to accept 1,000 rupees (about $20) in exchange for her daughter. But now, sitting on a cot made of woven rope outside her bamboo hut, she says that day was cursed.

"Deepa Das told us there is nothing to worry about," chimes in Kanika's 15-year-old sister, who steps out from the crowd of villagers in a ragged pink dress. "When we called her, she said only 'Kanika is not here.' We asked, 'Who has Kanika married?' But she did not say. Then, she told us Kanika died of some stomach problem, and hung up. But she never gave us the death certificate." Without the confirmation of a body or a proper cremation, Kanika's family refuses to believe she is dead. They suspect she has been resold, perhaps after failing to bear Pappu Singh a son. The police have not yet registered Kanika's case, and social workers despair that they will ever be able to trace her.

After pressure from the media and social workers, village elders mounted an investigation into the charge that Deepa Das was trafficking girls from Assam, but police officials stepped in to vouch for her. Some social workers and activists say it's police involvement in the girl trade that allows it to continue unabated, even alleging that police take kickbacks in exchange for their silence. When asked about the trend of trafficking girls into Haryana, Rajender Kumar, the police superintendent for one Haryana district, simply reiterates that it is not illegal to marry girls from outside the state. "You can't call it trafficking if the mediator charges money," he claims.

Recently, though, the Haryana police have begun cracking down. Last summer, they rescued four female minors from families, arrested the trafficker, and put him behind bars. Once rescued, however, the girls are offered few options. Rehana, a 13-year-old Assamese girl freed from a family after being repeatedly raped and beaten, has been languishing in a Haryana government home for months. Lacking a rehabilitation program, the government put her in a halfway house for female criminals, where she received no counseling.

In Meghalaya, the northeastern state that borders Assam, social worker Hasina Kharbhih has set up a working model that offers some hope. Her group, Impulse NGO Network, works closely with the state government and police to rehabilitate girls who have been trafficked out of the northeast and sold into families or brothels. After they receive counseling, they are taught a trade—usually handicraft or beautician skills. Eventually they are given a microcredit loan to start their own small businesses. They are reintegrated with their families, but not before the family and neighbors are educated about trafficking and sexual violation.

"The most important thing is they have to get back into society," says Hasina. She envisions a time when communities will band together to prevent their girls from being sold. In Kanika's village, such an awareness may already be growing, spurred by her unexplained disappearance. Her neighbors say they will never take money from a stranger for one of their daughters. They see Kanika's mother every evening, as dusk falls, waiting outside her bamboo shack for her daughter to come home.

Who Wants to Marry a Feminist?

Lisa Miya-Jervis (2000)

The winter I got engaged, a college friend was using some of my essays as course material for a Rhetoric 101 class she was teaching at a large Midwestern university. She couldn't wait to alert her students to my impending marriage. "They all think you're a lesbian," she told me. "One of them even asked if you hate men." I was blown over by the clichZ of it all—how had we come to the end of the twentieth century with such ridiculous, outmoded notions even partially intact? But I was, at least, pleased that my friend was able to use my story to banish the stereotype once and (I hoped) for all in the minds of 30 corn-fed first-years. "To a man?" they reportedly gasped when told the news.

I'd been married less than a year when a customer at the bookstore where my husband works approached the counter to buy a copy of the feminist magazine I edit. "You know," a staffer told her while ringing up the purchase, "the woman who does this magazine is married to a guy who works here." The customer, supposedly a long-time reader, was outraged at the news—I believe the phrase "betrayal of feminism" was uttered—and vowed never to buy the magazine again. These two incidents may be extreme, but they are nonetheless indicative. Although we are far from rare, young married feminists are still, for some, something of a novelty—like a dressed-up dog. We can cause a surprised "Oh, would you look at that" or a disappointed "Take that damned hat off the dog, it's just not right."

Let's take the disappointment first. Marriage's bad reputation among feminists is certainly not without reason. We all know the institution's tarnished history: women as property passed from father to husband; monogamy as the simplest way to assure paternity and thus produce "legitimate" children; a husband's legal entitlement to his wife's domestic and sexual services. With marriage rates falling and social sanctions against cohabitation falling away, why would a feminist choose to take part in such a retro, potentially oppressive, bigotedly exclusive institution?

Well, there are a lot of reasons, actually. Foremost are the emotional ones: love, companionship, the pure joy that meeting your match brings with it. But, because I'm wary of the kind of muddled romanticizing that has ill-served women in their heterosexual dealings for most of recorded history, I have plenty of other reasons. To reject marriage simply because of its history is to give in to that history; to argue against marriage by saying that a wife's identity is necessarily subsumed by her husband's is to do nothing more than second the notion.

And wasn't it feminists who fought so hard to procure the basic rights that used to be obliterated by marriage? Because of the women's rights movement, we can maintain our own bank accounts; we can make our own health care choices; we can refuse sex with our husbands and prosecute them if they don't comply. In the feminist imagination, "wife" can still conjure up images of cookie-baking, cookie-cutter Donna Reeds whose own desires have been forced to take a backseat to their stultifying helpmate duties. But it's neither 1750 nor 1950, and Donna Reed was a mythical figure even in her own time. Marriage, now, is potentially what we make it.

Which brings me to the "surprise" portion of our program. As long as the yeti of the antifeminist world—the hairy-legged man-hater (everyone claims to have seen her but actual evidence is sparse)—roams the earth, we need to counteract her image. And as long as wives are assumed—by anyone—to be obedient little women with no lives of their own, those of us who give the lie to this straw bride need to make ourselves as conspicuous as possible.

I want to take the good from marriage and leave the rest. I know it's not for everyone, but the "for as long as we both shall live" love and support thang really works for me. Sure, I didn't need the wedding to get that love and support, but neither does the fact of marriage automatically consign me and my man to traditional man-and-wife roles. Like so many relationships, married and un-, ours is a complex weave of support, independence, and sex. We achieve this privately—from the mundanities of you-have-to-cook-tonight-because-I-have-this-deadline-tomorrow to sleepy late-night discussions on more profound matters, like the meaning of life or how many steps it takes to link Kevin Bacon to John Gielgud by way of at least one vampire movie. But also publicly—with our name change, for example (explaining to folks like the Social Security Administration and whoever hands out passports that, yes, we both need new papers, because we each have added the other's name was, and I mean this quite seriously, a thrill). And it's this public nature of marriage that appeals. It's what allows me to take

a stab at all this change I've been yammering about.

I won't pretend I meet with success all the time. Disrupting other people's expectations is hard, and sometimes it's neither possible nor desirable to wear the workings of one's relationship on one's sleeve. An appropriate cocktail party introduction is not, "This is my husband, Christopher, who knows how to truss a turkey, which I don't, and who, by the way, doesn't mind at all that I make more money than him. Oh, and did I mention that the last time our toilet got scrubbed, it wasn't by me?"

Plus, some people's perceptions can only change so much. My 90-year-old grandfather, who has been nothing but open-minded and incredibly supportive of my feminist work, persists in asking what my husband is going to do for food whenever I leave town on my own. Each time, I say the same thing: "Christopher knows perfectly well how to feed himself. In fact, he's cooking dinner for me right now." And then my grandfather gives a little surprised chuckle: those crazy kids, what will they thing of next? And my accountant, who's been doing my taxes for years and knows my husband only as a Social Security number, automatically assigned Christopher the status of "taxpayer" and put me down as "spouse" on our first joint return. Yeah, it was a tad annoying, but so far it's the sum total of the eclipse of my identity by his. Not so bad, really.

By and large I do believe that we're culturally ready to accept changes in the way marriages are viewed. Increasing rates of cohabitation and the growing visibility of long-term same-sex partnerships are changing popular notions of relationships. Even trash TV holds promise: Fox's *Who Wants to Marry a Multi-Millionaire?* debacle laid bare many ugly things about American capitalism and media spectacle, but there was one fairly unexpected result. The show was presented as a display, however crass, of old-fashioned marital values—a trade of youth, beauty, and fecundity for wealth, security, and caretaking, complete with the groom's friends and family on hand for that lovely arranged-marriage feel. But it turned out to be nothing of the kind. The bride, as it happened, just wanted the lark of a free trip to Vegas, and the groom, a boost to his moribund show-biz career. That the concept saw the outside of a Fox conference room proves that modern marriage is in dire need of feminist attention. But the widely expressed outrage and disgust that followed the show are evidence that the general public is more than ready to discard the notion that a woman's ultimate goal is the altar.

It's true that the most important parts, the actual warp and weft of Christopher's and my relationship, could be achieved without a legal marriage (and I could have kept my third-wave street cred). In the end, though, the decision to marry or not to marry is—no matter how political the personal—an emotional one. I wanted to link my life to Christopher's, and, yes, I admit to taking advantage of the universally understood straight-shot-to-relationship-legitimacy that marriage offers. But it is a testament to the feminists who came before me, who offered up all those arguments about marriage's oppressive roots and worked tirelessly to ensure that my husband owns neither my body nor my paycheck, that I can indulge my emotion without fear of being caught in those roots. Instead, I can carry on their struggle and help forge a new vision of what marriage is.

R E A D I N G **55**

Don't Give Up Your Day Job
Leslie Bennetts on *The Feminine Mistake*

Heidi Bruggink (2007)

Prior to joining *Vanity Fair,* where she has been a contributing editor since 1988, Leslie Bennetts spent ten years at the *New York Times.* Bennetts started as a writer for the Style section and went on to cover national politics, metropolitan news, and City Hall, becoming the first woman ever to cover a presidential campaign for the *Times.* In her new book, *The Feminine Mistake,* Bennetts asserts that women's decisions to abandon their careers may save them stress in the short-term, but the repercussions are enormously dangerous—and women often fail to understand this until it's far too late. Further, she argues, the financial and psychological benefits of working outside the home are enormous. Bennetts herself serves as a prime example of this assertion, having crafted an enviable journalism career over the past thirty years while simultaneously raising a family. She spoke with the *Humanist,* shortly before her book's release.

The *Humanist:* What do you consider the main points you want readers to take away from your book?

Bennetts: This book was originally inspired by my exasperation with the whole issue of women quitting their jobs to stay home with children. It's covered in the media and in our culture as if it were simply a lifestyle choice. Nobody ever mentions money—the economic risks that women take on by becoming financially dependent on a man. And every time I read a story about how juggling work and a family is so stressful that women are quitting their careers to stay home I'd think, yes, but what about ten or fifteen years from now when their kids are grown up? Half these women will likely get divorced, others may lose their husbands due to premature death, or their husbands may lose their jobs. There are all kinds of risk factors that just weren't being discussed. People also cover this issue as if you can opt out of the labor force for *x* number of years and just waltz back in whenever you want to, and women are just disastrously unaware of how difficult the barriers to reentry are and what an enormous financial penalty they pay for time out. So I started this project with the purpose of warning women about the risks of economic dependency. That's the first takeaway.

The second part of this is the good news. For a variety of reasons, many of which have to do with the way they're socialized, women in our society are unaware of the many benefits of work, aside from the paycheck. Women are raised not to brag; blowing one's own horn is the male model, the Donald Trump model. So women don't talk about how great it is to be successful, how great it is to make a lot of money, how great it is to have power, and how empowering it is to take on new challenges.

The *Humanist:* How did you approach the writing of this book?

Bennetts: I interviewed all kinds of women from age seventeen to eighty, and I found that women are horrendously unaware of the risks they're taking until it's too late. They're making these choices usually in their twenties and thirties, and they have very rosy expectations of the future. If you interview women in their forties and fifties, many have found themselves on the wrong side of the odds: divorced, widowed, or suddenly thrust into the role of breadwinner and they know what a high price they've paid because they can't find a decent job.

In addition to researching all the risks of dependency, I've also researched the benefits of work for women, and the bottom line is that working women are happier and, believe it or not, working women are healthier. There are really fascinating longitudinal studies that show that multiple roles are in fact good for women.

The *Humanist:* I was really surprised by the health issue.

Bennetts: It's just amazing. And women don't know this because we've been bombarded for thirty

years with the same old story in the media about the unbearable stress of the juggling act. And so you tell people that long enough and they buy it. The truth is it isn't unbearable. All of my friends have really successful careers and really wonderful families. And I don't think we're anomalous. Millions of women out there manage this. They work, they put dinner on the table for their kids at night, and they manage to keep their families together and to bring in a second income, increasingly one that represents the major share.

The *Humanist:* How did women evolve to this reality?

Bennetts: I think there was a segment of the baby boomer generation that learned from their mothers—the women of the 1950s and Betty Friedan's *The Feminine Mystique*—who were left stranded when the divorce rate spiked in the 1970s. Many of them didn't have college educations or professional credentials because they had been housewives. One of the women I interviewed said to me, "I saw what happened to my mother and her friends, and I said to myself, that is never going to happen to me." And so some women like her went out and pursued careers. A great many others didn't, so what I see is a lot of women out there in their late forties or early fifties who are feeling really lost and frightened, and many of them don't have partners anymore. Like the *New York Times* recently reported, there are now more American women living without a partner than there are living with one. Marriage is no longer the normative state for women in this country, and yet we're still bringing girls up to believe that it is and that there's always going to be a man around to take care of them, which, in fact, isn't the case.

Moreover, women are living longer these days, so that marriage is coming to represent just a segment of a woman's life. It's a very scary prospect for society as well as for individuals if women don't take responsibility for ensuring that they can support themselves throughout a life, not just a part of it.

One of the things younger women today don't seem to understand is how relatively finite the period of intensive mothering is over the course of a lifetime. In my book I call it the "fifteen-year paradigm" because if you have a couple of kids and they're two or three years apart, it's less than fifteen years that you spend really consumed by the demands of mothering. And over the course of a fifty-year work life, what's fifteen years? So because of the short-term demands of mothering small children, women are making this fatal choice that's going to compromise their interests and leave them with very little after their children grow up.

If you look at women in midlife, the ones who are really happy and excited about the future are the ones who have their own careers. The difference is so dramatic. They pay for it with a certain amount of stress early on, when their kids are young and they're juggling like mad, but as the years go on the benefits increase exponentially for working women, and the penalties increase exponentially for women who have given up their careers.

The *Humanist*: Right before I graduated from college, it seemed that suddenly everyone was talking about their fears that there was no way to have it all. I was shocked that after successfully juggling responsibilities from morning to midnight for years, many young women suddenly thought that it was impossible to handle a family and a career.

Bennetts: They've been brainwashed. There are so many messages in this culture that have been telling bright, ambitious young women that you really can't have it all. And the tragedy is that they believe it. It's true that you can't have it all in the sense that you can't have every area of your life be perfect at every moment along the way, but it depends on how you define having it all. Can you have a meaningful career and a stable marriage and wonderful children? Absolutely.

The *Humanist*: How do you address women's issues with perfectionism?

Bennetts: Perfectionism is the bane of women's existence. Everything out there is just harping on women to perfect various aspects of themselves. The message is always: you should be better, and it's the wrong message. We're focusing on the trivia

instead of the substance. There are so many girls out there—smart girls—who spend more time planning their wedding than they do planning how they're going to support themselves for the rest of their lives, because somehow they've absorbed the message that if you're a girl you don't really have to think about that. My message is, "Guess what? You really do have to think about that."

The *Humanist*: It seems that a big part of a woman's ability to continue having a fulfilling professional life while raising a family is finding an understanding employer.

Bennetts: It isn't just finding an understanding employer; it's recognizing that you may need to make compromises. No, you can't be a good mother of small children if you're going to have one of these "extreme" jobs that just take everything, but that doesn't mean that you have to give up your whole career. Those are just not the choices. There are many ways to continue to work and have a meaningful professional life. For many women that means working for themselves. An awful lot of women have found ways to work from the home, which is an ideal way, or work from home part time. Some of the most successful women I know do that, and increasingly employers in a lot of fields don't care where you're working, as long as the job gets done.

The *Humanist*: What are the implications on children when their mothers don't work, in terms of gender and family structure?

Bennetts: As one of the sociologists in my book said, this issue has been researched every which way for close to forty years, and it always comes out a wash. But the way it's framed by the "Can-you-be-a-good-mother-if-you-work?" syndrome makes working mothers feel horribly guilty. I talked to plenty of school principals and teachers and psychologists who said, "I see plenty of stay-at-home mothers who aren't emotionally available to their kids and plenty of working mothers who are." The difference isn't whether or not you work. The most important variables are completely different ones.

I'm the first one to admit that the needs of your children should come first. I put the needs of my children first. But I think that women who don't work are teaching their children dangerous lessons that they are often unaware of until later on. They act as dancing attendants to their kids around the clock, and that doesn't necessarily have a good effect on their kids from what I've seen, and from what I have been told by many child development experts. The children of working mothers are often more resourceful and self-sufficient because they've been encouraged to be. I think stay-at-home moms may unconsciously need to justify their own presence at home by making their children depend on them. When my kids were in preschool, I'd see kids who should've outgrown the stroller, but the mothers would still be strolling these oversized children along the street instead of saying "Get out and walk!" And that to me is a metaphor for what went on. The kids of working mothers were tying their own shoelaces because their mothers were busy and had taught them how, but the stay-at-home mothers were still tying their kids' shoelaces for them. If that kind of thing continues as children grow up and mature, I don't think it does kids any favors.

The other thing that kids learn from a mother who's basically dedicated her life to providing unpaid services for the children, the household, and the husband is that that's what women do. We service people. That doesn't breed the best possible respect for women. The sociologist I spoke to said that the daughters of working mothers had more of a sense of their own ambitions and goals and abilities, that it was empowering to have a working mother, and that their boys don't just automatically assume that all the housework is going to be done by a female.

I think there are huge benefits to egalitarian marriages that often aren't discussed. There's a lot of propaganda out there trying to convince people that traditional gender roles work better for people in the home, but there's a great deal of social science that contradicts this. It's a supported claim that is very threatening to people who are heavily invested in conventional gender roles. The evangelical religions, for example, typically believe in biblically ordained family hierarchies, and a lot of conservative ideologues also believe that women should "know their place." But the truth is, as I document in my book, egalitarian marriage works extremely well for people, and it protects women, because if men are assuming their share of the burden of childrearing and domestic tasks, that frees up their wives to maintain their careers, rather than being crushed by the burden of not only doing their jobs, but the dreaded second shift. That's what really drives women out of the workforce.

The *Humanist:* But as you say in your book, even in the more egalitarian marriages, women are considered lucky if they have a spouse who does his share.

Bennetts: I just don't understand why women aren't insisting on it. My attitude was, "I'm not interested in marrying or having kids with anybody who's not going to be an equal partner. What's really important here is to overcome the dual message. Men grow up assuming they're going to have a family and a career. Nobody ever tells them that they have to choose, and in the twenty-first century we need to raise women the same way. Women have to be mindful about their needs for both components of an adult life: work and love.

We can't expect it to fall easily into place, either. I remember an old t-shirt that featured a cartoon woman saying, "Oops, I forgot to have children." You can't forget about the fact that your fertile years are finite, and you can't put off thinking about what you're going to do with your life. What's really important is for women to be mindful of both goals, to consider how they're going to integrate them, and to understand that it's in their best interests to find a way rather than choose.

The *Humanist:* Are you planning to lecture on the college circuit to share your message?

Bennetts: Absolutely. The people that I'm most anxious to reach are the young women who haven't yet made a choice, because I think they have strong misperceptions and assumptions about these issues. It's time to set the record straight: nobody is going to take care of you but yourself.

Partners as Parents
Challenges Faced by Gays Denied Marriage

Charlene Gomes (2003)

*If the right of privacy means anything, it is the
right of the individual, married or single, to be free
from unwarranted governmental intrusion into
matters so fundamentally affecting a person as the
decision whether to bear or beget a child.*

—*Supreme Court Justice William Brennan,*
Eisenstadt v. Baird, *1972*

I had just read these words in my constitutional law class in 1997 when a coworker of mine shared with me his and his partner's struggles to have a child. They, together with a lesbian couple with whom they were close, had made numerous attempts at pregnancy "the old-fashioned way"—by tracking ovulation and inserting the sperm with a turkey baster—to no avail. They had recently begun to explore artificial insemination and were again frustrated to realize they would have to travel quite far from their Virginia home to get to a state where the procedure was legally available to them. A Virginia statute restricts the procedure to couples who are husband and wife. Numerous other states have similarly restrictive statutes. It seems that these laws aren't constitutional in light of the Supreme Court's 1972 decision in *Eisenstadt v. Baird*. Although the *Eisenstadt* ruling dealt specifically with laws restricting the use of contraceptives to married couples, the language of the decision was broad enough to encompass efforts to have a child as well as to avoid having a child.

In the past several years, issues regarding gay marriage and gay families have become a regular part of the national debate and, to a lesser extent, political debate. In 1996 Congress passed the Defense of Marriage Act (DOMA) in response to a Hawaii law that granted same-sex couples the right to marry (the law was later overturned by the Hawaii state legislature). Since then, thirty-seven states have passed their own DOMAs.

At the same time, it has become progressively easier for gay families to gain custody of biological children, conceive biological children through various fertilization methods and services, and adopt children. Yet President George W. Bush, many religious conservatives, and even some Democratic presidential hopefuls have reaffirmed their belief that marriage by definition applies only to unions between one man and one woman.

Given all the national rhetoric about the sanctity of marriage and the importance of raising children within a legally recognized relationship, one would assume that legislators would take note of the growing numbers of young children being raised by gay parents and get to work passing legislation legitimizing their parents' relationship. Yet nothing could be further from the truth. Despite Canada's recent move toward legalizing same-sex marriages, the United States continues to show every intention of fighting tooth and nail against this broadening of marriage laws, including a recently proposed constitutional amendment barring same-sex marriage. Unfortunately, the opposite mood has prevailed.

Data from the 2000 U.S. census reveal that approximately one in three lesbian/bisexual couples and 22 percent of gay/bisexual couples are raising children. According to the National Gay and Lesbian Task Force (NGLTF), estimates of the total number of children with at least one gay or lesbian parent range from six million to fourteen million. Yet these numbers only track gays who were willing to self-report on the census; many remain unwilling to reveal their sexual orientation to the federal government, as the government offers them no protection from discrimination. Thus, the numbers certainly underestimate the true number of gays raising children. Married heterosexual couples with children comprise only 23 percent of U.S. households.

Gay or straight, not all parents raise children equally. Parenting ability relies on a complex and unquantifiable mix of skills and emotions. Love, patience, empathy, and respect, along with the ability to provide necessities and discipline without being abusive, are a mere sampling of points along the infinite parenting spectrum. It is curious—and telling—that current debate focuses on the legal ability of gays to marry rather than their actual ability to maintain life partnerships and to raise productive, well-adjusted children.

Even so, gay parents face unique barriers in their efforts to care and provide for their children. According to the NGLTF, privileges enjoyed by heterosexual married couples but denied to gay parents include legal recognition of the parent-child relationship for children born during the relationship; recognition of parental status under the Family and Medical Leave Act; access to child support when the parental relationship ends; the right to petition for visitation and custody after the dissolution of a relationship; and (in some states) adoption and foster parenting.

PATHS TO PARENTHOOD

Same-sex couples become parents in a variety of ways. Some have children from previous heterosexual relationships while others are adoptive or foster parents. Lesbians may become pregnant through donor insemination, and gay male couples are turning more and more to surrogacy arrangements.

According to the NGLTF, donor insemination use among lesbian couples has increased since the 1980s. While insemination seems like an ideal solution, practical and legal barriers make it less so. Insemination is very expensive and results aren't always guaranteed. Insurance rarely covers these services—at least where lesbians are concerned—and clinical infertility hasn't been demonstrated. In addition, the majority of states have yet to address the issue of whether the sperm donor is the legal father of the child. This leaves the child's legal parentage to chance, opening the door for future legal problems. Also, the inability to prove paternity can be a stumbling block later on if one or both of the partners needs to be availed of public benefits.

Likewise, the NGLTF reports that the use of surrogacy among gay men has been on the rise in recent years. Unlike donor insemination, a generally accepted practice across the social and professional landscape, surrogacy is often considered controversial. Many states discourage the practice and two prohibit it outright. Other states prohibit payment to the surrogate mother. As with insemination, the law is unclear as to who are considered the legal parents of the offspring. Some states recognize the surrogate and her spouse while others attribute parentage to the couple contracting with the surrogate.

ADOPTION

Only Florida specifically prohibits individual lesbians and gay men or same-sex couples from adopting children. Mississippi only prohibits same-sex couples from adopting, and some states, such as Utah, prioritize heterosexual married couples as adoptive and foster parents. Other states that don't make it a specific consideration in adoption determinations often take sexual orientation into account if raised in the course of the proceeding. Even so, many states allow gays to adopt as individuals and many—including California, Connecticut, the District of Columbia, Massachusetts, New Jersey, New York, and Vermont—now allow joint adoptions by same-sex couples.

What is truly harmful for children of gay parents is the lack of legal protection arising out of a failure to recognize same-sex marriage or to allow adoption by nonbiological life partners. The situation of nonbiological same-sex partners is most similar to that of stepparents in heterosexual marriages. Generally, if the noncustodial biological parent consents, stepparents may adopt the children. Yet, in the same situation, same-sex life partners usually require rigorous home visits and family studies. Most states have recognized that in some limited circumstances stepparents can adopt even without the noncustodial biological parent's consent, yet this doesn't hold for same-sex life partners.

The child suffers needlessly when the nonbiological partner is unable to establish a legal relationship, especially should the biological parent die or the relationship otherwise dissolve. The child isn't entitled to financial support or inheritance rights if there is no will. Lack of legal protections for the nonbiological partner include custody and visitation privileges, consent to emergency medical treatment, and permission to attend parent-teacher conferences.

Children with an adoptive stepparent enjoy other benefits not available to children living with a same-sex parent who is unable to adopt. Some state worker's compensation programs and the federal Social Security survivor benefit program now permit minor stepchildren living with and dependent upon a stepparent to receive benefits after the stepparent's death. Additionally, the Family and Medical Leave Act allows unpaid leave to care for a stepchild. Extending these benefits and protections to same-sex couples by legitimizing their relationships would ensure that the children of these couples will be treated equally with children of heterosexual married couples. The benefits of according these protections to all children easily outweigh the externalities imposed on third parties disapproving of homosexual relationships.

The landscape is somewhat different in cases of second-parent adoption, where one member of a same-sex couple is a biological parent and the nonbiological partner wishes also to become a legal parent. Stepparents in heterosexual marriages encounter little or no barriers when it comes to adopting the child of the biological parent. The law assumes that such an arrangement is in the child's best interests. Approximately twenty-five states allow same-sex second-parent adoptions, but the adoptions are costly and littered with invasive and time-consuming procedures. Unlike heterosexual couples in the same situation, same-sex couples are subjected to numerous home visits and intensive social work assessments to determine the suitability of the adoption.

Because heterosexual couples are often the preferred placements for adoptive children, many gay and lesbian couples willingly adopt the least "adoptable" children. Most married couples seek to adopt healthy babies. As a result, children with physical or mental disabilities often spend their lives being shuffled around between countless foster homes. By the time they are of school age, finding adoptive parents for them becomes next to impossible. According to Allison Beers' 1997 article "Gay Men and Lesbians, Building Loving Families," published by the Adoption Resource Exchange for Single Parents, many of these children are now placed in stable, loving homes with gay individuals or gay couples. Beers cites the example of Elmy Martinez, who adopted five special-needs children. At the time the article was written, four out of the five children had graduated from high school, two went on to the army, one received vocational training and was holding a steady job, and one had completed two years of community college. As proud as any parent, Martinez states in the article, "These kids have made a big difference in my life. You take them away from me and what am I?"

That gays are more readily allowed to adopt special-needs children raises an interesting question: why are the people who some label as "unfit to parent" often given children needing the most care? Where are the protests from heterosexual couples and conservative groups that proclaim homosexual relationships to be both immoral and illegal? Why aren't they rushing in to rescue these children from adoption by parents who suffer from what the Family Research Council has called a "pathological condition"?

CUSTODY

As challenging as it might sometimes be for same-sex couples to create a family, keeping the family together can be equally challenging. For gay and lesbian parents, custody disputes, by nature emotionally charged and often contentious, pose additional threats not faced by their heterosexual counterparts. Although the laws governing custody vary from state to state, two universal principles govern: that the court should consider the "best interests" of the child when determining custody and that there is a strong preference for placing the child with a natural parent as opposed to a third party. Courts considering custody disputes between two natural parents have generally followed one of three approaches for determining the fitness of gay and lesbian parents: the nexus approach, the nexus approach as a minor factor, and the per se approach.

The nexus approach is used by the majority of states. It asks the court to consider the causal connection between the conduct of the parent and any adverse effect on the child. The court inquires into the abilities of the parent rather than deeming the parent per se unfit based on sexual orientation. Of the three approaches, the nexus test is the most fact based, focusing on actual evidence of the child's best interests as opposed to stereotypes or presumptions about the parent. The parent's sexual orientation is considered only if harmful effects are proven. Currently, the District of Columbia is the only jurisdiction in which sexual orientation in and of itself cannot be a conclusive factor in custody and visitation matters.

Similarly, the nexus as a minor factor approach has led some courts to maintain that the parent's sexual orientation is merely one of many considerations in determining the best interests of the child. It differs from the strict nexus approach in that courts using nexus as a minor factor will automatically consider the parent's homosexuality in determining the best interest of the child.

The per se approach holds that the parent's homosexuality presents a refutable presumption that the parent is unfit. It rests on the notion that children of homosexual parents cannot possibly thrive because of social stigma, peer harassment, and the threat to their own "normal" heterosexual development. For the most part, even very conservative courts have shifted away from this approach in recent years. The per se rule isn't without support, however. Noted family law scholar Lynn Wardle of Brigham Young University would apply a refutable presumption to all cases involving a homosexual parent. Wardle would allow the heterosexual ex-spouse who has been denied custody to use a gay parent's new relationship as grounds for modifying the custody agreement and thus grant custody to the formerly noncustodial ex-spouse.

Unfortunately, the per se rule ultimately harms the child it seeks to protect by fueling power struggles between parents and undermining the state's (and the child's) interest in the finality and continuity of the custody agreement. The per se approach effectively eradicates the requirement for the party seeking to gain custody to show a change in circumstances that would serve the child's best interests.

In addition, courts often impose restrictions on divorcing parents that typically deny economic support (and sometimes custody) to parents who are cohabiting with a partner to whom they aren't married. These restrictions unfairly burden gay parents because they aren't legally able to marry their partners like heterosexual parents can, forcing them to choose between their children and their partner.

For the most part, gay parents today have a much easier time gaining custody of their children than they have in the recent past. Cases denying gay parents custody on factors other than actual fitness stand out as an area that generally receives little attention. Two cases are worth nothing.

In the 1996 *Ward v. Ward* decision, the First District Court of Appeals for the district of Florida awarded the father's petition for a change in custody based on the mother being a lesbian, despite the fact that the father had been convicted of murdering his first wife. What's more, the father had been less than a model parent in following the original custody agreement: he declined the mother's offer to extend his summer visitation, didn't attend doctors' appointments or parent-teacher conferences, wasn't knowledgeable about the child's attention deficit disorder, and fulfilled his child support obligation only sporadically.

In *Bottoms v. Bottoms,* a Virginia court in 1994 denied the mother custody in favor of the maternal grandmother, finding that a lesbian was per se unfit to parent. Ignoring expert testimony concluding that the child wasn't adversely affected by his mother's relationship with her partner, the judge based his ruling on his personal belief that the mother's conduct was illegal and immoral. At the time the case was tried, a Virginia sodomy statute made oral and anal sex a felony offense. But the statute applied to heterosexuals as well as homosexuals, and while the judge thoroughly probed the nature of the mother's relationship with her lesbian partner in graphic detail, he never questioned the grandmother's sexual practices.

In the *Bottoms* case, both the mother and the grandmother were high school dropouts with no special skills or training. Sharon Bottoms, the child's mother, had been sexually molested by her mother's boyfriend from the age of twelve to seventeen. Up until two weeks before the custody proceedings began, the grandmother continued living with the boyfriend who she knew had molested her daughter. Despite this, she was granted custody of the grandchild because the judge felt that she was a better parent than any homosexual could ever be. The grandmother's history of cohabiting with a man known to be molesting her own child should clearly have reinforced the presumption for the natural parent. Instead, the judge allowed prejudice to subjugate the law and stripped Sharon Bottoms of her parental rights.

Despite legal advancements since the *Bottoms* case, lesbian mothers continue to face unique custody challenges. According to the NGLTF, approximately 30 percent of all lesbian and bisexual female parents have been threatened with a loss of custody. Among those seeking to obtain custody from lesbian mothers are biological fathers, sperm donors, female co-parents, grandparents, and other relatives.

In addition, many gay individuals and families live in poverty. Yet gay families who rely on public benefits often find themselves up against a welfare system that favors married heterosexual couples above all other families. According to the NGLTF, gay couples face challenges in all areas of public benefits—from housing assistance, where they are often unable to register as a family, to Temporary Assistance to Needy Families regulations that assume all children are the products of heterosexual unions. For example, lesbian mothers unable to establish paternity of their children risk losing a large percentage of benefits and may forfeit benefits altogether. Single fathers on the other hand aren't required to disclose the maternity of their children in order to receive benefits.

CHILDREN OF GAY PARENTS

In her 1997 *Family Advocate* article "Debunking Myths About Lesbian and Gay Parents and Their Children," Kathryn Kendall addresses the gender identity and sexual orientation of children raised by gay parents. Kendall points out that numerous studies conducted since 1978 have found that children raised by gay or lesbian parents are "indistinguishable from other children in terms of gender identity, gender role behavior, and general psychological health" and that the incidence of same-sex orientation among children of gay and lesbian parents is the same as for heterosexual parents. Likewise, Kendall found that in terms of self-esteem, divorce does more damage to children than does their parent's sexual orientation.

Another argument frequently made by conservatives is that gay parents will surely raise gender-confused children. However, studies have consistently shown that this isn't the case. Carlos Ball and Janice Farrell Pea surveyed a series of studies from 1978 to 1996 regarding the sexual orientation of children raised by homosexual parents. Their survey concluded that, with the exception of one study, the percentage of children of gays and lesbians who were identified as gay or lesbian ranged from zero to nine.

Perhaps the most widely used argument against allowing gays to marry, adopt, or retain custody of their children is the assumption that being raised by gay parents will cause children to "become" gay. But is this really the case? And if so, is it really harmful? We tend to think of heterosexuality as the norm, but the most conservative estimates allow that approximately 3 percent of the population is gay. Although 3 percent seems next to insignificant, a different picture is presented when translated into raw numbers. For example, if there are 1,674,000 self-identified same-sex couples in the United States, then there are at least 3,348,000 gay individuals in the United States. It is a lot harder to overlook three million than 3 percent. So, besides marginalizing the incidence of homosexuality, the fear that children will turn out to be gay assumes that being gay is in and of itself detrimental to the child.

THE MYTH OF HOMOSEXUALITY AND PEDOPHILIA

It is a common misperception that gays are more likely to molest children than heterosexuals. In fact, the vast majority of child molestation acts are perpetrated by heterosexual men. In her 1994 *Pediatrics* magazine article "Are Children at Risk for Sexual Abuse by Homosexuals?" Carole Jenny found that 94 percent of molested girls and 86 percent of molested boys were abused by men. Of the boys abused by an adult male, 74 percent were abused by someone in a heterosexual relationship with the child's mother, while only 2 percent of perpetrators could "possibly" be identified as homosexual.

Yet these unambiguous statistics on child molestation aren't at issue when heterosexual men seek physical custody of their children. And yet at least one family law scholar, Lynne Wardle, has argued that potential abuse is a factor to be considered when gays and lesbians seek custody. The disparity between stereotype and reality is indicative of the level of harm that can ensue by allowing prejudice to determine custody placements.

CONCLUSION

Issues addressing the rights of homosexuals appear daily in the news. Debates abound about gays' right to marry, raise children, and hold a leadership role in public, private, and religious entities. The fact that these issues have come to the fore and are being publicly discussed says much about current attitudes regarding homosexuals as people. As with previous civil rights struggles, the road to full personhood under the law is long and hard but worth the journey.

Those who continue to oppose the right of homosexuals to marry and otherwise be free from discrimination in employment, housing, inheritance, family matters, and the countless other rights that many heterosexuals take for granted base their objections largely on religious grounds. Hiding behind the facade of morality, they call upon "tradition" as their key witness for refusal to change. But tradition is a red herring attempting to disguise what is fundamentally a religious objection based on—as Bush so eloquently put it—the "sanctity of marriage," meaning a one-man/one-woman relationship for the purpose of creating and raising God's children.

But truth will ultimately trump tradition, and the truth is that God is an optional party to a marriage in the United States. The real foundation of a marriage is having a legally recognized relationship between two people that affords them numerous benefits and protections, along with a handful of duties. While many couples choose to marry in a religious ceremony and plan to raise a family together, neither of these options is required and a couple is just as married if they have a civil ceremony and never have children. So, how relevant is the "sanctity of marriage"? It is relevant only to those who choose to make it so within their own relationship.

Marriage is a wonderful and important societal institution. It signals to the community a dedicated respect, affection, and commitment to one's partner. It fosters a recognizable and familiar family structure that makes it possible to confer and enforce the legal benefits, protections, and responsibilities that go along with it. It provides stability and safety for one's partner and children in the event of tragedy or dissolution of the relationship. As such, it should be available to all people, regardless of their sexual orientation. Conception, adoption, and custody likewise shouldn't be compromised by an unfounded concern that exposure to homosexuality poses a danger to children. Rather, they should be based on the long-standing principle of the best interests of the child and a presumption in favor of the parents who choose to conceive, adopt, or otherwise raise the child.

As popular as ideas about the instability of gay families may be, they are based on fear and not on fact. Nearly all children are teased about something, whether it be the child's physical appearance, speech, ethnicity, race, religion, or economic status. Society will have its prejudices. In the 1984 case of *Palmore v. Sidoti,* the Supreme Court overturned a case refusing custody to a child's mother based on fear of harassment arising out of her interracial marriage, stating, "The Constitution cannot control such prejudices but neither can it tolerate them." Likewise, prejudice against gays' right to adopt is unconstitutional and should no longer be tolerated in the United States.

R E A D I N G *57*

Man Child
A Black Lesbian Feminist's Response

Audre Lorde (1984)

This article is not a theoretical discussion of Lesbian Mothers and their Sons, nor a how-to article. It is an attempt to scrutinize and share some pieces of that common history belonging to my son and to me. I have two children: a fifteen-and-a-half-year-old daughter, Beth, and a fourteen-year-old son, Jonathan. This is the way it was/is with me and Jonathan, and I leave the theory to another time and person. This is one woman's telling.

I have no golden message about the raising of sons for other lesbian mothers, no secret to transpose your questions into certain light. I have my own ways of rewording those same questions, hoping we will all come to speak those questions and pieces of our lives we need to share. We are women making contact within ourselves and with each other across the restrictions of a printed page, bent upon the use of our own/one another's knowledges.

The truest direction comes from inside. I give the most strength to my children by being willing to look within myself, and by being honest with them about what I find there, without expecting a response beyond their years. In this way they begin to learn to look beyond their own fears.

All our children are outriders for a queendom not yet assured.

My adolescent son's growing sexuality is a conscious dynamic between Jonathan and me. It would be presumptuous of me to discuss Jonathan's sexuality here, except to state my belief that whomever he chooses to explore this area with, his choices will be nonoppressive, joyful, and deeply felt from within, places of growth.

One of the difficulties in writing this piece has been temporal; this is the summer when Jonathan is becoming a man, physically. And our sons must become men—such men as we hope our daughters, born and unborn, will be pleased to live among. Our sons will not grow into women. Their way is more difficult than that of our daughters, for they must move away from us, without us. Hopefully, our sons have what they have learned from us, and a howness to forge it into their own image.

Our daughters have us, for measure or rebellion or outline or dream; but the sons of lesbians have to make their own definitions of self as men. This is both power and vulnerability. The sons of lesbians have the advantage of our blueprints for survival, but they must take what we know and transpose it into their own maleness. May the goddess be kind to my son, Jonathan.

Recently I have met young Black men about whom I am pleased to say that their future and their visions, as well as their concerns within the present, intersect more closely with Jonathan's than do my own. I have shared visions with these men as well as temporal strategies for our survivals, and I appreciate the spaces in which we could sit down together. Some of these men I met at the First Annual Conference of Third World Lesbians and Gays held in Washington D.C. in October 1979. I have met others in different places and do not know how they identify themselves sexually. Some of these men are raising families alone. Some have adopted sons. They are Black men who dream and who act and who own their feelings, questioning. It is heartening to know our sons do not step out alone.

When Jonathan makes me angriest, I always say he is bringing out the testosterone in me. What I mean is that he is representing some piece of myself as a woman that I am reluctant to acknowledge or explore. For instance, what does "acting like a man" mean? For me, what I reject? For Jonathan, what he is trying to redefine?

Raising Black children—female and male—in the mouth of a racist, sexist, suicidal dragon is perilous and chancy. If they cannot love and resist at the same time, they will probably not survive. And in order to survive they must let go. This is what mothers teach—love, survival—that is, self-definition and letting go. For each of these, the ability to feel strongly and to recognize those feelings is central: how to feel love, how to neither discount fear nor be overwhelmed by it, how to enjoy feeling deeply.

I wish to raise a Black man who will not be destroyed by, nor settle for, those corruptions called *power* by the white fathers who mean his destruction as surely as they mean mine. I wish to raise a Black man who will recognize that the legitimate objects of his hostility are not women, but the particulars of a structure that programs him to fear and despise women as well as his own Black self.

For me, this task begins with teaching my son that I do not exist to do his feeling for him.

Men who are afraid to feel must keep women around to do their feeling for them while dismissing us for the same supposedly "inferior" capacity to feel deeply. But in this way also, men deny themselves their own essential humanity, becoming trapped in dependency and fear.

As a Black woman committed to a liveable future, and as a mother loving and raising a boy who will become a man, I must examine all my possibilities of being within such a destructive system.

Jonathan was three-and-one-half when Frances, my lover, and I met; he was seven when we all began to live together permanently. From the start, Frances' and my insistence that there be no secrets in our household about the fact that we were lesbians has been the source of problems and strengths for both children. In the beginning, this insistence grew out of the knowledge, on both our parts, that whatever was hidden out of fear could always be used against either the children or ourselves—one imperfect but useful argument for honesty. The knowledge of fear can help make us free.

> for the embattled
> there is no place
> that cannot be
> home
> nor is.*

For survival, Black children in America must be raised to be warriors. For survival, they must also be raised to recognize the enemy's many faces. Black children of lesbian couples have an advantage because they learn, very early, that oppression comes in many different forms, none of which have anything to do with their own worth.

---

* From "School Note" in *The Black Unicorn* (W. W. Norton and Company, New York, 1978), p. 55.

To help give me perspective, I remember that for years, in the namecalling at school, boys shouted at Jonathan not—"your mother's a lesbian"—but rather—"your mother's a nigger."

When Jonathan was eight years old and in the third grade we moved, and he went to a new school where his life was hellish as a new boy on the block. He did not like to play rough games. He did not like to fight. He did not like to stone dogs. And all this marked him early on as an easy target.

When he came in crying one afternoon, I heard from Beth how the corner bullies were making Johathan wipe their shoes on the way home whenever Beth wasn't there to fight them off. And when I heard that the ringleader was a little boy in Jonathan's class his own size, an interesting and very disturbing thing happened to me.

My fury at my own long-ago impotence, and my present pain at his suffering, made me start to forget all that I knew about violence and fear, and blaming the victim, I started to hiss at the weeping child. "The next time you come in here crying...," and I suddenly caught myself in horror.

This is the way we allow the destruction of our sons to begin—in the name of protection and to ease our own pain. *My* son get beaten up? I was about to demand that he buy that first lesson in the corruption of power, that might makes right. I could hear myself beginning to perpetuate the age-old distortions about what strength and bravery really are.

And no, Jonathan didn't have to fight if he didn't want to, but somehow he did have to feel better about not fighting. An old horror rolled over me of being the fat kid who ran away, terrified of getting her glasses broken.

About that time a very wise woman said to me, "Have you ever told Jonathan that once you used to be afraid, too?"

The idea seemed far-out to me at the time, but the next time he came in crying and sweaty from having run away again, I could see that he felt shamed at having failed me, or some image he and I had created in his head of mother/woman. This image of woman being able to handle it all was bolstered by the fact that he lived in a household with three strong women, his lesbian parents

and his forthright older sister. At home, for Jonathan, power was clearly female.

And because our society teaches us to think in an either/or mode—kill or be killed, dominate or be dominated—this meant that he must either surpass or be lacking. I could see the implications of this line of thought. Consider the two western classic myth/models of mother/son relationships: Jocasta/Oedipus, the son who fucks his mother, and Clytemnestra/Orestes, the son who kills his mother.

It all felt connected to me.

I sat down on the hallway steps and took Jonathan on my lap and wiped his tears. "Did I ever tell you about how I used to be afraid when I was your age?"

I will never forget the look on that little boy's face as I told him the tale of my glasses and my after-school fights. It was a look of relief and total disbelief, all rolled into one.

It is as hard for our children to believe that we are not omnipotent as it is for us to know it, as parents. But that knowledge is necessary as the first step in the reassessment of power as something other than might, age, privilege, or the lack of fear. It is an important step for a boy, whose societal destruction begins when he is forced to believe that he can only be strong if he doesn't feel, or if he wins.

I thought about all this one year later when Beth and Jonathan, ten and nine, were asked by an interviewer how they thought they had been affected by being children of a feminist.

Jonathan said that he didn't think there was too much in feminism for boys, although it certainly was good to be able to cry if he felt like it and not to have to play football if he didn't want to. I think of this sometimes now when I see him practising for his Brown Belt in Tae Kwon Do.

The strongest lesson I can teach my son is the same lesson I teach my daughter: how to be who he wishes to be for himself. And the best way I can do this is to be who I am and hope that he will learn from this not how to be me, which is not possible, but how to be himself. And this means how to move to that voice from within himself, rather than to those raucous, persuasive, or threatening voices from outside, pressuring him to be what the world wants him to be.

And that is hard enough.

Jonathan is learning to find within himself some of the different faces of courage and strength, whatever he chooses to call them. Two years ago, when Jonathan was twelve and in the seventh grade, one of his friends at school who had been to the house persisted in calling Frances "the maid." When Jonathan corrected him, the boy then referred to her as "the cleaning woman." Finally Jonathan said, simply, "Frances is not the cleaning woman, she's my mother's lover." Interestingly enough, it is the teachers at this school who still have not recovered from his openness.

Frances and I were considering attending a Lesbian/Feminist conference this summer, when we were notified that no boys over ten were allowed. This presented logistic as well as philosophical problems for us, and we sent the following letter:

Sisters:

Ten years as an interracial lesbian couple has taught us both the dangers of an oversimplified approach to the nature and solutions of any oppression, as well as the danger inherent in an incomplete vision.

Our thirteen-year-old son represents as much hope for our future world as does our fifteen-year-old daughter, and we are not willing to abandon him to the killing streets of New York City while we journey west to help form a Lesbian-Feminist vision of the future world in which we can all survive and flourish. I hope we can continue this dialogue in the near future, as I feel it is important to our vision and our survival.

The question of separatism is by no means simple. I am thankful that one of my children is male, since that helps to keep me honest. Every line I write shrieks there are no easy solutions.

I grew up in largely female environments, and I know how crucial that has been to my own development. I feel the want and need often for the society of women, exclusively. I recognize that our own spaces are essential for developing and recharging.

As a Black woman, I find it necessary to withdraw into all-Black groups at times for exactly the same reasons—differences in stages of development and differences in levels of interaction. Frequently, when speaking with men and white women, I am reminded of how difficult and time-consuming it is to have to reinvent the pencil every time you want to send a message.

But this does not mean that my responsibility for my son's education stops at age ten, any more than it does for my daughter's. However, for each of them, that responsibility does grow less and less as they become more woman and man.

Both Beth and Jonathan need to know what they can share and what they cannot, how they are joined and how they are not. And Frances and I, as grown women and lesbians coming more and more into our power, need to relearn the experience that difference does not have to be threatening.

When I envision the future, I think of the world I crave for my daughters and my sons. It is thinking for survival of the species—thinking for life.

Most likely there will always be women who move with women, women who live with men, men who choose men. I work for a time when women with women, women with men, men with men, all share the work of a world that does not barter bread or self for obedience, nor beauty, nor love. And in that world we will raise our children free to choose how best to fulfill themselves. For we are jointly responsible for the care and raising of the young, since *that* they be raised is a function, ultimately, of the species.

Within that tripartite pattern of relating/existence, the raising of the young will be the joint responsibility of all adults who choose to be associated with children. Obviously, the children raised within each of these three relationships will be different, lending a special savor to that eternal inquiry into how best can we live our lives.

Jonathan was three-and-a-half when Frances and I met. He is now fourteen years old. I feel the living perspective that having lesbian parents has brought to Jonathan is a valuable addition to his human sensitivity.

Jonathan has had the advantage of growing up within a nonsexist relationship, one in which this society's pseudonatural assumptions of ruler/ruled are being challenged. And this is not only because

Frances and I are lesbians, for unfortunately there are some lesbians who are still locked into patriarchal patterns of unequal power relationships.

These assumptions of power relationships are being questioned because Frances and I, often painfully and with varying degrees of success, attempt to evaluate and measure over and over again our feelings concerning power, our own and others'. And we explore with care those areas concerning how it is used and expressed between us and between us and the children, openly and otherwise. A good part of our biweekly family meetings are devoted to this exploration.

As parents, Frances and I have given Jonathan our love, our openness, and our dreams to help form his visions. Most importantly, as the son of lesbians, he has had an invaluable model—not only of a relationship—but of relating.

Jonathan is fourteen now. In talking over this paper with him and asking his permission to share some pieces of his life, I asked Jonathan what he felt were the strongest negative and the strongest positive aspects for him in having grown up with lesbian parents.

He said the strongest benefit he felt he had gained was that he knew a lot more about people than most other kids his age that he knew, and that he did not have a lot of the hang-ups that some other boys did about men and women.

And the most negative aspect he felt, Jonathan said, was the ridicule he got from some kids with straight parents.

"You mean, from your peers?" I said.

"Oh no," he answered promptly. "My peers know better. I mean other kids."

R E A D I N G   **58**

Broken Transformers*

Bi Shumin (1992)

'Mum, let's go. I don't want a Transformer,' said my ten-year-old son.

We were standing in a newly opened department store. As mother of a low-income family I was used to steering my son firmly away from toy counters; but this store had taken me by surprise; its manager had shrewdly filled the entrance hall with brightly coloured playthings instead of the usual dull array of cosmetics.

I stood in the doorway, debating whether or not to leave. There had been a sign outside saying the store sold wool, and I desperately needed to knit myself a new hat and scarf. Still, wool could be bought elsewhere.

I gripped my son's hand and drew him towards me intending to make up some excuse to get him

out of the store, and thus out of temptation's way. Ten was an age, after all, at which innocence gradually begins to give way to questioning, and I didn't want him to become conscious too early of the power of money and thus of our limited supply. At the same time I hated the thought of his disappointment at not being able to have the toy he so adored. I felt like covering his eyes with my palm!

The last thing I expected him to say was, 'Mum, let's leave. I don't want a Transformer.' I was at a loss to know how to express my gratitude.

I hated the monstrous cartoon family which had my son glued to the TV set every Saturday and Sunday night; not only did it prevent me watching the news, but it had so captured the imagination of thousands of children that the toy replicas now pouring into the stores were sucking money from parents like locusts devouring crops.

---

* Translated by Shi Junbao

If we hadn't been in the crowded store I would have bent down and kissed his smooth brow, now covered with beads of salty sweet sweat. But it immediately became clear to me that my sense of relief was premature, for his feet were as though rooted to the spot. His neck twisted towards the counter and he stared, through long dark eyelashes, at the colourful range of robots which stared back at him in disdain.

My heart bled as I looked admiringly at his lithe young neck which, like the branch of a willow tree, seemed able to twist back endlessly without incurring discomfort. Was it only a matter of a hat and a scarf?

A perfect example of the trend towards 'late marriage and late birth' characteristic of the time, I had now passed the age of forty while my son was only ten. I had been through all the turmoil and confusion, whereas his was still to come. My troubles tended to be physical, like the fact that the first northern winter winds had nearly frozen my head off and, worse, I had discovered I was beginning to lose my hair which was, moreover, turning grey. This was not only thoroughly unattractive, but meant I was even less well insulated than before. I considered myself pretty good with my hands; as well as lathing machine parts I could also knit and sew. For some time now I had been planning to knit myself a really good hat and scarf and had even told my husband about it. He had, as a gesture towards financing the project, stubbed out his cigarette. I knew he wouldn't give up permanently, of that I had been convinced from the very first day I met him, no matter what other money-saving hobbies he might dispense with. We also saved by eating less meat at dinner, concentrating our chopsticks on vegetables and hoping our son wouldn't notice the decline.

Despite the fact that since the boy's birth cold winds tended to cause a painful throbbing in my head, I could still do without a hat; my old square scarf would suffice, though no doubt I would look odd, like a solemn Arab woman or Mother Hen from the children's cartoon series. But so what? As long as my son could get his beloved robot.

I glanced at the Transformers. They were so expensive that the price of a hat and scarf would be enough to cover maybe the leg of one of the larger models.

And what would my husband say? He had always maintained that I spoiled the child and warned me that ours was just an ordinary 'blue-collar family' which shouldn't aspire to the same heights of those better-off.

But was it to be the case that no 'blue-collar' worker should ever own a Transformer?

I had enough money with me for one of the smallest models available, and knew I could make up a story about the hat and scarf which would satisfy my husband and indicate that I didn't need them.

It was at this point, just as I had made up my mind to buy it, that my son suddenly turned towards the exit, saying resolutely, 'Mum, let's go. The paper says Transformers are only foreign kids' cast-offs. They move them into China to get our money.'

He tugged my hand with his little damp one and glanced back at the toys as though taking a last look at a corpse. Then he quickened his short legs and made for the door as if fearful the Transformers might otherwise snatch him back.

He sounded like an adult, the logic of his argument certainly exceeded anything I might have come up with and it occurred to me that in comparison with our boy, who was, moreover, a model student at school, my husband and I were selfish.

Spurred by this revelation I strode back to the counter and, without giving a second's thought as to who profited by my action, whether foreigners or Hong Kong Chinese, I impulsively took possession of the smallest Transformer money could buy. Suddenly I no longer cared about the pains I would get in my head and neck. This purchase was a token of appreciation for my son's understanding and an expression of our mutual love.

That evening he skipped dinner in order to play with his robot. He put a black toy pistol into its hand and the creature, with a twist and a turn, obligingly turned into an exquisite streamlined bomber. The thermo-coloured American trademark turned from red to blue and back to red in his warm little hands.

'Convertible Transformer fights for justice and freedom with an iron will . . .' he sang sweetly. It was the theme song from the TV series.

Although my husband had grumbled, I felt the purchase had been a wise one. True, Transformers were expensive, but the moments of happiness they gave were priceless. In the event of my son growing up to be an important public figure, I didn't want to have to read in his autobiography: I liked toys when I was little but my family was too poor to afford them, so I could only watch the other children playing with theirs . . .

Of course he might also simply turn out to be a blue-collar worker; either way I was loath to leave him with any regrets about his childhood. Children are, after all, easy to satisfy: the smallest Transformer intoxicates them.

'Don't neglect your homework now,' I cautioned in an unusually serious, perhaps overcompensatory, tone of voice. He earnestly promised not to.

Over the next few days I carried out spot checks on his homework and was satisfied to find that he had lost none of his willpower; he allowed himself to play with his toy only after finishing his work.

Winter finally arrived with a vengeance.

My husband prolonged his prohibition on cigarettes, and though I tried to reassure him that my old scarf was perfectly adequate, his response was gloomy. 'You should have a pair of warm boots,' he said.

I gave him a grateful smile and made a face indicating that it was indeed cold down there.

One evening I suddenly found my son playing with a different Transformer: this one was yellow, and much larger and fiercer than his own.

'What's this?' I asked, almost severely. All the guidebooks on 'parenting' warned us not to ignore any new tangents a child went off on.

'Transformer Giant,' he answered calmly, as though discussing a close relative.

Thanks to the protracted TV series, I was equipped with basic knowledge of the Transformer family and I knew that the Giant was one of the principal characters.

Be that as it may, its name was not important to me—its owner was. Without softening my voice

I demanded to know whose it was. His reply was matter-of-fact. 'One of my classmates',' he said, without registering my suspicion. 'Almost everybody has one and they're all different, so we trade to play.'

Although I felt a slight twinge of guilt about my tone of voice, I couldn't guarantee I wouldn't react in the same way in the future. Dishonesty was above all others the thing I feared most in children and I was constantly on the look-out for it.

The kids were clever. They traded like primitive tribes. It was a new phenomenon, and I wasn't sure whether to oppose or support it. 'Giant or not,' I said to my elated son, 'don't let it ruin your school work, and be careful with other people's toys.'

He nodded his assent. I could always rely on him to listen.

Somebody was tapping at the door.

My son ran over and hospitably pulled it wide open. But the visitor slowly closed it again as if he wished to remain outside. Presently a round head hesitantly pushed its way through the crack. It was my son's classmate, one who seemed to go by the name of Fatty and who regularly dropped by to get my son to help him with his homework. Only this time Fatty hadn't come for help. He neither entered nor retreated but remained hovering on the threshold facing my son and glancing up at me with a miserable expression on his face. Finally he stammered out in embarrassment, 'I'm so sorry . . . I broke your toy . . .'

The blood drained from my son's cheeks. I had never seen such an agonized look pass across his face. He took the dismantled toy from Fatty, held it before his eyes and blew on it softly, as though it were a wounded pigeon.

After the initial shock had subsided, my son looked at me to rescue him. For one bitter moment the sacrificed hat and scarf flashed across my mind, but there was nothing we could do except face it. Trying to avoid my son's eye, I said, 'It's up to you. It's your toy, what do you think we should do?'

Perhaps inhibited by my presence, he remained silent. I therefore discreetly moved into the inner room and listened intently. I could hear

Fatty wheezing in the silence and longed to put an end to his misery by running out and saying, 'Fatty, you may leave now.' But the verdict, whatever it was, had to come from my son.

'How did you smash it?' I heard him ask, with anger in his voice.

'I just . . . then, flop . . .' Fatty must have been gesticulating. An exasperated gurgle appeared to be my son's stifled response.

What was I to do? Maybe I should go out and intervene. Transformers cost money, but magnanimity is something that no amount of money can buy; and although I believed my son had absorbed the moral principles I had instilled in him over the years, I nevertheless recognized that to him a small Transformer was the equivalent of a colour TV set or a deluxe camera to an adult. The prolonged silence was agony, for him and for Fatty as well as for me.

Finally he spoke. He seemed to have covered a great deal of mental ground and his voice, though weak, was none the less clear: 'Don't worry . . .'

Fatty grasped the opportunity and fled, as though afraid that my son might otherwise change his mind.

I heaved a long sigh of relief, as if I too had just returned from a long journey. Emerging, I kissed my son's sweaty forehead.

'It's dead,' he said as his eyes filled with tears.

'I'll try and glue it together,' I said comfortingly, though with little hope of success.

I duly went flat out to fix it, drawing on all my resources of skill and ingenuity. After spending a great deal more time and effort on it than I would have spent knitting a hat, it finally became recognizable again as a toy. But though it looked all right, it was too delicate to touch and it could no longer change shapes.

My son, meanwhile, devoted himself to the Giant. A Transformer should change shape, he said, otherwise it was just a trinket. So saying, he deftly changed the shape of the toy he had in his hand. One has to admire the Americans. Who else would come up with the idea of turning the belly of a fighter into a robot's head and then proceed to create a machine that executes the transition so flawlessly?

A good toy attracts both children and grown-ups, but no sooner had I begun to move closer to watch him play than I heard an ominous crash and saw the toy collapse in pieces.

What had happened? We looked at each other in horror.

Unfortunately, though we could hardly believe it, the truth was all too painfully clear: he had broken the Giant.

For a while my son tried to fix it, but only ended up with more pieces than he had started with. Realizing the situation was hopeless, he gathered the pieces together, wrapped them in a sheet of paper and prepared to leave the house.

'Where are you going?' I asked, still in a state of shock.

'To return the toy and apologize,' he said, looking calm and prepared.

'Is it Fatty's?' I asked, with a glimmer of hope.

'No.' He then mentioned a name.

Hers! My heart plunged, then leapt into my throat.

The only impression I had ever been able to gain of this girl was that she was like a delicate flower and had a very arrogant mother. The family was well heeled—my husband would call them 'wealthy'—and it was entirely natural that they should have bought such a large and ferocious-looking toy for their daughter.

'You're going . . . like this?' I stammered.

'Should I take something with me?' he asked, confused.

I looked at his limpid eyes and refrained from further comment.

'OK, mum, I'm off.' He disappeared out the door.

'Come home soon,' I called after him apprehensively.

I knew he wouldn't dawdle, but he didn't return soon, and when he hadn't returned later either, my heart began to flutter like fish on a hook.

I should have warned him that people were all different, that he might not be pardoned, even though he himself had forgiven a similar accident. I should have prepared him better for the possibility of an unpleasant scene, otherwise he might cry.

On the other hand things might turn out OK. His classmate might have asked him hospitably to stay a little, while her mother peeled him an orange, which my son would naturally push back politely. He is a lovable boy. They would surely forgive him in the same manner in which we had forgiven little Fatty.

The more I thought about it the more I convinced myself that that could be the only possible outcome. Moreover I congratulated myself now on not having filled his heart with my own cynical suspicions.

But as time passed, no matter how I tried to reassure myself, I grew increasingly concerned.

At last he returned, his footstep so light that, deep in thought as I was, I didn't even notice he was there until he was standing right in front of me.

One look at him was enough to convince me that he had undergone a profound inner trauma. I could also tell that he had been crying and that he had already dried his tears in the cold wind so that I wouldn't notice. A child often reveals more when he is hiding something.

I did not have the heart to get him to go into details; it would have been too painful.

'Mum, they want us . . . to compensate . . .' he said finally, as large, cold teardrops rolled down his cheeks and on to my hand.

I now had to deal not only with a broken toy but with a broken heart.

'It's only natural,' I said, wiping away his tears, 'that they'd want to be compensated for their loss.'

'Then let me go and find Fatty and ask him to compensate me for mine. All he said was "I'm sorry." Next time I go shopping I won't take my money, I'll just say, "I'm sorry" Will that do?' he asked, jumping up to leave.

'Don't go!' I pulled him back. He struggled wildly, suddenly seeming to have acquired the strength of a calf.

'Why, mum? Tell me!' he demanded, lifting his head.

I didn't know how to respond. Sometimes principles are all very well and, like beautiful clothes can be very attractive, but they are not the stuff from which clothes are actually made.

I had to give him an answer. It is a cat's responsibility to teach her kitten how to catch mice. I had to provide my son with an explanation, no matter how impractical it might be.

'The words "I'm sorry" mean you are being courteous. Their value ought not to be counted in terms of money.'

He nodded quietly. I probably sounded like one of his teachers, so he forced himself to listen.

'You forgave Fatty when he broke your Transformer,' I continued, patiently trying to explain things in terms he would understand. 'He was relieved. That was a nice thing to do.'

'But mum, I haven't been forgiven for a similar mistake!' he protested. His sense of shame seemed to override my reasoned arguments.

'Well, son, there are many ways of solving a problem. Problems are like Transformers: they can either be a robot, a plane or a car . . . Understand?'

'Yeah.' He nodded reluctantly. I knew he was unconvinced, and just wanted to placate me.

I let go of his hand, exhausted.

He relaxed and stood aside.

The large broken toy was going to involve a hideous amount of money, and though we hadn't yet reached the stage where we needed to go to the pawn shop—which our street didn't have anyway—we were still pretty broke.

Sitting on the bad news, we waited for my husband to come home. My son looked at me pitifully. Was he hoping I would not tell him about the incident at all, or hoping I would do it quickly?

I dreaded the prospect, but knew it had to be done, and despite my inclination to postpone the reckoning I knew it would be better in the long run to get it over and done with immediately.

On hearing the news, my husband managed temporarily to retain his composure.

'Tell me,' he said calmly, 'how did you come to break the thing?' He couldn't bring himself to give it a name.

'I just twisted it, and "flop", it broke . . .' stammered my son, looking at me appealingly for support. I'd seen it happen, certainly, but I couldn't have said how.

But describing how it broke was in any event unimportant. The consequence was that our son would never again be able to play with such a costly toy.

My husband's eyebrows locked and the ferocity of his expression sent my son scurrying behind me for protection. Suddenly he exploded.

'Tell me,' he said, his voice rising in a crescendo, 'did you break it on purpose or deliberately?'

I frankly couldn't see what the difference was between 'on purpose' and 'deliberately,' but didn't dare interfere.

'I did it . . . on purpose. No, dad, I did it deliberately . . .' Desperately searching for whichever seemed the less incriminating, he lurched from one to the other, shrinking beneath his father's glare.

'You little wretch! A whole month's salary won't pay for this thing, yet you think you can go around lording it like the master of some grand mansion. I'll give you a hiding you'll never forget.'

With that he raised his arm, and as it came crashing down I lifted my own to intercept the blow. A blinding pain instantly spread from my side down to my fingers. He was a strong man, a labourer, and it was fortunate I had blocked him.

For a few moments my son was stunned, then he let out a sharp cry, as if it had been he who had been hit.

'You've got a nerve to blubber like that!' shouted my husband, breathing heavily. 'That damn thing your mother bought you already cost her her wool hat, and now that! That's our fuel and cabbage for the whole winter gone!' Then he turned to me and added, 'It's your fault for spoiling him!'

I let him rant. As long as he didn't resort to violence again I could cope. My son had never been beaten before.

That winter, on one particularly freezing day when the sun seemed to be emanating blasts of cold air instead of warmth, I arrived home to find that the stove was barely alight. My son was waiting for me, his face burning red and his eyes glittering like stars reflected in a pool. I was afraid he had a fever.

'Close your eyes, mum,' he said. That sweet tone of his voice reassured me that he was not ill.

I closed my eyes quietly. I thought he must have a little surprise for me: a perfect exam paper perhaps, or a toy he might have made out of paper and bottles.

'You can open your eyes now, mum.'

I kept my eyes closed, savouring the happy moment that only a mother can experience.

'Quick, mum!' he urged.

I opened my eyes on to what seemed at first like a meadow in springtime. It took me a moment to register that what my son was, in fact, holding in front of me was a bundle of green knitting wool.

'Do you like the colour, mum?' he asked, looking at me expectantly.

Green was my favourite.

'Yes, very much! How did you know I like it?'

'You must have forgotten. You've always knitted me green clothes ever since I was little. I would be able to pick out the colour among a thousand others.' He must have wondered how I could even ask such a question.

'Did dad take you there?'

'No, I went by myself,' he said proudly.

'Where did you get the money?' I asked in surprise.

He didn't answer, but stared at me motionlessly.

He could not have stolen it. The very thought of stealing was anathema to my young son. He must have got the money by recycling used paper or toothpaste tubes, but I hadn't noticed him returning home late with blackened fingers. Well, I'd have to ask him again.

'Tell me, where did you get the money?' I persisted, almost pleading with him to give me a satisfactory answer.

'I asked Fatty for it,' he answered clearly.

'You asked who?' I couldn't believe my ears. It was impossible that he could have done something like that. He had always been so obedient.

'Fatty!' he repeated, staring at me resolutely.

A loud buzzing sounded in my head. His bold expression seemed to come from a boy I didn't know.

'How did you get it from him?' I asked in a weak voice.

'The way those other people asked us for it,' he said dismissively, as though I was being pernickety.

He saw my hand rise and, thinking I was about to stroke his head, moved in closer. But I slapped him. Remembering, in the split second before my arm descended, an article I had read somewhere warning parents never to hit their children on the head. But it was too late. My hand slanted at an angle and landed on his neck.

He didn't flinch, but merely looked at me in astonishment.

I had never really hit him before, but now I felt certain that this would not be the last time.

Since then, every time a gust of wind pushes open the front door, I expect to see a little fellow with a round head appear. But Fatty has never been back. He paid for our Transformer and left it with us.

I fixed the big one with glue. Its bold appearance added a sense of wealth to our house.

Now we have two Transformers that do not transform.

My son has never touched them again.

DISCUSSION QUESTIONS FOR CHAPTER 7

1. What are some myths about the normative U.S. family? To what degree does your family reflect this norm? Has your family experienced discrimination in any ways based on deviation from this norm? What are some of the realities of the diversity of U.S. families?

2. How are families both places of comfort, security, and nurture and at the same time places of domination, conflict, and violence?

3. How do social institutions reinforce power relations in the family? How does the family often reflect power relations of the dominant social order? How do power relations operate in your family?

4. How does the difference between mothering and fathering reflect dominant social norms for women and men?

5. What tasks do various members of your family do within the home? Do these tasks reflect typical social norms?

SUGGESTIONS FOR FURTHER READING

Bem, Sandra Lipsitz. *An Unconventional Family*. New Haven, CT: Yale University Press, 2001.

Coontz, Stephanie. *Marriage, a History: From Obedience to Intimacy, or How Love Conquered Marriage*. New York: Viking, 2005.

Hequembourg, Amy. *Lesbian Motherhood: Stories of Becoming*. New York: Harrington Park Press, 2007.

Hertz, Rosanna. *Single by Chance, Mothers by Choice: How Women Are Choosing Parenthood without Marriage and Creating the New American Family*. New York: Oxford University Press, 2006.

Hull, Kathleen. *Same-Sex Marriage: The Cultural Politics of Love and Law.* New York: Cambridge University Press, 2006.

Mason, Mary Ann, Arlene Skolnick, and Stephen D. Sugarman, eds. *All Our Families: New Policies for a New Century.* 2nd ed. New York: Oxford University Press, 2002.

O' Reilly, Andrea. *Mother Outlaws: Theories and Practices of Empowered Mothering.* Toronto: University of Toronto Press, 2004.

Wolf, Naomi. *Misconceptions: Truth, Lies, and the Unexpected Journey to Motherhood.* New York: Anchor, 2003.

CHAPTER 8

Women's Work Inside and Outside the Home

There is an important truth in the saying "women's work is never done." In the United States and around the world, women work long hours because work for them often involves unpaid domestic labor and care of dependent family members as well as paid labor. In addition, when they do get paid for their work, women tend to earn lower wages compared with men and are less likely to have control over the things they produce and the wages they receive. When the United Nations World Conference on Women met in Beijing, China, in 1995, the Platform for Action prioritized strategies to promote economic autonomy for women, ensure their access to productive resources, and encourage equitable sharing of family responsibilities. This commitment was reiterated in the "Beijing Plus 10" meeting held in New York in 2005. In this chapter we examine both women's domestic unpaid labor and their employment in the labor force. In the latter the focus is on the global economy and the changing nature and patterns of women's labor force participation, the dual economy, and the gender gap in wages.

UNPAID LABOR IN THE HOME

The work women do in the home is often not considered work at all: It is something women do for love, or because they are women, and therefore it is the natural thing for women to do. The humorist Dave Barry, for example, declares that 85 percent of men in the United States are "cleaning impaired," satirizing the supposed ineptitude or lack of participation in domestic activities on the part of men as normalized or natural. The point, though, is that there is nothing natural about the fact that women on the average do over two-thirds of all household work. The fact that they may be better at it is only because of years of practice. Gender norms that associate women, the home, and domesticity reinforce the assumption that housework and childcare are women's work.

The classic reading by Pat Mainardi, written in 1970, focuses on the politics of housework (issues of power associated with household tasks such as who does what

LEARNING ACTIVITY　**Housework and Technology**

The conventional wisdom would suggest that modern household inventions have saved time and energy for homemakers. But is that the case? Have technological innovations freed women from household chores? Or have they created more work for women in the home?

Take a look at Susan Strasser's *Never Done: A History of American Housework* and Ruth Schwartz Cowan's *More Work for Mother: The Ironies of Household Technologies from the Open Hearth to the Microwave*. What do they suggest about the role of household inventions?

Use these books and a search engine on the Web to research the following household appliances. Have they saved time and energy for women?

- Vacuum cleaner
- Stove
- Washing machine
- Dryer
- Refrigerator
- Microwave

Watch a couple of hours of daytime television and take note of the advertisements. What sorts of household products are advertised? What do the ads suggest about how these products can make women more efficient homemakers? Do you think these items really improve women's lives? What do these ads imply about women's responsibilities in the home? Do the ads suggest that men are equally responsible for housework? Do they suggest household technologies can help men become more efficient homemakers?

and why). She shares the dialogue about housework in her home and makes suggestions for ways that "participatory democracy" might work at home (p. 450). In the reading "Maid to Order," Barbara Ehrenreich also focuses on the politics of housework in contemporary U.S. society. She emphasizes that housework is not degrading because it involves manual labor but, instead, because it is embedded in degrading relationships that have the potential to reproduce male domination from one generation to the next. She notes that a contemporary solution to the housework problem among those who can afford it is to hire someone else to do the work. That "someone" is most likely a woman and very often a woman of color. Paid domestic work is one occupation traditionally held by women of color; it is also an occupation that is usually nonunionized and has low pay, little power, and few or no benefits. In addition, workers who used to contract services directly with employers are now being replaced by corporate cleaning services that control a good portion of the housecleaning business. Ehrenreich emphasizes that this new relationship between cleaners and those who can afford to employ them abolishes the traditional "mistress-maid" relationship and allows middle-class people who are sensitive to the political issues involved with hiring servants to avoid confronting these issues and feel less guilt.

Women and Agriculture

- Women make up 51 percent of the agricultural labor force worldwide.
- A study of the household division of labor in Bangladeshi villages found that women worked almost 12 hours a day—compared with the 8 to 10 hours a day worked by men in the same villages.
- In many regions, women spend up to 5 hours a day collecting fuelwood and water and up to 4 hours preparing food.
- In Africa and Asia, women work about 13 hours more than men each week.
- In Southeast Asia, women provide up to 90 percent of the labor for rice cultivation.
- In Africa, 90 percent of the work of gathering water and wood, for the household and for food preparation, is done by women.
- In Pakistan, 50 percent of rural women cultivate and harvest wheat.
- In the world's least developed countries, 23 percent of rural households are headed by women.
- In sub-Saharan Africa, women produce up to 80 percent of basic foodstuffs both for household consumption and for sale.
- Women perform from 25 to 45 percent of agricultural field tasks in Colombia and Peru.
- Women constitute 53 percent of the agricultural labor in Egypt.
- Fewer than 10 percent of women farmers in India, Nepal, and Thailand own land.
- An analysis of credit schemes in five African countries found that women received less than 10 percent of the credit awarded to males who own small farms.
- Only 15 percent of the world's agricultural extension agents are women.

Sources: www.fao.org/gender/en/labb2-e.htm and www.fao.org/gender/en/agrib4-e.htm.

Most researchers who study household labor define it as all tasks involved in household maintenance, purchasing and preparing food, taking care of children and/or aging or sick family members, garden and yard work, and routine care and maintenance of vehicles. Family work also involves "kin keeping," discussed below, that includes taking care of the emotional needs of family members. Two major findings emerge in the data on housework. The first concerns the amount of time women and men spend on household work. A 2006 study conducted by Bianchi et al. found that married women spent approximately 19.4 hours a week doing housework (down from 34 hours in 1965 and reflecting the increase in women also working outside the home) compared with married men, who spent approximately 9.7 hours on housework (up from 4.4 hours in 1965). In other words, married women do approximately twice the amount of housework that married men do or about two-thirds of all household labor. Daughters are also more likely to do household work than their brothers. When wives earn a higher proportion of the family income, they perform less housework, husbands increase their share, and the difference between their household workloads decreases. Similarly, couples with higher levels of education tend to have more equitable divisions of household labor.

In her 2005 reissue of *The Second Shift,* sociologist Arlie Russell Hochschild writes of the "70-30" gender split associated with household work and sociologist Chloe Bird suggests that once married, women do about twice the amount of work in the home as their spouses, increasing their stress and anxiety. When women marry, unfortunately most gain an average of 14 hours a week of domestic labor, compared with men, who gain an average of 90 minutes. Husbands tend to create more work for wives than they perform. This can cause stress-related problems and mental and physical exhaustion for women trying to juggle family responsibilities and paid employment. Studies find that couples who are most contented have the most flexibility regarding work and commitment to sharing responsibilities. According to Neil Chethik in *VoiceMale* a book on husbands and marriage, men who do more housework and childcare report a better sex life with their wives, who have more energy for sexual intimacy when they have fewer dishes to wash and lunches to make. Women are more content with husbands who take an active role in the home and this encourages sexual intimacy.

Cross-national comparisons of the gender gap in housework drawing on data in Japan, North America, Scandinavia, Russia, and Hungary by the Institute for Social Research (ISR) indicate that North American men are less egalitarian (meaning equally sharing power) than Scandinavians (Swedish men do an average of 24 hours of housework a week), but more egalitarian than Japanese men. Russian women do the least amount of housework, although they work the most total hours (employed plus domestic work), and Hungarian women do the most housework and have the least amount of leisure time. All these comparative data must be interpreted with caution as questions are raised in terms of how household labor is defined, whether methods for reporting are standardized, and whether a discussion of "women doing less housework" means overall hours or as a proportion of total hours performed by women and men.

LEARNING ACTIVITY **Who Does the Work at Your School and in Your Home?**

Use the following charts to discover who does various kinds of work at your school and in your home. Discuss your findings with your classmates. What patterns do you notice? What do your findings suggest about how systems of inequality function in the institution of work, both inside and outside the home?

WHO DOES THE WORK AT YOUR SCHOOL?

Job Description	White Men	White Women	Men of Color	Women of Color
Top administration				
Teaching				
Secretarial				
Groundskeeping				
Electrical/carpentry				
Janitorial				
Food preparation				
Security				
Intercollegiate coaching				

WHO DOES THE WORK IN YOUR HOME?

Job Description	Person in the Family Who Generally Does This Job	Sex of Person Who Generally Does This Job	Hours per Week Spent in Doing This Job
Laundry			
Mowing the lawn			
Maintaining the car			
Buying the groceries			
Cooking			
Vacuuming			
Washing dishes			
Making beds			
Cleaning bathroom			

One of the most significant issues to consider in terms of the reliability of this housework data is that much family work is difficult to measure. This is especially true of the work involved in "kin keeping": remembering birthdays, sending cards, preparing for holidays, organizing vacations, keeping in touch with relatives, and providing "spousal career support" by entertaining, volunteering, and networking. These tasks

HISTORICAL MOMENT **Wages for Housework**

Women do two-thirds of the world's work but receive only 5 percent of the world's income. Worldwide, women's unpaid labor is estimated at $11 trillion. Early in the women's movement, feminists made the connection between women's unpaid labor and the profits accumulated by the businesses that relied on women's household and child-rearing work to support the waged laborers that produced goods and capital. They argued, then, that women should be compensated for the domestic labor that is taken for granted and yet depended on to maintain capitalist economies.

Several groups agitated for wages for housework, and in 1972 the International Wages for Housework (WFH) Campaign was organized by women in developing and industrialized countries to agitate for compensation for the unpaid work women do. They argued that this goal could best be reached by dismantling the military-industrial complex. In 1975 the International Black Women for Wages for Housework (IBWWFH) Campaign, an international network of women of color, formed to work for compensation for unwaged and low-waged work and to ensure that challenging racism was not separated from challenging sexism and other forms of discrimination.

Few American feminists advocated this position, although it constituted a significant position for feminists in Europe. Some feminists opposed the campaign, arguing that to pay women for housework would reinforce women's role in the home and strengthen the existing gendered division of labor.

Both the WFH and IBWWFH campaigns are still active, advocating change in the ways women's work is valued and rewarded. They have been involved in a campaign for pay equity and a global women's strike. For more information, check out these websites:

www.ourworld.compuserve.com/homepages/crossroadswomenscentre/WFH.html

www.payequity.net/WFHCampaign/wfhcpgn.htm

www.crossroadswomen.net/BWWFH/BWWHF.html

are time consuming and involve a lot of emotional work that is not easily quantified and is often invisible. Women tend to perform the bulk of this kin-keeping work. It is important to note that such work cannot easily be replaced with hired labor. Finally, when it comes to household work, women seem to be better at multitasking, and, as a result, often underreport the work they do because they are performing multiple tasks at the same time.

The second major finding concerns the gender division of household labor. This means that women and men (and girl and boy children) do different kinds of work in the home. Women tend to do the repetitive, ongoing, daily kinds of tasks, and men are more likely to perform the less repetitive or seasonal tasks, especially if these tasks involve the use of tools or machines. Some tasks are seen as more masculine and some as more feminine. In this way, gender plays a significant role in the types of housework men and women perform. Researchers find that while women invest almost ten times the work that men do in laundry, five times in cleaning the home, and approximately four times the effort in preparing and cleaning up after meals, men devote between a third and two-thirds more effort in paying bills and are more likely to do repairs and outside chores. The work women are more likely to perform takes more time (between 10 and 20 hours a week), compared with the "masculine" tasks that take between 4 and 7 hours a week. It is important to note that the "feminine," frequently performed tasks are less optional for families and are also more likely to be thought of as boring by both women and men.

Many readers are probably remembering their father doing the housework or have a partner who shares equally in domestic labor. Although there have been changes over the past decades with some men taking on greater household responsibilities and some assuming an equal share, unfortunately, many men do little to no housework and there is a large group who "help" to a greater or lesser extent. Note how the term *helping* assumes that it is someone else's responsibility. Nonetheless, it is important to state that housework, although often dreary and repetitive, can also be creative and more interesting than some paid labor. And, although raising children is among the hardest work of all, it is also full of rewards. Men who do not participate in household work and childcare miss the joys associated with this work even while they have the privilege of being free to do other things.

PAID LABOR

Trends and Legalities

The reading "A Brief History of Working Women" by sociologists Sharlene Hesse-Biber and Gregg Lee Carter overviews the changes in women's labor force participation over the past centuries for different groups of women. Briefly, as U.S. society became industrialized in the nineteenth century, the traditional subsistence economies of producing what families needed to survive from the home, taking in work (like spinning or washing), or working in others' homes or on their land were changed in favor of a more distinct separation between work and home. Factories were established, employees were congregated under one roof (and thus more easily controlled), and emerging technologies started mass-producing goods. Instead of making products in the home for family consumption, people were working outside the home and spending their earnings on these mass-produced goods. Urban centers grew up around these sites of production, and ordinary people tended to work long hours in often very poor conditions. These harsh conditions associated with women's wage labor coincided with continuing domestic servitude in the home. This double day of work was recognized by scholars over a hundred years ago and is still a central aspect of women's lives today.

At the same time that working-class women and children were working in factories, mines, and sweatshops, the middle-class home came to be seen as a haven from the cruel world, and middle-class women were increasingly associated with this sphere. From this developed the "cult of true womanhood"—prescriptions for femininity that included piety, purity, and domesticity. Although these notions of femininity could be achieved only by privileged White women, such norms came to influence women generally. At the same time, some women were starting to enter higher education. With the founding of Oberlin Collegial Institute in 1833, other women's colleges like Mount Holyoke, Bryn Mawr, and Wellesley were established as the century progressed. In addition, state universities (beginning with Utah in 1850) started admitting women. By the turn of the century, there were cohorts of (mostly privileged White) women who were educated to be full political persons and who helped shape the Progressive Era of the early twentieth century with a focus on reform and civic leadership. These women entered the labor force in relatively large numbers, and many chose a career over marriage and the family.

As the twentieth century progressed, more women entered the public sphere. The years of the Great Depression slowed women's advancement, and it was not until World War II that women were seen working in traditionally male roles in unprecedented numbers. The government encouraged this transition, and many women were, for the first time, enjoying decent wages. All this would end after the war as women were encouraged or forced to return to the home so that men could claim their jobs in the labor force. Childcare centers were dismantled, and the conservative messages of the 1950s encouraged women to stay home and partake in the rapidly emerging consumer society. The social and cultural upheavals of the 1960s and the civil rights and women's movements fought for legislation to help women gain more power in the workplace.

The most important legislative gains include, first, the Equal Pay Act of 1963, which protects men and women who perform substantially equal work in the same establishment from sex-based wage discrimination. This is the "equal pay for equal work" law. Second, Title VII of the Civil Rights Act of 1964 prohibits discrimination in employment based on race, color, religion, sex, and/or national origin in establishments with 15 or more employees. It makes it illegal for employers to discriminate against these protected classes in terms of the conditions and privileges of employment (hiring, firing, pay, promotion, etc.). Title VII said that gender could not be used as a criterion in employment except where there is a "bona fide occupational qualification," meaning it is illegal unless an employer can prove that gender is crucial to job performance (for example, hiring male janitors in men's bathrooms). For the most part, the law had little influence until the establishment of the Equal Employment Opportunity Commission in the early 1970s to enforce the law. The courts have fine-tuned Title VII over the years, and it remains the most important legislation that protects working women and people of color. There are time limits imposed on discrimination claims and a charge must be filed within 180 days from the date of the alleged violation or within 300 days if the charge also is covered by a state or local anti-discrimination law. In May 2007 the Supreme Court ruled that for pay discrimination cases this meant 180 days from the original discriminatory action and not from the last paycheck. This time limit has imposed a substantial burden on women and men bringing Title VII violation claims.

In 1976 the Supreme Court expanded the interpretation of Title VII to include discrimination on the basis of pregnancy as sex discrimination, and in 1993 the Family and Medical Leave Act was passsed. It protected all workers by guaranteeing unpaid leave and protection of employment as a result of caring for a sick family member or the birth or adoption of a child. In 1986 the Supreme Court declared

African American Women in the Workplace: Common Barriers for Advancement

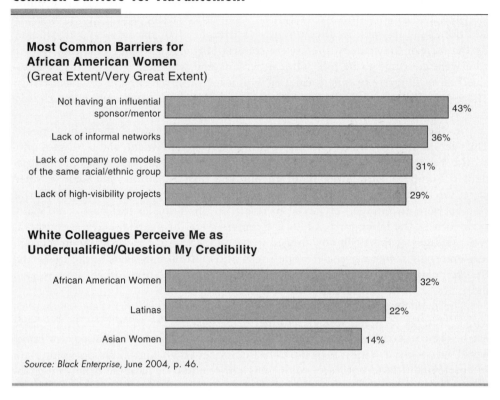

Most Common Barriers for African American Women
(Great Extent/Very Great Extent)

Not having an influential sponsor/mentor	43%
Lack of informal networks	36%
Lack of company role models of the same racial/ethnic group	31%
Lack of high-visibility projects	29%

White Colleagues Perceive Me as Underqualified/Question My Credibility

African American Women	32%
Latinas	22%
Asian Women	14%

Source: Black Enterprise, June 2004, p. 46.

sexual harassment a form of sex discrimination and in 1993 broadened this ruling by stating that women suing on the basis of sexual harassment did not have to prove that they had suffered "concrete psychological harm." Sexual harassment legislation made a distinction between *quid pro quo* (sexual favors are required in return for various conditions of employment) and *hostile work environment* (no explicit demand for an exchange of sexual acts for work-related conditions but being subjected to a pattern of harassment as part of the work environment). In a 2005 poll conducted by the *Wall Street Journal* and NBC, 44 percent of working women said they had been discriminated against because of their gender and one-third said they had experienced sexual harassment. In the reading "The Women's Movement Against Sexual Harassment," Carrie N. Baker traces the ways sexual harassment denied women sexual autonomy, "threatened their physical safety and integrity, deprived them of employment opportunities and, for women of color, was often a form of racism" (p. 486).

Third, the Age Discrimination in Employment Act that was enacted in 1968 and amended in 1978 and 1986, outlaws mandatory retirement and prohibits employers with 20 or more employees from discriminating on the basis of age, protecting individuals who are 40 years of age and older. In 2005 courts restricted this law by

What Is Sexual Harassment?

Sexual harassment is legally defined as unwelcome sexual advances or requests for sexual favors. It also includes any verbal or physical conduct of a sexual nature when the following criteria are met:

- Submission is made explicitly or implicitly a term or condition of an individual's employment.
- Submission to or rejection of such conduct by an individual is used as the basis for employment decisions affecting that individual.
- Such conduct has the purpose or effect of substantially interfering with an individual's work performance or creating an intimidating, hostile, or offensive working environment.

Sexual harassment may include physical conduct, verbal conduct, or nonverbal conduct such as sexual gestures or pornographic pictures.

TWO TYPES OF SEXUAL HARASSMENT

Quid Pro Quo

Unwelcome sexual advances, requests for sexual favors, and other verbal or physical conduct of a sexual nature constitute quid pro quo sexual harassment when:

Submission to such conduct is made either explicitly or implicitly a term or condition of an individual's employment or submission to or rejection of such conduct by an individual is used as the basis for employment decisions affecting that individual.

Hostile Work Environment

In determining whether or not an environment is hostile, it must be determined whether or not the conduct unreasonably interfered with an individual's work performance or created an intimidating, hostile, or offensive work environment.

The Equal Employment Opportunity Commission (EEOC) suggests that the courts look at the following criteria:

- Whether the conduct was verbal, physical, or both
- How frequently the conduct was repeated
- Whether the conduct was hostile or patently offensive
- Whether the alleged harasser was a coworker or a supervisor
- Whether others joined in perpetrating the harassment
- Whether the harassment was directed at more than one individual
- Whether the remarks were hostile and derogatory
- Whether the harasser singled out the charging party
- Whether the charging party participated in the exchange
- The relationship between the charging party and alleged harasser

(continued)

The Supreme Court established a two-pronged test for determining a hostile environment:

1. The conduct must "be severe or pervasive enough to create an objectively hostile or abusive environment that a reasonable person would find hostile or abusive."
2. The victim must "subjectively perceive the environment to be abusive."

Bernice Sandler of the National Association of Women in Education reports that surveys indicate that up to 30 percent of female college students and 70 percent of women in the workplace have been sexually harassed.

IDEAS FOR ACTIVISM

- Advocate with your elected representatives for an increase in the minimum wage.
- Encourage your school to analyze pay equity and to make corrections where needed.
- Write your elected representatives to encourage legislation and funding for childcare.
- Investigate exploitative employment practices of major national and multinational corporations and launch boycotts to demand improved conditions for workers.
- Encourage your elected representatives to support affirmative action.

interpreting it narrowly. Generally groups suing under Title VII of the Civil Rights Act of 1964 do not need to prove intentional discrimination and can declare "disparate impact" and claim they were disproportionately harmed by an employer's policy or behavior. Many courts now refuse to allow older workers to bring disparate-impact claims and require they prove intentional harm. Fourth, the Americans with Disabilities Act (ADA) of 1990 prohibits employment discrimination against qualified individuals with disabilities.

Finally, affirmative action policies that encouraged employers to take gender and race into account in terms of hiring were first initiated by President Kennedy in the 1960s. Since that time, affirmative action has helped diversify the workplace and encouraged the hiring of women and people of color. However, there is a lot of misunderstanding as well as serious hostility associated with affirmative action, as evidenced by the dismantling of affirmative action guidelines in many states. Basically, affirmative action creates positive steps to increase the representation of women and people of color in areas of employment, education, and government from which they may have been historically excluded. Affirmative action encourages the diversification of the job pool, but it does not encourage the hiring of unqualified women or people of color. It is a misunderstanding of these policies to think that White males now have a hard time getting jobs because they are being undercut by unqualified women or people of color.

The Dual Labor Market and the Changing Economy

At the beginning of the twenty-first century it is important to understand the changing nature of the workplace in the United States and the connections between U.S. corporate capitalism and the global economy. Capitalism is an economic system based on the pursuit of profit and the principle of private ownership. Such a system creates inequality because this profit comes in part from surplus value created from the labor of workers. In other words, workers produce more value than they receive in wages, this difference or surplus being reinvested into capital accumulation and corporate profit. The U.S. economy is able to maintain profit accumulation through the perpetuation of a "dual labor market" that provides a "primary" market, with relatively high wages and employee benefits and protections for workers, and a "secondary" market, where workers (disproportionately women and people of color) receive lower wages, fewer benefits, and less opportunity for advancement. The dual labor market also maintains profit through globalization strategies, discussed below.

In terms of the changing nature of the U.S. economy, three features stand out. First, new technologies (especially electronic communications) have revolutionized work and, in some cases, replaced workers and made some jobs obsolete. In cases where technology cannot replace workers, jobs have been exported overseas to take advantage of lower wages. Second, there has been a huge increase in the service sector and a shift from manufacturing to service-sector work. This has brought a change in the kinds of skills workers need in order to compete in this sector, reflecting the dual labor market and its distinctions between high-skilled service work (e.g., financial consultants, public relations) and low-paid and low-skilled service work (food service, child and elderly care). Women and people of color are more likely found in the latter part of the service sector, illustrating the ways the economy is a conduit for the maintenance of systems of inequality and privilege. Consequences of the dual labor market are discussed in the sections below on women's labor force participation and issues of pay equity.

Third, economies around the world are increasingly connected to, and positioned differently within, a global economy that operates in conjunction with such transnational organizations as the World Bank and the World Trade Organization. Critics emphasize how the latter organizations tend to function to maintain the power of "first world" nations like the United States. Multinational corporations have grown in size and influence, and mergers have resulted in a smaller number of corporations controlling a larger part of the market. They have immense power and influence and often no longer correspond to national borders, functioning outside the jurisdiction of nation states. Because many U.S.-based corporations rely on the cheaper, nonunionized labor force and looser environmental restrictions outside the United States, much manufacturing and increasingly service work is done overseas. Evelyn Hu-Dehart writes about the realities and consequences of these strategies in the reading "Surviving Globalization." She focuses on the work of immigrant women in both the formal economy of globalization (electronics and garment work) and the informal economy (child care, sex work, street vendoring) in the United States. As discussed in Chapter 11, the military has close ties to the economy, creating what scholars call the military-industrial complex. Military operations and the presence of international military forces in developing countries serve in part to "stabilize" these nations and protect foreign business interests such as oil or other resources, often

Global Employment Trends for Women

During the 1980s and 1990s women's participation in labour markets worldwide grew substantially. This gave rise to expectations that increased opportunities and economic autonomy for women would bring greater gender equality. To help determine the extent to which such hopes are being realized, it is necessary to analyse women's labour market trends in more detail. To this end, the *Global Employment Trends for Women* focuses on whether the tendency toward increased participation has continued more recently and whether women have found enough decent and productive jobs to really enable them to use their potential in the labour market and achieve economic independence.

The main findings are:

- In absolute numbers, more women than ever before are participating in labour markets worldwide. They are either in work or actively looking for a job.
- This overall figure only tells part of the story, however. During the past ten years, the labour force participation rate (the share of working-age women who work or are seeking work) stopped growing, with many regions registering declines. This reversal is notable, even though it partially reflects greater participation of young women in education.
- More women than ever before are actually in work.[1] The female share of total employment stayed almost unchanged at 40 percent in 2006 (from 39.7 percent 10 years ago).
- At the same time, more women than ever before are unemployed, with the rate of women's unemployment (6.6 percent) higher than that of men (6.1 percent).
- Women are more likely to work in low productivity jobs in agriculture and services. Women's share in industrial employment is much smaller than men's and has decreased over the last ten years.
- The poorer the region, the greater the likelihood that women work as unpaid contributing family members[2] or low-income own-account workers. Female contributing family workers, in particular, are not likely to be economically independent.
- The step from unpaid contributing family worker or low-paid own-account worker to wage and salaried employment is a major step toward freedom and self-determination for many women. The share of women in wage and salaried work grew during the past ten years from 42.9 percent in 1996 to 47.9 percent in 2006. However, especially in the world's poorest regions, this share is still smaller for women than for men.
- There is evidence that wage gaps persist. Throughout most regions and many occupations women get less money for the same job. But there is also some evidence that globalization can help close the wage gap for some occupations.
- Young women are more likely to be able to read and write than 10 years ago. But there is still a gap between female and male education levels. And there is considerable doubt that women get the same chances as men to develop their skills throughout their working lives.

[1] The expression "in work" summarizes all people employed according to the ILO definition, which includes self-employed, employed, employers as well as unpaid family members. The words "employed" and "in work" are used as synonyms in this *GET for Women Brief 2007*.
[2] The expressions "unpaid contributing family workers," "unpaid contributing family members," "contributing family workers," and "contributing family members" are used as synonyms.

These trends show that despite some progress, there is no cause for complacency. Policies to enhance women's chances to participate equally in labour markets are starting to pay off, but the pace with which gaps are closing is very slow. As a result, women are more likely than men to become discouraged and give up hope of being economically active. And for women who work, there is a greater likelihood to be among the working poor—they work but they do not earn enough to lift themselves and their families out of poverty. Given finally the persisting lack of socio-economic empowerment for women and unequal distribution of household responsibilities, there remains some way to go to achieve equality between men and women.

At a time when the world increasingly realizes that decent and productive work is the only sustainable way out of poverty, analyzing women's role in the world of work is particularly important. Progress on full, productive and decent employment, a new target within the Millennium Development Goals, will only be possible if the specific needs for women in labour markets are addressed.[3]

[3] This brief is a condensed version of the ILO working paper "Global Employment Trends for Women 2007."

in the name of forging "peace" or "democracy." The current crisis in the Middle East is a case in point.

The effects of the global economy often include profound inequalities between rich and poor nations as well as between rich and poor citizens within individual countries. Often these inequalities are based on older inequities resulting from nineteenth- and early-twentieth-century colonization and imperialism. For individual women, although multinational corporations do give women a wage, they often upset subsistence economies and cause migration and cultural dislocation, which encourages increasing consumerism, sex trading, and the pollution of fragile environments. Women often work in poor and unhealthy conditions for little pay. In addition, many thousands of U.S. workers have lost their jobs as corporations have moved productive processes overseas. These events are not random but part of a broader pattern of global capitalist expansion.

Women's Labor Force Participation

The major change in terms of trends in women's workforce participation has been the increase in the number of women who were in paid employment or looking for work as the last century progressed. The U.S. Bureau of Labor Statistics reports that this number grew from 5.3 million in 1900 to 18.4 million in 1950 and 70 million in 2006, when three-quarters of women worked full time. Women made up 18 percent of the labor force in 1900, almost 30 percent in 1950, and 46 percent in 2006. Approximately 55 percent of mothers with infant children are in the labor force today.

Given the large number of women working in the labor force, what kinds of work are they doing? The answer is everything. Women are doing all kinds of work and can be found in all segments of the labor force. At the same time, however, women are much more likely to be found in some sectors than others and are crowded into a

20 Leading Occupations of Employed Women

Full-Time Wage and Salary Workers,
2006 Annual Averages (employment in thousands)

Occupation	Percent Women	Women's Median Weekly Earnings (in dollars)
Preschool and kindergarten teachers	97.7	520
Secretaries and administrative assistants	96.9	559
Receptionists and information clerks	92.7	463
Teacher assistants	92.3	398
Registered nurses	91.3	930
Bookkeeping, accounting, and auditing clerks	90.3	551
Maid and housekeeping cleaners	90.3	328
Nurses, psychiatric and home health aides	88.9	385
Social workers	82.6	682
Elementary and middle school teachers	82.2	813
Office clerks, general	81.9	509
Cashiers	74.8	322
First-line supervisors/managers of office and administrative support workers	72.2	656
Waiters and waitresses	71.5	332
Customer service representatives	70.4	505
Accountants and auditors	60.2	784
Secondary school teachers	56.0	841
Financial managers	55.0	853
Retail sales workers	51.4	401
First-line supervisors/managers of retail sales workers	41.8	525

Source: U.S. Department of Labor, Bureau of Labor Statistics, *http://www.bls.gov.*

small number of fields, many of which are characterized as secondary sector jobs in the dual labor market. One aspect of segregating women and men into different jobs (known as *occupational segregation by gender*) is *horizontal segregation* (meaning segregation of women and men across different kinds of jobs). These jobs held by women are often called "pink-collar" and can be understood as an extension of women's work in the home.

As reported in the box above on occupations of employed women by the U.S. Department of Labor, almost 97 percent of secretaries and administrative assistants, 92 percent of registered nurses, and 98 percent of preschool and kindergarten teachers are women. Women congregate in clerical, retail, sales, and various service-sector jobs. In comparison, only about 2 percent of working women are employed in precision production, craft, and repair (down slightly from 1990), and 7 percent of working

Selected Nontraditional Occupations for Women*

Job Title	Total Employed (1,000s)	Women Employed (1,000s)	Percent Women
Police and detectives (supervisors)	103	16	15.5
Dentists	196	44	22.6
Architects	221	49	22.2
Farming, fishing, and forestry occupations	961	211	22.0
Logging	78	0.16	0.2
Driver/sales workers and truck drivers	3,475	174	5.2
Industrial truck and tractor operators	574	41	7.2
Aircraft pilots and flight engineers	115	2	2.2
Firefighters	253	9	3.5
Automotive service technicians and mechanics	875	14	1.6
Refuse and recyclable material collectors	91	6	6.1
Construction and extraction occupations	9,507	295	3.1
Taxi drivers and chauffeurs	282	45	16.0

*Nontraditional occupations are any that women constitute 25 percent or less of the total employed.
Source: U.S. Department of Labor.

women are employed as operators, fabricators, and laborers (with a more significant decline from 8.5 percent on 1990). Despite these traditional patterns, women's presence in certain once-male-dominated professions has increased. In 1970, 9 percent of practicing physicians were female, compared with about 30 percent in 2007; almost half of medical schools' graduating class of 2007 was female. Numbers have also increased for women dentists (19 percent), with women making up about a third of the 2007 graduating class from dental schools. Women attorneys make up about a third of all practicing attorneys, and 44 percent of law students. Female pharmacists also increased from 30 percent in 1985 to almost half in 2006. One of the most female-segregated jobs is sex work such as prostitution, where women workers have often struggled to control the conditions of their work against the demoralization and abuse by customers, pimps, and police. Kimberly Klinger's article, "Prostitution, Humanism, and a Woman's Choice," discusses prostitution, the legalities surrounding it, and the necessity of finding a common ground to support women's choice.

The term *blue collar* implies working class or involved with industrial, production, and factory work and can be contrasted with *white collar,* which means office or professional work and usually refers to middle-class occupations. Note the slippage between industrial work and male-segregated work such that blue collar means working class but also implies male-segregated work with its use of the word *blue* as opposed to *pink*. The Bureau of Labor Statistics reports the following occupations as the most male segregated: engineers, mechanics and drivers, carpenters and construction trades, firefighters, airline pilots and navigators, and forestry and logging work. You will note the obvious ways feminine jobs involve working with people, children, cleaning, and

ACTIVIST PROFILE   **Dolores Huerta**

Dolores Huerta is one of the most powerful and influential labor leaders in the United States. Born in Dawson, New Mexico, in 1930, Huerta grew up in Stockton, California, and eventually earned a teaching certificate from Stockton College. After one year of teaching, however, she quit to work with Community Service Organization (CSO). She thought she could do more to help the hungry children she saw at school by helping organize their farmworker parents.

While with CSO, she met César Chavez, and in 1962 they founded the United Farm Workers of America (UFW). Although Chavez was more comfortable in the fields organizing workers, Huerta became the voice of the union, becoming the first woman and first Chicana negotiator in labor history. The UFW met with great success in the 1965 Delano Grape Strike, which won the first collective bargaining agreement for farmworkers, and Huerta was instrumental in the negotiations. She also became consciously involved with the feminist movement when she met Gloria Steinem in 1968, although she had always focused on issues specific to women farmworkers.

In 1972 she co-chaired the California delegation to the Democratic Convention, and she led the struggle for unemployment insurance, collective bargaining rights, and immigration rights for farmworkers under the 1985 amnesty legalization program. She was the first Latina inducted into the National Women's Hall of Fame, and she received the National Organization for Women's Woman of Courage Award and the American Civil Liberties Union's Bill of Rights Award. She continues to struggle for farmworkers through the UFW and serve as a role model for Chicanas in their fight against discrimination.

administrative support, whereas masculine employment tends to involve working with machines and inanimate objects. There are other differences too, such as that wages for the heavily male-segregated jobs tend to be higher than wages for the female-segregated, pink-collar work. That is because these jobs are valued more, and they are more likely to be unionized, which tends to pay more. In 2006, almost half of all union members were female and unionized women workers earned 24 percent more than nonunion women workers and received better health and pension benefits: Union membership narrows the gender wage gap.

Another important aspect of occupational segregation by gender is that there is gender segregation even within the same job type. This is termed *vertical segregation* (segregation *within* jobs), and, like horizontal segregation, it functions as a result of sexism and racism and other systems of inequality and privilege. For example, although the number of women physicians is increasing as already mentioned,

LEARNING ACTIVITY **Working Women and Unions**

Visit the Web page of the AFL-CIO at *www.aflcio.org* to learn more about women in the workforce. What are some of the key issues for working women identified by the AFL-CIO? What legislative issues does the AFL-CIO identify that would be beneficial to working women? What is a union? What benefits do unions provide? Why are unions important for working women? What steps would people take to form a union at their workplace?

women are still overwhelmingly found in certain specialties such as pediatrics, dermatology, and public health work, and are less likely to be found in surgical specialties, orthopedics, and more entrepreneurial positions. For example, women's presence has increased dramatically in some specialties (in 1970 only 5 percent of doctors in obstetrics and gynecology were female; by 2005 this number had risen to about 70 percent) and more slowly in other specialties (about 10 percent of orthopedic surgeons and neurosurgeons were women in 2005). Observers note that the growing proportion of U.S. physicians who are female is improving the quality of medical care through more emotionally focused and patient-centered practice, although as discussed in the following section, it is lowering physicians' average salaries overall. (As an aside, research at Harvard Medical School has shown that female physicians have a higher rate of suicide than any other women professionals.) Female physicians on the average earned between 60 and 70 percent of what male physicians made in 2006.

Similarly, female lawyers are less likely to be in criminal law and are more likely to practice family law and make about 70 percent of male lawyers' salaries. Male teachers are more likely to teach sciences and are more likely to be with older children; female professors are more typically in the humanities and the social sciences and found in smaller number in the physical and applied sciences and technical fields. Usually specialties and fields that men occupy are more prestigious and the salaries are higher. In this way, women and men do not just tend to perform different jobs, but the jobs that they do are valued differently and have different levels of status and power and bring different problems associated with integration and advancement. This differential is related to sexism in society generally as well as to other systems of inequality and privilege.

Barriers to advancement in the labor force (what is often called the *glass ceiling*) have been challenged by women, by the courts, and by the women's movement. And, although these barriers are beginning to come down, they are still holding strong in many areas. Women tend not to be promoted at the same rate as men and they also continue to face obstacles when trying to enter the most prestigious and best-paid occupations. While women are increasingly moving into middle management positions, 2006 data show their relative absence in top leadership positions. Only 10 Fortune 500 companies (2 percent) have women CEOs or presidents and another 20 women CEOs are in the Fortune 1000 (again, 2 percent). Finally, although women

"Whatever happened to a good cry in the Ladies Room?"

Reprinted with permission from Carol Simpson Labor Cartoons.

make up more than 60 percent of the nonprofit workplace, they still lack access to top management positions, share of foundation dollars, and board positions. Women of color are relatively absent in the higher echelons of corporate power in all sectors. The reading "Power Plays" by Martha Burk explains the six ways the corporate elite keeps women down, emphasizing the power dynamics of the corporate world that continue to maintain the status quo.

Alongside consideration of the problems associated with the glass ceiling, it is important to recognize what researchers have called the *glass escalator* and the *glass precipice.* The glass escalator refers to the practices whereby men who go into traditionally female-dominated professions like teaching, nursing, and social work are disproportionately advanced into management and administrative positions where they receive more prestige, pay, and power than women. The glass precipice is the process whereby women are encouraged into leadership positions in failing organizations and companies and are disproportionately set up to fail professionally.

Finally, it is interesting to look at how the development of certain occupations as female segregated has affected the status and conditions of work. For example, clerical work, although low prestige, was definitely a man's job until the turn of the twentieth century, when women quickly became associated with this work. This was due to the following factors: There was a large pool of women with few other opportunities; clerical work's low status made it easier for women to be accepted; typewriter manufacturers began promoting the typewriter as something women used; and the personal service aspect of the work fit gender norms about the feminine aspect of secretarial work. As more women entered this profession, the gap between clerical wages and blue-collar wages generally increased, and the status of the clerical profession fell. A more recent example is the field of pharmacy. Two trends—the increasing number of pharmacies attached to chain drugstores and the increasing number of female pharmacists—have been seen as the reasons why the status of pharmacy has fallen as a profession. It remains to be seen whether the increase of women in human and animal medicine, and in the sciences generally, will decrease the status of these professions.

Wages and Comparable Worth

The most disparate wage gap in the United States is that between those who head corporations and those who work for corporations. A 2007 report from the Institute for Policy Studies compares the average compensation of full-time, year-round workers in nonmanagerial jobs (approximately $40,000/year) to CEO pay (approximately $10.8 million/year). The latter make almost 300 times the former, and this does not include the value of many perks CEOs receive, which averaged an additional almost half a million dollars, nor their pension benefits. The report emphasizes that this gap increases to 364 times when the top 20 U.S. companies are used (average CEO salary rises to approximately $36.4 million/year) and the average salary for all workers is employed (average salary falls to about $30,000/year). Such CEO compensation far exceeds leaders in other fields and in other countries. Top managers in the United States made three times more than those in similar European companies, even though the Europeans tended to have higher sales numbers than their U.S. counterparts. It is important to keep in mind that only 2 percent, or 20, of the top 1,000 U.S. companies are led by women. Most of these women are White.

The *gender wage gap* is an index of the status of women's earnings relative to men's and is expressed as a percentage (e.g., in 2005, women earned 77 percent as much as men) and is calculated by dividing the median annual earnings for women by the median annual earnings for men. These data include only full-time, year-round workers and exclude all part-time or seasonal workers. Because a large number of women work part-time jobs, the inclusion of these would lower the numbers discussed below because part-time work tends to be lower paid and these workers receive fewer job-related benefits and are less likely to be unionized. The most recent U.S. Census figures available as of this writing include 2005 data that report the gender wage gap of annual earnings at 77 percent. Census figures from 2006 that use median weekly earnings report a gender wage gap of 81 percent. African American women, however, earn just 70 cents to every dollar earned by White men, and for Hispanic women that figure drops to merely 59 cents per dollar. The wage gap is also more pronounced for older women. In addition, the return on education for women compared with men is significantly lower, with median annual earnings of a female high school graduate about 34 percent less, women with bachelor's degrees and graduate degrees almost a third less, and women with a doctoral degree 29 percent less than their male counterparts.

If working women earned the same as men (those who work the same number of hours; have the same education, age, and union status; and live in the same region of the country), their annual family incomes would rise by $4,000 and poverty rates would be cut in half. The Institute for Policy Research reports that over a lifetime of work, the average 25-year-old woman who works full-time, year-round, until she retires at age 65 years will earn on the average almost a half million dollars less than the average working man. Currently 13 percent of men and 4 percent of women earn over $75,000 a year, while a little more than 19 percent of men and 9 percent of women earn between $50,000 and $75,000 a year.

Copyright © Nicole Hollander. Used by permission of Nicole Hollander.

As you might imagine, there are many more women in the United States living in poverty (at about $19,350 a year for a family of four in 2005) than there are men. While almost 12 percent of the population is below the poverty level, rates are highest for families headed by single women, particularly women of color. As life earnings are calculated, the number of women over 65 years of age in poverty is more than double that of men (U.S. Census, 2002). Finally, women are nearly 60 percent of all social security beneficiaries generally and about 70 percent of beneficiaries over 85 years old. For many elderly women, Social Security is all they have; the future direction of Social Security will disproportionately affect women. Because women earn less when they work, they receive smaller Social Security benefits when they retire. In 2005, the U.S. Census reported that the average Social Security benefit was almost a third smaller for women than for men.

So, why do women earn less money than men on the average? The gender wage gap is explained by several factors. First, it is explained by the horizontal segregation of the labor force: Women and men tend to work in different kinds of jobs and the jobs women hold are valued and rewarded less. Such differences are not covered by the Equal Pay Act because women and men are engaged in different kinds of work. Second, the gap is explained by vertical segregation, or the ways women and men are in different specialties within the same occupation. Indeed, comparable wages are a problem in every occupational category, even in occupations in which women considerably outnumber men. In 2006, certain professions showed a significant gap. Women in professional and related occupations, sales and office occupations, for example, earned about a quarter less than their male counterparts. Female elementary and middle school teachers and registered nurses earned about 10 percent less than similarly employed men, despite comprising the majority of the field, and, as already noted, female physicians and surgeons earn about 38 percent less than male counterparts and female attorneys about 30 percent less. In higher education, women college and university professors in 2006 earned approximately 25 percent less than male professors. This vertical segregation implies that women and other marginalized workers are in specialties within these professions that are less valued and rewarded than more "masculine" specialties. Finally, the gender pay gap is explained by overt and covert discrimination against women and other marginalized workers.

After economists control for "human capital" variables (such as time spent in work, education, seniority, time since receipt of degree, prestige of institution awarding degree, etc.), there is still a proportion of unexplained variance between the wages of men and women in the same specialties and within the same occupational category. Norms about gender, race, age, and social class work to create patterns of institutionalized inequalities that reinforce ideas concerning women's and men's worth and the kinds of work people should do.

Comparable worth, also known as pay equity, is one means to pay women and men in different occupations comparably. Basically, comparable worth works to compare different jobs on experience, skill, training, and job conditions and assigns relative points on these indices in order to determine their worth. There is no federal-level comparable worth legislation, although many states have enacted laws demanding comparable worth comparisons in determining pay for state workers. In addition, the courts have ruled both for and against workers who have brought comparable worth suits against various corporations. When the courts have ruled in favor of plaintiffs, it has often meant a considerable amount of money in back pay to compensate female workers for years of financial inequities.

In this way inequality in women's work lives has important consequences for inequality in other spheres of life. Because most women work both inside and outside the home and spend a considerable part of their lives working, it is of central importance to understand the conditions under which women work as well as to strive for equality in the workplace.

The Politics of Housework

Pat Mainardi (1970)

Though women do not complain of the power of husbands, each complains of her own husband, or of the husbands of her friends. It is the same in all other cases of servitude; at least in the commencement of the emancipatory movement. The serfs did not at first complain of the power of the lords, but only of their tyranny.

—*John Staurt Mill*, On the Subjection of Women

Liberated women—very different from women's liberation! The first signals all kinds of goodies, to warm the hearts (not to mention other parts) of the most radical men. The other signals—*housework*. The first brings sex without marriage, sex before marriage, cozy housekeeping arrangements ("You see, I'm living with this chick") and the self-content of knowing that you're not the kind of man who wants a doormat instead of a woman. That will come later. After all, who wants that old commodity anymore, the Standard American Housewife, all husband, home and kids. The New Commodity, the Liberated Woman, has sex a lot and has a Career, preferably something that can be fitted in with the household chores—like dancing, pottery, or painting.

On the other hand is women's liberation—and housework. What? You say this is all trivial? Wonderful! That's what I thought. It seemed perfectly reasonable. We both had careers, both had to work a couple of days a week to earn enough to live on, so why shouldn't we share the housework? So I suggested it to my mate and he agreed—most men are too hip to turn you down flat. "You're right," he said. "It's only fair."

Then an interesting thing happened. I can only explain it by stating that we women have been brainwashed more than even we can imagine. Probably too many years of seeing television women in ecstasy over their shiny waxed floors or breaking down over their dirty shirt collars. Men have no such conditioning. They recognize the essential fact of housework right from the very beginning. Which is that it stinks. Here's my list of dirty chores: buying groceries, carting them home and putting them away; cooking meals and washing dishes and pots; doing the laundry, digging out the place when things get out of control; washing floors. The list could go on but the sheer necessities are bad enough. All of us have to do these things, or get someone else to do them for us. The longer my husband contemplated these chores the more repulsed he became, and so proceeded the change from the normally sweet considerate Dr. Jekyll into the crafty Mr. Hyde who would stop at nothing to avoid the horrors of—*housework*. As he felt himself backed into a corner laden with dirty dishes, brooms, mops, and reeking garbage, his front teeth grew longer and pointier, his fingernails haggled and his eyes grew wild. Housework trivial? Not on your life! Just try to share the burden.

So ensued a dialogue that's been going on for several years. Here are some of the high points:

"I don't mind sharing the housework, but I don't do it very well. We should each do the things we're best at."

Meaning: Unfortunately I'm no good at things like washing dishes or cooking. What I do best is a little light carpentry, changing light bulbs, moving furniture (*how often do you move furniture?*).

Also Meaning: Historically the lower classes (black men and us) have had hundreds of years experience doing menial jobs. It would be a waste of manpower to train someone else to do them now.

Also Meaning: I don't like the dull stupid boring jobs, so you should do them.

"I don't mind sharing the work, but you'll have to show me how to do it."

Meaning: I ask a lot of questions and you'll have to show me everything everytime I do it because I don't remember so good. Also don't try to sit down and read while I'm doing my jobs because I'm going to annoy hell out of you until it's easier to do them yourself.

"We used to be so happy!" (Said whenever it was his turn to do something.)

Meaning: I used to be so happy.

Meaning: Life without housework is bliss. (*No quarrel here. Perfect agreement.*)

"We have different standards, and why should I have to work to your standards. That's unfair."

Meaning: If I begin to get bugged by the dirt and crap I will say "This place sure is a sty" or "How can anyone live like this?" and wait for your reaction. I know that all women have a sore called "Guilt over a messy house" or "Household work is ultimately my responsibility." I know that men have caused that sore—if anyone visits and the place *is* a sty, they're not going to leave and say, "He sure is a lousy housekeeper." You'll take the rap in any case. I can outwait you.

Also Meaning: I can provoke innumerable scenes over the housework issue. Eventually doing all the housework yourself will be less painful to you than trying to get me to do half. Or I'll suggest we get a maid. She will do my share of the work. You will do yours. It's women's work.

"I've got nothing against sharing the housework, but you can't make me do it on your schedule."

Meaning: Passive resistance. I'll do it when I damned well please, if at all. If my job is doing dishes, it's easier to do them once a week. If taking out laundry, once a month. If washing the floors, once a year. If you don't like it, do it yourself oftener, and then I won't do it at all.

"I *hate* it more than you. You don't mind it so much."

Meaning: Housework is garbage work. It's the worst crap I've ever done. It's degrading and humiliating for someone of *my* intelligence to do it. But for someone of *your* intelligence . . .

"Housework is too trivial to even talk about."

Meaning: It's even more trivial to do. Housework is beneath my status. My purpose in life is to deal with matters of significance. Yours is to deal with matters of insignificance. You should do the housework.

"This problem of housework is not a man-woman problem! In any relationship between two people one is going to have a stronger personality and dominate."

Meaning: That stronger personality had better be *me*.

"In animal societies, wolves, for example, the top animal is usually a male even where he is not chosen for brute strength but on the basis of cunning and intelligence. Isn't that interesting?"

Meaning: I have historical, psychological, anthropological, and biological justification for keeping you down. How can you ask the top wolf to be equal?

"Women's liberation isn't really a political movement."

Meaning: The Revolution is coming too close to home.

Also Meaning: I am only interested in how *I* am oppressed, not how I oppress others. Therefore the war, the draft, and the university are political. Women's liberation is not.

"Man's accomplishments have always depended on getting help from other people, mostly women. What great man would have accomplished what he did if he had to do his own housework?"

Meaning: Oppression is built into the System and I, as the white American male receive the benefits of this System. I don't want to give them up.

POSTSCRIPT

Participatory democracy begins at home. If you are planning to implement your politics, there are certain things to remember.

1. He *is* feeling it more than you. He's losing some leisure and you're gaining it. The measure of your oppression is his resistance.
2. A great many American men are not accustomed to doing monotonous repetitive work which never ushers in any lasting let alone important achievement. This is why they would rather repair a cabinet than wash dishes. If human endeavors are like a pyramid with man's highest achievements at the top, then keeping oneself alive is at the bottom. Men have always had servants (us) to take care of this bottom strata of life while they have confined their efforts to the rarefied upper regions. It is thus ironic when they ask of women—where are your great painters, statesmen, etc? Mme. Matisse ran a millinery shop so he could paint. Mrs. Martin Luther King kept his house and raised his babies.
3. It is a traumatizing experience for someone who has always thought of himself as being against any oppression or exploitation of one human being by another to realize that in his daily life he has been accepting and implementing (and benefiting from) this exploitation; that his rationalization is little different from that of the racist who says "Black people don't feel pain" (women don't mind doing the shitwork); and that the oldest form of oppression in history has been the oppression of 50 percent of the population by the other 50 percent.
4. Arm yourself with some knowledge of the psychology of oppressed peoples everywhere, and a few facts about the animal kingdom. I admit playing top wolf or who runs the gorillas is silly but as a last resort men bring it up all the time. Talk about bees. If you feel really hostile bring up the sex life of spiders. They have sex. She bites off his head.

   The psychology of oppressed people is not silly. Jews, immigrants, black men, and all women have employed the same psychological mechanisms to survive: admiring the oppressor, glorifying the oppressor, wanting to be like the oppressor, wanting the oppressor to like them, mostly because the oppressor held all the power.

5. In a sense, all men everywhere are slightly schizoid—divorced from the reality of maintaining life. This makes it easier for them to play games with it. It is almost a cliché that women feel greater grief at sending a son off to war or losing him to that war because they bore him, suckled him, and raised him. The men who forment those wars did none of those things and have a more superficial estimate of the worth of human life. One hour a day is a low estimate of the amount of time one has to spend "keeping" oneself. By foisting this off on others, man gains seven hours a week—one working day more to play with his mind and not his human needs. Over the course of generations it is easy to see whence evolved the horrifying abstractions of modern life.
6. With the death of each form of oppression, life changes and new forms evolve. English aristocrats at the turn of the century were horrified at the idea of enfranchising working men—were sure that it signaled the death of civilization and a return to barbarism. Some working men were even deceived by this line. Similarly with the minimum wage, abolition of slavery, and female suffrage. Life changes but it goes on. Don't fall for any line about the death of everything if men take a turn at the dishes. They will imply that you are holding back the Revolution (their Revolution). But you are advancing it (your Revolution).
7. Keep checking up. Periodically consider who's actually *doing* the jobs. These things have a way of backsliding so that a year later once again the woman is doing everything. After a year make a list of jobs the man has rarely if ever done. You will find cleaning pots, toilets, refrigerators and ovens high on the list. Use time sheets if necessary. He will accuse you of being petty. He is above that sort of thing—(housework). Bear in mind what the worst jobs are, namely the ones that have to be done every day or several times a day. Also the ones that are dirty—it's more pleasant to pick up books, newspapers, etc. than to wash dishes. Alternate the bad jobs. It's the daily grind that gets you down. Also make sure that you don't have the responsibility for the housework

with occasional help from him. "I'll cook dinner for you tonight" implies it's really your job and isn't he a nice guy to do some of it for you.

8. Most men had a rich and rewarding bachelor life during which they did not starve or become encrusted with crud or buried under the litter. There is a taboo that says that women mustn't strain themselves in the presence of men: we haul around 50 pounds of groceries if we have to but aren't allowed to open a jar if there is someone around to do it for us. The reverse side of the coin is that men aren't supposed to be able to take care of themselves without a woman. Both are excuses for making women do the housework.

9. Beware of the double whammy. He won't do the little things he always did because you're now a "Liberated Woman," right? Of course he won't do anything else either . . .

I was just finishing this when my husband came in and asked what I was doing. Writing a paper on housework. Housework? He said, *Housework?* Oh my god how trivial can you get. A paper on housework.

R E A D I N G 60

A Brief History of Working Women

Sharlene Hesse-Biber and Gregg Lee Carter (1999)

WOMEN WORKERS IN PRE-INDUSTRIAL AMERICA

Seven hundred and fifty thousand Europeans came to America between 1600 and 1700. The bulk of them were from Britain, but the colonies also saw significant numbers from Holland, France, and Germany. Many came as indentured servants, exchanging their labor for the cost of passage to the American colonies. Indentured servants often worked from five to ten years to pay back their creditors. As early as the 1600s, prior to the slave trade, some Africans also came to the colonies as indentured servants; they often worked side by side with white indentured servants. Women's lives in this country differed drastically, depending on their race, class, and marital status.

White Women

European women usually arrived in the New World with their families, as daughters and wives, under the auspices of fathers or husbands. In the pre-industrial economy of the American colonial period (from the seventeenth century to the early eighteenth century), work was closely identified with home and family life. The family was the primary economic unit, and family members were dependent on one another for basic sustenance. Men performed the agricultural work, while women's work was done chiefly in the home, which was a center of production in colonial America. In addition to cooking, cleaning, and caring for children, women did spinning and weaving, and made lace, soap, candles, and shoes. Indeed, they manufactured nearly all articles used in daily life. This work was highly valued, and the colonies relied on the production of these "cottage industries."

Single women remained within the domestic sphere, living with relatives, often as "assistant homemakers." For married women, the nature of their work depended on the economic circumstances of their husbands:

In cash-poor homes and among frontier families, women bore the burden of filling most of the family's basic needs. They worked to reduce cash expenditures by growing vegetables in the kitchen garden and making the family's clothes, candles, soap and household furnishings. If a husband were a craftsman or the proprietor of a shop or tavern, his wife and children might also work in the business, in addition to all the other tasks. In contrast, the wife of a successful farmer, plantation owner, or merchant did little actual work; instead, she supervised household servants and slaves who purchased or made the goods the family needed, cooked the meals, and maintained the house.

The social codes of colonial America did not exclude a woman from working outside the home, and many did so. Colonial women engaged in a great range of occupations, and as old documents are discovered and new histories of women's work are written, that range appears greater still. Women were innkeepers, shopkeepers, crafts workers, nurses, printers, teachers, and landholders. In the city of Boston during 1690, for example, women ran approximately 40 percent of all taverns. During that year, city officials also granted more than thirty women the right to saw lumber and manufacture potash. Women acted as physicians and midwives in all the early settlements, producing medicines, salves, and ointments. Many of the women who worked outside their homes were widows with dependent children, who took their husbands' places in family enterprises. It seems that at one time or another, colonial women engaged in many of the occupations practiced by men. Indeed, most models of the "patriarchal family economy" ill fit the historical evidence; for example, eighteenth-century diaries describe "a world in which wives as well as husbands traded with their neighbors" and "young women felt themselves responsible for their own support." Not surprisingly, however, women's wages in this period were significantly lower than those of men.

For poor women, there were special incentives to work outside the home. Local poor laws encouraged single poor women to work rather than become recipients of relief. The choice of jobs was much more limited, and many poor women became laundresses, house servants, or cooks. Again, however, female laborers were paid approximately 30 percent less than the lowest-paid unskilled, free, white male workers and 20 percent less than hired-out male slaves.

The fact that some women worked in so-called "masculine fields"—that they were merchants, tavern owners, shopkeepers, and so on—has sometimes been interpreted to mean that the colonial period was a "golden age of equality" for women. Contemporary historians argue instead, however, that these jobs were exceptions to the rule, and that in fact "colonial times were characterized by a strict and simple division of labor between men and women, which assigned them to fields and house, or to the public and private spheres, respectively." The dominant ideology was still that a woman's place was at home, raising children. . . .

Women of Color

Historically, the experiences of women of color have differed dramatically from those of white women. If we consider only the present time period, it may appear that women of color and white women have certain experiences in common—relatively low economic position, being the target of discriminatory practices in education and in work, and overall marginality in the power structure. But women of color and white women have reached their present circumstances through very different histories. Although white women's status was clearly inferior to that of white men, they were treated with deference, and they shared in the status privileges of their husbands. African American women almost never had the option of choosing between work and leisure, as did some white women. They were not included in the image of the "colonial housewife." African American women were not considered "weak" females, but were treated more like beasts of burden. Thus these women of color suffered a double oppression of sexism and racism.

Nowhere is this double oppression more clearly demonstrated than within the institution of slavery, which became established in late seventeenth- and early eighteenth-century colonial society—

largely as a result of the demand for cheap agricultural labor, especially within the Southern plantation economy. Historians estimate the slave population in the United States, Caribbean, and Brazil consisted of 9.5 million blacks. More than double that number are estimated to have died in transit to the New World. Slave women in the Southern colonies were without doubt the most exploited of all women. They were exploited not only as workers but as breeders of slaves. The following advertisement was typical of the time:

> **Negroes for Sale:** A girl about twenty years of age (raised in Virginia) and her two female children, four and the other two years old—remarkably strong and healthy. Never having had a day's sickness with the exception of the smallpox in her life. She is prolific in her generating qualities and affords a rare opportunity to any person who wishes to raise a family of strong and healthy servants for their own use.

Slave women were also sometimes exploited as sex objects for white men. Like male slaves, they were considered intrinsically inferior. Slaves were property, not people. They faced severe cultural and legal restrictions: their family lives were controlled by their owners, their children were not their own, and their educational opportunities were almost nonexistent.

Sojourner Truth, formerly a slave and an activist in the abolitionist and women's rights movements, eloquently expressed the differences in treatment, under slavery, of black and white women: "That man over there says that women need to be helped into carriages and lifted over ditches, and to have the best place everywhere. Nobody ever helped me into carriages, or over mud puddles, or gives me any best place . . . and ain't I a woman?"

Before the Civil War, a black woman in one of the "cotton states," working on one of the larger plantations, would have been either a house servant or one of several million field hands who produced major cash crops. In the Southern plantation economy, we thus find a "bifurcated" concept of woman. The European woman became "the guardian of civilization," while the African American woman was "spared neither harsh labor nor harsh punishment," though the experience of slaves differed depending on the economic status and individual personality of the slave owner. Even pregnancy did not deter some slavemasters from cruel treatment: "One particular method of whipping pregnant slaves was used throughout the South; they were made to lie face down in a specially dug depression in the ground, a practice that provided simultaneously for the protection of the fetus and the abuse of its mother."

Some white women benefited from such slave labor and shared with their husbands the role of oppressor, although the slave-mistress relationship was psychologically complex: "In their role as labor managers, mistresses lashed out at slave women not only to punish them, but also to vent their anger on victims even more wronged than themselves. We may speculate that, in the female slave, the white woman saw the source of her own misery, but she also saw herself—a woman without rights or recourse, subject to the whims of an egotistical man." Conflict between white and African American women often resulted in violence, in which "mistresses were likely to attack with any weapon available—knitting needles, tongs, a fork, butcher knife, ironing board, or pan of boiling water." Yet, while the relationship was often filled with strife, white and African American women "also shared a world of physical and emotional intimacy that is uncommon among women of antagonistic classes and different races."

Slavery was justified by notions of race involving the "biological superiority" of the colonists. It was assumed that Europeans in the colonies made up an easily identifiable and discrete biological and social entity—a "natural" community of class interests, racial attributes, political and social affinities, and superior culture. This was of course not exactly true, but given that the differences between white skin and black skin were more noticeable than many of the differences among Europeans themselves, and given that whites were in dominant positions politically and socially, it could easily *seem* to be true.

Slave families often resisted the oppressive workloads by banding together to help one another in the fields and to lessen the workloads of older, weaker, or sicker workers. The extended family was of vital importance under the slave system. African American mothers labored most of the day, some of them caring for white women's families, while their own children were left under the care of grandmothers and old or disabled slaves. While the two-parent, nuclear family may have been the most typical form of slave cohabitation, close relatives were often very much involved in family life. Stevenson's study suggests that in colonial and antebellum Virginia, the slave family was a "malleable extended family that, when possible, provided its members with nurture, education, socialization, material support, and recreation in the face of the potential social chaos that the slaveholder imposed."

Even though African American men were unable to own property, to provide protection and support for their children, or to work within the public sphere, there was a sexual division within the slave household. Men collected the firewood and made furniture—beds, tables, chairs—and other articles of wood, such as animal traps, butter paddles, and ax handles. They also wove baskets and made shoes. African American women grew, prepared, and preserved foods; spun thread, wove and dyed cloth, and sewed clothes; and made soap and candles.

In the North, while slavery was an accepted practice, it was not nearly as widespread. Many African American women worked as free laborers as domestic servants; others worked as spinners, weavers, and printers.

Native American Women

The work and family life experience of Native American women prior to European colonization differed depending on the region of the country and the type of tribal society. But in every Native American nation, women played very important roles in the economic life of their communities:

> They had to be resourceful in utilizing every aspect of the environment to sustain life and engaging in cultural exchanges to incorporate new productive techniques. They gathered wild

plants for food, herbs for medicines and dyes, clay for pottery, bark and reeds for weaving cloth. In many nations, they also tilled the soil and sowed the seeds, cultivated and harvested, made cloth and clothing, dried vegetables, and ground grains for breads. In hunting societies, they cured the meats and dried the skins. They also assisted in the hunt in some cultures.

As a general rule, men hunted and women engaged in agricultural work. The more important hunting was to a community's survival, the more extensive the male power within the community; the greater the dependence on agriculture, the greater the power and independence of women. Women had the responsibility for raising children and maintaining hearth and home. Men engaged in hunting, fishing, and warfare.

In the East especially, many Indian communities were predominantly agricultural. Women constituted the agricultural labor force within these communities. An English woman who was held captive by a Seneca tribe observed that

> Household duties were simple and Seneca women, unlike English wives and daughters, were not slaves to the spinning wheel or the needle. In the summer, the women went out each morning to the fields, accompanied by their children, to work cooperatively and in the company of friends and relatives, planting and tending the corn, beans, and squash at a pace to their individual rhythms and skills rather than to the demands of an overseer. They moved from field to field, completing the same tasks in each before returning to the first.

Women within agricultural communities would often maintain control over tools and land—as well as any surplus foods they gathered from the land. This often enabled them (especially elderly women who were heads of households) to garner some political clout within their tribal communities. For instance, if Iroquois women opposed war on certain occasions, they might refuse to let the men have the cornmeal they would have needed to feed their raiding parties or armies. These communities often had a matrilineal family structure (inheritance and family name were through the female line, with family connections through the mother) and matrilocal residence (upon marriage a man lived with his mother-in-law's relatives).

Through the lens of the white colonist, the work roles and family structure of Native American society appeared deviant and, in some cases, perverse. After all, English society was characterized by a patriarchal family structure with patrilocal residence:

> To Europeans, Indian family patterns raised the specter of promiscuous women, freed from accountability to their fathers and husbands for the offspring they produced. . . . Equally incomprehensible—and thus perverse—to many Europeans were the work roles accepted by Indian men and women. In the world the English knew, farming was labor and farmers were male. Masculinity was linked, inexorably, to agriculture: household production and family reproduction defined femininity. That Indian men hunted was not a sufficient counterpoise, for, in the England of the seventeenth century, hunting was a sport, not an occupation. Many concluded that Indian men were effeminate, lazy; Indian women were beasts of burden, slaves to unmanly men.

European colonization and conquest pushed Native Americans off their land, depriving them of food and livelihood, culture and traditions. Disease or warfare demolished whole societies. Others were radically transformed, especially with regard to the traditional gender and work roles. Having used military force to remove Native Americans from their lands onto reservations, the U.S. government "began a systematic effort to destroy their cultures and replace them with the values and practices of middle-class whites."

Confined to relatively small reservations, Native American men could no longer hunt as extensively as before (nor, defeated by U.S. forces, could they any longer carry on warfare). They therefore needed to redefine their social roles and to find new economic activities. In many a Native American tribe, the men took over agriculture, traditionally the women's work. Family structure also changed, at the prompting of missionaries and others including government officials, to become more like that of the Europeans, with less emphasis on the matrilineal extended family and more on the nuclear family and the husband-wife relationship.

THE ARRIVAL OF INDUSTRIALIZATION

The transformation from an agrarian rural economy to an urban industrial society ushered in a new era in women's work. With the advent of industrialization, many of the products women made at home—clothes, shoes, candles—gradually came to be made instead in factories. For a while, women still performed the work at home, using the new machines. Merchants would contract for work to be done, supplying women with the machines and the raw materials to be made into finished articles. The most common of these manufacturing trades for women was sewing for the newly emerging clothing industry. Since women had always sewn for their families, this work was considered an extension of women's traditional role, and therefore a respectable activity. As the demand for goods increased, however, home production declined and gave way to the factory system, which was more efficient in meeting emerging needs.

The rise of factory production truly separated the home from the workplace. With the decline of the household unit as the center of industrial and economy activity, the importance of women's economic role also declined. Male and female spheres of activity became more separated, as did the definitions of men's and women's roles. Man's role continued to be primarily that of worker and provider; woman's role became primarily supportive. She was to maintain a smooth and orderly household, to be cheerful and warm, and thus to provide the husband with the support and services he needed to continue his work life. The industrial revolution created a set of social and economic conditions in which the basic lifestyle of white middle-class women more nearly approached society's expectations concerning woman's role. More and more middle-class women could now aspire to the status formerly reserved for the upper classes—that of "lady." The nineteenth-century concept of a lady was that of a fragile, idle, pure creature, submissive and subservient to her husband and to domestic needs. Her worth was based on her decorative value, a quality that embraced her beauty, her virtuous character, and her temperament. She was certainly not a paid employee. This ideal was later referred to as the "cult of true womanhood" because of its rigid, almost religious standards.

Biological and social arguments were also often used to justify women's exclusion from the labor force. Women were seen as too weak and delicate to participate in the rough work world of men. It was believed they lacked strength and stamina, that their brains were small, that the feminine perspective and sensitivity were liabilities in the marketplace. Such arguments rationalized women's accepting the roles of homemaker and mother almost exclusively, as the industrial revolution spread across the country.

During the early years of industrialization, however, because many men were still primarily occupied with agricultural work and were unavailable or unwilling to enter the early factories, male laborers were in short supply. American industry depended, then, on a steady supply of women workers. Yet how could society tolerate women's working in the factories, given the dominant ideology of the times, which dictated that a woman's place was at home? Single white women provided one answer. Their employment was viewed as a fulfillment of their family responsibilities, during an interlude before marriage.

The employment of young, single women in the early Lowell (Massachusetts) mills is a prime example of the reconciliation of ideology with the needs of industry. Francis Cabot Lowell devised a respectable route into employment for such women. Recruiting the daughters of farm families to work in his mill, which opened in 1821 in Lowell, he provided supervised boardinghouses, salaries sufficient to allow the young women to offer financial aid to their families or to save for their own trousseaux, and assurances to their families

that the hard work and discipline of the mill would help prepare them for marriage and motherhood.

In the early industrial era, working conditions were arduous and hours were long. By the late 1830s, immigration began to supply a strongly competitive, permanent workforce willing to be employed for low wages in the factories, under increasingly mechanized and hazardous conditions. By the late 1850s, most of the better-educated, single, native-born women had left the mills, leaving newly immigrated women (both single and married) and men to fill these positions.

While women thus played a crucial role in the development of the textile industry, the first important manufacturing industry in America, women also found employment in many other occupations during the process of industrialization. As railroads and other business enterprises expanded and consolidated, women went to work in these areas as well. In fact, the U.S. Labor Commissioner reported that by 1890 only 9 out of 360 general groups to which the country's industries had been assigned did not employ women.

By 1900, more than five million women or girls, or about one in every five of those 10 years old and over, had become a paid employee. The largest proportion (40%) remained close to home in domestic and personal service, but domestic service was on the decline for white working-class women at the turn of the century. About 25 percent (1.3 million) of employed women worked in the manufacturing industries: in cotton mills, in the manufacture of woolen and worsted goods, silk goods, hosiery, and knit wear. The third largest group of employed women (over 18%) were working on farms. Women in the trade and transportation industries (about 10%) worked as saleswomen, telegraph and telephone operators, stenographers, clerks, copyists, accountants, and bookkeepers. Women in the professions (about 9 percent, and typically young, educated, and single, of native-born parentage) were employed primarily in elementary and secondary teaching or nursing. Other professions—law, medicine, business, college teaching—tended to exclude women. The fastest growing of these occupational groups were manufacturing, trade, and transportation. In the last thirty years of the nineteenth century, the number of women working in trade and transportation rose from 19,000 to over half a million. These women also tended to be young, single, native-born Americans; immigrants and minority women were excluded from these white-collar positions.

. . .

By the turn of the century, the labor market had become clearly divided according to gender, race, and class. Fewer manufacturing jobs were being defined as suitable for white women, especially with the rising dominance of heavy industry employment for which female workers were considered too delicate. Working-class women were increasingly devalued by their continued participation in activities men had primarily taken over (such as factory work), because these activities were regarded as lacking in the Victorian virtue and purity called for by the "cult of true womanhood." As the economy expanded and prosperity came to more and more white middle-class families, middle-class women could "become ladies." A "woman's place" was still defined as at home. If these women did work outside the home, the appropriate occupation was a white-collar job (sales, clerical, and professional occupations). White women's occupations shifted from primarily domestic service—which became increasingly identified as "black women's work"—and from light manufacturing to the rapidly growing opportunities in office and sales work. These jobs were also considered more appropriate for feminine roles as defined by the cult of true womanhood. Women of color did not share in this occupational transformation. In 1910, for example, 90.5 percent of African American women worked as agricultural laborers or domestics, compared with 29.3 percent of white women.

The Legacy of Slavery

African American women were not part of the "cult of true womanhood." They were not sheltered or protected from the harsh realities, and "while many white daughters were raised in genteel refined circumstances, most black daughters were forced to

deal with poverty, violence and a hostile outside world from childhood on." After emancipation, their employment and economic opportunities were limited, in part because the skills they had learned on the plantation transferred to relatively few jobs, and those only of low pay and status.

African American women's concentration in service work—especially domestic work—was largely a result of limited opportunities available to them following the Civil War. The only factory employment open to them was in the Southern tobacco and textile industries, and until World War I most African American working women were farm laborers, domestics, or laundresses. . . .

Despite the limited range of job opportunities, a relatively large proportion of African American women were employed. The legacy of slavery may partly account for the relatively high labor-force participation rate of African American women. Although women's labor-force participation rate is generally lower than men's, African American women's participation rate was historically much higher than that of white women. Thus, for example, white women's labor-force participation in 1890 was 16.3 percent, while African American women's rate was 39.7 percent.

WORLD WAR I AND THE DEPRESSION

World War I accelerated the entry of white women into new fields of industry. The pressure of war production and the shortage of male industrial workers necessitated the hiring of women for what had been male-dominated occupations. Women replaced men at jobs in factories and business offices, and, in general, they kept the nation going, fed, and clothed. The mechanization and routinization of industry during this period enabled women to quickly master the various new skills. For the most part, this wartime pattern involved a reshuffling of the existing female workforce, rather than an increase in the numbers of women employed. Although the popular myth is that homemakers abandoned their kitchens for machine shops or airplane hangars, only about 5 percent of women workers were new to the labor force during the war years. . . .

Thus the wartime labor shortage temporarily created new job opportunities for women workers, and at higher wages than they had previously earned. This was not necessarily the case for African American women, however. Although World War I opened up some factory jobs to them, these were typically limited to the most menial, least desirable, and often the most dangerous jobs—jobs already rejected by white women. These jobs included some of the most dangerous tasks in industry, such as carrying glass to hot ovens in glass factories and dyeing furs in the furrier industry.

World War I produced no substantial or lasting change in women's participation in the labor force. The employment rate of women in 1920 was actually a bit lower (20.4%) than in 1910 (20.9%). The labor unions, the government, and the society at large were not ready to accept a permanent shift in women's economic role. Instead, women filled an urgent need during the wartime years and were relegated to their former positions as soon as peace returned. As the reformer Mary Von Kleeck wrote, "When the immediate dangers . . . were passed, the prejudices came to life once more."

When the men returned from the war, they were given priority in hiring, and although a number of women left the labor force voluntarily, many were forced out by layoffs. Those remaining were employed in the low-paying, low-prestige positions women had always occupied and in those occupations that had become accepted as women's domain. . . .

The Great Depression of the 1930s threw millions out of work. The severe employment problems during this period intensified the general attitude that a woman with a job was taking that job away from a male breadwinner. Yet during the 1930s, an increasing number of women went to work for the first time. The increase was most marked among younger, married women, who worked at least until the first child, and among older, married women, who reentered the marketplace because of dire economic need or in response to changing patterns of consumer demand. Most jobs held by women were part-time, seasonal,

and marginal. Women's labor-force participation increased slowly throughout this period and into the early 1940s . . . , except in the professions (including feminized professions such as elementary teaching, nursing, librarianship, and social work). The proportion of women in all professions declined from 14.2 percent to 12.3 percent during the Depression decade.

WORLD WAR II

The ordeal of World War II brought about tremendous change in the numbers and occupational distribution of working women. As during World War I, the shortage of male workers, who had gone off to fight, coupled with the mounting pressures of war production brought women into the workforce. A corresponding shift in attitudes about women's aptitudes and proper roles resulted. Women entered the munitions factories and other heavy industries to support the war effort. The War Manpower Commission instituted a massive advertising campaign to attract women to the war industries. Patriotic appeals were common.

. . .

Equal work did not mean equal pay for the women in these varied wartime occupations. Although the National War Labor Board issued a directive to industries that stipulated equal pay for equal work, most employers continued to pay women at a lower rate. Furthermore, women had little opportunity to advance in their new occupations.

World War II marked an important turning point in women's participation in the paid labor force. The social prohibition concerning married women working gave way under wartime pressure, and women wartime workers demonstrated that it was possible for women to maintain their households while also assuming the role of breadwinner with outside employment. More women than ever before learned to accommodate the simultaneous demands of family and work. The experience "pointed the way to a greater degree of choice for American women."

However, at the war's end, with the return of men to civilian life, there was a tremendous pressure on women to return to their former positions in the home. During this time, a new social ideology began to emerge; Betty Friedan later called it "the feminine mystique." This ideology drew in social workers, educators, journalists, and psychologists, all of whom tried to convince women that their place was again in the home. It was not until the "cult of true womanhood" advanced in the late 1800s to differentiate middle-class women from working-class women. As Friedan notes, in the fifteen years following World War II, the image of "women at home" rather than "at work" became a cherished and self-perpetuating core of contemporary American culture. A generation of young people were brought up to extol the values of home and family, and woman's role was defined as the domestic center around which all else revolved. Women were supposed to live like those in Norman Rockwell *Saturday Evening Post* illustrations. The idealized image was of smiling mothers baking cookies for their wholesome children, driving their station wagons loaded with freckled youngsters to an endless round of lessons and activities, returning with groceries and other consumer goods to the ranch houses they cared for with such pride. Women were supposed to revel in these roles and gladly leave the running of the world to men.

. . .

Yet, unlike the post–World War I period, after World War II women did not go back to the kitchens. Instead, women's labor-force participation continued to increase throughout the post–World War II decades, so that by the late 1960s, 40 percent of American women were in the labor force, and by the late 1990s, 60 percent were. Who were the women most likely to be part of this "new majority" of women at work?

AFTER WORLD WAR II: THE RISE OF THE MARRIED WOMAN WORKER

Between 1890 and the beginning of World War II, single women comprised at least half the female labor force. The others were mostly married African American, immigrant, or working-class women.

The decade of the 1940s saw a change in the type of woman worker, as increasing numbers of married women left their homes to enter the world of paid work. . . . Although single women continued to have the highest labor-force participation rates among women, during the 1940s the percentage of married women in the workforce grew more rapidly than any other category. Between 1940 and 1950, single women workers were in short supply because of low birthrates in the 1930s. Furthermore, those single women available for work were marrying at younger ages and leaving the labor market to raise their families. On the other hand, ample numbers of older, married women were available, and these women (who had married younger, had had fewer children, and were living longer) were eager for paid employment.

In 1940, about 15 percent of married women were employed; by 1950, 24 percent. This increase has continued: by 1960, 32 percent of married women; in 1970, over 41 percent; in 1980, 50 percent; and by 1995, 61 percent. Indeed, as the twentieth century comes to a close, we can see that labor-force participation rates of single and married women have become almost identical. . . .

During the 1940s, 1950s, and 1960s, it was mainly older, married women entering the workforce. In 1957, for example, the labor-force participation rate among women aged forty-five to forty-nine years exceeded the rate for twenty- to twenty-four-year-old women. During the 1960s, young married mothers with preschool- or school-age children began to enter the workforce. This trend continued for the next three decades; by 1995, more than three-quarters of married women with children between six and seventeen years of age were employed, and, most significantly, almost two-thirds of those women with children under the age of six were in the labor force. . . . In short, whereas before 1970 the overwhelming majority of married women stopped working after they had children, today the overwhelming majority of married women do not.

WOMEN OF COLOR

Denied entrance to the factories during the rise of industrialization and, for much of the twentieth century, facing discriminatory hiring practices that closed off opportunities in the newly expanded office and sales jobs, many women of color entered domestic service. From 1910 to 1940, the proportion of white women employed in clerical and sales positions almost doubled, and there was a decline in the numbers of white women in domestic work. Private household work then became the province of African American women: the percentage of African American household workers increased from 38.5 percent in 1910 to 59.9 percent in 1940. . . . For the next three decades, African American women remained the single largest group in domestic service.

African American women's economic status improved dramatically from 1940 through the 1960s, as a result of an increase in light manufacturing jobs, as well as changes in technology. African American women moved from private household work into manufacturing and clerical work, and made significant gains in the professions. Whereas in 1940, 60 percent of employed African American females worked in private households, by the late 1960s only 20 percent did. Their job prospects continued to improve, and by the 1980s, almost half of all working African American women were doing so in "white-collar" jobs—clerical and sales positions, as well as professional jobs in business, health care, and education. Through the 1990s, the historic, job-prestige gap between African American and white working women continued to close. Almost two-thirds of working African American women had jobs in the white-collar world by 1996, compared with nearly three-quarters of working white women. . . .

Other Women of Color at Work

Each minority group has had a different experience in American society and has faced different opportunities and obstacles. Women in each group share with African American women the concerns of all minority women; they share with the men of their ethnic groups the problems of discrimination against that particular ethnic minority.

Native American Women

As we noted earlier, gender roles in Native American communities were disrupted during the conquest and oppression by whites. For example, Navajo society was traditionally matrilineal, with extended families the norm; Navajo women owned property and played an important role in family decisions. But beginning in the 1930s, government policy disrupted this system by giving land only to males. As they could no longer make a sufficient living off the land, more and more Navajo men had to seek employment off the reservations. Nuclear families became the norm. Navajo women became dependent on male providers. With the men away much of the time, these women are often isolated and powerless. They often face divorce or desertion and thus economic difficulties, because the community frowns on women seeking work off the reservation.

Such disruption of the traditional Native American society left Native American women in very grim economic circumstances. But in recent decades, more and more of them have gotten jobs. Native American women's labor-force participation rate in 1970 was 35 percent (compared to 43% for all women). This rate rose sharply to 55 percent by the early 1990s and is now within a few percentage points of the rate for all women.

Like their African American counterparts over the past half century, Native American women have gradually moved out of low-skill farm and nonfarm work and domestic jobs into clerical, sales, professional, technical, and other "white-collar" jobs. In 1960, one in six working Native American women was employed as a domestic household worker; by the early 1990s only one in a hundred was. During the same period, the proportion of Native American women involved in agricultural work also went from ten to one in a hundred. Manufacturing work was increasingly replaced by white-collar work, reflecting the overall trends in the occupational structure; more specifically, while the percentage involved in factory work (much of it in textiles and traditional crafts) fell from 18.1 to 14.2, the percentage doing white-collar work soared from 28.9 to 61.3. Although many of these white-collar jobs are classified as "professional" (15.7% of all working Native American women) or "managerial" (9.4%), two-thirds of Native American women are still concentrated in the "secondary" sector of the labor market—which is characterized by low wages, few or no benefits, low mobility, and high instability. They are kept there because of the "stagnation of the reservation economy," discrimination, and their relatively low level of educational attainment. A significant number do not have a high school diploma (in 1990, more than one-third of all those over the age of 25, compared to one-fifth of white women).

Latina [Chicana] Women

. . . Large numbers of Chicanas migrated, usually with husband and children, from Mexico to the United States during the 1916–1920 labor shortage created by World War I. They found work in the sprawling "factory farms" of the Southwest, harvesting fruits, vegetables, and cotton in the Imperial and San Joaquin valleys of California, the Salt River valley of Arizona, and the Rio Grande valley of Texas. They also went to the Midwest, for instance to Michigan and Minnesota, to harvest sugar beets. Such migrant workers typically were exploited, spending long, tedious, and physically demanding hours in the fields for very low pay. Some became tenant farmers, which might seem a step up, except too often this system "created debt peonage; unable to pay the rent, tenants were unable to leave the land and remained virtually permanently indebted to their landlords."

During the 1920s, with a shortage of European immigration, new job opportunities opened up for Mexican Americans, and they began to migrate from rural, farm country to the urban, industrial centers, where they found work as domestics and factory workers. By 1930, one-third of working Chicanas were domestics and a quarter worked in manufacturing; at the time, the share employed in agriculture, forestry, and mining had fallen to 21 percent. Wage scales varied according to ethnicity, however. It was not uncommon to pay Chicana workers lower wages than "Anglo" (whites of European descent) women for doing the same job, whether as domestics, laundresses, or workers in the food-processing industries of the West and Southwest. Then the Depression years of the 1930s, with the general shortage of jobs, brought a backlash against Mexican American labor, and thousands of Mexicans were deported or pressured to leave.

World War II once again opened up the American labor market for Mexican migrants, as their labor was needed to offset wartime labor shortages. However, their treatment was deplorable by modern standards. In short, Mexican workers comprised a "reserve army" of exploited labor. Through the government-sponsored Bracero or "Manual Workers" program, Mexican workers were granted temporary work visas so that they could be employed on large corporate farms and elsewhere, but too often they were treated like slaves or prisoners.

World War II and the years following saw a massive shift in the occupational and geographical distribution of Chicana workers:

> Many left Texas for California, and the population became increasingly more urban. Women continued their move from the fields into garment factories throughout the Southwest. . . . [A] comparison of the 1930 and 1950 [census] data shows the magnitude of these shifts. For instance, the share of employed southwestern Chicanas working on farms dropped from 21 percent in 1930 to 6 percent in 1950, while the percentage in white-collar work doubled.

By the 1960s, the largest occupational category for Chicana workers was operatives, followed by clerical and service work. Chicanas became concentrated in particular industries—food processing, electronics (including telecommunications), and garments. Like their Native American counterparts, Chicana women have made some progress in entering professional and managerial occupations (primarily noncollege teaching, nursing, librarianship, and social work). In 1960, 8.6 percent were in these occupations; by 1980, 12.6 percent, and by the early 1990s 17.5 percent. However, like the Native Americans, Chicana women are still overwhelmingly found in the secondary labor market (75%)—much more so than women (60%) and men (32%) of white European heritage.

The dominant reasons behind the low occupational prestige of all minority groups are the same: discrimination and low educational attainment. In the case of Chicana women, over 15 percent "are illiterate by the standard measure (completion of less than five years of schooling)," but studies of functional illiteracy during the 1970s and 1980s suggest "much higher rates—perhaps as high as 56 percent." At the other end of the educational attainment spectrum, only 8.4 percent of Latina women have completed four or more years of college—compared with 21.0 percent of white women and 12.9 percent of blacks. However, education is only part of the formula for success in the U.S. occupational system: for when education is held constant, Latina women make only between 84 and 90 percent of what white women do.

Beyond lack of education, Chicana women face other important obstacles in the labor market. They have high rates of unemployment and underemployment. Many of the jobs they hold are seasonal and often nonunionized. This lack of advancement translates into higher poverty rates (23 percent for Chicana/os in the early 1990s). The median income for full-time Chicana workers is lower than that of any other U.S. racial-ethnic group. For Latina women (in general) with children and no husband present, the poverty rate is even worse: 49.4 percent compared with 26.6 percent of white women in this situation.

Increasingly, Chicana women, like many female workers of color around the globe, are doing service or assembly work for multi-national corporations, especially in the apparel, food-processing, and electronics industries. These women have often displaced men in assembly work because they can be paid less and many do not receive job benefits. The work hours are long, and women are often assigned monotonous tasks that are dangerous to their health.

. . .

Asian-American Women

. . . Asian Americans are considered to be the "model minority." . . . However, this is as much myth as fact. While many among both the native-born and the recent arrivals have high levels of education and professional skills and can readily fit into the labor market, others lack such advantages, often finding work only as undocumented laborers in low-paying jobs with long work days, little or no job mobility, and no benefits.

> We are told we have overcome our oppression, and that therefore we are the model minority. Model refers to the cherished dictum of capitalism that "pulling hard on your bootstraps" brings due rewards. . . . Asian American success stories . . . do little to illuminate the actual conditions of the majority of Asian Americans. Such examples conceal the more typical Asian American experience of unemployment, underemployment and struggle to survive. The model minority myth thus classically scapegoats Asian Americans. It labels us in a way that dismisses the real problems that many do face, while at the same time pitting Asians against other oppressed people of color.

In 1996, 37.3 percent of Asian women who were 25 years and over had at least a bachelor's degree, compared with 23.2 percent of non-Latina whites. Filipina American women secured the highest college graduation rate of all women, a rate 50 percent greater than that of white males. Following closely behind are Chinese American and Japanese American women, who exceed both the white male and female college graduation rates. Yet, these educational achievements bring lower returns for Asian women than for whites. Census data reveal a gap between achievement and economic reward for Asian

American women, who suffer from both race and sex discrimination within the labor market.

. . .

And it would be wrong to equate "Asian" with "well educated," because the majority of Asian women immigrating to the United States since 1980 have low levels of education. Though, as just noted, Asian women are much more likely to be college-educated than non-Latina white women, they are also much more likely—two and a half times more likely—to be grade-school dropouts: in 1996, 12.5 percent of Asian women had not gone beyond the eighth grade, compared to only 5.2 percent of their non-Latina white counterparts. This fact is linked to the other most obvious difference between Asian and white women . . . — the proportions working as "operators, fabricators, and laborers," where we find significantly more Asian women.

These women are most commonly employed as sewing machine operators at home or in small sweatshops in the Chinatowns of New York and San Francisco. Asian immigrant women are also heavily employed in the microelectronics industry. Women in general comprise 80 to 90 percent of assembly workers in this industry, and approximately "half of these assembly workers are recent immigrants from the Philippines, Vietnam, Korea, and South Asia." Within the microelectronics industry jobs are often "structured along racial and gender lines, with men and white workers earning higher wages and being much more likely to be promoted than women and workers of color." Karen Hossfeld's research on relationships between Third World immigrant women production workers and their white male managers in the high-tech Silicon Valley of California relates how immigrant women of color negotiate and often employ resistance to primarily white, middle-class management demands. One Filipina circuit board assembler in Silicon Valley puts it this way:

> The bosses here have this type of reasoning like a seesaw. One day it's "you're paid less because women are different than men," or "immigrants need less to get by." The next day it's "you're all just workers here—no special treatment just because you're female or foreigners."
>
> Well, they think they're pretty clever with their doubletalk, and that we're just a bunch of dumb aliens. But it takes two to use a seesaw. What we are gradually figuring out here is how to use their own logic against them.

As clerical or administrative support workers, Asian American women are disproportionately represented as cashiers, file clerks, office machine operators, and typists. They are less likely to obtain employment as secretaries or receptionists. Noting that there is an "overrepresentation of college-educated women in clerical work," Woo suggests that education functions less as a path toward mobility into higher occupational categories, and more as "a hedge against jobs as service workers and as machine operatives or assembly workers."

Asian American women with a college education who obtain professional employment are often restricted to the less prestigious jobs within this category. Asian American women "are more likely to remain marginalized in their work organization, to encounter a 'glass ceiling,' and to earn less than white men, Asian American men, and white women with comparable educational backgrounds." They are least represented in those male-dominated positions of physician, lawyer, and judge, and are heavily concentrated in the more female-dominated occupations of nursing and teaching.

Asian women have been subjected to a range of stereotypes. The "Lotus Blossom" stereotype depicts them as submissive and demure sex objects: "good, faithful, uncomplaining, totally compliant, self-effacing, gracious servants who will do anything and everything to please, entertain, and make them feel comfortable and carefree." At the opposite extreme, the Dragon Lady stereotype portrays Asian women as "promiscuous and untrustworthy,"

as the castrating Dragon Lady who, while puffing on her foot-long cigarette holder, could poison a man as easily as she could seduce him. "With her talon-like six-inch fingernails, her skin-tight satin dress slit to the thigh," the Dragon Lady is desirable, deceitful and dangerous.

Asian American feminist Germaine Wong notes how stereotypes concerning Asian women operate in the workplace, serving to deter their advancement into leadership roles and to increase their vulnerability to sexual harassment. Additionally, these stereotypes have fostered a demand for "X-rated films and pornographic materials featuring Asian women in bondage, for 'Oriental'

bathhouse workers in U.S. cities, and for Asian mail-order brides."

In sum, the notion of Asian Americans as the "model minority" deviates considerably from sociological reality. While Asian American women as a group have achieved some "success" in terms of high educational attainment, they receive lower returns on this investment compared to the white population. They have not "escaped the stigmatization of being minority and recent immigrants in a discriminatory job market."

R E A D I N G   **61**

Maid to Order
The Politics of Other Women's Work

Barbara Ehrenreich (2000)

In line with growing class polarization, the classic posture of submission is making a stealthy comeback. "We scrub your floors the old-fashioned way," boasts the brochure from Merry Maids, the largest of the residential-cleaning services that have sprung up in the last two decades, "on our hands and knees." This is not a posture that independent "cleaning ladies" willingly assume—preferring, like most people who clean their own homes, the sponge mop wielded from a standing position. In her comprehensive 1999 guide to homemaking, *Home Comforts,* Cheryl Mendelson warns: "Never ask hired housecleaners to clean your floors on their hands and knees; the request is likely to be regarded as degrading." But in a society in which 40 percent of the wealth is owned by 1 percent of households while the bottom 20 percent reports negative assets, the degradation of others is readily purchased. Kneepads entered American political discourse as a tool of the sexually subservient, but employees of Merry Maids,

The Maids International, and other corporate cleaning services spend hours every day on these kinky devices, wiping up the drippings of the affluent.

I spent three weeks in September 1999 as an employee of The Maids International in Portland, Maine, cleaning, along with my fellow team members, approximately sixty houses containing a total of about 250 scrubbable floors—bathrooms, kitchens, and entryways requiring the hands-and-knees treatment. It's a different world down there below knee level, one that few adults voluntarily enter. Here you find elaborate dust structures held together by a scaffolding of dog hair; dried bits of pasta glued to the floor by their sauce; the congealed remains of gravies, jellies, contraceptive creams, vomit, and urine. Sometimes, too, you encounter some fragment of a human being: a child's legs, stamping by in disgust because the maids are still present when he gets home from school; more commonly, the Joan & David–clad feet and electrolyzed calves of the female homeowner. Look up and you may find this person staring at you, arms folded, in anticipation of an overlooked stain. In rare instances she may try to help in some vague, symbolic way, by moving the cockatoo's cage, for example, or apologizing for the leaves shed by a miniature indoor tree. Mostly, though, she will not see you at all and may even sit down with her mail at a table in the very room you are cleaning, where she would remain completely unaware of your existence unless you were to crawl under that table and start gnawing away at her ankles.

Housework, as you may recall from the feminist theories of the Sixties and Seventies, was supposed to be the great equalizer of women. Whatever else women did—jobs, school, child care— we also did housework, and if there were some women who hired others to do it for them, they seemed too privileged and rare to include in the theoretical calculus. All women were workers, and the home was their workplace—unpaid and unsupervised, to be sure, but a workplace no less than the offices and factories men repaired to every morning. If men thought of the home as a site of leisure and recreation—a "haven in a heartless world"—this was to ignore the invisible female proletariat that kept it cozy and humming. We were on the march now, or so we imagined, united against a society that devalued our labor even as it waxed mawkish over "the family" and "the home." Shoulder to shoulder and arm in arm, women were finally getting up off the floor.

In the most eye-catching elaboration of the home-as-workplace theme, Marxist feminists Maria Rosa Dallacosta and Selma James proposed in 1972 that the home was in fact an economically productive and significant workplace, an extension of the actual factory, since housework served to "reproduce the labor power" of others, particularly men. The male worker would hardly be in shape to punch in for his shift, after all, if some woman had not fed him, laundered his clothes, and cared for the children who were his contribu-

tion to the next generation of workers. If the home was a quasi-industrial workplace staffed by women for the ultimate benefit of the capitalists, then it followed that "wages for housework" was the obvious demand.

But when most American feminists, Marxist or otherwise, asked the Marxist question *cui bono?* they tended to come up with a far simpler answer— men. If women were the domestic proletariat, then men made up the class of domestic exploiters, free to lounge while their mates scrubbed. In consciousness-raising groups, we railed against husbands and boyfriends who refused to pick up after themselves, who were unaware of housework at all, unless of course it hadn't been done. The "dropped socks," left by a man for a woman to gather up and launder, joined lipstick and spike heels as emblems of gender oppression. And if, somewhere, a man had actually dropped a sock in the calm expectation that his wife would retrieve it, it was a sock heard round the world. Wherever second-wave feminism took root, battles broke out between lovers and spouses over sticky countertops, piled-up laundry, and whose turn it was to do the dishes.

The radical new idea was that housework was not only a relationship between a woman and a dust bunny or an unmade bed; it also defined a relationship between human beings, typically husbands and wives. This represented a marked departure from the more conservative Betty Friedan, who, in *The Feminine Mystique,* had never thought to enter the male sex into the equation, as either part of the housework problem or part of an eventual solution. She raged against a society that consigned its educated women to what she saw as essentially janitorial chores, beneath "the abilities of a woman of average or normal human intelligence," and, according to unidentified studies she cited, "peculiarly suited to the capacities of feeble-minded girls." But men are virtually exempt from housework in *The Feminine Mystique*—why drag them down too? At one point she even disparages a "Mrs. G.," who "somehow couldn't get her housework done before her husband came home at night and was so tired then that he had to do it." Educated women would just have to become more efficient so that housework could no longer "expand to fill the time available."

Or they could hire other women to do it—an option approved by Friedan in *The Feminine Mystique* as well as by the National Organization for Women [NOW], which she had helped launch. At the 1973 congressional hearings on whether to extend the Fair Labor Standards Act to household workers, NOW testified on the affirmative side, arguing that improved wages and working conditions would attract more women to the field, and offering the seemingly self-contradictory prediction that "the demand for household help inside the home will continue to increase as more women seek occupations outside the home." One NOW member added, on a personal note: "Like many young women today, I am in school in order to develop a rewarding career for myself. I also have a home to run and can fully conceive of the need for household help as my free time at home becomes more and more restricted. Women know [that] housework is dirty, tedious work, and they are willing to pay to have it done. . . ." On the aspirations of the women paid to do it, assuming that at least some of them were bright enough to entertain a few, neither Friedan nor these members of NOW had, at the time, a word to say.

So the insight that distinguished the more radical, post-Friedan cohort of feminists was that when we talk about housework, we are really talking, yet again, about power. Housework was not degrading because it was manual labor, as Friedan thought, but because it was embedded in degrading relationships and inevitably served to reinforce them. To make a mess that another person will have to deal with—the dropped socks, the toothpaste sprayed on the bathroom mirror, the dirty dishes left from a late-night snack—is to exert domination in one of its more silent and intimate forms. One person's arrogance—or indifference, or hurry—becomes another person's occasion for toil. And when the person who is cleaned up after is consistently male, while the person who cleans up is consistently female, you

have a formula for reproducing male domination from one generation to the next.

Hence the feminist perception of housework as one more way by which men exploit women or, more neutrally stated, as "a symbolic enactment of gender relations." An early German women's liberation cartoon depicted a woman scrubbing on her hands and knees while her husband, apparently excited by this pose, approaches from behind, unzipping his fly. Hence, too, the second-wave feminists' revulsion at the hiring of maids, especially when they were women of color: At a feminist conference I attended in 1980, poet Audre Lorde chose to insult the all-too-white audience by accusing them of being present only because they had black housekeepers to look after their children at home. She had the wrong crowd; most of the assembled radical feminists would no sooner have employed a black maid than they would have attached Confederate flag stickers to the rear windows of their cars. But accusations like hers, repeated in countless conferences and meetings, reinforced our rejection of the servant option. There already were at least two able-bodied adults in the average home—a man and a woman—and the hope was that, after a few initial skirmishes, they would learn to share the housework graciously.

A couple of decades later, however, the average household still falls far short of that goal. True, women do less housework than they did before the feminist revolution and the rise of the two-income family: down from an average of 30 hours per week in 1965 to 17.5 hours in 1995, according to a July 1999 study by the University of Maryland. Some of that decline reflects a relaxation of standards rather than a redistribution of chores; women still do two thirds of whatever housework—including bill paying, pet care, tidying, and lawn care—gets done. The inequity is sharpest for the most despised of household chores, cleaning: in the thirty years between 1965 and 1995, men increased the time they spent scrubbing, vacuuming, and sweeping by 240 percent—all the way up to 1.7 hours per week—while women decreased their cleaning time by only 7 percent, to 6.7 hours per week. The averages conceal a variety of arrangements, of course, from minutely negotiated sharing to the most clichéd division of labor, as described by one woman to the *Washington Post:* "I take care of the inside, he takes care of the outside." But perhaps the most disturbing finding is that almost the entire increase in male participation took place between the 1970s and the mid-1980s. Fifteen years after the apparent cessation of hostilities, it is probably not too soon to announce the score: in the "chore wars" of the Seventies and Eighties, women gained a little ground, but overall, and after a few strategic concessions, men won.

Enter then, the cleaning lady as *dea ex machina,* restoring tranquillity as well as order to the home. Marriage counselors recommend her as an alternative to squabbling, as do many within the cleaning industry itself. A Chicago cleaning woman quotes one of her clients as saying that if she gives up the service, "my husband and I will be divorced in six months." When the trend toward hiring out was just beginning to take off, in 1988, the owner of a Merry Maids franchise in Arlington, Massachusetts, told the *Christian Science Monitor,* "I kid some women. I say, 'We even save marriages. In this new eighties period you expect more from the male partner, but very often you don't get the cooperation you would like to have. The alternative is to pay somebody to come in....'" Another Merry Maids franchise owner has learned to capitalize more directly on housework-related spats; he closes between 30 and 35 percent of his sales by making follow-up calls Saturday mornings, which is "prime time for arguing over the fact that the house is a mess." The micro-defeat of feminism in the household opened a new door for women, only this time it was the servants' entrance.

In 1999, somewhere between 14 and 18 percent of households employed an outsider to do the cleaning, and the numbers have been rising dramatically. Mediamark Research reports a 53 percent increase, between 1995 and 1999, in the number of households using a hired cleaner or service once a month or more, and Maritz Marketing finds that 30 percent of the people who hired help in 1999 did so for the first time that year. Among my middle-class, professional women friends and acquaintances, including some who made important contributions to the early feminist analysis of housework, the employment of a maid is now nearly universal. This sudden emergence of a servant class is consistent with what some economists have called the "Brazilianization" of the American economy: We are dividing along the lines of traditional Latin American societies—into a tiny overclass and a huge underclass, with the latter available to perform intimate household services for the former. Or, to put it another way, the home, or at least the affluent home, is finally becoming what radical feminists in the Seventies only imagined it was—a true "workplace" for women and a tiny, though increasingly visible, part of the capitalist economy. And the question is: As the home becomes a workplace for someone else, is it still a place where you would want to live?

. . .

The trend toward outsourcing the work of the home seems, at the moment, unstoppable. Two hundred years ago women often manufactured soap, candles, cloth, and clothing in their own homes, and the complaints of some women at the turn of the twentieth century that they had been "robbed by the removal of creative work" from the home sound pointlessly reactionary today. Not only have the skilled crafts, like sewing and cooking from scratch, left the home but many of the "white collar" tasks are on their way out, too. For a fee, new firms such as the San Francisco–based Les Concierges and Cross It Off Your List in Manhattan will pick up dry cleaning, baby-sit pets, buy groceries, deliver dinner, even do the Christmas shopping. With other firms and individuals offering to buy your clothes, organize your financial files, straighten out your closets, and wait around in your home for the plumber to show up, why would anyone want to hold on to the toilet cleaning?

Absent a major souring of the economy, there is every reason to think that Americans will become increasingly reliant on paid housekeepers and that this reliance will extend ever further down into the middle class. For one thing, the "time bind" on working parents shows no sign of loosening; people are willing to work longer hours at the office to pay for the people—housecleaners and baby-sitters—who are filling in for them at home. Children, once a handy source of household help, are now off at soccer practice or SAT prep classes; grandmother has relocated to a warmer climate or taken up a second career. Furthermore, despite the fact that people spend less time at home than ever, the square footage of new homes swelled by 33 percent between 1975 and 1998, to include "family rooms," home entertainment rooms, home offices, bedrooms, and often bathrooms for each family member. By the third quarter of 1999, 17 percent of new homes were larger than 3,000 square feet, which is usually considered the size threshold for household help, or the point at which a house becomes unmanageable to the people who live in it.

One more trend impels people to hire outside help, according to cleaning experts such as Aslett and Mendelson: fewer Americans know how to clean or even to "straighten up." I hear this from professional women defending their decision to hire a maid: "I'm just not very good at it myself" or "I wouldn't really know where to begin." Since most of us learn to clean from our parents (usually our mothers), any diminution of cleaning skills is transmitted from one generation to another, like a gene that can, in the appropriate environment, turn out to be disabling or lethal. Upper-middle-class children raised in the servant economy of the Nineties are bound to grow up as domestically incompetent as their parents and no less dependent on people to clean up after them. Mendelson sees this as a metaphysical loss, a "matter of no longer being physically centered in your environment." Having cleaned the rooms of many overly privileged teenagers in my stint with The Maids, I think the problem is a little more urgent than that. The American overclass is raising a generation of young people who will, without constant assistance, suffocate in their own detritus.

If there are moral losses, too, as Americans increasingly rely on paid household help, no one has been tactless enough to raise them. Almost everything we buy, after all, is the product of some other person's suffering and miserably underpaid labor. I clean my own house (though—full disclosure—I recently hired someone else to ready it for a short-term tenant), but I can hardly claim purity in any other area of consumption. I buy my jeans at The Gap, which is reputed to subcontract to sweatshops. I tend to favor decorative objects no doubt ripped off, by their purveyors, from scantily paid Third World craftspersons. Like everyone else, I eat salad greens just picked by migrant farm workers, some of them possibly children. And so on. We can try to minimize the pain that goes into feeding, clothing, and otherwise provisioning ourselves—by observing boycotts, checking for a union label, etc.—but there is no way to avoid it altogether without living in the wilderness on berries. Why should housework, among all the goods and services we consume, arouse any special angst?

And it does, as I have found in conversations with liberal-minded employers of maids, perhaps because we all sense that there are ways in which housework is different from other products and services. First, in its inevitable proximity to the activities that compose "private" life. The home that becomes a workplace for other people remains a home, even when that workplace has been minutely regulated by the corporate cleaning chains. Someone who has no qualms about purchasing rugs woven by child slaves in India or coffee picked by impoverished peasants in Guatemala might still hesitate to tell dinner guests that, surprisingly enough, his or her lovely home doubles as a sweatshop during the day. You can eschew the chain cleaning services of course, hire an independent cleaner at a generous hourly wage, and even encourage, at least in spirit, the unionization of the housecleaning industry. But this does not change the fact that someone is working in your home at a job she would almost certainly never have chosen for herself—if she'd had a college education, for example, or a little better luck along the way—and the place where she works, however enthusiastically or resentfully, is the same as the place where you sleep.

It is also the place where your children are raised, and what they learn pretty quickly is that some people are less worthy than others. Even better wages and working conditions won't erase the hierarchy between an employer and his or her domestic help, because the help is usually there only because the employer has "something better" to do with her time, as one report on the growth of cleaning services puts it, not noticing the obvious implication that the cleaning person herself has nothing better to do with her time. In a merely middle-class home, the message may be reinforced by a warning to the children that that's what they'll end up doing if they don't try harder in school. Housework, as radical feminists once proposed, defines a human relationship and, when unequally divided among social groups, reinforces preexisting inequalities. Dirt, in other words, tends to attach to the people who remove it—"garbagemen" and "cleaning ladies." Or, as cleaning entrepreneur Don Aslett told me with some bitterness—and this is a successful man, chairman of the board of an industrial cleaning service and frequent television guest—"The whole mentality out there is that if you clean, you're a scumball."

One of the "better" things employers of maids often want to do with their time is, of course, spend it with their children. But an underlying problem with post-nineteenth-century child-raising, as Deirdre English and I argued in our book *For Her Own Good* years ago, is precisely that it is unmoored in any kind of purposeful pursuit. Once "parenting" meant instructing the children in necessary chores; today it's more likely to center on one-sided conversations beginning with "So how was school today?" No one wants to put the kids to work again weeding and stitching; but in the void that is the modern home, relationships with children are often strained. A little "low-quality time" spent washing dishes or folding clothes together can provide a comfortable space for confidences—and give a child the dignity of knowing that he or she is a participant in, and not just the product of, the work of the home.

There is another lesson the servant economy teaches its beneficiaries and, most troubling, the children among them. To be cleaned up after is to achieve a certain magical weightlessness and immateriality. Almost everyone complains about violent video games, but paid housecleaning has the same consequence-abolishing effect: you blast the villain into a mist of blood droplets and move right along; you drop the socks knowing they will eventually levitate, laundered and folded, back to their normal dwelling place. The result is a kind of virtual existence, in which the trail of litter that follows you seems to evaporate all by itself. Spill syrup on the floor and the cleaning person will scrub it off when she comes on Wednesday. Leave *The Wall Street Journal* scattered around your airplane seat and the flight attendants will deal with it after you've deplaned. Spray toxins into the atmosphere from your factory's smokestacks and they will be filtered out eventually by the lungs of the breathing public. A servant economy breeds callousness and solipsism in the served, and it does so all the more effectively when the service is performed close up and routinely in the place where they live and reproduce.

Individual situations vary, of course, in ways that elude blanket judgment. Some people—the elderly and disabled, parents of new babies, asthmatics who require an allergen-free environment—may well need help performing what nursing-home staff call the "ADLs," or activities of daily living, and no shame should be attached to their dependency. In a more generous social order, housekeeping services would be subsidized for those who have health-related reasons to need them—a measure that would generate a surfeit of new jobs for the low-skilled people who now clean the homes of the affluent. And in a less-gender-divided social order, husbands and boyfriends would more readily do their share of the chores.

However we resolve the issue in our individual homes, the moral challenge is, put simply, to make work visible again: not only the scrubbing and vacuuming but all the hoeing, stacking, hammering, drilling, bending, and lifting that goes into creating and maintaining a livable habitat. In an ever more economically unequal culture, where so many of the affluent devote their lives to such ghostly pursuits as stock-trading, image-making, and opinion-polling, real work—in the old-fashioned sense of labor that engages hand as well as eye, that tires the body and directly alters the physical world—tends to vanish from sight. The feminists of my generation tried to bring some of it into the light of day, but, like busy professional women fleeing the house in the morning, they left the project unfinished, the debate broken off in midsentence, the noble intentions unfulfilled. Sooner or later, someone else will have to finish the job.

R E A D I N G   **62**

Surviving Globalization
Immigrant Women Workers in Late Capitalist America

Evelyn Hu-Dehart (2007)

Rosario Jocha, forty-nine, stands at the corner of Eighth Avenue and Thirty-seventh Street in Manhattan, in the heart of the fashion district, hoping to be picked up for a day's work. She said she had recently grabbed at the chance to cut threads from jackets for $5.75 an hour, twenty-four cents below New York State's minimum wage. The man who offered the job was a Chinese immigrant subcontractor who said he could not pay more. "What else is there to do if you have nothing to eat?" Rosario lamented, adding, "I've been here eleven years, and I still have not found a stable, steady job." Like Rosario, an immigrant from Ecuador, Rosa Yumbla supports four children left at home. She said, "We suffer the changing weather throughout the year, the heat of the sun and cold in winter, because where we wait to be picked up is on the street." And Nellie, thirty-two, also from Ecuador, pulls out a picture of the three children she left behind under her sister's care while she tries to earn enough money as a contingent worker doing casual work for the heart operation needed by her son, the youngest child. "The little I make here I send to him," she said. "Many times I just want to go to be with him, but I don't have the money to do so. It gives me a desperate feeling."[1] Immigrants waiting at urban street corners hoping to be picked up for a day or two of work at minimum wage or less is no longer just a male phenomenon, as the *New York Times* recently discovered; it is fast gaining a female dimension that can no longer be ignored.

Meanwhile, on the other coast in San Francisco, police broke up in early July 2005 a sex-trafficking operation that supplied Korean women for brothels and massage parlors in the Bay Area. All over Southern California, in cities like Santa Monica, Los Angeles, and Redondo Beach, hundreds of South Korean women worked as prostitutes, having also been smuggled into the country. These prostitutes were managed by an underground network of Korean "taxi" services that coordinated the prostitutes' daily schedules, working closely with brothel operators to deliver the women to their clients. The operators even arranged to fly prostitutes to work in Las Vegas, Dallas, New York, and Boston.[2]

These women are among the newly revealed faces of globalization moving from the Third World periphery or global South straight to the belly of the beast of the global North or core, the United States. This reading summarizes the considerable research on the system of global production and the role of immigrant women workers in the formal or visible economies, such as electronics and garment, while prying open the window on the less well studied and less visible informal economies of globalization, such as home, nursing, and elderly care; housecleaning; child care; sex work; and street vendoring. While many of these immigrant women workers came as part of the massive legal immigration flow, many others form part of the estimated 10 million undocumented workers in the United States.

DE-INDUSTRIALIZATION AND GLOBALIZATION

De-industrialization in the global core, the United States, was the other side of the coin of a restructured international economy, where an innovative development strategy called export-based industrialization (EBI) was adopted by the global periphery, the newly developing Asian countries soon dubbed NICs (newly industrializing country); that is, Taiwan, Hong Kong, Singapore, South Korea, followed by Thailand, Indonesia, and Vietnam. Japan was there at the beginning, but the sleeping communist giant, the People's Republic of China, would not get on the radar screen until later. And for reasons beyond the scope of this [reading] to explore, the highly populous India did not immediately join the switch from import-substitution industrialization to this new export-based industrialization, perhaps because, after hundreds of years of British colonial rule, and being more committed to establishing democracy than most of its neighbors, the ruling Congress Party did not relish the idea of being overwhelmed by foreign investment and consequent foreign control that inevitably accompanied this new development strategy. Essentially, the Asian NICs agreed to a new international division of labor with the United States by accepting large doses of U.S. investment to set up light manufacturing in jerry-built factories located on specially designated lands appropriately named "export processing zones" (EPZ) or "free trade zones" (FTZ). Here, the

largely authoritarian, staunchly anti-communist governments, some military in nature, offered the advanced, capitalist, multi- or transnational corporations cheap Third World labor to assemble finished products from materials supplied by first world investors, for export back to the first world nations.[3] Electronics, toys, athletic shoes, and apparel represent the majority of products in these EPZ factories. "The removal of barriers to free trade and the close integration of national economies," according to economist Joseph Stiglitz, is a good definition of globalization.[4]

Although many of these export zones are located on the Asia Pacific Rim, the prototype was the Border Industrialization Project (BIP), established in 1969 on the Mexican side of the U.S.-Mexican border, which gave rise to thousands of assembly plants called *maquiladoras* (or *maquilas,* for short), now transitioned into the backbone of the North American Free Trade Agreement (NAFTA) between Canada, the United States, and Mexico. During the past decade, maquilas have also moved well beyond the northern border zone deep into the heart of Mexico, all the way south to the Yucatán to take advantage of the cheap labor of indigenous Mayan women. In addition, EPZs have also proliferated all over Central America, in countries like Honduras, Guatemala, El Salvador, Nicaragua, as well as the Caribbean.[5] In addition to North Americans, other big corporate maquila investors come from Japan, South Korea, Taiwan, Hong Kong, and assorted European countries such as Germany.[6] The "giant sucking sound" that pierced Ross Perot's ears was that of jobs flowing southward to Mexico, the Caribbean, and Central America, and eastward across the Pacific as the United States eliminated industrial jobs. During this de-industrialization phase in the global core, the United States simultaneously experienced a rapid rise in service employment at both the high- and low-skilled end. In this country, the non-manufacturing labor force came to constitute 84.3 percent of the total (measured in hours) by 1996, or a growth of almost 30 million jobs since 1979.[7] In time, some Asian countries that had prospered from early export-based industrialization—notably Japan, Singapore, Taiwan, and Hong Kong (before re-integration with China)—themselves became exporters of finance capital, setting up assembly plants in poor and densely populated Asian countries such as Indonesia, Thailand, and China, as well as in Mexico, Central America, and the Caribbean, as noted above. In sum, globalization in late capitalism changes relations of production, marked by a labor strategy that stresses minimizing cost and maximizing flexibility. It is characterized by a shift from a Fordist or vertically integrated (characterized by the assembly line) system of production to a leaner and fragmented production process, with greater "spatial mobility" for both capital and labor.

THE GLOBAL SWEATSHOP: SUBCONTRACTING AND OUTSOURCING

Amazingly, global capital and production, in continuous and relentless search for cheap labor, manufacturing flexibility, and spatial mobility, have come full circle: the global assembly plant employing low-skill, low-cost female labor can now be found in abundance in the global core, the United States itself, in the form of hundreds of electronics assembly plants in the Silicon Valley of Northern California as well as factories in the apparel industry of Southern California, the San Francisco–Oakland area, and in and around New York's garment district and Chinatowns (in Manhattan and Queens). Although clothing manufacturing has constituted a mainstay of the Mexican maquilas and fly-by-night assembly plants set up in EPZs all over Asia itself, fast-changing designs and fluctuating market demands of the garment business have dictated the need to produce certain styles and quantities close to the retailers (big department stores), manufacturers (labels), and consumers in the United States.

Central to global production is the subcontracting system, a pyramid-shaped hierarchy consisting of a small number of U.S.-based manufacturers and retailers at the top, several thousand Third World-based contractors in the middle, and massive numbers of Third World workers at the bottom, most of them women. The exact same system is adapted to conditions in the United States, where outsourcing is localized, and subcontractors and workers co-exist in the same crowded urban space. Intense competition in this business has revitalized the garment sweatshop—defined as factories that fail to meet minimum wage, labor, and safety standards according to the law and state and local regulations—in New York and California. Mostly young female immigrants from Asia, Mexico, and Central America (legal and undocumented) have quickly filled the labor needs of hundreds of subcontractors operating small factories and sweatshops, doing the same work they would in their home countries had they not migrated to the United States.[8] Immigrant entrepreneurs, especially Koreans and Chinese, increasingly fill the ranks of subcontractors in New York and California.

While hidden for years from the American consuming public and the media, the revived American sweatshop is no longer a secret, its exposé helping to fuel the anti-globalization movement. The raid on the El Monte (California) underground sweatshop in August 1995 freed seventy-two Thai workers (sixty-seven women, five men) smuggled into the country by the Thai-Chinese owners, who contracted with several well-known U.S. brand-name manufacturers. Paid only $1.60 per hour, these workers were kept in a modern version of indentured servitude, denied their freedom to leave the barbed-wire compound, forced to pay off their passage, threatened with rape and retribution against family members back home if they disobeyed their captors. In January 1999, the media exposed another shameful sweatshop situation that resembled El Monte. Hundreds of sweatshops owned by Asians and Asian American subcontractors were found in the U.S. Pacific territory of Saipan, where workers, predominately young women from the Philippines, China, Thailand, and Bangladesh, worked twelve hours daily, seven days weekly, living seven to a room in "dreary barracks surrounded by inward-facing barbed wire."[9]

THE ELECTRONICS INDUSTRY: PROTOTYPE OF THE GLOBAL SWEATSHOP

An early form of the global sweatshop was actually not about clothes or shoes, but accompanied the rise of the U.S. electronics industry, based on revolutionary new technology of the 1960s and 1970s. Labor relations patterns established in this industry would re-appear later in other industries that relied heavily on immigrant, particularly immigrant women, labor. Renewed immigration from the Third World in the mid-1960s coincided with the postwar rise of the electronics/semiconductor industry, centered in the Silicon Valley of Santa Clara County, south of San Francisco and down the road from Stanford University, where much of the new technology was incubated. Its highly sophisticated technology notwithstanding, the semiconductor industry retained a component that is very labor intensive and requires "hand-eye coordination" in assembly work that is difficult to automate.[10] From the very beginning, much of this work was subcontracted out to export zones in Asia and Mexico, where docile, patient, manually dexterous, and, best of all, cheap labor, provided by young, unmarried "girls," was in abundance. As it turned out, the largely married and older women of the newly settled Asian immigrant communities in the emerging Silicon Valley proved equally adept and eager for this kind of work, in the absence of better paying jobs for new immigrants with little or no English skills.[11] Feminization of localized assembly plants occurred rapidly: in San Jose, from just 6,900 in 1966, the number of women workers rose to 18,288 by 1978.[12] For the entire Silicon Valley, some 70,000 women made up the bulk of the production workforce in the 1980s and held close to 90 percent of "operative" and "laborer" jobs on the factory floor. Of these women, 45 to 50 percent were Third World immigrant women, including undocumented ones from Mexico and Central America,[13] while white women moved into clerical and white-collar positions. From 1966 to 1978, Latina and Asian women in the workforce doubled, from 23 percent to 45 percent. During this period, the $4.91 hourly wage they earned fell behind the $5.69 bluecollar wages in other industries.[14] So while electronics production was being internationalized, the lowest-paid, least-skilled, most dead-end, highest turnover, least stable jobs were held by the same Third World women, whether they worked in the Third World itself or as immigrants to the United States.

Ironically, notes economist Linda Lim, "it is the *comparative disadvantage* of women [italics in original] in the wage labor market that gives them a *comparative advantage* [italics added] vis-à-vis men in the occupations and industries where they [women] are concentrated." These women-dominated niches became known as "female ghettos of employment," the jobs as "women's work."[15] By characterizing assembly-type manufacturing thus, the clear suggestion is that such jobs are somehow naturally or inherently more suited for women, or that women are innately more suited for the work, given their natural patience, dexterity, docility, discipline, and other similar traits. Further debasing and undervaluing women's work, managers in the Silicon Valley often suggested that the immigrant women workers were only "temporary" and their incomes "secondary," next to their spouses, and that they were, by choice, "mothers" first. Thus these women workers were deemed not "career-minded" and hence did not mind dead-end jobs with few advancement possibilities.[16] Furthermore, if these workers were induced to think of themselves as "temporary," and were seen by others as such, then they would not likely seek unionization, nor would unions be interested in them. Thus, a perfectly designed, segregated, segmented, and secondary labor market has been created for the downgraded manufacturing sector of the otherwise high-tech industry.[17] In the next section, we will see how critics expose these arguments as constructed or manufactured rationalizations for exploitation of immigrant women's work.

If most of the assembly jobs in the electronics industry were shifted overseas early, why did any have to remain in the Silicon Valley, where the mental and creative work of design and innovation is done? The reason is similar to why the garment industry also created production capacities closer to home: an ongoing need for "quickly available prototypic and short term products" in this fast-changing technological field.[18] But if it were not for the arrival of Third World immigrant women, Silicon Valley industries might not have been able to afford building a parallel assembly infrastructure right at home, given competition from cheap wages in the Third World. As it were, Silicon Valley, in fact, was able to replicate at the *core* a domestic version of the stratified system—by race, sex, and class—that has been euphemistically termed an "international division of labor" at the *periphery* of the restructured global economy.

THE UNDERSIDE OF GLOBALIZATION

The maquiladoras in Mexico, the export-processing factories in Asia and Central America, the electronic assembly plants and garment sweatshops in the United States—these are the unattractive public faces of globalization in late capitalist or de-industrialized America, appropriately and rather ominously dubbed by President George W. Bush as the New World Order. Do sweatshops represent the trickle-down dividends of globalization by creating jobs, as global boosters would have us believe,[19] or do they represent "lurid examples of random inhumanity," as critics such as William Greider charge?[20] Or, as Stiglitz alleges, U.S.-driven globalization has not only *not* reduced poverty around the world, but exacerbated the gap between rich and poor nations.[21]

There is now considerable research and published literature that supports Greider's and Stiglitz's observations and conclusions, especially when globalization is viewed from the perspective of immigrant women at the global periphery (Asia, Latin America, the Caribbean), many of whom, driven by growing poverty at home, have been moving to the global core (the United States). What follows is a discussion of what can be termed the underside of globalization—or globalization and its discontents, to borrow a term from Stiglitz—and how this perspective reframes the points raised above around subcon-tracting and outsourcing, immigration, free trade, and exploitation of female labor, especially in the informal sector.

Race to the Bottom

Corporate-led globalization depends on intense exploitation of labor, exacerbated by the subcontracting system that answers to the logic of a race to the bottom of the wage scale. To win a contract, the subcontractor must submit the lowest bid; he then squeezes the workers to make his profit. Third world women at home and immigrant women from these countries in the United States bear the brunt of this brutal logic. They are constantly fearful of losing their jobs to even more vulnerable women somewhere in the world who would work for even less wages under even more abysmal conditions. As Bonacich and Appelbaum conclude, "We believe that the current system of globalized, highly flexible production creates a new kind of labor regime and labor discipline. Workers are kept under control by the mobility and dispersal of the industry. This system, which constantly threatens job loss, and severely inhibits labor struggles, keeps workers toiling at breakneck speed for long hours and low wages. They do not require coercive oversight to achieve the desired effect."[22]

Third world women workers in their home countries and Third World immigrant women in the United States form one continuum in the same gendered and transnational workforce which lies at the base of globalization and its international subcontracting system. Whether they work in a Nike plant subcontracted to a Taiwanese factory owner in Indonesia or Vietnam or as contract workers in an Asian-owned Saipan factory, or in an unregistered, underground sweat- shop in Los Angeles operated by a Korean immigrant, or in a union shop in New York's Chinatown owned by a newly naturalized Chinese American, they may well be sewing the same style for the same manufacturer, affixing the same label on the finished garment. Given this, labor activists and immigrant rights advocates must adopt a globalized strategy of resistance to combat abuses in the workplace.[23]

Rationalizations for Low Wages

"Nimble fingers" and "bootstrap" myths have emerged to justify this intense exploitation of Third World women on the global periphery and immigrant women in the global core as natural, inevitable, and even desirable. These women are characterized as inherently, innately, and naturally suited for the kind of low-skill labor needed in light manufacturing, whether in Third World export-processing factories or in U.S. electronic assembly plants and sweatshops. Critics charge that this is nothing less than rationalization for low wages, not to mention justification for the perpetuation of the notion of Third World women's cognitive inferiority. It is not just the gendered quality of the division of labor that is so problematic, but that the gendered division is inferred and inscribed in a permanent hierarchy that is further reinforced by race, class, and nationality differences, as well as denial of immigration and citizenship rights in the case of the smuggled and undocumented.

What is so inherent about poor Third World women that should render them into "cheap and docile labor," cultural critic Laura Hyun Hi Kang pointedly asks, "as if depressed wages and workplace discipline were ontological properties unique to Asian women rather than historically specific, culturally dictated, and closely managed conditions." Can it be that the preponderance of young women employed in EPZs is less the result of a "natural supply" than "a consciously pursued strategy" on the part of transnational corporations (TNCs) and authoritarian governments alike? "The mobilization of disproportionate numbers of young Asian women in these TNC factories is thus revealed to be the modus operandi of corporate managers and not a sign of their innate fitness for these jobs," Kang concludes.[24] In short, we must begin to disabuse ourselves of believing in the inevitability of the grossly inequitable and exploitative gendered division of labor in the global assembly line, one in which the gendered position is fixed and immutable and usually not a transition to some better condition. More than just protesting abuses in the system, we must begin to question its rationality and logic in the first place.

Another kind of frequently voiced rhetoric rationalizing exploitation of immigrant women is the bootstrap myth: that sewing jobs are steps leading to the American dream, there for the ambitious Mexican women to grasp. As one Southern California manufacturer puts it in direct, no-nonsense terms: "We provide entry-level jobs for women, for Mexican women. These women have no other options; they can either do this or become dish washers. Working in a garment factory requires learning some skills. Maybe they are being taken advantage of, but they have a choice. No one is holding a gun to their heads. They come in at minimum wage, get some training, and can then put their children through college. It is the great American Dream!"[25] For a handful of Korean garment workers who immigrate with some capital and first enter the factory to learn the business, then quickly move on to being a subcontractor, the American dream may come true. But the reality for the vast majority of immigrant, particularly Latina, workers is closer to that of the thirty-five-year-old single mother Salvadoran garment-machine operative who worked in the same garment factory for fourteen years without ever receiving a raise.[26]

Not surprisingly, garment manufacturers are also stridently anti-union, advancing a logic similar to that employed to argue the bootstrap myth. Union drives by UNITE (Union of Needletrades, Industrial, and Textile Employees),[27] they argue, "may unwittingly serve to break the back of an industry that has been one of the key routes of upward mobility for immigrant entrepreneurs and workers"; and if union drives succeed, they warn, the LA garment "miracle" would become a "nightmare," with "tens of thousands of workers thrown into the street."[28]

The Rich Get Richer

Increased trade spurred on by decreased regulation and removal of all barriers does not necessarily produce better jobs. If anything, removal of regulations only serves to increase the power of wealthier nations (the North) over poorer ones (the South). Thus, unregulated global free trade will disproportionately benefit the already wealthy nations to the great disadvantage of the poor nations, enabling a few corporations and individuals to become fabulously, obscenely rich while deepening the misery of the world's multitudinous poor. Many new studies have demonstrated the growing gap *between* and *within* nations, with the United States a notable example of both kinds of inequalities.[29] As some critics have pointed out, contrary to the World Bank's bald assertion that accelerated globalization has produced greater world equality, the rising tide of globalization, far from lifting all boats, is "only lifting yachts!"[30] Today, the world's richest two hundred individuals have more wealth than 41 percent of the world's humanity.[31] Growing impoverishment in the global South is driving a "globalization of migration"—men, women, and children leaving for the global North in search of jobs and livelihood. In this context, immigration is not merely a simple matter of individuals or families making decisions to move and relocate, but becomes a de facto survival strategy. In the words of sociologist Arlie Hochschild, "migration has become a private solution to a public problem."[32]

Immigrants Are Indispensable

Immigrants are not only *not* a drain on the U.S. economy, but an absolute necessity, especially women immigrants, who comprise half or more of new immigrants to the United States. Immigrant labor is indispensable for the labor-intensive, service-dependent, restructured economy of the United States, as well as for the resurgent light manufacturing sector, captured at its worst by the image of the garment sweatshop.[33] Lately, well-educated and professionally trained immigrant labor is also in great demand in the computer programming sector of the Silicon Valley.[34] The role of the INS (since September 11, 2001, removed from the Justice Department and absorbed into Homeland Security as ICE, Immigration and Customs Enforcement) is not to stop the flow of immigration to the United States so much as to

regulate the level of that flow and to control the type of immigrants who come in at any given time.[35] When demand for new workers surges in any critical sector of the economy, as periodically happens in the high-tech industry of places like Silicon Valley or in the low-tech industries of agriculture in the West, meatpacking in the Midwest,[36] and poultry in the South,[37] the government is perfectly capable and willing to "look the other way."[38] In the booming economy of the Clinton years, with unemployment at just 4 percent and a strong demand for people to take jobs paying $8.00 an hour or less, which were 25 percent of all jobs, mostly immigrants—both legal and undocumented—made up the pool of applicants for these jobs.[39] Is U.S. immigration policy just an undetected contradiction or part and parcel of another unspoken logic in global capitalism, alongside the manic logic of the subcontracting system? Until very recently, even the U.S. labor movement subscribed to the arbitrary line invented by the government to differentiate between legal, thus good, immigrants and illegal, thus bad, immigrants. That colossal canard was finally laid to rest when the Service Employees International Union (SEIU) led its eighty-five hundred janitors, many of them "illegal aliens" from Mexico, Central America, and Asia, on successful strikes in downtown Chicago and Los Angeles, where they cleaned high-rise office buildings.[40] In the face of this new reality of globalized labor, AFL-CIO's leader, John Sweeney, finally proclaimed at the dawn of the new millennium a "new internationalism" for American unions.[41]

Informalization of Labor

Informalization of labor is a growing phenomenon under globalization, both in the global core (the United States) and the periphery (Mexico, Central America, the Caribbean, and Asia). Even more than other jobs, work in the informal economies mainly engages immigrant women, usually the poorest or most recent arrivals among them. Underground sweatshops, such as the infamous El Monte noted above, only scratch the surface of this hidden or invisible aspect of globalized labor. In fact, much of the work in informal economies is above ground and visible to anyone who cares to look and acknowledge benefits from the labor of those who toil in this sector. Hidden in plain sight, immigrant women workers are, indeed, everywhere, because for the most part, informal economies exist side by side with formal economies and are often different sides of the same coin. They are income-generating or income-substituting activities that hover under the radar screen of our collective consciousness.

In the informal economy, wages are paid in cash and thus not reported and not taxed. Employers own and operate very small enterprises, such as factories with ten or fewer workers. Work hours are flexible, and no labor, occupational health, or safety laws are observed. There are, of course, no benefits and no unions and no government oversight. In short, there is no contractual relationship between capital (employer) and labor (worker). Workers work "off the books" and are paid "under the table." Various types of the self-employed, like independent contractors and small business owners, can also be found in abundance in informal economies. Distinguished from criminal and illicit activities, such as drug running, they are, in fact, similar economic activities performed or produced in the formal sector but under conditions described above.[42]

In the garment industry, sweatshops, particularly underground sweatshops such as the notorious El Monte and Saipan examples, represent the informal sector of this economy because they flaunt wage and labor laws and other regulations. But while sweatshops have been exposed and denounced, there are other less visible instances of informal labor in garment and electronics assembly work. Called "industrial home work" when women workers moonlight after a regular workday in the plant by taking more work home, this is the most invisible kind of informal labor because it is performed in the privacy of the home. It is usually paid at piece rate, that is, by the number of completed tasks. In garment work, home work tasks usually entail finishing touches, such as cutting loose threads or sewing on buttons, tasks to which children can and do contribute.

In electronics, home work entails fusing components onto electronic boards or repairing and modifying older boards. Children and other family members, such as the elderly, often participate in speeding up production at home in order to maximize earnings, but unwittingly also share in the exposure to toxic chemicals from which they have no protection. For pregnant women who accept electronics home work, for obvious reasons the health consequences can be very severe. These low-tech and manual tasks of informal labor occur at home, alongside the highly automated assembly-floor jobs that pay regular wages. In fact, subcontractors recruit and sub-subcontract work to home workers; they deliver and collect work from the homes.[43]

To be sure, for some women, home work is one way to increase their income, an option they exercise along with job-hopping and working overtime. For those who have to juggle child care and other household duties, home work gives them more flexibility and perhaps a sense of greater control over their work. For other women who feel alienated from the oppressive environment on the job floor, home work may give them a chance to feel "independent," to earn what they want and work when they want, away from the prying eyes of supervisors. Of course, piece rate pay usually translates into less than minimum wage, no overtime, no breaks, no benefits, thus further downgrading the work of women for the industries. It means that they work at jobs, sometimes dangerous and toxic ones, totally eluding the scrutiny of government inspectors. Meanwhile, for managers and subcontractors, home work affords them a more flexible strategy to meet production goals and deadlines, reasons why they embrace the practice.[44] When home becomes a site for the global market under these totally unregulated conditions, immigrant women and families find themselves in a work situation not unlike a sweatshop.[45] Workers not only exploit themselves by speeding up work to earn more, but may need to exploit their family members, including children, without adequate remuneration.

Another category of informal labor can be grouped under the rubric of social reproductive work. If industrial home work is largely secluded and invisible, social reproductive work permeates the lives of middle- and upper-class families in America, especially when women of these families—mothers and wives—also work outside the home. While industrial home work is performed in the privacy of the worker's home, social reproductive labor is usually conducted in the client's space and delivered personally, sometimes intimately, and often emotionally. Whether working as nannies or housekeepers, in child care or elder care, for the sick or the young, as cooks or nurses, and as prostitutes, in massage parlors, even as mail-order brides, Third World immigrant women providing these services are not just making a living in low-paying, low-status occupational niches that require little English or few skills. In a very crucial way, they too are part of the new transnational division of labor, their paid labor replacing the previously unremunerated responsibilities of first world women in the social reproduction of daily and family life, in the renewal of intimacy and conveyance of emotional love. On a daily and intergenerational basis, they relieve professional first world women of much of the burden of the "second shift." Such social reproductive labor has always been associated with women's work and continues to be debased and devalued when industrialized or commodified, that is, performed for payment by Third World immigrant women for their largely white, first world "sisters" in a racial division of labor.[46] Barbara Ehrenreich has very aptly dubbed this kind of work "outsourcing the work of the home."[47]

Increasingly, American middle-class working women have joined upper-class women to access other women for social reproductive labor, with women performing such labor overwhelmingly Latina and Asian. The 1990 U.S. census recorded 28,859 domestics working as maids, housekeepers, and child care providers in private homes; over 80 percent identified as "Hispanics."[48] Because of the informality of such work, the actual numbers are probably many times higher. In sum, "most white middle class women could hire another woman—a recent immigrant, a working-class woman, a women of color, or all these—to perform much of the hard labor of household tasks" as they fulfill themselves in careers outside the home.[49] The "private sphere" responsibilities of class-privileged women are thereby transferred to racially and socially subordinate women.[50] Even immigrant women who find domestic employment through co-ethnic brokers remain largely informal or contingent workers, as they have little job security, irregular hours, and no benefits, can be hired or fired instantly, and are paid hourly or by the job.[51] Many of these maids and home caregivers, whether caring for children or the elderly, are undocumented; for them, informal work is their only option.[52]

This discussion on informal immigrant labor would not be complete without acknowledgment of sex work, perhaps the most contingent of informal labor. Asian women as preferred sex partners—paid or even unpaid in the case of military wives and mail-order (now Internet) brides—for some American men dates back to the days of America's serial military involvement in Asia, from World War II through the Korean War and the Vietnam War. "Militarized prostitution" developed around all the army bases in Asia, while American soldiers on furlough for "rest and relaxation" stimulated the development and growth of sex tourism to countries far beyond the battlegrounds, such as to Bangkok.[53] Just as American transnational capital has constructed Third World women, whether "over there" or after migration to the United States, as particularly adept at electronics and garment assembly work, so American men have imagined these same women as particularly seductive as girlfriends, attentive and submissive as wives, and, best of all, not "corrupted" by Western feminist ideas and values.

Some sex workers are self-employed in small businesses, such as massage parlors. Structurally, the massage parlor operates like an agency, with workers as "independent contractors" working with their own clients, sometimes off the books. Typically, masseuses are not paid a wage, nor guaranteed work, but provided with space at the parlor to meet their clients, with whom they negotiate desired services. The women pay the massage parlor owner a cut of their take from each customer.[54] U.S. morality laws criminalize sex workers by arresting them after sweeping streets or raiding massage parlors. Criminalization drives sex workers further underground to avoid detection and exposure, thus intensifying the already informal nature of sex work, making it even more difficult to address their right to be considered like other working people, deserving of decent wages and safe and humane working conditions.[55] Furthermore, criminalization adds another layer of oppression to the already multilayered system under which immigrant women labor, condemning them as noncitizen, criminal, and morally corrupt.[56]

Many types of self-employment can be found in informal economies, one of which has become well known as a Latino/Latina niche in Southern California. These are the street vendors—mostly Mexican and Central American women—who hock their food and other wares on freeway entry or exit ramps, in the center island divides of major boulevards, and on sidewalks of ethnic neighborhoods. They complement formal-sector food businesses such as supermarkets, restaurants, and bakeries.[57]

Informality is already highly feminized. It is likely to become more gendered and more likely to proliferate, spreading out from places like the U.S.-Mexican border, where it has always been prevalent and known, indeed, as the "Mexican solution."[58] To escape poverty, people on the border pursue multiple strategies with multiple earners in a household, sometimes straddling both sides of the border, often with one foot planted in a wage job and the other dallying in an informal economic activity. Many on the Mexican side may eventually choose migration as the ultimate solution, cross the border, and basically continue what they and so many other Mexicans have always done to survive globalization, pursuing the elusive *casa de mis sueños* (house of my dreams).[59]

CONCLUSION:
THE EVOLVING LOGIC OF GLOBALIZATION

We began this chapter with an emblematic story of contingent workers in an increasingly familiar kind of work associated with immigrant women, slowly unmasking the invisibility surrounding informal labor. We close with the next big story on the global horizon, one that has already taken the United States by storm, leaving much of the public perplexed and worried about their well-being. I am referring to the exporting of information-based service-sector jobs, previously thought immune to elimination from the American workscape under the logic of globalization.

This is a transnational story, like so many under globalization, but with a novel twist. On one side of the global divide, welfare recipients in Kansas, Arizona, Alabama, and Tennessee dial their usual toll-free number to inquire about their next check. Welfare mothers from New Jersey are especially anxious as they have been notified their checks will soon be cut off because they should be getting jobs. On the other side, in far off Bombay, India, a soft voice identifying herself as Megan takes the calls. "How can I help you?" she asks in her mild southern drawl as she attempts to answer questions about benefits and food stamp balances, patiently waiting out angry tirades, quietly listening to the sobs of stressed-out young single mothers at rope's end.

Megan is really Manisha Martin, twenty-seven, a worker at an Indian call center. Her employer is a subcontractor for a company based in Scottsdale, Arizona, which is in turn the subcontractor for various state welfare agencies to handle calls from their welfare recipients. Her training included learning a clearly identifiable American accent, hence the southern drawl, and learning to be vague about her location or other personal data if asked. Martin and others doing similar work earn about two hundred dollars a month, less than what the American welfare recipients receive but much higher than the five hundred dollar average yearly income in India. The over-educated Indian college graduate undoubtedly appreciates her significant economic uplift, but the problem is that the New Jersey welfare mother forced off the rolls and ordered to get work just saw one of the few jobs she was likely qualified to do slip away.[60] While one poor woman survived globalization, the other did not; ironically, the one who fell through the threadbare safety net lives in the United States, heart of the global core, very likely a woman of color herself.

On the other side of the U.S.-Mexican border, high-tech data work called "informatics" has also been outsourced from the United States. In these maquiladoras, as at similar sites in the Caribbean, China, the Philippines, South Korea, Sri Lanka, Malaysia, and Ghana, young women hunch over computer keyboards, "fingers flying" as they digitize U.S. and European market research surveys, insurance claims, airline tickets, package delivery invoices, credit card applications, even books, New York City parking tickets, U.S. medical doctors' scribbles, and a myriad of other data-processing work made possible by rapidly developing new satellite and telecommunications technology.[61] Again, these are jobs that U.S. women of color and immigrant women already here can perform, but Third World women can do them just as well and for much less. Will these jobs stem the tide of women pouring into the United States from India, China, the Philippines, and other parts of Asia and from Mexico? Probably not, as free trade continues to push more Mexicans deeper into poverty, and jobs are not created fast enough in India.[62]

NOTES

1. Nina Bernstein, "Invisible to Most, Immigrant Women Line up for Day Labor," *New York Times,* August 15, 2005 (online edition).
2. Jason Van Derbeken and Ryan Kim, "Alleged Sex-Trade Ring Broken up in Bay Area," *San Francisco Chronicle,* July 2, 2004, A1 and A9.
3. Swasti Mitter, *Common Fate, Common Bond: Women in the Global Economy.* (London: Pluto Press, 1986); Helen I. Safa, "Runaway Shops and Female Employment: The Search for Cheap Labor," *SIGNS: Journal of Women in Culture and Society* 7, no. 2 (1981): 418–433; David A. Smith, "Going South: Global Restructuring and Garment Production in Three East Asian Cases," *Asian Perspectives* 20, no. 2 (fall–winter 1996): 211–241; Saskia Sassen, *The Mobility of Labor and Capital. A Study in International Investment and Labor Flow* (New York: Cambridge University Press, 1988); Saskia Sassen-Koob, "Notes on the Incorporation of Third World Women into Wage Labor through Immigration and Off-Shore Production," *International Migration Review* 18, no. 4 (1983): 1144–1167; Paul Ong, Edna Bonacich, and Lucie Cheng, "The Political Economy of Capitalist Restructuring and the New Asian Immigrants," in *The New Asian Immigration in Los Angeles and Global Restructuring,* ed. Paul Ong, Edna Bonacich, and Lucie Cheng (Philadelphia: Temple University Press, 1992): 3–43; Gary Gereffi, "Global Sourcing and Regional Divisions of Labor in the Pacific Rim," in *What Is in a Rim? Critical Perspectives on the Pacific Region Idea,* 2nd. rev. ed., ed. Arif Dirlik (Lanham, Md.: Rowman & Littlefield, 1997), 143–161.
4. Joseph E. Stiglitz, *Globalization and Its Discontents* (New York: Norton, 2002), ix.
5. Evelyn Hu-DeHart, introduction to *Across the Pacific: Asian American Formations in the Age of Globalization,* ed. Evelyn Hu-DeHart (Philadelphia: Temple University Press, 2000), 1–28; Evelyn Hu DeHart, "Asian Women Immigrants in the U.S. Fashion Garment Industry," in *Women and Work in Globalising Asia,* ed. Dong-Sook S. Gills and Nicola Piper (London: Routledge, 2002), 209–230; Annette Fuentes and Barbara Ehrenreich, *Women in the Global Factory* (Boston: South End Press, 1983); Mary Beth Sheridan, "Riding Ripples of a Border Boom," *Los Angeles Times,* June 9, 1996, A1, A8; Leslie Kaufman and David González, "Labor Progress Clashes with Global Reality," *New York Times,* April 24, 1999, A1, A10; Elizabeth Becker, "Central American Deal Ignites a Trade Debate," *New York Times,* April 6, 2002, C1, C4.
6. Anthony DePalma, "Economic Lessons in a Border Town," *New York Times,* May 23, 1996, C1; Kelly Her, "Mexico's Leading Taiwan Investors," *Free China Journal,* September 13, 1995, 8; Barbara Stallings and Gabriel Szekely, eds., *Japan, the United States, and Latin America: Towards a Trilateral Relationship in the Western Hemisphere* (Baltimore: Johns Hopkins University Press, 1994).
7. Robert Brenner, "The Economics of Global Turbulence. A Special Report on the World Economy, 1950–98," *New Left Review* (special issue) 229 (1998): 204–205.
8. Hu-DeHart, "Asian Women Immigrants."

9. *Sweatshop Watch Newsletter,* http://sweatshopwatch .org, 1995 to 1999; Steven Greenhouse, "Janitors, Long Paid Little, Demand a Larger Slice," *New York Times,* April 28, 1999, A12.

10. June R. Keller, "The Division of Labor in Electronics," in *Women, Men, and the International Division of Labor,* ed. June Nash and María Patricia Fernández-Kelly (Albany: SUNY Press, 1983), 345–373.

11. Susan S. Green, "Silicon Valley's Women Workers: A Theoretical Analysis of Sex-Segregation in the Electronics Industry Labor Market," in Nash and Fernández-Kelly, *Women, Men, and the International Division of Labor,* 273–331.

12. Robert Snow, "The New International Division of Labor and the U.S. Work Force: The Case of the Electronics Industry," in June and Fernández-Kelly, *Women, Men, and the International Division of Labor.*

13. Naomi Katz and David S. Kemnitzer, "Fast Forward: The Internationalization of Silicon Valley," in Nash and Fernández-Kelly, *Women, Men, and the International Division of Labor,* 332–345.

14. Snow, "The New International Division of Labor."

15. Linda Y. C. Lim, "Capitalism, Imperialism, and Patriarchy: The Dilemma of Third-World Women Workers in Multinational Factories," in Nash and Fernández-Kelly, *Women, Men, and the International Division of Labor.*

16. Lim, "Capitalism, Imperialism, and Patriarchy"; Karen J. Hossfield, "Their Logic against Them: Contradictions of Sex, Race, and Class in Silicon Valley," in *Women Workers and Global Restructuring,* ed. Kathryn Ward (Cornell: School of Industrial and Labor Relations (ILR) Press, 1990), 150–178.

17. Sassen, *The Mobility of Labor and Capital.*

18. Hossfield, "Their Logic against Them."

19. Jeffrey Sachs and Paul Krugman, "In Principle: A Case for More 'Sweatshops,'" *New York Times,* June 22, 1997 (Week in Review).

20. William Greider, *One World, Ready or Not: The Manic Logic of Global Capitalism* (New York: Simon & Schuster, 1997).

21. Stiglitz, *Globalization and Its Discontents.*

22. Edna Bonacich and Richard P. Appelbaum, *Behind the Label. Inequality in the Los Angeles Apparel Industry* (Berkeley: University of California Press, 2000), 198.

23. Kim Moody, *Workers in a Lean World: Unions in the International Economy* (London: Verso, 1997).

24. Laura Hyun Hi Kang, "Si(gh)ting Asian/American Women as Transnational Labor," *Positions* 5, no. 2 (fall 1994): 403–437.

25. Bonacich and Appelbaum, *Behind the Label,* 121.

26. Ibid., 182.

27. In 2004, UNITE merged with H.E.R.E., Hotel Employees and Restaurant Employees Union, to become UNITE HERE. Both unions represent low-paid, low-skilled service workers, who are largely immigrant and heavily women.

28. Bonacich and Appelbaum, *Behind the Label,* 124.

29. William Macklin, "Making Them Sweat: Students Step up Pressure to Hold Colleges Accountable for Apparel," *USA Today,* April 13, 2006, 19; Mary Williams Walsh, "Latinos Get Left out of Economic Boom," *Boulder Daily Camera,* March 25, 2005, 14A (from the *Los Angeles Times*); Stiglitz, *Globalization and Its Discontents.*

30. "Global Monoculture," *New York Times* (paid advertisement), November 15, 1999, A7.

31. Robert L. Borosage, "The Battle in Seattle," *Nation,* December 6, 1999, 20–21.

32. Arlie Russell Hochschild, "Love and Gold," in *Global Woman: Nannies, Maids, and Sex Workers in the New Economy,* ed. Arlie Russell Hochschild and Barbara Ehrenreich (New York: Metropolitan Books, 2001), 24.

33. Harold Meyerson, "Liberalism with a New Accent: Immigrants Are Helping to Create a Dynamic, Globally Focused Movement," *Nation,* October 11, 1996, 15–20.

34. William Branigan, "Visa Program, High-Tech Workers Exploited," *Washington Post,* July 26, 1998, A1; Marc Cooper, "Class War at Silicon Valley," *Nation,* May 27, 1996, 11–16.

35. James D. Cockcroft, *Outlaws in the Promised Land: Mexican Immigrant Workers and America's Future* (New York: Grove, 1986).

36. Louise Lamphere, Alex Stepick, and Guillermo Grenier, eds., *Newcomers in the Workplace: Immigrants and the Restructuring of the U.S. Economy* (Philadelphia: Temple University Press, 1993); Jane Slaughter, "Welcome to the Jungle," *In These Times,* August 22, 1996, 5–6.

37. Raymond A. Mohl, "Globalization, Latinization, and the Nuevo New South," *Journal of American Ethnic History* 22, no. 4 (summer 2002): 31–66.

38. Louis Uchitelle, "INS Is Looking the Other Way as Illegal Immigrants Fill Jobs," *New York Times,* March 9, 1998, A1.

39. Uchitelle, "INS Is Looking the Other Way"; John Markoff, "Influx of New Immigrants Found in Silicon Valley," *New York Times,* January 10, 2002, C2; Louis Freedberg, "Borderline Hypocrisy: Do

We Want Them Here, or Not?" *Washington Post,* February 6, 2000, B1.

40. Greenhouse, "Janitors, Long Paid Little."

41. David Bacon, "Labor's About Face," *Nation,* March 20, 2000, 6–7; William Greider, "Time to Rein in Global Finance," *Nation,* April 24, 2000, 13–20.

42. Marta López-Garza, "A Study of the Informal Economy and Latina/o Immigrants in Greater Los Angeles," in *Asian and Latino Immigrants in a Restructuring Economy: The Metamorphosis of Southern California,* ed. López-Garza, Marta Díaz, and David R. Diaz (Stanford: Stanford University Press, 2000), 144–145.

43. Tran Ngoc Angie, "Transnational Assembly Work: Vietnamese American Electronic and Vietnamese Garment Workers," *Amerasia Journal* 29, no. 1 (2003): 4–28.

44. Katz and Kemnitzer, "Fast Forward: The Internationalization of Silicon Valley."

45. Angie, "Transnational Assembly Work."

46. Evelyn Nakano Glenn, "From Servitude to Service Work: Historical Continuities in the Racial Division of Paid Reproductive Labor," *SIGNS: Journal of Women in Culture Society* 18, no. 1 (1992): 1–43; Thanh Dam Truong, "Gender, International Migration, and Social Reproduction: Implications for Theory, Policy, Research, and Networking," *Asian and Pacific Migration Journal* 5, no. 2 (1992): 27–52; Milyoung Cho, "Overcoming Our Legacy as Cheap Labor, Scabs, and Model Minorities: Asian Activists Fight for Community Empowerment," in *The State of Asian America,* ed. Karin Aguilar San Juan (Boston: South End Press, 1994), 253–273; Sassen-Koob, "Notes on the Incorporation of Third World Women"; Bridget Anderson, "Just Another Job? The Commodification of Domestic Labor," in Hochschild and Ehrenreich, *Global Women,* 104–114; Rhacel Salazar Parreñas, *Servants of Globalization: Women, Migration, and Domestic Work* (Stanford: Stanford University Press, 1998); Pierrette Hondegneu-Sotelo, *Doméstica: Immigrant Workers Cleaning and Caring in the Shadows of Affluence* (Berkeley: University of California Press, 2002); Mary Romero, *Maid in the U.S.A.,* 10th anniversary ed. (New York: Routledge, 2002); Grace Chang, *Disposable Domestics: Immigrant Women Workers in the Global Economy* (Cambridge: South End Press, 2000); Charlene Tung, "The Cost of Caring: The Social Reproductive Labor of Filipina Live-in Home Health Caregivers," *Frontiers. A Journal of Women Studies* 21, nos. 1 and 2 (1997): 61–82; Kristine M. Zentgraf,

"Through Economic Restructuring, Recession, and Rebound," in *Asian and Latino Immigrants in a Restructuring Economy: The Metamorphosis of Southern California,* ed. Marta López-Garza and David R. Díaz (Stanford: Stanford University Press, 1998), 46–74.

47. Barbara Ehrenreich, "Maid to Order," in Hochschild and Ehrenreich, *Global Women,* 85–103.

48. Grace A. Rosales, "Labor behind Front Door: Domestic Workers in Urban and Suburban Households," in López-Garza and Díaz, *Asian and Latinos Immigrants in a Restructuring Economy,* 169–187.

49. Glenn, "From Servitude to Service Work," 7.

50. Parreñas, *Servants of Globalization.*

51. Kristen Hill Maher, "Good Women 'Ready to Go,' Labor Brokers and the Transnational Maid Trade," *Labor* 1, no. 1 (spring 2004): 55–76.

52. Tung, "The Cost of Caring."

53. Alexandra Suh, "Militarized Prostitution in Asia and the U.S.," in *States of Confinement: Policing, Detention, and Prisons,* ed. Joy James (New York: St. Martin's Press, 1996).

54. Suh, "Militarized Prostitution."

55. Kamala Kempadoo and Jo Doezema, *Global Sex Workers: Rights, Resistance, and Redefinition* (New York: Routledge, 1994).

56. Suh, "Militarized Prostitution."

57. Normal Stoltz Chinchilla and Nora Hamilton, "Doing Business: Central American Enterprises in Los Angeles," in López-Garza and Díaz, *Asian and Latino Immigrants in a Restructuring Economy,* 188–214; Clair M. Weber, "Latino Street Vendors in Los Angeles," in López-Garza and Díaz, *Asian and Latino Immigrants in a Restructuring Economy,* 217–240.

58. Kathleen Staudt, *Free Trade? Informal Economies on the U.S.-Mexico Border* (Philadelphia: Temple University Press, 1997).

59. Peri Fletcher, *La Casa de Mis Sueños: Dreams of a Home in a Transnational Mexican Community* (Boulder: Westview, 1999).

60. Amy Waldman, "More 'Can I Help You?' Jobs Migrate from U.S. to India," *New York Times,* May 11, 2003, International Section, 4.

61. Debbie Nathan, "Sweating out the Words," *Nation,* February 21, 2000, 27–28.

62. Mary Jordan and Kevin Sullivan, "Very Little Trickles Down: Free Trade Has Failed to Lift Mexicans out of Poverty," *Washington Post National Weekly Edition,* March 30–April 6, 2004, 15; Amy Waldman, "Low-Tech or High, Jobs Are Scarce in India's Boom," *New York Times,* May 6, 2004, A3.

Power Plays
Six Ways the Male Corporate Elite Keeps Women Out

Martha Burk (2005)

Males, much more so than females, are conditioned almost from birth to view the world in terms of hierarchies, power relationships, and being winners.

In the business world, many symbols of power are built into the system, like merit badges in the Boy Scouts. In the early days of a career, power could get you an office with a window, later the corner office or the reserved parking space. As the career progresses, the badges change; they're now the high-priced car, the $2,000 suit, the right club membership, fatter cigars, better brandy, the bigger expense account, and blonder, younger, thinner women. At the CEO level, corporate jets, unlimited expense accounts, a phalanx of "yes men," and obscenely high salaries and stock options are the norm.

So how can your average billionaire CEO dealmaker wring one more shred of superiority and one-upmanship out of this situation? He gets something money can't buy—such as belonging to a golf club that is so exclusive you can't apply for membership. And once you've got this thing, boy, are you reluctant to give it up.

When groups achieve a certain level of power and influence, sometimes their original purpose is subverted in favor of holding on to the status and the exclusivity that the group has achieved. Within that particular sphere, they are a *power elite*. And if the power sphere happens to be business related and male dominated, that's where the problem comes in for working women.

The power dynamic manifests itself in a number of ways:

Power re-creates itself in its own image. Psychologists have long known that we're most comfortable with people who are like us, both in appearance and ways of thinking. It has been well documented that managers like to hire people who look like themselves. In most of corporate America, that still means white and male. That's why laws against employment discrimination were passed in the first place—women and minority men just weren't on the radar screens of the folks doing the hiring and promoting. The so-called neutral processes in corporations were firmly enforcing a white-male quota system. That is still true—most companies have "diversity" in management only to the extent that it does not threaten the traditional balance.

Despite claims by some that women and minority men have taken all the jobs, the results of this recreation process are fairly easy to see, even from casual observation. The numbers speak for themselves—and the higher you go in the hierarchy, the greater the enforcement of traditional quotas in favor of the dominant group. In most companies, there will be a fair number of women and minority men in the rank and file, fewer at lower management, and still fewer at middle management. At the very top level of the Fortune 500, there are only nine female CEOs. Even in companies like Citigroup, where *women* are a 56 percent majority overall, *men* hold 56 percent of the "officials and managers" jobs. There is only one female top executive. She is paid 50 percent of the average for men at her level.

Power elites enforce norms and systems that guarantee continued power. At the highest levels of business, the board of directors is a major enforcer of the status quo—in both its own makeup and that of the top management of the company.

Consider what happens when an individual is chosen to be on a corporate board for the first time. He (or in rare cases, she) is usually nominated by the CEO or someone already on the board, and brought into a new environment with its own culture and skill set. The nominator has an interest in seeing this individual succeed, as it will reflect well on his judgment and business acumen. The newcomer, at the same time, wants to belong, wants to overcome any notion that he is unworthy or an impostor. So the new member is "trained" through mentoring and role modeling, quickly picking up on the board culture and the behavior and knowledge necessary to succeed.

It is not hard for the new individual to figure out what is expected. Boat rockers don't last as board members. So for a person in the minority (a woman or a man of color) there is actually a disincentive to advocate bringing others like herself into the circle, as she is likely to be accused of "pushing an agenda" and not behaving like a "team player."

Power creates a sense of entitlement. Most men at some level know that maleness is valued over femaleness in the culture, and we are all taught in subtle ways that males have first claim on jobs, sports, and opportunities. (Women of color are the first to admit their brothers are sexist, too.) But for the ordinary man, the cultural valuation of all things male does not translate into the sense of super-entitlement that corporate power elites exhibit. That comes from a corporate system where value is placed on its leaders that is far out of proportion to their actual worth.

Consider CEO pay. In 2003 the average CEO pay in large companies was more than 300 times that of the average worker (up from 42-to-1 in 1982). The rise in compensation for the top dogs outstripped rises in inflation, profits, and the S&P 500. Conservative journalist Robert Samuelson had this to say: "The scandal of CEO pay is not that it ascended to stratospheric levels . . . [but that] so few CEOs have publicly raised their voices in criticism or rebuke. . . . [T]here's a widespread self-serving silence. If they can't defend what they're doing, then maybe what they're doing is indefensible."

These words could as easily have applied to the controversy over membership in Augusta National Golf Club. CEOs did not raise their voices against the club's exclusion of women; there was a conspiracy of self-serving silence. It was obvious they believed themselves exempt from society's standards against discrimination, immune to criticism from the public or discipline from their companies, even in the face of employee unrest and questions at stockholder meetings.

Power creates invulnerability, leading to a flaunting of society's standards. As individuals become more powerful, they are increasingly surrounded by others whose job they control and who tell them how clever, smart, and right they are. Power elites are also increasingly insulated from the sanctions that ordinary people are subject to when they misbehave. In fact, breaking the rules to get where you are is excused as nothing more than hard-nosed business, shrewd politics, or the result of occupational pressure.

We've seen this again and again as sports and entertainment figures get a pass on cocaine possession or beating up their girlfriends, politicians get a pass on dallying with interns or taking "contributions" that result in big government contracts, and executives who lose billions and squander the retirements of thousands of workers get a slap on the wrist as they jump out of harm's way with the aid of their "golden parachutes."

Loyalty to power overshadows other loyalties, including gender and race. Statistics show that when it comes to income, black men gain more from being male than they lose from being black, particularly at high levels. It is also well known in business that after women reach a certain level, they are less likely to want to help other women advance. Two dynamics are likely at work here. As association with a certain group conveys more power, individuals begin to identify more with that group and less with other groups to which they belong. They also seek personal validation by the power group (almost everyone feels like an impostor at some level—women more so than men). In the business world this means behaving like the others. Holding on to the power—and gaining more of it—inevitably becomes more important than loyalty to what is now a less important group. Since the power group in corporate America is still overwhelmingly male and white, the less important group in the woman executive's case is other women.

In the majority male's case, however, the power group aligns perfectly with his race and gender group. So these loyalties, far from being lessened, are actually reinforced. He doesn't have to make a choice between his race and/or gender group and the power elite—he doesn't even have to think about it. When he promotes a member of his group up the executive ranks, or proposes a new board member who is not only like him but like the majority, he is never accused of "pushing an agenda." His candidate's credentials are never questioned because the nomination may be the result of a "special interest" mentality. In fact, it's the opposite; his nomination is seen as merely "normal." So not only is his choice reinforced, but also *his entitlement to make that particular choice.*

Group loyalty combined with power can trump good judgment and override individual moral codes. All Americans, male and female, are inculcated with a strong value for loyalty to one's group. In the great majority of cases, group loyalty is a good thing. It fosters team spirit for athletics, cohesiveness in military units, productivity in business, and dedication to the public good in community service organizations. But most of us know "loyalty" is perverted when it serves a purpose counter to society's values. While we might stay in a group even if it occasionally took a stand we disagreed with, we wouldn't remain if the group stood for something society condemns (like discrimination) or if it conspired to break the law.

At the extremes, group loyalty can go terribly wrong. It can facilitate lawlessness under the cover of secrecy and lead to group actions and cover-ups of those actions that group members would never consider as individuals. Examples can range from illegal accounting schemes to harmful and sometimes fatal hazing by fraternity brothers, to gang rapes (too often by athletic team members), military atrocities, and terrorism. It is probably no accident that most of the excesses occur in male-dominated or exclusively male groups.

Obviously the average man does not participate in illegal, immoral, or harmful group actions. But the average man (much more so than the average woman) has been exposed, again and again, to the code of loyalty to a group that can lead to actions that are not in his best interests, nor in the best interests of society. It's about living in a culture that links masculinity to power, dominance and control. In everyday life it might never affect most, because they're not faced with the stark choice of taking a stand and doing what's right versus betraying an unspoken loyalty oath to the "brotherhood of men."

Women encounter these situations, too—it's just that they have not been conditioned to group allegiance in the same way, or to the same degree, that men have. It is also very rare that we hear of group actions by women that are comparable to fraternity hazings or gang rapes. But not necessarily because women are genetically predisposed to being kinder and gentler human beings, as many would argue. If women had had the same power, status, and conditioning that men have had over the centuries, we might see parallels in female group behavior. But these "antecedent conditions" have not existed historically, and they still don't exist, even in the most advanced societies. So we'll have to leave the genetic arguments to another planet or to another 10 millennia in the future.

The Women's Movement Against Sexual Harassment

Carrie N. Baker (2008)

Despite continuing struggles, the history of the movement against sexual harassment is in many ways an incredible success story. The movement against sexual harassment emerged at the intersection of multiple social movements percolating in American society in the 1970s—the women's movements, the civil rights movement, the labor movement, the gay and lesbian rights movement, and the sexual revolution. The sexual revolution brought about changes in sexual morality and behavior, ushering in more open and positive attitudes toward sex. But as the sexual revolution articulated the right to engage in sex, the antirape movement asserted women's right to say no to sex and, along with the battered women's movement, asserted women's right to be free from physical violence. The women's health movement, including the reproductive rights movement, articulated women's right to control their bodies—for women to understand their health and be able to make decisions regarding medical care, including childbearing decisions. The women's movement protested the sexual objectification and exploitation of women and the lesbian rights movement supported women's sexual autonomy by asserting the right of women to choose other women as sexual and life partners. More generally, the women's and civil rights movements promised equal employment opportunity, without regard to sex or race. These movements offered women hopes of economic independence and sexual autonomy.

But the reality of sexual coercion in the workplace cut to the heart of these hopes. Sexual harassment denied women sexual autonomy, threatened their physical safety and integrity, deprived them of employment opportunities and, for women of color, was often a form of racism. At a time when women heavily populated the lower rungs of the workforce, but many aspired to work their way up, sexual harassment was a particularly personal and insulting form of discrimination. Not only were women not taken seriously as workers, but they were treated as sexual objects. The issue of sexual coercion in the workplace was first raised by lesbian feminists and African-American women working in the civil rights movement, but quickly spread to women in a range of contexts, including nontraditional occupations and educational institutions. The strength of the movement was how this diverse group of women was able to work in coalition across differences to achieve major social change in American society. With roots in the civil rights movement, the women's movements, and the labor movement, activists against sexual harassment drew upon the ideologies, strategies, and constituencies of these movements in varied ways to articulate their experiences of sexual harassment and combat this behavior in a broad range of contexts. This diverse and committed group of grassroots activists succeeded in raising awareness of sexual harassment and shaping laws that addressed sexual harassment not only in the office, but in coal mines, on construction sites, in factories, and at educational institutions.

The movement against sexual harassment was shaped by the political opportunities, mobilizing structures, and framing processes employed by movement participants. The movement took advantage of the growing institutional structure created by governments in response to the civil rights and women's movements, particularly the agencies developed to enforce the equal opportunity laws. As a result of the civil rights and women's movements, the nation had an expanding system of federal and state equal employment opportunity offices, civil rights agencies, human rights commissions, and commissions on the status of women. These agencies and commissions were committed to advancing civil rights, equality, and employment opportunity in the United States. Activists against sexual harassment used this new institutional structure to articulate their grievances about sexual harassment. Women also took advantage of elite allies in government—the progressive judicial and executive agency appointments of presidents Johnson, Kennedy, and Carter. Judges Richey and Robinson, Commissioner Norton, and other importantly positioned government officials advanced the movement's agenda. Despite these political opportunities, the movement was constrained by its limited ability to achieve legislative change because of its lack of lobbying capacity and influence on political parties.

The movement also took advantage of the "expanding cultural opportunities" that increased the likelihood of movement activity.[1] The movement emerged out of the glaring contradiction between a "highly salient cultural value"—equal employment opportunity—and conventional social practices—sexual coercion and harassment of women in the workplace. In a relatively short period of time, women across the country were raising grievances about sexual harassment and these "suddenly imposed grievances" were confirmed as a widespread phenomena through surveys and studies, which dramatized the vulnerability or even illegitimacy of the system by calling into question the meritocracy of the workplace and the court's enforcement of equal employment opportunity in the American workplace. The movement created an innovative "master frame" for sexual harassment—the Title VII sexual harassment claim—within which subsequent challengers could map their own grievances and demands.

The movement was also shaped by the mobilizing structures through which activists sought to organize. Mobilizing structures are "the collective vehicles, informal as well as formal, through which people mobilize and engage in collective action."[2] The movement drew upon the resources of other social movements of the day. The civil rights movement, the women's movements, and the labor movement provided key mobilizing structures and resources through which activists organized the movement against sexual harassment. Through formal organizational structures and informal networks of these broader movements, sexual harassment activists were able to generate collective action. Multiple locations, including the workplace, employment associations, unions, and schools were grassroots settings from which the movement facilitated collective action. They created their own organizations . . . but also used existing organizations at the national, state, and local levels to further their cause. . . . They worked through organizations of the women's movement, but also organizations of other social movements of the day, such as the Mexican American Legal Defense Fund and unions. They also applied for grants from organizations such as the Ford Foundation, Ms. Foundation, and federal granting agencies for research grants. Using this wide range of resources, they were able to mobilize women from diverse constituencies to work together within the movement against sexual harassment.

The third important factor that shaped the movement against sexual harassment was the framing processes—"the collective processes of interpretation, attribution, and social construction that mediate between opportunity and action."[3] Frames help define a problem and suggest actions to remedy the problem. For a social movement to arise, people must feel "both aggrieved about some aspect of their lives and optimistic that, acting collectively, they can redress the problem."[4] . . . [T]he movement against sexual harassment drew heavily upon ideas of the women's and civil rights movements to frame the issue of sexual harassment as a gendered phenomenon that violated women's civil rights. By highlighting the contradiction between the principle of sex equality and women's experience of sexual coercion in the workplace, activists were able to challenge prevailing understandings of sexual coercion in the workplace as a private problem and recast this behavior as a barrier to equal opportunity for women.[5] Drawing on the rhetoric of the civil rights and women's movements, activists invoked the powerful ideology of human equality and equal opportunity as well as sexual autonomy and bodily integrity to argue that sexual harassment was a basic violation of women's economic and physical well-being. By coining the term "sexual harassment" and characterizing it as a violation of equal employment opportunity, the movement offered "cognitive liberation"[6] from the indignities women suffered in the workplace as well as an avenue for action to address these violations. Movement participants fashioned a shared understanding that sexual coercion in the workplace was a violation of Title VII, thereby legitimating and motivating collective action. Activists framed the issue of sexual harassment dramatically as "economic rape" and as a manifestation of male domination in the workplace and society at large. Activists invoked radical feminist theory to argue that sexual harassment was a manifestation of male domination, antiracist theory to analyze the racist manifestations and causes of sexual harassment, and socialist analysis to understand the class-based implications of the behavior. Activists effectively used the media to communicate their understanding of the issue and bring more people into the movement.

The strength of the movement against sexual harassment stemmed from its racial and economic diversity. Women of color were critical contributors to the movement against sexual harassment, acting both individually and collectively to combat sexual coercion on the job and at educational institutions. African-American women brought most of the early precedent-setting sexual harassment cases, including the first successful Title VII cases in the federal district court (Diane Williams), the federal courts of appeals (Paulette Barnes), and the Supreme Court (Mechelle Vinson), and the first successful cases involving a student (Pamela Price), co-worker harassment (Willie Ruth Hawkins), and hostile environment harassment at the federal appellate level (Sandra Bundy). Plaintiffs in three of the first six published sexual harassment cases were

young African-American women (Diane Williams, Paulette Barnes, and Margaret Miller). The case of another African-American woman (Maxine Munford) inspired one of the early statewide campaigns to address the issue of sexual harassment, leading to the passage in 1980 of one of the first and most progressive state laws against sexual harassment. The significance of these cases was that they established the movement's framework by successfully articulating sexual harassment as discrimination based on sex and as a violation of women's civil rights under Titles VII and IX. This framework focused liability on employers rather than harassers—a more systemic approach that had a wider impact by encouraging institutions to take preventative action against sexual harassment.

African-American women's identities and backgrounds were significant in how they experienced sexual harassment, how they articulated the issue, and the methods they used to seek relief. Several of the women had experience with race discrimination or had experience in the civil rights movement, and hence had some knowledge of the mechanisms for relief from discrimination. Two of the plaintiffs in early precedent-setting sexual harassment cases—Diane Williams and Paulette Barnes—were African-American women who worked in government agencies established to combat race discrimination, so they had an understanding of civil rights concepts and processes. They felt a great sense of indignation at being sexually harassed by people who were supposed to be fighting discrimination. Both Williams and Barnes obtained counsel through LCCRUL, a private organization in Washington, D.C. that provided free counsel in civil rights cases and made referrals to cooperating attorneys who handled cases on a *pro bono* or contingency basis. The white male attorneys who represented Williams and Barnes—Warwick Furr and Michael Hausfeld—both had backgrounds in civil rights law. Sandra Bundy, who brought the first successful hostile environment sexual harassment case in the federal appellate courts, had a long history of participation in the civil rights movement in the 1960s. She had attended marches and demonstrations and had helped to organize a union that worked to end racial segregation in the workplace. Both Williams and Bundy spoke out about the issue in the media and testified at federal hearings on sexual harassment. Finally, Chilean exile Ximena Bunster's case at Clark University spurred the growing trend of educational institutions to adopt sexual harassment policies. Anita Hill brought the issue to the attention of the mainstream public when she testified against Clarence Thomas before Congress.

. . .

Many have commented on the prominent role African-American women have played in the development of sexual harassment law. About the prevalence of African-American women among early sexual harassment plaintiffs, Eleanor Holmes Norton has said, "With black women's historic understanding of slavery and rape, it is not surprising to me."[7] Judy Trent Ellis, the first African-American professor of law at SUNY Buffalo, has argued that African-American women's activism in protecting themselves against sexual harassment was probably due both to the greater or more severe harassment visited upon them and their long familiarity with discrimination and willingness to seek redress through the courts. Ellis has argued that African-American women were extremely vulnerable to sexual harassment because of their unique position in American history and mythology. First, the history of slavery still marked African-American women as sexually available, sexually promiscuous, and unprotected by African-American men. Second, African-American women's history of slavery and oppression created conditions of extreme economic vulnerability for them.[8]

Similarly, law professor Kimberlé Crenshaw has argued that the disproportionate representation of African-American women plaintiffs in early cases was perhaps due to the "racialization of sexual harassment"—"a merging of racist myths with their vulnerability as women." Crenshaw argued, "Racism may well provide the clarity to see that sexual harassment is neither a flattering gesture nor a misguided social overture but an act of intentional discrimination that is insulting, threatening, and debilitating."[9] Others have argued

that African-American women were less likely than white women to view sexual harassment as a personal problem "because sexual exploitation had been integral to racial oppression in this country."[10] The author of a 1981 article in *Essence* magazine, Yla Eason, argued that African-American women were "sensitized to discriminatory acts on the job and thus more aware of and less conditioned to abiding by them."[11]

. . .

[These women] used their backgrounds in the women's movement to understand sexual harassment and organize against it. They applied feminist theory on rape to understand sexual harassment as a form of sexual coercion. They applied socialist feminist understandings of the interaction of capitalism, racism, and patriarchy to understand women's vulnerability to sexual harassment. They applied feminist legal theory to develop remedies for sexual harassment. In addition to feminist theory, they used strategies and techniques from the women's movements, such as holding speak-outs, writing press releases, publishing newsletters, and developing myth/fact sheets. They used their education to articulate the experience of sexual harassment and promote public awareness of the issue through the media. They had all attended college, and several had attended graduate school. With this educational background, they were able to conduct surveys, develop a theoretical analysis of sexual harassment, and write and publish articles on the issue. . . .

The third leg of the movement against sexual harassment was the activism of women working in male-dominated fields. As women began to break into nontraditional blue-collar occupations in the late 1970s, many experienced tremendous hostility from men who resented women's encroachment upon traditionally masculine spheres of activity. Blue-collar women experienced harassment not only from supervisors but also from co-workers, in forms sometimes sexual, but also often misogynist and violent, including physical assault and work sabotage. Drawing upon the resources of unions and working women's organizations, blue-collar women organized against sexual harassment. They contributed to the movement by broadening the public understandings of sexual harassment to include not just *quid pro quo* harassment but also hostile environment harassment.

Blue-collar women brought several of the early precedent-setting sexual harassment cases. Phyllis Brown, a civilian police dispatcher, won the first successful hostile environment claim under Title VII in May of 1980. Factory worker Willie Ruth Hawkins won the first successful co-worker harassment case in July of 1980. Barbara Henson, also a police dispatcher, brought the precedent-setting hostile environment sexual harassment case, *Henson v. City of Dundee,* decided by the Eleventh Circuit in 1982. In the late 1970s and early 1980s, women working in a broad range of blue-collar occupations filed claims for sexual harassment, including janitors, security guards, police officers, and assembly-line workers. In addition, women in traditionally male occupations, such as construction and coal mining, brought sex discrimination lawsuits including allegations of sexual harassment. In response to a 1976 lawsuits brought by female construction workers, the DOL issued the first federal regulations on harassment in the workplace in 1978. Several organizations representing female construction workers participated in the lawsuit and in the process leading to the adoption of the federal regulations, including Advocates for Women in San Francisco, Women in Trades in Seattle, United Trade Workers Association in Tacoma, Washington, Wider Opportunities for Women and Women Working in Construction, both based in Washington, D.C., and the Coalition of Labor Union Women. In 1978, women coal miners brought a suit against Consolidated Coal Company of Pittsburgh, the largest coal company in the United States, leading to a federal investigation of the entire coal mining industry and resulting in an out-of-court settlement that called for hiring quotas, back pay, and affirmative programs to protect female miners from discrimination and harassment underground.

Blue-collar women and organizations representing them not only brought lawsuits to protest sexual harassment but also were extensively involved in raising awareness about sexual harassment.

Jean McPheeters, a letter carrier, served as chair of Working Women United, which included many blue-collar women. In New York City, the Clearinghouse on Blue Collar Women of Women for Racial and Economic Equality surveyed blue-collar women about sexual harassment in 1978, and the CEP later surveyed female coal miners about their experiences of harassment. Blue-collar women won attention to the issue of sexual harassment through media coverage of their cases, which often involved extreme violence and clear discriminatory intent. For example, sexual harassment of female coal miners was covered extensively in the press in the early 1980s. This coverage provided a very sympathetic case to convince people that men used sexual harassment to keep women out of the workplace.

Female union members also worked on the issue of sexual harassment. . . . Women and men in unions around the country supported victims of sexual harassment and worked to raise awareness of the issue by surveying union members, publishing and distributing information on harassment, providing educational programs, and fighting for clauses against sexual harassment in union contracts. Women's activism within the United Mine Workers of American led in 1979 to President Arnold Miller making a public commitment to eradicating sexual harassment in the mines.

. . .

The grassroots diversity of the movement against sexual harassment led to strong, broad-based public policy against sexual harassment. The movement's diffuse participants—individuals, organizations, and informal groups—arose from multiple locations, but intersected at critical junctures, before Congress and the Supreme Court. With the perspectives of differing constituencies represented in the political discourse around sexual harassment, public policy developed in such a way as to incorporate the experiences of a diverse array of women working in a wide range of contexts, including white- and blue-collar work settings and educational institutions. This activism came together in the sexual harassment lawsuits filed around the country in the 1970s and early 1980s.

...

Prohibitions on sexual harassment led to sexual harassment training in workplaces across the country, raising the issue with thousands people in a broad range of occupations. These training workshops provided a forum to discuss women's status in the workplace, gender roles, and sexual stereotypes. In this training, women's right to participate in the workplace on an equal footing with men was assumed, challenging traditional and persisting notions that women were not serious participants in the workplace. By the 1990s, most employers had policies against harassment, and many offered training to sensitize workers. Women were challenging sexual harassment across the country in a broad range of occupations and sometimes even winning large verdicts in sexual harassment cases. Through these successes, the movement had come a long way in achieving [its] goal of claiming the right of women to enter the public sphere, both political spaces as well as workplaces and schools. The movement achieved social change not only by achieving legal changes through court houses and legislatures, but also by achieving cultural changes in workplaces and educational institutions. The movement raised consciousness about women's right to enter the workplace and function there free from sexual coercion and molestation. Women are no longer outsiders or interlopers, but have a central place in these institutions, a shift for which the movement against sexual harassment deserves significant credit.

This success, however, is tempered by the continuing high rates of sexual harassment and the persisting stereotypes used against women who resist harassment. Rates of sexual harassment are similar to what they were twenty-five years ago when reliable studies of the phenomenon first appeared.[12] The public/private sphere ideology that historically justified and reinforced male dominance and that undergirded courts' early denials of sexual harassment claims continues to shape public discussion of sexual harassment.[13] The issue is often still seen as a matter of private sexual conduct, not abuse of power. Longstanding stereotypes blaming women for sexual harassment or accusing them of lying about it, existing from the earliest days of this country's history, still plague women who bring accusations of sexual harassment. According to political science professor Gwendolyn Mink, women complaining of sexual harassment face a "regime of disbelief."[14] Powerful biases against women continue to shape public opinion and court opinions on sexual harassment.

Furthermore, the conceptualization of sexual harassment primarily as a legal claim, in particular a claim of sex discrimination, placed the issue squarely within a highly contentious adversarial framework that has often not led to satisfactory solutions to the problem, especially for women who do not have the resources to use the legal system. The bureaucratic and legalistic procedures for addressing sexual harassment are often slow, costly, and contentious, and women have often felt victimized again by these processes. Although employers are providing training on sexual harassment, many are motivated more out of concerns for liability rather than integration of women into the workplace. Workers often resent the threat of lawsuits and the close oversight of employers seeking to avoid liability. The framing of the issue as a legal question narrowed the strategic options available to women resisting sexual coercion in the workplace, leaving many women without recourse.

Early feminist activists did not achieve their larger goal of undermining the system of dominance that produced sexual harassment. [They] had viewed sexual harassment as part of a larger struggle against sexism, classism, and racism and they understood sexual harassment to be symptomatic of a deeply flawed patriarchal, capitalist, racist system. They hoped to use the issue to inspire collective action to fight the root causes of injustice and transform society. In arguing that sexual harassment was sex discrimination, they conceptualized sexual harassment as a group harm. They argued that sexual harassment harmed not just individual women but women as a class by reinforcing sex segregation and subordination of women in the workforce. By focusing on employer liability for sexual harassment, feminists attempted to address this harm to women.

Despite this approach, individualized solutions to sexual harassment came to dominate the movement's agenda. As has been true in other areas, the legal remedies were a valuable tool for individuals seeking relief from sexual harassment, but they undermined collective efforts that might have led to deeper societal transformation and reached the root causes of sexual harassment in society.[15] Despite feminist hopes to challenge broader injustices in America, liberal legal gains eclipsed these radical hopes in the 1980s. The movement against sexual harassment shifted away from collective protest and toward individual legal solutions to sexual harassment. Although legal solutions have offered much, and the recent possibility of class action suits is promising, they have left in place the basic societal structure that allows sexual harassment to continue. As Joan Hoff has argued, the Supreme Court's 1986 decision in *Meritor Savings Bank v. Vinson* was a "bright legal light on the gender horizon" but that this decision "did not have any redistributive or fundamentally unsettling economic or moral impact on American society."[16]

Nevertheless, the movement was a powerful step toward claiming the right of women to enter the public sphere, both political spaces as well as workplaces. Women have growing economic power—some have risen from the lowest rungs of the American workplace—but they rarely achieve the highest rungs, the workplace is still highly segregated, the wage gap persists, and women still experience high rates of sexual harassment. And although sexual harassment law has provided some protection for women in the workplace, the sexual objectification of women in the broader culture has increased significantly and is being increasingly internalized by girls and women.[17] The issue of sexual harassment is often degendered and, in practice, is often disconnected from the feminist analysis of systems of privilege, domination, and oppression so that the underlying power relationships remain obscured.[18] The challenge is to reanalyze sexual harassment in the context of interlocking systems of oppression, to regender the issue by analyzing the ways American culture still embraces hegemonic discourses of male sexual dominance, and to challenge that discourse collectively both inside and outside the workplace. Remembering the origins of the movement against sexual harassment and understanding the theories and tactics of the movement's founders will help us to meet this challenge today.

NOTES

1. McAdam, McCarthy, and Zald, *Comparative Perspectives,* 25.
2. Ibid.
3. Ibid. at 2.
4. Ibid. at 5.
5. Lacking the information and perspective that others afford, isolated individuals would seem especially likely to explain their troubles on the basis of personal rather than system attributions. The movement provided "system attributions" that afforded the necessary rationale for resistance. Ibid. at 9.
6. Ibid.
7. Susan Brownmiller and Delores Alexander, "How We Got From Here: From Carmita Wood to Anita Hill," *Ms.,* January/February 1992, 71.
8. Ellis, "Sexual Harassment and Race."
9. Kimberlé Crenshaw, "Race, Gender, and Sexual Harassment," *Southern California Law Review* 65 (1992): 1467, 1469–70; Crenshaw, "Mapping the Margins," 93–118.
10. John Beckwith and Barbara Beckwith, "Sexual Harassment: Your Body or Your Job," *Science for the People* (July/August 1980): 6.
11. Yla Eason, "When Your Boss Wants Sex," *Essence,* March 1981, 82. Eason also argued that, as the last hired and the first fired, African-American women have the least to lose, noting that the most oppressed people tended to be in the forefront of civil uprisings.
12. The Merit System Protection Board studies on sexual harassment in 1981, 1988, and 1995 produced similar rates of sexual harassment. Merit Systems Protection Board, *Sexual Harassment in the Federal Workplace: Is It A Problem;* Merit System Protection Board, *Sexual Harassment of Federal Workers: An Update;* Merit System Protection Board, *Sexual Harassment in the Federal Workplace: Trends, Progress, Continuing Challenges* (Washington, D.C.: Government Printing Office, 1995). Rates of sexual harassment at educational institutions remain high also.

Michelle L. Kelley and Beth Parsons, "Sexual Harassment in the 1990s: A University-Wide Survey of Faculty, Administrators, Staff, and Students," *Journal of Higher Education 71* (2000): 548–69 (between 19% and 43% of females at Ohio State University reported sexual harassment). Despite these high rates of harassment Freada Klein believes that sexual harassment is generally not as egregious today it was in the 1970s. Klein, telephone interview, 26 March 2001.

13. Mary F. Rogers, "Clarence Thomas, Patriarchal Discourse and Public/Private Spheres," *Sociological Quarterly 39* (1998): 289–308 (describing how Thomas used arguments about privacy to avoid inquiries into whether he sexually harassed Anita Hill). Bill Clinton did the same thing. Both men also attributed political motives to their accusers.

14. Mink, *Hostile Environment, 77*, 115.

15. See, for example, Geoghegan, *Which Side Are You On?*.

16. Hoff, *Law, Gender, and Injustice,* 255. She noted that the treatment of the female employee in *Meritor* was so blatant that it would be difficult to apply to "'normal,' on-the-job examples of gender-biased harassment of female employees in the workplace." Ibid., 258–59.

17. Pamela Paul, *Pornified: How Pornography is Transforming Our Lives, Our Relationships, and Our Families* (New York: Times Books, 2005); Ariel Levy, *Female Chauvinist Pigs: Women and the Rise of Raunch Culture* (New York: Free Press, 2005).

18. Nan Stein, "Bullying or Sexual Harassment? The Missing Discourse of Rights in an Era of Zero Tolerance," *Arizona Law Review* 45 (Fall 2003): 783–99; James E. Gruber and Phoebe Morgan, eds., *In the Company of Men: Male Dominance and Sexual Harassment* (Boston: Northeastern University Press, 2005), x.

R E A D I N G **65**

Prostitution, Humanism, and a Woman's Choice

Kimberly Klinger (2003)

Driving home in the early morning hours after a night out in Washington, D.C., I turn from 14th to L Street near downtown. I'm only on the street for a block before I hit the clogged artery of Massachusetts Avenue, and this particular area seems devoid of important business or commerce. Except for the prostitutes.

Almost every weekend night I can spot women walking up and down the street—sometimes between the cars and quite near to my own. They're stereotypically wearing the tiniest slivers of fabric masquerading as dresses, swishing their hips as they teeter on high heels. I don't recall ever seeing any possible pimps nearby and wonder if these women operate independently. I wonder about a lot of things, actually. Are they happy? Are they safe? Are they making good money? Are they feminists?

That last question may seem incongruous, but to me it's relevant. As a third wave feminist, I find sex and sex work to be important issues—ones which are being addressed in ways unheard of by our foremothers. We third wavers are, in many cases, the lip-gloss wearing, *BUST* magazine reading, pro-sex women of the new millennium. We have taken the liberties of the second wave and run with them, demanding even more freedom as we struggle to find our new identities in the ever-dominating patriarchy. We don't hold consciousness-raising sessions; we hold safe-sex fairs. We still march on Washington, but we have punk rock bands helping us to raise the funds to get there. We're more multicultural and diverse, yet we continue to fight the white face— the opinion that feminism is a white women's movement—put upon us by the media.

We've also had to fight the awful stereotype that feminists are frigid, man-hating, anti-sex zealots. The second wave made incredible changes in how the United States deals with rape and domestic violence, and while we still have a long way to go, these issues are at least taken much more seriously. However, in the process, feminists have been labeled and demonized, thus creating a huge chasm between sexuality and feminism. Women are still the same sexual beings they always were, but to outsiders they have been considered strictly buzz-kills (no fun) or—gasp—lesbians. In 1983 Andrea Dworkin and Catharine A. MacKinnon wrote major antipornography bills that negatively labeled feminists as anti-sex instead of pro–human rights.

In the third wave, pornography, sex, and prostitution aren't presented as black and white issues. For instance, pornography isn't simply seen as degrading sexual imagery made by men, for men. There are female filmmakers and feminist porn stars who want to reclaim their right to enjoy sexual images without violence and negativity. Sex is more widely discussed than ever and taboos are being broken every day. The third wave hopes to expand definitions of sexuality. For women to be liberated sexually, they must be able to live as they choose, to break out of narrow ideas of sexuality, to be sexual and still be respected, and essentially to be whole. Feminism and sex work aren't therefore mutually exclusive. Choice is key here—women need to have the right and freedom to choose how to live their lives as sexual beings. This includes prostitution.

Prostitution. The word normally calls to mind women down on their luck, pitied cases who walk the streets at night with little protection or rights—essentially women who have no other choice. And unfortunately this often isn't far from the truth. In the United States and worldwide, many women turn to or are forced into sexual prostitution because they have limited options. But there are other situations, even in the United States, where women turn to this profession and other sex work because they want to. They are fortunate to have real choices and select this path because it suits them, while practicing prostitution safely and respectfully.

In the United States it is possible to find a number of organizations of sex workers who defend each other, work alongside international groups to decriminalize prostitution and protect prostitutes, and share the common experiences of choosing and enjoying this form of labor. There are advocacy and rights organizations, international conferences, and famous porn stars who all regard prostitution and other sex work as just that: a job and a way to earn a living. They argue that it should be treated as such—protected under the law with safety guidelines, unions, networks, and all the rest. Furthermore, taking a third wave feminist view, they maintain that women need to have the right and freedom to choose how to live their lives as sexual beings, including taking up "the world's oldest profession."

No matter what wave of feminism is applied, all feminists agree that forced, coerced, poverty-based, trafficked, and unprotected prostitution should be opposed. In countries where prostitution is illegal, such as in forty-nine of fifty states in the United States, women have no protection, socially or legally. The situation is messy at best and, at worst, violent, dangerous, and all but devoid of human rights. For example, most American prostitutes have to work for pimps or out of brothels, never seeing much of the money they have earned. If they are streetwalkers they live in fear of criminal assault or arrest—and in some cases, sexual abuse by police. They may be forced to deal with customers they are afraid of or who harm them. If they are raped, police will generally disregard their suffering, not even considering what in any other profession would be recognized as criminal assault and the forced rendering of service without pay. Beyond that, the victimized woman may even be arrested for practicing prostitution. The situation is even worse in poor countries where it is all too common for young girls to be forced into prostitution and where men from wealthier nations travel specifically to have sex with them.

Second wave feminist author MacKinnon has essentially deemed prostitution sexual slavery, arguing that the relevant laws immensely harm women, classifying them as criminals and denying them their basic civil rights. MacKinnon admits in an essay, "Prostitution and Civil

Rights," published in the *Michigan Journal of Gender and Law* (1993, 13:1) that she isn't sure about what to do legally concerning prostitution but that international initiatives and policy responses can help to put the power back in women's hands where it belongs. Does this mean all prostitution would disappear if women had their say? Not if the numerous prostitute rights groups and their sympathizers are any indication.

For many who have thought about this question, dismissing the entire sex industry as abusive and immoral only exacerbates existing problems and tosses the concerns of sex workers aside. Therefore many feminists, civil rights workers, and human rights activists argue for the decriminalization—not necessarily the legalization—of prostitution. Internationally, conferences are held that address decriminalization. The World Charter for Prostitutes Rights is one outcome. Created in 1985 this document is a template used by human rights groups all over the world—it makes certain basic demands abundantly clear:

1. Decriminalize all aspects of adult prostitution resulting from individual decision. This includes regulation of third parties (business managers) according to standard business codes.
2. Strongly enforce all laws against fraud, coercion, violence, child sexual abuse, child labor, rape, and racism everywhere and across national boundaries, whether or not in the context of prostitution.
3. Guarantee prostitutes all human rights and civil liberties, including the freedom of speech, travel, immigration, work, marriage, and motherhood and the right to unemployment insurance, health insurance, and housing.
4. Ensure that prostitutes' rights are protected.
5. Allow prostitutes to unionize.

Decriminalization essentially means the removal of laws against this and other forms of sex work. The Prostitutes Education Network clarifies that decriminalization is usually used to refer to total decriminalization—that is, the repeal of all

laws against consensual adult sexual activity in both commercial and noncommercial contexts. This allows the individual prostitute to choose whether or not she is managed and protects her from fraud, abuse, and coercion.

By contrast the term *legalization* usually refers to a system of governmental regulation of prostitutes wherein prostitutes are licensed and required to work in specific ways. When Jesse Ventura was running for the Minnesota governorship in 1998, he proposed that Minnesotans should consider legalizing prostitution in order to have governmental control and keep it out of residential areas. This is the practice in Nevada, the only state in the United States where brothels are legal. Although legalization can also imply a decriminalized, autonomous system of prostitution, the reality is that in most "legalized" systems the police control prostitution with criminal codes. Laws regulate prostitutes' businesses and lives, prescribing health checks and registration of health status. According to the International Union of Sex Workers, legalized systems often include special taxes, the restriction of prostitutes to working in brothels or in certain zones, licenses, registration of prostitutes and the consequent keeping of records of each individual in the profession, and health checks which often result in punitive quarantine. This is why the World Charter for Prostitutes Rights doesn't support mandatory health checks. This may be controversial but it fits with the general idea that prostitutes' lives should be protected but not regulated. Easier and more affordable access to health clinics where prostitutes don't feel stigmatized is of greater concern to these human rights groups because compulsory checks can frighten some prostitutes and actually prevent those who are most at risk from getting necessary medical checkups. Many groups that support sex workers have sexual health and disease control as their top priorities and provide education, contraception, and health care referrals.

A well-known example of legalized prostitution is that which has been practiced in the Netherlands since the 1800s; however, brothels were illegal until 2000. When the ban was lifted, forced prostitution came under harsher punishment. Brothels are now required to be licensed, and it is legal to organize the prostitution of another party, provided the prostitution isn't forced. According to the A. De Graaf Foundation, laws in the Netherlands now will control and regulate the exploitation of prostitution, improve the prosecution of involuntary exploitation, protect minors, protect the position of prostitutes, combat the criminal affairs related to prostitution, and combat the presence of illegal aliens in prostitution.

Designated streetwalking zones have also been established. While these aren't without their problems, they have essentially functioned as a safe community for women to work. The zones also offer the benefit of a shelter which affords prostitutes a place to meet with their colleagues, talk to health care professionals, and generally relax. This was a good solution for an occupation that had led both police and prostitutes to feel that frequent raids were only making matters worse. Women felt scared and were always on the run, and police thought they weren't succeeding at making the streets any safer. This system of legalization seems to have worked well because in the Netherlands social attitudes about sex and sex work are more liberal than in other parts of the world. There is a genuine effort to protect and respect the rights of Dutch sex workers.

But this sort of arrangement isn't found all over the world. Nor can one say that the Netherlands example should become a model for every other country. Some societies may benefit more from decriminalization while others are decades away from any regulation whatsoever. The latter seems to be the case in the United States, where puritanical attitudes about sex in general would make it nearly impossible to treat prostitution as just another business.

What, then, is the best choice for women? Put simply, the best choice for women is the choice that the individual woman makes for herself. Furthermore, a humanist perspective would naturally back up the right of women to choose how to live their lives as sexual beings. *Humanist Manifesto II* says:

In the area of sexuality, we believe that intolerant attitudes, often cultivated by orthodox religions and puritanical cultures, unduly repress sexual conduct. The right to birth control, abortion, and divorce should be recognized. While we do not approve of exploitive, denigrating forms of sexual expression, neither do we wish to prohibit, by law or social sanction, sexual behavior between consenting adults. The many varieties of sexual exploration should not in themselves be considered "evil." Without countenancing mindless permissiveness or unbridled promiscuity, a civilized society should be a tolerant one. Short of harming others or compelling them to do likewise, individuals should be permitted to express their sexual proclivities and pursue their lifestyles as they desire. We wish to cultivate the development of a responsible attitude toward sexuality, in which humans are not exploited as sexual objects, and in which intimacy, sensitivity, respect, and honesty in interpersonal relations are encouraged. Moral education for children and adults is an important way of developing awareness and sexual maturity.

As stated above, any variety of sexual exploration—as long as it isn't exploitative or harmful—can't be considered evil, yet that is exactly how prostitution is regarded. If a woman or man chooses to exchange sex for money and does it in a way that causes no harm to either party, then they should be free to do so.

In this new social environment, many of the prostitutes' rights groups build from the pro-sex ideals of the third wave. Groups such as COYOTE (Call Off Your Old Tired Ethics), the Blackstockings, and PONY (Prostitutes of New York) advocate for women who have chosen to be sex workers. Their Web sites are full of resources—from legal and medical referrals to commonsense safety tips—and they advocate tirelessly for the decriminalization of prostitution.

It would seem that decriminalization should be a key point in any humanistic feminist perspective on prostitution. Every woman's choices should be legally and socially respected whether a given woman chooses to be a wife, a CEO, or a prostitute.

And what is good for women in these instances becomes good for other sex workers, such as male prostitutes, exotic dancers of both sexes, and so on—this applies to both the gay and straight communities. Furthermore, what liberates those who make sex a profession also liberates everyone else who enjoys sex recreationally. General sexiness, for example, can take on more varied and open forms—so much so that no woman would need to fear that frank sexuality in manner or dress would any longer stigmatize her as a "slut" (or if it did, the word would have lost its sting).

Feminism has always advocated for women to enjoy freedom of choice. Women have made great strides in the courtrooms, the boardrooms, and the bedrooms. But there remains a long way to go. Negative attitudes toward sexuality, in particular, have made it hard for women to be fully liberated. But thanks to feminists, prostitute activists, and their supporters, things are slowly changing. Only when women have their sexual and personal choices protected and respected can they truly be free.

DISCUSSION QUESTIONS FOR CHAPTER 8

1. How are systems of inequality evident in women's work inside the home?

2. How do women experience sexism in the paid labor force? How does racism shape the ways women experience sexism in the paid labor force? Have you had experiences of discrimination in the workplace?

3. Why has legislation requiring equal pay and prohibiting discrimination failed to bring about equality for women in the workforce?

4. How has the perception of certain work as feminine affected women's work, both inside and outside the home?

5. What changes do you think need to occur to create equitable systems of work for all women?

SUGGESTIONS FOR FURTHER READING

Bennetts, Leslie. *The Feminine Mistake: Are We Giving Up Too Much?* New York: Voice, 2007.

Burk, Martha. *Cult of Power: Sex Discrimination in Corporate America and What Can Be Done About It.* New York: Scribner, 2005.

Hertz, Rosanna, and Nancy L. Marshall, eds. *Working Families: The Transformation of the American Home.* Berkeley: University of California Press, 2001.

Hirshman, Linda. *Get to Work: A Manifesto for Women of the World.* New York: Penguin, 2006.

Hochschild, Arlie, and Barbara Ehrenreich, eds. *Global Women: Nannies, Maids, and Sex Workers in the New Economy.* New York: Henry Holt, 2004.

Shields, Julie. *How to Avoid the Mommy Trap: A Roadmap for Sharing Parenting and Making It Work.* Sterling, VA: Capital Books, 2002.

CHAPTER 9

Women Confronting and Creating Culture

Although literature and the arts remain important cultural forms, various forms of popular culture—television, movies, music, magazines, and the Internet (including games, blogs, video blogs, and podcasting)—also play significant roles in reflecting, reinforcing, and sometimes subverting the dominant systems and ideologies that help shape gender. Popular cultural forms in particular are very seductive; they reflect and create societal needs, desires, anxieties, and hopes through consumption and participation. As emphasized in Chapter 5, popular culture plays a huge role in setting standards of beauty and encouraging certain bodily disciplinary practices. Popular culture *is* culture for many people; the various forms pop culture takes help shape identity and guide people's understandings of themselves and one another.

Popular culture provides stories and narratives that shape our lives and identities. They give us pleasure at the end of a long day and enable us to take our minds off work or other anxieties. In this regard, some scholars have suggested that popular culture regulates society by "soothing the masses," meaning that energy and opposition to the status quo is redirected in pursuit of the latest in athletic shoes or electronic gadgets. Of course, popular culture creates huge multi-million-dollar industries that themselves regulate society by providing markets for consumption, consolidating power and status among certain groups and individuals. Media conglomerates have merged technologies and fortunes in the last decade, consolidating resources and forming powerful corporations that control the flow of information to the public. In 2005, National Public Radio (NPR) reported that one film studio even managed to manipulate a scientific discovery to coincide with the release of a film on dinosaurs.

THE INTERNET

The Internet, a system of connecting computer technologies supporting the World Wide Web ("the Web"), is changing the ways people communicate, entertain, and gather information, making personal computers a necessity for communication, entertainment, and advertising. "Blackberries" and other types of personalized

Top Blogs on Feminism and Women's Rights

By Tom Head

Visit these feminist blogs and consider starting your own!

Feministing: *feministing.com*

Feministing is usually the first blog I read when I get up in the morning. Witty, irreverent, and profane (literally; don't read if you're F-bomb averse), it covers women's rights in America better than any other site on the 'net. Few controversial issues escape the attention of the site's twentysomething, grad-school educated bloggers, and no target is too sancrosanct for their sometimes jarring mix of snark and scholarship. You have been warned. Now click on the link already.

Blac(k)ademic: *blackademic.com*

The brainchild of doctoral student Kortney Ryan Ziegler, blac(k)ademic represents a perfect twenty-first-century, third-wave feminism. With no respect for the boundaries between feminism and antiracism, antiracism and antiheterosexism, et. al., blac(k)ademic is pure thought, pure expression—and some of the most mindblowing stuff you'll ever read. No matter how enlightened you *think* you are, this blog will open your eyes all over again.

The Happy Feminist: *happyfeminist.typepad.com*

Billed as "thoughts of a 30-something, married, Unitarian, dog-loving attorney," the Happy Feminist is probably one of the gentler feminist bloggers out there—but all this really means is that you can't tell right away how iconoclastic she really is. Take HF's recent entry on the *Debra Lafave* case. You start off nodding in agreement, you finish nodding in agreement, but somewhere in the middle she just changed your mind. And you never saw it coming.

Now What?!: *saveroe.com/blog*

Sponsored by Planned Parenthood's *Save Roe campaign,* this is the most active and well-rounded pro-choice blog on the Internet. Visit for the daily news updates; stay for the provocative analysis and commentary, which presents a far more robust and intellectually formidable pro-choice position than you're likely to encounter anywhere on the op-ed page of your favorite newspaper.

Echidne of the Snakes: *echidne of the snakes.blogspot.com*

This blog reminds me of Mary Wollstonecraft. A contemporary of Paine and Locke, she was one of the greatest political philosophers of the British Enlightenment but is remembered today as essentially a suffragist and nothing more. Why? Because she had the audacity to say important things *as a woman*. Echidne is not a feminism blog. It is a philosophy blog written by a serious feminist who takes her feminism with her on her philosophical adventures—and never leaves it in her luggage.

Alas, a blog: *amptoons.com/blog*

There's a definite *Alice in Wonderland* dimension to Alas. I don't know what gives it that dimension—maybe it's the odd title, the vaguely disconcerting cartoons, or the

(continued)

authors' offbeat sense of humor—but visiting this blog is like opening a window to a strange parallel universe, where the facts matter, where everyone makes sense (whether they want to or not), and where men are actually held accountable for their own sexism. The world needs more sensible nonsense like this.

Feministe: *feministe.us/blog*

Feministe is the Mayberry of feminist blogs. While many emphasize fierce debates and tough ideological questions, Feministe is a community—a friendly community with lots of cat blogging, shuffled iTunes playlists, and even a few antifeminist mascots. This is not to say that it's any less feminist, or any less relevant; just that it's less front line and more front porch. And in a field of civil liberties activism where the value of community-building is recognized, that's a powerful thing.

Hugo Schwyzer: *hugoschwyzer.net*

Male feminist bloggers want to be Hugo when they grow up. He has both an intuitive understanding of feminist values and an intuitive understanding of how to try to humbly live into those values as a heterosexual white man—dealing as much with the business of day-to-day life, and the day-to-day values and relationships that give it meaning, as he does with policy issues. And with rational humility, but without a hint of self-mortification, he makes it all look easy.

Majikthise: *majikthise.typepad.com*

Lindsay Beyerstein is another example of the Wollstonecraft Effect—a philosopher who is a feminist rather than a narrowly defined feminist philosopher. But Beyerstein's posts have a hard edge that seems rooted in a very potent secular humanism, an edge that screams out from the snarling photograph of herself on the front page of her site. In Tibetan Buddhism, there's a figure named Manjushri who carries a sword to cut through falsehoods. This is what Manjushri's blog might look like.

Source: http://civilliberty.about.com/od/gendersexuality/tp/blogs_feminist.htm?p=1

digital assistants can combine computing, telephone, fax, Internet, and networking features that often involve handwriting and voice-recognition technologies. The avid use of the search engine Google has even produced a new verb: "to google." People google each other before dates, employers google job candidates, and friends google friends. Although originally the Web was imagined as a utopian space where gender, race, class, and sexuality were neutral forces or where alternative subjectivities could be performed (this potential still remains), it mostly works to reinforce current social standards about gender and other identities. This occurs in two ways.

First, traditional standards are scripted through gendered and racialized content supported by advertising, entertainment, and pornography. Both women and men use the Internet for entertainment purposes, playing games, downloading music and videos, watching television shows online, and reading narratives about other people's lives and activities on social networking sites like MySpace and Facebook. Advertisements accompany most websites and a large percentage of Internet traffic is pornography related. This "content" is saturated with traditional ideas about gender and sexuality and provides important messages about the body.

Second, traditional ideas about gender are reinforced through the ways women and men use the Internet. Women are more likely than men to use it for communication, email, and the maintenance of relationships, whereas men are more inclined to use it for entertainment, information gathering, and problem solving. The Internet is a contested site where girls and women may experience marginalization, discrimination, abuse, and/or empowerment. Many women have fought to make a place for themselves in the technological world, developing their own activist websites, blogs, and computer games. Still, by far, these technologies remain a male domain.

Despite the fact that Internet technologies provide new opportunities and help people connect across wide geographical expanses, they have also encouraged a widening of the gap between the "haves" (those with resources to acquire and use the necessary technologies) and the "have-nots." The speed with which technology evolves or becomes obsolete, the "technology turnover" that pushes new gadget accessories through the marketplace at astonishing speeds, exacerbates these issues of equity associated with Internet technologies. For example, the price tag of the iPhone, *the* IT product of 2007, was beyond the reach of most people in the United States, despite the fact that it's price was lowered by almost one-third within months to entice new buyers during the holiday season and to compete with other phones launched on the market. In these ways, rather than challenging gendered behaviors and encouraging equity, Internet usage patterns, and the structure and practices of the medium, provide little resistance. In particular, it is important to understand the ways advertisers capitalize on the market saturation provided by the Internet. Websites accept sponsors to reduce maintenance costs in exchange for an advertising link, or banner, that decorates the page. Demographic information is collected from websites and is used to create site-specific advertisements to entice users.

This is not to say, however, that the Web lacks sites that dispute gendered and racialized patterns. Blogs, social networking sites, and wikis are constructing knowledge in new and accessible ways. Blogs (from Web logs) are online public (or private) journals where individuals (bloggers) can critique, rant, or provide social commentary on their lives or the world around them. Blogging has changed the face of publishing. Although bloggers are not formally trained as journalists or necessarily have professional credentials, they have been able to publish their opinions or beliefs about any number of subjects, appearing in school projects, activism websites, and on political web pages. Some blogs have a loyal reader following, while others are more obscure and are read only by friends. The power of the blog lies in the ability for anyone with access to the Web to create such a site. Blogger and LiveJournal are two of the most popular sites that have free blog hosting. Social network sites like MySpace, Facebook, and Friendster allow users to maintain relationships between friends and associates. These sites differ from social networking sites such as chat rooms, in which users are actively networking with other unknown people who have similar interests or needs. Agenda-specific websites like Match.com, VolunteerMatch.org, and CareerJournal.com are creating connections across the globe for social or need-based communities. Wikis are knowledge databanks in which any user can add, edit, and create definitions for common words, concepts, histories, or biographies. It is important to note that though wikis can be good sources of common information, they are not always accurate and should not be confused with academic databases! These sites reflect a democratic construction of knowledge to which individuals can contribute (the website Wikipedia is one example). At the same time, however, the technologies associated with blogging, social network sites, and Google raise issues about accountability as employers, friends, or strangers can gain unlimited access to information about the lives of the users. Employers who look at these pages can hold employees responsible for what they do or divulge. The military has found it necessary to limit active-duty enlistees' posting of photographs online, as such photographs could inappropriately disclose location details.

TELEVISION

Television is one of the most influential forms of media because it is so pervasive and its presence is taken for granted in most households in the United States. Television has changed family life because it encourages passive interaction, replacing alternative family interaction. In addition, television is a visual medium that broadcasts multiple images on a continual basis in digitized, high-density formats. These images come to be seen as representing the real world and influence people's understanding of others and the world around them. This is especially significant for children because it is estimated that most children, on the average, watch far more television than is good for them. Of course, the range and quality of television shows vary, and a case can be made for the benefits of educational television. Unfortunately, educational programming is only a small percentage of television viewing. The explosion of cable and satellite availability has resulted in an unlimited number of television channels. Such choice, however, has not meant greater access to a wide range of alternative images of women. Reality shows, and makeover shows in particular, reinforce dominant notions of women and standards of beauty.

Advertising sponsors control the content of most commercial television. During male sporting events, for example, the commercials are for beer, cars, electronic products, Internet commerce, and other products targeted at a male audience. During daytime soap operas or evening family sitcoms, on the other hand, the commercials are aimed at women and focus on beauty and household products. As a result, commercial sponsors have enormous influence over the content of television programming. If they want to sell a certain product, they are unlikely to air the commercial during a feature that could be interpreted as criticizing such products or consumerism generally. In this way, commercial sponsors shape television content.

Television messages about gender tend to be mostly traditional. In fact, the assumed differences between the genders very often drive the plot of television programming. The format of shows is also gendered. For example, daytime soap operas focus on relationships and family and employ rather fragmented narratives with plots weaving around without closure or resolution, enabling women to tune in and out as they go about multiple tasks. Daytime soaps are only part of the story. Primetime shows such as *Desperate Housewives* (see the Pozner and Seigel reading on this show), *The O.C., Gossip Girl,* and *The Real World* follow multiple plot lines and are targeted toward a younger audience. These nighttime soaps are aired

LEARNING ACTIVITY   **Talking About Talk Shows**

Watch several television talk shows. Keep a journal describing the topic of the show, the guests, and the commercial sponsors. How would you characterize the host? What do you notice about the interactions among host, guests, and audience? In what ways does gender operate in the shows? Do you think the shows are in any way empowering for the guests, audience members, or television viewers? How do you think these shows reflect either dominant or subordinate American cultures? How do you think these shows contribute to public discourse?

between 8 pm and 10 pm and serve a similar function. Women are often completing their second shift of work at this time. Scholars have pointed out that these shows reconcile women to the fragmented nature of their everyday lives and to male-dominated interpersonal relationships generally. In other words, shows produced with a female viewing audience in mind help enforce gendered social relations. Other scholars argue that these shows enable women viewers to actively critique blatant male-dominated situations in ways that help them reflect on their own lives.

A similar analysis can be made of evening family sitcoms. These shows are funny and entertaining because they are relatively predictable. The family or work group is made up of characters with distinct personalities and recognizable habits; each week this family is thrown into some kind of crisis, and the plot of the show is to resolve that crisis back to situation as usual. For the most part, the messages are typical in terms of gender, race, class, and other differences, and they often involve humor that denigrates certain groups of people and ultimately maintains the status quo. As already mentioned, reality television is especially influential. The appeal of shows like *Survivor, American Idol, The Biggest Loser,* and *The Amazing Race* rely on creative casting, scripting, and editing to make the shows seen spontaneous, and the incorporation of character traits and personalities that viewers love to hate and adore. These shows also rely on a cult of the celebrity, rampant in popular culture. Gay-themed decorating and personal styling shows may have helped normalize gay life for the broader society. On the other hand, they have often relied on and reinforced stereotypical representations of gay men and lesbians.

Increasingly, we are seeing shows and advertisements that resist the usual gendered representations, or at least show them with a new twist. Kristi Turnquist makes this point in the reading "A Woman's Role Is . . . on Television." She suggests that empowering roles for women are actually more likely to appear in television than in the movies because the former expects a female audience, whereas the latter relies on young male viewers. In addition, changes in society's views of gender have made sponsors realize that they have a new marketing niche. Often, unfortunately, these new representations involve the same old package tied up in new ways; typically they involve women and men resisting some of the old norms while keeping most intact. For example, although women are starting to be shown as competent, strong, athletic, and in control of their lives rather than ditsy housewives or sex symbols, they still are very physically attractive and are often highly sexualized. Examples abound in the recent popularity of crime dramas such as *Law and Order* and *CSI*. These shows provide strong, intelligent women as primary characters, but at the same time these women fulfill the stereotypical standards of beauty. They can track down criminals using forensic science and look gorgeous while doing it. Unfortunately, most of the victims are female, too. An increased visibility of larger-sized women in some advertising and in catalogs (although often "large" is size 12 or 14, a very "normal" size for U.S. women) has come about as a result of the capitalist-driven need to create a new marketing niche and sell clothing to large women as well as from pressures from fat women and the women's movement. At the same time, however, Dove (which includes positive advertisements) is owned by the same parent company as Slim Fast and Axe. The series *Desperate Housewives* provides an interesting case study of the conflicted presentation of women on TV. The "debate" between Jennifer L. Pozner and Jessica Seigel in "Desperately Debating *Housewives*" suggests various feminist readings of the show.

THE MOVIES

In her groundbreaking work on cinema, Laura Mulvey identifies the "male gaze" as a primary motif for understanding gender in filmmaking. Mulvey argues that movies are essentially made through and for the male gaze and fulfill a voyeuristic desire for men to look at women as objects. Viewers are encouraged to "see" the movie through the eyes of the male protagonist who carries the plot forward. Some feminist scholars have suggested the possibility for "subversive gazing" by viewers who refuse to gaze the way filmmakers expect and by making different kinds of movies.

Probably the best genre of film in which to observe gender is the romantic comedy or romantic drama. These films are packed with subtle and not-so-subtle notions of gender, and they are very seductive in the way that they offer fun entertainment. For example, *Pretty Woman* is a contemporary retelling of the Cinderella story, in which a young woman waits for her Prince Charming to rescue her from her undesirable situation. In this case, the prostitute-with-a-heart-of-gold is swept away in a white limousine by the older rich man who procured her services and then fell in love with her. Some films like *Enchanted* are trying to challenge the idea that all women need to be saved by a handsome prince. Other genres of films are also revealing in terms of norms about gender. Slasher films and horror movies are often spectacular in terms of their victimization of women. The killers in these movies, such as Norman Bates in the classic *Psycho,* are often sexually disturbed and hound and kill women who arouse them. This is also the subtext of other films like *The Texas Chainsaw Massacre* movies and *Motel Hell.* Often it is sexually active couples who are killed, either after sex or in anticipation of it, as in the case of the movie *Vacancy.* The killer usually watches, as in *Halloween II* or *Grindhouse,* as he impersonates the male lover before he then kills the female partner. Another plot of horror movies is the crazed and demanding mother who drives her offspring to psychosis, as in *Carrie,* where the mother gives birth to the spawn of Satan, and in *The Omen, Rosemary's Baby,* and others. Although both women and men claim to

LEARNING ACTIVITY   **Women Make Movies**

Very often the subjects that are important to women are ignored in popular film-making or are distorted by stereotypes or the male gaze. Despite lack of funding and major studio backing, independent women filmmakers worldwide persist in documenting the wide range of women's lives and experiences.

Visit the website of Women Make Movies at *www.wmm.com*. Browse the catalog and identify movies made by filmmakers outside the United States. What themes do they pursue? Are these themes also common in American women filmmakers' movies? In what ways do they also express cultural distinctions? How do these films differ from mainstream box office releases? Why is an organization like Women Make Movies important?

be entertained by these films, it is important to talk about the messages they portray about men, about women, and about the normalization of violence.

Pornography is an extreme example of the male gaze and the normalization of violence against women (discussed in Chapter 10). With its print media counterpart, pornography extends the sexualization and objectification of women's bodies for entertainment. In pornographic representations, women are often reduced to body parts and are shown deriving pleasure from being violated and dominated. Additionally, racism intersects with sexism in pornography as the "exotic other" is fetishized and portrayed in especially demeaning and animalistic ways. Although many feminists, ourselves included, oppose pornography, others, especially those described as "sex radicals," feel that pornography can be a form of sexual self-expression for women. They argue that women who participate in the production of pornography are taking control of their own sexuality and are profiting from control of their own bodies. Advertisers have targeted young girls with stripper and porn-inspired merchandise that creates a very narrow definition of what constitutes sexiness for women. Ariel Levy comments on the ways popular culture encourages young women to confuse their objectification and sexualization with empowerment in the reading "Female Chauvinist Pigs." She comments on the phenomena associated with "Girls Gone Wild," as does Jessica Valenti in the reading "Pop Culture Gone Wild." This essay addresses the increasing "pornification" of popular culture.

Some of the more pervasive and lasting gender images in American culture derive from Walt Disney feature films. Disney heroines live, however, not only on the big screen but also as dolls in little girls' rooms, on their sheets and curtains, on their lunchboxes, and even on their t-shirts. On the whole, Disney characters reflect White, heterosexual, middle-class, patriarchal norms. Later representations in Disney movies have attempted to be more inclusive, but still rely on these traditional norms.

As women have made societal gains, Hollywood filmmaking has also changed and become more inclusive of new norms about gender. In some instances, as in *Terminator 2: Judgment Day* and *Aliens*, women are shown to be powerful, although in both movies the heroines are beautiful, fit, and often scantily clad. In other instances, especially when women have more control over the film as in a number of independent movies, films become more reflective of women's actual lives and concerns.

CONTEMPORARY MUSIC AND MUSIC VIDEOS

Popular music like rock, grunge, punk, heavy metal, techno, and rap are contemporary cultural forms targeted at youth. Often this music offers resistance to traditional cultural forms and contains a lot of teenage angst attractive to young people who are figuring out who they are in relation to their parents and other adults in positions of authority in their lives. In this way, such music serves as contemporary resistance and can work to mobilize people politically. Certainly music functions to help youth shape notions of identity. The various musical forms offer different kinds of identities from which young people can pick and choose to sculpt their own sense of self. In this way, music has played, and continues to play, a key role in the consolidation of youth cultures in society. There is a huge music industry in the United States, and it works in tandem with television, film, video, radio, and, of course, advertising. The Internet and personalized music devices like the iPod allow people to download music and create their own personalized collections rather than purchasing complete CDs. This has changed industries and listening practices.

Just as rock music was an essential part of mobilizing the youth of the 1960s to rebel against traditional norms, oppose the war, and work for civil rights, rap music (and hip-hop culture generally) has been influential in recent decades as a critique of racial cultural politics. Originating in African American urban street culture of the late 1970s, rap was influenced by rhythm and blues and rock and quickly spread beyond its roots into television, fashion, film, and, in particular, music videos. At the same time that the rap music industry has been able to raise the issue of racism, poverty, and social violence in the context of its endorsement of Black nationalism, rap has also perpetuated misogyny and violence against women in its orientation and musical lyrics. There are Black women performers in hip-hop and new female rappers are receiving much more attention, but their status in the industry is far below the male bands. Aya de Leon reflects on this in her poem "If Women Ran Hip Hop." The appeal of hip-hop music is not just an American phenomenon, however, and in "Growing the Size of the Black Woman," Ronni Armstead discusses the debates about gender, identity, and politics that are being carried out in popular music.

About 30 years after the advent of rock music, the combination of music with visual images gave rise to the music video genre, which gained immense popularity with the prominence of MTV, a music video station that has now branched into specialized programming. Music videos are unique in blending television programming with commercials such that while the viewer is actually watching a commercial, the illusion is of programmatic entertainment. Music videos are essentially advertisements for record company products and focus on standard rock music, although

IDEAS FOR ACTIVISM

- Write letters to encourage networks to air television shows that depict the broad diversity of women.
- Write letters to sponsors to complain about programs that degrade or stereotype women.
- Form a reading group to study novels by female authors.
- Sponsor a media awareness event on campus to encourage other students to be aware of media portrayals of women.

different musical genres like country-western also have their own video formatting. Most music videos are fairly predictable in the ways they sexualize women, sometimes in violent ways. As in movies, women are generally present in music videos to be looked at. In fact, music videos featuring male musicians are aired in greater numbers than those featuring female musicians.

Nonetheless, we could also argue that the music video industry has allowed women performers to find their voice (literally) and to script music videos from their perspective. This opportunity has given women audience recognition and industry backing. Music videos have also helped produce a feminine voice that has the potential to disrupt the traditional gendered perspective. At its peak in the mid-1980s, MTV helped such women as Tina Turner, Cyndi Lauper, and Madonna find success. Madonna is especially interesting because she was cast simultaneously as both a feminist nightmare perpetuating gendered stereotypes about sexualized women and an important role model for women who want to be active agents in their lives. On the latter, she has been regarded as someone who returns the male gaze by staring right back at the patriarchy. Newer artists like Christina Aguilera, Missy Elliot, Lil' Kim, and Pink are celebrated for being both sexual and assertively feminist in much the same way.

New technologies have also provided more ways for women to express themselves. Performing rock music has generally been seen as a male activity, despite the presence of women rockers from the genre's beginnings in the 1950s. The male-dominated record industry has tended to exclude women rockers and tried to force women musicians into stereotypical roles as singers and sex objects. But the advent of new, accessible technologies has allowed women greater control of their own music. Now, instead of needing a recording contract with one of the big labels, an aspiring rocker can write, record, produce, and distribute her own music (see the box "Rock 'n' Roll Camp for Girls"). For years, independent artists sold most of their music out of the back of a van, but now the Internet has made global distribution possible for just about every musician—without a large budget, agent, manager, or record label. MySpace, for example, and YouTube are websites where new musicians can display their music and image for free. This allows them to break out of the expected norms for women in music.

Rock 'n' Roll Camp for Girls

It all started as a women's studies senior project at Portland State University, but it grew into a feminist nonprofit agency that provides a summer camp and an after-school program for girls and a spring camp for women—who want to rock. Women's studies student Misty McElroy originally intended for her rock camp to be a one-time event in the summer of 2000, but the response was so overwhelming that she continued the project.

Why rock? Rock lets girls be loud—something they're not supposed to be. It lets them express themselves and try out their voices. And it's something that's traditionally male dominated. Rock camp teaches girls to play rock music. They spend a week with women musicians who teach them guitar, bass, drum, or vocals. They learn to create zines, write lyrics, and run sound. And they learn about feminist issues such as body image and self-defense. At the end of the week, they perform in a local Portland club to the cheers of family and friends. Because the camp was so successful, McElroy also launched an institute that provides training after school. Her hope was that local girls can use this option, freeing space for more national and international participants in the summer camp. The Ladies Rock Camp is a fundraiser for scholarships for the girls camp. This camp allows women the chance to try their hands at playing rock 'n' roll. Check out the camp's website at *www.girlsrockcamp.org*.

The empowerment envisioned by Rock 'n' Roll Camp for Girls works hand in hand with a recent technological possibility for musicians—DIY (do it yourself). Because of increasing access to computers and other musical technological innovations, aspiring artists can create and distribute their own CDs. DIY allows musicians to retain complete control over their music, and the advice many veterans of the recording scene offer to newcomers is to do it themselves. Perhaps the most famous do-it-yourselfer is Ani DiFranco, whose Righteous Babe Records has demonstrated the possibility of commercial success for music and musicians who don't follow the mainstream pop formula. Indigo Girl Amy Ray, who herself has achieved success on a large label, used her assets and know-how to found Daemon Records, a small label that gives new artists the opportunity to produce a recording. What's most astounding about Daemon is that it is a nonprofit—something unique in the recording industry. And when Amy Ray recorded a solo album on the Daemon label, she limited her expenses to what the label spends on any other artist.

Check out Righteous Babe and Daemon at *www.righteousbabe.com* and *www.daemonrecords.com*.

PRINT MEDIA

No discussion of popular culture is complete without a discussion of print media. These mass media forms include magazines, newspapers, comic books, and other periodicals. Like other media, they are a mix of entertainment, education, and advertising. Fashion magazines are heavy on advertising, whereas comic books tend to be geared toward entertainment and rely more on product sales of the comic books themselves. Newspapers fall somewhere in between.

LEARNING ACTIVITY **Looking Good, Feeling Sexy, Getting a Man**

Collect a number of women's magazines, such as *Cosmopolitan, Vogue, Elle, Mirabella, Redbook,* and *Woman's Day.* Read through the magazines and fill in the chart listing the number of articles you find about each topic. What do you observe from your analysis? What messages about gender are these magazines presenting?

Magazine Title	Makeup	Clothes	Hair	Sex/ Dating	Dieting	Food/ Recipes	Home Decoration	Work	Politics

Women's magazines are an especially fruitful subject of study for examining how gender works in contemporary U.S. society. As discussed in Chapter 5, women's magazines are a central part of the multi-billion-dollar industries that produce cosmetics and fashion and help shape the social construction of "beauty." Alongside these advertising campaigns are bodily standards against which women are encouraged to measure themselves. Because almost no one measures up to these artificially created and often computer-generated standards, the message is to buy these products and your life will improve.

Generally, women's magazines can be divided into three distinct types. First are the fashion magazines that focus on beauty, attracting and satisfying men, self-improvement, and (occasionally) work and politics. Examples are *Vogue* (emphasizing fashion and makeup), *Cosmopolitan* (emphasizing sexuality and relationships with men), and *Self* (emphasizing self-improvement and employment), although the latter two are also heavy on beauty and fashion and the former is also preoccupied with sex. Most of these magazines have a White audience in mind; *Ebony* is one similar kind of magazine aimed at African American women. Note that there are also a number of junior magazines in this genre, such as *Seventeen,* aimed at teenage women. However, although its title suggests the magazine might be oriented toward 17-year-olds, it is mostly read by younger teenagers and even preadolescent girls. Given the focus of teen magazines on dating, fashion, and makeup, the effects of such copy and advertisements on young girls are significant.

The second genre of women's magazines includes those oriented toward the family, cooking, household maintenance and decoration, and keeping the man you already have. Examples include *Good Housekeeping, Redbook,* and *Better Homes and Gardens.* These magazines (especially those like *Good Housekeeping*) also include articles and advertising on fashion and cosmetics, although the representations of these products are different. Instead of the seductive model dressed in a shiny, revealing garment (as is usually featured on the cover of *Cosmo*), *Redbook,* for example, usually features a less glamorous woman (although still very beautiful) in more conservative clothes, surrounded by other graphics or captions featuring various desserts, crafts, and so forth. The focus is off sex and onto the home.

HISTORICAL MOMENT *SI* for Women

By Lindsay Schnell

Featuring a variety of male athletes, marketed to men and written (mostly) by men, *Sports Illustrated (SI)* magazine has never done a consistent job of covering and featuring female athletes. It's easy to see why: *SI* primarily covers professional sports, and a small percentage of professional athletes are women. For years, female athletes struggled to get a fair shake in media coverage, often being touted more for their looks than their abilities on the playing field.

That all changed in the spring of 1999 with the debut of *Sports Illustrated for Women*. Featuring teen basketball phenom Seimone Augustus—who went on to star at Louisiana State University and become the number-one pick of the 2006 WNBA draft—on its first cover, *SI for Women* catered to female athletes of all ages and skill levels. The magazine offered tips on eating like a professional athlete, previews of college and professional teams, in-depth features on known and unknown females making an impact in the world of sport, and much more. One issue even had a sports horoscope for its readers! *SI for Women* also had an answer to its parent magazine's hottest-selling issue annually: a swimsuit issue of its own, with male athletes showing off the bodies they had worked so hard for. Finally, women had a sports magazine just for them that celebrated their athletic accomplishments instead of just their looks.

One of the earliest covers featured Julie Foudy, a member of the 1999 Women's World Cup soccer team. Foudy and her teammates became known across the nation after a thrilling 5–4 shootout victory over China in the Rose Bowl for the '99 Cup title. Brandi Chastain's "shot heard 'round the world" and subsequent act of ripping off her shirt and falling to her knees in ecstasy became one of the most iconic sports images of the twentieth century.

Coupled with the success of the '99 World Cup team, *SI for Women* helped athletes like soccer great Mia Hamm and basketball superstar Sheryl Swoopes become household names. Unfortunately, *SI for Women* wasn't a hot seller on the newsstands, and lasted just 18 issues. It folded in 2002, but in the two-and-a-half years that *SI for Women* was in print it helped give a face—or faces—to a generation hungry for strong female role models.

In 2008 Winter X Games star Gretchen Bleiler told *ESPN The Magazine*, "It sucks. When you're a woman in sports, people want you to show some skin." Though it's no longer in print, *SI for Women* helped prove female athletes didn't have to show skin to get some pub. And with female athletic participation at an all-time high since Title XI was passed in 1972, is there any better news we can give to our friends, teammates, sisters, and daughters?

The third genre of women's magazines is the issue periodical that focuses on some issue or hobby that appeals to many women. *Parents* magazine is an example of an issue periodical aimed at women (although not exclusively). *Ms.* magazine is one aimed at feminists, as are the periodicals *Bitch* and *Bust*. Examples of hobby-type periodicals include craft magazines on needlework or crochet and fitness magazines. There are many specialized issue periodicals aimed at men (such as hunting and fishing and outdoor activities periodicals, computer and other electronic-focused magazines, car and motorcycle magazines, and various sports periodicals). The best known of the latter is *Sports Illustrated,* famous also for its "swimsuit edition," which always produces record sales in its sexualization of female athletes' bodies. That there are more issue periodicals for men reflects the fact that men are assumed to work and have specialized interests and that women are assumed to be preoccupied with looking good, working on relationships, and keeping a beautiful home.

Again, as in music, technology has also provided a way for women to express their voices through publishing. "Zines" are quick, cheap, cut-and-paste publications that have sprung up both in print form and on the World Wide Web in recent years. These publications, which range in quality, often provide a forum for alternative views on a wide variety of subjects, especially pop culture. As Jennifer Bleyer notes in "Cut-and-Paste Revolution," zines have provided an opportunity for young feminists to resist the ideas in mainstream publications that sustain women's subordination.

LITERATURE AND THE ARTS

In "Thinking About Shakespeare's Sister," Virginia Woolf responds to the question "Why has there been no female Shakespeare?" Similarly, in the early 1970s, Linda Nochlin wrote a feminist critique of art history that sought to answer the question "Why have there been no great women artists?" Woolf and Nochlin reached very similar conclusions. According to Nochlin, the reason there had been no great women artists was not that no woman had been capable of producing great art but that the social conditions of women's lives prevented such artistic endeavors.

Woolf wrote her essay in the late 1920s, but still today many critics and professors of literature raise the same questions about women's abilities to create great literature. Rarely, for example, does a seventeenth- or eighteenth-century British literature course give more than a passing nod to women authors of the periods. Quite often, literature majors graduate having read perhaps only Virginia Woolf, George Eliot, Jane Austen, or Emily Dickinson. The usual justification is that women simply have not written the great literature that men have or that to include

Virginia Woolf Talks to the Landlady

I JUST NATURALLY ASSUMED THERE WOULD BE A BED OF ONE'S OWN, A DESK OF ONE'S OWN, A RUG OF ONE'S OWN...

T.O. SYLVESTER

Copyright © 2000 T.O. Sylvester. Sylvester is the pseudonym for Sylvia Mollick (artist) and Terry Ryan (writer). They live in San Francisco.

women would mean leaving out the truly important works of the literary canon (those written by White men).

In her essay, Woolf argues that it would have been impossible due to social constraints for a woman to write the works of Shakespeare in the age of Shakespeare. Although women did write, even in the time of Shakespeare, their works were often neglected by the arbiters of the literary canon because they fell outside the narrowly constructed definitions of great literature. For example, women's novels often dealt with the subjects of women's lives—family, home, love—subjects not deemed lofty enough for the canon of literature. Additionally, women often did not follow accepted forms, writing in fragments rather than unified texts. As the canon was defined according to White male norms, women's writing and much of the writing of both women and men of color were omitted.

Yet, toward the end of the twentieth century, more women began to publish novels and poetry, and these have been slowly introduced into the canon. These works have dealt with the realities of women's lives and have received wide acclaim. For example, writers such as Toni Morrison (who received the Nobel Prize for literature), Alice Walker, and Maya Angelou have written about the dilemmas and triumphs faced by Black women in a White, male-dominated culture. Annie Dillard won a Pulitzer Prize at the age of 29 for her nature essays about a year spent living by Tinker Creek. Feminist playwrights such as Wendy Wasserstein, Suzan Lori-Parks, Lynn Nottage, Migdalia Cruz, and Eve Ensler; performance artists like Lily Tomlin and Lori Anderson; and feminist comedians such as Suzanne Westenhoffer, Tracey Ullman, and Margaret Cho have also been very influential in providing new scripts for women's lives. In the readings, Audre Lorde and Gloria Anzaldúa write about the importance of literature for women.

Just as female writers have been ignored, misrepresented, and trivialized, so too female artists and musicians have faced similar struggles. Women's art has often been labeled "crafts" rather than art. This is because women, who were often barred from entering the artistic establishment, have tended to create works of art that were useful and were excluded from the category of art. Often, female artists, like their sisters who

ACTIVIST PROFILE **Maxine Hong Kingston**

As a young girl, Maxine Hong Kingston could not find herself in the images in the books she read. The public library in her hometown of Stockton, California, had no stories of Chinese Americans and very few that featured girls. For Kingston, this meant a significant need and open space for the telling of her stories.

Kingston was born in Stockton in 1940 to Chinese immigrant parents. Her mother was trained as a midwife in China, and her father was a scholar and teacher. Arriving in the United States, Tom Hong could not find work and eventually ended up working in a gambling business. Maxine was named after a successful blonde gambler who frequented her father's establishment.

Growing up in a Chinese American community, Kingston heard the stories of her culture that would later influence her own storytelling. By earning 11 scholarships, she was able to attend the University of California at Berkeley, where she earned a B.A. in literature. She married in 1962, and she and her new husband moved to Hawaii, where they both taught for the next 10 years.

In 1976 Kingston published her first book, *The Woman Warrior: Memoirs of a Girlhood Among Ghosts*. This story of a young Chinese American girl who finds her own voice won the National Book Critic's Circle Award. Kingston's portrayal of the girl's struggle with silence was met with a great deal of criticism from many Chinese men who attacked Kingston's exploration of critical gender and race issues among Chinese Americans.

Kingston followed *Woman Warrior* with *China Men* in 1980, which also won the National Book Critic's Circle Award. This book explored the lives of the men in Kingston's family who came to the United States, celebrating their achievements and documenting the prejudices and exploitation they faced. Her 1989 novel, *Tripmaster Monkey: His Fake Book*, continued her explorations of racism and oppression of Chinese Americans. Although some critics have accused Kingston of selling out because her stories have not reflected traditional notions of Chinese culture, she has maintained her right to tell her story in her own words with her own voice.

The Fifth Book of Peace, published in 2003, uses her personal tragedy of losing her house, possessions, and an unfinished novel in the Oakland-Berkeley fire of 1991 as a metaphor for war. She asks repeatedly the questions "Why war? Why not peace?"

HISTORICAL MOMENT   **The NEA Four**

Chartered by the U.S. Congress in 1965, the National Endowment for the Arts (NEA) provides funding for artists to develop their work. In 1990 Congress passed legislation that forced the NEA to consider "standards of decency" in awarding grants. Four performance artists—Karen Finley, Holly Hughes, John Fleck, and Tim Miller—had been selected to receive NEA grants, but following charges by conservatives, particularly Senator Jesse Helms (R–North Carolina), that the artists' works were obscene, the NEA denied their grants. All but Finley are gay, and Finley herself is an outspoken feminist.

Finley's work deals with raw themes of women's lives. She gained notoriety for a performance in which she smeared herself with chocolate to represent the abuse of women. Latching onto this image, conservatives referred to Finley as "the chocolate-smeared woman." Her work is shocking, but she uses the shocking images to explore women's horrific experiences of misogyny, and she uses her body in her performances in ways that reflect how society uses her body against her will.

Hughes' work explores lesbian sexuality, and, in revoking her NEA grant, then-NEA chairman John Frohnmeyer specifically referenced Hughes's lesbianism as one of the reasons she had lost her grant. Some of her performances have included "Well of Horniness," "Lady Dick," and "Dress Suits to Hire."

Following the revocation of their grant, the four sued the U.S. government, and in 1992 a lower court ruled in favor of the plaintiffs, reinstating the grants. The government appealed in 1994 and lost again. Then, in a surprise move, the Clinton administration appealed the decision to the U.S. Supreme Court. In 1998 the Supreme Court overturned the lower court rulings and held that the "standards of decency" clause is constitutional. Since the ruling, the budget and staff of the NEA have been slashed, and artists like Finley and Hughes must seek funding from other sources to continue their performances.

If you're interested in finding out more about feminism and censorship, visit the website of Feminists for Free Expression at *www.ffeusa.org.*

were writing novels and poetry, used a male pen name and disguised their identity in order to have their work published or shown. With the influence of the women's movement, women's art is being reclaimed and introduced into the art history curriculum, although it is often taught in the context of "women's art." This emphasizes the ways the academy remains androcentric, with the contributions of "others" in separate courses. Female artists such as Georgia O'Keeffe and Judy Chicago have revitalized the art world by creating women-centered art and feminist critiques of masculine art forms.

The works of female composers and musicians have also been ignored, and very few women have been given the opportunity to conduct orchestras until recently. In fact, through the nineteenth century, only certain instruments such as the keyboard and harp were considered appropriate for women to play, and, even today, women are still directed away from some instruments and toward others. Women continue to produce literature and art and to redefine the canon. As in other male-dominated arenas, however, women have had to struggle to create a place for themselves. This place is ever-changing, providing women with opportunities for fame, empowerment, self-validation, and respect.

Thinking About Shakespeare's Sister

Virginia Woolf (1929)

... [I]t is a perennial puzzle why no woman wrote a word of extraordinary literature when every other man, it seemed, was capable of song or sonnet. What were the conditions in which women lived, I asked myself; for fiction, imaginative work that is, is not dropped like a pebble upon the ground, as science may be; fiction is like a spider's web, attached ever so lightly perhaps, but still attached to life at all four corners. Often the attachment is scarcely perceptible; Shakespeare's plays, for instance, seem to hang there complete by themselves. But when the web is pulled askew, hooked up at the edge, torn in the middle, one remembers that these webs are not spun in midair by incorporeal creatures, but are the work of suffering human beings, and are attached to grossly material things, like health and money and the houses we live in.

I went therefore, to the shelf where the stories stand and took down one of the latest, Professor Trevelyan's *History of England*. Once more I looked up Women, found "position of," and turned to the pages indicated. "Wifebeating," I read "was a recognized right of man, and was practiced without shame by high as well as low.... Similarly," this historian goes on, "the daughter who refused to marry the gentleman of her parents' choice was liable to be locked up, beaten and flung about the room, without any shock being inflicted on public opinion. Marriage was not an affair of personal affection, but of family avarice, particularly in the 'chivalrous' upper classes.... Betrothal often took place while one or both of the parties was in the cradle, and marriage when they were scarcely out of the nurses' charge." That was about 1470, soon after Chaucer's time. The next reference to the position of women is some two hundred years

later, in the time of the Stuarts. "It was still the exception for women of the upper and middle class to choose their own husbands, and when the husband had been assigned, he was lord and master, so far at least as law and custom could make him. Yet even so," Professor Trevelyan concludes, "neither Shakespeare's women nor those of authentic seventeenth-century memoirs, like the Vemeys and the Hutchinsons, seem wanting in personality and character." Certainly, if we consider it, Cleopatra must have had a way with her; Lady Macbeth, one would suppose, had a will of her own; Rosalind, one might conclude, was an attractive girl. Professor Trevelyan is speaking no more than the truth when he remarks that Shakespeare's women do not seem wanting in personality and character. Not being a historian, one might go even further and say that women have burnt like beacons in all the works of all the poets from the beginning of time— Clytemnestra, Antigone, Cleopatra, Lady Macbeth, Phèdre, Cressida, Rosalind, Desdemona, the Duchess of Malfi, among the dramatists; then among the prose writers: Millamant, Clarissa, Becky Sharp, Anna Karenina, Emma Bovary, Madame de Guermantes—the names flock to mind, nor do they recall women "lacking in personality and character." Indeed, if woman had no existence save in fiction written by men, one would imagine her a person of the utmost importance, very various; heroic and mean; splendid and sordid; infinitely beautiful and hideous in the extreme; as great as a man, some think even greater. But this is woman in fiction. In fact, as Professor Trevelyan points out, she was locked up, beaten and flung about the room.

A very queer, composite being thus emerges. Imaginatively she is of the highest importance;

practically she is completely insignificant. She pervades poetry from cover to cover; she is all but absent from history. She dominates the lives of kings and conquerors in fiction; in fact she was the slave of any boy whose parents forced a ring upon her finger. Some of the most inspired words, some of the most profound thoughts in literature fall from her lips; in real life she could hardly read, could scarcely spell, and was the property of her husband.

. . .

Be that as it may, I could not help thinking, as I looked at the works of Shakespeare on the shelf . . . it would have been impossible, completely and entirely, for any woman to have written the plays of Shakespeare in the age of Shakespeare. Let me imagine, since facts are so hard to come by, what would have happened had Shakespeare had a wonderfully gifted sister, called Judith, let us say. Shakespeare himself went, very probably—his mother was an heiress—to the grammar school, where he may have learnt Latin—Ovid, Virgil and Horace—and the elements of grammar and logic. He was, it is well known, a wild boy who poached rabbits, perhaps shot a deer, and had, rather sooner than he should have done, to marry a woman in the neighbourhood, who bore him a child rather quicker than was right. That escapade sent him to seek his fortune in London. He had, it seemed, a taste for the theatre; he began by holding horses at the stage door. Very soon he got work in the theatre, became a successful actor, and lived at the hub of the universe, meeting everybody, knowing everybody, practising his art on the boards, exercising his wits in the streets, and even getting access to the palace of the queen. Meanwhile his extraordinarily gifted sister, let us suppose, remained at home. She was as adventurous, as imaginative, as agog to see the world as he was. But she was not sent to school. She had no chance of learning grammar and logic, let alone of reading Horace and Virgil. She picked up a book now and then, one of her brother's perhaps, and read a few pages. But then her parents came in and told her to mend the stockings or mind the stew and not moon about with books and papers.

They would have spoken sharply but kindly, for they were substantial people who knew the conditions of life for a woman and loved their daughter—indeed, more likely than not she was the apple of her father's eye. Perhaps she scribbled some pages up in an apple loft on the sly, but was careful to hide them or set fire to them. Soon, however, before she was out of her teens, she was to be betrothed to the son of a neighbouring wool-stapler. She cried out that marriage was hateful to her, and for that she was severely beaten by her father. Then he ceased to scold her. He begged her instead not to hurt him, not to shame him in this matter of her marriage. He would give her a chain of beads or a fine petticoat, he said; and there were tears in his eyes. How could she disobey him? How could she break his heart? The force of her own gift alone drove her to it. She made up a small parcel of her belongings, let herself down by a rope one summer's night and took the road to London. She was not seventeen. The birds that sang in the hedge were not more musical than she was. She had the quickest fancy, a gift like her brother's, for the tune of words. Like him, she had a taste for the theatre. She stood at the stage door; she wanted to act, she said. Men laughed in her face. The manager—a fat, loose-lipped man—guffawed. He bellowed something about poodles dancing and women acting—no woman, he said, could possibly be an actress. He hinted—you can imagine what. She could get no training in her craft. Could she even seek her dinner in a tavern or roam the streets at midnight? Yet her genius was for fiction and lusted to feed abundantly upon the lives of men and women and the study of their ways. At last—for she was very young, oddly like Shakespeare the poet in her face, with the same grey eyes and rounded brows—at last Nick Greene the actor-manager took pity on her; she found herself with child by that gentleman and so—who shall measure the heat and violence of the poet's heart when caught and tangled in a woman's body?—killed herself one winter's night and lies buried at some cross-roads where the omnibuses now stop outside the Elephant and Castle.

That, more or less, is how the story would run, I think, if a woman in Shakespeare's day had had Shakespeare's genius. . . .

This may be true or it may be false—who can say?—but what is true in it, so it seemed to me, reviewing the story of Shakespeare's sister as I had made it, is that any woman born with a great gift in the sixteenth century would certainly have gone crazed, shot herself, or ended her days in some lonely cottage outside the village, half witch, half wizard, feared and mocked at. For it needs little skill in psychology to be sure that a highly gifted girl who had tried to use her gift for poetry would have been so thwarted and hindered by other people, so tortured and pulled asunder by her own contrary instincts, that she must have lost her health and sanity to a certainty. No girl could have walked to London and stood at a stage door and forced her way into the presence of actor-managers without doing herself a violence and suffering an anguish which may have been irrational— for chastity may be a fetish invented by certain societies for unknown reasons—but were none the less inevitable. . . .

But for women, I thought, looking at the empty shelves, these difficulties were infinitely more formidable. In the first place, to have a room of her own, let alone a quiet room or a sound-proof room, was out of the question, unless her parents were exceptionally rich or very noble, even up to the beginning of the nineteenth century. Since her pin money, which depended on the good will of her father, was only enough to keep her clothed, she was debarred from such alleviations as came even to Keats or Tennyson or Carlyle, all poor men, from a walking tour, a little journey to France, from the separate lodging which, even if it were miserable enough, sheltered them from the claims and tyrannies of their families. Such material difficulties were formidable; but much worse were the immaterial. The indifference of the world which Keats and Flaubert and other men of genius have found so hard to bear was in her case not indifference but hostility. The world did not say to her as it said to them, Write if you choose; it makes no difference to me. The world said with a guffaw, Write? What's the good of your writing? . . .

R E A D I N G *67*

Poetry Is Not a Luxury

Audre Lorde (1982)

The quality of light by which we scrutinize our lives has direct bearing upon the product which we live, and upon the changes which we hope to bring about through those lives. It is within this light that we form those ideas by which we pursue our magic and make it realized. This is poetry as illumination, for it is through poetry that we give name to those ideas which are— until the poem—nameless and formless, about to be birthed, but already felt. That distillation of experience from which true poetry springs births thought as dream births concept, as feeling births idea, as knowledge births (precedes) understanding.

As we learn to bear the intimacy of scrutiny and to flourish within it, as we learn to use the products of that scrutiny for power within our living, those fears which rule our lives and form our silences begin to lose their control over us.

For each of us as women, there is a dark place within, where hidden and growing our true spirit rises, "beautiful/and tough as chestnut/stanchions against (y)our nightmare of weakness/"[1] and of impotence.

These places of possibility within ourselves are dark because they are ancient and hidden; they have survived and grown strong through that darkness. Within these deep places, each one of us holds an incredible reserve of creativity and power, of unexamined and unrecorded emotion and feeling. The woman's place of power within each of us is neither white nor surface; it is dark, it is ancient, and it is deep.

When we view living in the european mode only as a problem to be solved, we rely solely upon our ideas to make us free, for these were what the white fathers told us were precious.

But as we come more into touch with our own ancient, noneuropean consciousness of living as a situation to be experienced and interacted with, we learn more and more to cherish our feelings, and to respect those hidden sources of our power from where true knowledge and, therefore, lasting action comes.

At this point in time, I believe that women carry within ourselves the possibility for fusion of these two approaches so necessary for survival, and we come closest to this combination in our poetry. I speak here of poetry as a revelatory distillation of experience, not the sterile word play that, too often, the white fathers distorted the word *poetry* to mean—in order to cover a desperate wish for imagination without insight.

For women, then, poetry is not a luxury. It is a vital necessity of our existence. It forms the quality of the light within which we predicate our hopes and dreams toward survival and change, first made into language, then into idea, then into more tangible action. Poetry is the way we help give name to the nameless so it can be thought. The farthest horizons of our hopes and fears are cobbled by our poems, carved from the rock experiences of our daily lives.

As they become known to and accepted by us, our feelings and the honest exploration of them become sanctuaries and spawning grounds for the most radical and daring of ideas. They become a safe-house for that difference so necessary to change and the conceptualization of any meaningful action. Right now, I could name at least ten ideas I would have found intolerable or incomprehensible and frightening, except as they came after dreams and poems. This is not idle fantasy, but a disciplined attention to the true meaning of "it feels right to me." We can train ourselves to respect our feelings and to transpose them into a language so they can be shared. And where that language does not yet exist, it is our poetry which helps to fashion it. Poetry is not only dream and vision; it is the skeleton architecture of our lives. It lays the foundations for a future of change, a bridge across our fears of what has never been before.

Possibility is neither forever nor instant. It is not easy to sustain belief in its efficacy. We can sometimes work long and hard to establish one beachhead of real resistance to the deaths we are expected to live, only to have that beachhead assaulted or threatened by those canards we have been socialized to fear, or by the withdrawal of those approvals that we have been warned to seek for safety. Women see ourselves diminished or softened by the falsely benign accusations of childishness, of nonuniversality, of changeability, of sensuality. And who asks the question: Am I altering your aura, your ideas, your dreams, or am I merely moving you to temporary and reactive action? And even though the latter is no mean task, it is one that must be seen within the context of a need for true alteration of the very foundations of our lives.

The white fathers told us: I think, therefore I am. The Black mother within each of us—the poet— whispers in our dreams: I feel, therefore I can be free. Poetry coins the language to express and charter this revolutionary demand, the implementation of that freedom.

However, experience has taught us that action in the now is also necessary, always. Our children cannot dream unless they live, they cannot live unless they are nourished, and who else will feed them the real food without which their dreams will be no different from ours? "If you want us to change the world someday, we at least have to live long enough to grow up!" shouts the child.

Sometimes we drug ourselves with dreams of new ideas. The head will save us. The brain alone will set us free. But there are no new ideas still waiting in the wings to save us as women, as human. There are only old and forgotten ones, new combinations, extrapolations and recognitions from within ourselves—along with the renewed courage to try them out. And we must constantly encourage ourselves and each other to attempt the heretical actions that our dreams imply, and so many of our old ideas disparage. In the forefront of our move toward change, there is only poetry to hint at possibility made real. Our poems formulate the implications of ourselves, what we feel within and dare make real (or bring action into accordance with), our fears, our hopes, our most cherished terrors.

For within living structures defined by profit, by linear power, by institutional dehumanization, our feelings were not meant to survive. Kept around as unavoidable adjuncts or pleasant pastimes, feelings were expected to kneel to thought as women were expected to kneel to men. But

women have survived. As poets. And there are no new pains. We have felt them all already. We have hidden that fact in the same place where we have hidden our power. They surface in our dreams, and it is our dreams that point the way to freedom. Those dreams are made realizable through our poems that give us the strength and courage to see, to feel, to speak, and to dare.

If what we need to dream, to move our spirits most deeply and directly toward and through promise, is discounted as a luxury, then we give up the core—the fountain—of our power, our womanness; we give up the future of our worlds.

For there are no new ideas. There are only new ways of making them felt—of examining what those ideas feel like being lived on Sunday morning at 7 A.M., after brunch, during wild love, making war, giving birth, mourning our dead—while we suffer the old longings, battle the old warnings and fears of being silent and impotent and alone, while we taste new possibilities and strengths.

NOTE

1. From "Black Mother Woman," first published in *From A Land Where Other People Live* (Broadside Press, Detroit, 1973), and collected in *Chosen Poems: Old and New* (W. W. Norton and Company, New York, 1982), p. 53.

READING **68**

Tlilli, Tlapalli/ The Path of Red and Black Ink

Gloria Anzaldúa (1987)

Out of poverty, poetry;
out of suffering, song.

—*a Mexican saying*

When I was seven, eight, nine, fifteen, sixteen years old, I would read in bed with a flashlight under the covers, hiding my self-imposed insomnia from my mother. I preferred the world of the imagination to

the death of sleep. My sister, Hilda, who slept in the same bed with me, would threaten to tell my mother unless I told her a story.

I was familiar with *cuentos*—my grandmother told stories like the one about her getting on top of the roof while down below rabid coyotes were ravaging the place and wanting to get at her. My father told stories about a phantom giant dog that appeared out of nowhere and sped along the side of the pickup no matter how fast he was driving.

Nudge a Mexican and she or he will break out with a story. So, huddling under the covers, I made up stories for my sister night after night. After a while she wanted two stories per night. I learned to give her installments, building up the suspense with convoluted complications until the story climaxed several nights later. It must have been then that I decided to put stories on paper. It must have been then that working with images and writing became connected to night.

INVOKING ART

In the ethno-poetics and performance of the shaman, my people, the Indians, did not split the artistic from the functional, the sacred from the secular, art from everyday life. The religious, social and aesthetic purposes of art were all intertwined. Before the Conquest, poets gathered to play music, dance, sing and read poetry in open-air places around the *Xochicuahuitl, el Árbol Florido,* Tree-in-Flower. (The *Coaxihuitl* or morning glory is called the snake plant and its seeds, known as *ololiuhqui,* are hallucinogenic.[1]) The ability of story (prose and poetry) to transform the storyteller and the listener into something or someone else is shamanistic. The writer, as shape-changer, is a *nahual,* a shaman.

In looking at this book that I'm almost finished writing, I see a mosaic pattern (Aztec-like) emerging, a weaving pattern, thin here, thick there. I see a preoccupation with the deep structure, the underlying structure, with the gesso underpainting that is red earth, black earth. I can see the deep structure, the scaffolding. If I can get the bone structure right, then putting flesh on it proceeds without too many hitches. The problem is that the bones often do not exist prior to the flesh, but are shaped after a vague and broad shadow of its form is discerned or uncovered during beginning, middle and final stages of the writing. Numerous overlays of paint, rough surfaces, smooth surfaces make me realize I am preoccupied with texture as well. Too, I see the barely contained color threatening to spill over the boundaries of the object it represents and into other "objects" and over the borders of the frame. I see a hybridization of metaphor, different species of ideas popping up here, popping up there, full of variations and seeming contradictions, though I believe in an ordered structured universe where all phenomena are interrelated and imbued with spirit. This almost finished product seems an assemblage, a montage, a beaded work with several leitmotifs and with a central core, now appearing, now disappearing in a crazy dance. The whole thing has had a mind of its own, escaping me and insisting on putting together the pieces of its own puzzle with minimal direction from my will. It is a rebellious, willful entity, a precocious girl-child forced to grow up too quickly, rough, unyielding, with pieces of feather sticking out here and there, fur, twigs, clay. My child, but not for much longer. This female being is angry, sad, joyful, is *Coatlicue,* dove, horse, serpent, cactus. Though it is a flawed thing—a clumsy, complex, groping blind thing—for me it is alive, infused with spirit. I talk to it; it talks to me.

I make my offerings of incense and cracked corn, light my candle. In my head I sometimes will say a prayer—an affirmation and a voicing of intent. Then I run water, wash the dishes or my underthings, take a bath, or mop the kitchen floor. This "induction" period sometimes takes a few minutes, sometimes hours. But always I go against a resistance. Something in me does not want to do this writing. Yet once I'm immersed in it, I can go fifteen to seventeen hours in one sitting and I don't want to leave it.

My "stories" are acts encapsulated in time, "enacted" every time they are spoken aloud or read silently. I like to think of them as performances and not as inert and "dead" objects (as the aesthetics of Western culture think of art works). Instead, the work has an identity; it is a "who" or a "what" and contains the presences of persons, that is, incarnations of gods or ancestors or natural and cosmic powers. The work manifests the same needs as a person, it needs to be "fed," *la tengo que bañar y vestir.*

When invoked in rite, the object/event is "present;" that is, "enacted," it is both a physical thing and the power that infuses it. It is metaphysical in that it "spins its energies between gods and humans" and its task is to move the gods. This type of work dedicates itself to managing the universe and its energies. I'm not sure what it is when it is at rest (not in performance). It may or may not be a "work" then. A mask may only have the power of presence during a ritual dance and the rest of the time it may merely be a "thing." Some works exist forever invoked, always in performance. I'm thinking of totem poles, cave paintings. Invoked art is communal and speaks of everyday life. It is dedicated to the validation of humans; that is, it makes people hopeful, happy, secure, and it can have negative effects as well, which propel one towards a search for validation.[2]

The aesthetic of virtuosity, art typical of Western European cultures, attempts to manage the energies of its own internal system such as conflicts, harmonies, resolutions and balances. It bears the presences of qualities and internal meanings. It is dedicated to the validation of itself. Its task is to move humans by means of achieving mastery in content, technique, feeling. Western art is always whole and always "in power." It is individual (not communal). It is "psychological" in that it spins its energies between itself and its witness.[3]

Western cultures behave differently toward works of art than do tribal cultures. The "sacrifices" Western cultures make are in housing their art works in the best structures designed by the best architects; and in servicing them with insurance, guards to protect them, conservators to maintain them, specialists to mount and display them, and the educated and upper classes to "view" them. Tribal cultures keep art works in honored and sacred places in the home and elsewhere. They attend them by making sacrifices of blood (goat or chicken), libations of wine. They bathe, feed, and clothe them. The works are treated not just as objects, but also as persons. The "witness" is a participant in the enactment of the work in a ritual, and not a member of the privileged classes.[4]

Ethnocentrism is the tyranny of Western aesthetics. An Indian mask in an American museum is transposed into an alien aesthetic system where what is missing is the presence of power invoked through performance ritual. It has become a conquered thing, a dead "thing" separated from nature and, therefore, its power.

Modern Western painters have "borrowed," copied, or otherwise extrapolated the art of tribal cultures and called it cubism, surrealism, symbolism. The music, the beat of the drum, the Blacks' jive talk. All taken over. Whites, along with a good number of our own people, have cut themselves off from their spiritual roots, and they take our spiritual art objects in an unconscious attempt to get them back. If they're going to do it, I'd like them to be aware of what they are doing and to go about doing it the right way. Let's all stop importing Greek myths and the Western Cartesian split point of view and root ourselves in the mythological soil and soul of this continent. White America has only attended to the body of the earth in order to exploit it, never to succor it or to be nurtured in it. Instead of surreptitiously ripping off the vital energy of people of color and putting it to commercial use, whites could allow themselves to share and exchange and learn from us in a respectful way. By taking up *curanderismo,* Santeria, shamanism, Taoism, Zen and otherwise delving into the spiritual life and ceremonies of multi-colored people, Anglos would perhaps lose the white sterility they have in their kitchens, bathrooms, hospitals, mortuaries and missile bases. Though in the conscious mind, black and dark may be associated with death, evil and destruction, in the subconscious mind and in our dreams, white is associated with disease, death and hopelessness. Let us hope that the left hand, that of darkness, of femaleness, of "primitiveness," can divert the indifferent, right-handed, "rational" suicidal drive that, unchecked, could blow us into acid rain in a fraction of a millisecond.

NOTE

1. R. Gordon, Wasson, *The Wondrous Mushroom: Mycolatry in Mesoamerica* (New York, NY: McGraw-Hill Book Company, 1980), 59, 103.
2. Robert Plant Armstrong, *The Power of Presence: Consciousness, Myth, and Affecting Presence* (Philadelphia, PA: University of Pennsylvania Press, 1981), 11, 20.
3. Armstrong, 10.
4. Armstrong, 4.

Female Chauvinist Pigs

Ariel Levy (2005)

On the first warm day of spring 2000, the organization New York Women in Film & Television threw a brunch to honor Sheila Nevins, a twenty-six-year veteran of HBO and their president of documentary and family programming. It was held in a grand, street-level room off Park Avenue, in which they'd assembled an impressive selection of stylish women, seasonal berries, and high-end teas. Through the windows you could see the passing streams of yellow taxis sparkling in the midtown sunlight.

But the vibe was more *Lifetime Intimate Portrait* than *Sex and the City.* "I was growing up in a society where women were quiet so I got to listen," Nevins reflected from the podium, where she sat lovely and serene in a pale pink shawl. "I like to laugh, I like to cry, the rest is paperwork."

Nevins is a big deal. She was once profiled as one of the "25 Smartest Women in America" along with Tina Brown, Susan Sontag, and Donna Brazile in *Mirabella. Crain's* has called Nevins "a revered player." Under her stewardship, HBO programs and documentary films have won seventy-one Emmy awards, thirteen Oscars, and twenty-two George Foster Peabody awards, including Nevins's own personal Peabody. In 2000, Nevins was inducted into the Broadcasting and Cable Hall of Fame, and she has received Lifetime Achievement Awards from the International Documentary Association and the Banff Television Festival. In 2002, Nevins was named the National Foundation for Jewish Culture's "Woman of Inspiration." She is an elegant blonde with a husband and a son and a glamorous, lucrative career that even involves an intimidating level of gravitas: She has overseen the making of films about the Holocaust, cancer, and war orphans.

At that breezy spring breakfast, all the women wore glazed, reverential expressions as they picked at their melon wedges and admired Nevins's sharp wit, keen intellect, and zebra-printed slides. "Who opened your career doors for you?" one wanted to know.

"Me," Nevins replied.

A tweedy gentleman with a bow tie started his question with, "I'm just the token guy . . ."

Nevins gave a little snort and said, "You're all tokens," and everyone had a good laugh.

But then a curly-haired woman in the back brought up *G-String Divas,* a late-night "docu-soap" Nevins executive produced, which treated audiences to extended showings of T & A sandwiched between interviews with strippers about tricks of the trade and their real-life sexual practices. "Why would a woman—a middle-aged woman with a child—make a show about strippers?" the woman asked. Everyone was stunned.

Nevins whipped around in her chair. "You're talking fifties talk! Get with the program!" she barked. "I love the sex stuff, I love it! What's the big deal?"

In fact, there *was* something vaguely anachronistic about this woman compared to the rest with their blowouts and lip liner. She adjusted her eyeglasses, visibly shaken, but persisted. "Why is it still the case that if we're going to have a series about women on television, it has to be about their bodies and their sexuality?"

Nevins shook her head furiously. "Why is it that women will still go after women taking their clothes off and not after all the injustices in the workplace? I don't get it! As if women taking off their clothes is disgusting and degrading. Not being able to feed your kids, *that's* disgusting and degrading!"

"But . . ."

"Everyone has to bump and grind for what they want," Nevins interrupted. "Their bodies are their instruments and if I had that body I'd play it like a Stradivarius!"

"But . . ."

"The women are beautiful and the men are fools! What's the problem?"

"But you're not really answering my question."

Of course not. Because part of the answer is that nobody wants to be the frump at the back of the room anymore, the ghost of women past. It's just not cool. What *is* cool is for women to take a guy's-eye view of pop culture in general and live, nude girls in particular. *You're worried about strippers?* Nevins seemed on the verge of hollering at her inquisitor, *Honey, they could teach you a thing or two about where it's at!* Nevins was threatening something she clearly considered far worse than being objectified: being out of touch.

If you are too busy or too old or too short to make a Stradivarius of yourself, then the least you can do is appreciate that achievement in others, or so we are told. If you still suffer from the (hopelessly passé) conviction that valuing a woman on the sole basis of her hotness is, if not disgusting and degrading, then at least dehumanizing, if you still cling to the (pathetically deluded) hope that a more abundant enjoyment of the "sex stuff" could come from a reexamination of old assumptions, then you are clearly stuck in the past (and you'd better get a clue, but quick).

If I told you that I'd met someone who executive produces a reality show about strippers, who becomes irritable and dismissive when faced with feminist debate, and who is a ferocious supporter of lap dances, you might reasonably assume I was talking about a man—the kind of man we used to call a Male Chauvinist Pig. But no. I'm talking about the Jewish Woman of Inspiration. I'm talking about an urbane, articulate, extremely successful woman who sits on a high perch in the middle of the mainstream, and I *could* be talk- ing about any number of other women, because the ideas and emotions Nevins gave voice to are by no means uniquely her own: They are the status quo.

We decided long ago that the Male Chauvinist Pig was an unenlightened rube, but the Female Chauvinist Pig (FCP) has risen to a kind of exalted status. She is post-feminist. She is funny. She *gets it.* She doesn't mind cartoonish stereotypes of female sexuality, and she doesn't mind a cartoonishly macho response to them. The FCP asks: Why throw your boyfriend's *Playboy* in a freedom trash can when you could be partying at the Mansion? Why worry about *disgusting* or *degrading* when you could be giving—or getting—a lap dance yourself? Why try to beat them when you can join them?

There's a way in which a certain lewdness, a certain crass, casual manner that has at its core a me-Tarzan-you-Jane mentality can make people feel equal. It makes us feel that way because we are all Tarzan now, or at least we are all pretending to be. For a woman like Nevins, who "grew up in a society where women were quiet" and still managed to open all her career doors herself, this is nothing new. She has been functioning—with enormous success—in a man's world for decades. Somewhere along the line she had to figure out how to be one of the guys.

Nevins is (still) what used to be known as a "loophole woman," an exception in a male-dominated field whose presence supposedly proves its penetrability. (The phrase was coined by Caroline Bird in her book *Born Female: The High Cost of Keeping Women Down,* published in 1968.) Women in powerful positions in entertainment were a rare breed when Nevins started out, and they remain so today. In 2003, women held only 17 percent of the key roles—executive producers, producers, directors, writers, cinematographers, and editors—in making the top 250 domestic grossing films. (And progress is stalled: The percentage of women working on top films hasn't changed since 1998.) Meanwhile on television, men outnumbered women by approximately four to one in behind-the-scenes roles in the 2002–2003 prime-time season, which was also the case for the preceding four seasons. What the statistics indicate more clearly than the entertainment industry's permeability is a woman like Nevins's own vulnerability. To hang on to her position, she has to appear that much more confident, aggressive, and unconflicted about her choices—she has to do everything Fred Astaire does, backward, in heels.

Women who've wanted to be perceived as powerful have long found it more efficient to identify with men than to try and elevate the entire female sex to their level. The writers Mary McCarthy and Elizabeth Hardwick were famously contemptuous of "women's libbers," for example, and were untroubled about striving to "write like a man." Some of the most glamorous and intriguing women in our history have been compared to men, either by admirers or detractors. One of poet Edna St. Vincent Millay's many lovers, the young editor John Bishop, wrote to her in a letter, "I think really that your desire works strangely like a man's." In an August 2001 article for *Vanity Fair*, Hillary Clinton's biographer Gail Sheehy commented that "from behind, the silhouette of the freshman senator from New York looks like that of a man." A high school classmate of Susan Sontag's told her biographers Carl Rollyson and Lisa Paddock that young "Sue" maintained a "masculine kind of independence." Judith Regan, the most feared and famous executive in publishing—and the woman who brought us Jenna Jameson's best-selling memoir—is fond of bragging, "I have the biggest cock in the building!" at editorial meetings (and referring to her detractors as "pussies"). There is a certain kind of woman—talented, powerful, unrepentant—whom we've always found difficult to describe without some version of the phrase "like a man," and plenty of those women have never had a problem with that. Not everyone cares that this doesn't do much for the sisterhood.

Raunch provides a special opportunity for a woman who wants to prove her mettle. It's in fashion, and it is something that has traditionally appealed exclusively to men and actively offended women, so producing it or participating in it is a way both to flaunt your coolness and to mark yourself as different, tougher, looser, funnier—a new sort of loophole woman who is "not like other women," who is instead "like a man." Or, more precisely, like a Female Chauvinist Pig.

Sherry, Anyssa, and Rachel are a trio of friends who share a taste for raunch: *Maxim,* porn, Howard Stern, *Playboy,* you name it. All three are in their late twenties and, on the night we met, they had recently returned to New York City from a post-collegiate spring break. Rachel, a registered nurse, a tough, compact girl with short red hair, had brought the others a memento: a postcard picturing a woman's tumescent breasts against a background of blue sky with the words *Breast wishes from Puerto Rico!* scrawled in loopy cursive across the top.

"When I first moved to New York, I couldn't get over Robin Byrd," said Rachel. She was talking about New York City's local-access television sex queen. Byrd has been on cable since 1977, hosting a show in which male and female performers strip and plug their upcoming appearances in clubs or magazines or porn movies. The finale of each show is Byrd—herself a former adult film performer—going around and licking or fondling each of her guest's breasts or genitals. "I wouldn't go out till I watched Robin Byrd, and when I did go out, I would talk about Robin Byrd," Rachel said. "Watching Robin Byrd doesn't turn me on, though. It's for humor."

"Yeah, it's all comical to me," Sherry agreed. Sherry had just completed her first day at a new job as an advertising account executive, and Rachel gave her a little congratulatory gift: a thick red pencil with a rubber Farrah Fawcett head smiling on one end.

All three of them loved *Charlie's Angels* growing up, but more recently they had become "obsessed" with Nevins's show *G-String Divas.* "The other day we were on the subway and I wanted to dance on the pole in the middle," said Anyssa. "I could never be a stripper myself, but I think it would be so sexually liberating." Her looks were not holding her back. Anyssa was a Stradivarius . . . a built, beautiful young woman with milky skin and silky hair and a broad, lip-sticked mouth. She aspired to be an actress, but in the meantime she was working at a bar near Union Square. "When I'm bartending, I don't dress up though," she said. "Because I have to deal with enough assholes as it is. In college, Sherry and I, by day we would wear these guy outfits, and then at night we'd get dressed up, and people would be like, *Oh my God!* It's like a card . . . you pull out the hot card and let them look at you and it takes it to a whole different level." Anyssa smiled. "And maybe you get to *feel* like a stripper does."

Everyone was quiet for a moment, savoring that possibility.

I suggested there were reasons one might not want to feel like a stripper, that spinning greasily around a pole wearing a facial expression not found in nature is more a parody of female sexual power than an expression of it. That did not go over well.

"I can't feel bad for these women," Sherry snapped. "I think they're asking for it."

Sherry considered herself a feminist. "I'm very pro-woman," she said. "I like to see women succeed, whether they're using their minds to do it or using their tits." But she didn't mind seeing women fail, either, if they weren't using both effectively. . . .

"Yeah, we're all women, but are we supposed to band together?" said Anyssa. "Hell, no. I don't trust women. Growing up, I hung out with all guys . . . these are the first girls I ever hung out with who had the same mentality as me." . . .

Carrie Gerlach, then an executive at Sony Pictures in Los Angeles, wrote in an e-mail in 2001:

> My best mentors and teachers have always been men. Why? Because I have great legs, great tits, and a huge smile that God gave to me. Because I want to make my first million before the age of thirty-five. So of course I am a female chauvinist pig. Do you think those male mentors wanted me telling them how to better their careers, marketing departments, increase demographics? Hell no. They wanted to play in my secret garden. But I applied the Chanel war paint, pried the door open with Gucci heels, worked, struggled and climbed the ladder. And made a difference!!! And I did it all in a short Prada suit.

Gerlach made no bones about wanting to "climb the ladder" so she could enjoy life's ultimate riches, namely Prada, Gucci, and Chanel. The ends justify the means, and the means are "great legs" and "great tits."

"Everyone wants to make money," said Erin Eisenberg, the daughter of a pair of erstwhile hippies. ("My dad claims he was a socialist," she said skeptically.) Where her parents had misgivings about the system, Erin has doubts only about its lower rungs. Gone is the sixties-style concern (and lip service) about society as a whole. FCPs don't bother to question the criteria on which women are judged, they are too busy judging other women themselves.

"Who doesn't want to be looked at as a sex symbol?" said Shaina. "I always tell people, if I had a twenty-three-inch waist and a great body, I would pose in *Playboy*. You know all those guys are sitting there staring at you, *awe-ing* at you. That must be power."

. . .

Mary Wells Lawrence was one of the first women in this country to start her own advertising agencies, certainly the most successful, and the first woman CEO of a company listed on the New York Stock Exchange. She stands out as one of the great giants of her industry, male or female. Wells Lawrence came up with the "I Love New York" campaign, which many people credit with resuscitating the city's image during the seventies; she also invented the weirdly unforgettable "Plop Plop Fizz Fizz" Alka-Seltzer ads.

One of her earliest successes was a colorful marketing strategy for Braniff Airlines in the sixties that eventually prompted a transformation of the look of American airports. Wells Lawrence bucked the bland, military style of the times and had every Braniff plane painted a bright color. Then she hired Emilio Pucci to design riotous costumes for the flight "hostesses." One of her ads featured what she called the "air strip," the process by which Braniff stewardesses paired down their Pucci flight uniforms little by little on the way to tropical destinations. Pucci "even made teeny-weeny bikinis for them, an inch of cloth," Wells Lawrence wrote in her memoir, *A Big Life (in Advertising)*. These ads, with their focus on pretty young women in escalating stages of undress, may have been what prompted

Gloria Steinem to famously comment, "Mary Wells Uncle Tommed it to the top."

In her memoir, Wells Lawrence returned fire at Steinem. "What a silly woman," she wrote. "I wanted a big life. I worked as a man worked. I didn't preach it, I did it."

How scalding. How convincing. Who wouldn't pick action over nagging, succeeding over hand-wringing? Who doesn't want a big life?

There's just one thing: Even if you are a woman who achieves the ultimate and becomes *like a man,* you will still always be like a woman. And as long as womanhood is thought of as something to escape from, something less than manhood, you will be thought less of, too.

There is a variety program on Comedy Central called *The Man Show,* which concludes each episode with a segment of bouncing women appropriately called "Girls on Trampolines." The show's original hosts Jimmy Kimmel and Adam Carolla have left; Kimmel now has his own network talk show, *Jimmy Kimmel Live,* on ABC, and both Kimmel and Carolla executive produce *Crank Yankers* for Comedy Central. But when I went to visit their set in L.A. in 2000, *The Man Show* was one of the top shows on cable, and it was getting a lot of attention for its brand of self-described "chauvinistic fun." Thirty-eight percent of *The Man Show's* viewers were female. It was co-executive produced by two women.

Like Sheila Nevins, co-executive producer Jennifer Heftler was not who you'd expect to find as the wizard behind the curtain of a raunch operation. She was a big woman who wore batik and had a tattoo of a dragonfly on her wrist and another of a rose on her ankle. She described her program as "big, dumb, goofy fun."

"One of the perks to this job was that I wouldn't have to prove myself anymore," she said. "I could say, 'I worked at *The Man Show*' and no one would ever say, 'Oh, that prissy little woman' again." Heftler felt her female viewers' incentive for watching the program was very much like her own for making it. "It's like a badge," she said. "Women have always had to find ways to make guys comfortable with where we are, and this is just another way of doing that. If you can show you're one of the guys, it's good."

The night I went to a taping, there wasn't enough space to fit all the guys who had lined up outside the studio, and a team of heavy-limbed boys in matching green T-shirts from Chico State were pumped to make it into the audience.

Don, the bald audience fluffer, seemed to be looking directly at them when he yelled from the stage, "A few weeks ago we had trouble with guys touching the women here. You can't just grab their asses—you don't do that in real life, do you? [Beat.] Welllll . . . so do I!" The frat guys cheered, but not with the alarming gusto of the man in front of them, a scrawny computer technician who resembled one of the P's in Peter, Paul and Mary. "To the women," shouted Don, "today only, you're an honorary man! Grab your dick!"

Abby, a brunette in tight white jeans, was called up to the stage for her big chance to win a T-shirt. Honorary man status notwithstanding, she was asked to expose her breasts. Abby declined, but agreed brightly to kiss another girl instead. A pert redhead in her early twenties raced up from the audience to wrap her hands around Abby's back and put her tongue in the stranger's mouth. "Yeah! Yeah! You're making me hard," shrieked Peter/Paul. He was nearly hit in the head by the Chico Statesman behind him, who pumped his fist in the air in front of his crotch, semaphoring masturbation.

Soon after, the stage doors opened and out poured the Juggies, nine dancing girls in coordinating pornographic nursery rhyme costumes: Little Red Riding Hood in spike-heeled patent leather thigh-highs, Bo Peep in a push-up bra so aggressive you could almost see her nipples, and, of course, Puss 'n Boots.

They shimmied their way around the audience, and some did tricks on the poles like strippers. After the shouting died down, Adam Carolla and Jimmy Kimmel emerged from backstage, fresh as daisies in matching gingham shirts. "Who knows a good joke?" Carolla asked.

"How do you piss your girlfriend off when you're having sex?" a guy in the back volunteered. "Call her up and tell her."

Then they showed a pretaped spot about a mock clinic for wife evaluation, where a prospective bride was assessed based on her grasp of football and her aptitude for administering fellatio to pornographer Ron Jeremy.

. . .

"There's a side to boydom that's fun," Jen Heftler declared. "They get to fart, they get to be loud—and I think now we're saying we can fart and curse and go to strip clubs and smoke cigars just as easily and just as well." As for the Juggies, we are supposed to experience them as kitsch. "In the sixties, Dean Martin had his Golddiggers, and they were basically Juggies," Heftler said, "but the audience wasn't in on the joke. It was just pretty girls because that's what a guy would have. Then it was, you can never have that, you can't show a woman as a sex object, that's terrible. Now we're back to having it, but it's kind of commenting on that as opposed to just being that. The girls are in on it, and the women watching it are in on it."

But after sitting in that audience, I have to wonder what exactly we are in on. That women are ditzy and jiggly? That men would like us to be?

"Listen," Heftler countered, "our generation has gone past the point where *The Man Show* is going to cause a guy to walk into a doctor's office and say, 'Oh, my God! A woman doctor!'"

Her co-executive producer, Lisa Page, a sweet, quiet woman, said, "It doesn't need to threaten us anymore."

The night after the taping, I had dinner with Carolla, Kimmel, and *The Man Show's* cocreator and executive producer, Daniel Kellison, at the restaurant inside the W Hotel in Westwood. I asked them why they supposed 38 percent of their viewers were women.

"We did a little research," said Carolla, "and it turns out 38 percent of all women have a sense of humor."

I laughed. I wanted to be one of those women. The women at the W were like another species: lush curves bursting off of impossibly thin frames and miles of hairless, sand-colored skin as far as the eye could see.

"It's a whole power thing that you take advantage of and career women take advantage of," Kellison offered. "If you read *Gear* or watch our show or Howard Stern or whatever, you have an overview of a cultural phenomenon, you have power. You take responsibility for your life and you don't walk around thinking, *I'm a victim of the press! I'm a victim of pop culture!* So you can laugh at girls on trampolines." He smiled warmly. "You get it."

For a moment I allowed myself to feel vaguely triumphant.

Kimmel sucked an oyster out of its shell and then snickered. "At TCA," the annual Television Critics Association conference in Pasadena, "this woman asked, 'How does having a big-breasted woman in the Juggy dance squad differ from having black women in the darkie dance squad?' I said, 'First of all, that's the stupidest question I've ever heard.'"

"Then Adam said, 'Let me put your mind at ease: If we ever decide to put together a retarded dance squad, you'll be the first one in it,'" said Kellison, and all three of them laughed.

"What kind of women do you hang out with?" I asked them.

Kimmel looked at me like I was insane. "For the most part," he said, "*women* don't even want to hang out with their friends."

And there it is. The reason that being Robin Quivers or Jen Heftler or me, for that moment when *I got it,* is an ego boost but not a solution. It can be fun to feel exceptional—to be the loophole woman, to have a whole power thing, to be an honorary man. But if you are the exception that proves the rule, and the rule is that women are inferior, you haven't made any progress.

A Woman's Role Is . . . on Television

Kristi Turnquist (2008)

One night not too long ago, I was at home, plopped on the couch at about 10:30 p.m., deciding whether to stay up a while longer or be a good citizen and go to bed. Rebel that I am, I opted to stay up, and switched channels on the TV, looking for something to hold my interest.

A familiar stop: Turner Classic Movies. And a familiar movie: "Gone With the Wind," which TCM shows as often as possible, apparently, and which I've seen umpteen times. I don't really know how many times equals "umpteen," but I first saw the Southern spectacle when I was a kid in the '60s. It was a gala re-release engagement at the old J.J. Parker's Broadway theater in downtown Portland, back when you'd dress up for a special movie (I chose an orange-and-gold plaid skirt and matching gold tights, if memory serves).

I loved "Gone With the Wind," of course, and in my youthful film-nut way, I concluded that when Vivien Leigh's Scarlett O'Hara swore, "As God is mah witness, ah'll nevah be hungry again!" it was the greatest movie scene ever. Masses of subsequent movies broadened my perspective since then. And frankly, my dear, though I've watched "Gone With the Wind" many times over the years, I haven't thought much more about Miss Scarlett and her travails.

Until now.

Because it wasn't until that sleepy evening of watching "Gone With the Wind" play out in all its melodramatic, dated, racially insensitive glory, that I realized how radical—shocking, even—it would be to see a character with as many layers as Scarlett turn up in a contemporary movie.

It's not news that American movies are in a massive slump when it comes to giving women juicy, complex, fully imagined roles. But it's a sign of just how dismal things have gotten when the most compelling female character of the year is "Juno," the hyperverbal, pregnant 16-year-old played by Ellen Page in the sleeper hit movie. True, Juno is complicated, a fascinating blend of child and adult, with strong, mixed-up emotions, a biting wit and vast expertise in the work of slasher film director Dario Argento. But, she's a teenager, for crying out loud. Where are the grown-up women in film with this much oomph? Where are the Scarletts—passionate, selfish, romantic, pragmatic, strong, lovable one minute, hateful the next, but never boring?

I'll tell you where they are: on TV. Where movies, with few exceptions, define women characters by their relationships (to men, to parents, to their children), TV's heroines are all over the map. They scheme (Glenn Close in "Damages"). They mess up (Holly Hunter in "Saving Grace"). They stare down bad guys (Kyra Sedgwick in "The Closer"). They're action moms (Lena Headey in "Terminator: The Sarah Connor Chronicles"). Even when the shows are lousy, as in the "Sex and the City" clone, "Cashmere Mafia," the leading ladies are in charge, the men handsome satellites revolving around them.

Meanwhile, at the movies, you can see men fighting men ("No Country for Old Men"), men building empires ("There Will be Blood"), a fabulous actress *playing* a man (Cate Blanchett in "I'm Not There"), men bonding with men ("The Bucket List"), and so on. The exceptions—the intriguing, deeply flawed writer-to-be Briony, in "Atonement"—are few and far-between.

Two Target Audiences

Why the gap between the big screen and the small? Movies, at least the non-indie variety, have for the past decade relied heavily on young male viewers—they were the audience most likely to attend during the all-important opening weekend, and women were presumably dragged along as willing dates. As for movies focused on women, for every female-centric hit like "The Devil Wears Prada," the box office is littered with flameouts like "In Her Shoes," the female action duds "Catwoman" and "Aeon Flux," and Hilary Swank's post- "Million Dollar Baby" fizzles, "Freedom Writers" and "The Reaping."

Women, apparently, read reviews. And save their money.

In television, by contrast, female viewers are much desired, which is another reason why imitations of "Sex and the City"—a breakthrough in terms of showing just how loyal women viewers could be to a show they identified with—keep chugging down the pipeline (next up: "Lipstick Jungle"). And TV's most popular female characters are hardly role models.

Daring to Annoy

Consider Katherine Heigl. In "Knocked Up," her character represented responsibility; she was the grounded, realistic half of the romantic duo, leaving co-star Seth Rogen to be funny, irritating and all-too-human. On "Grey's Anatomy," Heigl's Izzie is a mess of conflicting emotions: she sleeps with another woman's husband, fumes that her friends are cutting her out, but is the soul of compassion when it comes to patient care. "Grey's Anatomy" is addictive for women viewers because creator Shonda Rimes' female characters dare to be annoying.

They're selfish; they're driven; they're confused. They are, dare I say, Scarlett O'Hara-esque.

Heigl's character in "Knocked Up" is undoubtedly the better person. But Izzie is a heck of a lot more fun to watch. She doesn't have to be a combination wife/mother, the role Leslie Mann embodied in "Knocked Up," forcing feckless hubby Paul Rudd to step up to the plate. Izzie's just a person, with all the maddening imperfections that implies.

Hope on the Horizon

So where does all this leave us? With, most likely, another slate of not-very-thrilling Oscar best-actress nominees. And unfortunately, among all the other turmoil caused by the writers' strike, TV shows like "Grey's Anatomy" running out of fresh episodes.

But I have a glimmer of hope. For one, more women are in the moviemaking mix now (including such talents as "Juno" writer Diablo Cody, "The Savages" director Tamara Jenkins and "Lars and the Real Girl" writer Nancy Oliver). Movie attendance by young males is trending down (competition from video games and other distractions), so studios are acknowledging the need for movies that appeal to broader audiences. Maybe, if the writers' strike ever gets settled, and the directors don't go on strike, and the actors don't go on strike, we may see more movies built around women who aren't a) noble; b) loving-and-or-worried wives; or c) eye candy.

If TV can do it, Hollywood, so can you. As Scarlett—ever the optimist—would say: "After all . . ." (cue swelling music), "tomorrow is another day."

Desperately Debating *Housewives*

Jennifer L. Pozner and Jessica Seigel (2005)

Dear Jessica,

Say it ain't so! I hear you love *Desperate House-wives,* ABC's hit series that cynically reinforces sexual, racial, and class stereotypes. If that's true, you're in some questionable company.

On the episode of CNN's *Crossfire* during which he mocked "grouchy feminists with mustaches," Tucker Carlson praised *Housewives* as "good entertainment." *Washington Times* columnist Suzanne Fields described it as "sophisticated, edgy television for the era of the values voters who kept George W. on Pennsylvania Avenue."

It's no wonder right-wing culture warriors such as Carlson and Fields love a show whose worldview harks back to a time when two-parent, middle-class families could comfortably thrive on single incomes, women's identities were primarily determined by the men they married and the children they raised, and husbands were not expected to trouble themselves with such pesky matters as child care and housework. *House-wives'* Wisteria Lane is even set on the same Hollywood back lot where *Leave It to Beaver* was filmed.

Hyped as a cunning parody, *Housewives* is light on actual satire and heavy on the sorts of cultural clichés that play well at red-state country clubs. Of the four main characters, three are white, all are wealthy, and only one has a job—divorced mom Susan (Teri Hatcher), supposedly a children's-book illustrator. The only nonwhite wife, Gabrielle (Eva Longoria), plays into every tired cliché about oversexed, "spicy" Latina gold diggers. On Wisteria Lane, female friendships are shallow and only superficially supportive, and the rare woman who doesn't conform to an ultrathin, waxed ideal of beauty gets strangled in her kitchen (literally, as happened to a plump, nosy neighbor).

Jessica, when you find yourself enjoying a show that the *Chicago Tribune* encouraged readers to watch by saying, "Women viewers may find it offensive to wives, mothers, suburbanites, and feminists alike. Definitely stay tuned," it may be time to reevaluate your analysis. Is there something I'm missing?

Desperately Hating Housewives,
Jenn

Dear Desperately Hating,

Yup, you're missing plenty, Jenn, like the delicious Sunday evenings I spend coffee-klatching with my best friend over this madcap send-up of the *Leave It to Beaver* American dream. This show doesn't "hark back" to the past—it skewers the myth of motherhood and suburban bliss with *Feminine Mystique*–inspired irony so sly that conservatives are as divided as liberals over whether to love it or hate it.

Its stealth feminism has not been lost on the "values" crowd, including Rev. Donald Wildmon's American Family Association (AFA), which predictably denounced the show as immoral. Not surprisingly, Wildmon's group condemned its adulterous antics but not the murderous ones, singling out Gabrielle's affair with a hunky teenaged gardener. Disgusting, isn't it? Adult women finally get to ogle hottie jailbait without feeling like Mrs. Robinson—a visual droit du seigneur long enjoyed by men.

Yeah, adultery is bad. I'm against it. But *girl talk?* The AFA condemns that, too, as spokesman Randy Sharp told the *Chicago Tribune:* "Our objection to *Desperate Housewives* is that . . . discussion of intimate details between individuals is open for 'girl talk,' for lack of a better phrase."

Real ladies, we know, shut up and suffer in silence. Girl talk, in fact—formalized as consciousness-raising groups—helped fuel the women's movement. The personal was political, then and now. *Desperate Housewives* dramatizes the "Second Shift" realities of an America in which even full-time working women do most of the housework and only 5 percent of men take primary responsibility for child care. Girl talk is subversive, and it's the emotional heart of *Housewives,* as our four heroines lean on each other to navigate troubled marriages, divorce, children, and romance. Male characters are peripheral on the show, which has resurrected the careers of three fine actresses over age 40—a rarity on sweet-young-thing-obsessed prime-time television.

I think you confuse the starring quartet's longtime, sometimes ambivalent friendships—as in real life—with their spicy conflicts with secondary characters such as the neighborhood biddy (true, the only fatty). Still, when men fight we call it politics; when women fight, it's derided as backbiting or catfighting—words that denigrate females jockeying for position and power.

This show exposes a *Diary of a Mad Housewife* reality *and* the power of sisterhood. For example, when former corporate honcho Lynette's (Felicity Huffman) four unruly children make her suicidal, she confesses to her buddies that motherhood is driving her crazy. "Why don't they tell us this stuff?" she whines. "Why don't we talk about this?"

So they talk. When we finally get to a prime-time hit about women's domestic struggles—previously relegated to sappy daytime soaps—why is it a lightning rod for everything *wrong* with TV and America, including racism, classism, and lookism? Jenn, come on, join our coffee klatch—but no talking except during commercials. Can't you see the winking subversion beneath the impossibly thin, nouveau-riche facade? Or are you lining up with family-values conservatives on this one, like some feminists did in the 1980s antipornography movement?

Desperately Loving Housewives,
Jess

Hey Jess,

If you want "family-values conservatives," don't look to me—look to *Desperate Housewives'* creator Marc Cherry, a gay Republican who believes the real problem facing today's post-feminist women is too much freedom. As he told the *Contra Costa Times,* "We've reached the point where we realize that no, you really can't have it all. . . . Long ago, it used to be easier: Society laid down the rules for you. Now, there are a lot of choices, but sometimes choices can lead to chaos."

Where, exactly, does the "skewering" come in? Certainly not from the show's majority-male writers, or from its creator, who says *Housewives* is darkly comic but not *satirical.* "Satire sounds like you're making fun of something. And the truth is, I'm not making fun of the suburbs," Cherry told The Associated Press, adding to *Entertainment Weekly,* "I love the values the suburbs represent. Family, community, God." But since "stuff happens," the "fun" comes from watching women "making bad choices" and suffering the repercussions.

That's not "stealth feminism," it's just vindictive. Nor is it new—the Right loves punishing female sinners. Sadly, you're buying into regressive stereotyping gussied up as female empowerment. It's fabulous that it illuminates the frustrations accompanying stay-at-home motherhood. But while writer Ellen Goodman points to Lynette as a "signpost of a slowly changing society" and the *Pittsburgh Post-Gazette* branded her a "Generation's Truthsayer," they (and you) are ignoring the show's fundamental premise that child care is solely women's responsibility. Doesn't it bother you that Lynette is the very model of silent suffering? In a key flashback, she nods in queasy acquiescence when her husband tells her to quit her career to stay home with her babies. And no matter how low she sinks under the pressure of raising four kids—popping their ADD pills, self-medicating with red wine—she never asks her husband to share the burden.

As the former hostess of weekly *Xena, Warrior Princess* and *Buffy the Vampire Slayer* parties,

I'd happily join a coffee klatch centered around subversive, kitschy girl power. Friendships between intelligent, fleshed-out female characters were powerful enough to save the world on those shows; in contrast, the *Housewives* keep secrets from—rather than lean on—each other.

Look, I appreciate a good comedy as much as the next gal, but this show is more dangerous than a simple guilty pleasure—it's backlash humor hawking conservative ideology. For example, biological determinism explains a PTA mom's backstabbing behavior: "It hasn't really changed since Girl Scouts. Girls smile at you to your face, but then behind your back they make fun of you," Susan complains.

"That never would have happened in Boy Scouts," answers Lynette. "A guy takes his opponent on face-to-face, and once he's won, he's top dog. It's primitive but fair."

"Isn't it sexist of us to generalize like this?" Gabrielle asks.

"It's science, Gabrielle," says Lynette. "Sociologists have documented this stuff."

"Well, who am I to argue with sociologists," Gabrielle shrugs.

This is what passes for "girl talk" on Wisteria Lane—too bad it sounds so much like the Best of Dr. Laura.

Desperately Missing Roseanne,
Jenn

Dear Jenn,

At least we agree that *Desperate Housewives* is "darkly comic." Webster's says comedy is "the representation of human error and weakness as provocative of amusement." That means screwups and bad choices—which you seem to see as "vindictive" to women. Does that mean Jerry Lewis, the Marx Brothers, and Three Stooges are "vindictive" to men? But I won't suggest you "lighten up," because "Can't you take a joke?" is often used to undermine legitimate social critique.

Instead, I will deconstruct the joke. On *Desperate,* we're in the land of camp, that often gay, exaggerated aesthetic the late Susan Sontag so brilliantly pegged in "Notes on 'Camp'" (1964).

Housewives is a textbook case, beginning with the "double sense in which some things can be taken"—a "private zany experience" for insiders. Sontag's characteristics of camp also include exaggerated sex roles, shallow characters, overweening passion, heightened glamour, even pleasure in the "psychopathology of affluence."

That's exactly life on Wisteria Lane: murder, suicide, pedophilia, adultery, prostitution and drug abuse, all on one fabulously landscaped suburban street. *Desperate* creator Marc Cherry—who began his career writing for another woman-centered camp classic, *The Golden Girls*—claims to be a gay Republican (what could be campier?) while creating a show that's cul-de-sac Sodom.

You "got" the tongue-in-cheek aesthetic of *Xena* and *Buffy* because you liked the subject of superheroes fighting evil. I loved them too. But you're so offended by stay-at-home moms that *Housewives'* camp style doesn't register. Yet it's crucial. The show is not making policy recommendations about child care any more than it is recommending fornication and a multitude of sins yet to come (stay tuned!).

But enough critical theory—let's get to the burrito sex scene, my favorite. To win back her husband, domestic diva Bree (Marcia Cross) arrives at his hotel room wearing only red lingerie under an overcoat. At that very moment, however, he is chowing down on a giant burrito. The husband takes the bait, but, no surprise, the burrito topples from the table and distracts her. His wife's concern with a teetering bean wrap symbolizes how she makes him feel stifled.

The camera steps in as feminist, zooming in on the cheesy mess about to hit the floor. Who could think of sex at a time like that? Not us. As Infuriated Husband escorts her out, Bree quips: "Obviously you've never had to clean a cheese stain off a carpet."

"You bet, honey," I tell the TV. I've also urged Lynette to go back to work part-time, even while I identify with her pleasure in feminine arts I love, like sewing. These are women's concerns in a fortysomething woman's world, so rarely seen on prime-time television. That's my "zany private" experience as a feminist who believes women are good enough to be bad.

Still Loving Housewives,
Jessica

Hey Jessica,

What's with your accusation that I'm "offended by stay-at-home moms," rather than by a show which treats them so shabbily? I'm surprised you'd dust off the tired, misguided media chestnut painting feminists as anti-mother. I never implied that mothers shouldn't stay home if they want to (and if they *can*—that choice is a luxury in today's economy).

Jess, I don't need you to deconstruct the joke for me—I just don't buy it. When Roseanne Barr wrestled Meryl Streep in the film *She Devil,* that was camp. But when a bunch of conservative guys create a show in which every female character is portrayed as self-indulgent and incompetent, that's just good old-fashioned Hollywood crap. Can you really be so elitist as to think that burrito stains and arts and crafts are the "woman's world" concerns that most deserve celluloid attention? As for Lynette's "pleasure" in sewing school-play costumes, *please*—that "feminine art" drove her to drugs!

The Golden Girls played by their own rules, letting no societal code (and no man) dictate their behavior. Twenty years later, Lynette lives her husband's choices, Gabrielle trades sex for jewelry, "good girl" Susan is pitted against the "town slut," and Bree would rather keep a cheap motel's carpet clean than have an orgasm.

Yet that's why corporate media finds Wisteria's women so appealing. Remember when *Time* cited neurotic, micro-miniskirted *Ally McBeal* as the poster girl for the supposed death of feminism in 1998? Seven years later, it's the same old story: Reviewers from *The Washington Post* to *The Jerusalem Post* insist *Housewives* represents "reality" in a "typical" American neighborhood, and proves feminism has "failed" or been "killed." By the time Oprah Winfrey and Dr. Phil paraded around "Real-Life Desperate Housewives," I was ready to throw up. This show and its '50s politics are being used against us; don't confuse that with feminism.

At least Buffy's on DVD,
Jenn

Dear Jenn—

You have tried to indict *Desperate Housewives* and its fans with charges of male oppression and elitism. I beg to differ.

Hardly a male cabal, the *Desperate* writing staff is one-third female—slightly exceeding the percentage of women in the Writer's Guild of America, and much higher than that of, say, the popular sitcom *Everybody Loves Raymond* (only one of 10 writers is a woman this season). As to elitism, in today's economy, stay-at-home parenting is no "luxury," as you claim, but a savings for many families, considering child-care costs, income taxes and commuting expenses. So much for housewives = haute bourgeoisie.

You also imply that sewing is elitist. Careerism and girl-power fantasy blind you to women's real experience and history. I learned sewing from my grandmother, who learned from her mother, a seamstress. Making my own clothes is a proud working-class legacy.

Yes, the backlash scolds women. But so do you. You cherry-pick grievances, first faulting a character's "silent suffering," then branding the *Housewives* as "self-indulgent." Which is it? Neither. They're cartoon characters. This is high camp, which Sontag calls a multilayered "mode of enjoyment, of appreciation—not judgment."

You're still welcome to come over for *Desperate* night—I'll teach you to sew (during commercials). We'll start simple: maybe an apron.

Yours in stitches—
Jessica

If Women Ran Hip Hop

Aya de Leon (2007)

If women ran hip hop
the beats & rhymes would be just as dope,
but there would never be a bad vibe when you
    walked in the place
& the clubs would be beautiful & smell good
& the music would never be too loud
but there would be free earplugs available anyway
& venues would have skylights and phat patios
and shows would run all day not just late at night
cuz If women ran hip-hop we would have nothing
    to be ashamed of
& there would be an African marketplace
with big shrines to Oya
Yoruba deity of the female warrior &
    entrepreneur
and women would sell & barter & prosper
If women ran hip hop
there would never be shootings
cuz there would be onsite conflict mediators
to help you work through all that negativity &
    hostility
& there would also be free condoms & dental dams
in pretty baskets throughout the place
as well as counselors to help you make the
    decision:
do I really want to have sex with him or her?
& there would be safe, reliable, low-cost 24 hour
    transportation home
& every venue would have on-site quality child care
where kids could sleep while grown folks danced
& all shows would be all ages

cause the economy of hip-hop wouldn't revolve
    around the sale of alcohol
If women ran hip hop
same gender-loving & transgender emcees
would be proportionally represented
& get mad love from everybody
& females would dress sexy if we wanted to
    celebrate our bodies
but it wouldn't be that important because
everyone would be paying attention to our minds,
    anyway
If women ran hip hop
men would be relieved because it's so draining
to keep up that front of toughness & power &
    control 24-7
If women ran hip hop
the only folks dancing in cages would be dogs &
    cats
from the local animal shelter
excited about getting adopted by pet lovers in the
    crowd
If women ran hip-hop
there would be social workers available to refer
    gangsta rappers
to 21-day detox programs where they could get
    clean & sober
from violence & misogyny
but best of all, if women ran hip hop
we would have the dopest female emcees ever
because all the young women afraid to bust
would unleash their brilliance on the world

"Growing the Size of the Black Woman"
Feminist Activism in Havana Hip Hop

Ronni Armstead (2007)

Black Cubans have long been told by Cuban authorities that they do not need places to express the problems of race and class because there are no such problems: they have all been solved by the Revolution. Nevertheless, Black Cubans do face all manners of discrimination in contemporary Cuba. With few formal political outlets open to young Black Cubans (Fernandes 2003), hip hop has emerged on the island as a powerful form of political expression: a kind of "theater of the oppressed" that addresses the racial and economic problems encountered by Black Cubans (Boal 1985). The all-female group Las Krudas stands out as particularly courageous within this hip-hop scene.

In 2003, I spent four months studying at the University of Havana. While in Cuba, my research partner and I recorded interviews with 23 women of African descent. The members of Las Krudas were among this group. I draw upon these interviews to sketch a portrait of a striking phenomenon: the emergence of a strongly oppositional, Black, feminist activist art in Cuba.

I first saw Las Krudas perform at a concert of women rappers; I was struck by their positive message, and they were kind enough to invite me to their home for an interview. We chatted like old friends before we began tape recording the interview. One of the first topics we addressed was how they see their intersecting identities. Olivia tells me:

> I'm Black, I'm a woman and I'm Cuban. *¿Entiendes?* I'm not *above all* Cuban. I am more than Cuban; I feel as a woman, I feel Black. . . . But there are moments when I don't know *what* it means to be Cuban. Many times in places like schools and things I'm treated like: 'yes, you're Cuban, but you are not representative of Cuba.' *¿Entiendes?* So then I ask myself, *¿Soy cubana o no soy cubana?* Am I Cuban or not?

Pelusa is a *guantanamera* by birth. She lived in Guantánamo until she was seventeen and then migrated to the capital city. She made her social location clear during the interview: "Principally, I am a woman. I wake up in the morning and I say: 'I am a woman.'" But she also identifies as an artist, an artist with strong ties to the Afro-Cuban community: "I say: 'I have a social responsibility to represent my new ideas and to make my art, on stilts [with her public theater project], in the street, in hip hop, in my poetry, in our painting . . . family too. We are family, in our community.'" For Pelusa, being family, being part of a community, also means being true to her African roots. She proudly insists that Las Krudas seek to incorporate their African roots into their daily lives as well as into their artistic projects, and rap has been a good way to do that: "This hip-hop movement is a really beautiful way to urbanize and modernize and bring up to date the Afro-descended culture that is here," she explained. And she insists on her class location as well.

> More than being Cuban, I am a poor Cuban. *¿Entiendes?* A more humble Cuban. Because they say that in Cuba there are not classes, that everybody is working class. But in Cuba there has been achieved a differentiation, let's say, of certain social scales; there are people [here] who have a car

and a house. There are people here who have neither car nor house. *¿Entiendes lo que estoy diciendo?* Do you understand what I'm saying? And I am one of those people who have neither car nor house. Nothing. So I wake up in the morning wondering if at night I'm going to sleep in the same [bed] where I'm living now. So I tell you that [I identify with the] poor, women, artists, Cuban, Black, hip hop.

I also asked the group: *¿Uds son feministas?* Are you feminists? Pelusa spoke up to clarify:

We think that for us it is absolutely necessary to be feminists. Here, in this context at least. Because to be feminists, for us—is the balance that we need to live in this society *tan machista* that is so sexist. If society were a little-more open and more balanced, maybe we'd be a little more balanced and less extremist; but we are in an extremist society, and women have to balance our lives, and so we are also extremists. We are absolutely feminists . . . we know that women in the world need a lot of support today from other women. We give much solidarity so that our self-esteem becomes higher and higher. Because historically, it has been lower every day, I do not know, at least here in Cuba. It is said that, for example, during the revolutionary process, Cuban women have made some social advances and have gone on to, shall we say, to claim their position in society. But we absolutely know that women in Cuba have the double responsibility to work in the street, whatever work she obtains and soon to arrive home and perhaps work even harder in the house. Because here the domestic customs are [such] that the woman is the one who works in house . . . the woman is working all the time. All the time.

LAS KRUDAS AND HIP HOP

Pelusa, Wanda, and Olivia—the three members of Las Krudas—are *raperas* and community performance artists. Every afternoon they perform in the streets of Habana Vieja (Old Havana) on stilts.

They also direct a camp, introducing children to performance and public art. Pelusa underscores the importance to them of participating in a variety of art forms.

We are actresses in addition to rappers. . . . [We are] in theater, but we have to do our own theater because we don't want to join the [established] Cuban theater. We don't like what [Cuban theater] is doing. We do our own, where the Black woman has the role of protagonist; because the rest of the time in Cuban theater it's not that way. [Black women play] the classic role of slaves, servants, domestics, of long-suffering women, housewives. We have never had the possibility to have plays where the Black woman is protagonist and her life is a victory. *¿Entiendes?* Understand? So then, we, through our theater projects try to grow the size of the Black woman.

Achieving this goal through their hip-hop practice has not been easy. Pelusa illustrates this point.

Only young men have much time in their lives to dedicate to listening to music, learning to dance, going to parties, or rapping on the corner. . . . Since we were girls we played in the house and when we arrived at adolescence, we had to preoccupy ourselves with learning how to clean the house, how to keep our kitchens correctly, and all that.

She says that she understands that as men were at the forefront of the hip-hop movement they deserve their due, but at the same time she feels excluded from promoting her own art and talents.

[We recognize] that men have opened paths, that they have been the warriors, the chief warriors of this tribe . . . we [Las Krudas and other female rappers] are a tribe within a tribe, and we are fighting to prove we are just as strong and that we are going to demonstrate that we are capable of continuing the struggle with as much force as they [the male rappers] are.

Hip hop made its way to Cuba in the late 1970s as an extension of the U.S. rap scene via the eastern outskirts of Havana, in Alamar, home to "one of the largest housing projects in the world" whose residents were and continue to be predominantly Black (Olavarria 2002, 1). U.S. rap music was pirated from Miami radio transmissions by innovative young Alamar residents. It gained very wide popularity in Cuba in the early 1990s, just as hip hop in the United States was taking on distinct regional flavors and spilling across national borders.

Lacking technology and recording equipment, Cuban rappers composed their own lyrics to popular American rap tracks taped from the radio. Because of rap music's immense youth appeal, it can be effectively shaped to accommodate most any message. As in the United States, Cuban rap communicates a youthful sense of struggle and rebellion, anger and aggression, aspirations for social mobility and material well-being, and an unswerving identification with the streets. As a musical form it also opens a space for creativity, dialogue, and criticism (George 1998, 155). Also as in U.S. rap, Cuban rappers sample liberally, calling upon a shared musical heritage and collective memory. Afro-Cuban music, including a strong drum beat and traditional rumba sounds, is blended and combined with rap to form something original acknowledging and paying homage to the legacy of Cuba's African musical heritage.

Rap music—in both the United States and Cuban contexts—speaks directly to the social traumas and dislocations suffered by African-descended peoples living in metropolitan centers. Despite the official, government proclamations of fairness, economic opportunity, social mobility, and racial equality, inequity is the rule for most Black Cubans (Rose 1994, 102). For example, many young Black Cubans experience targeted police repression. In establishments catering to foreign capital, Black Cubans in particular are regularly denied access.[1] Like poor Black Americans, Black Cubans are the overwhelming majority of the island's growing underclass as is evidenced by increasing rates of Black unemployment, crime, and incarceration.

During a time of deep uneasiness about Cuba's post-socialist future, many Cubans fear that racial problems may undermine the notion that all is well in Cuba's revolutionary society. Black Cubans active in the hip-hop movement personify the fissure between the real, lived experience of race and the official ideology promoting the notion that racial harmony has been achieved on the island.

Although Las Krudas cannot represent the experiences of all Black women on the island, they occupy a unique position within a growing Black hip-hop intelligentsia. While their activities and lyrics point to specific issues of contemporary concern around the politics of race and gender in Cuba, they differ from U.S. Black women rappers and their Cuban male contemporaries in that they unwaveringly advance a feminist agenda in which they seek to politicize the social and economic reality of being Black and female in Cuba. Las Krudas therefore calls attention to the situation of Black women in a social and political context that denies the existence of racism, sexism, status, and privilege.

Despite Las Krudas' members' increasingly important position as feminists within the Cuba hip-hop culture, they share with U.S. women rappers a frustrating invisibility. In both Cuba and in the United States, women as fans, advocates, and artists in hip hop are virtually ignored in discussions of the phenomenon. Both in the United States and in Cuba, male artists have been touted for the political awareness and resistant nature of their rap lyrics. For example, male rappers in both the United States and Cuba protest and criticize the multiple ways the Black male body and masculinity is policed and surveilled. By contrast, many themes dominant in Black female rappers' lyrics in both the United States and Cuba articulate and/or question hegemonic notions of femininity and Black female sexuality.

Although in their lyrics many Black U.S. women rappers defend women against sexist assumptions and misogynist assertions made by their Black male counterparts, and they attempt to build their female audience's self-esteem and raise consciousness levels in efforts to encourage solidarity among women, most perceive feminism to be a movement specifically related to white women. Consequently, they are ambivalent about taking on a feminist label or stance for fear that assuming a feminist position will be perceived as "anti-Black male" (Rose 1994, 176). In solidarity with Black men, many U.S. Black women rappers refuse to identify or affiliate themselves with a movement that is perceived as speaking largely to heterosexual, white, upper middle-class women's concerns.

Unlike their North American counterparts, Las Krudas readily identify themselves as feminists and refuse to relinquish their strong critiques of the nature and effects of Cuban patriarchy on the lives of marginalized women. Las Krudas' lyrics encourage Black women to reject the racism and sexism of patriarchal notions of femininity, and they seek to raise the self-esteem of their female audiences. Many U.S. Black women rappers do the same. But Las Krudas' open embrace of feminist ideals makes them unique in the world of hip hop. This open embrace of feminism by Las Krudas has caused problems for them within the state-controlled music marketing entity. One example of the racially inflected sexism routinely experienced by the group occurred during the planning of the all-women's concert where I first saw them perform. The hip-hop agency that organized the concert is state-subsidized and run by a white man and a Black woman: together they manage eleven groups. Of these, only one group has a female member, Obseción (a husband and wife duo). The agency did not want to have to pay any of the groups or artists that they did not represent (which, in this case, included all the female *rapera* groups in this all women's concert). In addition, the director of the theater where the concert was taking place pushed for the inclusion of men on the stage even though the concert was intended to feature women artists exclusively. For instance, he tried to force the women rappers to incorporate male dancers and rappers into their acts, something Las Krudas resisted.

Ultimately, Las Krudas prevailed and successfully performed their own original, pro-woman songs, without the "enhancement" of male dancers. Olivia notes that the hip-hop world in Cuba is very sexist: "the rap world is (¡hmmmmph!) *tan fuerte,* so strong. *Muy machista, muy, muy, muy:* Very sexist, very, very." Olivia explained that she was annoyed and angered at the women's concert not only because of the way the organizers treated the women rappers but also because while the men (of the hip-hop world) showed up, their presence was perceived as counterproductive; the men never lent any real support to the women's cause according to Las Krudas. Also, regarding the other female rappers at the concert, Pelusa noted while the women were very good interpreters of text, *los textos* were not written by them but by men. Las Krudas agreed that the feminist movement as well as the hip-hop movement in Cuba has a "long way to go. Long, long, long."

GROWING THE SIZE OF THE BLACK WOMAN

Like their male counterparts, in their lyrics, Las Krudas defend the marginalized social location of the rapper and endeavor to dignify the rappers' claim that their music is authentically Cuban (Hernández 2004, 11). However, Las Krudas' artistic content diverges from Cuban male rappers in significant ways. Embedded in Las Krudas' lyrics and philosophy is a feminist stance that refuses to accept the sexist oppression of Black women. Las Krudas have used their music to speak openly about issues of racial and sexual identity that are not often aired publicly.

The first cut on their demo album, *Cubensi Hip Hop,* deals with the *momentos difíciles* (the difficult moments) women must live through. Those moments are eclipsed by a national discourse calling on all Cubans to sacrifice while asking women and African-descended peoples to sacrifice the most for the goals of the Revolution. In the opening song, *"Vamos a Vence,"* (We Will Overcome), Pasa Kruda announces the liberatory commitment of Las Krudas.

> *Vivimos momentos difíciles/ pero seguimos*
> *pa'lante*
> *Luchando nuestro derecho/ pa'lante me tiendo el*
> *pecho*
> *No obstante el camino estrecho/ juntas sabiendo*
> *la brecha*
> *Krudas, ¡prender la mecha!*

We live [through] difficult moments/ but we
  continue forward
Struggling [for] our right/ I turn my chest
  [facing] forward
No matter how narrow the path/ together,
  knowing the injustices
Krudas, light the torch! (Las Krudas 2004)

To Las Krudas, struggle is neither ugly, nor violent, nor done resentfully. The group promotes liberatory struggle "because life is a flower, small and delicate/ we will take care of it because it's very precious/ we will maintain it because it's beautiful, we will" *(porque la vida es como una florecita, pequeña y delicada/vamos a cuidarla porque es muy preciada/vamos a costarla porque es bonita, vamos)* (Las Krudas 2004).

It is because life is so precious and delicate and beautiful that Las Krudas urges their audience to *vencer la dificultad, "overcome the difficulty."* Concluding the song, Las Krudas sing the following.

Vamo' a vencer, orgullo arriba, comunidad,
Vamo' a vencer, Afrocubana viva prosperidad,
Vamo' a vencer, Krudas son parte de tu identidad,
Vamo' a vencer, mucha salud y felicidad . . .
Sexo feminino siempre relegado/pero Las Krudas el
  molde han quebrado.

We will overcome, raise your pride, community,
We will overcome, *Afrocubana* live [your] prosperity,
We will overcome, *Krudas* are a part of your
  identity,
We will overcome, with health and happiness . . .
Feminine sex, always relegated/but Las Krudas
  have broken the mold. (Las Krudas 2004)

By struggling to overcome the difficult moments that they face as Black women, and articulating this struggle as *raperas,* Las Krudas are paying homage to those artists who have gone before them, demanding that their presence in the hip-hop world be taken seriously and encouraging their audiences to take heart.

Las Krudas directly address and challenge their listeners. The group's lyrics remind and exhort their listeners to raise up their pride of self, to embrace the "crude" message of resistance, while securing a space for dialogue, empowerment, and self-definition and breaking the silence about the nature and effects of Cuban patriarchy and racism. The use in this song of the phrase "Vamos a Vence" carries a particularly pungent reference to the Cuban Revolution's long-standing slogan, "Venceremos!" (variously translatable as "We shall overcome," "We shall prevail," or "We will win/conquer"), which continues to be used during all official gatherings, by Fidel Castro during speeches and in countless other situations. This sly turn of phrase by Las Krudas transforms the fading battle cry of the revolution's warriors into a feminist exhortation to refuse sexist oppression.

In the second song on the demo album, *Pa'ketenteres* (*So that You Know*), Las Krudas allude to the stereotype of the long-suffering Cuban woman, destabilizing it by giving voice to her (their) experience(s). The chorus of the song points out that women play games with their lives, often for their very survival, as in the case of *jineteras,* female hustlers, and sex workers. Las Krudas sing the following.

Pa'ketenteres, asére/ y sepan el juego jugamos las
  mujeres
Pa'ketentere y no se desespere/ mi krudeza es la que
  tu mente quiere

So that you know, *asére/* that you might know the
  games we women play
So that you know and don't despair/ my crudeness
  is what your mind wants. (Las Krudas 2004)

While this lyric in particular might suggest that Las Krudas have constructed their audience to be male, the group raps primarily to female audiences, seeking to help women in the audience name their struggles and recognize the way patriarchy shapes "the games they play" and thus their oppression(s).

As *Pa'ketenteres* continues, the lyrics demonstrate that Las Krudas have as their goal nothing less than the liberation of Black Cuban women. They urge their listeners to embrace their independence and recognize the deeper implications of the experiences they share as Black women, exhorting them to struggle alongside Las Krudas as they rap.

Más que uds conocemos la discriminación/ somos clase humildes

Somos color/ pero demás somos mujeres/ necesitamos amor

Conocemos el sudor/ discutamos nuestro error

Cierra las piernas/ más hijo de la perra/ si protestas eres diabla

Cerebro de mosquito/ secretaria, salario bajito/ de las mas altas/ orgullo poquito

Hasta dónde/ contra la pared/somos personas/ siempre el mismo drama

El macho pa' la calle/ la hembra pa' la cama

[. . .]mujer, eres dueña de ti mismo/ de tu destino/ eres tu quien determina

cómo sigue tu camino/ eliges a quien amar/ eliges como pensar

eliges con quien soñar/ la dueña de la tierra y de la mar

mujer poderosa/ mujer hermosa/ mujer diosa/

femenina criatura sagrada, divina/ eres dueña de ti/ de la cabeza.

More than you, we [women] know discrimination
we are [a] humble class/ we are [of] color
but what's more, we are women/ we need love
we know sweat/ we discuss our error[s]

close your legs/ son of a bitch/ if you protest,
   you're [a] she-devil
brain of a mosquito/ secretary, low salary/ from
   the higher [salaried positions
there is] little pride/ where does it lead/ back
   against the wall/ we are people
always the same drama/ the man for the street/
   and the women for the bed

[. . .] woman, you rule yourself/ your destiny
you are the one who determines/ how to follow
   your path
choose who to love/ choose how to think/ choose
   with whom to dream
the ruler of the earth and the sea/ powerful woman
beautiful woman/ goddess woman/ sacred
   feminine creature, divine

you rule yourself/ of your [own] head. (Las
   Krudas 2004)

In *Pa'ketenteres,* Las Krudas reach beyond stereotypes of women as long-suffering or hyper-sexualized. They refer pointedly to the gendered contradictions implicit in Cuban society. They ask, drawing attention to the low wages of female clerical work, "where does this lead?" They respond with: our backs "against the wall." Las Krudas are never resigned to discrimination. They exhort their female audiences to recognize their power to be their own "ruler," to control their own lives. A good example here is the way the group invokes female deities and goddesses in their lyrics. This incorporation of Afro-Cuban cultural and religious references is a distinctive feature of Las Krudas's message of female dignity and self-determination.

Las Krudas's "Eres Bella" (You are Beautiful) is another anthem to the dignity of the Black Cuban woman. Significantly, Las Krudas dedicated this rap to solidarity with an imagined, global community of women.

Dedicado a todas las mujeres del mundo

A todas las mujeres que como nosotras están luchando

A todas las guerreras campesinas, urbanas

A todas las hermanas

Especialmente a las más negras

Especialmente a las más pobres

Especialmente a las más gordas

Soy yo . . .

Dedicated to all the women in the world,
To all the women who, like us, are struggling,
To all the rural, urban warriors,
To all of the sisters,
Especially the most Black,
Especially the most poor,
Especially the most fat,
I am . . . (Las Krudas 2004)

Dedicated to the most marginalized women of the world, "Eres Bella" strongly rejects the old Cuban adage that Black women are strictly for work, while *mulatas* are for the love. Las Krudas rap to their "sisters."

Eres bella siendo tú, ébano en flor, negra luz
Eres bella siendo tú, cuerpo no es única virtud
Eres bella siendo tú, ébano en flor, negra luz
Eres bella siendo tú, inteligencia es tu virtud.

You are beautiful being you, ebony in flower,
    Black light
You are beautiful being you, [your] body isn't
    [your] only virtue
You are beautiful being you, ebony in flower,
    Black light
You are beautiful being you, intelligence is your
    virtue. (Las Krudas 2004)

Las Krudas also demonstrate here a deep understanding of the plight of Black women involved in the world of *jineterismo.* Their lyrics make clear that hustling for dollars is, in many instances, an individual strategy for survival as well as a national one. Las Krudas make the point that even if a woman is caught up in hustling as a way to "get by," using whatever means available to her, her humanity, her personhood are nonetheless deserving of respect.

Ya no seguimos, siendo objeto de valorización
que nos queda/ prostitución, seducción
esto es solo una costumbre de dar
pa' ayudar a nuestra gente económicamente
en este mundo tan material/ no somos nalgas y
    pechos solamente
tenemos cerebros/ mujeres siente, siente

We will no longer continue to be objects to be
    devalued
What does that leave us/ prostitution, seduction
[but] this is just a custom to give/ in order to
    help our people economically
in this world [that is] so material/ we are not simply
    ply buttocks and breasts
we have minds/ women feel, feel (Las Krudas 2004)

Las Krudas's rap lyrics reveal a very keen political analysis, one that recognizes that the viability and livelihood of the very state that oppresses Black women is dependent upon their sexual, domestic, and emotional labor. In contemporary Cuba prostitution, the "black" market and growing consumerism are now more than ever revealing the deficiencies that persist despite state-sponsored notions of egalitarian socialism. New awareness of the gap between official proclamations and living reality has led to unofficial radical movements such as Cuban hip hop and the feminist, oppositional lyrics of Las Krudas.

KRUDAS, LIGHT[ING] THE TORCH

In this essay, I have described how Black Cuban women like Las Krudas are beginning to lay claim to their own social spaces within hip hop, increasingly a powerful diasporic expressive form. I have argued that Las Krudas have created an activist art that uniquely fuses Black, Cuban, and feminist perspectives; they are in the process of creating a female audience for their unique version of rap and in so doing have encouraged criticism of and dialogue about the reality of life in Cuba among fans and tourists alike. By rapping *to* women, Las Krudas have helped to cultivate a space where women across the spectrum of race and class can express their own realities. I have proposed that Las Krudas are singularly engaged in revolutionary feminist activism through their art by giving voice to the harshness and inequities of Black female experience in Cuban society, a society which has prided itself on its egalitarianism. Las Krudas have stepped up as the vanguard of Black feminism in Cuba. No one else speaks out as they do on the ways in which race, gender, and class inform not only power relations but also socioeconomic status in Cuba. They multiply their activist effect through their youth theater camps and public performances, succeeding in imposing a unique oppositional identity onto public space that is otherwise difficult to achieve.

What the future may bring Las Krudas is uncertain. Now that the dollar has been rendered illegal in Cuba, it is possible that the government may crack down on *raperos* and *raperas,* even perhaps on the state-supported or so-called "commercial" rap artists. What will happen to Cuban "underground" rap like that of Las Krudas that so far has been tacitly supported by the government despite its rebellious spirit and expression of political awareness that often run counter to official dogmas? Perhaps Cuban rap of various stripes will become the sanctioned music of rebellion on the island? If so, does it follow that Black women will begin to gain access to more "official" channels of power and the political process?

Las Krudas as activists and artists use hip hop as a consciousness-raising forum in which truths are told and justice is sought, "put[ting] the Revolution to the Revolution" (Hernandez 2002). What remains to be seen is whether up and coming female *raperas* will follow Las Krudas' lead in breaking the mold or whether they will conform to the patriarchal, consumption-oriented style that is more typical of mainstream Cuban hip hop.

NOTE

1. As a visitor to the island, I discovered that the darker one's skin tone, the more likely one is to be deemed "Cuban" and ejected from these establishments. For instance, I was denied entry to the Cuba Libre Hotel on the suspicion that I was a prostitute.

REFERENCES

Boal, Augusto. 1985. *Theater of the Oppressed.* Charles A., and Maria-Odilia Leal McBride, trans. New York: Theater Communications Group.

Fernandes, Sujatha. 2003. "Fear of a Black Nation: Local Rappers, Transnational Crossings, and State Power in Contemporary Cuba," *Anthropological Quarterly* 76:575–609.

George, Nelson. 1998. *Hip Hop America.* New York: Viking.

Hernandez, Ariel. 2002. Interview with author, 4 January.

Hernández, Grisel. 2004. "Demo Krudas: Cubensi." *Movimiento: La Revista Cubana de Hip Hop* 2:11.

Las Krudas. 2004. *Cubensi,* Compact disc. Havana, Cuba.

——. 2003. Tape-recorded interview with author, Havana, Cuba, 15 December.

Olavarria, Margot. 2002. "Rap and Revolution: Hip-Hop comes to Cuba." *NACLA Report on the Americas.* Retrieved 22 September from http://www.nacla.org/art_display_printable. php? Art=2018.

Rose, Tricia. 1994. *Black Noise: Rap Music and Black Culture in Contemporary America.* Middletown, CT: Wesleyan University Press.

R E A D I N G   *74*

Cut-and-Paste Revolution
Notes from the Girl Zine Explosion

Jennifer Bleyer (2004)

When they started publishing *Cupsize* in 1994, most of the other zines that Sasha Cagen and Tara Emelye Needham had seen were "creepy things by boys who hung out in the East Village." The two friends had clicked with each other as disgruntled first-years at Amherst College in Massachusetts, and when circumstances and school transfers found them reunited in New York City a few years later, they knew that making a zine as sassy and smart as themselves was exactly the way to cement their friendship. Cagen was working, ironically, at a major women's glossy—the kind of magazine that runs stories like "Drop Twenty Pounds in Two Weeks!" and "Moves That Will Make Him Beg for Mercy!"—and thus had unlimited access to office equipment and supplies. Late at night Needham would come to Cagen's midtown office building, and the two would ride to the twenty-first floor and take over the corporate suite. Writing, cutting, gluing, and drawing, they would laugh riotously into the wee hours, looking out over the twinkling Manhattan skyline.

Cupsize was the conduit through which their inner censors were silenced and their deepest voices unearthed. They wrote weighty personal tomes about bisexuality and analyzed the virtues of public and private education. At the same time, they wrote jokey stories about excessive eyebrow tweezing and memoirs of their first visit to a porn shop. On the cover, they would photocopy a swatch from a favorite article of clothing that one of them owned, a final wink to this very personal collage. Cagen would surreptitiously make hundreds of copies of the zine at her office over the course of a month. People—especially teenage women, who ordered copies in droves—loved *Cupsize,* and Cagen and Needham loved making it. "I think one of our impulses was political, but on the deepest level it was creative," Cagen recalls, almost five years after the final issue came out. "Tara and I had a fabulous chemistry between us that was really unique. It was just this absolute freedom that we believed in each other and could put whatever we wanted on the page. It was such a unique time in our lives, not having to worry about meeting professional obligations or standards." Cagen, who is now thirty and publishes the magazine *To-Do List* in San Francisco, wistfully remembers the zine heyday as a sort of literary Wild West, in which the utter lack of rules could yield extraordinary results. "You wound up with some really sloppy stuff," she says, "but you also ended up with these beautiful unpolished gems like *Cupsize* that would never make it in a commercial context."

Cagen and Needham were not alone. From the late eighties to the mid-nineties, thousands of zines sprouted up like resilient weeds inside the cracks of the mainstream media's concrete. Like those of most underground phenomena, their origin is fuzzy and debatable. Some trace it to the political broadsheets of the anti–Vietnam War movement; others link it to the raunchy, edgy comix of the seventies and eighties. One thing is certain, however: after Xerox machines became widely accessible and before the explosion of the Internet, there was a brief moment during which people realized that they could make their own rudimentary publications on copy paper, fasten them with staples, and send them out along the zine distribution thoroughfares that coursed across the country, without any permission or guidance whatsoever. There were gay zines, travel zines, country music zines, and film noir zines. There were socialist zines, stripper zines, bicycle zines, and radical environmental zines. As Sasha Cagen explains it, the homemade publications were not bound by any particular standards of quality—sophomoric writing, lunatic ravings, and bizarre obsessions were more common than not—yet there was something beautifully democratic about letting readers sift through it all on their own, instead of having an armada of elite publishers, editors, and critics do it for them. In many ways zines predicted what would soon happen on the Web, and although the comparison is akin to that between a firecracker pop and a nuclear bomb, they helped pave the way for a culture that would allow anyone with anything to say, to say it. Zines demonstrated what by the end of the twentieth century became a credo: Free speech on demand and without apology.

The zine world, as it turned out, was as susceptible to sexism as the larger society from which its niche was carved. Sarah Dyer was the only woman in a collective of male friends working on a music zine in the late eighties, and she was constantly aggravated that people calling about the zine would instinctually ask to speak with someone else when she answered the phone. Even when she branched off to start her own zine, *Mad Planet,* Dyer realized that many people couldn't quite accept that a woman could be doing this on her own. "It got really frustrating," she recalls. "A guy who wrote one review of one comic would somehow get credited with editing my whole zine." During a trip to London, she met another girl zinester who told her about some girl zines in the United States that she had never heard of, and the need for a networking device became obvious. In 1992 Dyer started the *Action Girl* newsletter. It was one of the first resources for girl zines—a single photocopied page with the names and addresses of the few other zines made by young women at the time, folded in thirds, addressed, and mailed off with a single stamp to girls voraciously looking for their own zine community. Coincidentally, Riot Grrrl was born a few months later in Olympia, Washington, and what resulted, given the climate of free expression already engendered by the larger zine community, was a media revolution of unprecedented proportion.

Riot Grrrl, of course, was that anarchic web of punk girls who were outcasts a couple of seasons before "outcast" was "in," who decided that slumber parties and hand-holding were revolutionary activities, and who were rightfully delirious from their collective peeling away of the pretenses of American teenage girlhood. It was a grassroots movement of young women who decided that mosh pits, bands, fanzines, and revolution were not just for boys. They used the same organizational tools that feminists had wielded for decades—a cool name, a manifesto, a tattered phone list, meetings in crowded living rooms—to confront not only myriad problems in their punk scenes, high schools, and dysfunctional families but also the dogma of mainstream feminism and society.

Zines were the perfect outlet for expressing discontent and new beliefs, and thousands of them materialized alongside the Riot Grrrl juggernaut. . . .

. . . Alice Marwick found out about zines through *Sassy* magazine in 1992, when the edgy teen magazine started running a regular feature on zines. Marwick, now twenty-four, went to high school in upstate New York, where she and her friends would order the zines in *Sassy* for the cost of copying and stamps, and devour them as soon as they arrived. "Zines connected me to a lot of things I couldn't find in my hometown, to a larger like-minded community," she says. "It definitely fostered my own feminist consciousness by proving that feminism wasn't something for people my mother's age only, or a dead movement altogether. That was the feeling you got growing up where I did—as if feminism didn't have anything to offer anyone young, that it was something that had happened and was done. But finding out about girl bands and underground feminist filmmaking through zines made it something that was still going on. It was a huge inspiration to me."

Integral to reading zines was the implicit challenge to turn around and write them. Zines made clear that they were not just another product to be consumed but were unique contributions to a vast conversation which everyone was expected to join. Girls who wrote zines did so because it was activism, it was therapy, and it was fun. They did so, as Sasha Cagen and Tara Emelye Needham of *Cupsize* did, to make emblems of their friendship and beliefs. They did it to respond to other girls' zines and to engage in the larger discussion about what exactly constituted "Revolution Girl Style." . . .

. . .

Like Alice Marwick, I found out about zines through *Sassy,* and hunted relentlessly for the Riot Grrrl community that was generating these magical creations. I recall with extraordinary fondness staying up all night in high school making zines with others from my local Riot Grrrl collective. Our backpacks and Glue Stics and stolen copy cards strewn all over the floor of Kinko's, we would scour books picked up from yard sales—housewife manuals, Girl Scout guides, Barbie coloring books, anatomical diagrams—for the most ironic graphics. We were dizzying crucibles of emotion, creating ourselves as well as creating our zines—the two seemed interchangeable. Between the ages of seventeen and nineteen, I published my own zine called *Gogglebox:* a rather candid and often explicit record of my travels back and forth across the country. *Gogglebox* achieved a respectable stature in the zine community, having been named editor's choice by the now-defunct zine bible *Factsheet 5.* It generated tons of mail from girls all around the country, who poured their hearts out to me and who bought three thousand copies of the last issue. For a young writer and feminist, it was an exhilarating experience. Zines basically represented pure freedom; there were no ideological police to say that women's liberation couldn't be alternately sexy, angry, emotional, feminine, combative, childish—and unapologetically contradictory.

Revolution Girl Style was touted with an almost religious fervor. It seemed that if we only churned out enough zines and screamed loud enough, people would listen and society would quake. I do think this happened, in the way that small revolutions happen whenever people challenge the status quo and demonstrate alternative models of living in the world. But there are ways in which zines were not revolutionary, ways that are instructive for those of us committed to writing and publishing as a positive force for social change. One major detraction was how the mainstream media, with its interminable fetish for the salient and absurd, quickly pounced on zines. "Get ready for Riot Grrrl magazines," warned *USA Today.* "Hundreds of small, photocopied pamphlets now circulate, offering gut-wrenching confessional poetry and angry honest prose on topics such as rape, feeling ugly, boys, sex, and masturbation."[1] *The Dallas Morning News* leveled that "girlzines have their downside—bad spelling and layout, an excess of concert reviews, and a tendency toward self-indulgence."[2] Indeed, it was only a matter of time before Riot Grrrl was effectively subsumed by the cultural zeitgeist, and the girl zines it helped inspire became little more than social curios and collectors' items. Of course, they continued to be produced, but the much portended Revolution Girl Style that had seemed so imminent when girl zines, bands, and collectives first exploded soon seemed like little more than a blip on the radar of feminist history, a mere footnote to social trends of the nineties.

Besides the impact of being sensationalized, there was the weakening effect of capitalization. The entire zine movement was effectively over, one could say, almost as soon as it began, having been swallowed up by the great maw of popular culture with dollar signs flashing in its eyes. Like hip-hop, grunge, and punk rock, the language and style of Riot Grrrl were absorbed, repackaged, and marketed back to us in the most superficial form of its origin. Whereas Riot Grrrl's "grrrl power" was about doing it yourself and questioning authority, pop culture appropriated the message to sell a sanitized version of "girl power" that was essentially capitalism dressed up in baby doll dresses, blue nail polish, and mall-bought nose rings. Indeed, the values— fearlessness, independence, daring, and a solid

middle finger to the patriarchy—on which many girls zines were built, and for which their writers were denigrated as "angry" and "self-indulgent," were flipped on their heads and used to sell everything from cars and cigarettes to athletic shoes. The selling of girl power illustrated, as Naomi Klein wrote in *No Logo,* how "the cool hunters reduce vibrant cultural ideas to the status of archeological artifacts, and drain away whatever meaning they once held for the people who lived with them."[3]

Girl power, harnessed for its market potential and translated into consumer culture, had something for everyone. For the little girls, there were the Spice Girls and their endless records, collectibles, and concert tickets. For the bigger girls, there was *Sex and the City* and a bevy of books, movies, and magazines affirming, as Michelle Goldberg wrote, that "shopping-and-fucking feminism jibes precisely with the message of consumer society, [saying] that freedom means more—hotter sex, better food, ever-multiplying pairs of Manolo Blahnik shoes, drawers full of Betsey Johnson skirts, Kate Spade bags, and MAC lipsticks."[4] . . .

Both the denigration and the appropriation of zine style certainly did something to preempt the movement. Both were attacks from the outside in which zinesters essentially became caricatures of their own vision. A deeper blemish, however, was one that actually grew from within: the movement's virtual homogeneity. Despite pools of copier ink spilled in earnest discussions of race and class, girl zines were largely a hobby of white, middle-class young women. Riding on the heels of a feminist movement that had long stood rightly accused of excluding women of color and poor women, Riot Grrrl and its attendant zinesters was still a young version of a ladies' lunch society—except that the ladies have blue hair and weird clothes. Participating in girl zine culture requires that one have the leisure time to create zines, a life generally uncluttered with the rudiments of survival, access to copy machines and other equipment, money for stamps and supplies, and enough self-esteem and encouragement to believe that one's thoughts are worth putting down for public consumption—all marks of a certain level of privilege.

Although they were the exception to the rule, zines by young women of color or working-class backgrounds still found their way to fruition, and they were excellent. *Bamboo Girl,* which is still in print, features sassy, smart indictments of the exoticization of Asian-American women, interviews with Filipina authors on queerness, and analyses of "superwomen of color" in Japanese comix. The writer of *Discharge* zine recounts coming from a working-class, alcoholic, gambling family in Detroit to the D.C. Riot Grrrl community, where the most pressing concern often seemed the achievement of an equal opportunity mosh pit. Claudia von Vacano, a Latina Riot Grrrl in New York, wrote scathing indictments in her zines of Riot Grrrl's failure to confront its own internalized racism—which was for many the first time they had ever heard the phrase. *HUES* (Hear Us Emerging Sisters) was one of the most successful and respected girl zines (though more of a regular magazine than a zine) made by, for, and about young women of every color and shape. However, its content made it seem less a peripheral element of the white-dominated zine scene than a literary element of the growing multicultural scene.

Many of my fellow zinesters never saw or spoke of excellent zines like *Bamboo Girl* and *HUES,* suggesting that even within the self-proclaimed "underground," there is both a mainstream underground and an underground underground. To be fair, the girls in the former category were often writing zines about genuinely difficult things in their lives. But even so, it is difficult to feel completely vested in a slogan like "Revolution Girl Style Now" when the girls shouting it almost all look the same.

I might be giving the impression that zines are a phenomenon that came and went, that their effects were briefly felt, and that they no longer exist, or that Riot Grrrl and the motivations behind the "girl zine explosion" have also petered out. None of these statements is true. Riot Grrrl chapters still exist all over the country, in third- or fourth-generation incarnations, many churning

out zines as they always have. Do-It-Yourself (DIY) zine distributions are still operated out of bedrooms and living rooms, selling zines that reflect the distributors' personal favorites. Anarchist infoshops, independent record stores, and many small bookstores still carry racks of new zine titles. Bigger magazines (some of which have their roots as zines) like *Giant Robot* and *Bust* review new zines and tell people where to send their concealed dollar or two for a copy. . . .

Still, zines are not quite what they used to be, and the most compelling explanation of what happened to them can be told in one word: Internet. Since the Net blew up to unpredictable proportions in the mid-nineties, the essence of zines—namely, that anyone with anything to say can say it to the world—was codified and implemented en masse online. Everyone got a homepage, and e-zines became the electronic equivalents of their paper predecessors. Alice Marwick, who had already been involved with the zine community for several years, started *I Reclaim Wack* online in 1995 and loved the worldwide distribution, instant responses from readers, ability to change and update content, and absolutely free production. Like so many others, she taught herself HTML and learned the rudiments of Web design as an outlet for her creative energy and personal expression, and she has relished watching so many others do the same. "I think it's really good that there are so many e-zines," she says. "And actually, even though there are a lot of feminist girls online, I don't find that most of the e-zines by young women have a feminist slant at all. Yes, some are explicitly feminist, but many of them are just personal zines about girls' lives. If I was fourteen years old and growing up now, I would be so excited to find that community online."

Marwick's view is an important commentary not just on the status of girl e-zines but on the status of feminism as well. She's right that most e-zines for young women—even of the fierce, seemingly feminist variety—don't mention the F word outright. But a quick perusal of content shows that they are largely smart, challenging, socially aware, and independent—in short, feminist in every sense. . . .

It would seem, then, that the Internet and the advent of e-zines have been nothing short of a miracle for girls who previously had to scrounge around indie record stores and punk shows for a portal into the zine underground. Positive things have clearly come from the proliferation of online zines, not least, as Marwick mentions, the ease with which isolated young women pining for like-minded peers can now find them. And although some zine aficionados may lament having lost the exciting sense of tree-house-club secrecy that once shrouded the zine culture, there is something equally exciting about their enormous visibility online. How vindicating is it that e-zines like *My Boot Against the World* and *BratGirl* can be located as easily as the webpage for, say, Amazon? The blank URL bar of an Internet window has proven itself in many ways to be the great cultural equalizer. A Google search for "girl zine" turns up thousands of results; "pro-choice zine" hundreds. The question nowadays is not where to find a good girl zine but rather how to begin sloshing through the glut of them.

And the girls and women making e-zines? Their motivations vary as much online as they do in print. Deanna Zandt never made a print zine and didn't even know they existed until she was in college. As the publisher of *GenerationGrrl*, however, she values helping younger girls foster a sense of themselves by offering an alternative to what she calls the "bullshit of glossy magazines." She says, "I remember reading those and thinking anything from 'I will never have skin that smooth!' to 'I will never have the money to spend two hundred dollars on a pair of jeans!' and also thinking that those things were really inherent to my self-worth as a person. Not to mention the zero-lesbian-visibility factor. Please! We are real girls and women producing these things, telling our life stories—we give life to our words through our designs and pictures. In a very broad sense, it's like being the big sister who shows you how to navigate the world, not just what lipstick to buy." Others see their e-zines more as conduits through which to connect with peers. After producing *Bunnies on Strike* as a paper zine in Holland for several years, Tanja put it online with the help of a Web designer friend.[5]

Since then she has been able to connect with Riot Grrrls and like-minded young feminists all over Europe and North America, and in some parts of Asia and Africa. "E-zines themselves are just a step further in the already existing revolution of paper zines," Tanja explains. "Being online just makes your zine available to more people. It can be revolutionary once you meet other girls through the Internet and decide to take action."

Revolutionary is a powerful term, however, and one that just doesn't apply to what many girls are doing online. Homepages, for example, are pretty closely related to zines—rants, raves, diary entries, some photographs, perhaps some poetry, yet often nothing politicized. In this light, not everyone agrees that the realization of a soapbox for every young woman is the pinnacle of feminist achievement. The website gURL.com hosts around half a million homepages, and its co-founder Esther Drill suggests that while they may be an important rite of self-expression for teenage girls, they may also have gone overboard. "It's great if these girls are smart and have something to say, but if they're talking about stupid things, then it's just one more extraneous voice added to everything," she says. "Girls put up their diaries all the time, and after a while, I wonder if that's a good development. There are other important things for people to talk about besides themselves, and in general, the homepages are really self-focused. For all the good things, I also want to say, 'Guess what, girls, you're not the most important people in the world.'"

More troubling even than the possible over-abundance of homepages and e-zines is the complete absence of them for those without access. The technological landscape reflects the homogeneity of zine makers. The 2000 U.S. census reported that among families with incomes of $25,000 or less, only 19 percent had access to the Internet, compared with 75 percent among families with incomes of $75,000 or higher. Only 33 percent of black homes and 34 percent of Latinos had Internet access, while 53 percent of white non-Hispanics had access, as did 65 percent of Asians and Pacific Islanders.[6] More recent reports, however, show that both the racial and class gaps are closing. By 2001 there were reports that Internet use among blacks had grown at an annual rate of 31 percent, while use among whites grew by 19 percent. During the same period that home access to the Internet increased among blacks, it increased as well for poor people of all races.[7]

Young women of color who do have Internet access are using the information superhighway to build community, express themselves, discover its infinite possibilities, and connect with people both similar to and different from themselves. The resources are certainly not anywhere as abundant as they should be, but they seem to be increasingly present, ranging from *Colorlines* magazine's information on the rampant incarceration of urban youth to Black Grrrl Revolution's *Problackgrrrlfesto,* which states that "still being ingrained in society's consciousness by academia [is] that black only equates African-American and male, and that woman only equates white"[8]— both hopeful signs that when the numbers of young women of color online increase, there will be something there for them beyond Backstreet Boys fanpages and Caucasian beauty tips.

As technology activists continue working to narrow the digital divide, the critical imperative to do so shows no signs of letting up. Beyond zines and e-zines, young women are making films, producing music, publishing books, and otherwise carving space for the DIY ethic in the feminist sphere. Kara Herold interviewed forty-five girl zinesters for her film *Grrlyshow,* a documentary about girl zines and their relationship to contemporary feminism, and found that many identified as strongly as media activists as they did as feminists. "Since just a few corporations essentially own all the magazines, the whole point is getting your writing out there into the culture, even if it's just to ten other people," Herold explains. "If you have something different to say than the mainstream, it's feminist just by virtue of believing that what you have to say is important. That's why I think girl zines and e-zines will continue, because, really, you have to create your own venues. Nobody else is going to do it for you."

NOTES

1. Elizabeth Snead, "Feminist Riot Girls Don't Just Wanna Have Fun," *USA Today,* 7 August 1992, 5D.
2. Margot Mifflin, "Girlzines Attract New Feminist Breed," *Dallas Morning News,* 26 November 1995, 5F.
3. Naomi Klein, *No Logo* (New York: Picador, 1999), 72–73.
4. Michelle Goldberg, "Feminism for Sale," *Alternet,* 8 January 2001, http://www.alternet.org/story .html?StoryID=10306.
5. Tanja's last name was unavailable.
6. U.S. Department of Commerce, *Falling Through the Net: Toward Digital Inclusion* (Washington, D.C., 2000).
7. National Telecommunications and Information Administration, *A Nation Online: How Americans Are Expanding Their Use of the Internet,* 5 February 2002 (Washington, D.C.), http://www.ntia.doc .gov/ntiahome/dn/html/toc.htm.
8. See http://www.thirdwavefoundation.org/programs/ summer00.pdf for more information about Black Grrrl Revolution.

Pop Culture Gone Wild

Jessica Valenti (2007)

It's not exactly news that pop culture is all sex all the time. But it's not just "sex"—it's us girls. Pop culture sex is sugar and spice, tits and ass. Sexuality itself seems to be defined as distinctly female in our culture. After all, while billboards and magazine ads may feature a ripped guy from time to time, it's mostly women who make up what sexy is supposed to be.

And it's not just sexy—it's straight-up sex. Pop culture is becoming increasingly "pornified."[1] As pornography becomes more culturally acceptable, and the more we're inundated with sexual messages—most of which are targeted at younger women—the more hardcore these messages become. Yes, I know, sex sells and always has. But do you think that twenty years ago little girls would be taking *Playboy* pencil cases to school, or that teen girls would be vying to take their tops off for little more than a moment of "fame"?

. . .

THAT'S (NOT) HOT

It's pretty well established that girls want to be considered hot. I mean, when you're brought up to think that your hotness quotient is pretty much your entire worth, that becomes pretty damn important. Don't get me wrong, I think wanting to be desired is a really understandable thing. Who doesn't want to be wanted? The problem is *who* defines "hot"—and therefore desirability. Hint: It's not women.

Unattainable beauty standards for women aren't a new thing. Magazines, TV shows, and movies have been shoving a certain kind of woman down our throats for decades. White, skinny waist, big boobs, long legs, full lips, great hair—a conglomeration of body parts put together to create the "perfect" woman we're all supposed to be. And if we're not, we're scorned. Nothing worse than being the ugly girl, right?

But it's not just looks that make you "hot"—beauty standards are a whole other conversation. It's being accessible—to men, in particular. To be truly hot in this never-never land of tits and ass, we have to be constantly available—to be looked at, touched, and fucked. Sounds harsh, I know, but it's true. We're only as hot as our willingness to put on a show for guys.

And the "show" is everywhere. In magazines like *Maxim* and *Playboy*. And in the insanity of *Girls Gone Wild*, with teens putting on fake lesbian make-out sessions so guys will think they're hot. We're on display—everywhere. We couldn't escape it if we wanted to. (And maybe some of us don't. More on this later.)

Hot and available is everywhere. *Maxim* magazine—kind of like *Playboy* with more clothes—is the number-one best-selling men's magazine in the nation. *Maxim* not only puts out an annual "hot list" (just in case you forgot how you don't measure up), but also has a VH1 special and is in talks to start *Maxim* hotels and lounges.

Playboy is even worse. All you have to do is go to the local mall to see how normalized *Playboy* has become in American culture. Teens buy *Playboy* shirts before they even have boobs. The E! channel has a reality show, *The Girls Next Door*, based on the lives of several *Playboy* Bunnies who are also magazine founder Hugh Hefner's live-in "girlfriends." MTV has even featured teenagers getting plastic surgery in order to look like (and be) *Playboy* Bunnies. And again—*Playboy* pencil cases. 'Nuff said.

But there's probably no better example of Porn Gone Wild in pop culture than the ubiquitous

Girls Gone Wild (GGW). What started as voyeuristic porn lite—girls flashing their boobs to cameras during Mardi Gras and spring break—is now an empire. The company that owns *GGW* claims $40 million in yearly sales, and the founder, Joe Francis, has said he's working on a film, *GGW* ocean cruises, a clothing line, and a restaurant chain (I'm imagining Hooters Gone Wild).

When people think of the way porn culture has oozed into the mainstream in recent years, *Girls Gone Wild* is usually the first thing to come up. After all, *GGW* is where porn meets real life—you don't have to be a porn star to be in one of its videos. You just have to be willing.

I remember the first time I saw one of *GGW*'s late-night commercials, featuring girls lifting their shirts to reveal Mardi Gras beads and little else—maybe a *GGW* logo across their nipples. (Classy, right?) This was back when the girls featured were still largely unaware that their images would be used to make up a tit montage. I mean, really, these were girls who were "caught" on camera in a drunken moment—not girls who sought out the camera breasts first. I felt bad for them; I even recognized a couple of girls. I had gone to Tulane University in New Orleans my freshman year of college; my classmates' getting drunk and flashing on Bourbon Street wasn't exactly out of the ordinary. And while tourists were around and there were the occasional camera flashes, I don't think anyone figured their momentary drunk exhibitionism would be forever captured on film to be sold on a mass scale.

But now girls are lining up to be part of *Girls Gone Wild*—flashing their breasts (and more), masturbating, and having girl-on-girl action, all for fifteen minutes of fame and maybe a *Girls Gone Wild* hat or thong. I'm not going to lie—this bothers me. I mean, why in the world would you potentially ruin the rest of your life just so—for a minute—some guy thinks you're hot?

Ariel Levy, who wrote the popular *Female Chauvinist Pigs: Women and the Rise of Raunch Culture*, argues that a new generation of feminists (ahem) is objectifying ourselves and each other by participating in things like *GGW*.

You see, Levy is part of a group of feminist thinkers who aren't too pleased with some of the theory coming from younger feminists—some of whom say that things like sex work or stripping can be empowering, because it's subversive or because hey, it's fun. We're making the choice to participate; therefore, it's powerful. But Levy says that the joke is on us, and that we're really just fooling ourselves.

Maybe.

I understand why *GGW* is so controversial (or *Maxim* and *Playboy*, for that matter). And like I said, it really bothers me. But the assumption that *all* girls who enjoy the "show" are stupid or being fooled bothers me just as much. Not to mention that for a lot of women, developing a sexual identity is a process.

In response to Levy's book, Jennifer Baumgardner, third-wave feminist icon and coauthor of *Manifesta*, brought up a supergood point that I think resonates with a lot of women.

> If pressed, I'd venture that at least half of my sexual experiences make me cringe when I think about them today. Taking top honors is the many times I made out with female friends in bars when I was in my early twenties, a rite of passage Levy much disdains throughout the book. I'm embarrassed about the kiss-around-the-circles, but if I didn't have those moments, I'm not sure I ever would have found my way to the real long-term relationship I have today. If all my sexual behavior had to be evolved and reciprocal and totally revolutionary before I had it, I'd never have had sex.[2]

Ain't that the truth. I've had more than a couple of embarrassing moments in my life and sexual history—but isn't that what makes us who we are? Do we really have to be on point and thinking politics *all* the time? Sometimes doing silly, disempowering, sexually vapid things when you're young is just part of getting to the good stuff.

I guess what I've come to—and this is what works for me—is that you have to find your own middle ground. There has to be space for young women to figure it out on their own. And I think most times young women do figure it out.

In a recent Salon.com article about the trend of straight girls making out with each other for male attention, one young woman came to an epiphany while talking to reporter Whitney Joiner:

> "A lot of girls who do want long-term boyfriends will still settle for the hookup because it gives them that temporary feeling of being taken care of and being close to someone," Julie says. "It's sad to see that this is what it's come to—that guys will raise the bar and girls will scramble to meet it. Women just want to know what they have to do to get these guys to fall in love with them. And if guys will take them home after kissing a girl, then that's what they're going to do, because it's better than going home alone." She pauses. "Now that I'm saying it out loud, I'm like, Huh—that's a sad way of going about it."[3]

See? I really think it doesn't take all that much for us to work through the pop culture nonsense—we just have to talk it out, hopefully with each other and with women who have been there and done that. Okay, so maybe it won't be quite *that* easy. But it's a start. And it's a much better alternative than calling each other sluts, that's for damn sure.

LIKE A VIRGIN, AND OTHER POP CONTRADICTIONS

Never mind trying to find an authentic sexuality in our fake-orgasm pop culture—it's near impossible to find *anything* that makes sense. There are all of these contradictions in porn/pop culture that blow my mind and make it all the more difficult for young women to find an authentic sexual identity. It hurts the head to talk about them too much, but unfortunately it's necessary if we really want to get a grasp on what is being expected of women: the impossible.

Be a Virgin . . . But Be Sexy

We already know that we're supposed to be virginal (lest we mar our purity), but when it comes to pop culture, the virginity thing gets more complicated.

Since I'd probably date myself by talking about Madonna's "Like a Virgin," I won't go there. Think Britney Spears (pre-K-Fed) and Jessica Simpson (pre-*Newlyweds*). They both claimed to be "saving themselves" for marriage and spoke out against premarital sex (while simultaneously presenting themselves in the most sexual way possible, of course). Naturally, it later came out that Spears (before her two weddings) had sex; it was rumored that Simpson managed to wait till the night before her wedding. I can't think of a better example of how we expect girls to be sexy but not have sex. It's the *idea* of virginity that's popular, not the reality of being chaste. Look sexy, act as if you're having sex, but if you do it . . . whore! You can even look at the newfound popularity of "revirginization" surgeries—you know, getting your hymen "repaired." It's the lie and the performance of being a virgin, not the reality. Truly baffling. And impossible to recreate. Unless you feel like getting a new hymen.

Be Available . . . But Unattainable

Like I mentioned earlier about hotness: It's about accessibility. We're expected to be available to men, but we're also expected to be "mysterious." Much in the same way we're supposed to be sexy but not give it up. Think about a *Maxim* cover girl—she's totally unattainable but simultaneously available for consumption. No guy who reads the magazine will ever meet her or talk to her—but he gets to look at her half-naked and jerk off to her if he wants, which is something he can't always get from the women he meets in his everyday life. So in that way, she's the "perfect" girl. Again, impossible for real women to live up to.

Like Sex . . . But Don't Come

The prevalence of porn has led to this really weird point in American society where the sexual ideal for younger women is a porn star. Internet porn and the normalization of pornography have spawned a whole new generation of guys who were raised thinking that porn sex equals normal sex. Not to mention a generation of girls who think porn sex is the only way to please guys. So we're expected to—once again—put on the "show." This means a whole load of screaming, dirty-talking, and sex-loving madness. But the problem is that we're expected to imitate something that's *acted.* Most porn stars aren't really getting off. So the best sex is fake sex? Think about what this does to younger people trying to develop their sexuality! Terrifying.

Be a Lesbian . . . Who Likes Men

Being a lesbian is totally acceptable—so long as there's a man around to watch it—and you're young and "hot," of course. The absence of any real images of lesbians in pop culture is kind of crazy. I mean, even Showtime's *The L Word* features a bevy of sexy gals and storylines that fit pretty neatly into the girl-on-girl male fantasy. This isn't to say that there aren't outed women in the mainstream—there are. But the pop culture, sexed-up version of lesbians is what reigns supreme. Just think of the appropriation of lesbianism by straight male porn. . . . While a lesbian makeout session may be a fake expression of lust to some, it's an awesome, authentic experience to others, so if you want to make out with a girl, go for it. It's about the consciousness behind your decisions. Many younger women *know* what we want and go for it. And that's nothing to apologize for. But if you're doing something you wouldn't normally want to do, or if the only thought behind something sexual is *Please god, let him like me,* you may be in trouble. If you're doing something that mimics someone else's sexual choices—for someone else's benefit or because you feel pressured—then you might want to consider how empowered that choice actually is.

Be a Woman of Color . . . But Only In Stereotypes, Please

Women who aren't white (or at least aren't on the fair side) are nearly invisible in pop culture—unless they're adhering to the most vile racial stereotypes. Sure, *Maxim* or *Playboy* will occasionally

feature women of color on their pages, but they're generally as Caucasian-looking as possible. And you don't have to look far for the tired old stereotypes. Black women are bitchy! And if there's an overweight black woman, she's going to be all sassy! Asian women are docile and bow a lot! Latinas are spicy hot hot hot! It's not just in the sexual stereotyping of women of color in magazines—but in television shows, movies, and even porn listings. . . .

What all of these contradictions add up to are insanely impossible expectations of women. (And yes, I'm aware that pop culture puts expectations on men as well. But really, not like it does on women.) These baffling expectations mean that any authentic expression of yourself is near impossible. How do you act like yourself when you're constantly putting on a show?

PERFORMANCE VS. REALITY

Contradictions aside, what all this porn/pop culture has in common is performance. Sometimes performance can be a cool thing when it comes to sexuality.

Rachel Kramer Bussel, a feminist sex columnist at *The Village Voice,* says that younger women are claiming a public space for their sexuality.

> I think we have to move beyond the overly simplistic "empowered" or "exploited" debate. We can acknowledge that our motivations for putting our bodies "out there" may not be the same as what's taken away by certain consumers, but we wrestle with and confront those contradictions. Instead of attacking women for the choices they make, we should be working toward creating a more accepting, welcoming culture that values sexual diversity. I see many positive signs that sexual culture is flourishing and thriving among the younger generation in ways that are more egalitarian, open, and honest, whether it's indie porn magazine *Sweet Action,* the many college sex magazines and columns, or the thriving burlesque scenes happening across

the country which celebrate curvy girls, striptease, double entendre, and sexuality. Some even have male dancers and you can really see with the new burlesque how "sexy" does not have to equal "exploited." Sexy can be aggressive, alluring, entertaining, and even thought-provoking all at once.[4]

The difference between what Rachel is talking about—in my opinion—and stuff like *Girls Gone Wild* is that some performances are thought out and some are, well, not. (Especially when you consider the inebriation factor for those less-thought-out times.)

Can a performance really be a subversive way of playing with your sexuality? Sure. But I think it's a really individual thing and depends on how much you're buying in to the bullshit notions of what sexy is. Rachel is clearly not buying in.

. . .

SO WHAT'S A GIRL TO DO?

It shouldn't be that hard to develop an authentic sexuality—or even personhood, for that matter. But the prevalence of porn/pop makes it pretty frigging difficult to negotiate how we separate good kinds of performance from bad and how we develop an identity that isn't mired in all of this ridiculous crap.

Some suggestions that have worked for me:

Stop Getting So Drunk

I'm well aware that going out and partying is fun. But my college years taught me well about drinking and participating in sexual activities (whether it's actual sex, flashing, make-out sessions, whatever). If you wouldn't do it sober, don't do it drunk. 'Cause I guarantee if it's something that really turns you on, it will be more fun sober. Plus, if you're sober, you can't use the liquor as an excuse for your actions—because, again, if it's fun and something you want to do, you shouldn't have to make excuses. Ever. . . .

Are You Having Fun?

Serious fun. Not "this seems like a good idea" fun. And definitely not "well, they're egging me on" non-fun. So much of our personalities get caught up in trying to adhere to what we're "supposed" to be like, it's hard to just, you know, relax. When you're trying to be sexy, virginal, available but not, appropriately lesbian but still straight, skinny, hot, and so on, all of a sudden life ain't so fun anymore. It takes a lot of work to remain in pop culture character. So make it easy on yourself. . . .

Does It Feel Good?

Yeah, I'm dirty. But you get what I'm saying. Because I really can't imagine that whole porn-performance thing is too orgasm friendly—after all, performing *does* mean faking it.

Why Do You Want It?

Obviously, everything we do is affected to a certain degree by social norms and what pop culture demands of us. I think it's fine to go along with these things to a certain extent, so long as you're always cognizant of why you're doing it. For example, I wear makeup. I love it. But I recognize that the reason I love it sooo much is that the larger world tells me I need it to be pretty. Would it be revolutionary of me to throw all of my makeup away? Yup. But I don't want to. I wear it, but I'm aware of why I do.

. . .

NOTES

1. This term was coined by Pamela Paul in her new book by the same name. Pamela Paul. *Pornified: How Pornography Is Transforming Our Lives, Our Relationships, and Our Families* (New York: Henry Holt, 2005).
2. Jennifer Baumgardner. "Feminism Is a Failure, and Other Myths," AlterNet, November 17, 2005.
3. Whitney Joiner. "Live girl-on-girl action!" Salon.com, June 20, 2006.
4. From a Feministing interview with Rachel Kramer Bussel.

DISCUSSION QUESTIONS FOR CHAPTER 9

1. How do you think cultural forms shape gender? How might cultural forms function subversively to challenge traditional gender norms?

2. How do some television shows reflect changing gender norms while at the same time keeping most other norms intact? Can you name some examples?

3. What are some recent movies you've seen? How are women depicted in these movies? How is the gaze constructed in these movies?

4. How does pornography as a cultural form influence gender norms in U.S. society?

5. Why do you think some critics suggest there has never been a female Shakespeare or a female da Vinci? Do you agree with this assessment? Why or why not?

SUGGESTIONS FOR FURTHER READING

Carson, Mina, Tisa Lewis, and Susan M. Shaw. *Girls Rock! Fifty Years of Women Making Music.* Lexington: University Press of Kentucky, 2004.

Hogshead-Makar, Nancy, and Andrew Zimbalist, eds. *Equal Play: Title IX and Social Change.* Philadelphia: Temple University Press, 2007.

Jervis, Lisa, and Andi Zeisler, eds. *BITCHfest: Ten Years of Cultural Criticism from the Pages of* Bitch *Magazine.* New York: Farrar, Straus and Giroux, 2006.

Johnson, Lisa, ed. *Third Wave Feminism and Television: Jane Puts It in a Box.* New York: I. B. Tauris & Co., Ltd., 2007.

Kord, Susanne. *Hollywood Divas, Indice Queens, and TV Heroines: Contemporary Screen Images of Women.* Lanham, MD: Rowman & Littlefield, 2004.

Pohl-Weary, Emily. *Girls Who Bite Back: Witches, Mutants, Slayers, and Freaks.* Toronto: Sumach, 2004.

Resisting Violence Against Women

Gendered violence in the United States and around the world is an important public health and human rights issue. Violence, an assault on a person's control over her/his body and life, can take many forms and has varying consequences depending on the type of assault, its context and interpretation, the chronicity of violence, and the availability of support. *Gendered violence* implies that harm evolves from the imbalance in power between women and men. In most societies around the world, gendered violence usually occurs when masculine entitlements produce power that manifests itself in harm and injury (physical, sexual, emotional/psychological) toward women. Women are especially vulnerable in interpersonal relationships; most violence against them occurs in their own homes. Women are 10 times more likely than men to be victimized by an intimate partner. However, because violence is about the exercise of power over another person, both men and women can perpetrate violence and it occurs in both heterosexual and homosexual relationships. What do you think would be the societal response if women and girls routinely victimized men and boys?

The range of gendered violence includes acts of intimidation and harassment (stalking; voyeurism; online/chat room, street, school, and workplace harassment; road rage; and obscene phone calls), forcing someone to watch or participate in pornography, forced prostitution and other sex work, emotional/psychological, physical, and sexual abuse (that includes rape and attempted rape), and any other coercive act that harms and violates another person. Despite the fact that anyone can perpetrate violence, women are much more likely to be victims of violence by men because violence is a consequence of power relationships. Men are likely to suffer physical violence at the hands of other men. In childhood and adolescence, males are especially at risk for suffering physical abuse by female and male caretakers and sexual abuse by other males. Given the norms about masculine invulnerability, it is often hard for boys and men to talk about sexual abuse and seek help. As a result, men are more likely than women to be in denial about such experiences, and some men who have been abused try to "master" the abuse by identifying with the source of their victimization and avoiding the weaknesses associated with being a "victim."

The rates of violence against women in the United States are quite alarming, although compared to figures from the early 1990s, rates of rape and sexual assault have decreased somewhat. Because intimate violence is so underreported, accurate statistics are difficult to collect. Recent laws such as rape shield laws, which prevent a victim's sexual history from being used by defense attorneys, and various state reform laws have helped survivors. Mandatory arrest procedures in cases of domestic violence and the creation of temporary restraining orders have helped survivors of domestic abuse. In addition, the 1994 Violence Against Women Act (VAWA, passed as Title IV of the Violent Crime Control and Law Enforcement Act) provides some legal protections for women. It will be up for reauthorization in 2010.

The 2006 National Crime Victimization Survey of the U.S. Bureau of Justice reports that a sexual assault occurs about every 2 minutes, a rape about every 8 minutes, and approximately 56 women are victimized in some way by an intimate partner every hour. A 2006 U.S. Centers for Disease Control and Prevention fact sheet reports that nearly 25 percent of women and 8 percent of men said they were raped and/or physically assaulted by a current or former spouse, date, or intimate partner sometime in their lifetime. Recent statistics for teen violence are especially disturbing, although different studies ask about victimization in different ways and get different results. Some studies ask about current abuse and some survey past histories; some ask only about physical abuse, while others include questions about emotional or psychological abuse and sexual abuse. It is important to consider whether consent for sexual intimacy can occur in a relationship where physical violence and intimidation are present. According to national statistics published by the National Center for Victims of Crime (2004), one in five high school girls in the United States reported being abused physically and/or sexually by a boyfriend, and 50 to 80 percent of teenagers reported knowing others in violent relationships. Estimates of physical and sexual dating violence among high school students typically range from one in ten to one in four. A 2007 study of women college students reported almost a fifth of them experiencing sexual victimization in a two-year period. The reading by Joetta L. Carr, "Campus Sexual Violence," underscores these data.

Although girls are more likely to be sexually abused than boys and the latter are more likely to be sexually abused by other males, both male and female adolescents report being victims of physical violence in relationships. Some relationships involve mutual abuse, with both partners using violence against each other. However, it is clear that male and female adolescents use force for different reasons and with different results. Researchers have found that girls suffer more from relationship violence, emotionally and physically. They are more likely than males to have serious injuries and report being terrified. In contrast, male victims seldom fear violence by their girlfriends and often say the attacks did not hurt or that they found the violence amusing (National Youth Violence Prevention Resource Center, 2005). Rape victims are 4 times more likely to contemplate suicide and 13 times more likely to actually make a suicide attempt. Helpful links for fact sheets on intimate partner violence, "warning signs" for abusive relationships, and other information can be found at *www.cdc.gov/ncipc/factsheets/ipvfacts.htm; www.ojp.usdoj.gov/vawo;* and *www.ojp.usdoj.gov/bjs/abstract/ipv.htm.*

Another disturbing trend is the increase in stalking behavior directed at women (see the box in this chapter "Cyberstalking"). The National College Women Sexual

HISTORICAL MOMENT **The Violence Against Women Act of 1994**

For decades feminist activists had worked to gain recognition of the extent and severity of violence against women in the United States. On the whole, violence against women had not been fully recognized as a serious crime within the criminal justice system.

Often reports of sexual assault were greeted with skepticism or victim-blaming. Prior to feminist activism in the 1970s, women had to present evidence of resistance to sexual assault; rules of evidence allowed consideration of a victim's entire sexual history; and husbands were exempt from charges of raping their wives. Following the opening of the first rape crisis centers in 1972, grassroots advocacy managed not only to provide care and services to victims, but also to change these laws.

Generally, domestic violence was considered by law enforcement to be a "family matter," and so police, prosecutors, and judges were often reluctant to "interfere." The first domestic violence shelters opened in the mid-1970s, but not until the 1980s did this problem receive widespread attention. Thanks to activists, laws did change in the 1980s to codify domestic violence as criminal conduct, to provide increased penalties, to create civil protection orders, and to mandate training about domestic violence for law enforcement.

Following a Washington, D.C., meeting of representatives from various groups advocating for victims of sexual assault and domestic violence in the 1980s, activists turned their attention to ensuring federal legislation to protect women through interstate enforcement of protection orders, to provide funding for shelters and other programs for victims, and to provide prevention efforts. By demonstrating the need for these protections and programs, grassroots advocates and the National Organization for Women (NOW) Legal Defense Fund were able to develop bipartisan support in Congress and to pass the Violence Against Women Act (VAWA) in 1994. The four subtitles of the Act describe the target areas of concern: Safe Streets, Safe Homes for Women, Civil Rights for Women and Equal Justice for Women in the Courts, and Protections of Battered Immigrant Women and Children. VAWA changed rules of evidence, police procedures, penalties, and court procedures. It also authorized funding for prevention, education, and training.

Since 1994, VAWA has been reauthorized and modified several times. The Act was most recently reauthorized in 2005. To find out more about VAWA, visit the website of the U.S. Department of Justice's Violence Against Women Office at *www.ojp.usdoj.gov/vawo*.

Victimization (NCWSV) survey published in 2000 by Fisher et al., found that 13 percent of female college students had been stalked since school began that year and that four in five women knew their stalkers. Of these known stalkers, most were boyfriends or ex-boyfriends, classmates, acquaintances, or coworkers. Stalking incidents lasted an average of 2 months and included unwanted, repeated telephoning (78 percent), offenders waiting outside or inside places (48 percent), victims being watched from afar (44 percent), being followed (42 percent), being sent letters

(30 percent), and receiving unwanted, repeated e-mails (25 percent). Ten percent of women stalked reported that the offender forced or attempted sexual contact; the most common consequence for women was fear and emotional and psychological trauma. These data are also reported in the reading by Joetta Carr.

Violence against girls and women is a persistent problem all over the world and is increasingly understood as a human rights issue. The wars of the twentieth century and the new conflicts of the twenty-first, the increase in globalization and scope of global commerce and communications, have all facilitated an increase in global violence against women and children. The 2005 Population Report indicates that around the world, one in three women is beaten, coerced into sex, and otherwise abused. As the reading "War Crimes" by Helen Clarkson reports, sexual violence is a weapon of war all over the world. These issues are addressed by the recent "Beijing Plus" meetings, five years and a decade after violence against women was declared a central tenet of the "Platform for Action" of the 1995 conference. Some countries condone or legalize such crimes, and others accept violence against women as a consequence of war and/or civil unrest and ethnic cleansing. The increasing militarism in such postindustrial societies as the United States has important consequences for the safety of women and children in target societies and facilitates prostitution and the international sex traffic in girls and women. Alice Leuchtag in "Human Rights: Sex Trafficking and Prostitution" writes about sex slavery and sex tourism and discusses global responses to this global problem. She addresses the UN General Assembly's adoption of a convention and protocol on sex trafficking, as well as the U.S. Victims of Trafficking and Violence Act, both passed in 2005.

Similarly, Diana Washington Valdez's short piece, "Deaths That Cry Out" discusses the rape/murders of young women in Ciudad Juárez, Mexico, who worked in the maquiladoras where U.S. and European companies hire cheap female labor. In this way the history of colonialism reveals the complex interactions of race and nation and the ways this is gendered and implicated in the politics of globalization. In addition, the status of women, for example, has often been used as a marker of the level of "civilization" of a society, just as cultural interventions have been justified in part in the name of improving the status of women (as was most recently shown with the U.S. attacks on Afghanistan as "liberating" women from the Taliban, discussed briefly in the reading by Andrea Smith, "Beyond the Politics of Inclusion," and with other discussions on the status of Muslim women associated with the war in Iraq). This creates complexity for feminist activism as women and men in these countries seeking to address nationalist, patriarchal problems can be interpreted as "traitors"; similarly, it causes problems for feminists in North America and Europe whose activism can be interpreted as ethnocentric meddling or support for the militarist strategies of their own societies.

Any discussion attempting to address the issue of violence against women must involve several key points. First, violence against women must be understood in the context of socially constructed notions of gender. If boys are raised to hide emotion, see sensitivity as a weakness, and view sexual potency as wound up with interpersonal power, and girls are raised to be dependent and support masculine entitlement, then interpersonal violence should be no surprise. As Debra Anne Davis explains in the reading "Betrayed by the Angel," women are raised in ways that may

Cyberstalking

- A U.S. Department of Justice report estimates that there may be tens or even hundreds of thousands of cyberstalking victims in the United States (Report on Cyberstalking, 1999).
- A 1997 nationwide survey conducted by the University of Cincinnati found that almost 25 percent of stalking incidents among college-age women involved cyberstalking (Report on Cyberstalking, 1999).

DEFINITION

Cyberstalking can be defined as threatening behavior or unwanted advances directed at another using the Internet and other forms of online and computer communications.

OVERVIEW

Cyberstalking is a relatively new phenomenon. With the decreasing expense and thereby increased availability of computers and online services, more individuals are purchasing computers and "logging onto" the Internet, making another form of communication vulnerable to abuse by stalkers.

Cyberstalkers target their victims through chat rooms, message boards, discussion forums, and e-mail. Cyberstalking takes many forms such as threatening or obscene e-mail; spamming (in which a stalker sends a victim a multitude of junk e-mail); live chat harassment or flaming (online verbal abuse); leaving improper messages on message boards or in guest books; sending electronic viruses; sending unsolicited e-mail; tracing another person's computer and Internet activity; and electronic identity theft.

Similar to stalking off-line, online stalking can be a terrifying experience for victims, placing them at risk of psychological trauma and possible physical harm. Many cyberstalking situations do evolve into off-line stalking, and a victim may experience abusive and excessive phone calls, vandalism, threatening or obscene mail, trespassing, and physical assault.

CYBERSTALKING AND THE LAW

With personal information becoming readily available to an increasing number of people through the Internet and other advanced technology, state legislators are addressing the problem of stalkers who harass and threaten their victims over the World Wide Web. Stalking laws and other statutes criminalizing harassment behavior currently in effect in many states may already address this issue by making it a crime to communicate by any means with the intent to harass or alarm the victim.

States have begun to address the use of computer equipment for stalking purposes by including provisions prohibiting such activity in both harassment and anti-stalking

(*continued*)

legislation (Riveira, 1,2). A handful of states, such as Alabama, Arizona, Connecticut, Hawaii, Illinois, New Hampshire, and New York, have specifically included prohibitions against harassing electronic, computer, or e-mail communications in their harassment legislation. Alaska, Oklahoma, Wyoming, and, more recently, California have incorporated electronically communicated statements as conduct potentially constituting stalking in their anti-stalking laws. A few states have both stalking and harassment statutes that criminalize threatening and unwanted electronic communications. Other states have laws other than harassment or anti-stalking statutes that prohibit misuse of computer communications and e-mail, while others have passed laws containing broad language that can be interpreted to include cyberstalking behaviors (Gregorie).

Recent federal law has addressed cyberstalking as well. The Violence Against Women Act, reauthorized in 2000, made cyberstalking a part of the federal interstate stalking statute. Other federal legislation that addresses cyberstalking has been introduced recently, but no such measures have yet been enacted. Consequently, there remains a lack of legislation at the federal level to specifically address cyberstalking, leaving the majority of legislative prohibitions against cyberstalking at the state level (wiredpatrol.org).

IF YOU ARE A VICTIM OF CYBERSTALKING

- Experts suggest that in cases where the offender is known, victims should send the stalker a clear written warning. Specifically, victims should communicate that the contact is unwanted and ask the perpetrator to cease sending communications of any kind. Victims should do this only once. Then, no matter the response, victims should under no circumstances ever communicate with the stalker again. Victims should save copies of this communication in both electronic and hard-copy form.
- If the harassment continues, the victim may wish to file a complaint with the stalker's Internet service provider, as well as with their own service provider. Many Internet service providers offer tools that filter or block communications from specific individuals.
- As soon as individuals suspect they are victims of online harassment or cyberstalking, they should start collecting all evidence and document all contact made by the stalker. Save all e-mail, postings, or other communications in both electronic and hard-copy form. If possible, save all of the header information from e-mails and newsgroup postings. Record the dates and times of any contact with the stalker.
- Victims may also want to start a log of each communication explaining the situation in more detail. Victims may want to document how the harassment is affecting their lives and what steps they have taken to stop the harassment.
- Victims may want to file a report with local law enforcement or contact their local prosecutor's office to see what charges, if any, can be pursued. Victims should save copies of police reports and record all contact with law enforcement officials and the prosecutor's office.
- Victims who are being continually harassed may want to consider changing their e-mail address, Internet service provider, and home phone number, and should examine the possibility of using encryption software or privacy protection programs. Any local computer store can offer a variety of protective software,

options, and suggestions. Victims may also want to learn how to use the filtering capabilities of e-mail programs to block e-mails from certain addresses.

- Furthermore, victims should contact online directory listings such as *www.four11.com*, *www.switchboard.com,* and *www.whowhere.com* to request removal from specific directories.
- Finally, under no circumstances should victims agree to meet with the perpetrator face to face to "work it out" or "talk." No contact should ever be made with the stalker. Meeting a stalker in person can be very dangerous.

REFERENCES

U.S. Department of Justice. (August 1999). *Cyberstalking: A New Challenge for Law Enforcement and Industry—A Report from the Attorney General to the Vice President.* Washington, D.C.: U.S. Department of Justice, pp. 2, 6.

Gregorie, Trudy. *Cyberstalking: Dangers on the Information Superhighway.* The Stalking Resource Center, The National Center for Victims of Crime. Online.

Riveira, Diane. (September/October 2000). "Internet Crimes Against Women," *Sexual Assault Report,* 4 (1).

Wired Patrol. "US Federal Laws—Cyberstalking." Accessed 15 April 2003. *http://www.wiredpatrol.org/stalking/federal.html.*

encourage victimization. Second, violence by men is a power issue and must be seen as related to masculine dominance in society generally as represented in interpersonal relationships and in the control of political systems that address crime and create policy. Indeed, entitlements associated with masculinity produce a range that some scholars term the *rape spectrum.* This means that all sexist behaviors are arranged along a continuum from unexamined feelings of superiority over women, for example, on one end to rape on the other. In this sense, all these behaviors, even though they are so very different in degree, are connected at some level. In addition, scholars emphasize that these behaviors are also connected to the "backlash" or resistance to the gains made by women and other marginalized peoples. Though many men today support these gains and are working on ways to address interpersonal power and violence, hoping to enjoy egalitarian relationships with women, some men have not responded well to these gains. They have responded with anger and feelings of powerlessness and insecurity. Interpersonal violence occurs as men attempt to reestablish power they believe they have lost as a direct result of the gains of women.

Third, male sexual violence is related to the ways violence is eroticized and sexuality is connected to violence. Although pornography is the best example of this problem in its role in eroticizing power differences, women's magazines and advertising generally are rampant with these themes. John Stoltenberg addresses this in the reading "Pornography and Freedom." Finally, we must understand violence

against women in terms of the normalization of violence in society. We live in a society where violence is used to solve problems every day, the media is saturated with violence, and militarism is a national policy.

Consider the following story told to us. The woman, a White professional in her early 30s, had been having a drink with her colleagues one early evening after work. A well-dressed man struck up a conversation with her, and they chatted a while. When she was leaving with her colleagues, the man asked if he could call her sometime, and she gave him her business card that listed only work information. He called her at work within the next week and asked her to have dinner with him, and, seeing no reason not to, she agreed to meet him at a particular restaurant after work. She was careful to explain to us that on both occasions, she was dressed in her professional work clothes and it was early evening in a public space. There was nothing provocative, she emphasized, about her clothes or her demeanor. At some point during the meal she started feeling uncomfortable. The man was very pushy; he chose and ordered her food for her and started telling her that if she wanted to date him, he had certain requirements about how his girlfriends dressed and acted. She panicked and felt a strong need to get away from him, so, at some point she quietly excused herself saying she needed to visit the ladies' room. She then did a quick exit and did not return to the table. Unfortunately, this was not the end of the story.

The man found out where her home was and started to stalk her. One evening he forced his way into her apartment and beat her badly. Fortunately, he did not rape her. Although she took out a restraining order on him, he managed to gain entrance into her apartment building again and beat her senseless one more time in the hallway outside her apartment.

This story is a tragic illustration of misogyny and masculine entitlement. The man felt he had the right to define the reality of women in his life and expected them to be subordinate. He believed it was his entitlement. He was so full of rage that when a woman snubbed him, he would have to subdue her. In addition, the woman's telling of the story is illustrative of societal norms that blame women for their own victimization. When tearfully sharing her story, she had felt the shame and humiliation that comes with such an experience; she wanted it to be known that she had not been "asking for it." He had given no indication that he was anything but clean-cut and upstanding, she was dressed appropriately, she took no risks other than accepting a date, she gave him only her work numbers, and she agreed to meet him in a public place. What more could she have done except be wary of all men she might meet?

Abused women are disproportionately represented among the homeless and suicide victims, and they have been denied insurance in some states because they are considered to have a "pre-existing condition" (i.e., having resided with a batterer). It is important to remember that alongside the sheer physical and emotional costs of violence against women, the Centers for Disease Control and Prevention estimated in 2006 that the health-related financial costs of rape, physical assault, stalking, and homicide against women by intimate partners exceeds $5.8 billion annually. Women who are battered have more than twice the health care needs and costs than those who are never battered. This figure does not include lost wages and productivity. In this chapter we discuss sexual assault and rape, physical abuse, and incest and end with a discussion of pornography as a form of violence against women. Because many forms of pornography are legal, some people object to thinking about pornography in the context of sexual violence and claim instead that it is a legitimate type of entertainment. Despite these concerns, we have decided to discuss it in the context of sexual violence because pornography eroticizes unequal power relations between women and men and often involves representations of coercive sex. Men are the major consumers of pornography, and women's bodies tend to be the ones on display. Pornography thus represents a particular aspect of gender relations that reflects the issue of male sexual violence against women.

RAPE

Although rape can be broadly defined as sex without consent, it is understood as a crime of aggression because the focus is on hurting and dominating. More specifically, it is the penetration of any bodily orifice by a penis or object without consent. Someone who is asleep, passed out, or incapacitated by alcohol or drugs cannot give consent. Silence, or lack of continued resistance, does not mean consent. Likewise, consent is not the same as giving in to pressure and intimidation. Women are often victims of *altruistic sex* (motivation for consent involves feeling sorry for the other person, or feeling guilty about resisting sexual advances) and *compliant sex* (where the consequences of not doing it are worse than doing it). Neither of these forms of sexual intimacy involve complete consent. Consent is a freely made choice that is clearly communicated. *Consensual sex* is negotiated through communication where individuals express their feelings and desires and are able to listen to and respect others' feelings and desires. Rape can happen to anyone—babies who are months old to women in their 90s, people of all races, ethnicities, and socioeconomic status. Both women and men are raped, and, as already discussed, overwhelmingly it is a problem of men raping women and other men. Rape occurs relatively frequently in prisons; dominant men rape men they perceive as inferior. Often dominant inmates refer to the victims as "women." In this way, rape is about power, domination, and humiliation and must be understood in this context.

Individuals may be sexually assaulted without being raped. Sexual assault can be defined as any sexual contact without consent and/or that involves the use of force. Like rape, sexual assault is an act of power, control, and domination. The terms can get confusing because sexual assault, sexual abuse, and rape are often used interchangeably. Basically, rape is a form of sexual assault and sexual abuse, but sexual assault and abuse do not necessarily imply rape. The sexual abuse of children is often termed *molestation,* which may or may not involve rape. When children are molested or raped by family members, it is termed *incest.* Although the rates of rape are very high, sexual assault rates generally (which include but are not limited to rape) are even higher.

As already mentioned, current statistics suggest that about 95 percent of reported sexual assaults are against females, with 1 in 3 to 1 in 4 women experiencing sexual assault in their lifetime. In addition, half of all females raped are under the age of 18 years, and about one-fifth are under 12 years old. Among college women in the

LEARNING ACTIVITY **How Safe Is Your Campus?**

Investigate the safety and security of your campus by asking these questions:

- How many acts of violence were reported on your campus last year?
- Does your campus have a security escort service?
- What resources does your campus provide to ensure safety?
- What training and educational opportunities about safety does your college provide?
- What specialized training about violence is offered to fraternities and sports teams on your campus?
- How does your school encourage the reporting of violence?
- What support services does your school offer to victims of violence?
- What is your school administration's official protocol for dealing with complaints of violence?
- How does your school's code of conduct address violence?
- Are there dark areas of your campus that need additional lighting?
- Are emergency phones available around your campus?

NCWSV survey that was sponsored by the U.S. Department of Justice, it was reported that women at a university with 10,000 female students could experience about 350 rapes a year "with serious policy implications for college administrators." More than one-third of these college women said they had unwanted or uninvited sexual contacts, and 10 percent said they had experienced rape. In this study, 9 in 10 offenders were known to the women. Survivors are more likely to report a rape or sexual assault when the assailant is someone they do not know, and indeed, among the college women in the NCWSV sample, less than 5 percent of completed or attempted rapes were reported to law enforcement officials and about one-third of victims did not tell anyone. The U.S. Bureau of Justice Statistics (2005) adds that about 7 in 10 female rape or sexual assault victims stated that the offender was an intimate, relative, friend, or acquaintance, and other studies have estimated that about 75 percent of sexual assaults are committed by a friend, acquaintance, husband, or family member. In this way, acquaintance rape (often called date rape), in which each person is known to the other, is the most frequent form of rape, and is the most underreported.

Rapes on college campuses (especially gang rapes) sometimes occur by fraternity members, and may be part of male bonding rituals. This does not mean, of course, that all fraternities are dangerous places for women, only that the conditions for the abuse of women can occur in these male-only living spaces, especially when alcohol is present. About 70 to 80 percent of campus rapes generally involve alcohol or other drugs (with alcohol most pervasive among all drugs). The most common "date rape" or predatory drugs are rohypnol (commonly known as "roofies"), ketamine (commonly known as "special k"), and GHB (gamma hydroxybutyrate). These drugs are odorless when dissolved and are indiscernible when put in beverages. They metabolize quickly and make a person incapable of resisting sexual advances. Memory impairment is associated with these drugs, and a survivor may not be aware of such an attack until 8 to 12 hours after it has occurred. In addition, there may be little evidence to support the claim that drugs were used to facilitate the attack because of the speed at which these predatory drugs metabolize. It is imperative to be vigilant at social occasions where such attacks might happen; do not leave a drink unattended, get your own drinks from an unopened container, and watch out for your friends. A buddy system that includes a designated driver is essential!

In 1990 Congress passed the Campus Security Act, which mandated colleges and universities participating in federal student aid programs to complete and distribute security reports on campus practices and crime statistics. This was amended in 1992 to include the Campus Sexual Assault Victim's Bill of Rights to provide policies and statistics and to ensure basic rights to survivors of sexual assault. This act was amended again in 1998 to provide for more extensive security-related provisions, and, since then, the U.S. Department of Justice has given substantial grants to colleges and universities to address sexual and physical assault, harassment, and stalking on campus.

One specific form of "acquaintance rape" is marital rape. A recent national study reported that 10 percent of all sexual assault cases involve a husband or ex-husband, and the National Resource Center on Domestic Violence suggests that taking into account the underreporting that occurs as women are less likely to label such actions as rape, 10 to 14 percent of married women in the United States have been raped by their husbands. Historically, rape has been understood as a property crime against men as women were considered the property of husbands and fathers. As a result, it was considered impossible to violate something that was legally considered your property, and rape laws defined rape as forced intercourse with a woman who was not your wife. In 1993 marital rape became a crime in all 50 states, even though some states still do not consider it as serious as other forms of rape and include some forms of marital rape exemption (for example, if a spouse has an illness causing an inability to sexually respond, the other spouse may engage her/him in sexual relations without criminal liability). In the United States, statutory rape laws do not go into effect if a spouse is under the age of consent for that state. Women who are raped by their husbands are likely to be raped many times. They experience not only vaginal rape, but also oral and anal rape. Researchers generally categorize marital rape into three types: force-only rape, when a husband uses only enough force to enact the rape; battering rape, in which rape occurs in the context of an ongoing physically abusive relationship; and sadistic/obsessive rape, where husbands use torture or perverse acts to humiliate and harm their wives. Pornography is often involved in the latter case. Women are at particularly high risk for being raped by their partners when they are married to domineering men who view them as "property," when they are pregnant, ill physically or mentally, or recovering from surgery, and when they are separated or divorced.

As will be discussed in Chapter 11, political institutions in the United States have historically supported men's access to women as sexual property, and the history of racism and the lynching of Black men for fabricated rapes of White women have influenced how our society and the courts deal with the interaction of race and sexual violence. Although most rapes are *intra-racial* (they occur within racial groups), women of color are especially vulnerable as victims of sexual violence because of their marginalized status. They also have less credibility in the courtroom when rape cases have gone to trial. Men of color accused of rape are more likely to get media attention, are more likely to get convicted, and receive longer sentences. While these differences result from the racism of society that sees Black men in particular as more violent or dangerous, they also are related to class differences whereby men of color are generally less able to acquire superior legal counsel. As Andrea Smith explains in the reading "Beyond the Politics of Inclusion," gender violence functions as a tool of racism and colonialism for women of color. She emphasizes the need to make the needs of marginalized women central in the anti-violence movement and implores writers and activists to understand the intersectionality of racism and sexism in social movements for ending violence and supporting racial justice.

Very often, women realize that a past sexual encounter was actually a rape, and, as a result, they begin to think about the experience differently. They may have left the encounter hurt, confused, or angry but without being able to articulate what happened. Survivors need to talk about what occurred and get support. It is never too late to get support from people who care. Feeling ashamed, dirty, or stupid is a typical reaction for those who have experienced sexual assault. It is not their/your/our fault.

Social myths about rape that encourage these feelings include the following:

- *Rape happens less frequently in our society than women believe. Feminists in particular blow this out of proportion by focusing on women's victimization, and women make up rape charges as a way to get attention.* This is false; rape happens at an alarming rate and is underreported. Rape is considered a crime

THE CONSEQUENCES OF INTIMATE PARTNER VIOLENCE

The consequences of abuse are profound, extending beyond the health and happiness of individuals to affect the well-being of entire communities. Living in a violent relationship affects a woman's sense of self-esteem and her ability to participate in the world. Studies have shown that abused women are routinely restricted in the way they can gain access to information and services, take part in public life, and receive emotional support from friends and relatives. Not surprisingly, such women are often unable properly to look after themselves and their children or to pursue jobs and careers.

IMPACT ON HEALTH

A growing body of research evidence is revealing that sharing her life with an abusive partner can have a profound impact on a woman's health. Violence has been linked to a host of different health outcomes, both immediate and long term. The list below draws on the scientific literature to summarize the consequences that have been associated with intimate partner violence. Although violence can have direct health consequences, such as injury, being a victim of violence also increases a woman's risk of future ill health. As with the consequences of tobacco and alcohol use, being a victim of violence can be regarded as a risk factor for a variety of diseases and conditions.

. . .

Health Consequences of Intimate Partner Violence

Physical

- Abdominal/thoracic injuries
- Bruises and welts
- Chronic pain syndromes
- Disability
- Fibromyalgia
- Fractures
- Gastrointestinal disorders
- Irritable bowel syndrome
- Lacerations and abrasions
- Ocular damage
- Reduced physical functioning

Sexual and Reproductive

- Gynecological disorders
- Infertility
- Pelvic inflammatory disease
- Pregnancy complications/miscarriage
- Sexual dysfunction
- Sexually transmitted diseases, including HIV/AIDS
- Unsafe abortion
- Unwanted pregnancy

Psychological and Behavioral

- Alcohol and drug abuse
- Depression and anxiety
- Eating and sleep disorders
- Feelings of shame and guilt
- Phobias and panic disorder
- Physical inactivity
- Poor self-esteem
- Post-traumatic stress disorder
- Psychosomatic disorders
- Smoking
- Suicidal behavior and self-harm
- Unsafe sexual behavior

Fatal Health Consequences

- AIDS-related mortality
- Maternal mortality
- Homicide
- Suicide

Source: World Report on Violence and Health *www.who.int/violence_injury_prevention/global_campaign/en/chap4.pdf.*

against the state and rape survivors are witnesses to the crime. As a result, the credibility of the "witness" is challenged in rape cases, and women are often retraumatized as a result of rape trials. This is among the many reasons why rape is underreported, and, as a proportion of total rapes committed, charges are rarely pressed and assailants rarely convicted. The FBI reports that the rate of false reporting for rape and sexual assault is the same as for other violent crimes: less than 3 percent. Although feminists care about the victimization of women, we focus on surviving, becoming empowered, and making changes to stop rapes from happening.

- *Women are at least partly responsible for their victimization in terms of their appearance and behavior (encouraging women to feel guilty when they are raped).* This is false; rape is the only violent crime in which the victim is not de facto perceived as innocent. Consider the suggestion that a person who has just been robbed was asking to have his/her wallet stolen.
- *Men are not totally responsible for their actions. If a woman comes on to a man sexually, it is impossible for him to stop.* This is false; men are not driven by uncontrollable biological urges, and it is insulting to men to assume that this is how they behave. Likewise it is wrong to assume a woman has "to finish what she started." Everyone has the right to stop sexual behaviors at any time. Note how this myth is related to the previous one that blames the victim.

These myths not only support masculine privilege concerning sexuality and access to women and therefore support some men's tendency to sexually abuse women, but are also important means for controlling women's lives. Recall again the discussion of *sexual terrorism* in Chapter 2. Such terrorism limits women's activities and keeps us in line by the threat of potential sexual assault. Research on rapists in the early 1980s revealed that, although there are few psychological differences between men who have raped and those who have not, the former group were more likely to believe in the rape myths, were more misogynous and tolerant of the interpersonal domination of women generally, showed higher levels of sexual arousal around depictions of rape, and were more prone to use violence.

BATTERING AND PHYSICAL ABUSE

Although women are less likely than men to be victims of violent crimes overall, women are 5 to 8 times more likely to be victimized by an intimate partner. Intimate partner violence is primarily a crime against women and all races are equally vulnerable. In 2007, the Bureau of Justice reported that 96 percent of women experiencing nonfatal partner violence were victimized by a male and about 85 percent of all victims were female. According to FBI statistics, every day about four women (approximately 1,400 a year) die in the United States as a result of domestic violence. Although about half a million reports of physical assault by intimates officially reach federal officials each year, it is estimated that 2 to 4 million women are battered each year; about one every 20 seconds or so. Women of all races and classes are battered, although rates are 5 times higher among families below poverty levels, and severe spouse abuse is twice as likely to be committed by unemployed men as by those

IDEAS FOR ACTIVISM

- Volunteer at a local domestic violence shelter.
- Organize a food, clothing, and toiletries drive to benefit your local domestic violence shelter.
- Interrupt jokes about violence against women.
- Organize Domestic Violence Awareness Month (October) activities on your campus.
- Create and distribute materials about violence against women on your campus.

working full time. These differences reflect economic vulnerability and lack of resources, as well as the ways these families have more contact with authorities like social services that increases opportunities for reporting. Women who are pregnant are especially at risk of violence. Approximately 17 percent of pregnant women report having been battered, and the results include miscarriages, stillbirths, and a two- to fourfold greater likelihood of bearing a low birth weight baby. Sadly, the impact of violence in families on children is severe. More than half of all female victims of intimate partner violence live in households with children under 12 years, and studies indicate that between 3 and 10 million children witness some form of domestic violence every year. Approximately half of men who abuse female partners also abuse the children in those homes. Of course, women may abuse their children, too. Violent juvenile offenders are four times more likely than nonoffenders to have grown up in homes where they saw violence. Children who have witnessed violence at home are also five times more likely to commit or suffer violence when they become adults.

Women who are physically abused are also always emotionally abused because they experience emotional abuse by virtue of being physically terrorized. Emotional abuse, however, does not always involve physical abuse. A man, for example, who constantly tells his partner that she is worthless, stupid, or ugly can emotionally abuse without being physically abusive. Sometimes the scars of emotional abuse take longer to heal than physical abuse and help explain why women might stay with abusive partners.

Why do some men physically abuse women or abuse other men? They abuse because they have internalized sexism and the right to dominate women (or others they perceive as subordinate) in their lives, have learned to use violence as a way to deal with conflict, and have repressed anger. Given this, how is it possible to explain why some women abuse men or abuse other women? Abusive behavior is an act of domination. Women too can internalize domination and can see men in their interpersonal relationships as subordinate to them, even though there is little support for that in society generally. Women in romantic relationships with other women can likewise negotiate dominance and subordination in their relationships and act this out. Battering is a problem in the lesbian community.

Why do women so often stay in abusive relationships? The research on this question suggests that when women leave abusive relationships they return about 5 to 7 times before actually leaving for good. There are several complex and interconnected

Check Up on Your Relationship

DOES YOUR PARTNER

Constantly put you down?

Call you several times a night or show up to make sure you are where you said you would be?

Embarrass or make fun of you in front of your friends or family?

Make you feel like you are nothing without him/her?

Intimidate or threaten you? "If you do that again, I'll . . ."

Always say that it's your fault?

Pressure you to have sex when you don't want to?

Glare at you, give you the silent treatment, grab, shove, kick, or hit you?

DO YOU

Always do what your partner wants instead of what you want?

Fear how your partner will act in public?

Constantly make excuses to other people for your partner's behavior?

Feel like you walk on eggshells to avoid your partner's anger?

Believe if you just tried harder, submitted more, that everything would be okay?

Stay with your partner because you fear what your partner would do if you broke up?

These indicators suggest potential abuse in your relationship. If you've answered yes to any of these questions, talk to a counselor about your relationship. Remember, when one person scares, hurts, or continually puts down the other person, it's abuse.

Created by the President's Commission on the Status of Women, Oregon State University.

reasons why women stay. First, emotional abuse often involves feelings of shame, guilt, and low self-esteem. Women in these situations (like rape survivors generally) often believe that the abuse is their fault. They may see themselves as worthless and have a difficult time believing that they deserve better. Low self-esteem encourages women to stay with or return to abusive men. Second, some women who are repeatedly abused become desensitized to the violence; they may see it as a relatively normal aspect of gender relationships and therefore something to tolerate.

A third reason women stay in abusive relationships is that men who abuse women tend to physically isolate them from others. This often involves a pattern where women are prevented from visiting or talking to family and friends, are left without

The Cycle of Violence

Domestic violence may seem unpredictable, but it actually follows a typical pattern no matter when it occurs or who is involved. Understanding the cycle of violence and the thinking of the abuser helps survivors recognize they are not to blame for the violence they have suffered—and that *the abuser is the one responsible*.

1. *Tension building* The abuser might set up the victim so that she is bound to anger him. The victim, knowing her abuser is likely to erupt, is apologetic. She may even defend his actions.
2. *The abuse* The batterer behaves violently, inflicting pain and abuse on the victim.
3. *Guilt and fear of reprisal* After the violence, the abuser may have feelings of "guilt"—not normal guilt, in which he'd feel sorry for hurting another person, but actually a fear of getting caught. He might blame alcohol for his outburst.
4. *Blaming the victim* The abuser can't stand any kind of guilt feeling for long, so he quickly rationalizes his actions and blames the victim for causing him to hurt her. He might tell her that her behavior "asked for it."
5. *"Normalcy"* At this point, the batterer exhibits kind and loving behavior. Welcomed by both parties, an unusual calm will surround the relationship. He may bring gifts and promise the violence will never happen again.
6. *Fantasy/set-up* Batterers and abusers fantasize about their past and future abuses. These fantasies feed the abuser's anger. He begins to plan another attack by placing his victim in situations that he knows will anger him.

Reprinted from *Take Care: A Guide for Violence-Free Living,* a publication of Raphael House of Portland.

transportation, and/or have no access to a telephone. Notice how, when women are abused, the shame associated with this situation can encourage women to isolate themselves. An outcome of this isolation is that women do not get the reality check they need about their situation. Isolation thus helps keep self-esteem low, prevents support, and minimizes women's options in terms of leaving the abusive situation.

A fourth reason women stay is that they worry about what people will think, and this worry keeps them in abusive situations as a consequence of the shame they feel. Most women in abusive relationships worry about this to some extent, although middle-class women probably feel it the most. The myth that this is a lower-class problem and that it does not happen to "nice" families who appear to have everything going for them is part of the problem. And, indeed, the question about what people will think is a relevant one: Some churches tell abused women to submit to their husbands and hide the abuse, neighbors often look the other way, mothers worry about their children being stigmatized at school, and certainly there is embarrassment associated with admitting your husband or boyfriend hits you. For men this issue is even more pertinent, and the shame and embarrassment may be even greater for abused men.

A fifth reason women stay is that they cannot afford to leave. Women in this situation fear for the economic welfare of themselves and their children should they leave the abusive situation. These women tend to have less education and to have

ACTIVIST PROFILE **Del Martin**

In the 1950s, few lesbians were able to be out about their sexual identity. In fact, in most places homosexual sex was illegal, and lesbians and gay men were easy targets for violence, even by police. Nonetheless, in 1955 Del Martin (left), her partner Phyllis Lyon, and six other women co-founded the Daughters of Bilitis. The group started as a social club for lesbians seeking to meet and socialize with other lesbians, but before long it expanded its mission to include social reform, and chapters of the organization were launched around the country. Martin was president of the national organization from 1957 to 1960.

Martin became involved in the feminist movement in the early 1970s and in 1976 wrote *Battered Wives,* a revolutionary examination of the experiences of victims of domestic violence. One of the most significant contributions of the book was identifying the origins of domestic violence in the patriarchal structure of the nuclear family. She wrote, "The nuclear family is the building block of American society, and the social, religious, educational and economic institutions of society are designed to maintain, support and strengthen family ties even if the people involved can't stand the sight of one another." Martin advocated collective thinking among members of government, social agencies, religious institutions, and political action groups. Her vision led to the creation of a movement addressing the problem of battered women.

In 1975 she helped found the Coalition for Justice for Battered Women. She also co-founded *La Casa de las Madres,* a refuge for battered women in San Francisco. She helped write the protocol for the San Francisco criminal justice system and served 3 years on the California Commission on Crime Control and Violence Prevention.

Partners since 1953, in the late 1990s, Martin and Lyon continued to work for issues of justice, particularly those related to aging. In 1995 they were appointed delegates to the White House Conference on Aging. For more than 50 years they have worked tirelessly on behalf of marginalized people in order to bring about a more just world.

dependent children. They understand that the kind of paid work they could get would not be enough to support the family. Reason six is that some survivors believe that children need a father—and that even a bad father might be better than no father. Although this belief is erroneous in our view, it does keep women in abusive situations "for the sake of the children." Interestingly, the primary reason women do permanently leave an abusive relationship is also the children: When women see that their children are being hurt, this is the moment when they are most likely to leave for good.

Another reason women stay is that there is often nowhere to go. Although the increase in the numbers of crisis lines and emergency housing shelters is staggering given their absence only a few decades ago, some women still have a difficult time imagining an alternative to the abusive situation. This is especially true of women who live in rural areas and who are isolated from friends and family. Reason eight is that battered women often believe their partner will change. Part of the cycle of violence noted by scholars in this area is the "honeymoon phase" after the violent episode. First comes the buildup of tension when violence is brewing, second is the violent episode, and third is the honeymoon phase when men tend to be especially remorseful—even horrified that they could have done such a thing—and ask for forgiveness. Given that the profile of many batterers is charm and manipulation, such behavior during this phase can be especially persuasive. Women are not making it up when they think their partner will change.

Finally, women stay because they believe their partner might kill them—or hurt or kill the children—should they leave. Again, his past violence is often enough to make women realize this is no idle threat. Men do kill in these situations and often after wives and girlfriends have fled and brought restraining orders against them.

INCEST

This topic is especially poignant as the poem by Grace Caroline Bridges, "Lisa's Ritual, Age 10," demonstrates. Incest is the sexual abuse (molestation, inappropriate touching, rape, being forced to watch or perform sexual acts on others) of children by a family member or someone with a kinship role in a child's life. There is now an evolving definition of incest that takes into account betrayals of trust and power imbalances, expanding the definition to include sexual abuse by anyone who has power or authority over the child. Perpetration might include baby-sitters, schoolteachers, Boy Scout leaders, priests/ministers, family friends, as well as immediate and extended family members. It is estimated that in about 90 percent of cases where children are raped it is by someone they know. Studies suggest that one in every three to five girls have experienced some kind of childhood sexual abuse by the time they are 16 years old. For boys this number is one in six to ten, although this may be underestimated because boys are less likely to admit that they are survivors. Again, like other forms of abuse, incest crosses all ethnic, class, and religious lines. Power is always involved in incest, and, because children are the least powerful group in society, the effects on them can be devastating. Approximately a third of all juvenile victims of sexual abuse are younger than 6 years old. Children who are abused often have low self-esteem and may find it difficult to trust.

Violence Against Women: Selected Human Rights Documents

International human rights documents encompass formal written documents, such as conventions, declarations, conference statements, guidelines, resolutions, and recommendations. Treaties are legally binding on States that have ratified or acceded to them, and their implementation is observed by monitoring bodies, such as the Committee on the Elimination of Discrimination Against Women (CEDAW).

GLOBAL DOCUMENTS

The Universal Declaration of Human Rights (1948) has formed the basis for the development of international human rights conventions. Article 3 states that everyone has the right of life, liberty, and security of the person. According to article 5, no one shall be subjected to torture or to cruel, inhuman, or degrading treatment or punishment. Therefore, any form of violence against a woman that is a threat to her life, liberty, or security of person or that can be interpreted as torture or cruel, inhuman, or degrading treatment violates the principles of this Declaration.

The International Covenant on Economic, Social and Cultural Rights (1966), together with the *International Covenant on Civil and Political Rights*, prohibits discrimination on the basis of sex. Violence detrimentally affects women's health; therefore, it violates the right to the enjoyment of the highest attainable standard of physical and mental health (article 12). In addition, article 7 provides the right to the enjoyment of just and favorable conditions of work which ensure safe and healthy working conditions. This provision encompasses the prohibition of violence and harassment of women in the workplace.

The International Covenant on Civil and Political Rights (1966) prohibits all forms of violence. Article 6.1 protects the right to life. Article 7 prohibits torture and inhuman or degrading treatment or punishment. Article 9 guarantees the right to liberty and security of person.

The Convention Against Torture and Other Cruel, Inhuman or Degrading Treatment or Punishment (1984) provides protection for all persons, regardless of their sex, in a more detailed manner than the International Covenant on Civil and Political Rights. States should take effective measures to prevent acts of torture (article 2).

The Convention on the Elimination of All Forms of Discrimination Against Women (1979) is the most extensive international instrument dealing with the rights of women. Although violence against women is not specifically addressed in the Convention, except in relation to trafficking and prostitution (article 6), many of the anti-discrimination clauses protect women from violence. States Parties have agreed to a policy of eliminating discrimination against women, and to adopt legislative and other measures prohibiting all discrimination against women (article 2). In 1992, CEDAW, which monitors the implementation of this Convention, formally included gender-based violence under gender-based discrimination. General Recommendation No. 19, adopted at the 11th session (June 1992), deals entirely with violence against women and the measures taken to eliminate such violence. As for health issues, it recommends that States should provide support services for all victims of gender-based violence, including refuges, specially trained health workers, and rehabilitation and counseling services.

The International Convention on the Elimination of All Forms of Racial Discrimination (1965) declares that States Parties undertake to prohibit and to eliminate racial discrimination in all its forms and to guarantee the enjoyment of the right to security of the person and protection by the State against violence or bodily harm, whether inflicted by government officials or by any individual group or institution (article 5).

The four *1949 Geneva Conventions* and two additional Protocols form the cornerstone of international humanitarian law. The Geneva Conventions require that all persons taking no active part in hostilities shall be treated humanely, without adverse distinction on any of the usual grounds, including sex (article 3). They offer protection to all civilians against sexual violence, forced prostitution, sexual abuse, and rape.

Regarding international armed conflict, *Additional Protocol I* to the 1949 Geneva Conventions creates obligations for parties to a conflict to treat humanely persons under their control. It requires that women shall be protected against rape, forced prostitution, and indecent assault. *Additional Protocol II,* applicable during internal conflicts, also prohibits rape, enforced prostitution, and indecent assault.

The Convention on the Rights of the Child (1989) declares that States Parties take appropriate legislative, administrative, social, and educational measures to protect the child from physical or mental violence, abuse, maltreatment, or exploitation (article 19). States shall act accordingly to prevent the exploitative use of children in prostitution or other unlawful sexual practices, and the exploitative use of children in pornographic performances and materials (article 34).

The International Convention on the Protection of the Rights of All Migrant Workers and Members of Their Families (adopted by the General Assembly in 1990 and went into force in 2003) contains the right of migrant workers and their family members to liberty and security of person as proclaimed in other international instruments. They shall be entitled to effective protection by the State against violence, physical injury, threats, and intimidation, whether by public officials or by private individuals, groups, or institutions (article 16).

Incest can be both direct and indirect. Direct forms include vaginal, oral, and rectal penetration; sexual rubbing; excessive, inappropriate hugging; body and mouth kissing; bouncing a child on a lap against an erection; and sexual bathing. Direct incest also includes forcing children to watch or perform these acts on others. Indirect incest includes sexualizing statements or joking, speaking to the child as a surrogate spouse, inappropriate references to a child's body, or staring at the child's body. Examples also include intentionally invading children's privacy in the bathroom or acting inappropriately jealous when adolescents start dating. These indirect forms of incest involve sexualizing children and violating their boundaries.

Often siblings indulge in relatively normal uncoerced sexual play with each other that disappears over time. When this involves a child who is several years older or one who uses threats or intimidation, the behavior can be characterized as incestuous. Indicators of abuse in childhood include excessive crying, anxiety, night fears and sleep disturbances, depression and withdrawal, clinging behaviors, and physical problems like urinary tract infections and trauma to the mouth and/or perineal area. Adolescent symptoms often include eating disorders, psychosomatic complaints, suicidal thoughts, and depression. Survivors of childhood sexual violence may get involved in self-destructive behaviors like alcohol and drug abuse or cutting on their bodies as they turn their anger inward, or they may express their anger through acting out or promiscuous behavior. In particular, girls internalize their worthlessness and their role as sexual objects used by others; boys often have more anger because they were dominated, an anger that is sometimes projected onto their future sexual partners as well as onto themselves. Although it takes time, we can heal from being sexually violated. Jane Fonda makes this point in the reading "Reclaiming Our Mojo." She writes about her mother's experience of childhood sexual abuse and the ways she hopes to turn that knowledge into successful empowerment of survivors.

PORNOGRAPHY

Pornography involves the sexualization and objectification of women's bodies and parts of bodies for entertainment value. According to feminist legal scholar Catharine MacKinnon, who has written on and debated the issue of pornography at length, pornography can be defined as the graphic, sexually explicit subordination of women through pictures and/or words. She says pornography includes one or more of the following: women presented as dehumanized sexual objects, things, or commodities; shown as enjoying humiliation, pain, or sexual assault; tied up, mutilated, or physically hurt; depicted in postures or positions of sexual submission or servility; shown with body parts—including though not limited to vagina, breasts, or buttocks—exhibited such that women are reduced to those parts; women penetrated by animals or objects; and women presented in scenarios of degradation, humiliation, or torture, shown as filthy or inferior, bleeding, bruised, or hurt in a context that makes these conditions sexual. MacKinnon adds that the use of men, children, or transsexuals in the place of women is also pornography. Note the definition includes the caveat that because a person has consented to being harmed, abused, or subjected to coercion does not alter the degrading character of the behavior.

Just as there are degrees of objectification and normalization of violence in pop culture forms, so too in pornography there is a continuum from the soft porn of *Playboy* to the hard-core *Hustler* and along to illegal forms of representation like child pornography and snuff films. Snuff films are illegal because women are actually murdered in the making of these films. The Internet is one of the largest sites for pornography. There are thousands of pornography sites on the Web, including those of "fantasy rape" that depict women being raped, and "sex" is still the top search word. In addition to Internet pornography there is the problem of Internet prostitution where technology is utilized for the global trafficking and the sexual exploitation of women and children.

Many people do not oppose pornography because they feel that it represents free speech, or because they feel that the women have chosen to be part of it, or because they like the articles in these magazines. This is especially true of soft porn like

Playboy. Some see pornography as a mark of sexual freedom and characterize those who would like to limit pornography as prudish. In the reading "Pornography and Freedom," John Stoltenberg explains how sexual freedom requires sexual justice and suggests that pornography is a violation of this justice rather than an expression of it. He writes about pornography in the context of gender and male domination in society.

Some people make a distinction between hard-core and soft porn and feel that the former is harmful and the latter relatively harmless. Others oppose pornography entirely as a violation of women's rights against objectification and sexualization for male pleasure and believe that people's rights to consume such materials are no longer rights when they violate the rights of others. This is an important debate that has brought about some interesting coalitions among those who normally do not work together, such as feminists and conservative religious groups.

In this way, acts of violence and the threat of violence have profound and lasting effects on all women's lives. We tend to refer to those who have survived violence as "survivors" rather than "victims" to emphasize that it is possible to go on with our lives after such experiences, difficult though that might be. Understanding and preventing violence against women has become a worldwide effort, bringing women and men together to make everyone safer.

Beyond the Politics of Inclusion
Violence Against Women of Color and Human Rights

Andrea Smith (2004)

What was disturbing to so many U.S. citizens about the September 11, 2001, attacks on the World Trade Center is that these attacks disrupted their sense of safety at "home." Terrorism is something that happens in other countries; our "home," the U.S.A., is supposed to be a place of safety. Similarly, mainstream U.S. society believes that violence against women only occurs "out there" and is perpetrated by a few crazed men whom we simply need to lock up. However, the anti-violence movement has always contested this notion of safety at home. The notion that violence only happens "out there," inflicted by the stranger in the dark alley makes it difficult to recognize that the home is in fact the place of greatest danger for women. In response to this important piece of analysis, the anti-violence movement has, ironically, based its strategies on the premise that the criminal legal system is the primary tool with which to address violence against women. However, when one-half of women will be battered in their lifetimes and nearly one-half of women will be sexually assaulted in their lifetimes, it is clear that we live in a rape culture that prisons, themselves a site of violence and control, cannot change.

Similarly, the notion that terrorism happens in other countries makes it difficult to grasp that the United States is built on a history of genocide, slavery, and racism. Our "home" has never been a safe place for people of color. Because many mainstream feminist organizations are white-dominated, they often do not see themselves as potential victims in Bush's war in the U.S. and abroad. However, those considered "alien" in the United States and hence deserving of repressive policies and overt attack are not only people of color. Since 9/11, many organizations in LGBT communities have reported sharp increases in attacks, demonstrating the extent to which gays and lesbians are often seen as "alien" because their sexuality seems to threaten the white nuclear family thought to be the building block of U.S. society.

Furthermore, many mainstream feminist organizations, particularly anti-violence organizations, have applauded the U.S. attacks on Afghanistan for "liberating" Arab women from the repressive policies of the Taliban. Apparently, bombing women in Afghanistan somehow elevates their status. However, the Revolutionary Association of the Women from Afghanistan (RAWA), the organization comprised of members most affected by the policies of the Taliban, has condemned U.S. intervention and has argued that women cannot expect an improvement in their status under the regime of the Northern Alliance with which the United States has allied itself. This support rests entirely on the problematic assumption that state violence can secure safety and liberation for women and other oppressed groups. Clearly, alternative approaches to provide true safety and security for women must be developed, both at "home" and abroad.

BEYOND INCLUSION: CENTERING WOMEN OF COLOR IN THE ANTI-VIOLENCE MOVEMENT

The central problem is that as the anti-violence movement has attempted to become more "inclusive" these attempts at multicultural interventions have unwittingly strengthened the white supremacy within the anti-violence movement. That is, inclusivity has come to mean taking on a domestic violence model that was developed largely with the interests of white, middle class women in mind, and simply adding to it a multicultural component. However, if we look at the histories of women of color in the United States, as I have done in other work, it is clear that gender violence functions as a tool for racism and colonialism for women of color in general (Smith 2002). The racial element of gender violence points to the necessity of an alternative approach that goes beyond mere inclusion to actually centering women of color in the organizing and analysis. That is, if we do not make any assumptions about what a domestic violence program should look like but, instead, ask what would it take to end violence against women of color, then what would this movement look like?

In fact, Beth Richie suggests we go beyond just centering women of color, to centering those most marginalized within the category of "women of color." She writes:

> We have to understand that the goal of our antiviolence work is not for diversity, and not inclusion. It is for liberation. If we're truly committed to ending violence against women, then we must start in the hardest places, the places like jails and prisons and other correctional facilities. The places where our work has not had an impact yet. . . . [W]e have to stop being the friendly colored girls as some of our anti-violence programs require us to be. We must not deny the part of ourselves and the part of our work that is least acceptable to the mainstream public. We must not let those who really object to all of us and our work co-opt some of us and the work we're trying to do. As if this anti-violence movement could ever really be legitimate in a patriarchal, racist society. . . . Ultimately the movement needs to be accountable not to those in power, but to the powerless. (Richie 2000)

When we center women of color in the analysis, it becomes clear that we must develop approaches that address interpersonal and state violence simultaneously. In addition, we find that by centering women of color in the analysis, we may actually build a movement that more effectively ends violence not just for women of color, but for all peoples.

HUMAN RIGHTS FRAMEWORK FOR ADDRESSING VIOLENCE

Developing strategies to address state violence, then, suggests the importance of developing a human rights approach toward ending violence. By human rights I mean those rights seen under international law to be inalienable and not dependent on any particular government structure. When we limit our struggles around changes in domestic legislation within the United States, we forget that the United States government itself perpetrates more violence against women than any other actor in the world. While we may use a variety of rhetorical and organizing tools, our overall strategy should not be premised on the notion that the United States should or will always continue to exist—to do so is to fundamentally sanction the continuing genocide of indigenous peoples on which this government is based.

One organization that avoids this problem is the American Indian Boarding School Healing Project, which organizes against gender violence from a human rights perspective. During the nineteenth century and into the twentieth century, American Indian children were abducted from their homes to attend Christian boarding schools as a matter of state policy that again demonstrates the links between sexual violence and state violence. This system was later imported to Canada in the form of the residential school system. Because the worst of the abuses happened to an older generation, there is simply not sufficient documentation or vocal outcry against boarding school abuses.

Responding to this need, the International Human Rights Association of American Minorities issued a report documenting the involvement of mainline churches and the federal government in the murder of over 50,000 Native children through the Canadian residential school system (Annet 2001). The list of offenses committed by church officials includes murder by beating, poisoning, hanging, starvation, strangulation, and medical experimentation. In addition, the report found that church, police, business, and government officials maintained pedophile rings using children from residential schools. Several schools are also charged with concealing on their grounds the unmarked graves of children who were murdered, particularly children killed after being born as a result of rapes of Native girls by priests and other church officials. While some churches in Canada have taken some minimal steps towards addressing their involvement in this genocidal policy, churches in the United States have not.

As a result of boarding school policies, an epidemic of child sexual abuse now exists in Native communities. The shame attached to abuse has allowed no space in which to address this problem. Consequently, child abuse passes from one generation to the next. The American Indian Boarding School Healing Project provides an entryway to addressing this history of child sexual abuse by framing it not primarily as an example of individual and community dysfunction, but instead as the continuing effect of human rights abuses perpetrated by state policy. This project seeks to take the shame away from talking about abuse and provide the space for communities to address the problem and heal.

A human rights approach can even be of assistance to traditional service providers for survivors of violence. The human rights approach provides an organizing strategy to protest John Ashcroft's dramatic cuts in funding for anti-violence programs, particularly indigenous programs. Adequate funding for indigenous-controlled programs and services is not a privilege for States to curtail in times of economic crises. Rather, as international human rights law dictates, states are mandated to address the continuing effects of human rights violations.

Hence, the United States violates international human rights law when it de-funds anti-violence programs. For indigenous women and women of color in general, sexual and domestic violence are clearly the continuing effects of human rights violations perpetrated by U.S. state policy.

CONCLUSION

For too long, women of color have been forced to choose between racial justice and gender justice. Yet, it is precisely through sexism and gender violence that colonialism and white supremacy have been successful. This failure to see the intersectionality of racism and sexism in racial justice movements was evident at the UN World Conference Against Racism, where the types of racism that women of color face in reproductive rights policies, for example, failed to even register on the UN radar screen. Women of color are often suspicious of human rights strategies because white-dominated human rights organizations often pursue the imperialist agenda of organizing around the human rights violations of women in other countries while ignoring the human rights violations of women of color in the United States. Nonetheless, an anti-colonial human rights strategy can be helpful in highlighting the violence perpetrated by U.S. state policy and combating U.S. exceptionalism on the global scale—as well as right here at home.

REFERENCES

Annett, Kevin. 2001. "The Truth Commission into the Genocide in Canada." Accessed August 31, 2003 (http://annett55.freewebsites.com/genocide.pdf).

Richie, Beth. 2000. Plenary Address, "Color of Violence: Violence Against Women of Color" Conference, Santa Cruz, CA.

Smith, Andrea. 2002. "Better Dead than Pregnant: The Colonization of Native Women's Reproductive Health." In *Policing the National Body: Race, Gender, and Criminalization,* ed. Jael Silliman and Anannya Bhattacharjee. Cambridge: South End Press.

Human Rights
Sex Trafficking and Prostitution

Alice Leuchtag (2003)

Despite laws against slavery in practically every country, an estimated twenty-seven million people live as slaves. Kevin Bales, in his book *Disposable People: New Slavery in the Global Economy* (University of California Press, Berkeley, 1999), describes those who endure modern forms of slavery. These include indentured servants, persons held in hereditary bondage, child slaves who pick plantation crops, child soldiers, and adults and children trafficked and sold into sex slavery.

A LIFE NARRATIVE

Of all forms of slavery, sex slavery is one of the most exploitative and lucrative with some 200,000 sex slaves worldwide bringing their slaveholders an annual profit of $10.5 billion. Although the great preponderance of sex slaves are women and girls, a smaller but significant number of males—both adult and children—are enslaved for homosexual prostitution.

The life narrative of a Thai girl named Siri, as told to Bales, illustrates how sex slavery happens to vulnerable girls and women. Siri is born in northeastern Thailand to a poor family that farms a small plot of land, barely eking out a living. Economic policies of structural adjustment pursued by the Thai government under the aegis of the World Bank and the International Monetary Fund have taken former government subsidies away from rice farmers, leaving them to compete against imported, subsidized rice that keeps the market price artificially depressed.

Siri attends four years of school, then is kept at home to help care for her three younger siblings.

When Siri is fourteen, a well-dressed woman visits her village. She offers to find Siri a "good job," advancing her parents $2,000 against future earnings. This represents at least a year's income for the family. In a town in another province the woman, a trafficker, "sells" Siri to a brothel for $4,000. Owned by an "investment club" whose members are business and professional men—government bureaucrats and local politicians—the brothel is extremely profitable. In a typical thirty-day period it nets its investors $88,000.

To maintain the appearance that their hands are clean, members of the club's board of directors leave the management of the brothel to a pimp and a bookkeeper. Siri is initiated into prostitution by the pimp who rapes her. After being abused by her first "customer," Siri escapes, but a policeman—who gets a percentage of the brothel profits—brings her back, whereupon the pimp beats her up. As further punishment, her "debt" is doubled from $4,000 to $8,000. She must now repay this, along with her monthly rent and food, all from her earnings of $4 per customer. She will have to have sex with three hundred men a month just to pay her rent. Realizing she will never be able to get out of debt, Siri tries to build a relationship with the pimp simply in order to survive.

The pimp uses culture and religion to reinforce his control over Siri. He tells her she must have committed terrible sins in a past life to have been born a female; she must have accumulated a karmic debt to deserve the enslavement and abuse to which she must reconcile herself. Gradually Siri begins to see herself from the point of view of the slaveholder—as someone unworthy and deserving of punishment. By age fifteen she no longer protests or runs away. Her physical enslavement has become psychological as well, a common occurrence in chronic abuse.

Siri is administered regular injections of the contraceptive drug Depo-Provera for which she is charged. As the same needle is used for all the girls, there is a high risk of HIV and other sexual diseases from the injections. Siri knows that a serious illness threatens her and she prays to Buddha at the little shrine in her room, hoping to earn merit so he will protect her from the dreaded disease. Once a month she and the others, at their own expense, are tested for HIV. So far Siri's tests have been negative. When Siri tries to get the male customers to wear condoms—distributed free to brothels by the Thai Ministry of Health—some resist wearing them and she can't make them do so.

As one of an estimated 35,000 women working as brothel slaves in Thailand—a country where 500,000 to one million prostituted women and girls work in conditions of degradation and exploitation short of brothel slavery—Siri faces at least a 40 percent chance of contracting the HIV virus. If she is lucky, she can look forward to five more years before she becomes too ill to work and is pushed out into the street.

THAILAND'S SEX TOURISM

Though the Thai government denies it, the World Health Organization finds that HIV is epidemic in Thailand, with the largest segment of new cases among wives and girlfriends of men who buy prostitute sex. Viewing its women as a cash crop to be exploited, and depending on sex tourism for foreign exchange dollars to help pay interest on the foreign debt, the Thai government can't acknowledge the epidemic without contradicting the continued promotion of sex tourism and prostitution.

By encouraging investment in the sex industry, sex tourism creates a business climate conducive to the trafficking and enslavement of vulnerable girls such as Siri. In 1996 nearly five million sex tourists from the United States, Western Europe,

Australia, and Japan visited Thailand. These transactions brought in about $26.2 billion—thirteen times more than Thailand earned by building and exporting computers.

In her 1999 report *Pimps and Predators on the Internet: Globalizing the Sexual Exploitation of Women and Children,* published by the Coalition Against Trafficking in Women (CATW), Donna Hughes quotes from postings on an Internet site where sex tourists share experiences and advise one another. The following is one man's description of having sex with a fourteen-year-old prostituted girl in Bangkok:

> Even though I've had a lot of better massages . . . after fifteen minutes, I was much more relaxed. . . . Then I asked for a condom and I fucked her for another thirty minutes. Her face looked like she was feeling a lot of pain. . . . She blocked my way when I wanted to leave the room and she asked for a tip. I gave her 600 bath. Altogether, not a good experience.

Hughes says, "To the men who buy sex, a 'bad experience' evidently means not getting their money's worth, or that the prostituted woman or girl didn't keep up the act of enjoying what she had to do. . . . [O]ne glimpses the humiliation and physical pain most girls and women in prostitution endure."

Nor are the men oblivious to the existence of sexual slavery. One customer states, "Girls in Bangkok virtually get sold by their families into the industry; they work against their will." His knowledge of their sexual slavery and lack of sensitivity thereof is evident in that he then names the hotels in which girls are kept and describes how much they cost!

As Hughes observes, sex tourists apparently feel they have a right to prostitute sex, perceiving prostitution only from a self-interested perspective in which they commodify and objectify women of other cultures, nationalities, and ethnic groups. Their awareness of racism, colonialism, global economic inequalities, and sexism seems limited to the way these realities benefit them as sex consumers.

SEX TRAFFICKERS CAST THEIR NETS

According to the *Guide to the New UN Trafficking Protocol* by Janice Raymond, published by the CATW in 2001, the United Nations estimates that sex trafficking in human beings is a $5 billion to $7 billion operation annually. Four million persons are moved illegally from one country to another and within countries each year, a large proportion of them women and girls being trafficked into prostitution. The United Nations International Children's Emergency Fund (UNICEF) estimates that some 30 percent of women being trafficked are minors, many under age thirteen. The International Organization on Migration estimates that some 500,000 women per year are trafficked into Western Europe from poorer regions of the world. According to *Sex Trafficking of Women in the United States: International and Domestic Trends,* also published by the CATW in 2001, some 50,000 women and children are trafficked into the United States each year, mainly from Asia and Latin America.

Because prostitution as a system of organized sexual exploitation depends on a continuous supply of new "recruits" trafficking is essential to its continued existence. When the pool of available women and girls dries up, new women must be procured. Traffickers cast their nets ever wider and become ever more sophisticated. The Italian Camorra, Chinese Triads, Russian Mafia, and Japanese Yakuza are powerful criminal syndicates consisting of traffickers, pimps, brothel keepers, forced labor lords, and gangs which operate globally.

After the breakdown of the Soviet Union, an estimated five thousand criminal groups formed the Russian Mafia, which operates in thirty countries. The Russian Mafia traffics women from African countries, the Ukraine, the Russian Federation, and Eastern Europe into Western Europe, the United States, and Israel. The Triads traffic women from China, Korea, Thailand, and other Southeast Asian countries into the United States and Europe. The Camorra traffics women from Latin America into Europe. The Yakuza traffics women from the Phillipines, Thailand, Burma, Cambodia, Korea, Nepal, and Laos into Japan.

A GLOBAL PROBLEM MEETS A GLOBAL RESPONSE

Despite these appalling facts, until recently no generally agreed upon definition of trafficking in human beings was written into international law. In Vienna, Austria, during 1999 and 2000, 120 countries participated in debates over a definition of trafficking. A few nongovernmental organizations (NGOs) and a minority of governments—including Australia, Canada, Denmark, Germany, Ireland, Japan, the Netherlands, Spain, Switzerland, Thailand, and the United Kingdom—wanted to separate issues of trafficking from issues of prostitution. They argued that persons being trafficked should be divided into those who are forced and those who give their consent, with the burden of proof being placed on persons being trafficked. They also urged that the less explicit means of control over trafficked persons—such as abuse of a victim's vulnerability—not be included in the definition of trafficking and that the word *exploitation* not be used. Generally supporters of this position were wealthier countries into which large numbers of women were being trafficked and countries in which prostitution was legalized or sex tourism encouraged.

The CATW—along with 140 other NGOs in the International Human Rights Network plus many governments (including those of Algeria, Bangladesh, Belgium, China, Colombia, Cuba, Egypt, Finland, France, India, Mexico, Norway, Pakistan, the Philippines, Sweden, Syria, Venezuela, and Vietnam)—maintains that trafficking can't be separated from prostitution. Persons being trafficked shouldn't be divided into those who are forced and those who give their consent because trafficked persons are in no position to give meaningful consent. The subtler methods used by traffickers, such as abuse of a victim's vulnerability, should be included in the definition of trafficking and the word *exploitation* be an essential part of the definition. Generally supporters of this majority view were poorer countries from which large numbers of women were being trafficked or countries in which strong feminist, anti-colonialist, or socialist influences existed. The United States, though initially critical of the majority position, agreed to support a definition of trafficking that would be agreed upon by consensus.

The struggle—led by the CATW to create a definition of trafficking that would penalize traffickers while ensuring that all victims of trafficking would be protected—succeeded when a compromise proposal by Sweden was agreed to. A strongly worded and inclusive *UN Protocol to Prevent, Suppress, and Punish Trafficking in Persons*—especially women and children—was drafted by an ad hoc committee of the UN as a supplement to the Convention Against Transnational Organized Crime. The UN protocol specifically addresses the trade in human beings for purposes of prostitution and other forms of sexual exploitation, forced labor or services, slavery or practices similar to slavery, servitude, and the removal of organs. The protocol defines trafficking as

> The recruitment, transportation, transfer, harboring or receipt of persons, by means of the threat or use of force or other forms of coercion, of abduction, of fraud, of deception, of the abuse of power or of a position of vulnerability or of the giving or receiving of payments or benefits to achieve the consent of a person having control over another person, for the purpose of exploitation.

While recognizing that the largest amount of trafficking involves women and children, the wording of the UN protocol clearly is gender and age neutral, inclusive of trafficking in both males and females, adults and children.

In 2000 the UN General Assembly adopted this convention and its supplementary protocol; 121 countries signed the convention and eighty countries signed the protocol. For the convention and protocol to become international law, forty countries must ratify them.

HIGHLIGHTS

Some highlights of the new convention and protocol are:

For the first time there is an accepted international definition of trafficking and an agreed upon set of prosecution, protection, and prevention mechanisms on which countries can base their national legislation.

- The various criminal means by which trafficking takes place, including indirect and subtle forms of coercion, are covered.
- Trafficked persons, especially women in prostitution and child laborers, are no longer viewed as illegal migrants but as victims of a crime.
- The convention doesn't limit its scope to criminal syndicates but defines an organized criminal group as "any structured group of three or more persons which engages in criminal activities such as trafficking and pimping."
- All victims of trafficking in persons are protected, not just those who can prove that force was used against them.
- The consent of a victim of trafficking is meaningless and irrelevant.
- Victims of trafficking won't have to bear the burden of proof.
- Trafficking and sexual exploitation are intrinsically connected and not to be separated.
- Because women trafficked domestically into local sex industries suffer harmful effects similar to those experienced by women trafficked transnationally, these women also come under the protections of the protocol.
- The key element in trafficking is the exploitative purpose rather than the movement across a border.

The protocol is the first UN instrument to address the demand for prostitution sex, a demand that results in the human rights abuses of women and children being trafficked. The protocol recognizes an urgent need for governments to put the buyers of prostitution sex on their policy and legislative agendas, and it calls upon countries to take or strengthen legislative or other measures to discourage demand, which fosters all the forms of sexual exploitation of women and children.

As Raymond says in the *Guide to the New UN Trafficking Protocol*:

> The least discussed part of the prostitution and trafficking chain has been the men who buy women for sexual exploitation in prostitution. . . . If we are to find a permanent path to ending these human rights abuses, then we cannot just shrug our shoulders and say, "men are like this," or "boys will be boys," or "prostitution has always been around." Or tell women and girls in prostitution that they must continue to do what they do because prostitution is inevitable. Rather, our responsibility is to make men change their behavior, by all means available—educational, cultural and legal.

Two U.S. feminist human rights organizations—Captive Daughters and Equality Now—have been working toward that goal. Surita Sandosham of Equality Now says that when her organization asked women's groups in Thailand and the Philippines how it could assist them, the answer came back, "Do something about the demand." Since then the two organizations have legally challenged sex tours originating in the United States and have succeeded in closing down at least one operation.

REFUGEES, NOT ILLEGAL ALIENS

In October 2000 the U.S. Congress passed a bill, the Victims of Trafficking and Violence Protection Act of 2000, introduced by New Jersey republican representative Chris Smith. Under this law penalties for traffickers are raised and protections for victims increased. Reasoning that desperate women are unable to give meaningful consent to their own sexual exploitation, the law adopts a broad definition of sex trafficking so as not to exclude so-called consensual prostitution or trafficking that occurs solely within the United States. In these respects the new federal law conforms to the UN protocol.

Two features of the law are particularly noteworthy:

- In order to pressure other countries to end sex trafficking, the U.S. State Department is to make a yearly assessment of other countries' anti-trafficking efforts and to rank them according to how well they discourage trafficking. After two years of failing to meet even minimal standards, countries are subject to sanctions, although not sanctions on humanitarian aid. "Tier 3" countries—those failing to meet even minimal standards—include Greece, Indonesia, Israel, Pakistan, Russia, Saudi Arabia, South Korea, and Thailand.

- Among persons being trafficked into the United States, special T-visas will be provided to those who meet the criteria for having suffered the most serious trafficking abuses. These visas will protect them from deportation so they can testify against their traffickers. T-1 non-immigrant status allows eligible aliens to remain in the United States temporarily and grants specific non-immigrant benefits. Those acquiring T-1 non-immigrant status will be able to remain for a period of three years and will be eligible to receive certain kinds of public assistance—to the same extent as refugees. They will also be issued employment authorization to "assist them in finding safe, legal employment while they attempt to retake control of their lives."

A DEBATE RAGES

A worldwide debate rages about legalization of prostitution fueled by a 1998 International Labor Organization (ILO) report entitled *The Sex Sector: The Economic and Social Bases of Prostitution in Southeast Asia*. The report follows years of lobbying by the sex industry for recognition of prostitution as "sex work." Citing the sex industry's unrecognized contribution to the gross domestic product of four countries in Southeast Asia, the ILO urges governments to officially recognize the "sex sector" and "extend taxation nets to cover many of the lucrative activities connected with it." Though the ILO report says it stops short of calling for legalization of prostitution, official recognition of the sex industry would be impossible without it.

Raymond points out that the ILO's push to redefine prostitution as sex work ignores legislation demonstrating that countries can reduce organized sexual exploitation rather than capitulate to it. For example, Sweden prohibits the purchase of sexual services with punishments of stiff fines or imprisonment, thus declaring that prostitution isn't a desirable economic and labor sector. The government also helps women getting out of prostitution to rebuild their lives. Venezuela's Ministry of Labor has ruled that prostitution can't be considered work because it lacks the basic elements of dignity and social justice. The Socialist Republic of Vietnam punishes pimps, traffickers, brothel owners, and buyers—sometimes publishing buyer's names in the mass media. For women in prostitution, the government finances medical, educational, and economic rehabilitation.

Raymond suggests that instead of transforming the male buyer into a legitimate customer, the ILO should give thought to innovative programs that make the buyer accountable for his sexual exploitation. She cites the Sage Project, Inc. (SAGE) program in San Francisco, California, which educates men arrested for soliciting women in prostitution about the risks and impacts of their behavior.

Legalization advocates argue that the violence, exploitation, and health effects suffered by women in prostitution aren't inherent to prostitution but simply result from the random behaviors of bad pimps or buyers, and that if prostitution were regulated by the state these harms would diminish. But examples show these arguments to be false.

In the pamphlet entitled *Legalizing Prostitution Is Not the Answer: The Example of Victoria, Australia,* published by the CATW in 2001, Mary Sullivan and Sheila Jeffreys describe the way legalization in Australia has perpetuated and strengthened the culture of violence and exploitation inherent in prostitution. Under legalization, legal and illegal brothels have proliferated, and trafficking in women has accelerated to meet the increased demand. Pimps, having even more power, continue threatening and brutalizing the women they control. Buyers continue to abuse women, refuse to wear condoms, and spread the HIV virus—and other sexually transmitted diseases—to their wives and girlfriends. Stigmatized by identity cards and medical inspections, prostituted women are even more marginalized and tightly locked into the system of organized sexual exploitation while the state, now an official party to the exploitation, has become the biggest pimp of all.

The government of the Netherlands has legalized prostitution, doesn't enforce laws against pimping, and virtually lives off taxes from the earnings of prostituted women. In the book *Making the Harm Visible* (published by the CATW in 1999), Marie-Victoire Louis describes the effects on prostituted women of municipal regulation of brothels in Amsterdam and other Dutch cities. Her article entitled "Legalizing Pimping, Dutch Style" explains the way immigration policies in the Netherlands are shaped to fit the needs of the prostitution industry so that traffickers are seldom prosecuted and a continuous supply of women is guaranteed. In Amsterdam's 250 officially listed brothels, 80 percent of the prostitutes have been trafficked in from other countries and 70 percent possess no legal papers. Without money, papers, or contact with the outside world, these immigrant women live in terror. Instead of being protected by the regulations governing brothels, prostituted women are frequently beaten up and raped by pimps. These "prostitution managers" have practically been given a free hand by the state and by buyers who, as "consumers of prostitution," feel themselves entitled to abuse the women they buy. Sadly and ironically the "Amsterdam model" of legalization and regulation is touted by the Netherlands and Germany as "self-determination and empowerment for women." In reality it simply legitimizes the "right" to buy, sexually use, and profit from the sexual exploitation of someone else's body.

A HUMAN RIGHTS APPROACH

As part of a system of organized sexual exploitation, prostitution can be visualized along a continuum of abuse with brothel slavery at the furthest extreme. All along the continuum, fine lines divide the degrees of harm done to those caught up in the system. At the core lies a great social injustice no cosmetic reforms can right: the setting aside of a segment of people whose bodies can be purchased for sexual use by others. When this basic injustice is legitimized and regulated by the state and when the state profits from it, that injustice is compounded.

In her book *The Prostitution of Sexuality* (New York University Press, 1995), Kathleen Barry details a feminist human rights approach to prostitution that points the way to the future. Ethically it recognizes prostitution, sex trafficking, and the globalized industrialization of sex as massive violations of women's human rights. Sociologically it considers how and to what extent prostitution promotes sex discrimination against individual women, against different racial categories of women, and against women as a group. Politically it calls for decriminalizing prostitutes while penalizing pimps, traffickers, brothel owners, and buyers.

Understanding that human rights and restorative justice go hand in hand, the feminist human rights approach to prostitution addresses the harm and the need to repair the damage. As Barry says:

> Legal proposals to criminalize customers, based on the recognition that prostitution violates and harms women, must ... include social-service, health and counseling and job retraining programs. Where states would be closing down brothels if customers were criminalized, the economic resources poured into the former prostitution areas could be turned toward producing gainful employment for women.

With the help of women's projects in many countries—such as Buklod in the Philippines and the Council for Prostitution Alternatives in the United States—some women have begun to confront their condition by leaving prostitution, speaking out against it, revealing their experiences, and helping other women leave the sex industry.

Ending the sexual exploitation of trafficking and prostitution will mean the beginning of a new chapter in building a humanist future—a more peaceful and just future in which men and women can join together in love and respect, recognizing one another's essential dignity and humanity. Humanity's sexuality then will no longer be hijacked and distorted.

R E A D I N G   **78**

Deaths That Cry Out

Diana Washington Valdez (2006)

It was the brutality with which they killed the young women that first caught my attention. That winter's day of 1999, I stayed up into the early morning hours reading narratives that described death after horrible death. Despite what the Mexican authorities said, the murders were not normal. And, they were many.

Dating back to 1993, girls in their adolescent and teenage years suffered unspeakable atrocities, including gang rape and mutilation. Between 1993 and 2005, approximately 470 girls and women died violently in Juarez, Mexico—far more than the 379 deaths the Mexican Federal Attorney General reported for that period. They were killed in various ways: strangled, stabbed, bludgeoned, shot to death. Dozens more are missing.

Janeth Fierro, one of the early victims, was only twelve years old in 1994 when she was abducted. The authorities recovered her strangled body and determined she had been raped. In September 1995, the body of Silvia Rivera Morales, a seventeen-year-old student, was dumped in Lote Bravo, just south of the Juarez International Airport. Her right breast was severed and her left breast mauled by human teeth. That was the year authorities discovered the bodies of several other young women at the same site. All of them were killed with the same ferocity.

Seventeen-year-old Sagragrio Gonzalez Flores disappeared in April of 1998, after finishing her shift at a maquiladora. Later, someone passing by a grassy patch in another part of Juarez saw her body and called the police. The site was about ten miles east of her assembly plant, where hundreds of men and women turned out electronics components by the thousands.

She, too, had been raped, stabbed and strangled. In 1996, more bodies were discovered in the northwest desert region known as Lomas de Poleo. During a visit to Juarez in March 1999, FBI profilers analyzed the Mexican case files for Lote Bravo and Lomas de Poleo. The FBI sent the experts a month after U.S. President Bill Clinton and Mexican President Ernesto Zedillo met in Merida, Mexico.

Five years later, two new presidents, Vicente Fox and George W. Bush, also discussed the Juarez murders. According to Mexican authorities, a large triangle had been marked on the backs of several of the victims with a knife or other sharp instrument. In some regions of the world, a triangle is associated with ultra right-wing politics. Some secret societies, lodges and even the Nazis use it as a symbol.

The accounts I read that night in 1999 were disturbing. Although not all the murders were related, almost all of them involved extreme violence. The victims also shared striking similarities. It was apparent that the crimes involved a selection process and highly organized abductions. Young women were disappearing in the city's downtown without anyone seeing or hearing anything.

At first, it seemed as though the systematic slayings were the work of depraved criminals with police protection and ties to the underworld. There were indications of that. But back then I never imagined that something far more sinister was behind this harvest of death.

In time, I learned that some of the killers were powerful men with links to the highest levels of the Mexican government. Police officials who knew they were preying on young women from poor families did nothing to stop them. Dr. Rita Laura Segato, a social anthropologist, said such cabals and their accomplices act as fraternities that use deaths "to mark their territory and seal their pacts of silence." Dr. Julia Monarrez Fragoso, a sociologist in Juarez, referred to the deaths in Juarez as *femicides*—gender murders. Serial killers, vicious gangs and drug dealers also were getting away with the murders of women in Juarez.

The crime wave that transformed Mexico's largest border city into a global symbol for women's murders did not occur overnight. The unsolved slayings and disappearances had their roots in Mexico's "dirty war," and in alliances with drug cartels that gave rise to extensive networks of corrupt business leaders, soldiers, police and government officials.

Powerful drug lords and their protectors bribed and intimidated those involved in the investigations. Under pressure to solve the crimes, authorities jailed a dozen people who were framed or tortured until they confessed to several of the murders.

The authorities had no scientific proof against any of the suspects in four of the most notorious multiple homicide cases. Because of the impunity that prevailed in Juarez, similar murders and disappearances spread to other places, including the Chihuahua State capital.

In 2003, Cynthia Kiecker, an American citizen from Minnesota, and her husband, Ulises Perzabal, were accused of killing one of the young femicide victims of Chihuahua City. The U.S. State Department was convinced the couple had been tortured into confessing to the girl's murder.

The rampant violence perpetrated by the Carrillo Fuentes drug cartel, which ravaged and terrorized Juarez during this period, served to cloak powerful people who used the slayings to protect their economic interests. A group of men known as "juniors" (slang for the children of wealthy families) also was involved in several of the murders, and for many years, these people remained in the background.

Slowly, however, the veil was pulled back, and it shook them. "The juniors are worried," a source cautioned. "They don't want their names divulged." A concerned government source warned that a Mexican official had launched an operation to silence a Mexico City journalist who was helping to investigate the murders. The official hatched the plan after an influential citizen complained that we were getting too close.

In late 2003, *La Jornada* published an abstract of this manuscript, and several Mexican police sent a message to cease my investigation. Several collaborators and I began to receive telephone calls with strange background noises, including that of an electric saw and a child's voice crying, "Mommy, no!" A U.S. federal officer in EI Paso, Texas, received similar messages. We traced the calls back to Mexico. An American women from El Paso who appeared in a British documentary about the murders received threats, too.

Since the beginning, threats and intimidation have been a part of this odyssey. In Juarez, experts have come and gone. And, nothing changes. Mexico's government has refused to permit the FBI, which previously provided important leads, to investigate the murders directly. Amnesty International, the Inter-American Commission on Human Rights and the United Nations registered protests with the Mexican government for failing to stop the murders. Periodic pronouncements by Mexican officials that they solved the crimes bewildered the families of victims who still seek justice. In some cases, the government offered the families compensation in exchange for their silence.

Mexican lawyers Mario Escobedo Anaya and Sergio Dante Almaraz, who defended two men accused unjustly of murdering eight women in 2001, were gunned down in the streets of Juarez. Although their deaths occurred four years apart, the brazen attacks served notice to everyone involved in this issue.

Juarez is not a dusty border town. It is Mexico's largest border city with nearly two million souls and about 300 assembly plants known as *maquiladoras,* most of them owned by Fortune 500 companies. People work and carry out the normal activities of life. Yet, high-order criminals also operate in the city, and they appear to have free rein. Heavily armed commandos roam the streets, abducting and executing people in broad daylight. The police never arrest anyone for those brazen crimes. While police look the other way, U.S. corporations go about their business, ignoring the atrocities. Even the Mexican federal government seems powerless to do anything. The explanation for all this terror would come much later, seven years after that winter's night in 1999. It involved a pact that destined people in the border city to unspeakable violence and horror. It condemned women to fear for their lives.

The pattern of brutal murders of women has spread to other parts of Mexico and Central America. The deaths are occurring where crime lords from Colombia to the U.S.-Mexican border are fighting over coveted corridors of drug, arms and human trafficking. Juarez is but one such corridor, albeit an important one.

In February 2006, the Mexican Federal Attorney General's Office released its final report on the issue of the Juarez women's murders. The 420-page report said the crimes were vastly exaggerated, there were no serial murders, family violence was the primary cause for them. And, most of the slayings were solved. Human rights groups viewed the report as a whitewash. Without international intervention, the second decade may prove deadlier than the first for the women of Juarez.

Betrayed by the Angel
What Happens When Violence Knocks and Politeness Answers?

Debra Anne Davis (2004)

Mrs. W. arranged us alphabetically, so I spent my entire third-grade year sitting next to a sadist named Hank C. Every day, several times a day, whenever the teacher wasn't looking, Hank would jab his pencil into my arm. He was shorter than me, and I'd look down on his straight brown hair and he'd glance up at me with a crooked smile and then he'd do it: jab jab jab.

He'd get up from his seat often to sharpen the point; I'd sit in my seat in dread, listening to the churn of the pencil sharpener in the back of the room, knowing the pencil tip would be dulled not by paper but by my skin. I'd go home with little gray circles, some with dots of red in the center, Hank's own bull's-eye, all up and down my left arm. I remember it was my left arm because I can see myself sitting next to him, wearing one of the outfits, not just a dress, but an *outfit*—matching socks, hair ribbon, even underwear—that my mother would put me in each morning. I look at him and hope *maybe not this time, please no more,* and he glances at me (or doesn't—he got so good at it that after a while he could find my arm without looking) and: jab jab jab. Each time I hope he won't and each time he does.

Mostly I'd just endure. *This is what is happening; there's nothing I can do about it.* One day after school I decided that I couldn't take it anymore. I decided that I would tell the teacher the very next time he did it. Of course I'd have to wait for him to do it again first. I felt relief.

When I went to school the next day, we had a substitute teacher instead of Mrs. W. I lost some of my resolve, but not all of it. Hank seemed in better spirits than usual. He started in soon after the bell rang while we were doing work-books. Jab jab jab. I stood and walked to the front of the room, my lime green dress brushing against the gray metal of the teacher's desk. "Hank always pokes me with the pencil," I told the stranger. My voice was much smaller than I'd hoped. I'd said it like a whisper; I'd meant to sound mad.

"You go back to your seat and tell me if he does it again," she said. And that was it. I never could work up the nerve again to walk the 15 feet to the big desk and blurt out the nature of the boy's crime: Always, he pokes me. I continued going home each day with pencil wounds.

The problem, I think, was that I simply wasn't mad at him. When I went to tell the teacher, my voice wasn't loud in a burst of righteous anger; it was demure. I didn't want to bother her. Maybe I didn't want to see Hank punished. Maybe I didn't think I deserved not to be hurt. Maybe it just didn't seem that big an aberration. Even though no one else was being poked at every day, maybe this was just my lot in life.

I'm 25 years old. I'm alone in my apartment. I hear a knock. I open the door and see a face I don't know. The man scares me, I don't know why. My first impulse is to shut the door. But I stop myself: You can't do something like that. It's rude.

I don't invite him in, but suddenly he is pushing the door and stepping inside. I don't want him to come in; he hasn't waited to be invited. I push the door to close it, but I don't push very hard; I keep remembering that it's not polite to slam a door in someone's face.

He is inside. He slams the door shut himself and pushes me against the wall. My judgment: He is *very* rude. I make this conscious decision: Since he is being rude, it is okay for me to be rude back. I reach for the doorknob; I want to open the door and shove him outside and then slam the door in his face, rude or not, I don't care now. But frankly, I don't push him aside with much determination. I've made the mental choice to be rude, but I haven't been able to muster the physical bluntness the act requires.

Or maybe I realize the game is lost already. He is stronger than I am, I assume, as men have always been stronger. I have no real chance of pushing him aside. No real chance of it unless I am *very* angry. And I'm not very angry. I'm a little bit angry.

But, despite the fact that I didn't shove with much force, *he* is angry with *me*. I know why: It's because I've been rude to him. He is insulted. I am a bit ashamed.

We fall into our roles quite easily, two people who have never met each other, two people raised in the same culture, a man and a woman. As it turns out, a rapist and his victim.

I asked my students, college freshmen, these two questions once: What did your parents teach you that you will teach your own kids? What did they teach you that you won't teach your kids?

One young woman said, "My parents always told me to be kind to everyone. I won't teach my children that. It's not always good to be kind to everyone."

She was so young, but she knew this. Why did it take me so long to learn?

Working on this stuff makes me a little crazy. Sitting at my computer typing for hours about being raped and how it made me feel and makes me feel makes me distracted, jittery—both because I drink too much strong coffee and because writing goes beyond imagining into reliving.

I decided I needed to reread Virginia Woolf. I'd been making notes to myself for a while—"angel" or just "Woolf" scribbled on scraps of paper on my desk and in the front pocket of my backpack, to go buy the book, the book with the angel in it. (I could feel her hovering as I typed; I know the exact color and texture of her flowing gown.)

What could be easier than to write articles and to buy Persian cats with the profits? But wait a moment. Articles have to be about something. Mine, I seem to remember, was about a novel by a famous man. And while I was writing this review, I discovered that if I were going to review books I should need to do battle with a certain phantom. And the phantom was a woman, and when I came to know her better I called her after the heroine of a famous poem. "The Angel in the House." It was she who used to come between me and my paper when I was writing reviews. It was she who bothered me and wasted my time and so tormented me that at last I killed her.

—*"Professions for Women"*
Virginia Woolf (1931)

There was TV. Reruns of reruns of *I Love Lucy* and *The Flintstones. I Dream of Jeannie. Bewitched.* I can't even think of a show from my youth that had a single female character who was smart, self-confident, and respected by others. My sister and I would lie on our stomachs, heads propped on fuzzy cotton pillows with leopard-skin covers, watching, indiscriminate, mildly entertained, for hours.

Samantha was smarter than Darrin, it was obvious, but she hid her intelligence just as she hid her magical powers, powers Darrin didn't have, powers that made him angry. Samantha's mother, Endora, used her powers with confidence and even flair, but she cackled and wore flowing bright green dresses and too much makeup; she was a mother-in-law. I was supposed to learn how to be like Samantha, not like Endora, and I did.

None of this is news, of course; we can all see those sexist stereotypes quite easily now. But just because I can see, understand, and believe that something is false, that it's not right, now, doesn't mean it won't continue to be a part of me, always.

(Barbara Eden calling Larry Hagman "Master." How many times did I hear *that?*)

"It's big," I say. I turn my head up. I smile. Why do I say this? I ask myself, even then. Well it is big. . . .

And I want to flatter him, so he won't hurt me any more than he already plans to. I, yes, I am trying to flirt with him. I've learned about flirting and how it works and what it can do. (It can get people to like you, to do things for you, to treat you well.) It's a skill I have honed. And I'm using it now. To save my life. (And, hey, it worked! Unless of course he hadn't planned to kill me in the first place.)

He smiles down at me (I'm on my knees, naked, leaning against my own bed, my hands tied behind me, my head in his crotch) proudly.

You who come of a younger and happier generation may not have heard of her—you may not know what I mean by the Angel in the House. I will describe her as shortly as I can. She was intensely sympathetic. She was immensely charming. She was utterly unselfish. She excelled in the difficult arts of family life. She sacrificed herself daily. If there was chicken, she took the leg; if there was a draught she sat in it—in short she was so constituted that she never had a mind or a wish of her own, but preferred to sympathize always with the minds and wishes of others.

Back when he was pulling my jeans off, this is what happened: He kneeled behind me, reached around the waistband to the fly, and pulled until all the buttons popped open. Then he crawled back a few feet and began to pull the jeans off from the ankles—a stupid way to try to take someone else's pants off, but I didn't say anything.

He was having a little trouble because the pants weren't slipping off as, obviously, he'd envisioned they would. He tugged and then began yanking. "Stop fighting!" he growled at me. Ooh, *that* pissed me off! "I'm *not fighting!*" I sassed back at him. And I wasn't. How dare he! Accuse me, I mean. Of fighting.

Above all—I need not say it—she was pure. Her purity was supposed to be her chief beauty—her blushes, her great grace. In those days—the last of Queen Victoria—every house had its Angel. And when I came to write I encountered her with the very first words. The shadow of her wings fell on my page; I heard the rustling of her skirts in

the room. Directly, that is to say, I took my pen in hand to review that novel by a famous man, she slipped behind me and whispered: "My dear, you are a young woman. You are writing about a book that has been written by a man. Be sympathetic; be tender; flatter; deceive; use all the arts and wiles of our sex. Never let anybody guess that you have a mind of your own. Above all, be pure."

One thing being raped did to me: It caused me to be sometimes rude to strangers. Not out of anger, though, but out of fear.

I was 25 when I was raped. I'm 35 now. This happened last week.

I was in a coffee shop, reading a textbook for a class I'm teaching. After a while, I took a little break and brought my now-empty cup back to the counter. There was a guy at the counter waiting for his drink. "What are you reading?" he asked. He had a big smile on his face, a friendly smile. He wasn't creepy; he was being friendly. I sensed these things. "It's a textbook," I answered. I was looking at the floor now, not at his face any longer.

"Oh! What class are you studying for?" he asked.

"It's a class I'm teaching," I said. Oh no.

"Where do you teach? At _____ College?"

"No," I said flatly and tried to smile a little. I felt nervous, pinned. I knew the conversation wasn't over, but I simply turned and went back to my little table. He stood there at the counter, probably watching me walk away and wondering why I wouldn't answer his question, why, against the unspoken code of our culture, I hadn't at least finished the exchange with a friendly word or a wave. But there was no way I would tell him (or *you,* notice) where I taught or what I taught or anything else about me. And there was no way I could explain this to him courteously; the whole exchange made me too nervous. I certainly wasn't angry at him, but I was a bit afraid. And right there in the coffee shop, I felt the presence of my angel, the rustling of her skirts: "Be sympathetic," I heard her reprimand me, sweetly. "Be tender. And pure." I couldn't be polite, but I did feel guilty.

Though I wasn't finished with my reading, when I got back to the table, I gathered up my things and left.

I turned upon her and caught her by the throat. I did my best to kill her. My excuse, if I were to be had up in a court of law, would be that I acted in self-defense. Had I not killed her she would have killed me.

He bent down to gently arrange the towel over my bare and oozing body, after it was all over with. "You were so good-looking, I just couldn't resist," he told me.

And for the first time in my life, I didn't enjoy being complimented on my physical appearance. Why, I wondered at that moment, had I ever wanted to be considered pretty—or kind, or good? Compliments mean nothing. Or worse, compliments mean this. What good does such a compliment do *me*?

Thus, whenever I felt the shadow of her wing or the radiance of her halo upon my page, I took up the inkpot and flung it at her. She died hard. Her fictitious nature was of great assistance to her. It is far harder to kill a phantom than a reality.

I haven't killed her. Yet. Maybe I need to go out and get an inkpot to fling at her. Hmm, I wonder how she'd hold up against a flying laptop. I can imagine hurling this 10-pound black plastic box at her (she's up in the corner, to my right). It easily tears through the soft blue, rough cotton of her ankle-length gown (she has a long, thin white lace apron tied around her waist). The computer crashes into the space where the walls and ceiling meet; she falls to the carpet. And then what? She's dead. And how do I feel about that? Guilty? Relieved? Well, I don't think I'd want to stuff my pockets with rocks and wade into a river. (Did Woolf ever really kill her angel? Or is it the angel that killed her?)

What I want to know is this: If I'm ever physically attacked again, will I fight to save myself? And will I be fighting out of righteous anger or out of unstrung fear?

What I need to know is this: Is the angel really the one who needs to die?

"I guess I'll get twenty years in the penitentiary for this," he says and waves his hand across the room at me.

Twenty years? Just for this? Just for doing this to me? Twenty years is a really long time.

In fact, he got 35 years. On a plea bargain. The police, the lawyers, the judge—the state, the legal system—even he, the criminal, the rapist, thought he deserved decades in jail for what he'd done to me. Why didn't I?

READING 80

Campus Sexual Violence

Joetta L. Carr (2005)

SCOPE OF THE PROBLEM

There are approximately 16 million students enrolled in 4,200 colleges and universities (U.S. Department of Education, 2002). . . . According to the Violent Victimization of College Students report (Baum & Klaus, 2005), between 1995 and 2002, college students ages 18–24 were victims of approximately 479,000 crimes of violence annually: rape/sexual assault, robbery, aggravated assault, and simple assault. . . . During this seven-year period, students experienced crimes at a lower average rate than nonstudents ages 18–24, except for rape/sexual assault. . . .

- Approximately 15–20 percent of female college students have experienced forced intercourse (rape) in their life time (Douglas et al., 1997; Koss, Gidycz, & Wisniewski, 1987).
- Approximately 20–25 percent of college women are projected to be the victims of an attempted or completed rape during their college careers (Fisher, Cullen, & Turner, 2000).
- Approximately 5–15 percent of college men have acknowledged committing rape (Koss et al., 1987; Rapaport & Burkhart, 1984).
- Approximately one out of every 14 U.S. men have been physically assaulted or raped by an intimate partner (Tjaden & Thoennes, 2000).
- Simple assault accounted for about two-thirds of college student violent crimes (63 percent), while rape/sexual assault accounted for around 6 percent.
- Approximately 5 percent of completed and attempted rapes committed against students were reported to police (Fisher et al., 2000).
- Rape/sexual assault was the only violent crime against students more likely to be committed by a person the victim knew. Non-strangers committed 79 percent of the rape/sexual assaults against students.
- Alcohol and other drugs were implicated in approximately 55–74 percent of sexual assaults on campuses (Lisak & Roth, 1990; Muehlenhard & Linton, 1987).

Campus crime statistics have been found to be flawed due to a significant underreporting among victims (Sloan, Fisher, & Cullen, 1997). In an important study of 3,400 students randomly selected from 12 colleges and universities stratified by student enrollment and location, Sloan et al. found that only 25 percent of campus crimes were reported to *any* authority across all offenses. Only 22 percent of rapes and 18 percent of sexual assaults were reported.

. . .

Sexual harassment is defined as unwelcome sexual conduct which is related to any condition of employment or evaluation of student performance. It includes unwarranted sex-related comments, sexually explicit comments or graphics, unwelcome touching, etc. This harassment can take the form of making derogatory jokes based on sex, speaking crude or offensive language, spreading rumors about a person's sexuality, placing a compromising photo on the web, or ogling. These behaviors cause the recipient discomfort or humiliation, and continue after the recipient has made clear that they want them to stop (Sandler & Shoop, 1997).

Sexual assault on campus is far more extensive than reported in official statistics, and the large majority of rapists are never apprehended (Carr & VanDeusen, 2004). The ACHA-National College Health Assessment (ACHA-NCHA) found that the incidence of rape and attempted rape in female college students within the last academic year was 5.8 percent, with 11.9 percent reporting unwanted sexual touching (ACHA, 2004). Colleges with 10,000 college women could experience more than 350 rapes per academic year and the vast majority of rapes occur in living quarters (Fisher et al., 2000). Surveys have consistently reported that college men acknowledged committing rape at a rate of 5–15 percent (Koss et al., 1987; Rapaport & Burkhart, 1984) and sexual aggression at a rate of 25 percent (Koss et al., 1987).

Cross-cultural studies of rape and studies of rape-prone versus rape-free campus cultures identify sex role socialization, rape myths, lack of sanctions for woman abuse, male peer group support, pornography, and all-male membership groups such as fraternities and sports teams as contributors to sexual violence (Berkowitz, 1992; Carr & VanDeusen, 2004; Quackenbush, 1989; Sanday, 1996; Schwartz & DeKeseredy, 1997; Warshaw & Parrot, 1991).

Stalking is defined as "the willful, repeated, and malicious following, harassing, or threatening of another person" (Melton, 2000, p. 248). Results from a national survey of women attending two- and four-year colleges in the U.S. (Fisher et al., 2000) revealed four out of every five college-aged female victims know their stalkers. Stalkers were most often a boyfriend or ex-boyfriend (42.5 percent), classmate (24.5 percent), acquaintance (10.3 percent), friend (5.6 percent), or co-worker (5.6 percent). Only a small percentage of stalkers are strangers to the victim (McGuire & Wraith, 2000). The most common stalking behaviors reported by Fisher et al. were being telephoned (77.7 percent), being waited for outside or inside places (47.9 percent), being watched from afar (44 percent), being followed (42 percent), being sent letters (30.7 percent), and being e-mailed (24.7 percent).

Research suggests that stalking victimization may be greater among female college students than in the general population. Fisher et al. (2000) found 13.1 percent of female college students in their sample had been stalked since the school year began (almost seven months prior to the survey). Mustaine and Tewsbury (1999) found a similar incidence in their study of women attending nine institutions of higher learning; 10 percent of the female students participating in this study reported being stalked in the previous six months. Other studies have revealed between 25 and 30 percent of college women and between 11 and 17 percent of college men have ever been stalked (Bjerregaard, 2000; Fremouw, Westrup, & Pennypacker, 1996).

Ravensberg and Miller (2003) identified two possible reasons why stalking victimization rates are higher among college-aged individuals than in the general population. First, stalkers may have "developmental deficits in social skills" (p. 458). That is, college-aged individuals are so young that they are still learning how to handle, and act in, complex social relationships and situations. These individuals may simply not recognize their behavior as stalking. Second, the nature of student life and structure of college campuses may contribute to higher stalking victimization rates among college-aged individuals. College students typically live in close proximity to each other (e.g., in residence halls, fraternities, and sororities), as well as have flexible schedules and a large amount of unstructured discretionary time. Additionally, students "are not accountable to an authority figure for their daily activities and they are working to establish themselves socially" (p. 459).

Stalking can result in emotional or psychological injury, physical harm, or sexual assault. Fisher et al. (2000) reported that, according to respondents, 10.3 percent of stalking incidents resulted in forced or attempted sexual contact. The most common impact of stalking on victims, however, was psychological—30 percent of victims in their sample reported being injured emotionally or psychologically.

Very little research has been conducted to determine the effectiveness of methods to deal with stalkers. Fisher et al. (2000) stated that victims reported the stalking incident to the police in 17 percent of incidents. Most victims, however, reported avoiding the stalker (43.2 percent). Only 16.3 percent of victims confronted their stalker. Other responses to stalkers included ignoring messages or e-mails, moving residence, seeking a restraining order, filing a grievance with university officials, getting caller ID, improving residential security, traveling with a companion, and buying a weapon.

For legal considerations regarding stalking and recommended campus anti-stalking policy, see Jordan, Quinn, Jordan, and Daileader (1999–2000) and Romeo (2001), respectively. Stalking laws vary from state to state.

Campus dating violence is the actual or threatened physical or sexual violence or psychological and emotional abuse directed toward a current or former dating partner. Intimate partners may be heterosexual, bisexual, or homosexual.

College is a major arena for dating violence and the college setting provides opportunities for primary and secondary prevention of Intimate Partner Violence (IPV) (Carr & VanDeusen, 2002). A recent longitudinal study of dating violence among adolescent and college women found that women who were physically assaulted as adolescents by a romantic partner were at greater risk for being revictimized during their freshman year and subsequent years of college (Smith, White, & Holland, 2003).

In addition, women who were physically abused in any year were more likely to be sexually assaulted that same year. ACHA-NCHA data indicated that 15.0 percent of women and 9.2 percent of men report being in emotionally abusive relationships within the last school year. ACHA-NCHA data also revealed 2.4 percent of women and 1.3 percent of men have been in a physically abusive relationship during the last school year, and 1.7 percent of women and 1.0 percent of men have been in a sexually abusive relationship in that time frame (ACHA, 2004).

According to the National Violence Against Women Survey, one out of four U.S. women have been physically assaulted or raped by an intimate partner; one out of every 14 U.S. men reported such an experience (Tjaden & Thoennes, 2000). Nearly two-thirds of women who reported being raped, physically assaulted, or stalked since age 18 were victimized by a current or former husband, cohabitating partner, boyfriend, or date (Tjaden & Thoennes). Among women who are physically assaulted or raped by an intimate partner, one in three is injured. Each year, more than 500,000 women injured as a result of IPV require medical treatment (Tjaden & Thoennes). Women ages 20 to 29 years are at greatest risk of being killed by an intimate partner (Paulozzi, Saltzman, Thompson, & Holmgreen, 2001).

Specific to the LGBT population, according to the National Center for Victims of Crime (2004) there were 5,046 reported incidents of IPV in 2001, an increase of 25 percent over LGBT cases reported in 2000.

Intimate Partner Violence is often repetitive. Two-thirds of both men and women physically assaulted by an intimate partner experienced multiple incidents, and half of all women raped by intimates reported victimization by the same partner 2–9 times. Relationship physical assault involves 10 or more incidents for 19.8 percent of women and 10.6 percent of men. Relationship rape involves 10 or more incidents for 15.2 percent of women (Tjaden & Thoennes, 2000).

Perpetrators of IPV may lack some social skills, such as communication skills, particularly in the context of problematic situations with their intimate partners (Holtzworth-Monroe et al., 1997). A high proportion of IPV perpetrators report more depression, lower self-esteem, and more aggression than non-violent intimate partners. Evidence indicates that violent intimate partners may be more likely to have personality disorders, such as schizoidal/borderline personality, antisocial or narcissistic behaviors, and dependency and attachment problems (Holtzworth-Monroe et al.).

Alcohol use is frequently associated with violence between intimate partners. It is estimated that in 45 percent of cases of IPV, men had been drinking, and in about 20 percent of cases, women had been drinking (Roizen, 1993). As the consumption of alcohol by either the victim or perpetrator increases, the rate of serious injuries associated with IPV also increases (Makepeace, 1988).

. . .

UNDERLYING ISSUES RELATED TO CAMPUS VIOLENCE

In his book on teaching college men about gender, Kilmartin (2001) discussed the importance of enlisting men in changing the destructive aspects of masculine culture and helping college students see how this culture is created and maintained. He views:

> . . . rape and other partner violence as the worst symptom of a larger problem: a continuum of disrespect toward women. This continuum includes men's display of negative attitudes through misogynist jokes, demeaning pornography . . . and runs to the most extreme form of violence: gender-motivated murder. Such an analysis also emphasizes power imbalances between the sexes and the social forces that create and maintain these imbalances. (Kilmartin, 2001, p. 3)

Some campus violence is a reflection of society's sexism, racism, and homophobia. Students are acculturated in the dominant ideologies and cultural practices of the times before they come to college. The media and popular culture play a decisive role in how students view gender, race, ethnicity, sexual identity, sexual orientation, alcohol and drug use, and interpersonal relationships.

Sports culture can promote competition, aggression, and male privilege. "The locker room is a breeding ground for male aggression and the denigration of women" (Barnett & DiSabato, 2000, p. 201). The recruiting trip experience can reinforce this culture, as athletes and coaches seek to impress the new recruit and demonstrate the benefits of team membership and camaraderie (Barnett & DiSabato). Competition, status, bonding, entitlements, hypermasculinity, power, and sexual conquest can be promoted in this culture. However, not all sports cultures exhibit such extremes.

. . .

Alcohol is a major factor in campus violence. Presley, Meilman, and Cashin (1997) reported that students were under the influence of alcohol or other drugs in 13 percent of incidents of ethnic harassment, 46 percent of incidents of theft involving force or threat of force, 51 percent of threats of physical assault, 64 percent of physical assaults, 71 percent of forced sexual touching, and 79 percent of unwanted sexual intercourse.

First-year students are particularly vulnerable to victimization, since they have new freedoms, lack parental control for the first time, may be inexperienced in self-protection and boundaries, and are thrust into residence halls where living density is high and social experimentation is common. In addition, more students are entering college with severe mental health disorders and conduct disorders with violent components. Treatment for these problems can be disrupted or cease when students enter college and are no longer supervised by parents or guardians (Kitzrow, 2003).

. . .

Campus Sexual Assault Victims' Bill of Rights (1992). This law requires that all colleges and universities, both public and private, that participate in federal student aid programs afford sexual assault survivors certain basic rights. The accuser and accused must have the same opportunity to have others present at judicial hearings. Both

parties shall be informed of the outcome of any disciplinary proceeding. Survivors shall be informed of their options to notify law enforcement. Survivors shall be notified of counseling services and of options for changing academic and living situations.

Campus Sex Crimes Prevention Act (2000). This act provides for the collection and disclosure of information about convicted, registered sex offenders either enrolled in or employed at institutions of higher education.

. . .

INNOVATIVE PROGRAMS

Promising and innovative sexual violence prevention programs have been developed that are intended for college males only, females only, mixed-gendered audiences, athletes, fraternity members, and other targeted campus groups. Many programs utilize a variety of modalities, including general education regarding violence, theatre productions, poster contests, and involvement in community activities (Harner, 2003). However, according to Söchting, Fairbrother, and Koch (2004), sexual violence prevention programs on the American college campus maintain a limited focus. "Almost exclusively, rape prevention programs have, to date, been designed to change beliefs and attitudes assumed to increase the probability of men perpetrating a sexual crime and of women failing to take sufficient precaution" (Söchting et al., 2004, p. 74). Few studies evaluating these prevention programs have documented actual attitude changes among program participants, and fewer studies have even assessed changes in student behaviors (i.e., a reduction in sexual assault). For an in-depth review and discussion of promising or innovative sexual violence prevention programs, see Wolfe and Jaffe (2003), Söchting et al., Katz (1995), Kilmartin (2001), Foubert (2000), Banyard, Plante, and Moynihan (2004), Schewe (2002), and Lonsway (1996).

. . .

REFERENCES

American College Health Association. (2004). *National college health assessment: Reference group executive summary spring 2004.* Baltimore, MD: American College Health Association.

Banyard, V. L., Plante, E. G., & Moynihan, M. M. (2004). Bystander education: Bringing a broader community perspective to sexual violence prevention. *Journal of Community Psychology, 32*(1), 61–79.

Barnett, N. D., & DiSabato, M. (2000). Training camp: Lessons in masculinity. In J. Gold & S. Villari (Eds.), *Just sex: Students rewrite the rules on sex, violence, activism and equality* (pp. 197–210). Lanham, MD: Rowman & Littlefield.

Baum, K., & Klaus, P. (2005, January). *Violent victimization of college students, 1995–2002.* (NCJ Publication No. 206836). Washington, DC: U.S. Department of Justice, Office of Justice Programs, Bureau of Justice Statistics).

Berkowitz, A. (1992). College men as perpetrators of acquaintance rape and sexual assault: A review of recent research. *Journal of American College Health, 40*(4), 175–181.

Bjerregaard, B. (2000). An empirical study of stalking victimization. *Violence and Victims, 15*(4), 389–406.

Campus Sexual Assault Victims' Bill of Rights, Pub. L. No. 102–135, § 486(c), (1992).

Campus Sex Crimes Prevention Act, Pub. L. No. 106–386, § 1601, (2000).

Carr, J. L., & VanDeusen, K. (2002). The relationship between family of origin violence and dating violence in college men. *Journal of Interpersonal Violence, 17*(6), 630–646.

Carr, J. L., & VanDeusen, K. (2004). Risk factors for male sexual aggression on college campuses. *Journal of Family Violence, 19*(5), 279–289.

Douglas, K.A., Collins, J. L. Warren, C. Kann, L. Gold, R. Clayton, S. Rass, J. G., & Kolbe, L. J. (1997). Results from the 1995 national college health risk behavior survey. *Journal of American College Health, 46*(9), 55–66.

Fisher, B. S., Cullen, F. T., & Turner, M. G. (2000). *The Sexual Victimization of College Women* (NCJRS Publication No. 182369). Washington, DC: U.S. Department of Justice, National Criminal Justice Reference Service.

Foubert, J. D. (2000). The longitudinal effects of a rape-prevention program on fraternity men's attitudes, behavioral intent, and behavior. *Journal of American College Health, 48*(4), 158–163.

Fremouw, W. J., Westrup, D., & Pennypacker, J. (1996). Stalking on campus: The prevalence and strategies for coping with stalking. *Journal of Forensic Sciences, 42*(4), 666–669.

Harner, H. (2003, May). *Sexual Violence and Adolescence.* Retrieved April 8, 2004, from http://www.vaw.umn.edu/documents/vawnet/ adolescent/aradolescent.html

Holtzworth-Monroe, A., Bates, L., Smutzler, N., & Sandin, E. (1997). A brief review of the research on husband violence: Part 1: Maritally violent vs. nonviolent men. *Aggression and Violent Behavior, 2*(1), 65–99.

Jordan, C. E., Quinn, K., Jordan, B., & Daileader, C. R. (1999–2000). Stalking: Cultural, clinical and legal considerations. *Brandeis Law Journal, 38,* 513–579.

Katz, J. (1995). Reconstructing masculinity in the locker room: The mentors in violence prevention project. *Harvard Educational Review, 65*(2), 163–174.

Kilmartin, C. (2001). *Sexual assault in context: Teaching college men about gender.* Holmes Beach, FL: Learning Publications, Inc.

Kitzrow, M.A. (2003). The mental health needs of today's college students: Challenges and recommendations. *NASPA Journal, 41*(1), 167–181.

Koss, M. P., Gidycz, C. A., & Wisniewski, N. (1987). The scope of rape: Incidence and prevalence of sexual aggression and victimization in a national sample of higher education students. *Journal of Consulting and Clinical Psychology, 55,* 64–170.

Lisak, D., & Roth, S. (1990). Motives and psychodynamics of self-reported, unincarcerated rapists. *American Journal of Orthopsychiatry. 60,* 268–280.

Lonsway, K. A. (1996). Preventing acquaintance rape through education: What do we know? *Psychology of Women Quarterly, 20,* 229–265.

Makepeace, J. M. (1988). The severity of courtship violence and the effectiveness of individual precautions. In G. T. Hotaling, D. Finkelhor, J. T. Kirkpatrick, & M. A. Straus (Eds.), *Family abuse and its consequences. New directions in research* (pp. 297–311). Sage Publishers, London.

McGuire, B., & Wraith, A. (2000). Legal and psychological aspects of stalking: A review. *The Journal of Forensic Psychiatry, 11*(2), 316–327.

Melton, H. C. (2000). Stalking: A review of the literature and direction for the future. *Criminal Justice Review, 25*(2), 246–252.

Muelenhard, C., & Linton, M. (1987). Date rape and sexual aggression in dating situations: Incidence and risk factors. *Journal of Counseling Psychology,* 34, 186–196.

Mustaine, E. E., & Tewsbury, R. (1999). A routine activity theory explanation of women's stalking victimizations. *Violence Against Women,* 5(1), 43–62.

Paulozzi, L. J., Saltzman, L. A., Thompson, M. J., & Holmgreen, P. (2001). Surveillance for States, 1981–1998. *CDC Surveillance Summaries,* 50(SS-3), 1–16.

Presley, C. A., Meilman, P. W., & Cashin, J. R. (1997). Weapon carrying and substance abuse among college students. *Journal of American College Health,* 46(1), 3–8.

Quackenbush, R. L. (1989). A comparison of androgynous, masculine sex-typed, and undifferentiated males on dimensions of attitudes toward rape. *Journal of Research in Personality,* 23, 318–342.

Rapaport, K. & Burkhart, B.R. (1984). Personality and attitudinal characteristics of sexually coercive college males. *Journal of Abonormal Psychology,* 93(2), 216–221.

Ravensberg, V., & Miller, C. (2003). Stalking among young adults: A review of the preliminary research. *Aggression and Violent Behavior,* 8, 455–469.

Roizen, J. (1993). Issues in the epidemiology of alcohol and violence. In S. E. Martin (Ed.), *Alcohol and interpersonal violence: Fostering multidisciplinary perspectives* (pp. 3–36; NIAAA Research Monograph No. 24). Bethesda, MD: National Institutes of Health, National Institute on Alcohol Abuse and Alcoholism.

Sandler, B. R., & Shoop, R. J. (Eds.) (1997). *Sexual harassment on campus: a guide for administrators, faculty and students.* Boston, MA: Allyn and Bacon.

Schewe, P. A. (2002). *Preventing violence in relationships: Interventions across the lifespan.* Washington, DC: American Psychological Association.

Schwartz, M. D., & DeKeseredy, W. (1997). *Sexual assault on the college campus: The role of male peer support.* Thousand Oaks, CA: Sage Publications, Inc.

Sloan, J. J., Fisher, B. S., & Cullen, F. T. (1997). Assessing the student right-to-know and campus security act of 1990: An analysis of the victim reporting practices of college and university students. *Crime & Delinquency,* 43(2), 148–168.

Smith, P. H., White, J. W., & Holland, L. J. (2003). A longitudinal perspective on dating violence among adolescent and college-age women. *American Journal of Public Health,* 93(7), 1104–1109.

Söchting, I., Fairbrother, N., & Koch, W. J. (2004). Sexual assault of women: Prevention efforts and risk factors. *Violence Against Women,* 10(1), 73–93.

Tjaden, P., & Thoennes, N. (2000, July). *Extent, nature, and consequences of intimate partner violence: Findings from the National Violence Against Women Survey* (NCJRS Publication No. 181867). Washington, DC: U.S. Department of Justice, National Criminal Justice Reference Service.

U.S. Department of Education. (2002). *Integrated postsecondary education data system (IPEDS) enrollment survey, spring 2002.* National Center for Education Statistics. Retrieved November 12, 2004, from http://nces.ed.gov/pubsearch/pubsinfo.asp?pubid=2003168

Warshaw, R., & Parrot, A. (1991). The contribution of sex-role socialization to acquaintance rape. In A. Parrot & L. Bechhofer (Eds.), *Acquaintance rape: The hidden crime* (pp. 73–82). New York: John Wiley and Sons, Inc.

Wolfe, D. A., & Jaffe, P. G. (2003, January). *Prevention of domestic violence and sexual assault.* Retrieved April 8, 2004, from http://www.vaw.umn.edu/documents/vawnet/arprevent/arprevent.html

Lisa's Ritual, Age 10

Grace Caroline Bridges (1994)

Afterwards when he has finished
lots of mouthwash helps
to get rid of her father's cigarette taste.
She runs a hot bath
   to soak away the pain
      like red dye leaking from her
         school dress in the washtub.

She doesn't cry
When the bathwater cools she adds more hot.
She brushes her teeth for a long time.

Then she finds the corner of her room,
curls against it. There the wall is
hard and smooth
as teacher's new chalk, white
as a clean bedsheet. Smells
fresh. Isn't sweaty, hairy, doesn't stick
to skin. Doesn't hurt much
when she presses her small backbone
into it. The wall is steady
while she falls   away:
   first the hands   lost

arms dissolving   feet gone
   the legs   dis-   jointed
     body cracking down
       the center like a fault
       she falls inside
         slides down like
dust   like kitchen dirt
        slips off
the dustpan into
        noplace
a place where
nothing happens,
nothing ever happened.

When she feels the cool
wall against her cheek
she doesn't want to
come back. Doesn't want to
think about it.
The wall is quiet, waiting.
It is tall like a promise
only better.

Pornography and Freedom

John Stoltenberg (1989)

There is a widespread belief that sexual freedom is an idea whose time has come. Many people believe that in the last few decades we have gotten more and more of it—that sexual freedom is something you can carve out against the forces of sexual repressiveness, and that significant gains have been won, gains we dare not give up lest we backslide into the sexual dark ages, when there wasn't sexual freedom, there was only repression.

Indeed, many things seem to have changed. But if you look closely at what is supposed to be sexual freedom, you can become very confused. Let's say, for instance, you understand that a basic principle of sexual freedom is that people should be free to be sexual and that one way to guarantee that freedom is to make sure that sex be free from imposed restraint. That's not a bad idea, but if you happen to look at a magazine photograph in which a woman is bound and gagged and lashed down on a plank with her genital area open to the camera, you might well wonder: Where is the freedom from restraint? where's the sexual freedom?

Let's say you understand that people should be free to be sexual and that one way to guarantee that freedom is to make sure people can feel good about themselves and each other sexually. That's not a bad idea. But if you happen to read random passages from books such as the following, you could be quite perplexed:

> Baby, you're gonna get fucked tonight like you ain't never been fucked before, he hissed evilly down at her as she struggled fruitlessly against her bonds. The man wanted only to abuse and ravish her till she was totally broken and subservient to him. He knelt between her wide-spread legs and gloated over the cringing little pussy he was about to ram his cock into.

. . .

After reading that, you might well ask: Where's the freedom from hatred? where's the freedom from degradation? where's the sexual freedom?

Let's say you understand people should be free to be sexual and that one way to guarantee that freedom is to make sure people are not punished for the individuality of their sexuality. And then you find a magazine showing page after page of bodies with their genitals garroted in baling wire and leather thongs, with their genitals tied up and tortured, with heavy weights suspended from rings that pierce their genitals, and the surrounding text makes clear that this mutilation and punishment are experienced as sex acts. And you might wonder in your mind: Why must this person suffer punishment in order to experience sexual feelings? why must this person be humiliated and disciplined and whipped and beaten until he bleeds in order to have access to his homoerotic passion? why have the Grand Inquisitor's most repressive and sadistic torture techniques become what people do to each other and call sex? where's the sexual freedom?

If you look back at the books and magazines and movies that have been produced in this country in the name of sexual freedom over the past decade, you've got to wonder: *Why has sexual freedom come to look so much like sexual repression? why has sexual freedom come to look so much like unfreedom?* The answer, I believe, has to do with the relationship between freedom and justice, and specifically the relationship between *sexual* freedom and *sexual* justice. When we think of freedom in any other sense, we think of freedom as *the result* of justice. We know that there can't truly *be* any freedom until justice has happened, until justice exists. For any people in history who have struggled for freedom, those people have understood that their freedom exists on the future side of justice. The notion of freedom *prior to* justice is understood to be meaningless. Whenever people do not have freedom, they have understood freedom to be that which you arrive at by achieving justice. If you told them they should try to have their freedom without there being justice, they would laugh in your face. Freedom *always* exists on the far side of justice. That's perfectly understood—except when it comes to sex.

The popular concept of sexual freedom in this country has never meant sexual justice. Sexual-freedom advocates have cast the issue only in terms of having sex that is free from suppression and restraint. Practically speaking, that has meant advocacy of sex that is free from institutional interference; sex that is free from being constrained by legal, religious, and medical ideologies; sex that is free from any outside intervention. Sexual freedom on a more personal level has meant sex that is free from fear, guilt, and shame—which in practical terms has meant advocacy of sex that is free from value judgments, sex that is free from responsibility, sex that is free from consequences, sex that is free from ethical distinctions, sex that is essentially free from any obligation to take into account in one's consciousness that the other person is a *person*. In order to free sex from fear, guilt, and shame, it was thought that institutional restrictions on sex needed to be overthrown, but in fact what needed to be overthrown was any vestige of an interpersonal ethic in which people would be real to one another; for once people are real to one another, the consequences of one's acts matter deeply and personally; and particularly in the case of sex, one risks perceiving the consequences of one's acts in ways that feel *bad* because they do not feel *right*. This entire moral-feeling level of sexuality, therefore, needed to be undone. And it was undone, in the guise of an assault on institutional suppression.

Sexual freedom has never really meant that individuals should have sexual self-determination,

that individuals should be free to experience the integrity of their own bodies and be free to act out of that integrity in a way that is totally within their own right to choose. Sexual freedom has never really meant that people should have absolute sovereignty over their own erotic being. And the reason for this is simple: Sexual freedom has never really been about *sexual justice between men and women*. It has been about maintaining men's superior status, men's power over women; and it has been about sexualizing women's inferior status, men's subordination of women. Essentially, sexual freedom has been about preserving a sexuality that preserves male supremacy.

. . .

PORNOGRAPHY AND MALE SUPREMACY

Male-supremacist sexuality is important to pornography, and pornography is important to male supremacy. Pornography *institutionalizes* the sexuality that both embodies and enacts male supremacy. Pornography says about that sexuality, "Here's how": Here's how to act out male supremacy in sex. Here's how the action should go. Here are the acts that impose power over and against another body. And pornography says about that sexuality, "Here's who": Here's who you should do it to and here's who she is: your whore, your piece of ass, yours. Your penis is a weapon, her body is your target. And pornography says about that sexuality, "Here's why": Because men are masters, women are slaves; men are superior, women are subordinate; men are real, women are objects; men are sex machines, women are sluts.

Pornography institutionalizes male supremacy the way segregation institutionalizes white supremacy. It is a practice embodying an ideology of biological superiority; it is an institution that both expresses that ideology and enacts that ideology—makes it the reality that people believe is true, keeps it that way, keeps people from knowing any other possibility, keeps certain people powerful by keeping certain people *down*.

Pornography also *eroticizes* male supremacy. It makes dominance and subordination feel like sex; it makes hierarchy feel like sex; it makes force and violence feel like sex; it makes hate and terrorism feel like sex; it makes inequality feel like sex. Pornography keeps sexism sexy. It keeps sexism *necessary* for some people to have sexual feelings. It makes reciprocity make you go limp. It makes mutuality leave you cold. It makes tenderness and intimacy and caring make you feel like you're going to disappear into a void. It makes justice the opposite of erotic; it makes injustice a sexual thrill.

Pornography exploits every experience in people's lives that *imprisons* sexual feelings—pain, terrorism, punishment, dread, shame, powerlessness, self-hate—and would have you believe that it *frees* sexual feelings. In fact, the sexual freedom represented by pornography is the freedom of men to act sexually in ways that keep sex a basis for inequality.

You can't have authentic sexual freedom without sexual justice. It is only freedom for those in power; the powerless cannot be free. Their experience of sexual freedom becomes but a delusion borne of complying with the demands of the powerful. Increased sexual freedom under male supremacy has had to mean an increased tolerance for sexual practices that are predicated on eroticized injustice between men and women: treating women's bodies or body parts as merely sexual objects or things; treating women as utterly submissive masochists who enjoy pain and humiliation and who, if they are raped, enjoy it; treating women's bodies to sexualized beating, mutilation, bondage, dismemberment.... Once you have sexualized inequality, once it is a learned and internalized prerequisite for sexual arousal and sexual gratification, then anything goes. And that's what sexual freedom means on this side of sexual justice.

PORNOGRAPHY AND HOMOPHOBIA

Homophobia is absolutely integral to the system of sexualized male supremacy. Cultural homophobia expresses a whole range of antifemale revulsion: It expresses contempt for men who are sexual with men because they are believed to be "treated like a woman" in sex. It expresses contempt for women who are sexual with women just *because* they are women and also because they are perceived to be a rebuke to the primacy of the penis.

But cultural homophobia is not merely an expression of woman hating; it also works to protect men from the sexual aggression of other men. Homophobia keeps men doing to women what they would not want done to themselves. There's not the same sexual harassment of men that there is of women on the street or in the workplace or in the university; there's not nearly the same extent of rape; there's not the same demeaned social caste that is sexualized, as it is for women. And that's thanks to homophobia: Cultural homophobia keeps men's sexual aggression directed toward women. Homophobia keeps men acting in concert as male supremacists so that they won't be perceived as an appropriate target for male-supremacist sexual treatment. Male supremacy *requires* homophobia in order to keep men safe from the sexual aggression of men. Imagine this country *without* homophobia: A woman raped every three minutes *and a man* raped every three minutes. Homophobia keeps that statistic at a "manageable" level. The system is not foolproof, of course. There are boys who have been sexually molested by men. There are men who have been brutalized in sexual relationships with their male lovers, and they too have a memory of men's sexual violence. And there are many men in prison who are subject to the same sexual terrorism that women live with almost all the time. But for the most part—happily—homophobia serves male supremacy by protecting "real men" from sexual assault by other real men.

Pornography is one of the major enforcers of cultural homophobia. Pornography is rife with gay-baiting and effemiphobia. Portrayals of allegedly lesbian "scenes" are a staple of heterosexual pornography: The women with each other are there for the male viewer, the male voyeur; there is not the scantest evidence that they are there for each other. Through so-called men's-sophisticate magazines—the "skin" magazines—pornographers outdo one another in their attacks against feminists, who are typically derided as lesbians—"sapphic" at best, "bulldykes" at worst. The innuendo that a man is a "fairy" or a "faggot" is, in pornography, a kind of dare or a challenge to prove his cocksmanship. And throughout pornography, the male who is perceived to be the passive orifice in sex is tainted with the disdain that "normally" belongs to women.

. . .

PORNOGRAPHY AND MEN

Now this is the situation of men within male supremacy: Whether we are straight or gay, we have been looking for a sexual freedom that is utterly specious, and we have been looking for it through pornography, which perpetuates the very domination and subordination that stand in the way of sexual justice. Whether we are straight or gay, we have been looking for a notion of freedom that leaves out women; we have been looking for a sexuality that preserves men's power over women. So long as that is what we strive for, we cannot possibly feel freely, and no one can be free. Whatever sexual freedom might be, it must be after justice.

I want to speak directly to those of us who live in male supremacy as men, and I want to speak specifically to those of us who have come to understand that pornography does make sexism sexy; that pornography does make male supremacy sexy; and that pornography does define what is sexy in terms of domination and subordination, in terms that serve *us as men*—whether we buy it or not, whether we buy into it or not—because it serves male supremacy, which is exactly what it is for.

I want to speak to those of us who live in this setup as men and who recognize—in the world and in our very own selves—the power pornography can have over our lives: It can make men believe that our penises are like weapons. It can make men believe—for some moments of orgasm—that we are just like the men in pornography: virile, strong, tough, maybe cruel. It can make men believe that if you take it away from us, we won't have sexual feelings.

. . .

We've got to be telling our sons that if a man gets off by putting women down, *it's not okay*.

We've got to be telling merchants that if they peddle women's bodies and lives for men's consumption and entertainment, *it's not okay*.

We've got to be telling other men that if you let the pornographers lead you by the nose (or any other body part) into believing that women exist to be tied up and hung up and beaten and raped, *it's not okay*.

We've got to be telling the pornographers—Larry Flynt and Bob Guccione and Hugh Hefner and Al Goldstein and all the rest—that whatever they think they're doing in our names as men, as entertainment for men, for the sake of some delusion of so-called manhood . . . well, it's not okay. It's not okay with *us*.

War Crimes

Helen Clarkson (2004)

The town of Baraka sits on the shores of Lake Tanganyika in the South Kivu province of eastern Democratic Republic of Congo. It ought to be a prosperous town. The lake is full of fish, the land between the edge of the lake and the nearby mountains is arable, and the mountains hold gold and minerals that could be mined. Clearly this was once the case and buildings show the signs of the commerce they once supported—a photo shop, grocery stores, a smart tailor. But after years of civil war the buildings are crumbling, the roads are hidden beneath mud and grass, and the petrol station sign, riddled with bullet holes, swings in the breeze next to a forecourt that has long since disappeared.

Baraka is at the crossroads of armed groups—from Congo, Rwanda, and Burundi—who have used the area to support themselves economically. They have spread terror through the population by looting and burning villages and raping and murdering their inhabitants. Throughout the fighting many people fled into the bush, where they hid, afraid to come out.

In the Médecins Sans Frontières (MSF) hospital here, we see between 30 and 50 victims of sexual violence each week. Most are women but there are also men and children.

More than half the rapes took place in the fields, as one woman told us in October 2003: "One week ago I was working in the fields with my husband and two other women. Suddenly we saw a group of armed men approaching us. My husband managed to flee but two men caught me. They raped me and at the same time they hit me on the back."

Other rapes took place as part of a wider attack on the village, as another woman who was raped in March 2003 explained: "There was an attack on our village, five armed men entered our house . . . they caught me and took me to the bush . . . [W]hen they had done with me, they carried me back to the village. As it turned out my house had been burnt in the attack and my children had fled. My husband was not there any more either; later we found his body in the bush." Over 80 per cent of the women seen by MSF have been raped by between two and five attackers.

The medical consequences of these rapes are both pathological and psychological. The risk of catching sexually transmitted diseases including HIV/AIDS is high. And the trauma runs very deep. At the clinic the counsellors hear the psychological aftermath of rape: fear, anxiety, and intrusive memories. One young woman spoke of the sound of her sister being raped and killed: "I can still hear my young sister screaming beside me. I did not know what they were doing to her and I could not help her."

There are social consequences too. The stigma of rape leads some men to abandon their wives. As one man explained: "Rape or not rape, having sexual intercourse outside the conjugal house makes her husband ridiculous and for the woman, it means being definitely rejected outside of the house." Others report deteriorated relations between them and their husbands: "Whenever my husband and I have an argument he calls me the wife of the militia men who raped me," says one woman.

Furthermore, because the rapes often take place in the fields, the women are scared to go back to cultivate. "I would rather never go there again, because I felt so close to death," said one. Yet this is not a viable option for most women—they have many children and few other sources of income. Food is scarce in the area and malnutrition is high. Victims also report that after the rape the soldiers stole the food they were growing, and in some cases took control of the fields entirely.

As a weapon of war, sexual violence is highly effective. The outcome is a traumatized, impoverished population. The military groups achieve both power and material gain, particularly useful when their pay is erratic. The violence is conducted seemingly with impunity. Despite the truce, many attacks reported took place after the ceasefire commenced, suggesting that it is one weapon demobilized soldiers refuse to surrender.

The question for Baraka now is, with a peace accord in place and a ceasefire being followed, whether it can prosper again. It will depend on a lot of factors: it will need the peace process to last and the military groups to be kept under control; it will need international aid to restore essential services and provide economic assistance. And given the psychological trauma of the population, it will need a lot of time.

R E A D I N G **84**

Reclaiming Our Mojo

Jane Fonda (2007)

Every mother contains her daughter in herself and every daughter her mother and every mother extends backwards into her mother and forwards into her daughter

> —*Carl Jung and Carl Kerenyi,*
> Essays on a Science of Mythology*

It would have been easy to miss altogether. Just a short sentence tucked within the fifty or so pages of my mother's medical records:

"She spoke with considerable shame of being molested at age eight."

The moment I read it, I was filled with relief. Yes, sadness for her. Of course. Sadness. I wanted to hold her and rock her and tell her I understood and forgave her. But relief was there, too, flooding me as I lay shivering in the bed.

I was two years into writing my memoirs, *My Life So Far,* which I dedicated to my mother as a way to force myself to discover why she was the

way she was. Part of that research meant trying to obtain her records from the institute where she committed suicide in the late 1940s on her forty-second birthday. I was twelve.

The evening the records arrived, I had to climb into the bed and cover myself in blankets because I suddenly felt so cold. Here were the documents that would enable me to travel back in time into the reality that had been the last days of my mother's life. What I had not anticipated was that there, tucked away amid the daily reports from doctors and nurses about her deteriorating state, was her own eleven-page double-spaced autobiography. Could it contain the clues to the puzzle that I needed?

Perhaps other family members had read these documents before me and missed that one sentence. Or had read it and not paid it much heed. Not understood what she meant when, in recounting her middle and high school years, she wrote, "Boys, boys, boys." Not connected the dots upon reading that she'd had six abortions and plastic surgery before I was born in 1937, and that

---

*Bollingen Series 22 (Princeton: Princeton University Press, 1963), p. 162.

her psychiatric tests at the end were "replete with perceptual distortions many of them emphasizing bodily defects and deformities."

But I had been getting ready for this moment for years and could at last understand and forgive her and, in doing so, forgive myself.

All my adult life, I had wondered about my mother's childhood. The older I got and the more I understood about the long-term effects of early trauma, the more I intuited that something bad must have happened. Maybe that was why I had been drawn to studying childhood sexual abuse over the previous five years. Maybe that was why in 1995 I founded the Georgia Campaign for Adolescent Pregnancy Prevention and soon discovered that childhood sexual abuse was the single biggest predictor of teenage pregnancy. Sixty percent of teen mothers fifteen years old and younger have been victims of sexual abuse.

By the time I read my mother's reports, I knew that sexual abuse, be it a onetime trauma or a long-term violation, is not only a physical trauma but that its memories carry a powerful emotional and psychic charge and can lead to emotional and psychosomatic illnesses and difficulties with intimacy. The ability to connect deeply with others is broken, and it becomes difficult to experience trust, feel competent, have agency. I knew that sexual abuse robs a young person of a sense of autonomy. The boundaries of her personhood become porous, and she no longer feels the right to claim her psychic or bodily integrity. For this reason, it is not unusual for survivors to become promiscuous starting in adolescence. The message that abuse delivers to the fragile young one is "All that you have to offer is your sexuality, and you have no right to keep it off-limits." *Boys, boys, boys.*

Then there's the issue of guilt. It seems counterintuitive that a child would feel guilty about being abused by an adult whom they are incapable of fending off. But children, I learned, are developmentally unable to blame adults. They must believe that adults, on whom they depend for life and nurture, are trustworthy. Instead, guilt is internalized and carried in the body, often for a lifetime, often crossing generations—a dark,

free-floating anxiety and depression. Frequently, this leads to hatred of one's body, excessive plastic surgery, and self-mutilation (more and more, I feel they are the same).

But the most profound thing I learned—years before I'd read my mother's history of abuse—was that these feelings of guilt and shame, the sense of never being good enough, and hatred of one's body cast a long shadow that can span generations, carried on a cellular level to daughters and even granddaughters.

Mother saw many doctors and psychiatrists for a seemingly endless list of ailments. As a child, I had begun to believe that she liked being in hospitals more than she did being home. But in those days, if the doctors had thought to connect her medical issues with early sexual abuse, which was unlikely, they certainly wouldn't have known what to do about it.

The psychiatrists she saw would have been Freudian. She'd have lain on a couch, staring at the ceiling, with the doctor sitting silently behind her. Just what she didn't need. As Dana Crowley Jack has said, "the more traditional therapy reproduces a hierarchical relationship of authoritative (male) therapist and deferential (female) client which is not conducive to relationship."

Early on, Freud had discovered incest and sexual abuse as the root cause of what was then called "hysteria" among his first well-to-do female patients. When his theories about this were first published, he was ridiculed by his colleagues in the field, who said it was unthinkable, an impossibility. Doubting his conclusions and perhaps fearing they would prevent his rise within academia, he developed what became the classic Freudian theory: Children *want* to have sex with their parents, and when incest is reported by patients, it is to be seen as sexual fantasy.

From then until the 1970s, the psychiatric profession firmly believed that incidents of sexual abuse and incest were "one in a million." The frequency and effects of such trauma (and the ways to treat it) did not begin to surface until the arrival of a new wave of pioneering feminist psychologists such as Carol Gilligan, Jean Baker Miller, and Judith Lewis Herman. Only in the

1970s, when women began to eschew the old presuppositions (*one in a million!*) and listen to one another empathically, did the truth emerge: Childhood sexual abuse and incest were and are epidemic.

These women and their colleagues were also discovering that recovery required rebuilding bonds of trust and connection. Because so many survivors of childhood violence, sexual abuse, and incest have experienced trauma at the hands of a loved and trusted person, closeness to another can come to represent danger. Intimacy, for them, is too frightening, and so they cut off. We can cut off, deny, and be symptom-free, but the shadow is there, tamping down our potential juice—muting our mojo. The shadow becomes all the darker and more powerful when we deny it.

With the birth of relational psychology, the landscape of treatment for survivors of abuse has been transformed. Rather than the former neutral, impersonal form of psychotherapy, it is through the empowerment of a trusting, growth-fostering relationship that the damaged faculties allowing us to experience intimate connection can be brought back to life.

I often imagine how it might have been for my mother had she lived today and had the support of a community of women who could have heard her story, believed it, and been moved by it. The alchemy of their tears might have opened her heart to her own pain.

That's the crucial step.

I have a friend whom I love very much. He once told me about his childhood, describing without the slightest affect a litany of psychological and physical brutality. He seemed surprised when tears began rolling down my cheeks.

"But it was for my own good!" he declared, assuring me that the perpetrator was his "best friend." Try as I might, I was never able to help him move through the factual history and reconnect with his feelings as that young boy, so beaten and abandoned. Nor could any therapist he saw over time. Perhaps the wounds were too deep, the scar tissue too thick. Besides, to the world, he seemed to be getting along just fine—no visible symptoms. Only those who wanted a deep connection with him knew why he couldn't show up, why the empathy gene seemed to have been plucked from his heart. He could not experience empathy for others or for himself. As I've discovered, healing often has to start with self-empathy.

It is too late for my mother. But not for me. I feel blessed to have been given the truth about her history because it has enabled me to understand her as well as the nature and cause of my own shadow.

Isn't it our job in life to get out from under the shadow and reclaim our mojo, realize our full potential as human beings? Don't we—don't I—need to expose the shadow to the light? Isn't this the greatest legacy we can leave our children?

I have already made big strides. I have written my memoirs, my own historical narrative that reaches back to my ancestors and forward to my children and grandchildren—the remembering part. I feel this is a gift to them. When I die, or maybe even sooner than that, they can use my narrative, as I used my mother's, to shed light on their own.

My task now is to go beyond the narrative and to enter it experientially, emotionally. Memory reconnected to feeling.

I know many people who have been able, with help, to move beyond dissociation. I'm one of them, and I've learned it's an ongoing journey, not easy in a patriarchal culture that tells us it's better to stuff it. Maturity, we're told, means staying always in control.

But what's so great about control if your heart feels empty and the walls between you and others feel impenetrable? Step three in AA's twelve-step program is about giving up control to a higher power. For me, right now, my higher power is my own deep consciousness, my own Divine within that needs me to surrender to it the tightness and brittleness of control.

I'm in the last act of my life. What frightens me isn't the thought of dying but getting to the edge of life with regrets. I discovered in preparing for my act, at age sixty, that my biggest regret would be to have never experienced real intimacy. To do this, I saw, to finally overcome my fears, I would have to be willing to go that dark, shadowy place and experience it. To learn to acknowledge and handle the toxic parts of what I inherited from my mother but also embrace and embody the juicy, sensual, the wild, and beautiful parts of her. I can't do this if all I have is a relationship to the facts.

Knowing and healing aren't the same. We can talk about the facts of trauma, recount the chronology, and still continue to be cut off from the experience, unable to go back to the dark place and feel. Healing takes feeling.

Healing also takes courage, because it's painful.

But if you've ever exercised for physical fitness, you know the difference between the pain of hard muscular or anaerobic work and the pain of injury. The former has a positive payoff: increased strength and fitness.

So it is with the pain of the internal work required for recovery. Yes, it's painful to purpose-fully try to access the emotions of trauma. But out of the pain can come a new, deeper, freer life if you are in a safe place, with loving guidance from a knowledgeable, skillful therapist or with a pro-fessionally guided group of women on the same journey.

For many, bodywork and holotropic breath-work, as developed by Dr. Stanislav Grof, and other transpersonal psychotherapies can dislodge the blockages that prevent us from reexperiencing and integrating early trauma.

It's important to create an intentional commu-nity of love, friends who are also committed to living as fully and wholly as possible. Eve Ensler [creator of "The Vagina Monologues"] and I are part of each other's community of love. It was with her that I first witnessed the power of what I call therapeutic listening. We were visiting a shelter for abused and abandoned girls in Jerusa-lem. Eve had asked permission to interview five or six of the girls, and I was worried that in the brief several hours we had with them, we would be opening Pandora's box and then we'd be gone. That's not at all what happened.

I saw what is meant by "active listening." Eve pulled the girls into the act of remembering and encouraged them to go beyond the unspeakable facts of their traumas to what their feelings were. Her listening always held palpable respect and empathy. She shed tears for them, and a shift occurred. I could feel it: Each girl saw she was believed and began to hear her own story with empathy. For the first time, the girls heard one another's stories, and this, too, seemed therapeu-tic. A community had been created.

Serendipitously, I recently made a film that touches on the subject of incest. At dinner one evening with one of the producers, I was talking about the frequency of sexual abuse and incest and how so many women I know—most, in fact—have experienced this trauma.

"Why is this?" he asked. "Don't tell me it's about power."

Don't tell me it's about power.

I saw that evening how dissociation can happen not only to victims of trauma but on a mass social level. This is how we avoid seeing violence against women as an inherent part of male dominance—the drive to impose power over those society views as "less than," or the drive to ensure sub-mission of those whose power is feared.

A psychiatrist once said, "The general contrac-tor for the social construction of masculinity and femininity is psychological trauma, but the archi-tect is the system of dominance."*

In case you think that in the United States at the beginning of the twenty-first century women aren't viewed as less than, listen to how men put down other men by calling them "girls," "pussies." How men who exhibit wonderful qualities such as empathy, compassion, nurture, qualities associ-ated with women, are often scorned. And that's without going into issues like lower pay for com-parable work and far lower representation in the halls of corporate, media, and political power.

For survivors of violence, sexual abuse, and in-cest, part of what can lead them to self-repossession is to be drawn into the work of stopping the vio-lence. This can mean supporting shelters for vic-tims of rape and domestic violence, creating crisis hotlines and rape crisis centers where there are none. We must ensure the presence of victim

---

*Bessel A. Van der Kolk, "The Body Keeps the Score" (Cambridge, Mass: Harvard Medical School, 1994), p. 219.

advocates in the court system, and the enforcement of penalties against perpetrators.

Those are some of the immediate forms that healing activism can take. But we need to hold in our hearts a bigger vision of a world in which both men and women are able to be full human beings, in control of their bodies and their hearts, respecting others' bodies and hearts. And the more we achieve that within ourselves, the more effective we'll be at moving society into a post-dominant era.

DISCUSSION QUESTIONS FOR CHAPTER 10

1. How do violence and the threat of violence exert social control on women? Do you ever fear gender-based violence? How do you think your gender affects your answer to this question?

2. Why do you think many feminists suggest that acts of violence against women are actually hate crimes? Do you think these acts should be classified as hate crimes?

3. Why do you think violence against women is so prevalent in society? Why do you think violence against women is primarily perpetrated by men?

4. How do myths about violence against women silence women and perpetuate sexist systems of oppression?

5. What steps do you believe need to be taken in order to address the problem of violence against women?

SUGGESTIONS FOR FURTHER READING

Buchwald, Emilie, Pamela R. Fletcher, and Martha Roth, eds. *Transforming a Rape Culture.* Rev. ed. Minneapolis: Milkweed, 2005.

Giles, Wenona, and Jennifer Hyndman, eds. *Sites of Violence: Gender and Conflict Zones.* Berkeley: University of California Press, 2004.

Jessop, Carolyn, and Laura Palmer. *Escape.* New York: Broadway, 2007.

Jones, Ann. *Next Time, She'll Be Dead: Battering & How to Stop It.* Rev. ed. Boston: Beacon, 2000.

Ristock, Janice L. *No More Secrets: Violence in Lesbian Relationships.* New York: Routledge, 2002.

Smith, Merril D. *Sex Without Consent: Rape and Sexual Coercion in America.* New York: New York University Press, 2002.

Valdez, Diana. *The Killing Fields: Harvest of Women.* Los Angeles: Peace at the Border, 2006.

CHAPTER **11**

State, Law, and Social Policy

As we have noted in earlier chapters, societal institutions are established patterns of social behavior organized around particular needs and purposes. Gender, race, class, and other systems of inequality structure social institutions, creating different effects on different people. The state, the institution explored in this chapter, is a major social institution organized to maintain systems of legitimized power and authority in society. The state plays an important role in both teaching and enforcing social values. It is a very powerful institution that has profound implications for women's everyday lives.

The *state* is an abstract concept that refers to all forms of social organization representing official power in society: the government, law and social policy, the courts and the criminal justice system, the military, and the police. The state determines how people are selected to govern others and controls the systems of governance they must use. With considerable authority in maintaining social order, the state influences how power is exercised within society. The definition of *state* here is different from state as a geographic region, such as California or Ohio.

Because the state is a conduit for various patterns of social inequity, it does not always fairly regulate and control social order. Historically, White women and women and men of color have been treated poorly by the state, and there are still many problems and challenges at all levels of the political system. However, the state has also been a tool for addressing historical forms of social, political, and economic inequalities through laws and social policy (as evidenced by civil rights and affirmative action legislation). In this way, the state works both to maintain sources of inequality and as an avenue for social justice. A key focus of this chapter is the interaction between the state and gender relations in society.

As already discussed in Chapter 2, the state works with other institutions and assigns roles and distributes resources. In particular, it regulates other institutions and provides guidelines for expected behaviors (roles) and channels resources and power. For example, it regulates the family (such as the Family Leave Act or considering some families illegitimate and thus ineligible for state benefits), education (such as Title IX), the economic system (such as antitrust laws that prevent monopolies and

LEARNING ACTIVITY   **Women and the United Nations**

> Visit the website of United Nations Division for the Advancement of Women at *http://www.un.org/womenwatch/daw/index.html*. Follow the link to CEDAW (the Convention on the Elimination of All Forms of Discrimination Against Women), and then follow the link to Country Reports to read about various nations' implementation of the plan. Then visit the UN's WomenWatch site at *http://www.un.org/womenwatch* to learn more about the UN's promotion of gender equality and empowerment of women. Follow the link to Women of the World for region-specific information. Follow the link for Statistics and Indicators for reports, databases, and archives relating to gender equality and women's human rights. What do you notice are the pressing issues facing women worldwide? What is the United Nations doing to address these issues?

anti-discrimination policies), and religion (such as state rules for the separation of church and state). The state as nation-state also participates in international policy-making that has important implications for global stability and development. When the United States refuses to ratify international treaties such as CEDAW (the Convention on the Elimination of All Forms of Discrimination Against Women) or the Kyoto Treaty on environmental quality because it seeks to protect U.S. statutes and corporations, it has significant impact globally. The United States is often seen as a powerful symbol of urban secular decadence, with the emancipation of women a central feature. This highlights the importance of gender-sensitive conceptions of international aid and development.

Beyond national levels of state policy in the United States is the United Nations (UN), which has tremendous influence on global politics. Bay Fang writes about the U.S. involvement in Iraq in the reading "The Talibanization of Iraq" and reports on the status of women and the Organization for Women's Freedom in Iraq (OWFI). Although the right to gender equality has been affirmed in international law, still many nations explicitly discriminate against women (including the United States). In the reading "Demilitarizing Society in a Globalized World," Cynthia Enloe discusses how new thinking about gender has been integrated into UN Resolution 1325, understanding the need for UN regulations and a clear gender policy beyond the nation-state level.

GOVERNMENT AND REPRESENTATION

Although the terms *government* and *state* tend to be used interchangeably, the government is actually one of the institutions that make up the state. The government creates laws and procedures that govern society and is often referred to as the political system. Although the U.S. government or political system is purported to be a democracy based on the principle of equal representation, the government is not representative of all people, and those who participate as elected officials do not necessarily represent all interests equitably.

Women have had a complicated relationship to the Constitution. The liberal doctrine of representation first included women as rights-bearing citizens and represented them as members of the body politic. They came to be excluded for a variety of political reasons, justified in part because the dominant culture assumed that politics and citizenship were purely masculine domains. The founding fathers believed that women's political identity should be restricted because their presence in politics was immoral, corruptive, and potentially disruptive, and that women should be represented by fathers, husbands, or brothers. It was believed that women should be confined to the private sphere of the home where they would be dependent on men, and, as a result, they had no separate legal identity and were legal beings only through their relationship to a man. They had no claims to citizenship rights as women until well into the nineteenth century.

As you know from Chapter 1, the Seneca Falls convention in 1848 produced the Declaration of Sentiments and Resolutions that aimed to ensure citizenship rights for women. Women would have to wait until 1920 and the passage of the Nineteenth Amendment to the U.S. Constitution to receive the vote. In 1868, however, the Fourteenth Amendment was ratified, asserting that no state shall "make or enforce any law which will abridge the privileges or immunities of citizens of the United States, nor . . . deprive any person of life, liberty, or property without due process of law, nor deny to any person within its jurisdiction the equal protection of laws." This "person" was assumed to be male, and, as a result, women still could not vote, and the government did not (and, many people would argue, still does not) extend the same protection of the law to women as it does to men. Susan B. Anthony, one of the first feminists, who helped write the Declaration of Sentiments and Resolutions, wanted to test her belief that the Fourteenth Amendment should give women, as citizens, the right to vote. She voted in an election in Rochester, New York, and was fined. Hoping to push the case to the Supreme Court, Anthony refused to pay the fine. The case, however, was dropped in order to avoid this test of law. In the Anthony reading "Constitutional Argument," she argues her right to vote as a citizen under the terms guaranteed by the Fourteenth Amendment. This excerpt is from a speech Anthony gave in 1873.

In 1923 the Equal Rights Amendment (ERA) was introduced into Congress to counter the inadequacies of the Fourteenth Amendment concerning women and citizenship. The ERA affirms that both women and men hold equally all of the rights guaranteed by the U.S. Constitution. It would provide a remedy for gender discrimination for both women and men and, at the constitutional level, provide equal legal status to women for the first time in our country's history. It was rewritten in the 1940s to read: "Equality of rights under the law shall not be denied or abridged by the United States or by any state on account of sex"; and it eventually passed Congress (almost 50 years later) in 1972. Unfortunately, it failed to be ratified by the states and suffered a serious defeat in 1982. The most important effect of the ERA would have been to clarify the status of gender discrimination for the courts, whose decisions still show confusion about how to deal with such claims. For the first time, "sex" would have been a suspect classification like race. It would require the same high level of "strict scrutiny" and have to meet the same high level of justification—a "necessary" relation to a "compelling" state interest—as the classification of race.

Copyright © 1982 Nicole Hollander. Used by permission of Nicole Hollander.

Although survey after survey showed overwhelming public support for the ERA among women and men, it was officially defeated on June 30, 1982, when it failed to be ratified by the states. It fell three states short of the 38 states needed for ratification. Although the ERA continues to be introduced into each session of Congress, passage of the amendment has yet to regain the momentum it did during the 1970s (even though in 1988 a Harris poll showed 78 percent approval). In order for the ERA to be fully amended, two-thirds of each house in Congress must pass it first, followed by its ratification by 38 states. As opposition to the ERA grew, some states retracted their prior ratification, and others, such as Illinois, changed laws in order to make ratification more difficult. Indiana became the thirty-fifth and last state to ratify the ERA in 1977, and the Republican Party removed ERA support from its platform. Many years later, ratification efforts continue, with women and men in many of the unratified states working under the "three-state strategy." This strategy argues that because there was no actual time limit for ratification in the original ERA, the amendment remains only three states short of official ratification. A bill in the 108th Congress of 2003–2004 stipulated that the House of Representatives shall take any necessary action to verify ratification of the ERA when an additional three states ratify. In addition, 19 states have state ERAs or equal rights guarantees in their constitutions. At present, many groups are working together toward the legislation of the Equal Rights Amendment at all levels. These groups include the League of Women Voters U.S., American Association of University Women, Business & Professional Women/USA, National Organization for Women, National Women's Political Caucus, ERA Campaign, and the Equal Rights Amendment Organization.

Opponents of the ERA have mistakenly claimed that the amendment is anti-family, reporting that it would deny a woman's right to be supported by her husband and encourage women to desert motherhood. There was also worry that it would legislate abortion and gay and lesbian rights as well as send women into combat. In addition, anti-ERA sentiments were voiced by business interests (such as members of the insurance industry) that profited from gender discrimination. The media sensationalized the issue and did not accurately report about what the ERA would and would not do, and conservative political organizations spent a lot of money and many hours organizing against it.

LEARNING ACTIVITY **The League of Women Voters**

The League of Women Voters was founded by Carrie Chapman Catt in 1920 during the convention of the National American Woman Suffrage Association, just 6 months before the Nineteenth Amendment was ratified. In its early years, the league advocated for collective bargaining, child labor laws, minimum wage, compulsory education, and equal opportunity for women in government and industry. Today the league is still involved in advocacy for justice, working on such issues as Medicare reform, campaign finance reform, and environmental preservation, as well as continuing the work begun over 80 years ago to encourage women to use their political voices. To learn more about the League of Women Voters or to join the league, visit its website at *www.lwv.org*.

Most feminist leaders today agree that women would be better off if the ERA had been ratified in 1977. They would have received better opportunities for equality and would have been supported by stronger laws fighting gender discrimination in employment, education, and other areas of society. Some people feel that we no longer need a constitutional amendment because there have been piecemeal federal and state laws to protect against gender discrimination. However, as we have seen, federal laws are no longer as safe as they have been and can be repealed by a simple majority. Similarly, courts change policy as the makeup of the courts changes. A constitutional amendment requires three-quarters of the legislature to vote to repeal it. Although many people assume the continuity of women's rights, the U.S. Supreme Court is central in maintaining or potentially overturning several taken-for-granted rights. These rights include reproductive privacy, affirmative action, protection against gender-based discrimination, family and medical leave, and quality health care services.

An illustration of how the government has handled women and citizenship concerns the treatment of women who have married non-U.S. citizens. Prior to the mid-1920s, non-native-born women who married male U.S. citizens automatically became American, and native-born women who married male non-U.S. citizens automatically lost their citizenship and were expected to reside in their husband's country. They also lost their right to vote, once women had been given the vote in 1920. When laws were passed to retain women's citizenship in the mid-1920s, still only men were able to pass on citizenship to their children. Laws equalizing citizenship on these issues were eventually passed in the mid-1930s.

In addition to rights, citizenship also entails such obligations as taxation, jury duty, and military service. Although women have shared taxation with men, in the past they have been prevented from service and/or exempted from jury duty because of their role as mothers and housewives. It was not until the 1970s that the Supreme Court declared that juries had to be representative of the community. Even then juries were often racially biased such that it was not unusual for an African American to face a White jury. A 1986 Supreme Court ruling stated that juries could not be constituted on the basis of race, and a 1994 ruling declared that gender too could

ACTIVIST PROFILE **Wilma Mankiller**

With her election as chief of the Cherokee Nation, Wilma Mankiller took both a step forward and a step backward. Although Mankiller was the first woman to serve as chief of a major Native American tribe in modern times, her election recalled the importance women had among the Cherokee before colonization by Europeans. Precontact Cherokee society was matrifocal and matrilineal. Women owned the property and maintained the home and were intimately involved in tribal governance.

Mankiller first became committed to involvement in Native American rights in 1969 when Native activists, including some of her own siblings, occupied Alcatraz island in San Francisco Bay. The 19-month occupation became a turning point in Mankiller's life. She became director of the Native American Youth Center in Oakland, California, and in 1973 she watched as her brother joined other Native American activists as they held off FBI agents for 72 days at Wounded Knee, South Dakota.

Following a divorce, Mankiller returned to her family's land in Oklahoma and began to work for the Cherokee Nation; as an economic stimulus coordinator, she had the task of encouraging Cherokee people to train in environmental health and science and then return to their communities to put their knowledge to use. In 1981 she became director of the Cherokee Nation Community Development Department, and her work was so successful that she attracted the attention of Chief Ross Swimmer, who asked her to run as his deputy chief in 1983.

Despite sexist rhetoric and verbal threats from opponents, Swimmer and Mankiller won. In 1985 Swimmer was named head of the Bureau of Indian Affairs by President

Ronald Reagan, and Mankiller became chief of the Cherokee Nation. In 1987 Mankiller ran on her own and was elected chief in her own right. That year, *Ms.* magazine named her Woman of the Year. She was re-elected in 1991, winning by 83 percent of the vote. During her tenure as chief, Mankiller focused on addressing high unemployment and low education rates among Cherokee people, improving community health care, implementing housing initiatives and child and youth projects, and developing the economy of northeastern Oklahoma. She created the Institute for Cherokee Literacy, emphasizing the need for Cherokee people to retain their traditions. She did not run for re-election in 1995. In 1998 President Bill Clinton awarded her the Presidential Medal of Freedom.

not be used as a basis for jury competence. The obligation for military service, which many women have wanted to share with men, is outlined in more detail later in the chapter. Of course, women have served in auxiliary roles as nurses, transport drivers, and dispatchers for many years and are now able to participate in combat positions within most divisions of the armed services.

Although women tend to be as involved as men in electoral politics (and sometimes even more involved) in terms of voting, showing support, and volunteering for campaigns, there are markedly fewer women involved in official political positions associated with campaigns. Women still constitute a relatively small number of candidates for local, state, and national offices, and their presence is greater at the local than the national level. As political offices get more visible, higher level, better paid, and more authoritative or powerful, there are fewer women in these positions. There are several explanations for this gap. Although some suggest that women are just not interested and that they lack the credentials, the main reasons are conflict between family and work roles, lack of political financing, and discrimination and sexist attitudes toward women in politics.

The 109th Congress of 2004–2005 included 68 women (45 Democrats and 23 Republicans), or 15.5 percent in the House of Representatives; 14 women (9 Democrats and 5 Republicans), or 14 percent in the Senate; and 82 women total (54 Democrats and 28 Republicans), or 15 percent overall in Congress. Of these 82 women in Congress, 22, or 27 percent, are women of color. It is not clear how the 2008 Presidential election may change these figures, especially (as of this writing) given potential Democratic hopefuls. A Democratic presidential win over the Republican Party would change the political landscape in terms of women's issues, bringing a stronger focus on the needs and general welfare of women and children. The presence of women candidates to date, however, although much improved compared with pre-1990s statistics, is still alarming. These figures illustrate male and White domination in society and challenge the extent to which women and people of color are represented. However, remember that females do not necessarily represent women's interests, just as people of color do not necessarily support issues that improve the status of non-White groups. Many feminists vote for men in political office over opposing women candidates because they understand that a candidate's being female does not necessarily mean that her politics, or those of the party she

Where Women Rule: A Sample of Female Representatives in National Legislatures Worldwide

Simple statistics merely hint at complex stories. Rwandan genocide has increased the number of female representatives but so, it appears, has Scandinavian social democracy. It may be no surprise that Saudi Arabia trails the pack, but how do you explain the Islamic Republic of Pakistan beating out the United States? Note that in no country's national legislature have female reps been able to crack the 50 percent mark.

Rank	Country	Number of Seats	Number of Women	Percent Women
1	Rwanda	80	39	48.8
2	Sweden	349	165	47.3
3	Finland	200	84	42.0
4	Costa Rica	57	22	38.6
5	Norway	169	64	37.9
6	Denmark	179	66	36.9
7	Netherlands	150	55	36.7
8	Cuba	609	219	36.0
8	Spain	350	126	36.0
9	Mozambique	250	87	34.8
10	Belgium	150	52	34.7
25	Afghanistan	249	68	27.3
26	Namibia	78	21	26.9
27	Grenada	15	4	26.7
28	Viet Nam	493	127	25.8
29	Iraq	275	70	25.5
40	Mexico	500	113	22.6
41	United Arab Emirates	40	9	22.5
42	Philippines	237	53	22.4
43	Bulgaria	240	53	22.1
44	Eritrea	150	33	22.0
44	Senegal	150	33	22.0
45	Ethiopia	529	116	21.9
46	Estonia	101	22	21.8
46	Republic of Moldova	101	22	21.8
47	Croatia	152	33	21.7
48	Pakistan	342	73	21.3
64	Italy	630	109	17.3
64	Nepal	329	57	17.3
65	Mauritius	70	12	17.1
66	Bolivia	130	22	16.9
67	El Salvador	84	14	16.7
67	Panama	78	13	16.7
67	Zimbabwe	150	25	16.7

Rank	Country	Number of Seats	Number of Women	Percent Women
68	**United States of America**	**435**	**71**	**16.3**
69	Greece	300	48	16.0
69	Turkmenistan	50	8	16.0
70	Kazakhstan	107	17	15.9
71	Czech Republic	200	31	15.5
72	Burkina Faso	111	17	15.3
72	Cape Verde	72	11	15.3
132	Kuwait	65	1	1.5
133	Papua New Guinea	109	1	0.9
134	Yemen	301	1	0.3
135	Kyrgyzstan	72	0	0.0
135	Micronesia (Federal States of)	14	0	0.0
135	Oman	84	0	0.0
135	Palau	16	0	0.0
135	Qatar	35	0	0.0
135	Saudi Arabia	150	0	0.0

www.ipu.org/wmn-e/classif.htm

represents, are pro-women. In terms of the gender gap in voting, on the average women tend to lean toward the Democratic Party more than men do and are more likely to be concerned about such issues as education, welfare, health care, and the environment. Though there are exceptions, men are more likely as a group to vote for strong defense, anti-welfare, and anti–affirmative action policies: the stance of the Republican Party. This does not, of course, imply that all men are Republican, only that as a group, they are more likely to favor the issues put forward by this political party.

WOMEN AND THE LAW

The United States inherited British common law that utilized the doctrine of *femme couverte* (also known as *feme covert*), or covered women: Husband and wife were one person under law, and she was his sexual property. As a result, married women could not seek employment without the husband's consent, keep their own wages, own property, sue, exercise control over their children, and control their reproductive lives. As already discussed in Chapter 10, because husbands and wives were "one" in marriage, wives were sexual property of husbands, and rape within marriage was legally condoned. It was legally impossible to charge a husband with raping his wife because it would imply that the husband was raping himself. Although the Married Women's Property Act of 1848 allowed women to own and inherit property, the other constraints on their lives remained intact through the

HISTORICAL MOMENT **Shirley Chisholm for President**

Shirley Chisholm was born to a mother from Barbados and a father from British Guiana. She grew up in Barbados and Brooklyn and graduated with honors from Brooklyn College with a major in sociology. Following graduation, she worked at the Mt. Calvary Childcare Center in Harlem and became active in local politics. She completed a master's in education at Columbia University in 1952 and then managed daycare centers.

Chisholm ran for a state assembly seat in 1964 and won, serving in the New York General Assembly until 1968. While in the New York legislature, she focused on issues of education and daycare. In 1968 she ran for and won a seat in the U.S. Congress representing New York's Twelfth Congressional District, becoming the first Black woman in the House of Representatives. Chisholm quickly distinguished herself as an outspoken advocate for the poor and for women's and civil rights and against the war in Vietnam.

During a speech on equal rights for women before the House of Representatives in 1969, Chisholm pointed out, "More than half of the population of the United States is female. But women occupy only 2 percent of the managerial positions. They have not even reached the level of tokenism yet. No women sit on the AFL-CIO council or Supreme Court. There have been only two women who have held Cabinet rank, and at present there are none. Only two women now hold ambassadorial rank in the diplomatic corps. In Congress, we are down to 1 senator and 10 representatives.

Considering that there are about 3½ million more women in the United States than men, this situation is outrageous."

In January 1972, Chisholm announced her candidacy for the Democratic nomination for the presidency: "I stand before you today as a candidate for the Democratic nomination for the Presidency of the United States. I am not the candidate of Black America, although I am Black and proud. I am not the candidate of the women's movement of this country, although I am a woman, and I am equally proud of that. I am not the candidate of any political bosses or special interests. I am the candidate of the people."

Chisholm became the first woman considered for the presidential nomination. Although she was defeated, she did garner more than 150 votes from the delegates to the Democratic National Convention in Miami. She continued to serve in Congress until 1982. She wrote two books: *Unbossed and Unbought* and *The Good Fight.* She died January 1, 2005 at the age of 80.

twentieth century. Even with the passage of these property acts, the law allowed the husband to control community property (jointly owned legally by husband and wife) until the 1970s.

Prior to the 1960s most states decriminalized violence in the family (meaning violence within families was not legally understood as criminal acts), and operated marital rape exemption laws. It was not until the 1980s and 1990s that women had legal protections against violence; these protections include legislation such as the rape shield laws, mandatory arrest procedures in cases of domestic violence, public notification programs about convicted sex offenders in communities, the creation of protective or temporary restraining orders, state rape reform laws, and the 1994 Violence Against Women Act. Also prior to the 1960s, women's reproductive lives were a function of state control because the state had criminalized access to contraceptive information and procedures. As discussed in Chapter 6, before the passage of *Griswold v. Connecticut* in 1965, women had no legal right to contraceptives, and before the early 1970s with the passage of state abortion rulings and *Roe v. Wade,* they had no legal right to an abortion. The issue of reproductive rights is still controversial, and the legal arena is the site for many of these battles today, especially in the area of parental notification and consent.

In terms of work and employment, *Muller v. Oregon* in 1908 reaffirmed the state's justification for limiting women's employment. This legislation approved Oregon's right to prevent women from working in factories or similar facilities for more than 10 hours a day based on the state's interest in protecting the reproductive functions of women. It was considered important for the "well-being of the race" that women's ability to contract freely be limited. As discussed in Chapter 8, by the 1960s various civil rights legislation was passed including the Equal Pay Act and Title VII, preventing employers from discriminating against women and people of color in employment. Affirmative action legislation of the 1970s and sexual harassment legislation of the 1980s further attempted to dismantle gender- and race-based

"Uh, oh, Regina has her lawyer with her . . ."

Reprinted by permission of Dave Carpenter.

inequities in the labor force. Challenges remain in this area, however, as systems of inequality still shape labor force experiences.

The state also affects women through the institution of marriage. Women had access to divorce in the nineteenth century, although divorce was much more difficult to obtain. In addition, divorce carried a considerable stigma, especially to the divorced wife. Prior to the advent of no-fault divorce in the 1970s (divorce on demand by either or both parties), partners had to sue for divorce. Grounds to sue were based on a spouse's violation of the marriage contract such as by cruelty, abandonment, or adultery, and the courts needed to prove that someone had committed a crime. This procedure was difficult and expensive for women; it also tended to involve a double standard of behavior based on gender. Nonetheless, because this procedure allowed wives to show that husbands were "guilty," wives might receive relatively generous compensation. With the advent of no-fault divorce, this has changed because no one is charged with blame.

Likewise, *alimony,* the payment that women have traditionally received as compensation for their unpaid roles as wives and mothers, has been reduced or

Women in Elective Office

Visit the site of the Center for American Women in Politics at *www.rci.rutgers .edu/~cawp*. Follow the link to "Facts and Findings" and select "Women in Statewide Elective Office" from the pull-down menu to discover which women currently hold elective office in the United States. Next use the pull-down menu to discover who are the women of color currently in elective office. What elective positions do women in your state hold?

IDEAS FOR ACTIVISM

- Visit the home page for Women Leaders Online at *www.wlo.org*. Women Leaders Online (WLO) is the first and largest women's activist group on the Internet. WLO provides action alerts to make people aware of issues that need activism. The organization also promotes voter education and facilitates e-mail access to your U.S. senators and representatives.
- For more information about political issues of concern to women, visit the home page of the Feminist Majority Foundation at *www.feminist.org*. Follow the link to "Take Action" for ideas about what you can do to make a difference.

eliminated through various legislation since 1970. Although eliminating alimony indicates a more gender-neutral situation where women are not simply viewed as dependent wives and mothers and may even have higher earnings than husbands, it has caused problems. This is because despite the gender-neutral language and intentions, society is stratified regarding gender, and women still tend to be financially subordinate to men. Although financial loss after divorce is significant for both men and women, women continue to bear the brunt of a breakup financially. This is because women tend to have lower salaries and therefore have less to live on, and also because women are more likely to have custody of children and endure more financial costs associated with single parenting. Financial hardship is often exacerbated by court-mandated child support that does not get paid to women. Some states have enforced legislation to track errant child-support monies and enforce payment. Yet, even though the law affects women in myriad ways, many women feel that law has little to do with their lives. This is Catharine A. MacKinnon's point in the reading "Law in the Everyday Life of Women." She writes that laws tend not to be formulated by and for women and often do not meet their needs, especially in the "private" realm. She calls for putting power (law) in the hands of the powerless.

PUBLIC POLICY

State policies determine people's rights and privileges, and, as a result, the state has the power to exclude groups, discriminate against groups, and create policies in favor of groups. By maintaining inequality, the state reflects the interests of the dominant groups in society and supports policies that work in their interests and reinforce their power. Native Americans, for example, have suffered because of state policies that required forced relocation, and African Americans have been harmed by Jim Crow laws that helped enforce segregation in the South and prevented African Americans from voting. There were miscegenation laws in the United States that prevented interracial marriage and aimed to maintain racial purity and superiority, and many states instigated laws that prevented African Americans from residing in

Affirmative Action: Myths and Misconceptions

MYTH: Affirmative action is a form of reverse discrimination.

REALITY: Affirmative action does not mean giving preference to any group. In fact, it stands for just the opposite. Included in the concept of affirmative action is the idea that all individuals must be treated equally and that a position should be given to the candidate most qualified. However, a hiring committee *must* make a good-faith effort to create a pool of candidates that reflects the number of women and minorities who possess proper training for the position. Once the qualified candidates are identified, a candidate's ability to provide cultural diversity to a department, to serve as a role model, and to offer a range of perspectives should be major elements in the evaluation and selection progress.

MYTH: Affirmative action means establishing a "quota" system for women and minorities.

REALITY: There is a difference between goals and quotas. Ideally, the percentage of women and minorities working in the position should be similar to the percentage of women and minorities qualified for such positions. Affirmative action does not mean showing partiality but rather *reaching out to candidates and treating them with fairness and equity.* Quotas, on the other hand, are court assigned to redress a pattern of discriminatory hiring.

MYTH: Once you hire an affirmative action candidate, you can never fire him or her.

REALITY: The terms of employment are the same for women and minorities as they are for men and nonminorities. In fact, in terms of affirmative action principles, standards of achievement, job requirements, and job expectations should be applied equally to all individuals.

MYTH: To satisfy affirmative action responsibilities, all that needs to be done is to hire one or two women or minorities for dead-end jobs.

REALITY: This is called tokenism. Hiring women and minorities for positions that are terminal in terms of advancement does not satisfy the affirmative action goals. The same opportunities for employment and career advancement must exist for all individuals.

MYTH: Affirmative action will result in lowering the standards and reputation of a department.

REALITY: This will not happen if a qualified candidate is selected for a position. Diverse staff providing varying talents and points of view increases effectiveness and vitality and can lead to an enhanced reputation.

MYTH: Affirmative action and equal employment opportunity are the same things.

REALITY: Equal employment opportunity means that all individuals must be treated equally in the hiring process and in advancement once on the job. Each person is to be evaluated as an individual on his or her merits and not on a stereotypic conception of what members of specific groups are like. Affirmative action is a more proactive concept. It means that one will actively and aggressively seek to recruit women and minorities by making a positive and continuous effort in their recruitment, employment, retention, and promotion.

MYTH: Affirmative action means applying a double standard; one for white males and a somewhat lower one for women and minorities.

REALITY: Double standards are inconsistent with the principles and spirit of affirmative action. One standard should be applied to all candidates. This myth, of course, implies that women and minorities are inherently less qualified than white males.

> **MYTH:** Unqualified individuals are being hired and promoted for the sake of diversity/affirmative action.
>
> **REALITY:** Affirmative action plans that compromise valid job or educational qualifications are illegal. Plans must be flexible, realistic, reviewable, and fair. The U.S. Supreme Court has found that there are at least two permissible bases for voluntary affirmative action by employers under Title VII, the federal law that prohibits discrimination in employment on the basis of race, national origin, sex, or religion: (1) to remedy a clear and convincing history of past discrimination by the employer or union, and (2) to cure a manifest imbalance in the employer's workforce. Thus, affirmative action programs are intended to hire the most qualified individuals, while achieving equal opportunity for all.
>
> *Source: www.units.muohio.edu/oeeo/Myths.htm.*

certain communities and/or being in a town after sundown. Some of these laws were still on the books into the late twentieth century.

An example of how policy reinforces systems of inequality is seen in lesbian and gay plaintiffs who are in the court system for child custody, contract, or property disputes. It is also evident in current discussions concerning gay marriage and civil unions. Homophobia in the system tends to work against gays and lesbians. As discussed in Chapter 7, the 1996 Defense of Marriage Act, which allows states not to recognize gay unions performed in other states, prevents lesbians and gay men from enjoying the privilege of state recognition of marriage, although currently there are several states that recognize these partnerships as civil unions or domestic partnerships. Massachussetts endorses gay marriage (see Chapter 4).

Welfare policy is especially illustrative of the ways the state is a conduit for the perpetuation of systems of inequality. Poverty in the United States is powerfully structured by racial and gender inequities, and patterns of income and wealth are strongly skewed along these lines. In 2006 the U.S. poverty rate (estimated from a poverty threshold of $19,307 for a family of four) was 12.3 percent of all families, with about 36.5 million individuals, or 8 million families, living in poverty. In terms of race, these figures break down to about 10 percent of Asian Americans, 22 percent of Latinas/os, 25 percent of African Americans, and 9 percent of White Americans living in poverty. Almost one-fifth of children of all races live in poverty. Ideologies (recall from Chapter 2 that these are sets of beliefs that support institutions in society) about who is deserving of wealth rely on the individualistic notion that success is a result of hard work and ambition; thus, anyone who works hard and pushes him- or herself should succeed economically. The corollary of this, of course, is that the fault associated with lack of economic success rests with the individual. This was referred to in Chapter 2 as the *bootstrap myth*. This myth avoids looking at structural aspects of the labor force and social systems that perpetuate classism and instead focuses on the individual.

The bootstrap myth helps explain the stigma associated with welfare in the United States and the many stereotypes associated with women on welfare—that they are lazy, cheat the system, and have babies to increase their welfare check. Women on welfare often face a triple whammy: They are women facing lower-paid work, they are mothers and have domestic responsibilities and childcare expenses, and they are single with only one paycheck. Indeed, if women earned as much as comparable men, then single women generally would see a rise in their incomes and a substantial drop in poverty rates. If we applied this comparable situation to single mothers, poverty rates would be cut almost in half, from 25 percent to 13 percent. Having a job does not necessarily lift women out of poverty. Having a job does not also guarantee sufficient retirement income, as the contemporary debate on Social Security reveals. Women will be disproportionately affected by Social Security reforms, especially any possible privatization.

In 1996 the passing of the Personal Responsibility and Work Opportunity Reconciliation Act (PRWORA) terminated the major source of welfare, Aid to Families with Dependent Children (AFDC), and replaced it with Temporary Assistance to Needy Families (TANF). No person could receive welfare for more than 5 years. In addition, welfare was transferred to the state through a block grant system, allowing some states to set their own agenda for distribution of funds. Critics of this and other policies of the 1990s have argued that not only have such policies failed to make low-income families self-sufficient, but they have kept wages low and undermined women's independence. The Welfare Reform Bill of 2002 raises the number of hours mothers receiving welfare have to work outside the home, study, or be involved in training, from 30 to 40 hours, at the same time that daycare in most states is totally inadequate. President George W. Bush again reauthorized welfare reform with the Deficit Reduction Act of 2005, signed into law in 2006, which, among other things, reduced Medicare and Medicaid spending. He also attempted to provide incentives for women to marry (for example by supporting pro-marriage organizations) as a strategy for reducing welfare costs. Communities of color experience some of the most devastating consequences of poverty, and welfare "reform" has increased the vulnerability of individuals (especially single mothers and children) in these communities. In the reading "What This Nation Really Thinks of Motherhood," Ellen Bravo explores the myths of welfare and provides feminist solutions for poverty.

A most obvious example of policies working to favor dominant groups is the practice often called "wealthfare," "welfare for the rich," or "aid to dependent corporations" (a play on words regarding AFDC) by some scholars. These policies reflect the ties political leaders have to the economic system and the ways the government subsidizes corporations and reduces taxes and other payments to the state for some corporations and businesses. Wealthfare involves five major types: direct grants; allowing publicly funded research and development to be used free by private for-profit corporations; discounted fees for public resources (such as grazing fees on public land); tax breaks for the wealthy; and corporate tax reductions and loopholes. It has been estimated that more than $200 billion in corporate welfare could be saved over the next 5 years if policies reining in these favors were instigated. Neither Republican nor Democratic lawmakers want to do this because they fear losing donations to their respective parties.

THE CRIMINAL JUSTICE SYSTEM

Laws can be defined as formal aspects of social control that determine what is permissible and what is forbidden in a society. The court system was created to maintain the law through adjudicating conflicts that may be unlawful and deciding punishments for people who have broken the law. The role of the police is to enforce these laws and keep public order. Prisons are responsible for punishing those who have broken the law and protecting society from people who have committed crimes. All these fit together to maintain the control of the state.

Although women are especially likely to be victims of certain crimes, such as rape and battering, they constitute a small proportion of people arrested for crimes (about 20 percent) and a smaller number of those who are sent to prison (about 7 percent of prisoners are female). These figures are related to gendered forms of behavior that encourage more males into violence and risk-related activities as well as the perception by criminal justice officials that women (especially White women) are less dangerous than men. Among men, poor men and men of color are more likely to be considered a danger to society and tend to receive the longest sentences. The highest levels of incarceration are among African American males in their 20s. It is estimated that about 1 in 8 such young men is incarcerated. Even though women are less likely to be in the prison system, their numbers are increasing. In 2006, for example, the number of women imprisoned in the United States grew at a rate of more than 1.5 times the rate of growth for men. This increased rate of incarceration between 2000 and 2006 is also relatively higher for White women, even though overall African American women are imprisoned at 3 times the rate of White women. According to a Women's Prison Association analysis, almost two-thirds of women in state or federal prisons in 2004 were sentenced for nonviolent crimes, almost half of which were drug-related. Robin Templeton writes about this incarceration in "She Who Believes in Freedom," discussing its consequences for communities and the need to address the structural, socioeconomic causes of violence. She is active in a grassroots anti-incarceration movement to educate about and change criminal justice policy.

The rate of crime committed by women has increased in recent years, with the largest increase being drug-related criminal behavior. The Bureau of Justice Statistics reports that just under half of all women (and one-tenth of all men) in correctional facilities indicated physical and/or sexual abuse before their current sentence. A large number of these incidents occurred before the age of 18 years. Most of the homicides enacted by women involve male victims, and they are most likely to have taken place in the home, often in self-defense. Women are more likely to be first-time offenders than men, are less likely to use firearms, and are more likely to use kitchen knives and other household implements. This evidence again suggests that much female homicide is done in self-defense. Although prior to the 1980s women who killed in self-defense almost always lost their plea, today juries are more understanding of the experiences of battered women. Even so, it is still sometimes very difficult for women to convince a jury that they were being abused, especially in terms of the question of "imminent danger" when an abused woman kills a partner when he is sleeping or not behaving violently at that moment. Defendants must meet two criteria for claiming justifiable homicide as self-defense: reasonable fear or perception of danger (such that killing was the only course of action to protect the

Women in Prison

- In 2005, 107,518 women were in prison.
- The number of women prisoners increased 2.6 percent in 2005 (men increased by 1.9 percent).
- By the end of 2005, women accounted for 7.0 percent of all prisoners, up from 6.1 percent in 1995.
- Since 1995, the number of women prisoners has grown 57 percent.
- The largest number of women prisoners were held in Texas (13,506), followed by the federal system (12,422), and California (11,667). Together these three jurisdictions accounted for over one-third of women prisoners.
- Mississippi, Oklahoma, and Idaho had the highest incarceration rates for women. Rhode Island, Massachusetts, and Maine had the lowest.
- White women in prison numbered 45,800, Black women 29,900 and Latinas 15,900.
- Black women are twice as likely as Latinas and more than three times as likely than White women to be in prison.

Source: U.S. Dept. of Justice, *www.ojp.usdoj.gov/bjs/abstract/p05.htm.*

defendant's life) and the confrontation of the defendant with deadly force by an assailant.

Another example of the double standard concerning women as victims is U.S. asylum law that provides protection for immigrants fleeing their country if they are being persecuted because of race, religion, nationality, political opinion, or membership in a social group. Although there were important advancements in asylum law that have protected women fleeing abusive husbands with the introduction of a policy to provide political asylum for women suffering severe domestic abuse in their homeland, this legislation was repealed by the Bush administration and attached to a now-defunct immigration reform bill. Finally, all marginalized people (women and men) are at risk of being victimized by hate crimes, a constant problem in contemporary U.S. society.

THE MILITARY

The military, a branch of government that is constituted to defend against foreign and domestic conflict, is a central component of the state and political system. As mentioned in Chapter 2, the military has strong ties to the economic system through a military-industrial complex that supports industries that manufacture weapons. Military presence overseas (as well as civil wars) tend to be related to economic interests like the need for oil or control of other resources, including the need for political "stability" in nations to maintain global corporate endeavors and strategic defense. The Pentagon has connections to other state entities, especially the government and its representatives. The military is a male-dominated arena, not only in terms of actual personnel who serve but in terms of the ways it is founded upon

Women in the Military

Women have served in the U.S. armed forces since 1901, when the Army Nurse Corps was established. Currently, 350,000 women serve in the U.S. military, almost 15 percent of active duty personnel. Milestones affecting women:

1967   Military abolishes 2 percent cap on women serving in the armed forces.

1973   Draft ends. Armed forces seek more women.

1976   Women admitted to service academies.

1978   Women allowed permanent assignment to Navy support ships.

1981   U.S. Supreme Court rules that excluding women from the draft is constitutional.

1991   About 41,000 women are sent to the Gulf War. Five die from hostile fire.

1993   Defense Secretary Les Aspin orders combat aviation and combat surface ships opened to women.

1994   Rule changes open more than 80,000 Army and Marine positions to women. Combat assignments to infantry, armor, artillery, and special operations remain off-limits.

PERCENTAGE OF WOMEN IN MILITARY BRANCHES

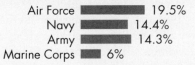

Air Force   19.5%
Navy   14.4%
Army   14.3%
Marine Corps   6%

PERCENTAGE OF MILITARY POSITIONS OPEN TO WOMEN

Air Force   99%
Navy   91%
Army   70%
Marine Corps   62%

NUMBER OF WOMEN WHO SERVED IN PREVIOUS CONFLICTS

World War I	33,000	Persian Gulf	41,000
World War II	400,000	Somalia	1,000
Korean War	120,000	Haiti	1,200
Vietnam	7,000	Bosnia	13,935
Grenada	170	Kosovo	5,660
Panama	770		

Sources: Defense Department, Women's Research and Education Institute. By Suzy Parker, *USA TODAY,* www.wrei.org/WomenMilitary.htm.

so-called masculine cultural traits like violence, aggression, hierarchy, competition, and conflict. The military has a history of misogynistic and homophobic attitudes to enforce highly masculine codes of behavior. In the reading "Demilitarizing Society in a Globalized World," Cynthia Enloe writes about the ways military culture is integrated, often unknowingly, into our everyday lives, such as through camouflage fashions and ROTC on college campuses. She calls for a demilitarization of society.

Throughout most of history, women were not allowed to serve in the military except in such auxiliary forces as nursing. It was not until World War II that women who served in any military capacity were given formal status and not until 1976 that women were allowed into the military academies. In terms of race, the armed forces were officially segregated until 1948. The percentage of military personnel who are people of color increased from 28 percent in 1995 to 38 percent in 2000 (with the overrepresentation of African Americans in particular), reflecting the relative lack of opportunities for people of color in the civilian realm. Between 2000 and 2005, however, the number of African American military personnel fell from almost a quarter to 14 percent. Despite their relatively high numbers in the service, people of color are less likely than Whites proportionately to be found in leadership positions. This is true for women of all races as well.

In 1981 the Supreme Court reaffirmed that it is constitutional to require registering men but not women for the draft. Currently, men are subject to conscription if a draft is in process and women are not, although women are allowed to serve if they wish. The rationale for the 1981 decision centered on the fact that women were not allowed in combat positions at that time, plus the notion that women have responsibilities in the home and family. After women's service in the Gulf War in 1991, there was pressure for President Clinton in 1993 to order a repeal of the ban on women in combat positions, and now most Navy and Air Force positions are open to women. The Army and Marines still preclude women from combat positions in field artillery, armor, infantry, submarines, and special units, although they are allowed to serve as pilots, supply officers, drivers, fuel handlers, interpreters, checkpoint workers, medics, and so on. In addition, as their service in the Iraq War has shown, although women are assigned to rear units, they are often temporarily assigned to combat units. As of 2008, 350,000 women were serving in the U.S. military, making up almost 15 percent of active duty personnel. Approximately 1 in 7 soldiers involved in the Iraq war is a woman, with African American women overrepresented in this ratio (in 2005 making up about a third of all women military personnel). About 45 percent of female soldiers in Iraq are mothers. Similar to the decrease in relative numbers of non-White personnel, the percentage of women in the military generally has decreased by 13 percent since 2005.

Sexualized violence and the harassment of women has been recognized as a widespread problem within the U.S. armed services. Recent history reveals the 1991. Tailhook scandal, in which more than 100 officers at a Navy convention sexually assaulted and harassed dozens of women, yet not one offender was convicted and an investigation found that Navy officials had tacitly approved these behaviors for years. In 1996, a series of sexual assaults at the Aberdeen Proving Ground in Maryland led to charges against a dozen Army drill instructors, and in 2004, three veterans of the Special Forces in Afghanistan killed their spouses. Studies show women entering the military often have histories as abuse survivors and men have violent pasts. Misogynous military

Women in Black: For Justice, Against War

Perhaps you've seen them—a small group of women dressed in black standing silently on a street corner or in some other public place and perhaps on your campus. They are Women in Black, part of a global network of women advocating for peace and opposing injustice, war, militarism, and other forms of violence. Women in Black began in Israel in 1988, as Israeli women stood in weekly vigils to protest the Israeli occupation of the West Bank. They did not chant or march. Rather, they stood at a busy intersection with a simple sign that read "Stop the Occupation." Bypassers shouted at them, calling them "whores" and "traitors." They did not shout back but maintained a silent dignity. Eventually, Women in Black vigils were organized around the world to support the women in Israel. As war came to Croatia and Bosnia in 1992, Women in Black groups began to oppose the violence there. And so the movement has continued to spread as women around the world have responded to war. In both the Gulf War and the wars in Afghanistan and Iraq, women across the globe and in the United States have stood in protest. Any group of women anywhere can hold a Women in Black vigil against any form of violence, militarism, or war. Women in Black also engage in nonviolent and nonaggressive action—blocking roads or entering military bases. To find out if there is already a vigil in your area or to learn how to start your own vigil, visit www.womeninblack.org.

culture normalizes violence, pornography is often readily available, and prostitution is abundant around military bases. As the events of the torture of prisoners at the Abu Ghraib prison in Iraq in 2004 testify, women also can act in violent ways when assimilated into military culture. The use of rape as a weapon of war, including by U.S. soldiers, illustrates one of the most extreme examples of interpersonal military violence. In addition, families of service personnel are also at risk as unique stresses such as relocations, long work tours, frequent family separations, and dangerous work assignments increase the risk for family violence and encourage alcohol and drug use and abuse. Studies show that combat stress after entry into the service increases the likelihood of males perpetrating abuse, especially when post-traumatic stress is involved. Abused female military personnel (and civilian spouses fearful of jeopardizing husbands' prospects for continued service and promotion) often resist reporting incidents out of fear of lack of confidentiality, retaliation, and lack of available services.

In response to these problems, in 2004 the Department of Defense (DOD) conducted a review of its sexual assault policies and programs and found reports of more than 1,000 incidents of sexual assault in 2003 alone, plus inconsistent policies and many barriers to reporting. Recommendations for improvement were presented to the Secretary of Defense in 2004. Change requires a transformation of sexist ideologies and practices and improvements in victim services (such as enhanced confidentiality, and the appointment of a central authority within the DOD to investigate and prosecute violent crimes), education to recognize and prevent abusive situations, increased funding of domestic violence shelters for military personnel, legislation to decrease the availability of firearms, and increased funding for research, treatment, and prevention.

Finally, the military has a long history of homophobia that has included the execution, persecution, and dismissal of gay soldiers. Although polls consistently show strong support for removing the current anti-gay ban (in a 2003 Gallup poll, 79 percent polled were in favor and that included 91 percent of 18- to 29-year-olds and 68 percent of those over 65 years old), arguments in favor of such prejudice mirror those proposing racial segregation in earlier times. These include: The morale and fighting spirit of military personnel will drop if openly gay and lesbian personnel are present, and gays and lesbians pose a national security threat. Through the 1980s, more than 15,000 military personnel were discharged because of homosexuality. By the mid-1990s President Clinton had created the "don't ask, don't tell" policy. It was supposed to be a compromise, although it has few supporters. Today discharges are still allowed under the policy, but numbers dropped by almost half between 2001 and 2007. Such figures routinely drop in times of war, reflecting the need for military personnel, or, perhaps, that gay and lesbian soldiers are not disclosing their identities. Some scholars have suggested that military authorities may no longer be choosing to discharge them. In this way, the government policy on lesbians and gays in the military illustrates how the state may have differential effects on some groups relative to others.

The state is a very powerful institution that has enormous effects upon women's everyday lives. It is important to understand how gender, race, and class mold and shape government, law, and policy, and how these institutions reflect and promote the needs of some groups over those of others.

Constitutional Argument

Susan B. Anthony (1898)

Friends and Fellow-Citizens:—I stand before you under indictment for the alleged crime of having voted at the last presidential election, without having a lawful right to vote. It shall be my work this evening to prove to you that in thus doing, I not only committed no crime, but instead simply exercised my citizen's right, guaranteed to me and all United States citizens by the National Constitution beyond the power of any State to deny.

Our democratic-republican government is based on the idea of the natural right of every individual member thereof to a voice and a vote in making and executing the laws. We assert the province of government to be to secure the people in the enjoyment of their inalienable rights. We throw to the winds the old dogma that government can give rights. No one denies that before governments were organized each individual possessed the right to protect his own life, liberty and property. When 100 or 1,000,000 people enter into a free government, they do not barter away their natural rights; they simply pledge themselves to protect each other in the enjoyment of them through prescribed judicial and legislative tribunals. They agree to abandon the methods of brute force in the adjustment of their differences and adopt those of civilization. Nor can you find a word in any of the grand documents left us by the fathers which assumes for government the power to create or to confer rights. The Declaration of Independence, the United States Constitution, the constitutions of the several States and the organic laws of the Territories, all alike propose to *protect* the people in the exercise of their God-given rights. Not one of them pretends to bestow rights.

All men are created equal, and endowed by the Creator with certain inalienable rights. Among these are life, liberty and the pursuit of happiness. To secure these, governments are instituted among men, deriving their just powers from the consent of the governed.

Here is no shadow of government authority over rights, or exclusion of any class from their full and equal enjoyment. Here is pronounced the right of all men, and "consequently," as the Quaker preacher said, "of all women," to a voice in the government. And here, in this first paragraph of the Declaration, is the assertion of the natural right of all to the ballot; for how can "the consent of the governed" be given, if the right to vote be denied? Again:

> Whenever any form of government becomes destructive of these ends, it is the right of the people to alter or abolish it, and to institute a new government, laying its foundations on such principles, and organizing its powers in such form, as to them shall seem most likely to effect their safety and happiness.

Surely the right of the whole people to vote is here clearly implied; for however destructive to their happiness this government might become, a disfranchised class could neither alter nor abolish it, nor institute a new one, except by the old brute force method of insurrection and rebellion. One-half of the people of this nation today are utterly powerless to blot from the statute books an unjust law, or to write there a new and a just one. The women, dissatisfied as they are with this form of government, that enforces taxation without representation—that compels them to obey laws to which they never have given their consent—that imprisons and hangs them without a trial by a jury of their peers— that robs them, in marriage, of the custody of their own persons, wages and children—are this half of the people who are left wholly at the mercy of the other half, in direct violation of the spirit and letter of the declarations of the framers of this government, every one of which was based on the immutable principle of equal rights to all. By these declarations, kings, popes, priests, aristocrats, all were alike dethroned and placed on a common level, politically, with the lowliest born subject or serf. By them, too, men, as such, were deprived of their divine right to rule and placed on a political level with women. By the practice of these declarations all class and caste distinctions would be abolished, and slave, serf, plebeian, wife, woman, all alike rise from their subject position to the broader platform of equality.

The preamble of the Federal Constitution says:

We, the people of the United States, in order to form a more perfect union, establish justice, insure domestic tranquillity, provide for the common defence, promote the general welfare and secure the blessings of liberty to ourselves and our posterity, do ordain and establish this Constitution for the United States of America.

It was we, the people, not we, the white male citizens, not we, the male citizens; but we, the whole people, who formed this Union. We formed it not to give the blessings of liberty but to secure them; not to the half of ourselves and the half of our posterity, but to the whole people—women as well as men. It is downright mockery to talk to women of their enjoyment of the blessings of liberty while they are denied the only means of securing them provided by this democratic-republican government—the ballot. . . .

R E A D I N G **86**

Law in the Everyday Life of Women

Catharine A. MacKinnon (2005)

For most women, life is little but everyday, a constant cycle of minutiae with few landmarks or dramatic demarcations of time, a litany of needs served but never satisfied, time spent but seldom occupied, lines drawn that, like the horizon, recede on approach. Across time and culture, and in individual biographies, the sameness in women's lives is as striking as the diversity of conditions under which it is lived. Men rise and fall. Their dynasties and revolutions and intellectual fashions come and go. Things happen. In the lives of women, men are served, children are cared for, home is made, work is done, the sun goes down.

Most women will tell you that law has little to do with their everyday lives. They seldom hit walls that look legal—they do not get that far. The lives of women in poverty are circumscribed by rules and regulations that they know are stacked and enforced against them and could be different, but nothing so majestic as "the law" is accessible to them. Many women encounter official obstacles, but few have the law in their hands. If a woman complains to the police of a crime against her, the law is in the hands of the prosecutor. On the civil side, it usually takes money to get the law to work for you. Even when a woman's injury is recognized by law, which is seldom, most women lack the resources to use it.

To most women, the law is a foreign country with an unintelligible tongue, alien mores, secret traps, uncontrollable and unresponsive dynamics, obscure but rigid dogmas, barbaric and draconian rituals, and consequences as scary as they are incomprehensible. Actually, this is true for most men as well.[1] The difference is that the people who can and do make law work for them, who designed it so it would work for them as if they were the whole world, are men—specifically, white upper-class men. Women reflect this reality in their view that if you try to use the law, it is as likely to blow up in your face as to help. Law is Kafka's trial, Dickens's *Bleak House.* Mostly women feel that the law is not about them, has no idea who they are or what they face or how they think or feel, has nothing to say to them, and can do nothing for them. When the law and their life collide, it is their life that gets the worst of it.

Women in conflict with the law show this relation in highest relief. Most become criminals for responding in kind to male violence against them, for crimes of poverty, for being involved with a man who committed a crime (what might be called first-degree bad choice of boyfriend), or for prostitution—being sold by men to men for what men value women for, and then being devalued and considered a criminal for it. On my observation, most imprisoned women who are not inside for crimes of self-defense *against* men who batter them are in for crimes committed *with* men who batter them.[2] The law does little to nothing about the crimes against women that position them to commit the crimes that do matter officially. For instance, women's imprisonment in their homes by violent men who batter them is not thought official, even though it is widely officially condoned.

The law operates most visibly in the lives of women in officially recognized captivity. They are surrounded, defined, debased, and confined by the law. Their everyday lives are taken over by it. It swallows them up: their liberties, their children, their bodies, their community ties, what initiative and self-respect they had managed to salvage, and sometimes their lives. To be in prison is what it is for women to live their everyday lives entirely inside the law. Even when women criminals do the same things and get the same sentences as men, which is not the norm,[3] their crimes are the crimes of women. They commit them as women, are punished as women, and, when the law is finished with them, are thrown back onto society's trash heap for women.

The law that is applied to them and to all women was not written by women, white or Black, rich or poor. It has not been based on women's experiences of life, everyday or otherwise. No one represented women's interests as women in creating it, and few have considered women's interests as women in applying it.[4] Unlike men, many of whom are also estranged from the law—especially unlike white upper-class men—no women had voice or representation in constituting this state or its laws, yet we are presumed to consent to its rule. It was not written for our benefit, and it shows.

The exclusion of women from a formative role in the law has meant that much legal intervention in women's lives is unconstructive, to say the least, while most of women's lives is carried out beneath explicit legal notice. Crimes and civil injuries do not imagine most harms distinctive to women, such as the stigma of female sexuality, which pervasively imposes inferiority on women in everyday life. Canons of legal interpretation in laws that might apply to real events in women's lives are shaped to assume the validity of the male point of view. An example in the law of sex discrimination is the "intent" requirement, which bases a finding of discrimination on the perspective of the alleged discriminator rather than on the consequences of his actions for the discriminated-against. Burdens of proof and evidentiary standards as well as substantive law tacitly presuppose the male experience as normative and credible and relevant. An example is the mens rea requirement in the law of rape, which bases its determination of rape on the perspective of the accused rapist as opposed to that of the victim. Proceeding by analogy, as the law does, means that new crimes and injuries committed against women must be like old ones (read: those committed against men) before they can be recognized as crimes and injuries at all. Crimes women distinctively commit, they seem to have figured out. When a woman tries to raise her voice, precedent often requires decisive deference to a law built on the silence of women, a law that originated when we were not even permitted to vote or to learn to read, in a society premised on women's subjection.

No law addresses the deepest, simplest, quietest, and most widespread atrocities of women's everyday lives. The law that purports to address them, like the law of sexual assault, does not reflect their realities or, like the law of domestic violence, is not enforced. It seems that either the law does not exist, does not apply, is applied to women's detriment, or is not applied at all. The deepest rules of women's lives are written beneath or between the lines, and on other pages.

Yet the actions and inactions of law construct and constrict women's lives, its consequences no less powerful for being offstage. Focusing on the areas the law abdicates, its gaps and silences and absences, one finds that women's everyday life has real rules, but they are not the formal ones. They have never been legislated or adjudicated. They have not had to be. They effectively prescribe what girls can be, what the community encourages and permits in a woman, what opportunities are available and hence what aspirations are developed, what shape of life is so expected that it is virtually never articulated. These rules go under the heading of socialization, pressure, religion, popular culture, masculinity and femininity, everyday life. The rules of everyday life, in this sense, are that law which is not one, the law for women where there is no law.

The content of the formal legal system, the output of legislatures and courts, has a real effect on these processes, but, from the vantage point of life being lived, it seems a distant one. Whether sex discrimination in athletics is illegal, whether women's supposed "interests" make occupational segregation nondiscriminatory,[5] whether pornography is protected by the state,[6] whether legal abortion is available[7]—all deeply shape women's realities, but from high up and a long way off. Women seldom have much say in these matters yet live their consequences every day in factories, behind counters, in beds, on streets, in their heads, and in the eyes and at the hands of men, where the everyday lives of most women are largely lived out. Women's exclusion from law and marginality within it does not make the law inactive in women's subordination day to day. The fact that women have nothing to say about a sphere of life does not mean that it does not affect us—to the contrary. Especially if one thinks of everyday life as not having to be the way it is, the role of law in keeping it the way it is becomes visible, compelling, imperative.

Of all of everyday life, sexual relations between women and men may seem the farthest from the reach of law. Sex occurs in private, in presumed consent, in everyday intimacy. Sex is thought of as a sphere to itself with its own rules, written by desire or individual taste or mutual negotiation or tolerance, not by law. Yet the law of sexual assault in the United States has a very real everyday impact on sexual life. Rape is supposedly illegal. Yet the rape that the law actually recognizes as illegal is a far cry from the sex forced on women in everyday life. The law's rape is by a stranger, in a strange location, with a weapon, which the woman resisted within an inch of her life. Preferably the woman is white, the rapist Black. Most rapes that actually happen are by someone the woman knows, of the same race, often to women of color. Rape happens at home or on a date, without weapons other than hands and a penis, and the woman is too surprised or too terrified or too learned in passivity or wants to get it over with too badly or has heard too much about men who kill women who resist to fight back. Or she does fight back and loses and is not believed, either by the rapist or in court, because sex is what a woman is for.

To the extent your reality does not fit the law's picture, your rape is not illegal. The implications of this for everyday sex life are that any man who knows a woman of the same race can probably get away with raping her. The better he knows her, the more likely he is to get away with it. Married women in states that do not have a law against marital rape are the ultimate example. Until the early 1970s, a woman was not considered a reliable witness about her own rape, but the defendant was.[8] Unless someone besides the woman saw it, it was not legally real. Many jurisdictions, like California and Canada and England, still require that the state prove that the accused rapist honestly believed that the woman did not consent, no matter how much force was used.[9]

What does all this mean for having no mean no? When no can legally mean yes, what does yes mean in everyday life? When rape passes legally as intercourse, what is sexual intimacy? The law of rape deeply affects sexual intimacy by making forced sex legally sex, not rape, every night. Every day, because women know this, they do not report rapes nine times out of ten.[10] When a woman does report, the media have the legal right to print her name and picture, making her into everyday pornography.[11] The racism of the criminal justice system is an everyday reality for women of color, who do not report their rapes by men of color because of it. In reality, there are no laws against what can be done to them. Many women, no matter how violated they were, do not call what happened to them rape if they do not think a court would agree with them. In this ultimate triumph of law over life, law tells women what happened to them and many of us believe it. When asked, "Have you ever been raped?" many women answer, "I don't know."[12]

A similar combination of utter neglect with malignant concern animates the law of reproduction. Women get pregnant every day without wanting to be and at the same time are prevented from having children they want to have. The question here is who controls the reproductive uses of women, a process to which controlling the fetus is instrumental. When a woman is sterilized against her will and even without her knowledge, as has most often been done to women of color and to "mentally disabled" women, no law prohibits it or even compensates it after the fact.[13] Does law then have no relation to each day of the rest of their lives, on which they now cannot have children? If a woman dies from a desperation-induced self-abortion because a funded, safe one is not available by law—and most such women have been Black or Hispanic[14]—did law not end her everyday life?

Pornography suffuses women's everyday life, crisp in cellophane at your child's eye level in the 7–11, dog-eared and hidden at the back of your boss's drawer at work, smack in your face on the wall of your car repair shop or your school's film society's trendy spring roster, soggy under your son's mattress. Under the law of obscenity, pornography is supposed to be against the law. In the real world of everyday life, it is effectively legal because it is pervasively there, available without sanction or fear of sanction. This is what a dead-letter law looks like: everyday life is lived as if it is not there. But the pretense of law being there also has a distinctive effect. The combination of pornography being putatively forbidden but totally available, decried in public but permitted and used in private, intrudes the law deeply into women's everyday lives. The allegedly forbidden quality of pornography sexualizes it by surrounding it with power and taboo and makes defending and using it appear to be an act of daring and danger, a blow for freedom against repression. Meantime, its actual availability belies the taboo and promotes the power, spreading it and supporting it as a model for women's everyday lives.

The everyday reality of pornography, particularly of adults, supersedes any formal law currently in force and becomes the real rules for women's lives, the sacred secret codebook with directions about what to do with a woman, what everything she says and does means, what a woman is. All the sexual abuses of women's everyday lives that are not recognized by the law are there in the pornography: the humiliation, the objectification, the forced access, the torture, the use of children, the sexualized racial hatred, the misogyny. As Andrea Dworkin has said, "Pornography is the law for women." Open your mouth this far. Spread your legs this wide. Put your arms like this. Talk dirty to me. Now smile.[15]

In this way, visual and physical intrusion on women—a normative experience of objectification and dehumanization made to seem deviant and marginal when medicalized as voyeurism and other exotic paraphilias—becomes the paradigm for sex. Sex in this sense is not just an activity at a time and place but a pervasive dimension of social life as lived every day. A woman's physical condition *(Knocked-Up Mamas, Milky Tits)*, occupation (lady lawyer, hot housewife), racial or ethnic or religious heritage *(Geisha Gashes, Black Bondage, I Was a Gestapo Sex Slave)*, age *(Cherry Tarts, Ten)*, family status *(Daddy's Girl)*, pets *(Doggie Girl)*, facts of everyday life to her, become sex to the consumer in the world pornography creates, along with everyday objects like telephones, cucumbers, beer cans, ropes, paper clips, razors, candle wax, police uniforms, plumber's helpers, lollipops, and teddy bears. In this process, the law helps constitute what is called desire by defining what amounts to sexual use and abuse of women and children as illegal and out of bounds and then doing nothing about it. Women realize that reporting sexual assaults is futile because this is a society that considers them freedom. When the state goes a step further and declares that pornography is affirmatively protected after all, and its harm to women is real but does not matter as much as the pornography of us matters,[16] women's despairing relation to the state and its laws—our belief that they will never see us as real—becomes total.

Even in the world pornography has made, it never occurs to most women, living their lives day to day, that having sex with a man to whom one is married is part of being a good mother. The law of child custody in general, of lesbian child custody in particular, reveals that there are sexual requirements for the legal adequacy of women's parenting. If a woman has a sexual relationship with a woman, she can lose her children,[17] "lesbian" being pornography for men, to which they do not think children should be exposed. The everyday sexuality of many women is thus controlled every day through fear due to the recently strengthened possibility of men seeking custody of children.[18] This is not to say that the men actually want the children, although sometimes they do. More commonly, they want to use the threat of challenging custody as a financial

lever to reduce support payments, and as control generally. The new norm of joint custody has a similar effect. Day to day, the mother has the major responsibility and does most of the work, but because of joint custody, the father can still control the big decisions. In other words, now not even divorce disturbs the power relation of marriage. And women who were raped in their marriages face sharing custody of their children with their rapist.

Family law keeps a lot of women in place and in line, fearful of altering their lives because of how it could be made to look in court. Some do not go public with past abuse through pornography for this reason. Many stay with men who abuse them because they fear the man would try to take their children away, and he would look better under existing legal standards—high income, intact new family, white picket fence—than they do. Most women feel they married an individual but find on considering divorce that he represents the law and the law represents him. He is the law of the state in the home.

The realm in which women's everyday life is lived, the setting for many of these daily atrocities, is termed "the private." Law defines the private as where law is not, that into which law does not intrude, where no harm is done other than by law's presence. In everyday life, the privacy is his. Obscenity is affirmatively protected in private. Wives are raped in private. Women's labor is exploited in private. Equality is not guaranteed in private. Prostitution, when acts of sex occur out of public view, is often termed private. In private, women who can afford abortions can get them, but those who cannot afford them get no public support, because private choices are not public responsibilities.[19]

Women in everyday life have no privacy in private. In private, women are objects of male subjectivity and male power. The private is that place where men can do whatever they want because women reside there. The consent that supposedly demarcates this private surrounds women and follows us wherever we go. Men seem to reside in public, where laws against harm exist—real harm, harm to men and whoever has the privilege to be hurt like men—and follow them wherever they go. Having arranged the law against rape and battering and sexual abuse of children so virtually nothing is done about them, and having supported male power in the home as a virtual absolute, the law then proclaims its profoundest self-restraint, its guarantee of liberty where it matters most, in "the right to be let alone."[20] This home is the place Andrea Dworkin has described from battered women's perspective as "that open grave where so many women lie waiting to die."[21] As a legal doctrine, privacy has become the affirmative triumph of the state's abdication of women.[22] Sanctified by the absolution of law, the private is the everyday domain of women in captivity, abandoned to their isolation and told it is what freedom really means.

This is to say that the law is complicit in the impoverishment of the average woman who makes nowhere near the income of the average man,[23] in the everyday aggression against the 44 percent of women who are victims of rape or attempted rape at least once in their lives,[24] in the assaults of the quarter to a third of women who are battered in their homes,[25] in the denial to women of the choice not to have children and the choice to have children and not to have them stolen, and in every act of violation or second-class citizenship that involves pornography. The law of rape collaborates with rapists to the extent it precludes recognition of the violations it purports to prohibit. The law of discrimination collaborates with perpetrators of discrimination to the extent its doctrines reproduce inequality rather than remedy it, requiring that equality already effectively exist before it can be guaranteed. The law of pornography collaborates with pornographers by protecting their right to abuse women behind the guarantee of freedom of speech, at the same time participating in their marketing strategy of sexualizing pornography by making it seem forbidden. The law of child custody collaborates with patriarchy in imposing male dominant values on women in the family, and the law of privacy collaborates with whoever has power by guaranteeing spheres of impunity in which the law leaves men to their own devices. Even when the law does nothing—and it does nothing in so many ways—

it is responsible for not working for women, whether law permits nothing when it pretends to do something, is inadequate, is not enforced, or does not exist at all. If it does not work for women, it does not work.

The same people who have power in life have had power in law, and the reverse. This relation is a process, though, not an inert or static fact, as one counterexample serves to reveal. Women have made at least one law: the law against sexual harassment. Before sexual harassment became actionable as a form of sex discrimination, it was just everyday life. The sex role norm that empowers men to initiate sex to women under conditions of inequality is intensified in sexual harassment. Women are pressured and intimidated into sexual compliance and raped as the price for economic survival. This has been done for centuries with virtual impunity. When women's experience was made the basis for the law against sexual harassment, everyday life altered as well. Men kept doing it, but the experience had a name, an analysis that placed it within the collective reality of gender, a forum for confrontation with some dignity and the possibility of relief. Most important, women's own sense of violation changed because the harm had legal expression and legitimacy and public sanction. Law told women back what they knew was true. Sexual harassment was against the law against treating women as unequals, the law of sex discrimination. This law told the truth: sex inequality is the problem, this problem. In going from everyday life to law, sexual harassment went from a gripe to a grievance, from a shameful story about a woman to actionable testimony about a man. Changing what could be done by law changed the way it felt to live through it in life, and the status of women took a step from victim to citizen.

. . .

Whoever says law cannot make change so we should not try might explain why the law should be exempt in the struggle for social transformation. Some of us suspect that women, in particular, are being told that not much can be done with law because a lot can be. If law were to be made to work for women, the relation of law to life, as well as its content, might have to change in the process. As more women become lawyers and maybe the law starts to listen to women, perhaps the legal profession will decline in prestige and power. Maybe women using law will delegitimize law, and male supremacy—in its endless adaptability and ingenuity—will have to find other guises for the dominance it currently exercises through law.

This is not to urge a top-down model of change or to advocate merely inverting or reshuffling the demographics of existing structures of power, or to say that law alone solves anything. It is to say that putting power in the hands of the powerless can change power as well as the situation of the powerless. It is also to urge a confrontational engagement with existing institutions: one that refuses to let power off the hook. Integral to a larger political movement on all levels, this is a demand that law recognize that women live here, too. Every day of our lives.

NOTES

This essay was first published in *Law in Everyday Life* 109 (Austin Sarat and Thomas R. Kearns eds., 1993).

1. See the evocative treatment by Austin Sarat, "'The Law Is All Over': Power, Resistance, and the Legal Ideology of the Welfare Poor," 2 *Yale Journal of Law and the Humanities* 343 (1990).
2. I learned this from working with women in prison in the United States and Canada, specifically at Niantic, Connecticut, and Kingston, Ontario.
3. Rita J. Simon and Jean Landis, *The Crimes Women Commit the Punishments They Receive* (1991).
4. There are striking exceptions like Wanrow v. State of Washington, 88 Wash. 2d 221, 559 P.2d 548 (1977).
5. EEOC v. Sears, 839 F.2d 302 (7th Cir. 1988).
6. Rabidue v. Osceola Refining, 548 F. Supp. 419 (E. D. Mich. 1984); but compare Robinson v. Jacksonville Shipyards, 760 F. Supp. 1486 (D. Fla. 1991).
7. Roe v. Wade, 410 U.S. 113 (1973) (abortion decriminalized); Webster v. Reproductive Health Services, 492 U.S. 490, 518, 529 (1989) (*Roe*'s decriminalization of abortion questioned). See also Planned Parenthood v. Casey, 505 U.S. 833 (1992) (*Roe*'s fundamental holding affirmed).
8. Of course, this would only be effective for the defendant permitted to testify in his own defense, a relatively recent development.
9. People v. Mayberry, 15 Cal. 3d 143, 542 P.2d 1337 (1975); Pappajohn v. The Queen, 11 D.L.R. 3d 1 (1980); DPP v. Morgan, 2411 E.R. 347 (1975).
10. Diana E. H. Russell, *Sexual Exploitation*, 36 (1984). ("[O]nly about 1 in 10 nonmarital rapes in the Russell sample were ever reported to the police.")
11. The Florida Star v. B.J.F., 491 U.S. 524 (1989).
12. See generally, *Senate Judiciary Committee, The Response to Rape: Detours on the Road to Equal Justice,* May 1993.
13. This is documented in Catharine A. MacKinnon, "Reflections on Sex Equality Under Law," 100 *Yale Law Journal* 1281, 1301 n.94 (1991).
14. See Laurie Nsiah-Jefferson, "Reproductive Laws, Women of Color and Low-Income Women," 11 *Women's Rights Law Reporter* 15 (1989).
15. Andrea Dworkin said this in many public speeches in 1982 and 1984. The analysis behind it was originally developed in her *Pornography: Men Possessing Women*, 70–100 (1979).
16. Hudnut v. American Booksellers Ass'n., Inc., 771 F.2d 323 (7th Cir. 1985).
17. See Dailey v. Dailey, 635 S.W.2d 391 (Tenn. Ct. App. 1982); Jacobson v. Jacobson, 314 N.W.2d 78 (N.D. 1981); L. v. D., 630 S.W.2d 240 (Mo. Ct. App. 1982); Constant A. v. Paul C.A., 496 A.2d 1 (Pa. Super. Ct. 1985). But cf. S.N.E. v. R.L.B., 699 P.2d 875 (Alaska 1985); Stroman v. Williams, 353 S.E.2d 704 (S.C. App. Ct. 1987). See also Roe v. Roe, 324 S.E.2d 691 (Va. 1985).
18. See Comment, "The Emerging Constitutional Protection of the Putative Father's Parental Rights," 70 *Michigan Law Review* 1581 (1972); Phyllis Chesler, *Mothers on Trial* (1989).
19. Harris v. McRae, 448 U.S. 297 (1980).
20. Roberson v. Rochester Folding Box Co., 171 N.Y. 538 (1902); Cooley, *Torts,* 4th ed. sec. 135 (1932). See also Samuel D. Warren and Louis D. Brandeis, "The Right to Privacy," 4 *Harvard Law Review* 193 (1890); Samuel Hofstadter and George Horowitz, *The Right to Privacy,* 1–2 (1964).
21. Andrea Dworkin, "A Battered Wife Survives," *Letters from a War Zone,* 100 (1988).
22. On the structural level, see, e.g., Harris v. McRae, 448 U.S. 297 (1980); Deshaney v. Winnebago County Dep't. of Social Services, 489 U.S. 189 (1989). For further discussion, see Catharine A. MacKinnon, *Toward a Feminist Theory of the State,* chap. 10 (1989). For an attempt to reconstruct the privacy right, see Anita Allen, *Uneasy Access: Privacy for Women in a Free Society* (1988).

23. U.S. Equal Employment Opportunity Commission, *Job Patterns for Minorities and Women in Private Industry 1986*, (1988) (occupational segregation by race and sex); Kevin L. Phillips, *The Politics of Rich and Poor*, 202–203 (1990).

24. Russell, *Sexual Exploitation*, 50.

25. Harold Lentzner and Marshall DeBerry, *Intimate Victims: A Study of Violence Among Friends and Relatives* (Bureau of Justice Statistics, U.S. Dept. of Justice, 1980).

R E A D I N G   **87**

What This Nation Really Thinks of Motherhood
Welfare Reform

Ellen Bravo (2007)

America . . . subsidizes births among poor women, who are also disproportionately at the low end of the intelligence distribution. We urge . . . that these policies, represented by the extensive network of cash and services for low-income women who have babies, be ended.

—*Charles Murray,* The Bell Curve[1]

When I was a kid, my father used to tell a riddle that drove me crazy. It went like this (you'll know from the amounts how old this story is): Three salesmen ask a hotel clerk for a shared room. "That'll be thirty dollars," says the clerk. Each man chips in ten bucks. Minutes later, the clerk realizes he's made a mistake—the room costs only twenty-five dollars. He gives the bellboy a five-dollar bill to take back to the men. On the elevator, the bellboy ponders how to divide the five among three people. He decides to give each man a single and keep the remaining two dollars himself.

"Okay," my dad would say, "how much did each man pay?"

"Ten dollars minus one dollar is nine dollars," my sister and I would answer, huddling together. After the first time, we knew what was coming.

"How much did they pay altogether?"

"Twenty-seven dollars."

"And how much does the busboy have?"

"Two dollars!" By now we'd be shrieking.

"Twenty-seven plus two is twenty-nine. Where's the other dollar?"

My sister and I scoured the entire hotel for that dollar, but we never found it. I still remember the day we figured it out—you had to *subtract* the two dollars from twenty-seven to get the actual price of the room (twenty-five), rather than *adding* the two dollars and comparing that to the incorrect price.

In the process, I learned a really important lesson: If you don't frame the problem correctly, you can never get the right solution.

This is just what happened with the disastrous experiment known as welfare reform.

MISDIAGNOSING THE WELFARE PROBLEM

In 1996 Congress passed the Personal Responsibility and Work Opportunity Reconciliation Act to "end welfare as we know it." Our political leaders defined the problem as women who "didn't work" and were "dependent" on taxpayer dollars. The solution: Require the women to work; any job would do. The measure of success would be reducing the numbers on the welfare rolls. The fewer people receiving assistance, the greater the success—regardless of the actual income level or well-being of those who left.

There was, of course, another way to frame the problem: Many mothers whose jobs were undependable and who lacked any other support had no choice but to endure the indignity of public assistance in order to take care of their families. The solution: Value the work of caregiving, reform work to pay a living wage and be flexible for family care, solve the health-care crisis, invest in childcare and education, tackle the root causes of domestic violence. The measure of success would be reduction in poverty and improvements in the living standards and stability of families.

What led the politicians to that first formulation? Almost without exception, those who voted to "end welfare as we know it" had never known welfare—or hunger or poverty or severe economic hardship.[2] Most had never even met an actual welfare recipient. In one fell swoop they ended the nation's commitment to poor children based not on their own experience or research or any sound data. Instead, they relied on the stereotype of welfare recipients as irresponsible women who refused to get a job—as Tommy Thompson put it, "these women [who] won't do their end of the deal by working."[3]

As for opportunity, the Personal Responsibility and Work Opportunity Reconciliation Act created plenty, but not for women and their children. It brought career opportunities for the politicians and a windfall for private contractors. And for some of the Big Boys, the new law represented the prospect of a steady supply of cheap labor.

Myth: The Welfare Queen

The central figure in this drama was the welfare "queen," a stereotype that is all-too-familiar: She starts collecting as a teenage mom, cruises in a Cadillac, pops out babies to haul in bigger bucks, spends her food stamps on drugs or hands the stamps over to her boyfriend so he can spend them on drugs. Too lazy to work, she passes the day watching soaps instead of her kids. She's never held a job. And she's black. Her lifestyle is bankrolled by huge amounts of taxpayer dollars.

Or so we were told. History tells a very different story about who's on welfare, why, for how long, and for what reason.

A little background is instructive. The public assistance program called welfare, formally known as Aid to Families with Dependent Children (AFDC), dates back to 1935. Its purpose was "to release from the wage-earning role the parent whose task is to raise children."[4] Taking care of kids, in short, was thought to be a job. The intended beneficiaries were almost exclusively mothers, but not *all* mothers trying to raise kids on their own. As journalist Jason DeParle points out, divorced and unmarried women were largely excluded, and in the South, so were most blacks.[5] "Southern members of Congress controlled the presiding committees," says DeParle, "and made sure the law did nothing to interfere with the South's supply of cheap field labor."

Things began to change in the 1960s. By then Congress had made it easier for widows to receive more generous Social Security benefits. A combination of the War on Poverty, high unemployment, and welfare rights activism led to greater access for many of those previously excluded, although states were still free to determine their own payment levels. By the time welfare reform was enacted nationwide, nearly four and a half million families were receiving AFDC. As DeParle points out, "while the program once conjured a West Virginia widow, it now brought to mind a black teen mother in a big-city ghetto."[6] The welfare queen stereotype began to take hold.

Reality: Undependable Work

When spinmeisters work their magic, facts tend to fall by the wayside. Here's look at the real story. At the time welfare was "ended," the racial breakdown of those receiving AFDC was about 40 percent white and 40 percent black.[7] The majority of families on welfare consisted of a mother with one or two kids.[8] Contrary to the image of lazy soap watchers, 70 percent of women on welfare were employed or looking for a job.[9] They were *cyclers* (on and off welfare) or *combiners* (people who combined work and welfare because they earned so little, they qualified for assistance). According to a study of six Midwest states by Northern Illinois University, only 6.3 percent of AFDC recipients had never worked; only 3.4 percent were under eighteen.[10]

A big part of the problem was the lack of jobs, even during good times. For every entry-level job in Wisconsin in 1996, there were 3 jobseekers, 7 for every such job in Milwaukee. Change the description to a living wage job and the numbers shot up to 18 jobseekers per opening in Wisconsin, 45 to 99 in Milwaukee.[11] I remember stories on TV showing hundreds of workers camping out and standing in line for hours when some manufacturer announced job openings. How did the politicians tune that out?

As for the cost and value of welfare, consider these numbers: At its peak, AFDC accounted for only 1 percent of the federal budget. Welfare checks did not approach the poverty level in any state in the United States, even combined with the value of food stamps. In 1992, for instance, the average total of a grant plus stamps fell nearly $4,000 below the official poverty line.[12] Not a very royal life.

Some women undoubtedly were guilty of welfare fraud. But when the press tried to track down the prototypical welfare queen, a Chicago woman Ronald Reagan claimed used eighty different names to collect $150,000 in benefits, they found she didn't exist.[13]

As for actual welfare recipients, what were they doing during the times they were on AFDC? Mostly, they were working. They just weren't getting paychecks for that labor, because they were caring for their kids. For the Big Boys, "taking care of children is real work" (as White House Director of Communications Karen Hughes indignantly noted after Teresa Heinz Kerry claimed that Laura Bush never held a "real job")[14]—except when it's done by women who are poor. Whether in the home or in paid jobs caring for other people's loved ones, caregiving is consistently devalued by those in power in the ways they count most—status and compensation.

Reality: Needing Time to Care

Anyone who's spent time among women receiving welfare has known people who wound up on AFDC because they were a good mother or daughter or niece. Clarence Thomas's sister, much maligned by him in a 1980 speech to conservative Republicans as someone who "gets mad when the mailman is late with her check—that's how dependent she is,"[15] in fact was taking time off her two minimum-wage jobs to care for *their* aunt, who'd had a stroke. Lack of leave or flexibility drove many women to public assistance when a loved one fell ill.

Women on welfare mostly found it humiliating.[16] But for low-wage workers ineligible for unemployment insurance, welfare was how you made do when you got laid off. For those unfamiliar with the law or unable to afford a lawyer, it was also where you turned when you got fired—including for being pregnant. For many, it gave a way out of violence, an end to dependence on a man who caused harm.[17] To some it represented a way to get health insurance for a kid, or to avoid having to leave young children home alone. And for others, it was simply the only way they could eat and feed their families.

Some women, of course, signed up for welfare simply because they could. It was one among many sources of income, none sufficient on its own. Some welfare recipients abused their children or were addicted to drugs—just like some middle-class and wealthy people. But the Big Boys painted them all with the same "bad mother" brush.

. . .

Myth: Dependency on a Handout

"Ending the cycle of dependency" is the mantra of welfare reform, as illustrated by the Clarence Thomas quote about his sister. The question is, Who's dependent on whom?

New York Times reporter Jason DeParle followed three Milwaukee area women over seven years to gauge the impact of welfare reform in Wisconsin. In the process, he traced a relative of two of the women back to the sharecropping system in the Mississippi Delta. Sharecropping, says DeParle, had "only one theme: The need for cheap and abundant (in this case, black) labor. . . . Perhaps nowhere was the prosperity of the white elite as dependent on perpetuating a large black underclass."[18]

Reality: Dependency on Cheap Labor

What do you know, welfare reform turns out to have the same driving force (or at least the same result)—reliable, you-don't-have-to-search-for-it, they-won't-raise-a-fuss-about-it cheap labor. Tommy Thompson, then governor of Wisconsin, said as much to a gathering of restaurant owners in 1988; excerpts of his address were broadcast on public radio.

At the time restaurants and other low-wage employers were having trouble finding enough people to work at minimum and near-minimum wages. What about the law of supply and demand?, you might ask. If employers can't find workers at the going rate, they'll have to pay more. This is how the market's supposed to work—unless the supply side can be manipulated. Instead of encouraging a pay adjustment, Tommy Thompson told his pals not to worry about how they'd fill those slots. Welfare reform, he assured them, would solve the problem. He was designing a program which would turn out to be the precursor to reform on the national level, one that demanded "work first"—or in plain language, "work or else." Women would be required to take a job, in most cases the first one offered. So much for the marketplace.

Angie and Jewell, two of the three women DeParle writes about, "succeeded" in moving off welfare under Thompson's plan. The problem was, their success amounted to finding low-wage jobs. They were still poor. They still had trouble paying the bills and scrounging up enough food. They needed to double up to afford housing. But unlike before, they were unavailable to their children, who suffered the consequences. Angie's four children all ran into problems, according to DeParle. The youngest, Darrell, suffered from unexplained seizures which a friend of Angie's thought might be "psychosomatic, a lonely boy's bid for attention."[19] Von, who did the best academically, finished his freshman year in high school with a grade point average of 0.2. His older brother, Redd, dropped out of school after failing ninth grade twice and began thinking about selling drugs, saying, "I'm tired of not having no money." Kesha, the firstborn, had a baby at seventeen and

left school. Jewell's son, Terrell, began cutting school and hanging out with what his mother considered the wrong crowd.

Angie, Jewell, and Opal, DeParle's third subject, had been on welfare for long stretches of time. Even if the average stay was two years or less, some people seemed to linger. Research shows that half of those long-term recipients had significant problems that could interfere with working, including severely limited cognitive abilities, depression, medical disabilities, and cocaine use (Opal fell into this category). Multiple problems were not uncommon.[20] Forced work would not cause these situations to improve.

For most women on welfare, in short, the problem was not "dependency," but the fact that employment and other systems like education, mental health, and substance abuse treatment were undependable, and that caregiving was not considered to be work.

A genuine system of reform would address all these problems. The one we have operates as if they didn't exist.

Why the New System Was Doomed to Fail

The program that replaced AFDC is known as Temporary Assistance for Needy Families, or TANF. Tommy Thompson, promoted to secretary of Health and Human Services under George W. Bush, proclaimed TANF the "greatest social policy change in this nation in 60 years."[21] And that it was, if by "great" we understand scale as opposed to value: The dismantling of the safety net was unprecedented. No longer would mothers (or fathers) raising children automatically be supported if they found themselves on their own and without sufficient income. States had the option of limiting assistance to two years; none could provide it for longer than five. In addition, for the first time, states were allowed to hand over the job of implementing such a program to private, for-profit agencies.

Ask the women who'd had to use public assistance and they'd tell you in a heartbeat that the system needed reform. But their wish list grew out of a clear goal: They wanted out of poverty.

Those who designed welfare reform had a different goal in mind. At best, they saw work as uplifting. At worst, they wanted a captive cheap labor force and a scapegoat—if taxpayers could focus their anger on the welfare queen, they might be less demanding about their own falling wages and rising health-care costs. Almost all who voted for "ending welfare" sought political capital by pandering to popular prejudice. Ending poverty, a path to decent jobs—these weren't part of the picture for most of those politicians.

Not surprisingly, TANF (and its precursor in Wisconsin, Wisconsin Works or W-2) failed to build in a method to track those who moved off assistance. The policymakers assumed that anyone no longer on the rolls was employed, and that employment was an end in itself. What if the jobs turned out to be low-wage, too few hours, unpredictable shifts? Not a problem to Jason Turner. He's the guy hired by Thompson in 1993 to redesign the welfare program in Milwaukee. As DeParle points out, "Turner's fascination with welfare began in a place where it didn't exist—the leafy precincts of Darien, Connecticut,"[22] when he happened to read an article in *U.S. News and World Report* about the growing number of people who "didn't work" and instead received "government charity." The news floored him. Jason Turner was twelve years old and attending prep school and he'd found his mission in life.

Later he would describe his belief in the power of work, no matter what kind, by asserting, "It's work that sets you free." (DeParle notes that Turner apparently didn't realize he was quoting the motto on the gates of Auschwitz.)[23] The architect of W-2 had no illusions about the quality of the jobs available to those receiving welfare. In fact, Turner told a gathering in Milwaukee, he modeled W-2 on the lives of low-wage workers.[24] If those women couldn't get a day off when their kids were sick, by golly, neither would anyone on W-2. If they had to scramble to figure out child-care for an evening shift, why should W-2 participants expect anything different?

Never mind that in the past those same low-wage workers had AFDC as a safety net between jobs.

Reality: Free Work

Turner and others extolled a feature of W-2 called "Community Service Jobs" or CSJs (known as workfare in other places). Typically CSJs were supposed to provide valuable work experience and skills to someone with little work history. Women would receive their W-2 grant rather than a wage, but in return they'd become more marketable.

Meet Venez Blackman, who in 2004 spent ten months working a CSJ in the emergency room of a major hospital in Milwaukee. At the age of thirty-four, Blackman has a high school diploma, some college courses, lots of workforce experience, and lots of spunk. She turned to W-2 "as a last last LAST resort"[25] after being laid off and seeing her unemployment payments run out. She'd already tried various temp jobs but needed something more reliable to support herself and her eight-year-old son.

Once on W-2, Blackman was required to attend various classes on job readiness. "They tell you, 'Don't talk slang or wear hootchie shorts to the interview,'" Blackman told the state's head of the W-2 program, "stuff I already knew. They don't ask you what your career goals are or get to know you as a person." Everyone seemed to be assigned to a CSJ regardless of work experience.

"The only reason I took that CSJ was that I thought it would lead to a job," Blackman insisted. But month after month, despite good reviews, hospital personnel said they just weren't hiring. They got ten months of free labor and Venez Blackman got ten months of time on her welfare clock—the amount of time she could receive W-2, which now had a lifetime limit of two years.

Shocking? Wait until you meet Jackie Caruso, also a veteran worker who ended up on W-2 after a layoff. Her CSJ was at McDonald's (how's that for community service!), where she was supposed to receive managerial training. "I never got past the cash register and fry maker," Caruso said.[26]

Many TANF recipients did find jobs, although they didn't always last very long. Gena Mitchell worked at a large postage meter company in Savannah, Georgia. She described a revolving door of hiring black women who'd been receiving public assistance—either welfare or, as in Mitchell's case, Supplemental Security Income (SSI) for a son with a medical disability.[27]

During the job interview, the personnel manager encouraged Mitchell to talk about her family situation and then offered sympathy for her son's situation, asking how Mitchell managed and whether she received any assistance from the government. "When I told them I got SSI," Mitchell explained, "she gave me what she said was a routine form that allows the government to know they will be employing someone with a very ill child. Only after I was fired did I find out they got $3,000 for me—that form got them a tax credit." Gena Mitchell also found out the company that year hired and fired 740 black women, most former welfare recipients, to get those tax credits. For each recipient hired, the company got the tax, no matter how long they kept them on.

. . .

Reality: Welfare for Business

Hmm, handouts of cash as entitlements, with almost no monitoring or accountability. Sounds like conservatives' descriptions of welfare. Except the recipients in this case are profit-making and often highly profitable enterprises.

In Wisconsin and many other states, the freebies extended to for-profit social-service agencies overseeing the TANF contracts. Many who left the welfare rolls under their watch didn't actually find jobs. Not to worry. Agencies were rewarded for lowering the number on welfare regardless of whether those "welfare leavers" were better or worse off. Wisconsin's program was set up with what was known as a "light touch"—translation: If they don't ask, we won't tell. Agency staff was to respond only to what applicants specifically requested. If someone didn't know to inquire about emergency housing assistance, for example, she shouldn't receive any information on that program, even if she were eligible and her chances at success would be enhanced by it.

The profit motive provided an ugly added attraction to deny people aid. It also meant that a much bigger chunk of the funding got swallowed up in administrative costs than was the case under AFDC. Peruse the Milwaukee press and you'll find headlines of huge executive salaries, financial mismanagement, corruption, and graft associated with W-2 agencies. For all the talk about cheating by welfare recipients and the need for stronger enforcement, most of the scandals involving the W-2 agencies brought no action or a mere slap on the wrist during the Thompson administration.[28]

Reality: Inadequate Work Supports

Everyone knew low-wage jobs in themselves couldn't provide a decent living. And most decision-makers had figured out that you couldn't expect women to work if their kids didn't have someone to watch them. As a result, work supports such as food stamps, childcare assistance, health-care programs, and the like were built into TANF.

But the shortsightedness about employment extended to work supports as well. Many women who are eligible for childcare subsidies are not taking advantage of them because they can't afford the co-payment. Fifty dollars a week seems like a dream payment to many parents, but for those earning less than $15,000 a year, it's a lot of money. A corporate manager encouraging employers to hire more women off welfare told me the story of a group of bakery workers in Detroit brought in to work the midnight shift. The owner of the bakery was quite pleased with the former welfare recipients' work ethic and competency. But he was puzzled by one thing: Every time they had a break, the women would go out to the parking lot, even when it was bitter cold. Turned out their kids were sleeping in the cars.

Other eligible for subsidies but not using them cite a lack of eligible providers in their community, or a lack of trust in the quality of care. These women would like to give the subsidy to a relative, but often these grandmothers and aunts aren't certified as childcare providers, and therefore are disqualified.

. . .

So how are things going in the post-welfare world? Some women got decent jobs, just as they had under AFDC. Given the limits on access to education, however, most welfare "leavers" who are employed are stuck in low-paying jobs. Half or more are still living in poverty, a greater number than before in extreme poverty.[29] More of these children are among the nearly 4 million middle school kids (and 40,000 kindergarteners) described as being in "self care"—that means they're home alone.[30] Many states have long waiting lists for childcare. Families may not be lining the streets, as some envisioned—but many are squeezed into housing where they double and triple up with relatives or friends. One grandmother told me how her daughter spent the night in the emergency room with horrible stomach pains. After hours of tests, the doctors told her the diagnosis: "You're starving." The woman hadn't wanted to ask her mother, who was already providing shelter and food for the babies, for anything more for herself.

The architects of welfare reform did achieve their goal of cutting the rolls—but they didn't save taxpayers money, especially given administrative costs and profits to private agencies, and they certainly didn't enhance the quality of life for most former recipients. Because they misdiagnosed the problem, their solution was doomed from the start.

FEMINIST SOLUTIONS

Solving the problem of welfare requires different premises, goals, and strategies from those the Big Boys used. For starters, the real objectives have to be ending poverty and supporting families. Given that most women end up on welfare because of problems with employment, the focus should be reform of *work*. Specifically, that means decent pay, flexibility for family care, universal health care, and quality childcare. Women moving off welfare, like all workers, need the right to organize. Workers earning low wages need greater access to income supports, but above all, we need to raise the wage floor. Improved transportation systems are crucial—but creating jobs where

people live, and affordable housing near outlying jobs, are even better solutions.

Any program to end poverty will target ways to create family-supporting jobs, as well as education and training aimed at linking people with such jobs. That requires careful partnerships with workforce investment programs and with technical and four-year colleges. It will also involve more on-the-job training and courses delivered at worksites on released time.

Supporting families means valuing the work of caring for family members. For those with infants or short-term emergency care situations, the answer is sufficient and affordable leave—and a safety net of public support for those who need it. Those tending to a disabled family member should be able to receive pay for providing that care at the same level the state pays a private care worker. If the caregiver is able to work part time, equitable treatment for part-time workers will help, but some people may need supplemental assistance if those wages falls short.

Enlarging the Caregiver Tax Credit and making it fully refundable for those without a taxable income will also help, as well as having Social Security cover years spent out of the workforce to care for a family member. These tax policies are ways to acknowledge that all the tasks involved with raising kids or nursing a sick loved one do, in fact, constitute work and should be supported by a society that values families.

The safety net that remains must be reasonable, humane, and inclusive, without time limits, and without excluding immigrants. Rather than assuming abuse, it will seek to help each person be successful. The program will take the advice of people who have known welfare firsthand. "Address the whole person," Venez Blackman urges. "We just want opportunity. Don't assume I'm going to make bad of an opportunity when you haven't given me one." Coaching and meaningful choices will accommodate most people.

For agencies providing service, states will have to ensure accountability related to effective outcomes. That means requiring a high bar for training that speaks to people's actual skills, health, and life situations. Once people are ready, it means demanding placements in good jobs and monitoring agencies carefully to make sure those standards are met.

For such changes to work, they must be linked to reform in other systems. Given the close association between domestic violence and women needing assistance, welfare reform needs to go hand-in-hand with efforts to end violence and foster equality in personal relationships. Child support programs must be strengthened—but they also have to help fathers find meaningful work, not just send them to jail, especially if they happen to be nonwhite.[31] Real economic development that slashes poverty, small class sizes and other educational reforms that increase graduation rates, greater access to higher education and to treatment for mental health problems and addiction—these and other changes will reduce the *need* for assistance.

. . .

NOTES

1. Richard J. Herrnstein and Charles Murray, *The Bell Curve: Intelligence and Class Structure in American Life* (New York: The Free Press 1994), 548.
2. Three exceptions come to mind—Cong. Lynn Woolsey, Cong. Barbara Leigh, and Sen. Patti Murray had each been on welfare at some point. They voted against the bill, known as the Personal Responsibility and Work Opportunity Reconciliation Act, or PRWORA.
3. Letter to then-archbishop Rembert Weakland, who had expressed concerns about W-2. See "Governor Tells Bishop to 'Read His Bible,'" *Christian Century*, Oracle Publishing Co. (July 17, 1996): 711.
4. 1935 Senate Finance Committee Report on the President's Economic Security Bill, *Social Security Online:* http://www.ssa.gov/history/reports/35seatereport .html. Cited in Jason DeParle, *American Dream: Three Women, Ten Kids, and a Nation's Drive to End Welfare* (New York: Viking Press, 2004), 86.
5. According to Jason DeParle, AFDC tried to make a national program out of a hodgepodge of Mothers' Pensions established in the states to keep poor children out of orphanages. Like those programs, it was intended for "fit" parents—meaning white and widowed. Congress allowed states to set payments as low as they wanted and to determine their own eligibility rules, eliminating language seen as prohibiting racial discrimination (*American Dream: Three Women, Ten Kids, and a Nation's Drive to End Welfare* [New York: Viking Press, 2004], 86).
6. Ibid., 92.
7. The racial breakdown for AFDC recipients in 1994 was as follows: White 37 percent, Black 36 percent, Hispanic 20 percent, Asian 3 percent, Native American 1 percent, and Unknown 2 percent. U.S. Department of Health and Human Services, Office of Family Assistance, 2004. Cited in Sanford F. Schram, "Contextualizing Racial Disparities in American Welfare Reform: Toward a New Poverty Research," in *Perspectives on Politics* 3, no. 2 (June 2005): 258.
8. "Welfare Myths: Fact of Fiction? Exploring the Truth about Welfare," National Center for Law and Economic Justice (Formerly the Welfare Law Center) (1986): http://www.welfarelaw.org/myths.html.
9. Roberta Spalter-Roth et al., *Welfare That Works: The Working Lives of AFDC Recipients* (Washington, DC: Institute for Women's Policy Research, 1995).
10. Paul Kleppner and Nikolas Theodore, *Work After Welfare: Is the Midwest's Booming Economy Creating Enough Jobs?* (Dekalb, IL: Midwest Job Gap Project, 1997).
11. Ibid.
12. Jason DeParle, *American Dream: Three Women, Ten Kids, and a Nation's Drive to End Welfare* (New York: Viking Press, 2004), 92.
13. Steve Kangas, "Poverty and Welfare," *Liberalism Resurgent* (1994): www.huppi.com/kangaroo/7Welfare .htm.
14. Heinz Kerry, who made the remark during the 2004 presidential campaign, quickly apologized. See "Teresa Heinz Kerry apologizes for Laura Bush comment," *USA Today* (October 20, 2004).
15. Quoted in Juan Williams, "A Question of Fairness," *Atlantic Monthly*, February 1987.
16. For two years, 9to5 and the Radcliffe Public Policy Center conducted research on low-wage workers in Boston, Denver, and Milwaukee to see how they "crossed the boundaries" between work, family, and community. Of the scores of women interviewed who had experience with welfare, not one wanted to be on assistance. See Lisa Dodson and Ellen Bravo, "Keeping Jobs and Raising Families in Low-Income America: It Just Doesn't Work" (Boston: Harvard University, 2002), http://www .radcliffe.edu/research/pubpol/boundaries.pdf.
17. Research shows that about 20 percent of women receiving cash assistance are current victims of domestic violence, while about 50 to 60 percent

have experienced domestic violence during their adulthood. Nisha Patel and Vicki Turetsky, "Safety in the Safety Net: TANF Reauthorization Provisions Relevant to Domestic Violence" Pub No. 04–48 (Washington, DC: Center on Law and Social Policy, October 22, 2004). DeParle notes that Newt Gingrich argued to end welfare by pointing to "twelve-year-olds having babies." Hattie Mae Crenshaw, the mother of one of the three women DeParle followed for several years, was "the rare woman who really did get pregnant at twelve"—after being raped. Hattie Mae did go on AFDC, and as a result, was able to move and get away from her rapist (Jason DeParle, *American Dream: Three Women, Ten Kids, and a Nation's Drive to End Welfare* [New York: Viking Press, 2004], 35).

18. In person interview, May 22, 2003, 26. Cheating is another common accusation leveled at women on welfare. They were all blamed for it, and some of them did, in fact, have jobs they didn't report while receiving a check. Given how little income welfare provided, this shouldn't surprise us. But abuse of the welfare system pales in comparison to the long history of cheating poor blacks. DeParle cites a 1939 work by anthropologist Hortense Powdermaker, who traveled extensively, examining the living conditions of blacks in the South. "She was startled at how openly planters talked of cheating," DeParle writes. "They justified it by arguing that 'the Negro is congenitally lazy and must be kept in debt in order to be made to work'" (Powdermaker, *After Freedom* [1939; repr., Madison: University of Wisconsin Press, 1993]: 22–23, cited in Jason DeParle).

19. Ibid.

20. One third have severely limited cognitive abilities, 13 percent near-daily bouts of depression, 10 percent medical disabilities, and 9 percent problems from cocaine use. Ibid., 93, citing Krista K. Olson and LaDonna Pavetti, "Personal and Family Challenges to the Successful Transition from Welfare to Work," The Urban Institute, May 17, 1996.

21. "Remarks by HHS Secretary Tommy G. Thompson: Presentation of The President's Fiscal Year 2003 Budget for the U.S. Department of Health and Human Services," *United States Department of Health and Human Services,* press release (February 4, 2002): http://www.hhs.gov/news/press/2002pres/20020204b.html.

22. Jason DeParle, *American Dream: Three Women, Ten Kids, and a Nation's Drive to End Welfare* (New York: Viking Press, 2004), 162 ff.

23. Ibid.

24. Forum on W-2 at the Italian Community Center in Milwaukee, sponsored by the Interfaith Conference of Greater Milwaukee, October 1, 2004.

25. Conversation with the head of Wisconsin's Workforce Solutions program, January 13, 2005.

26. Ibid.

27. Phone interview, June 15, 2001.

28. Department of Workforce Development is now working with advocates to develop accountability guidelines, but problems of discouraging applicants remain.

29. Gregory Acs and Pamela Loprest, "Final Synthesis Report of Findings from ASPE '"Leavers' Grants'" (Washington, DC: The Urban Institute, November 27, 2001). A 2005 report by the Legislative Audit Bureau in Wisconsin found that only 42.1 percent of those who left W-2 in 1999 earned more than the poverty level in 2003—and that's only when you count the state and federal earned income tax credits. During the first year after leaving the program, only one in five earned more than the poverty level (www.legis.state.wi.us/LAB/reports/05-6 Highlights.htm).

30. Gretchen Wright, "American After 3PM: First-Ever National Household Survey On How Kids Spend the After School Hours to be Released," *Afterschool Alliance,* news release (May 19, 2004): http://www.afterschoolalliance.org/press_archives/America_3pm.pdf. The group found that 25 percent of African American students from kindergarten through twelfth grade take care of themselves after the school day ends. See Gretchen Wright, "One in Four African American Students Care for Themselves After the School Day Ends, Study Finds," *Afterschool/Alliance,* news release (June 15, 2004): pdhttp://www.afterschoolalliance.org/press_archives/america_3pm/african_american_pr.pdf

31. Racism has been a problem in some programs to deal with "deadbeat dads." In Dane County, Wisconsin, for example, arrest rates for African Americans for nonpayment of child support have been shown to be 35 times those of white residents. Nearly one in two of those arrested for this reason were African Americans in a county whose 2000 African American population was 4 percent of the total county population. (Rebecca May and Marguerite Roulet, "A Look at Arrests of Low-Income Fathers for Child Support Nonpayment," *Center for Family Policy and Practice* [January 2005], http://www.cffpp.org/publications/pdfs/noncompliance.pdf.

She Who Believes in Freedom
Young Women Defy the Prison Industrial Complex

Robin Templeton (2004)

In 2001 the prison population in the United States exceeded 2 million people, most of them illiterate, most under- or unemployed, most in jail for non-violent crimes, and a vast majority people of color. The gargantuan total of 6.5 million people in the United States are under some form of correctional supervision.[1]

Twenty-three-year-old Alicia Yang is trying to lower those numbers by dedicating her life to fighting the prison industrial complex. She says, "I know we need to build a fierce, strategic movement to deal with the prison crisis, but I also know we need to take care of people, to reach into people's hearts. We need to heal communities. Ultimately, we need to create a society that's based on redemption, a society that would refuse to allow 2 million people, most of them poor, to be locked up in cages."

Yang's cousin became one of the numbers when he got a life sentence in a California penitentiary. Like many young women who share her opposition to mass incarceration, Yang is driven by more than political analysis. She says she was reborn as an anti-incarceration activist because her cousin's imprisonment is like having part of her soul locked away. Then, shifting in her seat, she raises her voice and ebulliently describes visiting her cousin behind bars and getting to know some of the men with whom he's jailed: "They showed me the resiliency of the human spirit and allowed me—for the first time in my life—to really taste freedom."

How does freedom taste? "It's not like a flavor but a focus," Yang explains. "I examined my own life and started taking freedom very seriously. This fight against the prison industrial complex is a freedom struggle. Because prisons destroy and enslave life, the focus of our work against prisons has to be restoring life, liberating life."

Like slavery, that other "peculiar institution," prisons decimate life by stealing people from their communities, forcing families apart, and converting human beings into disposable parts that generate immense profit for private interests. The punishment sector has been one of the fastest-growing and most lucrative industries in the United States. Most prisoners do some form of work under repressive conditions and earn pennies per hour. Prisoners provide a pool of cheap labor that can be infinitely filled and exponentially enlarged. Eighteen private prison companies do business in the United States—Corrections Corporation of America and Wackenhut are the largest, operating eighty-one and fifty-two prisons respectively—and hundreds more corporations contract with publicly "owned" prisons to sell goods and services, usually at inflated, "captive market" prices. All the while, the institution perpetuates its legitimacy by criminalizing and bestializing the very lives it controls.

Yang's prison visits became for her an experience of restoring dignity and resurrecting hope in the face of a machine that dehumanizes life at a scale that is nearly—considering that African-American men have a greater than one in four chance of being incarcerated—genocidal. Visits with her cousin led Yang to teach in a prison-based adult education program. Subsequently, she started organizing on police and prison-related issues with an organization in Oakland called Asian American Youth Promoting Advocacy and Leadership. She explains, "We'd present workshops breaking down the prison industrial complex—using all the economic arguments about how much it costs to lock someone up and the terrible statistics about how many people of color are behind bars. But more and more, I just wanted to talk to people in my community about healing. I really wanted to stop and say: 'We won't be whole until we bring our sisters and brothers home from prison; until we learn to trust and forgive each other.'"

SISTERS AT THE CENTER OF THE PRISON CRISIS

In the tenacity of her convictions as well as in her vacillation on what is to be done about the prison industrial complex, Alicia Yang is not alone. A new generation of young people is at the forefront of grassroots organizing against mass incarceration in the United States. They are demanding accountability from law enforcement and corrections agencies that are rife with abuse. And they are organizing toward investing prison funds in rebuilding eviscerated social programs, especially schools, instead.

According to data compiled by the Prison Activist Resource Center, over the past twenty years, at the local, state, and federal levels, spending on incarceration has increased 571 percent while spending on K–12 education has risen only 33 percent. The number of prison guards has increased 250 percent while the number of K–12 teachers has dropped by 8 percent. And over the past two decades, while the number of students graduating from high school has dropped by 2.7 percent, the number of people filling the nation's prisons and jails has increased by over 400 percent.[2]

Because the vast majority of these prisoners are incarcerated for nonviolent offenses, young antiprison activists say that prisons should not be a default public works program. People living in poverty and facing structural racism should have their basic human needs met, should have access to good schools and jobs, and should get treatment, not punishment, if they develop an addiction. But while the activists' goal is to create a society in which the prison industrial complex is unnecessary, they know that violent crime is a pernicious reality and that members of their communities need to be protected from it. In response to critics who say that violent criminals must be kept off the street, activists who want to shut down the prison industrial complex say that the priority should be changing the socioeconomic conditions which create violence. When asked about the child murderers, rapists, and serial killers, these activists do not readily contend that these few members of the population should not be kept away from the public. But, they underscore, people convicted of violent offenses are only a small fraction of those in prison and are illegitimately used to justify the buildup of a massive industry. And, they remind their critics, one of the most violent demographic groups in the United States is white men in their thirties, a segment of the population grossly underrepresented in the prison system.

Today women in general and young women in particular are the fastest-growing segments of the prison population in the United States. The prison crisis is for young women of color and poor women a double-edged sword: They have to take care of families, pick up the broken pieces, and earn income when men are removed from their communities. And they are increasingly entangled in the criminal justice system themselves. Dozens of criminal justice organizers have told me that the harder the system clamps down on young women, the harder they fight back. By founding grassroots organizations or taking control of preexisting ones in their communities, advocating that social services meet their and their children's needs so that they do not end up in the criminal justice system, and creating new forms of cultural expression that challenge criminalization, young women are disproportionately assuming leadership in the nascent movement against the prison industrial complex.

Largely as a result of their foremothers' work, young women are redefining grassroots leadership by ensuring that everyone is given credit for her work behind the scenes, building organizations from the bottom up, and constantly cultivating new leadership. But the scale of the prison crisis is also drawing on and pulling out something deeper. Young women are determined to fight prisons but also—at the risk of sounding biologically deterministic—to nurture human beings.

. . .

MEET THE INCARCERATION GENERATION

Third wave feminists are the daughters of the "baby boomer" women's libbers of the 1960s and '70s. Those of us in the "third wave" are now in our twenties and thirties. The spike in prison construction in the United States began in our formative years, exactly coinciding with our maturation. The number of prison inmates in the United States quadrupled from 1980 to 2000, from 500,000 to 2 million.[3] During this time the U.S. population grew only 20 percent. California particularly dramatizes the prison boom of the last two decades of the twentieth century. In 1980 the state had twelve prisons. By 1998 it was home to thirty-three prisons but had constructed only one new state university.[4] In other words, young women have grown up with the biggest, most catastrophic prison boom in world history. Young women of color and low-income young women bring to the antiprison movement knowledge that they must respond not only to the social and economic conditions of those whose lives are torn apart by the powers that punish but also to their personal and spiritual needs.

America imprisons more human beings per capita than any country on the planet, with the exception of Rwanda. It costs about $41 billion a year for the United States to warehouse its 2 million prisoners.[5] Even adjusting for inflation, overall criminal justice spending has nearly doubled since the mid-1980s. And relative to population growth, per capita prison spending increased 69 percent, from $217 to $366, from 1983 to 1995.[6] These increases are irrational because exorbitant prison spending is throwing money at a problem that does not exist. The last time crime rates increased in the United States was between 1965 and 1973. Since then general crime trends have been stable or declined. From 1991 to 1998, violent crime in the United States fell by 25 percent.[7]

Most of these tough-on-crime dollars are spent incapacitating people for nonviolent offenses. Over the past twenty years, the growth of the nonviolent prison population has far outpaced the incarceration rate for violent offenders: 77 percent of those entering prisons and jails are sentenced for nonviolent offenses. From 1980 to 1997, the number of prisoners charged with violent offenses doubled while the number of nonviolent prisoners tripled, and the number of people convicted for drug offenses increased elevenfold. These numbers are steeper still for women. Eighty-five percent of women are imprisoned for nonviolent offenses.[8]

The drive to lock up nonviolent prisoners is all the more pernicious given that prisons constitute one of the United States' most well-endowed public works programs. The prison industrial complex—fueled by the War on Crime and the War on Drugs much as the Cold War drove its military predecessor—delivers big profits to private prison contractors and service providers, economic development for depressed rural areas, and jobs to blue-collar workers facing a deindustrialized economy. Working people from urban areas are increasingly removed from their communities to work in far-flung rural communities. The runaway growth of the U.S. prison system also corresponds—not coincidentally—with the structural decimation of public policy responses to poverty and other social problems.

The California Bay Area youth organizer Raquel Laviña offers this economic analysis: "For young women of color and poor women, it's not only that we're getting harassed by police and more and more often going to prison, but that the community is a different place when so many people get taken away. There are so many young women without their babies' fathers because over half of the men in their community are either dead or in jail. Women of color feel a responsibility for the men in our community. We have to hold the liberation of men and women at the same time."

Laviña explains that the prison industrial complex is a primary point of struggle for her generation and for those coming up after her: "It's a symbol of the freedom we don't have. There are so many things impacting young people of color and poor youth—poverty, homelessness, substandard education. But the police coming at you and taking people away from your community is immediate and direct. The others are more slow-burn ways of killing you. You know the police aren't there to protect you but the business across the street."

WOMEN AND GIRLS ON LOCKDOWN

Hermon Getachew, twenty-one-year-old director of the organization Sister Outsider in the Brownsville and East Flatbush neighborhoods of Brooklyn, knows that many young women are motivated by their own experiences to organize for a just criminal justice system. "I've had a lot of encounters with the police," Getachew says. "It really hits home, the women you see in jail— they're just there on bench warrants, drug charges, and for self-defense. Girls end up in the system when they're just trying to support themselves. It just boils down to money. I know women who have to support themselves and their families at the age of fourteen, and no one is trying to give those women, especially those from immigrant communities, a job."

While prison spending siphons employment and education resources out of needy communities, "prisons do not disappear problems, they disappear human beings," charges the lifelong antiprison activist Angela Y. Davis.[9] Increasingly, prisons are disappearing "problematic" women. According to the National Council on Crime and Delinquency, twenty-five years ago women were virtually invisible in the criminal justice system. Today more than 140,000 women are in U.S. prisons and jails, nearly triple the number in 1985. The number of women imprisoned in California alone is nearly twice that of women incarcerated nationwide thirty years ago. African-American women, the fastest-growing segment of the U.S. prison population, are incarcerated at a rate eight times that of white women. Latina women are incarcerated at four times the rate of white women.

Seventy percent of women in prison have been convicted of nonviolent offenses, and 80 percent of adult women prisoners have children—most are single mothers of children under eighteen. Half of all women imprisoned in the United States are African-American. As a result of War on Drugs legislation like mandatory minimums, women are twice as likely as men to be incarcerated for drug-related offenses. Men, however, are more likely than women to receive drug treatment.[10]

From 1930 to 1950, a total of five women's prisons were built in the United States. During the 1980s alone, thirty-four were constructed. According to a recent Amnesty International report: "Even this could not keep pace with the swelling numbers of women in prison. Women's prisons are understaffed, overcrowded, lack recreation facilities, serve poor quality food, suffer chronic shortages of family planning counselors and services, obstetrics and gynecological specialists, drug treatment and childcare facilities, and transportation funds for family visits—which are necessary due to the remote locations of the women's prisons. A 2000 study by the General Accounting Office, commissioned by the Washington, D.C., congressional delegate Eleanor Holmes Norton, found that women in prison are more likely to suffer from HIV infection and mental illness than are incarcerated men.[11]

Like adult women, girls have become increasingly caught up in the criminal justice system in recent decades. Between 1993 and 1997, in almost every offense category, increases in arrests were greater—or decreases in arrests were smaller— for girls than for boys. Research on girls in detention consistently shows that girls rarely pose a threat to others' safety but that they are at the highest risk levels for becoming substance addicted and sexually active, and for failing out of school. "Tragically," says a report by the National Council on Crime and Delinquency, "these problems are almost always correlated with histories of violent victimization, poverty, and deeply fragmented families and public service systems."[12] According to the American Bar Association, between 1988 and 1997 delinquency cases involving girls jumped 83 percent. The spike was not in response to increased crime or violence by girls but rather "re-labeling of family conflicts as violent offenses, gender bias in the processing of minor offenses, changes in police practice . . . and a lack of services aimed at helping troubled girls."[13]

Further, the criminalization of poor people is a double-edged swipe at women, who are disproportionately poor. Two-thirds of adults living in poverty in the United States are women, and the poverty rate for children in female-headed households is over 50 percent. In fact, the wage gap between male and female workers is declining only because the real earnings of low-income men are falling. A female worker still earns seventy-two cents to a man's dollar.[14]

Suemyra Shah, a nineteen-year-old board member of the National Coalition to Abolish the Death Penalty, speaks to the prison system's dual attack on poor young women. "Young women are especially affected because we've always been the keepers of the family. Women have always played a central role, not only in leading political struggles but also in centering and preserving life. And it's escalating now, with the [criminal justice] system taking so many young people away from the community."

. . .

IN OUR HANDS

In response to the punitive zeal fueling the prison industrial complex, the leadership of the up-and-coming antiprison movement—with young women at the forefront—is decidedly interested in redemption. The inclusive style of leadership that young women bring to this seedling movement is rooted in a strong belief in community, passed down, perhaps, by grandmothers raising many of the 1.5 million children otherwise rendered parentless by prisons in this country. It is a method of leadership as

determined to tackle adversaries as it is to build hope by reclaiming human beings from a system that irredeemably labels them "criminal." The processes of hope, restoration, and bringing people back into their communities are personal. But they are also political acts because they reverse the cultural and socioeconomic process of criminalization that vilifies people who are desperate for resources and isolated from others. This is not to say that "criminalized" people do not perform criminal acts. But young women who critique the criminal justice system are saying—at their peers' parole hearings, when they talk to the media, in hip-hop lyrics, and in conversation over the dinner table—that criminal mistakes should not define the sum total of one's humanity.

. . .

Maintaining a relationship with a loved one or family member behind bars begins at the level of individual experience but extends into the realm of collective accountability. "You have no idea what it's like to love someone who is being tortured inside a prison. You never get used to living with so much horror," says asha bandele, an editor at *Essence* magazine and author of *The Prisoner's Wife*. bandele describes how this experience stretches into the domain of collective responsibility: "Whenever I hear of police and prison abuses, it doesn't matter if I know the person or not because it could always be happening to anyone I love.

"I've often wondered," bandele says, "out of all the social justice work that could be my calling, why this work? Why immerse myself in a world where I know that someone I love may be kept from me and the rest of the community forever? I'm finally coming to understand that I do this work because I want to be free."

The work that young women are doing embodies an emphasis on freedom, liberation, and humanity. Recently the Center for Young Women's Development in San Francisco spearheaded a dialogue with young women in juvenile hall about what issues they felt were most pressing. As Lateefah Simon puts it, "We thought it was important to do something in the system where we usually have no power, and could show youth in the hall that things could indeed be changed." Working with the young women in the hall, the center was able to uncover harassment of queer women. Simon notes that, "even though none of our leadership was out and queer, we took on this issue because it came up so much as an issue that was important to the girls in the hall. We are developing their voices and their vision. Recognizing and supporting the fullness of everyone's humanity is embedded in the culture of the organization."

The center organized a group of legal experts to help draft a model policy for the city of San Francisco to address the concerns of queer youth in juvenile detention. As a result of the group's advocacy, and after a long struggle, the mayoral commission on juvenile justice and probation recently adopted the policy the center created—the first of its kind in the nation. The policy stipulates that juvenile hall staff be trained to work with queer youth and that monitoring and oversight be implemented to ensure that the concerns and complaints of queer youth are heard and tended to. Additionally, two center staffers (fifteen and seventeen years old, both former sex workers) were part of a mayoral committee to research and make recommendations to the city council on practical alternatives to incarceration for young women who have been arrested for prostitution. Formerly incarcerated girls (sixteen to nineteen years old) also developed workshops on "how to stay out of the system," which they present as an ongoing program in San Francisco's juvenile hall—a precedent for the facility.

Recognizing the power of the collective efforts of young women, Simon notes, "Our power comes from the truth we speak. We are the first youth who have been through the system to serve on the juvenile probation commission. We told the commission real stories about real youth who have been in the hall. We could tell them which correction officers had been abusive, and we gave them testimony of the girls we work with. This issue is not sexy and it's not easy, but it's proof that we're really going to be doing this work on the inside for the long haul."

NOTES

1. Jerome Miller, "American Gulag," *YES! Magazine* 15 (February 2000), http://www.futurenet.org/15prisons/miller.htm.
2. Prison Activist Resource Center, "Education vs. Incarceration: A Stacked Deck," http://www.prisonactivist.org/factsheets/ed-vs-inc.pdf.
3. Fox Butterfield, "Study Finds Big Increase in Black Men as Inmates Since 1980," *New York Times*, 28 August 2002, late ed., A1.
4. "Class Dismissed: Higher Education vs. Corrections During the Wilson Years," Press Release, Center for Juvenile and Criminal Justice (2002), http://www.cjcj.org/pubs/classdis/classdis.html.
5. Alan Elsner, "U.S. Prison Population Social Costs Mount," Reuters, 23 January 2001.
6. Tracy L. Huling, "Prisons as a Growth Industry in Rural America: An Exploratory Discussion of the Effects on Young African American Men in the Inner Cities," paper presented at Consultation of the U.S. Commission on Civil Rights, April 15, 1999; also in "The Crisis of the Young African Male in the Inner Cities," U.S. Commission on Civil Rights, Washington, D.C., July 2000.
7. Elsner, "U.S. Prison Population Social Costs Mount."
8. John Irwin and Jason Ziedenberg, "America's One Million Nonviolent Prisoners," Press Release, Justice Policy Institute (March 1999).
9. Angela Y. Davis, "Masked Racism: Reflections on the Prison Industrial Complex," *Colorlines* 1, no. 2 (Fall 1998), 12.
10. Mandatory minimum laws remove judges' discretion to determine sentences according to the crime committed and according to its context. For example, a drug addict who is charged with drug possession may be best served by an effective treatment program; however, as a result of mandatory minimum laws, the judge is forced to sentence the addict to twenty years of hard time. Mandatory minimum sentences mostly and most unfairly apply to drug offenses. Organizations like Families Against Mandatory Minimums point out that both drug addicts and the partners of drug dealers—mostly women—are caught in the net of mandatory minimums.
11. Arthur Santana, "Female Prison Ranks Double; Citing Study, Norton Plans to Improve Conditions," *Washington Post*, 1 February 2000, A08.
12. Ibid.
13. Karen Gullo, "Report Decries Jailing Girls," *Chicago Tribune*, 16 May 2001, 8.

14. Real earnings are the real value of a dollar earned. Low-income male workers may make more in dollars today than they did ten years ago, but the value of that money is falling. This explains why a factory worker in 1965 might have been able to buy a new car or a house, but his twenty-first-century equivalent is taking the bus and renting.

Women made so much less than men in 1965 that their wages have risen relative to low-income men's but only because they were starting at such a deficit; the wage floor was very low. David Moberg, "Bridging the Gap: Why Women Still Don't Get Equal Pay," *In These Times,* 8 January 2001, 24.

R E A D I N G **89**

The Talibanization of Iraq

Bay Fang (2007)

Yanar Mohammed returned to Iraq after the fall of Saddam Hussein's regime because she thought the veil of tyranny had finally been lifted from her native country. She and two other women started the Organization for Women's Freedom in Iraq (OWFI), with the goal of fighting for women's rights.

But since those days, her OWFI cofounders have fled the country, and Mohammed herself has received numerous death threats for her work. OWFI, one of the few remaining nongovernmental organizations left in Iraq, has been forced to operate in complete secrecy.

"Because of the chaos on the streets and in the government, women have been forced to leave work and hide at home," says Mohammed, 47. "We live in a state of continuous fear—if our hair shows on the street, if we're not veiled enough at work," says Mohammed. "It's a new experience for women in Iraq. After four years, it's turned into Afghanistan under the Taliban."

Throughout much of recent history, Iraq was one of the most progressive countries in the Middle East for women. Saddam Hussein and his Baath party encouraged women to go to school and enter the workforce. The constitution drafted

in 1970 guaranteed women the right to vote, attend school, own property and run for political office.

The 1959 Law of Personal Status—which came into being thanks to a mobilization by Iraqi women after the end of British colonial rule— gave women equal rights to divorce, restricted polygamy, prohibited marriages under age 18 and ensured that men and women had the same inheritance rights.

These rights diminished somewhat after the 1991 Gulf War, partly because of Saddam Hussein's new embrace of Islamic tribal law as a way of consolidating power, and partly due to the United Nations' sanctions against the regime. After the sanctions were imposed, Human Rights Watch reports, the gender gap in school enrollment increased dramatically, as did female illiteracy (because, when faced with limited financial resources, many families chose to keep their girls home). According to the United Nations Educational, Scientific and Cultural Organization (UNESCO), in 1987 approximately 75 percent of Iraqi women were literate; by the end of 2000 that percentage had dropped to less than 25 percent.

Still, as bad as it was during Saddam's time, women's well-being and security have sharply deteriorated since the fall of his regime. Violence against women, both at home and on the streets, has spiked, as women are less protected legally and

---

Bay Fang is a correspondent for the *Chicago Tribune* who has been based in both China and Iraq.

institutionally and standards of living have gone down. From 2003 to 2005, says Mohammed, she could meet with groups of 200 or 300 women at factories or the railway station. "But this year is completely different. A woman can't even walk two to three blocks safely, much less [come to] a meeting."

Furthermore, extremists in both Sunni and Shiite areas have taken over pockets of the country and imposed their own Taliban-like laws on the population, requiring women to wear full-length veils, segregating the sexes in public and forbidding such activities as singing and dancing. Hair salons are bombed, and many have gone underground. Women college students are stopped and harassed on campuses, so going to school is a risk. "I don't have one woman friend who has not been harassed, or worse, on the street," says Mohammed. Women who work for OWFI are routinely threatened with beatings or rape if they aren't completely veiled. Islamist "misery gangs" regularly patrol the streets in many areas, beating and harassing women who are not "properly" dressed or behaved.

Zainab Salbi also grew up in Iraq, experiencing first-hand the oppression of Saddam Hussein's dictatorial regime as the daughter of Saddam's pilot. When Hussein was toppled, she too began traveling back to Iraq to work for women's rights. But when she compares the situation there today to how it was in her childhood, she says that now it is definitively worse.

"The violence during Saddam's time was . . . committed by the government, Saddam's family, people in power. Now the violence is . . . being committed by everyone around you," says Salbi, who founded the group Women for Women International in 1993. That organization now operates in nine countries to help women survivors of war and civil strife rebuild their lives; Iraq, says Salbi, is in the worst shape of them all.

Today, most of her friends have left Iraq. There are only a handful of organizations left in the country. Women for Women International has to keep its locations secret and take all sorts of security precautions. Unlike other countries in which the group operates, in Iraq it's responsible not only for helping needy women but also keeping its own staff alive.

Salbi herself stopped traveling back to her homeland two years ago because of the spike in targeted assassinations of professional women. "At first I was able to say I knew 10, 20 women who had been assassinated," she says. "Now, I've lost count. . . . They are pharmacists, professors, reporters, activists . . ."

The Human Rights Office of the U.N. Mission in Iraq has received reports of young women being abducted by armed sectarian militias and found days later sexually abused, tortured and murdered. It has also charted an increase in kidnapping and killing of women: "In late December, three female students from Mustansiriya University were reportedly kidnapped by Shiite militias," the report reads. "Despite the payment of a ransom, their bodies were found at the morgue on December 22 bearing signs of rape and torture. Official sources denied the incident but students from the University confirmed it did take place."

Many of the bodies of women and girls who are raped and killed are not getting claimed, because families are too fearful or ashamed to identify them. One day at the Baghdad morgue last November, OWFI activists were told that more than 150 unclaimed women's bodies had moved through over the previous 10 days, many of which were beheaded, disfigured or showed signs of torture.

"Often, the first salvo in a war for theocracy is a systematic attack on women and minorities who represent or demand an alternative or competing vision for society," wrote Yifat Susskind, communications coordinator of the international human and women's-rights organization MADRE, in a report she authored on "gender apartheid" in Iraq. "These initial targets are usually the most marginalized and, therefore, most vulnerable members of society, and once they are dealt with, fundamentalist forces then proceed towards less vulnerable targets."

Beyond negotiating their personal safety, women in the new Iraq are worried about whether fundamentalist forces will succeed in curtailing their legal freedoms. The new Iraqi constitution makes citizens "equal before the law without discrimination based on gender," yet the document also states that no law "that contradicts the established provisions of Islam may be established." But which version of Islam will prevail in the country's new legal system?

During Saddam's rule, the national personal status law governed such things as age of marriage, inheritance, divorce and custody of children. Women were able to settle suits in civil courts. Now, such law is the domain of religious courts, and judges and imams are free to make their own individual interpretations. In some parts of Baghdad, like the Shiite slum of Sadr City, religious courts following strict interpretations of sharia law have become the de facto authority in place of government courts. "We used to have a government that was almost secular. It had one dictator," says Yanar Mohammed. "Now we have almost 60 dictators—Islamists who think of women as forces of evil. This is what is called the democratization of Iraq."

During the January 2005 elections for the National Assembly, political parties were required to field electoral slates on which every third candidate was a woman, and as a result women captured 31 percent of the seats. But nearly half of the elected women parliamentarians ran on the list of the Shiite alliance, and they have had to toe the conservative line of their party. Some of the women parliamentarians could be forces for moderation and progress—such as Mayson al-Damluji, a former undersecretary of culture who has urged the prime minister to honor his pledge to improve women's rights—but the dangerous political environment of targeted assassinations has prevented them from being very outspoken.

Increased violence against women in the streets has had a parallel effect on the increase in domestic violence, including "honor" killings. With the destruction of the former Iraqi state, and the rise in the power of Islamists and conservative tribal authorities, lethal responses against women who are raped—and thus considered to have shamed their families—have become more common.

Also, in a situation that may be akin to honor killings, it was reported in December 2006 by the United Nations Assistance Mission for Iraq that in the Kurdish-governed north, 239 women burned themselves in the first eight months of 2006. A hospital source in the northeast city of Sulaimaniya

suspected that such cases are underreported because of fear of the social stigma, shame and culpable involvement of family members associated with honor crimes. Most cases have been investigated as "accidents" or "suicide attempts."

In response to the rise in honor killings and other domestic violence, OWFI has set up women's shelters in four cities around the country. If the shelters cannot protect a woman, an "underground railroad" network helps her escape the country, along with providing money and support to help her set up a new life.

For those remaining in Iraq, a recent survey by the United Nations Development Programme shows one-third live in poverty and 5 percent in extreme poverty—a sharp deterioration from before the 2003 invasion. Half the population is lacking in the supply of clean water, and more than 40 percent have inadequate sanitation. The price of certain essentials, like kerosene used for cooking, has shot up, in some cases from $1 per unit four years ago to $40 per unit today.

Such poverty has a harsh impact on women, as does the fact that very few jobs are available. Women generally have a harder time finding work in Iraq, and after years of war there are an estimated half million widows in the country, according to OWFI. The U.N. reports that the international community has not done enough to help: "Projects created to provide jobs for women were abandoned after the exodus of international NGOs from [Iraq in] October 2005. There is an urgent need for the international community to ensure projects aimed at job creation, especially for women, who now face a long struggle surviving and bringing up families on their own."

The few women activists who are still in Iraq feel that time is running out for them and their work. "Women are a bellwether for the direction of a society. Both violence and progress often start with women," says Salbi. "A classic example was with the Taliban—they started with violence against women, and everyone looked the other way . . . but eventually everyone suffered. We need to take this moment to raise the world's attention. Iraqi women are holding up, but they can't hold it on their own—they need us to help."

Demilitarizing Society in a Globalized World

Cynthia Enloe (2007)

The Women of Color Resource Center (WCRC) isn't what most experts think of as a site of research on militarization and demilitarization. But that oversight may be due to many militarization experts' narrow views of "expertise." The WCRC is an energetic organization located in downtown Oakland, California, that develops programs for Asian American, African American, Native American, and Latina women in the San Francisco Bay Area. As the director of the WCRC's small antimilitarism project, Christine Ahn wanted to find a topic that would engage these young women in thinking about their own possible complicity in the processes of militarization. In 2004, she began mulling over the meaning of "camo." Camo is the popular nickname for the fashion of turning the military's camouflaged designs into tank tops, shorts, pants, knapsacks, even condoms. Ahn wondered whether the many young people she knew who were buying and wearing this "hip" fashion—her peers—had thought about the implications of their style choices. Christine Ahn went into action. She organized what might have been the first-ever antimilitarism fashion show.

In late May 2005, the WCRC took over the refurbished theater in downtown Oakland. By 8:00 p.m., the lobby and the theater were alive with displays, music, performers, and the conversations of a lively audience. Christine Ahn had invited a wide array of Bay Area groups—ranging from young male hip-hop fashion designers to Code Pink, a network of feminist peace activists. They were all crowded into the lobby, displaying their wares and talking with other attendees. Inside the theater, the show was about to begin. The lights went down, and the disc jockey started to spin her records. The master of ceremonies was a tall African American woman, herself a performance poet. She was soon joined by local rappers talking about war and peace. The stage began to fill with camo. There was camo casual wear, there were camo ball gowns.

Then there were "blasts from the past." One participant told the story of khaki—how khaki wasn't coined by the Gap but was an Afghan word to describe the distinctive color of that country's stark hillsides, which the British imperial army adopted for their own uniform colors but only after their red-coated troops were defeated in their initial efforts to subdue the region's less dramatically attired tribal fighters. Khaki as Americans know it has its roots in military conquest. The lights then focused on a well-known and longtime Bay Area Latina activist who strode to the front of the stage wearing a classic 1940s outfit—hat, gloves, brass-buttoned coat, and pumps—all in patriotic red, white, and blue. She was followed by a slender young woman wearing nothing but a bikini. The audience cheered. Then the poet MC told them that the bikini was created by a designer who wanted to exploit the international popular interest in the U.S. atomic bomb testing in the Pacific, which rendered Bikini, an island, uninhabitable. The audience uttered a collective gasp.

That was the goal of Christine Ahn and her WCRC colleagues. She didn't want to lecture these California women and men about what to think about the camo in their closets. She hoped instead that the fashion show would start them thinking and developing their own thoughts about militarization and about their own personal relationships to militarization.

Thousands of miles away, in Turkey, other local activists were organizing their own innovative event—one they hoped would raise ordinary civilians' consciousness about the dailyness of militarization and generate new awareness of that often invisible process. They didn't choose a fashion show. These Turkish activists, women and men, many of them feminists and anticonscription activists, instead organized a militarism tour. They called their event "Militourism."

Taking people on bus and walking tours around Istanbul and Ankara, they pointed out buildings where every day some small or major strand of militarized Turkish life was woven. Most of these places were the sort that civilians passed every day without noticing and without thinking about what was going on inside, about what was being done there in their names, for their protection, for the "good of the nation." It is not as if Turkish women and men are unconscious of the central role that the military has played since the 1920s in shaping both public policy and national myths of unity, modernity, masculine duty, and the secular state. The Turkish military has made itself too prominent to be overlooked. Yet the organizers of the annual Militourism events wanted to make even clearer to their fellow citizens that both the military and practices of militarized living were more diverse and more "ordinary" than perhaps even the reader of the daily newspapers realized (Altinay 2004; Mater 2005).

In Israel, a small group of middle-aged Jewish women (and now several young women and men in their new youth group) have come together, one by one, and call themselves New Profile. Out of their concern that children's lives were becoming militarized, they tried to build bridges with Israeli academics involved in the country's educational system. It has turned out to be hard work. They also decided to take their messages about militarism into modest local sites. These women created a traveling exhibit to reveal how ideas about soldiering, about the country's recent past, about the military's centrality in Israeli life are even inserted into primary school children's education. The exhibit isn't flashy. It was assembled by the New Profile women themselves by looking at what their own children and grandchildren and nieces and nephews were being shown in schools and in contemporary children's books. They mounted their findings on five-foot-high folding boards. The women have to be able to carry these boards around the country, to Haifa and Tel Aviv, as well as to Jerusalem, and assemble the exhibit without fuss. A New Profile member sits by the exhibit wherever they get permission to set it up—in schools, in local community centers, at conferences. She doesn't lecture the people who come to look at its images and captions but is there to answer any questions or just to engage in conversation. At first glance, some people who come think that the exhibit is in praise of the military. Only on closer inspection do they see the problematic relationships and ideas being revealed. There is a guest book, too, in which anyone who comes to look at the exhibit can share their own reactions. Underlying the New Profile modest exhibit is an ambitious goal: to inspire their fellow citizens, especially their fellow Jewish citizens (15 percent of Israel's citizens are non-Jews, mostly Palestinian Israelis), to weigh the costs of having created or consented to such a deeply militarized public culture.

A fashion show, a tour, a small display of children's books. These are not the usual activities for analyzing militarization or laying out the steps for demilitarization. But the San Francisco, Oakland, Istanbul, Ankara, Tel Aviv, and Haifa activists who created these events did so because they had become convinced that if militarization took myriad and often unnoticed forms, then *de*militarization would start only when the invisible became visible, when the naturalized was made problematic.

Members of each group believed in the power of ideas—ideas about what is stylish, what is normal, what is educational. They believed that popularly held ideas—not just interests, policies, or institutions—were the source of militarization. Thus, all of these people working for demilitarization had become convinced that only through raising new questions in the minds of their fellow citizens could fresh conversations begin—conversations that might eventually turn into pressures for demilitarization.

Demilitarization. Today we are learning—often painfully, and usually reluctantly—that *demilitarization may be one of the toughest transformative processes to carry through in all its steps to completion. To demilitarize any society—or even to demilitarize just a town, an organization, a television network, a family, a school, or a sense of yourself—turns out to require changes many of us would rather avoid. We want to don our camo shorts if they are deemed fashionable. We want to walk around our cities without questioning what is going on in their bland-looking buildings. We want to trust that our young children are learning healthy lessons in their schools. We want to keep cashing our paychecks from our employers, even if their executives bid on defense contracts. We want to hold our marriages together without scrutinizing our partner's work. We want to continue to be accepted as patriotic.

Many demilitarizing actions go unnoticed. They are taken by individuals without fanfare. But that lack of public attention doesn't necessarily make demilitarizing steps easy to take, particularly if militarism's beliefs, values, and practices have become normal or even glorified:

- A South Korean prodemocracy activist decides to critique how she and her fellow activists adopted militaristic ideas and strategies even as they sought to topple the country's military regime (Kwon 2000).
- An American young soldier decides to refuse to return for a second tour of duty to Iraq because he has come to see the military's actions there as unjust (Laufer 2006).
- A Chilean middle-aged woman buys new sneakers for her elderly mother and aunt so they can take part in antimilitary rallies and run away from the tear gas.
- A nineteen-year-old Jewish Israeli woman decides to resist her army conscription notice, even while most of her friends are accepting theirs, because, she explains, after volunteering for local groups seeking to support abused women, she now realizes that by becoming a soldier she would violate her principles as a feminist (Halili 2006).
- A Puerto Rican woman tells the story of how in the early 2000s she gained new self-confidence by mobilizing with her neighbors

to force the U.S. Navy to withdraw from its military base and stop using her island of Vieques as a bombing range; her story is being circulated globally to women and men in Diego Garcia, Hawaii, Aruba, Guam, and other places with U.S. military bases (Lutz forthcoming; Ferguson and Mironesco forthcoming).

- An American mother and father together decide to sign the waiver, offered by their child's school in very small print on an official form, so that the name and home address of their son, a high school senior, will not automatically be sent by school officials, along with all the other seniors' names and addresses, to the Pentagon recruiting command. They decide that would be an invasion of their own and their child's privacy.
- An Argentine mother decides that even though the military has been ousted from power, she will not give up pressuring the now-civilian elected government to bring the generals to justice (Arditti 1999).
- An American career diplomat, after deciding that a preemptive invasion of Iraq violates her profession's principles and after thus deciding to give up the career she loves and to resign from the U.S. Foreign Service, writes a letter to the secretary of state not claiming vague "personal reasons" but spelling out her principled objections to the government's policy.
- A Canadian woman living in Winnipeg, Manitoba, decides to speak out against Ottawa's plan to conduct urban warfare military maneuvers in her city.
- Yugoslav parents take great personal risks to get their son out of the country, to Germany, so that he won't be conscripted into the army, which the then Milošević-led government is deploying to Bosnia to pursue its Serbian nationalist goals.
- The father of an American Latino soldier who was killed in Iraq decides that he cannot grieve in private, that he needs to go to high schools with large Latino enrollments to speak to students about the reasons Latino young people should not enlist in the U.S. military.

Some of these individual actions remain just that. The person may be scorned or admired now and then by his or her family and colleagues, but otherwise few people pay any attention to that person's decision and the reasoning behind it. Occasionally, however, enough individuals discover that they are not alone in their thinking and actions, that they can create a group; perhaps, over time, enough small groups connect with each other that they together become a more sprawling network, a "movement."

On even fewer occasions news of such individual and collective decisions and actions can travel across national boundaries and start to globalize. This happened with the Mothers and Grandmothers of the Plaza de Mayo, a group of older women who stood up to the military in Argentina, insisting after the end of military rule that senior officers be held accountable for their abuses. News of their actions traveled to Turkey, where it inspired Turkish women to organize as mothers calling on the militarized government to provide news of their missing sons and daughters (Baydar and Ivegen 2006). This is similar to what has happened over the last century as individuals (mostly men) in many countries have resisted compulsory military service ("conscription" or "the draft"), have compared experiences, and often joined by women supporters who become integral to the movement, have created international networks of support for conscientious objectors.

...

Today feminists in many countries are showing us that trying to demilitarize anything requires making difficult changes in relationships between women and men—as well as changes in relationships between men and the state and between women and the state and even between women and women. Some efforts at demilitarization thus take place within the most intimate relationships—for instance, two people trying to reduce the secrecy that has come to riddle their relationship because one of the partners works on a weapons manufacturer's classified project.

...

Demilitarization calls for more than silencing the cannons. Those working for demilitarization with feminist analytical tools have discovered that ideas about manliness have to be addressed (Munn forthcoming; Conway forthcoming). For example, one of the most widespread programs that the United Nations introduces in societies that are trying to implement precarious peace accords is called Disarmament, Demobilization, and Reintegration, or "DDR" as postconflict field workers routinely call it. Nowadays DDR is seen by its proponents as integral to international peacekeeping in countries around the world trying not just to bring wartime violence to an end but to lay the groundwork for a sustainable peace. DDR is a tough political assignment. When tried in Northern Ireland, El Salvador, East Timor, Congo, Liberia, Mozambique, Kosovo, it has met with resistance. People who have found safety, influence, and even a deep sense of identity in their possession of guns, sometimes walking and sleeping with those guns for years, are not likely to easily surrender them to international workers simply to garner what seem to be dubious offers of food, medical care, and training for new peacetime jobs. Guns have come to mean too much to those who hold them.

Conflict-zone officials and field workers until recently saw the gun holders to whom they were addressing their DDR appeals as just "soldiers" or "combatants" or "militiamen" or "insurgents." They didn't see them explicitly as men or as boys. It has taken interventions—not always welcomed—by feminists in nongovernmental organizations to expose what was missing in this conventional DDR approach: a questioning of masculinity. These soldiers, combatants, militiamen, and insurgents were not only those things but were men with anxieties about their reduced power in peacetime and pride in their status as gunholding masculinized men. Unless those ideas about—and needs for—masculinity were directly and effectively addressed, lasting disarmament, demobilization, and reintegration were not likely to be achieved. And thus demilitarization would be partial, superficial, and short lived (Farr and Gebre-Wold 2002; Farr 2006). Lepa Mladjenovic, one of the founders of the Belgrade Women in Black, is a longtime activist working to end violence against women. She explained to an audience in New York in 2005 how a decade after the signing of the Dayton Accords, the internationally brokered agreements intended to end the war in Bosnia, men's relationships to guns had changed in her city. As a volunteer in groups supporting women subjected to violence, she could see that over the past ten years of "peace" there had been an increase in men's use of guns and an increase in men's access to guns. As Lepa Mladjenovic explained to her American audience, "The gun is no longer in the cellar or the closet, it is now visible so that it can be used by the man in the home as an instrument of intimidation."

While too few of the planners and administrators of DDR have explicitly thought through what the politics of masculinity means for their actions, feminist activists and organizational workers have realized that most of these DDR planners and administrators do implicitly take for granted that DDR is about men and boys. That is, they have planned and carried out their programs as if all the people they will be dealing with in DDR camps would be men, although they avoid taking seriously in their operations the workings of ideas about manliness.

The reality in wars is more complicated. Feminist researchers working closely with local women's groups in conflict regions such as Uganda, Sierra Leone, Sri Lanka, Mozambique, and Liberia have had gender questions in the front of their minds. They have been wary of the vague term "child soldiers." The concept of the "child soldier"—and the reality it represents—has indeed aroused a new concern about children as young as eight being recruited, often forcibly, into armies. Nor have "child soldiers" been only those third world boys and girls who capture media attention because they are sent into conflict operations. The practice of turning children into soldiers, many activists contend, should include the more widely adopted and seemingly more benign government policy of authorizing, promoting, and funding voluntary school-age cadet corps (New Profile 2004).

A new public consciousness was created through global campaigning by the Coalition to Stop the Use of Child Soldiers. Founded in 1998 by Amnesty International, Human Rights Watch, the Quakers, the Jesuit Refugee Service, and several other organizations, the Coalition to Stop the Use of Child Soldiers helped mobilize international support for ratifying and implementing the UN Convention on the Rights of the Child, passed in 1989. By 1998, 117 governments had signed and ratified the historic convention (Singer 2006). Other governments, such as the British and the U.S. governments, have been reluctant to sign and ratify the convention because it might hamper their programs to introduce military cadet programs in high schools.

It is not that feminist-informed researchers and international peace workers criticize the use of the popular term "child soldier," they just don't think it is adequate. If one is committed to demilitarizing children who have been recruited into armies, then, they have found, one must ask when and how gender matters in how those children have experienced soldiering. So these feminist-informed researchers and practitioners have asked, "Where are the girls?" And following up on this innovative question, researchers discovered that girls have been recruited or coerced into fighting forces by all armed groups in a conflict and have been used by male commanders as porters, cooks, nurses, fighters, and sexual slaves (sometimes called "wives").

Moreover, these feminist researchers discovered that very few of these girls were receiving care from international or local organizations engaged in peacekeeping and national reconstruction. For instance, many of the agencies administering DDR camps made the handing in of a rifle the "ticket" for admission into the demobilization camps and the healthcare, job training, education, and psychological counseling those camps offered. But in most fighting forces, girls, while they played important roles in sustaining those forces, were only rarely issued guns. To make the DDR services accessible to girls trying to remake their lives after being used by fighting forces, the gun criterion would have to be eliminated. Furthermore, once one starts asking "Where are the girls?" one has to appropriate a lot more funding for the sort of post-traumatic stress syndrome care designed for girls who have endured sexual abuse, a lot more resources for girls who, while still only sixteen or seventeen years old themselves, have come out of the fighting forces with small children of their own as a result of having been used as older male commanders' "wives." "Girl-headed household" would have to be a concept used by any policymaker who hoped to implement a realistic and meaningful postwar peacekeeping and reconstruction program (McKay and Mazurana 2004; Fox 2004; Krosch 2005).

In 2000, a first-of-its-kind international policy decision was made that is making it sound less "odd" and more "reasonable" to ask "What about masculinity?" and "Where are the girls?" In October 2000, delegates to the UN Security Council passed Resolution 1325. For the first time in its fifty-five years, the UN Security Council passed a resolution specifically addressing the condition of women. Resolution 1325 called on all UN agencies and the officials of all of the 184 UN member states to do two things they had neglected or resisted doing.

First, Security Council Resolution 1325 called on both staff members of all UN agencies, as well as officials of all UN member governments, to pay explicit attention to the conditions and experiences and needs of women in war zones. No longer, according to Resolution 1325, could rapes of women—by anyone—be swept under the rug or dismissed as merely a natural phenomenon of war. No longer could "refugees" be planned for and administered as if distributing food rations through men as alleged "heads of households" had the same political consequences as distributing those supplies through women. No longer could "child soldiers" be treated as if girls and boys in a fighting force had had the identical experiences—and thus had the same postconflict traumas or socioeconomic prospects.

Second, Resolution 1325 called on UN and government agencies to make sure that women, especially in local women's organizations, had a voice in decision making at every step of the peace process. No longer should the negotiations to craft the conditions for a ceasefire among the warring

groups be an all-male affair. No longer should women be left out of the closed-door decision-making processes that constructed the new security forces, new legislature, new executive, new constitutional provisions. No longer should international and local male officials and leaders feel satisfied when they had considered women as mere victims. Under Resolution 1325, women, including those victimized by the warring parties, should be treated as political players.

...

Among the less anticipated consequences of the passage of—and interpretation and attempted application of—Resolution 1325 has been the shining of a bright light on the gender dynamics inside the international peacekeeping operations themselves. When more people began to take seriously the experiences, ideas, and organizational priorities of women and women's organizations in societies to which the United Nations and NATO were sending peacekeeping and reconstruction teams, they began to ask fresh questions about whether the international civilian aid providers and military peacekeepers themselves might be having a less-than-positive impact on local women's and girls' lives. This meant taking stock of the masculinized and racialized biases among "the good guys." Many people used to seeing themselves as the rational, well-meaning, civilized, altruistic actors were, not surprisingly, uncomfortable under this new scrutiny.

"Peacekeepers" suddenly could be seen as men—men with particular, often diverse notions of what it meant to be deployed as a soldier on a peacekeeping mission. That is, their own notions of masculinity were revealed as a significant factor in how they conducted their militarized peacekeeping operations. Women and girls in Cambodia, East Timor, Bosnia, Kosovo, and Liberia would have to figure out ways to cope with—and organize and strategize to confront—those notions and the men's behaviors that flowed from them. And local women in societies coming out of militarized conflict would have to confront men in international peacekeeping forces at the same time as they sought to challenge abusive behavior and arrogance of men in their own communities—men who often acted out their own sense of frustration, anger, and confusion with violence toward women in their households, communities, and refugee camps (Joshi 2005; Cockburn and Zarkov 2002).

When international aid workers, peacekeeping officials, and government and private foundation donors assumed that reaching out to "local leaders" meant working with the men who had influential positions in the postconflict societies—leaders of villages, town mayors, heads of political parties, clerical authorities—then the patriarchal hurdles that local women activists confronted in trying to have a voice in peacemaking and national reconstruction loomed even higher: those male "local leaders" were often no less scornful of women's policy ideas than the international officials reaching out to them. That is, "local leaders," when left ungendered, is not in itself a guarantee of the sort of representation that can move a society effectively toward sustainable demilitarization.

Many male soldiers chosen by their home governments for deployment on UN or NATO peacekeeping missions still attach the highest value to combat. The appeal of combat is why they joined the military. Combat experience is what would earn them the greatest respect (and maybe promotion and extra pay) from their military comrades and superiors and from their fellow citizens back home. Combat is what they had been trained for. Combat would earn them the sought-after status of "real men" (Whitworth 2004).

Further undermining many peacekeeping soldiers' ability to engage in effective peace building are their stereotypes about the women and the men in the country to which they are deployed—the women as needing their superior protection, the men as not being capable of protecting their women. They exchange needed food for a "date," not thinking of it as having anything to do with prostitution, but feeling that they, the manly men, are doing a good deed (Higate and Henry 2004).

Because serious consideration about the interplay of demilitarizing policies and the politics of militarized masculinity was not "on the agenda" prior to the passage of Resolution 1325 and only barely given the nod after the formal passage of Resolution 1325, peacekeeping has been experienced by many women as prostitution, sex trafficking, and sexual harassment (Refugees International 2005).

So much of this new global feminist-informed thinking about demilitarization—what it is, what undermines it, how it can be achieved and sustained—hinges on revising our ideas about *security*. Security turns out to be a broad, many-layered goal. It can no longer be imagined as simply synonymous with militarized security. Security, many women activists working to end armed conflict in various countries have concluded, has to be seen more realistically and more broadly, and that means it has to be seen as more complicated (Jacobson 2005). Security is one of the goals of demilitarization because so many people have discovered that militarization—that is, coming to see the world as dangerous, learning to be preoccupied with enemies, bolstering executive power in the name of fighting those enemies, starting to define one's patriotism and the criteria for belonging according to military service, or deferring to those who have done military service—has caused them to feel less, not more, secure. Security for many women and girls also comes, more are beginning to realize, less from fortifying the country's borders or driving out of their towns people of other ethnic groups than from finding ways to escape violent assaults perpetrated by men in their own homes.

Yet the familiar militarized ways of conceptualizing security remain stubbornly entrenched.

. . .

In Afghanistan one of the principal critiques articulated by local Afghan women's groups is that the U.S. occupying forces and their superiors in Washington depended heavily on the male commanders of the regional militias (referred to as the Northern Alliance) in their military invasion to topple the Taliban regime, without taking into account how militarized and patriarchal those commanders were. Consequently, now, with the new constitutional system's legislature and president (and his cabinet) struggling to exert their civilian authority, those conservative militarized commanders (often called "warlords") remain entrenched in positions of power as governors, police chiefs, and the dominant bloc in the newly elected legislature. One member of the new legislature, Malai Joya, a twenty-seven-year-old woman already active in a local women's organization, won a seat in the 2005 national elections. What made her famous among Afghans was her standing up in the new legislature in December 2005 to denounce those male legislators who were "criminal warlords . . . whose hands are stained with the blood of the people" (Coghan 2006; Coleman and Hunt 2006). In the wake of her public denunciation of the patriarchal and militarized warlords, principal players in the anti-Taliban Northern Alliance, Malai Joya was subjected to death threats.

What Malai Joya underscored in her dramatic speech was what Resolution 1325 also implies: demilitarization cannot be achieved unless women are empowered to the point that all the forms of maculinized militarization are exposed and rolled back. Most of those local and international officials determining how peace building and postconflict reconstruction will proceed do not think in these terms. In their planning for the U.S.-led invasion and occupation of Afghanistan, American officials did not think deeply about the causes of militarization or about what it would take to reverse it; they made forming alliances with the existing anti-Taliban warlords a priority. The ramifications of that U.S. decision continue to be felt in the lives of Afghan women and men (Enloe 2004).

. . .

Demilitarization efforts in so many countries—both developed and developing, both war-torn and war-waging—have been resisted by those individuals and groups who have realized—even if they do not say it out loud—that pushing a demilitarization process beyond tokenism would require dismantling patriarchal structures, not only in the public realm, but in the private sphere as well. Genuine, lasting, and thoroughgoing demilitarization, in other words, would have to alter the relationships between women and women, between women and men, between men and men, and between women and men and all the influential institutions of society—schools, legislatures, religious organizations, corporations, the media, the military, the offices of prime ministers and presidents.

Successful demilitarization calls for changing the relationships between masculine authority figures and feminized "dependents," awarding the education department as much political influence as the defense department, and withdrawing from male citizens—especially those claiming insider military knowledge—their privileged status as the citizens presumed to be "expert" on security issues.

REFERENCES

Altinay, Ayse Gul. 2004. *The Myth of the Military Nation: Militarism, Gender, and Education in Turkey.* New York: Palgrave Macmillan.

Arditti, Rita. 1999. *Searching for Life: The Grandmothers of the Plaza de Mayo and the Disappeared Children of Argentina.* Berkeley: University of California Press.

Cockburn, Cynthia, and Dubravka Zarkov, eds. 2002. *The Postwar Moment: Militaries, Masculinities, and International Peacekeeping.* London: Lawrence & Wishart.

Coghan, Tom. 2006, "Afghan MP Says She Will Not Be Silenced." Reprinted in *Women Living Under Muslim Law Newsletter* 18 (April): 4.

Coleman, Isobel, and Swanee Hunt. 2006. "Afghanistan Should Make Room for Its Female Leaders." *Christian Science Monitor,* April 24.

Enloe, Cynthia. 2004. *The Curious Feminist: Searching for Women in a New Age of Empire.* Berkeley: University of California Press.

Farr, Vanessa. 2006. "Gender Analysis as a Tool for Multilateral Negotiators in the Small Arms Context." In *Disarmament as Humanitarian Action,* ed. John Borrie and Vanessa Martin Randin, 109–136. Geneva: United Nations Institute for Desarmament Research.

Farr, Vanessa A., and Kiflemiriam Gebre-Wold, eds. 2002. *Gender Perspectives on Small Arms and Light Weapons.* Brief 24. Bonn, Germany: Bonn International Central for Conversion, July.

Ferguson, Kathy, and Monique Mironesco, eds. Forthcoming. *Gender and Globalization in Asia and the Pacific.* Honolulu: University of Hawaii Press.

Fox, Mary-Jane. 2004. "Girl Soldiers." *Security Dialogue* 35 (4) 465–480.

Halili, Idan. 2006. "Interview with Feminist Refusnik Idan Halili," Tel Aviv, Quaker Service.

Higate, Paul, and Marsha Henry. 2004. "Gender in Peace Support Operations." In "Gender and Security," ed.

Lene Hansen and Louise Olsson, special issue, *Security Dialogue* 35 (4): 481–498.

Jacobson, Agneta Soderberg. 2005. *Security on Whose Terms: If Men and Women Were Equal.* Stockholm: Kvinna Till Kvinna: Women's Empowerment Projects.

Joshi, Vijaya. 2005. "Building Opportunities: Women's Organizing, Militarism, and the United Nations Transitional Administration in East Timor." PhD diss., Clark University.

Krosch, Sara L. 2005. "'A New Race of Women': The Challenges of Reintegrating Eritrea's Demobilized Female Combatants." Research paper, Department of International Development, Community and Environment, Clark University.

Kwon, Insook. 2000. "Militarism in My Heart: Militarization of Women's Consciousness and Culture in South Korea." PhD diss., MA, Clark University.

Laufer, Peter. 2006, *Mission Rejected: US Soldiers Who Say No to Iraq.* White River Junction, VT: Chelsea Green.

Lutz, Catherine, ed. Forthcoming. *Undermining Empire: Social Movements against US Overseas Military Installations.* Ithaca: Cornell University Press.

Mater, Nadire. 2005. *Voices fom the Front: Turkish Soldiers on the War with Kurdish Guerrillas.* New York: Palgrave Macmillan.

McKay, Susan, and Dyan Mazurana. 2004. *Where Are the Girls? Girls in Fighting Forces in Northern Uganda, Sierra Leone, and Mozambique.* Montreal: Rights and Democracy.

Munn, Jamie. Forthcoming. "The Hegemonic Male and Kosovar Nationalism from 2000–2005." In "Hegemonic Masculinities in International Politics," ed. Juanita Elias, special issue, *Men and Masculinities.*

New Profile. 2004. *The New Profile Report on Child Recruitment in Israel.* Ramat Ha-Sharon, Israel: New Profile.

Refugees International. 2005. *Must Boys Be Boys?* Washington, DC: Refugees International.

Singer, P.W. 2006. *Children at War.* Berkeley: University of California Press.

Whitworth, Sandra. 2004. *Men, Militarism and UN Peacekeeping.* Boulder, CO: Lynne Rienner.

DISCUSSION QUESTIONS FOR CHAPTER 11

1. What are some of the ways the state maintains social inequality? Have you experienced discrimination by the state in any way?

2. How does the early American assumption that citizens were White men perpetuate contemporary social inequities?

3. Do you believe that full equality can be achieved under our present system of democracy and capitalism? Why or why not?

4. What myths that maintain inequity do you see operating in the state, the law, and social policies?

5. What changes do you believe should be made in order to create a more just state?

SUGGESTIONS FOR FURTHER READING

Enloe, Cynthia. *Maneuvers: The International Politics of Militarizing Women's Lives.* Berkeley: University of California Press, 2000.

———. *Globalization and Militarism: Feminists Make the Link.* Lanham, MD: Rowman & Littlefield Publishers, Inc., 2007.

Forrell, Caroline, and Donna Matthews. *A Law of Her Own: The Reasonable Woman as a Measure of Man.* New York: New York University Press, 2000.

LaDuke, Winona. *The Winona LaDuke Reader: A Collection of Essential Writings.* Stillwats, MN: Voyageur, 2002.

MacKinnon, Catharine. *Women's Lives, Men's Laws.* Cambridge, MA: Belknap Press, 2007.

Ricciutelli, Luciana, Angela Miles, and Margaret McFadden, eds. *Feminist Politics, Activism and Vision: Local and Global Challenges.* London: Zed Books, 2005.

Woods, Harriet. *Stepping Up to Power: The Political Journey of American Women.* Boulder, CO: Westview, 2000.

Religion and Spirituality in Women's Lives

Religion is a complex and complicating feature of women's lives. Although many women feel empowered by religion because it offers them a place of belonging, comfort, acceptance, and encouragement, others feel oppressed by religion because it excludes and sometimes denigrates women. In this way, as this chapter will explore, religion remains a significant personal and political force in women's lives. Many of the social and cultural battles raging in American society are cast in religious terms—abortion, gay marriage, sex education, racial violence, domestic violence, to name a few—and many women organize their lives around their religious convictions.

The Southern Baptist controversy illustrates the experiences of many women in religious traditions. Throughout the 1980s and early 1990s, Southern Baptists, the nation's largest Protestant denomination with more than 14 million members, were embroiled in a controversy between fundamentalist and moderate leaders. The Baptist battles began over the issue of inerrancy (the notion that the Bible is without error in history, science, or doctrine) but quickly expanded to include, and then emphasize, social issues such as abortion, homosexuality, and the role of women in the home and church. As the fundamentalists grew in political power, they led the Southern Baptist Convention to pass resolutions excluding women from pastoral leadership in the churches and encouraging wives to submit to their husbands. Fundamentalist victory, however, did not come without a long, bitter conflict in which many women, particularly women in ministry, left the denomination. Other women decided to stay and focus their efforts on the autonomous local churches that carried on in the Baptist tradition of dissent, unbound by convention resolutions. Many women became involved in alternative Baptist organizations that grew out of the controversy and promised women more visibility, opportunity, and support as seminary professors and denominational leaders. The women who found positions as seminary professors often faced resistance from students and misunderstanding from colleagues. Some became associate pastors in moderate Baptist churches, but very few were offered senior pastor positions. Women in the congregation heard the rhetoric of equality, but it came from the lips of the men who held the top positions in the churches and newly formed Baptist organizations.

LEARNING ACTIVITY   **Women of Faith**

Interview three women who actively participate in a religious community. Ask about their experiences as women in their faith. Use the following questions or develop your own interview protocol.

- What is your religious community's stance on women's roles in home, society, and the religious community itself?
- What roles do women fulfill in your religious community?
- In what activities do you participate in your religious community?
- In what ways has your religious community been empowering for you as a woman? Has your religious community ever been oppressive to you as a woman?
- What do you gain by your participation in your religious community?
- How might your religious community better serve women?

Gather the data obtained by several other students in your class and examine your findings. Do you see any common themes arising from your interviews? What do your data suggest about these women's experiences in their faith communities? Can you make any generalizations from the data about how women experience religion as both empowering and oppressive?

The willingness of so many moderate Southern Baptist women to stay in Baptist churches despite the anti-woman actions of the Southern Baptist Convention indicates the powerful pull of religion. Even women who strongly opposed the policy of the Southern Baptist Convention often became active participants in other Christian denominations: few left Christianity entirely. This simultaneous push and pull of religion, as exemplified by the experience of Southern Baptist women, merits careful feminist analysis. As both a force that can oppress and empower, religion has a dramatic potential to work politically—either to continue women's oppression or to support women's liberation. Understanding this complex dynamic involves a close reading of the discourse of religion.

RELIGION AS OPPRESSIVE TO WOMEN

Southern Baptists are not alone in Christianity, nor is Christianity alone in world religions, in functioning as an oppressive force to women. This section discusses four ways that religion as belief and institutional practice has helped subordinate women. First, central to religion's oppressive function is the premise of a divinely ordained order of creation in which females are deemed inferior and men not only are seen as superior to women but also closer to God. As discussed in the next section, gendered language about the deity reinforces male domination of women. The notion of women's inferiority is often supported by creation myths that embed woman's inferior status in the religious community's narrative of identity; these are the stories a religious community tells about itself in order to make itself known to both members and the outside community. For example, a common interpretation of the second Hebrew myth of creation (although feminist biblical scholars take issue with

IDEAS FOR ACTIVISM

- Invite a group of women pastors, ministers, priests, and rabbis to participate in a panel discussion of women in ministry.
- Organize a women's spirituality group.
- Organize an educational event to explore women in the world's religions. If possible, invite practitioners of various faiths to speak about women in their religious tradition.
- Investigate the official stance of your own religious tradition on women's roles and women's issues. Where there is room for improvement, write religious leaders to express your opinion.
- Organize an event to commemorate the women who died in the "burning times."

this interpretation) is that Eve is created after Adam because she is to serve him and be his inferior. Later in the Christian testament, writers argue that woman's secondary status is a result of Eve's role as temptress in the fall of humanity. As Elizabeth Cady Stanton pointed out in her "Introduction to *The Woman's Bible*" over a hundred years ago, the Bible has most often been used to maintain the oppression of women by excluding them from particular roles in church, family, and society.

Second, women's lower status is further maintained by excluding women from sacred rituals. Among the different world religions women have not been allowed to celebrate the Eucharist, pray in public, dance sacred dances, hear confession, make sacrifices, baptize, enter the holy of holies, read sacred scriptures aloud in public, preach, or teach men. One argument for the exclusion of women from priesthood has been that the priest stands as a representative of God, and a woman cannot represent God because she is female. The underlying assumption is that men are more Godlike than women. When worshippers see only men as representatives of God, it reinforces the notion that men are more Godlike, and women's exclusion continues.

Third, religions maintain women's oppression very directly through church laws that require wives to submit to their husbands, regulate women's sexuality, and which create highly defined gender performances for women and men. For example, these laws may keep women in abusive relationships or prevent them from having access to birth control and/or abortion. Women may be told by church authorities that their role in the home is to be the support person for the husband and to submit to his divinely ordained authority in the home. Then, when abuse occurs, a woman may be told that she is to continue to submit because that is her role and that God will change her husband because of her obedience to God's commandments. The husband's abusive behavior then becomes the wife's responsibility because his changing is contingent upon her submission. This situation is exacerbated by a prohibition on divorce in some denominations, preventing women from permanently leaving abusive or dysfunctional marriages.

Finally, historically and currently, religions also exercise power over women through church- and state-sanctioned control. During its early years, Christianity taught a spiritual unity that integrated the oppressiveness of Roman laws and gave women some status in the church (although women's place was still subordinate and

LEARNING ACTIVITY   **That Old-Time TV Religion**

Watch several episodes of religious programming on television, such as the *700 Club* and two or three televised worship services. Who are the key personalities? What is their message? In the worship services, who is speaking? Who is singing? Who is leading? What messages about gender are conveyed, not only in the words themselves but also in the roles played by different people? What messages about race, class, sexual identity, and/or ability are conveyed? Do you think these shows are helpful to people? Why or why not? Are they helpful to women? Who do you think benefits from these shows? Are there ways in which these shows reinforce the subordination of women and other nondominant groups? Keep a log of your observations to share with your classmates.

Jesus' teachings about equality did not manifest in the teachings and practices of the church). Some women found solace in devotional life of the convent where they could live a religious life as well as hold leadership positions and avoid the constraints of traditional femininity that included marriage and childbearing. In the "burning times" (between the eleventh and fourteenth centuries), millions of women in Europe were murdered as witches. For many of these women, "witchcraft" was simply the practice of traditional healing and spirituality and the refusal to profess Christianity. For other women, the charge of witchcraft had nothing to do with religious practices and everything to do with accusations rooted in jealousy, greed, and fear of female sexuality. But in the frenzy of the times, defending oneself against an accusation of witchcraft was practically impossible, and an accusation alone generally meant death.

Other examples include the ways Christian imperialism has proved destructive for women and men of color and reinforced racism and ethnocentrism, despite the fact that in the Bible the Apostle Paul in his letter to the Galations said that in Jesus Christ there is "neither Jew nor Greek, slave nor free, male nor female," interpreted as everyone is equal in the sight of God and should be treated so. The genocide of Native Americans was conducted with the underlying belief that it was the God-given destiny of Europeans to conquer the native peoples of the Americas. Without understanding African cultures, Christian missionaries insisted that indigenous African peoples adopt Western ways. The legacy of Christian racism continued in the American South, where many Christians defended slavery based on their reading of scripture. Following reconstruction, hate groups such as the Ku Klux Klan arose, calling for continued dominance by White, anglo Christians. This continues today with the messages of such groups as the Christian Identity Movement and the Aryan Nation (as well as the Klan). In Germany, thousands of Christians joined in Hitler's plan to build a master race and contributed directly to the genocide of 6 million Jews. In the 1950s and 1960s, while many Christians worked tirelessly for the civil rights movement and African American churches in particular became sites of resistance to racism, many others defended segregation and participated in acts of racial hatred. Only in 2000 did Bob Jones University, a fundamentalist institution of higher education in South Carolina, repeal its rule against interracial dating. Despite the many advances in the twentieth century, the twenty-first century began with the continuing problems of racism and intolerance by

many who profess Christianity. It continues with an association between the executive branch of government and policies providing a conduit for structured inequalities.

In India, many Hindu women are raised to see self-immolation as a high form of religious commitment. *Sati,* the act by which a wife throws herself on the burning pyre with her dead husband, was considered a great act of honor by the codifiers of Hindu law and became glorified in Hindu legends told to little girls. In the nineteenth century, the British who occupied and colonized India outlawed sati. Karen McCarthy Brown explains the story of Roop Kanwar, an 18-year-old woman who was burned alive on her husband's funeral pyre, as central in understanding fundamentalism in her essay titled "Fundamentalism and the Control of Women."

Currently the Religious Right, a political movement of religious conservatives in the United States that has received support from the political establishment, is attempting to exert control over women by influencing the U.S. legal system. Faith-based initiatives that provide government funds to religious institutions tend to blur the line between church and state, and often serve to reduce women's choice and autonomy. Religious influence on social policy has managed to chip away at abortion rights by convincing lawmakers to pass various restrictions on abortion, and attention has also been focused on limiting the gains made by the gay and lesbian rights movement. A particularly telling example of the power of the Religious Right to influence American politics came in the Defense of Marriage Act (DOMA), already mentioned, that allows states not to recognize gay unions performed in other states. DOMA was a significant departure from precedent in which every state recognized the legal contracts entered into by other states.

The Muslim practice of wearing the veil (*hijab*) presents an especially complex example of the simultaneously oppressive and empowering role of religion in women's lives. From a Western perspective, the practice of veiling is often viewed as absolutely oppressing. Although many Muslim women criticize this as coercion, they also see choosing to wear the veil as an empowering practice of ethnic and cultural identity in the face of Western influence. Muslim women often explain that they feel safer when veiled in public. The veil indicates that a woman is devout and virtuous, and therefore Muslim men will not objectify and sexualize a veiled woman. In fact, very often these women express sympathy for North American women, who must constantly fear sexual assault in public places. The veil, they claim, protects them and therefore allows them the freedom to move about publicly without fear, and, in some cases, it allows them to claim their identity and take a stand against the hegemonic forces of Western imperialism. In this discussion it is important to recognize the differences between the teachings of the Quran and the interpretation of these teachings in some Muslim societies with the goal of keeping women subordinate to men. As the reading by Asra Q. Nomani explains, there is a movement to address the ways rights granted by Islam to women have been denied in contemporary manifestations of the Muslim faith.

RELIGION AS EMPOWERING TO WOMEN

Despite religion's long history of oppression, women have also experienced profound support, encouragement, and satisfaction in religion. This section focuses on those aspects of empowerment. First, for many women religion provides an environment in which they experience real community with other women. Women in traditional marriages who work in the home may find their only real social outlet in the church. Here they build connections with other women and participate in personally meaningful experiences in a community context.

Second, religion may provide women with opportunities for building and exercising leadership skills within religious organizations. Particularly for women in traditional families, this allows them to develop skills they might not learn otherwise. For example, although Southern Baptists have generally excluded women from pastoral leadership in the churches, the Woman's Missionary Union (WMU), auxiliary to the Southern Baptist Convention, has provided thousands of women with the opportunity to become lay leaders in their churches, as well as in associational, state, and national WMU organizations. WMU is a missions education organization for women. In local church WMU organizations, women plan, budget, and implement programs for education and action. WMU curriculum materials teach young girls that they can do anything God calls them to do. The subversive power of this message is clear in talking to Southern Baptist women in ministry. Many of them report first experiencing their call to ministry in a WMU organization. Similarly, Catholic women have been empowered through convent experiences, in which they exercise leadership and enjoy community with other women.

Third, leadership within the church or religious organization may facilitate women's power within their local or regional communities as well as encourage their

HISTORICAL MOMENT   **Becoming a Bishop**

Until 1984, no Black woman had been elected bishop of a major religious denomination in the United States, but in that year, the Western Jurisdictional Conference of the United Methodist Church elected Leontine Kelly its first African American woman bishop and only the Church's second female bishop.

Both Kelly's father and brother were Methodist ministers. Kelly married and had three children but divorced in the early 1950s. She remarried a Methodist minister in 1956 and returned to college to earn a bachelor's degree and become a social studies teacher. Kelly was drawn to preaching and became a certified lay preacher. When her husband died in 1969, she accepted the church's invitation for her to become pastor. She earned a master of divinity (MDiv) from Wesley Theological Seminary in 1976 and became an ordained minister in the Methodist Church. From 1977 to 1983 she was pastor of Asbury–Church Hill United Methodist Church in Richmond, Virginia, and then became assistant general secretary of evangelism for the United Methodist General Board of Discipleship.

Kelly's nomination to the post of bishop by a group of California clergywomen was not without controversy. Some thought her unfit for the position because she was a Black woman. Others opposed her nomination because she was divorced. Nonetheless, she was elected and then named bishop for the San Francisco Bay area, making her the chief administrator and spiritual leader for more than 100,000 United Methodists in Northern California and Nevada. She remained at that post for 4 years until her retirement in 1988.

In the fall of 2000, the United Methodist Church elected three African American women as bishops, the first since Leontine Kelly: Violet Fisher, Linda Lee, and Beverly Shamana. Kelly commented, "I will always be the first African American woman bishop of the United Methodist Church, but praise God I am no longer the only."

participation in various forms of social activism. For example, in Santeria, a Caribbean religion, women who are healers, or *santeras*, have great personal power and hold immense social power in their communities. These women willingly enter into altered states of consciousness and allow the spirits to use them to bring about healing. When a person visits a *santera*, the *santera* sees all the spirits with that person, and the *santera* is often able to reveal to the person what she or he needs to do. This ability puts the *santera* in an extremely powerful position, especially when the person consulting her is a politician or government official, as is often the case. Furthermore, as Caribbean women visit *santeras*, they see women who wield power in their culture and who can act as role models for them.

Another example of the role of religion in encouraging social activism is that of Jesse Daniel Ames, who helped organize the antilynching movement in the early part of the twentieth century. She worked through women's missions organizations in Methodist and Baptist churches in the South. Black churches were at the heart of the 1950s and 1960s civil rights movement in which many early leaders of second wave feminism had their first experiences of political organizing. A key component of

Judaism is social justice, and Jewish women have long been actively involved in anti-defamation, anti-racist, anti-sexist, and anti-heterosexist work. Ernestine Louise Rose, who fought for women's rights and against slavery during the 1840s and 1850s, challenged New York state lawmakers in 1854 to allow women to retain their own property and have equal guardianship of children with their husbands. When male politicians urged women to postpone their quest for suffrage and focus on the rights of former slaves, Rose declared, "Emancipation from every kind of bondage is my principle." She also spoke out against anti-Semitism and set the tone for twentieth-century Jewish feminists' critique of Judaism's traditional attitudes toward women.

Finally, for many women, religion provides a place in which they find a sense of worth as a valued person. The poem "God Says Yes to Me" by Kaylin Haught illustrates an accepting, loving God that has the potential to empower women. In the early twenty-first century, many women participate in revivals of ancient woman-centered religions and have become empowered through the revaluing of the feminine implicit in this spirituality. *Wicca,* or witchcraft (although not the witches we popularly think of at Halloween), is a Goddess- and nature-oriented religion whose origins pre-date both Judaism and Christianity. Current Wiccan practice involves the celebration of the feminine, connection with nature, and the practice of healing. As Starhawk suggests in "Witchcraft and Women's Culture," witchcraft encourages women to be strong, confident, and independent and to love the Goddess, the earth, and other human beings. This notion of witchcraft is very different from the cultural norms associated with witches that are propagated in society.

WOMEN AND GOD-LANGUAGE

Many theorists contend that one of the most powerful influences in molding gender and maintaining gender oppression is language. The language religions use to talk about God is especially powerful in shaping the ways we think about men and women. Any language we use to talk about God is of necessity metaphorical. We create images that can only partially represent the full reality of the concept of God. Unfortunately, those images sometimes become understood in literal rather than metaphorical ways. So, instead of thinking of God *as* Father, we may come to think God *is* Father. Throughout Jewish and Christian history, the preponderance of images for God have been masculine—Father, King, Lord, Judge, Master—and the effect has been that many people imagine God as male even though, intellectually, they might know this is not true. God is often imagined as White too.

In ancient times, the image of the Great Mother Goddess was primary in many cultures, but as war-centered patriarchal cultures developed, the life-giving Goddess had to be defeated by the warring God. In ancient Babylonian mythology, Tiamat was the Great Mother, but she was eventually slaughtered by her son Marduk, the God of war. Yahweh, the God of the ancient Israelites, was originally a consort of the Canaanite Mother Goddess, but, as the Israelites moved toward a patriarchal monotheism (belief in just one God), Yahweh became prominent as the Great Father God, and worship of the Goddess was harshly condemned by Yahweh's priests. The prominence of a single masculine image of deity then became reflected in the exclusion of women from the priesthood and eventually from the concept of Israel itself.

LEARNING ACTIVITY   **How Well Do You Know the Goddess?**

Match the Goddess to her name.

_____ g   1. Odudua   a. Egyptian mother Goddess and Goddess of the underworld, the queen of heaven and mother of light.

_____   2. Coatlicue   b. "Queen of Heaven." Assyrian creator of life, mother and guardian. Goddess of fertility, love, sexuality, and justice.

_____   3. Izanami-no-kami   c. Celtic creator of life. Mother Goddess of the earth and moon. The mother of all heroes or deities.

_____ m   4. Demeter   d. Scandinavian creator of life. Leader of the Valkyries.

_____   5. Tho-og   e. "Great, Invincible, and Magnificent Founder and Savior, Commander and Guide, Legislator and Queen." Creator and mother Goddess of Anatolia.

_____ j   6. Kali   f. The mother of Hawaii. Mother and guardian, mother of Pele and the Hawaiian people.

_____ b   7. Astarte   g. Creator of life who brings fertility and love. Goddess of the Yoruba people of Nigeria.

_____   8. Kokyan Wuhti   h. Tibetan primordial being. The eternal mother who is self-formed. She is the preexisting space.

_____ d   9. Freyja   i. "The Great Mother Goddess." Mesopotamian Goddess of justice, earth, nature, and goodness.

_____   10. Haumea   j. Hindu Goddess. She who gives life and also destroys it. The symbol of eternal time.

_____   11. Po Ino Nogar   k. "Spider Grandmother." Hopi creator of life. Beneficent deity who created humans, plants, and animals.

_____ a   12. Hathor   l. "Serpent Skirt." Mother Goddess of all Aztec deities of Mexico, the ruler of life and death.

_____ c   13. Anu   m. Greek mother and guardian. One of the twelve great Greek Olympian deities. She has power over the productivity of the earth and the social order of humans.

_____   14. Asherah   n. "Female-Who-Invites." Japanese creator of life, earth and nature, heaven and hell.

_____ e   15. Artemis Ephesus   o. "Great One." Vietnamese creator of life. World fertility Goddess who brings rice to the people and protects the fields and harvests.

Answers: 1. g; 2. l; 3. n; 4. m; 5. h; 6. j; 7. b; 8. k; 9. d; 10. f; 11. o; 12. a; 13. c; 14. i; 15. e

Source: Martha Ann and Dorothy Myers Imel, *Goddesses in World Mythology: A Biographical Dictionary* (New York: Oxford University Press, 1993).

LEARNING ACTIVITY **Exploring New Metaphors for Deity**

Metaphors are images drawn from familiar human experiences, used in fresh ways to help explore realities that are not easily accessible in our everyday experience. All language about deity is metaphorical because no one image or analogy can capture the essence of deity. Throughout the history of Jewish and Christian faiths, in particular, deity has been variously imaged as Father, Shepherd, King, Lord, and Master. Originally, these metaphors helped many people explore and grapple with different aspects of the nature of deity. Many contemporary theologians, however, suggest the need for new metaphors for deity, shocking metaphors that will cause people to think about deity in new ways. Theologian Sallie McFague contends, "The best metaphors give both a shock and a shock of recognition." In good metaphors, we see something about reality, and we see it in new ways.

What are some of the metaphors for deity with which you are familiar? In what ways have those metaphors been helpful? In what ways are those metaphors limiting? What do you perceive as the consequences of taking these metaphors literally? Are there some metaphors you think have outlived their usefulness?

Following are a number of new metaphors for deity that are being utilized in current theological discussion. What do you think of these metaphors? In what new ways do they cause you to think about deity? What new ideas about deity do they suggest to you? In what ways do they call you to reappraise images of deity?

- God as mother
- God as lover
- God as companion
- God as gambler
- The earth and God's body

Can you think of any shocking new metaphors that help you think about deity in original ways?

In response to the hegemony of masculine images of God, feminist theologians have constructed alternative feminine images of deity. Some theologians, such as Virginia Mollenkott, have returned to the Jewish and Christian testaments to point out the existence of feminine images within scripture. Other theologians, such as Sallie McFague, have challenged people to develop new models of God such as God as mother, God as lover, and God as companion. And yet other women have returned to the ancient images of the Goddess herself. In "Grandmother of the Sun: The Power of Woman in Native America," Paula Gunn Allen explains Native American feminine images of deity.

The political nature of the decision to challenge normative God-language does not go unnoticed by traditionalists wishing to cling to male images. The Southern Baptist Convention issued a statement declaring that God is not *like* a father, but God *is* Father. And a group of mainline churchwomen created a furor within their denominations when at a conference they chose to call God "Sophia," a biblical, but feminine, name for deity.

[handwritten note: why does the belief not matter, only the name (male names) — still the same superdivine being]

REINTERPRETING
AND RECONSTRUCTING TRADITIONS

For those feminist women who have chosen to remain in religious traditions, the task of reworking oppressive elements has been great. Theology itself has been constructed with male experience as normative and has not taken into account the experiences of both men and women. Since the 1960s, feminist theologians have undertaken the task of rethinking traditional theological notions from the perspective of women's experiences. For example, the traditional notion of sin expressed in the story of the Fall in Genesis is that of pride and the centrality of the self. Redemption in the Christian testament then involves the restoration of what humans lack—sacrificial love. Yet the normative experience for women is not pride and self-centeredness, given that women are generally socialized to be self-negating for the sake of their families, and, in fact, encouraging women to be self-sacrificing as a form of redemption simply exacerbates women's situation. Feminist theology, as Alicia Ostriker suggests in her poem "Everywoman Her Own Theology," brings women's experiences to the center and reconstructs theological concepts in keeping with those experiences.

Because of the predominance of Christianity in the United States, the Bible and its various interpretations play a large role in shaping women's lives. Given this importance, feminist re-examinations of religion are on a continuum from reinterpretation to reconstruction. *Reinterpretation* involves recognizing the passages that are particularly problematic for women and highlighting and reintegrating the passages that extol equality between women and men. Proponents of such reinterpretation include Christian feminists who maintain a positive view of scripture as they continue to accept scripture as an authority in their lives. The goal of *reconstruction,* however, is to move beyond reinterpretation and recognize the patriarchal underpinnings of various interpretations and the ways they have been used to oppress women.

As an example of a reconstructionist account, Christian testament scholar Elisabeth Schüssler Fiorenza encourages readers of scripture to look for the presence of women in the margins and around the edges of the text. She calls for biblical readers to re-create the narratives of women that were left out of but hinted at in the text. In a similar fashion, the reading "Standing Again at Sinai" by Jewish feminist scholar Judith Plaskow calls for a reconceptualization of notions of God, Torah, and Israel that are inclusive of women. Other reconstructions of scripture include "womanist" biblical interpretations of women of color that analyze the Bible in light of both sexism and racism. In these accounts the Bible itself is subject to scrutiny in terms of its expressions of justice and injustice. Readers of the Bible with this perspective focus on the moral and ethical imperatives of justice contained therein and with an eye toward struggle for liberation for women of color.

Women have begun to challenge and reconstruct religious traditions as well as scripture. For example, Jewish women have developed feminist haggadahs, texts containing the ritual for celebrating the Passover seder. These feminist haggadahs commemorate the women of the Exodus, the liberation of the Israelites from slavery in

"... and so, then I said, 'You think that just because I'm a woman I can't preach, just because I'm a woman I can't hold office in the convention, just because I'm a woman I can't do evangelism, just because I'm a woman I can't teach theology!' And he said, 'Yes.'"

Reprinted with permission from Norma Young.

Egypt. In one haggadah, the four sons of the traditional ceremony become four daughters, and the lives of the women celebrating Passover are inserted in the ceremony to create a living history and a new story.

Perhaps one of the most contentious reconstructions of religious traditions is the ordination of women. Although feminist church historians have recovered a long tradition of women as rabbis, priests, pastors, bishops, and evangelists, most Christian denominations did not ordain women until the latter part of the twentieth century. Many still do not. One exception to this is the Quakers, who have a long and unique history of women's equality in the congregation. Although Quakers do not ordain anyone, some groups of Quakers do record ministers, and women have always been among the recorded. In silent Quaker meetings, women as well as men are assumed to be able to receive and speak a word from God. Beginning in the 1960s, many mainline Protestant churches began to ordain women ministers, although men still make up the larger percentage of senior pastors in almost every denomination. Roman Catholics still prohibit women from becoming priests, although there is a growing movement within Catholicism, particularly American Catholicism, to change this policy. Several churches, such as the United Church of Christ, the Unitarian Universalist Association, and the Episcopalians, ordain openly gay and lesbian clergy, although in the latter case this has caused tension between the Episcopalian churches inside and outside the United States because the latter resist such ordination of gay clergy.

ACTIVIST PROFILE **Nannie Helen Burroughs**

Nannie Helen Burroughs was only 21 years old when she delivered her stirring speech, "How the Sisters Are Hindered from Helping," at the 1900 National Baptist Convention in Richmond, Virginia. This speech proved to be instrumental in the formation of the Women's Convention Auxiliary to the National Baptist Convention, the largest African American women's organization in the country at that time. The Women's Convention promptly elected Burroughs its corresponding secretary and continued to re-elect her every year from 1900 to 1948. In 1948 she became the convention's president and served in that role until her death in 1961.

Burroughs was also a tireless activist—challenging lynching and segregation, denouncing employment discrimination, opposing European colonization of Africa, and promoting women's suffrage. After the Nineteenth Amendment was passed, she founded the National League of Republican Colored Women and worked to encourage African American women to become politically involved. She also established the Women's Industrial Club, which offered short-term housing to African American women and taught them basic domestic skills. The club also offered moderately priced lunches for downtown office workers. During the Depression, Burroughs formed Cooperative Industrial, Inc., which provided free facilities for a medical clinic, hair salon, and variety store.

One of Burroughs's driving passions was the education of African American women. In 1909, with the support of the National Baptist Convention, she opened the National Trade and Professional School for Women and Girls in Washington, D.C., and served as the institution's president. The school emphasized a close connection between education and religion. Its curriculum focused on the development of practical and professional skills and included a program in Black history in which every student was required to take a course. Burroughs's motto for the school was "We specialize in the wholly impossible." In 1964 the school was renamed the Nannie Burroughs School. In 1975 Mayor Walter E. Washington proclaimed May 10 Nannie Helen Burroughs Day in the District of Columbia in recognition of Burroughs's courage in advocating for education for African American women despite societal norms.

CREATING NEW SPIRITUAL TRADITIONS

Although some feminists believe in the reinterpretation and reconstruction of scriptures and choose to work within existing denominations, others prefer to create their own empowering religious texts and organizations. For some, traditional religious scriptures are so essentially androcentric, or male centered, that they can only reproduce patriarchal social relations. They see no possibility of liberation for women in scripture because even reconstruction of biblical texts cannot change the patriarchal core of, for example, the Bible. Rather, these reconstructions simply perpetuate the patriarchal order. Feminist philosopher Mary Daly argues that patriarchal language is not accidental or incidental to the Bible but is an essential element of it, rendering the Bible useless in the liberation of women. Women like Daly look beyond traditional scripture for spiritual insight and understanding. Wiccan groups, discussed above, fall into this category too.

In this way, although many women have expressed their spirituality within formal religious traditions, many others have created new forms of spiritual expression outside churches, synagogues, and mosques. Women's spirituality is an empowering force that has taken such various forms as meditation, poetry, art, prayer, ritual, and social action. Spirituality enables women to experience connection with creation, with other human beings, and with the divine within themselves.

For many feminists, spirituality is a central force in their politics. The awareness of the interconnectedness of all things motivates feminist action toward justice and peace and encourages women to work together across differences. Nature-based spiritualities affirm the connections among all living things and seek to protect the natural environment on which we all depend. Feminist spirituality values and affirms the diversity that makes up the unity of creation, and it challenges women to restructure the systems of power that create and maintain injustice. The reading "Religion and Feminism's Fourth Wave" by Pythia Peay demonstrates this commitment to change. It discusses an ecumenical group: a gathering of women across many different religious faiths who share a desire for spiritually informed activism. As Marge Piercy writes:

> Praise our choices, sisters, for each doorway
> open to us was taken by squads of fighting
> women who paid years of trouble and struggle,
> who paid their wombs, their sleep, their lives
> that we might walk through these gates upright.
> Doorways are sacred to women for we
> are the doorways of life and we must choose
> what comes in and what goes out. Freedom
> is our real abundance.*

---

* "The Sabbath of Mutual Respect," *The Moon Is Always Female* (New York: Knopf, 1980).

Introduction to *The Woman's Bible*

Elizabeth Cady Stanton (1895)

From the inauguration of the movement for woman's emancipation the Bible has been used to hold [woman] in the "divinely ordained sphere," prescribed in the Old and New Testaments.

The canon and civil law; church and state; priests and legislators; all political parties and religious denominations have alike taught that woman was made after man, of man, and for man, an inferior being, subject to man. Creeds, codes, Scriptures and statutes, are all based on this idea. The fashions, forms, ceremonies and customs of society, church ordinances and discipline all grow out of this idea.

. . .

The Bible teaches that woman brought sin and death into the world, that she precipitated the fall of the race, that she was arraigned before the judgment seat of Heaven, tried, condemned and sentenced. Marriage for her was to be a condition of bondage, maternity a period of suffering and anguish, and in silence and subjection, she was to play the role of a dependent on man's bounty for all her material wants, and for all the information she might desire on the vital questions of the hour, she was commanded to ask her husband at home. Here is the Bible position of woman briefly summed up.

. . .

These familiar texts are quoted by clergymen in their pulpits, by statesmen in the halls of legislation, by lawyers in the courts, and are echoed by the press of all civilized nations, and accepted by woman herself as "The Word of God." So perverted is the religious element in her nature, that with faith and works she is the chief support of the church and clergy; the very powers that make her emancipation impossible. When, in the early part of the Nineteenth Century, women began to protest against their civil and political degradation, they were referred to the Bible for an answer. When they protested against their unequal position in the church, they were referred to the Bible for an answer.

This led to a general and critical study of the Scriptures. Some, having made a fetish of these books and believing them to be the veritable "Word of God," with liberal translations, interpretations, allegories and symbols, glossed over the most objectionable features of the various books and clung to them as divinely inspired. Others, seeing the family resemblance between the Mosaic code, the canon law, and the old English common law, came to the conclusion that all alike emanated from the same source; wholly human in their origin and inspired by the natural love of domination in the historians. Others, bewildered with their doubts and fears, came to no conclusion. While their clergymen told them on the one hand that they owed all the blessings and freedom they enjoyed to the Bible, on the other, they said it clearly marked out their circumscribed sphere of action: that the demands for political and civil rights were irreligious, dangerous to the stability of the home, the state and the church. Clerical appeals were circulated from time to time conjuring members of their churches to take no part in the anti-slavery or woman suffrage movements, as they were infidel in their tendencies, undermining the very foundations of society. No wonder the majority of women stood still, and with bowed heads, accepted the situation.

683

God Says Yes to Me

Kaylin Haught (1995)

I asked God if it was okay to be melodramatic
and she said yes
I asked her if it was okay to be short
and she said it sure is
I asked her if I could wear nail polish
or not wear nail polish
and she said honey
she calls me that sometimes
she said you can do just exactly

what you want to
Thanks God I said
And is it even okay if I don't paragraph
my letters
Sweetcakes God said
who knows where she picked that up
what I'm telling you is
Yes Yes Yes

Fundamentalism and the Control of Women

Karen McCarthy Brown (1994)

Religious fundamentalism is very difficult to define; yet many of us—scholars and journalists in particular—think we know it when we see it. For those attuned to gender as a category of analysis, a stab of recognition is often occasioned by the presence of high degrees of religiously sanctioned control of women. In conservative religious movements around the world, women are veiled or otherwise covered; confined to the home or in some other way strictly limited in their access to the public sphere; prohibited from testifying in a court of law, owning property, or initiating divorce; and they are very often denied the authority to make their own reproductive choices.

I propose to take up the thread of the control of women and follow it into the center of the maze of contemporary fundamentalism. Yet I will not argue, as might be expected, that the need to control women is the main motivation for the rise of fundamentalism, but rather that aggravation of this age-old, widespread need is an inevitable side effect of a type of stress peculiar to our age.

I will suggest that the varieties of fundamentalism found throughout the world today are extreme responses to the failed promise of Enlightenment rationalism. Fundamentalism, in my view, is the religion of the stressed and the disoriented, of those for whom the world is overwhelming. More to the point, it is the religion of those at once seduced and betrayed by the promise that we human beings can comprehend and control our world. Bitterly disappointed by the politics of rationalized bureaucracies, the limitations of science, and the perversions of industrialization, fundamentalists seek to reject the modern world, while nevertheless holding onto its habits of mind: clarity, certitude, and control. Given these habits, fundamentalists necessarily operate with a limited view of human activity (including religious activity), one confined largely to consciousness and choice. They deny the power of those parts of the human psyche that are inaccessible to consciousness yet play a central role in orienting us in the world. Most of all they seek to control the fearsome, mute power of the flesh. This characteristic ensures that fundamentalism will always involve the control of women, for women generally carry the greater burden of human fleshliness.

This essay is an exploratory one. Its topic is huge and it ranges widely, crossing over into several academic disciplines other than my own. Occasionally I am forced to paint with a broad stroke and a quick hand. Writing that is preliminary and suggestive can be risky, but the connections I see between religious fundamentalism and other, larger aspects of our contemporary world seem compelling enough to lead me to take that risk. My argument begins close to home, in the United States, with Christian anti-abortion activism.

THE ANTI-ABORTION MOVEMENT IN THE UNITED STATES

The "pro-life movement" emerged in the 1970s as a new type of religio-political organization. It was a bottom-up movement that used sophisticated, top-down technology. In the early stages of the movement, the organizing work was done around kitchen tables. But the envelopes stuffed at those tables were sent to addresses on computer-generated mailing lists, the product of advanced market-research techniques. This blend of grass-roots organization and advanced technology quickly brought a minority movement[1] to a position of significant political power. The combination of traditional and modern methods also reveals an ambivalence toward the ways of the modern world

that I will later argue is characteristic of fundamentalist movements.

Many observers have noted an inconsistency in the pro-life position. The very groups who launch an emotional defense of the fetus's right to life are curiously indifferent to children outside the womb. As a rule, pro-lifers do not support social programs focused on issues such as child abuse, day care, foster care, or juvenile drug use. They oppose welfare programs in general and have taken no leadership in educational reform beyond concern with sex education, public school prayer, and the theory of evolution. Furthermore, their so-called pro-life argument is deeply compromised by staunch support for increased military spending and for the death penalty. It seems clear that the pro-life position is not a consistent theological or philosophical stance. A quite different kind of consistency emerges from the full range of this group's social policy positions. Their overriding concern is that of maintaining strong and clear social boundaries—boundaries between nation-states, between law-abiding citizens and criminals, between the righteous and the sinful, between life and death, and not coincidentally, between men and women. This is a group centrally concerned with social order and social control.

Beyond the trigger of the 1973 Supreme Court decision in *Roe v. Wade,* stresses with a broader historical range have contributed to a focus on boundary maintenance in the anti-abortion movement. The upheavals of the 1960s created the immediate historical context of the anti-abortion movement of the 1970s. Student activists of the 1960s questioned the authority of parents, educators, and politicians. Black activists challenged the cherished American myths of equal opportunity and equal protection under the law. And the Vietnam War not only raised questions about U.S. military prowess but also planted doubts about the moral valence of the international presence and policy of the United States. These are very specific reasons why Americans in the 1970s might have felt that the social and moral orders were becoming dangerously befuddled.

. . .

A WORLD SUDDENLY TOO BIG

From the mid-nineteenth century into the early decades of the twentieth, the writings of travelers, missionaries, and, eventually, anthropologists were popular bedside reading materials in the United States. Americans were fascinated by exotic "others." They were concerned about their own place in this expanding, newly complex world. Most of these books did more than titillate. With their implicit or explicit social Darwinism, they also carried deeply comforting messages of progress and of Western superiority. Such messages, coming from many sources, infused an air of optimism into an otherwise disorienting age. During the same general time span, the seeds of American fundamentalism were sown and came to fruition.

Some of the social forces that shaped this period—expanding knowledge of and contact with the larger world, and increased communication—had emerged over a relatively long period of time. Others, such as the burgeoning of cities, the dramatic increase in immigrant populations, and a series of shifts in women's roles, had occurred more recently.[2] All of these forces came together in the second half of the nineteenth century to contribute to a general sense of vertigo; the world was becoming too big, too complicated, and too chaotic to comprehend. Most important, each individual's own place in it was uncertain. Religion, given its basic orientational role in human life, emerged as a natural arena for dealing with the resulting stress.

From that period until this in the United States, conservative Christians have come under a double attack. On one level, they have had to deal with the general stress of the times; and on the other, with the direct challenge of Enlightenment rationalism in the form of biblical higher criticism and evolutionary theory. The reaction of some groups of Christians has been ironic: they have responded to the threat by mimicking Enlightenment rationalism. The religion-versus-science debate pits against one another groups who share a common intellectual style: each claims to possess the truth. Believers,

like rationalists, stress consciousness, clarity, and control.[3] Morality is codified; sacred narratives are taken literally and sometimes attempts are made to support them with "scientific evidence"; all sorts of truths are listed and enumerated; scripture becomes inerrant. Furthermore, conscious consent to membership in the community of belief, on the model of "making a decision for Christ," becomes increasingly important.

These are the religious groups we call fundamentalists. Their central aim is to make of their religion an Archimedean point in the midst of a changing world. But to do so, they must limit their religion's responsiveness to its social environment; and as a result they are left with little flexibility to respond to the complexity of their own feelings or to the challenge of a changing world. Sometimes they fall into aggressively defending brittle truths. This is what makes fundamentalism in the contemporary world problematic and, in some cases, dangerous.

. . .

FUNDAMENTALISM CROSS-CULTURALLY

Up to this point, I have been concerned with Christian fundamentalism in the United States, but in the process I have focused on dimensions of the story that serve, without denying the significance of local variations, to characterize fundamentalism around the globe. Religious fundamentalism is born in times and places where, for a variety of reasons, the world suddenly seems too complex to comprehend; and one's place in it, too precarious to provide genuine security.

One example is modern India, where the cult that developed around the recent immolation of a young woman on her husband's funeral pyre has been described as an instance of fundamentalism. John Hawley demonstrates that the background for the *sati* of Roop Kanwar was emerging Hindu nationalism in India augmented by a multitude of local destabilizing forces in Deorala, the site of the immolation. Furthermore, as Hawley and other authors have pointed out, Deorala is not a truly deprived area, and its residents are not traditionalists out of contact with the larger realities of modern India. I would therefore suggest, along with Hawley, that fundamentalism is not primarily a religion of the marginalized, as some have argued. Its more salient feature is that it develops among people caught off balance. Hence, fundamentalist groups often arise in situations where social, cultural, and economic power is up for grabs; many, like these groups now being referred to as Hindu fundamentalists, arise in postcolonial situations. Far from being essentially marginal to the societies in which they exist, fundamentalists are often directly involved in the political and economic issues of their time and place. And they often have a significant, if precarious, stake in them.

For the Rajputs in Deorala, traditional sources of pride and authority are being challenged by increasing contact with the cities of Jaipur and Delhi, and through them, all of India. These Rajputs are experiencing the disorientation of having to depend on economic and political systems beyond their control. Marwari merchants and industrialists, financial backers of the cult of the goddess Sati, are destabilized in another way. As their economic role expands throughout India, they risk their livelihood in a wider, less familiar, and less predictable world than the one in which earlier generations operated. The Marwari focus on the district around Jhunjhunu with its important Sati shrine gives them their emotionally saturated Archimedean point. The case of the Marwari businessmen suggests, even more directly than does that of the Rajputs, that fundamentalism is not a religion of the marginalized, but of the disoriented.

In the contemporary Indian context, rallying around the *sati* of Roop Kanwar (like anti-abortion activity in the United States) reasserts social control and demonstrates moral worth. It strengthens gender boundaries and provides an example of undiluted, innocent virtue that vicariously underwrites the virtue of Rajputs and Marwaris in general. Furthermore, as in the United States, insecurity about social control and moral rectitude is displaced onto the body of a woman. But in the *sati* ritual described by Hawley, the drive to kill the devouring, fleshly goddess and to enshrine the pure, spiritual one is much more painfully literal.

Both men and women attended the *sati* of Roop Kanwar, and both men and women subsequently revere her. At first glance this may seem difficult to understand, but the complicity of Indian women in the practice of *sati* has to be considered on more than one level. At the deepest level its explanation lies in the fear of women's will and women's flesh that men and women share, and in the relief that both feel when these forces are kept in check. But on another level there are explanations of a much more practical nature. Most Indian women's economic security heavily depends on marriage. A woman doing homage at a Sati shrine thus signals to her husband and to the world at large, as well as to herself, that she intends to be good and to do good, according to her society's standards. Thus she chooses to ignore any anger or fear she might feel about the practice, in the name of living a secure and ordered life. It is a herculean task for women to try to define the meaning and worth of their lives in terms different from those that prevail in their community. So some security can always be found in surrendering to, and even helping to strengthen, the accepted gender norms.

. . .

THE FAILED PROMISE
OF ENLIGHTENMENT RATIONALISM

Modern communications, transnational economic pressures, and wars waged from the opposite side of the globe have brought many populations intimate knowledge of the vastness and complexity of their worlds. In the late twentieth century, the others in relation to whom we must define ourselves are more available to our experience and imagination than ever before; yet few if any of us have a satisfactory model for understanding ourselves within this complex, stressful world.

We all live in and are defined by a world too big and unstable for intellect or belief to comprehend, and we all react to intimations—as well as a few pieces of hard evidence[4]—of the failed promise of the Enlightenment. Academics, politicians, and ordinary folk the world over are immersed in this challenge and most commonly react to it (as fundamentalists do) by assuming that, with sufficient effort, the chaos can be first comprehended and then managed. In this way fundamentalists are simply extreme versions of the rest of us.

An emphasis on the control of women is characteristic of fundamentalism, but there is some of it everywhere in the world. The anti-abortion movement in the United States arises out of a much broader context in which, among other signals of misogyny, public power and authority have been denied to women for centuries. And the Sati cult could not have become an issue in Indian nationalism if in general Indian women were not seen as sources of pollution as well as of blessing—as a result of which they have been subject to a variety of social controls through the ages. When the mind and the spirit are cut off from the body, women become magnets for the fear raised by everything in life that seems out of control. The degree to which control is exercised over women is therefore a key to the profundity of stresses felt by most persons and groups. Fundamentalism is a product of extreme social stress.

Religion, whose primary function is to provide a comprehensible model of the world and to locate the individual safely and meaningfully within it, is an obvious place for this type of stress to express itself and seek redress. But as long as religions deal with this stress by positing a world that can be directly known, and in which it is possible to determine one's own fate, they only reinforce the controlling tendencies of Enlightenment rationalism and do nothing to move us beyond it to whatever comes next. We should be suspicious of any religion that claims too much certainty or draws the social boundaries too firmly. In this period marked by the gradual breakdown of Enlightenment rationalism and Euro-American hegemony in the world, something more is necessary. We need help in accepting ourselves as organic creatures enmeshed in our world rather than continuing to posture as cerebral masters granted dominion over it. This requires that we learn to trust the wisdom of our mute flesh and accept the limitations inherent in our humanity. If we could do this, it would radically diminish our scapegoating of women and all the other "others" who provide a convenient screen on which to project fears.

The resurgence of religion that we are experiencing at the turn of this millennium should not be viewed in an entirely negative light. If any system of orientation in the world can help us now, it seems likely to be a religious one. There is no small comfort in knowing that, as the grand ambitions spawned by the Enlightenment falter in the present age, what is likely to emerge is not what several generations of social scientists predicted. It is not civilization marching toward increasing secularization and rationalization. What is slowly being revealed is the hubris of reason's pretense in trying to take over religion's role.

NOTES

1. From the beginning of the anti-abortion movement to the present, opinion polls have consistently shown that the majority of people in the United States favor a woman's right to have an abortion.
2. Betty A. DeBerg, *Ungodly Women: Gender and the First Wave of American Fundamentalism* (Minneapolis: Fortress Press, 1990), has an excellent discussion of the general changes—and particularly the changes in women's roles—attendant to the formation of fundamentalism in the United States. . . .
3. Often the only kind of control that fundamentalists can exercise over a chaotic and threatening world rests in their claim to have a privileged understanding of the deeper meaning of the chaos. Fundamentalists who engage in "end-time" thinking thus sometimes find themselves in the position of welcoming the signs of modern social decay because these signal the approach of the time when God will call home the chosen few.
4. The growing ecological crisis is one of the most tangible pieces of this evidence; it also reinforces the point that reason alone is an insufficient problem-solving tool, because we are incapable of holding in consciousness the full range of the interconnectedness of things.

Grandmother of the Sun
The Power of Woman in Native America

Paula Gunn Allen (1989)

There is a spirit that pervades everything, that is capable of powerful song and radiant movement, and that moves in and out of the mind. The colors of this spirit are multitudinous, a flowing, pulsing rainbow. Old Spider Woman is one name for this quintessential spirit, and Serpent Woman is another. Corn Woman is one aspect of her, and Earth Woman is another, and what they together have made is called Creation, Earth, creatures, plants, and light.

At the center of all is Woman, and no thing is sacred (cooked, ripe, as the Keres Indians of Laguna Pueblo say it) without her blessing, her thinking.

> . . . In the beginning Tse che nako, Thought Woman finished everything, thoughts, and the names of all things. She finished also all the languages. And then our mothers, Uretsete and Naotsete said they would make names and they would make thoughts. Thus they said: Thus they did.[1]

This spirit, this power of intelligence, has many names and many emblems. She appears on the plains, in the forests, in the great canyons, on the mesas, beneath the seas. To her we owe our very breath, and to her our prayers are sent blown on pollen, on corn meal, planted into the earth on feather-sticks, spit onto the water, burned and sent to her on the wind. Her variety and multiplicity testify to her complexity: she is the true Creatrix for she is thought itself, from which all else is born. She is the necessary precondition for material creation, and she, like all of her creation, is fundamentally female—potential and primary.

She is also the spirit that informs right balance, right harmony, and these in turn order all relationships in conformity with her law.

To assign to this great being the position of "fertility goddess" is exceedingly demeaning: it trivializes the tribes and it trivializes the power of woman. Woman bears, that is true. She also destroys. That is true. She also wars and hexes and mends and breaks. She creates the power of the seeds, and she plants them. As Anthony Purley, a Laguna writer, has translated a Keres ceremonial prayer, "She is mother of us all, after Her, mother earth follows, in fertility, in holding, and taking again us back to her breast."[2]

The Hopi account of their genatrix, Hard Beings Woman, gives the most articulate rendering of the difference between simple fertility cultism and the creative prowess of the Creatrix. Hard Beings Woman (Huruing Wuhti) is of the earth. But she lives in the worlds above where she "owns" (empowers) the moon and stars. Hard Beings Woman has solidity and hardness as her major aspects. She, like Thought Woman, does not give birth to creation or to human beings but breathes life into male and female effigies that become the parents of the Hopi—in this way she "creates" them. The male is Muingwu, the god of crops, and his sister-consort is Sand Altar Woman who is also known as Childbirth Water Woman. In Sand Altar Woman the mystical relationship between water, worship, and woman is established; she is also said to be the mother of the katsinas, those powerful messengers who relate the spirit world to the world of humankind and vice versa.[3]

Like Thought Woman, Hard Beings Woman lived in the beginning on an island which was the only land there was. In this regard she resembles a number of Spirit Woman Beings; the Spirit genatrix of the Iroquois, Sky Woman, also lived on an island in the void which only later became the earth. On this island, Hard Beings Woman is identified with or, as they say, "owns" all hard substances—moon, stars, beads, coral, shell, and so forth. She is a sea goddess as well, the single inhabitant of the earth, that island that floats alone in the waters of space. From this meeting of woman and water, earth and her creatures were born.[4] . . .

Contemporary Indian tales suggest that the creatures are born from the mating of sky father and earth mother, but that seems to be a recent interpolation of the original sacred texts. The revision may have occurred since the Christianizing influence on even the arcane traditions, or it may have predated Christianity. But the older, more secret texts suggest that it is a revision. It may be that the revision appears only in popular versions of the old mythic cycles on which ceremony and ritual are based; this would accord with the penchant in the old oral tradition for shaping tales to reflect present social realities, making the rearing and education of children possible even within the divergent worlds of the United States of America and the tribes.

According to the older texts (which are sacred, that is, power-engendering), Thought Woman is not a passive personage: her potentiality is dynamic and unimaginably powerful. She brought corn and agriculture, potting, weaving, social systems, religion, ceremony, ritual, building, memory, intuition, and their expressions in language, creativity, dance, human-to-animal relations, and she gave these offerings power and authority and blessed the people with the ability to provide for themselves and their progeny.

Thought Woman is not limited to a female role in the total theology of the Keres people. Since she is the supreme Spirit, she is both Mother and Father to all people and to all creatures. She is the only creator of thought, and thought precedes creation.[5]

Central to Keres theology is the basic idea of the Creatrix as She Who Thinks rather than She Who Bears, of woman as creation thinker and female thought as origin of material and non-material reality. In this epistemology, the perception of female power as confined to maternity is a limit on the power inherent in femininity. But "she is the supreme Spirit, . . . both Mother and Father to all people and to all creatures."[6] . . .

In Keres theology the creation does not take place through copulation. In the beginning existed Thought Woman and her dormant sisters, and Thought Woman thinks creation and sings her two sisters into life. After they are vital she instructs them to sing over the items in their baskets (medicine bundles) in such a way that those items will have life. After that crucial task is accomplished, the creatures thus vitalized take on the power to regenerate themselves—that is, they can reproduce others of their kind. But they are not in and of themselves self-sufficient; they depend for their being on the medicine power of the three great Witch creatrixes, Thought Woman, Uretsete, and Naotsete. The sisters are not related by virtue of having parents in common; that is, they are not alive because anyone bore them. Thought Woman turns up, so to speak, first as Creatrix and then as a personage who is acting out someone else's "dream." But there is no time when she did not exist. She has two bundles in her power, and these bundles contain Uretsete and Naotsete, who are not viewed as her daughters but as her sisters, her coequals who possess the medicine power to vitalize the creatures that will inhabit the earth. They also have the power to create the firmament, the skies, the galaxies, and the seas, which they do through the use of ritual magic.

. . .

THE HEART OF POWER

. . .

Pre-Conquest American Indian women valued their role as vitalizers. Through their own bodies they could bring vital beings into the world—a miraculous power whose potency does not diminish with industrial sophistication or time.

They were mothers, and that word did not imply slaves, drudges, drones who are required to live only for others rather than for themselves as it does so tragically for many modern women. The ancient ones were empowered by their certain knowledge that the power to make life is the source of all power and that no other power can gainsay it. Nor is that power simply of biology, as modernists tendentiously believe. When Thought Woman brought to life the twin sisters, she did not give birth to them in the biological sense. She sang over the medicine bundles that contained their potentials. With her singing and shaking she infused them with vitality. She gathered the power that she controlled and focused it on those bundles, and thus they were "born." Similarly, when the sister goddesses Naotsete and Uretsete wished to bring forth some plant or creature, they reached into the basket (bundle) that Thought Woman had given them, took out the effigy of the creature, and thought it into life. Usually they then instructed it in its proper role. They also meted out consequences to creatures (this included plants, spirits, and katsinas) who disobeyed them.

The water of life, menstrual or postpartum blood, was held sacred. Sacred often means taboo; that is, what is empowered in a ritual sense is not to be touched or approached by any who are weaker than the power itself, lest they suffer negative consequences from contact. The blood of woman was in and of itself infused with the power of Supreme Mind, and so women were held in awe and respect. The term *sacred,* which is connected with power, is similar in meaning to the term *sacrifice,* which means "to make sacred." What is made sacred is empowered. Thus, in the old way, sacrificing meant empowering, which is exactly what it still means to American Indians who adhere to traditional practice. Blood was and is used in sacrifice because it possesses the power to make something else powerful or, conversely, to weaken or kill it.

Pre-contact American Indian women valued their role as vitalizers because they understood that bearing, like bleeding, was a transformative ritual act. Through their own bodies they could bring vital beings into the world—a miraculous power unrivaled by mere shamanic displays. They were mothers, and that word implied the highest degree of status in ritual cultures. The status of mother was so high, in fact, that in some cultures Mother or its analogue, Matron, was the highest office to which a man or woman could aspire.

The old ones were empowered by their certain knowledge that the power to make life is the source and model for all ritual magic and that no other power can gainsay it. Nor is that power really biological at base; it is the power of ritual magic, the power of Thought, of Mind, that gives rise to biological organisms as it gives rise to social organizations, material culture, and transformations of all kinds—including hunting, war, healing, spirit communication, rain-making, and all the rest. . . .

A strong attitude integrally connects the power of Original Thinking or Creation Thinking to the power of mothering. That power is not so much the power to give birth, as we have noted, but the power to make, to create, to transform. Ritual means transforming something from one state or condition to another, and that ability is inherent in the action of mothering. It is the ability that is sought and treasured by adepts, and it is the ability that male seekers devote years of study and discipline to acquire. Without it, no practice of the sacred is possible, at least not within the Great Mother societies.

And as the cultures that are woman-centered and Mother-ritual based are also cultures that value peacefulness, harmony, cooperation, health, and general prosperity, they are systems of thought and practice that would bear deeper study in our troubled, conflict-ridden time.

NOTES

1. Anthony Purley, "Keres Pueblo Concepts of Deity," *American Indian Culture and Research Journal* 1 (Fall 1974): 29. The passage cited is Purley's literal translation from the Keres Indian language of a portion of the Thought Woman story. Purley is a native-speaker Laguna Pueblo Keres.
2. Ibid., 30–31.

3. Hamilton A. Tyler, *Pueblo Gods and Myths,* Civilization of the American Indian Series (Norman, OK: University of Oklahoma Press, 1964), 37. Evidently, Huruing Wuhti has other transformative abilities as well. Under pressure from patriarchal politics, she can change her gender, her name, and even her spiritual nature.

4. Ibid., 93.

5. Purley, "Keres Pueblo Concepts," 31.

6. Ibid.

R E A D I N G **95**

An Islamic Bill of Rights for Women in Mosques

Asra Q. Nomani (2005)

1. Women have an Islamic right to enter a mosque.
2. Women have an Islamic right to enter through the main door.
3. Women have an Islamic right to visual and auditory access to the *musalla* (main sanctuary).
4. Women have an Islamic right to pray in the musalla without being separated by a barrier, including in the front and in mixed-gender congregational lines.
5. Women have an Islamic right to address any and all members of the congregation.
6. Women have an Islamic right to hold leadership positions, including positions as prayer leaders and as members of the board of directors and management committees.
7. Women have an Islamic right to be full participants in all congregational activities.
8. Women have an Islamic right to lead and participate in meetings, study sessions, and other community activities without being separated by a barrier.
9. Women have an Islamic right to be greeted and addressed cordially.
10. Women have an Islamic right to respectful treatment and exemption from gossip and slander.

THE CONVENTION

CHICAGO—. . . I was committed to being honest about who I am. Most women, although not all, wore the hijab in Chicago. Even women who didn't ordinarily cover their hair did for the convention so that they wouldn't be the subject of gossip. I cover my hair only in the mosque, and I wasn't going to do it now just for public appearance.

After all of the other panelists had spoken—most with PowerPoint presentations—I took the podium. I gazed softly at the audience and thanked the Islamic Society of North America. I explained that the presentation was the result of almost two years of work inspired by the transformative experience of praying together with my family in Mecca on the holy pilgrimage of the hajj in February 2003. I had made that journey with the help of the Islamic Society of North America, and I thanked the society for that experience and the opportunity to speak at the convention. My points were simple. "Islam is at a crossroads much like the place where the prophet Muhammad found himself when he was on the cusp of a new dawn with his migration to Medina from Mecca. Medina became 'the City of Illumination' because of the wisdom with which the prophet nurtured his ummah. In much the same way, the Muslim world has the opportunity to rise to a place of deep and sincere enlightenment, inspired by the greatest teachings of Islam. It is our choice which path we take. It is our mandate to take action to ensure that we define our communities as tolerant, inclusive, and compassionate places that value and inspire all within our fold."

The problem was clear. "There are many model mosques that affirm women's rights. Yet women are systematically denied rights that Islam granted them in the seventh century in mosques throughout America. Islam grants all people inalienable rights to respect, dignity, participation, leadership, voice, knowledge, and worship. These rights must be granted to women, as well as men, in the mosques and Islamic centers that are a part of our Muslim communities. Islamic teaching seeks expressions of modesty between men and women. But many mosques in America and beyond have gone well beyond that principle by defining themselves with cultural traditions that perpetuate a system of separate accommodations that provides women with wholly unequal services for prayer and education. And yet, excluding women ignores the rights the prophet Muhammad gave them in the seventh century when he created a Muslim ummah in Medina and represents innovations that emerged after the prophet died."

I gave evidence of the rights denied in mosques throughout America and laid out the Islamic arguments that had empowered me to take action in my mosque in Morgantown. "It is

time for our communities to embody the essential principles of equity, tolerance, and inclusion within Islam," I said. "And it is incumbent upon each of us as Muslims to stand up for those principles."

I told them what I had come to realize in the two years since January 2001 when the Dalai Lama had set me on my path toward Mecca. Terrorists transformed our world into a more dangerous place when they attacked the World Trade Center and the Pentagon on September 11, 2001. Before we knew it, a minority of Islamic fundamentalists who preached hatred of the West were defining Islam in the world. Alas, moderates, including myself, have been a "silent majority," remaining largely quiet. A combination of fear, shame, and apathy has contributed to a culture of silence among even those of us who are discontented with the status quo in Muslim society. Moderate Muslims have a great responsibility to define Islam and their communities in the world. For me, this effort started at home when I walked up to the front door of my mosque for the first time on the eve of Ramadan 2003. It is time, I said, for us to reclaim the rights Islam granted to women in the seventh century. Toward that end, I humbly introduced my poster with the Islamic Bill of Rights for Women in Mosques.

The rights are simple: the right to enter a mosque; the right to use the main door; the right to have visual and auditory access to the *musalla* (the main sanctuary); the right to pray in the main sanctuary without being separated by a barrier; the right to address any and all members of the congregation; the right to hold leadership positions, including positions on the board of directors; the right to be greeted and addressed cordially; and the right to receive respectful treatment and to be exempt from gossip and slander.

After reading the rights, I told the audience, "Ultimately, it is incumbent upon Islamic organizations, community leaders, academics, and mosques to respond to this call for improved rights for women in mosques by endorsing and promoting a campaign, modeling it after their very successful educational and legal campaigns to protect the civil liberties of Muslim men and women in other areas. To do so would honor not only Muslim women but also Islam. The journey is never complete, and a long road remains in front of us, but we have as inspiration a time in the seventh century when a new day lay ahead of a caravan trader who had as much to fear as we do today but nonetheless transcended his doubts and fears to create an ummah to which we all belong today. Allow us all to rise to our highest potential."

With a deep breath, I sat down, not knowing what to expect next.

Although there were four other speakers, a torrent of questions came at me when members of the audience stood at the microphone.

There were three hecklers. One admonished me for not saying the code phrase "Peace be upon him" after the name of the prophet. Another part of our inside language is "Sall-Allahu aleyhi wa sallam" (May the peace and blessings of Allah be upon him, abbreviated as SAW), said after any mention of the prophet or an angel. "The Clans" in the Qur'an (33:56) says, "The Prophet is blessed by God and His angels. Bless him then, you that are true believers, and greet him with a worthy salutation."

At the dais, the director of the Long Island mosque, Faroque Khan, a physician originally from India, had just spoken about the powerful interfaith work his mosque had done after 9/11 by opening its doors, and he defended me from his seat. "She is a brave daughter of Islam. Do not criticize her for such little things." The critics were undeterred. A young man stood up and identified himself as a member of the Muslim Students' Association. "Where is your proof?" he demanded angrily, shaking his head, his beard a blur in front of me. I pointed to the seventy-four footnotes in the reprint of the article my father and I wrote for the *Journal of Islamic Law and Society*. "The Sunnah of the prophet will never change," he said, shaking his head fiercely again. I stared at his eyes, so wide and menacing. *I will never forget those eyes,* I told myself, not realizing how useful that observation would become when I confronted the young man's rage again, days later.

At that moment, though, I didn't know I'd ever cross paths with him again, and I actually felt sorry for him that he felt so threatened by the simple bill of rights. I wanted to scream: these rights *are* the Sunnah of the prophet. I knew what lay beneath his anger. Some men don't want to relinquish the power and control it has taken them centuries to accumulate. Some men think it is their God-given right to express this power and control over women. But the prophet gave women rights that men deny them today, and it is our Islamic duty to reclaim those rights so that we can be stronger citizens of the world.

A twenty-four-year-old African American woman from Boston, Nakia Jackson, stood up. The women in her mosque prayed in a urine-stained, rat-infested room that doubled as a storage closet. And they accepted the status quo. "I feel so alone. What advice do you have for someone like me?" she asked, her voice trembling.

"You are not alone," I told her. "So often I have stood physically alone in my mosque in Morgantown. But I have felt the spiritual press of so many kindred spirits who stand with me. I am with you. You are not alone."

Afterward, I was mobbed. I hugged so many women, young and old, that I lost count. And I received the encouragement of so many men, young and old, that my faith was renewed. "We did it!" I told my parents when I called home later.

THE PROFESSOR

LOS ANGELES—"The professor would like to invite you, your mother, and Shibli to visit him at his home," said Naheed Fakoor, an Afghan American woman who was the assistant extraordinaire to UCLA law professor Khalid Abou El Fadl. She mentioned delicately that he rarely invited anyone to his home. I understood the power of this invitation. In my estimation, we were getting an audience with the pope of tolerant Islam.

A year earlier I had not even known that this professor existed. It had taken me months to memorize all the syllables of his name and the order in which they are said. More often than not,

I referred to him as "Abou Khalid . . . oh, you know, the UCLA professor of law." My kindred spirits within the Muslim world knew of whom I spoke. When I told Dr. Alan Godlas, the Islamic studies professor at the University of Georgia, that I was going to be meeting "the Professor," as Naheed allowed me to call him, Dr. Godlas got excited. "He is the best hope for Islam in America," he said. Not only could the Professor speak to disenfranchised Muslims like me, but he had the grounding in Islamic jurisprudence and original texts to be able to communicate with the mainstream puritanical set who were in positions of authority in our communities. His students and friends had created a Web site for him called scholarofthehouse.org, inspired by an award he received by that name when he was a student at Yale University. They called him "the most important and influential Islamic thinker in the modern age."

. . .

What separated Khalid Abou El Fadl from many intellectuals was his training in Egypt and Kuwait in Islamic jurisprudence: he was a high-ranking sheikh. I didn't know about him until a friend sent me a copy of a book he had written, *The Place of Tolerance in Islam.* My mother read it first. When she was finished, she closed its cover with a sigh of relief. "Since my childhood days," she said, "I was told that only Muslims would go to heaven and no others. I would ask, 'Why?' We were born Muslim by accident. Why should others be denied heaven because they were born Christian, Jew, Buddhist, or Hindu? Nobody would answer me. They would tell me not to ask such stupid questions. For the first time, someone has answered my question and confirmed my belief that this assumption is wrong and that, in fact, the doors of heaven are open to all good people." She paused. "Khalid Abou El Fadl is a great man," my mother said. "He is the first person who helped me understand and *believe* in Islam." When I had called him to seek his guidance on the trial that I faced, I told him my mother's story. "Al-hamdulillah," he said, simply. Praise be to Allah.

It was enough to speak to him by phone. It was an honor to be beckoned for an audience. My response surprised even me. After all, I had met with senators, celebrities, and heads of state. What was a *professor?* But I knew I had to make this trip. I just didn't know why.

In Los Angeles I framed the Islamic Bill of Rights for Women in Mosques for the Professor and wrote below it two words: "In Gratitude." . . . I brought a copy of *Time* magazine with an essay in which I'd written about the struggle for the soul of Islam and an article in which the Professor argued against the theological logic that al-Qaeda leaders such as Abu Mousab al-Zarqawi use to sanction the beheading of prisoners. Since Danny's beheading, militants from Iraq to Saudi Arabia had turned to this execution-style brutality to kill hostages. The Professor told *Time,* "Al-Zarqawi searches for the trash that everyone threw out centuries ago and declares the trash to be Islam." His words resonated with me on so many levels, including in the battle to win rights for women in our Muslim world. Having some idea that the meeting would certainly be meaningful, but not knowing quite how, I departed for his home with curious anticipation.

After winding slowly through rush-hour traffic, we arrived at the Professor's house at the corner of a street in a Los Angeles suburb. It was surrounded by a security fence, a reminder of the danger in which he lived. He had taken on Wahhabi ideology with frontal attacks on their theology as flawed and un-Islamic. Even Muslim American organizations lashed out at him when he penned an op-ed for the *Los Angeles Times* after 9/11, criticizing Muslim leaders for not condemning the attacks.

The Professor's assistant, Naheed, warmly beckoned us through the gate. His wife, a gentle and beautiful woman by the appropriate name of Grace, welcomed us at the door with a smile and embrace. The door opened into rooms that swept into each other. The walls were lined from floor to ceiling with one thing: books. The books in some sets were lined up next to each other so that their bindings spelled words in Arabic. . . .

The Professor emerged in a flowing black cape, under which an embroidered collar peeked out from the traditional Arab gown he was wearing.

What struck me immediately was his physical vulnerability. He leaned on a cane and walked smoothly but slowly with small steps, extending his hand toward me gently. This in itself was significant. Saudi scholars had ruled that a man shaking hands with a woman was "evil" and *haram,* or unlawful. I took his hand gently. "Thank you for the honor of this invitation to visit you," I said. Not close enough to extend her hand to the Professor, my mother raised her cupped right hand to her forehead in a high-browed Indian Muslim gesture of respect between men and women. "Adhab," she said, in an Urdu greeting.

The Professor immediately lent me his support in the trial that my mosque had started against me. He reveled in the spirit of the Islamic Bill of Rights for Women in Mosques. "This is good," he said. And he cheered the writing that I was doing.

When it was time for prayer, the Professor did another remarkable thing. He prayed with his son on his left side and his wife on his right side. Naheed, my mother, and I lined up behind them. He needed help going into prostration and then standing up again, but his spatial arrangement was more than just practical. He believed in the intrinsic right of women to stand on a par with men.

In prayer at the Professor's house, I felt free for the first time in so long. Even though I was physically behind the Professor, I did not feel disrespected. Many Muslim men say they are expressing respect for women in their desire to protect them through segregation. But I knew the Professor didn't want to silence me. We sat around a circular dining table until late into the night, and he honored me when he revealed that he had read my first book and supported my voice. "It is a great victory that you are writing. You can only testify to the truth that you know," he said. "And you are doing that." He spoke with candor, even using the word *sucks,* and he lamented that Muslim leaders ran their communities as if they were playing Monopoly, collecting properties and building symbolic hotels of power.

The next night we returned, and my mother, Naheed, the Professor's wife, and I prayed in the same row as the Professor and his son. When we broke from prayer, the Professor led us through a tour of his library. To call it a library is an understatement. His books filled every wall in his room. ("Does he sell them?" my mother asked afterward, perplexed about why he collected so many books. "Mom!" I admonished her, but privately I could understand her curiosity.) He pored through Arabic texts to show me the works of the two thousand women jurists Islam has had since its inception in the seventh century. A year earlier I couldn't even name the century in which Islam was born. Now I knew the number of women jurists we've had. I was both amazed and astonished. On these shelves was the secret history of feminine power that centuries of male domination had erased. He pulled down a book published by a *madhab,* or school of jurisprudence, that had been destroyed. Both the school and its prayer had been led by a woman, he told me. "What?" I exclaimed. "A woman?"

"Yes, a woman."

I was surprised to see a familiar book on his shelves—my first book, *Tantrika.* And it was the hardcover edition with the image of a woman's bare torso on the front. Some Muslims had protested the cover when editor Ahmed Nassef put it on the Muslim WakeUp! Web site. I had put a yellow Post-it over the torso when I took the book to the Islamic Society of North America convention. But here it was, uncensored, beside the works of the great Muslim jurists. And to my shock, the Professor asked me to autograph the book. So many men—and even some women—within my religion had discounted me and discredited me because I wrote truthfully about the most intimate challenges in my life. But the Professor did not make me feel ashamed. Instead, he affirmed me.

I handed the book back to him with an inscription that couldn't capture the gift he had given me with the respect he had shown for my intellect, voice, and being. As he stood, he lost his balance and his cane slipped from his grip. My heart fell as I witnessed the physical vulnerability that accompanied the Professor's spiritual fortitude. Grace moved swiftly to help him regain his balance. Without pause, he looked me in the eye and took my hand, gently, in parting.

"Asra, do not let anyone deter you. Continue to be courageous," he said clearly. "You are on the right path."

"Thank you, Professor," I said quietly. Touched by his words and his sincere gestures of kindness and respect toward my family and me, my heart wept. He recognized that I had struggled hard to resolve the dissonance between the intimate areas of my life and my religion. So often we live with guilt about our sexual lives. But I had found a peace with the decisions I'd made about my body, and I had claimed the worthiness of my spirit. I could embrace Islam.

Religion isn't meant to destroy people. The Professor recognized that I had struggled to answer the question of who I am and where my faith rests in my identity as a Muslim woman. I knew he was not speaking just to me but to all people—women and men, girls and boys—who choose the path of honesty, justice, tolerance, and compassion. This has been my struggle, but it is the struggle of all people as well. . . .

R E A D I N G   **96**

Standing Again at Sinai

Judith Plaskow (1990)

EXPLORING THE TERRAIN OF SILENCE

. . . The central Jewish categories of Torah, Israel, and God are all constructed from male perspectives. Torah is revelation as men perceived it, the story of Israel told from their standpoint, the law unfolded according to their needs. Israel is the male collectivity, the children of a Jacob who had a daughter, but whose sons became the twelve tribes. God is named in the male image, a father and warrior much like his male offspring, who confirms and sanctifies the silence of his daughters. Exploring these categories, we explore the parameters of women's silence.

In Torah, Jewish teaching, women are not absent, but they are cast in stories told by men. As characters in narrative, women may be vividly characterized, as objects of legislation, singled out for attention. But women's presence in Torah does not negate their silence, for women do not decide the questions with which Jewish sources deal. When the law treats of women, it is often because their "abnormality" demands it. If women are central to plot, the plots are not about them. Women's interests and intentions must be unearthed from texts with other purposes, for both law and narrative serve to obscure them.

The most striking examples of women's silence come from texts in which women are most central, for there the normative character of maleness is especially jarring. In the family narratives of Genesis, for example, women figure prominently. The matriarchs of Genesis are all strong women. As independent personalities, fiercely concerned for their children, they often seem to have an intuitive knowledge of God's plans for their sons. Indeed, it appears from the stories of Sarah and Rebekah that they understand God better than their husbands. God defends Sarah when she casts out Hagar, telling Abraham to obey his wife (Gen. 21:12). Rebekah, knowing it is God's intent, helps deceive Isaac into accepting Jacob as his heir (Gen. 25:23; 27:5–17). Yet despite their intuitions, and despite their wiliness and resourcefulness, it is not the women who receive the covenant or who pass on its lineage. The establishment of patrilineal descent and the patriarchal family takes precedence over the matriarch's stories. Their relationship to God, in some way presupposed by the text, remains an undigested element in the narrative. What was the full theophany to Rebekah, and how is it related to the covenant with Isaac? The writer does not tell us; it is not sufficiently important. And so the covenant remains the covenant with Isaac, while Rebekah's experience floats at the margin of the story.

The establishment of patrilineal descent and patriarchal control, a subtext in Genesis, is an important theme in the legislation associated with Sinai. Here again, women figure prominently, but only as objects of male concerns. The laws pertaining to women place them firmly under the control of first fathers, then husbands, so that men can have male heirs they know are theirs. Legislation concerning adultery (Deut. 22:22, also Num. 5:11–31) and virginity (Deut. 22:13–21) speaks of women, but only to control female sexuality to male advantage. The *crime* of adultery is sleeping with another man's wife, and a man can bring his wife to trial even on suspicion of adultery, a right that is not reciprocal. Sleeping with a betrothed virgin constitutes adultery. A man who sleeps with a virgin who is not betrothed must simply marry her. A girl whose lack of virginity shames her father on her wedding night can be stoned to death for harlotry. A virgin who is raped must marry her assailant. The subject of these laws is women, but the interest behind them is the purity of the male line.

The process of projecting and defining women as objects of male concerns is expressed most fully not in the Bible, however, but in the Mishnah, an important second-century legal code. Part of the Mishnah's Order of Women (one of its six divisions) develops laws discussed in the Torah concerning certain problematic aspects of female sexuality. The subject of the division is the transfer of women—the regulation of women who are in states of transition, whose uncertain status threatens the stasis of the community. The woman who is about to enter into a marriage or who has just left one requires close attention. The law must regularize her irregularity, facilitate her transition to the normal state of wife and motherhood, at which point she no longer poses a problem. . . .

Thus Torah—"Jewish" sources, "Jewish" teaching—puts itself forward as *Jewish* teaching but speaks in the voice of only half the Jewish people. This scandal is compounded by another: The omission is neither mourned nor regretted; it is not even noticed. True, the rabbis were aware of the harshness of certain laws pertaining to women and sought to mitigate their effects. They tried to find ways to force a recalcitrant husband to divorce his wife, for example. But the framework that necessitated such mitigations went unquestioned. Women's Otherness was left intact. The Jewish passion for justice did not extend to Jewish women. As Cynthia Ozick puts it, one great "Thou shalt not"—"Thou shalt not lessen the humanity of women"—is missing from the Torah.

For this great omission, there is no historical redress. Indeed, where one might expect redress, the problem is compounded. The prophets, those great champions of justice, couch their pleas for justice in the language of patriarchal marriage. Israel in her youth is a devoted bride, subordinate and obedient to her husband/God (for example, Jer. 2:2). Idolatrous Israel is a harlot and adulteress, a faithless woman whoring after false gods (for example, Hos. 2,3). Transferring the hierarchy of male and female to God and his people, the prophets enshrine in metaphor the legal subordination of women. Those who might have named and challenged women's marginalization thus ignore and extend it.

The prophetic metaphors mark an end and a beginning. They confront us with the injustice of Torah; they link that injustice to other central Jewish ideas. If exploring Torah means exploring a terrain of women's silence, this is no less true of the categories of Israel or God.

Israel, the bride, the harlot, the people that is female (that is, subordinate) in relation to God is nonetheless male in communal self-perception. The covenant community is the community of the circumcised (Gen. 17:10), the community defined as male heads of household. Women are named through a filter of male experience: that is the essence of their silence. But women's experiences are not recorded or taken seriously because women are not perceived as normative Jews.

They are part of but do not define the community of Israel.

The same evidence that speaks to women's silence in the tradition, to the partiality of Torah, also reflects an understanding of Israel as a community of males. In the narratives of Genesis, for example, the covenant moves from father to son, from Abraham to Isaac to Jacob to Joseph. The matriarchs' relation to their husbands' God is sometimes assumed, sometimes passed over, but the women do not constitute the covenant people. Women's relation to the community is also ambiguous and unclear in biblical legislation. The law is couched in male grammatical forms, and its content too presupposes a male nation. "You shall not covet your neighbor's wife" (Ex. 20:17). Probably we cannot deduce from this verse that women are free to covet! Yet the injunction assumes that women's obedience is owed to fathers and husbands, who are the primary group addressed.

The silence of women goes deeper, however, than who defines Torah or Israel. It also finds its way into language about God. Our language about divinity is first of all male language; it is selective and partial. The God who supposedly transcends sexuality, who is presumably one and whole, comes to us through language that is incomplete and narrow. The images we use to describe God, the qualities we attribute to God, draw on male pronouns and experience and convey a sense of power and authority that is clearly male. The God at the surface of Jewish consciousness is a God with a voice of thunder, a God who as lord and king rules his people and leads them into battle, a God who forgives like a father when we turn to him. The female images that exist in the Bible and (particularly the mystical) tradition form an underground stream that occasionally reminds us of the inadequacy of our imagery without transforming its overwhelmingly male nature.

This male imagery is comforting and familiar— comforting because familiar—but it is an integral part of a system that consigns women to the margins. Since the experience of God cannot be directly conveyed in language, imagery for God is a vehicle that suggests what is actually impossible to describe. Religious experiences are expressed in a vocabulary drawn from the significant and valuable in a particular culture. To speak of God is to speak of what we most value. In attributing certain qualities to God, we both attempt to point to God and offer God's qualities to be emulated and admired. To say that God is just, for example, is to say both that God acts justly and that God demands justice. Justice belongs to God but is also ours to pursue. Similarly with maleness, to image God as male is to value the quality and those who have it. It is to define God in the image of the normative community and to bless men—but not women—with a central attribute of God.

But our images of God are not simply male images; they are images of a certain kind. The prophetic metaphors for the relation between God and Israel are metaphors borrowed from the patriarchal family—images of dominance softened by affection. God as husband and father of Israel demands obedience and monogamous love. He repays faithfulness with mercy and lovingkindness, but punishes waywardness, just as the wayward daughter can be stoned at her father's door (Deut. 22:21). When these family images are combined with political images of king and warrior, they reinforce a particular model of power and dominance. God is the power over us, the One out there over against us, the sovereign warrior with righteousness on his side. Family and political models of dominance and submission are recapitulated and rendered plausible by the dominance and submission of God and Israel. The silence and submission of women becomes part of a greater pattern that makes it appear fitting and right.

. . .

Clearly, the implications of Jewish feminism reach beyond the goal of equality to transform the bases of Jewish life. Feminism demands a new understanding of Torah, Israel, and God. It demands an understanding of Torah that begins by acknowledging the injustice of Torah and then goes on to create a Torah that is whole. The silence of women reverberates through the tradition, distorting the shape of narrative and skewing the content of the law. Only the deliberate recovery of women's hidden voices, the unearthing and invention of women's Torah, can give us Jewish teachings that are the product of the whole Jewish people and that reflect more fully its experiences of God.

Feminism demands an understanding of Israel that includes the whole of Israel and thus allows women to speak and name our experience for ourselves. It demands we replace a normative male voice with a chorus of divergent voices, describing Jewish reality in different accents and tones. Feminism impels us to rethink issues of community and diversity, to explore the ways in which one people can acknowledge and celebrate the varied experiences of its members. What would it mean for women *as women* to be equal participants in the Jewish community? How can we talk about difference without creating Others?

Feminism demands new ways of talking about God that reflect and grow out of the redefinition of Jewish humanity. The exclusively male naming of God supported and was rendered meaningful by a cultural and religious situation that is passing away. The emergence of women allows and necessitates that the long-suppressed femaleness of God be recovered and explored and reintegrated into the Godhead. But feminism presses us beyond the issue of gender to examine the nature of the God with male names. How can we move beyond images of domination to a God present *in* community rather than over it? How can we forge a God-language that expresses women's experience?

R E A D I N G **97**

Everywoman Her Own Theology

Alicia Suskin Ostriker (1986)

I am nailing them up to the cathedral door
Like Martin Luther. Actually, no,
I don't want to resemble that *Schmutzkopf*
(See Erik Erikson and N. O. Brown
On the Reformer's anal aberrations,
Not to mention his hatred of Jews and peasants),
So I am thumbtacking these ninety-five
Theses to the bulletin board in my kitchen.

My proposals, or should I say requirements,
Include at least one image of a god,
Virile, beard optional, one of a goddess,
Nubile, breast size approximating mine,
One divine baby, one lion, one lamb,
All nude as figs, all dancing wildly,
All shining. Reproducible
In marble, metal, in fact any material.

Ethically, I am looking for
An absolute endorsement of loving-kindness.
No loopholes except maybe mosquitoes.

Virtue and sin will henceforth be discouraged,
Along with suffering and martyrdom.
There will be no concept of infidels;
Consequently the faithful must entertain
Themselves some other way than killing infidels.

And so forth and so on. I understand
This piece of paper is going to be
Spattered with wine one night at a party
And covered over with newer pieces of paper.
That is how it goes with bulletin boards.
Nevertheless it will be there.
Like an invitation, like a chalk pentangle,
It will emanate certain occult vibrations.

If something sacred wants to swoop from the
    universe
Through a ceiling, and materialize,
Folding its silver wings,
In a kitchen, and bump its chest against mine,
My paper will tell this being where to find me.

Witchcraft and Women's Culture

Starhawk (1979)

From earliest times, women have been witches, *wicce*, "wise ones"—priestesses, diviners, midwives, poets, healers, and singers of songs of power. Woman-centered culture, based on the worship of the Great Goddess, underlies the beginnings of all civilization. Mother Goddess was carved on the walls of paleolithic caves, and painted in the shrines of the earliest cities, those of the Anatolian plateau. For her were raised the giant stone circles, the henges of the British Isles, the dolmens and cromlechs of the later Celtic countries, and for her the great passage graves of Ireland were dug. In her honor, sacred dancers leaped the bulls in Crete and composed lyric hymns within the colleges of the holy isles of the Mediterranean. Her mysteries were celebrated in secret rites at Eleusis, and her initiates included some of the finest minds of Greece. Her priestesses discovered and tested the healing herbs and learned the secrets of the human mind and body that allowed them to ease the pain of childbirth, to heal wounds and cure diseases, and to explore the realm of dreams and the unconscious. Their knowledge of nature enabled them to tame sheep and cattle, to breed wheat and corn from grasses and weeds, to forge ceramics from mud and metal from rock, and to track the movements of moon, stars, and sun.

Witchcraft, "the craft of the wise," is the last remnant in the west of the time of women's strength and power. Through the dark ages of persecution, the covens of Europe preserved what is left of the mythology, rituals, and knowledge of the ancient matricentric (mother-centered) times. The great centers of worship in Anatolia, Malta, Iberia, Brittany, and Sumeria are now only silent stones and works of art we can but dimly understand. Of the mysteries of Eleusis, we have literary hints; the poems of Sappho survive only in fragments. The great collections of early literature and science were destroyed by patriarchal forces—the library of Alexandria burnt by Caesar, Charlemagne's collection of lore burnt by his son Louis "the Pious," who was offended at its "paganism." But the craft remains, in spite of all efforts to stamp it out, as a living tradition of Goddess-centered worship that traces its roots back to the time before the triumph of patriarchy.

The old religion of witchcraft before the advent of Christianity was an earth-centered, nature-oriented worship that venerated the Goddess, the source of life, as well as her son-lover-consort, who was seen as the Horned God of the hunt and animal life. Earth, air, water, fire, streams, seas, wells, beasts, trees, grain, the planets, sun, and most of all, the moon, were seen as aspects of deity. On the great seasonal festivals—the solstices and equinoxes, and the eves of May, August, November, and February—all the countryside would gather to light huge bonfires, feast, dance, sing, and perform the rituals that assured abundance throughout the year.

When Christianity first began to spread, the country people held to the old ways, and for hundreds of years the two faiths coexisted quite peacefully. Many people followed both religions, and country priests in the twelfth and thirteenth centuries were frequently upbraided by church authorities for dressing in skins and leading the dance at the pagan festivals.

But in the thirteenth and fourteenth centuries, the church began persecution of witches, as well as Jews and "heretical" thinkers. Pope Innocent the VIII, with his Bull of 1484, intensified a campaign of torture and death that would take the lives of an estimated 9 million people, perhaps 80 percent of whom were women.

The vast majority of victims were not coven members or even necessarily witches. They were old widows whose property was coveted by someone else, young children with "witch blood," midwives who furnished the major competition to the male-dominated medical profession, freethinkers who asked the wrong questions.

An enormous campaign of propaganda accompanied the witch trials as well. Witches were said to have sold their souls to the devil, to practice obscene and disgusting rites, to blight crops and murder children. In many areas, the witches did worship a Horned God as the spirit of the hunt, of animal life and vitality, a concept far from the power of evil that was the Christian devil. Witches were free and open about sexuality—but their rites were "obscene" only to those who viewed the human body itself as filthy and evil. Questioning or disbelieving any of the slander was itself considered proof of witchcraft or heresy, and the falsehoods that for hundreds of years could not be openly challenged had their effect. Even today, the word *witch* is often automatically associated with "evil."

With the age of reason in the eighteenth century, belief in witches, as in all things psychic and supernatural, began to fade. The craft as a religion was forgotten; all that remained were the wild stories of broomstick flights, magic potions, and the summoning of spectral beings.

Memory of the true craft faded everywhere except within the hidden covens. With it went the memory of women's heritage and history, of our ancient roles as leaders, teachers, healers, seers. Lost, also, was the conception of the Great Spirit, as manifest in nature, in life, in woman. Mother Goddess slept, leaving the world to the less than gentle rule of the God-Father.

The Goddess has at last stirred from sleep, and women are reawakening to our ancient power. The feminist movement, which began as a political, economic, and social struggle, is opening to a spiritual dimension. In the process, many women are discovering the old religion, reclaiming the word *witch* and, with it, some of our lost culture.

Witchcraft, today, is a kaleidoscope of diverse traditions, rituals, theologies, and structures. But underneath the varying forms is a basic orientation common to all the craft. The outer forms of religion—the particular words said, the signs made, the names used—are less important to us than the inner forms, which cannot be defined or described but must be felt and intuited.

The craft is earth religion, and our basic orientation is to the earth, to life, to nature. There is no dichotomy between spirit and flesh, no split between Godhead and the world. The Goddess is manifest in the world; she brings life into being, *is* nature, *is* flesh. Union is not sought outside the world in some heavenly sphere or through dissolution of the self into the void beyond the senses. Spiritual union is found in life, within nature, passion, sensuality—through being fully human, fully one's self.

Our great symbol for the Goddess is the moon, whose three aspects reflect the three stages in women's lives and whose cycles of waxing and waning coincide with women's menstrual cycles. As the new moon or crescent, she is the Maiden, the Virgin—not chaste, but belonging to herself alone, not bound to any man. She is the wild child, lady of the woods, the huntress, free and untamed—Artemis, Kore, Aradia, Nimue. White is her color. As the full moon, she is the mature woman, the sexual being, the mother and nurturer, giver of life, fertility, grain, offspring, potency, joy—Tana, Demeter, Diana, Ceres, Mari. Her colors are the red of blood and the green of growth. As waning or dark moon, she is the old woman, past menopause, the hag or crone that is ripe with wisdom, patroness of secrets, prophecy, divination, inspiration, power—Hecate, Ceridwen, Kali, Anna. Her color is the black of night.

The Goddess is also earth—Mother Earth, who sustains all growing things, who is the body, our bones and cells. She is air—the winds that move in the trees and over the waves, breath. She is the fire of the hearth, of the blazing bonfire and the fuming volcano; the power of transformation and change. And she is water—the sea, original source of life; the rivers, streams, lakes and wells;

the blood that flows in the rivers of our veins. She is mare, cow, cat, owl, crane, flower, tree, apple, seed, lion, sow, stone, woman. She is found in the world around us, in the cycles and seasons of nature, and in mind, body, spirit, and emotions within each of us. Thou art Goddess. I am Goddess. All that lives (and all that is, lives), all that serves life, is Goddess.

Because witches are oriented to earth and to life, we value spiritual qualities that I feel are especially important to women, who have for so long been conditioned to be passive, submissive and weak. The craft values independence, personal strength, *self*—not petty selfishness but that deep core of strength within that makes us each a unique child of the Goddess. The craft has no dogma to stifle thought, no set of doctrines that have to be believed. Where authority exists, within covens, it is always coupled with the freedom every covener has, to leave at any time. When self is valued—in ourselves—we can see that self is everywhere.

Passion and emotion—that give depth and color and meaning to human life—are also valued.

Witches strive to be in touch with feelings, even if they are sometimes painful, because the joy and pleasure and ecstasy available to a fully alive person make it worth occasional suffering. So-called negative emotion—anger—is valued as well, as a sign that something is wrong and that action needs to be taken. Witches prefer to handle anger by taking action and making changes rather than by detaching ourselves from our feelings in order to reach some nebulous, "higher" state.

Most of all, the craft values love. The Goddess' only law is "Love unto all beings." But the love we value is not the airy flower power of the hippies or the formless, abstracted *agape* of the early Christians. It is passionate, sensual, personal love, *eros,* falling in love, mother-child love, the love of one unique human being for other individuals, with all their personal traits and idiosyncrasies. Love is not something that can be radiated out in solitary meditation—it manifests itself in relationships and interactions with other people. It is often said "You cannot be a witch alone"— because to be a witch is to be a lover, a lover of the Goddess, and a lover of other human beings.

R E A D I N G **99**

Religion and Feminism's Fourth Wave

Pythia Peay (2005)

On September 11, 2001, California psychotherapist Kathlyn Schaaf was overwhelmed by a powerful thought. Watching the violent images on television, she suddenly felt the time had come to "gather the women." She wasn't alone. Schaaf and 11 others who shared her response soon created Gather the Women, a Web site and communications hub that 5,000 women have used to chronicle their local events in support of world peace. As women assembled near the pyramids in Egypt and held potluck dinners in Alaska, staged candlelight vigils and other rituals in countries around the

world, it confirmed Schaaf's gut instinct that an untapped reserve of energy "lies like oil beneath the common ground the women share."

Since then, the group has organized a series of congresses to connect women's groups. Their work is one example of a new kind feminism, slowly growing for a decade and now bursting out everywhere. At its heart lies a new kind of political activism that's guided and sustained by spirituality. Some are calling it the long-awaited "fourth wave" of feminism—a fusion of spirituality and social justice reminiscent of the American civil rights movement and Gandhi's call for nonviolent change.

This phenomenon is most visible in the popular conferences organized by women spiritual and religious leaders. Just as important are those meeting privately to meditate and pray, to study the world, and to support each other in social action. These gatherings share a commitment to a universal spirituality that affirms women's bonds across ethnic and religious boundaries. They're also exploring a new feminine paradigm of power that's based on tolerance, mutuality, and reverence for nature—values they now see as crucial to curing the global pathologies of poverty and war.

Previous advances in American feminism have rarely happened smoothly; the gains of one generation have often both shaped and conflicted with the ambitions of the next. First-wave feminists fought for women's suffrage. Led in the 1970s by icons like Gloria Steinem and Betty Friedan, a second wave pushed for economic and legal gains. Their ideals would eventually clash with the spirited individualism of third-wave feminists, women in their 20s and 30s who still advocate for women's rights while embracing a "girlie culture" that celebrates sex, men, gay culture, and clothes.

But as never before, today's conservative political environment has united women across the feminist spectrum. The result differs from earlier forms of feminism in several ways. For one, it espouses a new activism based not in anger, but in joy. It also tends to be focused outward, beyond the individual to wider issues, often global in scope. In the words of author Carol Lee Flinders, "Feminism catches fire when it draws on its inherent spirituality," which means something else can happen as well. "When you get Jewish, Catholic, Buddhist, Hindu, and Sufi women all practicing their faith in the same room," she recently said, "another religion emerges, which is feminine spirituality."

Though Flinders and other writers have been calling on women to reconnect with the sacred for years, many agree that the tipping point was 9/11. Before then, a women's spirituality conference called Sacred Circles, held biannually at Washington National Cathedral in the nation's capital, had focused on *personal* spirituality. More recently, however, program director Grace Ogden said she felt compelled to use the gatherings to address religious violence. "There was this sense of something gone terribly wrong," she said, "of communities splitting apart and a growing suspicion of people of Arab descent or other traditions." Her planning committee has since become more interfaith than in the past. Recent Sacred Circles conferences have stressed the role of compassion and tolerance in addressing political, economic, and religious differences.

Appalled by the lack of women in positions of religious authority on 9/11, Dena Merriam, a New York arts writer and public relations executive, joined others trying to form an international network of women religious leaders from the major faiths. In October 2002, they launched the Global Peace Initiative of Women Religious and Spiritual Leaders in Geneva, Switzerland. Associated with the United Nations, the initiative wants to get religious leaders more involved in U.N. peace-building plans. Specific programs aim to help young women of different faiths to communicate in places like Jerusalem that have been torn by conflict.

Merriam, the group's convener, said that one of women's strengths in peace work stems from their greatest weakness—their long exile from authority inside mainstream institutions. "Suddenly women are beginning to realize that their outsider status is an asset," she said, leaving them free to act directly, outside institutional lines. Many women are following the fate of U.N. Resolution 1325, which, if passed, will mandate that women be involved in all peace negotiations.

Feminism's new direction was perhaps most striking at the Women & Power conference sponsored by the Omega Institute and V-Day in New York City last September. The 3,000 participants heard celebrity feminists like Jane Fonda, Sally Field, and Gloria Steinem herself note the shift. Playwright Eve Ensler, founder of V-Day, a movement to stop global violence against women and girls, addressed the need to change the face of power. Today, she said, our power is seen in terms of "country over country, tribe against tribe." The new paradigm, however, has to be about power "in the service of"—collaboration, not conquest.

The free flow of creative expression at these assemblies marks a radical departure from the church coffees of our mothers' era. Participants often join together in fashioning new rites and rituals from ancient traditions, shaping forms at once old and new. Organizers at the Women & Power conference draped one room in carpets and labeled it the Red Tent area, evoking the Jewish ritual popularized by the book of that name. Elizabeth Lesser, a co-founder of the Omega Institute, said the room was like "an ancient gathering place where women were laughing, crying, brushing each other's hair, praying, and meditating. It seemed to satisfy women's deepest longings and was spiritual in a very feminine way."

At gatherings big and small, many are realizing that putting themselves in the service of the world is feminism's next step. At a time when the United States is viewed with increasing distrust by other countries, feminism's shift toward cultivating a spiritually informed activism may help to repair our diplomatic ties. No less important is the depth that comes from quiet reflection closer to home. As Carol Lee Flinders notes, a "serious spiritual life with a strong inward dimension" is crucial in itself, releasing the energy that can turn visionary feminist theory into action.

Meanwhile, as feminism allows more women to reach positions of power in American culture, increasing numbers have discovered that material success does not satisfy their hunger for meaning and connection. Women are becoming increasingly clear and vocal about the need to integrate an emerging set of feminine-based values into the culture. As the Democratic Party searches for a guiding set of values, it might consider turning to the women's spirituality movement for inspiration.

DISCUSSION QUESTIONS FOR CHAPTER 12

1. Why do you think the control of women is a central component in many religions?

2. How do you think religion has been both empowering and oppressive for women?

3. How do you think the availability of a greater variety of images of God might impact religion and religion's influence on social life?

4. How might women work toward reform from within religious traditions? Why might some women feel the need to abandon religious traditions completely?

5. How have negative stereotypes of witchcraft served to perpetuate the oppression of women? Why do you think practices of women's spirituality were (and still are) perceived as such a threat?

6. How do nondominant religious traditions challenge the influence of hegemonic Christianity in U.S. society?

SUGGESTIONS FOR FURTHER READING

Armstrong, Karen. *The Spiral Staircase: My Climb Out of Darkness.* New York: Anchor, 2005.

Barazangi, Nimat Hafez. *Woman's Identity and the Qu'ran: A New Reading.* Gainesville: University Press of Florida, 2004.

Cochran, Pamela. *Evangelical Feminism: A History.* New York: New York University Press, 2004.

Higginbotham, Joyce, and River Higginbotham. *Paganism: An Introduction to Earth-Centered Religions.* St. Paul, MN: Llewellyn Publications, 2002.

Kidd, Sue. *The Dance of the Dissident Daughter: A Woman's Journey from Christian Tradition to the Sacred Feminine.* New York: HarperOne, 2006.

Mitchem, Stephanie. *Introducing Womanist Theology.* Maryknoll, NY: Orbis, 2002.

Nomani, Asra. *Standing Alone: An American Woman's Struggle for the Soul of Islam.* New York: HarperOne, 2006.

Plaskow, Judith, and Donna Berman, eds. *The Coming of Lilith: Essays on Feminism, Judaism, and Sexual Ethics, 1972–2003.* Boston: Beacon Press, 2005.

CHAPTER 13

Activism, Change, and Feminist Futures

THE PROMISE OF FEMINIST EDUCATION

In Chapter 1 we discussed the goals of women's studies as a discipline. These objectives include, first, an understanding of the social construction of gender and the intersection of gender with other systems of inequality in women's lives; second, a familiarity with women's status, contributions, and individual and collective actions for change; and third, an awareness of ways to improve women's status. A fourth objective of women's studies is that you will start thinking about patterns of privilege and discrimination in your own life and understand your position vis-à-vis systems of inequality. We hope you will learn to think critically about how societal institutions affect individual lives—especially your own. We hope you will gain new insights and confidence and that new knowledge will empower you.

Feminist educators attempt to give students more inclusive and socially just forms of knowledge and to support teachers using their power in nonexploitive ways. Women's studies usually involve nonhierarchical, egalitarian classrooms where teachers respect students and hope to learn from them as well as teach them. The focus is on the importance of the student voice and experience and encouraging both personal and social change. Most women's studies classes, however, are within colleges that do not necessarily share the same goals and objectives. Many feminist educators operate within the social and economic constraints of educational institutions that view "counter-hegemonic" education—that is, education that challenges the status quo—as problematic and/or subversive. Despite these constraints, feminist education, with its progressive and transformative possibilities, is an important feature on most campuses.

For many students, and perhaps for you too, the term *feminism* is still problematic. Many people object to the political biases associated with feminist education and believe knowledge should be objective and devoid of political values. It is important to emphasize that all knowledge is associated with power, as knowledge arises from communities with certain positions, resources, and understandings of the world. This means that all knowledge (and not just feminist knowledge) is ideological in that it is in some way associated with history and politics. To declare an unbiased objectivity or value neutrality is to ignore or mask the workings of power that are present in all forms of knowledge. Although feminist education is more explicit than other forms of knowledge in speaking of its relationship to power in society, this does not mean it is more biased or ideological than other forms of knowledge. It is important to note that some knowledge's claim to being objective, unbiased, and value neutral (these words mean the same thing) is related to the claim to a scientific "truth." Feminist knowledge emphasizes that science is a human product and therefore hardly unbiased or value free either: All truth claims are relative and must be understood in the context of history, culture, and politics. This means that all knowledge, whether feminist or not, is "political."

Many people support the justice-based goals of feminism but do not identify with the label. The reading by Lisa Marie Hogeland titled "Fear of Feminism: Why Young Women Get the Willies" addresses this issue. She also looks in depth at continuing resistance to feminism as politics and as a way of life. She makes the important distinction between *gender consciousness* and *feminist consciousness*, explains why one does not necessarily imply the other, and discusses the fear of reprisals and consequences associated with a feminist consciousness.

ACTIVISM

We live in a complex time. White women have made significant progress over the past decades and have begun the twenty-first century integrated into most societal institutions. Although the progress of women of color lags behind the gains made by White women, it too is beginning to be seen. Yet, the big picture is far from rosy, as society has not been transformed in its core values in ways feminists throughout the last century would have liked. An equitable sharing of power and resources in terms of gender, race, class, and other differences has not been actualized. In addition, as women receive more public power, they are encouraged to internalize more private constraints concerning the body and sexuality.

Many believe there is increasing prosperity in the United States, even though the gap between the rich and the poor is among the largest in industrialized nations and is increasing. Despite the widespread belief that the United States remains a more mobile society than some (meaning people can move out of poverty or move into more wealth), economists show that in recent decades the typical child starting out in poverty in the United States has less chance at prosperity than one in continental Europe or Canada. The United States and Britain stand out as the least mobile among postindustrial societies. In 2003 it was estimated that the top 1 percent of people in the United States own 40 percent of the country's wealth. U.S. Census data for 2005 show almost 20 percent of children under 18 years old live in poverty and one in five children goes to bed hungry. Economists and sociologists emphasize that personal debt is a major problem in the United States—it is currently at about 120 percent of personal income. Despite this, U.S. workers tend to work about 9 weeks more a year than their European counterparts. Violence is increasing in our society in all walks of life; women, people of color, and gays and lesbians are frequently the targets of

LEARNING ACTIVITY   **Feminist.com**

Visit the website *www.feminist.com* and follow the link to the activism page. There you'll find links to action alerts and legislative updates for a number of feminist organizations, including the National Organization for Women (NOW), Sisterhood Is Global, Women Organizing for Change, and Planned Parenthood. Follow these links to learn what actions you can take. The website also offers links to government resources and voter education and other activist resources.

hate and hostility; and the balance of power in the world seems fragile and in the hands of relatively few (often egocentric, delusional) men. Wars surround us. The picture is one of great optimism and yet simultaneous despair. Perhaps we can address the rage, cynicism, and often mean-spiritedness of this historical moment and come up with a transformational politics that encourages a consciousness shift and extends generosity and compassion toward others. Any movement for justice-based equalities must have a strong moral foundation based on love, human dignity, and community.

As Audre Lorde, one of the most eloquent writers of the feminist second wave, once declared, "Silence will not protect you." Lorde wrote about the need to be part of social change efforts, and she encouraged us to speak out and address the problems in our lives and communities. And, as the reading by Michael Kimmel, "Real Men Join the Movement," implies, speaking out and addressing inequities involves learning how to be an ally to people who are different from you and who do not enjoy the privileges you enjoy. Kimmel emphasizes the necessity of men joining with women to make this world better for everyone. In this sense, coalitions are a central aspect of social change efforts.

In the past four decades there has been significant resistance to the status quo, or established power, in U.S. society, despite enormous backlash from the conservative right and other groups that seeks to maintain this power. Response to this backlash is the focus of the reading by Ruth Rosen, "Epilogue: Beyond Backlash." The strength of justice-based resistance has been its multistrategic and multi-issue approach. *Multistrategic* means relying on working coalitions that mobilize around certain shared issues and involve different strategies toward a shared goal. *Multi-issue* means organizing on many fronts over a variety of different issues that include political, legal, and judicial changes, educational reform, welfare rights, elimination of violence, workplace reform, and reproductive issues. The reading "Reflections of a Human Rights Educator" by Dazón Dixon Diallo focuses on activism by "Sisterlove," a group that educates on the intersections of HIV/AIDS, sexism, racism, and human rights. The human rights framework encourages coalitions to apply human rights standards associated with justice and human dignity to individual and community problems.

As discussed in Chapter 1, some *liberal* or reformist activists have worked within the system and advocated change from within. Their approach locates the source of inequality in barriers to inclusion and advancement and they have worked to change

Size Does Matter and Nine Other Tips for Effective Protest

- *Size does matter.* The most memorable protests—and the ones the media tends to cover—are the big ones: Think of the 1968 March on Washington and the Million Man March in 1995. The best way to put masses of people on the streets? Forge coalitions in order to broaden your base of potential protesters.
- *Get organized.* A large crowd is not, ipso facto, an effective performance. In November 1997, the Disney/Haiti Justice Campaign pulled together a sizable number of protesters outside the Disney Store in Times Square to denounce the company's Haitian sweatshops, but organizers failed to start a picket line or lead energetic chants. Many in the crowd simply milled around with their hands in their pockets or sipping coffee.
- *Location, location, location.* Many large, well-organized protests happen outside corporate headquarters or foreign consulates. Unfortunately, those tend to be on side streets with little pedestrian traffic and no adjoining public spaces. Simply relocating the event to a busy nearby corner can increase the audience tenfold.
- *Distinguish yourself.* In December 1997, the East Timor Action Network marched up Madison Avenue to the Indonesian Consulate to protest the occupation of East Timor. Only a few carried signs; the rest were indistinguishable from other pedestrians on the crowded street. Solution? Form a picket line or sit down en masse on the busy sidewalk.
- *Get the crowd involved.* Successful protests encourage audience participation—appearing exclusive is a sure way to alienate onlookers from your cause. At a 1997 World AIDS Day vigil in New York, for example, organizers handed out chalk to passersby and asked them to write on a nearby fountain the names of loved ones who had died of AIDS.
- *Put it down on paper.* A simple, clearly written leaflet that explains who is protesting, why, and how to get involved is crucial. Sure, it may end up in the nearest trash can, but some people will read it, and a few might show up at the next event.
- *Manage the media.* Of course, the biggest prize for any protest is media coverage. Inform local newspapers and TV and radio stations (not just "progressive" media) a few days in advance.
- *Above all, be spectacular.* Eye-catching costumes, a sea of candles in a dark plaza, limp bodies being carried from a street to a police van—these telegenic images make for good press. At an August 1997 march prompted by the police beating of Haitian immigrant Abner Louima, many waved toilet plungers—the tool with which Louima was allegedly beaten and sodomized—transforming an ordinary object into an unforgettable symbol of violent racism.
- *Meteorology matters.* A wet and cold protester is usually a demoralized one. Plan for foul weather by establishing an alternative day; if timing is critical, find a nearby indoor or protected space to which protesters can retreat. To be sure, there are exceptions: A dedicated group braving the elements can convey a profound sense of commitment to a cause—assuming, of course, that someone's watching.
- *Use protest to beget protest.* Any single march or demonstration should be one link in a larger chain. Most political movements, after all, must endure for years

to attain their goals. So think about the morning after: How can the momentum generated (if any) be maintained? How soon is too soon for the next protest? What worked, what didn't? Protests should be carefully crafted performances designed to be unforgettable and moving for audiences and participants alike. Only meaningful and memorable protests can effectively challenge people to think differently and motivate still further protest in the days and years ahead.

Source: Jeff Goodwin, *Mother Jones*, March/April 1999.

women's working lives through comparable worth, sexual harassment policy, and parenting leaves. Legal attacks on abortion rights have been deflected by the work of liberal feminists working within the courts, and affirmative action and other civil rights legislation have similarly been the focus of scholars, activists, and politicians working in the public sphere. These organizations tend to be hierarchical with a centralized governing structure (president, advisory board, officers, and so forth) and local chapters around the country. Other strategies for change take a *radical* approach (for example, radical or cultural feminism) and attempt to transform the system rather than to adapt the existing system. Together these various strategies work to advocate justice-based forms of equality. Contemporary feminism (both self-identified third wave activism and others) uses both liberal and radical strategies to address problems and promote change.

Although differences in strategy are sometimes a source of divisiveness among activists and feminists, they are also a source of strength in being able to work on multiple issues from multiple approaches. Indeed, any given issue lends itself to both reformist and radical approaches. Lesbian and gay rights, for example, is something that can be tackled in the courts and in the voting booths as organizations work toward legislation to create domestic partner legislation or community civil protections. At the same time, consciousness-raising activities and grassroots demonstrations, such as candlelight vigils for victims of hate crimes and Queer Pride parades, work on the local level. Together, different strategies improve the quality of life. This is what is meant by *multistrategic*.

One important aspect to consider is that simply increasing women's participation and leadership does not necessarily imply a more egalitarian or feminist future. As you know, there are White women and women and men of color who are opposed to strategies for improving the general well-being of disenfranchised peoples. Changing the personnel—replacing men with women, for example—does not necessarily secure a different kind of future. Although in practice liberal feminism is more sophisticated than, for example, simply considering female leaders merely because they are women, it has been criticized for promoting women into positions of power and authority irrespective of their stance on the social relations of gender, race, class, and other differences. Still, the encouragement of women into leadership positions is a central aspect of feminist change. The reading by Alice Eagly and Linda L. Carli, "Women and Leadership," discusses the ways traditional organizations

IDEAS FOR ACTIVISM

- Organize an activism awareness educational event on your campus. Invite local activists to speak about their activism. Provide opportunities for students to volunteer for a wide variety of projects in your area.
- Find out about your school's recycling program. If there's not one in place, advocate with administrators to begin one. If one is in place, try to find ways to help it function more effectively and to encourage more participation in recycling. If recycling services are not provided in your local community, advocate with city and county officials to begin providing these services.
- Find out what the major environmental issues are in your state and what legislative steps need to be taken to address these concerns. Then organize a letter-writing campaign to encourage legislators to enact laws protecting the environment.
- Identify a major polluter in your community and organize a nonviolent protest outside that business demanding environmental reforms.
- Sponsor a workshop on conflict management and nonviolence for campus and community members.

disadvantage women's attempts at leadership and suggests organizational innovations to foster gender equality.

Contemporary U.S. feminism is concerned with issues that are increasingly global, inevitable in the context of a global economy and militarism worldwide. These concerns have resulted in the sponsorship of numerous international conferences and have promoted education about women's issues all over the world. And, as communication technologies have advanced, the difficulties of global organization have lessened. International feminist groups have worked against militarism, global capitalism, and racism, as well as supported issues identified by indigenous women around the world. This activism was demonstrated in 1995 with the United Nations Fourth World Conference on Women held in Beijing, China (the first conference was held in Mexico City in 1975, the second in Copenhagen in 1980, and the third in Nairobi in 1985). More than 30,000 women attended the Beijing conference and helped create the internationally endorsed Platform for Action. This platform is a call for concrete action involving human rights of women and girls as part of universal human rights, the eradication of poverty of women, the removal of obstacles to women's full participation in public life and decision making, the elimination of all forms of violence against women, the assurance of women's access to educational and health services, and actions to promote women's economic autonomy. The Platform for Action is also discussed in the reading by Ruth Rosen. Since the Beijing conference in 1995, conventions under the leadership of the Commission on the Status of Women have been held in 2000 and 2005 to re-formalize the platform in light of global changes since the conference. Activism continues for U.S. ratification of the Convention on the Elimination of All Forms of Discrimination Against Women (CEDAW), adopted in 1979 by the United Nations General Assembly

UN Millennium Development Goals

1. Eradicate extreme poverty and hunger
   - Reduce by half the proportion of people living on less than a dollar a day
   - Reduce by half the proportion of people who suffer from hunger

2. Achieve universal primary education
   - Ensure that all boys and girls complete a full course of primary schooling

3. Promote gender equality and empower women
   - Eliminate gender disparity in primary and secondary education preferably by 2005, and at all levels by 2015

4. Reduce child mortality
   - Reduce by two-thirds the mortality rate among children under five

5. Improve maternal health
   - Reduce by three-quarters the maternal mortality ratio

6. Combat HIV/AIDS, malaria, and other diseases
   - Halt and begin to reverse the spread of HIV/AIDS
   - Halt and begin to reverse the incidence of malaria and other major diseases

7. Ensure environmental sustainability
   - Integrate the principles of sustainable development into country policies and programmes; reverse loss of environmental resources
   - Reduce by half the proportion of people without sustainable access to safe drinking water
   - Achieve significant improvement in the lives of at least 100 million slum dwellers by 2020

8. Develop a global partnership for development
   - Develop further an open trading and financial system that is rule-based, predictable, and nondiscriminatory. Includes a commitment to good governance, development, and poverty reduction—nationally and internationally.
   - Address the least developed countries' special needs. This includes tariff- and quota-free access for their exports; enhanced debt relief for heavily indebted poor countries; cancellation of official bilateral debt; and more generous official development assistance for countries committed to poverty reduction.
   - Address the special needs of landlocked and small island developing States
   - Deal comprehensively with developing countries' debt problems through national and international measures to make debt sustainable in the long term
   - In cooperation with the developing countries, develop decent and productive work for youth
   - In cooperation with pharmaceutical companies, provide access to affordable essential drugs in developing countries
   - In cooperation with the private sector, make available the benefits of new technologies—especially information and communications technologies

By the year 2015 all 189 United Nations Member States have pledged to meet the above goals.

Source: http://www.un.org/millenniumgoals/index.html.

and discussed in Chapter 1. As an international bill of rights for women, it defies discrimination and sets up national agendas for change. As already mentioned, the United States has not ratified CEDAW in part because it fears treaty provisions would supercede U.S. laws and sovereignty.

FUTURE VISIONS

How might the future look? How will our knowledge of gender, race, and class-based inequalities be used? Does our future hold the promise of prosperity and peace or economic unrest and increased militarization? Will technology save us or hasten our destruction? Will feminist values be a part of future social transformation? Future visions are metaphors for the present; we anticipate the future in light of how we make sense of the present and have come to understand the past. This approach encourages us to look at the present mindfully, so that we are aware of its politics, and creatively, so that we can see the possibility for change. In her playful poem "Warning," Jenny Joseph looks to the future to offer some guidance in the present.

There are some social trends that have implications for the future. Given the higher fertility rates among the non-White population as well as immigration figures, Whites will eventually become a relatively smaller percentage of the population until they are no longer a majority in the United States. Latinas/os are the largest growing group, estimated to increase from the current 12.5 percent of the U.S. population to 18 percent by 2025. In addition, the rise in births between 1946 and 1960 (the baby boomer cohort) and the decline through the 1970s will mean a large percentage of the population will be over 65 years old within the next couple of decades. Census reports of 2005 suggest that by 2030 there will be about 70 million older persons (65 years and older): more than twice their number in 2000 and reaching approximately 20 percent of the population. Currently, persons 65 years and older represent about 13 percent of the population. And, although some people have always lived to be 80, 90, and 100 years old, the number of aged will grow in response to better nutrition and health care among certain segments of the population. As the baby boomers age, they will create stress on medical and social systems. They might also influence family systems as several generations of aged family members could require care at the same time. This is complicated by the fact that families are becoming smaller, and divorce and remarriage rates will probably continue at current rates. Ties between stepfamilies and other nonfamilial ties are most likely going to become more important in terms of care and support.

In our society, where the profit motive runs much of our everyday lives, where many citizens have lost respect for political and governmental institutions and are working longer hours and may feel disconnected from families and communities, the issue of integrity is something to consider. The definition of integrity has two parts: one, it is a moral positioning about the distinction between right and wrong, and two, it is a consistent stance on this morality such that we act out what we believe and attempt to live our ideals. "Do as I say and not as I do" is an example of the very opposite of integrity. What might it mean to live with feminist-inspired integrity as well as envision a future where feminist integrity is central? We'll discuss seven implications here.

ACTIVIST PROFILE   **Haunani-Kay Trask**

Haunani-Kay Trask is one of the world's foremost Hawaiian Studies scholars and a successful activist for indigenous rights. Trask was the first full-time director of the Center for Hawaiian Studies at the University of Hawai'i-Manoa and a founding member of Ka Lāhui Hawai'i, Hawai'i's largest sovereignty organization.

Hawai'i was independently ruled by a unified monarchy first organized under Kamehameha I in 1810 and recognized by the world community of nations as an independent nation. In 1893 the U.S. minister assigned to Hawai'i conspired with non-Hawai'ian residents to overthrow the government, and, though President Grover Cleveland acknowledged the wrong done and called for restoration of the monarchy, the U.S. government annexed Hawai'i in 1898. Native Hawai'ians have been fighting for sovereignty since then. In 1993, President Bill Clinton signed a resolution of apology to Native Hawai'ians on the 100th anniversary of the overthrow of the monarchy.

The calls for Hawai'ian independence continue, and Haunani-Kay Trask provides a respected voice in the sovereignty movement. She is the author of *From a Native Daughter: Colonialism & Sovereignty in Hawai'i* and *Eros and Power: The Promise of Feminist Theory* and two volumes of poetry, *Light in the Crevice Never Seen* and *Night Is a Sharkskin Drum*. She also wrote and co-produced a film, *Act of War: The Overthrow of the Hawaiian Nation*, and she has co-anchored a weekly television show that highlights Hawai'ian cultural and political issues. She has been a Fellow at the Pacific Basin Research Center at Harvard University, a National Endowment for the Arts Writer-in-Residence at Santa Fe, New Mexico, a Rockefeller Resident Fellow at the University of Colorado at Boulder, and an American Council of Learned Societies Research Fellow.

Principles of Environmental Justice

1. Environmental justice affirms the sacredness of Mother Earth, ecological unity and the interdependence of all species, and the right to be free from ecological destruction.

2. Environmental justice demands that public policy be based on mutual respect and justice for all peoples, free from any form of discrimination or bias.

3. Environmental justice mandates the right to ethical, balanced, and responsible uses of land and renewable resources in the interest of a sustainable planet for humans and other living things.

4. Environmental justice calls for universal protection from nuclear testing, extraction, production and disposal of toxic/hazardous wastes and poisons that threaten the fundamental right to clean air, land, water, and food.

5. Environmental justice affirms the fundamental right to political, economic, cultural, and environmental self-determination of all peoples.

6. Environmental justice demands the cessation of the production of all toxins, hazardous wastes, and radioactive materials, and that all past and current producers be held strictly accountable to the people for detoxification and containment at the point of production.

7. Environmental justice demands the right to participate as equal partners at every level of decision making, including needs assessment, planning, implementation, enforcement, and evaluation.

8. Environmental justice affirms the right of all workers to a safe and healthy work environment, without being forced to choose between an unsafe livelihood and unemployment. It also affirms the right of those who work at home to be free from environmental hazards.

9. Environmental justice protects the right of victims of environmental injustice to receive full compensation and reparations for damages as well as quality health care.

10. Environmental justice considers governmental acts of environmental injustice a violation of international law, the Universal Declaration on Human Rights, and the United Nations Convention on Genocide.

11. Environmental justice must recognize a special legal and natural relationship of Native Peoples to the U.S. government through treaties, agreements, compacts, and covenants affirming sovereignty and self-determination.

12. Environmental justice affirms the need for urban and rural ecological policies to clean up and rebuild our cities and rural areas in balance with nature, honoring the cultural integrity of all our communities, and providing fair access for all to the full range of resources.

13. Environmental justice calls for the strict enforcement of principles of informed consent and a halt to the testing of experimental reproductive and medical procedures and vaccinations on people of color.

14. Environmental justice opposes the destructive operations of multinational corporations.

15. Environmental justice opposes military occupation; repression and exploitation of lands, peoples and cultures, and other life forms.

16. Environmental justice calls for the education of present and future generations that emphasizes social and environmental issues, based on our experience and an appreciation of our diverse cultural perspectives.

17. Environmental justice requires that we, as individuals, make personal and consumer choices to consume as little of Mother Earth's resources and to produce as little waste as possible; and make the conscious decision to challenge and reprioritize our lifestyles to ensure the health of the natural world for present and future generations.

Source: People of Color Environmental Leadership Summit, 1991. *www.umich.edu/˜jrazer/nre/whatis.html.*

First, it is important to set feminist priorities and keep them. In a society where sound bites and multiple, fragmented pieces of information vie to be legitimate sources of knowledge, we must recognize that some things are more important than others. Priorities are essential. Postmodernism might have deconstructed notions of truth to the point where some argue that there is no such thing as the truth; yet, some things are truer than others. Figure out your truths and priorities based upon your own values and politics. Decide where to put your energy and figure out which battles are worth fighting. This also means developing personal resilience to weather the ups and downs (and, for some, the deeper trauma) of our lives. Survivors act not only from self-interest, but also in the interest of others. Having a relaxed awareness and the confidence that it brings allows us to prioritize and use our energy for things that really matter. Refusing to be controlled by improper laws or social standards,

Women Working for Peace

The International Peace Bureau (IPB) is the world's oldest and most comprehensive international peace federation. Founded in 1892, the organization won the Nobel Peace Prize in 1910. Its role is to support peace and disarmament initiatives. Current priorities include the abolition of nuclear weapons, conflict prevention and resolution, human rights, and women and peace. To learn more about the IPB, visit the website at *www.ipb.org.*

The Women's International League for Peace and Freedom (WILPF), founded in 1915 to protest the war in Europe, suggests ways to end war and to prevent war in the future; as well, it seeks to educate and mobilize women for action. The goals of the WILPF are political solutions to international conflicts, disarmament, promotion of women to full and equal participation in all society's activities, economic and social justice within and among states, elimination of racism and all forms of discrimination and exploitation, respect of fundamental human rights, and the right to development in a sustainable environment. For more information, including action alerts and readings, visit the WILPF homepage at *www.wilpf.org.*

Female Nobel Peace Laureates

Twelve women have been honored with the Nobel Peace Prize for their work for justice:

Baroness Bertha Von Suttner (1905) Austrian honored for her writing and work opposing war.

Jane Addams (1931) International President, Women's International League for Peace and Freedom.

Emily Greene Balch (1946) Honored for her pacifism and work for peace through a variety of organizations.

Betty Williams and Mairead Corrigan (1976) Founders of the Northern Ireland Peace Movement to bring together Protestants and Catholics to work for peace together.

Mother Teresa (1979) Honored for her "work in bringing help to suffering humanity" and her respect for individual human dignity.

Alva Myrdal (1982) Honored with Alfonso Garcia Robles for their work with the United Nations on disarmament.

Aung San Suu Kyi (1991) Burmese activist honored for nonviolent work for human rights in working for independence in Myanmar.

Rigoberta Menchú Tum (1992) Honored for her work for "ethno-cultural reconciliation based on respect for the rights of indigenous peoples."

Jody Williams (1997) Honored for her work with the International Campaign to Ban Landmines.

Shirin Ebadi (2003) Honored for her efforts to promote democracy and human rights.

Wangari Maathai (2004) Honored for her contribution to sustainable development, democracy, and peace.

Source: http://womenshistory.about.com/education/womenshistory/msubnobelpeace.htm.

yet choosing to abide by them for the sake of others and with an eye to changing these structures, is what Bernie Siegel in *Love, Medicine and Miracles* calls "cooperative nonconformity."

Second, it is important that we live and envision a society that balances personal freedom and identity with public and collective responsibility. Transformational politics call for living with communal values that teach how to honor the needs of the individual as well as the group. The United States is a culture that values individualism very highly and often forgets that although the Constitution says you have the right to do something, we also have the right to criticize you for it. Similarly, we might question the limitations associated with certain rights. Is your right still a right if it violates our rights or hurts a community? And, just because the Constitution says something is your right, that does not necessarily make that act a moral choice. Just because we

can do something doesn't mean we have to do it. Although the Constitution exists to protect choices and rights, it does not tell us which choices and rights are best.

Third, recognize that corporate capitalism does not function in everybody's interests. In this sense, economic *freedom* must not be confused with economic *democracy*. Because we can choose between 20 different kinds of breakfast cereal does not mean we have economic or political democracy. Many of us have learned that capitalist societies are synonymous with democracies and that other economic systems are somehow undemocratic in principle. We live in a society that attempts a political democracy at the same time that economic democracy, or financial equity for all peoples, is limited. Unfortunately, capitalism has had deleterious effects on both physical and human environments, and consumerism has changed families and communities by encouraging people to accumulate material possessions beyond their immediate needs. Perhaps a motto for the future might be "pack lightly."

Fourth, a present and future with a core value of feminist integrity is one that understands the limitations of technology as well as its liberating aspects. The future vision must be one of sustainability: finding ways to live in the present so that we do not eliminate options for the future. It is important to balance economic, environmental, and community needs in ways that do not jeopardize sustainability. This means being in control of technology so that it is used ethically and productively, an issue that is related to the previous point about capitalist expansion. Corporations have invested heavily in new technologies that do not always work for the collective good.

Fifth, feminist integrity requires advocating a sustainable physical environment. There is only one world and we share it; there is an interdependence of all species. Given this, it makes no sense to destroy our home through behaviors that bring about global climate change, environmental pollution, and species eradication. A source of clean and sustainable energy to replace reliance on oil and other fossil fuels is imperative at this moment. Sustainable environmental practices start with addressing issues associated with capitalist global expansion and technological development, as discussed previously. Is it possible to own the rivers and other natural resources of the land? What does it mean to turn precious resources into commodities and what might be the consequences? Could we imagine such resources as sustainable communal property held in trust to be used in equitable ways by future generations? If this were possible, might we see air pollution, for example, as a violation of community property rights? Central here is the need for *environmental justice* because the poor and communities of color have suffered disproportionately in terms of environmental pollution and degradation. Environmental justice calls for protection from nuclear testing, extraction, production, and disposal of toxic and hazardous wastes and poisons that threaten the fundamental right to clean air, land, water, and food. It also demands that workers have the right to safe and healthy work environments without being forced to choose between unsafe livelihood and unemployment.

Sixth, a peaceful and sustainable future is one that respects human dignity, celebrates difference and diversity, and yet recognizes that diversity does not necessarily imply equality. It is not enough to be tolerant of the differences among us, although that would be a good start; it is necessary to recognize everyone's right to a piece of the pie and work toward equality of outcome and not just equality of access. As Phyllis Rosser reports in the reading "Too Many Women in College?" the increasing numbers of women (especially low-income women) compared with men in institutions of higher education reflect women's successes. Such figures must not be interpreted as lack of opportunities for men, or failure on their part, except to acknowledge how lack of socio-economic resources affects working-class men. We believe we must create social movements that derive from an ethic of caring, empathy, and compassion for all people.

Seventh and finally, we believe it is important to have a sense of humor and to take the time to play and celebrate. As socialist labor reformer Emma Goldman once said, "If I can't dance, it's not my revolution!"

A justice-based politics of integrity embraces equality for all peoples. It is an ethic that has the potential to help create a peaceful and sustainable future, improving the quality of our lives and the future of our planet. An ethic that respects and values all forms of life and seeks ways to distribute resources equitably is one that moves away from dominance and uses peaceful solutions to environmental, societal, and global problems. As a blueprint for the future, a focus on justice and equality has much to offer. As Ruth Rosen writes in the reading "Epilogue: Beyond Backlash," in her reference to the movement for women's human rights, the struggle has begun and there is no end in sight!

Fear of Feminism
Why Young Women Get the Willies

Lisa Marie Hogeland (1994)

I began thinking about young women's fear of feminism, as I always do in the fall, while I prepared to begin another year of teaching courses in English and women's studies. I was further prodded when former students of mine, now graduate students elsewhere and teaching for the first time, phoned in to complain about their young women students' resistance to feminism. It occurred to me that my response—"Of course young women are afraid of feminism"—was not especially helpful. This essay is an attempt to trace out what that "of course" really means; much of it is based on my experience with college students, but many of the observations apply to other young women as well.

Some people may argue that young women have far less to lose by becoming feminists than do older women: they have a smaller stake in the system and fewer ties to it. At the same time, though, young women today have been profoundly affected by the demonization of feminism during the 12 years of Reagan and Bush—the time when they formed their understanding of political possibility and public life. Older women may see the backlash as temporary and changeable; younger women may see it as how things are. The economic situation for college students worsened over those 12 years as well, with less student aid available, so that young women may experience their situation as extremely precarious—too precarious to risk feminism.

My young women students often interpret critiques of marriage—a staple of feminist analysis for centuries—as evidence of their authors' dysfunctional families. This demonstrates another reality they have grown up with: the increased

tendency to pathologize any kind of oppositional politics. Twelve years of the rhetoric of "special interests versus family values" have created a climate in which passionate political commitments seem crazy. In this climate, the logical reasons why all women fear feminism take on particular meaning and importance for young women.

To understand what women fear when they fear feminism—and what they don't—it is helpful to draw a distinction between gender consciousness and feminist consciousness. One measure of feminism's success over the past three decades is that women's gender consciousness—our self-awareness as women—is extremely high. Gender consciousness takes two forms: awareness of women's vulnerability and celebration of women's difference. Fear of crime is at an all-time high in the United States; one of the driving forces behind this fear may well be women's sense of special vulnerability to the epidemic of men's violence. Feminists have fostered this awareness of violence against women, and it is to our credit that we have made our analysis so powerful; at the same time, however, we must attend to ways this awareness can be deployed for nonfeminist and even antifeminist purposes, and most especially to ways it can be used to serve a racist agenda. Feminists have also fostered an awareness of women's difference from men and made it possible for women (including nonfeminists) to have an appreciation of things pertaining to women—perhaps most visibly the kinds of "women's culture" commodified in the mass media (soap operas and romance, self-help books, talk shows, and the like). Our public culture in the U.S. presents myriad opportunities for women to take pleasure in being women—most often, however, that pleasure is used as an advertising or marketing strategy.

Gender consciousness is a necessary precondition for feminist consciousness, but they are not the same. The difference lies in the link between gender and politics. Feminism politicizes gender consciousness, inserts it into a systematic analysis of histories and structures of domination and privilege. Feminism asks questions—difficult and complicated questions, often with contradictory and confusing answers—about how gender consciousness can be used both for and against women, how vulnerability and difference help and hinder women's self-determination and freedom. Fear of feminism, then, is not a fear of gender, but rather a fear of politics. Fear of politics can be understood as a fear of living in consequences, a fear of reprisals.

The fear of political reprisals is very realistic. There are powerful interests opposed to feminism—let's be clear about that. It is not in the interests of white supremacy that white women insist on abortion rights, that women of color insist on an end to involuntary sterilization, that all women insist on reproductive self-determination. It is not in the interests of capitalism that women demand economic rights or comparable worth. It is not in the interests of many individual men or many institutions that women demand a non-exploitative sexual autonomy—the right to say and mean both no and yes on our own terms. What would our mass culture look like if it didn't sell women's bodies—even aside from pornography? It is not in the interests of heterosexist patriarchy that women challenge our understandings of events headlined MAN KILLED FAMILY BECAUSE HE LOVED THEM, that women challenge the notion of men's violence against women and children as deriving from "love" rather than power. It is not in the interests of any of the systems of domination in which we are enmeshed that we see how these systems work—that we understand men's violence, male domination, race and class supremacy, as systems of permission for both individual and institutional exercises of power, rather than merely as individual

pathologies. It is not in the interests of white supremacist capitalist patriarchy that women ally across differences.

Allying across differences is difficult work, and is often thwarted by homophobia—by fears both of lesbians and of being named a lesbian by association. Feminism requires that we confront that homophobia constantly. I want to suggest another and perhaps more subtle and insidious way that fear of feminism is shaped by the institution of heterosexuality. Think about the lives of young women—think about your own. What are the arenas for selfhood for young women in this culture? How do they discover and construct their identities? What teaches them who they are, who they want to be, who they might be? Our culture allows women so little scope for development, for exploration, for testing the boundaries of what they can do and who they can be, that romantic and sexual relationships become the primary, too often the only, arena for selfhood.

Young women who have not yet begun careers or community involvements too often have no public life, and the smallness of private life, of romance as an arena for selfhood, is particularly acute for them. Intimate relationships become the testing ground for identity, a reality that has enormously damaging consequences for teenage girls in particular (the pressures both toward and on sex and romance, together with the culturally induced destruction of girls' self-esteem at puberty, have everything to do with teenage pregnancy). The feminist insistence that the personal is political may seem to threaten rather than empower a girl's fragile, emergent self as she develops into a sexual and relational being.

Young women may believe that a feminist identity puts them out of the pool for many men, limits the options of who they might become with a partner, how they might decide to live. They may not be wrong either: how many young men feminists or feminist sympathizers do you know? A politics that may require making demands on a partner, or that may motivate particular choices in partners, can appear to foreclose rather than to open up options for identity, especially for women who haven't yet discovered that all relationships require negotiation and struggle. When you live on Noah's ark, anything that might make it more difficult to find a partner can seem to threaten your very survival. To make our case, feminists have to combat not just homophobia, but also the rule of the couple, the politics of Noah's ark in the age of "family values." This does not mean that heterosexual feminist women must give up their intimate relationships, but it does mean that feminists must continually analyze those pressures, be clear about how they operate in our lives, and try to find ways around and through them for ourselves, each other, and other women.

For women who are survivors of men's violence—perhaps most notably for incest and rape survivors—the shift feminism enables, from individual pathology to systematic analysis, is empowering rather than threatening. For women who have not experienced men's violence in these ways, the shift to a systematic analysis requires them to ally themselves with survivors—itself a recognition that *it could happen to me*. Young women who have not been victims of men's violence hate being asked to identify with it; they see the threat to their emergent sense of autonomy and freedom not in the fact of men's violence, but in feminist analyses that make them identify with it. This can also be true for older women, but it may be lessened by the simple statistics of women's life experience: the longer you live, the more likely you are to have experienced men's violence or to know women who are survivors of it, and thus to have a sense of the range and scope of that violence.

My women students, feminist and nonfeminist alike, are perfectly aware of the risks of going unescorted to the library at night. At the same time, they are appalled by my suggesting that such gender-based restrictions on their access to university facilities deny them an equal education. It's not that men's violence isn't real to them—but that they are unwilling to trace out its consequences and to understand its complexities. College women, however precarious their economic situation, and even despite the extent of sexual harassment and date rape on campuses all over the country, still insist on believing that women's equality has been achieved. And, in fact,

to the extent that colleges and universities are doing their jobs—giving women students something like an equal education—young women may experience relatively little overt or firsthand discrimination. Sexism may come to seem more the exception than the rule in some academic settings—and thus more attributable to individual sickness than to systems of domination.

Women of all ages fear the existential situation of feminism, what we learned from Simone de Beauvoir, what we learned from radical feminists in the 1970s, what we learned from feminist women of color in the 1980s: feminism has consequences. Once you have your "click!" moment, the world shifts, and it shifts in some terrifying ways. Not just heterosexism drives this fear of political commitment—it's not just fear of limiting one's partner-pool. It's also about limiting oneself—about the fear of commitment to something larger than the self that asks us to examine the consequences of our actions. Women fear anger, and change, and challenge—who doesn't? Women fear taking a public stand, entering public discourse, demanding—and perhaps getting—attention. And for what? To be called a "feminazi"? To be denounced as traitors to women's "essential nature"?

The challenge to the public-private division that feminism represents is profoundly threatening to young women who just want to be left alone, to all women who believe they can hide from feminist issues by not being feminists. The central feminist tenet that the personal is political is profoundly threatening to young women who don't want to be called to account. It is far easier to rest in silence, as if silence were neutrality, and as if neutrality were safety. Neither wholly cynical nor wholly apathetic, women who fear feminism fear living in consequences. Think harder, act more carefully; feminism requires that you enter a world supersaturated with meaning, with implications. And for privileged women in particular, the notion that one's own privilege comes at someone else's expense—that my privilege *is* your oppression—is profoundly threatening.

Fear of feminism is also fear of complexity, fear of thinking, fear of ideas—we live, after all, in a profoundly anti-intellectual culture. Feminism is one of the few movements in the U.S. that produce nonacademic intellectuals—readers, writers, thinkers, and theorists outside the academy, who combine and refine their knowledge with their practice. What other movement is housed so substantially in bookstores? All radical movements for change struggle against the anti-intellectualism of U.S. culture, the same anti-intellectualism, fatalism, and disengagement that make even voting too much work for most U.S. citizens. Feminism is work—intellectual work as surely as it is activist work—and it can be very easy for women who have been feminists for a long time to forget how hard-won their insights are, how much reading and talking and thinking and work produced them. In this political climate, such insights may be even more hard-won.

Feminism requires an expansion of the self—an expansion of empathy, interest, intelligence, and responsibility across differences, histories, cultures, ethnicities, sexual identities, othernesses. The differences between women, as Audre Lorde pointed out over and over again, are our most precious resources in thinking and acting toward change. Fear of difference is itself a fear of consequences: it is less other women's difference that we fear than our own implication in the hierarchy of differences, our own accountability to other women's oppression. It is easier to rest in gender consciousness, in one's own difference, than to undertake the personal and political analysis required to trace out one's own position in multiple and overlapping systems of domination.

Women have real reasons to fear feminism, and we do young women no service if we suggest to them that feminism itself is safe. It is not. To stand opposed to your culture, to be critical of institutions, behaviors, discourses—when it is so clearly *not* in your immediate interest to do so—asks a lot of a young person, of any person. At its best, the feminist challenging of individualism, of narrow notions of freedom, is transformative, exhilarating, empowering. When we do our best work in selling feminism to the unconverted, we make clear not only its necessity, but also its pleasures: the joys of intellectual and political work, the moral power of living in consequences, the surprises of coalition, the rewards of doing what is difficult. Feminism offers an arena for selfhood beyond personal relationships but not disconnected from them. It offers—and requires—courage, intelligence, boldness, sensitivity, relationality, complexity, a sense of purpose, and, lest we forget, a sense of humor as well. Of course young women are afraid of feminism—shouldn't they be?

Too Many Women in College?

Phyllis Rosser (2005)

Although American women still struggle for parity in many arenas, we have outpaced men in at least one: undergraduate college education. Currently, 57.4 percent of bachelor's degrees in the United States are earned by women, 42.6 percent by men. This is an almost exact reversal from 1970, when 56.9 percent of college graduates were males and 43.1 percent females.

We should be celebrated for this landmark achievement, but instead it has engendered fear. Read the headlines: "Falling Male College Matriculation an Alarming Trend," or "Admissions Officers

Weigh a Heretical Idea: Affirmative Action for Men." Notice, too, that a major focus of first lady Laura Bush's new anti-gang task force is education for boys. As she's been quoted, "The statistics are pretty alarming. Girls are going to college much more than boys."

Few worried when college students were two-thirds men. But as early as February 1999, *U.S. News & World Report* predicted that the rising tide of women college grads could close the salary gap and move women into positions of power as heads of corporations, presidents of universities and political leaders. At the other extreme, the article suggested, college education might become devalued—considered "a foolhardy economic decision"—as has happened in other fields after women begin to predominate.

STILL RARE AT THE TOP

What *U.S. News* failed to mention was that women are still a rare presence at the top ranks of the corporate and professional world despite earning more college degrees than men for 23 years. Women undertake stronger academic programs than men in high school, and receive higher average grades than men in both high school and college, but haven't been able to translate that success into equitable money and power. Consider these disparities as well:

- Women currently earn nearly 59 percent of master's degrees, but men outstrip women in advanced degrees for business, engineering and computer-science degrees—fields which lead to much higher-paying jobs than education, health and psychology, the areas where women predominate.
- Despite women's larger numbers as under-grads and in master's programs, men outnumber women in earning doctorates (54 percent) and professional degrees (53 percent).
- This year, the number of women applying to medical school outpaced men for the second

time, but they are only predicted to be 33 percent of doctors by 2010.
- Women comprise nearly half of the students entering law schools, but they're miles from parity as law partners, professors and judges.

TESTS DON'T TELL THE WHOLE TALE

Women may lose a step on the career ladder even before they enter college. That's because, despite their greater number of bachelor's and master's degrees, women remain at a disadvantage in college admissions testing—which affects their acceptance at elite schools. The main purpose of the SAT—on which women averaged 44 points lower than men last year—is to predict first-year grades. However, it consistently underpredicts the college performance of women, who earn higher college grades than men.

Women's lower scores on the SAT have been shown to arise from several factors biased toward male performance, including the fact that it's a timed test and rewards guessing—and men tend to be more confident and risk-taking than women in such test situations. Also, the SAT puts many of the questions in a male context (such as sports), which can further lower female confidence about knowing the material.

In an attempt to even the gender playing field, a writing section that includes language questions and an essay was added to the SAT this year, after the University of California insisted that the test be more attuned to the skills necessary for college success. This may raise women's SAT scores somewhat, since writing tests are an area in which they have traditionally outperformed males.

Lower SAT scores keep qualified women from both attending the most competitive schools and from receiving National Merit Scholarships and other awards based on PSAT and SAT scores. The test biases against women then continue in graduate education, with such instruments as the Graduate Record Exam (GRE), Graduate Management Admissions Test (GMAT) and Law School Admissions Test (LSAT).

Thus, women have yet to predominate at the most prestigious colleges and universities, where graduates are tracked toward top leadership positions in society. With enormous numbers of both sexes applying to these schools, the admissions offices can choose their gender ratio. In 2005, men outnumbered women at all the Ivy League schools except Brown and Columbia. Women are also significantly outnumbered at universities specializing in engineering and physical science, such as Massachusetts Institute of Technology in Cambridge and California Institute of Technology in Pasadena.

AFFIRMATIVE ACTION—FOR MEN?

The greater percentage of women earning bachelor's degrees has given rise to some reactionary theories explaining why. Conservative analyst Christina Hoff Sommers insists the gap takes root in the more "girl-friendly" elementary school environment where boys are turned off to learning.

In *The War Against Boys: How Misguided Feminism Is Harming Our Young Men* (Simon & Schuster, 2000), Hoff Sommers claims that schoolboys are "routinely regarded as protosexists, potential harassers and perpetuators of gender inequity" who "live under a cloud of censure."

Even higher-education policy analyst Tom Mortensen, who has a special concern with underrepresented populations in higher education, also sees the college gender gap as part of a larger societal problem for men and boys. Mortensen says K–12 teachers, 75 percent of whom are women, are not providing the role models and learning styles boys need. Of course, this was never an issue during the decades when college graduates were mainly men, and hasn't drawn much notice since the end of the Civil War—the time when women began their continuing predominance as elementary school teachers.

If these theories seem to spring from a blame-the-women viewpoint, there is a legitimate concern about the decline in male graduates at private colleges, where the gap has been greatest (although public universities have also been affected). Admissions officers worry that their colleges' value will be lowered by an imbalance of female students: The larger the female majority, some say, the less likely either males or females will want to apply.

Speaking at a College Board conference several years ago, admissions officers agreed that a 60-40 female-to-male gender ratio was their upper limit. After that, said former Macalester College president Michael McPherson, "students will take notice." Small private colleges are now using what can only be called "male affirmative action" to increase male enrollment: actively recruiting men by emphasizing their science, math and engineering courses, adding sports programs (in violation of Title IX), sending extra mailings designed to attract men and even calling men to remind them of the admissions deadline.

"Probably no one will admit it, but I know lots of places try to get some gender balance by having easier admissions standards for boys than for girls," said Columbia University Teachers College president Arthur Levine to *The New York Times* national correspondent Tamar Lewin. Robert Massa, vice president of Dickinson College in Carlisle, Penn., has said that the school now evaluates prospective male students less on grades and more on measures where they typically do better, such as SAT scores. Adds Goucher College admissions vice president Barbara Fritze, "Men are being admitted to schools they never got into before, and offered financial aid they hadn't gotten before."

Massa reported that the number of first-year males at Dickinson rose from 36 percent to 43 percent in 2001 after they took affirmative action toward men, who were admitted with lower grades but comparable SAT scores. Women, meanwhile, had to be much better than men to make the cut: Nearly 62 percent of the women accepted to the school ranked in the top 10 percent of their high school class, compared to 42 percent of the men.

This new form of affirmative action, even if begun with all good intentions, could lead to bad college-admissions policy. What if a university decides it doesn't just want more men in attendance, but more white men? The whole notion of affirmative action as a way to help disadvantaged populations succeed could be turned on its head.

THE INCOME GAP

The real reason behind the undergrad gender gap may have much less to do with one's sex and more to do with income, race and class.

Jacqueline King, director of the Center for Policy Analysis at the American Council on Education in Washington, D.C., decided that media stories about the decline of white male enrollment didn't intuitively jibe with what she saw happening, so she took a closer look at college student data, analyzing it by sex, age, race/ethnicity and socioeconomic status. She found the gender gap in college enrollment for students 18 to 24 years of age in 1995–96 occurred among low-income students of all racial/ethnic groups except Asian Americans.

In fact, since 1995, many more women than men from households making less than $30,000 attend college. The latest available data, from 2003–04, shows there is an even smaller percentage of low-income males attending college than there were in 1995, and they are from every racial/ethnic group. African American and Native American students have the largest gender gaps—males comprise just 37 percent of all low-income African American students and 36 percent of low-income Native Americans. Low-income Hispanic men reach a slightly higher 39 percent, and low-income white males 41 percent (a drop from 46 percent in 1995). Asian Americans have the smallest gender gap, with 47 percent of that group's low-income college students being male.

Middle-income ($30,000-$70,000) male students maintained gender parity with females 10 years ago, but since then the numbers have dropped somewhat. This may mean that fewer men from the lower end of this income bracket are attending college, says Eugene Anderson, senior research associate at the American Council on Education.

At the highest income level ($70,000 or more), though, men and women in all ethnic groups attend college in nearly equal numbers.

No studies have been done to determine why more low-income women than men attend college, but there are theories. Economist Lester Thurow suggests that low-income men have been lured to the comfortable salaries of mechanical maintenance jobs. Low-income women, on the other hand, don't have such opportunities, and without a college degree, see themselves getting trapped in low-pay sales or service jobs, says King. Also, more men than women work in computer support or high-tech factories—jobs that don't require bachelor's degrees.

Overall, an increasing number of poor and working-class people are dropping out of college because of such reasons as escalating tuition and the attraction of high-paying factory work, according to a May piece in *The New York Times* ("The College Dropout Boom: Diploma's Absence Strands Many in the Working Class"). Harvard president Lawrence H. Summers goes so far as to call this widening of the education gap between rich and poor our "most serious domestic problem"—and recent changes in federal grant formulas may exacerbate it even further.

UPRISING: MINORITIES AND OLDER WOMEN

On the bright side, ethnic minorities have made impressive gains as college students since 1976, increasing their percentage in the total student body from 10 percent to 23 percent. Minority men's share of all bachelor's degrees has gone from 5 percent to 9 percent. But, again, minority women have outstripped them, more than doubling their share of bachelor's degrees, from 5 percent to 14 percent of the total degrees awarded.

Not only is that statistic a contributing factor to the overall gender gap, but another contributing factor is that women are the majority of older (25+) students—and that demographic has been returning to college in record numbers. The "oldsters" now make up 27 percent of the undergraduate student body, and 61 percent of older students are women. King found that many of these students were African American or Latina, attending community colleges to improve future earnings in health-related fields.

"This story is not one of male failure, or even lack of opportunity," says King, "but rather one of increased academic opportunity and success among females and minorities." Indeed, there has been no decline in bachelor's degrees awarded to men; the numbers awarded to women have simply increased.

Feminists should continue to be concerned about encouraging low-income and minority students to attend college, using the current momentum to give these problems the attention they deserve. But in the meantime, we must remain vigilant about attempts to roll back our educational gains. The fact is, we're a long way from threatening corporate America, so don't put the onus on women. Maybe it's just time to let men try to catch up to us, for a change.

R E A D I N G   102

Real Men Join the Movement

Michael Kimmel (1997)

Cory Shere didn't go to Duke University to become a profeminist man. He was going to be a doctor, covering his bets with a double major in engineering and premed. But his experiences with both organic chemistry and feminist women conspired to lead this affable and earnest 20-year-old Detroit native in a different direction. Now in his junior year, he still has a double major—women's studies and psychology. And he works with a group of men to raise awareness about sexual assault and date rape.

Eric Freedman wasn't profeminist either, when he arrived at Swarthmore College three years ago. A 20-year-old junior literature major from Syracuse, New York, he became involved in a campus antiracism project and began to see the connections among different struggles for equality. At an antiracism workshop he helped organize, he suddenly found himself speaking about male privilege as well as white privilege. This fall, he's starting a men's group to focus on race and gender issues.

Who are these guys? And what are they doing in the women's movement?

They are among a growing number of profeminist men around the country. These aren't the angry divorcés who whine about how men are the new victims of reverse discrimination, nor are they the weekend warriors trooping off to a mythopoetic retreat. They're neither Promise Keepers nor Million Man Marchers vowing to be responsible domestic patriarchs on a nineteenth-century model.

You might think of profeminist men as the "other" men's movement, but I prefer to consider it the "real" men's movement, because by actively supporting women's equality on the job or on the streets and by quietly changing their lives to create that equality at home, profeminist men are also transforming the definition of masculinity. Perhaps this is the movement about which Gloria Steinem rhapsodized when she wrote how women "want a men's movement. We are literally dying for it."

Profeminist men staff the centers where convicted batterers get counseling, organize therapy for rapists and sex offenders in prison, do the workshops on preventing sexual harassment in the workplace or on confronting the impact of pornography in men's lives. On campus, they're organizing men's events during Take Back the Night marches; presenting programs on sexual assault to fraternities, dorms, and athletic teams; taking courses on masculinity; and founding campus groups with acronyms like MAC (Men Acting for Change), MOST (Men Opposed to Sexist Tradition), MASH (Men Against Sexual Harassment), MASA (Men Against Sexual Assault), and, my current favorite, MARS (Men Against Rape and Sexism). Maybe John Gray was right after all—real men *are* from Mars!

FEMINISM AND MEN'S LIVES

I first met Cory, Eric, and about a dozen other young profeminist men in April at the Young Feminist Summit, organized by NOW, in Washington, D.C. They were pretty easy to spot among the nearly one thousand young women from colleges all over the country. As we talked during an impromptu workshop, I heard them describe both the exhilaration and isolation of becoming part of the struggle for women's equality, the frustrations of dealing with other men, the active suspicions and passive indifference of other students.

It felt painfully familiar. I've spent nearly two decades in feminist politics, first as an activist in antirape and antibattery groups, and later helping to organize the National Organization for Men Against Sexism (NOMAS), a network of profeminist men and women around the country. More recently, I've tried to apply the insights of academic feminist theory to men's lives, developing courses on men, debating with Robert Bly and his followers, and writing a history of the idea of manhood in the United States.

Of course, men like Cory and Eric are a distinct minority on campus. They compete with the angry voice of backlash, those shrill interruptions that scream "Don't blame me, I never raped anyone! Leave me alone!" They compete with that now familiar men-as-victims whine. Men, we hear, are terrified of going to work or on a date, lest they be falsely accused of sexual harassment or date rape; they're unable to support their scheming careerist wives, yet are vilified as bad fathers if they don't provide enough child support to keep their ex-wives in Gucci and Donna Karan after the divorce.

In the public imagination, profeminist men also compete with the mythopoetic vision of the men's movement as a kind of summer-camp retreat, and the earnest evangelical Promise Keepers with their men-only sports-themed rallies, and the Million Man March's solemn yet celebratory

atonement. All offer men solace and soul-work, and promise to heal men's pain and enable them to become more nurturing and loving. All noble goals, to be sure. But to profeminist men, you don't build responsibility and democracy by exclusion—of women, or of gays and lesbians.

And profeminist men compete with the most deafening sound coming from the mouths of American men when the subject is feminism: silence. Most men, on campus and off, exude an aura of studied indifference to feminism. Like the irreverent second child at the Passover seder, they ask, "What has this to do with me?"

A lot. Sure, feminism is the struggle of more than one-half of the population for equal rights. But it's also about rethinking identities, our relationships, the meanings of our lives. For men, feminism is not only about what we *can't* do—like commit violence, harassment, or rape—or *shouldn't* do, like leave all the child care and housework to our wives. It's also about what we *can* do, what we *should* do, and even what we *want* to do—like be a better father, friend, or partner. "Most men know that it is to all of our advantage—women and men alike—for women to be equal," noted NOW President Patricia Ireland, in her Summit keynote address. Far from being only about the loss of power, feminism will also enable men to live the lives we say we want to live.

This isn't the gender cavalry, arriving in the nick of time to save the damsels from distress. "Thanks for bringing this sexism stuff to our attention, ladies," one might imagine them saying. "We'll take it from here." And it's true that some men declare themselves feminists just a bit too effortlessly, especially if they think it's going to help them get a date. (A friend calls it "premature self-congratulation," and it's just as likely to leave women feeling shortchanged.)

In part, this explains why I call them "profeminist men" and not "feminist men" or "male feminists." As an idea, it seems to me, feminism involves an empirical observation—that women are not equal—and the moral position that declares they should be. Of course, men may share this empirical observation and take this moral stance. And to that extent men support feminism as an ideal. But feminism as an identity also involves the felt experience of that inequality. And this men do not have, because men are privileged by sexism. To be sure, men may be oppressed—by race, class, ethnicity, sexuality, age, physical ability—but men are not oppressed *as men*. Since only women have that felt experience of oppression about gender, it seems sensible to make a distinction in how we identify ourselves. Men can support feminism and can call ourselves "antisexist" or "profeminist." I've chosen profeminist because, like feminism, it stresses the positive and forward-looking.

In a sense, I think of profeminist men as the Gentlemen's Auxiliary of Feminism. This honorable position acknowledges that we play a part in this social transformation, but not the most significant part. It's the task of the Gentlemen's Auxiliary to make feminism comprehensible to men, not as a loss of power—which has thus far failed to "trickle down" to most individual men anyway—but as a challenge to the false sense of entitlement we have to that power in the first place. Profeminism is about supporting both women's equality and other men's efforts to live more ethically consistent and more emotionally resonant lives.

. . .

The routes taken by today's profeminist men are as varied as the men themselves. But most do seem to have some personal experience that made gender inequality more concrete. For some, it involved their mother. (Remember President Clinton describing how he developed his commitment to women's equality when he tried to stop his stepfather from hitting his mother? Of course, one wishes that commitment had facilitated more supportive policy initiatives.) Max Sadler, a 17-year-old senior at Trinity High School in New York City, watched his professional mother hit her head on the glass ceiling at her high-powered corporate job—a job she eventually quit to join a company with more women in high-level positions. Max shared her frustration and also felt ashamed at the casual attitudes of her male colleagues.

Shehzad Nadeem, a 19-year-old student at James Madison University in Virginia, remembered the way his older sister described her experiences. "I could barely believe the stories she told me, yet something deep inside told me that they were not only true, but common. I realized that we men are actively or passively complicit in women's oppression, and that we have to take an active role in challenging other men." Shehzad joined MOST (Men Opposed to Sexist Tradition), which has presented workshops on violence and sexual assault at Madison dorms.

. . .

Or perhaps it was having a feminist girlfriend, or even just having women friends, that brought these issues to the fore for men. "I grew up with female friends who were as ambitious, smart, achieving, and confident as I thought I was—on a good day," recalls Jason Schultz, a founder of MAC at Duke, who now organizes men's programs to combat campus sexual assault. "When I got to college, these same women began calling themselves feminists. When I heard men call women 'dumb chicks' I knew something was wrong."

. . .

THE PROFEMINIST "CLICK!"

But there has to be more than the presence of feminist role models, challenges from girlfriends, brilliant assignments, or challenging support from professors. After all, we all have women in our lives, and virtually all of those women have had some traumatic encounter with sexism. There has to be something else.

Feminists call it the "click!"—that moment when they realize that their pain, fears, confusion, and anger are not theirs alone, but are shared with other women. Do profeminist men have "clicks!"? Yes, but they don't typically come from righteous indignation or fear, but rather from guilt and shame, a gnawing sense of implication in something larger and more pervasive than individual intention. It's that awful moment when you hear women complain about "men" in general and realize, even just a little bit, that you are what they're talking about. (Much of men's reactive defensiveness seems to be a hedge against these feelings of shame.)

Suddenly, it's not those "bad" men "out there" who are the problem—it's all men. Call it the Pogo revelation: "We have met the enemy, and he is us."

That's certainly the way it felt for Jeff Wolf (not his real name). A sexually naive college sophomore, he found himself growing closer and closer to a woman friend, Annie, during a study date. They talked long into the night and eventually kissed. One thing began to lead to another, and both seemed eager and pleased to be with the other. Just before penetration, though, Jeff felt Annie go limp. "Her eyes glazed over, and she went kind of numb," he recalled, still wincing at the memory.

This is the moment that many a college guy dreams of—her apparent surrender to his desire, even if it was induced by roofies or alcohol. It's a moment when men often space out, preferring to navigate the actual encounter on automatic pilot, fearing that emotional connection will lead to an early climax.

As Annie slipped into this mental coma, though, Jeff stayed alert, as engaged emotionally as he was physically. "What had been so arousing was the way we had been connecting intellectually and emotionally," he said. After some patient prodding, she finally confessed that she'd been raped as a high school sophomore, and ever since, had used this self-protective strategy to get through a sexual encounter without reliving her adolescent trauma. Jeff, it seemed, was the first guy who noticed.

. . .

Others say their "click!" experience happened later in life. In the 1970s, psychologist David Greene was deeply involved in political activism, when he and his wife had a baby. "Not that much changed for me; I still went around doing my thing, but now there was a baby in it." On the other hand, his wife's life was totally transformed by the realities of round-the-clock child care. She'd become a mother. "After several weeks of this, she sat me down and confronted me," he recalls. "The bankruptcy of my politics quickly became clear to me. I was an oppressor, an abuser of privilege—I'd become the enemy I thought I was fighting against." The couple meticulously divided housework and child care, and David learned that revolutions are fought out in people's kitchens as well as in the jungles of Southeast Asia. Terry Kupers, a 54-year-old psychiatrist, and author of *Revisioning Men's Lives*, remembers his first wife initiating some serious talks about the "unstated assumptions we were making about housework, cooking, and whose time was more valuable." Not only did Kupers realize that his wife was right, "but I also realized I liked things better the new way."

. . .

PROFEMINISM TODAY—AND TOMORROW

And just as sisterhood is global, so too are profeminist men active around the world. Men from nearly 50 countries—from Mexico to Japan—regularly contribute to a newsletter of international profeminist scholars and activists, according to its editor, Oystein Holter, a Norwegian researcher. Scandinavian men are working to implement a gender equity mandated by law. Liisa Husu, a senior advisor to Finland's gender equity commission, has developed a parliamentary subcommittee of concerned men. (When I met with them last fall, we spent our day discussing our mutual activities, after which they whisked me off to an all-male sauna resort on the shore of an icy Baltic Sea for a bit of male-bonding as a follow-up to all that equity work.) Scandinavian men routinely take parental leave; in fact, in Sweden and Norway they've introduced "Daddy days," an additional month of paid paternity leave for the men to have some time with their newborns after the mothers have returned to work. About half of Swedish men take paternal leave, according to fatherhood expert Lars Jalmert at the University of Stockholm.

The world's most successful profeminist organization must be Canada's White Ribbon Campaign. Begun in 1991 to coincide with the second anniversary of the Montreal Massacre—when a young man killed 14 women engineering students at the University of Montreal on December 6, 1989—its goal was to publicly and visibly declare opposition to men's violence against women by encouraging men to wear a white ribbon as a public pledge. "Within days, hundreds of thousands of men and boys across Canada wore a ribbon," noted Michael Kaufman, one of the campaign's founders. "It exceeded our wildest expectations—even the prime minister wore a ribbon." This year, WRC events are also planned for Norway, Australia, and several U.S. colleges; in Canada, events include an Alberta hockey team planning a skating competition to raise money for a local women's shelter. WRC organizers have also developed curricula for secondary schools to raise the issue for boys.

But just as surely, some of the most important and effective profeminist men's activities are taking place in American homes every day, as men increasingly share housework and child care, reorganize their schedules to be more responsive to the needs of their families, and even downsize their ambitions to develop a family strategy that does not revolve exclusively around *his* career path. "Housework remains the last frontier" for men to tame, argues sociologist Kathleen Gerson in her book *No Man's Land.* . . .

But the payoff is significant. If power were a scarce commodity or a zero-sum game, we might think that women's increased power would mean a decrease in men's. And since most men don't feel very powerful anyway, the possibilities of further loss are rather unappealing. But for most men, all the power in the world does not seem to have trickled down to enable individual men to live the lives we say we want to live—lives of intimacy, integrity, and individual expression. By demanding the redistribution of power along more equitable lines, feminism also seeks a dramatic shift in our social priorities, our choices about how we live, and what we consider important. Feminism is also a blueprint for men about how to become the men we want to be, and profeminist men believe that men will live happier, healthier, and more emotionally enriched lives by supporting women's equality.

Part of profeminist men's politics is to visibly and vocally support women's equality, and part of it is to quietly and laboriously struggle to implement that public stance into our own lives. And part of it must be to learn to confront and challenge other men, with care and commitment. "This cause is not altogether and exclusively woman's cause," wrote Frederick Douglass in 1848. "It is the cause of human brotherhood as well as human sisterhood, and both must rise and fall together."

R E A D I N G   103

Reflections of a Human Rights Educator

Dazón Dixon Diallo (2004)

In my early days as an activist, I spent a lot of my time examining the problems in the world, and dreaming of ways to eradicate the pain and suffering of life on Earth. So many forces work against the elimination of oppression, and so few choices exist for those of us who want a safer, saner, and more peaceful planet. Thus, I chose to be a fighter, although my weapons were (and are) education, organizing, and mobilizing. But still, I had to fight. The fight was against the marginalization of women of color in the feminist health movement. The fight was against a new disease with deadly consequences, and a strange penchant for already reviled and disrespected "minorities." The fight was, and still is, against the fear and hatred of difference and change. I had to fight against something, because I believed it was the only way to contribute to the social change that we all so desperately need.

As a woman of African descent born in the southern United States, I am among the masses of people who experience some form of oppression on a daily basis. I am from and in the grassroots, where change is essential for moving beyond survival to thriving. Whether the issue is HIV, sexual violence, gender discrimination, poverty, or lack of access, my own experience is inextricably intertwined with the struggle of millions of other souls throughout the world. Some of my struggle has resulted in the creation and development of an HIV/AIDS program for African-American women called SisterLove Women's AIDS project.

When we formed SisterLove in 1989, we were on the cutting edge of the HIV/AIDS tide that was sweeping through the lives and families of women in our communities. We thought, then, that if we provided enough education, intervention, and support services to women at greatest risk for HIV, and for those living with HIV or AIDS, maybe the disease wouldn't hit our communities as hard as it was hitting gay men all over the United States. By 1992, when we became incorporated, we had heard lots of women's stories of pain, fear, rejection, and immobilization. And it became clear that HIV needed to be articulated and addressed in the context of women's lives.

We had been dealing with women's lives in the context of HIV, and it was a flawed strategy. Holistically speaking, we were indirectly responding to a myriad of issues—substance abuse, violence, poverty, misogyny, internalized oppression, family neglect/abandonment . . . the list could go on and on—that were layered inside the iceberg, of which HIV was only the tip. We knew that HIV was the connecting point for a lot of these experiences, but getting folks, especially the mainstream feminist groups and the growing numbers of AIDS activists, to see the direct connection was difficult and as labor intensive as helping folks

understand HIV and its risks. We didn't have the tools or the language to pull these issues together.

In 1996, Loretta J. Ross founded the National Center for Human Rights Education (NCHRE), the first human rights education organization in the United States that focuses primarily on domestic human rights violations including civil, political, economic, social, cultural, developmental, environmental, and sexual rights. NCHRE's mission is to build a human rights movement in the United States by training community leaders and student activists to apply human rights standards to issues of injustice. Ms. Ross introduced these concepts to SisterLove staff and volunteers, and we found the framework within which the HIV/AIDS work we were already doing could be buoyed, strengthened, and articulated in a manner through which the humanity of those living with HIV/AIDS and those at risk could be defended, protected, respected, and valued.

SisterLove's introduction to human rights education was a revelation of sorts. What a simple notion: that if all of us working on social justice issues could define those issues and combat human suffering through a common framework, then we may just effect the change that is needed. As we began to use the human rights education approach, it became even clearer that a perverse reality prevails in the simplicity of this notion and the complexity of its meaning.

I recently illustrated this "simplicity in complexity" when I gave a presentation titled "HIV/AIDS, Gender, and Human Rights: Women and Girls at the Apex and the Intersection." I used a visual that looked more like a simple infant's crib mobile than a complex diagram. Yet, the simplicity of the child's mobile perfectly conveyed the complexity of the categories of issues and populations most affected by those issues. HIV is the apex of the experience, and the axis upon which the issues turn in people's lives. The issues are the hanging baubles that keep spinning in motion, while those who experience the pain from these issues are lying or sitting in the center looking up at all this action, just out of their reach.

Working at the intersection of HIV/AIDS, gender, and human rights is a challenging exercise in working on complex issues for the sake of simplifying the work of social change. When I consider the litany of issues that impede the health and development of women at risk and women living with HIV or AIDS, I often feel overwhelmed by the interconnectedness of the layers of possible responses and necessary actions that must take place. Simultaneously, I feel empowered by the simple notion that many of these issues could be eliminated, prevented, or abolished if human dignity was valued. This is not yet the situation in the United States.

While SisterLove formed initially to answer the needs of people with information about the impact and risks of HIV/AIDS, we quickly moved to include women's reproductive and sexual health and rights on our agenda. As we began to articulate HIV/AIDS issues in the context of the human rights framework, we were faced with the reality that human rights education was actually a more critical need than building an advocacy movement around HIV/AIDS in communities of color, because at that time more than 92 percent of the U.S. population had never heard of the UN Declaration of Human Rights (UNDHR).

Today's fight against HIV/AIDS requires not only continued medical research, education for prevention, and compassion for all individuals without imposing gender-based boundaries on who they love. The fight *also* requires us to examine our attitudes and beliefs about poverty and classism, racism, sexism, homophobia, and human rights. In addition to "finding a cure," our aptitude for halting the spread of HIV/AIDS rests upon our ability to convince those who have generally been unseen and unheard to fight for everyone's right to health information, ethical treatment, and responsive health care. Yet, it is impossible to expect people to fight for rights they do not know they have.

With so few human rights treaties ratified by the United States, and with nearly no existing legal recourse for retribution or compensation for victims of human rights violations, it is strategically important to focus on the moral imperative of creating a human rights culture in the United States. In a woman-only context, women coming into SisterLove are taught how to think about their rights. SisterLove focuses on learning and sharing black and African feminist theory because the "inclusion" of voices of color and their networks in the white-dominated mainstream human rights movements ignores the potential of the community of color to mobilize its own population and develop its own organization models. SisterLove recognizes the need to look outside the U.S. model of women's sexuality, which is based on white men's desire, to the international community to find models more suited to the experience of African-American women. In this way, HIV/AIDS was the centerpiece that helped define the myriad of interlocking reproductive health issues affecting Black women and other women of color—women marginalized by the broader society and even more so by the women's movement and its proponents.

SisterLove began to use the language of human rights in all of our programs and components, such as the Healthy Love Workshop and the LoveHouse, a transitional housing program for HIV+ women and their children. The Healthy Love Workshop is an interactive group-level intervention that addresses HIV and reproductive health information while providing women with practical tools and applications to negotiate safer sex or abstinence, to use condoms and other latex barriers in their sexual activity, and to understand the social and political context in which individual and community change must take place in order to stem the spread of HIV and the impact of AIDS. We incorporate the human rights education paradigm so that women can envision their participation in HIV prevention as an opportunity to effect social change in their own households as well as in the streets of their communities.

We use a similar strategy for the HIV+ residents in the LoveHouse, who learn how to incorporate their understanding of rights and entitlement to human dignity into their understanding of how the Social Security System works, how funding reaches (or doesn't!) their communities to provide the necessary services and support programs, and how to access the information and care they need for themselves and their families. This work develops grassroots leadership with a deep understanding of the bridges connecting what happens in the lives of women in the United States to what happens for women living in other communities in the world similar to our own.

Nowadays, as I continue this work, I spend a lot of time thinking of the world that I want to live in, and the things we need in order to live without pain and suffering. Learning how to use the human rights education framework shifted my paradigm of thinking about how I may affect change and build a just and peaceful existence for all of humanity and life on Earth. As my mother still says, "Education never stops, so you never stop educating." Human rights education provides the opportunity to mobilize groups by bridging isolated issues and individual lived experiences with the language and understanding of basic protections of the things all human beings need to live in dignity and have quality lives. Using the human rights framework has taught me that it is much more productive to strategize around that which you are fighting for, rather than what you are fighting against. Those of us who wear the idealist's "rose colored glasses" know that *"change gonna come"* because of the positive and productive energies of the young and the old, the black and the white, the homosexual and the heterosexual, the advantaged and the disadvantaged. This energy, which we call love, is what moves us at SisterLove to continue our work. The power of love knows no bounds.

R E A D I N G 104

Women and Leadership

Alice H. Eagly and Linda L. Carli (2007)

Most leaders are men. Predictably, people think about leadership mainly in masculine terms. These mental associations about leadership not only shape stereotypes about leaders but also influence organizational norms and practices. As managers follow precedents set by their colleagues, informal norms develop, consensus emerges about what is appropriate, and guidelines become hardened into bureaucratic rules. Over time, organizational leadership inevitably has come to embody the preferences, lifestyles, and responsibilities of the men who usually have held these leadership roles.[1] In this essay, we demonstrate that many of these organizational traditions disadvantage women.

Each organization has its own social structure—regular and predictable patterns of behavior—and its own culture—shared beliefs, values, symbols, and goals. Leadership is an important part of this social structure and culture. Because of both structural and cultural barriers, women generally have had less access than men to leadership roles in organizations. To attain these roles, women negotiate labyrinthine arrangements that present various kinds of obstructions, few of which were expressly designed to discriminate against women although they have this effect.

To reveal this portion of the labyrinth, we analyze those aspects of organizational structure and culture that disadvantage women. We show that considerable change would have to take place in organizations before women would enjoy equal access to leadership. This conclusion holds even though women have already gained much greater access than at any other period in history.[2]

To gain some initial insight into organizational practices that disadvantage women, consider the experiences of a woman attorney in a large law firm that serves corporate clients. This organization's work practices included legal work interspersed with long lunches with other attorneys and considerable chitchatting in one another's offices. These side activities, together with heavy task demands, prevented the associate attorneys from meeting the firm's normative requirements for *billable hours,* the time spent working on clients' cases, during the conventional 9-to-5 schedule. Therefore, most of the associate attorneys stayed very late at the office virtually every evening and also worked most of the weekend.

As a mother, this woman found that the system interfered with her family responsibilities. She instead focused on the legal work that had to be accomplished. Long lunches were infrequent, and casual socializing was kept short. Although her legal work received kudos all around and she turned in an above-average number of billable hours, she was told that, to achieve partner status, she should "get to know" more of the partners in the firm. Getting to know them presumably involved not only working on their cases but also devoting more time to the lunches and chitchatting that give associate attorneys opportunities to assure partners that their career goals are in harmony with the culture of the firm.

Almost all of the women associate attorneys who were or became mothers, including this particular woman, exited the firm's partner track. Some dropped out to become full-time homemakers. Others moved to part-time legal positions that provided considerably less income and virtually no possibility for advancement. The woman in our example, like many other female associates, found a full-time attorney position in the public sector. Even some of the firm's women partners abandoned their positions when they had a child. Although these exits might suggest that the women merely preferred less demanding work or a homemaker role, the fact remains that the firm's own culture undermined its explicit policy of increasing gender diversity.

Research on the careers of lawyers confirms these informal observations. A study of Chicago lawyers showed that women were no less likely than men to begin their careers at large firms but more likely to leave these firms for positions in the public sector or as counsels for corporations. Consequently, women were much less likely than men to hold the leadership positions in large law firms—the positions that are most highly paid and that confer (arguably) the highest prestige. The problems for the women were concentrated in work–family trade-offs. Among those relatively few women who did become partner, 60 percent had no children, and the minority who had children generally had delayed childbearing until after they attained partner status.[3]

It might seem that this outcome of fewer women attaining partner status is entirely fair, because it rewards those who devote themselves most fully to their law firms. However, any such conclusion is wrong. Research by sociologists Fiona Kay and John Hagan showed that higher standards were applied to female than male candidates for partner. Women had to demonstrate higher work commitment as well as especially enthusiastic advocacy of firm culture—that is, "to embody standards that are an exaggerated form of a partnership ideal."[4] Here is yet another demonstration of the double standard.

Women attorneys in law firms, like women in corporate and other executive positions, face at least two types of problems in achieving positions of authority. One barrier is that extreme time demands can make it difficult to combine employment obligations with a family life that involves more than minimal responsibility for children. The other barrier is that, to convince her colleagues that she is worthy of advancement, a woman is often held to standards that are set higher for women than men.[5]

ORGANIZATIONAL BARRIERS TO WOMEN'S ADVANCEMENT

When newcomers enter an established organization, its structure and culture are already in place, invented in the past and modified during the life of the organization. Organizational practices are held in place by their repeated implementation. Such practices evolve slowly, in a dynamic exchange with the beliefs of the individuals who inhabit these organizations. Organizational practices and individuals' beliefs continually shape one another. However, because most employees begin near the bottom of organizational hierarchies, it is much easier for them to accept existing practices than to lobby for change.

To many people who inhabit organizations, workplaces may not seem to be biased in favor of either sex. However, underlying this veneer of fairness there is often an implicit model of an ideal employee. Such an individual is continuously on call to work long hours and make other personal sacrifices for the good of the organization. Because this ideal presumes minimal outside encumbrances, the person who best matches this model is someone who has only limited family obligations. Men, even if married with children, can fit this model if they delegate most domestic responsibilities to their wives. Women typically fit the model less well because they are less able to shift family obligations to their spouses. Even those women who have no children do not fit the ideal employee model if they are seen as potential mothers.[6]

Demands for Long Hours, Travel, and Relocation

Organizations have become greedy in claiming employees' time in higher-level managerial positions as well as in many professional positions. Sociologist Lewis Coser wrote prophetically in the 1970s about the growing demands that organizations placed on managerial workers, requiring "exclusive and undivided loyalty" in addition to long hours.[7] The situation has only become more extreme in the intervening years. . . .

. . . . At the highest job levels, hours can become very long and therefore difficult to reconcile with family responsibilities. A study of women who had quit their high-level managerial and professional jobs found that 86 percent cited work-related factors as coercing their decision, especially norms dictating extremely long hours.[8] . . .

The demand for long hours affects women differently from men. Because of anticipated conflict of such work with childcare responsibilities, women in high-status careers tend to forgo or delay childbearing.[9] Men with wives who accept most domestic responsibilities are far less conflicted. Although work–family conflict should have eased for women because husbands have increased their domestic work, this gain has been offset by increasing time demands of most high-level careers as well as escalating pressures for intensive parenting. Both changes make it difficult for women in demanding careers to manage a family life that includes children. . . .

These norms about employment became entrenched when a far larger proportion of women were full-time homemakers. Among the dual-earner couples who now predominate, these norms create stresses for wives, who, more often than husbands, transport children to and from childcare or school, take children to doctors' appointments, participate in teacher conferences, stay home with sick children, and provide care for aging relatives. Of course, extreme commitment to paid work can be feasible for female employees who have few of these family responsibilities—mainly childless women or older women whose children are no longer at home.

The long-hours lifestyle is possible for women with children at home if they are willing and able to share childcare with husbands, other family members, or paid workers. However, decision makers often merely assume that mothers have domestic responsibilities that make it inappropriate to promote them to demanding positions. As one participant in a study of the federal workforce explained, "I mean, there were 2 or 3 names [of women] in the hat and they said, 'I don't want to talk about her because she has children who are still home in these [evening] hours.' Now they don't pose that thing about men on the list, many of whom also have children in that age group."[10]

. . .

Many elite workers, especially in management, face demands not only to travel frequently but also to relocate. Even a high-performing manager may have little possibility of advancement in his or her local office because no higher-level positions exist or are unfilled. When positions open up in other locations, fast-track employees may have to relocate or step off the fast track. This system of requiring employees to "move to get ahead" characterized the Sears organization, as revealed in the 1980s discrimination case of *EEOC v. Sears, Roebuck & Co.* Some employees relocated three or four times during a ten-year period, and such relocations resulted in promotions and significant salary increases.[11]

Men face less disruption in moving to a new location if their wives are homemakers or have careers that are secondary to their husbands' careers. Because most employed women have employed husbands who are co-breadwinners or primary breadwinners, a move for the wife's career could unacceptably compromise the husband's career or require that the couple live apart. For employed mothers, the complexities of moving may also involve terminating arrangements with trusted childcare providers. As a result, mothers can face great disruption when career advancement requires a move to a new city. At Sears, for example, the "move to get ahead" system tended to close women out of opportunities for promotion.[12] Demands for relocation as well as long hours extend the labyrinth that women negotiate as they attempt to rise in organizational hierarchies.

. . .

Challenges of Building Social Capital

The earlier example of the lawyer who was expected to spend time chatting and having long lunches may seem to lack bureaucratic rationality. However, such activities can serve organizations by building social relationships. The fact that managers and professionals spend considerable time in informal interactions coheres with social scientists' understanding of *social capital*, the relationships between people and the feelings of mutual obligation and support that these relationships create.[13] These informal ties are as essential to organizations as the human capital that allows competent work in the narrower, technical sense. Relationships build knowledge, trust, cooperation, and shared understanding.

People bond through networks both within their organizations and beyond them. Good relationships make it possible to call on others for support, ranging from getting advice and information to setting up deals and transactions. Empirical evidence has shown that managers' social capital, especially their relationships with people in other organizations, fosters their advancement.[14] Such relationships can yield valuable information, access to help and resources, and career sponsorship.

In a demonstration of the importance of social capital, one study yielded the following description of managers who advance rapidly in hierarchies: fast-track managers "spent relatively more time and effort socializing, politicking, and interacting with outsiders than did their less successful counterparts . . . [and] did not give much time or attention to the traditional management activities of planning, decision making, and controlling or to the human resource management activities of motivating/reinforcing, staffing, training/developing, and managing conflict."[15] It thus appears that social capital can be even more essential to managers' advancement than skillful performance of traditional managerial tasks.

Gender affects social capital: women usually have less of it. One interpretation is that men excel at strategically building crucial professional relationships. . . .

The perception that women are not as effectively networked as men is often accurate but mainly reflects causes other than women's lack of understanding of how organizations really work. One difficulty is that networking exacerbates the long work hours that present obstacles to women (and men) with family responsibilities. Managers with significant family responsibilities may fully realize the value of networking but merely decide not to "play the game." Consider a mother who is a manager or professional. Rather than go out for drinks after work, she picks up her child and often prepares a family dinner. She rarely joins a golf outing on the weekend.

Even during ordinary work hours, informal networking can be difficult if women are a small minority. As business journalist and former CEO Margaret Heffernan wrote, "It's still hard to resist the feeling that at meetings, at conferences, on golf courses, women are gatecrashers."[16] When women are a small minority, most networks, especially influential networks, are composed entirely or almost entirely of men. In these male-dominated networks, women usually have less legitimacy and influence and thus may benefit less than men from participation. In such contexts, women can gain from a strong and supportive mentoring relationship with a well-placed individual who possesses greater legitimacy—typically a man.[17]

Breaking into these male networks can be difficult, especially when men center their networks on masculine activities. As one woman in corporate finance remarked, "Sunday night was basketball night where everybody in the department goes and plays basketball. I don't play basketball . . . so there was a big social network there that revolved around men's sports and men's activities, and to be on the outside of that really impacted my ability to develop relationships with people."[18] At a motion picture production company, wheeling and dealing took place on a yearly raft trip—no "girls" allowed.[19]

. . .

Women of color can face even greater challenges than white women in gaining social capital, because both their gender and their race set them apart from the typical white male power holders. These women's strategies for networking are twofold: while attempting to join influential, mainly white male networks, they also network with others who share their race and gender. These strategies thus resemble those used by white women, except for the special effort to connect with women of their own race. This approach makes sense in terms of finding role models and sharing advice about advancing in the presence of barriers that can stem from both race and gender.[20]

Challenges of Fitting In with Organizational Culture

Related to the difficulties that women often experience in building social capital at work are challenges in fitting in with organizational culture.[21] In the survey of the Boston women in executive and professional positions, the barrier to advancement cited most frequently was "a male-dominated work culture." In the words of one of the partici-

pants in this study, "While men create the culture, women adapt to it."[22]

The culture of organizations involves shared, sometimes unspoken, values, meaning, and understanding. Culture is expressed through dress and office arrangements as well as through the symbols that represent organizations and the language that employees use to describe their work.[23] Many organizations are imbued with masculine values, sometimes including displays of competitive masculinity, especially among executives. The fun and games that lighten executives' work might involve, for example, late-night racing of rental cars around hotel parking lots.[24] One egregious example of especially negative aspects of masculine culture involved financial services corporation Smith Barney:

> Three women in the Garden City, N.Y., office of Smith Barney sued that firm in 1996, in what became known as the "Boom-Boom Room" case. Their male colleagues had set up a party room in the basement of what was otherwise a business office, hanging a toilet seat from the ceiling and mixing Bloody Marys and other drinks in a big plastic garbage bin. The men called it the Boom-Boom Room, but the women called it an example of frat-house behavior in a request for class action status in federal court.[25]

. . .

Wal-Mart has provided additional examples of masculine managerial culture. For example, an executive retreat took the form of a quail hunting expedition at Sam Walton's ranch in Texas. To make the masculine culture message clear, one executive received feedback that she probably would not advance in the company because she didn't hunt or fish. Middle managers' meetings included visits to strip clubs and Hooters restaurants, and a sales conference attended by thousands of store managers featured a football theme.[26]

. . .

Consistent with men's emphasis on action, masculine organizational culture is often expressed in language replete with sports and military terminology. Successful activity is termed a *slam-*

dunk or *home run* or *batting a thousand,* and good behavior involves *being a team player.* Militaristic language includes phrases such as *uphill battle, getting flak,* and *killing the competition.* Women can surely learn such vocabulary, facilitated by their increasing participation in athletics, but this language no doubt has remained more effortless for men.

 language is important

If men are more enthusiastic about masculine culture than women are, and there is evidence that this is the case, a masculine organizational culture can at least make many women uncomfortable and thus form part of the labyrinth that women negotiate.[27] Of course, sometimes women may merely figure out aspects of a masculine culture and accommodate to it. Dawn Steel, who became president of Columbia Pictures, exemplified this approach: "By habit, these guys wandered in and out of each other's offices. By the time they got to the weekly production meeting, all the really important decisions had already been made . . . I did not participate in these ad hoc meetings because I was not part of this herd of roaming men. The lesson here . . . Join the roamers." And that's exactly what Dawn Steel did.[28]

Challenges of Obtaining Desirable Assignments

Female managers frequently report difficulty in obtaining appropriately demanding assignments. Lack of access to such assignments, known as *developmental job experiences,* can disqualify women for promotions.[29] Meeting the challenges inherent in tough assignments and becoming recognized for having overcome these challenges are prerequisites to advancement to upper-level management, but social capital is a prerequisite for winning the chance to take on such projects.[30]

Demonstrating that women often back opportunities for appropriately demanding work, organizational psychologists Karen Lyness and Donna Thompson surveyed women and men who were in similar midlevel and senior executive positions in a large multinational financial services corporation. They found that the women had fewer international assignments and were less likely than men to have roles that gave them authority over others. In addition, the women encountered greater difficulty in obtaining demanding and important assignments and opportunities to relocate to a new location for a better position. They also performed fewer complex activities encompassing multiple functions, products, customers, and markets.[31]

More than one process may contribute to women's difficulties in obtaining challenging assignments. Under some circumstances, women apparently choose, or at least agree to perform, work that is not especially challenging, perhaps reacting to implicit expectations in their workplaces. Also, bosses are apparently less likely to assign challenging work to women, perhaps because they hold sexist but chivalrous attitudes that women should receive less stressful forms of work and men the "tougher" assignments.[32] For example, one woman noted how a colleague of hers was impeded from advancement by being denied travel opportunities: "She should have been the director of the office in about 1985 but what happened was that they brought some man in from another place and put him above her. They gave as a reason that she didn't travel. They never let her travel."[33]

Whatever the causes of women's lesser access to challenging work, the low-stakes assignments that they often receive do little to foster their careers. Working hard at routine assignments is not a route to advancement.

. . .

Women's difficulties in obtaining developmental job experiences are compounded by their occupancy of managerial roles that serve staff functions, such as human resources and public relations, rather than line functions, which are more critical to the success of organizations. Women are usually aware that their chances for advancement are limited by placement in staff positions. For example, a large multinational study of executives from major corporations found that women, more than men, complained about their limited opportunities for line management.[34] . . .

Why are women more confined than men to staff management roles? The most likely explanation is that women's stereotypical abilities and interests match staff positions more than line positions. Women are thought to be well endowed with qualities such as social sensitivity and interest in people, attributes that are seen as prerequisites to success in staff managerial roles. Men, in turn, are thought to be well endowed with qualities such as assertiveness and decisiveness, attributes that are seen as prerequisites to success in line managerial roles. When organizations develop stereotypical norms about which sex is optimal for various types of management, men are more often channeled into line management, with its better opportunities to ascend into senior leadership.[35]

Given these twists and turns in the corporate labyrinth, women, more often than men, feel that they have to leave their organizations to have an opportunity to advance.[36] Changing jobs to advance may also reflect the greater importance that women place on the intrinsic satisfaction provided by their jobs. So women may leave organizations not only because they end up with unexciting work but also because they are less satisfied than men would be with such assignments.

. . .

Despite women's difficulties in obtaining demanding assignments, there is also evidence that some women are placed, more often than comparable men, in highly risky positions. Organizational psychologists Michelle Ryan and Alexander Haslam refer to this phenomenon as the *glass cliff*.[37] They showed that companies in the United Kingdom are more likely to place women in high-level executive positions when the companies are experiencing financial downturns and declines in performance.

A U.S. example is the appointment of Anne Mulcahy as CEO of Xerox when the company was on the brink of bankruptcy and under investigation by the Securities and Exchange Commission for irregular accounting methods. In such especially precarious circumstances, executives face a fairly high likelihood of failing, although Mulcahy proved to be outstandingly successful. The reasons for this glass cliff phenomenon may include companies' greater willingness to risk sacrificing their female executives and women's greater willingness to take these positions, given their poorer prospects for obtaining more-desirable positions.

Ironically, then, women apparently have special access to managerial tasks that are virtually impossible as well as to tasks that are especially easy. The glass cliff and the lack of developmental job experiences are cut from the same cloth: both deny women access to the "good" assignments that offer reasonable opportunities for showing oneself as a high-potential manager.[38]

ORGANIZATIONAL INNOVATIONS TO FOSTER GENDER EQUALITY

There are many ways to remove barriers to women's advancement. However, attaining greater fairness is no simple matter. Who gets hired and promoted is a complex outcome of organizational practices interacting with market forces. Nonetheless, specific policies and practices that have a discriminatory impact on women, such as the requirement that managers relocate to advance, can be changed.[39]

A solution that is often proposed is for governments to implement and enforce antidiscrimination legislation and thereby require organizations to eliminate inequitable and discriminatory practices. However, legal remedies can be elusive when gender inequality results from norms that are embedded in organizational structure and culture. The courts often decide that such practices do not violate antidiscrimination legislation despite their adverse impact on women.[40]

Some of the most important organizational changes would confront the ways that the differing life situations of women and men interface with the characteristics of organizations. Women's lifestyles are in general different from men's, especially in their greater domestic responsibility.

Flexible Work

To address the disadvantage that women face from their larger share of domestic work, various proposals have been made to design jobs differently. For instance, managers (and professionals) might have positions that consume fewer hours per week, perhaps having a part-time schedule or even sharing a job with another manager. Also, some managers might work from home for at least a portion of the workweek.

The most famous proposal of this type appeared in *Harvard Business Review* in 1989 in an article written by Felice Schwartz. She was the founder and first president of Catalyst. Schwartz argued that most women in management careers are not "career-primary women" but "career-and-family women," who want both good careers and a family life that involves substantial participation in childrearing. Schwartz proposed that corporations provide flexible jobs for such women even though these jobs would have lower pay and slower advancement. In her view, this strategy would allow companies to retain valuable female executives who could at later points give greater priority to their careers.[41] Schwartz's article ignited a firestorm of criticism.

. . .

Despite the brouhaha that followed Schwartz's proposal, reactions to suggestions for flexible work have become more positive. Proposals include upgrading part-time work with greater responsibility and better wages. Full-time jobs could offer flexible hours. Allowing employees having significant parental responsibility more time to prove themselves worthy of promotion is another widely discussed option. Such parents (most often mothers) may need extra time to build their credentials, in many cases only an additional year or two. Their potential is thrown away if they are forced off the promotion path by lockstep rules about when they must be evaluated for higher-level positions. It is also important to allow high-performing women who step off the fast track an opportunity to return to responsible positions after a period out of the workforce.[42]

Family-friendly practices can allow women to stay in their jobs during the most demanding years of childrearing, build social capital, keep up-to-date in their fields, and eventually compete for higher positions. A study of seventy-two large U.S. firms thus showed that family-friendly human resource practices increased the proportion of women in senior management five years later, controlling for other organizational variables.[43]

Many organizations are incorporating such practices, which may encompass flex-time, job sharing, telecommuting, elder care provisions, adoption benefits, and dependent childcare options, sometimes including employee-sponsored on-site childcare. Although some people claim that such reforms are costly and inefficient, systematic analyses suggest that firms as well as employees can gain from such policies. The gains to individuals are obvious, and the gains to firms can include retaining and recruiting talented employees, increasing employee motivation, reducing turnover, and gaining a favorable public image as a "good place to work."[44]

Despite these advantages, dangers lurk in family-friendly benefits that are taken only by women, as Schwartz's critics correctly discerned. The exercise of options such as generous parental leave and part-time work slows the careers of those women who take such benefits. More profoundly, having many more women than men take such benefits can harm the careers of women in general because of the expectation that they may well exercise such options. A system of family friendliness directed only to women can make it harder for women to gain access to essential managerial roles.[45]

More-profound changes would challenge the long-hours norm of many higher managerial and professional jobs. Critics of these practices point out that it is not necessarily true that the best employees are those who spend the longest hours at work. Face time and constant availability are not the same thing as excellence of performance. Organizations can change the emphasis on long hours by placing more value on the quality of work and by planning for efficient use of employees' time. Reasonable work hours can improve employees' morale and family life, reduce their stress, and enhance their performance. Such reforms have the potential for increasing organizations' competitiveness.[46]

Other Progressive Innovations

There are many innovations, in addition to changing the long-hours norm, that would facilitate women's advancement in organizations. All of these proposals involve making organizations fairer, so that they reward individuals' merit and accomplishment.

Reforming Performance Evaluations and Recruitment

To ensure fairness, the evaluation of candidates for promotion should become less subjective than it has traditionally been. Promotions should be based on explicit, valid performance evaluations that limit the influence of decision makers' conscious and unconscious biases. In addition, recruitment from outside of organizations should involve open processes such as advertising and using employment agencies rather than informal social networks and referrals. Recruitment from within organizations also should be transparent, with posting of open positions in appropriate venues. Research has shown that these open personnel practices increase the numbers of women in managerial roles.[47]

. . .

Legitimizing Women's Contributions as Leaders

By conveying respect for and confidence in women as leaders, organizations can lessen the resistance to female leadership. An initial step is to emphasize the promotion and development of female as well as male employees and to make sure that women are included among those who are given training opportunities. In fact, a general emphasis on development of all employees can yield larger numbers of women in top management positions.[48]

Once a woman is chosen for a leadership position, it is important to convey that she was selected on the basis of her demonstrated ability and not on some other basis such as demands to fulfill diversity goals.[49] Still, some suspicion often remains that she does not really have what it takes for an important leadership position. . . .

To allay these suspicions, executives can signal their confidence in women's effectiveness as leaders. In an experiment testing this proposition, participants received information that for the tasks their group was assigned, women often serve as leaders because they are particularly

effective. In groups that received this information, female leaders overcame the disadvantage they otherwise suffered and became as influential and effective as male leaders.[50] In organizations, too, legitimizing women's authority is helpful because women can lack the built-in legitimacy that men more often possess.

. . .

Reducing Tokenism

In many settings, it is a breakthrough to appoint even one woman, and such first steps are important. However, because token women receive extra scrutiny, it is essential to move beyond token representation. Token women are often subjected to intense performance pressures. As Katharine Graham, former CEO of the *Washington Post*, wrote, "Each time I was the only woman in a room full of men, I suffered lest I appear stupid or ignorant."[51] In addition, token women tend to end up in narrow stereotypical roles such as "seductress," "mother," "pet," or "Iron Maiden." As one woman banker remarked, "When you start out in banking, you are a slut or a geisha. The pretty young things fresh off of the college campus. And you get all kinds of attention because you are fit and cute."[52]

Such treatment of women limits their options and makes it difficult for them to rise to positions of responsibility. Having a critical mass of women in executive positions—not just one or two women—can lessen this problem. When women are not a small minority, their identities as women become less salient, and colleagues are more likely to react to them in terms of their individual competencies.[53]

. . .

CHANGES IN ORGANIZATIONAL NORMS OF GOOD LEADERSHIP

A major component of the labyrinth that women must negotiate to become leaders derives from the fact that leadership has long been associated with men and masculine characteristics. Therefore, women can be regarded with suspicion when they occupy leadership roles. However, the qualities that constitute good leadership have changed in ways that lessen this role incongruity for women.[54] Consider the following confident assertion by journalist, author, and political adviser David Gergen:

> Women leaders, it turns out, seem perfectly tailored for this new style . . . When we describe the new leadership, we employ terms like *consensual, relational, web-based, caring, inclusive, open, transparent*—all qualities that we associate with the "feminine" style of leadership. One can argue whether this feminine style is in women's genes or is created by socialization. It doesn't matter much . . . The key point . . . is that women are knocking at the door of leadership at the very moment when their talents are especially well matched with the requirements of the day.[55]

. . .

New models of good leadership make sense, given that many managers no longer focus mainly on the traditional functions of planning, organizing, directing, and controlling. Instead, they primarily support teams of employees who execute tasks. Facilitating the work of a team demands solving many interpersonal as well as technical problems and dealing with the details of performance reviews and sometimes with budgetary issues. "Command and control" has little place in many of these positions, but instead managers' days are filled with communicating, listening, monitoring, teaching, and encouraging.

. . .

CONCLUSION

Critical components of the labyrinth that women encounter in trying to advance derive from organizational traditions and practices, which in turn reflect the traditional family division of labor. The extremely long hours on the job that are normative for many managers and professionals conflict with women's domestic responsibilities (and sometimes those of men). Aside from these work-life issues, organizations often embody a many-

sided masculine culture that can hinder women from accumulating the social capital they need to advance. In these settings, preferences of executives to work with people similar to themselves, along with beliefs that executive positions require masculine qualities, compound women's difficulties in advancing.

Managerial roles are in flux because of broader changes in the economy and society, so now is an excellent time to propose and try out innovations that may make organizations more hospitable to female managers and executives. In addition, many men are becoming receptive to family-friendly changes in workplaces, because they have accepted more domestic responsibility than in the past. We have provided many suggestions for reforming organizations so that they become as welcoming to women as to men. Implementing such suggestions requires thoughtful analysis by the women and men who hold positions in organizations. Moving forward with progressive proposals requires activism on the part of those who desire organizations with greater gender integration and families with more equal male and female roles.

NOTES

1. Although this analysis often refers to organizational norms and practices, related processes can occur in smaller units such as groups or teams and in larger units such as governments and nations.
2. For wide-ranging discussions of organizational factors relevant to the advancement of women as leaders, see Ely, Scully, and Foldy, 2003; Powell and Graves, 2003, 2006; Ragins and Sundstrom, 1989; Reskin and McBrier, 2000.
3. Hull and Nelson, 2000. The sample consisted of 788 randomly sampled lawyers practicing in Chicago in 1995. See also Noonan and Corcoran, 2004, for a study of differences in the promotion of men and women to partnership among University of Michigan Law School graduates.
4. Kay and Hagan, 1998, p. 741. This study was based on a sample of 905 Canadian lawyers in firm practice. See also Kay and Hagan, 1999; Spurr, 1990.
5. See P. Y. Martin, 2003, for observations of similar corporate work patterns that disadvantage women.
6. J. Williams, 2000, provided extensive analysis of ideal worker norms. See also Acker, 1990.

7. Coser, 1974; see also Maier, 1999.

8. Stone and Lovejoy, 2004, p. 68.

9. Among the younger cohort of women surveyed by Hewlett, 2002, only 45 percent had a child by age thirty-five. For related studies, see Catalyst, 2003; Fagenson and Jackson, 1994; Goldin, 1997; Swiss, 1996.

10. Naff, 1994, p. 511.

11. For discussion of the Sears discrimination case, see Nelson and Bridges, 1999.

12. Nelson and Bridges, 1999.

13. See Putnam's book, *Bowling Alone* (2000), which provides extensive discussion of social capital. For the implications of social capital in organizations, see Brass, 2001.

14. See Burt, 1992; Seibert, Kraimer, and Liden, 2001.

15. Luthans, 1988, p. 130. For this study, see Luthans, Hodgetts, and Rosenkrantz, 1988. See also Ellemers, de Gilder, and van den Heuvel, 1998, for distinctions between three types of work commitment: career oriented, team oriented, and organizational.

16. Heffernan, 2004, p. 62. For general discussion of gender and social capital, see Tharenou, 1999; Timberlake, 2005.

17. See G. Moore, 1988, for evidence that women are excluded from powerful networks, and G. Moore, 1990, for evidence that women have smaller job networks than men. See also Davies-Netzley, 1998.

18. Roth, 2006, p. 85.

19. Steel, 1993, p. 133.

20. Catalyst, 2006a.

21. Lyness and Thompson, 2000.

22. Manuel, Shefte, and Swiss, 1999, p. 9.

23. See Alvesson and Billing, 1992, for discussion of gender and organizational culture.

24. Heffernan, 2002.

25. Antilla, 2004.

26. Featherstone, 2004. Hooters restaurants, designed for male customers, emphasize the sex appeal of scantily clad female servers, called Hooters girls.

27. See van Vianen and Fischer, 2002, for evidence of greater preference for masculine culture among men than women.

28. Steel, 1993, p. 141.

29. See Kelleher, Finestone, and Lowy, 1986; M. W. McCall, Lombardo, and Morrison, 1988; Morrison, 1992.

30. For discussion of the importance of challenging work experiences to managerial development, see M. W. McCall, Lombardo, and Morrison, 1988; McCauley et al., 1994.

31. Lyness and Thompson, 2000. Other studies showing similar effects include de Pater and Van Vianen, 2006; Ohlott, Ruderman, and McCauley, 1994.

32. See de Pater, 2005, for studies giving some evidence that women may choose or accept less-challenging work, and de Pater and van Vianen, 2006, for evidence that supervisors assign women less-challenging work. For discussion of the sexism that could underlie such supervisor behavior, see Glick and Fiske, 1996, 2001a, 2001b.

33. Erkut, 2001, p. 26.

34. Galinsky et al., 2003; Ibarra, 1997; Nadis, 1999.

35. See Ragins and Sundstrom, 1989, for further discussion of this point; and Lyness and Heilman, 2006, for empirical evidence.

36. Tharenou, 1999. However, among MBA graduates, changing one's employer appears to increase compensation only for white men and not for white women or minority men or women (Brett and Stroh, 1997; Dreher and Cox, 2000).

37. M. K. Ryan and Haslam, 2005a, 2005b, 2007. These researchers have documented this glass cliff phenomenon in controlled experiments as well as studies of organizations.

38. For discussion of the barriers that prevent women from achieving elective political office, see Fox and Lawless, 2004.

39. See Nelson and Bridges, 1999, for analysis of wage setting in organizations. Consideration of job evaluation and affirmative action is beyond the scope of this book. For review of job evaluation and comparable worth, see England, 1992. For review of affirmative action, see Crosby, 2004; Crosby, Iyer, and Sincharoen, 2006; Harper and Reskin, 2005.

40. See Nelson and Bridges, 1999, for evidence that litigation has proven to be decreasingly effective for remedying organizational discrimination.

41. F. N. Schwartz, 1989.

42. See, for example, Crittenden, 2004; Hewlett, 2002; Hewlett and Luce, 2005; J. Williams, 2000. Lawrence and Corwin, 2003, discuss integrating part-time professionals into organizations.

43. Dreher, 2003.

44. See Wax, 2004, for discussion of firms' potential to adopt and maintain family-friendly reforms. See also Crosby, Iyer, and Sincharoen, 2006; Kossek and Lee, 2005; Roehling, Roehling, and Moen, 2001. Osterman, 1995, presented data on the prevalence of various work–family options in private sector establishments. Flex-time was most common, and

childcare options such as on-site childcare were relatively rare.

45. For a cross-national study suggesting that mother-friendly employment policies exacerbate occupational gender inequality, see Mandel and Semyonov, 2005. See also D. Gupta, Oaxaca, and Smith, 2006.

46. For discussion, see Meyerson and Fletcher, 2000; Rapoport et al., 2002. See also Brett and Stroh, 2003.

47. Reskin and McBrier, 2000. See also Bernardin et al., 1998; Gelfand et al., 2005.

48. J. S. Goodman, Fields, and Blum, 2003, reported data consistent with this principle in a study of 228 private sector establishments in Georgia.

49. Beliefs that an individual was hired or promoted to fulfill affirmative action or diversity goals can increase the perception that the individual lacks competence. See Heilman, 1996.

50. Lucas, 2003. This experiment had undergraduate research participants. See also Yoder, Schleicher, and McDonald, 1998.

51. Graham, 1997, p. 420.

52. Heffernan, 2004, p. 28. See Kanter, 1977, for discussion of stereotypical female work roles.

53. For discussion, see Elsass and Graves, 1997; Kanter, 1977; Reskin, McBrier, and Kmec, 1999; Yoder, 2002. See Taylor and Fiske, 1978, for experimental evidence. See also Ely, 1995, for evidence that gender is construed more traditionally in organizations with few senior women, and Bell and Nkomo, 2001, for evidence of different stereotypical roles applied to black women than white women.

54. Not all experts agree with this view. See, for example, Fletcher, 2004; R. M. Kramer, 2006; Wajcman, 1998, for alternative claims.

55. Gergen, 2005, p. xxi.

R E A D I N G **105**

Epilogue
Beyond Backlash

Ruth Rosen (2000)

"If you're on the right track, you can expect some pretty savage criticism," veteran feminist Phyllis Chesler warned young women at the close of the twentieth century. "Trust it. Revel in it. It is the truest measure of your success." Words of wisdom from one of the pioneer activists who understood the meaning of a fierce backlash.

No movement could have challenged so many ideas and customs without threatening vast numbers of women and men. Some activists viewed the backlash as either a political conspiracy or a media plot hatched to discredit feminists. But the backlash, in fact, reflected a society deeply divided and disturbed by rapid changes in men's and women's lives, at home and at work.

Abortion genuinely polarized American women. Working women, as sociologist Kristin Luker discovered, tended to support abortion rights, while homemakers, who depended on a breadwinner's income, were more likely to regard children as a means of keeping husbands yoked to their families and so opposed it. The backlash, which had grown alongside the women's movement, gained strength in 1973 after the Supreme Court, in its *Roe v. Wade* decision, made abortion legal. The Catholic Church—and later the evangelical Christian Right—quickly mobilized to reverse that decision. By 1977, Congress had passed the Hyde Amendment, which banned the use of taxpayers' money to fund abortions for poor women. By 1980, the New Right had successfully turned abortion into a litmus test for political candidates, Cabinet officials, and Supreme Court justices. By 1989, the Supreme Court's *William L. Webster v. Reproductive Health*

Services decision began the process of chipping away at women's right to abortion.

A long, drawn-out struggle over the Equal Rights Amendment also helped consolidate opposition to the women's movement. Passed quickly by Congress in a burst of optimism in 1972, the ERA needed to be ratified by thirty-eight state legislatures in order to become a part of the Constitution. Within a year, the ERA received swift ratification or support from thirty states, but then it stalled, and in 1978, proponents extracted a reluctant extension from Congress. By 1982, the ERA, unable to gain more state ratifications, had been buried, a victim of the rising symbolic politics of a triumphant political movement of the Right.

The ten-year battle over the ERA and the escalating struggle over abortion helped mobilize conservative women. Ironically, women of the Right learned from the women's movement, even if in opposition to it. In a kind of mirror-image politicking, they began to form their own all-female organizations, including Happiness of Motherhood Eternal (HOME), Women Who Want to Be Women (WWWW), American Women Against the Ratification of the ERA (AWARE), Females Opposed to Equality (FOE), and the Eagle Forum. Soon, they engaged in their own kinds of local and national consciousness-raising activities. Their tactics, like those of the women's movement, included polite protest and lobbying in Washington, as well as more militant rallies and protests. But unlike the women's movement, the fringes engaged in actual terrorism at abortion clinics.

The political struggle also catapulted several conservative women to national prominence. Among them was Phyllis Schlafly, a shrewd attorney who nonetheless—like Betty Friedan almost two decades earlier—described herself as "just a housewife," and founded Stop ERA, which she credited with defeating the ERA. An influential if little-known member of the conservative Right, Schlafly had written a book, *The Power of the Positive Woman* (1977), which attacked feminists for their negative assessments of women's condition in the United States. Schlafly also blamed "limousine liberals," "the cosmopolitan elite," and "chic fellow travelers" for living in a rarefied world that cared little about the traditional family and its values. Schlafly used her antifeminism as a vehicle for reinventing herself as a national celebrity. Thanks to the media, her name soon became a household word.

The growing engagement of women in the religious and secular New Right legitimated an increasing fusillade of attacks on feminism by right-wing male religious and political leaders. In *The New Right: We're Ready to Lead*, Richard Viguerie, one of those leaders, announced that the New Right had to fight "anti-family organizations like the National Organization for Women and to resist laws like the Equal Rights Amendment that attack families and individuals." Schlafly, Viguerie, and other leaders of the New Right blamed the hedonistic values of American culture on feminists. For them, an independent woman was by definition a selfish, self-absorbed creature who threatened the nation's "traditional values."

Support for the growing backlash came from many directions, including many women who were not members of any New Right organization. Some of those disgruntled women now felt overwhelmed by the double responsibilities they bore at home and at work; they blamed feminism for their plight. The media took its cue from such women. A new formulaic narrative appeared in the print media, that of the repentant career woman who finally realizes that feminism had very nearly ruined her life. Editors began to dispatch reporters in search of professional women who had quit their high-status jobs and returned home with great sighs of relief to care for their husbands and children.

Like the "first woman" stories of the 1970s, these cautionary tales of the 1980s obscured the actual lives of the vast majority of women in the labor force, for whom there was no choice but to get up every morning and go to work. Most working mothers labored at low-paid jobs, and husbands generally avoided even a reasonable share of the housework from their now-employed spouses. So women daily returned home to what sociologist Arlie Hochschild dubbed the "second shift." Even successful professional women were discovering that they, too, had no choice but to enter careers on men's terms. Their new employers expected them to be available "25 hours a day, seven days a week" and their husbands, too, expected the same services they would have received from an unemployed wife. To secure promotions, career women—but not men—felt compelled to choose whether to dedicate their prime child-bearing years to their careers and remain childless, or to face the daunting prospect of trying to do it all.

Despite the difficulties women and men experienced as they tried to adjust to this newly configured home life, it's important to recognize that the women's movement did not invariably pit men against women. This was not a battle between the sexes; it was part of the highly gendered and racialized cultural wars that polarized Americans in the wake of the 1960s. Men and women fought *together* on both sides of the divide, for this was a struggle between social and cultural ideals.

. . .

Feminist responses to the backlash began to appear in literature as well. During the heady years of the 1970s, feminist utopian novels had become the *genre du jour*. Some of the most prominent novels—Marge Piercy's *Woman on the Edge of Time* or Ursula Le Guin's *The Left Hand of Darkness*—had played with gender and sexual identity and optimistically imagined new ways of achieving gender equality. In the wake of the backlash, the Canadian novelist Margaret Atwood published a bleak dystopian novel, *The Handmaid's Tale* (1986), which quickly became a bestseller. This chilling novel took the destructive potential of the religious backlash seriously and offered a scary answer to the question: "What if the religious Right actually gained political power?"

Despite the sense of gloom and defeat that many feminists experienced at the time, American women were, in fact, increasingly embracing the goals of the women's movement. Reasons were not hard to fathom. Growing numbers of women were falling into poverty. Diana Pearce's 1978 phrase "the feminization of poverty" caught a startling and unexpected reality of American life. Divorce rates, which had doubled since 1965, had created a new cohort of women who joined the poor when their marriages ended. By 1984, working women began to outnumber women who worked at home and the glamorization of the superwoman and her career choice had eroded the prestige of homemaking. The growing tendency of middle-class women to postpone marriage and motherhood, combined with an increase in single mothers and divorced mothers, created a critical mass of women who now wondered how they were going to support themselves and their children. Polls steadily revealed what the much-publicized backlash obscured, that a majority of women now looked favorably upon the goals of the women's movement.

Women's attitudes had, in fact, changed rapidly. In a 1970 Virginia Slims opinion poll, 53 percent of women cited being a wife and mother as "one of the best parts of being a woman." By 1983, that figure had dropped to 26 percent. In 1970, very few women expressed concern over discrimination. By 1983, one-third of women agreed that "male chauvinism, discrimination, and sexual stereotypes ranked as their biggest problem"; while 80 percent agreed that "to get ahead a woman has to be better at what she does than a man." Nor did women still believe they lived privileged lives, as they had in 1975, when one-third of Americans viewed men's lives as far more difficult. By 1990, nearly half of all adults assumed that men had the easier life.

At the height of the backlash, in short, more American women, not fewer, grasped the importance of the goals of the women's movement. In 1986, a Gallup poll asked women, "Do you consider yourself a feminist?" At a time when identifying yourself as a feminist felt like a risky admission, 56 percent of American women were willing to do so (at least privately to Gallup's pollsters). Women of all classes were also becoming aware of the ways in which gender shaped their lives. Sixty-seven percent of all women, including those who earned under $12,500 *and* those who made more than $50,000, favored a strong women's movement. Pollsters consistently found that more African-American women approved of the goals of the women's movement than did white women. A 1989 poll found that 51 percent of all men, 64 percent of white women, 72 percent of Hispanic women, and 85 percent of African-American women agreed with the statement "The United States continues to need a strong women's movement to push for changes that benefit women."

In 1989, *Time* magazine ushered in a new decade with yet one more pronouncement of the death of feminism. Its cover story, "Women Face the '90s," bore the subtitle "During the '80s, they tried to have it all. Now they've just plain had it. Is there a future for feminism?" But, inside, the reader discovered quite a different story. Feminism was endangered, *Time* magazine suggested, not because it had failed, but precisely because it had been so successful. "In many ways," the article declared,

> feminism is a victim of its own resounding achievements. Its triumphs—in getting women into the workplace, in elevating their status in society and in shattering "the feminine mystique" that defined female success only in terms of being a wife and a mother—have rendered it obsolete, at least in its original form and rhetoric.

The growth of gender consciousness had, in fact, altered society and culture in countless ways. In August 1980, a *New York Times* editorial declared that the women's movement, once viewed as a group of "extremists and trouble-makers," had turned into an "effective political force." The editorial concluded that "the battle for women's rights is no longer lonely or peripheral. It has moved where it belongs—to the center of American politics." In 1984, commenting on legislation that would grant child support for all families and give wives access to their husbands' pensions, the *Times* editorialized that "'Women's Issues' have already become everyone's." And so they had. Perhaps the important legacy was precisely that "women's issues" had entered mainstream national politics, where they had changed the terms of political debate.

Everyday life had changed in small but significant ways. Strangers addressed a woman as Ms.; meteorologists named hurricanes after *both* men and women; schoolchildren learned about sexism before they became teenagers; language became more gender-neutral; popular culture saturated society with comedies, thrillers, and mysteries that turned on changing gender roles; and two decades after the movement's first years, the number of women politicians doubled. Even more significantly, millions of women had entered jobs that had once been reserved for men.

Although women had not gained the power to change institutions in fundamental ways, they had joined men in colleges and universities in unprecedented numbers. In the 1950s, women had constituted only 20 percent of college undergraduates, and their two most common aspirations, according to polls of the time, were to become the wife of a prominent man and the mother of several accomplished children. By 1990, women constituted 54 percent of undergraduates and they wanted to do anything and everything. Women had also joined men in both blue-collar and professional jobs in startling numbers. In 1960, 35 percent of women had worked outside the home; by 1990, that figure had jumped to 58 percent. During the same period, the number of female lawyers and judges leaped from 7,500 to 108,200; and female doctors from 15,672 to 174,000.

The cumulative impact of decades of revelations, education, debates, scandals, controversies, and high-profile trials raised women's gender consciousness, which in turn eventually showed up in a long-awaited political "gender gap." In 1871, Susan B. Anthony had prematurely predicted that once women got the right to vote, they would vote as a bloc. A gender gap did not appear until 1980, when more men than women voted for Ronald Reagan, whose opposition to the Equal Rights Amendment and abortion may have moved some women into the Democratic column. More important was Reagan's pledge to dismantle the welfare state, which nudged even more women toward the Democrats, the party more likely (theoretically) to preserve the safety net. Eventually, the gender gap would cause at least a temporary realignment of national politics. In 1996, 16 percent more women than men voted for Bill Clinton for president. Some political analysts now believed that women were voting their interests as workers, family caregivers, or as single or divorced mothers.

Gender gap or not, the rightward tilt of American politics led to the demonization of poor women and their children. As some middle-class women captured meaningful and well-paid work, ever more women slid into poverty and homelessness, which, on balance, the women's movement did too little, too late, to change. On the other hand, the lives of many ordinary working women, who had not become impoverished, improved in dramatic ways. In 1992, a *Newsweek* article described how twenty years of the women's movement had changed Appleton, Wisconsin (the hometown of Joseph McCarthy and the John Birch Society). Women, the magazine reported, had taken on significant roles in local politics. In addition, the article observed,

> There are women cops and women firefighters, and there are women in managerial jobs in local business and government. There is firm community consensus, and generous funding with local tax dollars, for Harbor House, a shelter for battered women. And there is an active effort, in the Appleton public schools, to eliminate the invidious stereotyping that keeps young women in the velvet straitjacket of traditional gender roles.

GLOBAL FEMINISM

As ideas from the Western women's movement traveled across the Atlantic, American feminists learned more than they taught. On October 25, 1985, President Vigdis Finnbogadottir of Iceland joined tens of thousands of women who had walked off the job in a twenty-four-hour protest against male privilege on the island. She also refused to sign a bill that would have ordered striking flight attendants back to work. Iceland's telephone system collapsed, travel came to a halt, and groups of men crowded into hotels for the breakfast their wives refused to cook for them.

As feminism began spreading beyond industrialized nations, American feminists also encountered new definitions of "women's issues." Sometimes "freedom" meant better access to fuel and water, toppling a ruthless dictator, or ending a genocidal civil war. The gradual emergence of global women's networks made such encounters and confrontations inevitable.

Many of these networks grew out of the United Nations' 1975 International Women's Year. At the first World Conference on Women in Mexico, delegates urged the UN to proclaim the years between 1975 and 1985 "The Decade for Women." At each subsequent UN conference, there were two parallel meetings—one for delegates who represented their governments and another for women who participated in the nongovernmental organization (NGO) meetings. The numbers of NGO participants mushroomed. Six thousand women participated in the second conference, held in 1980 at Copenhagen; fourteen thousand attended the third in 1985 in Nairobi; and a startling thirty thousand arrived in Huairou, China, for the fourth in 1995.

What President Kennedy's Commission on the Status of Women had done for American women activists, the UN's World Conferences now did at a global level. Proximity bred intimacy and spread knowledge. The thousands of women rubbing shoulders or debating in Mexico, Denmark, Kenya, or China were learning from and teaching each other about their lives. Aside from their differences, they were also discovering the ubiquity of certain kinds of shared oppression—violence and poverty that had once seemed local, rather than global. And, in the process, they were nurturing and legitimating a global feminism, which was quite literally being born at UN conferences as they watched.

That didn't mean that women everywhere interpreted the information newly available to them in the same way. From the start, the NGO forum meetings witnessed serious clashes between "First" and "Third" World women, and between women whose nations were at war. Over time, the atmosphere began to improve. Western feminists began to *listen,* rather than *lecture,* and women from developing countries, who had formerly viewed Western concerns over clitoridectomies, dowry deaths, wife-beatings, and arranged marriages as so many instances of cultural imperialism—the urge of developed countries to impose their values and customs on underdeveloped nations—began the painful process of redefining their own customs as crimes.

Here was the essence of global feminism—addressing the world's problems *as if women mattered*. Human rights organizations, for instance, had traditionally focused exclusively on state-sanctioned violence against political activists. But most women encountered violence not in prison or at protests, but in their homes and communities. Viewed as customs rather than crimes, wife-beating, rape, genital excision, dowry deaths, and arranged marriages had never been certified as violations of women's human rights.

At a 1993 UN World Conference on Human Rights in Vienna, women from all over the globe movingly testified to the various forms of violence that had devastated their lives. Feminists successfully made their case; the conference passed a resolution that recognized violence against women and girls as a violation of their human rights. One immediate consequence of this historic redefinition of human rights was that Western nations could now grant *political* asylum to women fleeing certain violence or death from husbands or other relatives.

Two years later, at a 1995 UN Conference on Development and Population in Cairo, feminists criticized accepted development policies that promoted massive industrial or hydroelectric projects as *the* way to improve the standard of living of developing nations. Such projects, they argued, irreversibly damaged the human and natural ecology, provided work for indigenous men, but not for women, and undermined women's traditional economic role and social authority. Instead, they advocated small-scale cottage industries, through which women could earn money for their education. They also attacked those population experts who took it, as an article of faith, that population growth automatically declined when industrial development lifted people out of poverty. Citing the failure of

such policies, feminists countered that educating women and giving them control over their reproductive decisions was a far more effective way of controlling population growth. As one reporter wrote, "The deceptively simple idea of a woman making a decision about her future is one of the cornerstones of the emerging debate on global population policy."

The "Platform for Action," the document that emerged from the Beijing conference in 1995, asked the nations of the world to see social and economic development through the eyes of women. Although the "Platform" recognized the differences that separated women, it also emphasized the universal poverty and violence that crippled the lives of so many of the world's women. In addition to affirming women's rights as human rights, the conference also declared three preconditions for women's advancement; equality, development, and peace. To many participants, the event seemed like a miracle, a moment existing out of time, when the world's women imagined a different kind of future, even if they had little power to implement it.

By publicizing even more gender consciousness, the 1995 Fourth World Conference on Women probably encouraged greater numbers of the world's women to challenge traditional forms of patriarchal authority. In the years following the conference, feminist activists and scholars began the process of redefining rape (when it occurred during a military conflict) as a war crime, publicizing the particular plight of refugees (most of whom were women), and rethinking the role women might play in reconstructing societies ravaged by war.

At the same time, women in both developed and developing nations began debating the impact of feminism itself on global culture and economics. Was feminism yoked only to concepts of individual rights? Was it simply an inevitable by-product of Western consumer capitalism, whose effects would rupture the ties that bound families and communities together—and to the land? Or could feminism help protect the rights of women as they left family and land behind and entered the global wage economy? Could women's rights, redefined as human rights, provide a powerful new stance from which to oppose totalitarian societies of both the Right and the Left? Many theories proliferated, heated debates took place, but the answers—even many of the questions— lay in the future.

There is no end to this story. Over a hundred years ago, the suffragist Matilda Gage turned her gaze toward the future. The work of her generation of activists, she wrote, was not for them alone,

> but for all women of all time. The hopes of posterity were in their hands, and they were determined to place on record for the daughters of 1976, the fact that their mothers of 1876 had thus asserted their equality of rights, and thus impeached the government of today for its injustice towards women.

Nearly a century later, veteran feminist Robin Morgan, along with thousands of other twentieth-century "daughters," took up the unfinished agenda left by the suffrage movement. Morgan, too, realized that she struggled for future daughters and worried that her generation might squander precious opportunities.

> I fear for the women's movement falling into precisely the same trap as did our foremothers, the suffragists: creating a bourgeois feminist movement that never quite dared enough, never questioned enough, never really reached out beyond its own class and race.

As women in developing countries become educated and enter the marketplace as wage-earners, they will invariably intensify existing cultural conflicts between religious and secular groups, and between those sectors of society living under preindustrial conditions and those who connect through cyberspace in a postmodern global society. Like small brushfires, these cultural wars may circle the globe, igniting a wild and frightening firestorm. Inevitably, some women will feel defeated as they encounter wave after wave of backlash. But in the darkness of their despair, they should remember that resistance is

not a sign of defeat, but rather evidence that women are challenging a worldview that now belongs to an earlier era of human history.

Each generation of women activists leaves an unfinished agenda for the next generation. First Wave suffragists fought for women's citizenship, created international organizations, dedicated to universal disarmament, but left many customs and beliefs unchallenged. Second Wave feminists questioned nearly everything, transformed much of American culture, expanded the idea of democracy by insisting that equality had to include the realities of its women citizens, and catapulted women's issues onto a global stage. Their greatest accomplishment was to change the terms of debate, so that women mattered. But they left much unfinished as well. They were unable to change most institutions, to gain greater economic justice for poor women, or to convince society that child care is the responsibility of the whole society. As a result, American women won the right to "have it all," but only if they "did it all."

It is for a new generation to identify what they need in order to achieve greater equality. It may even be their solemn duty. In the words of nineteenth-century suffragist Abigail Scott Duniway:

> The young women of today, free to study, to speak, to write, to choose their occupation, should remember that every inch of this freedom was bought for them at a great price. It is for them to show their gratitude by helping onward the reforms of their own times, by spreading the light of freedom and truth still wider. The debt that each generation owes to the past it must pay to the future.

The struggle for women's human rights has just begun. As each generation shares its secrets, women learn to see the world through their own eyes and discover, much to their surprise, that they are not the first and that they are not alone. The poet Muriel Rukeyser once asked, "What would happen if one woman told the truth about her life?" Her answer: "The world would split open." And so it has. A revolution is under way, and there is no end in sight.

Warning

Jenny Joseph (1992)

When I am an old woman I shall wear purple
With a red hat which doesn't go, and doesn't suit
 me.
And I shall spend my pension on brandy and
 summer gloves
And satin sandals, and say we've no money for
 butter.
I shall sit down on the pavement when I'm tired
And gobble up samples in shops and press alarm
 bells

And run my stick along the public railings
And make up for the sobriety of my youth.
I shall go out in my slippers in the rain
And pick the flowers in other people's gardens
And learn to spit.

You can wear terrible shirts and grow more fat
And eat three pounds of sausages at a go
Or only bread and pickle for a week
And hoard pens and pencils and beermats and
 things in boxes.

But now we must have clothes that keep us dry
And pay our rent and not swear in the street
And set a good example for the children.
We must have friends to dinner and read the
 papers.
But maybe I ought to practise a little now?
So people who know me are not too shocked or
 surprised
When suddenly I am old, and start to wear
 purple.

DISCUSSION QUESTIONS FOR CHAPTER 13

1. How has your experience in a feminist classroom had on impact on you?

2. What do you consider important factors for building a "beloved community"?

3. How do you envision a just future? How do you think we can get there?

4. What does integrity mean to you? How does integrity affect your work for justice?

5. What impact might a "transformational politics" have on our society?

6. Why are peace and the environment important women's issues?

7. What will you take away from this class to help you make your way in the world?

SUGGESTIONS FOR FURTHER READING

Aptheker, Bettina. *Intimate Politics: How I Grew Up Red, Fought for Free Speech, and Became a Feminist Rebel.* Berkeley, CA: Seal Press, 2006.

Braithwaite, Ann, Susan Heald, Susanne Luhmann, and Sharon Rosenberg. *Troubling Women's Studies: Pasts, Presents, and Possibilities.* Toronto: Sumach Press, 2005.

Daly, Mary. *Amazon Grace: Re-Calling the Courage to Sin Big.* New York: Palgrave Macmillan, 2006.

Eisenstein, Zillah. *Against Empire: Feminisms, Racism, and "the" West.* London: Zed Books, 2004.

Kennedy, Elizabeth Lapovsky, and Agatha Beins. *Women's Studies for the Future.* Piscataway, NJ: Rutgers University Press, 2005.

Pollitt, Katha. *Virginity or Death! And Other Social and Political Issues of Our Time.* New York: Random House Trade Paperbacks, 2006.

Schrepfer, Susan R. *Nature's Altars: Mountains, Gender, and American Environmentalism.* Lawrence: University Press of Kansas, 2005.

Seely, Megan. *Fight Like a Girl: How to Be a Fearless Feminist.* New York: NYU Press, 2007.

Shiva, Vandana. *Earth Democracy: Justice, Sustainability, and Peace.* Boston: South End, 2005.

Credits

Index